Thesaurus

Collins Gem

Thesaurus
A dictionary of synonyms

Harper*Resource*

An Imprint of HarperCollins*Publishers*

second edition 2002

© HarperCollins Publishers 1990, 2002

latest reprint 2003

HarperCollins Publishers
Westerhill Road, Bishopbriggs, Glasgow G64 2QT
Great Britain

www.collins.co.uk

Collins Gem® and Bank of English® are registered trademarks
of HarperCollins Publishers Limited

Collins Gem and HarperResource are imprints
of HarperCollins Publishers

HarperCollins Publishers, Inc.
10 East 53rd Street, New York, NY 10022

ISBN 0-06-008567-3

Library of Congress Cataloging-in-Publication Data
has been applied for

HarperCollins books may be purchased for educational,
business, or sales promotional use. For information, please write to:
Special Markets Department, HarperCollins Publishers Inc.
10 East 53rd Street, New York, NY 10022

www.harpercollins.com

---

*Computing support and typesetting by Stewart C Russell
and John Podbielski*

Printed and bound in Great Britain by Charles Letts & Company Ltd

Editorial Staff

US Editor
Jennifer Sagala

Editor
Lorna Gilmour

Publishing Manager
Elaine Higgleton

Series Editor
Lorna Sinclair Knight

BANK *of* ENGLISH

This book has been compiled by referring to the Bank of English, a unique database of the English language with examples of over 400 million words taken from a very wide range of American and international books, newspapers, magazines, radio, TV, letters and talks, reflecting the whole spectrum of English today. This database enables Collins lexicographers to analyze how American English is actually used today and how it is changing.

The Bank of English was set up as a joint initiative by HarperCollins Publishers and Birmingham University to be a resource for language research and lexicography. Its size and range make it an unequalled source of information and the purpose-built software for its analysis is unique to Collins English Dictionaries.

This ensures that Collins Dictionaries accurately reflect English as it is used today in a way that is most helpful to the user, as well as including the full range of rarer and historical words and meanings.

Foreword

The American edition of the **Collins Gem Thesaurus**, which was first published in 1990, has proved to be an immensely popular language resource. It allows you to look up a word and find a useful selection of alternatives that can replace it. It is, therefore, tremendously helpful when you are trying to find different ways of expressing yourself, as well as being an invaluable aid for crosswords and puzzles.

Collins thesauruses are designed to give the user as much help as possible in finding the right word for any occasion. Because the **Gem Thesaurus** has its main entry words arranged in A-Z form, you can go straight to the word you want without having to resort to an index, just as if you were looking it up in a dictionary. In this new edition, the number of main entry words has been increased, giving you an even greater chance of finding the word you want. At the same time, the list of alternative words (synonyms) for each main entry has been reviewed so that the most helpful alternatives are included in each case. The new edition also takes account of recent changes in the language, with terms like *gridlock, dweeb,* and *Internet* included as main entry words for the first time, and words like *twenty-four-seven, phat, wannabe,* and *scuzzbucket* being found among the synonyms.

This new edition further demonstrates Collins' commitment to helping the user. As part of an innovative design, key synonyms have been put in capital letters and placed first in each list. This layout enables you to see at once which sense of the word is being referred to, which is particularly helpful when a main entry word has a number of different senses. It also gives you an idea of which synonym is the closest alternative to the word you have looked up.

These innovations mean that the American edition of the **Collins Gem Thesaurus** continues to provide the user with a treasury of useful words arranged in the most helpful format possible.

Guide to the Text

Headword

Synonyms
words, listed in
alphabetical order,
that can be used in
place of the headword

Part of speech labels

Labels
a label in brackets
applies only to the
word preceding it

Key Synonyms
given first and highlighted

abnormality *noun* ODDITY,
deformity, exception,
irregularity, peculiarity,
singularity, strangeness

abode *noun* HOME, domicile,
dwelling, habitat, habitation,
house, lodging, pad (*slang*,
dated), quarters, residence

abolish *verb* DO AWAY WITH,
annul, cancel, destroy,
eliminate, end, eradicate, put
an end to, quash, rescind,
revoke, stamp out

abolition *noun* ENDING,
cancellation, destruction,
elimination, end,
extermination, termination,
wiping out

abominable *adjective* TERRIBLE,
despicable, detestable,
disgusting, hateful, horrible,
horrid, lousy (*slang*), repulsive,
revolting, scuzzy (*slang*), vile

abort *verb* 1 TERMINATE (*a
pregnancy*), miscarry 2 STOP,
arrest, ax (*informal*), call off,
check, end, fail, halt, terminate

abortion *noun* TERMINATION,
deliberate miscarriage,
miscarriage

abortive *adjective* FAILED,
fruitless, futile, ineffectual,
miscarried, unsuccessful,
useless, vain

abound *verb* BE PLENTIFUL,
flourish, proliferate, swarm,
swell, teem, thrive

abounding *adjective* PLENTIFUL,
abundant, bountiful, copious,
full, profuse, prolific, rich

about *preposition* 1 REGARDING, as
regards, concerning, dealing

x

Guide to the Text

with, on, referring to, relating to **2** NEAR, adjacent to, beside, circa (*used with dates*), close to, nearby ▶ *adverb* **3** NEARLY, almost, approaching, approximately, around, close to, more or less, roughly

above *preposition* OVER, beyond, exceeding, higher than, on top of, upon

above board *adjective* HONEST, fair, genuine, legitimate, square, straight

abrasion *noun Medical* GRAZE, chafe, scrape, scratch, scuff, surface injury

abrasive *adjective* **1** UNPLEASANT, caustic, cutting, galling, grating, irritating, rough, sharp **2** ROUGH, chafing, grating, scraping, scratchy

abreast *adjective* **1** ALONGSIDE, beside, side by side **2 abreast of** INFORMED ABOUT, acquainted with, *au courant* with, *au fait* with, conversant with, familiar with, in the picture about, in touch with, keeping one's finger on the pulse of, knowledgeable about, up to date with, up to speed with

abridge *verb* SHORTEN, abbreviate, condense, cut, decrease, reduce, summarize

abroad *adverb* OVERSEAS, in foreign lands, out of the country

abrupt *adjective* **1** SUDDEN, precipitate, quick, surprising, unexpected **2** CURT, brusque, gruff, impatient, rude, short, terse

Labels
a label which is not in brackets relates to the whole of that particular sense

Foreign words and phrases

Phrases and idioms

Sense Numbers
synonyms divided according to meaning to help you find the sense you want

A a

abandon verb **1** LEAVE, desert, forsake, strand **2** GIVE UP, relinquish, surrender, yield ▶noun **3** WILDNESS, recklessness

abandonment noun LEAVING, dereliction, desertion, forsaking

abashed adjective EMBARRASSED, ashamed, chagrined, disconcerted, dismayed, humiliated, mortified, shamefaced, taken aback

abate verb DECREASE, decline, diminish, dwindle, fade, lessen, let up, moderate, relax, slacken, subside, weaken

abbey noun MONASTERY, convent, friary, nunnery, priory

abbreviate verb SHORTEN, abridge, compress, condense, contract, cut, reduce, summarize

abbreviation noun SHORTENING, abridgment, contraction, reduction, summary, synopsis

abdicate verb GIVE UP, abandon, quit, relinquish, renounce, resign, step down (informal)

abdication noun GIVING UP, abandonment, quitting, renunciation, resignation, retirement, surrender

abduct verb KIDNAP, carry off, seize, snatch (slang)

abduction noun KIDNAPING, carrying off, seizure

aberration noun ODDITY, abnormality, anomaly, defect, irregularity, lapse, peculiarity, quirk

abet verb HELP, aid, assist, connive at, support

abeyance noun **in abeyance** SHELVED, hanging fire, on ice (informal), pending, suspended

abhor verb HATE, abominate, detest, loathe, shrink from, shudder at

abhorrent adjective HATEFUL, abominable, disgusting, distasteful, hated, horrid, loathsome, offensive, repulsive, scuzzy (slang)

abide verb TOLERATE, accept, bear, endure, put up with, stand, suffer

abide by verb OBEY, agree to, comply with, conform to, follow, observe, submit to

abiding adjective EVERLASTING, continuing, enduring, lasting, permanent, persistent, unchanging

ability noun SKILL, aptitude, capability, competence, expertise, proficiency, talent

abject adjective **1** MISERABLE, deplorable, forlorn, hopeless, pitiable, wretched **2** SERVILE, cringing, degraded, fawning, grovelling, submissive

ablaze adjective ON FIRE, aflame, alight, blazing, burning, fiery, flaming, ignited, lighted

able adjective CAPABLE, accomplished, competent, efficient, proficient, qualified, skillful

able-bodied adjective STRONG, fit, healthy, robust, sound, sturdy

abnormal adjective UNUSUAL,

atypical, exceptional, extraordinary, irregular, odd, peculiar, strange, uncommon

abnormality noun ODDITY, deformity, exception, irregularity, peculiarity, singularity, strangeness

abode noun HOME, domicile, dwelling, habitat, habitation, house, lodging, pad (slang, dated), quarters, residence

abolish verb DO AWAY WITH, annul, cancel, destroy, eliminate, end, eradicate, put an end to, quash, rescind, revoke, stamp out

abolition noun ENDING, cancellation, destruction, elimination, end, extermination, termination, wiping out

abominable adjective TERRIBLE, despicable, detestable, disgusting, hateful, horrible, horrid, lousy (slang), repulsive, revolting, scuzzy (slang), vile

abort verb 1 TERMINATE (a pregnancy), miscarry 2 STOP, arrest, ax (informal), call off, check, end, fail, halt, terminate

abortion noun TERMINATION, deliberate miscarriage, miscarriage

abortive adjective FAILED, fruitless, futile, ineffectual, miscarried, unsuccessful, useless, vain

abound verb BE PLENTIFUL, flourish, proliferate, swarm, swell, teem, thrive

abounding adjective PLENTIFUL, abundant, bountiful, copious, full, profuse, prolific, rich

about preposition 1 REGARDING, as regards, concerning, dealing with, on, referring to, relating to 2 NEAR, adjacent to, beside, circa (used with dates), close to, nearby ▶ adverb 3 NEARLY, almost, approaching, approximately, around, close to, more or less, roughly

above preposition OVER, beyond, exceeding, higher than, on top of, upon

above board adjective HONEST, fair, genuine, legitimate, square, straight

abrasion noun Medical GRAZE, chafe, scrape, scratch, scuff, surface injury

abrasive adjective 1 UNPLEASANT, caustic, cutting, galling, grating, irritating, rough, sharp 2 ROUGH, chafing, grating, scraping, scratchy

abreast adjective 1 ALONGSIDE, beside, side by side 2 abreast of INFORMED ABOUT, acquainted with, au courant with, au fait with, conversant with, familiar with, in the picture about, in touch with, keeping one's finger on the pulse of, knowledgeable about, up to date with, up to speed with

abridge verb SHORTEN, abbreviate, condense, cut, decrease, reduce, summarize

abroad adverb OVERSEAS, in foreign lands, out of the country

abrupt adjective 1 SUDDEN, precipitate, quick, surprising, unexpected 2 CURT, brusque, gruff, impatient, rude, short, terse

abscond verb FLEE, clear out, disappear, escape, make off, run off, steal away

absence noun **1** NONATTENDANCE, absenteeism, truancy **2** LACK, deficiency, need, omission, unavailability, want

absent adjective **1** MISSING, away, elsewhere, gone, nonexistent, out, unavailable **2** ABSENT-MINDED, blank, distracted, inattentive, oblivious, preoccupied, vacant, vague ▶ verb **3** absent oneself STAY AWAY, keep away, play truant, withdraw

absent-minded adjective VAGUE, distracted, dreaming, forgetful, inattentive, preoccupied, unaware

absolute adjective **1** TOTAL, complete, outright, perfect, pure, sheer, thorough, utter **2** SUPREME, full, sovereign, unbounded, unconditional, unlimited, unrestricted

absolutely adverb TOTALLY, completely, entirely, fully, one hundred per cent, perfectly, utterly, wholly

absolution noun FORGIVENESS, deliverance, exculpation, exoneration, mercy, pardon, release

absolve verb FORGIVE, deliver, exculpate, excuse, let off, pardon, release, set free

absorb verb **1** SOAK UP, consume, digest, imbibe, incorporate, receive, suck up, take in **2** PREOCCUPY, captivate, engage, engross, fascinate, rivet

absorbed adjective **1** PREOCCUPIED, captivated, engrossed, fascinated, immersed, involved, lost, rapt, riveted, wrapped up **2** DIGESTED, assimilated, incorporated, received, soaked up

absorbent adjective PERMEABLE, porous, receptive, spongy

absorbing adjective FASCINATING, captivating, engrossing, gripping, interesting, intriguing, riveting, spellbinding

absorption noun **1** SOAKING UP, assimilation, consumption, digestion, incorporation, sucking up **2** CONCENTRATION, fascination, immersion, intentness, involvement, preoccupation

abstain verb REFRAIN, avoid, decline, deny (oneself), desist, fast, forbear, forgo, give up, keep from

abstemious adjective SELF-DENYING, ascetic, austere, frugal, moderate, sober, temperate

abstention noun REFUSAL, abstaining, abstinence, avoidance, forbearance, refraining, self-control, self-denial, self-restraint

abstinence noun SELF-DENIAL, abstemiousness, avoidance, forbearance, moderation, self-restraint, soberness, teetotalism, temperance

abstinent adjective SELF-DENYING, abstaining, abstemious, forbearing, moderate, self-controlled, sober, temperate

abstract adjective **1** THEORETICAL, abstruse, general, hypothetical, indefinite, notional, recondite ▶ noun **2** SUMMARY, abridgment, digest, epitome, outline, précis, résumé, synopsis ▶ verb **3** SUMMARIZE, abbreviate, abridge, condense, digest, epitomize, outline, précis,

shorten 4 REMOVE, detach,
extract, isolate, separate, take
away, take out, withdraw

abstraction noun 1 IDEA,
concept, formula,
generalization, hypothesis,
notion, theorem, theory,
thought 2 ABSENT-MINDEDNESS,
absence, dreaminess,
inattention, pensiveness,
preoccupation, remoteness,
woolgathering

abstruse adjective OBSCURE,
arcane, complex, deep,
enigmatic, esoteric, recondite,
unfathomable, vague

absurd adjective RIDICULOUS,
crazy (informal), farcical,
foolish, idiotic, illogical, inane,
incongruous, irrational,
ludicrous, nonsensical,
preposterous, senseless, silly,
stupid, unreasonable

absurdity noun RIDICULOUSNESS,
farce, folly, foolishness,
incongruity, joke, nonsense,
silliness, stupidity

abundance noun PLENTY,
affluence, bounty, copiousness,
exuberance, fullness, profusion

abundant adjective PLENTIFUL,
ample, bountiful, copious,
exuberant, filled, full, luxuriant,
profuse, rich, teeming

abuse noun 1 ILL-TREATMENT,
damage, exploitation, harm,
hurt, injury, maltreatment,
manhandling 2 INSULTS, blame,
castigation, censure,
defamation, derision,
disparagement, invective,
reproach, scolding, vilification
3 MISUSE, misapplication ▶ verb
4 ILL-TREAT, damage, exploit,
harm, hurt, injure, maltreat,

misuse, take advantage of
5 INSULT, castigate, curse,
defame, disparage, malign,
scold, vilify

abusive adjective 1 INSULTING,
censorious, defamatory,
disparaging, libelous, offensive,
reproachful, rude, scathing
2 HARMFUL, brutal, cruel,
destructive, hurtful, injurious,
rough

abysmal adjective TERRIBLE,
appalling, awful, bad, dire,
dreadful

abyss noun PIT, chasm, crevasse,
fissure, gorge, gulf, void

academic adjective 1 SCHOLARLY,
bookish, erudite, highbrow,
learned, literary, studious
2 HYPOTHETICAL, abstract,
conjectural, impractical,
notional, speculative,
theoretical ▶ noun 3 SCHOLAR,
academician, don, fellow,
lecturer, master, professor, tutor

accede verb 1 AGREE, accept,
acquiesce, admit, assent,
comply, concede, concur,
consent, endorse, grant
2 INHERIT, assume, attain, come
to, enter upon, succeed,
succeed to (as heir)

accelerate verb SPEED UP,
advance, expedite, further,
hasten, hurry, quicken

acceleration noun SPEEDING UP,
hastening, hurrying,
quickening, stepping up
(informal)

accent noun 1 PRONUNCIATION,
articulation, brogue,
enunciation, inflection,
intonation, modulation, tone
2 EMPHASIS, beat, cadence,
force, pitch, rhythm, stress,

timbre ▸ verb 3 EMPHASIZE, accentuate, stress, underline, underscore

accentuate verb EMPHASIZE, accent, draw attention to, foreground, highlight, stress, underline, underscore

accept verb 1 RECEIVE, acquire, gain, get, obtain, secure, take 2 · AGREE TO, admit, approve, believe, concur with, consent to, cooperate with, recognize

acceptable adjective SATISFACTORY, adequate, admissible, all right, fair, moderate, passable, tolerable

acceptance noun 1 ACCEPTING, acquiring, gaining, getting, obtaining, receipt, securing, taking 2 AGREEMENT, acknowledgment, acquiescence, admission, adoption, approval, assent, concurrence, consent, cooperation, recognition

accepted adjective AGREED, acknowledged, approved, common, conventional, customary, established, normal, recognized, traditional

access noun ENTRANCE, admission, admittance, approach, entry, passage, path, road

accessibility noun 1 HANDINESS, availability, nearness, possibility, readiness 2 APPROACHABILITY, affability, cordiality, friendliness, informality 3 OPENNESS, susceptibility

accessible adjective 1 HANDY, achievable, at hand, attainable, available, near, nearby, obtainable, reachable

2 APPROACHABLE, affable, available, cordial, friendly, informal 3 OPEN, exposed, liable, susceptible, vulnerable, wide-open

accessory noun 1 ADDITION, accompaniment, adjunct, adornment, appendage, attachment, decoration, extra, supplement, trimming 2 ACCOMPLICE, abettor, assistant, associate (in crime), colleague, confederate, helper, partner

accident noun 1 MISFORTUNE, calamity, collision, crash, disaster, misadventure, mishap 2 CHANCE, fate, fluke, fortuity, fortune, hazard, luck

accidental adjective UNINTENTIONAL, casual, chance, fortuitous, haphazard, inadvertent, incidental, random, unexpected, unforeseen, unlooked-for, unplanned

accidentally adverb UNINTENTIONALLY, by accident, by chance, fortuitously, haphazardly, inadvertently, incidentally, randomly, unwittingly

acclaim verb 1 PRAISE, applaud, approve, celebrate, cheer, clap, commend, exalt, hail, honor, salute ▸ noun 2 PRAISE, acclamation, applause, approval, celebration, commendation, honor, kudos

acclamation noun PRAISE, acclaim, adulation, approval, ovation, plaudit, tribute

acclimatization noun ADAPTATION, adjustment, habituation, inurement, naturalization

acclimatize verb ADAPT, accommodate, accustom, adjust, get used to, habituate, inure, naturalize

accolade noun PRAISE, acclaim, applause, approval, commendation, compliment, ovation, recognition, tribute

accommodate verb 1 HOUSE, cater for, entertain, lodge, put up, shelter 2 HELP, aid, assist, oblige, serve 3 ADAPT, adjust, comply, conform, fit, harmonize, modify, reconcile, settle

accommodating adjective HELPFUL, considerate, cooperative, friendly, hospitable, kind, obliging, polite, unselfish, willing

accommodation noun HOUSING, board, house, lodging(s), quarters, shelter

accompaniment noun 1 SUPPLEMENT, accessory, companion, complement 2 BACKING MUSIC, backing

accompany verb 1 GO WITH, attend, chaperon, conduct, convoy, escort, hold (someone's) hand 2 OCCUR WITH, belong to, come with, follow, go together with, supplement

accompanying adjective ADDITIONAL, associated, attached, attendant, complementary, related, supplementary

accomplice noun HELPER, abettor, accessory, ally, assistant, associate, collaborator, colleague, henchman, partner

accomplish verb DO, achieve, attain, bring about, carry out, complete, effect, execute, finish, fulfill, manage, perform, produce

accomplished adjective SKILLED, expert, gifted, masterly, polished, practiced, proficient, talented

accomplishment noun 1 COMPLETION, bringing about, carrying out, conclusion, execution, finishing, fulfillment, performance 2 ACHIEVEMENT, act, coup, deed, exploit, feat, stroke, triumph

accord noun 1 AGREEMENT, conformity, correspondence, harmony, rapport, sympathy, unison ▶verb 2 FIT, agree, conform, correspond, harmonize, match, suit, tally

accordingly adverb 1 APPROPRIATELY, correspondingly, fitly, properly, suitably 2 CONSEQUENTLY, as a result, ergo, hence, in consequence, so, therefore, thus

according to adverb 1 AS STATED BY, as believed by, as maintained by, in the light of, on the authority of, on the report of 2 IN KEEPING WITH, after, after the manner of, consistent with, in accordance with, in compliance with, in line with, in the manner of

accost verb APPROACH, buttonhole, confront, greet, hail

account noun 1 DESCRIPTION, explanation, narrative, report, statement, story, tale, version 2 Commerce STATEMENT, balance, bill, books, charge, invoice, reckoning, register, score, tally 3 IMPORTANCE, consequence, honor, note, significance, standing, value, worth ▶ *verb* **4** CONSIDER, count, estimate, judge, rate, reckon, regard, think, value

accountability *noun* RESPONSIBILITY, answerability, chargeability, culpability, liability

accountable *adjective* RESPONSIBLE, amenable, answerable, charged with, liable, obligated, obliged

accountant *noun* AUDITOR, bean counter (*informal*), book-keeper

account for *verb* EXPLAIN, answer for, clarify, clear up, elucidate, illuminate, justify, rationalize

accredited *adjective* AUTHORIZED, appointed, certified, empowered, endorsed, guaranteed, licensed, official, recognized

accrue *verb* INCREASE, accumulate, amass, arise, be added, build up, collect, enlarge, flow, follow, grow

accumulate *verb* COLLECT, accrue, amass, build up, gather, hoard, increase, pile up, store

accumulation *noun* COLLECTION, build-up, gathering, heap, hoard, increase, mass, pile, stack, stock, stockpile, store

accuracy *noun* EXACTNESS, accurateness, authenticity, carefulness, closeness, correctness, fidelity, precision, strictness, truthfulness, veracity

accurate *adjective* EXACT, authentic, close, correct, faithful, precise, scrupulous, strict, true, unerring

accurately *adverb* EXACTLY,

authentically, closely, correctly, faithfully, precisely, scrupulously, strictly, to the letter, truly, unerringly

accursed *adjective* **1** CURSED, bewitched, condemned, damned, doomed, hopeless, ill-fated, ill-omened, jinxed, unfortunate, unlucky, wretched **2** HATEFUL, abominable, despicable, detestable, execrable, hellish, horrible, lousy (*slang*), scuzzy (*slang*)

accusation *noun* CHARGE, allegation, complaint, denunciation, incrimination, indictment, recrimination

accuse *verb* CHARGE, blame, censure, denounce, impeach, impute, incriminate, indict

accustom *verb* ADAPT, acclimatize, acquaint, discipline, exercise, familiarize, train

accustomed *adjective* **1** USUAL, common, conventional, customary, established, everyday, expected, habitual, normal, ordinary, regular, traditional **2** USED, acclimatized, acquainted, adapted, familiar, familiarized, given to, in the habit of, trained

ace *noun* **1** Cards, dice, etc. ONE, single point **2** *Informal* EXPERT, champion, master, star, virtuoso, wizard (*informal*)

ache *verb* **1** HURT, pain, pound, smart, suffer, throb, twinge ▶ *noun* **2** PAIN, hurt, pang, pounding, soreness, suffering, throbbing

achieve *verb* ATTAIN, accomplish, acquire, bring about, carry out, complete, do, execute, fulfill, gain, get, obtain, perform

achievement noun
ACCOMPLISHMENT, act, deed, effort, exploit, feat, feather in one's cap, stroke

acid adjective **1** SOUR, acerbic, acrid, pungent, tart, vinegary **2** SHARP, biting, bitter, caustic, cutting, harsh, trenchant, vitriolic

acidity noun **1** SOURNESS, acerbity, pungency, tartness **2** SHARPNESS, bitterness, harshness

acknowledge verb **1** ACCEPT, admit, allow, concede, confess, declare, grant, own, profess, recognize, yield **2** GREET, address, hail, notice, recognize, salute **3** REPLY TO, answer, notice, react to, recognize, respond to, return

acknowledged adjective
ACCEPTED, accredited, approved, confessed, declared, professed, recognized, returned

acknowledgment noun
1 ACCEPTANCE, admission, allowing, confession, declaration, profession, realization, yielding **2** GREETING, addressing, hail, hailing, notice, recognition, salutation, salute **3** APPRECIATION, answer, credit, gratitude, kudos, reaction, recognition, reply, response, return, thanks

acquaint verb TELL, disclose, divulge, enlighten, familiarize, inform, let (someone) know, notify, reveal

acquaintance noun **1** ASSOCIATE, colleague, contact **2** KNOWLEDGE, awareness, experience, familiarity,

fellowship, relationship, understanding

acquainted with adjective
FAMILIAR WITH, alive to, apprised of, au fait with, aware of, conscious of, experienced in, informed of, knowledgeable about, versed in

acquiesce verb AGREE, accede, accept, allow, approve, assent, comply, concur, conform, consent, give in, go along with, submit, yield

acquiescence noun AGREEMENT, acceptance, approval, assent, compliance, conformity, consent, giving in, obedience, submission, yielding

acquire verb GET, amass, attain, buy, collect, earn, gain, gather, obtain, receive, secure, win

acquisition noun **1** POSSESSION, buy, gain, prize, property, purchase **2** ACQUIRING, attainment, gaining, procurement

acquisitive adjective GREEDY, avaricious, avid, covetous, grabbing, grasping, predatory, rapacious

acquit verb **1** CLEAR, discharge, free, liberate, release, vindicate **2** BEHAVE, bear, comport, conduct, perform

acquittal noun CLEARANCE, absolution, deliverance, discharge, exoneration, liberation, release, relief, vindication

acrid adjective PUNGENT, bitter, caustic, harsh, sharp, vitriolic

acrimonious adjective BITTER, caustic, irascible, petulant, rancorous, spiteful, splenetic, testy

acrimony noun BITTERNESS, harshness, ill will, irascibility, rancor, virulence

act noun 1 DEED, accomplishment, achievement, action, exploit, feat, performance, undertaking 2 LAW, bill, decree, edict, enactment, measure, ordinance, resolution, statute 3 PERFORMANCE, routine, show, sketch, turn 4 PRETENSE, affectation, attitude, front, performance, pose, posture, show ▶verb 5 DO, carry out, enact, execute, function, operate, perform, take effect, work 6 PERFORM, act out, impersonate, mimic, play, play or take the part of, portray, represent

act for verb STAND IN FOR, cover for, deputize for, fill in for, replace, represent, substitute for, take the place of

acting noun 1 PERFORMANCE, characterization, impersonation, performing, playing, portrayal, stagecraft, theater ▶adjective 2 TEMPORARY, interim, pro tem, provisional, substitute, surrogate

action noun 1 DEED, accomplishment, achievement, act, exploit, feat, performance 2 LAWSUIT, case, litigation, proceeding, prosecution, suit 3 ENERGY, activity, force, liveliness, spirit, vigor, vim, vitality 4 MOVEMENT, activity, functioning, motion, operation, process, working 5 BATTLE, clash, combat, conflict, contest, encounter, engagement, fight, skirmish, sortie

activate verb START, arouse, energize, galvanize, initiate, mobilize, move, rouse, set in motion, stir

active adjective 1 BUSY, bustling, hard-working, involved, occupied, on the go (informal), on the move, strenuous 2 ENERGETIC, alert, animated, industrious, lively, quick, sprightly, spry, vigorous 3 IN OPERATION, acting, at work, effectual, in action, in force, operative, working

activist noun MILITANT, organizer, partisan

activity noun 1 ACTION, animation, bustle, exercise, exertion, hustle, labor, motion, movement 2 PURSUIT, hobby, interest, pastime, project, scheme

actor noun PERFORMER, actress, player, Thespian

actress noun PERFORMER, actor, leading lady, player, starlet, Thespian

actual adjective DEFINITE, concrete, factual, physical, positive, real, substantial, tangible

actually adverb REALLY, as a matter of fact, indeed, in fact, in point of fact, in reality, in truth, literally, truly

act up verb Informal MAKE A FUSS, have a fit, horse around, misbehave, raise Cain, raise hell

acumen noun JUDGMENT, astuteness, cleverness, ingenuity, insight, intelligence, perspicacity, shrewdness

acute adjective 1 SERIOUS, critical, crucial, dangerous, grave, important, severe, urgent

2 SHARP, excruciating, fierce, intense, piercing, powerful, severe, shooting, violent
3 PERCEPTIVE, astute, clever, insightful, keen, observant, sensitive, sharp, smart

acuteness noun **1** SERIOUSNESS, gravity, importance, severity, urgency **2** PERCEPTIVENESS, astuteness, cleverness, discrimination, insight, perspicacity, sharpness

adamant adjective DETERMINED, firm, fixed, obdurate, resolute, stubborn, unbending, uncompromising

adapt verb ADJUST, acclimatize, accommodate, alter, change, conform, convert, modify, remodel, tailor

adaptability noun FLEXIBILITY, changeability, resilience, versatility

adaptable adjective FLEXIBLE, adjustable, changeable, compliant, easy-going, plastic, pliant, resilient, versatile

adaptation noun
1 ACCLIMATIZATION, familiarization, naturalization
2 CONVERSION, adjustment, alteration, change, modification, transformation, variation, version

add verb **1** COUNT UP, add up, compute, reckon, total, tot up
2 INCLUDE, adjoin, affix, append, attach, augment, supplement

addendum noun ADDITION, appendage, appendix, attachment, extension, extra, postscript, supplement

addict noun **1** JUNKIE (informal), fiend (informal), freak (informal)

2 FAN, adherent, buff (informal), devotee, enthusiast, follower, nut (slang)

addicted adjective HOOKED (slang), absorbed, accustomed, dedicated, dependent, devoted, habituated

addiction noun DEPENDENCE, craving, enslavement, habit, obsession

addition noun **1** INCLUSION, adding, amplification, attachment, augmentation, enlargement, extension, increasing **2** EXTRA, addendum, additive, appendage, appendix, extension, gain, increase, increment, supplement **3** COUNTING UP, adding up, computation, totalling, totting up **4 in addition (to)** AS WELL (AS), additionally, also, besides, into the bargain, moreover, over and above, to boot, too

additional adjective EXTRA, added, fresh, further, new, other, spare, supplementary

address noun **1** LOCATION, abode, dwelling, home, house, residence, situation, whereabouts **2** SPEECH, discourse, dissertation, lecture, oration, sermon, talk ▶ verb **3** SPEAK TO, approach, greet, hail, talk to **4 address (oneself) to** CONCENTRATE ON, apply (oneself) to, attend to, devote (oneself) to, engage in, focus on, take care of

add up verb COUNT UP, add, compute, count, reckon, total, tot up

adept adjective **1** SKILLFUL, able, accomplished, adroit, expert, practiced, proficient, skilled, versed ▸ *noun* 2 EXPERT, genius, hotshot (*informal*), master

adequacy *noun* SUFFICIENCY, capability, competence, fairness, suitability, tolerability

adequate *adjective* ENOUGH, competent, fair, satisfactory, sufficient, tolerable, up to scratch (*informal*)

adhere *verb* STICK, attach, cleave, cling, fasten, fix, glue, hold fast, paste

adherent *noun* SUPPORTER, admirer, devotee, disciple, fan, follower, upholder

adhesive *adjective* 1 STICKY, clinging, cohesive, gluey, glutinous, tenacious ▸ *noun* 2 GLUE, cement, gum, paste

adieu *noun* GOOD-BYE, farewell, leave-taking, parting, valediction

adjacent *adjective* NEXT, adjoining, beside, bordering, cheek by jowl, close, near, neighboring, next door, touching

adjoin *verb* CONNECT, border, join, link, touch

adjoining *adjective* CONNECTING, abutting, adjacent, bordering, neighboring, next door, touching

adjourn *verb* POSTPONE, defer, delay, discontinue, interrupt, put off, suspend

adjournment *noun* POSTPONEMENT, delay, discontinuation, interruption, putting off, recess, suspension

adjudicate *verb* JUDGE, adjudge, arbitrate, decide, determine, mediate, referee, settle, umpire

adjudication *noun* JUDGMENT,

arbitration, conclusion, decision, finding, pronouncement, ruling, settlement, verdict

adjust *verb* ALTER, accustom, adapt, make conform, modify

adjustable *adjective* ALTERABLE, adaptable, flexible, malleable, modifiable, movable

adjustment *noun* 1 ALTERATION, adaptation, modification, redress, regulation, settling 2 ACCLIMATIZATION, orientation, settling in

ad-lib *verb* IMPROVISE, busk, extemporize, make up, speak off the cuff, wing it (*informal*)

administer *verb* 1 MANAGE, conduct, control, direct, govern, handle, oversee, run, supervise 2 GIVE, apply, dispense, impose, mete out, perform, provide

administration *noun* MANAGEMENT, application, conduct, control, direction, government, running, supervision

administrative *adjective* MANAGERIAL, directorial, executive, governmental, organizational, regulatory, supervisory

administrator *noun* MANAGER, bureaucrat, executive, official, organizer, supervisor

admirable *adjective* EXCELLENT, commendable, exquisite, fine, laudable, praiseworthy, wonderful, worthy

admiration *noun* REGARD, amazement, appreciation, approval, esteem, praise, respect, wonder

admire *verb* 1 RESPECT,

appreciate, approve, esteem, look up to, praise, prize, think highly of, value 2 MARVEL AT, appreciate, delight in, take pleasure in, wonder at

admirer noun 1 SUITOR, beau, boyfriend, lover, sweetheart, wooer 2 FAN, devotee, disciple, enthusiast, follower, partisan, supporter

admissible adjective PERMISSIBLE, acceptable, allowable, passable, tolerable

admission noun 1 ENTRANCE, acceptance, access, admittance, entrée, entry, initiation, introduction 2 CONFESSION, acknowledgment, allowance, declaration, disclosure, divulgence, revelation

admit verb 1 CONFESS, acknowledge, declare, disclose, divulge, fess up (informal), own, reveal 2 ALLOW, agree, grant, let, permit, recognize 3 LET IN, accept, allow, give access, initiate, introduce, receive, take in

admonish verb REPRIMAND, berate, chide, rebuke, scold, slap on the wrist, tell off (informal)

adolescence noun 1 YOUTH, boyhood, girlhood, minority, teens 2 YOUTHFULNESS, childishness, immaturity

adolescent adjective 1 YOUNG, boyish, girlish, immature, juvenile, puerile, teenage, youthful ▸ noun 2 YOUTH, juvenile, minor, teenager, youngster

adopt verb 1 FOSTER, take in 2 CHOOSE, assume, espouse,

follow, maintain, take up

adoption noun 1 FOSTERING, adopting, taking in 2 CHOICE, appropriation, assumption, embracing, endorsement, espousal, selection, taking up

adorable adjective LOVABLE, appealing, attractive, charming, cute, dear, delightful, fetching, pleasing

adore verb LOVE, admire, cherish, dote on, esteem, exalt, glorify, honor, idolize, put on a pedestal (informal), revere, worship

adoring adjective LOVING, admiring, affectionate, devoted, doting, fond

adorn verb DECORATE, array, embellish, festoon

adornment noun DECORATION, accessory, embellishment, festoon, frill, frippery, ornament, supplement, trimming

adrift adjective 1 DRIFTING, afloat, unanchored, unmoored 2 AIMLESS, directionless, goalless, purposeless ▸ adverb 3 WRONG, amiss, astray, off course

adroit adjective SKILLFUL, adept, clever, deft, dexterous, expert, masterful, neat, proficient, skilled

adulation noun WORSHIP, fawning, fulsome praise, servile flattery, sycophancy

adult noun 1 GROWN-UP, grown or grown-up person (man or woman), person of mature age ▸ adjective 2 FULLY GROWN, full grown, fully developed, grown-up, mature, of age, ripe

advance verb 1 PROGRESS, come

forward, go on, hasten, make inroads, proceed, speed **2** BENEFIT, further, improve, prosper **3** SUGGEST, offer, present, proffer, put forward, submit **4** LEND, pay beforehand, supply on credit ▶ noun **5** PROGRESS, advancement, development, forward movement, headway, inroads, onward movement **6** IMPROVEMENT, breakthrough, gain, growth, progress, promotion, step **7** LOAN, credit, deposit, down payment, prepayment, retainer **8 advances** OVERTURES, approach, approaches, moves, proposals, proposition ▶ adjective **9** PRIOR, beforehand, early, in front **10 in advance** BEFOREHAND, ahead, earlier, previously

advanced adjective FOREMOST, ahead, avant-garde, forward, higher, leading, precocious, progressive

advancement noun PROMOTION, betterment, gain, improvement, preferment, progress, rise

advantage noun BENEFIT, ascendancy, dominance, good, help, lead, precedence, profit, superiority, sway

advantageous adjective **1** BENEFICIAL, convenient, expedient, helpful, of service, profitable, useful, valuable, worthwhile **2** SUPERIOR, dominant, dominating, favorable, win-win (informal)

adventure noun ESCAPADE, enterprise, experience, exploit, incident, occurrence, undertaking, venture

adventurer noun **1** MERCENARY, charlatan, fortune-hunter, gambler, opportunist, rogue, speculator **2** HERO, daredevil, heroine, knight-errant, traveler, voyager

adventurous adjective DARING, bold, daredevil, enterprising, intrepid, reckless

adversary noun OPPONENT, antagonist, competitor, contestant, enemy, foe, rival

adverse adjective UNFAVORABLE, contrary, detrimental, hostile, inopportune, negative, opposing

adversity noun HARDSHIP, affliction, bad luck, disaster, distress, hard times, misfortune, reverse, trouble

advertise verb PUBLICIZE, announce, inform, make known, notify, plug (informal), promote, tout

advertisement noun NOTICE, ad (informal), announcement, blurb, circular, commercial, plug (informal), poster

advice noun GUIDANCE, counsel, help, opinion, recommendation, suggestion

advisability noun WISDOM, appropriateness, aptness, desirability, expediency, fitness, propriety, prudence, suitability

advisable adjective WISE, appropriate, desirable, expedient, fitting, politic, prudent, recommended, seemly, sensible

advise verb **1** RECOMMEND, admonish, caution, commend, counsel, prescribe, suggest, urge **2** NOTIFY, acquaint, apprise, inform, make known, report, tell, warn

adviser noun GUIDE, aide, confidant or (fem.) confidante, consultant, counselor, helper, mentor, right-hand man

advisory adjective ADVISING, consultative, counseling, helping, recommending

advocate verb 1 RECOMMEND, advise, argue for, campaign for, champion, commend, encourage, promote, propose, support, uphold ▶ noun 2 SUPPORTER, campaigner, champion, counselor, defender, promoter, proponent, spokesman, upholder 3 Law LAWYER, attorney, barrister, counsel

affable adjective FRIENDLY, amiable, amicable, approachable, congenial, cordial, courteous, genial, pleasant, sociable, urbane

affair noun 1 EVENT, activity, business, episode, happening, incident, matter, occurrence 2 RELATIONSHIP, amour, intrigue, liaison, romance

affect[1] verb 1 INFLUENCE, act on, alter, bear upon, change, concern, impinge upon, relate to 2 MOVE, disturb, overcome, perturb, stir, touch, upset

affect[2] verb PUT ON, adopt, aspire to, assume, contrive, feign, imitate, pretend, simulate

affectation noun PRETENSE, act, artificiality, assumed manners, façade, insincerity, pose, pretentiousness, show

affected adjective PRETENDED, artificial, contrived, feigned, insincere, mannered, phoney or phony (informal), put-on,

unnatural

affecting adjective MOVING, pathetic, pitiful, poignant, sad, touching

affection noun FONDNESS, attachment, care, feeling, goodwill, kindness, liking, love, tenderness, warmth

affectionate adjective FOND, attached, caring, devoted, doting, friendly, kind, loving, tender, warm-hearted

affiliate verb JOIN, ally, amalgamate, associate, band together, combine, incorporate, link, unite

affinity noun 1 ATTRACTION, fondness, inclination, leaning, liking, partiality, rapport, sympathy 2 SIMILARITY, analogy, closeness, connection, correspondence, kinship, likeness, relationship, resemblance

affirm verb DECLARE, assert, certify, confirm, maintain, pronounce, state, swear, testify

affirmation noun DECLARATION, assertion, certification, confirmation, oath, pronouncement, statement, testimony

affirmative adjective AGREEING, approving, assenting, concurring, confirming, consenting, corroborative, favorable, positive

afflict verb TORMENT, distress, grieve, harass, hurt, oppress, pain, plague, trouble

affliction noun SUFFERING, adversity, curse, disease, hardship, misfortune, ordeal, plague, scourge, torment, trial, trouble, woe

affluence noun WEALTH, abundance, fortune, opulence, plenty, prosperity, riches

affluent adjective WEALTHY, loaded (slang), moneyed, opulent, prosperous, rich, well-heeled (informal), well-off, well-to-do

afford verb 1 As in **can afford** SPARE, bear, manage, stand, sustain 2 GIVE, offer, produce, provide, render, supply, yield

affordable adjective INEXPENSIVE, cheap, economical, low-cost, moderate, modest, reasonable

affront noun 1 INSULT, offense, outrage, provocation, slap in the face (informal), slight, slur ▶verb 2 OFFEND, anger, annoy, displease, insult, outrage, provoke, slight

aflame adjective BURNING, ablaze, alight, blazing, fiery, flaming, lit, on fire

afoot adverb GOING ON, abroad, brewing, current, happening, in preparation, in progress, on the go (informal), up (informal)

afraid adjective 1 SCARED, apprehensive, cowardly, faint-hearted, fearful, frightened, nervous, wired (slang) 2 SORRY, regretful, unhappy

afresh adverb AGAIN, anew, newly, once again, once more, over again

after adverb FOLLOWING, afterwards, behind, below, later, subsequently, succeeding, thereafter

aftermath noun EFFECTS, aftereffects, consequences, end result, outcome, results, sequel, upshot, wake

again adverb 1 ONCE MORE, afresh, anew, another time 2 ALSO, besides, furthermore, in addition, moreover

against preposition 1 BESIDE, abutting, facing, in contact with, on, opposite to, touching, upon 2 OPPOSED TO, anti (informal), averse to, hostile to, in defiance of, in opposition to, resisting, versus 3 IN PREPARATION FOR, in anticipation of, in expectation of, in provision for

age noun 1 TIME, date, day(s), duration, epoch, era, generation, lifetime, period, span 2 OLD AGE, advancing years, decline (of life), majority, maturity, senescence, senility, seniority ▶verb 3 GROW OLD, decline, deteriorate, mature, mellow, ripen

aged adjective OLD, ancient, antiquated, antique, elderly, getting on, gray

agency noun 1 BUSINESS, bureau, department, office, organization 2 Old-fashioned MEDIUM, activity, means, mechanism

agenda noun LIST, calendar, diary, plan, program, schedule, timetable

agent noun 1 REPRESENTATIVE, envoy, go-between, negotiator, rep (informal), surrogate 2 WORKER, author, doer, mover, operator, performer 3 FORCE, agency, cause, instrument, means, power, vehicle

aggravate verb 1 MAKE WORSE, exacerbate, exaggerate, increase, inflame, intensify, magnify, worsen 2 Informal

ANNOY, bother, get on one's nerves (*informal*), irritate, nettle, provoke

aggravation noun 1 WORSENING, exacerbation, exaggeration, heightening, increase, inflaming, intensification, magnification 2 *Informal* ANNOYANCE, exasperation, gall, grief (*informal*), hassle (*informal*), irritation, provocation

aggregate noun 1 TOTAL, accumulation, amount, body, bulk, collection, combination, mass, pile, sum, whole ▶ adjective 2 TOTAL, accumulated, collected, combined, composite, cumulative, mixed ▶ verb 3 COMBINE, accumulate, amass, assemble, collect, heap, mix, pile

aggression noun 1 HOSTILITY, antagonism, belligerence, destructiveness, pugnacity 2 ATTACK, assault, injury, invasion, offensive, onslaught, raid

aggressive adjective 1 HOSTILE, belligerent, destructive, offensive, pugnacious, quarrelsome 2 FORCEFUL, assertive, bold, dynamic, energetic, enterprising, militant, pushy (*informal*), vigorous

aggressor noun ATTACKER, assailant, assaulter, invader

aggrieved adjective HURT, afflicted, distressed, disturbed, harmed, injured, unhappy, wronged

aghast adjective HORRIFIED, amazed, appalled, astonished, astounded, awestruck,

confounded, shocked, startled, stunned

agile adjective 1 NIMBLE, active, brisk, lithe, quick, sprightly, spry, supple, swift 2 ACUTE, alert, bright (*informal*), clever, lively, quick-witted, sharp

agility noun NIMBLENESS, litheness, liveliness, quickness, suppleness, swiftness

agitate verb 1 UPSET, disconcert, distract, excite, fluster, perturb, trouble, unnerve, worry 2 STIR, beat, convulse, disturb, rouse, shake, toss

agitation noun 1 TURMOIL, clamor, commotion, confusion, disturbance, excitement, ferment, trouble, upheaval 2 TURBULENCE, convulsion, disturbance, shaking, stirring, tossing

agitator noun TROUBLEMAKER, agent provocateur, firebrand, instigator, rabble-rouser, revolutionary, stirrer (*informal*)

agog adjective EAGER, avid, curious, enthralled, enthusiastic, excited, expectant, impatient, in suspense, wired (*slang*)

agonize verb SUFFER, be distressed, be in agony, be in anguish, go through the mill, labor, strain, struggle, worry

agony noun SUFFERING, anguish, distress, misery, pain, throes, torment, torture

agree verb 1 CONSENT, assent, be of the same opinion, comply, concur, see eye to eye 2 GET ON (TOGETHER), coincide, conform, correspond, match, tally

agreeable adjective 1 PLEASANT,

delightful, enjoyable, gratifying, likable or likeable, pleasing, satisfying, to one's taste **2** CONSENTING, amenable, approving, complying, concurring, in accord, onside (*informal*), sympathetic, well-disposed, willing

agreement *noun* **1** ASSENT, agreeing, compliance, concord, concurrence, consent, harmony, union, unison **2** CORRESPONDENCE, compatibility, conformity, congruity, consistency, similarity **3** CONTRACT, arrangement, bargain, covenant, deal (*informal*), pact, settlement, treaty, understanding

agricultural *adjective* FARMING, agrarian, country, rural, rustic

agriculture *noun* FARMING, cultivation, culture, husbandry, tillage

aground *adverb* BEACHED, ashore, foundered, grounded, high and dry, on the rocks, stranded, stuck

ahead *adverb* IN FRONT, at an advantage, at the head, before, in advance, in the lead, leading, to the fore, winning

aid *noun* **1** HELP, assistance, benefit, encouragement, favor, promotion, relief, service, support ▸ *verb* **2** HELP, assist, encourage, favor, promote, serve, subsidize, support, sustain

aide *noun* ASSISTANT, attendant, helper, right-hand man, second, supporter

ailing *adjective* ILL, indisposed, infirm, poorly, sick, under the

weather (*informal*), unwell, weak

ailment *noun* ILLNESS, affliction, complaint, disease, disorder, infirmity, malady, sickness

aim *verb* **1** INTEND, attempt, endeavor, mean, plan, point, propose, seek, set one's sights on, strive, try ▸ *noun* **2** INTENTION, ambition, aspiration, desire, goal, objective, plan, purpose, target

aimless *adjective* PURPOSELESS, directionless, pointless, random, stray

air *noun* **1** ATMOSPHERE, heavens, sky **2** WIND, breeze, draft, zephyr **3** MANNER, appearance, atmosphere, aura, demeanor, impression, look, mood **4** TUNE, aria, lay, melody, song ▸ *verb* **5** PUBLICIZE, circulate, display, exhibit, express, give vent to, make known, make public, reveal, voice **6** VENTILATE, aerate, expose, freshen

airborne *adjective* FLYING, floating, gliding, hovering, in flight, in the air, on the wing

airing *noun* **1** VENTILATION, aeration, drying, freshening **2** EXPOSURE, circulation, display, dissemination, expression, publicity, utterance, vent

airless *adjective* STUFFY, close, heavy, muggy, oppressive, stifling, suffocating, sultry

airs *plural noun* AFFECTATION, arrogance, haughtiness, hauteur, pomposity, pretensions, superciliousness

airy *adjective* **1** WELL-VENTILATED, fresh, light, open, spacious, uncluttered **2** LIGHT-HEARTED, blithe, cheerful, high-spirited, jaunty, lively, sprightly

aisle noun PASSAGEWAY, alley, corridor, gangway, lane, passage, path

alacrity noun EAGERNESS, alertness, enthusiasm, promptness, quickness, readiness, speed, willingness, zeal

alarm noun 1 FEAR, anxiety, apprehension, consternation, fright, nervousness, panic, scare, trepidation 2 DANGER SIGNAL, alarm bell, alert, bell, distress signal, hooter, siren, warning ▶ verb 3 FRIGHTEN, daunt, dismay, distress, give (someone) a fright (informal), panic, scare, startle, unnerve

alarming adjective FRIGHTENING, daunting, distressing, disturbing, scaring, shocking, startling, unnerving

alcoholic noun 1 DRUNKARD, dipsomaniac, drinker, drunk, inebriate, tippler, toper, wino (informal) ▶ adjective 2 INTOXICATING, brewed, distilled, fermented, hard, strong

alcove noun RECESS, bay, compartment, corner, cubbyhole, cubicle, niche, nook

alert adjective 1 WATCHFUL, attentive, awake, circumspect, heedful, observant, on guard, on one's toes, on the lookout, vigilant, wide-awake ▶ noun 2 WARNING, alarm, signal, siren ▶ verb 3 WARN, alarm, forewarn, inform, notify, signal

alertness noun WATCHFULNESS, attentiveness, heedfulness, liveliness, vigilance

alias adverb 1 ALSO KNOWN AS, also called, otherwise, otherwise known as ▶ noun 2 PSEUDONYM, assumed name, nom de guerre, nom de plume, pen name, stage name

alibi noun EXCUSE, defense, explanation, justification, plea, pretext, reason

alien adjective 1 FOREIGN, exotic, incongruous, strange, unfamiliar ▶ noun 2 FOREIGNER, newcomer, outsider, stranger

alienate verb SET AGAINST, disaffect, estrange, make unfriendly, shut out, turn away

alienation noun SETTING AGAINST, disaffection, estrangement, remoteness, separation, turning away

alight^1 verb 1 GET OFF, descend, disembark, dismount, get down 2 LAND, come down, come to rest, descend, light, perch, settle, touch down

alight^2 adjective 1 ON FIRE, ablaze, aflame, blazing, burning, fiery, flaming, lighted, lit 2 LIT UP, bright, brilliant, illuminated, shining

align verb 1 ALLY, affiliate, agree, associate, cooperate, join, side, sympathize 2 LINE UP, even up, order, range, regulate, straighten

alignment noun 1 ALLIANCE, affiliation, agreement, association, cooperation, sympathy, union 2 LINING UP, adjustment, arrangement, evening up, order, straightening up

alike adjective 1 SIMILAR, akin, analogous, corresponding, identical, of a piece, parallel, resembling, the same ▶ adverb 2 SIMILARLY, analogously, correspondingly, equally, evenly, identically, uniformly

alive *adjective* **1** LIVING, animate, breathing, in the land of the living (*informal*), subsisting **2** IN EXISTENCE, active, existing, extant, functioning, in force, operative **3** LIVELY, active, alert, animated, energetic, full of life, vital, vivacious

all *adjective* **1** THE WHOLE OF, every bit of, the complete, the entire, the sum of, the totality of, the total of **2** EVERY, each, each and every, every one of, every single **3** COMPLETE, entire, full, greatest, perfect, total, utter ▶ *adverb* **4** COMPLETELY, altogether, entirely, fully, totally, utterly, wholly ▶ *noun* **5** WHOLE AMOUNT, aggregate, entirety, everything, sum total, total, totality, utmost

allegation *noun* CLAIM, accusation, affirmation, assertion, charge, declaration, statement

allege *verb* CLAIM, affirm, assert, charge, declare, maintain, state

alleged *adjective* **1** STATED, affirmed, asserted, declared, described, designated **2** SUPPOSED, doubtful, dubious, ostensible, professed, purported, so-called, unproved

allegiance *noun* LOYALTY, constancy, devotion, faithfulness, fidelity, obedience

allegorical *adjective* SYMBOLIC, emblematic, figurative, symbolizing

allegory *noun* SYMBOL, fable, myth, parable, story, symbolism, tale

allergic *adjective* SENSITIVE,

affected by, hypersensitive, susceptible

allergy *noun* SENSITIVITY, antipathy, hypersensitivity, susceptibility

alleviate *verb* EASE, allay, lessen, lighten, moderate, reduce, relieve, soothe

alley *noun* PASSAGE, alleyway, backstreet, lane, passageway, pathway, walk

alliance *noun* UNION, affiliation, agreement, association, coalition, combination, confederation, connection, federation, league, marriage, pact, partnership, treaty

allied *adjective* UNITED, affiliated, associated, combined, connected, in league, linked, related

allocate *verb* ASSIGN, allot, allow, apportion, budget, designate, earmark, mete, set aside, share out

allocation *noun* ASSIGNMENT, allotment, allowance, lot, portion, quota, ration, share

allot *verb* ASSIGN, allocate, apportion, budget, designate, earmark, mete, set aside, share out

allotment *noun* **1** PLOT, kitchen garden, patch, tract **2** ASSIGNMENT, allocation, allowance, grant, portion, quota, ration, share, stint

all-out *adjective* TOTAL, complete, exhaustive, full, full-scale, maximum, thoroughgoing, undivided, unremitting, unrestrained

allow *verb* **1** PERMIT, approve, authorize, enable, endure, let, sanction, stand, suffer, tolerate

2 GIVE, allocate, allot, assign, grant, provide, set aside, spare **3** ACKNOWLEDGE, admit, concede, confess, grant, own

allowable adjective PERMISSIBLE, acceptable, admissible, all right, appropriate, suitable, tolerable

allowance noun **1** PORTION, allocation, amount, grant, lot, quota, ration, share, stint **2** CONCESSION, deduction, discount, rebate, reduction

allow for verb TAKE INTO ACCOUNT, consider, make allowances for, make concessions for, make provision for, plan for, provide for, take into consideration

alloy noun **1** MIXTURE, admixture, amalgam, blend, combination, composite, compound, hybrid ▶verb **2** MIX, amalgamate, blend, combine, compound, fuse

all right adjective **1** SATISFACTORY, acceptable, adequate, average, fair, O.K. or okay (informal), standard, up to scratch (informal) **2** O.K. or OKAY (informal), healthy, safe, sound, unharmed, uninjured, well, whole

allude verb REFER, hint, imply, intimate, mention, suggest, touch upon

allure noun **1** ATTRACTIVENESS, appeal, attraction, charm, enchantment, enticement, glamour, lure, persuasion, seductiveness, temptation ▶verb **2** ATTRACT, captivate, charm, enchant, entice, lure, persuade, seduce, tempt, win over

alluring adjective ATTRACTIVE, beguiling, captivating, come-hither, fetching, glamorous, seductive, tempting

allusion noun REFERENCE, casual remark, hint, implication, innuendo, insinuation, intimation, mention, suggestion

ally noun **1** PARTNER, accomplice, associate, collaborator, colleague, friend, helper, homeboy (slang), homegirl (slang) ▶verb **2** UNITE, associate, collaborate, combine, join, join forces, unify

almighty adjective **1** ALL-POWERFUL, absolute, invincible, omnipotent, supreme, unlimited **2** Informal GREAT, enormous, excessive, intense, loud, severe, terrible

almost adverb NEARLY, about, approximately, close to, just about, not quite, on the brink of, practically, virtually

alone adjective BY ONESELF, apart, detached, isolated, lonely, only, separate, single, solitary, unaccompanied

aloof adjective DISTANT, detached, haughty, remote, standoffish, supercilious, unapproachable, unfriendly

aloud adverb OUT LOUD, audibly, clearly, distinctly, intelligibly, plainly

already adverb BEFORE NOW, at present, before, by now, by then, even now, heretofore, just now, previously

also adverb TOO, additionally, and, as well, besides, further, furthermore, in addition, into the bargain, moreover, to boot

alter verb CHANGE, adapt, adjust,

amend, convert, modify,
reform, revise, transform, turn,
vary

alteration noun CHANGE,
adaptation, adjustment,
amendment, conversion,
difference, modification,
reformation, revision,
transformation, variation

alternate verb **1** CHANGE, act
reciprocally, fluctuate,
interchange, oscillate, rotate,
substitute, take turns ▶ adjective
2 EVERY OTHER, alternating, every
second, interchanging, rotating

alternative noun **1** CHOICE,
option, other (of two),
preference, recourse, selection,
substitute ▶ adjective **2** DIFFERENT,
alternate, another, other,
second, substitute

alternatively adverb OR, as an
alternative, if not, instead, on
the other hand, otherwise

although conjunction THOUGH,
albeit, despite the fact that,
even if, even though,
notwithstanding, while

altogether adverb **1** COMPLETELY,
absolutely, fully, perfectly,
quite, thoroughly, totally,
utterly, wholly **2** ON THE WHOLE,
all in all, all things considered,
as a whole, collectively,
generally, in general **3** IN TOTAL,
all told, everything included, in
all, in sum, taken together

altruistic adjective SELFLESS,
benevolent, charitable,
generous, humanitarian,
philanthropic, public-spirited,
self-sacrificing, unselfish

always adverb CONTINUALLY,
consistently, constantly,
eternally, evermore, every

time, forever, invariably,
perpetually, repeatedly,
twenty-four-seven (slang),
without exception

amalgamate verb COMBINE, ally,
blend, fuse, incorporate,
integrate, merge, mingle, unite

amalgamation noun
COMBINATION, blend, coalition,
compound, fusion, joining,
merger, mixture, union

amass verb COLLECT, accumulate,
assemble, compile, gather,
hoard, pile up

amateur noun NONPROFESSIONAL,
dabbler, dilettante, layman

amateurish adjective
UNPROFESSIONAL, amateur,
bungling, clumsy, crude,
inexpert, unaccomplished

amaze verb ASTONISH, alarm,
astound, bewilder,
dumbfound, shock, stagger,
startle, stun, surprise

amazement noun ASTONISHMENT,
admiration, bewilderment,
confusion, perplexity, shock,
surprise, wonder

amazing adjective ASTONISHING,
astounding, breathtaking,
eye-opening, overwhelming,
staggering, startling, stunning,
surprising

ambassador noun REPRESENTATIVE,
agent, consul, deputy,
diplomat, envoy, legate,
minister

ambiguity noun VAGUENESS,
doubt, dubiousness,
equivocation, obscurity,
uncertainty

ambiguous adjective UNCLEAR,
dubious, enigmatic, equivocal,
inconclusive, indefinite,
indeterminate, obscure, vague

ambition noun **1** ENTERPRISE, aspiration, desire, drive, eagerness, longing, striving, yearning, zeal **2** GOAL, aim, aspiration, desire, dream, hope, intent, objective, purpose, wish

ambitious adjective ENTERPRISING, aspiring, avid, eager, hopeful, intent, purposeful, striving, zealous

ambivalent adjective UNDECIDED, contradictory, doubtful, equivocal, in two minds, uncertain, wavering

amble verb STROLL, dawdle, meander, mosey (informal), ramble, saunter, walk, wander

ambush noun **1** TRAP, lying in wait, waylaying ▶ verb **2** TRAP, attack, bushwhack (U.S.), ensnare, surprise, waylay

amenable adjective RECEPTIVE, able to be influenced, acquiescent, agreeable, open, persuadable, responsive, susceptible

amend verb CHANGE, alter, correct, fix, improve, mend, modify, reform, remedy, repair, revise

amendment noun **1** CHANGE, alteration, correction, emendation, improvement, modification, reform, remedy, repair, revision **2** ALTERATION, addendum, addition, attachment, clarification

amends plural noun As in **make amends for** COMPENSATION, atonement, recompense, redress, reparation, restitution, satisfaction

amenity noun FACILITY, advantage, comfort, convenience, service

amiable adjective PLEASANT, affable, agreeable, charming, congenial, engaging, friendly, genial, likable or likeable, lovable

amicable adjective FRIENDLY, amiable, civil, cordial, courteous, harmonious, neighborly, peaceful, sociable

amid, amidst preposition IN THE MIDDLE OF, among, amongst, in the midst of, in the thick of, surrounded by

amiss adverb **1** WRONGLY, erroneously, improperly, inappropriately, incorrectly, mistakenly, unsuitably **2** As in **take (something) amiss** AS AN INSULT, as offensive, out of turn, wrongly ▶ adjective **3** WRONG, awry, faulty, incorrect, mistaken, untoward

ammunition noun MUNITIONS, armaments, explosives, powder, rounds, shells, shot

amnesty noun GENERAL PARDON, absolution, dispensation, forgiveness, immunity, remission (of penalty), reprieve

amok, amuck adverb As in **run amok** MADLY, berserk, destructively, ferociously, in a frenzy, murderously, savagely, uncontrollably, violently, wildly

among, amongst preposition **1** IN THE MIDST OF, amid, amidst, in the middle of, in the thick of, surrounded by, together with, with **2** IN THE GROUP OF, in the class of, in the company of, in the number of, out of **3** TO EACH OF, between

amorous adjective LOVING, erotic, impassioned, in love, lustful, passionate, tender

amount noun QUANTITY, expanse, extent, magnitude, mass, measure, number, supply, volume

amount to verb ADD UP TO, become, come to, develop into, equal, mean, total

ample adjective PLENTY, abundant, bountiful, copious, expansive, extensive, full, generous, lavish, plentiful, profuse

amplify verb **1** EXPLAIN, develop, elaborate, enlarge, expand, flesh out, go into detail **2** INCREASE, enlarge, expand, extend, heighten, intensify, magnify, strengthen, widen

amply adverb FULLY, abundantly, completely, copiously, generously, profusely, richly

amputate verb CUT OFF, curtail, lop, remove, separate, sever, truncate

amuck see AMOK

amuse verb ENTERTAIN, charm, cheer, delight, interest, please, tickle

amusement noun **1** ENTERTAINMENT, cheer, enjoyment, fun, merriment, mirth, pleasure **2** ENTERTAINMENT, diversion, game, hobby, joke, pastime, recreation, sport

amusing adjective FUNNY, comical, droll, enjoyable, entertaining, humorous, interesting, witty

analogy noun SIMILARITY, comparison, correlation, correspondence, likeness, parallel, relation, resemblance

analysis noun EXAMINATION, breakdown, dissection, inquiry,

investigation, perusal, scrutiny, sifting, test

analytic, analytical adjective RATIONAL, inquiring, inquisitive, investigative, logical, organized, problem-solving, systematic

analyze verb **1** EXAMINE, evaluate, investigate, research, test, work over **2** BREAK DOWN, dissect, divide, resolve, separate, think through

anarchic adjective LAWLESS, chaotic, disorganized, rebellious, riotous, ungoverned

anarchist noun REVOLUTIONARY, insurgent, nihilist, rebel, terrorist

anarchy noun LAWLESSNESS, chaos, confusion, disorder, disorganization, revolution, riot

anatomy noun **1** EXAMINATION, analysis, dissection, division, inquiry, investigation, study **2** STRUCTURE, build, composition, frame, framework, make-up

ancestor noun FOREFATHER, forebear, forerunner, precursor, predecessor

ancient adjective OLD, aged, antique, archaic, old-fashioned, primeval, primordial, timeworn

ancillary adjective SUPPLEMENTARY, additional, auxiliary, extra, secondary, subordinate, subsidiary, supporting

and conjunction ALSO, along with, as well as, furthermore, in addition to, including, moreover, plus, together with

anecdote noun STORY, reminiscence, short story, sketch, tale, urban legend, yarn

anemic adjective PALE, ashen, colorless, feeble, pallid, sickly, wan, weak

anesthetic noun **1** PAINKILLER, analgesic, anodyne, narcotic, opiate, sedative, soporific ▶*adjective* **2** PAIN-KILLING, analgesic, anodyne, deadening, dulling, numbing, sedative, soporific

angel noun **1** DIVINE MESSENGER, archangel, cherub, seraph **2** *Informal* DEAR, beauty, darling, gem, jewel, paragon, saint, treasure

angelic *adjective* **1** PURE, adorable, beautiful, entrancing, lovely, saintly, virtuous **2** HEAVENLY, celestial, cherubic, ethereal, seraphic

anger noun **1** RAGE, annoyance, displeasure, exasperation, fury, ire, outrage, resentment, temper, wrath ▶*verb* **2** MADDEN, annoy, displease, enrage, exasperate, gall, incense, infuriate, outrage, rile, vex

angle[1] noun **1** INTERSECTION, bend, corner, crook, edge, elbow, knee, point **2** POINT OF VIEW, approach, aspect, outlook, perspective, position, side, slant, standpoint, viewpoint

angle[2] *verb* FISH, cast

angry *adjective* FURIOUS, annoyed, cross, displeased, enraged, exasperated, incensed, infuriated, irate, mad, outraged, resentful

angst noun ANXIETY, apprehension, unease, worry

anguish noun SUFFERING, agony, distress, grief, heartache, misery, pain, sorrow, torment, woe

animal noun **1** CREATURE, beast, brute **2** *Applied to a person* BRUTE, barbarian, beast, monster, savage, wild man ▶*adjective* **3** PHYSICAL, bestial, bodily, brutish, carnal, gross, sensual

animate *verb* **1** ENLIVEN, energize, excite, fire, inspire, invigorate, kindle, move, stimulate ▶*adjective* **2** LIVING, alive, alive and kicking, breathing, live, moving

animated *adjective* LIVELY, ebullient, energetic, enthusiastic, excited, passionate, spirited, vivacious, wired (*slang*)

animation noun LIVELINESS, ebullience, energy, enthusiasm, excitement, fervor, passion, spirit, verve, vivacity, zest

animosity noun HOSTILITY, acrimony, antipathy, bitterness, enmity, hatred, ill will, malevolence, malice, rancor, resentment

annals *plural noun* RECORDS, accounts, archives, chronicles, history

annex *verb* **1** SEIZE, acquire, appropriate, conquer, occupy, take over **2** JOIN, add, adjoin, attach, connect, fasten

annihilate *verb* DESTROY, abolish, decimate, eradicate, exterminate, extinguish, obliterate, wipe out

announce *verb* MAKE KNOWN, advertise, broadcast, declare, disclose, proclaim, report, reveal, tell

announcement noun STATEMENT, advertisement, broadcast, bulletin, communiqué, declaration, proclamation, report, revelation

announcer noun PRESENTER, broadcaster, commentator, master of ceremonies, newscaster, newsreader, reporter

annoy verb IRRITATE, anger, bother, displease, disturb, exasperate, get on one's nerves (*informal*), hassle (*informal*), madden, molest, pester, plague, trouble, vex

annoyance noun 1 IRRITATION, anger, bother, hassle (*informal*), nuisance, trouble 2 NUISANCE, bore, bother, drag (*informal*), pain (*informal*)

annoying adjective IRRITATING, disturbing, exasperating, maddening, troublesome

annual adjective YEARLY, once a year, yearlong

annually adverb YEARLY, by the year, once a year, per annum, per year

annul verb INVALIDATE, abolish, cancel, declare or render null and void, negate, nullify, repeal, retract

anoint verb CONSECRATE, bless, hallow, sanctify

anomalous adjective UNUSUAL, abnormal, eccentric, exceptional, incongruous, inconsistent, irregular, odd, peculiar

anomaly noun IRREGULARITY, abnormality, eccentricity, exception, incongruity, inconsistency, oddity, peculiarity

anonymous adjective UNNAMED, incognito, nameless, unacknowledged, uncredited, unidentified, unknown,

unsigned

answer verb 1 REPLY, explain, react, resolve, respond, retort, return, solve ▶ noun 2 REPLY, comeback, defense, explanation, reaction, rejoinder, response, retort, return, riposte, solution

answerable adjective (usually with for or to) RESPONSIBLE, accountable, amenable, chargeable, liable, subject, to blame

answer for verb BE RESPONSIBLE FOR, be accountable for, be answerable for, be chargeable for, be liable for, be to blame for

antagonism noun HOSTILITY, antipathy, conflict, discord, dissension, friction, opposition, rivalry

antagonist noun OPPONENT, adversary, competitor, contender, enemy, foe, rival

antagonistic adjective HOSTILE, at odds, at variance, conflicting, incompatible, in dispute, opposed, unfriendly

antagonize verb ANNOY, anger, get on one's nerves (*informal*), hassle (*informal*), irritate, offend

anthem noun 1 HYMN, canticle, carol, chant, chorale, psalm 2 SONG OF PRAISE, paean

anthology noun COLLECTION, compendium, compilation, miscellany, selection, treasury

anticipate verb EXPECT, await, foresee, foretell, hope for, look forward to, predict, prepare for

anticipation noun EXPECTATION, expectancy, foresight, forethought, premonition, prescience

anticlimax noun DISAPPOINTMENT, bathos, comedown (*informal*), letdown

antics plural noun CLOWNING, escapades, elderliness, mischief, playfulness, pranks, tomfoolery, tricks

antidote noun CURE, countermeasure, remedy

antipathy noun HOSTILITY, aversion, bad blood, dislike, enmity, hatred, ill will

antiquated adjective OBSOLETE, antique, archaic, dated, old-fashioned, out-of-date, passé

antique noun 1 PERIOD PIECE, bygone, heirloom, relic
▶ adjective 2 VINTAGE, antiquarian, classic, olden 3 OLD-FASHIONED, archaic, obsolete, outdated

antiquity noun 1 OLD AGE, age, ancientness, elderliness, oldness 2 DISTANT PAST, ancient times, olden days, time immemorial

antiseptic adjective 1 HYGIENIC, clean, germ-free, pure, sanitary, sterile, uncontaminated ▶ noun 2 DISINFECTANT, germicide, purifier

antisocial adjective 1 UNSOCIABLE, alienated, misanthropic, reserved, retiring, uncommunicative, unfriendly, withdrawn 2 DISRUPTIVE, antagonistic, belligerent, disorderly, hostile, menacing, rebellious, uncooperative

antithesis noun OPPOSITE, contrary, contrast, converse, inverse, reverse

anxiety noun UNEASINESS, angst, apprehension, concern, foreboding, misgiving, nervousness, tension, trepidation, worry

anxious adjective 1 UNEASY, apprehensive, concerned, fearful, in suspense, nervous, on tenterhooks, tense, troubled, wired (*slang*), worried 2 EAGER, desirous, impatient, intent, keen, yearning

apart adverb 1 TO PIECES, asunder, in bits, in pieces, to bits 2 SEPARATE, alone, aside, away, by oneself, isolated, to one side 3 **apart from** EXCEPT FOR, aside from, besides, but, excluding, not counting, other than, save

apartment noun ROOM, accommodation, flat, living quarters, penthouse, quarters, rooms, suite

apathetic adjective UNINTERESTED, cool, indifferent, passive, phlegmatic, unconcerned

apathy noun LACK OF INTEREST, coolness, indifference, inertia, nonchalance, passivity, torpor, unconcern

apex noun HIGHEST POINT, crest, crown, culmination, peak, pinnacle, point, summit, top

apiece adverb EACH, for each, from each, individually, respectively, separately, to each

aplomb noun SELF-POSSESSION, calmness, composure, confidence, level-headedness, poise, sang-froid, self-assurance, self-confidence

apocryphal adjective DUBIOUS, doubtful, legendary, mythical, questionable, unauthenticated, unsubstantiated

apologetic *adjective* REGRETFUL, contrite, penitent, remorseful, rueful, sorry

apologize *verb* SAY SORRY, ask forgiveness, beg pardon, express regret

apology *noun* 1 DEFENSE, acknowledgment, confession, excuse, explanation, justification, plea 2 *As in* **an apology for** MOCKERY, caricature, excuse, imitation, travesty

apostle *noun* 1 EVANGELIST, herald, messenger, missionary, preacher 2 SUPPORTER, advocate, champion, pioneer, propagandist, proponent

apotheosis *noun* DEIFICATION, elevation, exaltation, glorification, idealization, idolization

appall *verb* HORRIFY, alarm, daunt, dishearten, dismay, frighten, outrage, shock, unnerve

appalling *adjective* HORRIFYING, alarming, awful, daunting, dreadful, fearful, frightful, horrible, shocking, terrifying

apparatus *noun* 1 EQUIPMENT, appliance, contraption (*informal*), device, gear, machinery, mechanism, tackle, tools 2 ORGANIZATION, bureaucracy, chain of command, hierarchy, network, setup (*informal*), structure, system

apparent *adjective* 1 OBVIOUS, discernible, distinct, evident, manifest, marked, unmistakable, visible 2 SEEMING, ostensible, outward, superficial

apparently *adverb* IT APPEARS

THAT, it seems that, on the face of it, ostensibly, outwardly, seemingly, superficially

apparition *noun* GHOST, chimera, phantom, specter, spirit, wraith

appeal *verb* 1 PLEAD, ask, beg, call upon, entreat, pray, request 2 ATTRACT, allure, charm, entice, fascinate, interest, please, tempt ▶ *noun* 3 PLEA, application, entreaty, petition, prayer, request, supplication 4 ATTRACTION, allure, beauty, charm, fascination

appealing *adjective* ATTRACTIVE, alluring, charming, desirable, engaging, winsome

appear *verb* 1 COME INTO VIEW, be present, come out, come to light, crop up (*informal*), emerge, occur, show up (*informal*), surface, turn up 2 LOOK (LIKE OR AS IF), occur, seem, strike one as

appearance *noun* 1 ARRIVAL, coming, emergence, introduction, presence 2 LOOK, demeanor, expression, figure, form, looks, manner, mien (*literary*) 3 IMPRESSION, front, guise, illusion, image, outward show, pretense, semblance

appease *verb* 1 PACIFY, calm, conciliate, mollify, placate, quiet, satisfy, soothe 2 EASE, allay, alleviate, calm, relieve, soothe

appeasement *noun* 1 PACIFICATION, accommodation, compromise, concession, conciliation, mollification, placation 2 EASING, alleviation, lessening, relieving, soothing

appendage noun ATTACHMENT, accessory, addition, supplement

appendix noun SUPPLEMENT, addendum, addition, adjunct, appendage, postscript

appetite noun DESIRE, craving, demand, hunger, liking, longing, passion, relish, stomach, taste, yearning

appetizing adjective DELICIOUS, appealing, inviting, mouthwatering, palatable, succulent, tasty, tempting, yummy (informal)

applaud verb CLAP, acclaim, approve, cheer, commend, compliment, encourage, extol, praise

applause noun OVATION, accolade, approval, big hand, cheers, clapping, hand, praise

appliance noun DEVICE, apparatus, gadget, implement, instrument, machine, mechanism, tool

applicable adjective APPROPRIATE, apt, fitting, pertinent, relevant, suitable, useful

applicant noun CANDIDATE, claimant, inquirer

application noun 1 REQUEST, appeal, claim, inquiry, petition, requisition 2 EFFORT, commitment, dedication, diligence, hard work, industry, perseverance

apply verb 1 REQUEST, appeal, claim, inquire, petition, put in, requisition 2 USE, bring to bear, carry out, employ, exercise, exert, implement, practice, utilize 3 PUT ON, cover with, lay on, paint, place, smear, spread on 4 BE RELEVANT, be applicable, be appropriate, bear upon, be

fitting, fit, pertain, refer, relate 5 apply oneself TRY, be diligent, buckle down (informal), commit oneself, concentrate, dedicate oneself, devote oneself, persevere, work hard

appoint verb 1 ASSIGN, choose, commission, delegate, elect, name, nominate, select 2 DECIDE, allot, arrange, assign, choose, designate, establish, fix, set 3 EQUIP, fit out, furnish, provide, supply

appointed adjective 1 ASSIGNED, chosen, delegated, elected, named, nominated, selected 2 DECIDED, allotted, arranged, assigned, chosen, designated, established, fixed, set 3 EQUIPPED, fitted out, furnished, provided, supplied

appointment noun 1 MEETING, arrangement, assignation, date, engagement, interview, rendezvous 2 SELECTION, assignment, choice, election, naming, nomination 3 JOB, assignment, office, place, position, post, situation 4 appointments FITTINGS, fixtures, furnishings, gear, outfit, paraphernalia, trappings

apportion verb DIVIDE, allocate, allot, assign, dispense, distribute, dole out, ration out, share

apportionment noun DIVISION, allocation, allotment, assignment, dispensing, distribution, doling out, rationing out, sharing

apposite adjective APPROPRIATE, applicable, apt, fitting, pertinent, relevant, suitable, to the point

appraisal noun ASSESSMENT, estimate, estimation, evaluation, judgment, opinion

appraise verb ASSESS, estimate, evaluate, gauge, judge, rate, review, value

appreciable adjective SIGNIFICANT, considerable, definite, discernible, evident, marked, noticeable, obvious, pronounced, substantial

appreciate verb 1 VALUE, admire, enjoy, like, prize, rate highly, respect, treasure 2 BE AWARE OF, perceive, realize, recognize, sympathize with, take account of, understand 3 BE GRATEFUL FOR, be appreciative, be indebted, be obliged, be thankful for, give thanks for 4 INCREASE, enhance, gain, grow, improve, rise

appreciation noun 1 GRATITUDE, acknowledgment, gratefulness, indebtedness, obligation, thankfulness, thanks 2 AWARENESS, admiration, comprehension, enjoyment, perception, realization, recognition, sensitivity, sympathy, understanding 3 INCREASE, enhancement, gain, growth, improvement, rise

appreciative adjective 1 GRATEFUL, beholden, indebted, obliged, thankful 2 AWARE, admiring, enthusiastic, respectful, responsive, sensitive, sympathetic, understanding

apprehend verb 1 ARREST, capture, catch, seize, take prisoner 2 UNDERSTAND, comprehend, conceive, get the picture, grasp, perceive, realize, recognize

apprehension noun 1 ANXIETY, alarm, concern, dread, fear, foreboding, suspicion, trepidation, worry 2 ARREST, capture, catching, seizure, taking 3 AWARENESS, comprehension, grasp, perception, understanding

apprehensive adjective ANXIOUS, concerned, foreboding, nervous, uneasy, wired (slang), worried

apprentice noun TRAINEE, beginner, learner, novice, probationer, pupil, student

approach verb 1 MOVE TOWARDS, come close, come near, draw near, near, reach 2 MAKE A PROPOSAL TO, appeal to, apply to, make overtures to, sound out 3 SET ABOUT, begin work on, commence, embark on, enter upon, make a start, undertake ▶ noun 4 COMING, advance, arrival, drawing near, nearing 5 (often plural) PROPOSAL, advance, appeal, application, invitation, offer, overture, proposition 6 ACCESS, avenue, entrance, passage, road, way 7 WAY, manner, means, method, style, technique 8 LIKENESS, approximation, semblance

approachable adjective 1 FRIENDLY, affable, congenial, cordial, open, sociable 2 ACCESSIBLE, attainable, reachable

appropriate adjective 1 SUITABLE, apt, befitting, fitting, pertinent, relevant, to the point, well-suited ▶ verb 2 SEIZE, commandeer, confiscate, impound, take possession of, usurp 3 STEAL, embezzle, filch,

misappropriate, pilfer, pocket
4 SET ASIDE, allocate, allot,
apportion, assign, devote,
earmark

approval noun **1** CONSENT,
agreement, assent,
authorization, blessing,
endorsement, permission,
recommendation, sanction
2 FAVOR, acclaim, admiration,
applause, appreciation, esteem,
good opinion, praise, respect

approve verb **1** FAVOR, admire,
commend, have a good
opinion of, like, praise, regard
highly, respect **2** AGREE TO,
allow, assent to, authorize,
consent to, endorse, pass,
permit, ratify, recommend,
sanction

approximate adjective **1** CLOSE,
near **2** ROUGH, estimated,
inexact, loose ▶ verb **3** COME
CLOSE, approach, border on,
come near, reach, resemble,
touch, verge on

approximately adverb ALMOST,
about, around, circa (used with
dates), close to, in the region
of, just about, more or less,
nearly, roughly

approximation noun GUESS,
conjecture, estimate,
estimation, guesswork, rough
calculation, rough idea

apron noun PINAFORE

apt adjective **1** INCLINED,
disposed, given, liable, likely,
of a mind, prone, ready
2 APPROPRIATE, fitting, pertinent,
relevant, suitable, to the point
3 GIFTED, clever, quick, sharp,
smart, talented

aptitude noun **1** TENDENCY,
inclination, leaning,

predilection, proclivity,
propensity **2** GIFT, ability,
capability, faculty, intelligence,
proficiency, talent

arable adjective PRODUCTIVE,
farmable, fertile, fruitful

arbiter noun JUDGE,
adjudicator, arbitrator, referee,
umpire **2** AUTHORITY, controller,
dictator, expert, governor,
lord, master, pundit, ruler

arbitrary adjective RANDOM,
capricious, chance, erratic,
inconsistent, personal,
subjective, whimsical

arbitrate verb SETTLE, adjudicate,
decide, determine, judge,
mediate, pass judgment,
referee, umpire

arbitration noun SETTLEMENT,
adjudication, decision,
determination, judgment

arbitrator noun JUDGE,
adjudicator, arbiter, referee,
umpire

arc noun CURVE, arch, bend,
bow, crescent, half-moon

arcade noun GALLERY, cloister,
colonnade, portico

arcane adjective MYSTERIOUS,
esoteric, hidden, occult,
recondite, secret

arch¹ noun **1** CURVE, archway,
dome, span, vault **2** CURVE, arc,
bend, bow, hump, semicircle
▶ verb **3** CURVE, arc, bend, bow,
bridge, span

arch² adjective PLAYFUL,
frolicsome, mischievous, pert,
roguish, saucy, sly, waggish

archaic adjective **1** OLD, ancient,
antique, bygone, olden
(archaic), primitive
2 OLD-FASHIONED, antiquated,
behind the times, obsolete,

outmoded, out of date, passé

archetypal *adjective* **1** TYPICAL, classic, ideal, model, standard **2** ORIGINAL, prototypic *or* prototypical

archetype *noun* **1** STANDARD, model, paradigm, pattern, prime example **2** ORIGINAL, prototype

architect *noun* DESIGNER, master builder, planner

architecture *noun* **1** DESIGN, building, construction, planning **2** STRUCTURE, construction, design, framework, make-up, style

archive *noun* **1** RECORD OFFICE, museum, registry, repository **2** *archives* RECORDS, annals, chronicles, documents, papers, rolls

arctic *adjective Informal* FREEZING, chilly, cold, frigid, frozen, glacial, icy

Arctic *adjective* POLAR, far-northern, hyperborean

ardent *adjective* **1** PASSIONATE, amorous, hot-blooded, impassioned, intense, lusty **2** ENTHUSIASTIC, avid, eager, keen, zealous

ardor *noun* **1** PASSION, fervor, intensity, spirit, vehemence, warmth **2** ENTHUSIASM, avidity, eagerness, keenness, zeal

arduous *adjective* DIFFICULT, exhausting, fatiguing, grueling, laborious, onerous, punishing, rigorous, strenuous, taxing, tiring

area *noun* **1** REGION, district, locality, neighborhood, zone **2** PART, portion, section, sector **3** FIELD, department, domain, province, realm, sphere,

territory

arena *noun* **1** RING, amphitheater, bowl, enclosure, field, ground, stadium **2** SPHERE, area, domain, field, province, realm, sector, territory

argue *verb* **1** DISCUSS, assert, claim, debate, dispute, maintain, reason, remonstrate **2** QUARREL, bicker, disagree, dispute, fall out (*informal*), fight, squabble

argument *noun* **1** QUARREL, clash, controversy, disagreement, dispute, feud, fight, row, squabble **2** DISCUSSION, assertion, claim, debate, dispute, plea, questioning, remonstration **3** REASON, argumentation, case, defense, dialectic, ground(s), line of reasoning, logic, polemic, reasoning

argumentative *adjective* QUARRELSOME, belligerent, combative, contentious, contrary, disputatious, litigious, opinionated

arid *adjective* **1** DRY, barren, desert, parched, sterile, torrid, waterless **2** BORING, dreary, dry, dull, tedious, tiresome, uninspired, uninteresting

arise *verb* **1** HAPPEN, begin, emerge, ensue, follow, occur, result, start, stem **2** GET UP, get to one's feet, go up, rise, stand up, wake up

aristocracy *noun* UPPER CLASS, elite, gentry, nobility, patricians, peerage, ruling class

aristocrat *adjective* NOBLE, grandee, lady, lord, patrician, peer, peeress

aristocratic *noun* UPPER-CLASS,

blue-blooded, elite, gentlemanly, lordly, noble, patrician, titled

arm[1] noun UPPER LIMB, appendage, limb

arm[2] verb Especially with weapons EQUIP, accouter, array, deck out, furnish, issue with, provide, supply

armada noun FLEET, flotilla, navy, squadron

armaments plural noun WEAPONS, ammunition, arms, guns, materiel, munitions, ordnance, weaponry

armed adjective CARRYING WEAPONS, equipped, fitted out, primed, protected

armistice noun TRUCE, ceasefire, peace, suspension of hostilities

armor noun PROTECTION, armor plate, covering, sheathing, shield

armored adjective PROTECTED, armor-plated, bombproof, bulletproof, ironclad, mailed, steel-plated

arms plural noun 1 WEAPONS, armaments, firearms, guns, instruments of war, ordnance, weaponry 2 HERALDRY, blazonry, crest, escutcheon, insignia

army noun 1 SOLDIERS, armed force, legions, military, military force, soldiery, troops 2 VAST NUMBER, array, horde, host, multitude, pack, swarm, throng

aroma noun SCENT, bouquet, fragrance, odor, perfume, redolence, savor, smell

aromatic adjective FRAGRANT, balmy, perfumed, pungent, redolent, savory, spicy, sweet-scented, sweet-smelling

around preposition 1 SURROUNDING, about, encircling, enclosing, encompassing, on all sides of, on every side of 2 APPROXIMATELY, about, circa (used with dates), roughly ▶adverb 3 EVERYWHERE, about, all over, here and there, in all directions, on all sides, throughout, to and fro 4 NEAR, at hand, close, close at hand, nearby, nigh (archaic or dialect)

arouse verb 1 STIMULATE, excite, incite, instigate, provoke, spur, stir up, summon up, whip up 2 AWAKEN, rouse, waken, wake up

arrange verb 1 PLAN, construct, contrive, devise, fix up, organize, prepare 2 AGREE, adjust, come to terms, compromise, determine, settle 3 PUT IN ORDER, classify, group, line up, order, organize, position, sort 4 ADAPT, instrument, orchestrate, score

arrangement noun 1 (often plural) PLAN, organization, planning, preparation, provision, schedule 2 AGREEMENT, adjustment, compact, compromise, deal, settlement, terms 3 ORDER, alignment, classification, form, organization, structure, system 4 ADAPTATION, instrumentation, interpretation, orchestration, score, version

array noun 1 ARRANGEMENT, collection, display, exhibition, formation, line-up, parade, show, supply 2 Poetic CLOTHING, apparel, attire, clothes, dress, finery, garments, regalia ▶verb 3 ARRANGE, display, exhibit, group, parade, range, show

4 DRESS, adorn, attire, clothe, deck, decorate, festoon

arrest verb **1** CAPTURE, apprehend, catch, detain, seize, take prisoner **2** STOP, block, delay, end, inhibit, interrupt, obstruct, slow, suppress **3** GRIP, absorb, engage, engross, fascinate, hold, intrigue, occupy ▶noun **4** CAPTURE, bust (informal), detention, seizure **5** STOPPING, blockage, delay, end, hindrance, interruption, obstruction, suppression

arresting adjective STRIKING, cool (informal), engaging, impressive, noticeable, outstanding, phat (slang), remarkable, stunning, surprising

arrival noun **1** COMING, advent, appearance, arriving, entrance, happening, occurrence, taking place **2** NEWCOMER, caller, entrant, incomer, visitor

arrive verb **1** COME, appear, enter, get to, reach, show up (informal), turn up **2** Informal SUCCEED, become famous, make good, make it (informal), make the grade (informal)

arrogance noun CONCEIT, disdainfulness, haughtiness, high-handedness, insolence, pride, superciliousness, swagger

arrogant adjective CONCEITED, disdainful, haughty, high-handed, overbearing, proud, scornful, supercilious

arrow noun **1** DART, bolt, flight, quarrel, shaft (archaic) **2** POINTER, indicator

arsenal noun ARMORY, ammunition dump, arms depot, ordnance depot, stockpile, store, storehouse, supply

art noun SKILL, craft, expertise, ingenuity, mastery, virtuosity

artful adjective CUNNING, clever, crafty, shrewd, sly, smart, wily

article noun **1** PIECE, composition, discourse, essay, feature, item, paper, story, treatise **2** THING, commodity, item, object, piece, substance, unit **3** CLAUSE, item, paragraph, part, passage, point, portion, section

articulate adjective **1** EXPRESSIVE, clear, coherent, eloquent, fluent, lucid, well-spoken ▶verb **2** EXPRESS, enunciate, pronounce, say, speak, state, talk, utter, voice

artifice noun **1** TRICK, contrivance, device, machination, maneuver, stratagem, subterfuge, tactic **2** CLEVERNESS, ingenuity, inventiveness, skill

artificial adjective **1** SYNTHETIC, man-made, manufactured, non-natural, plastic **2** FAKE, bogus, counterfeit, imitation, mock, sham, simulated **3** INSINCERE, affected, contrived, false, feigned, forced, phoney or phony (informal), unnatural

artillery noun BIG GUNS, battery, cannon, cannonry, gunnery, ordnance

artisan noun CRAFTSMAN, journeyman, mechanic, skilled workman, technician

artistic adjective CREATIVE, aesthetic, beautiful, cultured, elegant, refined, sophisticated, stylish, tasteful

artistry noun SKILL, brilliance,

craftsmanship, creativity, finesse, mastery, proficiency, virtuosity

artless adjective
1 STRAIGHTFORWARD, frank, guileless, open, plain **2** NATURAL, homely, plain, pure, simple, unadorned, unaffected, unpretentious

as conjunction **1** WHEN, at the time that, during the time that, just as, while **2** IN THE WAY THAT, in the manner that, like **3** WHAT, that which **4** SINCE, because, considering that, seeing that **5** FOR INSTANCE, like, such as ▶preposition **6** BEING, in the character of, in the role of, under the name of

ascend verb MOVE UP, climb, go up, mount, scale

ascent noun **1** RISE, ascending, ascension, climb, mounting, rising, scaling, upward movement **2** UPWARD SLOPE, gradient, incline, ramp, rise, rising ground

ascertain verb FIND OUT, confirm, determine, discover, establish, learn

ascetic noun **1** MONK, abstainer, hermit, nun, recluse ▶adjective **2** SELF-DENYING, abstinent, austere, celibate, frugal, puritanical, self-disciplined

ascribe verb ATTRIBUTE, assign, charge, credit, impute, put down, refer, set down

ashamed adjective EMBARRASSED, distressed, guilty, humiliated, mortified, remorseful, shamefaced, sheepish, sorry

ashen adjective PALE, colorless, gray, leaden, like death warmed over (informal), pallid, wan, white

ashore adverb ON LAND, aground, landwards, on dry land, on the beach, on the shore, shorewards, to the shore

aside adverb **1** TO ONE SIDE, apart, beside, on one side, out of the way, privately, separately, to the side ▶noun **2** INTERPOLATION, parenthesis

asinine adjective STUPID, fatuous, foolish, idiotic, imbecilic, moronic, senseless

ask verb **1** INQUIRE, interrogate, query, question, quiz **2** REQUEST, appeal, beg, demand, plead, seek **3** INVITE, bid, summon

askew adverb **1** CROOKEDLY, aslant, awry, obliquely, off-center, to one side ▶adjective **2** CROOKED, awry, cockeyed (informal), lopsided, oblique, off-center

asleep adjective SLEEPING, dormant, dozing, fast asleep, napping, slumbering, snoozing (informal), sound asleep

aspect noun **1** FEATURE, angle, facet, side **2** POSITION, outlook, point of view, prospect, scene, situation, view **3** APPEARANCE, air, attitude, bearing, condition, demeanor, expression, look, manner

asphyxiate verb SUFFOCATE, choke, smother, stifle, strangle, strangulate, throttle

aspiration noun AIM, ambition, desire, dream, goal, hope, objective, wish

aspire verb AIM, desire, dream, hope, long, seek, set one's heart on, wish

aspiring adjective HOPEFUL, ambitious, eager, longing,

wannabe (*informal*), would-be

ass noun 1 DONKEY 2 FOOL, blockhead, dork (*slang*), halfwit, idiot, jackass, oaf, schmuck (*slang*)

assail verb ATTACK, assault, fall upon, set upon

assailant noun ATTACKER, aggressor, assailer, assaulter, invader

assassin noun MURDERER, executioner, hatchet man (*slang*), hit man (*slang*), killer, liquidator, slayer

assassinate verb MURDER, eliminate (*slang*), hit (*slang*), kill, liquidate, slay, take out (*slang*)

assault noun 1 ATTACK, charge, invasion, offensive, onslaught ▶ verb 2 ATTACK, beset, fall upon, set about, set upon, strike at

assemble verb 1 GATHER, amass, bring together, call together, collect, come together, congregate, meet, muster, rally 2 PUT TOGETHER, build up, connect, construct, fabricate, fit together, join, piece together, set up

assembly noun 1 GATHERING, collection, company, conference, congress, council, crowd, group, mass, meeting 2 PUTTING TOGETHER, building up, connecting, construction, piecing together, setting up

assent noun 1 AGREEMENT, acceptance, approval, compliance, concurrence, consent, permission, sanction ▶ verb 2 AGREE, allow, approve, consent, grant, permit

assert verb 1 STATE, affirm, declare, maintain, profess, pronounce, swear 2 INSIST UPON, claim, defend, press, put forward, stand up for, stress, uphold 3 **assert oneself** BE FORCEFUL, exert one's influence, make one's presence felt, put oneself forward, put one's foot down (*informal*)

assertion noun 1 STATEMENT, claim, declaration, pronouncement 2 INSISTENCE, maintenance, stressing

assertive adjective CONFIDENT, aggressive, domineering, emphatic, feisty (*informal*), forceful, insistent, positive, pushy (*informal*), strong-willed

assess verb 1 JUDGE, appraise, estimate, evaluate, rate, size up (*informal*), value, weigh 2 EVALUATE, fix, impose, levy, rate, tax, value

assessment noun 1 JUDGMENT, appraisal, estimate, evaluation, rating, valuation 2 EVALUATION, charge, fee, levy, rating, toll, valuation

asset noun 1 BENEFIT, advantage, aid, blessing, boon, feather in one's cap, help, resource, service 2 **assets** PROPERTY, capital, estate, funds, goods, money, possessions, resources, wealth

assiduous adjective DILIGENT, hard-working, indefatigable, industrious, persevering, persistent, unflagging

assign verb 1 SELECT, appoint, choose, delegate, designate, name, nominate 2 GIVE, allocate, allot, apportion, consign, distribute, give out, grant 3 ATTRIBUTE, accredit, ascribe, put down

assignation noun 1 SECRET MEETING, clandestine meeting, illicit meeting, rendezvous, tryst 2 SELECTION, appointment, assignment, choice, delegation, designation, nomination

assignment noun TASK, appointment, commission, duty, job, mission, position, post, responsibility

assimilate verb 1 LEARN, absorb, digest, incorporate, take in 2 ADJUST, adapt, blend in, mingle

assist verb HELP, abet, aid, cooperate, lend a helping hand, serve, support

assistance noun HELP, aid, backing, cooperation, helping hand, support

assistant noun HELPER, accomplice, aide, ally, colleague, right-hand man, second, supporter

associate verb 1 CONNECT, ally, combine, identify, join, link, lump together 2 MIX, accompany, consort, hobnob, mingle, socialize ▶noun 3 PARTNER, collaborator, colleague, confederate, co-worker 4 FRIEND, ally, companion, comrade, homeboy (slang), homegirl (slang)

association noun 1 GROUP, alliance, band, club, coalition, federation, league, organization, society 2 CONNECTION, blend, combination, joining, juxtaposition, mixture, pairing, union

assorted adjective VARIOUS, different, diverse, miscellaneous, mixed, motley, sundry, varied

assortment noun VARIETY, array, choice, collection, jumble, medley, mixture, selection

assume verb 1 TAKE FOR GRANTED, believe, expect, fancy, imagine, infer, presume, suppose, surmise, think 2 TAKE ON, accept, enter upon, put on, shoulder, take over 3 PUT ON, adopt, affect, feign, imitate, impersonate, mimic, pretend to, simulate

assumed adjective 1 FALSE, bogus, counterfeit, fake, fictitious, made-up, make-believe 2 TAKEN FOR GRANTED, accepted, expected, hypothetical, presumed, presupposed, supposed, surmised

assumption noun 1 PRESUMPTION, belief, conjecture, guess, hypothesis, inference, supposition, surmise 2 TAKING ON, acceptance, acquisition, adoption, entering upon, putting on, shouldering, takeover, taking up 3 TAKING, acquisition, appropriation, seizure, takeover

assurance noun 1 ASSERTION, declaration, guarantee, oath, pledge, promise, statement, vow, word 2 CONFIDENCE, boldness, certainty, conviction, faith, nerve, poise, self-confidence

assure verb 1 PROMISE, certify, confirm, declare confidently, give one's word to, guarantee, pledge, swear, vow 2 CONVINCE, comfort, embolden, encourage, hearten, persuade, reassure 3 MAKE CERTAIN, clinch, complete, confirm, ensure, guarantee, make sure, seal, secure

assured *adjective* **1** CONFIDENT, certain, poised, positive, self-assured, self-confident, sure of oneself **2** CERTAIN, beyond doubt, confirmed, ensured, fixed, guaranteed, in the bag (*slang*), secure, settled, sure

astonish *verb* AMAZE, astound, bewilder, confound, daze, dumbfound, stagger, stun, surprise

astonishing *adjective* AMAZING, astounding, bewildering, breathtaking, brilliant, sensational (*informal*), staggering, stunning, surprising

astonishment *noun* AMAZEMENT, awe, bewilderment, confusion, consternation, surprise, wonder, wonderment

astounding *adjective* AMAZING, astonishing, bewildering, breathtaking, brilliant, cool (*informal*), impressive, phat (*slang*), sensational (*informal*), staggering, stunning, surprising

astray *adjective, adverb* OFF THE RIGHT TRACK, adrift, amiss, lost, off, off course, off the mark, off the subject

astute *adjective* INTELLIGENT, canny, clever, crafty, cunning, perceptive, sagacious, sharp, shrewd, subtle

asylum *noun* **1** REFUGE, harbor, haven, preserve, retreat, safety, sanctuary, shelter **2** *Old-fashioned* MENTAL HOSPITAL, funny farm (*slang*), hospital, institution, madhouse (*informal*), psychiatric hospital, psychiatric ward

atheism *noun* NONBELIEF, disbelief, godlessness, heathenism, infidelity, irreligion, paganism, skepticism, unbelief

atheist *noun* NONBELIEVER, disbeliever, heathen, infidel, pagan, skeptic, unbeliever

athlete *noun* SPORTSPERSON, competitor, contestant, gymnast, player, runner, sportsman, sportswoman

athletic *adjective* FIT, active, energetic, muscular, powerful, strapping, strong, sturdy

athletics *plural noun* SPORTS, contests, exercises, gymnastics, races, track and field events

atmosphere *noun* **1** AIR, aerosphere, heavens, sky **2** FEELING, ambience, character, climate, environment, mood, spirit, surroundings, tone

atom *noun* PARTICLE, bit, dot, molecule, speck, spot, trace

atone *verb* (usually with *for*) MAKE AMENDS, compensate, do penance, make redress, make reparation, make up for, pay for, recompense, redress

atonement *noun* AMENDS, compensation, penance, recompense, redress, reparation, restitution

atrocious *adjective* **1** CRUEL, barbaric, brutal, fiendish, infernal, monstrous, savage, vicious, wicked **2** *Informal* SHOCKING, appalling, detestable, grievous, horrible, horrifying, terrible

atrocity *noun* **1** CRUELTY, barbarity, brutality, fiendishness, horror, savagery, viciousness, wickedness **2** ACT

OF CRUELTY, abomination, crime, evil, horror, outrage

attach verb **1** CONNECT, add, couple, fasten, fix, join, link, secure, stick, tie **2** PUT, ascribe, assign, associate, attribute, connect

attached adjective **1** SPOKEN FOR, accompanied, engaged, married, partnered **2 attached to** FOND OF, affectionate towards, devoted to, full of regard for

attachment noun **1** FONDNESS, affection, affinity, attraction, liking, regard **2** ACCESSORY, accoutrement, extension, extra, fitting, fixture, supplement

attack verb **1** ASSAULT, invade, raid, set upon, storm, strike (at) **2** CRITICIZE, abuse, blame, censure, put down, vilify ▶ noun **3** ASSAULT, campaign, charge, foray, incursion, invasion, offensive, onslaught, raid, strike **4** CRITICISM, abuse, blame, censure, denigration, stick (slang), vilification **5** BOUT, convulsion, fit, paroxysm, seizure, spasm, stroke

attacker noun ASSAILANT, aggressor, assaulter, intruder, invader, raider

attain verb ACHIEVE, accomplish, acquire, complete, fulfill, gain, get, obtain, reach

attainment noun ACHIEVEMENT, accomplishment, completion, feat

attempt verb **1** TRY, endeavor, seek, strive, undertake, venture ▶ noun **2** TRY, bid, crack (informal), effort, go (informal), shot (informal), stab (informal), trial

attend verb **1** BE PRESENT, appear, frequent, go to, haunt, put in an appearance, show oneself, turn up, visit **2** LOOK AFTER, care for, mind, minister to, nurse, take care of, tend **3** PAY ATTENTION, hear, heed, listen, mark, note, observe, pay heed **4 attend to** APPLY ONESELF TO, concentrate on, devote oneself to, get to work on, look after, occupy oneself with, see to, take care of

attendance noun **1** PRESENCE, appearance, attending, being there **2** TURNOUT, audience, crowd, gate, house, number present

attendant noun **1** ASSISTANT, aide, companion, escort, follower, guard, helper, servant ▶ adjective **2** ACCOMPANYING, accessory, associated, concomitant, consequent, related

attention noun **1** CONCENTRATION, deliberation, heed, intentness, mind, scrutiny, thinking, thought **2** NOTICE, awareness, consciousness, consideration, observation, recognition, regard **3** CARE, concern, looking after, ministration, treatment

attentive adjective **1** INTENT, alert, awake, careful, concentrating, heedful, mindful, observant, studious, watchful **2** CONSIDERATE, courteous, helpful, kind, obliging, polite, respectful, thoughtful

attic noun LOFT, garret

attire noun CLOTHES, apparel, costume, dress, garb, garments, outfit, robes, wear

attitude noun 1 DISPOSITION, approach, frame of mind, mood, outlook, perspective, point of view, position, stance 2 POSITION, pose, posture, stance

attract verb APPEAL TO, allure, charm, draw, enchant, entice, lure, pull (informal), tempt

attraction noun APPEAL, allure, charm, enticement, fascination, lure, magnetism, pull (informal), temptation

attractive adjective APPEALING, alluring, charming, fair, fetching, good-looking, handsome, inviting, lovely, pleasant, pretty, tempting

attribute verb 1 ASCRIBE, assign, charge, credit, put down to, refer, set down to, trace to ▶noun 2 QUALITY, aspect, character, characteristic, facet, feature, peculiarity, property, trait

attune verb ACCUSTOM, adapt, adjust, familiarize, harmonize, regulate

audacious adjective 1 DARING, bold, brave, courageous, fearless, intrepid, rash, reckless 2 CHEEKY, brazen, defiant, impertinent, impudent, insolent, presumptuous, shameless

audacity noun 1 DARING, boldness, bravery, courage, fearlessness, nerve, rashness, recklessness 2 CHEEK, chutzpah (informal), effrontery, impertinence, impudence, insolence, nerve

audible adjective CLEAR, detectable, discernible, distinct, hearable, perceptible

audience noun 1 SPECTATORS, assembly, crowd, gallery, gathering, listeners, onlookers, turnout, viewers 2 INTERVIEW, consultation, hearing, meeting, reception

aura noun AIR, ambience, atmosphere, feeling, mood, quality, tone

auspicious adjective FAVORABLE, bright, encouraging, felicitous, hopeful, promising

austere adjective 1 STERN, forbidding, formal, serious, severe, solemn, strict 2 ASCETIC, abstemious, puritanical, self-disciplined, sober, solemn, strait-laced, strict 3 PLAIN, bleak, harsh, homely, simple, spare, Spartan, stark

austerity noun 1 STERNNESS, formality, inflexibility, rigor, seriousness, severity, solemnity, stiffness, strictness 2 ASCETICISM, puritanism, self-denial, self-discipline, sobriety 3 PLAINNESS, simplicity, starkness

authentic adjective GENUINE, actual, authoritative, bona fide, legitimate, pure, real, true-to-life, valid

authenticity noun GENUINENESS, accuracy, certainty, faithfulness, legitimacy, purity, truthfulness, validity

author noun 1 WRITER, composer, creator 2 CREATOR, architect, designer, father, founder, inventor, originator, producer

authoritarian adjective 1 STRICT, autocratic, dictatorial, doctrinaire, dogmatic, severe, tyrannical ▶noun 2 DISCIPLINARIAN, absolutist, autocrat, despot, dictator, tyrant

authoritative adjective
1 RELIABLE, accurate, authentic, definitive, dependable, trustworthy, valid
2 COMMANDING, assertive, imperious, imposing, masterly, self-assured

authority noun **1** POWER, command, control, direction, influence, supremacy, sway, weight **2** (usually plural) POWERS THAT BE, administration, government, management, officialdom, police, the Establishment **3** EXPERT, connoisseur, judge, master, professional, specialist

authorization noun PERMISSION, a blank check, approval, leave, license, permit, warrant

authorize verb **1** EMPOWER, accredit, commission, enable, entitle, give authority **2** PERMIT, allow, approve, give authority for, license, sanction, warrant

autocracy noun DICTATORSHIP, absolutism, despotism, tyranny

autocrat noun DICTATOR, absolutist, despot, tyrant

autocratic adjective DICTATORIAL, absolute, all-powerful, despotic, domineering, imperious, tyrannical

automatic adjective
1 MECHANICAL, automated, mechanized, push-button, self-propelling **2** INVOLUNTARY, instinctive, mechanical, natural, reflex, spontaneous, unconscious, unwilled

autonomous adjective SELF-RULING, free, independent, self-determining,

self-governing, sovereign

autonomy noun INDEPENDENCE, freedom, home rule, self-determination, self-government, self-rule, sovereignty

auxiliary adjective
1 SUPPLEMENTARY, back-up, emergency, fall-back, reserve, secondary, subsidiary, substitute **2** SUPPORTING, accessory, aiding, ancillary, assisting, helping ▶ noun **3** BACKUP, reserve **4** HELPER, assistant, associate, companion, subordinate, supporter

avail verb **1** BENEFIT, aid, assist, be of advantage, be useful, help, profit ▶ noun **2** BENEFIT, advantage, aid, good, help, profit, use

availability noun ACCESSIBILITY, attainability, handiness, readiness

available adjective ACCESSIBLE, at hand, at one's disposal, free, handy, on tap, ready, to hand

avalanche noun **1** SNOW-SLIDE, landslide, landslip **2** FLOOD, barrage, deluge, inundation, torrent

avant-garde adjective PROGRESSIVE, experimental, ground-breaking, innovative, pioneering, unconventional

avarice noun GREED, covetousness, meanness, miserliness, niggardliness, parsimony, stinginess

avaricious adjective GRASPING, covetous, greedy, mean, miserly, niggardly, parsimonious, stingy

avenge verb GET REVENGE FOR, get

even for (*informal*), hit back, punish, repay, retaliate

avenue noun STREET, approach, boulevard, course, drive, passage, path, road, route, way

average noun **1** USUAL, mean, medium, midpoint, norm, normal, par, standard **2 on average** USUALLY, as a rule, for the most part, generally, normally, typically ▸ *adjective* **3** USUAL, commonplace, fair, general, normal, ordinary, regular, standard, typical **4** MEAN, intermediate, median, medium, middle ▸ *verb* **5** MAKE ON AVERAGE, balance out to, be on average, do on average, even out to

averse *adjective* OPPOSED, disinclined, hostile, ill-disposed, loath, reluctant, unwilling

aversion noun HATRED, animosity, antipathy, disinclination, dislike, hostility, revulsion, unwillingness

avert *verb* **1** TURN AWAY, turn aside **2** WARD OFF, avoid, fend off, forestall, frustrate, preclude, prevent, stave off

aviator noun PILOT, aeronaut, airman, flyer

avid *adjective* **1** ENTHUSIASTIC, ardent, devoted, eager, fanatical, intense, keen, passionate, zealous **2** INSATIABLE, grasping, greedy, hungry, rapacious, ravenous, thirsty, voracious

avoid *verb* **1** REFRAIN FROM, dodge, duck (out of) (*informal*), eschew, fight shy of, shirk **2** PREVENT, avert **3** KEEP AWAY FROM, bypass, dodge, elude, escape, evade, shun,

steer clear of

avoidance noun EVASION, dodging, eluding, escape, keeping away, shunning, steering clear

avowed *adjective* **1** DECLARED, open, professed, self-proclaimed, sworn **2** CONFESSED, acknowledged, admitted

await *verb* **1** WAIT FOR, abide, anticipate, expect, look for, look forward to, stay for **2** BE IN STORE FOR, attend, be in readiness for, be prepared for, be ready for, wait for

awake *adjective* **1** NOT SLEEPING, aroused, awakened, aware, conscious, wakeful, wide-awake **2** ALERT, alive, attentive, aware, heedful, observant, on the lookout, vigilant, watchful ▸ *verb* **3** WAKE UP, awaken, rouse, wake **4** ALERT, arouse, kindle, provoke, revive, stimulate, stir up

awaken *verb* **1** AWAKE, arouse, revive, rouse, wake **2** ALERT, kindle, provoke, stimulate, stir up

awakening noun WAKING UP, arousal, revival, rousing, stimulation, stirring up

award *verb* **1** GIVE, bestow, confer, endow, grant, hand out, present ▸ *noun* **2** PRIZE, decoration, gift, grant, trophy

aware *adjective* **1** aware of KNOWING ABOUT, acquainted with, conscious of, conversant with, familiar with, mindful of **2** INFORMED, enlightened, in the picture, knowledgeable

awareness noun KNOWLEDGE, consciousness, familiarity,

perception, realization, recognition, understanding

away *adverb* **1** OFF, abroad, elsewhere, from here, from home, hence **2** AT A DISTANCE, apart, far, remote **3** ASIDE, out of the way, to one side **4** CONTINUOUSLY, incessantly, interminably, relentlessly, repeatedly, uninterruptedly, unremittingly ▶ *adjective* **5** NOT PRESENT, abroad, absent, elsewhere, gone, not at home, not here, out

awe *noun* **1** WONDER, admiration, amazement, astonishment, dread, fear, horror, respect, reverence, terror ▶ *verb* **2** IMPRESS, amaze, astonish, frighten, horrify, intimidate, stun, terrify

awesome *adjective* **1** AWE-INSPIRING, amazing, astonishing, breathtaking, cool (*informal*), formidable, impressive, intimidating, phat (*slang*), stunning **2** *Informal* FIRST-CLASS, choice, elite, excellent, first-rate, hand-picked, superior, world-class

awful *adjective* TERRIBLE, abysmal, appalling, deplorable, dreadful, frightful, ghastly, horrendous

awfully *adverb* **1** BADLY, disgracefully, dreadfully, reprehensibly, unforgivably, unpleasantly, woefully, wretchedly **2** *Informal* VERY, dreadfully, exceedingly, exceptionally, extremely, greatly, immensely, terribly

awkward *adjective* **1** CLUMSY, gauche, gawky, inelegant, lumbering, uncoordinated, ungainly **2** UNMANAGEABLE,

clunky (*informal*), cumbersome, difficult, inconvenient, troublesome, unwieldy **3** EMBARRASSING, delicate, difficult, ill at ease, inconvenient, uncomfortable

awkwardness *noun* **1** CLUMSINESS, gawkiness, inelegance, ungainliness **2** UNWIELDINESS, difficulty, inconvenience **3** EMBARRASSMENT, delicacy, difficulty, inconvenience

ax *noun* **1** HATCHET, adz, chopper **2 the ax** *Informal* DISMISSAL, termination, the boot (*slang*), the chop (*slang*) ▶ *verb* **3** *Informal* CUT BACK, cancel, dismiss, dispense with, eliminate, fire (*informal*), get rid of, remove, sack (*informal*)

axiom *noun* PRINCIPLE, adage, aphorism, dictum, maxim, precept, truism

axiomatic *adjective* SELF-EVIDENT, accepted, assumed, certain, given, granted, manifest, understood

axis *noun* PIVOT, axle, center line, shaft, spindle

axle *noun* SHAFT, axis, pin, pivot, rod, spindle

B b

babble *verb* **1** GABBLE, burble, chatter, jabber, prattle **2** GIBBER, gurgle ▶ *noun* **3** GABBLE, burble, drivel, gibberish

baby *noun* **1** INFANT, babe, babe in arms, child, newborn child ▶ *adjective* **2** SMALL, little, mini,

miniature, minute,
teeny-weeny, tiny, wee

babyish *adjective* CHILDISH,
foolish, immature, infantile,
juvenile, puerile, sissy, spoiled

back *noun* 1 REAR, end, far end,
hind part, hindquarters,
reverse, stern, tail end
2 behind one's back SECRETLY,
covertly, deceitfully, sneakily,
surreptitiously ▶ *verb* 3 MOVE
BACK, back off, backtrack, go
back, retire, retreat, reverse,
turn tail, withdraw 4 SUPPORT,
advocate, assist, champion,
endorse, promote, sponsor
▶ *adjective* 5 REAR, end, hind,
hindmost, posterior, tail
6 PREVIOUS, delayed, earlier,
elapsed, former, overdue, past

backbiting *noun* SLANDER,
bitchiness (*slang*), cattiness
(*informal*), defamation,
disparagement, gossip, malice,
scandalmongering, spitefulness

backbone *noun* 1 *Medical* SPINAL
COLUMN, spine, vertebrae,
vertebral column 2 STRENGTH OF
CHARACTER, character, courage,
determination, fortitude, grit,
nerve, pluck, resolution

backbreaking *adjective*
EXHAUSTING, arduous, crushing,
grueling, hard, laborious,
punishing, strenuous

back down *verb* GIVE IN, accede,
admit defeat, back-pedal,
concede, surrender, withdraw,
yield

backer *noun* SUPPORTER,
advocate, angel (*informal*),
benefactor, patron, promoter,
second, sponsor, subscriber

backfire *verb* FAIL, boomerang,
disappoint, flop (*informal*),

miscarry, rebound, recoil

background *noun* HISTORY,
circumstances, culture,
education, environment,
grounding, tradition,
upbringing

backing *noun* SUPPORT, aid,
assistance, encouragement,
endorsement, moral support,
patronage, sponsorship

backlash *noun* REACTION,
counteraction, recoil,
repercussion, resistance,
response, retaliation

backlog *noun* BUILD-UP,
accumulation, excess, hoard,
reserve, stock, supply

back out *verb* (often with *of*)
WITHDRAW, abandon, cancel,
excuse oneself, give up, go
back on, quit, resign, retreat,
wimp out (*slang*)

backslide *verb* RELAPSE, go
astray, go wrong, lapse, revert,
slip, stray, weaken

backslider *noun* RELAPSER,
apostate, deserter, recidivist,
recreant, renegade, turncoat

back up *verb* SUPPORT, aid, assist,
bolster, confirm, corroborate,
reinforce, second, stand by,
substantiate

backward *adjective* SLOW,
behind, dull, retarded,
subnormal, underdeveloped,
undeveloped

backwards, backward *adverb*
TOWARDS THE REAR, behind, in
reverse, rearward

bacteria *plural noun*
MICROORGANISMS, bacilli, bugs
(*slang*), germs, microbes,
pathogens, viruses

bad *adjective* 1 INFERIOR,
defective, faulty, imperfect,

inadequate, lousy (*slang*), poor, substandard, unsatisfactory **2** HARMFUL, damaging, dangerous, deleterious, detrimental, hurtful, ruinous, unhealthy **3** EVIL, corrupt, criminal, immoral, mean, sinful, wicked, wrong **4** NAUGHTY, disobedient, mischievous, unruly **5** ROTTEN, decayed, moldy, putrid, rancid, sour, spoiled **6** UNFAVORABLE, adverse, distressing, gloomy, grim, troubled, unfortunate, unpleasant

badge *noun* MARK, brand, device, emblem, identification, insignia, sign, stamp, token

badger *verb* PESTER, bully, goad, harass, hound, importune, nag, plague, torment

badinage *noun* WORDPLAY, banter, mockery, pleasantry, repartee, teasing

badly *adverb* **1** POORLY, carelessly, imperfectly, inadequately, incorrectly, ineptly, wrongly **2** UNFAVORABLY, unfortunately, unsuccessfully **3** SEVERELY, deeply, desperately, exceedingly, extremely, greatly, intensely, seriously

bad-mouth *verb* Slang CRITICIZE, abuse, deride, insult, malign, mock, slander

baffle *verb* PUZZLE, bewilder, confound, confuse, flummox, mystify, nonplus, perplex, stump

bag *noun* **1** CONTAINER, receptacle, sac, sack ▶ *verb* **2** CATCH, acquire, capture, kill, land, shoot, trap

baggage *noun* LUGGAGE, accoutrements, bags,

belongings, equipment, gear, paraphernalia, suitcases, things

baggy *adjective* LOOSE, bulging, droopy, floppy, ill-fitting, oversize, roomy, sagging, slack

bail *noun Law* SECURITY, bond, guarantee, pledge, surety, warranty

bail out *verb* **1** HELP, aid, relieve, rescue, save (someone's) bacon (*informal*) **2** ESCAPE, quit, retreat, withdraw

bait *noun* **1** LURE, allurement, attraction, decoy, enticement, incentive, inducement, snare, temptation ▶ *verb* **2** TEASE, annoy, bother, harass, hassle (*informal*), hound, irritate, persecute, torment

baked *adjective* DRY, arid, desiccated, parched, scorched, seared, sun-baked, torrid

balance *noun* **1** STABILITY, composure, equanimity, poise, self-control, self-possession, steadiness **2** EQUILIBRIUM, correspondence, equity, equivalence, evenness, parity, symmetry **3** REMAINDER, difference, residue, rest, surplus ▶ *verb* **4** STABILIZE, level, match, parallel, steady **5** COMPARE, assess, consider, deliberate, estimate, evaluate, weigh **6** *Accounting* CALCULATE, compute, settle, square, tally, total

balcony *noun* **1** TERRACE, veranda **2** UPPER CIRCLE, gallery, gods

bald *adjective* **1** HAIRLESS, baldheaded, depilated **2** PLAIN, blunt, direct, forthright, straightforward, unadorned, unvarnished

balderdash noun NONSENSE, claptrap (informal), drivel, garbage (informal), gibberish, hogwash, hot air (informal), rubbish

baldness noun 1 HAIRLESSNESS, alopecia (Pathology), baldheadedness 2 PLAINNESS, austerity, bluntness, severity, simplicity

balk verb 1 RECOIL, evade, flinch, hesitate, jib, refuse, resist, shirk, shrink from 2 FOIL, check, counteract, defeat, frustrate, hinder, obstruct, prevent, thwart

ball noun SPHERE, drop, globe, globule, orb, pellet, spheroid

ballast noun COUNTERBALANCE, balance, counterweight, equilibrium, sandbag, stability, stabilizer, weight

balloon verb SWELL, billow, blow up, dilate, distend, expand, grow rapidly, inflate, puff out

ballot noun VOTE, election, poll, polling, voting

ballyhoo noun FUSS, babble, commotion, hubbub, hue and cry, hullabaloo, noise, racket, to-do

balm noun 1 OINTMENT, balsam, cream, embrocation, emollient, lotion, salve, unguent 2 COMFORT, anodyne, consolation, curative, palliative, restorative, solace

balmy adjective MILD, clement, pleasant, summery, temperate

baloney noun Informal NONSENSE, claptrap (informal), crap (slang), drivel, garbage, hogwash, poppycock (informal), rubbish, stuff and nonsense, trash, tripe (informal)

bamboozle verb Informal 1 CHEAT, con (informal), deceive, dupe, fool, hoodwink, swindle, trick 2 PUZZLE, baffle, befuddle, confound, confuse, mystify, perplex, stump

ban verb 1 PROHIBIT, banish, bar, block, boycott, disallow, disqualify, exclude, forbid, outlaw ▸ noun 2 PROHIBITION, boycott, disqualification, embargo, restriction, taboo

banal adjective UNORIGINAL, hackneyed, humdrum, mundane, pedestrian, stale, stereotyped, trite, unimaginative

band¹ noun 1 ENSEMBLE, combo, group, orchestra 2 GANG, body, company, group, party, posse (informal)

band² noun STRIP, belt, bond, chain, cord, ribbon, strap

bandage noun 1 DRESSING, compress, gauze, plaster ▸ verb 2 DRESS, bind, cover, swathe

bandit noun ROBBER, desperado, highwayman, marauder, outlaw, thief

bane noun PLAGUE, bête noire, curse, nuisance, pest, ruin, scourge, torment

bang noun 1 EXPLOSION, clang, clap, clash, pop, slam, thud, thump 2 BLOW, bump, cuff, knock, punch, smack, stroke, whack ▸ verb 3 HIT, belt (informal), clatter, knock, slam, strike, thump 4 EXPLODE, boom, clang, resound, thump, thunder ▸ adverb 5 HARD, abruptly, headlong, noisily, suddenly 6 STRAIGHT, precisely, slap, smack

banish verb 1 EXPEL, deport,

eject, evict, exile, outlaw **2** GET
RID OF, ban, cast out, discard,
dismiss, oust, remove

banishment noun EXPULSION,
deportation, exile, expatriation,
transportation

banisters plural noun RAILING,
balusters, balustrade, handrail,
rail

bank[1] noun **1** STOREHOUSE,
depository, repository **2** STORE,
accumulation, fund, hoard,
reserve, reservoir, savings,
stock, stockpile ▶ verb **3** SAVE,
deposit, keep

bank[2] noun **1** MOUND, banking,
embankment, heap, mass, pile,
ridge **2** SIDE, brink, edge,
margin, shore ▶ verb **3** PILE,
amass, heap, mass, mound,
stack **4** TILT, camber, cant, heel,
incline, pitch, slant, slope, tip

bank[3] noun ROW, array, file,
group, line, rank, sequence,
series, succession

bankrupt adjective INSOLVENT,
broke (informal), destitute,
impoverished, in queer street,
in the red, ruined, wiped out
(informal)

bankruptcy noun INSOLVENCY,
disaster, failure, liquidation, ruin

banner noun FLAG, colors,
ensign, pennant, placard,
standard, streamer

banquet noun FEAST, dinner,
meal, repast, revel, treat

banter verb **1** JOKE, jest, kid
(informal), rib (informal), taunt,
tease ▶ noun **2** JOKING,
badinage, jesting, kidding
(informal), repartee, teasing,
wordplay

baptism noun Christianity
CHRISTENING, immersion,

purification, sprinkling

baptize verb Christianity PURIFY,
cleanse, immerse

bar noun **1** ROD, paling,
palisade, pole, rail, shaft, stake,
stick **2** OBSTACLE, barricade,
barrier, block, deterrent,
hindrance, impediment,
obstruction, stop **3** PUBLIC
HOUSE, canteen, counter, inn,
saloon, tavern, watering hole
(facetious slang) ▶ verb **4** FASTEN,
barricade, bolt, latch, lock,
secure **5** OBSTRUCT, hinder,
prevent, restrain **6** EXCLUDE,
ban, black, blackball, forbid,
keep out, prohibit

Bar noun the Bar Law BARRISTERS,
body of lawyers, counsel,
court, judgment, tribunal

barb noun **1** DIG, affront, cut,
gibe, insult, sarcasm, scoff,
sneer **2** POINT, bristle, prickle,
prong, quill, spike, spur, thorn

barbarian noun **1** SAVAGE, brute,
yahoo **2** LOUT, bigot, boor,
philistine

barbaric adjective **1** UNCIVILIZED,
primitive, rude, wild **2** BRUTAL,
barbarous, coarse, crude, cruel,
fierce, inhuman, savage

barbarism noun SAVAGERY,
coarseness, crudity

barbarous adjective
1 UNCIVILIZED, barbarian, brutish,
primitive, rough, rude, savage,
uncouth, wild **2** BRUTAL,
barbaric, cruel, ferocious,
heartless, inhuman, monstrous,
ruthless, vicious

barbed adjective **1** CUTTING,
critical, hostile, hurtful, nasty,
pointed, scathing, unkind
2 SPIKED, hooked, jagged,
prickly, spiny, thorny

bare adjective 1 NAKED, nude, stripped, unclad, unclothed, uncovered, undressed, without a stitch on (*informal*) 2 PLAIN, bald, basic, sheer, simple, stark, unembellished 3 SIMPLE, austere, homely, spare, spartan, unadorned, unembellished

barefaced adjective 1 OBVIOUS, blatant, flagrant, open, transparent, unconcealed 2 SHAMELESS, audacious, bold, brash, brazen, impudent, insolent

barely adverb ONLY JUST, almost, at a push, by the skin of one's teeth, hardly, just, scarcely

barf verb Slang VOMIT, heave, puke (*slang*), retch, spew, throw up (*informal*), toss one's cookies (*slang*) ▶ noun VOMIT, puke, sick

bargain noun 1 AGREEMENT, arrangement, contract, pact, pledge, promise 2 GOOD BUY, (cheap) purchase, discount, giveaway, good deal, reduction, steal (*informal*) ▶ verb 3 NEGOTIATE, agree, contract, covenant, promise, stipulate, transact

barge noun CANAL BOAT, flatboat, lighter, narrow boat

bark[1] noun, verb YAP, bay, growl, howl, snarl, woof, yelp

bark[2] noun COVERING, casing, cortex (*Anatomy, botany*), crust, husk, rind, skin

barracks plural noun CAMP, billet, encampment, garrison, quarters

barrage noun 1 TORRENT, burst, deluge, hail, mass, onslaught, plethora, stream 2 Military

BOMBARDMENT, battery, cannonade, fusillade, gunfire, salvo, shelling, volley

barren adjective 1 INFERTILE, childless, sterile, unproductive 2 UNPRODUCTIVE, arid, desert, desolate, dry, empty, unfruitful, waste

barricade noun 1 BARRIER, blockade, bulwark, fence, obstruction, palisade, rampart, stockade ▶ verb 2 BAR, block, blockade, defend, fortify, obstruct, protect, shut in

barrier noun 1 BARRICADE, bar, blockade, boundary, fence, obstacle, obstruction, wall 2 HINDRANCE, difficulty, drawback, handicap, hurdle, obstacle, restriction, stumbling block

barter verb TRADE, bargain, drive a hard bargain, exchange, haggle, sell, swap, traffic

base[1] noun 1 BOTTOM, bed, foot, foundation, pedestal, rest, stand, support 2 BASIS, core, essence, heart, key, origin, root, source 3 CENTER, camp, headquarters, home, post, settlement, starting point, station ▶ verb 4 FOUND, build, construct, depend, derive, establish, ground, hinge 5 PLACE, locate, post, station

base[2] adjective 1 DISHONORABLE, contemptible, despicable, disreputable, evil, immoral, lousy (*slang*), scuzzy (*slang*), shameful, sordid, wicked 2 COUNTERFEIT, alloyed, debased, fake, forged, fraudulent, impure

baseless adjective UNFOUNDED, groundless, unconfirmed, uncorroborated, ungrounded, unjustified, unsubstantiated, unsupported

bash verb Informal HIT, belt (informal), smash, sock (slang), strike, wallop (informal)

bashful adjective SHY, blushing, coy, diffident, reserved, reticent, retiring, timid

basic adjective ESSENTIAL, elementary, fundamental, key, necessary, primary, vital

basically adverb ESSENTIALLY, at heart, fundamentally, inherently, in substance, intrinsically, mostly, primarily

basics plural noun ESSENTIALS, ABCs, brass tacks (informal), fundamentals, nitty-gritty (informal), nuts and bolts (informal), principles, rudiments

basis noun FOUNDATION, base, bottom, footing, ground, groundwork, support

bask verb LIE IN, laze, loll, lounge, relax, sunbathe, swim in

bass adjective DEEP, deep-toned, low, low-pitched, resonant, sonorous

bastard noun 1 Informal, offensive ROGUE, miscreant, reprobate, scoundrel, villain, wretch 2 ILLEGITIMATE CHILD, love child, natural child

bastion noun STRONGHOLD, bulwark, citadel, defense, fortress, mainstay, prop, rock, support, tower of strength

bat noun, verb HIT, bang, smack, strike, swat, thump, wallop (informal), whack

batch noun GROUP, amount, assemblage, bunch, collection, crowd, lot, pack, quantity, set

bath noun 1 WASH, cleansing, douche, scrubbing, shower, soak, tub ▸ verb 2 WASH, bathe, clean, douse, scrub down, shower, soak

bathe verb 1 WASH, cleanse, rinse, soak 2 COVER, flood, immerse, steep, suffuse

baton noun STICK, club, crook, mace, rod, scepter, staff, truncheon, wand

batten verb (usually with down) FASTEN, board up, clamp down, cover up, fix, nail down, secure, tighten

batter verb BEAT, buffet, clobber (slang), pelt, pound, pummel, thrash, wallop (informal)

battery noun ARTILLERY, cannon, cannonry, gun emplacements, guns

battle noun 1 FIGHT, action, attack, combat, encounter, engagement, hostilities, skirmish 2 CONFLICT, campaign, contest, crusade, dispute, struggle ▸ verb 3 STRUGGLE, argue, clamor, dispute, fight, lock horns, strive, war

battlefield noun BATTLEGROUND, combat zone, field, field of battle, front

battleship noun WARSHIP, gunboat, man-of-war

batty adjective CRAZY, absent-minded, bonkers (informal), daft (informal), eccentric, mad, odd, peculiar

bauble noun TRINKET, bagatelle, gewgaw, gimcrack, knick-knack, plaything, toy, trifle

baulk see BALK

bawdy adjective RUDE, coarse, dirty, indecent, lascivious, lecherous, lewd, ribald, salacious, smutty

bawl verb **1** CRY, blubber, sob, wail, weep **2** SHOUT, bellow, call, clamor, howl, roar, yell

bay[1] noun INLET, bight, cove, gulf, natural harbor, sound

bay[2] noun RECESS, alcove, compartment, niche, nook, opening

bay[3] verb HOWL, bark, clamor, cry, growl, yelp

bazaar noun **1** FAIR, bring-and-buy, fête, sale of work **2** MARKET, exchange, marketplace

be verb EXIST, be alive, breathe, inhabit, live

beach noun SHORE, coast, sands, seashore, seaside, water's edge

beached adjective STRANDED, abandoned, aground, ashore, deserted, grounded, high and dry, marooned, wrecked

beacon noun SIGNAL, beam, bonfire, flare, lighthouse, sign, watchtower

bead noun DROP, blob, bubble, dot, droplet, globule, pellet, pill

beady adjective BRIGHT, gleaming, glinting, glittering, sharp, shining

beak noun BILL, mandible, neb (archaic or dialect), nib

beam noun **1** SMILE, grin **2** RAY, gleam, glimmer, glint, glow, shaft, streak, stream **3** RAFTER, girder, joist, plank, spar, support, timber ▸ verb **4** SMILE, grin **5** RADIATE, gleam, glitter, glow, shine **6** SEND OUT, broadcast, emit, transmit

bear verb **1** SUPPORT, have, hold, maintain, possess, shoulder, sustain, uphold **2** CARRY, bring, convey, move, take, transport **3** PRODUCE, beget, breed, bring

forth, engender, generate, give birth to, yield **4** TOLERATE, abide, allow, brook, endure, permit, put up with (informal), stomach, suffer

bearable adjective TOLERABLE, admissible, endurable, manageable, passable, sufferable, supportable, sustainable

bearer noun CARRIER, agent, conveyor, messenger, porter, runner, servant

bearing noun (usually with on or upon) RELEVANCE, application, connection, import, pertinence, reference, relation, significance **2** MANNER, air, aspect, attitude, behavior, demeanor, deportment, posture

bearings plural noun POSITION, aim, course, direction, location, orientation, situation, track, way, whereabouts

bear out verb SUPPORT, confirm, corroborate, endorse, justify, prove, substantiate, uphold, vindicate

beast noun **1** ANIMAL, brute, creature **2** BRUTE, barbarian, fiend, monster, ogre, sadist, savage, swine

beastly adjective UNPLEASANT, awful, disagreeable, horrid, mean, nasty, rotten

beat verb **1** HIT, bang, batter, buffet, knock, pound, strike, thrash **2** FLAP, flutter **3** THROB, palpitate, pound, pulsate, quake, thump, vibrate **4** DEFEAT, conquer, outdo, overcome, overwhelm, surpass, vanquish ▸ noun **5** THROB, palpitation, pulsation, pulse **6** ROUTE, circuit, course, path, rounds, way **7** RHYTHM, accent, cadence, meter, stress, time

beaten adjective **1** STIRRED, blended, foamy, frothy, mixed, whipped, whisked **2** DEFEATED, cowed, overcome, overwhelmed, thwarted, vanquished

beat up verb Informal ASSAULT, attack, batter, beat the living daylights out of (informal), knock about or around, pound, pulverize, thrash

beau noun **1** Old-fashioned BOYFRIEND, admirer, fiancé, lover, suitor, sweetheart **2** DANDY, coxcomb, fop, gallant, ladies' man

beautiful adjective ATTRACTIVE, charming, delightful, exquisite, fair, fine, gorgeous, handsome, lovely, pleasing

beautify verb MAKE BEAUTIFUL, adorn, decorate, embellish, festoon, garnish, glamorize, ornament

beauty noun **1** ATTRACTIVENESS, charm, comeliness, elegance, exquisiteness, glamour, grace, handsomeness, loveliness **2** BELLE, good-looker, lovely (slang), stunner (informal)

becalmed adjective STILL, motionless, settled, stranded, stuck

because conjunction SINCE, as, by reason of, in that, on account of, owing to, thanks to

beckon verb GESTURE, bid, gesticulate, motion, nod, signal, summon, wave at

become verb **1** COME TO BE, alter to, be transformed into, change into, develop into, grow into, mature into, ripen into **2** SUIT, embellish, enhance, fit, flatter, set off

becoming adjective **1** APPROPRIATE, compatible, fitting, in keeping, proper, seemly, suitable, worthy **2** FLATTERING, attractive, comely, enhancing, graceful, neat, pretty, tasteful

bed noun **1** BEDSTEAD, berth, bunk, cot, couch, divan **2** PLOT, area, border, garden, patch, row, strip **3** BOTTOM, base, foundation, groundwork

bedevil verb **1** TORMENT, afflict, distress, harass, plague, trouble, vex, worry **2** CONFUSE, confound

bedlam noun PANDEMONIUM, chaos, commotion, confusion, furor, tumult, turmoil, uproar

bedraggled adjective MESSY, dirty, dishevelled, disordered, muddied, scuzzy (slang), unkempt, untidy

bedridden adjective CONFINED TO BED, confined, flat on one's back, incapacitated, laid up (informal)

bedrock noun **1** BOTTOM, bed, foundation, rock bottom, substratum, substructure **2** BASICS, basis, core, essentials, fundamentals, nuts and bolts (informal), roots

beefy adjective Informal BRAWNY, bulky, hulking, muscular, stocky, strapping, sturdy, thickset

befall verb HAPPEN, chance, come to pass, fall, occur, take place, transpire (informal)

befitting adjective APPROPRIATE, apposite, becoming, fit, fitting, proper, right, seemly, suitable

before preposition 1 AHEAD OF, in advance of, in front of 2 EARLIER THAN, in advance of, prior to 3 IN THE PRESENCE OF, in front of ▶adverb 4 PREVIOUSLY, ahead, earlier, formerly, in advance, sooner 5 IN FRONT, ahead

beforehand adverb IN ADVANCE, ahead of time, already, before, earlier, in anticipation, previously

befriend verb HELP, aid, assist, back, encourage, side with, stand by, support, welcome

beg verb 1 SCROUNGE, cadge, seek charity, solicit charity, sponge on 2 IMPLORE, beseech, entreat, petition, plead, request, solicit

beggar noun TRAMP, bag lady, bum (informal), down-and-out, pauper, vagrant

beggarly adjective POOR, destitute, impoverished, indigent, needy, poverty-stricken

begin verb 1 START, commence, embark on, initiate, instigate, institute, prepare, set about 2 HAPPEN, appear, arise, come into being, emerge, originate, start

beginner noun NOVICE, amateur, apprentice, learner, neophyte, rookie (informal), starter, trainee, tyro

beginning noun 1 START, birth, commencement, inauguration, inception, initiation, onset, opening, origin, outset 2 SEED, fount, germ, root

begrudge verb RESENT, be jealous, be reluctant, be stingy, envy, grudge

beguile verb 1 FOOL, cheat, deceive, delude, dupe, hoodwink, mislead, take for a ride (informal), trick 2 CHARM, amuse, distract, divert, engross, entertain, occupy

beguiling adjective CHARMING, alluring, attractive, bewitching, captivating, enchanting, enthralling, intriguing

behave verb 1 ACT, function, operate, perform, run, work 2 CONDUCT ONESELF PROPERLY, act correctly, keep one's nose clean, mind one's manners

behavior noun 1 CONDUCT, actions, bearing, demeanor, deportment, manner, manners, ways 2 ACTION, functioning, operation, performance

behind preposition 1 AFTER, at the back of, at the heels of, at the rear of, following, later than 2 CAUSING, at the bottom of, initiating, instigating, responsible for 3 SUPPORTING, backing, for, in agreement, on the side of ▶adverb 4 AFTER, afterwards, following, in the wake (of), next, subsequently 5 OVERDUE, behindhand, in arrears, in debt ▶noun 6 Informal BOTTOM, butt (informal), buttocks, posterior

behold verb LOOK AT, observe, perceive, regard, survey, view, watch, witness

beholden adjective INDEBTED, bound, grateful, obliged, owing, under obligation

being noun 1 EXISTENCE, life, reality 2 NATURE, entity, essence, soul, spirit, substance 3 CREATURE, human being, individual, living thing

belated adjective LATE,

behindhand, behind time, delayed, late in the day, overdue, tardy

belch verb 1 BURP (*informal*), hiccup 2 EMIT, discharge, disgorge, erupt, give off, spew forth, vent

beleaguered adjective 1 HARASSED, badgered, hassled (*informal*), persecuted, pestered, plagued, put upon, vexed 2 BESIEGED, assailed, beset, blockaded, hemmed in, surrounded

belief noun 1 TRUST, assurance, confidence, conviction, feeling, impression, judgment, notion, opinion 2 FAITH, credo, creed, doctrine, dogma, ideology, principles, tenet

believable adjective CREDIBLE, authentic, imaginable, likely, plausible, possible, probable, trustworthy

believe verb 1 ACCEPT, be certain of, be convinced of, credit, depend on, have faith in, rely on, swear by, trust 2 THINK, assume, gather, imagine, judge, presume, reckon, speculate, suppose

believer noun FOLLOWER, adherent, convert, devotee, disciple, supporter, upholder, zealot

belittle verb DISPARAGE, decry, denigrate, deprecate, deride, scoff at, scorn, sneer at

belligerent adjective 1 AGGRESSIVE, bellicose, combative, hostile, pugnacious, unfriendly, warlike, warring ▶ noun 2 FIGHTER, combatant, warring nation

bellow noun, verb SHOUT, bawl,

clamor, cry, howl, roar, scream, shriek, yell

belly noun 1 STOMACH, abdomen, gut, insides (*informal*), paunch, potbelly, tummy ▶ verb 2 SWELL OUT, billow, bulge, fill, spread, swell

bellyful noun SURFEIT, enough, excess, glut, plateful, plenty, satiety, too much

belonging noun RELATIONSHIP, acceptance, affinity, association, attachment, fellowship, inclusion, loyalty, rapport

belongings plural noun POSSESSIONS, accouterments, chattels, effects, gear, goods, paraphernalia, personal property, stuff, things

belong to verb 1 BE THE PROPERTY OF, be at the disposal of, be held by, be owned by 2 BE A MEMBER OF, be affiliated to, be associated with, be included in

beloved adjective DEAR, admired, adored, darling, loved, pet, precious, prized, treasured, worshipped

below preposition 1 LESSER, inferior, subject, subordinate 2 LESS THAN, lower than ▶ adverb 3 LOWER, beneath, down, under, underneath

belt noun 1 WAISTBAND, band, cummerbund, girdle, girth, sash 2 Geography ZONE, area, district, layer, region, stretch, strip, tract

bemoan verb LAMENT, bewail, deplore, grieve for, mourn, regret, rue, weep for

bemused adjective PUZZLED, at sea, bewildered, confused, flummoxed, muddled, nonplussed, perplexed

bench noun 1 SEAT, form, pew, settle, stall 2 WORKTABLE, board, counter, table, trestle table, workbench 3 **the bench** COURT, courtroom, judges, judiciary, magistrates, tribunal

benchmark noun REFERENCE POINT, criterion, gauge, level, measure, model, norm, par, standard, yardstick

bend verb 1 CURVE, arc, arch, bow, lean, turn, twist, veer ▸noun 2 CURVE, angle, arc, arch, bow, corner, loop, turn, twist

beneath preposition 1 UNDER, below, lower than, underneath 2 INFERIOR TO, below, less than 3 UNWORTHY OF, unbefitting ▸adverb 4 UNDERNEATH, below, in a lower place

benefactor noun SUPPORTER, backer, donor, helper, patron, philanthropist, sponsor, well-wisher

beneficial adjective HELPFUL, advantageous, benign, favorable, profitable, useful, valuable, wholesome, win-win (informal)

beneficiary noun RECIPIENT, heir, inheritor, payee, receiver

benefit noun 1 HELP, advantage, aid, asset, assistance, favor, good, profit ▸verb 2 HELP, aid, assist, avail, enhance, further, improve, profit

benevolent adjective KIND, altruistic, benign, caring, charitable, generous, philanthropic

benign adjective 1 KINDLY, amiable, friendly, genial, kind, obliging, sympathetic

2 Medical HARMLESS, curable, remediable

bent adjective 1 CURVED, angled, arched, bowed, crooked, hunched, stooped, twisted 2 **bent on** DETERMINED TO, disposed to, fixed on, inclined to, insistent on, predisposed to, resolved on, set on ▸noun 3 INCLINATION, ability, aptitude, leaning, penchant, preference, propensity, tendency

bequeath verb LEAVE, bestow, endow, entrust, give, grant, hand down, impart, pass on, will

bequest noun LEGACY, bestowal, endowment, estate, gift, inheritance, settlement

berate verb SCOLD, castigate, censure, chide, criticize, harangue, rebuke, reprimand, reprove, tell off (informal), upbraid

bereavement noun LOSS, affliction, death, deprivation, misfortune, tribulation

bereft adjective DEPRIVED, devoid, lacking, parted from, robbed of, wanting

berserk adverb CRAZY, amok, enraged, frantic, frenzied, mad, raging, wild

berth noun 1 BUNK, bed, billet, hammock 2 Nautical ANCHORAGE, dock, harbor, haven, pier, port, quay, wharf ▸verb 3 Nautical ANCHOR, dock, drop anchor, land, moor, tie up

beseech verb BEG, ask, call upon, entreat, implore, plead, pray, solicit

beset verb PLAGUE, bedevil, harass, pester, trouble

beside preposition 1 NEXT TO,

abreast of, adjacent to, alongside, at the side of, close to, near, nearby, neighboring **2 beside oneself** DISTRAUGHT, apoplectic, at the end of one's tether, demented, desperate, frantic, frenzied, out of one's mind, unhinged

besides adverb **1** TOO, also, as well, further, furthermore, in addition, into the bargain, moreover, otherwise, what's more ▶preposition **2** APART FROM, barring, excepting, excluding, in addition to, other than, over and above, without

besiege verb **1** SURROUND, blockade, encircle, hem in, lay siege to, shut in **2** HARASS, badger, harry, hassle (*informal*), hound, nag, pester, plague

besotted adjective INFATUATED, doting, hypnotized, smitten, spellbound

best adjective **1** FINEST, foremost, leading, most excellent, outstanding, pre-eminent, principal, supreme, unsurpassed ▶adverb **2** MOST HIGHLY, extremely, greatly, most deeply, most fully ▶noun **3** FINEST, cream, crème de la crème, elite, flower, pick, prime, top

bestial adjective BRUTAL, barbaric, beastly, brutish, inhuman, savage, sordid

bestow verb PRESENT, award, commit, give, grant, hand out, impart, lavish

bet noun **1** GAMBLE, long shot, risk, speculation, stake, venture, wager ▶verb **2** GAMBLE, chance, hazard, risk, speculate, stake, venture, wager

betoken verb INDICATE, bode, denote, promise, represent, signify, suggest

betray verb **1** BE DISLOYAL, be treacherous, be unfaithful, break one's promise, double-cross (*informal*), inform on or against, sell out (*informal*), stab in the back **2** GIVE AWAY, disclose, divulge, expose, let slip, reveal, uncover, unmask

betrayal noun **1** DISLOYALTY, deception, double-cross (*informal*), sell-out (*informal*), treachery, treason, trickery **2** GIVING AWAY, disclosure, divulgence, revelation

better adjective **1** SUPERIOR, excelling, finer, greater, higher-quality, more desirable, preferable, surpassing **2** WELL, cured, fully recovered, on the mend (*informal*), recovering, stronger ▶adverb **3** IN A MORE EXCELLENT MANNER, in a superior way, more advantageously, more attractively, more competently, more effectively **4** TO A GREATER DEGREE, more completely, more thoroughly ▶verb **5** IMPROVE, enhance, further, raise

between preposition AMIDST, among, betwixt, in the middle of, mid

beverage noun DRINK, liquid, liquor, refreshment

bevy noun GROUP, band, bunch (*informal*), collection, company, crowd, gathering, pack, troupe

bewail verb LAMENT, bemoan, cry over, deplore, grieve for, moan, mourn, regret

beware verb BE CAREFUL, be

cautious, be wary, guard against, heed, look out, mind, take heed, watch out

bewilder verb CONFOUND, baffle, bemuse, confuse, flummox, mystify, nonplus, perplex, puzzle

bewildered adjective CONFUSED, at a loss, at sea, baffled, flummoxed, mystified, nonplussed, perplexed, puzzled

bewitch verb ENCHANT, beguile, captivate, charm, enrapture, entrance, fascinate, hypnotize

bewitched adjective ENCHANTED, charmed, entranced, fascinated, mesmerized, spellbound, under a spell

beyond preposition 1 PAST, above, apart from, at a distance, away from, over 2 EXCEEDING, out of reach of, superior to, surpassing

bias noun 1 PREJUDICE, favoritism, inclination, leaning, partiality, tendency ▸verb 2 PREJUDICE, distort, influence, predispose, slant, sway, twist, warp, weight

biased adjective PREJUDICED, distorted, one-sided, partial, slanted, weighted

bicker verb QUARREL, argue, disagree, dispute, fight, squabble, wrangle

bid verb 1 OFFER, proffer, propose, submit, tender 2 SAY, call, greet, tell, wish 3 TELL, ask, command, direct, instruct, order, require ▸noun 4 OFFER, advance, amount, price, proposal, sum, tender 5 ATTEMPT, crack (informal), effort, go (informal), stab (informal), try

bidding noun ORDER, beck and

call, command, direction, instruction, request, summons

big adjective 1 LARGE, enormous, extensive, great, huge, immense, massive, substantial, vast 2 IMPORTANT, eminent, influential, leading, main, powerful, prominent, significant 3 GROWN-UP, adult, elder, grown, mature 4 GENEROUS, altruistic, benevolent, gracious, magnanimous, noble, unselfish

big cheese noun Informal MANAGER, boss (informal), bossman (slang), foreman, head honcho (slang), overseer, superintendent, supervisor

bighead noun Informal BOASTER, braggart, know-all (informal)

bigheaded adjective BOASTFUL, arrogant, cocky, conceited, egotistic, immodest, overconfident, swollen-headed

bigot noun FANATIC, racist, sectarian, zealot

bigoted adjective INTOLERANT, biased, dogmatic, narrow-minded, opinionated, prejudiced, sectarian

bigotry noun INTOLERANCE, bias, discrimination, dogmatism, fanaticism, narrow-mindedness, prejudice, sectarianism

bill[1] noun 1 CHARGES, account, invoice, reckoning, score, statement, tally 2 PROPOSAL, measure, piece of legislation, projected law 3 ADVERTISEMENT, bulletin, circular, handbill, handout, leaflet, notice, placard, poster 4 LIST, agenda, card, catalog, inventory, listing, program, roster, schedule ▸verb 5 CHARGE, debit, invoice

6 ADVERTISE, announce, give advance notice of, post

bill² noun BEAK, mandible, neb (archaic or dialect), nib

billet verb 1 QUARTER, accommodate, berth, station ▶noun 2 QUARTERS, accommodation, barracks, lodging

billow noun 1 WAVE, breaker, crest, roller, surge, swell, tide ▶verb 2 SURGE, balloon, belly, puff up, rise up, roll, swell

bind verb 1 SECURE, fasten, hitch, lash, strap, tie 2 OBLIGE, compel, constrain, engage, force, necessitate, require ▶noun Informal 3 NUISANCE, bore, drag (informal), pain in the neck (informal) 4 DIFFICULTY, dilemma, quandary, spot (informal)

binding adjective COMPULSORY, indissoluble, irrevocable, mandatory, necessary, obligatory, unalterable

binge noun Informal BOUT, feast, fling, orgy, spree

biography noun LIFE STORY, account, curriculum vitae, CV, life, memoir, profile, record

birth noun 1 CHILDBIRTH, delivery, nativity, parturition 2 ANCESTRY, background, blood, breeding, lineage, parentage, pedigree, stock

bisect verb CUT IN TWO, cross, cut across, divide in two, halve, intersect, separate, split

bit¹ noun PIECE, crumb, fragment, grain, morsel, part, scrap, speck

bit² noun CURB, brake, check, restraint, snaffle

bitch noun 1 Informal COMPLAINT, gripe (informal), grouse, grumble, objection, protest ▶verb 2 Informal COMPLAIN, bemoan, gripe (informal), grouse, grumble, lament, object

bitchy adjective Informal SPITEFUL, backbiting, catty (informal), mean, nasty, snide, vindictive

bite verb 1 CUT, chew, gnaw, nip, pierce, pinch, snap, tear, wound ▶noun 2 WOUND, nip, pinch, prick, smarting, sting, tooth marks 3 SNACK, food, light meal, morsel, mouthful, piece, refreshment, taste

biting adjective 1 PIERCING, bitter, cutting, harsh, penetrating, sharp 2 SARCASTIC, caustic, cutting, incisive, mordant, scathing, stinging, trenchant, vitriolic

bitter adjective 1 SOUR, acid, acrid, astringent, harsh, sharp, tart, unsweetened, vinegary 2 RESENTFUL, acrimonious, begrudging, hostile, sore, sour, sullen 3 FREEZING, biting, fierce, intense, severe, stinging

bitterness noun 1 SOURNESS, acerbity, acidity, sharpness, tartness 2 RESENTMENT, acrimony, animosity, asperity, grudge, hostility, rancor, sarcasm

bizarre adjective STRANGE, eccentric, extraordinary, fantastic, freakish, ludicrous, outlandish, peculiar, unusual, weird, zany

blab verb TELL, blurt out, disclose, divulge, give away, let slip, let the cat out of the bag, reveal, spill the beans (informal)

black adjective 1 DARK, dusky, ebony, jet, raven, sable, swarthy **2** HOPELESS, depressing, dismal, foreboding, gloomy, ominous, sad, somber **3** ANGRY, furious, hostile, menacing, resentful, sullen, threatening **4** WICKED, bad, evil, iniquitous, nefarious, villainous ▶*verb* **5** BOYCOTT, ban, bar, blacklist

blacken *verb* **1** DARKEN, befoul, begrime, cloud, dirty, make black, smudge, soil **2** DISCREDIT, defame, denigrate, malign, slander, smear, smirch, vilify

blacklist *verb* EXCLUDE, ban, bar, boycott, debar, expel, reject, snub

black magic *noun* WITCHCRAFT, black art, diabolism, necromancy, sorcery, voodoo, wizardry

blackmail *noun* **1** THREAT, extortion, hush money (*slang*), intimidation, ransom ▶*verb* **2** THREATEN, coerce, compel, demand, extort, hold to ransom, intimidate, squeeze

blackness *noun* DARKNESS, duskiness, gloom, murkiness, swarthiness

blackout *noun*
1 UNCONSCIOUSNESS, coma, faint, loss of consciousness, oblivion, swoon **2** NONCOMMUNICATION, censorship, radio silence, secrecy, suppression, withholding news

blame *verb* **1** HOLD RESPONSIBLE, accuse, censure, chide, condemn, criticize, find fault with, reproach ▶*noun* **2** RESPONSIBILITY, accountability, culpability, fault, guilt, liability, onus

blameless *adjective* INNOCENT, above suspicion, clean, faultless, guiltless, immaculate, impeccable, irreproachable, perfect, unblemished, virtuous

blameworthy *adjective* REPREHENSIBLE, discreditable, disreputable, indefensible, inexcusable, iniquitous, reprehensible, shameful

bland *adjective* DULL, boring, flat, humdrum, insipid, tasteless, unexciting, uninspiring, vapid

blank *adjective* **1** UNMARKED, bare, clean, clear, empty, plain, void, white **2** EXPRESSIONLESS, deadpan, empty, impassive, poker-faced (*informal*), vacant, vague ▶*noun* **3** EMPTY SPACE, emptiness, gap, nothingness, space, vacancy, vacuum, void

blanket *noun* **1** COVER, coverlet, rug **2** COVERING, carpet, cloak, coat, layer, mantle, sheet ▶*verb* **3** COVER, cloak, coat, conceal, hide, mask, obscure, suppress

blare *verb* SOUND OUT, blast, clamor, clang, resound, roar, scream, trumpet

blasé *adjective* INDIFFERENT, apathetic, lukewarm, nonchalant, offhand, unconcerned

blaspheme *verb* CURSE, abuse, damn, desecrate, execrate, profane, revile, swear

blasphemous *adjective* IRREVERENT, godless, impious, irreligious, profane, sacrilegious, ungodly

blasphemy *noun* IRREVERENCE, cursing, desecration, execration, impiety, profanity, sacrilege, swearing

blast *noun* **1** EXPLOSION, bang,

burst, crash, detonation, discharge, eruption, outburst, salvo, volley **2** GUST, gale, squall, storm, strong breeze, tempest **3** BLARE, blow, clang, honk, peal, scream, toot, wail ▶*verb* **4** BLOW UP, break up, burst, demolish, destroy, explode, put paid to, ruin, shatter

blatant *adjective* OBVIOUS, brazen, conspicuous, flagrant, glaring, obtrusive, ostentatious, overt

blaze *noun* **1** FIRE, bonfire, conflagration, flames **2** GLARE, beam, brilliance, flare, flash, gleam, glitter, glow, light, radiance ▶*verb* **3** BURN, fire, flame **4** SHINE, beam, flare, flash, glare, gleam, glow

bleach *verb* WHITEN, blanch, fade, grow pale, lighten, wash out

bleak *adjective* **1** EXPOSED, bare, barren, desolate, unsheltered, weather-beaten, windswept **2** DISMAL, cheerless, depressing, discouraging, dreary, gloomy, grim, hopeless, joyless, somber

bleary *adjective* DIM, blurred, blurry, foggy, fuzzy, hazy, indistinct, misty, murky

bleed *verb* **1** LOSE BLOOD, flow, gush, ooze, run, shed blood, spurt **2** DRAW *or* TAKE BLOOD, extract, leech **3** *Informal* EXTORT, drain, exhaust, fleece, milk, squeeze

blemish *noun* **1** MARK, blot, defect, disfigurement, fault, flaw, imperfection, smudge, stain, taint ▶*verb* **2** STAIN, damage, disfigure, impair, injure, mar, mark, spoil, sully,

taint, tarnish

blend *verb* **1** MIX, amalgamate, combine, compound, merge, mingle, unite **2** GO WELL, complement, fit, go with, harmonize, suit ▶*noun* **3** MIXTURE, alloy, amalgamation, combination, compound, concoction, mix, synthesis, union

bless *verb* **1** SANCTIFY, anoint, consecrate, dedicate, exalt, hallow, ordain **2** GRANT, bestow, favor, give, grace, provide

blessed *adjective* HOLY, adored, beatified, divine, hallowed, revered, sacred, sanctified

blessing *noun* **1** BENEDICTION, benison, commendation, consecration, dedication, grace, invocation, thanksgiving **2** APPROVAL, backing, consent, favor, good wishes, leave, permission, sanction, support **3** BENEFIT, favor, gift, godsend, good fortune, help, kindness, service, windfall

blight *noun* **1** CURSE, affliction, bane, contamination, corruption, evil, plague, pollution, scourge, woe **2** DISEASE, canker, decay, fungus, infestation, mildew, pest, pestilence, rot ▶*verb* **3** FRUSTRATE, crush, dash, disappoint, mar, ruin, spoil, undo, wreck

blind *adjective* **1** SIGHTLESS, eyeless, unseeing, unsighted, visionless **2** UNAWARE OF, careless, heedless, ignorant, inattentive, inconsiderate, indifferent, insensitive, oblivious, unconscious of **3** UNREASONING, indiscriminate, prejudiced ▶ noun 4 COVER, camouflage, cloak, façade, feint, front, mask, masquerade, screen, smoke screen

blindly adverb 1 THOUGHTLESSLY, carelessly, heedlessly, inconsiderately, recklessly, senselessly 2 AIMLESSLY, at random, indiscriminately, instinctively

blink verb 1 WINK, bat, flutter 2 FLICKER, flash, gleam, glimmer, shine, twinkle, wink ▶ noun 1 **on the blink** Slang NOT WORKING (PROPERLY), faulty, malfunctioning, out of action, out of order, playing up

bliss noun JOY, beatitude, blessedness, blissfulness, ecstasy, euphoria, felicity, gladness, happiness, heaven, nirvana, paradise, rapture

blissful adjective JOYFUL, ecstatic, elated, enraptured, euphoric, happy, heavenly (informal), rapturous

blister noun SORE, abscess, boil, carbuncle, cyst, pimple, pustule, swelling

blithe adjective HEEDLESS, careless, casual, indifferent, nonchalant, thoughtless, unconcerned, untroubled

blitz noun ATTACK, assault, blitzkrieg, bombardment, campaign, offensive, onslaught, raid, strike

blizzard noun SNOWSTORM, blast, gale, squall, storm, tempest

bloat verb PUFF UP, balloon, blow up, dilate, distend, enlarge, expand, inflate, swell

blob noun DROP, ball, bead, bubble, dab, droplet, globule, lump, mass

bloc noun GROUP, alliance, axis, coalition, faction, league, union

block noun 1 PIECE, bar, brick, chunk, hunk, ingot, lump, mass 2 OBSTRUCTION, bar, barrier, blockage, hindrance, impediment, jam, obstacle ▶ verb 3 OBSTRUCT, choke, clog, close, plug, stem the flow, stop up 4 STOP, bar, check, halt, hinder, impede, obstruct, thwart

blockade noun STOPPAGE, barricade, barrier, block, hindrance, impediment, obstacle, obstruction, restriction, siege

blockage noun OBSTRUCTION, block, impediment, occlusion, stoppage

blockhead noun IDIOT, chump (informal), dork (slang), dunce, fool, nitwit, schmuck (slang), thickhead

blond, blonde adjective FAIR, fair-haired, fair-skinned, flaxen, golden-haired, light, tow-headed

blood noun 1 LIFEBLOOD, gore, vital fluid 2 FAMILY, ancestry, birth, descent, extraction, kinship, lineage, relations

bloodcurdling adjective TERRIFYING, appalling, chilling, dreadful, fearful, frightening, hair-raising, horrendous, horrifying, scaring, spine-chilling

bloodshed noun KILLING, blood bath, blood-letting, butchery, carnage, gore, massacre, murder, slaughter, slaying

bloodthirsty adjective CRUEL, barbarous, brutal, cut-throat, ferocious, gory, murderous, savage, vicious, warlike

bloody adjective 1 BLOODSTAINED, bleeding, blood-soaked, blood-spattered, gaping, raw 2 CRUEL, ferocious, fierce, sanguinary, savage

bloom noun 1 FLOWER, blossom, blossoming, bud, efflorescence, opening (of flowers) 2 PRIME, beauty, flourishing, freshness, glow, health, heyday, luster, radiance, vigor ▶ verb 3 BLOSSOM, blow, bud, burgeon, open, sprout 4 FLOURISH, develop, fare well, grow, prosper, succeed, thrive, wax

blossom noun 1 FLOWER, bloom, bud, floret, flowers ▶ verb 2 FLOWER, bloom, burgeon 3 GROW, bloom, develop, flourish, mature, progress, prosper, thrive

blot noun 1 SPOT, blotch, mark, patch, smear, smudge, speck, splodge 2 STAIN, blemish, defect, fault, flaw, scar, spot, taint ▶ verb 3 STAIN, disgrace, mark, smirch, smudge, spoil, spot, sully, tarnish 4 SOAK UP, absorb, dry, take up 5 **blot out: a** OBLITERATE, darken, destroy, eclipse, efface, obscure, shadow **b** ERASE, cancel, expunge

blow[1] verb 1 CARRY, buffet, drive, fling, flutter, move, sweep, waft 2 EXHALE, breathe, pant, puff 3 PLAY, blare, mouth, pipe, sound, toot, trumpet, vibrate

blow[2] noun 1 KNOCK, bang, clout (informal), punch, smack, sock (slang), stroke, thump, wallop (informal), whack 2 SETBACK, bombshell, calamity,

catastrophe, disappointment, disaster, misfortune, reverse, shock

blow out verb 1 PUT OUT, extinguish, snuff 2 BURST, erupt, explode, rupture, shatter

blow up verb 1 EXPLODE, blast, blow sky-high, bomb, burst, detonate, rupture, shatter 2 INFLATE, bloat, distend, enlarge, expand, fill, puff up, pump up, swell 3 Informal LOSE ONE'S TEMPER, become angry, erupt, fly off the handle (informal), hit the roof (informal), rage, see red (informal)

bludgeon noun 1 CLUB, cudgel, truncheon ▶ verb 2 CLUB, beat up, cudgel, knock down, strike 3 BULLY, bulldoze (informal), coerce, force, railroad (informal), steamroller

blue adjective 1 AZURE, cerulean, cobalt, cyan, navy, sapphire, sky-colored, ultramarine 2 DEPRESSED, dejected, despondent, downcast, low, melancholy, sad, unhappy 3 SMUTTY, indecent, lewd, obscene, risqué, X-rated (informal)

blueprint noun PLAN, design, draft, outline, pattern, pilot scheme, prototype, sketch

blues plural noun DEPRESSION, doldrums, dumps (informal), gloom, low spirits, melancholy, unhappiness

bluff[1] verb 1 DECEIVE, con, delude, fake, feign, mislead, pretend, pull the wool over someone's eyes ▶ noun 2 DECEPTION, bluster, bravado, deceit, fraud, humbug, pretense, sham, subterfuge

bluff² noun **1** PRECIPICE, bank, cliff, crag, escarpment, headland, peak, promontory, ridge ▶ adjective **2** HEARTY, blunt, blustering, genial, good-natured, open, outspoken, plain-spoken

blunder noun **1** MISTAKE, bloomer (informal), faux pas, foul-up (slang), indiscretion **2** ERROR, fault, inaccuracy, mistake, oversight, slip, slip-up (informal) ▶ verb **3** MAKE A MISTAKE, botch, bungle, err, foul up (slang), slip up (informal) **4** STUMBLE, bumble, flounder

blunt adjective **1** DULL, dulled, edgeless, pointless, rounded, unsharpened **2** FORTHRIGHT, bluff, brusque, frank, outspoken, plain-spoken, rude, straightforward, tactless ▶ verb **3** DULL, dampen, deaden, numb, soften, take the edge off, water down, weaken

blur verb **1** MAKE INDISTINCT, cloud, darken, make hazy, make vague, mask, obscure ▶ noun **2** INDISTINCTNESS, confusion, fog, haze, obscurity

blurt out verb EXCLAIM, disclose, let the cat out of the bag, reveal, spill the beans (informal), tell all, utter suddenly

blush verb **1** TURN RED, color, flush, go red (as a beetroot), redden, turn scarlet ▶ noun **2** REDDENING, color, flush, glow, pink tinge, rosiness, rosy tint, ruddiness

bluster verb **1** ROAR, bully, domineer, hector, rant, storm ▶ noun **2** HOT AIR (informal), bluff, bombast, bravado

blustery adjective GUSTY, boisterous, inclement, squally, stormy, tempestuous, violent, wild, windy

board noun **1** PLANK, panel, piece of timber, slat, timber **2** DIRECTORS, advisers, committee, conclave, council, panel, trustees **3** MEALS, daily meals, provisions, victuals ▶ verb **4** GET ON, embark, enter, mount **5** LODGE, put up, quarter, room

boast verb **1** BRAG, blow one's own trumpet, crow, strut, swagger, talk big (slang), vaunt **2** POSSESS, be proud of, congratulate oneself on, exhibit, flatter oneself, pride oneself on, show off ▶ noun **3** BRAG, avowal

boastful adjective BRAGGING, cocky, conceited, crowing, egotistical, full of oneself, swaggering, swollen-headed, vaunting

bob verb DUCK, bounce, hop, nod, oscillate, wiggle, wobble

bode verb PORTEND, augur, be an omen of, forebode, foretell, predict, signify, threaten

bodily adjective PHYSICAL, actual, carnal, corporal, corporeal, material, substantial, tangible

body noun **1** PHYSIQUE, build, figure, form, frame, shape **2** TORSO, trunk **3** CORPSE, cadaver, carcass, dead body, remains, stiff (slang) **4** ORGANIZATION, association, band, bloc, collection, company, confederation, congress, corporation, society **5** MAIN PART, bulk, essence, mass, material, matter, substance

bog *noun* MARSH, fen, mire, morass, quagmire, slough, swamp, wetlands

bogey *noun* BUGBEAR, bête noire, bugaboo, nightmare

bogus *adjective* FAKE, artificial, counterfeit, false, forged, fraudulent, imitation, phoney or phony (*informal*), sham

bohemian *adjective*
1 UNCONVENTIONAL, alternative, artistic, arty (*informal*), left bank, nonconformist, offbeat, unorthodox ▶ *noun*
2 NONCONFORMIST, beatnik, dropout, hippie, iconoclast

boil¹ *verb* BUBBLE, effervesce, fizz, foam, froth, seethe

boil² *noun* PUSTULE, blister, carbuncle, gathering, swelling, tumor, ulcer

boisterous *adjective* UNRULY, disorderly, loud, noisy, riotous, rollicking, rowdy, unrestrained, vociferous, wild

bold *adjective* **1** FEARLESS, adventurous, audacious, brave, courageous, daring, enterprising, heroic, intrepid, valiant **2** IMPUDENT, barefaced, brazen, cheeky, confident, forward, insolent, rude, shameless

bolster *verb* SUPPORT, augment, boost, help, reinforce, shore up, strengthen

bolt *noun* **1** BAR, catch, fastener, latch, lock, sliding bar **2** PIN, peg, rivet, rod ▶ *verb* **3** RUN AWAY, abscond, dash, escape, flee, fly, make a break (for it), run for it **4** LOCK, bar, fasten, latch, secure **5** GOBBLE, cram, devour, gorge, gulp, guzzle,

stuff, swallow whole, wolf

bomb *noun* **1** EXPLOSIVE, device, grenade, mine, missile, projectile, rocket, shell, torpedo ▶ *verb* **2** BLOW UP, attack, blow sky-high, bombard, destroy, shell, strafe, torpedo

bombard *verb* **1** BOMB, assault, blitz, fire upon, open fire, pound, shell, strafe **2** ATTACK, assail, beset, besiege, harass, hound, pester

bombardment *noun* BOMBING, assault, attack, barrage, blitz, fusillade, shelling

bombastic *adjective* GRANDILOQUENT, grandiose, high-flown, inflated, pompous, verbose, wordy

bona fide *adjective* GENUINE, actual, authentic, honest, kosher (*informal*), legitimate, real, true

bond *noun* **1** FASTENING, chain, cord, fetter, ligature, manacle, shackle, tie **2** TIE, affiliation, affinity, attachment, connection, link, relation, union **3** AGREEMENT, contract, covenant, guarantee, obligation, pledge, promise, word ▶ *verb* **4** HOLD TOGETHER, bind, connect, fasten, fix together, glue, paste

bondage *noun* SLAVERY, captivity, confinement, enslavement, imprisonment, subjugation

bonus *noun* EXTRA, dividend, gift, icing on the cake, plus, premium, prize, reward

bony *adjective* THIN, emaciated, gaunt, lean, scrawny, skin and bone, skinny

book *noun* **1** WORK, publication,

title, tome, tract, volume **2** NOTEBOOK, album, diary, exercise book, jotter, pad ▸verb **3** RESERVE, arrange for, charter, engage, make reservations, organize, program, schedule **4** NOTE, enter, list, log, mark down, put down, record, register, write down

booklet noun BROCHURE, leaflet, pamphlet

boom verb **1** BANG, blast, crash, explode, resound, reverberate, roar, roll, rumble, thunder **2** FLOURISH, develop, expand, grow, increase, intensify, prosper, strengthen, swell, thrive ▸noun **3** BANG, blast, burst, clap, crash, explosion, roar, rumble, thunder **4** EXPANSION, boost, development, growth, improvement, increase, jump, upsurge, upswing, upturn

boon noun BENEFIT, advantage, blessing, favor, gift, godsend, manna from heaven, windfall

boorish adjective LOUTISH, churlish, coarse, crude, oafish, uncivilized, uncouth, vulgar

boost noun **1** HELP, encouragement, praise, promotion **2** RISE, addition, expansion, improvement, increase, increment, jump ▸verb **3** INCREASE, add to, amplify, develop, enlarge, expand, heighten, raise **4** ADVERTISE, encourage, foster, further, hype, plug (informal), praise, promote

boot verb KICK, drive, drop-kick, knock, punt, shove

booty noun PLUNDER, gains, haul, loot, prey, spoils, swag (slang),

takings, winnings

border noun **1** FRONTIER, borderline, boundary, line, march **2** EDGE, bounds, brink, limits, margin, rim, verge ▸verb **3** EDGE, bind, decorate, fringe, hem, rim (informal)

bore¹ verb DRILL, burrow, gouge out, mine, penetrate, perforate, pierce, sink, tunnel

bore² verb **1** TIRE, be tedious, fatigue, jade, pall on, send to sleep, wear out, weary ▸noun **2** NUISANCE, geek (slang), pain (informal) **3** PAIN (informal), yawn (informal)

bored adjective FED UP, listless, tired, uninterested, wearied

boredom noun TEDIUM, apathy, ennui, flatness, monotony, sameness, tediousness, weariness, world-weariness

boring adjective UNINTERESTING, dull, flat, humdrum, mind-numbing, monotonous, tedious, tiresome

borrow verb **1** TAKE ON LOAN, cadge, scrounge (informal), use temporarily **2** STEAL, adopt, copy, obtain, plagiarize, take, usurp

bosom noun **1** BREAST, bust, chest ▸adjective **2** INTIMATE, boon, cherished, close, confidential, dear, very dear

boss¹ noun Informal HEAD, chief, director, employer, leader, manager, master, supervisor

boss² noun STUD, knob, point, protuberance, tip

boss around verb Informal DOMINEER, bully, dominate, oppress, order, push around (slang)

bossy adjective DOMINEERING,

arrogant, authoritarian, autocratic, dictatorial, hectoring, high-handed, imperious, overbearing, tyrannical

botch verb 1 SPOIL, blunder, bungle, foul up (slang), mar, mess up, screw up (informal) ▶ noun 2 MESS, blunder, bungle, failure

bother verb 1 TROUBLE, alarm, concern, disturb, harass, hassle (informal), inconvenience, pester, plague, worry ▶ noun 2 TROUBLE, difficulty, fuss, hassle (informal), inconvenience, irritation, nuisance, problem, worry

bottleneck noun HOLD-UP, block, blockage, congestion, impediment, jam, obstacle, obstruction

bottle up verb SUPPRESS, check, contain, curb, keep back, restrict, shut in, trap

bottom noun 1 LOWEST PART, base, bed, depths, floor, foot, foundation 2 UNDERSIDE, lower side, sole, underneath 3 BUTTOCKS, backside, behind (informal), posterior, rear, rump, seat, tush (slang) ▶ adjective 4 LOWEST, last

bottomless adjective UNLIMITED, boundless, deep, fathomless, immeasurable, inexhaustible, infinite, unfathomable

bounce verb 1 REBOUND, bob, bound, jump, leap, recoil, ricochet, spring ▶ noun 2 Informal LIFE, dynamism, energy, go (informal), liveliness, vigor, vivacity, zip (informal) 3 SPRINGINESS, elasticity, give, recoil, resilience, spring

bound¹ adjective 1 TIED, cased, fastened, fixed, pinioned, secured, tied up 2 CERTAIN, destined, doomed, fated, sure 3 OBLIGED, beholden, committed, compelled, constrained, duty-bound, forced, pledged, required

bound² verb LIMIT, confine, demarcate, encircle, enclose, hem in, restrain, restrict, surround

bound³ verb, noun LEAP, bob, bounce, gambol, hurdle, jump, skip, spring, vault

boundary noun LIMITS, barrier, border, borderline, brink, edge, extremity, fringe, frontier, margin

boundless adjective UNLIMITED, endless, immense, incalculable, inexhaustible, infinite, unconfined, untold, vast

bounds plural noun BOUNDARY, border, confine, edge, extremity, limit, rim, verge

bountiful adjective Literary 1 PLENTIFUL, abundant, ample, bounteous, copious, exuberant, lavish, luxuriant, prolific 2 GENEROUS, liberal, magnanimous, open-handed, prodigal, unstinting

bounty noun Literary 1 GENEROSITY, benevolence, charity, kindness, largesse or largess, liberality, philanthropy 2 REWARD, bonus, gift, present

bouquet noun 1 BUNCH OF FLOWERS, buttonhole, corsage, garland, nosegay, posy, spray, wreath 2 AROMA, fragrance, perfume, redolence, savor, scent

bourgeois adjective MIDDLE-CLASS,

conventional, hidebound, materialistic, traditional

bout noun **1** PERIOD, fit, spell, stint, term, turn **2** FIGHT, boxing match, competition, contest, encounter, engagement, match, set-to, struggle

bow[1] verb **1** BEND, bob, droop, genuflect, nod, stoop **2** GIVE IN, acquiesce, comply, concede, defer, kowtow, relent, submit, succumb, surrender, yield ▶noun **3** BENDING, bob, genuflexion, kowtow, nod, obeisance

bow[2] noun Nautical PROW, beak, fore, head, stem

bowels plural noun **1** GUTS, entrails, innards (informal), insides (informal), intestines, viscera, vitals **2** DEPTHS, belly, core, deep, hold, inside, interior

bowl[1] noun BASIN, dish, vessel

bowl[2] verb THROW, fling, hurl, pitch

box[1] noun **1** CONTAINER, carton, case, casket, chest, pack, package, receptacle, trunk ▶verb **2** PACK, package, wrap

box[2] verb FIGHT, exchange blows, spar

boxer noun FIGHTER, prizefighter, pugilist, sparring partner

boy noun LAD, fellow, junior, schoolboy, stripling, youngster, youth

boycott verb EMBARGO, ban, bar, black, exclude, outlaw, prohibit, refuse, reject

boyfriend noun SWEETHEART, admirer, beau, date, lover, man, suitor

boyish adjective YOUTHFUL, adolescent, childish, immature,

juvenile, puerile, young

brace noun **1** SUPPORT, bolster, bracket, buttress, prop, reinforcement, stay, strut, truss ▶verb **2** SUPPORT, bolster, buttress, fortify, reinforce, steady, strengthen

bracing adjective REFRESHING, brisk, crisp, exhilarating, fresh, invigorating, stimulating

brag verb BOAST, blow one's own trumpet, bluster, crow, swagger, talk big (slang), vaunt

braggart noun BOASTER, bigmouth (slang), bragger, show-off (informal)

braid verb INTERWEAVE, entwine, interlace, intertwine, lace, plait, twine, weave

brainless adjective STUPID, foolish, idiotic, inane, mindless, senseless, thoughtless, witless

brains plural noun INTELLIGENCE, intellect, sense, understanding

brainy adjective Informal INTELLIGENT, bright, brilliant, clever, smart

brake noun **1** CONTROL, check, constraint, curb, rein, restraint ▶verb **2** SLOW, check, decelerate, halt, moderate, reduce speed, slacken, stop

branch noun **1** BOUGH, arm, limb, offshoot, shoot, spray, sprig **2** DIVISION, chapter, department, office, part, section, subdivision, subsection, wing

brand noun **1** LABEL, emblem, hallmark, logo, mark, marker, sign, stamp, symbol, trademark **2** KIND, cast, class, grade, make, quality, sort, species, type, variety ▶verb **3** MARK, burn, burn in, label, scar, stamp **4** STIGMATIZE, censure, denounce, discredit, disgrace, expose, mark

brandish verb WAVE, display, exhibit, flaunt, flourish, parade, raise, shake, swing, wield

brash adjective BOLD, brazen, cocky, impertinent, impudent, insolent, pushy (informal), rude

bravado noun SWAGGER, bluster, boastfulness, boasting, bombast, swashbuckling, vaunting

brave adjective **1** COURAGEOUS, bold, daring, fearless, heroic, intrepid, plucky, resolute, valiant ▸verb **2** CONFRONT, defy, endure, face, stand up to, suffer, tackle, withstand

bravery noun COURAGE, boldness, daring, fearlessness, fortitude, heroism, intrepidity, mettle, pluck, spirit, valor

brawl noun **1** FIGHT, affray (Law), altercation, clash, dispute, fracas, fray, melee or mêlée, rumpus, scuffle, skirmish ▸verb **2** FIGHT, scrap (informal), scuffle, tussle, wrestle

brawn noun MUSCLE, beef (informal), might, muscles, power, strength, vigor

brawny adjective MUSCULAR, beefy (informal), hefty (informal), lusty, powerful, strapping, strong, sturdy, well-built

brazen adjective BOLD, audacious, barefaced, brash, defiant, impudent, insolent, shameless, unabashed, unashamed

breach noun **1** NONOBSERVANCE, contravention, infraction, infringement, noncompliance, transgression, trespass, violation **2** CRACK, cleft, fissure, gap, opening, rift, rupture, split

bread noun **1** FOOD, fare, nourishment, sustenance **2** Slang MONEY, cash, dough (slang)

breadth noun **1** WIDTH, broadness, latitude, span, spread, wideness **2** EXTENT, compass, expanse, range, scale, scope

break verb **1** SEPARATE, burst, crack, destroy, disintegrate, fracture, fragment, shatter, smash, snap, split, tear **2** DISOBEY, breach, contravene, disregard, infringe, renege on, transgress, violate **3** REVEAL, announce, disclose, divulge, impart, inform, let out, make public, proclaim, tell **4** STOP, abandon, cut, discontinue, give up, interrupt, pause, rest, suspend **5** WEAKEN, demoralize, dispirit, subdue, tame, undermine **6** Of a record, etc. BEAT, better, exceed, excel, go beyond, outdo, outstrip, surpass, top ▸noun **7** DIVISION, crack, fissure, fracture, gap, hole, opening, split, tear **8** REST, breather (informal), hiatus, interlude, intermission, interruption, interval, let-up (informal), lull, pause, respite **9** Informal STROKE OF LUCK, advantage, chance, fortune, opening, opportunity

breakable adjective FRAGILE, brittle, crumbly, delicate, flimsy, frail, frangible, friable

breakdown noun COLLAPSE, disintegration, disruption, failure, mishap, stoppage

break down verb **1** COLLAPSE,

come unstuck, fail, seize up, stop, stop working **2** BE OVERCOME, crack up (*informal*), go to pieces

break-in noun BURGLARY, breaking and entering, robbery

break off verb **1** DETACH, divide, part, pull off, separate, sever, snap off, splinter **2** STOP, cease, desist, discontinue, end, finish, halt, pull the plug on, suspend, terminate

break out verb BEGIN, appear, arise, commence, emerge, happen, occur, set in, spring up, start

breakthrough noun DEVELOPMENT, advance, discovery, find, invention, leap, progress, quantum leap, step forward

break up verb **1** SEPARATE, dissolve, divide, divorce, part, scatter, sever, split **2** STOP, adjourn, disband, dismantle, end, suspend, terminate

breast noun BOSOM, bust, chest, front, teat, udder

breath noun RESPIRATION, breathing, exhalation, gasp, gulp, inhalation, pant, wheeze

breathe verb **1** INHALE AND EXHALE, draw in, gasp, gulp, pant, puff, respire, wheeze **2** WHISPER, murmur, sigh

breather noun *Informal* REST, break, breathing space, halt, pause, recess, respite

breathless adjective **1** OUT OF BREATH, gasping, gulping, panting, short-winded, spent, wheezing **2** EXCITED, eager, on tenterhooks, open-mouthed, wired (*slang*), with bated breath

breathtaking adjective AMAZING, astonishing, awe-inspiring, cool (*informal*), exciting, impressive, magnificent, phat (*slang*), sensational, stunning (*informal*), thrilling

breed verb **1** REPRODUCE, bear, bring forth, hatch, multiply, procreate, produce, propagate **2** BRING UP, cultivate, develop, nourish, nurture, raise, rear **3** PRODUCE, arouse, bring about, cause, create, generate, give rise to, stir up ▶noun **4** VARIETY, pedigree, race, species, stock, strain, type **5** KIND, brand, sort, stamp, type, variety

breeding noun **1** UPBRINGING, ancestry, cultivation, development, lineage, nurture, raising, rearing, reproduction, training **2** REFINEMENT, conduct, courtesy, cultivation, culture, polish, sophistication, urbanity

breeze noun **1** LIGHT WIND, air, breath of wind, current of air, draft, gust, waft, zephyr ▶verb **2** MOVE BRISKLY, flit, glide, hurry, pass, sail, sweep

breezy adjective **1** WINDY, airy, blowy, blustery, fresh, gusty, squally **2** CAREFREE, blithe, casual, easy-going, free and easy, jaunty, light-hearted, lively, sprightly

brevity noun **1** SHORTNESS, briefness, impermanence, transience, transitoriness **2** CONCISENESS, crispness, curtness, economy, pithiness, succinctness, terseness

brew verb **1** MAKE (*beer*), boil, ferment, infuse (*tea*), soak, steep, stew **2** DEVELOP, foment, form, gather, start, stir up ▶noun **3** DRINK, beverage, blend, concoction, infusion, liquor, mixture, preparation

bribe verb **1** BUY OFF, corrupt, grease the palm or hand of (slang), pay off (informal), reward, suborn ▶noun **2** INDUCEMENT, allurement, backhander (slang), enticement, kickback, pay-off (informal), sweetener (slang)

bribery noun BUYING OFF, corruption, inducement, palm-greasing (slang), payola (informal)

bric-a-brac noun KNICK-KNACKS, baubles, curios, ornaments, trinkets

bridal adjective MATRIMONIAL, conjugal, connubial, marital, marriage, nuptial, wedding

bridge noun **1** ARCH, flyover, overpass, span, viaduct ▶verb **2** CONNECT, join, link, span

bridle noun **1** CURB, check, control, rein, restraint ▶verb **2** GET ANGRY, be indignant, bristle, draw (oneself) up, get one's back up, raise one's hackles, rear up

brief adjective **1** SHORT, ephemeral, fleeting, momentary, quick, short-lived, swift, transitory ▶noun **2** SUMMARY, abridgment, abstract, digest, epitome, outline, précis, sketch, synopsis ▶verb **3** INFORM, advise, explain, fill in (informal), instruct, keep posted, prepare, prime, put (someone) in the picture (informal)

briefing noun INSTRUCTIONS, conference, directions, guidance, information, preparation, priming, rundown

briefly adverb SHORTLY, concisely,

hastily, hurriedly, in a nutshell, in brief, momentarily, quickly

brigade noun GROUP, band, company, corps, force, organization, outfit, squad, team, troop, unit

bright adjective **1** SHINING, brilliant, dazzling, gleaming, glowing, luminous, lustrous, radiant, shimmering, vivid **2** INTELLIGENT, astute, aware, clever, inventive, quick-witted, sharp, smart, wide-awake **3** SUNNY, clear, cloudless, fair, limpid, lucid, pleasant, translucent, transparent, unclouded

brighten verb MAKE BRIGHTER, gleam, glow, illuminate, lighten, light up, shine

brightness noun SHINE, brilliance, glare, incandescence, intensity, light, luminosity, radiance, vividness **2** INTELLIGENCE, acuity, cleverness, quickness, sharpness, smartness

brilliance noun **1** BRIGHTNESS, dazzle, intensity, luminosity, luster, radiance, sparkle, vividness **2** TALENT, cleverness, distinction, excellence, genius, greatness, inventiveness, wisdom **3** SPLENDOR, éclat, glamour, grandeur, illustriousness, magnificence

brilliant adjective **1** SHINING, bright, dazzling, glittering, intense, luminous, radiant, sparkling, vivid **2** SPLENDID, celebrated, famous, glorious, illustrious, magnificent, notable, outstanding, superb **3** INTELLIGENT, clever, expert, gifted, intellectual, inventive, masterly, penetrating, profound, talented

brim noun 1 RIM, border, brink, edge, lip, margin, skirt, verge ▶verb 2 BE FULL, fill, fill up, hold no more, overflow, run over, spill, well over

bring verb 1 TAKE, bear, carry, conduct, convey, deliver, escort, fetch, guide, lead, transfer, transport 2 CAUSE, contribute to, create, effect, inflict, occasion, produce, result in, wreak

bring about verb CAUSE, accomplish, achieve, create, effect, generate, give rise to, make happen, produce

bring off verb ACCOMPLISH, achieve, carry off, execute, perform, pull off, succeed

bring up verb 1 REAR, breed, develop, educate, form, nurture, raise, support, teach, train 2 MENTION, allude to, broach, introduce, move, propose, put forward, raise

brink noun EDGE, border, boundary, brim, fringe, frontier, limit, lip, margin, rim, skirt, threshold, verge

brisk adjective LIVELY, active, bustling, busy, energetic, quick, sprightly, spry, vigorous

briskly adverb QUICKLY, actively, apace, efficiently, energetically, promptly, rapidly, readily, smartly

bristle noun 1 HAIR, barb, prickle, spine, stubble, thorn, whisker ▶verb 2 STAND UP, rise, stand on end 3 BE ANGRY, bridle, flare up, rage, see red, seethe

bristly adjective HAIRY, prickly, rough, stubbly

brittle adjective FRAGILE, breakable, crisp, crumbling, crumbly, delicate, frail, frangible, friable

broach verb 1 BRING UP, introduce, mention, open up, propose, raise the subject, speak of, suggest, talk of, touch on 2 OPEN, crack, draw off, pierce, puncture, start, tap, uncork

broad adjective 1 WIDE, ample, expansive, extensive, generous, large, roomy, spacious, vast, voluminous, widespread 2 GENERAL, all-embracing, comprehensive, encyclopedic, inclusive, sweeping, wide, wide-ranging

broadcast noun 1 TRANSMISSION, program, show, telecast ▶verb 2 TRANSMIT, air, beam, cable, put on the air, radio, relay, show, televise 3 MAKE PUBLIC, advertise, announce, circulate, proclaim, publish, report, spread

broaden verb EXPAND, develop, enlarge, extend, increase, spread, stretch, supplement, swell, widen

broad-minded adjective TOLERANT, free-thinking, indulgent, liberal, open-minded, permissive, unbiased, unbigoted, unprejudiced

broadside noun ATTACK, assault, battering, bombardment, censure, criticism, denunciation, diatribe

brochure noun BOOKLET, advertisement, circular, folder, handbill, hand-out, leaflet, mailshot, pamphlet

broke adjective Informal PENNILESS, bankrupt, bust (informal), down and out, down on one's luck (informal), impoverished, insolvent, in the red, ruined, short

broken adjective 1 SMASHED, burst, fractured, fragmented, ruptured, separated, severed, shattered 2 INTERRUPTED, discontinuous, erratic, fragmentary, incomplete, intermittent, spasmodic 3 NOT WORKING, defective, imperfect, kaput (informal), on the blink (slang), out of order 4 IMPERFECT, disjointed, halting, hesitating, stammering

brokenhearted adjective HEARTBROKEN, desolate, devastated, disconsolate, grief-stricken, inconsolable, miserable, sorrowful, wretched

broker noun DEALER, agent, factor, go-between, intermediary, middleman, negotiator

bronze adjective REDDISH-BROWN, brownish, chestnut, copper, rust, tan

brood noun 1 OFFSPRING, clutch, family, issue, litter, progeny ▶verb 2 THINK UPON, agonize, dwell upon, mope, mull over, muse, ponder, ruminate

brook noun STREAM, beck, rill, rivulet, watercourse

brother noun 1 SIBLING, blood brother, kin, kinsman, relation, relative 2 MONK, cleric, friar

brotherhood noun 1 FELLOWSHIP, brotherliness, camaraderie, companionship, comradeship, friendliness, kinship 2 ASSOCIATION, alliance, community, fraternity, guild, league, order, society, union

brotherly adjective KIND, affectionate, altruistic, amicable, benevolent, cordial, fraternal, friendly, neighborly, philanthropic, sympathetic

browbeat verb BULLY, badger, coerce, dragoon, hector, intimidate, ride roughshod over, threaten, tyrannize

brown adjective 1 BRUNETTE, auburn, bay, bronze, chestnut, chocolate, coffee, dun, hazel, sunburned, tan, tanned, tawny, umber ▶verb 2 FRY, cook, grill, sauté, sear, seal

browse verb 1 SKIM, dip into, examine cursorily, flip through, glance at, leaf through, look round, look through, peruse, scan, survey 2 GRAZE, chow down (slang), eat, feed, nibble

bruise verb 1 DISCOLOR, damage, injure, mar, mark, pound ▶noun 2 DISCOLORATION, black mark, blemish, contusion, injury, mark, swelling

brunt noun FULL FORCE, burden, force, impact, pressure, shock, strain, stress, thrust, violence

brush¹ noun 1 BROOM, besom, sweeper 2 ENCOUNTER, clash, conflict, confrontation, skirmish, tussle ▶verb 3 CLEAN, buff, paint, polish, sweep, wash 4 TOUCH, flick, glance, graze, kiss, scrape, stroke, sweep

brush² noun SHRUBS, brushwood, bushes, copse, scrub, thicket, undergrowth

brush off verb Slang IGNORE, blow off (slang), disdain, dismiss, disregard, reject, repudiate, scorn, snub, spurn

brush up verb REVISE, bone up (informal), cram, go over, polish up, read up, refresh one's memory, relearn, study

brusque adjective CURT, abrupt, discourteous, gruff, impolite, sharp, short, surly, terse

brutal adjective 1 CRUEL, bloodthirsty, heartless, inhuman, ruthless, savage, uncivilized, vicious 2 HARSH, callous, gruff, impolite, insensitive, rough, rude, severe

brutality noun CRUELTY, atrocity, barbarism, bloodthirstiness, ferocity, inhumanity, ruthlessness, savagery, viciousness

brute noun 1 SAVAGE, barbarian, beast, devil, fiend, monster, sadist, swine 2 ANIMAL, beast, creature, wild animal ▶ adjective 3 MINDLESS, bodily, carnal, fleshly, instinctive, physical, senseless, unthinking

bubble noun 1 AIR BALL, bead, blister, blob, drop, droplet, globule ▶ verb 2 FOAM, boil, effervesce, fizz, froth, percolate, seethe, sparkle 3 GURGLE, babble, burble, murmur, ripple, trickle

bubbly adjective 1 LIVELY, animated, bouncy, elated, excited, happy, merry, sparky, wired (slang) 2 FROTHY, carbonated, effervescent, fizzy, foamy, sparkling

buccaneer noun PIRATE, corsair, freebooter, privateer, sea-rover

buckle noun 1 FASTENER, catch, clasp, clip, hasp ▶ verb 2 FASTEN, clasp, close, hook, secure 3 DISTORT, bend, bulge, cave in,

collapse, contort, crumple, fold, twist, warp

bud noun 1 SHOOT, embryo, germ, sprout ▶ verb 2 DEVELOP, burgeon, burst forth, grow, shoot, sprout

budding adjective DEVELOPING, beginning, burgeoning, embryonic, fledgling, growing, incipient, nascent, potential, promising

budge verb MOVE, dislodge, push, shift, stir

budget noun 1 ALLOWANCE, allocation, cost, finances, funds, means, resources ▶ verb 2 PLAN, allocate, apportion, cost, estimate, ration

buff¹ adjective 1 YELLOWISH-BROWN, sandy, straw, tan, yellowish ▶ verb 2 POLISH, brush, burnish, rub, shine, smooth

buff² noun Informal EXPERT, addict, admirer, aficionado, connoisseur, devotee, enthusiast, fan

buffer noun SAFEGUARD, bulwark, bumper, cushion, fender, intermediary, screen, shield, shock absorber

buffet¹ noun SNACK BAR, brasserie, café, cafeteria, refreshment counter, sideboard

buffet² verb BATTER, beat, bump, knock, pound, pummel, strike, thump, wallop (informal)

buffoon noun CLOWN, comedian, comic, fool, harlequin, jester, joker, wag

bug noun 1 Informal ILLNESS, disease, infection, virus 2 FAULT, defect, error, flaw, glitch, gremlin ▶ verb 3 Informal ANNOY, bother, disturb, get on

bugbear one's nerves (*informal*), hassle (*informal*), irritate, pester, vex **4** TAP, eavesdrop, listen in, spy

bugbear noun PET HATE, bane, bête noire, bogey, dread, horror, nightmare

build verb **1** CONSTRUCT, assemble, erect, fabricate, form, make, put up, raise ▶noun **2** PHYSIQUE, body, figure, form, frame, shape, structure

building noun STRUCTURE, domicile, dwelling, edifice, house

build-up noun INCREASE, accumulation, development, enlargement, escalation, expansion, gain, growth

bulbous adjective BULGING, bloated, convex, rounded, swelling, swollen

bulge noun **1** SWELLING, bump, hump, lump, projection, protrusion, protuberance **2** INCREASE, boost, intensification, rise, surge ▶verb **3** SWELL OUT, dilate, distend, expand, project, protrude, puff out, stick out

bulk noun **1** SIZE, dimensions, immensity, largeness, magnitude, substance, volume, weight **2** MAIN PART, better part, body, lion's share, majority, mass, most, nearly all, preponderance

bulky adjective LARGE, big, cumbersome, heavy, hulking, massive, substantial, unwieldy, voluminous, weighty

bulldoze verb DEMOLISH, flatten, level, raze

bullet noun PROJECTILE, ball, missile, pellet, shot, slug

bulletin noun ANNOUNCEMENT, account, communication, communiqué, dispatch, message, news flash, notification, report, statement

bully noun **1** PERSECUTOR, browbeater, bully boy, coercer, intimidator, oppressor, ruffian, tormentor, tough ▶verb **2** PERSECUTE, browbeat, coerce, domineer, hector, intimidate, oppress, push around (*slang*), terrorize, tyrannize

bulwark noun **1** FORTIFICATION, bastion, buttress, defense, embankment, partition, rampart **2** DEFENSE, buffer, guard, mainstay, safeguard, security, support

bumbling adjective CLUMSY, awkward, blundering, bungling, incompetent, inefficient, inept, maladroit, muddled

bump verb **1** KNOCK, bang, collide (with), crash, hit, slam, smash into, strike **2** JERK, bounce, jolt, rattle, shake ▶noun **3** KNOCK, bang, blow, collision, crash, impact, jolt, thud, thump **4** LUMP, bulge, contusion, hump, nodule, protuberance, swelling

bumper adjective EXCEPTIONAL, abundant, bountiful, excellent, jumbo (*informal*), massive, whopping (*informal*)

bumpkin noun YOKEL, country bumpkin, hick (*informal*), hillbilly, peasant, redneck (*slang*), rustic

bumptious adjective COCKY, arrogant, brash, conceited, forward, full of oneself, overconfident, pushy (*informal*), self-assertive

bumpy *adjective* ROUGH, bouncy, choppy, jarring, jerky, jolting, rutted, uneven

bunch *noun* **1** NUMBER, assortment, batch, bundle, clump, cluster, collection, heap, lot, mass, pile **2** GROUP, band, crowd, flock, gang, gathering, party, team ▶ *verb* **3** GROUP, assemble, bundle, cluster, collect, huddle, mass, pack

bundle *noun* **1** BUNCH, assortment, batch, collection, group, heap, mass, pile, stack ▶ *verb* **2** (with *out, off, into,* etc.) PUSH, hurry, hustle, rush, shove, throw, thrust

bundle up *verb* WRAP UP, swathe

bungle *verb* MESS UP, blow (*slang*), blunder, botch, foul up, make a mess of, muff, ruin, spoil

bungling *adjective* INCOMPETENT, blundering, clumsy, inept, maladroit

bunk, bunkum *noun* Informal NONSENSE, balderdash, baloney (*informal*), garbage (*informal*), hogwash, hot air (*informal*), moonshine, poppycock (*informal*), rubbish, stuff and nonsense, twaddle

buoy *noun* **1** MARKER, beacon, float, guide, signal ▶ *verb* **2 buoy up** ENCOURAGE, boost, cheer, cheer up, hearten, keep afloat, lift, raise, support, sustain

buoyancy *noun* **1** LIGHTNESS, weightlessness **2** CHEERFULNESS, animation, bounce (*informal*), good humor, high spirits, liveliness

buoyant *adjective* **1** FLOATING, afloat, light, weightless **2** CHEERFUL, carefree, chirpy (*informal*), happy, jaunty, light-hearted, upbeat (*informal*)

burden *noun* **1** LOAD, encumbrance, weight **2** TROUBLE, affliction, millstone, onus, responsibility, strain, weight, worry ▶ *verb* **3** WEIGH DOWN, bother, handicap, load, oppress, saddle with, tax, worry

bureau *noun* **1** OFFICE, agency, branch, department, division, service **2** DESK, writing desk

bureaucracy *noun* **1** GOVERNMENT, administration, authorities, civil service, corridors of power, officials, the system **2** RED TAPE, officialdom, regulations

bureaucrat *noun* OFFICIAL, administrator, civil servant, functionary, mandarin, officer, public servant

burglar *noun* HOUSEBREAKER, cat burglar, filcher, pilferer, robber, sneak thief, thief

burglary *noun* BREAKING AND ENTERING, break-in, housebreaking, larceny, robbery, stealing, theft, thieving

burial *noun* INTERMENT, entombment, exequies, funeral, obsequies

buried *adjective* **1** INTERRED, entombed, laid to rest **2** HIDDEN, concealed, private, sequestered, tucked away

burlesque *noun* **1** PARODY, caricature, mockery, satire, spoof (*informal*), travesty ▶ *verb* **2** SATIRIZE, ape, caricature, exaggerate, imitate, lampoon, make a monkey out of, make fun of, mock, parody, ridicule, spoof (*informal*), travesty

burly adjective BRAWNY, beefy (*informal*), big, bulky, hefty, hulking, stocky, stout, sturdy, thickset, well-built

burn verb 1 BE ON FIRE, be ablaze, blaze, flame, flare, glow, go up in flames, smoke 2 SET ON FIRE, char, ignite, incinerate, kindle, light, parch, scorch, sear, singe, toast 3 BE PASSIONATE, be angry, be aroused, be inflamed, fume, seethe, simmer, smolder

burning adjective 1 INTENSE, ardent, eager, fervent, impassioned, passionate, vehement 2 CRUCIAL, acute, compelling, critical, essential, important, pressing, significant, urgent, vital 3 BLAZING, fiery, flaming, flashing, gleaming, glowing, illuminated, scorching, smoldering

burnish verb POLISH, brighten, buff, furbish, glaze, rub up, shine, smooth

burrow noun 1 HOLE, den, lair, retreat, shelter, tunnel ▶ verb 2 DIG, delve, excavate, hollow out, scoop out, tunnel

burst verb 1 EXPLODE, blow up, break, crack, puncture, rupture, shatter, split, tear apart 2 RUSH, barge, break, break out, erupt, gush forth, run, spout ▶ noun 3 EXPLOSION, bang, blast, blowout, break, crack, discharge, rupture, split 4 RUSH, gush, gust, outbreak, outburst, outpouring, spate, spurt, surge, torrent ▶ adjective 5 RUPTURED, flat, punctured, rent, split

bury verb 1 INTER, consign to the grave, entomb, inhume, lay to rest 2 EMBED, engulf, submerge 3 HIDE, conceal, cover, enshroud, secrete, stow away

bush noun 1 SHRUB, hedge, plant, shrubbery, thicket 2 **the bush** THE WILD, backwoods, brush, scrub, scrubland, woodland

bushy adjective THICK, bristling, fluffy, fuzzy, luxuriant, rough, shaggy, unruly

busily adverb ACTIVELY, assiduously, briskly, diligently, energetically, industriously, purposefully, speedily, strenuously

business noun 1 TRADE, bargaining, commerce, dealings, industry, manufacturing, selling, transaction 2 ESTABLISHMENT, company, concern, corporation, enterprise, firm, organization, venture 3 PROFESSION, career, employment, function, job, line, occupation, trade, vocation, work 4 CONCERN, affair, assignment, duty, problem, responsibility, task

businesslike adjective EFFICIENT, methodical, orderly, organized, practical, professional, systematic, thorough, well-ordered

businessman noun EXECUTIVE, capitalist, employer, entrepreneur, financier, industrialist, merchant, tradesman, tycoon

bust¹ noun BOSOM, breast, chest, front, torso

bust² *Informal* ▶ verb 1 BREAK,

bustle burst, fracture, rupture **2** ARREST, catch, raid, search ▶ adjective **3 go bust** GO BANKRUPT, become insolvent, be ruined, fail

bustle verb **1** HURRY, fuss, hasten, rush, scamper, scurry, scuttle ▶ noun **2** ACTIVITY, ado, commotion, excitement, flurry, fuss, hurly-burly, stir, to-do

bustling adjective BUSY, active, buzzing, crowded, full, humming, lively, swarming, teeming

busy adjective **1** OCCUPIED, active, employed, engaged, hard at work, industrious, on duty, rushed off one's feet, working **2** LIVELY, energetic, exacting, full, hectic, hustling ▶ verb **3** OCCUPY, absorb, employ, engage, engross, immerse, interest

busybody noun NOSY ROSY (U.S. informal), gossip, meddler, snooper, stirrer (informal), troublemaker

but conjunction **1** HOWEVER, further, moreover, nevertheless, on the contrary, on the other hand, still, yet ▶ preposition **2** EXCEPT, bar, barring, excepting, excluding, notwithstanding, save, with the exception of ▶ adverb **3** ONLY, just, merely, simply, singly, solely

butcher noun **1** MURDERER, destroyer, killer, slaughterer, slayer ▶ verb **2** SLAUGHTER, carve, clean, cut, cut up, dress, joint, prepare **3** KILL, assassinate, cut down, destroy, exterminate, liquidate, massacre, put to the sword, slaughter, slay

butt¹ noun **1** END, haft, handle, hilt, shaft, shank, stock **2** STUB, cigarette end, leftover, tip **3** Informal BUTTOCKS, behind (informal), bottom, derrière (euphemistic), rump (informal), tush (slang)

butt² noun TARGET, dupe, laughing stock, victim

butt³ verb, noun **1** With or of the head or horns KNOCK, bump, poke, prod, push, ram, shove, thrust ▶ verb **2 butt in** INTERFERE, chip in (informal), cut in, interrupt, intrude, meddle, put one's oar in, stick one's nose in

butt⁴ noun CASK, barrel

buttonhole verb DETAIN, accost, bore, catch, grab, importune, take aside, waylay

buttress noun **1** SUPPORT, brace, mainstay, prop, reinforcement, stanchion, strut ▶ verb **2** SUPPORT, back up, bolster, prop up, reinforce, shore up, strengthen, sustain, uphold

buxom adjective PLUMP, ample, bosomy, busty, curvaceous, healthy, voluptuous, well-rounded

buy verb **1** PURCHASE, acquire, get, invest in, obtain, pay for, procure, shop for ▶ noun **2** PURCHASE, acquisition, bargain, deal

by preposition **1** VIA, by way of, over **2** THROUGH, through the agency of **3** NEAR, along, beside, close to, next to, past ▶ adverb **4** NEAR, at hand, close, handy, in reach **5** PAST, aside, away, to one side

bygone adjective PAST, antiquated, extinct, forgotten, former, lost, of old, olden

bypass verb GO ROUND, avoid, circumvent, depart from, detour round, deviate from, get round, give a wide berth to, pass round

bystander noun ONLOOKER, eyewitness, looker-on, observer, passer-by, spectator, viewer, watcher, witness

byword noun SAYING, adage, maxim, motto, precept, proverb, slogan

C c

cab noun TAXI, hackney carriage, minicab, taxicab

cabal noun 1 CLIQUE, caucus, conclave, faction, league, party, set 2 PLOT, conspiracy, intrigue, machination, scheme

cabin noun 1 ROOM, berth, compartment, quarters 2 HUT, chalet, cottage, lodge, shack, shanty, shed

cabinet noun CUPBOARD, case, chiffonier, closet, commode, dresser, escritoire, locker

Cabinet noun COUNCIL, administration, assembly, counselors, ministry

caddish adjective UNGENTLEMANLY, despicable, ill-bred, lousy (slang), low, scuzzy (slang), unmannerly

café noun SNACK BAR, brasserie, cafeteria, coffee bar, coffee shop, lunchroom, restaurant, tearoom

cage noun ENCLOSURE, pen, pound

cagey adjective Informal WARY, careful, cautious, chary, discreet, guarded, noncommittal, shrewd, wily

cajole verb PERSUADE, brown-nose (slang), coax, flatter, seduce, sweet-talk (informal), wheedle

cake noun 1 BLOCK, bar, cube, loaf, lump, mass, slab ▶ verb 2 ENCRUST, bake, coagulate, congeal, solidify

calamitous adjective DISASTROUS, cataclysmic, catastrophic, deadly, devastating, dire, fatal, ruinous, tragic

calamity noun DISASTER, cataclysm, catastrophe, misadventure, misfortune, mishap, ruin, tragedy, tribulation

calculate verb 1 WORK OUT, compute, count, determine, enumerate, estimate, figure, reckon 2 PLAN, aim, design, intend

calculated adjective DELIBERATE, considered, intended, intentional, planned, premeditated, purposeful

calculating adjective SCHEMING, crafty, cunning, devious, Machiavellian, manipulative, sharp, shrewd, sly

calculation noun 1 WORKING OUT, answer, computation, estimate, forecast, judgment, reckoning, result 2 PLANNING, contrivance, deliberation, discretion, foresight, forethought, precaution

caliber noun 1 WORTH, ability, capacity, distinction, merit, quality, stature, talent 2 DIAMETER, bore, gauge, measure

call verb 1 NAME, christen,

describe as, designate, dub, entitle, label, style, term **2** CRY, arouse, hail, rouse, shout, yell **3** PHONE, telephone ▶*noun* **4** SUMMON, assemble, convene, gather, muster, rally ▶*verb* **5** CRY, hail, scream, shout, signal, whoop, yell **6** SUMMONS, appeal, command, demand, invitation, notice, order, plea, request **7** NEED, cause, excuse, grounds, justification, occasion, reason

call for *verb* **1** REQUIRE, demand, entail, involve, necessitate, need, occasion, suggest **2** FETCH, collect, pick up

calling *noun* PROFESSION, career, life's work, mission, trade, vocation

call on *verb* VISIT, drop in on, look in on, look up, see

callous *adjective* HEARTLESS, cold, hard-boiled, hardened, hardhearted, insensitive, uncaring, unfeeling

callow *adjective* INEXPERIENCED, green, guileless, immature, naive, raw, unsophisticated

calm *adjective* **1** COOL, collected, composed, dispassionate, relaxed, sedate, self-possessed, unemotional **2** STILL, balmy, mild, quiet, serene, smooth, tranquil, windless ▶*noun* **3** PEACEFULNESS, hush, peace, quiet, repose, serenity, stillness ▶*verb* **4** QUIETEN, hush, mollify, placate, relax, soothe

calmness *noun* **1** COOLNESS, composure, cool (*slang*), equanimity, impassivity, poise, sang-froid, self-possession **2** PEACEFULNESS, calm, hush, quiet, repose, restfulness, serenity, stillness, tranquillity

camouflage *noun* **1** DISGUISE, blind, cloak, concealment, cover, mask, masquerade, screen, subterfuge ▶*verb* **2** DISGUISE, cloak, conceal, cover, hide, mask, obfuscate, obscure, screen, veil

camp[1] *noun* CAMP SITE, bivouac, camping ground, encampment, tents

camp[2] *adjective* *Informal* EFFEMINATE, affected, artificial, mannered, ostentatious, posturing

campaign *noun* OPERATION, attack, crusade, drive, expedition, movement, offensive, push

canal *noun* WATERWAY, channel, conduit, duct, passage, watercourse

cancel *verb* **1** CALL OFF, abolish, abort, annul, delete, do away with, eliminate, erase, expunge, obliterate, repeal, revoke **2 cancel out** MAKE UP FOR, balance out, compensate for, counterbalance, neutralize, nullify, offset

cancellation *noun* ABANDONMENT, abolition, annulment, deletion, elimination, repeal, revocation

cancer *noun* GROWTH, corruption, malignancy, pestilence, sickness, tumor

candid *adjective* HONEST, blunt, forthright, frank, open, outspoken, plain, straightforward, truthful

candidate *noun* CONTENDER, applicant, claimant, competitor, contestant, entrant, nominee, runner

candor *noun* HONESTY, directness, forthrightness,

frankness, openness, outspokenness, straightforwardness, truthfulness

canker *noun* DISEASE, bane, blight, cancer, corruption, infection, rot, scourge, sore, ulcer

cannon *noun* GUN, big gun, field gun, mortar

canny *adjective* SHREWD, astute, careful, cautious, clever, judicious, prudent, wise

canon *noun* 1 RULE, criterion, dictate, formula, precept, principle, regulation, standard, statute, yardstick 2 LIST, catalog, roll

canopy *noun* AWNING, covering, shade, sunshade

cant¹ *noun* 1 HYPOCRISY, humbug, insincerity, lip service, pretense, pretentiousness, sanctimoniousness 2 JARGON, argot, lingo, patter, slang, vernacular

cant² *verb* TILT, angle, bevel, incline, rise, slant, slope

cantankerous *adjective* BAD-TEMPERED, choleric, contrary, disagreeable, grumpy, irascible, irritable, testy, waspish

canter *noun* 1 JOG, amble, dogtrot, lope ▸ *verb* 2 JOG, amble, lope

canvass *verb* 1 CAMPAIGN, electioneer, solicit, solicit votes 2 POLL, examine, inspect, investigate, scrutinize, study ▸ *noun* 3 POLL, examination, investigation, scrutiny, survey, tally

cap *verb* BEAT, better, crown, eclipse, exceed, outdo, outstrip, surpass, top, transcend

capability *noun* ABILITY, capacity, competence, means, potential, power, proficiency, qualification(s), wherewithal

capable *adjective* ABLE, accomplished, competent, efficient, gifted, proficient, qualified, talented

capacious *adjective* SPACIOUS, broad, commodious, expansive, extensive, roomy, sizable or sizeable, substantial, vast, voluminous, wide

capacity *noun* 1 SIZE, amplitude, compass, dimensions, extent, magnitude, range, room, scope, space, volume 2 ABILITY, aptitude, aptness, capability, competence, facility, genius, gift 3 FUNCTION, office, position, post, province, role, sphere

cape *noun* HEADLAND, head, peninsula, point, promontory

caper *noun* 1 ESCAPADE, antic, high jinks, jape, lark (*informal*), mischief, practical joke, prank, stunt ▸ *verb* 2 DANCE, bound, cavort, frolic, gambol, jump, skip, spring, trip

capital *noun* 1 MONEY, assets, cash, finances, funds, investment(s), means, principal, resources, wealth, wherewithal ▸ *adjective* 2 PRINCIPAL, cardinal, major, prime, vital 3 Old-fashioned FIRST-RATE, excellent, fine, splendid, sterling, superb

capitalism *noun* PRIVATE ENTERPRISE, free enterprise, laissez faire *or* laisser faire, private ownership

capitalize on *verb* TAKE ADVANTAGE OF, benefit from, cash in on (*informal*), exploit, gain from, make the most of, profit from

capitulate *verb* GIVE IN, come to terms, give up, relent, submit, succumb, surrender, yield

caprice *noun* WHIM, fad, fancy, fickleness, impulse, inconstancy, notion, whimsy

capricious *adjective* UNPREDICTABLE, changeful, erratic, fickle, fitful, impulsive, inconsistent, inconstant, mercurial, variable, wayward, whimsical

capsize *verb* OVERTURN, invert, keel over, tip over, turn over, turn turtle, upset

capsule *noun* 1 PILL, lozenge, tablet 2 *Botany* POD, case, receptacle, seed case, sheath, shell, vessel

captain *noun* LEADER, boss (*informal*), chief, commander, head, master, skipper

captivate *verb* CHARM, allure, attract, beguile, bewitch, enchant, enrapture, enthrall, entrance, fascinate, infatuate, mesmerize

captive *noun* 1 PRISONER, convict, detainee, hostage, internee, prisoner of war, slave ▶*adjective* 2 CONFINED, caged, enslaved, ensnared, imprisoned, incarcerated, locked up, penned, restricted, subjugated

captivity *noun* CONFINEMENT, bondage, custody, detention, imprisonment, incarceration, internment, slavery

capture *verb* 1 CATCH, apprehend, arrest, bag, collar (*informal*), secure, seize, take,

take prisoner ▶*noun* 2 CATCHING, apprehension, arrest, imprisonment, seizure, taking, taking captive, trapping

car *noun* 1 VEHICLE, auto, automobile, clunker (*informal*), jalopy (*informal*), machine, motor, motorcar, wheels (*informal*) 2 (RAILWAY) CARRIAGE, buffet car, cable car, coach, dining car, sleeping car, van

carcass *noun* BODY, cadaver (*Medical*), corpse, dead body, framework, hulk, remains, shell, skeleton

cardinal *adjective* PRINCIPAL, capital, central, chief, essential, first, fundamental, key, leading, main, paramount, primary

care *verb* 1 BE CONCERNED, be bothered, be interested, mind ▶*noun* 2 CAUTION, attention, carefulness, consideration, forethought, heed, management, pains, prudence, vigilance, watchfulness 3 PROTECTION, charge, control, custody, guardianship, keeping, management, supervision 4 WORRY, anxiety, concern, disquiet, perplexity, pressure, responsibility, stress, trouble

career *noun* 1 OCCUPATION, calling, employment, life's work, livelihood, pursuit, vocation ▶*verb* 2 RUSH, barrel (along) (*informal*), bolt, dash, hurtle, race, speed, tear

care for *verb* LOOK AFTER, attend, foster, mind, minister to, nurse, protect, provide for, tend, watch over LIKE, be fond of, desire, enjoy, love, prize, take to, want

carefree *adjective* UNTROUBLED, blithe, breezy, cheerful, easy-going, halcyon, happy-go-lucky, light-hearted

careful *adjective* **1** CAUTIOUS, chary, circumspect, discreet, prudent, scrupulous, thoughtful, thrifty **2** THOROUGH, conscientious, meticulous, painstaking, particular, precise

careless *adjective* **1** SLAPDASH, cavalier, inaccurate, irresponsible, lackadaisical, neglectful, offhand, slipshod, sloppy (*informal*) **2** NEGLIGENT, absent-minded, forgetful, hasty, remiss, thoughtless, unthinking **3** NONCHALANT, artless, casual, unstudied

carelessness *noun* NEGLIGENCE, indiscretion, irresponsibility, laxity, neglect, omission, slackness, sloppiness (*informal*), thoughtlessness

caress *verb* **1** STROKE, cuddle, embrace, fondle, hug, kiss, make out (*informal*), neck (*informal*), nuzzle, pet ▶ *noun* **2** STROKE, cuddle, embrace, fondling, hug, kiss, pat

caretaker *noun* WARDEN, concierge, curator, custodian, janitor, keeper, porter, superintendent, watchman

cargo *noun* LOAD, baggage, consignment, contents, freight, goods, merchandise, shipment

caricature *noun* **1** PARODY, burlesque, cartoon, distortion, farce, lampoon, satire, travesty ▶ *verb* **2** PARODY, burlesque, distort, lampoon, mimic, mock, ridicule, satirize

carnage *noun* SLAUGHTER, blood bath, bloodshed, butchery, havoc, holocaust, massacre, mass murder, murder, shambles

carnal *adjective* SEXUAL, erotic, fleshly, lascivious, lewd, libidinous, lustful, sensual

carnival *noun* FESTIVAL, celebration, fair, fête, fiesta, gala, holiday, jamboree, jubilee, merrymaking, revelry

carol *noun* SONG, chorus, ditty, hymn, lay

carp *verb* FIND FAULT, cavil, complain, criticize, pick holes, quibble, reproach

carpenter *noun* JOINER, cabinet-maker, woodworker

carriage *noun* **1** VEHICLE, cab, coach, conveyance **2** BEARING, air, behavior, comportment, conduct, demeanor, deportment, gait, manner, posture

carry *verb* **1** TRANSPORT, bear, bring, conduct, convey, fetch, haul, lug, move, relay, take, transfer **2** WIN, accomplish, capture, effect, gain, secure

carry on *verb* CONTINUE, endure, keep going, last, maintain, perpetuate, persevere, persist

carry out *verb* PERFORM, accomplish, achieve, carry through, effect, execute, fulfill, implement, realize

carton *noun* BOX, case, container, pack, package, packet

cartoon *noun* **1** DRAWING, caricature, comic strip, lampoon, parody, satire, sketch **2** ANIMATION, animated cartoon, animated film

cartridge *noun* **1** SHELL, charge, round **2** CONTAINER, capsule, case, cassette, cylinder, magazine

carve verb CUT, chip, chisel, engrave, etch, hew, mold, sculpt, slice, whittle

cascade noun 1 WATERFALL, avalanche, cataract, deluge, downpour, falls, flood, fountain, outpouring, shower, torrent ▶ verb 2 FLOW, descend, fall, flood, gush, overflow, pitch, plunge, pour, spill, surge, teem, tumble

case¹ noun 1 INSTANCE, example, illustration, occasion, occurrence, specimen 2 SITUATION, circumstance(s), condition, context, contingency, event, position, state 3 Law LAWSUIT, action, dispute, proceedings, suit, trial

case² noun 1 CONTAINER, box, canister, carton, casket, chest, crate, holder, receptacle, suitcase, tray 2 COVERING, capsule, casing, envelope, jacket, sheath, shell, wrapper

cash noun MONEY, coinage, currency, dough (slang), funds, notes, ready money, silver

cashier¹ noun TELLER, bank clerk, banker, bursar, clerk, purser, treasurer

cashier² verb DISMISS, discard, discharge, drum out, expel, give the boot to (slang)

casket noun BOX, case, chest, coffer, jewel box

cast noun 1 ACTORS, characters, company, dramatis personae, players, troupe 2 TYPE, complexion, manner, stamp, style ▶ verb 3 CHOOSE, allot, appoint, assign, name, pick, select 4 GIVE OUT, bestow, deposit, diffuse, distribute,

emit, radiate, scatter, shed, spread 5 FORM, found, model, mold, set, shape 6 THROW, fling, hurl, launch, pitch, sling, thrust, toss

caste noun CLASS, estate, grade, order, rank, social order, status, stratum

castigate verb REPRIMAND, berate, censure, chastise, criticize, lambast(e), rebuke, scold

cast-iron adjective CERTAIN, copper-bottomed, definite, established, fixed, guaranteed, settled

castle noun FORTRESS, chateau, citadel, keep, palace, stronghold, tower

cast-off adjective 1 UNWANTED, discarded, rejected, scrapped, surplus to requirements, unneeded, useless ▶ noun 2 REJECT, discard, failure, outcast, second

castrate verb NEUTER, emasculate, geld

casual adjective 1 CARELESS, blasé, cursory, lackadaisical, nonchalant, offhand, relaxed, unconcerned 2 OCCASIONAL, accidental, chance, incidental, irregular, random, unexpected 3 INFORMAL, non-dressy, sporty

casualty noun VICTIM, death, fatality, loss, sufferer, wounded

cat noun FELINE, kitty (informal), puss (informal), pussy (informal), tabby

catacombs plural noun VAULT, crypt, tomb

catalog noun 1 LIST, directory, gazetteer, index, inventory, record, register, roll, roster, schedule ▶ verb 2 LIST, accession, alphabetize, classify, file, index, inventory, register, tabulate

catapult noun **1** SLING, slingshot (U.S.) ▶verb **2** SHOOT, heave, hurl, pitch, plunge, propel

catastrophe noun DISASTER, adversity, calamity, cataclysm, fiasco, misfortune, tragedy, trouble

catcall noun JEER, boo, gibe, hiss, raspberry, whistle

catch verb **1** SEIZE, clutch, get, grab, grasp, grip, lay hold of, snatch, take **2** CAPTURE, apprehend, arrest, ensnare, entrap, snare **3** DISCOVER, catch in the act, detect, expose, find out, surprise, take unawares, unmask **4** CONTRACT, develop, get, go down with, incur, succumb to, suffer from **5** MAKE OUT, comprehend, discern, get, grasp, hear, perceive, recognize, sense, take in ▶noun **6** FASTENER, bolt, clasp, clip, latch **7** DRAWBACK, disadvantage, fly in the ointment, hitch, snag, stumbling block, trap, trick

catching adjective INFECTIOUS, communicable, contagious, transferable, transmittable

catch on verb UNDERSTAND, comprehend, find out, get the picture, grasp, see, see through

catchword noun SLOGAN, byword, motto, password, watchword

catchy adjective MEMORABLE, captivating, haunting, popular

categorical adjective ABSOLUTE, downright, emphatic, explicit, express, positive, unambiguous, unconditional,

unequivocal, unqualified, unreserved

category noun CLASS, classification, department, division, grade, grouping, heading, section, sort, type

cater verb PROVIDE, furnish, outfit, purvey, supply

cattle plural noun COWS, beasts, bovines, livestock, stock

catty adjective SPITEFUL, backbiting, bitchy (informal), malevolent, malicious, rancorous, shrewish, snide, venomous

cause noun **1** ORIGIN, agent, beginning, creator, genesis, mainspring, maker, producer, root, source, spring **2** REASON, basis, grounds, incentive, inducement, justification, motivation, motive, purpose **3** AIM, belief, conviction, enterprise, ideal, movement, principle ▶verb **4** PRODUCE, bring about, create, generate, give rise to, incite, induce, lead to, result in

caustic adjective **1** BURNING, acrid, astringent, biting, corroding, corrosive, mordant, vitriolic **2** SARCASTIC, acrimonious, cutting, pungent, scathing, stinging, trenchant, virulent, vitriolic

caution noun **1** CARE, alertness, carefulness, circumspection, deliberation, discretion, forethought, heed, prudence, vigilance, watchfulness **2** WARNING, admonition, advice, counsel, injunction ▶verb **3** WARN, admonish, advise, tip off, urge

cautious adjective CAREFUL, cagey

(*informal*), chary, circumspect, guarded, judicious, prudent, tentative, wary

cavalcade noun PARADE, array, march-past, procession, spectacle, train

cavalier adjective HAUGHTY, arrogant, disdainful, lofty, lordly, offhand, scornful, supercilious

cavalry noun HORSEMEN, horse, mounted troops

cave noun HOLLOW, cavern, cavity, den, grotto

cavern noun CAVE, hollow, pothole

cavernous adjective DEEP, hollow, sunken, yawning

cavity noun HOLLOW, crater, dent, gap, hole, pit

cease verb STOP, break off, conclude, discontinue, end, finish, halt, leave off, refrain, terminate

ceaseless adjective CONTINUAL, constant, endless, eternal, everlasting, incessant, interminable, never-ending, nonstop, perpetual, twenty-four-seven (*slang*), unremitting

cede verb SURRENDER, concede, hand over, make over, relinquish, renounce, resign, transfer, yield

celebrate verb 1 REJOICE, commemorate, drink to, keep, kill the fatted calf, observe, put the flags out, toast 2 PERFORM, bless, honor, solemnize

celebrated adjective WELL-KNOWN, acclaimed, distinguished, eminent, famous, illustrious, notable, popular, prominent, renowned

celebration noun 1 PARTY, festival, festivity, gala, jubilee, merrymaking, red-letter day, revelry 2 PERFORMANCE, anniversary, commemoration, honoring, observance, remembrance, solemnization

celebrity noun 1 PERSONALITY, big name, big shot (*informal*), dignitary, luminary, star, superstar, V.I.P. 2 FAME, distinction, notability, prestige, prominence, renown, reputation, repute, stardom

celestial adjective HEAVENLY, angelic, astral, divine, ethereal, spiritual, sublime, supernatural

celibacy noun CHASTITY, continence, purity, virginity

cell noun 1 ROOM, cavity, chamber, compartment, cubicle, dungeon, stall 2 UNIT, caucus, core, coterie, group, nucleus

cement noun 1 MORTAR, adhesive, glue, gum, paste, plaster, sealant ▶ verb 2 STICK TOGETHER, attach, bind, bond, combine, glue, join, plaster, seal, unite, weld

cemetery noun GRAVEYARD, burial ground, churchyard, God's acre, necropolis

censor verb CUT, blue-pencil, bowdlerize, expurgate

censorious adjective CRITICAL, captious, carping, cavilling, condemnatory, disapproving, disparaging, fault-finding, hypercritical, scathing, severe

censure noun 1 DISAPPROVAL, blame, condemnation, criticism, obloquy, rebuke, reprimand, reproach, reproof, stick (*slang*) ▶ verb 2 CRITICIZE, blame, castigate, condemn, denounce, rap over the knuckles, rebuke, reprimand, reproach, scold, slap on the wrist

center noun 1 MIDDLE, core, focus, heart, hub, kernel, midpoint, nucleus, pivot ▶ *verb* 2 FOCUS, cluster, concentrate, converge, revolve

central *adjective* 1 MIDDLE, interior, inner, mean, median, mid 2 MAIN, chief, essential, focal, fundamental, key, primary, principal

centralize *verb* UNIFY, concentrate, condense, incorporate, rationalize, streamline

ceremonial *adjective* 1 RITUAL, formal, liturgical, ritualistic, solemn, stately ▶ *noun* 2 RITUAL, ceremony, formality, rite, solemnity

ceremonious *adjective* FORMAL, civil, courteous, deferential, dignified, punctilious, solemn, stately, stiff

ceremony noun 1 RITUAL, commemoration, function, observance, parade, rite, service, show, solemnities 2 FORMALITY, ceremonial, decorum, etiquette, niceties, pomp, propriety, protocol

certain *adjective* 1 SURE, assured, confident, convinced, positive, satisfied 2 KNOWN, conclusive, incontrovertible, irrefutable, true, undeniable, unequivocal 3 INEVITABLE, bound, definite, destined, fated, inescapable, sure 4 FIXED, decided, definite, established, settled

certainly *adverb* DEFINITELY,

assuredly, indisputably, indubitably, surely, truly, undeniably, undoubtedly, without doubt

certainty noun 1 SURENESS, assurance, confidence, conviction, faith, positiveness, trust, validity 2 FACT, reality, sure thing (*informal*), truth

certificate noun DOCUMENT, authorization, credential(s), diploma, license, testimonial, voucher, warrant

certify *verb* CONFIRM, assure, attest, authenticate, declare, guarantee, testify, validate, verify

chafe *verb* 1 RUB, abrade, rasp, scrape, scratch 2 BE ANNOYED, be impatient, fret, fume, rage, worry

chaff[1] noun WASTE, dregs, husks, refuse, remains, rubbish, trash

chaff[2] *verb* TEASE, mock, rib (*informal*), ridicule, scoff, taunt

chain noun 1 LINK, bond, coupling, fetter, manacle, shackle 2 SERIES, progression, sequence, set, string, succession, train ▶ *verb* 3 BIND, confine, enslave, fetter, handcuff, manacle, restrain, shackle, tether

chairman noun DIRECTOR, chairperson, chairwoman, master of ceremonies, president, speaker, spokesman

challenge noun 1 TEST, confrontation, provocation, question, trial, ultimatum ▶ *verb* 2 TEST, confront, defy, dispute, object to, question, tackle, throw down the gauntlet

chamber noun 1 ROOM, apartment, bedroom,

compartment, cubicle, enclosure, hall **2** COUNCIL, assembly, legislative body, legislature

champion noun **1** WINNER, conqueror, hero, title holder, victor **2** DEFENDER, backer, guardian, patron, protector, upholder ▶ verb **3** SUPPORT, advocate, back, commend, defend, encourage, espouse, fight for, promote, uphold

chance noun **1** PROBABILITY, likelihood, odds, possibility, prospect **2** OPPORTUNITY, occasion, opening, time **3** LUCK, accident, coincidence, destiny, fate, fortune, providence **4** RISK, gamble, hazard, jeopardy, speculation, uncertainty ▶ verb **5** RISK, endanger, gamble, hazard, jeopardize, stake, try, venture, wager

chancy adjective Slang DANGEROUS, difficult, hazardous, perilous, risky

change noun **1** ALTERATION, difference, innovation, metamorphosis, modification, mutation, revolution, transformation, transition **2** VARIETY, break (informal), departure, diversion, novelty, variation **3** EXCHANGE, conversion, interchange, substitution, swap, trade ▶ verb **4** ALTER, convert, modify, mutate, reform, reorganize, restyle, shift, transform, vary **5** EXCHANGE, barter, convert, interchange, replace, substitute, swap, trade

changeable adjective VARIABLE, erratic, fickle, inconstant, irregular, mobile, mutable,

protean, shifting, unsettled, unstable, volatile, wavering

channel noun **1** ROUTE, approach, artery, avenue, course, means, medium, path, way **2** PASSAGE, canal, conduit, duct, furrow, groove, gutter, route, strait ▶ verb **3** DIRECT, conduct, convey, guide, transmit

chant verb **1** SING, carol, chorus, descant, intone, recite, warble ▶ noun **2** SONG, carol, chorus, melody, psalm

chaos noun DISORDER, anarchy, bedlam, confusion, disorganization, lawlessness, mayhem, pandemonium, tumult

chaotic adjective DISORDERED, anarchic, confused, deranged, disorganized, lawless, riotous, topsy-turvy, tumultuous, uncontrolled

chap noun Informal FELLOW, character, guy (informal), individual, man, person

chaperone noun **1** ESCORT, companion ▶ verb **2** ESCORT, accompany, attend, protect, safeguard, shepherd, watch over

chapter noun SECTION, clause, division, episode, part, period, phase, stage, topic

character noun **1** NATURE, attributes, caliber, complexion, disposition, personality, quality, temperament, type **2** REPUTATION, honor, integrity, rectitude, strength, uprightness **3** ROLE, part, persona, portrayal **4** ECCENTRIC, card (informal), oddball (informal), original **5** SYMBOL, device, figure, hieroglyph, letter, mark, rune, sign

characteristic noun 1 FEATURE, attribute, faculty, idiosyncrasy, mark, peculiarity, property, quality, quirk, trait ▶*adjective* 2 TYPICAL, distinctive, distinguishing, idiosyncratic, individual, peculiar, representative, singular, special, symbolic, symptomatic

characterize verb IDENTIFY, brand, distinguish, indicate, mark, represent, stamp, typify

charade noun PRETENSE, fake, farce, pantomime, parody, travesty

charge verb 1 ACCUSE, arraign, blame, impeach, incriminate, indict 2 RUSH, assail, assault, attack, stampede, storm 3 FILL, load 4 COMMAND, bid, commit, demand, entrust, instruct, order, require ▶*noun* 5 PRICE, amount, cost, expenditure, expense, outlay, payment, rate, toll 6 ACCUSATION, allegation, imputation, indictment 7 RUSH, assault, attack, onset, onslaught, sortie, stampede 8 CARE, custody, duty, office, responsibility, safekeeping, trust 9 WARD 10 INSTRUCTION, command, demand, direction, injunction, mandate, order, precept

charisma noun CHARM, allure, attraction, lure, magnetism, personality

charismatic adjective CHARMING, alluring, attractive, enticing, influential, magnetic

charitable adjective 1 TOLERANT, considerate, favorable, forgiving, humane, indulgent,

kindly, lenient, magnanimous, sympathetic, understanding 2 GENEROUS, beneficent, benevolent, bountiful, kind, lavish, liberal, philanthropic

charity noun 1 DONATIONS, assistance, benefaction, contributions, endowment, fund, gift, hand-out, help, largesse or largess, philanthropy, relief 2 KINDNESS, altruism, benevolence, compassion, fellow feeling, generosity, goodwill, humanity, indulgence

charlatan noun FRAUD, cheat, con man (informal), fake, impostor, phoney or phony (informal), pretender, quack, sham, swindler

charm noun 1 ATTRACTION, allure, appeal, fascination, magnetism 2 SPELL, enchantment, magic, sorcery 3 TALISMAN, amulet, fetish, trinket ▶*verb* 4 ATTRACT, allure, beguile, bewitch, captivate, delight, enchant, enrapture, entrance, fascinate, mesmerize, win over

charming adjective ATTRACTIVE, appealing, captivating, cute, delightful, fetching, likable or likeable, pleasing, seductive, winsome

chart noun 1 TABLE, blueprint, diagram, graph, map, plan ▶*verb* 2 PLOT, delineate, draft, map out, outline, shape, sketch

charter noun 1 DOCUMENT, contract, deed, license, permit, prerogative ▶*verb* 2 HIRE, commission, employ, lease, rent 3 AUTHORIZE, sanction

chase verb 1 PURSUE, course, follow, hunt, run after, stalk,

track 2 DRIVE AWAY, drive, expel, hound, put to flight ▸ *noun* **3** PURSUIT, hunt, hunting, race

chasm *noun* GULF, abyss, crater, crevasse, fissure, gap, gorge, ravine

chaste *adjective* PURE, immaculate, innocent, modest, simple, unaffected, undefiled, virtuous

chasten *verb* SUBDUE, chastise, correct, discipline, humble, humiliate, put in one's place, tame

chastise *verb* **1** SCOLD, berate, castigate, censure, correct, discipline, upbraid **2** *Old-fashioned* BEAT, flog, lash, lick (*informal*), punish, scourge, whip

chastity *noun* PURITY, celibacy, continence, innocence, maidenhood, modesty, virginity, virtue

chat *noun* **1** TALK, chatter, conversation, gossip, heart-to-heart, natter, tête-à-tête ▸ *verb* **2** TALK, chatter, chew the fat (*slang*), gossip, jaw (*slang*), natter

chatter *noun* **1** PRATTLE, babble, blather, chat, gab (*informal*), gossip ▸ *verb* **2** PRATTLE, babble, blather, chat, chew the fat (*slang*), gab (*informal*), gossip, schmooze (*slang*)

cheap *adjective* **1** INEXPENSIVE, bargain, cut-price, economical, keen, low-cost, low-priced, reasonable, reduced **2** INFERIOR, common, poor, second-rate, shoddy, tatty, tawdry, two a penny, worthless

cheapen *verb* DEGRADE, belittle, debase, demean, denigrate,

depreciate, devalue, discredit, disparage, lower

cheat *verb* **1** DECEIVE, beguile, con (*informal*), defraud, double-cross (*informal*), dupe, fleece, fool, mislead, rip off (*slang*), swindle, trick ▸ *noun* **2** DECEIVER, charlatan, con man (*informal*), double-crosser (*informal*), shark, sharper, swindler, trickster **3** DECEPTION, deceit, fraud, rip-off (*slang*), scam (*slang*), swindle, trickery

check *verb* **1** EXAMINE, inquire into, inspect, investigate, look at, make sure, monitor, research, scrutinize, study, test, vet **2** STOP, delay, halt, hinder, impede, inhibit, limit, obstruct, restrain, retard ▸ *noun* **3** EXAMINATION, inspection, investigation, once-over (*informal*), research, scrutiny, test **4** STOPPAGE, constraint, control, curb, damper, hindrance, impediment, limitation, obstacle, obstruction, restraint

cheeky *adjective* IMPUDENT, audacious, disrespectful, forward, impertinent, insolent, insulting, pert, saucy

cheer *verb* **1** APPLAUD, acclaim, clap, hail **2** CHEER UP, brighten, buoy up, comfort, encourage, gladden, hearten, uplift ▸ *noun* **3** APPLAUSE, acclamation, ovation, plaudits

cheerful *adjective* HAPPY, buoyant, cheery, chirpy (*informal*), enthusiastic, jaunty, jolly, light-hearted, merry, optimistic, upbeat

cheerfulness *noun* HAPPINESS, buoyancy, exuberance, gaiety, geniality, good cheer, good humor, high spirits, jauntiness, light-heartedness

cheerless adjective GLOOMY, bleak, desolate, dismal, drab, dreary, forlorn, miserable, somber, woeful

cheer up verb 1 COMFORT, encourage, enliven, gladden, hearten 2 TAKE HEART, buck up (informal), perk up, rally

cheery adjective CHEERFUL, breezy, carefree, chirpy (informal), genial, good-humored, happy, jovial, upbeat (informal)

chemist noun PHARMACIST, apothecary (obsolete), dispenser

cherish verb 1 CLING TO, cleave to, encourage, entertain, foster, harbor, hold dear, nurture, prize, sustain, treasure 2 CARE FOR, comfort, hold dear, love, nurse, shelter, support

chest noun BOX, case, casket, coffer, crate, strongbox, trunk

chew verb BITE, champ, chomp, crunch, gnaw, grind, masticate, munch

chewy adjective TOUGH, as tough as old boots, leathery

chic adjective STYLISH, cool (informal), elegant, fashionable, phat (slang), smart, trendy (informal)

chide verb Old-fashioned SCOLD, admonish, berate, censure, criticize, lecture, rebuke, reprimand, reproach, reprove, tell off (informal)

chief noun 1 HEAD, boss (informal), captain, commander, director, governor, leader, manager, master, principal, ruler ▶ adjective 2 PRIMARY, foremost,

highest, key, leading, main, predominant, pre-eminent, premier, prime, principal, supreme, uppermost

chiefly adverb 1 ESPECIALLY, above all, essentially, primarily, principally 2 MAINLY, in general, in the main, largely, mostly, on the whole, predominantly, usually

child noun YOUNGSTER, babe, baby, juvenile, kid (informal), minor, offspring, toddler, tot

childbirth noun CHILD-BEARING, confinement, delivery, labor, lying-in, parturition, travail

childhood noun YOUTH, boyhood or girlhood, immaturity, infancy, minority, schooldays

childish adjective IMMATURE, boyish or girlish, foolish, infantile, juvenile, puerile, young

childlike adjective INNOCENT, artless, guileless, ingenuous, naive, simple, trusting

chill noun 1 COLD, bite, coldness, coolness, crispness, frigidity, nip, rawness, sharpness ▶ verb 2 COOL, freeze, refrigerate 3 DISHEARTEN, dampen, deject, depress, discourage, dismay ▶ adjective 4 COLD, biting, bleak, chilly, freezing, frigid, raw, sharp, wintry

chilly adjective 1 COOL, brisk, crisp, drafty, fresh, nippy, penetrating, sharp 2 UNFRIENDLY, frigid, hostile, unresponsive, unsympathetic, unwelcoming

chime verb, noun RING, clang, jingle, peal, sound, tinkle, toll

china noun POTTERY, ceramics,

crockery, porcelain, service, tableware, ware

chink noun OPENING, aperture, cleft, crack, cranny, crevice, fissure, gap

chip noun 1 SCRATCH, fragment, nick, notch, shard, shaving, sliver, wafer ▶ verb 2 NICK, chisel, damage, gash, whittle

chirp verb CHIRRUP, cheep, peep, pipe, tweet, twitter, warble

chivalrous adjective COURTEOUS, bold, brave, courageous, gallant, gentlemanly, honorable, valiant

chivalry noun COURTESY, courage, gallantry, gentlemanliness, knight-errantry, knighthood, politeness

choice noun 1 OPTION, alternative, pick, preference, say 2 SELECTION, range, variety ▶ adjective 3 BEST, elite, excellent, exclusive, prime, rare, select

choke verb 1 STRANGLE, asphyxiate, gag, overpower, smother, stifle, suffocate, suppress, throttle 2 BLOCK, bar, bung, clog, congest, constrict, obstruct, stop

choose verb PICK, adopt, designate, elect, opt for, prefer, select, settle upon

choosy adjective FUSSY, discriminating, faddy, fastidious, finicky, particular, picky (informal), selective

chop verb CUT, cleave, fell, hack, hew, lop, sever

chore noun TASK, burden, duty, errand, job

chortle verb, noun CHUCKLE, cackle, crow, guffaw

chorus noun 1 CHOIR, choristers, ensemble, singers, vocalists 2 REFRAIN, burden, response, strain 3 UNISON, accord, concert, harmony

christen verb 1 BAPTIZE 2 NAME, call, designate, dub, style, term, title

Christmas noun FESTIVE SEASON, Noel, Xmas, Yule, Yuletide

chronicle noun 1 RECORD, account, annals, diary, history, journal, narrative, register, story ▶ verb 2 RECORD, enter, narrate, put on record, recount, register, relate, report, set down, tell

chubby adjective PLUMP, buxom, flabby, portly, rotund, round, stout, tubby

chuckle verb LAUGH, chortle, crow, exult, giggle, snigger, titter

chum noun Informal FRIEND, companion, comrade, crony, homeboy (slang), homegirl (slang), pal (informal)

chunk noun PIECE, block, dollop (informal), hunk, lump, mass, nugget, portion, slab

churlish adjective RUDE, brusque, harsh, ill-tempered, impolite, sullen, surly, uncivil

churn verb STIR UP, agitate, beat, convulse, swirl, toss

cinema noun FILMS, big screen (informal), flicks (slang), motion pictures, movies, pictures

cipher noun 1 CODE, cryptograph 2 NOBODY, nonentity

circle noun 1 RING, disc, globe, orb, sphere 2 GROUP, clique, club, company, coterie, set, society ▶ verb 3 GO ROUND, circumnavigate, circumscribe,

circuit noun encircle, enclose, envelop, ring, surround

circuit noun COURSE, journey, lap, orbit, revolution, route, tour, track

circuitous adjective INDIRECT, labyrinthine, meandering, oblique, rambling, roundabout, tortuous, winding

circular adjective 1 ROUND, ring-shaped, rotund, spherical 2 ORBITAL, circuitous, cyclical ▶ noun 3 ADVERTISEMENT, notice

circulate verb 1 SPREAD, broadcast, disseminate, distribute, issue, make known, promulgate, publicize, publish 2 FLOW, gyrate, radiate, revolve, rotate

circulation noun 1 BLOODSTREAM 2 FLOW, circling, motion, rotation 3 DISTRIBUTION, currency, dissemination, spread, transmission

circumference noun BOUNDARY, border, edge, extremity, limits, outline, perimeter, periphery, rim

circumstance noun EVENT, accident, condition, contingency, happening, incident, occurrence, particular, respect, situation

circumstances plural noun SITUATION, means, position, state, state of affairs, station, status

cistern noun TANK, basin, reservoir, sink, vat

citadel noun FORTRESS, bastion, fortification, keep, stronghold, tower

cite verb QUOTE, adduce, advance, allude to, enumerate, extract, mention, name, specify

citizen noun INHABITANT, denizen, dweller, resident, subject, townsman

city noun TOWN, conurbation, metropolis, municipality

civic adjective PUBLIC, communal, local, municipal

civil adjective 1 CIVIC, domestic, municipal, political 2 POLITE, affable, courteous, obliging, refined, urbane, well-mannered

civilization noun 1 CULTURE, advancement, cultivation, development, education, enlightenment, progress, refinement, sophistication 2 SOCIETY, community, nation, people, polity

civilize verb CULTIVATE, educate, enlighten, refine, sophisticate, tame

civilized adjective CULTURED, educated, enlightened, humane, polite, sophisticated, tolerant, urbane

claim verb 1 ASSERT, allege, challenge, insist, maintain, profess, uphold 2 DEMAND, ask, call for, insist, need, require ▶ noun 3 ASSERTION, affirmation, allegation, pretension, privilege, protestation 4 DEMAND, application, call, petition, request, requirement 5 RIGHT, title

clairvoyant noun 1 PSYCHIC, diviner, fortune-teller, visionary ▶ adjective 2 PSYCHIC, extrasensory, second-sighted, telepathic, visionary

clamber verb CLIMB, claw, scale, scrabble, scramble, shin

clammy adjective MOIST, close, damp, dank, sticky, sweaty

clamor noun NOISE, commotion,

din, hubbub, outcry, racket, shouting, uproar

clamp noun 1 VICE, bracket, fastener, grip, press ▶verb 2 FASTEN, brace, fix, make fast, secure

clan noun FAMILY, brotherhood, faction, fraternity, group, society, tribe

clandestine adjective SECRET, cloak-and-dagger, concealed, covert, furtive, private, stealthy, surreptitious, underground

clap verb APPLAUD, acclaim, cheer

clarification noun EXPLANATION, elucidation, exposition, illumination, interpretation, simplification

clarify verb EXPLAIN, clear up, elucidate, illuminate, interpret, make plain, simplify, throw or shed light on

clarity noun CLEARNESS, definition, limpidity, lucidity, precision, simplicity, transparency

clash verb 1 CONFLICT, cross swords, feud, grapple, lock horns, quarrel, war, wrangle 2 CRASH, bang, clang, clank, clatter, jangle, jar, rattle ▶noun 3 CONFLICT, brush, collision, confrontation, difference of opinion, disagreement, fight, showdown (informal)

clasp noun 1 FASTENING, brooch, buckle, catch, clip, fastener, grip, hook, pin 2 GRASP, embrace, grip, hold, hug ▶verb 3 GRASP, clutch, embrace, grip, hold, hug, press, seize, squeeze 4 FASTEN, connect

class noun 1 GROUP, category, division, genre, kind, set, sort, type ▶verb 2 CLASSIFY, brand,

categorize, designate, grade, group, label, rank, rate

classic adjective 1 DEFINITIVE, archetypal, exemplary, ideal, model, quintessential, standard 2 TYPICAL, characteristic, regular, standard, time-honored, usual 3 BEST, consummate, finest, first-rate, masterly, world-class 4 LASTING, abiding, ageless, deathless, enduring, immortal, undying ▶noun 5 STANDARD, exemplar, masterpiece, model, paradigm, prototype 6 comical Informal HILARIOUS, hysterical, ludicrous, uproarious

classical adjective PURE, elegant, harmonious, refined, restrained, symmetrical, understated, well-proportioned

classification noun CATEGORIZATION, analysis, arrangement, grading, sorting, taxonomy

classify verb CATEGORIZE, arrange, catalog, grade, pigeonhole, rank, sort, systematize, tabulate

classy adjective Informal HIGH-CLASS, elegant, exclusive, ritzy, stylish, superior, swanky, top-drawer, up-market

clause noun SECTION, article, chapter, condition, paragraph, part, passage

claw noun 1 NAIL, pincer, talon, tentacle ▶verb 2 SCRATCH, dig, lacerate, maul, rip, scrape, tear

clean adjective 1 PURE, flawless, fresh, immaculate, impeccable, spotless, unblemished, unsullied 2 HYGIENIC, antiseptic, decontaminated, purified, sterile, sterilized, uncontaminated, unpolluted 3 MORAL, chaste, decent, good, honorable, innocent, pure, respectable, upright, virtuous **4** COMPLETE, conclusive, decisive, entire, final, perfect, thorough, total, unimpaired, whole ▶verb **5** CLEANSE, disinfect, launder, purge, purify, rinse, sanitize, scour, scrub, wash

cleanse verb CLEAN, absolve, clear, purge, purify, rinse, scour, scrub, wash

cleanser noun DETERGENT, disinfectant, purifier, scourer, soap, solvent

clear adjective **1** CERTAIN, convinced, decided, definite, positive, resolved, satisfied, sure **2** OBVIOUS, apparent, blatant, comprehensible, conspicuous, distinct, evident, manifest, palpable, plain, pronounced, recognizable, unmistakable **3** TRANSPARENT, crystalline, glassy, limpid, pellucid, see-through, translucent **4** BRIGHT, cloudless, fair, fine, light, luminous, shining, sunny, unclouded **5** UNOBSTRUCTED, empty, free, open, smooth, unhindered, unimpeded **6** UNBLEMISHED, clean, immaculate, innocent, pure, untarnished ▶verb **7** UNBLOCK, disentangle, extricate, free, loosen, open, rid, unload **8** PASS OVER, jump, leap, miss, vault **9** BRIGHTEN, break up, lighten **10** CLEAN, cleanse, erase, purify, refine, sweep away, tidy (up), wipe **11** ABSOLVE, acquit, excuse, exonerate, justify, vindicate **12** GAIN, acquire, earn, make, reap, secure

clear-cut adjective

STRAIGHTFORWARD, black-and-white, cut-and-dried (informal), definite, explicit, plain, precise, specific, unambiguous, unequivocal

clearly adverb OBVIOUSLY, beyond doubt, distinctly, evidently, markedly, openly, overtly, undeniably, undoubtedly

clergy noun PRIESTHOOD, churchmen, clergymen, clerics, holy orders, ministry, the cloth

clergyman noun MINISTER, chaplain, cleric, man of God, man of the cloth, padre, parson, pastor, priest, vicar

clever adjective INTELLIGENT, bright, gifted, ingenious, knowledgeable, quick-witted, resourceful, shrewd, smart, talented

cleverness noun INTELLIGENCE, ability, brains, ingenuity, quick wits, resourcefulness, shrewdness, smartness

cliché noun PLATITUDE, banality, commonplace, hackneyed phrase, stereotype, truism

client noun CUSTOMER, applicant, buyer, consumer, patient, patron, shopper

clientele noun CUSTOMERS, business, clients, following, market, patronage, regulars, trade

cliff noun ROCK FACE, bluff, crag, escarpment, overhang, precipice, scar, scarp

climactic adjective CRUCIAL, critical, decisive, paramount, peak

climate noun WEATHER, temperature

climax noun CULMINATION, height, highlight, high point, peak, summit, top, zenith

climb verb ASCEND, clamber, mount, rise, scale, shin up, soar, top

climb down verb 1 DESCEND, dismount 2 BACK DOWN, eat one's words, retract, retreat

clinch verb SETTLE, conclude, confirm, decide, determine, seal, secure, set the seal on, sew up (informal)

cling verb STICK, adhere, clasp, clutch, embrace, grasp, grip, hug

clinical adjective UNEMOTIONAL, analytic, cold, detached, dispassionate, impersonal, objective, scientific

clip¹ verb 1 TRIM, crop, curtail, cut, pare, prune, shear, shorten, snip ▶ noun, verb 2 Informal SMACK, clout (informal), cuff, knock, punch, strike, thump, wallop (informal), whack

clip² verb ATTACH, fasten, fix, hold, pin, staple

clique noun GROUP, cabal, circle, coterie, faction, gang, set

cloak noun 1 CAPE, coat, mantle, wrap ▶ verb 2 COVER, camouflage, conceal, disguise, hide, mask, obscure, screen, veil

clog verb OBSTRUCT, block, congest, hinder, impede, jam

close¹ verb 1 SHUT, bar, block, lock, plug, seal, secure, stop up 2 END, cease, complete, conclude, finish, shut down, terminate, wind up 3 CONNECT, come together, couple, fuse, join, unite ▶ noun 4 END, completion, conclusion, culmination, denouement, ending, finale, finish

close² adjective 1 NEAR, adjacent, adjoining, at hand, cheek by jowl, handy, impending, nearby, neighboring, nigh 2 INTIMATE, attached, confidential, dear, devoted, familiar, inseparable, loving 3 CAREFUL, detailed, intense, minute, painstaking, rigorous, thorough 4 COMPACT, congested, crowded, dense, impenetrable, jam-packed, packed, tight 5 STIFLING, airless, heavy, humid, muggy, oppressive, stuffy, suffocating, sweltering 6 SECRETIVE, private, reticent, secret, taciturn, uncommunicative 7 MEAN, miserly, stingy

closed adjective 1 SHUT, fastened, locked, out of service, sealed 2 EXCLUSIVE, restricted 3 FINISHED, concluded, decided, ended, over, resolved, settled, terminated

cloth noun FABRIC, material, textiles

clothe verb DRESS, array, attire, cover, drape, equip, fit out, garb, robe, swathe

clothes plural noun CLOTHING, apparel, attire, costume, dress, garb, garments, gear (informal), outfit, wardrobe, wear

clothing noun CLOTHES, apparel, attire, costume, dress, garb, garments, gear (informal), outfit, wardrobe, wear

cloud noun 1 MIST, gloom, haze, murk, vapor ▶ verb 2 OBSCURE, becloud, darken, dim, eclipse, obfuscate, overshadow, shade, shadow, veil 3 CONFUSE, disorient, distort, impair, muddle, muddy the waters

cloudy adjective **1** DULL, dim, gloomy, leaden, louring or lowering, overcast, somber, sunless **2** OPAQUE, muddy, murky

clout Informal ▸ noun **1** INFLUENCE, authority, power, prestige, pull, weight ▸ verb **2** HIT, clobber (slang), punch, sock (slang), strike, thump, wallop (informal)

clown noun **1** COMEDIAN, buffoon, comic, fool, harlequin, jester, joker, prankster ▸ verb **2** PLAY THE FOOL, act the fool, jest, mess about

club noun **1** ASSOCIATION, company, fraternity, group, guild, lodge, set, society, union **2** STICK, bat, bludgeon, cudgel, truncheon ▸ verb **3** BEAT, bash, batter, bludgeon, hammer, pummel, strike

clue noun INDICATION, evidence, hint, lead, pointer, sign, suggestion, suspicion, trace

clueless adjective STUPID, dim, dull, half-witted, simple, slow, thick, unintelligent, witless

clump noun **1** CLUSTER, bunch, bundle, group, mass ▸ verb **2** STOMP, lumber, plod, thud, thump, tramp

clumsy adjective AWKWARD, bumbling, gauche, gawky, lumbering, maladroit, ponderous, uncoordinated, ungainly, unwieldy

cluster noun **1** GATHERING, assemblage, batch, bunch, clump, collection, group, knot ▸ verb **2** GATHER, assemble, bunch, collect, flock, group

clutch verb SEIZE, catch, clasp, cling to, embrace, grab, grasp, grip, snatch

clutches plural noun POWER, claws, control, custody, grasp, grip, hands, keeping, possession, sway

clutter verb **1** LITTER, scatter, strew ▸ noun **2** UNTIDINESS, confusion, disarray, disorder, jumble, litter, mess, muddle

coach noun **1** BUS, car, carriage, charabanc, vehicle **2** INSTRUCTOR, handler, teacher, trainer, tutor ▸ verb **3** INSTRUCT, drill, exercise, prepare, train, tutor

coalesce verb BLEND, amalgamate, combine, fuse, incorporate, integrate, merge, mix, unite

coalition noun ALLIANCE, amalgamation, association, bloc, combination, conjunction, confederation, conjunction, fusion, merger, union

coarse adjective **1** ROUGH, crude, homespun, impure, unfinished, unpolished, unprocessed, unpurified, unrefined **2** VULGAR, earthy, improper, indecent, indelicate, ribald, rude, smutty

coarseness noun **1** ROUGHNESS, crudity, unevenness **2** VULGARITY, bawdiness, crudity, earthiness, indelicacy, ribaldry, smut, uncouthness

coast noun **1** SHORE, beach, border, coastline, seaboard, seaside ▸ verb **2** CRUISE, drift, freewheel, glide, sail, taxi

coat noun **1** FUR, fleece, hair, hide, pelt, skin, wool **2** LAYER, coating, covering, overlay ▸ verb **3** COVER, apply, plaster, smear, spread

coax verb PERSUADE, allure, cajole, entice, prevail upon, sweet-talk (*informal*), talk into, wheedle

cocktail noun MIXTURE, blend, combination, mix

cocky adjective OVERCONFIDENT, arrogant, brash, cocksure, conceited, egotistical, full of oneself, swaggering, vain

code noun 1 CIPHER, cryptograph 2 PRINCIPLES, canon, convention, custom, ethics, etiquette, manners, maxim, regulations, rules, system

cogent adjective CONVINCING, compelling, effective, forceful, influential, potent, powerful, strong, weighty

cogitate verb THINK, consider, contemplate, deliberate, meditate, mull over, muse, ponder, reflect, ruminate

coherent adjective 1 CONSISTENT, logical, lucid, meaningful, orderly, organized, rational, reasoned, systematic 2 INTELLIGIBLE, articulate, comprehensible

coil verb WIND, curl, loop, snake, spiral, twine, twist, wreathe, writhe

coin noun 1 MONEY, cash, change, copper, silver, specie ▶ verb 2 INVENT, create, fabricate, forge, make up, mint, mold, originate

coincide verb 1 OCCUR SIMULTANEOUSLY, be concurrent, coexist, synchronize 2 AGREE, accord, concur, correspond, harmonize, match, square, tally

coincidence noun 1 CHANCE, accident, fluke, freak of chance accident, luck, stroke of luck 2 COINCIDING, concurrence, conjunction, correlation, correspondence

coincidental adjective CHANCE, accidental, casual, fluky (*informal*), fortuitous, unintentional, unplanned

cold adjective 1 CHILLY, arctic, bleak, cool, freezing, frigid, frosty, frozen, icy, wintry 2 UNFRIENDLY, aloof, distant, frigid, indifferent, reserved, standoffish ▶ noun 3 COLDNESS, chill, frigidity, frostiness, iciness

cold-blooded adjective CALLOUS, dispassionate, heartless, ruthless, steely, stony-hearted, unemotional, unfeeling

collaborate verb 1 WORK TOGETHER, cooperate, join forces, participate, play ball (*informal*), team up 2 CONSPIRE, collude, cooperate, fraternize

collaboration noun TEAMWORK, alliance, association, cooperation, partnership

collaborator noun 1 CO-WORKER, associate, colleague, partner, team-mate 2 TRAITOR, fraternizer, quisling, turncoat

collapse verb 1 FALL DOWN, cave in, crumple, fall, fall apart at the seams, give way, subside 2 FAIL, come to nothing, fold, founder, go belly-up (*informal*) ▶ noun 3 FALLING DOWN, cave-in, disintegration, falling apart, ruin, subsidence 4 FAILURE, downfall, flop, slump 5 FAINT, breakdown, exhaustion, prostration

collar verb Informal SEIZE, apprehend, arrest, capture, catch, grab, nail (*informal*)

colleague noun FELLOW WORKER, ally, assistant, associate,

collaborator, comrade, helper, partner, team-mate, workmate

collect *verb* **1** ASSEMBLE, cluster, congregate, convene, converge, flock together, rally **2** GATHER, accumulate, amass, assemble, heap, hoard, save, stockpile

collected *adjective* CALM, composed, cool, poised, self-possessed, serene, unperturbed, unruffled

collection *noun* **1** ACCUMULATION, anthology, compilation, heap, hoard, mass, pile, set, stockpile, store **2** GROUP, assembly, assortment, cluster, company, crowd **3** CONTRIBUTION, alms, offering, offertory

collective *adjective* COMBINED, aggregate, composite, corporate, cumulative, joint, shared, unified, united

collide *verb* **1** CRASH, clash, come into collision, meet head-on **2** CONFLICT, clash

collision *noun* **1** CRASH, accident, bump, impact, pile-up (*informal*), smash **2** CONFLICT, clash, confrontation, encounter, opposition, skirmish

colloquial *adjective* INFORMAL, conversational, demotic, everyday, familiar, idiomatic, vernacular

colony *noun* SETTLEMENT, community, dependency, dominion, outpost, possession, province, satellite state, territory

color *noun* HUE, colorant, dye, paint, pigment, shade, tint ▶*verb* **2** PAINT, dye, stain, tinge, tint **3** BLUSH, flush, redden

colorful *adjective* **1** BRIGHT, brilliant, multicolored, psychedelic, variegated **2** INTERESTING, distinctive, graphic, lively, picturesque, rich, vivid

colorless *adjective* **1** DRAB, achromatic, anemic, ashen, bleached, faded, wan, washed out **2** UNINTERESTING, characterless, dreary, dull, insipid, lackluster, vapid

colossal *adjective* HUGE, enormous, gigantic, immense, mammoth, massive, monumental, prodigious, vast

column *noun* **1** PILLAR, obelisk, post, shaft, support, upright **2** LINE, cavalcade, file, procession, rank, row

coma *noun* UNCONSCIOUSNESS, oblivion, stupor, trance

comb *verb* **1** UNTANGLE, arrange, dress, groom **2** SEARCH, forage, hunt, rake, ransack, rummage, scour, sift

combat *noun* **1** FIGHT, action, battle, conflict, contest, encounter, engagement, skirmish, struggle, war, warfare ▶*verb* **2** FIGHT, defy, do battle with, oppose, resist, withstand

combatant *noun* FIGHTER, adversary, antagonist, enemy, opponent, soldier, warrior

combination *noun* **1** MIXTURE, amalgamation, blend, coalescence, composite, connection, mix **2** ASSOCIATION, alliance, coalition, confederation, consortium, federation, syndicate, union

combine *verb* JOIN TOGETHER, amalgamate, blend, connect, integrate, link, merge, mix, pool, unite

come verb 1 MOVE TOWARDS, advance, approach, draw near, near 2 ARRIVE, appear, enter, materialize, reach, show up (informal), turn up (informal) 3 HAPPEN, fall, occur, take place 4 RESULT, arise, emanate, emerge, flow, issue, originate 5 REACH, extend 6 BE AVAILABLE, be made, be offered, be on offer, be produced

come about verb HAPPEN, arise, befall, come to pass, occur, result, take place, transpire (informal)

come across verb FIND, bump into (informal), chance upon, discover, encounter, meet, notice, stumble upon, unearth

comeback noun 1 Informal RETURN, rally, rebound, recovery, resurgence, revival, triumph 2 RESPONSE, rejoinder, reply, retaliation, retort, riposte

come back verb RETURN, reappear, recur, re-enter

comedian noun COMIC, card (informal), clown, funny man, humorist, jester, joker, wag, wit

comedown noun 1 DECLINE, deflation, demotion, reverse 2 Informal DISAPPOINTMENT, anticlimax, blow, humiliation, letdown

comedy noun HUMOR, farce, fun, hilarity, jesting, joking, light entertainment

comfort noun 1 LUXURY, cosiness, ease, opulence, snugness, wellbeing 2 RELIEF, compensation, consolation, help, succor, support ▶verb 3 CONSOLE, commiserate with, hearten, reassure, soothe

comfortable adjective 1 RELAXING, agreeable, convenient, cozy, homely, homey, pleasant, restful, snug 2 HAPPY, at ease, at home, contented, gratified, relaxed, serene 3 Informal WELL-OFF, affluent, in clover (informal), prosperous, well-to-do

comforting adjective CONSOLING, cheering, consolatory, encouraging, heart-warming, reassuring, soothing

comic adjective 1 FUNNY, amusing, comical, droll, farcical, humorous, jocular, witty ▶ noun 2 COMEDIAN, buffoon, clown, funny man, humorist, jester, wag, wit

comical adjective FUNNY, amusing, comic, droll, farcical, hilarious, humorous, priceless, side-splitting

coming adjective 1 APPROACHING, at hand, forthcoming, imminent, impending, in store, near, nigh ▶noun 2 ARRIVAL, advent, approach

command verb 1 ORDER, bid, charge, compel, demand, direct, require 2 HAVE AUTHORITY OVER, control, dominate, govern, handle, head, lead, manage, rule, supervise ▶noun 3 ORDER, commandment, decree, demand, directive, instruction, requirement, ultimatum 4 AUTHORITY, charge, control, government, management, mastery, power, rule, supervision

commandeer verb SEIZE, appropriate, confiscate, requisition, sequester, sequestrate

commander noun OFFICER, boss (*informal*), captain, chief, commanding officer, head, leader, ruler

commanding adjective CONTROLLING, advantageous, decisive, dominant, dominating, superior

commemorate verb REMEMBER, celebrate, honor, immortalize, pay tribute to, salute

commemoration noun REMEMBRANCE, ceremony, honoring, memorial service, tribute

commence verb BEGIN, embark on, enter upon, initiate, open, originate, start

commend verb PRAISE, acclaim, applaud, approve, compliment, extol, recommend, speak highly of

commendable adjective PRAISEWORTHY, admirable, creditable, deserving, estimable, exemplary, laudable, meritorious, worthy

commendation noun PRAISE, acclaim, acclamation, approbation, approval, credit, encouragement, good opinion, kudos, panegyric, recommendation

comment noun 1 REMARK, observation, statement 2 NOTE, annotation, commentary, explanation, exposition, illustration ▶ verb 3 REMARK, mention, note, observe, point out, say, utter 4 ANNOTATE, elucidate, explain, interpret

commentary noun 1 NARRATION, description, voice-over 2 NOTES, analysis, critique, explanation, review, treatise

commentator noun 1 REPORTER, special correspondent, sportscaster 2 CRITIC, annotator, interpreter

commerce noun TRADE, business, dealing, exchange, traffic

commercial adjective 1 MERCANTILE, trading 2 MATERIALISTIC, mercenary, profit-making ▶ noun 3 ADVERTISEMENT, ad (*informal*), announcement, plug (*informal*)

commiserate verb SYMPATHIZE, console, feel for, pity

commission noun 1 DUTY, errand, mandate, mission, task 2 FEE, cut, percentage, rake-off (*slang*), royalties 3 COMMITTEE, board, commissioners, delegation, deputation, representatives ▶ verb 4 APPOINT, authorize, contract, delegate, depute, empower, engage, nominate, order, select

commit verb 1 DO, carry out, enact, execute, perform, perpetrate 2 PUT IN CUSTODY, confine, imprison

commitment noun 1 DEDICATION, devotion, involvement, loyalty 2 RESPONSIBILITY, duty, engagement, liability, obligation, tie

common adjective 1 AVERAGE, commonplace, conventional, customary, everyday, familiar, frequent, habitual, ordinary, regular, routine, standard, stock, usual 2 POPULAR, accepted, general, prevailing, prevalent, universal, widespread 3 COLLECTIVE, communal, popular, public, social 4 VULGAR, coarse, inferior, plebeian

commonplace adjective
1 EVERYDAY, banal, common, humdrum, mundane, obvious, ordinary, widespread ▶noun
2 CLICHÉ, banality, platitude, truism

common sense noun GOOD SENSE, horse sense, level-headedness, native intelligence, prudence, sound judgment, wit

commotion noun DISTURBANCE, disorder, excitement, furor, fuss, hue and cry, rumpus, tumult, turmoil, upheaval, uproar

communal adjective PUBLIC, collective, general, joint, shared

commune noun COMMUNITY, collective, cooperative, kibbutz

commune with verb CONTEMPLATE, meditate on, muse on, ponder, reflect on

communicate verb MAKE KNOWN, convey, declare, disclose, impart, inform, pass on, proclaim, transmit

communication noun 1 PASSING ON, contact, conversation, correspondence, dissemination, link, transmission 2 MESSAGE, announcement, disclosure, dispatch, information, news, report, statement, word

communicative adjective TALKATIVE, chatty, expansive, forthcoming, frank, informative, loquacious, open, outgoing, voluble

Communism noun SOCIALISM, Bolshevism, collectivism, Marxism, state socialism

Communist noun SOCIALIST, Bolshevik, collectivist, Marxist, Red (informal)

community noun SOCIETY, brotherhood, commonwealth, company, general public, people, populace, public, residents, state

commuter noun DAILY TRAVELER, straphanger (informal), suburbanite

compact¹ adjective 1 CLOSELY PACKED, compressed, condensed, dense, pressed together, solid, thick 2 BRIEF, compendious, concise, succinct, terse, to the point ▶verb 3 PACK CLOSELY, compress, condense, cram, stuff, tamp

compact² noun AGREEMENT, arrangement, bargain, bond, contract, covenant, deal, pact, treaty, understanding

companion noun 1 FRIEND, accomplice, ally, associate, colleague, comrade, consort, homeboy (slang), homegirl (slang), mate (informal), partner 2 ESCORT, aide, assistant, attendant, chaperon, squire

companionship noun FELLOWSHIP, camaraderie, company, comradeship, conviviality, esprit de corps, friendship, rapport, togetherness

company noun 1 BUSINESS, association, concern, corporation, establishment, firm, house, partnership, syndicate 2 GROUP, assembly, band, collection, community, crowd, gathering, party, set 3 GUESTS, callers, party, visitors

comparable adjective 1 ON A PAR, a match for, as good as, commensurate, equal, equivalent, in a class with, on a level playing field (*informal*), proportionate, tantamount **2** SIMILAR, akin, alike, analogous, cognate, corresponding, cut from the same cloth, of a piece, related

comparative *adjective* RELATIVE, by comparison, qualified

compare *verb* **1** WEIGH, balance, contrast, juxtapose, set against **2** (usually with *with*) BE ON A PAR WITH, approach, bear comparison, be in the same class as, be the equal of, compete with, equal, hold a candle to, match **3 compare to** LIKEN TO, correlate to, equate to, identify with, mention in the same breath as, parallel, resemble

comparison *noun* CONTRAST, distinction, juxtaposition **2** SIMILARITY, analogy, comparability, correlation, likeness, resemblance

compartment *noun* SECTION, alcove, bay, berth, booth, carriage, cubbyhole, cubicle, locker, niche, pigeonhole

compass *noun* RANGE, area, boundary, circumference, extent, field, limit, reach, realm, scope

compassion *noun* SYMPATHY, condolence, fellow feeling, humanity, kindness, mercy, pity, sorrow, tender-heartedness, tenderness, understanding

compassionate *adjective* SYMPATHETIC, benevolent, charitable, humane, humanitarian, kind-hearted, merciful, pitying, tender-hearted, understanding

compatibility *noun* HARMONY, affinity, agreement, concord, empathy, like-mindedness, rapport, sympathy

compatible *adjective* HARMONIOUS, adaptable, congruous, consistent, in harmony, in keeping, suitable

compel *verb* FORCE, coerce, constrain, dragoon, impel, make, oblige, railroad (*informal*)

compelling *adjective* **1** FASCINATING, enchanting, enthralling, gripping, hypnotic, irresistible, mesmeric, spellbinding **2** PRESSING, binding, coercive, imperative, overriding, peremptory, unavoidable, urgent **3** CONVINCING, cogent, conclusive, forceful, irrefutable, powerful, telling, weighty

compensate *verb* **1** RECOMPENSE, atone, make amends, make good, refund, reimburse, remunerate, repay **2** CANCEL (OUT), balance, counteract, counterbalance, make up for, offset, redress

compensation *noun* RECOMPENSE, amends, atonement, damages, reimbursement, remuneration, reparation, restitution, satisfaction

compete *verb* CONTEND, be in the running, challenge, contest, fight, strive, struggle, vie

competence *noun* ABILITY, capability, capacity, expertise, fitness, proficiency, skill, suitability

competent *adjective* ABLE, adequate, capable, fit, proficient, qualified, suitable

competition noun 1 RIVALRY, opposition, strife, struggle 2 CONTEST, championship, event, head-to-head, puzzle, quiz, tournament 3 OPPOSITION, challengers, field, rivals

competitive adjective 1 CUT-THROAT, aggressive, antagonistic, at odds, dog-eat-dog, opposing, rival 2 AMBITIOUS, combative

competitor noun CONTESTANT, adversary, antagonist, challenger, opponent, rival

compilation noun COLLECTION, accumulation, anthology, assemblage, assortment, treasury

compile verb PUT TOGETHER, accumulate, amass, collect, cull, garner, gather, marshal, organize

complacency noun SELF-SATISFACTION, contentment, satisfaction, smugness

complacent adjective SELF-SATISFIED, contented, pleased with oneself, resting on one's laurels, satisfied, serene, smug, unconcerned

complain verb FIND FAULT, bemoan, bewail, carp, deplore, groan, grouse, grumble, lament, moan, whine

complaint noun 1 CRITICISM, charge, grievance, gripe (informal), grouse, grumble, lament, moan, protest 2 ILLNESS, affliction, ailment, disease, disorder, malady, sickness, upset

complement noun 1 COMPLETION, companion, consummation, counterpart, finishing touch, rounding-off, supplement 2 TOTAL, aggregate, capacity, entirety, quota, totality, wholeness ▶ verb 3 COMPLETE, cap (informal), crown, round off, set off

complementary adjective COMPLETING, companion, corresponding, interdependent, interrelating, matched, reciprocal

complete adjective 1 TOTAL, absolute, consummate, outright, thorough, thoroughgoing, utter 2 FINISHED, accomplished, achieved, concluded, ended 3 ENTIRE, all, faultless, full, intact, plenary, unbroken, whole ▶ verb 4 FINISH, close, conclude, crown, end, finalize, round off, settle, wind up (informal), wrap up (informal)

completely adverb TOTALLY, absolutely, altogether, entirely, every inch, fully, hook, line and sinker, in full, lock, stock and barrel, one hundred per cent, perfectly, thoroughly, utterly, wholly

completion noun FINISHING, bitter end, close, conclusion, culmination, end, fruition, fulfillment

complex adjective 1 COMPOUND, composite, heterogeneous, manifold, multifarious, multiple 2 COMPLICATED, convoluted, elaborate, intricate, involved, labyrinthine, tangled, tortuous ▶ noun 3 STRUCTURE, aggregate, composite, network, organization, scheme, system 4 OBSESSION, fixation, fixed idea, idée fixe, phobia, preoccupation

complexion noun 1 SKIN, color, coloring, hue, pigmentation, skin tone **2** NATURE, appearance, aspect, character, guise, light, look, make-up

complexity noun COMPLICATION, elaboration, entanglement, intricacy, involvement, ramification

complicate verb MAKE DIFFICULT, confuse, entangle, involve, muddle, ravel

complicated adjective
1 DIFFICULT, involved, perplexing, problematic, puzzling, troublesome
2 INVOLVED, complex, convoluted, elaborate, intricate, labyrinthine

complication noun
1 COMPLEXITY, confusion, entanglement, intricacy, web
2 PROBLEM, difficulty, drawback, embarrassment, obstacle, snag

compliment noun **1** PRAISE, bouquet, commendation, congratulations, eulogy, flattery, honor, tribute ▶ verb **2** PRAISE, brown-nose (slang), commend, congratulate, extol, flatter, pay tribute to, salute, speak highly of

complimentary adjective
1 FLATTERING, appreciative, approving, commendatory, congratulatory, laudatory
2 FREE, courtesy, donated, gratis, gratuitous, honorary, on the house

compliments plural noun GREETINGS, good wishes, regards, remembrances, respects, salutation

comply verb OBEY, abide by, acquiesce, adhere to, conform to, follow, observe, submit, toe the line

component noun **1** PART, constituent, element, ingredient, item, piece, unit ▶ adjective **2** CONSTITUENT, inherent, intrinsic

compose verb **1** PUT TOGETHER, build, comprise, constitute, construct, fashion, form, make, make up **2** CREATE, contrive, devise, invent, produce, write **3** CALM, collect, control, pacify, placate, quiet, soothe **4** ARRANGE, adjust

composed adjective CALM, at ease, collected, cool, level-headed, poised, relaxed, sedate, self-possessed, serene, unflappable

composition noun **1** CREATION, compilation, fashioning, formation, formulation, making, production, putting together **2** DESIGN, arrangement, configuration, formation, layout, make-up, organization, structure **3** ESSAY, exercise, literary work, opus, piece, treatise, work

composure noun CALMNESS, aplomb, equanimity, poise, sang-froid, self-assurance, self-possession, serenity

compound noun **1** COMBINATION, alloy, amalgam, blend, composite, fusion, medley, mixture, synthesis ▶ verb **2** COMBINE, amalgamate, blend, intermingle, mix, synthesize, unite **3** INTENSIFY, add to, aggravate, augment, complicate, exacerbate, heighten, magnify, worsen ▶ adjective **4** COMPLEX, composite, intricate, multiple

comprehend verb UNDERSTAND, apprehend, conceive, fathom, grasp, know, make out, perceive, see, take in

comprehensible *adjective* UNDERSTANDABLE, clear, coherent, conceivable, explicit, intelligible, plain

comprehension *noun* UNDERSTANDING, conception, discernment, grasp, intelligence, perception, realization

comprehensive *adjective* BROAD, all-embracing, all-inclusive, blanket, complete, encyclopedic, exhaustive, full, inclusive, thorough

compress *verb* SQUEEZE, abbreviate, concentrate, condense, contract, crush, press, shorten, squash

comprise *verb* 1 BE COMPOSED OF, consist of, contain, embrace, encompass, include, take in 2 MAKE UP, compose, constitute, form

compromise *noun* 1 GIVE-AND-TAKE, accommodation, adjustment, agreement, concession, settlement, trade-off ▶ *verb* 2 MEET HALFWAY, adjust, agree, concede, give and take, go fifty-fifty (*informal*), settle, strike a balance 3 DISHONOR, discredit, embarrass, expose, jeopardize, prejudice, weaken

compulsion *noun* 1 URGE, drive, necessity, need, obsession, preoccupation 2 FORCE, coercion, constraint, demand, duress, obligation, pressure, urgency

compulsive *adjective* IRRESISTIBLE, compelling, driving, neurotic, obsessive, overwhelming, uncontrollable, urgent

compulsory *adjective* OBLIGATORY, binding, *de rigueur*, forced, imperative, mandatory, required, requisite

compute *verb* CALCULATE, add up, count, enumerate, figure out, reckon, tally, total

comrade *noun* COMPANION, ally, associate, colleague, co-worker, fellow, friend, homeboy (*slang*), homegirl (*slang*), partner

con *Informal* ▶ *noun* 1 SWINDLE, deception, fraud, scam (*slang*), sting (*informal*), trick ▶ *verb* 2 SWINDLE, cheat, deceive, defraud, double-cross (*informal*), dupe, hoodwink, rip off (*slang*), trick

concave *adjective* HOLLOW, indented

conceal *verb* HIDE, bury, camouflage, cover, disguise, mask, obscure, screen

concede *verb* 1 ADMIT, accept, acknowledge, allow, confess, grant, own 2 GIVE UP, cede, hand over, relinquish, surrender, yield

conceit *noun* SELF-IMPORTANCE, arrogance, egotism, narcissism, pride, swagger, vanity

conceited *adjective* SELF-IMPORTANT, arrogant, bigheaded (*informal*), cocky, egotistical, full of oneself, immodest, narcissistic, too big for one's boots or breeches, vain

conceivable *adjective* IMAGINABLE, believable, credible, possible, thinkable

conceive *verb* 1 IMAGINE, believe, comprehend, envisage,

fancy, suppose, think,
understand **2** THINK UP,
contrive, create, design, devise,
formulate **3** BECOME PREGNANT,
become impregnated

concentrate verb **1** FOCUS ONE'S
ATTENTION ON, be engrossed in,
put one's mind to, rack one's
brains **2** FOCUS, bring to bear,
center, cluster, converge
3 GATHER, accumulate, cluster,
collect, congregate, huddle

concentrated adjective
1 INTENSE, all-out (informal),
deep, hard, intensive
2 CONDENSED, boiled down,
evaporated, reduced, rich,
thickened, undiluted

concentration noun
1 SINGLE-MINDEDNESS, absorption,
application, heed **2** FOCUSING,
bringing to bear,
centralization, centring,
consolidation, convergence,
intensification **3** CONVERGENCE,
accumulation, aggregation,
cluster, collection, horde, mass

concept noun IDEA, abstraction,
conception, conceptualization,
hypothesis, image, notion,
theory, view

conception noun **1** IDEA,
concept, design, image,
notion, plan **2** IMPREGNATION,
fertilization, germination,
insemination

concern noun **1** WORRY, anxiety,
apprehension, burden, care,
disquiet, distress **2** IMPORTANCE,
bearing, interest, relevance
3 BUSINESS, affair, interest, job,
responsibility, task **4** BUSINESS,
company, corporation,
enterprise, establishment, firm,
organization ▶ verb **5** WORRY,
bother, disquiet, distress,

disturb, make anxious, perturb,
trouble **6** BE RELEVANT TO, affect,
apply to, bear on, interest,
involve, pertain to, regard,
touch

concerned adjective **1** INVOLVED,
active, implicated, interested,
mixed up, privy to **2** WORRIED,
anxious, bothered, distressed,
disturbed, troubled, uneasy,
upset

concerning preposition
REGARDING, about, apropos of,
as regards, on the subject of,
re, relating to, respecting,
touching, with reference to

concession noun **1** GRANT,
adjustment, allowance, boon,
compromise, indulgence,
permit, privilege, sop
2 CONCEDING, acknowledgment,
admission, assent, confession,
surrender, yielding

conciliate verb PACIFY, appease,
clear the air, mediate, mollify,
placate, reconcile, soothe, win
over

conciliation noun PACIFICATION,
appeasement, mollification,
placation, reconciliation,
soothing

conciliatory adjective PACIFYING,
appeasing, mollifying, pacific,
peaceable, placatory

concise adjective BRIEF,
compendious, condensed,
laconic, pithy, short, succinct,
terse

conclude verb **1** DECIDE, assume,
deduce, gather, infer, judge,
surmise, work out **2** END, cease,
close, complete, finish, round
off, terminate, wind up
3 ACCOMPLISH, bring about,
carry out, effect, pull off

conclusion noun **1** DECISION, conviction, deduction, inference, judgment, opinion, verdict **2** END, bitter end, close, completion, ending, finale, finish, result, termination **3** OUTCOME, consequence, culmination, end result, result, upshot

conclusive adjective DECISIVE, clinching, convincing, definite, final, irrefutable, ultimate, unanswerable

concoct verb MAKE UP, brew, contrive, devise, formulate, hatch, invent, prepare, think up

concoction noun MIXTURE, blend, brew, combination, compound, creation, preparation

concrete adjective **1** SPECIFIC, definite, explicit **2** REAL, actual, factual, material, sensible, substantial, tangible

concur verb AGREE, acquiesce, assent, consent

condemn verb **1** DISAPPROVE, blame, censure, damn, denounce, reproach, reprove, upbraid **2** SENTENCE, convict, damn, doom, pass sentence on

condemnation noun **1** DISAPPROVAL, blame, censure, denunciation, reproach, reproof, stricture **2** SENTENCE, conviction, damnation, doom, judgment

condensation noun **1** DISTILLATION, liquefaction, precipitate, precipitation **2** ABRIDGMENT, contraction, digest, précis, synopsis **3** CONCENTRATION, compression, consolidation, crystallization, curtailment, reduction

condense verb **1** ABRIDGE, abbreviate, compress, concentrate, epitomize, shorten, summarize **2** CONCENTRATE, boil down, reduce, thicken

condensed adjective **1** ABRIDGED, compressed, concentrated, shortened, shrunken, slimmed-down, summarized **2** CONCENTRATED, boiled down, reduced, thickened

condescend verb **1** PATRONIZE, talk down to **2** LOWER ONESELF, bend, deign, humble or demean oneself, see fit, stoop

condescending adjective PATRONIZING, disdainful, lofty, lordly, snobbish, snooty (informal), supercilious, superior

condition noun **1** STATE, circumstances, lie of the land, position, shape, situation, state of affairs **2** REQUIREMENT, limitation, prerequisite, proviso, qualification, restriction, rider, stipulation, terms **3** HEALTH, fettle, fitness, kilter, order, shape, state of health, trim **4** AILMENT, complaint, infirmity, malady, problem, weakness ▶ verb **5** ACCUSTOM, adapt, equip, prepare, ready, tone up, train, work out

conditional adjective DEPENDENT, contingent, limited, provisional, qualified, subject to, with reservations

conditions plural noun CIRCUMSTANCES, environment, milieu, situation, surroundings, way of life

condone verb OVERLOOK, excuse, forgive, let pass, look the other way, make allowance for, pardon, turn a blind eye to

conduct noun **1** BEHAVIOR, attitude, bearing, demeanor, deportment, manners, ways **2** MANAGEMENT, administration, control, direction, guidance, handling, organization, running, supervision ▶ verb **3** CARRY OUT, administer, control, direct, handle, manage, organize, preside over, run, supervise **4** BEHAVE, acquit, act, carry, comport, deport **5** ACCOMPANY, convey, escort, guide, lead, steer, usher

confederacy noun UNION, alliance, coalition, confederation, federation, league

confer verb **1** DISCUSS, consult, converse, deliberate, discourse, talk **2** GRANT, accord, award, bestow, give, hand out, present

conference noun MEETING, colloquium, congress, consultation, convention, discussion, forum, seminar, symposium

confess verb **1** ADMIT, acknowledge, come clean (informal), concede, confide, disclose, divulge, fess up (informal), own up **2** DECLARE, affirm, assert, confirm, profess, reveal

confession noun ADMISSION, acknowledgment, disclosure, exposure, revelation, unbosoming

confidant, confidante noun CLOSE FRIEND, alter ego, bosom friend, crony, familiar, intimate

confide verb **1** TELL, admit, confess, disclose, divulge, impart, reveal, whisper

2 Formal ENTRUST, commend, commit, consign

confidence noun **1** TRUST, belief, credence, dependence, faith, reliance **2** SELF-ASSURANCE, aplomb, assurance, boldness, courage, firmness, nerve, self-possession **3 in confidence** IN SECRECY, between you and me (and the gatepost), confidentially, privately

confident adjective **1** CERTAIN, convinced, counting on, positive, satisfied, secure, sure **2** SELF-ASSURED, assured, bold, dauntless, fearless, self-reliant

confidential adjective SECRET, classified, hush-hush (informal), intimate, off the record, private, privy

confidentially adverb IN SECRET, behind closed doors, between ourselves, in camera, in confidence, personally, privately, sub rosa

confine verb RESTRICT, cage, enclose, hem in, hold back, imprison, incarcerate, intern, keep, limit, shut up

confinement noun IMPRISONMENT, custody, detention, incarceration, internment

confines plural noun LIMITS, boundaries, bounds, circumference, edge, precincts

confirm verb **1** PROVE, authenticate, bear out, corroborate, endorse, ratify, substantiate, validate, verify **2** STRENGTHEN, buttress, establish, fix, fortify, reinforce

confirmation noun PROOF, authentication, corroboration, evidence, substantiation, testimony, validation,

confirmed verification 2 SANCTION, acceptance, agreement, approval, assent, endorsement, ratification

confirmed adjective LONG-ESTABLISHED, chronic, dyed-in-the-wool, habitual, hardened, ingrained, inveterate, seasoned

confiscate verb SEIZE, appropriate, commandeer, impound, sequester, sequestrate

confiscation noun SEIZURE, appropriation, forfeiture, impounding, sequestration, takeover

conflict noun 1 OPPOSITION, antagonism, difference, disagreement, discord, dissension, friction, hostility, strife 2 BATTLE, clash, combat, contest, encounter, fight, strife, war ▶verb 3 BE INCOMPATIBLE, be at variance, clash, collide, differ, disagree, interfere

conflicting adjective INCOMPATIBLE, antagonistic, clashing, contradictory, contrary, discordant, inconsistent, opposing, paradoxical

conform verb 1 COMPLY, adapt, adjust, fall in with, follow, obey, toe the line 2 AGREE, accord, correspond, harmonize, match, suit, tally

conformist noun TRADITIONALIST, stick-in-the-mud (informal), yes man

conformity noun COMPLIANCE, conventionality, observance, orthodoxy, traditionalism

confound verb BEWILDER, astound, baffle, confuse, dumbfound, flummox, mystify, nonplus, perplex

confront verb FACE, accost, challenge, defy, encounter, oppose, stand up to, tackle

confrontation noun CONFLICT, contest, encounter, fight, head-to-head, showdown (informal)

confuse verb 1 MIX UP, disarrange, disorder, jumble, mingle, muddle, ravel 2 BEWILDER, baffle, bemuse, faze, flummox, mystify, nonplus, perplex, puzzle 3 DISCONCERT, discompose, disorient, fluster, rattle (informal), throw off balance, unnerve, upset

confused adjective 1 BEWILDERED, at sea, baffled, disorientated, flummoxed, muddled, nonplussed, perplexed, puzzled, taken aback 2 DISORDERED, chaotic, disorganized, in disarray, jumbled, mixed up, topsy-turvy, untidy

confusing adjective BEWILDERING, baffling, contradictory, disconcerting, misleading, perplexing, puzzling, unclear

confusion noun 1 BEWILDERMENT, disorientation, mystification, perplexity, puzzlement 2 DISORDER, chaos, commotion, jumble, mess, muddle, shambles, turmoil, untidiness, upheaval

congenial adjective 1 PLEASANT, affable, agreeable, companionable, favorable, friendly, genial, kindly 2 COMPATIBLE, kindred, like-minded, sympathetic, well-suited

congenital adjective INBORN,

immanent, inbred, inherent, innate, natural

congested *adjective*
1 OVERCROWDED, crowded, teeming 2 CLOGGED, blocked-up, crammed, jammed, overfilled, overflowing, packed, stuffed

congestion *noun*
1 OVERCROWDING, crowding
2 CLOGGING, bottleneck, jam, surfeit

congratulate *verb* COMPLIMENT, pat on the back, wish joy to

congratulations *plural noun, interjection* GOOD WISHES, best wishes, compliments, felicitations, greetings

congregate *verb* COME TOGETHER, assemble, collect, convene, converge, flock, gather, mass, meet

congregation *noun* ASSEMBLY, brethren, crowd, fellowship, flock, multitude, throng

congress *noun* MEETING, assembly, caucus, conclave, conference, convention, council, legislature, parliament

conjecture *noun* 1 GUESS, hypothesis, shot in the dark, speculation, supposition, surmise, theory ▶ *verb* 2 GUESS, hypothesize, imagine, speculate, suppose, surmise, theorize

conjugal *adjective* MARITAL, bridal, connubial, married, matrimonial, nuptial, wedded

conjure *verb* PERFORM TRICKS, juggle

conjurer, conjuror *noun* MAGICIAN, illusionist, sorcerer, wizard

conjure up *verb* BRING TO MIND,

contrive, create, evoke, produce as if by magic, recall, recollect

connect *verb* LINK, affix, attach, couple, fasten, join, unite

connected *adjective* LINKED, affiliated, akin, allied, associated, combined, coupled, joined, related, united

connection *noun* 1 ASSOCIATION, affinity, bond, liaison, link, relationship, relevance, tie-in
2 LINK, alliance, association, attachment, coupling, fastening, junction, tie, union
3 CONTACT, acquaintance, ally, associate, friend, homeboy (*slang*), homegirl (*slang*), sponsor

connivance *noun* COLLUSION, abetting, complicity, conspiring, tacit consent

connive *verb* 1 CONSPIRE, collude, cook up (*informal*), intrigue, plot, scheme
2 **connive at** TURN A BLIND EYE TO, abet, disregard, let pass, look the other way, overlook, wink at

connoisseur *noun* EXPERT, aficionado, appreciator, authority, buff (*informal*), devotee, judge

conquer *verb* 1 DEFEAT, beat, crush, get the better of, master, overcome, overpower, overthrow, quell, subjugate, vanquish 2 SEIZE, acquire, annex, obtain, occupy, overrun, win

conqueror *noun* WINNER, conquistador, defeater, master, subjugator, vanquisher, victor

conquest *noun* 1 DEFEAT, mastery, overthrow, rout,

triumph, victory **2** TAKEOVER, annexation, coup, invasion, occupation, subjugation

conscience noun PRINCIPLES, moral sense, scruples, sense of right and wrong, still small voice

conscientious adjective THOROUGH, careful, diligent, exact, faithful, meticulous, painstaking, particular, punctilious

conscious adjective **1** AWARE, alert, alive to, awake, responsive, sensible, sentient **2** DELIBERATE, calculated, intentional, knowing, premeditated, self-conscious, studied, willful

consciousness noun AWARENESS, apprehension, knowledge, realization, recognition, sensibility

consecrate verb SANCTIFY, dedicate, devote, hallow, ordain, set apart, venerate

consecutive adjective SUCCESSIVE, in sequence, in turn, running, sequential, succeeding, uninterrupted

consensus noun AGREEMENT, assent, common consent, concord, general agreement, harmony, unanimity, unity

consent noun **1** AGREEMENT, acquiescence, approval, assent, compliance, go-ahead (informal), O.K. or okay (informal), permission, sanction ▶ verb **2** AGREE, acquiesce, allow, approve, assent, concur, permit

consequence noun **1** RESULT, effect, end result, issue, outcome, repercussion, sequel, upshot **2** IMPORTANCE, account,

concern, import, moment, significance, value, weight

consequent adjective FOLLOWING, ensuing, resultant, resulting, subsequent, successive

consequently adverb AS A RESULT, accordingly, ergo, hence, subsequently, therefore, thus

conservation noun PROTECTION, guardianship, husbandry, maintenance, preservation, safeguarding, safekeeping, saving, upkeep

conservative adjective **1** TRADITIONAL, cautious, conventional, die-hard, hidebound, reactionary, sober ▶ noun **2** TRADITIONALIST, reactionary, stick-in-the-mud (informal)

conserve verb PROTECT, hoard, husband, keep, nurse, preserve, save, store up, take care of, use sparingly

consider verb **1** THINK, believe, deem, hold to be, judge, rate, regard as **2** THINK ABOUT, cogitate, contemplate, deliberate, meditate, ponder, reflect, ruminate, turn over in one's mind, weigh **3** BEAR IN MIND, keep in view, make allowance for, reckon with, remember, respect, take into account

considerable adjective LARGE, appreciable, goodly, great, marked, noticeable, plentiful, sizable or sizeable, substantial

considerably adverb GREATLY, appreciably, markedly, noticeably, remarkably, significantly, substantially, very much

considerate *adjective*
THOUGHTFUL, attentive, concerned, kindly, mindful, obliging, patient, tactful, unselfish

consideration *noun* **1** THOUGHT, analysis, deliberation, discussion, examination, reflection, review, scrutiny **2** FACTOR, concern, issue, point **3** THOUGHTFULNESS, concern, considerateness, kindness, respect, tact **4** PAYMENT, fee, recompense, remuneration, reward, tip

considering *preposition* TAKING INTO ACCOUNT, in the light of, in view of

consignment *noun* SHIPMENT, batch, delivery, goods

consist *verb* **1** consist of BE MADE UP OF, amount to, be composed of, comprise, contain, embody, include, incorporate, involve **2** consist in LIE IN, be expressed by, be found or contained in, inhere in, reside in

consistency *noun* **1** TEXTURE, compactness, density, firmness, thickness, viscosity **2** CONSTANCY, evenness, regularity, steadfastness, steadiness, uniformity

consistent *adjective* **1** UNCHANGING, constant, dependable, persistent, regular, steady, true to type, undeviating **2** AGREEING, coherent, compatible, congruous, consonant, harmonious, logical

consolation *noun* COMFORT, cheer, encouragement, help, relief, solace, succor, support

console *verb* COMFORT, calm, cheer, encourage, express sympathy for, soothe

consolidate *verb* **1** STRENGTHEN, fortify, reinforce, secure, stabilize **2** COMBINE, amalgamate, federate, fuse, join, unite

consort *verb* **1** ASSOCIATE, fraternize, go around with, hang about, around or out with, keep company, mix ▶*noun* **2** SPOUSE, companion, husband, partner, wife

conspicuous *adjective* **1** OBVIOUS, blatant, clear, evident, noticeable, patent, salient **2** NOTEWORTHY, illustrious, notable, outstanding, prominent, remarkable, salient, signal, striking

conspiracy *noun* PLOT, collusion, intrigue, machination, scheme, treason

conspirator *noun* PLOTTER, conspirer, intriguer, schemer, traitor

conspire *verb* **1** PLOT, contrive, intrigue, machinate, maneuver, plan, scheme **2** WORK TOGETHER, combine, concur, contribute, cooperate, tend

constant *adjective* **1** CONTINUOUS, ceaseless, incessant, interminable, nonstop, perpetual, sustained, twenty-four-seven (*slang*), unrelenting **2** UNCHANGING, even, fixed, invariable, permanent, stable, steady, uniform, unvarying **3** FAITHFUL, devoted, loyal, stalwart, staunch, true, trustworthy, trusty

constantly *adverb* CONTINUOUSLY,

all the time, always, continually, endlessly, incessantly, interminably, invariably, nonstop, perpetually, twenty-four-seven (*slang*)

consternation *noun* DISMAY, alarm, anxiety, distress, dread, fear, trepidation

constituent *noun* 1 VOTER, elector 2 COMPONENT, element, factor, ingredient, part, unit ▶ *adjective* 3 COMPONENT, basic, elemental, essential, integral

constitute *verb* MAKE UP, compose, comprise, establish, form, found, set up

constitution *noun* 1 HEALTH, build, character, disposition, physique 2 STRUCTURE, composition, form, make-up, nature

constitutional *adjective* 1 STATUTORY, chartered, vested ▶ *noun* 2 WALK, airing, stroll, turn

constrain *verb* 1 FORCE, bind, coerce, compel, impel, necessitate, oblige, pressurize 2 RESTRICT, check, confine, constrict, curb, restrain, straiten

constraint *noun* 1 RESTRICTION, check, curb, deterrent, hindrance, limitation, rein 2 FORCE, coercion, compulsion, necessity, pressure, restraint

construct *verb* BUILD, assemble, compose, create, fashion, form, make, manufacture, put together, shape

construction *noun* 1 BUILDING, composition, creation, edifice 2 INTERPRETATION, explanation, inference, reading, rendering

constructive *adjective* HELPFUL, positive, practical, productive,

useful, valuable

consult *verb* ASK, compare notes, confer, pick (someone's) brains, question, refer to, take counsel, turn to

consultant *noun* SPECIALIST, adviser, authority

consultation *noun* SEMINAR, appointment, conference, council, deliberation, dialogue, discussion, examination, hearing, interview, meeting, session

consume *verb* 1 EAT, chow down (*slang*), devour, eat up, gobble (up), put away, swallow 2 USE UP, absorb, dissipate, exhaust, expend, spend, squander, waste 3 DESTROY, annihilate, demolish, devastate, lay waste, ravage 4 (often *passive*) OBSESS, absorb, dominate, eat up, engross, monopolize, preoccupy

consumer *noun* BUYER, customer, purchaser, shopper, user

consummate *verb* 1 COMPLETE, accomplish, conclude, crown, end, finish, fulfill ▶ *adjective* 2 SKILLED, accomplished, matchless, perfect, polished, practiced, superb, supreme 3 COMPLETE, absolute, conspicuous, extreme, supreme, total, utter

consumption *noun* 1 USING UP, depletion, diminution, dissipation, exhaustion, expenditure, loss, waste 2 *Old-fashioned* TUBERCULOSIS, T.B.

contact *noun* 1 COMMUNICATION, association, connection 2 TOUCH, contiguity 3 ACQUAINTANCE, connection

▶*verb* **4** GET *or* BE IN TOUCH WITH, approach, call, communicate with, reach, speak to, write to

contagious *adjective* INFECTIOUS, catching, communicable, spreading, transmissible

contain *verb* **1** HOLD, accommodate, enclose, have capacity for, incorporate, seat **2** INCLUDE, comprehend, comprise, consist of, embody, embrace, involve **3** RESTRAIN, control, curb, hold back, hold in, keep a tight rein on, repress, stifle

container *noun* HOLDER, receptacle, repository, vessel

contaminate *verb* POLLUTE, adulterate, befoul, corrupt, defile, infect, stain, taint, tarnish

contamination *noun* POLLUTION, contagion, corruption, defilement, impurity, infection, poisoning, taint

contemplate *verb* **1** THINK ABOUT, consider, deliberate, meditate, muse over, ponder, reflect upon, ruminate (upon) **2** CONSIDER, envisage, expect, foresee, intend, plan, think of **3** LOOK AT, examine, eye up, gaze at, inspect, regard, stare at, study, survey, view

contemporary *adjective* **1** COEXISTING, concurrent, contemporaneous **2** MODERN, à la mode, current, newfangled, present, present-day, recent, up-to-date ▶*noun* **3** PEER, fellow

contempt *noun* SCORN, derision, disdain, disregard, disrespect, mockery, neglect, slight

contemptible *adjective* DESPICABLE, detestable, ignominious, lousy (*slang*), measly, paltry, pitiful, scuzzy (*slang*), shameful, worthless

contemptuous *adjective* SCORNFUL, arrogant, condescending, derisive, disdainful, haughty, sneering, supercilious, withering

contend *verb* **1** COMPETE, clash, contest, fight, jostle, strive, struggle, vie **2** ARGUE, affirm, allege, assert, dispute, hold, maintain

content[1] *noun* **1** MEANING, essence, gist, significance, substance **2** AMOUNT, capacity, load, measure, size, volume

content[2] *adjective* **1** SATISFIED, agreeable, at ease, comfortable, contented, fulfilled, willing to accept ▶*verb* **2** SATISFY, appease, humor, indulge, mollify, placate, please ▶*noun* **3** SATISFACTION, comfort, contentment, ease, gratification, peace of mind, pleasure

contented *adjective* SATISFIED, comfortable, content, glad, gratified, happy, pleased, serene, thankful

contentious *adjective* ARGUMENTATIVE, bickering, captious, cavilling, disputatious, quarrelsome, querulous, wrangling

contentment *noun* SATISFACTION, comfort, content, ease, equanimity, fulfillment, happiness, peace, pleasure, serenity

contents *plural noun* CONSTITUENTS, elements, ingredients, load

contest *noun* **1** COMPETITION, game, match, tournament, trial

2 STRUGGLE, battle, combat, conflict, controversy, dispute, fight ▸ *verb* **3** DISPUTE, argue, call in or into question, challenge, debate, doubt, object to, oppose, question **4** COMPETE, contend, fight, strive, vie

contestant *noun* COMPETITOR, candidate, contender, entrant, participant, player

context *noun* **1** CIRCUMSTANCES, ambience, conditions, situation **2** FRAME OF REFERENCE, background, connection, framework, relation

contingency *noun* POSSIBILITY, accident, chance, emergency, event, eventuality, happening, incident

continual *adjective* CONSTANT, frequent, incessant, interminable, recurrent, regular, repeated, twenty-four-seven (*slang*), unremitting

continually *adverb* CONSTANTLY, all the time, always, forever, incessantly, interminably, nonstop, persistently, repeatedly, twenty-four-seven (*slang*)

continuation *noun* **1** CONTINUING, perpetuation, prolongation, resumption **2** ADDITION, extension, furtherance, postscript, sequel, supplement

continue *verb* **1** REMAIN, abide, carry on, endure, last, live on, persist, stay, survive **2** KEEP ON, carry on, go on, maintain, persevere, persist in, stick at, sustain **3** RESUME, carry on, pick up where one left off, proceed,

recommence, return to, take up

continuing *adjective* LASTING, enduring, in progress, ongoing, sustained

continuity *noun* SEQUENCE, cohesion, connection, flow, progression, succession

continuous *adjective* CONSTANT, extended, prolonged, twenty-four-seven (*slang*), unbroken, unceasing, undivided, uninterrupted

contraband *noun* **1** SMUGGLING, black-marketing, bootlegging, trafficking ▸ *adjective* **2** SMUGGLED, banned, bootleg, forbidden, hot (*informal*), illegal, illicit, prohibited, unlawful

contract *noun* **1** AGREEMENT, arrangement, bargain, commitment, covenant, pact, settlement ▸ *verb* **2** AGREE, bargain, come to terms, commit oneself, covenant, negotiate, pledge **3** SHORTEN, abbreviate, curtail, diminish, dwindle, lessen, narrow, reduce, shrink, shrivel **4** CATCH, acquire, be afflicted with, develop, get, go down with, incur

contraction *noun* SHORTENING, abbreviation, compression, narrowing, reduction, shrinkage, shriveling, tightening

contradict *verb* DENY, be at variance with, belie, challenge, controvert, fly in the face of, negate, rebut

contradiction *noun* DENIAL, conflict, contravention, incongruity, inconsistency, negation, opposite

contradictory *adjective*

INCONSISTENT, conflicting, contrary, incompatible, opposed, opposite, paradoxical

contraption noun Informal DEVICE, apparatus, contrivance, gadget, instrument, mechanism

contrary noun **1** OPPOSITE, antithesis, converse, reverse ▶ adjective **2** OPPOSED, adverse, clashing, contradictory, counter, discordant, hostile, inconsistent, opposite, paradoxical **3** PERVERSE, awkward, cantankerous, difficult, disobliging, intractable, obstinate, unaccommodating

contrast noun **1** DIFFERENCE, comparison, disparity, dissimilarity, distinction, divergence, foil, opposition ▶ verb **2** DIFFERENTIATE, compare, differ, distinguish, oppose, set in opposition, set off

contribute verb **1** GIVE, add, bestow, chip in (informal), donate, provide, subscribe, supply **2 contribute to** be PARTLY RESPONSIBLE FOR, be conducive to, be instrumental in, help, lead to, tend to

contribution noun GIFT, addition, donation, grant, input, offering, subscription

contributor noun GIVER, donor, patron, subscriber, supporter

contrite adjective SORRY, chastened, conscience-stricken, humble, penitent, regretful, remorseful, repentant, sorrowful

contrivance noun **1** DEVICE, apparatus, appliance, contraption, gadget, implement, instrument, invention, machine,

mechanism **2** PLAN, intrigue, machination, plot, ruse, scheme, stratagem, trick

contrive verb **1** BRING ABOUT, arrange, effect, manage, maneuver, plan, plot, scheme, succeed **2** DEVISE, concoct, construct, create, design, fabricate, improvise, invent, manufacture

contrived adjective FORCED, artificial, elaborate, labored, overdone, planned, strained, unnatural

control noun **1** POWER, authority, charge, command, guidance, management, oversight, supervision, supremacy **2** RESTRAINT, brake, check, curb, limitation, regulation ▶ verb **3** HAVE POWER OVER, administer, command, direct, govern, handle, have charge of, manage, manipulate, supervise **4** RESTRAIN, check, constrain, contain, curb, hold back, limit, repress, subdue

controls plural noun INSTRUMENTS, console, control panel, dash, dashboard, dials

controversial adjective DISPUTED, at issue, contentious, debatable, disputable, open to question, under discussion

controversy noun ARGUMENT, altercation, debate, dispute, quarrel, row, squabble, wrangling

convalescence noun RECOVERY, improvement, recuperation, rehabilitation, return to health

convalescent adjective RECOVERING, getting better, improving, mending, on the mend, recuperating

convene verb GATHER, assemble, bring together, call, come together, congregate, convoke, meet, summon

convenience noun 1 AVAILABILITY, accessibility, advantage, appropriateness, benefit, fitness, suitability, usefulness, utility 2 APPLIANCE, amenity, comfort, facility, help, labor-saving device

convenient adjective 1 USEFUL, appropriate, fit, handy, helpful, labor-saving, serviceable, suitable, timely 2 NEARBY, accessible, at hand, available, close at hand, handy, just round the corner, within reach

convention noun 1 CUSTOM, code, etiquette, practice, propriety, protocol, tradition, usage 2 AGREEMENT, bargain, contract, pact, protocol, treaty 3 ASSEMBLY, conference, congress, convocation, council, meeting

conventional adjective 1 ORDINARY, accepted, customary, normal, orthodox, regular, standard, traditional, usual 2 UNORIGINAL, banal, hackneyed, prosaic, routine, stereotyped

converge verb COME TOGETHER, coincide, combine, gather, join, meet, merge

conversation noun TALK, chat, conference, dialogue, discourse, discussion, gossip, tête-à-tête

converse[1] verb TALK, chat, chew the fat (slang), commune, confer, discourse, exchange views

converse[2] noun 1 OPPOSITE, antithesis, contrary, obverse, other side of the coin, reverse ▶adjective 2 OPPOSITE, contrary, counter, reverse, reversed, transposed

conversion noun 1 CHANGE, metamorphosis, transformation 2 ADAPTATION, alteration, modification, reconstruction, remodeling, reorganization

convert verb 1 CHANGE, alter, transform, transpose, turn 2 ADAPT, apply, customize, modify, remodel, reorganize, restyle, revise 3 REFORM, convince, proselytize ▶noun 4 NEOPHYTE, disciple, proselyte

convex adjective ROUNDED, bulging, gibbous, protuberant

convey verb 1 COMMUNICATE, disclose, impart, make known, relate, reveal, tell 2 CARRY, bear, bring, conduct, fetch, guide, move, send, transport

convict verb 1 FIND GUILTY, condemn, imprison, pronounce guilty, sentence ▶noun 2 PRISONER, criminal, culprit, felon, jailbird, lag (slang)

conviction noun 1 BELIEF, creed, faith, opinion, persuasion, principle, tenet, view 2 CONFIDENCE, assurance, certainty, certitude, firmness, reliance

convince verb PERSUADE, assure, bring round, prevail upon, satisfy, sway, win over

convincing adjective PERSUASIVE, cogent, conclusive, credible, impressive, plausible, powerful, telling

convulse verb SHAKE, agitate, churn up, derange, disorder, disturb, twist, work

convulsion noun SPASM, contraction, cramp, fit, paroxysm, seizure

cool adjective 1 COLD, chilled, chilly, nippy, refreshing 2 CALM, collected, composed, relaxed, sedate, self-controlled, self-possessed, unemotional, unruffled 3 UNFRIENDLY, aloof, distant, indifferent, lukewarm, offhand, standoffish, unenthusiastic, unwelcoming 4 Informal FASHIONABLE, hip, phat (slang), trendy (informal) 5 CHILL, cool off, freeze, lose heat, refrigerate ▶noun 6 Slang CALMNESS, composure, control, poise, self-control, self-discipline, self-possession, temper

cooperate verb WORK TOGETHER, collaborate, combine, conspire, coordinate, join forces, pool resources, pull together

cooperation noun TEAMWORK, collaboration, combined effort, esprit de corps, give-and-take, unity

cooperative adjective 1 HELPFUL, accommodating, obliging, onside (informal), responsive, supportive 2 SHARED, collective, combined, joint

coordinate verb BRING TOGETHER, harmonize, integrate, match, organize, synchronize, systematize

cope verb 1 MANAGE, carry on, get by (informal), hold one's own, make the grade, struggle through, survive 2 cope with DEAL WITH, contend with, grapple with, handle, struggle with, weather, wrestle with

copious adjective ABUNDANT, ample, bountiful, extensive, full, lavish, plentiful, profuse

copy noun 1 REPRODUCTION, counterfeit, duplicate, facsimile, forgery, imitation, likeness, model, replica ▶verb 2 REPRODUCE, counterfeit, duplicate, replicate, transcribe 3 IMITATE, ape, emulate, follow, mimic, mirror, repeat

cord noun ROPE, line, string, twine

cordial adjective WARM, affable, agreeable, cheerful, congenial, friendly, genial, hearty, sociable

cordon noun 1 CHAIN, barrier, line, ring ▶verb 2 cordon off SURROUND, close off, encircle, enclose, fence off, isolate, picket, separate

core noun CENTER, crux, essence, gist, heart, kernel, nub, nucleus, pith

corner noun 1 ANGLE, bend, crook, joint 2 SPACE, hideaway, hideout, nook, retreat ▶verb 3 TRAP, run to earth 4 As in **corner the market** MONOPOLIZE, dominate, engross, hog (slang)

corny adjective Slang UNORIGINAL, banal, dull, hackneyed, old-fashioned, old hat, stale, stereotyped, trite

corporation noun 1 BUSINESS, association, corporate body, society 2 TOWN COUNCIL, civic authorities, council, municipal authorities

corps noun TEAM, band, company, detachment, division, regiment, squadron, troop, unit

corpse noun BODY, cadaver, carcass, remains, stiff (slang)

correct adjective 1 TRUE,

accurate, exact, faultless, flawless, O.K. *or* okay (*informal*), precise, right **2** PROPER, acceptable, appropriate, fitting, kosher (*informal*), O.K. *or* okay (*informal*), seemly, standard ▸ *verb* **3** RECTIFY, adjust, amend, cure, emend, redress, reform, remedy, right **4** PUNISH, admonish, chasten, chastise, chide, discipline, rebuke, reprimand, reprove

correction *noun* **1** RECTIFICATION, adjustment, alteration, amendment, emendation, improvement, modification **2** PUNISHMENT, admonition, castigation, chastisement, discipline, reformation, reproof

correctly *adverb* RIGHTLY, accurately, perfectly, precisely, properly, right

correctness *noun* **1** TRUTH, accuracy, exactitude, exactness, faultlessness, fidelity, preciseness, precision, regularity **2** DECORUM, civility, good breeding, propriety, seemliness

correspond *verb* **1** BE CONSISTENT, accord, agree, conform, fit, harmonize, match, square, tally **2** COMMUNICATE, exchange letters, keep in touch, write

correspondence *noun* **1** LETTERS, communication, mail, post, writing **2** RELATION, agreement, coincidence, comparison, conformity, correlation, harmony, match, similarity

correspondent *noun* **1** LETTER WRITER, pen friend *or* pal **2** REPORTER, contributor,

journalist

corresponding *adjective* RELATED, analogous, answering, complementary, equivalent, matching, reciprocal, similar

corridor *noun* PASSAGE, aisle, alley, hallway, passageway

corroborate *verb* SUPPORT, authenticate, back up, bear out, confirm, endorse, ratify, substantiate, validate

corrode *verb* EAT AWAY, consume, corrupt, erode, gnaw, oxidize, rust, wear away

corrosive *adjective* CORRODING, caustic, consuming, erosive, virulent, vitriolic, wasting, wearing

corrupt *adjective* **1** DISHONEST, bent (*slang*), bribable, crooked (*informal*), fraudulent, unprincipled, unscrupulous, venal **2** DEPRAVED, debased, degenerate, dissolute, profligate, vicious **3** DISTORTED, altered, doctored, falsified ▸ *verb* **4** BRIBE, buy off, entice, fix (*informal*), grease (someone's) palm (*slang*), lure, suborn **5** DEPRAVE, debauch, pervert, subvert **6** DISTORT, doctor, tamper with

corruption *noun* **1** DISHONESTY, bribery, extortion, fraud, shady dealings (*informal*), unscrupulousness, venality **2** DEPRAVITY, decadence, evil, immorality, perversion, vice, wickedness **3** DISTORTION, doctoring, falsification

corset *noun* GIRDLE, belt, bodice

cosmetic *adjective* BEAUTIFYING, nonessential, superficial, surface

cosmic *adjective* UNIVERSAL, stellar

cosmopolitan *adjective*

1 SOPHISTICATED, broad-minded, catholic, open-minded, universal, urbane, well-traveled, worldly-wise ▶ noun **2** MAN or WOMAN OF THE WORLD, jet-setter, sophisticate

cost noun **1** PRICE, amount, charge, damage (informal), expense, outlay, payment, worth **2** LOSS, damage, detriment, expense, harm, hurt, injury, penalty, sacrifice, suffering ▶ verb **3** SELL AT, come to, command a price of, set (someone) back (informal) **4** LOSE, do disservice to, harm, hurt, injure

costly adjective **1** EXPENSIVE, dear, exorbitant, extortionate, highly-priced, steep (informal), stiff **2** DAMAGING, catastrophic, deleterious, disastrous, harmful, loss-making, ruinous

costs plural noun EXPENSES, budget, outgoings, overheads

costume noun OUTFIT, apparel, attire, clothing, dress, ensemble, garb, livery, uniform

cottage noun CABIN, chalet, hut, lodge, shack

cough noun **1** FROG or TICKLE IN ONE'S THROAT, bark, hack ▶ verb **2** CLEAR ONE'S THROAT, bark, hack

council noun GOVERNING BODY, assembly, board, cabinet, committee, conference, congress, convention, panel, parliament

counsel noun **1** ADVICE, direction, guidance, information, recommendation, suggestion, warning **2** LEGAL ADVISER, advocate, attorney, barrister, lawyer ▶ verb **3** ADVISE, advocate, exhort, instruct,

recommend, urge, warn

count verb **1** ADD (UP), calculate, compute, enumerate, number, reckon, tally, tot up **2** MATTER, be important, carry weight, rate, signify, tell, weigh **3** CONSIDER, deem, judge, look upon, rate, regard, think **4** TAKE INTO ACCOUNT or CONSIDERATION, include, number among ▶ noun **5** CALCULATION, computation, enumeration, numbering, poll, reckoning, sum, tally

counter verb **1** RETALIATE, answer, hit back, meet, oppose, parry, resist, respond, ward off ▶ adverb **2** OPPOSITE TO, against, at variance with, contrariwise, conversely, in defiance of, versus

counteract verb ACT AGAINST, foil, frustrate, negate, neutralize, offset, resist, thwart

counterbalance verb OFFSET, balance, compensate, make up for, set off

counterfeit adjective **1** FAKE, bogus, false, forged, imitation, phoney or phony (informal), sham, simulated ▶ noun **2** FAKE, copy, forgery, fraud, imitation, phoney or phony (informal), reproduction, sham ▶ verb **3** FAKE, copy, fabricate, feign, forge, imitate, impersonate, pretend, sham, simulate

countermand verb CANCEL, annul, override, repeal, rescind, retract, reverse, revoke

counterpart noun OPPOSITE NUMBER, complement, equal, fellow, match, mate, supplement, tally, twin

countless adjective INNUMERABLE, endless, immeasurable,

incalculable, infinite, legion, limitless, myriad, numberless, uncountable, untold

count on or **upon** verb DEPEND ON, bank on, believe (in), lean on, pin one's faith on, reckon on, rely on, take for granted, take on trust, trust

country noun 1 NATION, commonwealth, kingdom, people, realm, state 2 TERRITORY, land, region, terrain 3 PEOPLE, citizens, community, inhabitants, nation, populace, public, society 4 COUNTRYSIDE, backwoods, farmland, green belt, outback (Austral. & N.Z.), provinces, sticks (informal)

countryside noun COUNTRY, farmland, green belt, outback (Austral. & N.Z.), outdoors, sticks (informal)

count up verb ADD, reckon up, sum, tally, total

county noun PROVINCE, shire

coup noun MASTERSTROKE, accomplishment, action, deed, exploit, feat, maneuver, stunt

couple noun 1 PAIR, brace, duo, two, twosome ▶ verb 2 LINK, connect, hitch, join, marry, pair, unite, wed, yoke

coupon noun SLIP, card, certificate, ticket, token, voucher

courage noun BRAVERY, daring, fearlessness, gallantry, heroism, mettle, nerve, pluck, resolution, valor

courageous adjective BRAVE, bold, daring, fearless, gallant, gritty, intrepid, lion-hearted, stouthearted, valiant

courier noun 1 GUIDE, representative 2 MESSENGER, bearer, carrier, envoy, runner

course noun 1 CLASSES, curriculum, lectures, program, schedule 2 PROGRESSION, development, flow, movement, order, progress, sequence, unfolding 3 ROUTE, direction, line, passage, path, road, track, trajectory, way 4 RACECOURSE, cinder track, circuit 5 PROCEDURE, behavior, conduct, manner, method, mode, plan, policy, program 6 PERIOD, duration, lapse, passage, passing, sweep, term, time 7 of course NATURALLY, certainly, definitely, indubitably, needless to say, obviously, undoubtedly, without a doubt ▶ verb 8 RUN, flow, gush, race, speed, stream, surge 9 HUNT, chase, follow, pursue, stalk

court noun 1 LAW COURT, bar, bench, tribunal 2 COURTYARD, cloister, piazza, plaza, quad (informal), quadrangle, square, yard 3 PALACE, hall, manor 4 ROYAL HOUSEHOLD, attendants, cortege, entourage, retinue, suite, train ▶ verb 5 WOO, date, go (out) with, run after, serenade, set one's cap at, take out, walk out with 6 CULTIVATE, brown-nose (slang), curry favor with, fawn upon, flatter, pander to, seek, solicit 7 INVITE, attract, bring about, incite, prompt, provoke, seek

courteous adjective POLITE, affable, attentive, civil, gallant, gracious, refined, respectful, urbane, well-mannered

courtesy noun 1 POLITENESS, affability, civility, courteousness, gallantry, good

manners, graciousness,
urbanity **2** FAVOR, benevolence,
indulgence, kindness

courtier noun ATTENDANT,
follower, squire

courtly adjective CEREMONIOUS,
chivalrous, dignified, elegant,
formal, gallant, polished,
refined, stately, urbane

courtyard noun YARD, enclosure,
quad, quadrangle

cove noun BAY, anchorage, inlet,
sound

covenant noun **1** PROMISE,
agreement, arrangement,
commitment, contract, pact,
pledge ▶ verb **2** PROMISE, agree,
contract, pledge, stipulate,
undertake

cover verb **1** CLOTHE, dress,
envelop, put on, wrap
2 OVERLAY, coat, daub, encase,
envelop **3** SUBMERGE, engulf,
flood, overrun, wash over
4 CONCEAL, cloak, disguise,
enshroud, hide, mask, obscure,
shroud, veil **5** TRAVEL OVER, cross,
pass through or over, traverse
6 PROTECT, defend, guard,
shield **7** REPORT, describe,
investigate, narrate, relate, tell
of, write up ▶ noun **8** COVERING,
canopy, case, coating,
envelope, jacket, lid, top,
wrapper **9** DISGUISE, façade,
front, mask, pretext, screen,
smoke screen, veil
10 PROTECTION, camouflage,
concealment, defense, guard,
shelter, shield **11** INSURANCE,
compensation, indemnity,
protection, reimbursement

covering adjective
1 EXPLANATORY, accompanying,
descriptive, introductory ▶ noun

2 COVER, blanket, casing,
coating, layer, wrapping

cover-up noun CONCEALMENT,
complicity, conspiracy, front,
smoke screen, whitewash
(informal)

cover up verb CONCEAL, draw a
veil over, hide, hush up,
suppress, sweep under the
carpet, whitewash (informal)

covet verb LONG FOR, aspire to,
crave, desire, envy, lust after,
set one's heart on, yearn for

covetous adjective ENVIOUS,
acquisitive, avaricious,
close-fisted, grasping, greedy,
jealous, rapacious, yearning

coward noun WIMP (informal),
chicken (slang), scaredy-cat
(informal), yellow-belly (slang)

cowardice noun
FAINT-HEARTEDNESS, fearfulness,
spinelessness, weakness

cowardly adjective FAINT-HEARTED,
chicken (slang), craven, fearful,
scared, soft, spineless,
timorous, weak, yellow
(informal)

cowboy noun COWHAND,
cattleman, drover, gaucho (S.
American), herdsman, rancher,
stockman

cower verb CRINGE, draw back,
flinch, grovel, quail, shrink,
tremble

coy adjective SHY, bashful,
demure, modest, reserved,
retiring, shrinking, timid

cozy adjective SNUG,
comfortable, comfy (informal),
homely, homey, intimate,
sheltered, tucked up, warm

crack verb **1** BREAK, burst, cleave,
fracture, snap, splinter, split
2 SNAP, burst, crash, detonate,

explode, pop, ring **3** GIVE IN, break down, collapse, give way, go to pieces, lose control, succumb, yield **4** Informal HIT, clip (informal), clout (informal), cuff, slap, smack, whack **5** SOLVE, decipher, fathom, get the answer to, work out ▸ noun **6** SNAP, burst, clap, crash, explosion, pop, report **7** BREAK, chink, cleft, cranny, crevice, fissure, fracture, gap, rift **8** Informal BLOW, clip (informal), clout (informal), cuff, slap, smack, whack **9** Informal JOKE, dig, funny remark, gag (informal), jibe, quip, wisecrack (informal), witticism

crackdown noun SUPPRESSION, clampdown, crushing, repression

cracked adjective BROKEN, chipped, damaged, defective, faulty, flawed, imperfect, split

cradle noun **1** CRIB, bassinet, cot **2** BIRTHPLACE, beginning, fount, fountainhead, origin, source, spring, wellspring ▸ verb **3** HOLD, lull, nestle, nurse, rock, support

craft noun **1** OCCUPATION, business, employment, handicraft, pursuit, trade, vocation, work **2** SKILL, ability, aptitude, art, artistry, expertise, ingenuity, know-how (informal), technique, workmanship **3** VESSEL, aircraft, boat, plane, ship, spacecraft

craftsman noun SKILLED WORKER, artisan, maker, master, smith, technician, wright

craftsmanship noun WORKMANSHIP, artistry, expertise, mastery, technique

crafty adjective CUNNING, artful, calculating, devious, sharp, shrewd, sly, subtle, wily

crag noun ROCK, bluff, peak, pinnacle, tor

cram verb **1** STUFF, compress, force, jam, pack in, press, shove, squeeze **2** OVEREAT, glut, gorge, satiate, stuff **3** STUDY, bone up (informal), review

cramp[1] noun SPASM, ache, contraction, convulsion, pain, pang, stitch, twinge

cramp[2] verb RESTRICT, constrain, hamper, handicap, hinder, impede, inhibit, obstruct

cramped adjective CLOSED IN, confined, congested, crowded, hemmed in, overcrowded, packed, uncomfortable

cranny noun CREVICE, chink, cleft, crack, fissure, gap, hole, opening

crash noun **1** COLLISION, accident, bump, pile-up (informal), smash, wreck **2** SMASH, bang, boom, clang, clash, clatter, din, racket, thunder **3** COLLAPSE, debacle, depression, downfall, failure, ruin ▸ verb **4** COLLIDE, bump (into), crash-land (an aircraft), drive into, have an accident, hit, plow into, wreck **5** COLLAPSE, be ruined, fail, fold, fold up, go belly up (informal), go bust (informal), go to the wall, go under **6** HURTLE, fall headlong, give way, lurch, overbalance, plunge, topple

crass adjective INSENSITIVE, boorish, gross, indelicate, oafish, stupid, unrefined, witless

crate noun CONTAINER, box, case, packing case, tea chest

crater noun HOLLOW, depression, dip

crave verb 1 LONG FOR, desire, hanker after, hope for, lust after, want, yearn for 2 BEG, ask, beseech, entreat, implore, petition, plead for, pray for, seek, solicit, supplicate

craving noun LONGING, appetite, desire, hankering, hope, hunger, thirst, yearning, yen (*informal*)

crawl verb 1 CREEP, advance slowly, inch, slither, worm one's way, wriggle, writhe 2 GROVEL, brown-nose (*slang*), creep, fawn, humble oneself, kiss ass (*slang*), toady 3 BE FULL OF, be alive, be overrun (*slang*), swarm, teem

craze noun FAD, enthusiasm, fashion, infatuation, mania, rage, trend, vogue

crazy adjective 1 RIDICULOUS, absurd, foolish, idiotic, ill-conceived, ludicrous, nonsensical, preposterous, senseless 2 FANATICAL, devoted, enthusiastic, infatuated, mad, passionate, wild (*informal*) 3 INSANE, crazed, demented, deranged, mad, nuts (*slang*), out of one's mind, unbalanced

creak verb SQUEAK, grate, grind, groan, scrape, scratch, screech

cream noun 1 LOTION, cosmetic, emulsion, essence, liniment, oil, ointment, paste, salve, unguent 2 BEST, crème de la crème, elite, flower, pick, prime
▶ adjective OFF-WHITE, yellowish-white

creamy adjective SMOOTH, buttery, milky, rich, soft, velvety

crease noun 1 LINE, corrugation,

fold, groove, ridge, wrinkle
▶ verb 2 WRINKLE, corrugate, crumple, double up, fold, rumple, screw up

create verb 1 MAKE, compose, devise, formulate, invent, originate, produce, spawn 2 CAUSE, bring about, lead to, occasion 3 APPOINT, constitute, establish, install, invest, make, set up

creation noun 1 MAKING, conception, formation, generation, genesis, procreation 2 SETTING UP, development, establishment, formation, foundation, inception, institution, production 3 INVENTION, achievement, brainchild (*informal*), concoction, handiwork, magnum opus, pièce de résistance, production 4 UNIVERSE, cosmos, nature, world

creative adjective IMAGINATIVE, artistic, clever, gifted, ingenious, inspired, inventive, original, visionary

creativity noun IMAGINATION, cleverness, ingenuity, inspiration, inventiveness, originality

creator noun MAKER, architect, author, designer, father, inventor, originator, prime mover

creature noun 1 LIVING THING, animal, beast, being, brute 2 PERSON, human being, individual, man, mortal, soul, woman

credentials plural noun CERTIFICATION, authorization, document, license, papers, passport, reference(s), testimonial

credibility noun BELIEVABILITY, integrity, plausibility, reliability, trustworthiness

credible adjective **1** BELIEVABLE, conceivable, imaginable, likely, plausible, possible, probable, reasonable, thinkable **2** RELIABLE, dependable, honest, sincere, trustworthy, trusty

credit noun **1** PRAISE, acclaim, acknowledgment, approval, commendation, honor, kudos, recognition, tribute **2** As in be a credit to SOURCE OF SATISFACTION or PRIDE, feather in one's cap, honor **3** PRESTIGE, esteem, good name, influence, position, regard, reputation, repute, standing, status **4** BELIEF, confidence, credence, faith, reliance, trust **5** on credit ON ACCOUNT, by deferred payment, by installments, on the card ▶verb **6** BELIEVE, accept, have faith in, rely on, trust **7** credit with ATTRIBUTE TO, ascribe to, assign to, impute to

creditable adjective PRAISEWORTHY, admirable, commendable, honorable, laudable, reputable, respectable, worthy

credulity noun GULLIBILITY, blind faith, credulousness, naivety

creed noun BELIEF, articles of faith, catechism, credo, doctrine, dogma, principles

creek noun STREAM, bayou, brook, rivulet, runnel, tributary, watercourse

creep verb **1** SNEAK, approach unnoticed, skulk, slink, steal, tiptoe **2** CRAWL, glide, slither,

squirm, wriggle, writhe ▶noun **3** Slang BROWN-NOSER (slang), crawler (slang), scuzzbucket (slang), sneak, sycophant, toady **4** Slang JERK, loser, lowlife, pervert, scumbag (slang), scuzzbucket (slang)

creeper noun CLIMBING PLANT, rambler, runner, trailing plant, vine

creeps plural noun **give one the creeps** Informal DISGUST, frighten, make one's hair stand on end, make one squirm, repel, repulse, scare

creepy adjective Informal DISTURBING, eerie, frightening, hair-raising, macabre, menacing, scary (informal), sinister

crescent noun MENISCUS, new moon, sickle

crest noun **1** TOP, apex, crown, highest point, peak, pinnacle, ridge, summit **2** TUFT, comb, crown, mane, plume **3** EMBLEM, badge, bearings, device, insignia, symbol

crestfallen adjective DISAPPOINTED, dejected, depressed, despondent, discouraged, disheartened, downcast, downhearted

crevice noun GAP, chink, cleft, crack, cranny, fissure, hole, opening, slit

crew noun **1** (SHIP'S) COMPANY, hands, (ship's) complement **2** TEAM, corps, gang, posse, squad **3** Informal CROWD, band, bunch (informal), gang, horde, mob, pack, set

crib noun **1** CRADLE, bassinet, bed, cot **2** MANGER, rack, stall ▶verb **3** Informal COPY, cheat, pirate, plagiarize, purloin, steal

crime noun **1** OFFENSE, felony, misdeed, misdemeanor, transgression, trespass, unlawful act, violation **2** LAWBREAKING, corruption, illegality, misconduct, vice, wrongdoing

criminal noun **1** LAWBREAKER, convict, crook (informal), culprit, felon, offender, sinner, villain ▶ adjective **2** UNLAWFUL, corrupt, crooked (informal), illegal, illicit, immoral, lawless, wicked, wrong **3** DISGRACEFUL, deplorable, foolish, preposterous, ridiculous, scandalous, senseless

cringe verb SHRINK, cower, draw back, flinch, recoil, shy, wince

cripple verb **1** DISABLE, hamstring, incapacitate, lame, maim, paralyze, weaken **2** DAMAGE, destroy, impair, put out of action, put paid to, ruin, spoil

crippled adjective DISABLED, challenged, handicapped, incapacitated, laid up (informal), lame, paralyzed

crisis noun **1** CRITICAL POINT, climax, crunch (informal), crux, culmination, height, moment of truth, turning point **2** EMERGENCY, deep water, dire straits, meltdown (informal), panic stations (informal), plight, predicament, trouble

crisp adjective **1** CRUNCHY, brittle, crispy, crumbly, firm, fresh **2** CLEAN, neat, smart, spruce, tidy, trim, well-groomed, well-pressed **3** BRACING, brisk, fresh, invigorating, refreshing

criterion noun STANDARD, bench

mark, gauge, measure, principle, rule, test, touchstone, yardstick

critic noun **1** JUDGE, analyst, authority, commentator, connoisseur, expert, pundit, reviewer **2** FAULT-FINDER, attacker, detractor, knocker (informal)

critical adjective **1** CRUCIAL, all-important, decisive, pivotal, precarious, pressing, serious, urgent, vital **2** DISPARAGING, captious, censorious, derogatory, disapproving, fault-finding, nagging, nit-picking (informal), scathing **3** ANALYTICAL, discerning, discriminating, fastidious, judicious, penetrating, perceptive

criticism noun **1** FAULT-FINDING, bad press, censure, character assassination, disapproval, disparagement, flak (informal), stick (slang) **2** ANALYSIS, appraisal, appreciation, assessment, comment, commentary, critique, evaluation, judgment

criticize verb FIND FAULT WITH, carp, censure, condemn, disapprove of, disparage, knock (informal), put down

croak verb SQUAWK, caw, grunt, utter or speak huskily, wheeze

crook noun CRIMINAL, cheat, racketeer, robber, rogue, shark, swindler, thief, villain

crooked adjective **1** BENT, curved, deformed, distorted, hooked, irregular, misshapen, out of shape, twisted, warped, zigzag **2** AT AN ANGLE, askew, awry, lopsided, off-center, slanting, squint, uneven

3 DISHONEST, bent (*slang*), corrupt, criminal, fraudulent, illegal, shady (*informal*), underhand, unlawful

croon verb SING, hum, purr, warble

crop noun **1** PRODUCE, fruits, gathering, harvest, reaping, vintage, yield ▶verb **2** CUT, clip, lop, pare, prune, shear, snip, trim **3** GRAZE, browse, nibble

crop up verb HAPPEN, appear, arise, emerge, occur, spring up, turn up

cross verb **1** GO ACROSS, bridge, cut across, extend over, move across, pass over, span, traverse **2** INTERSECT, crisscross, intertwine **3** OPPOSE, block, impede, interfere, obstruct, resist **4** INTERBREED, blend, crossbreed, cross-fertilize, cross-pollinate, hybridize, intercross, mix, mongrelize ▶noun **5** CRUCIFIX, rood **6** CROSSROADS, crossing, intersection, junction **7** MIXTURE, amalgam, blend, combination **8** TROUBLE, affliction, burden, grief, load, misfortune, trial, tribulation, woe, worry ▶adjective **9** ANGRY, annoyed, grumpy, ill-tempered, in a bad mood, irascible, put out, short **10** TRANSVERSE, crosswise, diagonal, intersecting, oblique

cross-examine verb QUESTION, grill (*informal*), interrogate, pump, quiz

cross out or **off** verb STRIKE OFF or OUT, blue-pencil, cancel, delete, eliminate, score off or out

crouch verb BEND DOWN, bow, duck, hunch, kneel, squat, stoop

crow verb GLOAT, blow one's own trumpet, boast, brag, exult, strut, swagger, triumph

crowd noun **1** MULTITUDE, army, horde, host, mass, mob, pack, swarm, throng **2** GROUP, bunch (*informal*), circle, clique, lot, set **3** AUDIENCE, attendance, gate, house, spectators ▶verb **4** FLOCK, congregate, gather, mass, stream, surge, swarm, throng **5** SQUEEZE, bundle, congest, cram, pack, pile

crowded adjective PACKED, busy, congested, cramped, full, jam-packed, swarming, teeming

crown noun **1** CORONET, circlet, diadem, tiara **2** LAUREL WREATH, garland, honor, laurels, prize, trophy, wreath **3** HIGH POINT, apex, crest, pinnacle, summit, tip, top ▶verb **4** HONOR, adorn, dignify, festoon **5** CAP, be the climax or culmination of, complete, finish, perfect, put the finishing touch to, round off, top **6** Slang STRIKE, belt (*informal*), box, hit over the head, punch

Crown noun **1** MONARCHY, royalty, sovereignty **2** MONARCH, emperor or empress, king or queen, ruler, sovereign

crucial adjective **1** VITAL, essential, high-priority, important, momentous, pressing, urgent **2** CRITICAL, central, decisive, pivotal

crucify verb EXECUTE, persecute, torment, torture

crude adjective **1** PRIMITIVE, clumsy, makeshift, rough, rough-and-ready, rudimentary, unpolished **2** VULGAR, coarse, dirty, gross, indecent, obscene, off-color, scuzzy (*slang*), smutty, tasteless, uncouth **3** UNREFINED, natural, raw, unprocessed

crudely *adverb* VULGARLY, bluntly, coarsely, impolitely, roughly, rudely, tastelessly

crudity *noun* **1** ROUGHNESS, clumsiness, crudeness **2** VULGARITY, coarseness, impropriety, indecency, indelicacy, obscenity, smuttiness

cruel *adjective* **1** BRUTAL, barbarous, callous, hard-hearted, heartless, inhuman, malevolent, sadistic, spiteful, unkind, vicious **2** MERCILESS, pitiless, ruthless, unrelenting

cruelly *adverb* **1** BRUTALLY, barbarously, callously, heartlessly, in cold blood, mercilessly, pitilessly, sadistically, spitefully **2** BITTERLY, deeply, fearfully, grievously, monstrously, severely

cruelty *noun* BRUTALITY, barbarity, callousness, depravity, fiendishness, inhumanity, mercilessness, ruthlessness, spitefulness

cruise *noun* **1** SAIL, boat trip, sea trip, voyage ▶ *verb* **2** SAIL, coast, voyage **3** TRAVEL ALONG, coast, drift, keep a steady pace

crumb *noun* BIT, fragment, grain, morsel, scrap, shred, soupçon

crumble *verb* **1** DISINTEGRATE, collapse, decay, degenerate, deteriorate, fall apart, go to pieces, go to rack and ruin, tumble down **2** CRUSH, fragment, granulate, grind,

pound, powder, pulverize

crummy *adjective Informal* **1** DESPICABLE, contemptible, lousy (*slang*), mean, scuzzy (*slang*) **2** INFERIOR, deficient, inadequate, lousy (*slang*), of poor quality, poor, substandard **3** UNWELL, below par, off color, under the weather (*informal*)

crumple *verb* **1** CRUSH, crease, rumple, screw up, scrumple, wrinkle **2** COLLAPSE, break down, cave in, fall, give way, go to pieces

crunch *verb* **1** CHOMP, champ, chew noisily, grind, munch ▶ *noun* **2** *Informal* CRITICAL POINT, crisis, crux, emergency, moment of truth, test

crusade *noun* CAMPAIGN, cause, drive, movement, push

crush *verb* **1** SQUASH, break, compress, press, pulverize, squeeze **2** OVERCOME, conquer, overpower, overwhelm, put down, quell, stamp out, subdue **3** HUMILIATE, abash, mortify, put down (*slang*), quash, shame ▶ *noun* **4** CROWD, huddle, jam

crust *noun* LAYER, coating, covering, shell, skin, surface

crusty *adjective* **1** CRISPY, hard **2** IRRITABLE, cantankerous, cross, gruff, prickly, short-tempered, testy

cry *verb* **1** WEEP, blubber, shed tears, snivel, sob **2** SHOUT, bawl, bellow, call out, exclaim, howl, roar, scream, shriek, yell ▶ *noun* **3** WEEPING, blubbering, snivelling, sob, sobbing, weep **4** SHOUT, bellow, call, exclamation, howl, roar,

scream, screech, shriek, yell
5 APPEAL, plea

cub noun YOUNG, offspring,
whelp

cuckoo adjective Slang INSANE,
bonkers (informal), crazy, daft
(informal), foolish, idiotic, nuts
(slang), out of one's mind,
stupid

cuddle verb HUG, bill and coo,
cosset, embrace, fondle, pet,
snuggle

cudgel noun CLUB, baton,
bludgeon, stick, truncheon

cue noun SIGNAL, catchword,
hint, key, prompting,
reminder, sign, suggestion

cul-de-sac noun DEAD END, blind
alley

culminate verb END UP, climax,
close, come to a climax, come
to a head, conclude, finish,
wind up

culmination noun CLIMAX, acme,
conclusion, consummation,
finale, peak, pinnacle, zenith

culpable adjective BLAMEWORTHY,
at fault, found wanting, guilty,
in the wrong, to blame, wrong

culprit noun OFFENDER, criminal,
evildoer, felon, guilty party,
miscreant, transgressor,
wrongdoer

cult noun **1** SECT, clique, faction,
religion, school **2** DEVOTION,
idolization, worship

cultivate verb **1** FARM, plant,
plow, tend, till, work **2** DEVELOP,
foster, improve, promote,
refine **3** COURT, dance
attendance upon, run after,
seek out

cultivation noun **1** FARMING,
gardening, husbandry,
planting, plowing, tillage

2 DEVELOPMENT, encouragement,
fostering, furtherance, nurture,
patronage, promotion, support

cultural adjective ARTISTIC,
civilizing, edifying, educational,
enlightening, enriching,
humane, liberal

culture noun **1** CIVILIZATION,
customs, lifestyle, mores,
society, way of life
2 REFINEMENT, education,
enlightenment, good taste,
sophistication, urbanity
3 FARMING, cultivation,
husbandry

cultured adjective REFINED,
educated, enlightened,
highbrow, sophisticated,
urbane, well-informed,
well-read

culvert noun DRAIN, channel,
conduit, gutter, watercourse

cumbersome adjective AWKWARD,
bulky, burdensome, heavy,
unmanageable, unwieldy,
weighty

cunning adjective **1** CRAFTY,
artful, devious, Machiavellian,
sharp, shifty, sly, wily **2** SKILLFUL,
imaginative, ingenious ▶ noun
3 CRAFTINESS, artfulness,
deviousness, guile, slyness,
trickery **4** SKILL, artifice,
cleverness, ingenuity, subtlety

cup noun **1** MUG, beaker, bowl,
chalice, goblet, teacup **2** TROPHY

cupboard noun CABINET, press

curb noun **1** RESTRAINT, brake,
bridle, check, control,
deterrent, limitation, rein ▶ verb
2 RESTRAIN, check, control,
hinder, impede, inhibit,
restrict, retard, suppress

cure verb **1** MAKE BETTER, correct,
ease, heal, mend, relieve,

remedy, restore **2** PRESERVE, dry, pickle, salt, smoke ▶*noun* **3** REMEDY, antidote, medicine, nostrum, panacea, treatment

curiosity *noun* **1** INQUISITIVENESS, interest, nosiness (*informal*), prying, snooping (*informal*) **2** ODDITY, freak, novelty, phenomenon, rarity, sight, spectacle, wonder

curious *adjective* **1** INQUIRING, inquisitive, interested, questioning, searching **2** INQUISITIVE, meddling, nosy (*informal*), prying **3** UNUSUAL, bizarre, extraordinary, mysterious, novel, odd, peculiar, rare, strange, unexpected

curl *verb* **1** TWIRL, bend, coil, curve, loop, spiral, turn, twist, wind ▶*noun* **2** TWIST, coil, kink, ringlet, spiral, whorl

curly *adjective* CURLING, crinkly, curled, frizzy, fuzzy, wavy, winding

currency *noun* **1** MONEY, coinage, coins, notes **2** ACCEPTANCE, circulation, exposure, popularity, prevalence, vogue

current *adjective* **1** PRESENT, contemporary, cool (*informal*), fashionable, in fashion, in vogue, phat (*slang*), present-day, trendy (*informal*), up-to-date **2** PREVALENT, accepted, common, customary, in circulation, popular, topical, widespread ▶*noun* **3** FLOW, course, draft, jet, progression, river, stream, tide, undertow **4** MOOD, atmosphere, feeling, tendency, trend, undercurrent

curse *verb* **1** SWEAR, blaspheme, cuss (*informal*), take the Lord's name in vain **2** DAMN, anathematize, excommunicate ▶*noun* **3** OATH, blasphemy, expletive, obscenity, swearing, swearword **4** DENUNCIATION, anathema, ban, excommunication, hoodoo (*informal*), jinx **5** AFFLICTION, bane, hardship, plague, scourge, torment, trouble

cursed *adjective* DAMNED, accursed, bedevilled, doomed, ill-fated

curt *adjective* SHORT, abrupt, blunt, brief, brusque, gruff, monosyllabic, succinct, terse

curtail *verb* CUT SHORT, cut back, decrease, diminish, dock, lessen, reduce, shorten, truncate

curtain *noun* HANGING, drape

curve *noun* **1** BEND, arc, curvature, loop, trajectory, turn ▶*verb* **2** BEND, arc, arch, coil, hook, spiral, swerve, turn, twist, wind

curved *adjective* BENT, arched, bowed, rounded, serpentine, sinuous, twisted

cushion *noun* **1** PILLOW, beanbag, bolster, hassock, headrest, pad ▶*verb* **2** SOFTEN, dampen, deaden, muffle, stifle, suppress

custody *noun* **1** SAFEKEEPING, care, charge, keeping, protection, supervision **2** IMPRISONMENT, confinement, detention, incarceration

custom *noun* **1** TRADITION, convention, policy, practice, ritual, rule, usage **2** HABIT, practice, procedure, routine,

way, wont 3 CUSTOMERS, patronage, trade

customary *adjective* USUAL, accepted, accustomed, common, conventional, established, normal, ordinary, routine, traditional

customer *noun* CLIENT, buyer, consumer, patron, purchaser, regular (*informal*), shopper

customs *plural noun* DUTY, import charges, tariff, tax, toll

cut *verb* **1** PENETRATE, chop, pierce, score, sever, slash, slice, slit, wound **2** DIVIDE, bisect, dissect, slice, split **3** TRIM, clip, hew, lop, mow, pare, prune, shave, snip **4** ABRIDGE, abbreviate, condense, curtail, delete, shorten **5** REDUCE, contract, cut back, decrease, diminish, lower, slash, slim (down) **6** SHAPE, carve, chisel, engrave, fashion, form, sculpt, whittle **7** HURT, insult, put down, snub, sting, wound ▶*noun* **8** INCISION, gash, laceration, nick, slash, slit, stroke, wound **9** REDUCTION, cutback, decrease, fall, lowering, saving **10** *Informal* SHARE, percentage, piece, portion, section, slice **11** STYLE, fashion, look, shape

cutback *noun* REDUCTION, cut, decrease, economy, lessening, retrenchment

cut down *verb* **1** FELL, hew, level, lop **2** REDUCE, decrease, lessen, lower

cute *adjective* APPEALING, attractive, charming, delightful, engaging, lovable, sweet, winning, winsome

cut in *verb* INTERRUPT, break in,

butt in, intervene, intrude

cut off *verb* **1** SEPARATE, isolate, sever **2** INTERRUPT, disconnect, intercept

cut out *verb* STOP, cease, give up, refrain from

cutthroat *adjective*
1 COMPETITIVE, dog-eat-dog, fierce, relentless, ruthless, unprincipled ▶*noun* **2** MURDERER, assassin, butcher, executioner, hit man (*slang*), killer

cutting *adjective* HURTFUL, acrimonious, barbed, bitter, caustic, malicious, sarcastic, scathing, vitriolic, wounding

cycle *noun* ERA, circle, period, phase, revolution, rotation

cynic *noun* SKEPTIC, doubter, misanthrope, misanthropist, pessimist, scoffer

cynical *adjective* SKEPTICAL, contemptuous, derisive, distrustful, misanthropic, mocking, pessimistic, scoffing, scornful, unbelieving

cynicism *noun* SKEPTICISM, disbelief, doubt, misanthropy, pessimism

D d

dab *verb* **1** PAT, daub, stipple, tap, touch ▶*noun* **2** SPOT, bit, drop, pat, smudge, speck **3** PAT, flick, stroke, tap, touch

dabble *verb* **1** PLAY AT, dip into, potter, tinker, trifle (with) **2** SPLASH, dip

daft *adjective* *Informal* **1** FOOLISH, absurd, asinine, bonkers (*informal*), crackpot (*informal*), crazy, idiotic, silly, stupid, witless **2** CRAZY, bonkers (*slang*), demented, deranged, insane, nuts (*slang*), touched, unhinged

dagger noun KNIFE, bayonet, dirk, stiletto

daily adjective **1** EVERYDAY, diurnal, quotidian ▸ adverb **2** EVERY DAY, day by day, once a day

dainty adjective DELICATE, charming, elegant, exquisite, fine, graceful, neat, petite, pretty

dam noun **1** BARRIER, barrage, embankment, obstruction, wall ▸ verb **2** BLOCK UP, barricade, hold back, obstruct, restrict

damage verb **1** HARM, hurt, impair, injure, ruin, spoil, weaken, wreck ▸ noun **2** HARM, destruction, detriment, devastation, hurt, injury, loss, suffering **3** *Informal* COST, bill, charge, expense

damages plural noun *Law* COMPENSATION, fine, reimbursement, reparation, satisfaction

damaging adjective HARMFUL, deleterious, detrimental, disadvantageous, hurtful, injurious, ruinous

dame noun NOBLEWOMAN, baroness, dowager, *grande dame*, lady, peeress

damn verb **1** CONDEMN, blast, censure, criticize, denounce, put down **2** SENTENCE, condemn, doom

damnation noun CONDEMNATION, anathema, damning, denunciation, doom

damned adjective **1** DOOMED, accursed, condemned, lost

2 *Slang* DETESTABLE, confounded, hateful, infernal, loathsome

damp adjective **1** MOIST, clammy, dank, dewy, drizzly, humid, soggy, sopping, wet ▸ noun **2** MOISTURE, dampness, dankness, drizzle ▸ verb **3** MOISTEN, dampen, wet **4 damp down** REDUCE, allay, check, curb, diminish, inhibit, pour cold water on, stifle

dampen verb **1** REDUCE, check, dull, lessen, moderate, restrain, stifle **2** MOISTEN, make damp, spray, wet

damper noun As in **put a damper on** DISCOURAGEMENT, cold water (*informal*), hindrance, restraint, wet blanket (*informal*)

dance verb **1** PRANCE, hop, jig, skip, sway, trip, whirl ▸ noun **2** BALL, disco, discotheque, hop (*informal*, *dated*), social

dancer noun BALLERINA, Terpsichorean

danger noun PERIL, hazard, jeopardy, menace, pitfall, risk, threat, vulnerability

dangerous adjective PERILOUS, breakneck, chancy (*informal*), hazardous, insecure, precarious, risky, unsafe, vulnerable

dangerously adverb PERILOUSLY, alarmingly, hazardously, precariously, recklessly, riskily, unsafely

dangle verb **1** HANG, flap, hang down, sway, swing, trail **2** WAVE, brandish, flaunt, flourish

dapper adjective NEAT, smart, soigné or soignée, spruce, spry, trim, well-groomed, well turned out

dare verb 1 RISK, hazard, make bold, presume, venture 2 CHALLENGE, defy, goad, provoke, taunt, throw down the gauntlet ▶noun 3 CHALLENGE, provocation, taunt

daredevil noun 1 ADVENTURER, desperado, exhibitionist, show-off (informal), stunt man ▶adjective 2 DARING, adventurous, audacious, bold, death-defying, reckless

daring adjective 1 BRAVE, adventurous, audacious, bold, daredevil, fearless, intrepid, reckless, venturesome ▶noun 2 BRAVERY, audacity, boldness, courage, fearlessness, nerve (informal), pluck, temerity

dark adjective 1 DIM, dingy, murky, shadowy, shady, sunless, unlit 2 BLACK, dark-skinned, dusky, ebony, sable, swarthy 3 GLOOMY, bleak, dismal, grim, morose, mournful, sad, somber 4 EVIL, foul, infernal, sinister, vile, wicked 5 SECRET, concealed, hidden, mysterious ▶noun 6 DARKNESS, dimness, dusk, gloom, murk, obscurity, semi-darkness 7 NIGHT, evening, nightfall, night-time, twilight

darken verb MAKE DARK, blacken, dim, obscure, overshadow

darkness noun DARK, blackness, duskiness, gloom, murk, nightfall, shade, shadows

darling noun 1 BELOVED, dear, dearest, love, sweetheart, truelove ▶adjective 2 BELOVED, adored, cherished, dear, precious, treasured

darn verb 1 MEND, cobble up, patch, repair, sew up, stitch ▶noun 2 MEND, invisible repair, patch, reinforcement

dart verb DASH, fly, race, run, rush, shoot, spring, sprint, tear

dash verb 1 RUSH, bolt, fly, hurry, race, run, speed, sprint, tear 2 THROW, cast, fling, hurl, slam, sling 3 CRASH, break, destroy, shatter, smash, splinter 4 FRUSTRATE, blight, foil, ruin, spoil, thwart, undo ▶noun 5 RUSH, dart, race, run, sortie, sprint, spurt 6 LITTLE, bit, drop, hint, pinch, soupçon, sprinkling, tinge, touch 7 STYLE, brio, élan, flair, flourish, panache, spirit, verve

dashing adjective 1 BOLD, debonair, gallant, lively, spirited, swashbuckling 2 STYLISH, elegant, flamboyant, jaunty, showy, smart, sporty

data noun INFORMATION, details, facts, figures, statistics

date noun 1 TIME, age, epoch, era, period, stage 2 APPOINTMENT, assignation, engagement, meeting, rendezvous, tryst 3 PARTNER, escort, friend ▶verb 4 PUT A DATE ON, assign a date to, fix the period of 5 BECOME OLD-FASHIONED, be dated, show one's age 6 date from or date back to COME FROM, bear a date of, belong to, exist from, originate in

dated adjective OLD-FASHIONED, obsolete, old hat, outdated, outmoded, out of date, passé, unfashionable

daub verb SMEAR, coat, cover, paint, plaster, slap on (informal)

daunting adjective INTIMIDATING, alarming, demoralizing, disconcerting, discouraging, disheartening, frightening, unnerving

dauntless adjective FEARLESS, bold, doughty, gallant, indomitable, intrepid, resolute, stouthearted, undaunted, unflinching

dawdle verb WASTE TIME, dally, delay, drag one's feet or heels, hang about, idle, loaf, loiter, trail

dawn noun 1 DAYBREAK, aurora (poetic), cockcrow, crack of dawn, daylight, morning, sunrise, sunup 2 BEGINNING, advent, birth, emergence, genesis, origin, rise, start ▶ verb 3 GROW LIGHT, break, brighten, lighten 4 BEGIN, appear, develop, emerge, originate, rise, unfold 5 dawn on or upon HIT, become apparent, come into one's head, come to mind, occur, register (informal), strike

day noun 1 TWENTY-FOUR HOURS, daylight, daytime 2 POINT IN TIME, date, time 3 TIME, age, epoch, era, heyday, period, zenith

daybreak noun DAWN, break of day, cockcrow, crack of dawn, first light, morning, sunrise, sunup

daydream noun 1 FANTASY, dream, fancy, imagining, pipe dream, reverie, wish ▶ verb 2 FANTASIZE, dream, envision, fancy, imagine, muse

daylight noun SUNLIGHT, light of day, sunshine

daze verb 1 STUN, benumb, numb, paralyze, shock, stupefy ▶ noun 2 SHOCK, bewilderment,

confusion, distraction, stupor, trance, trancelike state

dazed adjective SHOCKED, bewildered, confused, disorientated, dizzy, muddled, punch-drunk, staggered, stunned

dazzle verb 1 IMPRESS, amaze, astonish, bowl over (informal), overpower, overwhelm, take one's breath away 2 BLIND, bedazzle, blur, confuse, daze ▶ noun 3 SPLENDOR, brilliance, glitter, magnificence, razzmatazz (slang), sparkle

dazzling adjective SPLENDID, brilliant, glittering, glorious, scintillating, sensational (informal), sparkling, stunning, virtuoso

dead adjective 1 DECEASED, defunct, departed, extinct, late, passed away, perished 2 NOT WORKING, inactive, inoperative, stagnant, unemployed, useless 3 NUMB, inert, paralyzed 4 TOTAL, absolute, complete, outright, thorough, unqualified, utter 5 Informal EXHAUSTED, spent, tired, worn out 6 BORING, dull, flat, uninteresting ▶ noun 7 MIDDLE, depth, midst

deaden verb REDUCE, alleviate, blunt, cushion, diminish, dull, lessen, muffle, smother, stifle, suppress, weaken

deadline noun TIME LIMIT, cutoff point, limit, target date

deadlock noun 1 DRAW, dead heat, tie 2 IMPASSE, gridlock, stalemate, standoff, standstill

deadlocked adjective 1 EVEN, equal, level, neck and neck, on a level playing field (informal)

2 GRIDLOCKED, at an impasse, at a standstill

deadly adjective LETHAL, dangerous, death-dealing, deathly, fatal, malignant, mortal

deadpan adjective EXPRESSIONLESS, blank, impassive, inexpressive, inscrutable, poker-faced, straight-faced

deaf adjective **1** HARD OF HEARING, stone deaf, without hearing **2** OBLIVIOUS, indifferent, unconcerned, unhearing, unmoved

deafen verb MAKE DEAF, din, drown out, split or burst the eardrums

deafening adjective EAR-PIERCING, booming, ear-splitting, overpowering, piercing, resounding, ringing, thunderous

deal noun **1** AGREEMENT, arrangement, bargain, contract, pact, transaction, understanding **2** AMOUNT, degree, extent, portion, quantity, share ▶ verb **3** SELL, bargain, buy and sell, do business, negotiate, stock, trade, traffic

dealer noun TRADER, merchant, purveyor, supplier, tradesman, wholesaler

deal out verb DISTRIBUTE, allot, apportion, assign, dispense, dole out, give, mete out, share

deal with verb **1** HANDLE, attend to, cope with, get to grips with, manage, see to, take care of, treat **2** BE CONCERNED WITH, consider

dear noun **1** BELOVED, angel, darling, loved one, precious, treasure ▶ adjective **2** BELOVED, cherished, close, favorite, intimate, precious, prized, treasured **3** EXPENSIVE, at a premium, costly, high-priced, overpriced, pricey (informal)

dearly adverb **1** VERY MUCH, extremely, greatly, profoundly **2** AT GREAT COST, at a high price

dearth noun SCARCITY, deficiency, inadequacy, insufficiency, lack, paucity, poverty, shortage, want

death noun **1** DYING, demise, departure, end, exit, passing **2** DESTRUCTION, downfall, extinction, finish, ruin, undoing

deathly adjective DEATHLIKE, ghastly, grim, pale, pallid, wan

debacle noun DISASTER, catastrophe, collapse, defeat, fiasco, reversal, rout

debase verb DEGRADE, cheapen, devalue, lower, reduce

debatable adjective DOUBTFUL, arguable, controversial, dubious, moot, problematical, questionable, uncertain

debate noun **1** DISCUSSION, argument, contention, controversy, dispute ▶ verb **2** DISCUSS, argue, dispute, question **3** CONSIDER, deliberate, ponder, reflect, ruminate, weigh

debauchery noun DEPRAVITY, dissipation, dissoluteness, excess, indulgence, intemperance, lewdness, overindulgence

debonair adjective ELEGANT, charming, courteous, dashing, refined, smooth, suave, urbane, well-bred

debrief verb INTERROGATE, cross-examine, examine, probe, question, quiz

debris noun REMAINS, bits, detritus, fragments, rubble, ruins, waste, wreckage

debt noun 1 DEBIT, commitment, liability, obligation 2 **in debt** OWING, in arrears, in the red (*informal*), liable

debtor noun BORROWER, mortgagor

debunk verb EXPOSE, cut down to size, deflate, disparage, mock, ridicule, show up

debut noun INTRODUCTION, beginning, bow, coming out, entrance, first appearance, initiation, presentation

decadence noun DEGENERATION, corruption, decay, decline, deterioration, dissipation, dissolution

decadent adjective DEGENERATE, corrupt, decaying, declining, dissolute, immoral, self-indulgent

decapitate verb BEHEAD, execute, guillotine

decay verb 1 DECLINE, crumble, deteriorate, disintegrate, dwindle, shrivel, wane, waste away, wither 2 ROT, corrode, decompose, perish, putrefy ▶ noun 3 DECLINE, collapse, degeneration, deterioration, fading, failing, wasting, withering 4 ROT, caries, decomposition, gangrene, putrefaction

decease noun Formal DEATH, demise, departure, dying, release

deceased adjective DEAD, defunct, departed, expired, former, late, lifeless

deceit noun DISHONESTY,

cheating, chicanery, deception, fraud, lying, pretense, treachery, trickery

deceitful adjective DISHONEST, deceptive, down and dirty (*informal*), false, fraudulent, sneaky, treacherous, two-faced, untrustworthy

deceive verb DUPE (*informal*), cheat, con (*informal*), fool, hoodwink, mislead, swindle, trick

deceiver noun LIAR, cheat, con man (*informal*), double-dealer, fraud, impostor, swindler, trickster

decency noun RESPECTABILITY, civility, correctness, courtesy, decorum, etiquette, modesty, propriety

decent adjective 1 REASONABLE, adequate, ample, fair, passable, satisfactory, sufficient, tolerable 2 RESPECTABLE, chaste, decorous, modest, proper, pure 3 PROPER, appropriate, becoming, befitting, fitting, seemly, suitable 4 Informal KIND, accommodating, courteous, friendly, generous, gracious, helpful, obliging, thoughtful

deception noun 1 TRICKERY, cunning, deceit, fraud, guile, legerdemain, treachery 2 TRICK, bluff, decoy, hoax, illusion, lie, ruse, subterfuge

deceptive adjective MISLEADING, ambiguous, deceitful, dishonest, false, fraudulent, illusory, unreliable

decide verb REACH or COME TO A DECISION, adjudge, adjudicate, choose, conclude, determine, make up one's mind, resolve

decidedly adverb DEFINITELY,

clearly, distinctly, downright, positively, unequivocally, unmistakably

decimate verb DEVASTATE, ravage, wreak havoc on

decipher verb FIGURE OUT (*informal*), crack, decode, deduce, interpret, make out, read, solve

decision noun 1 JUDGMENT, arbitration, conclusion, finding, resolution, ruling, sentence, verdict 2 DECISIVENESS, determination, firmness, purpose, resolution, resolve, strength of mind *or* will

decisive adjective 1 INFLUENTIAL, conclusive, critical, crucial, fateful, momentous, significant 2 RESOLUTE, decided, determined, firm, forceful, incisive, strong-minded, trenchant

deck verb DECORATE, adorn, array, beautify, clothe, dress, embellish, festoon

declaim verb 1 ORATE, harangue, hold forth, lecture, proclaim, rant, recite, speak 2 **declaim against** PROTEST AGAINST, attack, decry, denounce, inveigh, rail

declaration noun 1 STATEMENT, acknowledgment, affirmation, assertion, avowal, disclosure, protestation, revelation, testimony 2 ANNOUNCEMENT, edict, notification, proclamation, profession, pronouncement

declare verb 1 STATE, affirm, announce, assert, claim, maintain, proclaim, profess, pronounce, swear, utter 2 MAKE KNOWN, confess, disclose, reveal, show

decline verb 1 LESSEN, decrease, diminish, dwindle, ebb, fade, fall off, shrink, sink, wane 2 DETERIORATE, decay, degenerate, droop, languish, pine, weaken, worsen 3 REFUSE, abstain, avoid, reject, say 'no', turn down ▶noun 4 LESSENING, downturn, drop, dwindling, falling off, recession, slump 5 DETERIORATION, decay, degeneration, failing, weakening, worsening

decode verb DECIPHER, crack, decrypt, interpret, solve, unscramble, work out

decompose verb ROT, break up, crumble, decay, fall apart, fester, putrefy

decor noun DECORATION, color scheme, furnishing style, ornamentation

decorate verb 1 ADORN, beautify, embellish, festoon, grace, ornament, trim 2 RENOVATE, do up (*informal*), color, furbish, paint, paper, wallpaper 3 PIN A MEDAL ON, cite, confer an honor on *or* upon

decoration noun 1 ADORNMENT, beautification, elaboration, embellishment, enrichment, ornamentation, trimming 2 ORNAMENT, bauble, frill, garnish, trimmings 3 MEDAL, award, badge, ribbon, star

decorative adjective ORNAMENTAL, beautifying, fancy, nonfunctional, pretty

decorous adjective PROPER, becoming, correct, decent, dignified, fitting, polite, seemly, well-behaved

decorum noun PROPRIETY,

decency, dignity, etiquette, good manners, politeness, protocol, respectability

decoy noun 1 LURE, bait, enticement, inducement, pretense, trap ▶verb 2 LURE, deceive, ensnare, entice, entrap, seduce, tempt

decrease verb 1 LESSEN, cut down, decline, diminish, drop, dwindle, lower, reduce, shrink, subside ▶noun 2 LESSENING, contraction, cutback, decline, dwindling, falling off, loss, reduction, subsidence

decree noun 1 LAW, act, command, edict, order, proclamation, ruling, statute ▶verb 2 ORDER, command, demand, ordain, prescribe, proclaim, pronounce, rule

decrepit adjective 1 WEAK, aged, doddering, feeble, frail, infirm 2 WORN-OUT, battered, beat-up (informal), broken-down, dilapidated, ramshackle, rickety, run-down, tumbledown, weather-beaten

decry verb CONDEMN, belittle, criticize, denigrate, denounce, discredit, disparage, put down, run down

dedicate verb 1 DEVOTE, commit, give over to, pledge, surrender 2 INSCRIBE, address

dedicated adjective DEVOTED, committed, enthusiastic, purposeful, single-minded, wholehearted, zealous

dedication noun 1 DEVOTION, adherence, allegiance, commitment, faithfulness, loyalty, single-mindedness, wholeheartedness 2 INSCRIPTION, address, message

deduce verb CONCLUDE, draw, gather, glean, infer, reason, take to mean, understand

deduct verb SUBTRACT, decrease by, knock off (informal), reduce by, remove, take away, take off

deduction noun 1 SUBTRACTION, decrease, diminution, discount, reduction, withdrawal 2 CONCLUSION, assumption, finding, inference, reasoning, result

deed noun 1 ACTION, achievement, act, exploit, fact, feat, performance 2 Law DOCUMENT, contract, title

deep adjective 1 WIDE, bottomless, broad, far, profound, unfathomable, yawning 2 MYSTERIOUS, abstract, abstruse, arcane, esoteric, hidden, obscure, recondite, secret 3 INTENSE, extreme, grave, great, profound, serious (informal), unqualified 4 ABSORBED, engrossed, immersed, lost, preoccupied, rapt 5 DARK, intense, rich, strong, vivid 6 LOW, bass, booming, low-pitched, resonant, sonorous ▶noun 7 the deep Poetic OCEAN, briny (informal), high seas, main, sea

deepen verb INTENSIFY, grow, increase, magnify, reinforce, strengthen

deeply adverb 1 THOROUGHLY, completely, gravely, profoundly, seriously, severely, to the core, to the heart, to the quick 2 INTENSELY, acutely, affectingly, distressingly, feelingly, mournfully, movingly, passionately, sadly

deface verb VANDALIZE, damage,

deform, disfigure, mar, mutilate, spoil, tarnish

de facto *adverb* 1 IN FACT, actually, in effect, in reality, really ▸ *adjective* 2 ACTUAL, existing, real

defame *verb* SLANDER, bad-mouth (*slang*), cast aspersions on, denigrate, discredit, disparage, knock (*informal*), libel, malign, smear

default *noun* 1 FAILURE, deficiency, dereliction, evasion, lapse, neglect, nonpayment, omission ▸ *verb* 2 FAIL, dodge, evade, neglect

defeat *verb* 1 BEAT, conquer, crush, master, overwhelm, rout, trounce, vanquish, wipe the floor with (*informal*) 2 FRUSTRATE, baffle, balk, confound, foil, get the better of, ruin, thwart ▸ *noun* 3 CONQUEST, beating, overthrow, rout 4 FRUSTRATION, failure, rebuff, reverse, setback, thwarting

defeatist *noun* 1 PESSIMIST, prophet of doom, quitter ▸ *adjective* 2 PESSIMISTIC

defect *noun* 1 IMPERFECTION, blemish, blotch, error, failing, fault, flaw, spot, taint ▸ *verb* 2 DESERT, abandon, change sides, go over, rebel, revolt, walk out on (*informal*)

defection *noun* DESERTION, apostasy, rebellion

defective *adjective* FAULTY, broken, deficient, flawed, imperfect, not working, on the blink (*slang*), out of order

defector *noun* DESERTER, apostate, renegade, turncoat

defend *verb* 1 PROTECT, cover, guard, keep safe, preserve, safeguard, screen, shelter, shield 2 SUPPORT, champion, endorse, justify, speak up for, stand up for, stick up for (*informal*), uphold, vindicate

defendant *noun* THE ACCUSED, defense, offender, prisoner at the bar, respondent

defender *noun* 1 PROTECTOR, bodyguard, escort, guard 2 SUPPORTER, advocate, champion, sponsor

defense *noun* 1 PROTECTION, cover, guard, immunity, resistance, safeguard, security, shelter 2 SHIELD, barricade, bulwark, buttress, fortification, rampart 3 ARGUMENT, excuse, explanation, justification, plea, vindication 4 *Law* PLEA, alibi, denial, rebuttal, testimony

defenseless *adjective* HELPLESS, exposed, naked, powerless, unarmed, unguarded, unprotected, vulnerable, wide open

defensive *adjective* ON GUARD, on the defensive, protective, uptight (*informal*), watchful

defer[1] *verb* POSTPONE, delay, hold over, procrastinate, put off, put on ice, shelve, suspend

defer[2] *verb* COMPLY, accede, bow, capitulate, give in, give way to, submit, yield

deference *noun* RESPECT, attention, civility, consideration, courtesy, honor, politeness, regard, reverence

deferential *adjective* RESPECTFUL, ingratiating, obedient, obeisant, obsequious, polite, reverential, submissive

defiance *noun* RESISTANCE,

confrontation, contempt, disobedience, disregard, insolence, insubordination, opposition, rebelliousness

defiant adjective RESISTING, audacious, bold, daring, disobedient, insolent, insubordinate, mutinous, provocative, rebellious

deficiency noun 1 LACK, absence, dearth, deficit, scarcity, shortage 2 FAILING, defect, demerit, fault, flaw, frailty, imperfection, shortcoming, weakness

deficient adjective 1 LACKING, inadequate, insufficient, meager, scant, scarce, short, skimpy, wanting 2 UNSATISFACTORY, defective, faulty, flawed, impaired, imperfect, incomplete, inferior, lousy (slang), weak

deficit noun SHORTFALL, arrears, deficiency, loss, shortage

define verb 1 DESCRIBE, characterize, designate, explain, expound, interpret, specify, spell out 2 MARK OUT, bound, circumscribe, delineate, demarcate, limit, outline

definite adjective 1 CLEAR, black-and-white, cut-and-dried (informal), exact, fixed, marked, particular, precise, specific 2 CERTAIN, assured, decided, guaranteed, positive, settled, sure

definitely adverb CERTAINLY, absolutely, categorically, clearly, positively, surely, undeniably, unmistakably, unquestionably, without doubt

definition noun 1 EXPLANATION, clarification, elucidation,

exposition, statement of meaning 2 SHARPNESS, clarity, contrast, distinctness, focus, precision

definitive adjective 1 FINAL, absolute, complete, conclusive, decisive 2 AUTHORITATIVE, exhaustive, perfect, reliable, ultimate

deflate verb 1 COLLAPSE, empty, exhaust, flatten, puncture, shrink 2 HUMILIATE, chasten, disconcert, dispirit, humble, mortify, put down (slang), squash 3 Economics REDUCE, depress, devalue, diminish

deflect verb TURN ASIDE, bend, deviate, diverge, glance off, ricochet, swerve, veer

deflection noun DEVIATION, bend, divergence, swerve

deform verb 1 DISTORT, buckle, contort, gnarl, mangle, misshape, twist, warp 2 DISFIGURE, deface, maim, mar, mutilate, ruin, spoil

deformity noun ABNORMALITY, defect, disfigurement, malformation

defraud verb CHEAT, con (informal), embezzle, fleece, pilfer, rip off (slang), swindle, trick

deft adjective SKILLFUL, adept, adroit, agile, dexterous, expert, neat, nimble, proficient

defunct adjective 1 DEAD, deceased, departed, extinct, gone 2 OBSOLETE, bygone, expired, inoperative, invalid, nonexistent, out of commission

defy verb RESIST, brave, confront, disregard, flout, scorn, slight, spurn

degenerate adjective

1 DEPRAVED, corrupt,
debauched, decadent,
dissolute, immoral, low,
perverted ▸ verb **2** WORSEN,
decay, decline, decrease,
deteriorate, fall off, lapse, sink,
slip

degradation noun **1** DISGRACE,
discredit, dishonor,
humiliation, ignominy,
mortification, shame
2 DETERIORATION, decline,
degeneration, demotion,
downgrading

degrade verb **1** DISGRACE,
debase, demean, discredit,
dishonor, humble, humiliate,
shame **2** DEMOTE, downgrade,
lower

degrading adjective DEMEANING,
dishonorable, humiliating,
shameful, undignified,
unworthy

degree noun STAGE, grade,
notch, point, rung, step, unit

deity noun GOD, divinity,
goddess, godhead, idol,
immortal, supreme being

dejected adjective DOWNHEARTED,
crestfallen, depressed,
despondent, disconsolate,
disheartened, downcast, glum,
miserable, sad

dejection noun LOW SPIRITS,
depression, despair,
despondency, doldrums,
downheartedness, gloom,
melancholy, sadness, sorrow,
unhappiness

de jure adverb LEGALLY, by right,
rightfully

delay verb **1** PUT OFF, defer, hold
over, postpone, procrastinate,
shelve, suspend **2** HOLD UP, bog
down, detain, hinder, hold

back, impede, obstruct, set
back, slow up ▸ noun **3** PUTTING
OFF, deferment, postponement,
procrastination, suspension
4 HOLD-UP, hindrance,
impediment, interruption,
interval, setback, stoppage, wait

delegate noun **1** REPRESENTATIVE,
agent, ambassador,
commissioner, deputy, envoy,
legate ▸ verb **2** ENTRUST, assign,
consign, devolve, give, hand
over, pass on, transfer
3 APPOINT, accredit, authorize,
commission, depute,
designate, empower, mandate

delegation noun **1** DEPUTATION,
commission, contingent,
embassy, envoys, legation,
mission **2** DEVOLUTION,
assignment, commissioning,
committal

delete verb REMOVE, cancel,
cross out, efface, erase,
expunge, obliterate, rub out,
strike out

deliberate adjective
1 INTENTIONAL, calculated,
conscious, planned,
prearranged, premeditated,
purposeful, willful **2** UNHURRIED,
careful, cautious, circumspect,
measured, methodical,
ponderous, slow, thoughtful
▸ verb **3** CONSIDER, cogitate,
consult, debate, discuss,
meditate, ponder, reflect,
think, weigh

deliberately adverb
INTENTIONALLY, by design,
calculatingly, consciously, in
cold blood, knowingly, on
purpose, willfully, wittingly

deliberation noun
1 CONSIDERATION, calculation,
circumspection, forethought,

meditation, reflection, thought
2 DISCUSSION, conference,
consultation, debate

delicacy noun **1** FINENESS,
accuracy, daintiness, elegance,
exquisiteness, lightness,
precision, subtlety **2** FRAGILITY,
flimsiness, frailty, slenderness,
tenderness, weakness **3** TREAT,
dainty, luxury, savory, tidbit
4 FASTIDIOUSNESS, discrimination,
finesse, purity, refinement,
sensibility, taste **5** SENSITIVITY,
sensitiveness, tact

delicate adjective **1** FINE, deft,
elegant, exquisite, graceful,
precise, skilled, subtle **2** SUBTLE,
choice, dainty, delicious, fine,
savory, tender, yummy
(informal) **3** FRAGILE, flimsy, frail,
slender, slight, tender, weak
4 CONSIDERATE, diplomatic,
discreet, sensitive, tactful

delicately adverb **1** FINELY,
daintily, deftly, elegantly,
exquisitely, gracefully,
precisely, skillfully, subtly
2 TACTFULLY, diplomatically,
sensitively

delicious adjective DELECTABLE,
appetizing, choice, dainty,
mouthwatering, savory, tasty,
toothsome, yummy (informal)

delight noun **1** PLEASURE, ecstasy,
enjoyment, gladness, glee,
happiness, joy, rapture ▶verb
2 PLEASE, amuse, charm, cheer,
enchant, gratify, thrill
3 delight in TAKE PLEASURE IN,
appreciate, enjoy, feast on,
like, love, relish, revel in, savor

delighted adjective PLEASED,
ecstatic, elated, enchanted,
happy, joyous, jubilant,
overjoyed, thrilled

delightful adjective PLEASANT,
agreeable, charming,
delectable, enchanting,
enjoyable, pleasurable,
rapturous, thrilling

delinquent noun CRIMINAL,
culprit, lawbreaker, miscreant,
offender, villain, wrongdoer

delirious adjective **1** MAD, crazy,
demented, deranged,
incoherent, insane, raving,
unhinged **2** ECSTATIC, beside
oneself, carried away, excited,
frantic, frenzied, hysterical,
wild, wired (slang)

delirium noun **1** MADNESS,
derangement, hallucination,
insanity, raving **2** FRENZY,
ecstasy, fever, hysteria, passion

deliver verb **1** CARRY, bear,
bring, cart, convey, distribute,
transport **2** HAND OVER, commit,
give up, grant, make over,
relinquish, surrender, transfer,
turn over, yield **3** GIVE,
announce, declare, present,
read, utter **4** RELEASE,
emancipate, free, liberate,
loose, ransom, rescue, save
5 STRIKE, administer, aim, deal,
direct, give, inflict, launch

deliverance noun RELEASE,
emancipation, escape,
liberation, ransom,
redemption, rescue, salvation

delivery noun **1** HANDING OVER,
consignment, conveyance,
dispatch, distribution,
surrender, transfer,
transmission **2** SPEECH,
articulation, elocution,
enunciation, intonation,
utterance **3** CHILDBIRTH,
confinement, labor, parturition

delude verb DECEIVE, beguile,

dupe, fool, hoodwink, kid (*informal*), mislead, trick

deluge noun 1 FLOOD, cataclysm, downpour, inundation, overflowing, spate, torrent 2 RUSH, avalanche, barrage, flood, spate, torrent ▶verb 3 FLOOD, douse, drench, drown, inundate, soak, submerge, swamp 4 OVERWHELM, engulf, inundate, overload, overrun, swamp

delusion noun MISCONCEPTION, error, fallacy, false impression, fancy, hallucination, illusion, misapprehension, mistake

deluxe adjective LUXURIOUS, costly, exclusive, expensive, grand, opulent, select, special, splendid, superior

delve verb RESEARCH, burrow, explore, ferret out, forage, investigate, look into, probe, rummage, search

demagogue noun AGITATOR, firebrand, rabble-rouser

demand verb 1 REQUEST, ask, challenge, inquire, interrogate, question 2 REQUIRE, call for, cry out for, entail, involve, necessitate, need, want 3 CLAIM, exact, expect, insist on, order ▶noun 4 REQUEST, inquiry, order, question, requisition 5 NEED, call, claim, market, requirement, want

demanding adjective DIFFICULT, challenging, exacting, hard, taxing, tough, trying, wearing

demarcation noun DELIMITATION, differentiation, distinction, division, separation

demean verb LOWER, abase, debase, degrade, descend, humble, stoop

demeanor noun BEHAVIOR, air, bearing, carriage, comportment, conduct, deportment, manner

demented adjective MAD, crazed, crazy, deranged, frenzied, insane, maniacal, unbalanced, unhinged

demise noun 1 FAILURE, collapse, downfall, end, fall, ruin 2 *Euphemistic* DEATH, decease, departure

democracy noun SELF-GOVERNMENT, commonwealth, republic

democratic adjective SELF-GOVERNING, autonomous, egalitarian, popular, populist, representative

demolish verb 1 KNOCK DOWN, bulldoze, destroy, dismantle, flatten, level, raze, tear down 2 DEFEAT, annihilate, destroy, overthrow, overturn, undo, wreck

demolition noun KNOCKING DOWN, bulldozing, destruction, explosion, levelling, razing, tearing down, wrecking

demon noun 1 EVIL SPIRIT, devil, fiend, ghoul, goblin, malignant spirit 2 WIZARD, ace (*informal*), fiend, master

demonic, demoniac, demoniacal adjective 1 DEVILISH, diabolic, diabolical, fiendish, hellish, infernal, satanic 2 FRENZIED, crazed, frantic, frenetic, furious, hectic, maniacal, manic

demonstrable adjective PROVABLE, evident, irrefutable, obvious, palpable, self-evident, unmistakable, verifiable

demonstrate verb 1 PROVE,

display, exhibit, indicate, manifest, show, testify to **2** SHOW HOW, describe, explain, illustrate, make clear, teach **3** MARCH, parade, picket, protest, rally

demonstration noun **1** MARCH, mass lobby, parade, picket, protest, rally, sit-in **2** EXPLANATION, description, exposition, presentation, test, trial **3** PROOF, confirmation, display, evidence, exhibition, expression, illustration, testimony

demoralize verb DISHEARTEN, deject, depress, discourage, dispirit, undermine, unnerve, weaken

demote verb DOWNGRADE, degrade, kick downstairs (slang), lower in rank, relegate

demur verb **1** OBJECT, balk, dispute, hesitate, protest, refuse, take exception, waver ▶ noun **2** As in without demur OBJECTION, compunction, dissent, hesitation, misgiving, protest, qualm

demure adjective SHY, diffident, modest, reserved, reticent, retiring, sedate, unassuming

den noun **1** LAIR, cave, cavern, haunt, hideout, hole, shelter **2** Chiefly U.S. STUDY, cubbyhole, hideaway, living room, retreat, sanctuary, sanctum

denial noun **1** NEGATION, contradiction, dissent, renunciation, repudiation, retraction **2** REFUSAL, prohibition, rebuff, rejection, repulse, veto

denigrate verb DISPARAGE, bad-mouth (slang), belittle,

knock (informal), malign, run down, slander, vilify

denomination noun **1** RELIGIOUS GROUP, belief, creed, persuasion, school, sect **2** UNIT, grade, size, value

denote verb INDICATE, betoken, designate, express, imply, mark, mean, show, signify

denounce verb CONDEMN, accuse, attack, censure, denunciate, revile, stigmatize, vilify

dense adjective **1** THICK, close-knit, compact, condensed, heavy, impenetrable, opaque, solid **2** STUPID, dull, obtuse, slow-witted, stolid, thick

density noun TIGHTNESS, bulk, compactness, consistency, denseness, impenetrability, mass, solidity, thickness

dent noun **1** HOLLOW, chip, crater, depression, dimple, dip, impression, indentation, pit ▶ verb **2** MAKE A DENT IN, gouge, hollow, press in, push in

deny verb **1** CONTRADICT, disagree with, disprove, rebuff, rebut, refute **2** REFUSE, begrudge, disallow, forbid, reject, turn down, withhold **3** RENOUNCE, disclaim, disown, recant, repudiate, retract

depart verb **1** LEAVE, absent (oneself), disappear, exit, go, go away, quit, retire, retreat, withdraw **2** DEVIATE, differ, digress, diverge, stray, swerve, turn aside, vary, veer

department noun SECTION, branch, bureau, division, office, station, subdivision, unit

departure noun **1** LEAVING, exit,

exodus, going, going away, leave-taking, removal, retirement, withdrawal **2** DIVERGENCE, deviation, digression, variation **3** SHIFT, change, difference, innovation, novelty, whole new ball game (*informal*)

depend *verb* **1** TRUST IN, bank on, count on, lean on, reckon on, rely upon, turn to **2** BE DETERMINED BY, be based on, be contingent on, be subject to, be subordinate to, hang on, hinge on, rest on, revolve around

dependable *adjective* RELIABLE, faithful, reputable, responsible, staunch, steady, sure, trustworthy, trusty, unfailing

dependant *noun* RELATIVE, child, minor, protégé, subordinate

dependent *adjective* **1** RELYING ON, defenseless, helpless, reliant, vulnerable, weak **2 dependent on** *or* **upon** DETERMINED BY, conditional on, contingent on, depending on, influenced by, subject to

depict *verb* **1** DRAW, delineate, illustrate, outline, paint, picture, portray, sketch **2** DESCRIBE, characterize, narrate, outline, represent

depiction *noun* REPRESENTATION, delineation, description, picture, portrayal, sketch

deplete *verb* USE UP, consume, drain, empty, exhaust, expend, impoverish, lessen, reduce

deplorable *adjective* **1** REGRETTABLE, grievous, lamentable, pitiable, sad, unfortunate, wretched **2** DISGRACEFUL, dishonorable,

reprehensible, scandalous, shameful

deplore *verb* DISAPPROVE OF, abhor, censure, condemn, denounce, object to, take a dim view of

deploy *verb* POSITION, arrange, set out, station, use, utilize

deployment *noun* POSITION, arrangement, organization, spread, stationing, use, utilization

deport *verb* **1** EXPEL, banish, exile, expatriate, extradite, oust **2 deport oneself** BEHAVE, acquit oneself, act, bear oneself, carry oneself, comport oneself, conduct oneself, hold oneself

depose *verb* **1** REMOVE FROM OFFICE, demote, dethrone, dismiss, displace, oust **2** *Law* TESTIFY, avouch, declare, make a deposition

deposit *verb* **1** PUT, drop, lay, locate, place **2** STORE, bank, consign, entrust, lodge ▶ *noun* **3** DOWN PAYMENT, installment, part payment, pledge, retainer, security, stake **4** SEDIMENT, accumulation, dregs, lees, precipitate, silt

depot *noun* **1** STOREHOUSE, depository, repository, warehouse **2** BUS STATION, garage, terminus

depraved *adjective* CORRUPT, degenerate, dissolute, evil, immoral, sinful, vicious, vile, wicked

depravity *noun* CORRUPTION, debauchery, evil, immorality, sinfulness, vice, wickedness

depreciate *verb* **1** DEVALUE, decrease, deflate, lessen, lose value, lower, reduce

2 DISPARAGE, belittle, denigrate, deride, detract, run down, scorn, sneer at

depreciation noun
  1 DEVALUATION, deflation, depression, drop, fall, slump
  2 DISPARAGEMENT, belittlement, denigration, depreciation, detraction

depress verb **1** SADDEN, deject, discourage, dishearten, dispirit, make despondent, oppress, weigh down **2** LOWER, cheapen, depreciate, devalue, diminish, downgrade, lessen, reduce **3** PRESS DOWN, flatten, level, lower, push down

depressed adjective
  1 LOW-SPIRITED, blue, dejected, despondent, discouraged, dispirited, downcast, downhearted, fed up, sad, unhappy **2** POVERTY-STRICKEN, deprived, disadvantaged, needy, poor, run-down **3** LOWERED, cheapened, depreciated, devalued, weakened **4** SUNKEN, concave, hollow, indented, recessed

depressing adjective BLEAK, discouraging, disheartening, dismal, dispiriting, gloomy, harrowing, sad, saddening

depression noun **1** LOW SPIRITS, dejection, despair, despondency, downheartedness, dumps (informal), gloominess, melancholy, sadness, the blues **2** RECESSION, economic decline, hard or bad times, inactivity, slump, stagnation **3** HOLLOW, bowl, cavity, dent, dimple, dip, indentation, pit, valley

deprivation noun
  1 WITHHOLDING, denial,

dispossession, expropriation, removal, withdrawal **2** WANT, destitution, distress, hardship, need, privation

deprive verb WITHHOLD, bereave, despoil, dispossess, rob, strip

deprived adjective POOR, bereft, destitute, disadvantaged, down at heel, in need, lacking, needy

depth noun **1** DEEPNESS, drop, extent, measure **2** INSIGHT, astuteness, discernment, penetration, profoundness, profundity, sagacity, wisdom

deputation noun DELEGATION, commission, embassy, envoys, legation

deputize verb STAND IN FOR, act for, take the place of, understudy

deputy noun SUBSTITUTE, delegate, legate, lieutenant, number two, proxy, representative, second-in-command, surrogate

deranged adjective MAD, crazed, crazy, demented, distracted, insane, irrational, unbalanced, unhinged

derelict adjective **1** ABANDONED, deserted, dilapidated, discarded, forsaken, neglected, ruined ▶ noun **2** TRAMP, bag lady, down-and-out, outcast, vagrant

deride verb MOCK, disdain, disparage, insult, jeer, ridicule, scoff, scorn, sneer, taunt

derisory adjective RIDICULOUS, contemptible, insulting, laughable, lousy (slang), ludicrous, outrageous, preposterous

derivation noun ORIGIN, beginning, foundation,

root, source

derive from verb COME FROM,
arise from, emanate from, flow
from, issue from, originate
from, proceed from, spring
from, stem from

derogatory adjective
DISPARAGING, belittling,
defamatory, offensive,
slighting, uncomplimentary,
unfavorable, unflattering

descend verb 1 MOVE DOWN,
drop, fall, go down, plummet,
plunge, sink, subside, tumble
2 SLOPE, dip, incline, slant
3 LOWER ONESELF, degenerate,
deteriorate, stoop 4 **be
descended** ORIGINATE, be
handed down, be passed
down, derive, issue, proceed,
spring 5 **descend on** ATTACK,
arrive, invade, raid, swoop

descent noun 1 COMING DOWN,
drop, fall, plunge, swoop
2 SLOPE, declivity, dip, drop,
incline, slant 3 ANCESTRY,
extraction, family tree,
genealogy, lineage, origin,
parentage 4 DECLINE,
degeneration, deterioration

describe verb 1 RELATE, depict,
explain, express, narrate,
portray, recount, report, tell
2 TRACE, delineate, draw, mark
out, outline

description noun 1 ACCOUNT,
depiction, explanation,
narrative, portrayal, report,
representation, sketch 2 KIND,
brand, category, class, order,
sort, type, variety

descriptive adjective GRAPHIC,
detailed, explanatory,
expressive, illustrative, pictorial,
picturesque, vivid

desert[1] noun WILDERNESS,
solitude, waste, wasteland,
wilds

desert[2] verb ABANDON, abscond,
forsake, jilt, leave, leave
stranded, maroon, quit, strand,
walk out on (informal)

deserted adjective ABANDONED,
derelict, desolate, empty,
forsaken, neglected,
unoccupied, vacant

deserter noun DEFECTOR,
absconder, escapee, fugitive,
renegade, runaway, traitor,
truant

desertion noun ABANDONMENT,
absconding, apostasy, betrayal,
defection, dereliction, escape,
evasion, flight, relinquishment

deserve verb MERIT, be entitled
to, be worthy of, earn, justify,
rate, warrant

deserved adjective WELL-EARNED,
due, earned, fitting, justified,
merited, proper, rightful,
warranted

deserving adjective WORTHY,
commendable, estimable,
laudable, meritorious,
praiseworthy, righteous

design verb 1 PLAN, draft, draw,
outline, sketch, trace 2 CREATE,
conceive, fabricate, fashion,
invent, originate, think up
3 INTEND, aim, mean, plan,
propose, purpose ▶ noun
4 PLAN, blueprint, draft,
drawing, model, outline,
scheme, sketch 5 ARRANGEMENT,
construction, form,
organization, pattern, shape,
style 6 INTENTION, aim, end,
goal, object, objective,
purpose, target

designate verb 1 NAME, call,

dub, entitle, label, style, term **2** APPOINT, assign, choose, delegate, depute, nominate, select

designation noun NAME, description, label, mark, title

designer noun CREATOR, architect, deviser, inventor, originator, planner

desirable adjective
1 WORTHWHILE, advantageous, advisable, beneficial, good, preferable, profitable, win-win (informal) **2** ATTRACTIVE, adorable, alluring, fetching, glamorous, seductive, sexy (informal)

desire verb **1** WANT, crave, hanker after, hope for, long for, set one's heart on, thirst for, wish for, yearn for ▶ noun **2** WISH, aspiration, craving, hankering, hope, longing, thirst, want **3** LUST, appetite, libido, passion

desist verb STOP, break off, cease, discontinue, end, forbear, leave off, pause, refrain from

desolate adjective **1** UNINHABITED, bare, barren, bleak, dreary, godforsaken, solitary, wild **2** MISERABLE, dejected, despondent, disconsolate, downcast, forlorn, gloomy, wretched ▶ verb **3** LAY WASTE, depopulate, despoil, destroy, devastate, lay low, pillage, plunder, ravage, ruin **4** DEJECT, depress, discourage, dishearten, dismay, distress, grieve

desolation noun **1** RUIN, destruction, devastation, havoc **2** BLEAKNESS, barrenness,

isolation, solitude **3** MISERY, anguish, dejection, despair, distress, gloom, sadness, woe, wretchedness

despair noun **1** DESPONDENCY, anguish, dejection, depression, desperation, gloom, hopelessness, misery, wretchedness ▶ verb **2** LOSE HOPE, give up, lose heart

despairing adjective HOPELESS, dejected, desperate, despondent, disconsolate, frantic, grief-stricken, inconsolable, miserable, wretched

despatch see DISPATCH

desperado noun CRIMINAL, bandit, lawbreaker, outlaw, villain

desperate adjective **1** RECKLESS, audacious, daring, frantic, furious, risky **2** GRAVE, drastic, extreme, urgent

desperately adverb **1** GRAVELY, badly, dangerously, perilously, seriously, severely **2** HOPELESSLY, appallingly, fearfully, frightfully, shockingly

desperation noun
1 RECKLESSNESS, foolhardiness, frenzy, impetuosity, madness, rashness **2** MISERY, agony, anguish, despair, hopelessness, trouble, unhappiness, worry

despicable adjective CONTEMPTIBLE, detestable, disgraceful, hateful, lousy (slang), mean, scuzzy (slang), shameful, sordid, vile, worthless, wretched

despise verb LOOK DOWN ON, abhor, detest, loathe, revile, scorn

despite preposition IN SPITE OF,

against, even with, in the face of, in the teeth of, notwithstanding, regardless of, undeterred by

despondency noun DEJECTION, depression, despair, desperation, gloom, low spirits, melancholy, misery, sadness

despondent adjective DEJECTED, depressed, disconsolate, disheartened, dispirited, downhearted, glum, in despair, sad, sorrowful

despot noun TYRANT, autocrat, dictator, oppressor

despotic adjective TYRANNICAL, authoritarian, autocratic, dictatorial, domineering, imperious, oppressive

despotism noun TYRANNY, autocracy, dictatorship, oppression, totalitarianism

destination noun JOURNEY'S END, haven, resting-place, station, stop, terminus

destined adjective FATED, bound, certain, doomed, intended, meant, predestined

destiny noun FATE, doom, fortune, karma, kismet, lot, portion

destitute adjective PENNILESS, down and out, down on one's luck (informal), impoverished, indigent, insolvent, moneyless, penurious, poor, poverty-stricken

destroy verb RUIN, annihilate, crush, demolish, devastate, eradicate, shatter, wipe out, wreck

destruction noun RUIN, annihilation, demolition, devastation, eradication, extermination, havoc,

slaughter, wreckage

destructive adjective DAMAGING, calamitous, catastrophic, deadly, devastating, fatal, harmful, lethal, ruinous

detach verb SEPARATE, cut off, disconnect, disengage, divide, remove, sever, tear off, unfasten

detached adjective 1 SEPARATE, disconnected, discrete, unconnected 2 UNINVOLVED, disinterested, dispassionate, impartial, impersonal, neutral, objective, reserved, unbiased

detachment noun
1 INDIFFERENCE, aloofness, coolness, nonchalance, remoteness, unconcern
2 IMPARTIALITY, fairness, neutrality, objectivity 3 Military UNIT, body, force, party, patrol, squad, task force

detail noun 1 POINT, aspect, component, element, fact, factor, feature, particular, respect 2 FINE POINT, nicety, particular, triviality 3 Military PARTY, assignment, body, detachment, duty, fatigue, force, squad ▶ verb 4 LIST, catalog, enumerate, itemize, recite, recount, rehearse, relate, tabulate 5 APPOINT, allocate, assign, charge, commission, delegate, send

detailed adjective COMPREHENSIVE, blow-by-blow, exhaustive, full, intricate, minute, particular, thorough

detain verb 1 DELAY, check, hinder, hold up, impede, keep back, retard, slow up (or down) 2 HOLD, arrest, confine, intern, restrain

detect verb 1 NOTICE, ascertain,

identify, note, observe, perceive, recognize, spot
2 DISCOVER, find, track down, uncover, unmask

detective noun INVESTIGATOR, cop (slang), gumshoe (slang), private eye, private investigator, sleuth (informal)

detention noun IMPRISONMENT, confinement, custody, incarceration, quarantine

deter verb DISCOURAGE, dissuade, frighten, inhibit from, intimidate, prevent, put off, stop, talk out of

detergent noun CLEANER, cleanser

deteriorate verb DECLINE, degenerate, go downhill (informal), lower, slump, worsen

determination noun TENACITY, dedication, doggedness, fortitude, perseverance, persistence, resolve, single-mindedness, steadfastness, willpower

determine verb **1** SETTLE, conclude, decide, end, finish, ordain, regulate **2** FIND OUT, ascertain, detect, discover, learn, verify, work out **3** DECIDE, choose, elect, make up one's mind, resolve

determined adjective RESOLUTE, dogged, firm, intent, persevering, persistent, single-minded, steadfast, tenacious, unwavering

deterrent noun DISCOURAGEMENT, check, curb, disincentive, hindrance, impediment, obstacle, restraint

detest verb HATE, abhor, abominate, despise, dislike intensely, loathe, recoil from

detonate verb EXPLODE, blast,

blow up, discharge, set off, trigger

detour noun DIVERSION, bypass, circuitous or indirect route, roundabout way

detract verb LESSEN, devaluate, diminish, lower, reduce, take away from

detriment noun DAMAGE, disadvantage, disservice, harm, hurt, impairment, injury, loss

detrimental adjective DAMAGING, adverse, deleterious, destructive, disadvantageous, harmful, prejudicial, unfavorable

devastate verb DESTROY, demolish, lay waste, level, ravage, raze, ruin, sack, wreck

devastating adjective OVERWHELMING, cutting, overpowering, savage, trenchant, vitriolic, withering

devastation noun DESTRUCTION, demolition, desolation, havoc, ruin

develop verb **1** ADVANCE, evolve, flourish, grow, mature, progress, prosper, ripen **2** FORM, breed, establish, generate, invent, originate **3** EXPAND, amplify, augment, broaden, elaborate, enlarge, unfold, work out

development noun **1** GROWTH, advance, evolution, expansion, improvement, increase, progress, spread **2** EVENT, happening, incident, occurrence, result, turn of events, upshot

deviant adjective **1** PERVERTED, kinky (slang), sick (informal), twisted, warped ▶noun **2** PERVERT, freak, misfit

deviate verb DIFFER, depart,

diverge, stray, swerve, veer, wander

deviation noun DEPARTURE, digression, discrepancy, disparity, divergence, inconsistency, irregularity, shift, variation

device noun 1 GADGET, apparatus, appliance, contraption, implement, instrument, machine, tool 2 PLOY, gambit, maneuver, plan, scheme, stratagem, trick, wile

devil noun 1 **the Devil** SATAN, Beelzebub, Evil One, Lucifer, Mephistopheles, Prince of Darkness 2 BRUTE, beast, demon, fiend, monster, ogre, terror 3 SCAMP, rascal, rogue, scoundrel 4 PERSON, beggar, creature, thing, wretch

devilish adjective FIENDISH, atrocious, damnable, detestable, diabolical, hellish, infernal, satanic, wicked

devious adjective 1 SLY, calculating, deceitful, dishonest, double-dealing, insincere, scheming, surreptitious, underhand, wily 2 INDIRECT, circuitous, rambling, roundabout

devise verb WORK OUT, conceive, construct, contrive, design, dream up, formulate, invent, think up

devoid adjective LACKING, bereft, deficient, destitute, empty, free from, wanting, without

devote verb DEDICATE, allot, apply, assign, commit, give, pledge, reserve, set apart

devoted adjective DEDICATED, ardent, committed, constant,

devout, faithful, loyal, staunch, steadfast, true

devotee noun ENTHUSIAST, adherent, admirer, aficionado, buff (informal), disciple, fan, fanatic, follower, supporter

devotion noun 1 DEDICATION, adherence, allegiance, commitment, constancy, faithfulness, fidelity, loyalty 2 LOVE, affection, attachment, fondness, passion 3 DEVOUTNESS, godliness, holiness, piety, reverence, spirituality 4 **devotions** PRAYERS, church service, divine office, religious observance

devour verb 1 EAT, chow down (slang), consume, gobble, gulp, guzzle, polish off (informal), swallow, wolf 2 DESTROY, annihilate, consume, ravage, waste, wipe out 3 ENJOY, read compulsively or voraciously, take in

devout adjective RELIGIOUS, godly, holy, orthodox, pious, prayerful, pure, reverent, saintly

dexterity noun 1 SKILL, adroitness, deftness, expertise, finesse, nimbleness, proficiency, touch 2 CLEVERNESS, ability, aptitude, ingenuity

diabolical adjective Informal DREADFUL, abysmal, appalling, atrocious, hellish, outrageous, shocking, terrible

diagnose verb IDENTIFY, analyze, determine, distinguish, interpret, pinpoint, pronounce, recognize

diagnosis noun 1 EXAMINATION, analysis, investigation, scrutiny 2 OPINION, conclusion, interpretation, pronouncement

diagonal *adjective* SLANTING, angled, cross, crossways, crosswise, oblique

diagonally *adverb* ASLANT, at an angle, cornerwise, crosswise, obliquely

diagram *noun* PLAN, chart, drawing, figure, graph, representation, sketch

dialect *noun* LANGUAGE, brogue, idiom, jargon, patois, provincialism, speech, vernacular

dialogue *noun* CONVERSATION, communication, conference, discourse, discussion

diary *noun* JOURNAL, appointment book, chronicle, daily record, engagement book, Filofax (*Trademark*)

dictate *verb* 1 SPEAK, read out, say, utter 2 ORDER, command, decree, demand, direct, impose, lay down the law, pronounce ▶ *noun* 3 COMMAND, decree, demand, direction, edict, fiat, injunction, order 4 PRINCIPLE, code, law, rule

dictator *noun* ABSOLUTE RULER, autocrat, despot, oppressor, tyrant

dictatorial *adjective* 1 ABSOLUTE, arbitrary, autocratic, despotic, totalitarian, tyrannical, unlimited, unrestricted 2 DOMINEERING, authoritarian, bossy (*informal*), imperious, oppressive, overbearing

dictatorship *noun* ABSOLUTE RULE, absolutism, authoritarianism, autocracy, despotism, totalitarianism, tyranny

diction *noun* PRONUNCIATION, articulation, delivery, elocution, enunciation, fluency, inflection, intonation, speech

dictionary *noun* WORDBOOK, glossary, lexicon, vocabulary

die *verb* 1 PASS AWAY, breathe one's last, croak (*slang*), expire, give up the ghost, kick the bucket (*slang*), perish, snuff it (*slang*) 2 DWINDLE, decay, decline, fade, sink, subside, wane, wilt, wither 3 STOP, break down, fade out or away, fail, fizzle out, halt, lose power, peter out, run down 4 be dying LONG, ache, be eager, desire, hunger, pine for, yearn

die-hard *noun* REACTIONARY, fanatic, old fogey, stick-in-the-mud (*informal*)

diet¹ *noun* 1 FOOD, fare, nourishment, nutriment, provisions, rations, sustenance, victuals 2 REGIME, abstinence, fast, regimen ▶ *verb* 3 SLIM, abstain, eat sparingly, fast, lose weight

diet² *noun* COUNCIL, chamber, congress, convention, legislature, meeting, parliament

differ *verb* 1 BE DISSIMILAR, contradict, contrast, depart from, diverge, run counter to, stand apart, vary 2 DISAGREE, clash, contend, debate, demur, dispute, dissent, oppose, take exception, take issue

difference *noun* 1 DISSIMILARITY, alteration, change, contrast, discrepancy, disparity, diversity, variation, variety 2 DISAGREEMENT, argument, clash, conflict, contretemps, debate, dispute, quarrel 3 REMAINDER, balance, rest, result

different *adjective* 1 UNLIKE, altered, changed, contrasting, disparate, dissimilar, divergent, inconsistent, opposed **2** VARIOUS, assorted, diverse, miscellaneous, sundry, varied **3** UNUSUAL, atypical, distinctive, extraordinary, peculiar, singular, special, strange, uncommon

differentiate verb **1** DISTINGUISH, contrast, discriminate, make a distinction, mark off, separate, set off or apart, tell apart **2** MAKE DIFFERENT, adapt, alter, change, convert, modify, transform

difficult adjective **1** HARD, arduous, demanding, formidable, laborious, onerous, strenuous, uphill **2** PROBLEMATICAL, abstruse, baffling, complex, complicated, intricate, involved, knotty, obscure **3** HARD TO PLEASE, demanding, fastidious, fussy, perverse, refractory, unaccommodating

difficulty noun **1** LABORIOUSNESS, arduousness, awkwardness, hardship, strain, strenuousness, tribulation **2** PREDICAMENT, dilemma, embarrassment, hot water (informal), jam (informal), mess, plight, quandary, trouble **3** PROBLEM, complication, hindrance, hurdle, impediment, obstacle, pitfall, snag, stumbling block

diffidence noun SHYNESS, bashfulness, hesitancy, insecurity, modesty, reserve, self-consciousness, timidity

diffident adjective SHY, bashful, doubtful, hesitant, insecure, modest, reserved, self-conscious, timid, unassertive, unassuming

dig verb **1** EXCAVATE, burrow, delve, hollow out, mine, quarry, scoop, tunnel **2** INVESTIGATE, delve, dig down, go into, probe, research, search **3** (with out or up) FIND, discover, expose, uncover, unearth, uproot **4** POKE, drive, jab, prod, punch, thrust ▶ noun **5** POKE, jab, prod, punch, thrust **6** CUTTING REMARK, barb, gibe, insult, jeer, sneer, taunt, wisecrack (informal)

digest verb **1** INGEST, absorb, assimilate, dissolve, incorporate **2** TAKE IN, absorb, consider, contemplate, grasp, study, understand ▶ noun **3** SUMMARY, abridgment, abstract, epitome, précis, résumé, synopsis

digestion noun INGESTION, absorption, assimilation, conversion, incorporation, transformation

dignified adjective DISTINGUISHED, formal, grave, imposing, noble, reserved, solemn, stately

dignitary noun PUBLIC FIGURE, high-up (informal), notable, personage, pillar of society, V.I.P., worthy

dignity noun **1** DECORUM, courtliness, grandeur, gravity, loftiness, majesty, nobility, solemnity, stateliness **2** HONOR, eminence, importance, rank, respectability, standing, status **3** SELF-IMPORTANCE, pride, self-esteem, self-respect

digress verb WANDER, depart, deviate, diverge, drift, get off the point or subject, go off at a tangent, ramble, stray

digression noun DEPARTURE, aside, detour, deviation,

divergence, diversion, straying, wandering

dilapidated *adjective* RUINED, broken-down, crumbling, decrepit, in ruins, ramshackle, rickety, run-down, tumbledown

dilate *verb* ENLARGE, broaden, expand, puff out, stretch, swell, widen

dilatory *adjective* TIME-WASTING, delaying, lingering, procrastinating, slow, sluggish, tardy, tarrying

dilemma *noun* PREDICAMENT, difficulty, mess, plight, problem, puzzle, quandary, spot (*informal*)

dilettante *noun* AMATEUR, aesthete, dabbler, trifler

diligence *noun* APPLICATION, attention, care, industry, laboriousness, perseverance

diligent *adjective* HARD-WORKING, assiduous, attentive, careful, conscientious, industrious, painstaking, persistent, studious, tireless

dilute *verb* 1 WATER DOWN, adulterate, cut, make thinner, thin (out), weaken 2 REDUCE, attenuate, decrease, diffuse, diminish, lessen, mitigate, temper, weaken

dim *adjective* 1 POORLY LIT, cloudy, dark, gray, overcast, shadowy, tenebrous 2 UNCLEAR, bleary, blurred, faint, fuzzy, ill-defined, indistinct, obscured, shadowy 3 take a dim view DISAPPROVE, be displeased, be skeptical, look askance, reject, suspect, take exception, view with disfavor ▶ *verb* 4 DULL, blur, cloud, darken, fade, obscure

dimension *noun* (often plural) MEASUREMENT, amplitude, bulk, capacity, extent, proportions, size, volume

diminish *verb* 1 DECREASE, curtail, cut, lessen, lower, reduce, shrink 2 DWINDLE, decline, die out, recede, subside, wane

diminutive *adjective* SMALL, little, mini, miniature, minute, petite, tiny, undersized

din *noun* 1 NOISE, clamor, clatter, commotion, crash, pandemonium, racket, row, uproar ▶ *verb* 2 **din (something) into (someone)** INSTILL, drum into, go on at, hammer into, inculcate, instruct, teach

dine *verb* EAT, banquet, chow down (*slang*), feast, lunch, sup

dingy *adjective* DULL, dark, dim, drab, dreary, gloomy, murky, obscure, somber

dinner *noun* MEAL, banquet, feast, main meal, repast, spread (*informal*)

dip *verb* 1 PLUNGE, bathe, douse, duck, dunk, immerse 2 SLOPE, decline, descend, drop (down), fall, lower, sink, subside ▶ *noun* 3 PLUNGE, douche, drenching, ducking, immersion, soaking 4 BATHE, dive, plunge, swim 5 HOLLOW, basin, concavity, depression, hole, incline, slope 6 DROP, decline, fall, lowering, sag, slip, slump

dip into *verb* SAMPLE, browse, glance at, peruse, skim

diplomacy *noun* 1 STATESMANSHIP, international negotiation, statecraft 2 TACT, artfulness, craft, delicacy, discretion, finesse, savoir-faire, skill, subtlety

diplomat noun NEGOTIATOR, conciliator, go-between, mediator, moderator, politician, tactician

diplomatic adjective TACTFUL, adept, discreet, polite, politic, prudent, sensitive, subtle

dire adjective 1 DISASTROUS, awful, calamitous, catastrophic, horrible, ruinous, terrible, woeful 2 DESPERATE, critical, crucial, drastic, extreme, now or never, pressing, urgent 3 GRIM, dismal, dreadful, fearful, gloomy, ominous, portentous

direct adjective 1 STRAIGHT, nonstop, not crooked, shortest, through, unbroken, uninterrupted 2 IMMEDIATE, face-to-face, first-hand, head-on, personal 3 HONEST, candid, frank, open, plain-spoken, straight, straightforward, upfront (informal) 4 EXPLICIT, absolute, blunt, categorical, downright, express, plain, point-blank, unambiguous, unequivocal ▶verb 5 CONTROL, conduct, guide, handle, lead, manage, oversee, run, supervise 6 ORDER, bid, charge, command, demand, dictate, instruct 7 GUIDE, indicate, lead, point in the direction of, point the way, show 8 ADDRESS, label, mail, route, send 9 AIM, focus, level, point, train

direction noun 1 WAY, aim, bearing, course, line, path, road, route, track 2 MANAGEMENT, administration, charge, command, control, guidance, leadership, order, supervision

directions plural noun INSTRUCTIONS, briefing, guidance, guidelines, plan, recommendation, regulations

directive noun ORDER, command, decree, edict, injunction, instruction, mandate, regulation, ruling

directly adverb 1 STRAIGHT, by the shortest route, exactly, in a beeline, precisely, unswervingly, without deviation 2 HONESTLY, openly, plainly, point-blank, straightforwardly, truthfully, unequivocally 3 AT ONCE, as soon as possible, forthwith, immediately, promptly, right away, straightaway

director noun CONTROLLER, administrator, chief, executive, governor, head, leader, manager, supervisor

dirge noun LAMENT, dead march, elegy, funeral song, requiem, threnody

dirt noun 1 FILTH, dust, grime, impurity, muck, mud 2 SOIL, clay, earth, loam 3 OBSCENITY, indecency, pornography, sleaze, smut

dirty adjective 1 FILTHY, foul, grimy, grubby, messy, mucky, muddy, polluted, scuzzy (slang), soiled, unclean 2 DISHONEST, crooked, fraudulent, illegal, lowdown (slang), scuzzy (slang), treacherous, unfair, unscrupulous, unsporting 3 OBSCENE, blue, indecent, pornographic, salacious, scuzzy (slang), sleazy, smutty, X-rated 4 As in **a dirty look** ANGRY, annoyed, bitter, choked, indignant, offended, resentful, scorching ▶ verb **5** SOIL, blacken, defile, foul, muddy, pollute, smirch, spoil, stain

disability noun **1** HANDICAP, affliction, ailment, complaint, defect, disorder, impairment, infirmity, malady **2** INCAPACITY, inability, unfitness

disable verb **1** HANDICAP, cripple, damage, enfeeble, immobilize, impair, incapacitate, paralyze **2** DISQUALIFY, invalidate, render or declare incapable

disabled adjective HANDICAPPED, challenged (informal), crippled, incapacitated, infirm, lame, paralyzed, weakened

disadvantage noun **1** HARM, damage, detriment, disservice, hurt, injury, loss, prejudice **2** DRAWBACK, downside, handicap, inconvenience, nuisance, snag, trouble

disagree verb **1** DIFFER (IN OPINION), argue, clash, cross swords, dispute, dissent, object, quarrel, take issue with **2** CONFLICT, be dissimilar, contradict, counter, differ, diverge, run counter to, vary **3** MAKE ILL, bother, discomfort, distress, hurt, nauseate, sicken, trouble, upset

disagreeable adjective **1** NASTY, disgusting, displeasing, distasteful, objectionable, obnoxious, offensive, repugnant, repulsive, scuzzy (slang), unpleasant **2** RUDE, bad-tempered, churlish, difficult, disobliging, irritable, surly, unpleasant

disagreement noun

1 INCOMPATIBILITY, difference, discrepancy, disparity, dissimilarity, divergence, incongruity, variance **2** ARGUMENT, altercation, clash, conflict, dispute, dissent, quarrel, row, squabble

disallow verb REJECT, disavow, dismiss, disown, rebuff, refuse, repudiate

disappear verb **1** VANISH, evanesce, fade away, pass, recede **2** CEASE, die out, dissolve, evaporate, leave no trace, melt away, pass away, perish

disappearance noun VANISHING, departure, eclipse, evanescence, evaporation, going, melting, passing

disappoint verb LET DOWN, disenchant, disgruntle, dishearten, disillusion, dismay, dissatisfy, fail

disappointed adjective LET DOWN, cast down, despondent, discouraged, disenchanted, disgruntled, dissatisfied, downhearted, frustrated

disappointing adjective UNSATISFACTORY, depressing, disconcerting, discouraging, inadequate, insufficient, lousy (slang), sad, sorry

disappointment noun **1** FRUSTRATION, chagrin, discontent, discouragement, disenchantment, disillusionment, dissatisfaction, regret **2** LETDOWN, blow, calamity, choker (informal), misfortune, setback

disapproval noun DISPLEASURE, censure, condemnation, criticism, denunciation, dissatisfaction, objection, reproach

disapprove verb CONDEMN, deplore, dislike, find unacceptable, frown on, look down one's nose at (*informal*), object to, reject, take a dim view of, take exception to

disarm verb 1 RENDER DEFENSELESS, disable 2 WIN OVER, persuade, set at ease 3 DEMILITARIZE, deactivate, demobilize, disband

disarmament noun ARMS REDUCTION, arms limitation, de-escalation, demilitarization, demobilization

disarming adjective CHARMING, irresistible, likable or likeable, persuasive, winning

disarrange verb DISORDER, confuse, disorganize, disturb, jumble (up), mess (up), scatter, shake (up), shuffle

disarray noun 1 CONFUSION, disorder, disorganization, disunity, indiscipline, unruliness 2 UNTIDINESS, chaos, clutter, jumble, mess, muddle, shambles

disaster noun CATASTROPHE, adversity, calamity, cataclysm, misfortune, ruin, tragedy, trouble

disastrous adjective TERRIBLE, calamitous, cataclysmic, catastrophic, devastating, fatal, ruinous, tragic

disbelief noun SKEPTICISM, distrust, doubt, dubiety, incredulity, mistrust, unbelief

discard verb GET RID OF, abandon, cast aside, dispense with, dispose of, drop, dump (*informal*), jettison, reject, throw away or out

discharge verb 1 RELEASE, allow to go, clear, free, liberate, pardon, set free 2 DISMISS, cashier, discard, expel, fire (*informal*), oust, remove, sack (*informal*) 3 FIRE, detonate, explode, let loose (*informal*), let off, set off, shoot 4 POUR FORTH, dispense, emit, exude, give off, leak, ooze, release 5 CARRY OUT, accomplish, do, execute, fulfill, observe, perform 6 PAY, clear, honor, meet, relieve, satisfy, settle, square up ▸ noun 7 RELEASE, acquittal, clearance, liberation, pardon 8 DISMISSAL, demobilization, ejection 9 FIRING, blast, burst, detonation, explosion, report, salvo, shot, volley 10 EMISSION, excretion, ooze, pus, secretion, seepage, suppuration

disciple noun FOLLOWER, adherent, apostle, devotee, pupil, student, supporter

disciplinarian noun AUTHORITARIAN, despot, martinet, stickler, taskmaster, tyrant

discipline noun 1 TRAINING, drill, exercise, method, practice, regimen, regulation 2 PUNISHMENT, castigation, chastisement, correction 3 SELF-CONTROL, conduct, control, orderliness, regulation, restraint, strictness 4 FIELD OF STUDY, area, branch of knowledge, course, curriculum, speciality, subject ▸ verb 5 TRAIN, bring up, drill, educate, exercise, prepare 6 PUNISH, bring to book, castigate, chasten, chastise, correct, penalize, reprimand, reprove

disclose verb 1 MAKE KNOWN,

broadcast, communicate, confess, divulge, let slip, publish, relate, reveal **2** SHOW, bring to light, expose, lay bare, reveal, uncover, unveil

disclosure noun REVELATION, acknowledgment, admission, announcement, confession, declaration, divulgence, leak, publication

discolor verb STAIN, fade, mark, soil, streak, tarnish, tinge

discomfort noun **1** PAIN, ache, hurt, irritation, malaise, soreness **2** UNEASINESS, annoyance, distress, hardship, irritation, nuisance, trouble

disconcert verb DISTURB, faze, fluster, perturb, rattle (informal), take aback, unsettle, upset, worry

disconcerting adjective DISTURBING, alarming, awkward, bewildering, confusing, distracting, embarrassing, perplexing, upsetting

disconnect verb CUT OFF, detach, disengage, divide, part, separate, sever, take apart, uncouple

disconnected adjective ILLOGICAL, confused, disjointed, incoherent, jumbled, mixed-up, rambling, unintelligible

disconsolate adjective INCONSOLABLE, crushed, dejected, desolate, forlorn, grief-stricken, heartbroken, miserable, wretched

discontent noun DISSATISFACTION, displeasure, envy, regret, restlessness, uneasiness, unhappiness

discontented adjective

DISSATISFIED, disaffected, disgruntled, displeased, exasperated, fed up, unhappy, vexed

discontinue verb STOP, abandon, break off, cease, drop, end, give up, quit, suspend, terminate

discord noun **1** DISAGREEMENT, conflict, dissension, disunity, division, friction, incompatibility, strife **2** DISHARMONY, cacophony, din, dissonance, harshness, jarring, racket, tumult

discordant adjective **1** DISAGREEING, at odds, clashing, conflicting, contradictory, contrary, different, incompatible **2** INHARMONIOUS, cacophonous, dissonant, grating, harsh, jarring, shrill, strident

discount verb **1** LEAVE OUT, brush off (slang), disbelieve, disregard, ignore, overlook, pass over **2** DEDUCT, lower, mark down, reduce, take off ▶ noun **3** DEDUCTION, concession, cut, rebate, reduction

discourage verb **1** DISHEARTEN, dampen, deject, demoralize, depress, dispirit, intimidate, overawe, put a damper on **2** PUT OFF, deter, dissuade, inhibit, prevent, talk out of

discouraged adjective PUT OFF, crestfallen, deterred, disheartened, dismayed, dispirited, downcast, down in the mouth, glum

discouragement noun **1** LOSS OF CONFIDENCE, dejection, depression, despair, despondency, disappointment,

dismay, downheartedness
2 DETERRENT, damper,
disincentive, hindrance,
impediment, obstacle,
opposition, setback

discouraging adjective
DISHEARTENING, dampening,
daunting, depressing,
disappointing, dispiriting,
unfavorable

discourse noun **1** CONVERSATION,
chat, communication,
dialogue, discussion, seminar,
speech, talk **2** SPEECH,
dissertation, essay, homily,
lecture, oration, sermon,
treatise ▶ verb **3** HOLD FORTH,
expatiate, speak, talk

discourteous adjective RUDE,
bad-mannered, boorish,
disrespectful, ill-mannered,
impolite, insolent, offhand,
ungentlemanly, ungracious

discourtesy noun **1** RUDENESS,
bad manners, disrespectfulness,
impertinence, impoliteness,
incivility, insolence **2** INSULT,
affront, cold shoulder, kick in
the teeth (slang), rebuff, slight,
snub

discover verb **1** FIND, come
across, come upon, dig up,
locate, turn up, uncover,
unearth **2** FIND OUT, ascertain,
detect, learn, notice, perceive,
realize, recognize, uncover

discovery noun **1** FINDING,
detection, disclosure,
exploration, location,
revelation, uncovering
2 BREAKTHROUGH, find,
innovation, invention, secret

discredit verb **1** DISGRACE, bring
into disrepute, defame,
dishonor, disparage, slander,

smear, vilify **2** DOUBT,
challenge, deny, disbelieve,
discount, dispute, distrust,
mistrust, question ▶ noun
3 DISGRACE, dishonor, disrepute,
ignominy, ill-repute, scandal,
shame, stigma

discreditable adjective
DISGRACEFUL, dishonorable,
ignominious, reprehensible,
scandalous, shameful, unworthy

discreet adjective TACTFUL,
careful, cautious, circumspect,
considerate, diplomatic,
guarded, judicious, prudent,
wary

discrepancy noun DISAGREEMENT,
conflict, contradiction,
difference, disparity,
divergence, incongruity,
inconsistency, variation

discretion noun **1** TACT,
carefulness, caution,
consideration, diplomacy,
judiciousness, prudence,
wariness **2** CHOICE, inclination,
pleasure, preference, volition,
will

discriminate verb **1** SHOW
PREJUDICE, favor, show bias,
single out, treat as inferior,
treat differently, victimize
2 DIFFERENTIATE, distinguish, draw
a distinction, segregate,
separate, tell the difference

discriminating adjective
DISCERNING, cultivated,
fastidious, particular, refined,
selective, tasteful

discrimination noun **1** PREJUDICE,
bias, bigotry, favoritism,
intolerance, unfairness
2 DISCERNMENT, judgment,
perception, refinement,
subtlety, taste

discuss verb TALK ABOUT, argue, confer, consider, converse, debate, deliberate, examine

discussion noun TALK, analysis, argument, conference, consultation, conversation, debate, deliberation, dialogue, discourse, exchange

disdain noun 1 CONTEMPT, arrogance, derision, haughtiness, scorn, superciliousness ▶ verb 2 SCORN, deride, disregard, look down on, reject, slight, sneer at, spurn

disdainful adjective CONTEMPTUOUS, aloof, arrogant, derisive, haughty, proud, scornful, sneering, supercilious, superior

disease noun ILLNESS, affliction, ailment, complaint, condition, disorder, infection, infirmity, malady, sickness

diseased adjective SICK, ailing, infected, rotten, sickly, unhealthy, unsound, unwell, unwholesome

disembark verb LAND, alight, arrive, get off, go ashore, step out of

disenchanted adjective DISILLUSIONED, cynical, disappointed, indifferent, jaundiced, let down, sick of, soured

disenchantment noun DISILLUSIONMENT, disappointment, disillusion, rude awakening

disengage verb RELEASE, disentangle, extricate, free, loosen, set free, unloose, untie

disentangle verb UNTANGLE, disconnect, disengage, extricate, free, loose, unravel

disfavor noun DISAPPROVAL, disapprobation, dislike, displeasure

disfigure verb DAMAGE, blemish, deface, deform, distort, mar, mutilate, scar

disgorge verb VOMIT, discharge, eject, empty, expel

disgrace noun 1 SHAME, degradation, dishonor, disrepute, ignominy, infamy, odium, opprobrium 2 STAIN, blemish, blot, reproach, scandal, slur, stigma ▶ verb 3 BRING SHAME UPON, degrade, discredit, dishonor, humiliate, shame, sully, taint

disgraceful adjective SHAMEFUL, contemptible, detestable, dishonorable, disreputable, ignominious, lousy (slang), scandalous, shocking, unworthy

disgruntled adjective DISCONTENTED, annoyed, displeased, dissatisfied, grumpy, irritated, peeved, put out, vexed

disguise verb 1 HIDE, camouflage, cloak, conceal, cover, mask, screen, shroud, veil 2 MISREPRESENT, fake, falsify ▶ noun 3 COSTUME, camouflage, cover, mask, screen, veil 4 FAÇADE, deception, dissimulation, front, pretense, semblance, trickery, veneer

disguised adjective IN DISGUISE, camouflaged, covert, fake, false, feigned, incognito, masked, undercover

disgust noun 1 LOATHING, abhorrence, aversion, dislike, distaste, hatred, nausea, repugnance, repulsion, revulsion ▶ verb 2 SICKEN, displease, nauseate, offend, put off, repel, revolt

disgusted adjective SICKENED, appalled, nauseated, offended, repulsed, scandalized

disgusting adjective SICKENING, foul, gross, loathsome, nauseating, offensive, repellent, repugnant, revolting

dish noun 1 BOWL, plate, platter, salver 2 FOOD, fare, recipe

dishearten verb DISCOURAGE, cast down, deject, depress, deter, dismay, dispirit, put a damper on

disheveled adjective UNTIDY, bedraggled, disordered, messy, ruffled, rumpled, tousled, uncombed, unkempt

dishonest adjective DECEITFUL, bent (slang), cheating, corrupt, crooked (informal), disreputable, double-dealing, false, lying, treacherous

dishonesty noun DECEIT, cheating, chicanery, corruption, fraud, treachery, trickery, unscrupulousness

dishonor verb 1 SHAME, debase, debauch, defame, degrade, discredit, disgrace, sully ▶noun 2 SHAME, discredit, disgrace, disrepute, ignominy, infamy, obloquy, reproach, scandal 3 INSULT, abuse, affront, discourtesy, indignity, offense, outrage, sacrilege, slight

dishonorable adjective 1 SHAMEFUL, contemptible, despicable, discreditable, disgraceful, ignominious, infamous, lousy (slang), scandalous, scuzzy (slang) 2 UNTRUSTWORTHY, corrupt, disreputable, shameless,

treacherous, unprincipled, unscrupulous

disillusioned adjective DISENCHANTED, disabused, disappointed, enlightened, undeceived

disinclination noun RELUCTANCE, aversion, dislike, hesitance, objection, opposition, repugnance, resistance, unwillingness

disinclined adjective RELUCTANT, averse, hesitating, loath, not in the mood, opposed, resistant, unwilling

disinfect verb STERILIZE, clean, cleanse, decontaminate, deodorize, fumigate, purify, sanitize

disinfectant noun ANTISEPTIC, germicide, sterilizer

disinherit verb Law CUT OFF, disown, dispossess, oust, repudiate

disintegrate verb BREAK UP, break apart, crumble, fall apart, go to pieces, separate, shatter, splinter

disinterest noun IMPARTIALITY, detachment, fairness, neutrality

disinterested adjective IMPARTIAL, detached, dispassionate, even-handed, impersonal, neutral, objective, unbiased, unprejudiced

disjointed adjective INCOHERENT, confused, disconnected, disordered, rambling

dislike verb 1 BE AVERSE TO, despise, detest, disapprove, hate, loathe, not be able to bear or abide or stand, object to, take a dim view of ▶noun 2 AVERSION, animosity, antipathy, disapproval, disinclination, displeasure, distaste, enmity, hostility, repugnance

dislodge verb DISPLACE, disturb, extricate, force out, knock loose, oust, remove, uproot

disloyal adjective TREACHEROUS, faithless, false, subversive, traitorous, two-faced, unfaithful, untrustworthy

disloyalty noun TREACHERY, breach of trust, deceitfulness, double-dealing, falseness, inconstancy, infidelity, treason, unfaithfulness

dismal adjective GLOOMY, bleak, cheerless, dark, depressing, discouraging, dreary, forlorn, somber, wretched

dismantle verb TAKE APART, demolish, disassemble, strip, take to pieces

dismay verb 1 ALARM, appall, distress, frighten, horrify, paralyze, scare, terrify, unnerve 2 DISAPPOINT, daunt, discourage, dishearten, disillusion, dispirit, put off ▶ noun 3 ALARM, anxiety, apprehension, consternation, dread, fear, horror, trepidation 4 DISAPPOINTMENT, chagrin, discouragement, disillusionment

dismember verb CUT INTO PIECES, amputate, dissect, mutilate, sever

dismiss verb 1 SACK (informal), ax (informal), cashier, discharge, fire (informal), give notice to, give (someone) their marching orders, lay off, remove 2 LET GO, disperse, dissolve, free, release, send away 3 PUT OUT OF ONE'S MIND, banish, discard, dispel, disregard, lay aside, reject,

set aside

dismissal noun THE SACK (informal), expulsion, marching orders (informal), notice, removal, the boot (slang)

disobedience noun DEFIANCE, indiscipline, insubordination, mutiny, noncompliance, nonobservance, recalcitrance, revolt, unruliness, waywardness

disobedient adjective DEFIANT, contrary, disorderly, insubordinate, intractable, naughty, refractory, undisciplined, unruly, wayward

disobey verb REFUSE TO OBEY, contravene, defy, disregard, flout, ignore, infringe, rebel, violate

disorder noun 1 UNTIDINESS, chaos, clutter, confusion, disarray, jumble, mess, muddle, shambles 2 DISTURBANCE, commotion, riot, turmoil, unrest, unruliness, uproar 3 ILLNESS, affliction, ailment, complaint, disease, malady, sickness

disorderly adjective 1 UNTIDY, chaotic, confused, disorganized, jumbled, messy 2 UNRULY, disruptive, indisciplined, lawless, riotous, rowdy, tumultuous, turbulent, ungovernable

disorganized adjective MUDDLED, chaotic, confused, disordered, haphazard, jumbled, unsystematic

disown verb DENY, cast off, disavow, disclaim, reject, renounce, repudiate

disparage verb RUN DOWN, belittle, denigrate, deprecate, deride, malign, put down, ridicule, slander, vilify

dispassionate adjective
1 UNEMOTIONAL, calm, collected, composed, cool, imperturbable, serene, unruffled **2** OBJECTIVE, detached, disinterested, fair, impartial, impersonal, neutral, unbiased, unprejudiced

dispatch, despatch verb
1 SEND, consign, dismiss, hasten **2** CARRY OUT, discharge, dispose of, finish, perform, settle **3** MURDER, assassinate, execute, kill, slaughter, slay ▸noun **4** MESSAGE, account, bulletin, communication, communiqué, news, report, story

dispel verb DRIVE AWAY, banish, chase away, dismiss, disperse, eliminate, expel

dispense verb **1** DISTRIBUTE, allocate, allot, apportion, assign, deal out, dole out, share **2** PREPARE, measure, mix, supply **3** ADMINISTER, apply, carry out, discharge, enforce, execute, implement, operate **4 dispense with: a** DO AWAY WITH, abolish, brush aside, cancel, dispose of, get rid of **b** DO WITHOUT, abstain from, forgo, give up, relinquish

disperse verb **1** SCATTER, broadcast, diffuse, disseminate, distribute, spread, strew **2** BREAK UP, disband, dissolve, scatter, separate

dispirited adjective DISHEARTENED, crestfallen, dejected, depressed, despondent, discouraged, downcast, gloomy, glum, sad

displace verb **1** MOVE, disturb, misplace, shift, transpose **2** REPLACE, oust, succeed, supersede, supplant, take the place of

display verb **1** SHOW, demonstrate, disclose, exhibit, expose, manifest, present, reveal **2** SHOW OFF, flaunt, flourish, parade, vaunt ▸noun **3** EXHIBITION, array, demonstration, presentation, revelation, show **4** SHOW, flourish, ostentation, pageant, parade, pomp, spectacle

displease verb ANNOY, anger, irk, irritate, offend, pique, put out, upset, vex

displeasure noun ANNOYANCE, anger, disapproval, dissatisfaction, distaste, indignation, irritation, resentment

disposable adjective
1 THROWAWAY, biodegradable, nonreturnable **2** AVAILABLE, consumable, expendable

disposal noun **1** THROWING AWAY, discarding, dumping (informal), ejection, jettisoning, removal, riddance, scrapping **2 at one's disposal** AVAILABLE, at one's service, consumable, expendable, free for use

dispose verb ARRANGE, array, distribute, group, marshal, order, place, put

dispose of verb **1** GET RID OF, destroy, discard, dump (informal), jettison, scrap, throw out or away, unload **2** DEAL WITH, decide, determine, end, finish with, settle

disposition noun **1** CHARACTER, constitution, make-up, nature, spirit, temper, temperament

2 TENDENCY, bent, bias, habit, inclination, leaning, proclivity, propensity **3** ARRANGEMENT, classification, distribution, grouping, ordering, organization, placement

disproportion noun INEQUALITY, asymmetry, discrepancy, disparity, imbalance, lopsidedness, unevenness

disproportionate adjective UNEQUAL, excessive, inordinate, out of proportion, unbalanced, uneven, unreasonable

disprove verb PROVE FALSE, contradict, discredit, expose, give the lie to, invalidate, negate, rebut, refute

dispute noun **1** DISAGREEMENT, altercation, argument, conflict, feud, quarrel **2** ARGUMENT, contention, controversy, debate, discussion, dissension ▶ verb **3** DOUBT, challenge, contest, contradict, deny, impugn, question, rebut **4** ARGUE, clash, cross swords, debate, quarrel, squabble

disqualification noun BAN, elimination, exclusion, ineligibility, rejection

disqualified adjective INELIGIBLE, debarred, eliminated, knocked out, out of the running

disqualify verb BAN, debar, declare ineligible, preclude, prohibit, rule out

disquiet noun **1** UNEASINESS, alarm, anxiety, concern, disturbance, foreboding, nervousness, trepidation, worry ▶ verb **2** MAKE UNEASY, bother, concern, disturb, perturb, trouble, unsettle, upset, worry

disregard verb **1** IGNORE, brush aside or away, discount, make light of, neglect, overlook, pass over, pay no heed to, turn a blind eye to ▶ noun **2** INATTENTION, contempt, disdain, disrespect, indifference, neglect, negligence, oversight

disrepair noun DILAPIDATION, collapse, decay, deterioration, ruination

disreputable adjective DISCREDITABLE, dishonorable, ignominious, infamous, louche, notorious, scandalous, shady (informal), shameful

disrepute noun DISCREDIT, disgrace, dishonor, ignominy, ill repute, infamy, obloquy, shame, unpopularity

disrespect noun CONTEMPT, cheek, impertinence, impoliteness, impudence, insolence, irreverence, lack of respect, rudeness, sauce

disrespectful adjective CONTEMPTUOUS, cheeky, discourteous, impertinent, impolite, impudent, insolent, insulting, irreverent, rude

disrupt verb **1** DISTURB, confuse, disorder, disorganize, spoil, upset **2** INTERRUPT, break up or into, interfere with, intrude, obstruct, unsettle, upset

disruption noun DISTURBANCE, interference, interruption, stoppage

disruptive adjective DISTURBING, disorderly, distracting, troublesome, unruly, unsettling, upsetting

dissatisfaction noun DISCONTENT, annoyance, chagrin, disappointment, displeasure, frustration, irritation, resentment, unhappiness

dissatisfied adjective
DISCONTENTED, disappointed, disgruntled, displeased, fed up, frustrated, unhappy, unsatisfied

dissect verb **1** CUT UP or APART, anatomize, dismember, lay open **2** ANALYZE, break down, explore, inspect, investigate, research, scrutinize, study

disseminate verb SPREAD, broadcast, circulate, disperse, distribute, publicize, scatter

dissension noun DISAGREEMENT, conflict, discord, dispute, dissent, friction, quarrel, row, strife

dissent verb **1** DISAGREE, differ, object, protest, refuse, withhold assent or approval
▶ noun **2** DISAGREEMENT, discord, dissension, objection, opposition, refusal, resistance

dissenter noun OBJECTOR, dissident, nonconformist

dissertation noun THESIS, critique, discourse, disquisition, essay, exposition, treatise

disservice noun BAD TURN, harm, injury, injustice, unkindness, wrong

dissident adjective **1** DISSENTING, disagreeing, discordant, heterodox, nonconformist
▶ noun **2** PROTESTER, agitator, dissenter, rebel

dissimilar adjective DIFFERENT, disparate, divergent, diverse, heterogeneous, unlike, unrelated, various

dissipate verb **1** SQUANDER, consume, deplete, expend, fritter away, run through, spend, waste **2** DISPERSE,

disappear, dispel, dissolve, drive away, evaporate, scatter, vanish

dissipation noun **1** DISPERSAL, disappearance, disintegration, dissolution, scattering, vanishing **2** DEBAUCHERY, dissoluteness, excess, extravagance, indulgence, intemperance, prodigality, profligacy, wantonness, waste

dissociate verb **1** BREAK AWAY, break off, part company, quit **2** SEPARATE, detach, disconnect, distance, divorce, isolate, segregate, set apart

dissolute adjective IMMORAL, debauched, degenerate, depraved, dissipated, profligate, rakish, wanton, wild

dissolution noun **1** BREAKING UP, disintegration, division, parting, separation **2** ADJOURNMENT, discontinuation, end, finish, suspension, termination

dissolve verb **1** MELT, deliquesce, fuse, liquefy, soften, thaw **2** END, break up, discontinue, suspend, terminate, wind up

dissuade verb DETER, advise against, discourage, put off, remonstrate, talk out of, warn

distance noun **1** SPACE, extent, gap, interval, length, range, span, stretch **2** RESERVE, aloofness, coldness, coolness, remoteness, restraint, stiffness **3 in the distance** FAR OFF, afar, far away, on the horizon, yonder ▶ verb **4 distance oneself** SEPARATE ONESELF, be distanced from, dissociate oneself

distant *adjective* **1** FAR-OFF, abroad, far, faraway, far-flung, outlying, out-of-the-way, remote **2** APART, dispersed, distinct, scattered, separate **3** RESERVED, aloof, cool, reticent, standoffish, unapproachable, unfriendly, withdrawn

distaste *noun* DISLIKE, aversion, disgust, horror, loathing, odium, repugnance, revulsion

distasteful *adjective* UNPLEASANT, disagreeable, objectionable, offensive, repugnant, repulsive, scuzzy (*slang*), uninviting, unpalatable, unsavory

distill *verb* EXTRACT, condense, purify, refine

distinct *adjective* **1** DIFFERENT, detached, discrete, individual, separate, unconnected **2** DEFINITE, clear, decided, evident, marked, noticeable, obvious, palpable, unmistakable, well-defined

distinction *noun*
1 DIFFERENTIATION, discernment, discrimination, perception, separation **2** FEATURE, characteristic, distinctiveness, individuality, mark, particularity, peculiarity, quality **3** DIFFERENCE, contrast, differential, division, separation **4** EXCELLENCE, eminence, fame, greatness, honor, importance, merit, prominence, repute

distinctive *adjective* CHARACTERISTIC, idiosyncratic, individual, original, peculiar, singular, special, typical, unique

distinctly *adverb* DEFINITELY, clearly, decidedly, markedly, noticeably, obviously, patently, plainly, unmistakably

distinguish *verb* **1** DIFFERENTIATE, ascertain, decide, determine, discriminate, judge, tell apart, tell the difference **2** CHARACTERIZE, categorize, classify, mark, separate, set apart, single out **3** MAKE OUT, discern, know, perceive, pick out, recognize, see, tell

distinguished *adjective* EMINENT, acclaimed, celebrated, famed, famous, illustrious, noted, renowned, well-known

distort *verb* **1** MISREPRESENT, bias, color, falsify, pervert, slant, twist **2** DEFORM, bend, buckle, contort, disfigure, misshape, twist, warp

distortion *noun*
1 MISREPRESENTATION, bias, falsification, perversion, slant **2** DEFORMITY, bend, buckle, contortion, crookedness, malformation, twist, warp

distract *verb* **1** DIVERT, draw away, sidetrack, turn aside **2** AMUSE, beguile, engross, entertain, occupy

distracted *adjective* AGITATED, at sea, flustered, harassed, in a flap (*informal*), perplexed, puzzled, troubled

distraction *noun* **1** DIVERSION, disturbance, interference, interruption **2** ENTERTAINMENT, amusement, diversion, pastime, recreation **3** AGITATION, bewilderment, commotion, confusion, discord, disorder, disturbance

distraught *adjective* FRANTIC, agitated, beside oneself, desperate, distracted, distressed, out of one's mind, overwrought, worked-up

distress noun **1** WORRY, grief, heartache, misery, pain, sorrow, suffering, torment, wretchedness **2** NEED, adversity, difficulties, hardship, misfortune, poverty, privation, trouble ▶ verb **3** UPSET, disturb, grieve, harass, sadden, torment, trouble, worry

distressed adjective **1** UPSET, agitated, distracted, distraught, tormented, troubled, worried, wretched **2** POVERTY-STRICKEN, destitute, down at heel, indigent, needy, poor, straitened

distressing adjective UPSETTING, disturbing, harrowing, heart-breaking, painful, sad, worrying

distribute verb **1** HAND OUT, circulate, convey, deliver, pass round **2** SHARE, allocate, allot, apportion, deal, dispense, dole out

distribution noun **1** DELIVERY, dealing, handling, mailing, transportation **2** SHARING, allocation, allotment, apportionment, division **3** CLASSIFICATION, arrangement, grouping, organization, placement

district noun AREA, locale, locality, neighborhood, parish, quarter, region, sector, vicinity

distrust verb **1** SUSPECT, be suspicious of, be wary of, disbelieve, doubt, mistrust, question, smell a rat (informal) ▶ noun **2** SUSPICION, disbelief, doubt, misgiving, mistrust, question, skepticism, wariness

disturb verb **1** INTERRUPT, bother, butt in on, disrupt, interfere with, intrude on, pester **2** UPSET, alarm, distress, fluster, harass, perturb, trouble, unnerve, unsettle, worry **3** MUDDLE, disarrange, disorder

disturbance noun **1** INTERRUPTION, annoyance, bother, distraction, intrusion **2** DISORDER, brawl, commotion, fracas, fray, rumpus

disturbed adjective **1** Psychiatry UNBALANCED, disordered, maladjusted, neurotic, troubled, upset **2** WORRIED, anxious, apprehensive, bothered, concerned, nervous, troubled, uneasy, upset, wired (slang)

disturbing adjective WORRYING, alarming, disconcerting, distressing, frightening, harrowing, startling, unsettling, upsetting

disuse noun NEGLECT, abandonment, decay, idleness

ditch noun **1** CHANNEL, drain, dyke, furrow, gully, moat, trench, watercourse ▶ verb **2** Slang GET RID OF, abandon, discard, dispose of, drop, dump (informal), jettison, scrap, throw out or overboard

dither verb **1** VACILLATE, hesitate, hum and haw, shillyshally (informal), teeter, waver ▶ noun **2** FLUTTER, flap (informal), fluster, tizzy (informal)

dive verb **1** PLUNGE, descend, dip, drop, duck, nose-dive, plummet, swoop ▶ noun **2** PLUNGE, jump, leap, lunge, nose dive, spring

diverge verb **1** SEPARATE, branch, divide, fork, part, split, spread **2** DEVIATE, depart, digress, meander, stray, turn aside, wander

diverse *adjective* **1** VARIOUS, assorted, manifold, miscellaneous, of every description, several, sundry, varied **2** DIFFERENT, discrete, disparate, dissimilar, distinct, divergent, separate, unlike, varying

diversify *verb* VARY, branch out, change, expand, have a finger in every pie, spread out

diversion *noun* PASTIME, amusement, distraction, entertainment, game, recreation, relaxation, sport

diversity *noun* DIFFERENCE, distinctiveness, diverseness, heterogeneity, multiplicity, range, variety

divert *verb* **1** REDIRECT, avert, deflect, switch, turn aside **2** DISTRACT, draw *or* lead away from, lead astray, sidetrack **3** ENTERTAIN, amuse, beguile, delight, gratify, regale

diverting *adjective* ENTERTAINING, amusing, beguiling, enjoyable, fun, humorous, pleasant

divide *verb* **1** SEPARATE, bisect, cut (up), part, partition, segregate, split **2** SHARE, allocate, allot, deal out, dispense, distribute **3** CAUSE TO DISAGREE, break up, come between, estrange, split

dividend *noun* BONUS, cut (*informal*), divvy (*informal*), extra, gain, plus, portion, share, surplus

divine *adjective* **1** HEAVENLY, angelic, celestial, godlike, holy, spiritual, superhuman, supernatural **2** SACRED,

consecrated, holy, religious, sanctified, spiritual **3** *Informal* WONDERFUL, beautiful, excellent, glorious, marvelous, perfect, splendid, superlative ▶ *verb* **4** INFER, apprehend, deduce, discern, guess, perceive, suppose, surmise

divinity *noun* **1** THEOLOGY, religion, religious studies **2** GOD *or* GODDESS, deity, guardian spirit, spirit **3** GODLINESS, deity, divine nature, holiness, sanctity

divisible *adjective* DIVIDABLE, separable, splittable

division *noun* **1** SEPARATION, cutting up, dividing, partition, splitting up **2** SHARING, allotment, apportionment, distribution **3** PART, branch, category, class, department, group, section **4** DISAGREEMENT, difference of opinion, discord, rupture, split, variance

divorce *noun* **1** SEPARATION, annulment, dissolution, split-up ▶ *verb* **2** SEPARATE, disconnect, dissociate, dissolve (*marriage*), divide, part, sever, split up

divulge *verb* MAKE KNOWN, confess, declare, disclose, let slip, proclaim, reveal, tell

dizzy *adjective* **1** GIDDY, faint, light-headed, off balance, reeling, shaky, swimming, wobbly, woozy (*informal*) **2** CONFUSED, at sea, befuddled, bemused, bewildered, dazed, dazzled, muddled

do *verb* **1** PERFORM, accomplish, achieve, carry out, complete, execute **2** BE ADEQUATE, be sufficient, cut the mustard, pass muster, satisfy, suffice **3** GET READY, arrange, fix, look

after, prepare, see to **4** SOLVE,
decipher, decode, figure out,
puzzle out, resolve, work out
5 CAUSE, bring about, create,
effect, produce

do away with verb **1** KILL,
exterminate, murder, slay **2** GET
RID OF, abolish, discard,
discontinue, eliminate, put an
end to, put paid to, remove

docile adjective SUBMISSIVE,
amenable, biddable,
compliant, manageable,
obedient, pliant

docility noun SUBMISSIVENESS,
compliance, manageability,
meekness, obedience

dock[1] noun **1** WHARF, harbor,
pier, quay, waterfront ▶ verb
2 MOOR, anchor, berth, drop
anchor, land, put in, tie up
3 Of spacecraft LINK UP, couple,
hook up, join, rendezvous,
unite

dock[2] verb **1** DEDUCT, decrease,
diminish, lessen, reduce,
subtract, withhold **2** CUT OFF,
clip, crop, curtail, cut short,
shorten

doctor noun **1** G.P., general
practitioner, medic (informal),
medical practitioner, physician
▶ verb **2** CHANGE, alter, disguise,
falsify, misrepresent, pervert,
tamper with **3** ADD TO,
adulterate, cut, dilute, mix
with, spike, water down

doctrinaire adjective DOGMATIC,
biased, fanatical, inflexible,
insistent, opinionated, rigid

doctrine noun TEACHING, article
of faith, belief, conviction,
creed, dogma, opinion,
precept, principle, tenet

document noun **1** PAPER,

certificate, record, report ▶ verb
2 SUPPORT, authenticate, certify,
corroborate, detail,
substantiate, validate, verify

dodge verb **1** DUCK, dart,
sidestep, swerve, turn aside
2 EVADE, avoid, elude, get out
of, shirk

dog noun **1** HOUND, canine, cur,
man's best friend, pooch
(slang) **2 go to the dogs**
Informal GO TO RUIN,
degenerate, deteriorate, go
down the drain, go to pot
▶ verb **3** TROUBLE, follow, haunt,
hound, plague, pursue, stalk,
track, trail

dogged adjective DETERMINED,
indefatigable, obstinate,
persistent, resolute, steadfast,
stubborn, tenacious,
unflagging, unshakable

dogma noun DOCTRINE, belief,
credo, creed, opinion, teachings

dogmatic adjective OPINIONATED,
arrogant, assertive, doctrinaire,
emphatic, obdurate,
overbearing

doldrums noun **the doldrums**
INACTIVITY, depression, dumps
(informal), gloom, listlessness,
malaise

dole verb **dole out** GIVE OUT,
allocate, allot, apportion,
assign, dispense, distribute,
hand out

dollop noun LUMP, helping,
portion, scoop, serving

dolt noun IDIOT, ass, blockhead,
chump (informal), dope
(informal), dork (slang), dunce,
fool, oaf, schmuck (slang)

domestic adjective **1** HOME,
family, household, private
2 HOME-LOVING, domesticated,

homely, housewifely,
stay-at-home **3** DOMESTICATED,
house-trained, pet, tame,
trained **4** NATIVE, indigenous,
internal ▸ *noun* **5** SERVANT,
charwoman, daily, help, maid

dominant *adjective*
1 CONTROLLING, assertive,
authoritative, commanding,
governing, ruling, superior,
supreme **2** MAIN, chief,
predominant, pre-eminent,
primary, principal, prominent

dominate *verb* **1** CONTROL,
direct, govern, have the whip
hand over, monopolize, rule,
tyrannize **2** TOWER ABOVE, loom
over, overlook, stand head and
shoulders above, stand over,
survey

domination *noun* CONTROL,
ascendancy, authority,
command, influence, power,
rule, superiority, supremacy

domineering *adjective*
OVERBEARING, arrogant,
authoritarian, bossy (*informal*),
dictatorial, high-handed,
imperious, oppressive,
tyrannical

dominion *noun* **1** CONTROL,
authority, command,
jurisdiction, power, rule,
sovereignty, supremacy
2 KINGDOM, country, domain,
empire, realm, territory

don *verb* PUT ON, clothe oneself
in, dress in, get into, pull on,
slip on *or* into

donate *verb* GIVE, contribute,
make a gift of, present,
subscribe

donation *noun* CONTRIBUTION,
gift, grant, hand-out, offering,
present, subscription

donor *noun* GIVER, benefactor,
contributor, donator,
philanthropist

doom *noun* **1** DESTRUCTION,
catastrophe, downfall, fate,
fortune, lot, ruin ▸ *verb*
2 CONDEMN, consign, damn,
destine, sentence

doomed *adjective* CONDEMNED,
bewitched, cursed, fated,
hopeless, ill-fated, ill-omened,
luckless, star-crossed

door *noun* OPENING, doorway,
entrance, entry, exit

dope *noun* **1** Slang DRUG,
narcotic, opiate **2** Informal
IDIOT, dimwit (*informal*), doofus
(*slang*), dork (*slang*), dunce,
dweeb (*slang*), fool, nitwit
(*informal*), schmuck (*slang*)
▸ *verb* **3** DRUG, anesthetize,
knock out, narcotize, sedate,
stupefy

dork *noun* Slang IDIOT, doofus
(*slang*), dope (*slang*), dunce,
dweeb (*slang*), fool, geek
(*slang*), nerd

dormant *adjective* INACTIVE,
asleep, hibernating, inert,
inoperative, latent, sleeping,
slumbering, suspended

dose *noun* QUANTITY, dosage,
draft, measure, portion,
potion, prescription

dot *noun* **1** SPOT, fleck, jot,
mark, point, speck, speckle
2 on the dot ON TIME, exactly,
on the button (*informal*),
precisely, promptly, punctually,
to the minute ▸ *verb* **3** SPOT,
dab, dabble, fleck, speckle,
sprinkle, stipple, stud

dotage *noun* SENILITY,
decrepitude, feebleness,
imbecility, old age, second

childhood, weakness

dote on or **upon** verb ADORE, admire, hold dear, idolize, lavish affection on, prize, treasure

doting adjective ADORING, devoted, fond, foolish, indulgent, lovesick

double adjective 1 TWICE, coupled, dual, duplicate, in pairs, paired, twin, twofold ▶ verb 2 MULTIPLY, duplicate, enlarge, grow, increase, magnify ▶ noun 3 TWIN, clone, dead ringer (slang), Doppelgänger, duplicate, lookalike, replica, spitting image (informal) 4 **at** or **on the double** QUICKLY, at full speed, briskly, immediately, posthaste, without delay

double-cross verb BETRAY, cheat, defraud, hoodwink, mislead, swindle, trick, two-time (informal)

doubt noun 1 UNCERTAINTY, hesitancy, hesitation, indecision, irresolution, lack of conviction, suspense 2 SUSPICION, apprehension, distrust, misgiving, mistrust, qualm, skepticism ▶ verb 3 BE UNCERTAIN, be dubious, demur, fluctuate, hesitate, scruple, vacillate, waver 4 SUSPECT, discredit, distrust, fear, lack confidence in, mistrust, query, question

doubtful adjective 1 UNLIKELY, debatable, dubious, equivocal, improbable, problematic(al), questionable, unclear 2 UNSURE, distrustful, hesitating, in two minds (informal), skeptical, suspicious, tentative, uncertain, unconvinced, wavering

doubtless adverb 1 CERTAINLY, assuredly, indisputably, of course, surely, undoubtedly, unquestionably, without doubt 2 PROBABLY, apparently, most likely, ostensibly, presumably, seemingly, supposedly

dour adjective GLOOMY, dismal, dreary, forbidding, grim, morose, sour, sullen, unfriendly

dowdy adjective FRUMPY, dingy, drab, dumpy (informal), frowzy, homely (U.S.), shabby, unfashionable

do without verb MANAGE WITHOUT, abstain from, dispense with, forgo, get along without, give up, kick (informal)

down adjective 1 DEPRESSED, dejected, disheartened, downcast, low, miserable, sad, unhappy ▶ verb 2 Informal SWALLOW, drain, drink (down), gulp, put away, toss off ▶ noun 3 **be down on** Informal BE ANTAGONISTIC or HOSTILE TO, bear a grudge towards, be prejudiced against, be set against, have it in for (slang)

down-and-out noun 1 TRAMP, bag lady, beggar, derelict, pauper, vagabond, vagrant ▶ adjective 2 DESTITUTE, derelict, down on one's luck (informal), impoverished, penniless, short, without two pennies to rub together (informal)

downcast adjective DEJECTED, crestfallen, depressed, despondent, disappointed, disconsolate, discouraged, disheartened, dismayed, dispirited

downer noun Informal MOANER, killjoy, pessimist, prophet of doom, sourpuss (*informal*), spoilsport, wet blanket (*informal*)

downfall noun RUIN, collapse, destruction, disgrace, fall, overthrow, undoing

downgrade verb DEMOTE, degrade, humble, lower or reduce in rank, take down a peg (*informal*)

downhearted adjective DEJECTED, crestfallen, depressed, despondent, discouraged, disheartened, dispirited, downcast, sad, unhappy

downpour noun RAINSTORM, cloudburst, deluge, flood, inundation, torrential rain

downright adjective COMPLETE, absolute, out-and-out, outright, plain, thoroughgoing, total, undisguised, unqualified, utter

down-to-earth adjective SENSIBLE, matter-of-fact, no-nonsense, plain-spoken, practical, realistic, sane, unsentimental

downtrodden adjective OPPRESSED, exploited, helpless, subjugated, subservient, tyrannized

downward adjective DESCENDING, declining, earthward, heading down, sliding, slipping

doze verb 1 SLEEP, nod off (*informal*), sleep, slumber, snooze (*informal*) ▶ noun 2 NAP, catnap, forty winks (*informal*), shuteye (*slang*), siesta, snooze (*informal*)

drab adjective DULL, dingy, dismal, dreary, flat, gloomy, shabby, somber

draft[1] noun 1 OUTLINE, abstract,

plan, rough, sketch, version 2 ORDER, bill (*of exchange*), check, postal order ▶ verb 3 OUTLINE, compose, design, draw, draw up, formulate, plan, sketch

draft[2] noun 1 BREEZE, current, flow, movement, puff 2 DRINK, cup, dose, potion, quantity

drag verb 1 PULL, draw, haul, lug, tow, trail, tug 2 **drag on** or **out** LAST, draw out, extend, keep going, lengthen, persist, prolong, protract, spin out, stretch out ▶ noun 3 *Informal* NUISANCE, annoyance, bore, bother, downer (*informal*), pain (*informal*), pest

dragoon verb FORCE, browbeat, bully, coerce, compel, constrain, drive, impel, intimidate, railroad (*informal*)

drain noun 1 PIPE, channel, conduit, culvert, ditch, duct, sewer, sink, trench 2 REDUCTION, depletion, drag, exhaustion, sap, strain, withdrawal ▶ verb 3 REMOVE, bleed, draw off, dry, empty, pump off or out, tap, withdraw 4 FLOW OUT, effuse, exude, leak, ooze, seep, trickle, well out 5 DRINK UP, finish, gulp down, quaff, swallow 6 EXHAUST, consume, deplete, dissipate, empty, sap, strain, use up

drama noun 1 PLAY, dramatization, show, stage show 2 THEATER, acting, dramaturgy, stagecraft 3 EXCITEMENT, crisis, histrionics, scene, spectacle, turmoil

dramatic adjective 1 THEATRICAL, dramaturgical, Thespian 2 POWERFUL, expressive, impressive, moving, striking, vivid **3** EXCITING, breathtaking, climactic, electrifying, melodramatic, sensational, suspenseful, tense, thrilling

dramatist noun PLAYWRIGHT, dramaturge, screenwriter, scriptwriter

dramatize verb EXAGGERATE, lay it on (thick) (*slang*), overdo, overstate, play to the gallery

drape verb COVER, cloak, fold, swathe, wrap

drastic adjective EXTREME, desperate, dire, forceful, harsh, radical, severe, strong

draw verb **1** SKETCH, depict, design, map out, mark out, outline, paint, portray, trace **2** PULL, drag, haul, tow, tug **3** TAKE OUT, extract, pull out **4** ATTRACT, allure, elicit, entice, evoke, induce, influence, invite, persuade **5** DEDUCE, derive, infer, make, take ▶ *noun* **6** *Informal* ATTRACTION, enticement, lure, pull (*informal*) **7** TIE, dead heat, deadlock, gridlock, impasse, stalemate

drawback noun DISADVANTAGE, deficiency, difficulty, downside, flaw, handicap, hitch, snag, stumbling block

drawing noun PICTURE, cartoon, depiction, illustration, outline, portrayal, representation, sketch, study

drawn adjective TENSE, haggard, pinched, stressed, tired, worn

draw on verb MAKE USE OF, employ, exploit, extract, fall back on, have recourse to, rely on, take from, use

draw out verb EXTEND, drag out, lengthen, make longer, prolong, protract, spin out,

stretch, string out

draw up verb **1** DRAFT, compose, formulate, frame, prepare, write out **2** HALT, bring to a stop, pull up, stop

dread verb **1** FEAR, cringe at, have cold feet (*informal*), quail, shrink from, shudder, tremble ▶ *noun* **2** FEAR, alarm, apprehension, dismay, fright, horror, terror, trepidation

dreadful adjective TERRIBLE, abysmal, appalling, atrocious, awful, fearful, frightful, hideous, horrible, shocking

dream noun **1** VISION, delusion, hallucination, illusion, imagination, trance **2** DAYDREAM, fantasy, pipe dream **3** AMBITION, aim, aspiration, desire, goal, hope, wish **4** DELIGHT, beauty, gem, joy, marvel, pleasure, treasure ▶ *verb* **5** HAVE DREAMS, conjure up, envisage, fancy, hallucinate, imagine, think, visualize **6** DAYDREAM, build castles in the air *or* in Spain, fantasize, stargaze

dreamer noun IDEALIST, daydreamer, escapist, fantasist, utopian, visionary, Walter Mitty

dreamy adjective **1** VAGUE, absent, abstracted, daydreaming, faraway, pensive, preoccupied, with one's head in the clouds **2** IMPRACTICAL, airy-fairy, fanciful, imaginary, quixotic, speculative

dreary adjective DULL, boring, drab, humdrum, monotonous, tedious, tiresome, uneventful, wearisome

dregs plural noun **1** SEDIMENT, deposit, dross, grounds, lees, residue, residuum, scum, waste

2 SCUM, good-for-nothings, rabble, riffraff

drench verb SOAK, drown, flood, inundate, saturate, souse, steep, swamp, wet

dress noun **1** FROCK, gown, outfit, robe **2** CLOTHING, apparel, attire, clothes, costume, garb, garments, togs ▶ verb **3** PUT ON, attire, change, clothe, don, garb, robe, slip on or into **4** BANDAGE, bind up, plaster, treat **5** ARRANGE, adjust, align, get ready, prepare, straighten

dressmaker noun SEAMSTRESS, couturier, tailor

dribble verb **1** RUN, drip, drop, fall in drops, leak, ooze, seep, trickle **2** DROOL, drivel, slaver, slobber

drift verb **1** FLOAT, be carried along, coast, go (aimlessly), meander, stray, waft, wander **2** PILE UP, accumulate, amass, bank up, drive, gather ▶ noun **3** PILE, accumulation, bank, heap, mass, mound **4** MEANING, direction, gist, import, intention, purport, significance, tendency, thrust

drifter noun WANDERER, beachcomber, bum (informal), hobo, itinerant, rolling stone, vagrant

drill noun **1** BORING TOOL, bit, borer, gimlet **2** TRAINING, discipline, exercise, instruction, practice, preparation, repetition ▶ verb **3** BORE, penetrate, perforate, pierce, puncture, sink in **4** TRAIN, coach, discipline, exercise, instruct, practice, rehearse, teach

drink verb **1** SWALLOW, gulp, guzzle, imbibe, quaff, sip, suck, sup **2** BOOZE (informal), hit the bottle (informal), tipple, tope ▶ noun **3** BEVERAGE, liquid, potion, refreshment **4** ALCOHOL, booze (informal), hooch or hootch, liquor, spirits, the bottle (informal) **5** GLASS, cup, draft

drip verb **1** DROP, dribble, exude, plop, splash, sprinkle, trickle ▶ noun **2** DROP, dribble, leak, trickle **3** Informal WEAKLING, mama's boy (informal)

drive verb **1** OPERATE, direct, guide, handle, manage, motor, ride, steer, travel **2** GOAD, coerce, constrain, force, press, prod, prompt, spur **3** PUSH, herd, hurl, impel, propel, send, urge **4** PUSH, hammer, ram, thrust ▶ noun **5** RUN, excursion, jaunt, journey, outing, ride, spin (informal), trip **6** CAMPAIGN, action, appeal, crusade, effort, push (informal) **7** INITIATIVE, ambition, energy, enterprise, get-up-and-go (informal), motivation, vigor, zip (informal)

drivel noun **1** NONSENSE, garbage (informal), gibberish, hogwash, hot air (informal), poppycock (informal), rubbish, trash ▶ verb **2** BABBLE, blether, gab (informal), prate, ramble

driving adjective FORCEFUL, compelling, dynamic, energetic, sweeping, vigorous, violent

drizzle noun **1** FINE RAIN, mist ▶ verb **2** RAIN, shower, spot or spit with rain, spray, sprinkle

droll adjective AMUSING, comical, entertaining, funny, humorous, jocular, waggish, whimsical

drone verb **1** HUM, buzz, purr, thrum, vibrate, whirr **2 drone on** SPEAK MONOTONOUSLY, be boring, chant, intone, spout, talk interminably ▶noun **3** HUM, buzz, murmuring, purr, thrum, vibration, whirring

drool verb **1** DRIBBLE, drivel, salivate, slaver, slobber, water at the mouth **2 drool over** GLOAT OVER, dote on, gush, make much of, rave about (informal)

droop verb SAG, bend, dangle, drop, fall down, hang (down), sink

drop verb **1** FALL, decline, descend, diminish, plummet, plunge, sink, tumble **2** DRIP, dribble, fall in drops, trickle **3** DISCONTINUE, ax (informal), give up, kick (informal), quit, relinquish ▶noun **4** DROPLET, bead, bubble, drip, globule, pearl, tear **5** DASH, mouthful, shot (informal), sip, spot, swig (informal), trace, trickle **6** DECREASE, cut, decline, deterioration, downturn, fall-off, lowering, reduction, slump **7** FALL, descent, plunge

drop off verb **1** SET DOWN, deliver, leave, let off **2** Informal FALL ASLEEP, doze (off), have forty winks (informal), nod (off), snooze (informal) **3** DECREASE, decline, diminish, dwindle, fall off, lessen, slacken

drop out verb LEAVE, abandon, fall by the wayside, give up, quit, stop, withdraw

drought noun DRY SPELL, aridity, dehydration, dryness

drove noun HERD, collection, company, crowd, flock, horde, mob, multitude, swarm, throng

drown verb **1** DRENCH, deluge, engulf, flood, go under, immerse, inundate, sink, submerge, swamp **2** OVERPOWER, deaden, muffle, obliterate, overcome, overwhelm, stifle, swallow up, wipe out

drowsy adjective SLEEPY, dopey (slang), dozy, half asleep, heavy, lethargic, somnolent, tired, torpid

drudge noun MENIAL, factotum, servant, slave, toiler, worker

drudgery noun MENIAL LABOR, donkey-work, grind (informal), hard work, labor, slog, toil

drug noun **1** MEDICATION, medicament, medicine, physic, poison, remedy **2** DOPE (slang), narcotic, opiate, stimulant ▶verb **3** DOSE, administer a drug, dope (slang), medicate, treat **4** KNOCK OUT, anesthetize, deaden, numb, poison, stupefy

drum verb **1** BEAT, pulsate, rap, reverberate, tap, tattoo, throb **2 drum into** DRIVE HOME, din into, hammer away, harp on, instill into, reiterate

drunk adjective **1** INTOXICATED, drunken, inebriated, plastered (slang), tipsy, under the influence (informal) ▶noun **2** DRUNKARD, alcoholic, boozer (informal), inebriate, lush (slang), wino (informal)

drunkard noun DRINKER, alcoholic, dipsomaniac, drunk, lush (slang), tippler, wino (informal)

drunkenness noun INTOXICATION, alcoholism, bibulousness, dipsomania, inebriation, insobriety, intemperance

dry adjective 1 DEHYDRATED, arid, barren, desiccated, dried up, parched, thirsty 2 DULL, boring, dreary, monotonous, plain, tedious, tiresome, uninteresting 3 SARCASTIC, deadpan, droll, low-key, sly ▶verb 4 DEHYDRATE, dehumidify, desiccate, drain, make dry, parch, sear

dry out or up verb BECOME DRY, harden, shrivel up, wilt, wither, wizen

dual adjective TWOFOLD, binary, double, duplex, duplicate, matched, paired, twin

dubious adjective 1 SUSPECT, fishy (informal), questionable, suspicious, unreliable, untrustworthy 2 UNSURE, doubtful, hesitant, skeptical, uncertain, unconvinced, undecided, wavering

duck verb 1 BOB, bend, bow, crouch, dodge, drop, lower, stoop 2 PLUNGE, dip, dive, douse, dunk, immerse, souse, submerge, wet 3 Informal DODGE, avoid, escape, evade, shirk, shun, sidestep

dud Informal ▶noun 1 FAILURE, flop (informal), washout (informal) ▶adjective 2 USELESS, broken, failed, inoperative, worthless

dudgeon noun in high dudgeon INDIGNANT, angry, choked, fuming, offended, resentful, ticked off (informal), vexed

due adjective 1 EXPECTED, scheduled 2 PAYABLE, in arrears, outstanding, owed, owing, unpaid 3 FITTING, appropriate, deserved, justified, merited, proper, rightful, suitable,

well-earned ▶noun 4 RIGHT(S), deserts, merits, privilege ▶adverb 5 DIRECTLY, dead, exactly, straight, undeviatingly

duel noun 1 SINGLE COMBAT, affair of honor 2 CONTEST, clash, competition, encounter, engagement, fight, head-to-head, rivalry ▶verb 3 FIGHT, clash, compete, contend, contest, lock horns, rival, struggle, vie with

dues plural noun MEMBERSHIP FEE, charge, charges, contribution, fee, levy

dull adjective 1 BORING, dreary, dumpy (informal), flat, frowzy, homely (U.S.), humdrum, monotonous, plain, tedious, uninteresting 2 STUPID, dense, dim-witted (informal), slow, thick, unintelligent 3 CLOUDY, dim, dismal, gloomy, leaden, overcast 4 LIFELESS, apathetic, blank, indifferent, listless, passionless, unresponsive 5 BLUNT, blunted, unsharpened ▶verb 6 RELIEVE, allay, alleviate, blunt, lessen, moderate, soften, take the edge off

duly adverb 1 PROPERLY, accordingly, appropriately, befittingly, correctly, decorously, deservedly, fittingly, rightfully, suitably 2 ON TIME, at the proper time, punctually

dumb adjective 1 MUTE, mum, silent, soundless, speechless, tongue-tied, voiceless, wordless 2 Informal STUPID, asinine, dense, dim-witted (informal), dull, foolish, thick, unintelligent

dumbfounded adjective AMAZED, astonished, astounded, flabbergasted (informal), lost for words, nonplussed, overwhelmed, speechless, staggered, stunned

dummy noun 1 MODEL, figure, form, manikin, mannequin 2 COPY, counterfeit, duplicate, imitation, sham, substitute 3 Slang FOOL, blockhead, dork (slang), dunce, idiot, nitwit (informal), oaf, schmuck (slang), simpleton ▸ adjective 4 IMITATION, artificial, bogus, fake, mock, phoney or phony (informal), sham, simulated

dump verb 1 DROP, deposit, fling down, let fall, throw down 2 GET RID OF, dispose of, ditch (slang), empty out, jettison, scrap, throw away or out, tip, unload ▸ noun 3 RUBBISH TIP, junkyard, refuse heap, rubbish heap, tip 4 Informal PIGSTY, hovel, mess, slum

dumpy adjective Informal DOWDY, frowzy, frumpy, homely (U.S.), unfashionable

dunce noun SIMPLETON, blockhead, dunderhead, ignoramus, moron, thickhead

dungeon noun PRISON, cage, cell, oubliette, vault

duplicate adjective 1 IDENTICAL, corresponding, matched, matching, twin, twofold ▸ noun 2 COPY, carbon copy, clone, double, facsimile, photocopy, replica, reproduction ▸ verb 3 COPY, clone, double, repeat, replicate, reproduce

durability noun DURABLENESS, constancy, endurance, imperishability, permanence, persistence

durable adjective LONG-LASTING, dependable, enduring, hard-wearing, persistent, reliable, resistant, strong, sturdy, tough

duration noun LENGTH, extent, period, span, spell, stretch, term, time

duress noun PRESSURE, coercion, compulsion, constraint, threat

dusk noun TWILIGHT, dark, evening, eventide, gloaming (Scot. or poetic), nightfall, sundown, sunset

dusky adjective 1 DARK, dark-complexioned, sable, swarthy 2 DIM, cloudy, gloomy, murky, obscure, shadowy, shady, tenebrous, twilit

dust noun 1 GRIME, grit, particles, powder ▸ verb 2 SPRINKLE, cover, dredge, powder, scatter, sift, spray, spread

dusty adjective DIRTY, grubby, scuzzy (slang), sooty, unclean, unswept

dutiful adjective CONSCIENTIOUS, devoted, obedient, respectful, reverential, submissive

duty noun 1 RESPONSIBILITY, assignment, function, job, obligation, role, task, work 2 LOYALTY, allegiance, deference, obedience, respect, reverence 3 TAX, excise, levy, tariff, toll 4 on duty AT WORK, busy, engaged, on active service

dwarf verb 1 TOWER ABOVE or OVER, diminish, dominate, overshadow ▸ adjective 2 MINIATURE, baby, bonsai, diminutive, small, tiny, undersized ▸ noun 3 MIDGET, Lilliputian, pygmy or pigmy,

Tom Thumb

dweeb noun Slang IDIOT, doofus (*slang*), dope (*slang*), dunce, fool, geek, slang, nerd

dwell verb LIVE, abide, inhabit, lodge, reside

dwelling noun HOME, abode, domicile, habitation, house, lodging, pad (*slang*), quarters, residence

dwindle verb LESSEN, decline, decrease, die away, diminish, fade, peter out, shrink, subside, taper off, wane

dye noun 1 COLORING, color, colorant, pigment, stain, tinge, tint ▶ verb 2 COLOR, pigment, stain, tinge, tint

dying adjective EXPIRING, at death's door, failing, *in extremis*, moribund, not long for this world

dynamic adjective ENERGETIC, forceful, go-ahead, go-getting (*informal*), high-powered, lively, powerful, vital

dynasty noun EMPIRE, government, house, regime, rule, sovereignty

— **E e** —

each adjective 1 EVERY ▶ pronoun 2 EVERY ONE, each and every one, each one, one and all ▶ adverb 3 APIECE, for each, individually, per capita, per head, per person, respectively, to each

eager adjective KEEN, agog, anxious, athirst, avid, enthusiastic, fervent, gung ho

(*slang*), hungry, impatient, longing

eagerness noun KEENNESS, ardor, enthusiasm, fervor, hunger, impatience, thirst, yearning, zeal

ear noun SENSITIVITY, appreciation, discrimination, perception, taste

early adjective 1 PREMATURE, advanced, forward, untimely 2 PRIMITIVE, primeval, primordial, undeveloped, young ▶ adverb 3 TOO SOON, ahead of time, beforehand, in advance, in good time, prematurely

earmark verb SET ASIDE, allocate, designate, flag, label, mark out, reserve

earn verb 1 MAKE, bring in, collect, gain, get, gross, net, receive 2 DESERVE, acquire, attain, be entitled to, be worthy of, merit, rate, warrant, win

earnest adjective 1 SERIOUS, grave, intent, resolute, resolved, sincere, solemn, thoughtful ▶ noun 2 As in **in earnest** SERIOUSNESS, sincerity, truth

earnings plural noun INCOME, pay, proceeds, profits, receipts, remuneration, salary, takings, wages

earth noun 1 WORLD, globe, orb, planet, sphere 2 SOIL, clay, dirt, ground, land, turf

earthenware noun CROCKERY, ceramics, pots, pottery, terracotta

earthly adjective WORLDLY, human, material, mortal, secular, temporal

earthy adjective CRUDE, bawdy, coarse, raunchy (slang), ribald, robust, uninhibited, unsophisticated

ease noun 1 EASINESS, effortlessness, facility, readiness, simplicity 2 CONTENT, comfort, happiness, peace, peace of mind, quiet, serenity, tranquillity 3 REST, leisure, relaxation, repose, restfulness ▶ verb 4 RELIEVE, alleviate, calm, comfort, lessen, lighten, relax, soothe 5 MOVE CAREFULLY, edge, inch, maneuver, slide, slip

easily adverb WITHOUT DIFFICULTY, comfortably, effortlessly, readily, smoothly, with ease, with one hand tied behind one's back

easy adjective 1 NOT DIFFICULT, a piece of cake (informal), child's play (informal), effortless, no trouble, painless, plain sailing, simple, straightforward, uncomplicated, undemanding 2 CAREFREE, comfortable, leisurely, peaceful, quiet, relaxed, serene, tranquil, untroubled 3 TOLERANT, easy-going, indulgent, lenient, mild, permissive, unoppressive

easy-going adjective RELAXED, carefree, casual, easy, even-tempered, happy-go-lucky, laid-back (informal), nonchalant, placid, tolerant, undemanding

eat verb 1 CONSUME, chew, devour, gobble, ingest, munch, scoff (slang), swallow 2 HAVE A MEAL, chow down (slang), dine, feed, take nourishment 3 DESTROY, corrode, decay, dissolve, erode, rot, waste away, wear away

eavesdrop verb LISTEN IN, monitor, overhear, snoop (informal), spy

ebb verb 1 FLOW BACK, go out, recede, retire, retreat, subside, wane, withdraw 2 DECLINE, decrease, diminish, dwindle, fade away, fall away, flag, lessen, peter out ▶ noun 3 FLOWING BACK, going out, low tide, low water, retreat, subsidence, wane, withdrawal

eccentric adjective 1 ODD, freakish, idiosyncratic, irregular, outlandish, peculiar, quirky, strange, unconventional ▶ noun 2 CRANK (informal), character (informal), nonconformist, oddball (informal), weirdo or weirdie (informal)

eccentricity noun ODDITY, abnormality, caprice, capriciousness, foible, idiosyncrasy, irregularity, peculiarity, quirk

ecclesiastic noun 1 CLERGYMAN, churchman, cleric, holy man, man of the cloth, minister, parson, pastor, priest ▶ adjective 2 Also **ecclesiastical** CLERICAL, divine, holy, pastoral, priestly, religious, spiritual

echo noun 1 REPETITION, answer, reverberation 2 COPY, imitation, mirror image, parallel, reflection, reiteration, reproduction ▶ verb 3 REPEAT, resound, reverberate 4 COPY, ape, imitate, mirror, parallel, recall, reflect, resemble

eclipse noun 1 OBSCURING, darkening, dimming, extinction, shading ▶ verb 2 SURPASS, exceed, excel, outdo, outshine, put in the shade (informal), transcend

economic adjective **1** FINANCIAL, commercial, industrial **2** PROFITABLE, money-making, productive, profit-making, remunerative, viable

economical adjective **1** THRIFTY, careful, frugal, prudent, scrimping, sparing **2** COST-EFFECTIVE, efficient, money-saving, sparing, time-saving **3** INEXPENSIVE, cheap, low-priced, modest, reasonable

economize verb CUT BACK, be economical, be frugal, draw in one's horns, retrench, save, scrimp, tighten one's belt

economy noun THRIFT, frugality, husbandry, parsimony, prudence, restraint

ecstasy noun RAPTURE, bliss, delight, elation, euphoria, fervor, joy, seventh heaven

ecstatic adjective RAPTUROUS, blissful, elated, enraptured, entranced, euphoric, in seventh heaven, joyous, on cloud nine (informal), overjoyed

eddy noun **1** SWIRL, counter-current, counterflow, undertow, vortex, whirlpool ▶ verb **2** SWIRL, whirl

edge noun **1** BORDER, brink, fringe, limit, outline, perimeter, rim, side, verge **2** SHARPNESS, bite, effectiveness, force, incisiveness, keenness, point **3** As in **have the edge on** ADVANTAGE, ascendancy, dominance, lead, superiority, upper hand **4** on edge NERVOUS, apprehensive, edgy, ill at ease, impatient, irritable, keyed up, on tenterhooks, tense, wired (slang) ▶ verb

5 BORDER, fringe, hem **6** INCH, creep, ease, sidle, steal

edgy adjective NERVOUS, anxious, ill at ease, irritable, keyed up, on edge, on tenterhooks, restive, tense, wired (slang)

edible adjective EATABLE, digestible, fit to eat, good, harmless, palatable, wholesome

edict noun DECREE, act, command, injunction, law, order, proclamation, ruling

edifice noun BUILDING, construction, erection, house, structure

edify verb INSTRUCT, educate, enlighten, guide, improve, inform, nurture, school, teach

edit verb REVISE, adapt, condense, correct, emend, polish, rewrite

edition noun VERSION, copy, impression, issue, number, printing, program (TV, Radio), volume

educate verb TEACH, civilize, develop, discipline, enlighten, improve, inform, instruct, school, train, tutor

educated adjective **1** TAUGHT, coached, informed, instructed, nurtured, schooled, tutored **2** CULTURED, civilized, cultivated, enlightened, knowledgeable, learned, refined, sophisticated

education noun TEACHING, development, discipline, enlightenment, instruction, nurture, schooling, training, tuition

educational adjective INSTRUCTIVE, cultural, edifying, educative, enlightening, improving, informative

eerie adjective FRIGHTENING,

creepy (*informal*), ghostly, mysterious, scary (*informal*), spooky (*informal*), strange, uncanny, unearthly, weird

efface verb OBLITERATE, blot out, cancel, delete, destroy, eradicate, erase, expunge, rub out, wipe out

effect noun 1 RESULT, conclusion, consequence, end result, event, outcome, upshot 2 OPERATION, action, enforcement, execution, force, implementation 3 IMPRESSION, essence, impact, sense, significance, tenor ▶verb 4 BRING ABOUT, accomplish, achieve, complete, execute, fulfill, perform, produce

effective adjective 1 EFFICIENT, active, adequate, capable, competent, productive, serviceable, useful 2 IN OPERATION, active, current, in effect, in force, operative 3 POWERFUL, cogent, compelling, convincing, forceful, impressive, persuasive, telling

effects plural noun BELONGINGS, gear, goods, paraphernalia, possessions, property, things

effeminate adjective WOMANLY, camp (*informal*), feminine, sissy, soft, tender, unmanly, weak, womanish

effervescent adjective 1 BUBBLING, carbonated, fizzy, foaming, frothy, sparkling 2 LIVELY, animated, bubbly, ebullient, enthusiastic, irrepressible, vivacious

effete adjective DECADENT, dissipated, enfeebled, feeble,

ineffectual, spoiled, weak

efficacious adjective EFFECTIVE, adequate, efficient, operative, potent, powerful, productive, successful, useful

efficiency noun COMPETENCE, adeptness, capability, economy, effectiveness, power, productivity, proficiency

efficient adjective COMPETENT, businesslike, capable, economic, effective, organized, productive, proficient, well-organized, workmanlike

effigy noun LIKENESS, dummy, figure, guy, icon, idol, image, picture, portrait, representation, statue

effluent noun WASTE, effluvium, pollutant, sewage

effort noun 1 EXERTION, application, elbow grease (*facetious*), endeavor, energy, pains, struggle, toil, trouble, work 2 ATTEMPT, endeavor, essay, go (*informal*), shot (*informal*), stab (*informal*), try

effortless adjective EASY, painless, plain sailing, simple, smooth, uncomplicated, undemanding

effrontery noun INSOLENCE, arrogance, audacity, brazenness, cheek (*informal*), impertinence, impudence, nerve, presumption, temerity

effusive adjective DEMONSTRATIVE, ebullient, expansive, exuberant, gushing, lavish, unreserved, unrestrained

egg on verb ENCOURAGE, exhort, goad, incite, prod, prompt, push, spur, urge

egocentric adjective SELF-CENTERED, egoistic,

egoistical, egotistic, egotistical, selfish

egotism, egoism noun
SELF-CENTEREDNESS, conceitedness, narcissism, self-absorption, self-esteem, self-importance, self-interest, selfishness, vanity

egotist, egoist noun
EGOMANIAC, bighead (*informal*), boaster, braggart, narcissist

egotistic, egotistical, egoistic or **egoistical** adjective
SELF-CENTERED, boasting, conceited, egocentric, full of oneself, narcissistic, self-absorbed, self-important, vain

egress noun Formal EXIT, departure, exodus, way out, withdrawal

eject verb THROW OUT, banish, drive out, evict, expel, oust, remove, turn out

ejection noun EXPULSION, banishment, deportation, eviction, exile, removal

eke out verb BE SPARING WITH, economize on, husband, stretch out

elaborate adjective **1** DETAILED, intricate, minute, painstaking, precise, studied, thorough **2** COMPLICATED, complex, fancy, fussy, involved, ornamented, ornate ▶ verb **3** EXPAND (UPON), add detail, amplify, develop, embellish, enlarge, flesh out

elapse verb PASS, glide by, go by, lapse, roll by, slip away

elastic adjective **1** STRETCHY, plastic, pliable, pliant, resilient, rubbery, springy, supple, tensile **2** ADAPTABLE, accommodating, adjustable, compliant, flexible, supple,

tolerant, variable, yielding

elated adjective JOYFUL, delighted, ecstatic, euphoric, exhilarated, gleeful, jubilant, overjoyed

elation noun JOY, bliss, delight, ecstasy, euphoria, exhilaration, glee, high spirits, jubilation, rapture

elbow noun **1** JOINT, angle ▶ verb **2** PUSH, jostle, knock, nudge, shove

elbow room noun SCOPE, freedom, latitude, leeway, play, room, space

elder adjective **1** OLDER, first-born, senior ▶ noun **2** OLDER PERSON, senior

elect verb CHOOSE, appoint, determine, opt for, pick, prefer, select, settle on, vote

election noun VOTING, appointment, choice, judgment, preference, selection, vote

elector noun VOTER, constituent, selector

electric adjective CHARGED, dynamic, exciting, rousing, stimulating, stirring, tense, thrilling

electrify verb STARTLE, astound, excite, galvanize, invigorate, jolt, shock, stir, thrill

elegance noun STYLE, dignity, exquisiteness, grace, gracefulness, grandeur, luxury, refinement, taste

elegant adjective STYLISH, chic, delicate, exquisite, fine, graceful, handsome, polished, refined, tasteful

element noun **1** COMPONENT, constituent, factor, ingredient, part, section, subdivision, unit

2 As in **in one's element** ENVIRONMENT, domain, field, habitat, medium, milieu, sphere

elementary adjective SIMPLE, clear, easy, plain, rudimentary, straightforward, uncomplicated

elements plural noun **1** BASICS, essentials, foundations, fundamentals, nuts and bolts (informal), principles, rudiments **2** WEATHER CONDITIONS, atmospheric conditions, powers of nature

elevate verb **1** RAISE, heighten, hoist, lift, lift up, uplift **2** PROMOTE, advance, aggrandize, exalt, prefer, upgrade

elevated adjective HIGH-MINDED, dignified, exalted, grand, high-flown, inflated, lofty, noble, sublime

elevation noun **1** PROMOTION, advancement, aggrandizement, exaltation, preferment, upgrading **2** ALTITUDE, height

elicit verb **1** BRING ABOUT, bring forth, bring out, bring to light, call forth, cause, derive, evolve, give rise to **2** OBTAIN, draw out, evoke, exact, extort, extract, wrest

eligible adjective QUALIFIED, acceptable, appropriate, desirable, fit, preferable, proper, suitable, worthy

eliminate verb GET RID OF, cut out, dispose of, do away with, eradicate, exterminate, remove, stamp out, take out

elite noun BEST, aristocracy, cream, crème de la crème, flower, nobility, pick, upper class

elitist adjective SNOBBISH,

exclusive, selective

elixir noun PANACEA, nostrum

elocution noun DICTION, articulation, declamation, delivery, enunciation, oratory, pronunciation, speech, speechmaking

elongate verb MAKE LONGER, draw out, extend, lengthen, prolong, protract, stretch

elope verb RUN AWAY, abscond, bolt, decamp, disappear, escape, leave, run off, slip away, steal away

eloquence noun EXPRESSIVENESS, expression, fluency, forcefulness, oratory, persuasiveness, rhetoric, way with words

eloquent adjective **1** SILVER-TONGUED, articulate, fluent, forceful, moving, persuasive, stirring, well-expressed **2** EXPRESSIVE, meaningful, suggestive, telling, vivid

elsewhere adverb IN OR TO ANOTHER PLACE, abroad, away, hence (archaic), not here, somewhere else

elucidate verb CLARIFY, clear up, explain, explicate, expound, illuminate, illustrate, make plain, shed or throw light upon, spell out

elude verb **1** ESCAPE, avoid, dodge, duck (informal), evade, flee, get away from, outrun **2** BAFFLE, be beyond (someone), confound, escape, foil, frustrate, puzzle, stump, thwart

elusive adjective **1** DIFFICULT TO CATCH, shifty, slippery, tricky **2** INDEFINABLE, fleeting, intangible, subtle, transient, transitory

emaciated adjective SKELETAL, cadaverous, gaunt, haggard, lean, pinched, scrawny, thin, undernourished, wasted

emanate verb FLOW, arise, come forth, derive, emerge, issue, originate, proceed, spring, stem

emancipate verb FREE, deliver, liberate, release, set free, unchain, unfetter

emancipation noun FREEDOM, deliverance, liberation, liberty, release

embalm verb PRESERVE, mummify

embargo noun 1 BAN, bar, boycott, interdiction, prohibition, restraint, restriction, stoppage ▶ verb 2 BAN, bar, block, boycott, prohibit, restrict, stop

embark verb 1 GO ABOARD, board ship, take ship 2 **embark on** or **upon** BEGIN, commence, enter, launch, plunge into, set about, set out, start, take up

embarrass verb SHAME, discomfit, disconcert, distress, fluster, humiliate, mortify, show up (informal)

embarrassed adjective ASHAMED, awkward, blushing, discomfited, disconcerted, humiliated, mortified, red-faced, self-conscious, sheepish

embarrassing adjective HUMILIATING, awkward, compromising, discomfiting, disconcerting, mortifying, sensitive, shameful, toe-curling (informal), uncomfortable

embarrassment noun 1 SHAME, awkwardness, bashfulness, distress, humiliation, mortification, self-consciousness, showing up (informal) 2 PREDICAMENT, bind (informal), difficulty, mess, pickle (informal), scrape (informal)

embellish verb DECORATE, adorn, beautify, elaborate, embroider, enhance, enrich, festoon, ornament

embellishment noun DECORATION, adornment, elaboration, embroidery, enhancement, enrichment, exaggeration, ornament, ornamentation

embezzle verb MISAPPROPRIATE, appropriate, filch, misuse, peculate, pilfer, purloin, rip off (slang), steal

embezzlement noun MISAPPROPRIATION, appropriation, filching, fraud, misuse, peculation, pilfering, stealing, theft

embittered adjective RESENTFUL, angry, bitter, disaffected, disillusioned, rancorous, soured, with a chip on one's shoulder (informal)

emblem noun SYMBOL, badge, crest, image, insignia, mark, sign, token

embodiment noun PERSONIFICATION, epitome, example, exemplar, expression, incarnation, representation, symbol

embody verb 1 PERSONIFY, exemplify, manifest, represent, stand for, symbolize, typify 2 INCORPORATE, collect, combine, comprise, contain, include

embolden verb ENCOURAGE, fire,

inflame, invigorate, rouse, stimulate, stir, strengthen

embrace verb **1** HUG, clasp, cuddle, envelop, hold, seize, squeeze, take *or* hold in one's arms **2** ACCEPT, adopt, espouse, seize, take on board, take up, welcome **3** INCLUDE, comprehend, comprise, contain, cover, encompass, involve, take in ▶ *noun* **4** HUG, clasp, clinch (*slang*), cuddle, squeeze

embroil verb INVOLVE, enmesh, ensnare, entangle, implicate, incriminate, mire, mix up

embryo noun GERM, beginning, nucleus, root, rudiment

emend verb REVISE, amend, correct, edit, improve, rectify

emendation noun REVISION, amendment, correction, editing, improvement, rectification

emerge verb **1** COME INTO VIEW, appear, arise, come forth, emanate, issue, rise, spring up, surface **2** BECOME APPARENT, become known, come out, come out in the wash, come to light, crop up, transpire

emergence noun COMING, advent, appearance, arrival, development, materialization, rise

emergency noun CRISIS, danger, difficulty, extremity, necessity, plight, predicament, quandary, scrape (*informal*)

emigrate verb MOVE ABROAD, migrate, move

emigration noun DEPARTURE, exodus, migration

eminence noun PROMINENCE, distinction, esteem, fame,

greatness, importance, note, prestige, renown, repute

eminent adjective PROMINENT, celebrated, distinguished, esteemed, famous, high-ranking, illustrious, noted, renowned, well-known

emission noun GIVING OFF *or* OUT, discharge, ejaculation, ejection, exhalation, radiation, shedding, transmission

emit verb GIVE OFF, cast out, discharge, eject, emanate, exude, radiate, send out, transmit

emotion noun FEELING, ardor, excitement, fervor, passion, sensation, sentiment, vehemence, warmth

emotional adjective **1** SENSITIVE, demonstrative, excitable, hot-blooded, passionate, sentimental, temperamental **2** MOVING, affecting, emotive, heart-warming, poignant, sentimental, stirring, touching

emotive adjective SENSITIVE, controversial, delicate, touchy

emphasis noun STRESS, accent, attention, force, importance, priority, prominence, significance, weight

emphasize verb STRESS, accentuate, dwell on, give priority to, highlight, lay stress on, play up, press home, underline

emphatic adjective FORCEFUL, categorical, definite, insistent, positive, pronounced, resounding, unequivocal, unmistakable, vigorous

empire noun KINGDOM, commonwealth, domain, realm

empirical adjective FIRST-HAND,

experiential, experimental, observed, practical, pragmatic

employ verb **1** HIRE, commission, engage, enlist, retain, take on **2** KEEP BUSY, engage, fill, make use of, occupy, take up, use up **3** USE, apply, bring to bear, exercise, exert, make use of, ply, put to use, utilize ▶ noun **4** As in **in the employ of** SERVICE, employment, engagement, hire

employed adjective WORKING, active, busy, engaged, in a job, in employment, in work, occupied

employee noun WORKER, hand, job-holder, staff member, wage-earner, workman

employer noun BOSS (informal), company, firm, owner, patron, proprietor

employment noun **1** TAKING ON, engagement, enlistment, hire, retaining **2** USE, application, exercise, exertion, utilization **3** JOB, line, occupation, profession, trade, vocation, work

emporium noun Old-fashioned SHOP, bazaar, market, mart, store, warehouse

empower verb ENABLE, allow, authorize, commission, delegate, entitle, license, permit, qualify, sanction, warrant

emptiness noun **1** BARENESS, blankness, desolation, vacancy, vacuum, void, waste **2** PURPOSELESSNESS, banality, futility, hollowness, inanity, meaninglessness, senselessness, vanity, worthlessness **3** INSINCERITY, cheapness,

hollowness, idleness

empty adjective **1** BARE, blank, clear, deserted, desolate, hollow, unfurnished, uninhabited, unoccupied, vacant, void **2** PURPOSELESS, banal, fruitless, futile, hollow, inane, meaningless, senseless, vain, worthless **3** INSINCERE, cheap, hollow, idle ▶ verb **4** EVACUATE, clear, drain, exhaust, pour out, unload, vacate, void

empty-headed adjective SCATTERBRAINED, brainless, dizzy (informal), featherbrained, harebrained, silly, vacuous

emulate verb IMITATE, compete with, copy, echo, follow, mimic, rival

enable verb ALLOW, authorize, empower, entitle, license, permit, qualify, sanction, warrant

enact verb **1** ESTABLISH, authorize, command, decree, legislate, ordain, order, proclaim, sanction **2** PERFORM, act out, depict, play, play the part of, portray, represent

enamored adjective IN LOVE, captivated, charmed, enraptured, fond, infatuated, smitten, taken

encampment noun CAMP, base, bivouac, camping ground, campsite, cantonment, quarters, tents

encapsulate verb SUM UP, abridge, compress, condense, digest, epitomize, précis, summarize

enchant verb FASCINATE, beguile, bewitch, captivate, charm, delight, enrapture, enthrall, ravish, spellbind

enchanter noun SORCERER, conjurer, magician, magus, necromancer, warlock, witch, wizard

enchanting adjective FASCINATING, alluring, attractive, bewitching, captivating, charming, delightful, entrancing, lovely, pleasant

enclose verb 1 SURROUND, bound, encase, encircle, fence, hem in, shut in, wall in 2 SEND WITH, include, insert, put in

encompass verb 1 SURROUND, circle, encircle, enclose, envelop, ring 2 INCLUDE, admit, comprise, contain, cover, embrace, hold, incorporate, take in

encounter verb 1 MEET, bump into (informal), chance upon, come upon, confront, experience, face, run across ▶ noun 2 MEETING, brush, confrontation, rendezvous 3 BATTLE, clash, conflict, contest, head-to-head, run-in (informal)

encourage verb 1 INSPIRE, buoy up, cheer, comfort, console, embolden, hearten, reassure 2 SPUR, advocate, egg on, foster, promote, prompt, support, urge

encouragement noun INSPIRATION, cheer, incitement, promotion, reassurance, stimulation, stimulus, support

encouraging adjective PROMISING, bright, cheerful, comforting, good, heartening, hopeful, reassuring, rosy

encroach verb INTRUDE, impinge, infringe, invade, make inroads,

overstep, trespass, usurp

encumber verb BURDEN, hamper, handicap, hinder, impede, inconvenience, obstruct, saddle, weigh down

end noun 1 EXTREMITY, boundary, edge, extent, extreme, limit, point, terminus, tip 2 FINISH, cessation, close, closure, ending, expiration, expiry, stop, termination 3 CONCLUSION, culmination, denouement, ending, finale, resolution 4 REMNANT, butt, fragment, leftover, oddment, remainder, scrap, stub 5 DESTRUCTION, death, demise, doom, extermination, extinction, ruin 6 PURPOSE, aim, goal, intention, object, objective, point, reason ▶ verb 7 FINISH, cease, close, conclude, culminate, stop, terminate, wind up

endanger verb PUT AT RISK, compromise, imperil, jeopardize, put in danger, risk, threaten

endearing adjective ATTRACTIVE, captivating, charming, cute, engaging, lovable, sweet, winning

endearment noun LOVING WORD, sweet nothing

endeavor verb 1 TRY, aim, aspire, attempt, labor, make an effort, strive, struggle, take pains ▶ noun 2 EFFORT, attempt, enterprise, trial, try, undertaking, venture

ending noun FINISH, cessation, close, completion, conclusion, culmination, denouement, end, finale

endless adjective ETERNAL, boundless, continual,

everlasting, incessant, infinite, interminable, unlimited

endorse verb 1 APPROVE, advocate, authorize, back, champion, promote, ratify, recommend, support 2 SIGN, countersign

endorsement noun 1 APPROVAL, advocacy, approbation, authorization, backing, favor, ratification, recommendation, seal of approval, support 2 SIGNATURE, countersignature

endow verb PROVIDE, award, bequeath, bestow, confer, donate, finance, fund, give

endowment noun PROVISION, award, benefaction, bequest, donation, gift, grant, legacy

endurable adjective BEARABLE, acceptable, sufferable, sustainable, tolerable

endurance noun 1 STAYING POWER, fortitude, patience, perseverance, persistence, resolution, stamina, strength, tenacity, toleration 2 PERMANENCE, continuity, durability, duration, longevity, stability

endure verb 1 BEAR, cope with, experience, stand, suffer, sustain, undergo, withstand 2 LAST, continue, live on, persist, remain, stand, stay, survive

enduring adjective LONG-LASTING, abiding, continuing, lasting, perennial, persistent, steadfast, unfaltering, unwavering

enemy noun FOE, adversary, antagonist, competitor, opponent, rival, the opposition, the other side

energetic adjective VIGOROUS, active, animated, dynamic, forceful, indefatigable, lively, strenuous, tireless

energy noun VIGOR, drive, forcefulness, get-up-and-go (informal), liveliness, pep, stamina, verve, vitality

enforce verb IMPOSE, administer, apply, carry out, execute, implement, insist on, prosecute, put into effect

engage verb 1 PARTICIPATE, embark on, enter into, join, set about, take part, undertake 2 OCCUPY, absorb, engross, grip, involve, preoccupy 3 CAPTIVATE, arrest, catch, fix, gain 4 EMPLOY, appoint, enlist, enroll, hire, retain, take on 5 Military BEGIN BATTLE WITH, assail, attack, encounter, fall on, join battle with, meet, take on 6 SET GOING, activate, apply, bring into operation, energize, switch on

engaged adjective 1 BETROTHED (archaic), affianced, pledged, promised, spoken for 2 OCCUPIED, busy, employed, in use, tied up, unavailable

engagement noun 1 APPOINTMENT, arrangement, commitment, date, meeting 2 BETROTHAL, troth (archaic) 3 BATTLE, action, combat, conflict, encounter, fight

engaging adjective CHARMING, agreeable, attractive, fetching (informal), likable or likeable, pleasing, winning, winsome

engender verb PRODUCE, breed, cause, create, generate, give rise to, induce, instigate, lead to

engine noun MACHINE, mechanism, motor

engineer verb BRING ABOUT, contrive, create, devise, effect, mastermind, plan, plot, scheme

engrave verb 1 CARVE, chisel, cut, etch, inscribe 2 FIX, embed, impress, imprint, ingrain, lodge

engraving noun CARVING, etching, inscription, plate, woodcut

engross verb ABSORB, engage, immerse, involve, occupy, preoccupy

engrossed adjective ABSORBED, caught up, enthralled, fascinated, gripped, immersed, lost, preoccupied, rapt, riveted

engulf verb IMMERSE, envelop, inundate, overrun, overwhelm, submerge, swallow up, swamp

enhance verb IMPROVE, add to, boost, heighten, increase, lift, reinforce, strengthen, swell

enigma noun MYSTERY, conundrum, problem, puzzle, riddle, teaser

enigmatic adjective MYSTERIOUS, ambiguous, cryptic, equivocal, inscrutable, obscure, puzzling, unfathomable

enjoy verb TAKE PLEASURE IN or FROM, appreciate, be entertained by, be pleased with, delight in, like, relish 2 HAVE, be blessed or favored with, experience, have the benefit of, own, possess, reap the benefits of, use

enjoyable adjective PLEASURABLE, agreeable, delightful, entertaining, gratifying, pleasant, satisfying, to one's liking

enjoyment noun PLEASURE, amusement, delectation, delight, entertainment, fun, gratification, happiness, joy, relish

enlarge verb 1 INCREASE, add to, amplify, broaden, expand, extend, grow, magnify, swell, widen 2 **enlarge on** EXPAND ON, descant on, develop, elaborate on, expatiate on, give further details about

enlighten verb INFORM, advise, cause to understand, counsel, edify, educate, instruct, make aware, teach

enlightened adjective INFORMED, aware, civilized, cultivated, educated, knowledgeable, open-minded, reasonable, sophisticated

enlightenment noun UNDERSTANDING, awareness, comprehension, education, insight, instruction, knowledge, learning, wisdom

enlist verb 1 JOIN UP, enroll, enter (into), join, muster, register, sign up, volunteer 2 OBTAIN, engage, procure, recruit

enliven verb CHEER UP, animate, excite, inspire, invigorate, pep up, rouse, spark, stimulate, vitalize

enmity noun HOSTILITY, acrimony, animosity, bad blood, bitterness, hatred, ill will, malice

ennoble verb DIGNIFY, aggrandize, elevate, enhance, exalt, glorify, honor, magnify, raise

enormity noun 1 WICKEDNESS, atrocity, depravity, monstrousness, outrageousness, vileness, villainy 2 ATROCITY, abomination, crime, disgrace, evil, horror, monstrosity, outrage **3** *Informal* HUGENESS, greatness, immensity, magnitude, vastness

enormous *adjective* HUGE, colossal, gigantic, gross, immense, mammoth, massive, mountainous, tremendous, vast

enough *adjective* **1** SUFFICIENT, abundant, adequate, ample, plenty ▸ *noun* **2** SUFFICIENCY, abundance, adequacy, ample supply, plenty, right amount ▸ *adverb* **3** SUFFICIENTLY, abundantly, adequately, amply, reasonably, satisfactorily, tolerably

enquire see INQUIRE

enquiry see INQUIRY

enrage *verb* ANGER, exasperate, incense, inflame, infuriate, madden

enrich *verb* **1** ENHANCE, augment, develop, improve, refine, supplement **2** MAKE RICH, make wealthy

enroll *verb* ENLIST, accept, admit, join up, recruit, register, sign up or on, take on

enrollment *noun* ENLISTMENT, acceptance, admission, engagement, matriculation, recruitment, registration

en route *adverb* ON or ALONG THE WAY, in transit, on the road

ensemble *noun* **1** WHOLE, aggregate, collection, entirety, set, sum, total, totality **2** OUTFIT, costume, get-up (*informal*), suit **3** GROUP, band, cast, chorus, company, troupe

ensign *noun* FLAG, banner, colors, jack, pennant, pennon, standard, streamer

ensue *verb* FOLLOW, arise, come next, derive, flow, issue, proceed, result, stem

ensure *verb* **1** MAKE CERTAIN, certify, confirm, effect, guarantee, make sure, secure, warrant **2** PROTECT, guard, make safe, safeguard, secure

entail *verb* INVOLVE, bring about, call for, demand, give rise to, necessitate, occasion, require

entangle *verb* **1** TANGLE, catch, embroil, enmesh, ensnare, entrap, implicate, snag, snare, trap **2** MIX UP, complicate, confuse, jumble, muddle, perplex, puzzle

enter *verb* **1** COME or GO IN or INTO, arrive, make an entrance, pass into, penetrate, pierce **2** JOIN, commence, embark upon, enlist, enroll, set out on, start, take up **3** RECORD, inscribe, list, log, note, register, set down, take down

enterprise *noun* **1** FIRM, business, company, concern, establishment, operation **2** UNDERTAKING, adventure, effort, endeavor, operation, plan, program, project, venture **3** INITIATIVE, adventurousness, boldness, daring, drive, energy, enthusiasm, resourcefulness

enterprising *adjective* RESOURCEFUL, adventurous, bold, daring, energetic, enthusiastic, go-ahead, intrepid, spirited

entertain *verb* **1** AMUSE, charm, cheer, delight, please, regale **2** SHOW HOSPITALITY TO, accommodate, be host to, harbor, have company, lodge, put up, treat **3** CONSIDER, conceive, contemplate, imagine, keep in mind, think about

entertaining adjective ENJOYABLE, amusing, cheering, diverting, funny, humorous, interesting, pleasant, pleasurable

entertainment noun ENJOYMENT, amusement, fun, leisure activity, pastime, pleasure, recreation, sport, treat

enthrall verb FASCINATE, captivate, charm, enchant, enrapture, entrance, grip, mesmerize

enthusiasm noun KEENNESS, eagerness, fervor, interest, passion, relish, zeal, zest

enthusiast noun LOVER, aficionado, buff (informal), devotee, fan, fanatic, follower, supporter

enthusiastic adjective KEEN, avid, eager, fervent, gung ho (slang), passionate, vigorous, wholehearted, zealous

entice verb ATTRACT, allure, cajole, coax, lead on, lure, persuade, seduce, tempt

entire adjective WHOLE, complete, full, gross, total

entirely adverb COMPLETELY, absolutely, altogether, fully, in every respect, thoroughly, totally, utterly, wholly

entitle verb 1 GIVE THE RIGHT TO, allow, authorize, empower, enable, license, permit 2 CALL, christen, dub, label, name, term, title

entity noun THING, being, creature, individual, object, organism, substance

entourage noun RETINUE, associates, attendants, company, court, escort,

followers, staff, train

entrails plural noun INTESTINES, bowels, guts, innards (informal), insides (informal), offal, viscera

entrance[1] noun 1 WAY IN, access, door, doorway, entry, gate, opening, passage 2 APPEARANCE, arrival, coming in, entry, introduction 3 ADMISSION, access, admittance, entrée, entry, permission to enter

entrance[2] verb 1 ENCHANT, bewitch, captivate, charm, delight, enrapture, enthrall, fascinate 2 MESMERIZE, hypnotize, put in a trance

entrant noun COMPETITOR, candidate, contestant, entry, participant, player

entreaty noun PLEA, appeal, earnest request, exhortation, petition, prayer, request, supplication

entrenched adjective FIXED, deep-rooted, deep-seated, ineradicable, ingrained, rooted, set, unshakable, well-established

entrepreneur noun BUSINESSMAN or BUSINESSWOMAN, impresario, industrialist, magnate, tycoon

entrust verb GIVE CUSTODY OF, assign, commit, confide, delegate, deliver, hand over, turn over

entry noun 1 WAY IN, access, door, doorway, entrance, gate, opening, passage 2 COMING IN, appearance, entering, entrance, initiation, introduction 3 ADMISSION, access, entrance, entrée, permission to enter 4 RECORD, account, item, listing, note

entwine verb TWIST, interlace,

interweave, knit, plait, twine, weave, wind

enumerate verb LIST, cite, itemize, mention, name, quote, recite, recount, relate, spell out

enunciate verb 1 PRONOUNCE, articulate, enounce, say, sound, speak, utter, vocalize, voice 2 STATE, declare, proclaim, promulgate, pronounce, propound, publish

envelop verb ENCLOSE, cloak, cover, encase, encircle, engulf, shroud, surround, wrap

envelope noun WRAPPING, case, casing, cover, covering, jacket, wrapper

enviable adjective DESIRABLE, advantageous, favored, fortunate, lucky, privileged, to die for (informal), win-win (informal)

envious adjective COVETOUS, green with envy, grudging, jealous, resentful

environment noun SURROUNDINGS, atmosphere, background, conditions, habitat, medium, setting, situation

environmental adjective ECOLOGICAL, green

environmentalist noun CONSERVATIONIST, ecologist, green

environs plural noun SURROUNDING AREA, district, locality, neighborhood, outskirts, precincts, suburbs, vicinity

envisage verb 1 IMAGINE, conceive (of), conceptualize, contemplate, fancy, picture, think up, visualize 2 FORESEE, anticipate, envision, predict, see

envoy noun MESSENGER, agent, ambassador, courier, delegate, diplomat, emissary, intermediary, representative

envy noun 1 COVETOUSNESS, enviousness, jealousy, resentfulness, resentment ▸ verb 2 COVET, be envious (of), begrudge, be jealous (of), grudge, resent

ephemeral adjective BRIEF, fleeting, momentary, passing, short-lived, temporary, transient, transitory

epidemic noun SPREAD, contagion, growth, outbreak, plague, rash, upsurge, wave

epigram noun WITTICISM, aphorism, bon mot, quip

epilogue noun CONCLUSION, coda, concluding speech, postscript

episode noun 1 EVENT, adventure, affair, escapade, experience, happening, incident, matter, occurrence 2 PART, chapter, installment, passage, scene, section

epistle noun LETTER, communication, message, missive, note

epitaph noun MONUMENT, inscription

epithet noun NAME, appellation, description, designation, moniker or monicker (slang), nickname, sobriquet, tag, title

epitome noun PERSONIFICATION, archetype, embodiment, essence, quintessence, representation, type, typical example

epitomize verb TYPIFY, embody, exemplify, illustrate, personify, represent, symbolize

epoch noun ERA, age, date, period, time

equable adjective EVEN-TEMPERED, calm, composed, easy-going, imperturbable, level-headed, placid, serene, unflappable (informal)

equal adjective **1** IDENTICAL, alike, corresponding, equivalent, the same, uniform **2** REGULAR, symmetrical, uniform, unvarying **3** EVEN, balanced, evenly matched, fifty-fifty (informal) **4** FAIR, egalitarian, even-handed, impartial, just, on a level playing field (informal), unbiased **5** equal to CAPABLE OF, competent to, fit for, good enough for, ready for, strong enough, suitable for, up to ▶ noun **6** MATCH, counterpart, equivalent, rival, twin ▶ verb **7** MATCH, amount to, be tantamount to, correspond to, equate, level, parallel, tie with

equality noun **1** SAMENESS, balance, correspondence, equivalence, evenness, identity, likeness, similarity, uniformity **2** FAIRNESS, egalitarianism, equal opportunity, parity

equalize verb MAKE EQUAL, balance, equal, even up, level, match, regularize, smooth, square, standardize

equate verb MAKE or BE EQUAL, be commensurate, compare, correspond with or to, liken, mention in the same breath, parallel

equation noun EQUATING, comparison, correspondence, parallel

equilibrium noun STABILITY, balance, equipoise, evenness, rest, steadiness, symmetry

equip verb SUPPLY, arm, array, fit out, furnish, provide, stock

equipment noun TOOLS, accoutrements, apparatus, gear, paraphernalia, stuff, supplies, tackle

equitable adjective FAIR, even-handed, honest, impartial, just, proper, reasonable, unbiased

equivalence noun EQUALITY, correspondence, evenness, likeness, parity, sameness, similarity

equivalent noun **1** EQUAL, counterpart, match, opposite number, parallel, twin ▶ adjective **2** EQUAL, alike, commensurate, comparable, corresponding, interchangeable, of a piece, on a level playing field (informal), same, similar, tantamount

equivocal adjective AMBIGUOUS, evasive, indefinite, indeterminate, misleading, oblique, obscure, uncertain, vague

era noun AGE, date, day or days, epoch, generation, period, time

eradicate verb WIPE OUT, annihilate, destroy, eliminate, erase, exterminate, extinguish, obliterate, remove, root out

erase verb WIPE OUT, blot, cancel, delete, expunge, obliterate, remove, rub out

erect verb **1** BUILD, construct, put up, raise, set up **2** FOUND, create, establish, form, initiate, institute, organize, set up ▶ adjective **3** UPRIGHT, elevated, perpendicular, pricked-up, stiff, straight, vertical

erode verb WEAR DOWN or AWAY, abrade, consume, corrode, destroy, deteriorate, disintegrate, eat away, grind down

erosion noun DETERIORATION, abrasion, attrition, destruction, disintegration, eating away, grinding down, wearing down or away

erotic adjective SEXUAL, amatory, carnal, lustful, seductive, sensual, sexy (informal), voluptuous

err verb MAKE A MISTAKE, blunder, go wrong, miscalculate, misjudge, mistake, slip up (informal)

errand noun JOB, charge, commission, message, mission, task

erratic adjective UNPREDICTABLE, changeable, inconsistent, irregular, uneven, unreliable, unstable, variable, wayward

erroneous adjective INCORRECT, fallacious, false, faulty, flawed, invalid, mistaken, unsound, wrong

error noun MISTAKE, bloomer (informal), blunder, miscalculation, oversight, slip, solecism

erstwhile adjective FORMER, bygone, late, old, once, one-time, past, previous, sometime

erudite adjective LEARNED, cultivated, cultured, educated, knowledgeable, scholarly, well-educated, well-read

erupt verb 1 EXPLODE, belch forth, blow up, burst out, gush, pour forth, spew forth or

out, spout, throw off 2 Medical BREAK OUT, appear

eruption noun 1 EXPLOSION, discharge, ejection, flare-up, outbreak, outburst 2 Medical INFLAMMATION, outbreak, rash

escalate verb INCREASE, expand, extend, grow, heighten, intensify, mount, rise

escapade noun ADVENTURE, antic, caper, prank, scrape (informal), stunt

escape verb 1 GET AWAY, abscond, bolt, break free or out, flee, fly, make one's getaway, run away or off, slip away 2 AVOID, dodge, duck, elude, evade, pass, shun, slip 3 LEAK, emanate, exude, flow, gush, issue, pour forth, seep ▶ noun 4 GETAWAY, break, break-out, flight 5 AVOIDANCE, circumvention, evasion 6 RELAXATION, distraction, diversion, pastime, recreation 7 LEAK, emanation, emission, seepage

escort noun 1 GUARD, bodyguard, convoy, cortege, entourage, retinue, train 2 COMPANION, attendant, beau, chaperon, guide, partner ▶ verb 3 ACCOMPANY, chaperon, conduct, guide, lead, partner, shepherd, usher

especial adjective Formal EXCEPTIONAL, noteworthy, outstanding, principal, special, uncommon, unusual

especially adverb EXCEPTIONALLY, conspicuously, markedly, notably, outstandingly, remarkably, specially, strikingly, uncommonly, unusually

espionage noun SPYING,

counter-intelligence, intelligence, surveillance, undercover work

espousal noun SUPPORT, adoption, advocacy, backing, championing, championship, defense, embracing, promotion, taking up

espouse verb SUPPORT, adopt, advocate, back, champion, embrace, promote, stand up for, take up, uphold

essay noun 1 COMPOSITION, article, discourse, dissertation, paper, piece, tract, treatise ▶ verb 2 Formal ATTEMPT, aim, endeavor, try, undertake

essence noun 1 FUNDAMENTAL NATURE, being, core, heart, nature, quintessence, soul, spirit, substance 2 CONCENTRATE, distillate, extract, spirits, tincture

essential adjective 1 VITAL, crucial, important, indispensable, necessary, needed, requisite 2 FUNDAMENTAL, basic, cardinal, elementary, innate, intrinsic, main, principal ▶ noun 3 PREREQUISITE, basic, fundamental, must, necessity, rudiment, sine qua non

establish verb 1 CREATE, constitute, form, found, ground, inaugurate, institute, settle, set up 2 PROVE, authenticate, certify, confirm, corroborate, demonstrate, substantiate, verify

establishment noun 1 CREATION, formation, foundation, founding, inauguration, installation, institution, organization, setting up

2 ORGANIZATION, business, company, concern, corporation, enterprise, firm, institution, outfit (informal) 3 **the Establishment** THE AUTHORITIES, ruling class, the powers that be, the system

estate noun 1 LANDS, area, domain, holdings, manor, property 2 Law PROPERTY, assets, belongings, effects, fortune, goods, possessions, wealth

esteem noun 1 RESPECT, admiration, credit, estimation, good opinion, honor, kudos, regard, reverence, veneration ▶ verb 2 RESPECT, admire, love, prize, regard highly, revere, think highly of, treasure, value 3 CONSIDER, believe, deem, estimate, judge, reckon, regard, think, view

estimate verb 1 CALCULATE ROUGHLY, assess, evaluate, gauge, guess, judge, number, reckon, value 2 FORM AN OPINION, believe, conjecture, consider, judge, rank, rate, reckon, surmise ▶ noun 3 APPROXIMATE CALCULATION, assessment, ballpark figure (informal), guess, guesstimate (informal), judgment, valuation 4 OPINION, appraisal, assessment, belief, estimation, judgment

estimation noun OPINION, appraisal, appreciation, assessment, belief, consideration, considered opinion, judgment, view

estuary noun INLET, creek, firth, fjord, mouth

et cetera adverb 1 AND SO ON, and so forth ▶ noun 2 AND THE REST, and others, and the like, et al.

etch verb CUT, carve, eat into, engrave, impress, imprint, inscribe, stamp

etching noun PRINT, carving, engraving, impression, imprint, inscription

eternal adjective **1** EVERLASTING, endless, immortal, infinite, never-ending, perpetual, timeless, unceasing, unending **2** PERMANENT, deathless, enduring, immutable, imperishable, indestructible, lasting, unchanging

eternity noun **1** INFINITY, ages, endlessness, immortality, perpetuity, timelessness **2** Theology THE AFTERLIFE, heaven, paradise, the hereafter, the next world

ethical adjective MORAL, conscientious, fair, good, honorable, just, principled, proper, right, upright, virtuous

ethics plural noun MORAL CODE, conscience, morality, moral philosophy, moral values, principles, rules of conduct, standards

ethnic adjective CULTURAL, folk, indigenous, national, native, racial, traditional

etiquette noun GOOD or PROPER BEHAVIOR, civility, courtesy, decorum, formalities, manners, politeness, propriety, protocol

euphoria noun ELATION, ecstasy, exaltation, exhilaration, intoxication, joy, jubilation, rapture

evacuate verb CLEAR, abandon, desert, forsake, leave, move out, pull out, quit, vacate, withdraw

evade verb **1** AVOID, dodge, duck, elude, escape, get away from, sidestep, steer clear of **2** AVOID ANSWERING, equivocate, fend off, fudge, hedge, parry

evaluate verb ASSESS, appraise, calculate, estimate, gauge, judge, rate, reckon, size up (informal), weigh

evaporate verb **1** DRY UP, dehydrate, desiccate, dry, vaporize **2** DISAPPEAR, dematerialize, dissolve, fade away, melt away, vanish

evasion noun **1** AVOIDANCE, dodging, escape **2** DECEPTION, equivocation, evasiveness, prevarication

evasive adjective DECEPTIVE, cagey (informal), equivocating, indirect, oblique, prevaricating, shifty, slippery

eve noun **1** NIGHT BEFORE, day before, vigil **2** BRINK, edge, point, threshold, verge

even adjective **1** LEVEL, flat, horizontal, parallel, smooth, steady, straight, true, uniform **2** REGULAR, constant, smooth, steady, unbroken, uniform, uninterrupted, unvarying, unwavering **3** EQUAL, comparable, fifty-fifty (informal), identical, level, like, matching, neck and neck, on a level playing field (informal), on a par, similar, tied **4** CALM, composed, cool, even-tempered, imperturbable, placid, unruffled, well-balanced **5 get even (with)** PAY BACK, give tit for tat, reciprocate, repay, requite, retaliate

evening noun DUSK, gloaming (Scot. or poetic), twilight

event noun 1 INCIDENT, affair, business, circumstance, episode, experience, happening, occasion, occurrence 2 COMPETITION, bout, contest, game, tournament

even-tempered adjective CALM, composed, cool, imperturbable, level-headed, placid, tranquil, unexcitable, unruffled

eventful adjective EXCITING, active, busy, dramatic, full, lively, memorable, remarkable

eventual adjective FINAL, concluding, overall, ultimate

eventuality noun POSSIBILITY, case, chance, contingency, event, likelihood, probability

eventually adverb IN THE END, after all, at the end of the day, finally, one day, some time, ultimately, when all is said and done

ever adverb 1 AT ANY TIME, at all, at any period, at any point, by any chance, in any case, on any occasion 2 ALWAYS, at all times, constantly, continually, evermore, for ever, perpetually, twenty-four-seven (slang)

everlasting adjective ETERNAL, endless, immortal, indestructible, never-ending, perpetual, timeless, undying

evermore adverb FOR EVER, always, eternally, ever, to the end of time

every adjective EACH, all, each one

everybody pronoun EVERYONE, all and sundry, each one, each person, every man, one and all, the whole world

everyday adjective COMMON, customary, mundane, ordinary, routine, stock, usual, workaday

everyone pronoun EVERYBODY, all and sundry, each one, each person, every person, one and all, the whole world

everything pronoun ALL, each thing, the lot, the whole lot

everywhere adverb TO or IN EVERY PLACE, all around, all over, far and wide or near, high and low, in every nook and cranny, the world over, ubiquitously

evict verb EXPEL, boot out (informal), eject, kick out (informal), oust, remove, throw out, turn out

evidence noun 1 PROOF, confirmation, corroboration, demonstration, grounds, indication, sign, substantiation, testimony ▸verb 2 SHOW, demonstrate, display, exhibit, indicate, prove, reveal, signify, witness

evident adjective OBVIOUS, apparent, clear, manifest, noticeable, perceptible, plain, unmistakable, visible

evidently adverb 1 OBVIOUSLY, clearly, manifestly, plainly, undoubtedly, unmistakably, without question 2 APPARENTLY, ostensibly, outwardly, seemingly, to all appearances

evil noun 1 WICKEDNESS, badness, depravity, malignity, sin, vice, villainy, wrongdoing 2 HARM, affliction, disaster, hurt, ill, injury, mischief, misfortune, suffering, woe ▸adjective 3 WICKED, bad, depraved, immoral, malevolent, malicious, sinful, villainous 4 HARMFUL, calamitous, catastrophic, destructive, dire, disastrous, pernicious, ruinous **5** OFFENSIVE, foul, noxious, pestilential, unpleasant, vile

evoke verb RECALL, arouse, awaken, call, give rise to, induce, rekindle, stir up, summon up

evolution noun DEVELOPMENT, expansion, growth, increase, maturation, progress, unfolding, working out

evolve verb DEVELOP, expand, grow, increase, mature, progress, unfold, work out

exact adjective **1** ACCURATE, correct, definite, faultless, precise, right, specific, true, unerring ▸ verb **2** DEMAND, claim, command, compel, extort, extract, force

exacting adjective DEMANDING, difficult, hard, harsh, rigorous, severe, strict, stringent, taxing, tough

exactly adverb **1** PRECISELY, accurately, correctly, explicitly, faithfully, scrupulously, truthfully, unerringly **2** IN EVERY RESPECT, absolutely, indeed, precisely, quite, specifically, to the letter

exactness noun PRECISION, accuracy, correctness, exactitude, rigorousness, scrupulousness, strictness, veracity

exaggerate verb OVERSTATE, amplify, embellish, embroider, enlarge, overemphasize, overestimate

exaggeration noun OVERSTATEMENT, amplification, embellishment, enlargement, hyperbole, overemphasis, overestimation

exalt verb **1** PRAISE, acclaim, extol, glorify, idolize, set on a pedestal, worship **2** RAISE, advance, elevate, ennoble, honor, promote, upgrade

exaltation noun **1** PRAISE, acclaim, glorification, idolization, reverence, tribute, worship **2** RISE, advancement, elevation, ennoblement, promotion, upgrading

exalted adjective HIGH-RANKING, dignified, eminent, grand, honored, lofty, prestigious

examination noun **1** INSPECTION, analysis, exploration, interrogation, investigation, research, scrutiny, study, test **2** QUESTIONING, inquiry, inquisition, probe, quiz, test

examine verb **1** INSPECT, analyze, explore, investigate, peruse, scrutinize, study, survey **2** QUESTION, cross-examine, grill (informal), inquire, interrogate, quiz, test

example noun **1** SPECIMEN, case, illustration, instance, sample **2** MODEL, archetype, ideal, paradigm, paragon, prototype, standard **3** WARNING, caution, lesson

exasperate verb IRRITATE, anger, annoy, enrage, incense, inflame, infuriate, madden, pique

exasperation noun IRRITATION, anger, annoyance, fury, pique, provocation, rage, wrath

excavate verb DIG OUT, burrow, delve, dig up, mine, quarry, tunnel, uncover, unearth

exceed verb **1** SURPASS, beat, better, cap (informal), eclipse, outdo, outstrip, overtake, pass, top **2** GO OVER THE LIMIT OF, go over the top, overstep

exceedingly adverb EXTREMELY, enormously, exceptionally, extraordinarily, hugely, superlatively, surpassingly, unusually, very

excel verb **1** BE SUPERIOR, beat, eclipse, outdo, outshine, surpass, transcend **2 excel in** or **at** BE GOOD AT, be proficient in, be skillful at, be talented at, shine at, show talent in

excellence noun HIGH QUALITY, distinction, eminence, goodness, greatness, merit, pre-eminence, superiority, supremacy

excellent adjective OUTSTANDING, brilliant, exquisite, fine, first-class, first-rate, good, great, superb, superlative, world-class

except preposition **1** Also **except for** APART FROM, barring, besides, but, excepting, excluding, omitting, other than, saving, with the exception of ▸ verb **2** EXCLUDE, leave out, omit, pass over

exception noun **1** SPECIAL CASE, anomaly, deviation, freak, inconsistency, irregularity, oddity, peculiarity **2** EXCLUSION, leaving out, omission, passing over

exceptional adjective **1** SPECIAL, abnormal, atypical, extraordinary, irregular, odd, peculiar, strange, unusual **2** REMARKABLE, excellent, extraordinary, marvelous, outstanding, phenomenal, prodigious, special, superior

excerpt noun EXTRACT, fragment, part, passage, piece, quotation, section, selection

excess noun **1** SURFEIT, glut, overload, superabundance, superfluity, surplus, too much **2** OVERINDULGENCE, debauchery, dissipation, dissoluteness, extravagance, intemperance, prodigality

excessive adjective IMMODERATE, disproportionate, exaggerated, extreme, inordinate, overmuch, superfluous, too much, undue, unfair, unreasonable

exchange verb **1** INTERCHANGE, barter, change, convert into, swap, switch, trade ▸ noun **2** INTERCHANGE, barter, quid pro quo, reciprocity, substitution, swap, switch, tit for tat, trade

excitable adjective NERVOUS, emotional, highly strung, hot-headed, mercurial, quick-tempered, temperamental, volatile, wired (slang)

excite verb AROUSE, animate, galvanize, inflame, inspire, provoke, rouse, stir up, thrill

excitement noun AGITATION, action, activity, animation, commotion, furor, passion, thrill

exciting adjective STIMULATING, dramatic, electrifying, exhilarating, rousing, sensational, stirring, thrilling

exclaim verb CRY OUT, call out, declare, proclaim, shout, utter, yell

exclamation noun CRY, call, interjection, outcry, shout, utterance, yell

exclude verb **1** KEEP OUT, ban, bar, boycott, disallow, forbid, prohibit, refuse, shut out **2** LEAVE OUT, count out, eliminate, ignore, omit, pass over, reject, rule out, set aside

exclusion noun **1** BAN, bar, boycott, disqualification, embargo, prohibition, veto **2** ELIMINATION, omission, rejection

exclusive adjective **1** SOLE, absolute, complete, entire, full, total, undivided, whole **2** LIMITED, confined, peculiar, restricted, unique **3** SELECT, chic, cliquish, cool (informal), fashionable, phat (slang), restricted, snobbish, up-market

excommunicate verb EXPEL, anathematize, ban, banish, cast out, denounce, exclude, repudiate

excruciating adjective AGONIZING, harrowing, insufferable, intense, piercing, severe, unbearable, violent

exculpate verb ABSOLVE, acquit, clear, discharge, excuse, exonerate, pardon, vindicate

excursion noun TRIP, day trip, expedition, jaunt, journey, outing, pleasure trip, ramble, tour

excusable adjective FORGIVABLE, allowable, defensible, justifiable, pardonable, permissible, understandable, warrantable

excuse noun **1** JUSTIFICATION, apology, defense, explanation, grounds, mitigation, plea, reason, vindication ▶ verb **2** JUSTIFY, apologize for, defend, explain, mitigate, vindicate **3** FORGIVE, acquit, exculpate, exonerate, make allowances for, overlook, pardon, tolerate,

turn a blind eye to **4** FREE, absolve, discharge, exempt, let off, release, relieve, spare

execute verb **1** PUT TO DEATH, behead, electrocute, guillotine, hang, kill, shoot **2** CARRY OUT, accomplish, administer, discharge, effect, enact, implement, perform, prosecute

execution noun **1** CARRYING OUT, accomplishment, administration, enactment, enforcement, implementation, operation, performance, prosecution **2** KILLING, capital punishment, hanging

executioner noun **1** HANGMAN, headsman **2** KILLER, assassin, exterminator, hit man (slang), liquidator, murderer, slayer

executive noun **1** ADMINISTRATOR, director, manager, official **2** ADMINISTRATION, directorate, directors, government, hierarchy, leadership, management ▶ adjective **3** ADMINISTRATIVE, controlling, decision-making, directing, governing, managerial

exemplary adjective **1** IDEAL, admirable, commendable, excellent, fine, good, model, praiseworthy **2** WARNING, cautionary

exemplify verb SHOW, demonstrate, display, embody, exhibit, illustrate, represent, serve as an example of

exempt adjective **1** IMMUNE, excepted, excused, free, not liable, released, spared ▶ verb **2** GRANT IMMUNITY, absolve, discharge, excuse, free, let off, release, relieve, spare

exemption noun IMMUNITY,

absolution, discharge, dispensation, exception, exoneration, freedom, release

exercise noun 1 EXERTION, activity, effort, labor, toil, training, work, work-out 2 TASK, drill, lesson, practice, problem 3 USE, application, discharge, fulfillment, implementation, practice, utilization ▶ verb 4 PUT TO USE, apply, bring to bear, employ, exert, use, utilize 5 TRAIN, practice, work out

exert verb 1 USE, apply, bring to bear, employ, exercise, make use of, utilize, wield 2 exert oneself MAKE AN EFFORT, apply oneself, do one's best, endeavor, labor, strain, strive, struggle, toil, work

exertion noun EFFORT, elbow grease (facetious), endeavor, exercise, industry, strain, struggle, toil

exhaust verb 1 TIRE OUT, debilitate, drain, enervate, enfeeble, fatigue, sap, weaken, wear out 2 USE UP, consume, deplete, dissipate, expend, run through, spend, squander, waste

exhausted adjective 1 WORN OUT, debilitated, done in (informal), drained, fatigued, spent, tired out 2 USED UP, consumed, depleted, dissipated, expended, finished, spent, squandered, wasted

exhausting adjective TIRING, backbreaking, debilitating, grueling, laborious, punishing, sapping, strenuous, taxing

exhaustion noun 1 TIREDNESS, debilitation, fatigue, weariness 2 DEPLETION, consumption,

emptying, using up

exhaustive adjective THOROUGH, all-embracing, complete, comprehensive, extensive, full-scale, in-depth, intensive

exhibit verb DISPLAY, demonstrate, express, indicate, manifest, parade, put on view, reveal, show

exhibition noun DISPLAY, demonstration, exposition, performance, presentation, representation, show, spectacle

exhilarating adjective EXCITING, breathtaking, enlivening, invigorating, stimulating, thrilling

exhort verb URGE, advise, beseech, call upon, entreat, persuade, press, spur

exhume verb DIG UP, disentomb, disinter, unearth

exigency noun NEED, constraint, demand, necessity, requirement

exile noun 1 BANISHMENT, deportation, expatriation, expulsion 2 EXPATRIATE, deportee, émigré, outcast, refugee ▶ verb 3 BANISH, deport, drive out, eject, expatriate, expel

exist verb 1 BE, be present, endure, live, occur, survive 2 SURVIVE, eke out a living, get along or by, keep one's head above water, stay alive, subsist

existence noun BEING, actuality, life, subsistence

existent adjective IN EXISTENCE, alive, existing, extant, living, present, standing, surviving

exit noun 1 WAY OUT, door, gate, outlet 2 DEPARTURE, exodus, farewell, going, good-bye, leave-taking, retreat, withdrawal ▶ *verb* **3** DEPART, go away, go offstage (*Theatre*), go out, leave, make tracks, retire, retreat, take one's leave, withdraw

exodus *noun* DEPARTURE, evacuation, exit, flight, going out, leaving, migration, retreat, withdrawal

exonerate *verb* CLEAR, absolve, acquit, discharge, exculpate, excuse, justify, pardon, vindicate

exorbitant *adjective* EXCESSIVE, extortionate, extravagant, immoderate, inordinate, outrageous, preposterous, unreasonable

exorcise *verb* DRIVE OUT, cast out, deliver (from), expel, purify

exotic *adjective* **1** UNUSUAL, colorful, fascinating, glamorous, mysterious, strange, striking, unfamiliar **2** FOREIGN, alien, external, imported, naturalized

expand *verb* **1** INCREASE, amplify, broaden, develop, enlarge, extend, grow, magnify, swell, widen **2** SPREAD (OUT), diffuse, stretch (out), unfold, unfurl, unravel, unroll **3 expand on** GO INTO DETAIL ABOUT, amplify, develop, elaborate on, embellish, enlarge on, expatiate on, expound on, flesh out

expanse *noun* AREA, breadth, extent, range, space, stretch, sweep, tract

expansion *noun* INCREASE, amplification, development, enlargement, growth, magnification, opening out, spread

expansive *adjective* **1** WIDE, broad, extensive, far-reaching, voluminous, wide-ranging, widespread **2** TALKATIVE, affable, communicative, effusive, friendly, loquacious, open, outgoing, sociable, unreserved

expatriate *adjective* **1** EXILED, banished, emigrant, émigré ▶ *noun* **2** EXILE, emigrant, émigré, refugee

expect *verb* **1** THINK, assume, believe, imagine, presume, reckon, suppose, surmise, trust **2** LOOK FORWARD TO, anticipate, await, contemplate, envisage, hope for, predict, watch for **3** REQUIRE, call for, demand, insist on, want

expectant *adjective* **1** EXPECTING, anticipating, apprehensive, eager, hopeful, in suspense, ready, watchful **2** PREGNANT, expecting (*informal*), gravid

expectation *noun* **1** PROBABILITY, assumption, belief, conjecture, forecast, likelihood, presumption, supposition **2** ANTICIPATION, apprehension, expectancy, hope, promise, suspense

expediency *noun* SUITABILITY, advisability, benefit, convenience, pragmatism, profitability, prudence, usefulness, utility

expedient *noun* **1** MEANS, contrivance, device, makeshift, measure, method, resort, scheme, stopgap ▶ *adjective* **2** ADVANTAGEOUS, appropriate, beneficial, convenient, effective, helpful, opportune, practical, suitable, useful, win-win (*informal*)

expedition noun JOURNEY, excursion, mission, quest, safari, tour, trek, voyage

expel verb 1 DRIVE OUT, belch, cast out, discharge, eject, remove, spew 2 DISMISS, ban, banish, chuck out (*slang*), drum out, evict, exclude, exile, throw out

expend verb SPEND, consume, dissipate, exhaust, go through, pay out, use (up)

expendable adjective DISPENSABLE, inessential, nonessential, replaceable, unimportant, unnecessary

expenditure noun SPENDING, consumption, cost, expense, outgoings, outlay, output, payment

expense noun COST, charge, expenditure, loss, outlay, payment, spending

expensive adjective DEAR, costly, exorbitant, extravagant, high-priced, lavish, overpriced, steep (*informal*), stiff

experience noun 1 KNOWLEDGE, contact, exposure, familiarity, involvement, participation, practice, training 2 EVENT, adventure, affair, encounter, episode, happening, incident, occurrence ▶verb 3 UNDERGO, encounter, endure, face, feel, go through, live through, sample, taste

experienced adjective KNOWLEDGEABLE, accomplished, expert, practiced, seasoned, tested, tried, veteran, well-versed

experiment noun 1 TEST, examination, experimentation, investigation, procedure, proof, research, trial, trial run ▶verb 2 TEST, examine, investigate, put to the test, research, sample, try, verify

experimental adjective TEST, exploratory, pilot, preliminary, probationary, provisional, speculative, tentative, trial, trial-and-error

expert noun 1 MASTER, authority, connoisseur, past master, professional, specialist, virtuoso ▶adjective 2 SKILLFUL, adept, adroit, experienced, masterly, practiced, professional, proficient, qualified, virtuoso

expertise noun SKILL, adroitness, command, facility, judgment, know-how (*informal*), knowledge, mastery, proficiency

expire verb 1 FINISH, cease, close, come to an end, conclude, end, lapse, run out, stop, terminate 2 BREATHE OUT, emit, exhale, expel 3 DIE, depart, kick the bucket (*informal*), pass away or on, perish

explain verb 1 MAKE CLEAR or PLAIN, clarify, clear up, define, describe, elucidate, expound, resolve, teach 2 ACCOUNT FOR, excuse, give a reason for, justify

explanation noun 1 REASON, account, answer, excuse, justification, motive, vindication 2 DESCRIPTION, clarification, definition, elucidation, illustration, interpretation

explanatory adjective DESCRIPTIVE, illustrative, interpretive

explicit adjective CLEAR,

categorical, definite, frank, precise, specific, straightforward, unambiguous

explode verb **1** BLOW UP, burst, detonate, discharge, erupt, go off, set off, shatter **2** DISPROVE, debunk, discredit, give the lie to, invalidate, refute, repudiate

exploit verb **1** TAKE ADVANTAGE OF, abuse, manipulate, milk, misuse, play on or upon **2** MAKE THE BEST USE OF, capitalize on, cash in on (informal), profit by or from, use, utilize ▶ noun **3** FEAT, accomplishment, achievement, adventure, escapade, attainment, deed, escapade, stunt

exploitation noun MISUSE, abuse, manipulation

exploration noun **1** INVESTIGATION, analysis, examination, inquiry, inspection, research, scrutiny, search **2** EXPEDITION, reconnaissance, survey, tour, travel, trip

exploratory adjective INVESTIGATIVE, experimental, fact-finding, probing, searching, trial

explore verb **1** INVESTIGATE, examine, inquire into, inspect, look into, probe, research, search **2** TRAVEL, reconnoiter, scout, survey, tour

explosion noun **1** BANG, blast, burst, clap, crack, detonation, discharge, report **2** OUTBURST, eruption, fit, outbreak

explosive adjective **1** UNSTABLE, volatile **2** VIOLENT, fiery, stormy, touchy, vehement

exponent noun **1** ADVOCATE, backer, champion, defender,

promoter, proponent, supporter, upholder **2** PERFORMER, player

expose verb **1** UNCOVER, display, exhibit, present, reveal, show, unveil **2** MAKE VULNERABLE, endanger, imperil, jeopardize, lay open, leave open, subject

exposed adjective **1** UNCONCEALED, bare, on display, on show, on view, revealed, uncovered **2** UNSHELTERED, open, unprotected **3** VULNERABLE, in peril, laid bare, susceptible, wide open

exposure noun PUBLICITY, display, exhibition, presentation, revelation, showing, uncovering, unveiling

expound verb EXPLAIN, describe, elucidate, interpret, set forth, spell out, unfold

express verb **1** STATE, articulate, communicate, declare, phrase, put into words, say, utter, voice, word **2** SHOW, convey, exhibit, indicate, intimate, make known, represent, reveal, signify, stand for, symbolize ▶ adjective **3** EXPLICIT, categorical, clear, definite, distinct, plain, unambiguous **4** SPECIFIC, clear-cut, especial, particular, singular, special **5** FAST, direct, high-speed, nonstop, rapid, speedy, swift

expression noun **1** STATEMENT, announcement, communication, declaration, utterance **2** INDICATION, demonstration, exhibition, manifestation, representation, show, sign, symbol, token **3** LOOK, air, appearance, aspect, countenance, face

4 PHRASE, idiom, locution, remark, term, turn of phrase, word

expressive adjective VIVID, eloquent, moving, poignant, striking, telling

expressly adverb **1** DEFINITELY, categorically, clearly, distinctly, explicitly, in no uncertain terms, plainly, unambiguously **2** SPECIFICALLY, especially, particularly, specially

expulsion noun EJECTION, banishment, dismissal, eviction, exclusion, removal

exquisite adjective **1** BEAUTIFUL, attractive, charming, comely, lovely, pleasing, striking **2** FINE, beautiful, dainty, delicate, elegant, lovely, precious **3** INTENSE, acute, keen, sharp

extempore adverb, adjective IMPROMPTU, ad lib, freely, improvised, offhand, off the cuff (*informal*), spontaneously, unpremeditated, unprepared

extend verb **1** MAKE LONGER, drag out, draw out, lengthen, prolong, spin out, spread out, stretch **2** LAST, carry on, continue, go on **3** WIDEN, add to, augment, broaden, enhance, enlarge, expand, increase, supplement **4** OFFER, confer, impart, present, proffer

extension noun **1** ANNEX, addition, appendage, appendix, supplement **2** LENGTHENING, broadening, development, enlargement, expansion, increase, spread, widening

extensive adjective WIDE, broad, far-flung, far-reaching, large-scale, pervasive, spacious, vast, voluminous, widespread

extent noun SIZE, amount, area, breadth, expanse, length, stretch, volume, width

extenuating adjective MITIGATING, justifying, moderating, qualifying

exterior noun **1** OUTSIDE, coating, covering, façade, face, shell, skin, surface ▶adjective **2** OUTSIDE, external, outer, outermost, outward, surface

exterminate verb DESTROY, abolish, annihilate, eliminate, eradicate

external adjective **1** OUTER, exterior, outermost, outside, outward, surface **2** OUTSIDE, alien, extrinsic, foreign

extinct adjective DEAD, defunct, gone, lost, vanished

extinction noun DYING OUT, abolition, annihilation, destruction, eradication, extermination, obliteration, oblivion

extinguish verb **1** PUT OUT, blow out, douse, quench, smother, snuff out, stifle **2** DESTROY, annihilate, eliminate, end, eradicate, exterminate, remove, wipe out

extol verb PRAISE, acclaim, commend, eulogize, exalt, glorify, sing the praises of

extort verb FORCE, blackmail, bully, coerce, extract, squeeze

extortionate adjective EXORBITANT, excessive, extravagant, inflated, outrageous, preposterous, sky-high, unreasonable

extra adjective **1** ADDITIONAL, added, ancillary, auxiliary, further, more, supplementary

2 SURPLUS, excess, leftover, redundant, spare, superfluous, unused ▶ *noun* **3** ADDITION, accessory, attachment, bonus, extension, supplement ▶ *adverb* **4** EXCEPTIONALLY, especially, extraordinarily, extremely, particularly, remarkably, uncommonly, unusually

extract *verb* **1** PULL OUT, draw, pluck out, pull, remove, take out, uproot, withdraw **2** DERIVE, draw, elicit, glean, obtain ▶ *noun* **3** PASSAGE, citation, clipping, cutting, excerpt, quotation, selection **4** ESSENCE, concentrate, distillation, juice

extraneous *adjective* IRRELEVANT, beside the point, immaterial, inappropriate, off the subject, unconnected, unrelated

extraordinary *adjective* UNUSUAL, amazing, exceptional, fantastic, outstanding, phenomenal, remarkable, strange, uncommon

extravagance *noun* **1** WASTE, lavishness, overspending, prodigality, profligacy, squandering, wastefulness **2** EXCESS, exaggeration, outrageousness, preposterousness, wildness

extravagant *adjective* **1** WASTEFUL, lavish, prodigal, profligate, spendthrift **2** EXCESSIVE, outrageous, over the top (*slang*), preposterous, reckless, unreasonable

extreme *adjective* **1** MAXIMUM, acute, great, highest, intense, severe, supreme, ultimate, utmost **2** SEVERE, drastic, harsh, radical, rigid, strict, uncompromising **3** EXCESSIVE, fanatical, immoderate, radical

4 FARTHEST, far-off, most distant, outermost, remotest ▶ *noun* **5** LIMIT, boundary, edge, end, extremity, pole

extremely *adverb* VERY, awfully (*informal*), exceedingly, exceptionally, extraordinarily, severely, terribly, uncommonly, unusually

extremist *noun* FANATIC, die-hard, radical, zealot

extremity *noun* **1** LIMIT, border, boundary, edge, extreme, frontier, pinnacle, tip **2** CRISIS, adversity, dire straits, disaster, emergency, exigency, trouble **3** extremities HANDS AND FEET, fingers and toes, limbs

extricate *verb* FREE, disengage, disentangle, get out, release, remove, rescue, wriggle out of

extrovert *adjective* OUTGOING, exuberant, gregarious, sociable

exuberance *noun* **1** HIGH SPIRITS, cheerfulness, ebullience, enthusiasm, liveliness, spirit, vitality, vivacity, zest **2** LUXURIANCE, abundance, copiousness, lavishness, profusion

exuberant *adjective* **1** HIGH-SPIRITED, animated, cheerful, ebullient, energetic, enthusiastic, lively, spirited, vivacious **2** LUXURIANT, abundant, copious, lavish, plentiful, profuse

exult *verb* BE JOYFUL, be overjoyed, celebrate, jump for joy, rejoice

eye *noun* **1** EYEBALL, optic (*informal*) **2** APPRECIATION, discernment, discrimination, judgment, perception, recognition, taste ▶ *verb* **3** LOOK

AT, check out (*informal*), contemplate, inspect, study, survey, view, watch

eyesight noun VISION, perception, sight

eyesore noun MESS, blemish, blot, disfigurement, horror, monstrosity, sight (*informal*)

eyewitness noun OBSERVER, bystander, onlooker, passer-by, spectator, viewer, witness

— **F f** —

fable noun 1 STORY, allegory, legend, myth, parable, tale 2 FICTION, fabrication, fantasy, fish story (*informal*), invention, tall tale (*informal*), urban legend, yarn (*informal*)

fabric noun 1 CLOTH, material, stuff, textile, web 2 FRAMEWORK, constitution, construction, foundations, make-up, organization, structure

fabricate verb 1 MAKE UP, concoct, devise, fake, falsify, feign, forge, invent, trump up 2 BUILD, assemble, construct, erect, form, make, manufacture, shape

fabrication noun 1 FORGERY, concoction, fake, falsehood, fiction, invention, lie, myth 2 CONSTRUCTION, assembly, building, erection, manufacture, production

fabulous adjective 1 Informal WONDERFUL, brilliant, fantastic (*informal*), marvellous, out-of-this-world (*informal*), sensational (*informal*),

spectacular, superb 2 ASTOUNDING, amazing, breathtaking, inconceivable, incredible, phenomenal, unbelievable 3 LEGENDARY, apocryphal, fantastic, fictitious, imaginary, invented, made-up, mythical, unreal

façade noun APPEARANCE, exterior, face, front, guise, mask, pretense, semblance, show

face noun 1 COUNTENANCE, features, mug (*slang*), visage 2 EXPRESSION, appearance, aspect, look 3 SCOWL, frown, grimace, pout, smirk 4 FAÇADE, appearance, display, exterior, front, mask, show 5 SIDE, exterior, front, outside, surface 6 SELF-RESPECT, authority, dignity, honor, image, prestige, reputation, standing, status ▶ verb 7 MEET, brave, come up against, confront, deal with, encounter, experience, oppose, tackle 8 LOOK ONTO, be opposite, front onto, overlook 9 COAT, clad, cover, dress, finish

faceless adjective IMPERSONAL, anonymous, remote

facet noun ASPECT, angle, face, part, phase, plane, side, slant, surface

facetious adjective FUNNY, amusing, comical, droll, flippant, frivolous, humorous, jocular, playful, tongue in cheek

face up to verb ACCEPT, acknowledge, come to terms with, confront, cope with, deal with, meet head-on, tackle

facile adjective SUPERFICIAL, cursory, glib, hasty, shallow, slick

facilitate verb PROMOTE, expedite, forward, further, help, make easy, pave the way for, speed up

facility noun 1 SKILL, ability, adroitness, dexterity, ease, efficiency, effortlessness, fluency, proficiency 2 (often plural) EQUIPMENT, advantage, aid, amenity, appliance, convenience, means, opportunity, resource

facsimile noun COPY, carbon copy, duplicate, fax, photocopy, print, replica, reproduction, transcript

fact noun 1 EVENT, act, deed, fait accompli, happening, incident, occurrence, performance 2 TRUTH, certainty, reality

faction noun 1 GROUP, bloc, cabal, clique, contingent, coterie, gang, party, set, splinter group 2 DISSENSION, conflict, disagreement, discord, disunity, division, infighting, rebellion

factor noun ELEMENT, aspect, cause, component, consideration, influence, item, part

factory noun WORKS, mill, plant

factual adjective TRUE, authentic, correct, exact, genuine, precise, real, true-to-life

faculties plural noun POWERS, capabilities, intelligence, reason, senses, wits

faculty noun 1 ABILITY, aptitude, capacity, facility, power, propensity, skill 2 DEPARTMENT, school

fad noun CRAZE, fashion, mania, rage, trend, vogue, whim

fade verb 1 PALE, bleach, discolor, lose color, wash out 2 DWINDLE, decline, die away, disappear, dissolve, melt away, vanish, wane

faded adjective DISCOLORED, bleached, dull, indistinct, pale, washed out

fading adjective DECLINING, decreasing, disappearing, dying, on the decline, vanishing

fail verb 1 BE UNSUCCESSFUL, bite the dust, break down, come to grief, come unstuck, fall, fizzle out (informal), flop (informal), founder, miscarry, misfire 2 DISAPPOINT, abandon, desert, forget, forsake, let down, neglect, omit 3 GIVE OUT, conk out (informal), cut out, die, peter out, stop working 4 GO BANKRUPT, become insolvent, close down, fold (informal), go broke (informal), go bust (informal), go into receivership, go out of business, go to the wall, go under ▸ noun 5 without fail REGULARLY, conscientiously, constantly, dependably, like clockwork, punctually, religiously, twenty-four-seven (slang), without exception

failing noun 1 WEAKNESS, blemish, defect, deficiency, drawback, fault, flaw, imperfection, shortcoming ▸ preposition 2 IN THE ABSENCE OF, in default of, lacking

failure noun 1 DEFEAT, breakdown, collapse, downfall, fiasco, lack of success, miscarriage, overthrow 2 LOSER, dead duck (slang), disappointment, dud (informal), flop (informal), nonstarter, washout (informal)

3 BANKRUPTCY, crash, downfall, insolvency, liquidation, ruin

faint *adjective* **1** DIM, distant, faded, indistinct, low, muted, soft, subdued, vague **2** SLIGHT, feeble, remote, unenthusiastic, weak **3** DIZZY, exhausted, giddy, light-headed, muzzy, weak, woozy (*informal*) ▶ *verb* **4** PASS OUT, black out, collapse, keel over (*informal*), lose consciousness, swoon (*literary*) ▶ *noun* **5** BLACKOUT, collapse, swoon (*literary*), unconsciousness

faintly *adverb* **1** SOFTLY, feebly, in a whisper, indistinctly, weakly **2** SLIGHTLY, a little, dimly, somewhat

fair[1] *adjective* **1** UNBIASED, above board, equitable, even-handed, honest, impartial, just, lawful, legitimate, proper, unprejudiced **2** LIGHT, blond, blonde, fair-haired, flaxen-haired, towheaded **3** RESPECTABLE, adequate, average, decent, moderate, O.K. or okay (*informal*), passable, reasonable, satisfactory, tolerable **4** BEAUTIFUL, bonny, comely, handsome, lovely, pretty **5** FINE, bright, clear, cloudless, dry, sunny, unclouded

fair[2] *noun* CARNIVAL, bazaar, festival, fête, gala, show

fairly *adverb* **1** MODERATELY, adequately, pretty well, quite, rather, reasonably, somewhat, tolerably **2** DESERVEDLY, equitably, honestly, impartially, justly, objectively, properly, without fear or favor **3** POSITIVELY, absolutely, really

fairness *noun* IMPARTIALITY, decency, disinterestedness, equitableness, equity, justice, legitimacy, rightfulness

fairy *noun* SPRITE, brownie, elf, imp, leprechaun, peri, pixie, Robin Goodfellow

fairy tale *or* **fairy story** *noun* **1** FOLK TALE, romance **2** LIE, cock-and-bull story (*informal*), fabrication, fiction, invention, tall tale (*informal*), untruth

faith *noun* **1** CONFIDENCE, assurance, conviction, credence, credit, dependence, reliance, trust **2** RELIGION, belief, church, communion, creed, denomination, dogma, persuasion **3** ALLEGIANCE, constancy, faithfulness, fidelity, loyalty

faithful *adjective* **1** LOYAL, constant, dependable, devoted, reliable, staunch, steadfast, true, trusty **2** ACCURATE, close, exact, precise, strict, true

faithless *adjective* DISLOYAL, false, fickle, inconstant, traitorous, treacherous, unfaithful, unreliable

fake *verb* **1** FORGE, copy, counterfeit, fabricate, feign, pretend, put on, sham, simulate ▶ *noun* **2** IMPOSTOR, charlatan, copy, forgery, fraud, hoax, imitation, reproduction, sham ▶ *adjective* **3** ARTIFICIAL, counterfeit, false, forged, imitation, mock, phoney *or* phony (*informal*), sham

fall *verb* **1** DESCEND, cascade, collapse, dive, drop, plummet, plunge, sink, subside, tumble **2** DECREASE, decline, diminish, drop, dwindle, go down,

lessen, slump, subside **3** BE
OVERTHROWN, capitulate, pass
into enemy hands, succumb,
surrender **4** DIE, be killed, meet
one's end, perish **5** OCCUR,
befall, chance, come about,
come to pass, happen, take
place **6** SLOPE, fall away, incline
7 LAPSE, err, go astray, offend,
sin, transgress, trespass ▸*noun*
8 DESCENT, dive, drop, nose
dive, plummet, plunge, slip,
tumble **9** DECREASE, cut, decline,
dip, drop, lessening, lowering,
reduction, slump **10** COLLAPSE,
capitulation, defeat,
destruction, downfall,
overthrow, ruin **11** LAPSE, sin,
transgression

fallacy *noun* ERROR, delusion,
falsehood, flaw,
misapprehension,
misconception, mistake, untruth

fallible *adjective* IMPERFECT,
erring, frail, ignorant,
uncertain, weak

fall out *verb* ARGUE, clash, come
to blows, differ, disagree, fight,
quarrel, squabble

fallow *adjective* UNCULTIVATED,
dormant, idle, inactive, resting,
unplanted, unused

false *adjective* **1** INCORRECT,
erroneous, faulty, inaccurate,
inexact, invalid, mistaken,
wrong **2** UNTRUE, lying,
unreliable, unsound, untruthful
3 ARTIFICIAL, bogus, counterfeit,
fake, forged, imitation, sham,
simulated **4** DECEPTIVE, deceitful,
fallacious, fraudulent,
hypocritical, misleading,
trumped up

falsehood *noun*
1 UNTRUTHFULNESS, deceit,
deception, dishonesty,

dissimulation, mendacity **2** LIE,
fabrication, fib, fiction, story,
untruth

falsify *verb* FORGE, alter,
counterfeit, distort, doctor,
fake, misrepresent, tamper with

falter *verb* HESITATE, stammer,
stumble, stutter, totter,
vacillate, waver

faltering *adjective* HESITANT,
broken, irresolute, stammering,
tentative, timid, uncertain, weak

fame *noun* PROMINENCE, celebrity,
glory, honor, kudos, renown,
reputation, repute, stardom

familiar *adjective* **1** WELL-KNOWN,
accustomed, common,
customary, frequent, ordinary,
recognizable, routine
2 FRIENDLY, amicable, close,
easy, intimate, relaxed
3 DISRESPECTFUL, bold, forward,
impudent, intrusive,
presumptuous

familiarity *noun* **1** ACQUAINTANCE,
awareness, experience, grasp,
understanding **2** FRIENDLINESS,
ease, informality, intimacy,
openness, sociability
3 DISRESPECT, boldness,
forwardness, presumption

familiarize *verb* ACCUSTOM,
habituate, instruct, inure,
school, season, train

family *noun* **1** RELATIONS, folk
(*informal*), household, kin, kith
and kin, one's nearest and
dearest, one's own flesh and
blood, relatives **2** CLAN,
dynasty, house, race, tribe
3 GROUP, class, genre, network,
subdivision, system

famine *noun* HUNGER, dearth,
scarcity, starvation

famished *adjective* STARVING,

ravenous, voracious

famous adjective WELL-KNOWN, acclaimed, celebrated, distinguished, eminent, illustrious, legendary, noted, prominent, renowned

fan[1] noun 1 BLOWER, air conditioner, ventilator ▸ verb 2 BLOW, air-condition, cool, refresh, ventilate

fan[2] noun SUPPORTER, admirer, aficionado, buff (informal), devotee, enthusiast, follower, lover

fanatic noun EXTREMIST, activist, bigot, militant, zealot

fanatical adjective PASSIONATE, bigoted, extreme, fervent, frenzied, immoderate, obsessive, overenthusiastic, wild, zealous

fanciful adjective UNREAL, imaginary, mythical, romantic, visionary, whimsical, wild

fancy adjective 1 ELABORATE, baroque, decorative, embellished, extravagant, intricate, ornamental, ornate ▸ noun 2 WHIM, caprice, desire, humor, idea, impulse, inclination, notion, thought, urge 3 DELUSION, chimera, daydream, dream, fantasy, vision ▸ verb 4 SUPPOSE, believe, conjecture, imagine, reckon, think, think likely 5 WISH FOR, crave, desire, hanker after, hope for, long for, thirst for, yearn for

fantasize verb DAYDREAM, dream, envision, imagine

fantastic adjective 1 Informal EXCELLENT, awesome (slang), first-rate, marvelous, sensational (informal), superb, wonderful 2 STRANGE, fanciful, grotesque, outlandish 3 UNREALISTIC, extravagant, far-fetched, ludicrous, ridiculous, wild 4 IMPLAUSIBLE, absurd, cock-and-bull (informal), incredible, preposterous, unlikely

fantasy noun 1 IMAGINATION, creativity, fancy, invention, originality 2 DAYDREAM, dream, flight of fancy, illusion, mirage, pipe dream, reverie, vision

far adverb 1 A LONG WAY, afar, a good way, a great distance, deep, miles 2 MUCH, considerably, decidedly, extremely, greatly, incomparably, very much ▸ adjective 3 REMOTE, distant, faraway, far-flung, far-off, outlying, out-of-the-way

farce noun 1 COMEDY, buffoonery, burlesque, satire, slapstick 2 MOCKERY, joke, nonsense, parody, sham, travesty

farcical adjective LUDICROUS, absurd, comic, derisory, laughable, nonsensical, preposterous, ridiculous, risible

fare noun 1 CHARGE, price, ticket money 2 FOOD, provisions, rations, sustenance, victuals ▸ verb 3 GET ON, do, get along, make out, manage, prosper

farewell noun GOOD-BYE, adieu, departure, leave-taking, parting, sendoff (informal), valediction

far-fetched adjective UNCONVINCING, cock-and-bull (informal), fantastic, implausible, incredible, preposterous, unbelievable, unlikely, unrealistic

farm noun **1** SMALLHOLDING, farmstead, grange, homestead, plantation, ranch ▸ verb **2** CULTIVATE, plant, work

fascinate verb INTRIGUE, absorb, beguile, captivate, engross, enthrall, entrance, hold spellbound, rivet, transfix

fascinating adjective GRIPPING, alluring, captivating, compelling, engaging, engrossing, enticing, intriguing, irresistible, riveting

fascination noun ATTRACTION, allure, charm, enchantment, lure, magic, magnetism, pull

fashion noun STYLE, craze, custom, fad, look, mode, rage, trend, vogue **2** METHOD, manner, mode, style, way ▸ verb **3** MAKE, construct, create, forge, form, manufacture, mold, shape

fashionable adjective POPULAR, à la mode, chic, cool (informal), in (informal), in vogue, modern, phat (slang), stylish, trendy (informal), up-to-date, with it (informal)

fast[1] adjective **1** QUICK, brisk, fleet, flying, hasty, rapid, speedy, swift **2** FIXED, close, fastened, firm, immovable, secure, sound, steadfast, tight **3** DISSIPATED, dissolute, extravagant, loose, profligate, reckless, self-indulgent, wanton, wild ▸ adverb **4** QUICKLY, hastily, hurriedly, in haste, like lightning, rapidly, speedily, swiftly **5** SOUNDLY, deeply, firmly, fixedly, securely, tightly

fast[2] verb **1** GO HUNGRY, abstain,

deny oneself, go without food ▸ noun **2** FASTING, abstinence

fasten verb FIX, affix, attach, bind, connect, join, link, secure, tie

fat adjective **1** OVERWEIGHT, corpulent, heavy, obese, plump, portly, rotund, stout, tubby **2** FATTY, adipose, greasy, oily, oleaginous ▸ noun **3** FATNESS, blubber, bulk, corpulence, flab, flesh, lard (slang), obesity, paunch, spare tire (informal)

fatal adjective **1** LETHAL, deadly, final, incurable, killing, malignant, mortal, terminal **2** RUINOUS, baleful, baneful, calamitous, catastrophic, disastrous

fatality noun DEATH, casualty, loss, mortality

fate noun **1** DESTINY, chance, divine will, fortune, kismet, nemesis, predestination, providence **2** FORTUNE, cup, horoscope, lot, portion, stars

fated adjective DESTINED, doomed, foreordained, inescapable, inevitable, predestined, preordained, sure, written

fateful adjective **1** CRUCIAL, critical, decisive, important, portentous, significant **2** DISASTROUS, deadly, destructive, fatal, lethal, ominous, ruinous

father noun **1** PARENT, dad (informal), daddy (informal), old man (informal), pa (informal), papa (old-fashioned informal), pater (old-fashioned informal, chiefly Brit.), pop (informal), sire **2** FOREFATHER, ancestor, forebear,

predecessor, progenitor
3 FOUNDER, architect, author,
creator, inventor, maker,
originator, prime mover
4 PRIEST, padre (informal),
pastor ▶ verb **5** SIRE, beget, get,
procreate

fatherland noun HOMELAND,
motherland, native land

fatherly adjective PATERNAL,
affectionate, benevolent,
benign, kindly, patriarchal,
protective, supportive

fathom verb UNDERSTAND,
comprehend, get to the
bottom of, grasp, interpret

fatigue noun **1** TIREDNESS,
heaviness, languor, lethargy,
listlessness ▶ verb **2** TIRE, drain,
exhaust, take it out of
(informal), weaken, wear out,
weary

fatten verb **1** GROW FAT, expand,
gain weight, put on weight,
spread, swell, thicken **2** (often
with up) FEED UP, build up, feed,
nourish, overfeed, stuff

fatty adjective GREASY, adipose,
fat, oily, oleaginous, rich

fatuous adjective FOOLISH,
brainless, idiotic, inane,
ludicrous, mindless, moronic,
silly, stupid, witless

fault noun **1** FLAW, blemish,
defect, deficiency, failing,
imperfection, shortcoming,
weakness, weak point
2 MISTAKE, blunder, error,
indiscretion, lapse, oversight,
slip **3** RESPONSIBILITY,
accountability, culpability,
liability **4** at fault GUILTY,
answerable, blamable,
culpable, in the wrong,
responsible, to blame **5** find

fault with CRITICIZE, carp at,
complain, pick holes in, pull to
pieces, quibble, take to task
6 to a fault EXCESSIVELY,
immoderately, in the extreme,
overmuch, unduly ▶ verb
7 CRITICIZE, blame, censure, find
fault with, hold (someone)
responsible, impugn

faultless adjective FLAWLESS,
correct, exemplary, foolproof,
impeccable, model, perfect,
unblemished

faulty adjective DEFECTIVE, broken,
damaged, flawed, impaired,
imperfect, incorrect,
malfunctioning, out of order,
unsound

favor noun **1** APPROVAL,
approbation, backing, good
opinion, goodwill, patronage,
support **2** GOOD TURN, benefit,
boon, courtesy, indulgence,
kindness, service ▶ verb **3** SIDE
WITH, indulge, reward, smile
upon **4** ADVOCATE, approve,
champion, commend,
encourage, incline towards,
prefer, support

favorable adjective
1 ADVANTAGEOUS, auspicious,
beneficial, encouraging,
helpful, opportune, promising,
propitious, suitable, win-win
(informal) **2** POSITIVE, affirmative,
agreeable, approving,
encouraging, enthusiastic,
reassuring, sympathetic

favorably adverb
1 ADVANTAGEOUSLY, auspiciously,
conveniently, fortunately,
opportunely, profitably, to
one's advantage, well
2 POSITIVELY, approvingly,
enthusiastically, helpfully, with
approval

favorite adjective 1 PREFERRED, best-loved, choice, dearest, esteemed, favored ▶ noun 2 DARLING, beloved, blue-eyed boy (informal), idol, pet, teacher's pet, the apple of one's eye

fawn[1] verb (often with on or upon) CURRY FAVOR, brown-nose (slang), crawl, creep, cringe, dance attendance, flatter, grovel, ingratiate oneself, kiss ass (slang), kowtow, pander to

fawn[2] adjective BEIGE, buff, grayish-brown, neutral

fawning adjective OBSEQUIOUS, crawling, cringing, deferential, flattering, grovelling, servile, sycophantic

fear noun 1 ALARM, apprehensiveness, dread, fright, horror, panic, terror, trepidation 2 BUGBEAR, bête noire, bogey, horror, nightmare, specter ▶ verb 3 BE AFRAID, dread, shake in one's shoes, shudder at, take fright, tremble at 4 **fear for** WORRY ABOUT, be anxious about, feel concern for

fearful adjective 1 SCARED, afraid, alarmed, frightened, jumpy, nervous, timid, timorous, uneasy, wired (slang) 2 FRIGHTFUL, awful, dire, dreadful, gruesome, hair-raising, horrendous, horrific, terrible

fearfully adverb 1 NERVOUSLY, apprehensively, diffidently, timidly, timorously, uneasily 2 VERY, awfully, exceedingly, excessively, frightfully, terribly, tremendously

fearless adjective BRAVE, bold, courageous, dauntless, indomitable, intrepid, plucky, unafraid, undaunted, valiant

fearsome adjective TERRIFYING, awe-inspiring, daunting, formidable, frightening, horrifying, menacing, unnerving

feasible adjective POSSIBLE, achievable, attainable, likely, practicable, reasonable, viable, workable

feast noun 1 BANQUET, dinner, repast, spread (informal), treat 2 FESTIVAL, celebration, fête, holiday, holy day, red-letter day, saint's day 3 TREAT, delight, enjoyment, gratification, pleasure ▶ verb 4 EAT ONE'S FILL, gorge, gormandize, indulge, overindulge, pig out (slang), wine and dine

feat noun ACCOMPLISHMENT, achievement, act, attainment, deed, exploit, performance

feathers plural noun PLUMAGE, down, plumes

feature noun 1 ASPECT, characteristic, facet, factor, hallmark, peculiarity, property, quality, trait 2 HIGHLIGHT, attraction, main item, speciality 3 ARTICLE, column, item, piece, report, story ▶ verb 4 SPOTLIGHT, emphasize, foreground, give prominence to, play up, present, star

features plural noun FACE, countenance, lineaments, physiognomy

feckless adjective IRRESPONSIBLE, good-for-nothing, hopeless, incompetent, ineffectual, shiftless, worthless

federation noun UNION, alliance,

amalgamation, association, coalition, combination, league, syndicate

fed up adjective DISSATISFIED, bored, depressed, discontented, down in the mouth, glum, sick and tired (informal), tired

fee noun CHARGE, bill, payment, remuneration, toll

feeble adjective 1 WEAK, debilitated, doddering, effete, frail, infirm, puny, sickly, weedy (informal) 2 UNCONVINCING, flimsy, inadequate, insufficient, lame, lousy (slang), paltry, pathetic, poor, tame, thin

feebleness noun WEAKNESS, effeteness, frailty, infirmity, languor, lassitude, sickliness

feed verb 1 CATER FOR, nourish, provide for, provision, supply, sustain, victual, wine and dine 2 (sometimes with on) EAT, chow down (slang), devour, exist on, live on, partake of ▶noun 3 FOOD, fodder, pasturage, provender 4 Informal MEAL, feast, repast, spread (informal)

feel verb 1 TOUCH, caress, finger, fondle, handle, manipulate, paw, stroke 2 EXPERIENCE, be aware of, notice, observe, perceive 3 SENSE, be convinced, intuit 4 BELIEVE, consider, deem, hold, judge, think ▶noun 5 TEXTURE, finish, surface, touch 6 IMPRESSION, air, ambience, atmosphere, feeling, quality, sense

feeler noun 1 ANTENNA, tentacle, whisker 2 APPROACH, advance, probe

feeling noun 1 EMOTION, ardor, fervor, intensity, passion, sentiment, warmth 2 IMPRESSION, hunch, idea, inkling, notion, presentiment, sense, suspicion 3 OPINION, inclination, instinct, point of view, view 4 SYMPATHY, compassion, concern, empathy, pity, sensibility, sensitivity, understanding 5 SENSE OF TOUCH, perception, sensation 6 ATMOSPHERE, air, ambience, aura, feel, mood, quality

fell verb CUT DOWN, cut, demolish, hew, knock down, level

fellow noun 1 MAN, chap (informal), character, guy (informal), individual, person 2 ASSOCIATE, colleague, companion, comrade, partner, peer

fellowship noun 1 CAMARADERIE, brotherhood, companionship, sociability 2 SOCIETY, association, brotherhood, club, fraternity, guild, league, order

feminine adjective WOMANLY, delicate, gentle, ladylike, soft, tender

femme fatale noun SEDUCTRESS, enchantress, siren, succubus, vamp (informal)

fen noun MARSH, bog, morass, quagmire, slough, swamp

fence noun 1 BARRIER, barricade, defense, hedge, palisade, railings, rampart, wall ▶verb 2 (often with in or off) ENCLOSE, bound, confine, encircle, pen, protect, surround 3 EVADE, dodge, equivocate, parry

ferment noun COMMOTION,

ferocious *adjective* **1** FIERCE, predatory, rapacious, ravening, savage, violent, wild **2** CRUEL, barbaric, bloodthirsty, brutal, ruthless, vicious

ferocity *noun* SAVAGERY, bloodthirstiness, brutality, cruelty, fierceness, viciousness, wildness

ferret out *verb* TRACK DOWN, dig up, discover, elicit, root out, search out, trace, unearth

ferry *noun* **1** FERRY BOAT, packet, packet boat ▶*verb* **2** CARRY, chauffeur, convey, run, ship, shuttle, transport

fertile *adjective* RICH, abundant, fecund, fruitful, luxuriant, plentiful, productive, prolific, teeming

fertility *noun* FRUITFULNESS, abundance, fecundity, luxuriance, productiveness, richness

fertilizer *noun* COMPOST, dressing, dung, manure

fervent, fervid *adjective* ARDENT, devout, earnest, enthusiastic, heartfelt, impassioned, intense, vehement

fervor *noun* INTENSITY, ardor, enthusiasm, excitement, passion, vehemence, warmth, zeal

fester *verb* **1** DECAY, putrefy, suppurate, ulcerate **2** INTENSIFY, aggravate, smolder

festival *noun* **1** CELEBRATION, carnival, entertainment, fête, gala, jubilee **2** HOLY DAY, anniversary, commemoration, feast, fête, fiesta, holiday,

disruption, excitement, frenzy, furor, stir, tumult, turmoil, unrest, uproar

red-letter day, saint's day

festive *adjective* CELEBRATORY, cheery, convivial, happy, jovial, joyful, joyous, jubilant, merry

festivity *noun* (*often plural*) CELEBRATION, entertainment, festival, party

festoon *verb* DECORATE, array, deck, drape, garland, hang, swathe, wreathe

fetch *verb* **1** BRING, carry, convey, deliver, get, go for, obtain, retrieve, transport **2** SELL FOR, bring in, earn, go for, make, realize, yield

fetching *adjective* ATTRACTIVE, alluring, captivating, charming, cute, enticing, winsome

fetish *noun* **1** FIXATION, mania, obsession, thing (*informal*) **2** TALISMAN, amulet

feud *noun* **1** HOSTILITY, argument, conflict, disagreement, enmity, quarrel, rivalry, row, vendetta ▶*verb* **2** QUARREL, bicker, clash, contend, dispute, fall out, row, squabble, war

fever *noun* EXCITEMENT, agitation, delirium, ferment, fervor, frenzy, restlessness

feverish *adjective* **1** HOT, febrile, fevered, flushed, inflamed, pyretic (*Medical*) **2** EXCITED, agitated, frantic, frenetic, frenzied, overwrought, restless, wired (*slang*)

few *adjective* NOT MANY, meager, negligible, rare, scanty, scarcely any, sparse, sporadic

fiasco *noun* DEBACLE, catastrophe, disaster, failure, mess, washout (*informal*)

fib *noun* LIE, fiction, story, untruth, white lie

fiber noun 1 THREAD, filament, pile, strand, texture, wisp 2 ESSENCE, nature, quality, spirit, substance 3 As in *moral fiber* RESOLUTION, stamina, strength, toughness

fickle adjective CHANGEABLE, capricious, faithless, inconstant, irresolute, temperamental, unfaithful, variable, volatile

fiction noun 1 TALE, fantasy, legend, myth, novel, romance, story, yarn (*informal*) 2 LIE, cock and bull story (*informal*), fabrication, falsehood, invention, tall tale (*informal*), untruth, urban legend

fictional adjective IMAGINARY, invented, legendary, made-up, nonexistent, unreal

fictitious adjective FALSE, bogus, fabricated, imaginary, invented, made-up, make-believe, mythical, untrue

fiddle verb 1 FIDGET, finger, interfere with, mess about or around, play, tamper with, tinker ▶ noun 2 VIOLIN 3 **fit as a fiddle** HEALTHY, blooming, hale and hearty, in fine fettle, in good form, in good shape, in rude health, in the pink, sound, strong

fiddling adjective TRIVIAL, futile, insignificant, pettifogging, petty, trifling

fidelity noun 1 LOYALTY, allegiance, constancy, dependability, devotion, faithfulness, staunchness, trustworthiness 2 ACCURACY, closeness, correspondence, exactness, faithfulness, precision, scrupulousness

fidget verb 1 MOVE RESTLESSLY,

fiddle (*informal*), fret, squirm, twitch ▶ noun 2 **the fidgets** RESTLESSNESS, fidgetiness, jitters (*informal*), nervousness, unease, uneasiness

fidgety adjective RESTLESS, antsy (*slang*), impatient, jittery (*informal*), jumpy, nervous, on edge, restive, twitchy (*informal*), uneasy, wired (*slang*)

field noun 1 MEADOW, grassland, green, lea (*poetic*), pasture 2 COMPETITORS, applicants, candidates, competition, contestants, entrants, possibilities, runners 3 SPECIALITY, area, department, discipline, domain, line, province, territory ▶ verb 4 RETRIEVE, catch, pick up, return, stop 5 DEAL WITH, deflect, handle, turn aside

fiend noun 1 DEMON, devil, evil spirit 2 BRUTE, barbarian, beast, ghoul, monster, ogre, savage 3 *Informal* ENTHUSIAST, addict, fanatic, freak (*informal*), maniac

fiendish adjective WICKED, cruel, devilish, diabolical, hellish, infernal, malignant, monstrous, satanic, unspeakable

fierce adjective 1 WILD, brutal, cruel, dangerous, ferocious, fiery, menacing, savage, vicious 2 STRONG, furious, howling, inclement, powerful, raging, stormy, tempestuous, violent 3 INTENSE, cut-throat, keen, relentless, strong

fiercely adverb FEROCIOUSLY, furiously, passionately, savagely, tempestuously, tigerishly, tooth and nail, viciously, with no holds barred

fiery adjective 1 BURNING, ablaze,

afire, aflame, blazing, flaming, on fire **2** EXCITABLE, fierce, hot-headed, impetuous, irascible, irritable, passionate

fight verb **1** BATTLE, box, clash, combat, do battle, grapple, spar, struggle, tussle, wrestle **2** OPPOSE, contest, defy, dispute, make a stand against, resist, stand up to, withstand **3** ENGAGE IN, carry on, conduct, prosecute, wage ▶ noun **4** CONFLICT, battle, clash, contest, dispute, duel, encounter, struggle, tussle **5** RESISTANCE, belligerence, militancy, pluck, spirit

fighter noun **1** SOLDIER, fighting man, man-at-arms, warrior **2** BOXER, prize fighter, pugilist

fight off verb REPEL, beat off, keep or hold at bay, repress, repulse, resist, stave off, ward off

figure noun **1** NUMBER, character, digit, numeral, symbol **2** AMOUNT, cost, price, sum, total, value **3** SHAPE, body, build, frame, physique, proportions **4** DIAGRAM, design, drawing, illustration, pattern, representation, sketch **5** CHARACTER, big name, celebrity, dignitary, personality ▶ verb **6** CALCULATE, compute, count, reckon, tally, tot up, work out **7** (usually with *in*) FEATURE, act, appear, be featured, contribute to, play a part

figurehead noun FRONT MAN, mouthpiece, puppet, titular or nominal head

figure out verb **1** CALCULATE, compute, reckon, work out **2** UNDERSTAND, comprehend,

decipher, fathom, make out, see

filch verb STEAL, embezzle, misappropriate, pilfer, pinch (*informal*), take, thieve, walk off with

file[1] noun **1** FOLDER, case, data, documents, dossier, information, portfolio **2** LINE, column, queue, row ▶ verb **3** REGISTER, document, enter, pigeonhole, put in place, record **4** MARCH, parade, troop

file[2] verb SMOOTH, abrade, polish, rasp, rub, scrape, shape

fill verb **1** STUFF, cram, crowd, glut, pack, stock, supply, swell **2** SATURATE, charge, imbue, impregnate, pervade, suffuse **3** PLUG, block, bung, close, cork, seal, stop **4** PERFORM, carry out, discharge, execute, fulfill, hold, occupy ▶ noun **5** one's **fill** SUFFICIENT, all one wants, ample, enough, plenty

filler noun PADDING, makeweight, stopgap

fill in verb **1** INFORM, acquaint, apprise, bring up to date, give the facts or background **2** REPLACE, deputize, represent, stand in, sub, substitute, take the place of

filling noun **1** STUFFING, contents, filler, inside, insides, padding, wadding ▶ adjective **2** SATISFYING, ample, heavy, square, substantial

fill out verb COMPLETE, answer, fill in, fill up

film noun **1** MOVIE, flick (*slang*), motion picture **2** LAYER, coating, covering, dusting, membrane, skin, tissue ▶ verb **3** PHOTOGRAPH, shoot, take, video, videotape

filter noun 1 SIEVE, gauze, membrane, mesh, riddle, strainer ▶ verb 2 PURIFY, clarify, filtrate, refine, screen, sieve, sift, strain, winnow 3 TRICKLE, dribble, escape, exude, leak, ooze, penetrate, percolate, seep

filth noun 1 DIRT, excrement, grime, muck, refuse, sewage, slime, sludge, squalor 2 OBSCENITY, impurity, indecency, pornography, smut, vulgarity

filthy adjective 1 DIRTY, foul, polluted, putrid, slimy, squalid, unclean 2 MUDDY, begrimed, blackened, grimy, grubby, scuzzy (slang) 3 OBSCENE, corrupt, depraved, impure, indecent, lewd, licentious, pornographic, smutty, X-rated

final adjective 1 LAST, closing, concluding, latest, terminal, ultimate 2 DEFINITIVE, absolute, conclusive, decided, definite, incontrovertible, irrevocable, settled

finale noun ENDING, climax, close, conclusion, culmination, denouement, epilogue

finalize verb COMPLETE, clinch, conclude, decide, settle, tie up, wind up, work out, wrap up (informal)

finally adverb 1 EVENTUALLY, at last, at length, at long last, in the end, lastly, ultimately 2 IN CONCLUSION, in summary, to conclude

finance noun 1 ECONOMICS, accounts, banking, business, commerce, investment, money ▶ verb 2 FUND, back, bankroll, guarantee, pay for, subsidize,

support, underwrite

finances plural noun RESOURCES, affairs, assets, capital, cash, funds, money, wherewithal

financial adjective ECONOMIC, fiscal, monetary, pecuniary

find verb 1 DISCOVER, come across, encounter, hit upon, locate, meet, recognize, spot, uncover 2 PERCEIVE, detect, discover, learn, note, notice, observe, realize ▶ noun 3 DISCOVERY, acquisition, asset, bargain, catch, good buy

find out verb 1 LEARN, detect, discover, note, observe, perceive, realize 2 DETECT, catch, disclose, expose, reveal, uncover, unmask

fine[1] adjective 1 EXCELLENT, accomplished, exceptional, exquisite, first-rate, magnificent, masterly, outstanding, splendid, superior 2 SUNNY, balmy, bright, clear, clement, cloudless, dry, fair, pleasant 3 SATISFACTORY, acceptable, all right, convenient, good, O.K. or okay (informal), suitable 4 DELICATE, dainty, elegant, expensive, exquisite, fragile, quality 5 SUBTLE, abstruse, acute, hairsplitting, minute, nice, precise, sharp 6 SLENDER, diaphanous, flimsy, gauzy, gossamer, light, sheer, thin

fine[2] noun 1 PENALTY, damages, forfeit, punishment ▶ verb 2 PENALIZE, punish

finery noun SPLENDOR, frippery, gear (informal), glad rags (informal), ornaments, showiness, Sunday best, trappings, trinkets

finesse noun SKILL, adeptness, adroitness, craft, delicacy, diplomacy, discretion, savoir-faire, sophistication, subtlety, tact

finger verb TOUCH, feel, fiddle with (*informal*), handle, manipulate, maul, paw (*informal*), toy with

finish verb 1 STOP, cease, close, complete, conclude, end, round off, terminate, wind up, wrap up (*informal*) 2 CONSUME, devour, dispose of, eat, empty, exhaust, use up 3 DESTROY, bring down, defeat, dispose of, exterminate, overcome, put an end to, put paid to, rout, ruin 4 PERFECT, polish, refine 5 COAT, gild, lacquer, polish, stain, texture, veneer, wax ▶ noun 6 END, cessation, close, completion, conclusion, culmination, denouement, finale, run-in 7 DEFEAT, annihilation, curtains (*informal*), death, end, end of the road, ruin 8 SURFACE, luster, patina, polish, shine, smoothness, texture

finished adjective 1 POLISHED, accomplished, perfected, professional, refined 2 OVER, closed, complete, done, ended, finalized, through 3 SPENT, done, drained, empty, exhausted, used up 4 RUINED, defeated, done for (*informal*), doomed, lost, through, undone, wiped out

finite adjective LIMITED, bounded, circumscribed, delimited, demarcated, restricted

fire noun 1 FLAMES, blaze, combustion, conflagration, inferno 2 BOMBARDMENT,

barrage, cannonade, flak, fusillade, hail, salvo, shelling, sniping, volley 3 PASSION, ardor, eagerness, enthusiasm, excitement, fervor, intensity, sparkle, spirit, verve, vigor ▶ verb 4 SHOOT, detonate, discharge, explode, let off, pull the trigger, set off, shell 5 INSPIRE, animate, enliven, excite, galvanize, impassion, inflame, rouse, stir 6 DISMISS, cashier, discharge, make redundant, sack (*informal*), show the door

firebrand noun RABBLE-ROUSER, agitator, demagogue, incendiary, instigator, tub-thumper

fireworks plural noun 1 PYROTECHNICS, illuminations 2 RAGE, hysterics, row, storm, trouble, uproar

firm¹ adjective 1 HARD, dense, inflexible, rigid, set, solid, solidified, stiff, unyielding 2 SECURE, embedded, fast, fixed, immovable, rooted, stable, steady, tight, unshakable 3 DEFINITE, adamant, inflexible, resolute, resolved, set on, unbending, unshakable, unyielding

firm² noun COMPANY, association, business, concern, conglomerate, corporation, enterprise, organization, partnership

firmly adverb 1 SECURELY, immovably, like a rock, steadily, tightly, unflinchingly, unshakably 2 RESOLUTELY, staunchly, steadfastly, unchangeably, unwaveringly

firmness noun 1 HARDNESS, inelasticity, inflexibility,

resistance, rigidity, solidity, stiffness **2** RESOLVE, constancy, inflexibility, resolution, staunchness, steadfastness

first adjective **1** FOREMOST, chief, head, highest, leading, pre-eminent, prime, principal, ruling **2** EARLIEST, initial, introductory, maiden, opening, original, premier, primordial **3** ELEMENTARY, basic, cardinal, fundamental, key, primary, rudimentary ▸ noun **4** As in **from the first** START, beginning, commencement, inception, introduction, outset, starting point ▸ adverb **5** BEFOREHAND, at the beginning, at the outset, firstly, initially, in the first place, to begin with, to start with

first-rate adjective EXCELLENT, crack (slang), elite, exceptional, first class, outstanding, superb, superlative, top-notch (informal), world-class

fishy adjective **1** Informal SUSPICIOUS, dubious, funny (informal), implausible, odd, questionable, suspect, unlikely **2** FISHLIKE, piscatorial, piscatory, piscine

fissure noun CRACK, breach, cleft, crevice, fault, fracture, opening, rift, rupture, split

fit¹ verb **1** MATCH, accord, belong, conform, correspond, meet, suit, tally **2** PREPARE, arm, equip, fit out, provide **3** ADAPT, adjust, alter, arrange, customize, modify, shape ▸ adjective **4** APPROPRIATE, apt, becoming, correct, fitting, proper, right, seemly, suitable **5** HEALTHY, able-bodied, hale, in good shape, robust, strapping,

trim, well

fit² noun **1** SEIZURE, attack, bout, convulsion, paroxysm, spasm **2** OUTBREAK, bout, burst, outburst, spell

fitful adjective IRREGULAR, broken, desultory, disturbed, inconstant, intermittent, spasmodic, sporadic, uneven

fitness noun **1** APPROPRIATENESS, aptness, competence, eligibility, propriety, readiness, suitability **2** HEALTH, good condition, good health, robustness, strength, vigor

fitting adjective **1** APPROPRIATE, apposite, becoming, correct, decent, proper, right, seemly, suitable ▸ noun **2** ACCESSORY, attachment, component, part, piece, unit

fix verb **1** PLACE, embed, establish, implant, install, locate, plant, position, set **2** FASTEN, attach, bind, connect, link, secure, stick, tie **3** DECIDE, agree on, arrange, arrive at, determine, establish, set, settle, specify **4** REPAIR, correct, mend, patch up, put to rights, see to **5** FOCUS, direct **6** Informal MANIPULATE, influence, rig ▸ noun **7** Informal PREDICAMENT, difficulty, dilemma, embarrassment, mess, pickle (informal), plight, quandary

fixation noun PREOCCUPATION, complex, hang-up (informal), idée fixe, infatuation, mania, obsession, thing (informal)

fixed adjective **1** PERMANENT, established, immovable, rigid, rooted, secure, set **2** INTENT, resolute, steady, unwavering **3** AGREED, arranged, decided, definite, established, planned, resolved, settled

fix up verb 1 ARRANGE, agree on, fix, organize, plan, settle, sort out 2 (often with *with*) PROVIDE, arrange for, bring about, lay on

fizz verb BUBBLE, effervesce, fizzle, froth, hiss, sparkle, sputter

fizzy adjective BUBBLY, bubbling, carbonated, effervescent, gassy, sparkling

flabbergasted adjective ASTONISHED, amazed, astounded, dumbfounded, lost for words, overwhelmed, speechless, staggered, stunned

flabby adjective LIMP, baggy, drooping, flaccid, floppy, loose, pendulous, sagging

flag¹ noun 1 BANNER, colors, ensign, pennant, pennon, standard, streamer ▶ verb 2 MARK, indicate, label, note 3 (sometimes with *down*) HAIL, signal, warn, wave

flag² verb WEAKEN, abate, droop, fade, languish, peter out, sag, wane, weary, wilt

flagging adjective FADING, declining, deteriorating, faltering, waning, weakening, wilting

flagrant adjective OUTRAGEOUS, barefaced, blatant, brazen, glaring, heinous, scandalous, shameless

flagstone noun PAVING STONE, block, flag, slab

flail verb THRASH, beat, thresh, windmill

flair noun 1 ABILITY, aptitude, faculty, feel, genius, gift, knack, mastery, talent 2 STYLE, chic, dash, discernment,

elegance, panache, stylishness, taste

flake noun 1 WAFER, layer, peeling, scale, shaving, sliver ▶ verb 2 BLISTER, chip, peel (off)

flake out verb COLLAPSE, faint, keel over, pass out

flamboyant adjective 1 EXTRAVAGANT, dashing, elaborate, florid, ornate, ostentatious, showy, swashbuckling, theatrical 2 COLORFUL, brilliant, dazzling, glamorous, glitzy (*slang*)

flame noun 1 FIRE, blaze, brightness, light 2 *Informal* SWEETHEART, beau, boyfriend, girlfriend, heart-throb (*Brit.*), lover ▶ verb 3 BURN, blaze, flare, flash, glare, glow, shine

flaming adjective BURNING, ablaze, blazing, fiery, glowing, raging, red-hot

flank noun 1 SIDE, hip, loin, thigh 2 WING, side

flap verb 1 FLUTTER, beat, flail, shake, thrash, vibrate, wag, wave ▶ noun 2 FLUTTER, beating, shaking, swinging, swish, waving

flare verb 1 BLAZE, burn up, flicker, glare 2 WIDEN, broaden, spread out ▶ noun 3 FLAME, blaze, burst, flash, flicker, glare

flare up verb LOSE ONE'S TEMPER, blow one's top (*informal*), boil over, explode, fly off the handle (*informal*), throw a tantrum

flash noun 1 BLAZE, burst, dazzle, flare, flicker, gleam, shimmer, spark, streak 2 MOMENT, instant, jiffy (*informal*), second, split second, trice, twinkling of an eye ▶ verb

3 BLAZE, flare, flicker, glare, gleam, shimmer, sparkle, twinkle **4** SPEED, dart, dash, fly, race, shoot, streak, whistle, zoom **5** SHOW, display, exhibit, expose, flaunt, flourish

flashy adjective SHOWY, flamboyant, garish, gaudy, glitzy (slang), jazzy (informal), ostentatious, snazzy (informal)

flat¹ adjective **1** EVEN, horizontal, level, levelled, low, smooth **2** DULL, boring, dead, lackluster, lifeless, monotonous, tedious, tiresome, uninteresting **3** ABSOLUTE, categorical, downright, explicit, out-and-out, positive, unequivocal, unqualified **4** PUNCTURED, blown out, burst, collapsed, deflated, empty ▶ adverb **5** COMPLETELY, absolutely, categorically, exactly, point blank, precisely, utterly **6 flat out** AT FULL SPEED, all out, at full tilt, for all one is worth

flat² noun APARTMENT, rooms

flatly adverb ABSOLUTELY, categorically, completely, positively, unhesitatingly

flatness noun **1** EVENNESS, smoothness, uniformity **2** DULLNESS, monotony, tedium

flatten verb LEVEL, compress, even out, iron out, raze, smooth off, squash, trample

flatter verb **1** PRAISE, brown-nose (slang), butter up, compliment, pander to, sweet-talk (informal), wheedle **2** SUIT, become, do something for, enhance, set off, show to advantage

flattering adjective **1** BECOMING,

effective, enhancing, kind, well-chosen **2** INGRATIATING, adulatory, complimentary, fawning, fulsome, laudatory

flattery noun OBSEQUIOUSNESS, adulation, blandishment, fawning, servility, sweet-talk (informal), sycophancy

flaunt verb SHOW OFF, brandish, display, exhibit, flash about, flourish, parade, sport (informal)

flavor noun **1** TASTE, aroma, flavoring, piquancy, relish, savor, seasoning, smack, tang, zest **2** QUALITY, character, essence, feel, feeling, style, tinge, tone ▶ verb **3** SEASON, ginger up, imbue, infuse, leaven, spice

flaw noun WEAKNESS, blemish, chink in one's armor, defect, failing, fault, imperfection, weak spot

flawed adjective DAMAGED, blemished, defective, erroneous, faulty, imperfect, unsound

flawless adjective PERFECT, faultless, impeccable, spotless, unblemished, unsullied

flee verb RUN AWAY, bolt, depart, escape, fly, make one's getaway, take flight, take off (informal), take to one's heels, turn tail

fleet noun NAVY, armada, flotilla, task force

fleeting adjective MOMENTARY, brief, ephemeral, passing, short-lived, temporary, transient, transitory

flesh noun **1** MEAT, brawn, fat, tissue, weight **2** HUMAN NATURE, carnality, flesh and blood **3 one's own flesh and blood**

FAMILY, blood, kin, kinsfolk, kith and kin, relations, relatives

flexibility noun ADAPTABILITY, adjustability, elasticity, give (informal), pliability, pliancy, resilience, springiness

flexible adjective **1** PLIABLE, elastic, lithe, plastic, pliant, springy, stretchy, supple **2** ADAPTABLE, adjustable, discretionary, open, variable

flick verb **1** STRIKE, dab, flip, hit, tap, touch **2** flick through BROWSE, flip through, glance at, skim, skip, thumb

flicker verb **1** TWINKLE, flare, flash, glimmer, gutter, shimmer, sparkle **2** FLUTTER, quiver, vibrate, waver ▶ noun **3** GLIMMER, flare, flash, gleam, spark **4** TRACE, breath, glimmer, iota, spark

flight[1] noun **1** Of air travel JOURNEY, trip, voyage **2** AVIATION, aeronautics, flying **3** FLOCK, cloud, formation, squadron, swarm, unit

flight[2] noun ESCAPE, departure, exit, exodus, fleeing, getaway, retreat, running away

flimsy adjective **1** FRAGILE, delicate, frail, insubstantial, makeshift, rickety, shaky **2** THIN, gauzy, gossamer, light, sheer, transparent **3** UNCONVINCING, feeble, implausible, inadequate, lousy (slang), pathetic, poor, unsatisfactory, weak

flinch verb RECOIL, cower, cringe, draw back, quail, shirk, shrink, shy away, wince

fling verb **1** THROW, cast, catapult, heave, hurl, propel, sling, toss ▶ noun **2** BINGE

(informal), bash, good time, party, spree

flip verb, noun TOSS, flick, snap, spin, throw

flippancy noun FRIVOLITY, impertinence, irreverence, levity, pertness, sauciness

flippant adjective FRIVOLOUS, cheeky, disrespectful, glib, impertinent, irreverent, offhand, superficial

flirt verb **1** LEAD ON, hit on (slang), make advances, make eyes at, philander **2** (usually with with) TOY WITH, consider, dabble in, entertain, expose oneself to, give a thought to, play with, trifle with ▶ noun **3** TEASE, coquette, heart-breaker, hussy, philanderer

flirtatious adjective TEASING, amorous, come-hither, coquettish, coy, enticing, flirty, provocative, sportive

float verb **1** BE BUOYANT, hang, hover **2** GLIDE, bob, drift, move gently, sail, slide, slip along **3** LAUNCH, get going, promote, set up

floating adjective **1** BUOYANT, afloat, buoyed up, sailing, swimming **2** FLUCTUATING, free, movable, unattached, variable, wandering

flock noun **1** HERD, colony, drove, flight, gaggle, skein **2** CROWD, collection, company, congregation, gathering, group, herd, host, mass ▶ verb **3** GATHER, collect, congregate, converge, crowd, herd, huddle, mass, throng

flog verb BEAT, flagellate, flay, lash, scourge, thrash, trounce, whack, whip

flood noun 1 DELUGE, downpour, inundation, overflow, spate, tide, torrent 2 ABUNDANCE, flow, glut, profusion, rush, stream, torrent ▶ verb 3 IMMERSE, drown, inundate, overflow, pour over, submerge, swamp 4 ENGULF, overwhelm, surge, swarm, sweep 5 OVERSUPPLY, choke, fill, glut, saturate

floor noun 1 TIER, level, stage, story ▶ verb 2 KNOCK DOWN, deck (slang), prostrate 3 Informal BEWILDER, baffle, confound, defeat, disconcert, dumbfound, perplex, puzzle, stump, throw (informal)

flop verb 1 FALL, collapse, dangle, droop, drop, sag, slump 2 Informal FAIL, come unstuck, fall flat, fold (informal), founder, go belly-up (slang), misfire ▶ noun 3 Informal FAILURE, debacle, disaster, fiasco, nonstarter, washout (informal)

floppy adjective DROOPY, baggy, flaccid, limp, loose, pendulous, sagging, soft

floral adjective FLOWERY, flower-patterned

florid adjective 1 FLUSHED, blowsy, high-colored, rubicund, ruddy 2 FLOWERY, baroque, flamboyant, fussy, high-flown, ornate, overelaborate

flotsam noun DEBRIS, detritus, jetsam, junk, odds and ends, wreckage

flounder verb FUMBLE, grope, struggle, stumble, thrash, toss

flourish verb 1 PROSPER, bloom, blossom, boom, flower, grow,

increase, succeed, thrive 2 WAVE, brandish, display, flaunt, shake, wield ▶ noun 3 WAVE, display, fanfare, parade, show 4 ORNAMENTATION, curlicue, decoration, embellishment, plume, sweep

flourishing adjective SUCCESSFUL, blooming, going places, in the pink, luxuriant, prospering, rampant, thriving

flout verb DEFY, laugh in the face of, mock, scoff at, scorn, sneer at, spurn

flow verb 1 RUN, circulate, course, move, roll 2 POUR, cascade, flood, gush, rush, stream, surge, sweep 3 RESULT, arise, emanate, emerge, issue, proceed, spring ▶ noun 4 TIDE, course, current, drift, flood, flux, outpouring, spate, stream

flower noun 1 BLOOM, blossom, efflorescence 2 ELITE, best, cream, crème de la crème, pick ▶ verb 3 BLOSSOM, bloom, flourish, mature, open, unfold

flowery adjective ORNATE, baroque, embellished, fancy, florid, high-flown

flowing adjective 1 STREAMING, falling, gushing, rolling, rushing, smooth, sweeping 2 FLUENT, continuous, easy, smooth, unbroken, uninterrupted

fluctuate verb CHANGE, alternate, oscillate, seesaw, shift, swing, vary, veer, waver

fluency noun EASE, articulateness, assurance, command, control, facility, glibness, readiness, slickness, smoothness

fluent adjective SMOOTH,

articulate, easy, effortless, flowing, natural, voluble, well-versed

fluff noun FUZZ, down, nap, pile

fluffy adjective SOFT, downy, feathery, fleecy, fuzzy

fluid noun 1 LIQUID, liquor, solution ▶ adjective 2 LIQUID, flowing, liquefied, melted, molten, runny, watery

fluke noun LUCKY BREAK, accident, chance, coincidence, quirk of fate, serendipity, stroke of luck

flurry noun 1 COMMOTION, ado, bustle, disturbance, excitement, flutter, fuss, stir 2 GUST, squall

flush[1] verb 1 BLUSH, color, glow, go red, redden 2 RINSE OUT, cleanse, flood, hose down, wash out ▶ noun 3 BLUSH, color, glow, redness, rosiness

flush[2] adjective 1 LEVEL, even, flat, square, true 2 Informal WEALTHY, in the money (informal), moneyed, rich, well-heeled (informal), well-off

flushed adjective BLUSHING, crimson, embarrassed, glowing, hot, red, rosy, ruddy

fluster verb 1 UPSET, agitate, bother, confuse, disturb, perturb, rattle (informal), ruffle, unnerve ▶ noun 2 TURMOIL, disturbance, dither, flap (informal), flurry, flutter, furor

flutter verb 1 BEAT, flap, palpitate, quiver, ripple, tremble, vibrate, waver ▶ noun 2 VIBRATION, palpitation, quiver, shiver, shudder, tremble, tremor, twitching 3 AGITATION, commotion, confusion, dither, excitement, fluster

fly verb 1 TAKE WING, flit, flutter,

hover, sail, soar, wing 2 PILOT, control, maneuver, operate 3 DISPLAY, flap, float, flutter, show, wave 4 PASS, elapse, flit, glide, pass swiftly, roll on, run its course, slip away 5 RUSH, career, dart, dash, hurry, race, shoot, speed, sprint, tear 6 FLEE, escape, get away, run for it, skedaddle (informal), take to one's heels

flying adjective HURRIED, brief, fleeting, hasty, rushed, short-lived, transitory

foam noun 1 FROTH, bubbles, head, lather, spray, spume, suds ▶ verb 2 BUBBLE, boil, effervesce, fizz, froth, lather

focus noun 1 CENTER, focal point, heart, hub, target ▶ verb 2 CONCENTRATE, aim, center, direct, fix, pinpoint, spotlight, zoom in

foe noun ENEMY, adversary, antagonist, opponent, rival

fog noun MIST, gloom, miasma, murk, smog

foggy adjective MISTY, cloudy, dim, hazy, indistinct, murky, smoggy, vaporous

foil[1] verb THWART, balk, counter, defeat, disappoint, frustrate, nullify, stop

foil[2] noun CONTRAST, antithesis, complement

foist verb IMPOSE, fob off, palm off, pass off, sneak in, unload

fold verb 1 BEND, crease, double over 2 Informal GO BANKRUPT, collapse, crash, fail, go bust (informal), go to the wall, go under, shut down ▶ noun 3 CREASE, bend, furrow, overlap, pleat, wrinkle

folder noun FILE, binder,

envelope, portfolio

folk noun PEOPLE, clan, family, kin, kindred, race, tribe

follow verb 1 COME AFTER, come next, succeed, supersede, supplant, take the place of 2 PURSUE, chase, dog, hound, hunt, shadow, stalk, track, trail 3 ACCOMPANY, attend, escort, tag along 4 OBEY, be guided by, conform, heed, observe 5 UNDERSTAND, appreciate, catch on (*informal*), comprehend, fathom, grasp, realize, take in 6 RESULT, arise, develop, ensue, flow, issue, proceed, spring 7 BE INTERESTED IN, cultivate, keep abreast of, support

follower noun SUPPORTER, adherent, apostle, devotee, disciple, fan, pupil

following adjective 1 NEXT, consequent, ensuing, later, subsequent, succeeding, successive ▶ noun 2 SUPPORTERS, clientele, coterie, entourage, fans, retinue, suite, train

folly noun FOOLISHNESS, imprudence, indiscretion, lunacy, madness, nonsense, rashness, stupidity

fond adjective 1 LOVING, adoring, affectionate, amorous, caring, devoted, doting, indulgent, tender, warm 2 FOOLISH, deluded, delusive, empty, naive, overoptimistic, vain 3 **fond of** KEEN ON, addicted to, attached to, enamored of, having a soft spot for, hooked on, into (*informal*), partial to

fondle verb CARESS, cuddle, dandle, pat, pet, stroke

fondly adverb 1 LOVINGLY, affectionately, dearly, indulgently, possessively, tenderly, with affection 2 FOOLISHLY, credulously, naively, stupidly, vainly

fondness noun 1 LIKING, attachment, fancy, love, partiality, penchant, soft spot, taste, weakness 2 DEVOTION, affection, attachment, kindness, love, tenderness

food noun NOURISHMENT, cuisine, diet, fare, grub (*slang*), nutrition, rations, refreshment

fool noun 1 SIMPLETON, blockhead, dork (*slang*), dunce, halfwit, idiot, ignoramus, imbecile (*slang*), schmuck (*slang*) 2 DUPE, fall guy (*informal*), laughing stock, mug (*Brit. slang*), stooge (*slang*), sucker (*slang*) 3 CLOWN, buffoon, harlequin, jester ▶ verb 4 DECEIVE, beguile, con (*informal*), delude, dupe, hoodwink, mislead, take in, trick

foolhardy adjective RASH, hot-headed, impetuous, imprudent, irresponsible, reckless

foolish adjective UNWISE, absurd, ill-judged, imprudent, injudicious, senseless, silly

foolishly adverb UNWISELY, idiotically, ill-advisedly, imprudently, injudiciously, mistakenly, stupidly

foolishness noun STUPIDITY, absurdity, folly, imprudence, indiscretion, irresponsibility, silliness, weakness

foolproof adjective INFALLIBLE, certain, guaranteed, safe, sure-fire (*informal*), unassailable, unbreakable

footing noun 1 BASIS, foundation, groundwork 2 RELATIONSHIP, grade, position, rank, standing, status

footstep noun STEP, footfall, tread

forage verb 1 SEARCH, cast about, explore, hunt, rummage, scour, seek ▸ noun 2 Cattle, etc. FODDER, feed, food, provender

foray noun RAID, incursion, inroad, invasion, sally, sortie, swoop

forbear verb REFRAIN, abstain, cease, desist, hold back, keep from, restrain oneself, stop

forbearance noun PATIENCE, long-suffering, moderation, resignation, restraint, self-control, temperance, tolerance

forbearing adjective PATIENT, forgiving, indulgent, lenient, long-suffering, merciful, moderate, tolerant

forbid verb PROHIBIT, ban, disallow, exclude, outlaw, preclude, rule out, veto

forbidden adjective PROHIBITED, banned, outlawed, out of bounds, proscribed, taboo, vetoed

forbidding adjective THREATENING, daunting, frightening, hostile, menacing, ominous, sinister, unfriendly

force noun 1 POWER, energy, impulse, might, momentum, pressure, strength, vigor 2 COMPULSION, arm-twisting (informal), coercion, constraint, duress, pressure, violence 3 INTENSITY, emphasis, fierceness, vehemence, vigor 4 ARMY, host, legion, patrol, regiment, squad, troop, unit 5 in force: a VALID, binding, current, effective, in operation, operative, working b IN GREAT NUMBERS, all together, in full strength ▸ verb 6 COMPEL, coerce, constrain, dragoon, drive, impel, make, oblige, press, pressurize 7 BREAK OPEN, blast, prise, wrench, wrest 8 PUSH, propel, thrust

forced adjective 1 COMPULSORY, conscripted, enforced, involuntary, mandatory, obligatory 2 FALSE, affected, artificial, contrived, insincere, labored, stiff, strained, unnatural, wooden

forceful adjective POWERFUL, cogent, compelling, convincing, dynamic, effective, persuasive

forcible adjective 1 VIOLENT, aggressive, armed, coercive, compulsory 2 STRONG, compelling, energetic, forceful, potent, powerful, weighty

forebear noun ANCESTOR, father, forefather, forerunner, predecessor

foreboding noun DREAD, anxiety, apprehension, apprehensiveness, chill, fear, misgiving, premonition, presentiment

forecast verb 1 PREDICT, anticipate, augur, divine, foresee, foretell, prophesy ▸ noun 2 PREDICTION, conjecture, guess, prognosis, prophecy

forefather noun ANCESTOR, father, forebear, forerunner, predecessor

forefront noun LEAD, center,

fore, foreground, front, prominence, spearhead, vanguard

foregoing adjective PRECEDING, above, antecedent, anterior, former, previous, prior

foreign adjective ALIEN, exotic, external, imported, remote, strange, unfamiliar, unknown

foreigner noun ALIEN, immigrant, incomer, stranger

foremost adjective LEADING, chief, highest, paramount, pre-eminent, primary, prime, principal, supreme

forerunner noun PRECURSOR, envoy, harbinger, herald, prototype

foresee verb ANTICIPATE, envisage, forecast, foretell, predict, prophesy

foreshadow verb PREDICT, augur, forebode, indicate, portend, prefigure, presage, promise, signal

foresight noun ANTICIPATION, far-sightedness, forethought, precaution, preparedness, prescience, prudence

foretell verb PREDICT, forecast, forewarn, presage, prognosticate, prophesy

forethought noun ANTICIPATION, far-sightedness, foresight, precaution, providence, provision, prudence

forever adverb 1 EVERMORE, always, for all time, for keeps, in perpetuity, till Doomsday, till the cows come home (informal) 2 CONSTANTLY, all the time, continually, endlessly, eternally, incessantly, interminably, perpetually, twenty-four-seven (slang),

unremittingly

forewarn verb CAUTION, advise, alert, apprise, give fair warning, put on guard, tip off

forfeit noun 1 PENALTY, damages, fine, forfeiture, loss ▶ verb 2 LOSE, be deprived of, be stripped of, give up, relinquish, renounce, say good-bye to, surrender

forge verb 1 CREATE, construct, devise, fashion, form, frame, make, mold, shape, work 2 FALSIFY, copy, counterfeit, fake, feign, imitate

forgery noun 1 FRAUDULENCE, coining, counterfeiting, falsification, fraudulent imitation 2 FAKE, counterfeit, falsification, imitation, phoney or phony (informal), sham

forget verb NEGLECT, leave behind, lose sight of, omit, overlook

forgetful adjective ABSENT-MINDED, careless, inattentive, neglectful, oblivious, unmindful, vague

forgive verb EXCUSE, absolve, acquit, condone, exonerate, let bygones be bygones, let off (informal), pardon

forgiveness noun PARDON, absolution, acquittal, amnesty, exoneration, mercy, remission

forgiving adjective MERCIFUL, clement, compassionate, forbearing, lenient, magnanimous, soft-hearted, tolerant

forgo verb GIVE UP, abandon, do without, relinquish, renounce, resign, surrender, waive, yield

forgotten adjective LEFT BEHIND, bygone, lost, omitted, past, past recall, unremembered

fork verb BRANCH, bifurcate, diverge, divide, part, split

forked adjective BRANCHING, angled, bifurcate(d), branched, divided, pronged, split, zigzag

forlorn adjective MISERABLE, disconsolate, down in the dumps (informal), helpless, hopeless, pathetic, pitiful, unhappy, woebegone, wretched

form noun 1 SHAPE, appearance, configuration, formation, pattern, structure 2 TYPE, kind, sort, style, variety 3 CONDITION, fettle, fitness, health, shape, trim 4 PROCEDURE, convention, custom, etiquette, protocol 5 DOCUMENT, application, paper, sheet 6 CLASS, grade, rank ▶ verb 7 MAKE, build, construct, create, fashion, forge, mold, produce, shape 8 ARRANGE, combine, draw up, organize 9 TAKE SHAPE, appear, become visible, come into being, crystallize, grow, materialize, rise 10 DEVELOP, acquire, contract, cultivate, pick up 11 CONSTITUTE, compose, comprise, make up

formal adjective 1 OFFICIAL, ceremonial, ritualistic, solemn 2 CONVENTIONAL, affected, correct, precise, stiff, unbending

formality noun 1 CONVENTION, custom, procedure, red tape, rite, ritual 2 CORRECTNESS, decorum, etiquette, protocol

format noun STYLE, appearance, arrangement, construction, form, layout, look, make-up, plan, type

formation noun 1 ESTABLISHMENT, constitution, development,

forming, generation, genesis, manufacture, production 2 PATTERN, arrangement, configuration, design, grouping, structure

formative adjective DEVELOPMENTAL, influential

former adjective PREVIOUS, earlier, erstwhile, one-time, prior

formerly adverb PREVIOUSLY, at one time, before, lately, once

formidable adjective 1 INTIMIDATING, daunting, dismaying, fearful, frightful, menacing, terrifying, threatening 2 IMPRESSIVE, awesome, cool (informal), great, mighty, phat (slang), powerful, redoubtable, terrific (informal), tremendous

formula noun METHOD, blueprint, precept, principle, procedure, recipe, rule

formulate verb 1 DEFINE, detail, express, frame, give form to, set down, specify, systematize 2 DEVISE, develop, forge, invent, map out, originate, plan, work out

forsake verb 1 DESERT, abandon, disown, leave in the lurch, strand 2 GIVE UP, forgo, relinquish, renounce, set aside, surrender, yield

forsaken adjective DESERTED, abandoned, disowned, forlorn, left in the lurch, marooned, outcast, stranded

fort noun 1 FORTRESS, blockhouse, camp, castle, citadel, fortification, garrison, stronghold 2 hold the fort STAND IN, carry on, keep things on an even keel, take over the reins

forte noun SPECIALITY, gift, métier, strength, strong point, talent

forth adverb FORWARD, ahead, away, onward, out, outward

forthcoming adjective
1 APPROACHING, coming, expected, future, imminent, impending, prospective, upcoming **2** ACCESSIBLE, at hand, available, in evidence, obtainable, on tap (informal), ready **3** COMMUNICATIVE, chatty, expansive, free, informative, open, sociable, talkative, unreserved

forthright adjective OUTSPOKEN, blunt, candid, direct, frank, open, plain-spoken, straightforward, upfront (informal)

forthwith adverb AT ONCE, directly, immediately, instantly, quickly, right away, straightaway, without delay

fortification noun **1** DEFENSE, bastion, fastness, fort, fortress, protection, stronghold
2 STRENGTHENING, reinforcement

fortify verb STRENGTHEN, augment, buttress, protect, reinforce, shore up, support

fortitude noun COURAGE, backbone, bravery, fearlessness, grit, perseverance, resolution, strength, valor

fortress noun CASTLE, citadel, fastness, fort, redoubt, stronghold

fortunate adjective **1** LUCKY, favored, in luck, successful, well-off **2** FAVORABLE, advantageous, convenient, expedient, felicitous, fortuitous, helpful, opportune, providential, timely, win-win (informal)

fortunately adverb LUCKILY, by a happy chance, by good luck, happily, providentially

fortune noun **1** WEALTH, affluence, opulence, possessions, property, prosperity, riches, treasure
2 LUCK, chance, destiny, fate, kismet, providence **3 fortunes** DESTINY, adventures, experiences, history, lot, success

forward adjective **1** LEADING, advance, first, foremost, front, head **2** PRESUMPTUOUS, bold, brash, brazen, cheeky, familiar, impertinent, impudent, pushy (informal) **3** WELL-DEVELOPED, advanced, precocious, premature ▶ adverb **4** AHEAD, forth, on, onward ▶ verb
5 PROMOTE, advance, assist, expedite, further, hasten, hurry **6** SEND, dispatch, post, send on

foster verb **1** PROMOTE, cultivate, encourage, feed, nurture, stimulate, support, uphold
2 BRING UP, mother, nurse, raise, rear, take care of

foul adjective **1** DIRTY, fetid, filthy, funky (slang), malodorous, nauseating, putrid, repulsive, scuzzy (slang), squalid, stinking, unclean **2** OBSCENE, abusive, blue, coarse, indecent, lewd, profane, scurrilous, vulgar **3** OFFENSIVE, abhorrent, despicable, detestable, disgraceful, lousy (slang), scandalous, scuzzy (slang), shameful, wicked **4** UNFAIR, crooked, dishonest, fraudulent, shady (informal), underhand, unscrupulous ▶ verb **5** POLLUTE, besmirch, contaminate, defile, dirty, stain, sully, taint

found verb ESTABLISH, constitute, create, inaugurate, institute, organize, originate, set up, start

foundation noun
1 GROUNDWORK, base, basis, bedrock, bottom, footing, substructure, underpinning
2 SETTING UP, endowment, establishment, inauguration, institution, organization, settlement

founder[1] noun INITIATOR, architect, author, beginner, father, inventor, originator

founder[2] verb 1 SINK, be lost, go down, go to the bottom, submerge 2 FAIL, break down, collapse, come to grief, come unstuck, fall through, miscarry, misfire 3 STUMBLE, lurch, sprawl, stagger, trip

foundling noun STRAY, orphan, outcast, waif

fountain noun 1 JET, font, fount, reservoir, spout, spray, spring, well 2 SOURCE, cause, derivation, fount, fountainhead, origin, wellspring

foyer noun ENTRANCE HALL, antechamber, anteroom, lobby, reception area, vestibule

fracas noun BRAWL, affray (Law), disturbance, melee or mêlée, riot, rumpus, scuffle, skirmish

fraction noun PIECE, part, percentage, portion, section, segment, share, slice

fractious adjective IRRITABLE, captious, cross, petulant, querulous, refractory, testy, tetchy, touchy

fracture noun 1 BREAK, cleft, crack, fissure, opening, rift,

rupture, split ▶ verb 2 BREAK, crack, rupture, splinter, split

fragile adjective DELICATE, breakable, brittle, dainty, fine, flimsy, frail, frangible, weak

fragment noun 1 PIECE, bit, chip, particle, portion, scrap, shred, sliver ▶ verb 2 BREAK, break up, come apart, come to pieces, crumble, disintegrate, shatter, splinter, split up

fragmentary adjective INCOMPLETE, bitty, broken, disconnected, incoherent, partial, piecemeal, scattered, scrappy, sketchy

fragrance noun SCENT, aroma, balm, bouquet, fragrancy, perfume, redolence, smell, sweet odor

fragrant adjective PERFUMED, aromatic, balmy, odorous, redolent, sweet-scented, sweet-smelling

frail adjective WEAK, delicate, feeble, flimsy, fragile, infirm, insubstantial, puny, vulnerable

frailty noun FEEBLENESS, fallibility, frailness, infirmity, susceptibility, weakness

frame noun 1 CASING, construction, framework, shell, structure 2 PHYSIQUE, anatomy, body, build, carcass 3 frame of mind MOOD, attitude, disposition, humor, outlook, state, temper ▶ verb 4 CONSTRUCT, assemble, build, make, manufacture, put together 5 DRAFT, compose, devise, draw up, formulate, map out, sketch 6 MOUNT, case, enclose, surround

framework noun STRUCTURE, foundation, frame,

groundwork, plan, shell, skeleton, the bare bones

frank *adjective* 1 HONEST, blunt, candid, direct, forthright, open, outspoken, plain-spoken, sincere, straightforward, truthful

frankly *adverb* 1 HONESTLY, candidly, in truth, to be honest 2 OPENLY, bluntly, directly, freely, plainly, without reserve

frankness *noun* OUTSPOKENNESS, bluntness, candor, forthrightness, openness, plain speaking, truthfulness

frantic *adjective* 1 FURIOUS, at the end of one's tether, berserk, beside oneself, distracted, distraught, wild 2 HECTIC, desperate, fraught (*informal*), frenetic, frenzied

fraternity *noun* 1 CLUB, association, brotherhood, circle, company, guild, league, union 2 COMPANIONSHIP, brotherhood, camaraderie, fellowship, kinship

fraternize *verb* ASSOCIATE, consort, cooperate, hobnob, keep company, mingle, mix, socialize

fraud *noun* 1 DECEPTION, chicanery, deceit, double-dealing, duplicity, sharp practice, swindling, treachery, trickery 2 IMPOSTOR, charlatan, fake, fraudster, hoaxer, phoney or phony (*informal*), pretender, swindler

fraudulent *adjective* DECEITFUL, crooked (*informal*), dishonest, double-dealing, duplicitous, sham, swindling, treacherous

fray *verb* WEAR THIN, chafe, rub, wear

freak *noun* 1 ODDITY, aberration, anomaly, malformation, monstrosity, weirdo or weirdie (*informal*) 2 ENTHUSIAST, addict, aficionado, buff (*informal*), devotee, fan, fanatic, fiend (*informal*), nut (*slang*) ▶ *adjective* 3 ABNORMAL, exceptional, unparalleled, unusual

free *adjective* 1 FOR NOTHING, complimentary, for free (*informal*), free of charge, gratis, gratuitous, on the house, unpaid, without charge 2 AT LIBERTY, at large, footloose, independent, liberated, loose, on the loose, unfettered 3 ALLOWED, able, clear, permitted, unimpeded, unrestricted 4 AVAILABLE, empty, idle, spare, unemployed, unoccupied, unused, vacant 5 GENEROUS, lavish, liberal, unsparing, unstinting ▶ *verb* 6 RELEASE, deliver, let out, liberate, loose, set free, turn loose, unchain, untie 7 EXTRICATE, cut loose, disengage, disentangle, rescue

freedom *noun* 1 LIBERTY, deliverance, emancipation, independence, release 2 OPPORTUNITY, a blank check, carte blanche, discretion, free rein, latitude, license

free-for-all *noun* FIGHT, brawl, fracas, melee or mêlée, riot, row, scrimmage

freely *adverb* 1 WILLINGLY, of one's own accord, of one's own free will, spontaneously, voluntarily, without prompting 2 OPENLY, candidly, frankly, plainly, unreservedly, without reserve 3 ABUNDANTLY, amply, copiously, extravagantly, lavishly, liberally, unstintingly

freeze verb **1** CHILL, harden, ice over or up, stiffen **2** SUSPEND, fix, hold up, inhibit, peg, stop

freezing adjective ICY, arctic, biting, bitter, chill, frosty, glacial, raw, wintry

freight noun **1** TRANSPORTATION, carriage, conveyance, shipment **2** CARGO, burden, consignment, goods, load, merchandise, payload

French adjective GALLIC

frenzied adjective FURIOUS, distracted, feverish, frantic, frenetic, rabid, uncontrolled, wild

frenzy noun FURY, derangement, hysteria, paroxysm, passion, rage, seizure

frequent adjective **1** COMMON, customary, everyday, familiar, habitual, persistent, recurrent, repeated, usual ▶ verb **2** VISIT, attend, be found at, hang out at (informal), haunt, patronize

frequently adverb OFTEN, commonly, habitually, many times, much, not infrequently, repeatedly

fresh adjective **1** NEW, different, modern, novel, original, recent, up-to-date **2** ADDITIONAL, added, auxiliary, extra, further, more, other, supplementary **3** INVIGORATING, bracing, brisk, clean, cool, crisp, pure, refreshing, unpolluted **4** LIVELY, alert, energetic, keen, refreshed, sprightly, spry, vigorous **5** NATURAL, unprocessed **6** Informal CHEEKY, disrespectful, familiar, forward, impudent, insolent, presumptuous

freshen verb REFRESH, enliven,

freshen up, liven up, restore, revitalize

freshness noun **1** NOVELTY, inventiveness, newness, originality **2** CLEANNESS, brightness, clearness, glow, shine, sparkle, vigor, wholesomeness

fret verb WORRY, agonize, brood, grieve, lose sleep over, upset or distress oneself

fretful adjective IRRITABLE, crotchety, edgy, fractious, querulous, short-tempered, testy, touchy, uneasy

friction noun **1** RUBBING, abrasion, chafing, grating, rasping, resistance, scraping **2** HOSTILITY, animosity, bad blood, conflict, disagreement, discord, dissension, resentment

friend noun **1** COMPANION, buddy (informal), chum (informal), comrade, homeboy (informal), homegirl (slang), pal (informal), playmate **2** SUPPORTER, ally, associate, patron, well-wisher

friendliness noun KINDLINESS, affability, amiability, congeniality, conviviality, geniality, neighborliness, sociability, warmth

friendly adjective SOCIABLE, affectionate, amicable, buddy-buddy (informal), close, familiar, helpful, intimate, neighborly, on good terms, pally (informal), sympathetic, welcoming

friendship noun GOODWILL, affection, amity, attachment, concord, familiarity, friendliness, harmony, intimacy

fright noun FEAR, alarm,

consternation, dread, horror, panic, scare, shock, trepidation

frighten verb SCARE, alarm, intimidate, petrify, shock, startle, terrify, terrorize, unnerve

frightened adjective AFRAID, alarmed, petrified, scared, scared stiff, startled, terrified, terrorized, terror-stricken

frightening adjective TERRIFYING, alarming, fearful, fearsome, horrifying, menacing, scary (informal), shocking, unnerving

frightful adjective TERRIFYING, alarming, awful, dreadful, fearful, ghastly, horrendous, horrible, terrible, traumatic

frigid adjective 1 COLD, arctic, frosty, frozen, glacial, icy, wintry 2 FORBIDDING, aloof, austere, formal, unapproachable, unfeeling, unresponsive

frills plural noun TRIMMINGS, additions, bells and whistles, embellishments, extras, frippery, fuss, ornamentation, ostentation

fringe noun 1 BORDER, edging, hem, trimming 2 EDGE, borderline, limits, margin, outskirts, perimeter, periphery ▶ adjective 3 UNOFFICIAL, unconventional, unorthodox

frisk verb 1 FROLIC, caper, cavort, gambol, jump, play, prance, skip, trip 2 SEARCH, check, inspect, run over, shake down (U.S. slang)

frisky adjective LIVELY, coltish, frolicsome, high-spirited, kittenish, playful, sportive

fritter away verb WASTE, dissipate, idle away, misspend, run through, spend like

water, squander

frivolity noun FUN, flippancy, frivolousness, gaiety, levity, light-heartedness, silliness, superficiality, triviality

frivolous adjective 1 FLIPPANT, childish, foolish, idle, juvenile, puerile, silly, superficial 2 TRIVIAL, minor, petty, shallow, trifling, unimportant

frolic verb 1 PLAY, caper, cavort, frisk, gambol, lark, make merry, romp, sport ▶ noun 2 REVEL, antic, game, lark, romp, spree

frolicsome adjective PLAYFUL, coltish, frisky, kittenish, lively, merry, sportive

front noun 1 EXTERIOR, façade, face, foreground, frontage 2 FOREFRONT, front line, head, lead, vanguard 3 DISGUISE, blind, cover, cover-up, façade, mask, pretext, show ▶ adjective 4 FIRST, foremost, head, lead, leading, topmost ▶ verb 5 FACE ONTO, look over or onto, overlook

frontier noun BOUNDARY, borderline, edge, limit, perimeter, verge

frost noun HOARFROST, freeze, rime

frosty adjective 1 COLD, chilly, frozen, icy, wintry 2 UNFRIENDLY, discouraging, frigid, standoffish, unenthusiastic, unwelcoming

froth noun 1 FOAM, bubbles, effervescence, head, lather, scum, spume, suds ▶ verb 2 FIZZ, bubble over, come to a head, effervesce, foam, lather

frothy adjective FOAMY, foaming, sudsy

frown verb 1 SCOWL, glare, glower, knit one's brows, look daggers, lour or lower 2 frown on DISAPPROVE OF, discourage, dislike, look askance at, take a dim view of

frozen adjective ICY, arctic, chilled, frigid, frosted, icebound, ice-cold, ice-covered, numb

frugal adjective THRIFTY, abstemious, careful, economical, niggardly, parsimonious, prudent, sparing

fruit noun 1 PRODUCE, crop, harvest, product, yield 2 RESULT, advantage, benefit, consequence, effect, end result, outcome, profit, return, reward

fruitful adjective USEFUL, advantageous, beneficial, effective, productive, profitable, rewarding, successful, win-win (informal), worthwhile

fruition noun MATURITY, attainment, completion, fulfillment, materialization, perfection, realization, ripeness

fruitless adjective USELESS, futile, ineffectual, pointless, profitless, unavailing, unproductive, unprofitable, unsuccessful, vain

frustrate verb THWART, balk, block, check, counter, defeat, disappoint, foil, forestall, nullify, stymie

frustrated adjective DISAPPOINTED, discouraged, disheartened, embittered, resentful

frustration noun 1 OBSTRUCTION, blocking, circumvention, foiling, thwarting 2 ANNOYANCE, disappointment, dissatisfaction, grievance, irritation, resentment, vexation

fuel noun INCITEMENT, ammunition, provocation

fugitive noun 1 RUNAWAY, deserter, escapee, refugee ▶adjective 2 MOMENTARY, brief, ephemeral, fleeting, passing, short-lived, temporary, transient, transitory

fulfill verb 1 ACHIEVE, accomplish, carry out, complete, perform, realize, satisfy 2 COMPLY WITH, answer, conform to, fill, meet, obey, observe

fulfillment noun ACHIEVEMENT, accomplishment, attainment, completion, consummation, implementation, realization

full adjective 1 SATURATED, brimming, complete, filled, loaded, replete, satiated, stocked 2 PLENTIFUL, abundant, adequate, ample, comprehensive, exhaustive, extensive, generous 3 RICH, clear, deep, distinct, loud, resonant, rounded 4 PLUMP, buxom, curvaceous, rounded, voluptuous 5 LOOSE, baggy, capacious, large, puffy, voluminous ▶noun 6 in full COMPLETELY, in its entirety, in total, without exception

full-blooded adjective VIGOROUS, hearty, lusty, red-blooded, virile

fullness noun 1 PLENTY, abundance, copiousness, fill, profusion, satiety, saturation, sufficiency 2 RICHNESS, clearness, loudness, resonance, strength

full-scale adjective MAJOR, all-out, comprehensive, exhaustive, in-depth, sweeping, thorough, thoroughgoing, wide-ranging

fully adverb TOTALLY, altogether, completely, entirely, in all respects, one hundred per cent, perfectly, thoroughly, utterly, wholly

fulsome adjective INSINCERE, excessive, extravagant, immoderate, inordinate, sycophantic, unctuous

fumble verb GROPE, feel around, flounder, scrabble

fume verb RAGE, get hot under the collar (informal), rant, see red (informal), seethe, smolder, storm

fumes plural noun SMOKE, exhaust, gas, pollution, smog, vapor

fumigate verb DISINFECT, clean out or up, cleanse, purify, sanitize, sterilize

fuming adjective ANGRY, enraged, in a rage, incensed, on the warpath (informal), raging, seething, up in arms

fun noun 1 ENJOYMENT, amusement, entertainment, jollity, merriment, mirth, pleasure, recreation, sport 2 **make fun of** MOCK, lampoon, laugh at, parody, poke fun at, ridicule, satirize ▸ adjective 3 ENJOYABLE, amusing, convivial, diverting, entertaining, lively, witty

function noun 1 PURPOSE, business, duty, job, mission, raison d'être, responsibility, role, task 2 RECEPTION, affair, gathering, social occasion ▸ verb 3 WORK, act, behave, do duty, go, operate, perform, run

functional adjective 1 PRACTICAL, hard-wearing, serviceable, useful, utilitarian 2 WORKING, operative

fund noun 1 RESERVE, kitty, pool, stock, store, supply ▸ verb 2 FINANCE, pay for, subsidize, support

fundamental adjective 1 ESSENTIAL, basic, cardinal, central, elementary, key, primary, principal, rudimentary, underlying ▸ noun 2 PRINCIPLE, axiom, cornerstone, law, rudiment, rule

fundamentally adverb ESSENTIALLY, at bottom, at heart, basically, intrinsically, primarily, radically

funds plural noun MONEY, capital, cash, finance, ready money, resources, savings, the wherewithal

funeral noun BURIAL, cremation, inhumation, interment, obsequies

funnel verb CHANNEL, conduct, convey, direct, filter, move, pass, pour

funny adjective 1 HUMOROUS, amusing, comic, comical, droll, entertaining, hilarious, riotous, side-splitting, witty 2 PECULIAR, curious, mysterious, odd, queer, strange, suspicious, unusual, weird

furious adjective 1 ANGRY, beside oneself, enraged, fuming, incensed, infuriated, livid (informal), raging, up in arms 2 VIOLENT, fierce, intense, savage, turbulent, unrestrained, vehement

furnish verb 1 DECORATE, equip, fit out, stock 2 SUPPLY, give, grant, hand out, offer, present, provide

furniture noun HOUSEHOLD

GOODS, appliances, fittings, furnishings, goods, possessions, things (*informal*)

furor *noun* DISTURBANCE, commotion, hullabaloo, outcry, stir, to-do, uproar

furrow *noun* 1 GROOVE, channel, crease, hollow, line, rut, seam, trench, wrinkle ▶ *verb* 2 WRINKLE, corrugate, crease, draw together, knit

further *adverb* 1 IN ADDITION, additionally, also, besides, furthermore, into the bargain, moreover, to boot ▶ *adjective* 2 ADDITIONAL, extra, fresh, more, new, other, supplementary ▶ *verb* 3 PROMOTE, advance, assist, encourage, forward, help, lend support to, work for

furthermore *adverb* BESIDES, additionally, as well, further, in addition, into the bargain, moreover, to boot, too

furthest *adjective* MOST DISTANT, extreme, farthest, furthermost, outmost, remotest, ultimate

furtive *adjective* SLY, clandestine, conspiratorial, secretive, sneaky, stealthy, surreptitious, underhand, under-the-table

fury *noun* 1 ANGER, frenzy, impetuosity, madness, passion, rage, wrath 2 VIOLENCE, ferocity, fierceness, force, intensity, savagery, severity, vehemence

fuss *noun* 1 BOTHER, ado, commotion, excitement, palaver, stir, to-do 2 ARGUMENT, complaint, furor, objection, row, squabble, trouble ▶ *verb* 3 WORRY, fidget, fret, get worked up, take pains

fussy *adjective* 1 HARD TO PLEASE, choosy (*informal*), difficult, fastidious, finicky, nit-picking (*informal*), particular, picky (*informal*) 2 OVERELABORATE, busy, cluttered, overworked, rococo

fusty *adjective* STALE, airless, damp, mildewed, moldering, musty, stuffy

futile *adjective* USELESS, fruitless, ineffectual, unavailing, unprofitable, unsuccessful, vain, worthless

futility *noun* USELESSNESS, emptiness, hollowness, ineffectiveness

future *noun* 1 HEREAFTER, time to come 2 OUTLOOK, expectation, prospect ▶ *adjective* 3 FORTHCOMING, approaching, coming, fated, impending, later, subsequent, to come

fuzzy *adjective* 1 FLUFFY, downy, frizzy, woolly 2 INDISTINCT, bleary, blurred, distorted, ill-defined, obscure, out of focus, unclear, vague

G g

gabble *verb* 1 PRATTLE, babble, blabber, gibber, gush, jabber, spout ▶ *noun* 2 GIBBERISH, babble, blabber, chatter, drivel, prattle, twaddle

gadabout *noun* PLEASURE-SEEKER, gallivanter, rambler, rover, wanderer

gadget *noun* DEVICE, appliance, contraption (*informal*), contrivance, gizmo (*slang*), instrument, invention, thing, tool

gaffe *noun* BLUNDER, bloomer

(*informal*), faux pas, indiscretion, lapse, mistake, slip, solecism

gag[1] verb 1 SUPPRESS, curb, muffle, muzzle, quiet, silence, stifle, stop up 2 RETCH, barf (*slang*), heave, puke (*slang*), spew, throw up (*informal*), toss one's cookies (*slang*), vomit

gag[2] noun JOKE, crack (*slang*), funny (*informal*), hoax, jest, wisecrack (*informal*), witticism

gaiety noun 1 CHEERFULNESS, blitheness, exhilaration, glee, high spirits, jollity, light-heartedness, merriment, mirth 2 MERRYMAKING, conviviality, festivity, fun, jollification, revelry

gaily adverb 1 CHEERFULLY, blithely, gleefully, happily, joyfully, light-heartedly, merrily 2 COLORFULLY, brightly, brilliantly, flamboyantly, flashily, gaudily, showily

gain verb 1 OBTAIN, acquire, attain, capture, collect, gather, get, land, pick up, secure, win 2 REACH, arrive at, attain, come to, get to 3 gain on GET NEARER, approach, catch up with, close, narrow the gap, overtake
▶ noun 4 PROFIT, advantage, benefit, dividend, return, yield 5 INCREASE, advance, growth, improvement, progress, rise

gainful adjective PROFITABLE, advantageous, beneficial, fruitful, lucrative, remunerative, rewarding, useful, win-win (*informal*), worthwhile

gains plural noun PROFITS, earnings, prize, proceeds, revenue, takings, winnings

gainsay verb CONTRADICT, contravene, controvert, deny, disagree with, dispute, rebut, retract

gait noun WALK, bearing, carriage, pace, step, stride, tread

gala noun FESTIVAL, carnival, celebration, festivity, fête, jamboree, pageant

gale noun 1 STORM, blast, cyclone, hurricane, squall, tempest, tornado, typhoon 2 OUTBURST, burst, eruption, explosion, fit, howl, outbreak, peal, shout, shriek

gall[1] noun 1 Informal IMPUDENCE, brazenness, cheek (*informal*), chutzpah (*informal*), effrontery, impertinence, insolence, nerve (*informal*) 2 BITTERNESS, acrimony, animosity, bile, hostility, rancor

gall[2] verb 1 SCRAPE, abrade, chafe, irritate 2 ANNOY, exasperate, irk, irritate, provoke, rankle, vex

gallant adjective 1 BRAVE, bold, courageous, heroic, honorable, intrepid, manly, noble, valiant 2 CHIVALROUS, attentive, courteous, gentlemanly, gracious, noble, polite

gallantry noun 1 BRAVERY, boldness, courage, heroism, intrepidity, manliness, spirit, valor 2 ATTENTIVENESS, chivalry, courteousness, courtesy, gentlemanliness, graciousness, nobility, politeness

galling adjective ANNOYING, bitter, exasperating, irksome, irritating, provoking, vexatious

gallivant verb WANDER, gad about, ramble, roam, rove

gallop verb RUN, bolt, career, dash, hurry, race, rush, speed, sprint

galore adverb IN ABUNDANCE, all over the place, aplenty, everywhere, in great quantity, in great numbers, in profusion, to spare

galvanize verb STIMULATE, electrify, excite, inspire, invigorate, jolt, provoke, spur, stir

gamble verb 1 BET, game, play, wager 2 RISK, chance, hazard, speculate, stick one's neck out (informal), take a chance ▶noun 3 RISK, chance, leap in the dark, lottery, speculation, uncertainty, venture 4 BET, wager

gambol verb 1 FROLIC, caper, cavort, frisk, hop, jump, prance, skip ▶noun 2 FROLIC, caper, hop, jump, prance, skip

game noun 1 PASTIME, amusement, distraction, diversion, entertainment, lark, recreation, sport 2 MATCH, competition, contest, event, head-to-head, meeting, tournament 3 WILD ANIMALS, prey, quarry 4 SCHEME, design, plan, plot, ploy, stratagem, tactic, trick ▶adjective 5 BRAVE, courageous, gallant, gritty, intrepid, persistent, plucky, spirited 6 WILLING, desirous, eager, interested, keen, prepared, ready

gamut noun RANGE, area, catalog, compass, field, scale, scope, series, sweep

gang noun GROUP, band, clique, club, company, coterie, crowd, mob, pack, squad, team

gangling adjective TALL, angular, awkward, lanky, rangy, rawboned, spindly

gangster noun RACKETEER, crook (informal), hood (slang), hoodlum, mobster (slang)

gap noun 1 OPENING, break, chink, cleft, crack, hole, space 2 INTERVAL, breathing space, hiatus, interlude, intermission, interruption, lacuna, lull, pause, respite 3 DIFFERENCE, disagreement, disparity, divergence, inconsistency

gape verb 1 STARE, gawk, goggle, wonder 2 OPEN, crack, split, yawn

gaping adjective WIDE, broad, cavernous, great, open, vast, wide open, yawning

garbage noun RUBBISH, litter, refuse, trash, waste

garbled adjective JUMBLED, confused, distorted, double-Dutch, incomprehensible, mixed up, unintelligible

garish adjective GAUDY, brash, brassy, flashy, loud, showy, tacky (informal), tasteless, vulgar

garland noun 1 WREATH, bays, chaplet, crown, festoon, honors, laurels ▶verb 2 ADORN, crown, deck, festoon, wreathe

garments plural noun CLOTHES, apparel, attire, clothing, costume, dress, garb, gear (slang), outfit, uniform

garner verb COLLECT, accumulate, amass, gather, hoard, save, stockpile, store, stow away

garnish verb 1 DECORATE, adorn, embellish, enhance, ornament, set off, trim ▶noun

2 DECORATION, adornment, embellishment, enhancement, ornamentation, trimming

garrison noun **1** TROOPS, armed force, command, detachment, unit **2** FORT, base, camp, encampment, fortification, fortress, post, station, stronghold ▶ verb **3** STATION, assign, position, post, put on duty

garrulous adjective TALKATIVE, chatty, gossiping, loquacious, prattling, verbose, voluble

gash verb **1** CUT, gouge, lacerate, slash, slit, split, tear, wound ▶ noun **2** CUT, gouge, incision, laceration, slash, slit, split, tear, wound

gasp verb **1** GULP, blow, catch one's breath, choke, pant, puff ▶ noun **2** GULP, exclamation, pant, puff, sharp intake of breath

gate noun BARRIER, door, entrance, exit, gateway, opening, passage, portal

gather verb **1** ASSEMBLE, accumulate, amass, collect, garner, mass, muster, stockpile **2** LEARN, assume, conclude, deduce, hear, infer, surmise, understand **3** PICK, cull, garner, glean, harvest, pluck, reap, select **4** INTENSIFY, deepen, expand, grow, heighten, increase, rise, swell, thicken **5** FOLD, pleat, tuck

gathering noun ASSEMBLY, company, conclave, congress, convention, crowd, group, meeting

gauche adjective AWKWARD, clumsy, ill-mannered, inelegant, tactless,

unsophisticated

gaudy adjective GARISH, bright, flashy, loud, showy, tacky (informal), tasteless, vulgar

gauge verb **1** MEASURE, ascertain, calculate, check, compute, count, determine, weigh **2** JUDGE, adjudge, appraise, assess, estimate, evaluate, guess, rate, reckon, value ▶ noun **3** INDICATOR, criterion, guide, guideline, measure, meter, standard, test, touchstone, yardstick

gaunt adjective EMACIATED, angular, anorexic, bony, cadaverous, lean, pinched, scrawny, skeletal, skinny, spare

gawky adjective AWKWARD, clumsy, gauche, loutish, lumbering, maladroit, ungainly

gay adjective **1** HOMOSEXUAL, bent (informal, derogatory), lesbian, queer (informal, derogatory) **2** CAREFREE, blithe, cheerful, jovial, light-hearted, lively, merry, sparkling **3** COLORFUL, bright, brilliant, flamboyant, flashy, rich, showy, vivid ▶ noun **4** HOMOSEXUAL, lesbian

gaze verb **1** STARE, gape, look, regard, view, watch, wonder ▶ noun **2** STARE, fixed look, look

gazette noun NEWSPAPER, journal, news-sheet, paper, periodical

gear noun **1** COG, cogwheel, gearwheel **2** MECHANISM, cogs, machinery, works **3** EQUIPMENT, accouterments, apparatus, instruments, paraphernalia, supplies, tackle, tools **4** CLOTHING, clothes, costume, dress, garments, outfit, togs, wear ▶ verb **5** EQUIP, adapt, adjust, fit

geek noun Slang BORE, anorak (informal), dork (slang), drip (informal), obsessive, trainspotter (informal), wonk (informal)

gelatinous adjective JELLY-LIKE, gluey, glutinous, gummy, sticky, viscous

gelid adjective COLD, arctic, chilly, freezing, frigid, frosty, frozen, glacial, ice-cold, icy

gem noun 1 PRECIOUS STONE, jewel, stone 2 PRIZE, jewel, masterpiece, pearl, treasure

general adjective 1 COMMON, accepted, broad, extensive, popular, prevalent, public, universal, widespread 2 IMPRECISE, approximate, ill-defined, indefinite, inexact, loose, unspecific, vague 3 UNIVERSAL, across-the-board, blanket, collective, comprehensive, indiscriminate, miscellaneous, sweeping, total

generally adverb 1 USUALLY, as a rule, by and large, customarily, normally, on the whole, ordinarily, typically 2 COMMONLY, extensively, popularly, publicly, universally, widely

generate verb PRODUCE, breed, cause, create, engender, give rise to, make, propagate

generation noun 1 PRODUCTION, creation, formation, genesis, propagation, reproduction 2 AGE GROUP, breed, crop 3 AGE, epoch, era, period, time

generic adjective COLLECTIVE, blanket, common, comprehensive, general, inclusive, universal, wide

generosity noun 1 CHARITY, beneficence, bounty, kindness, largesse or largess, liberality, munificence, open-handedness 2 UNSELFISHNESS, goodness, high-mindedness, magnanimity, nobleness

generous adjective 1 CHARITABLE, beneficent, bountiful, hospitable, kind, lavish, liberal, open-handed, unstinting 2 UNSELFISH, big-hearted, good, high-minded, lofty, magnanimous, noble 3 PLENTIFUL, abundant, ample, copious, full, lavish, liberal, rich, unstinting

genesis noun BEGINNING, birth, creation, formation, inception, origin, start

genial adjective CHEERFUL, affable, agreeable, amiable, congenial, friendly, good-natured, jovial, pleasant, warm

geniality noun CHEERFULNESS, affability, agreeableness, amiability, conviviality, cordiality, friendliness, good cheer, joviality, warmth

genius noun 1 MASTER, brainbox, expert, hotshot (informal), maestro, mastermind, savant, virtuoso, whiz (informal) 2 BRILLIANCE, ability, aptitude, bent, capacity, flair, gift, knack, talent

genre noun TYPE, category, class, group, kind, sort, species, style

genteel adjective REFINED, courteous, cultured, elegant, gentlemanly, ladylike, polite, respectable, urbane, well-mannered

gentle adjective 1 SWEET-TEMPERED, compassionate, humane, kindly, meek, mild, placid, tender **2** MODERATE, light, mild, muted, slight, soft, soothing **3** GRADUAL, easy, imperceptible, light, mild, moderate, slight, slow **4** TAME, biddable, broken, docile, manageable, placid, tractable

gentlemanly *adjective* POLITE, civil, courteous, gallant, genteel, honorable, refined, urbane, well-mannered

gentleness *noun* TENDERNESS, compassion, kindness, mildness, softness, sweetness

gentry *noun* NOBILITY, aristocracy, elite, upper class, upper crust (*informal*)

genuine *adjective* **1** AUTHENTIC, actual, bona fide, legitimate, real, the real McCoy, true, veritable **2** SINCERE, candid, earnest, frank, heartfelt, honest, unaffected, unfeigned

germ *noun* **1** MICROBE, bacterium, bug (*informal*), microorganism, virus **2** BEGINNING, embryo, origin, root, rudiment, seed, source, spark

germane *adjective* RELEVANT, apposite, appropriate, apropos, connected, fitting, material, pertinent, related, to the point or purpose

germinate *verb* SPROUT, bud, develop, generate, grow, originate, shoot, swell, vegetate

gesticulate *verb* SIGNAL, gesture, indicate, make a sign, motion, sign, wave

gesture *noun* **1** SIGNAL, action, gesticulation, indication, motion, sign ▶ *verb* **2** SIGNAL, gesticulate, indicate, motion, sign, wave

get *verb* **1** OBTAIN, acquire, attain, fetch, gain, land, net, pick up, procure, receive, secure, win **2** CONTRACT, catch, come down with, fall victim to, take **3** CAPTURE, grab, lay hold of, seize, take **4** BECOME, come to be, grow, turn **5** UNDERSTAND, catch, comprehend, fathom, follow, perceive, see, take in, work out **6** PERSUADE, convince, induce, influence, prevail upon **7** *Informal* ANNOY, bug (*informal*), gall, irritate, upset, vex

get across *verb* **1** CROSS, ford, negotiate, pass over, traverse **2** COMMUNICATE, bring home to, convey, impart, make clear or understood, put over, transmit

get along *verb* BE FRIENDLY, agree, be compatible, click (*slang*), concur, hit it off (*informal*)

get at *verb* **1** GAIN ACCESS TO, acquire, attain, come to grips with, get hold of, reach **2** IMPLY, hint, intend, lead up to, mean, suggest **3** CRITICIZE, attack, blame, find fault with, nag, pick on

getaway *noun* ESCAPE, break, break-out, flight

get by *verb* MANAGE, cope, exist, fare, get along, keep one's head above water, make both ends meet, survive

get off *verb* LEAVE, alight, depart, descend, disembark, dismount, escape, exit

get on *verb* BOARD, ascend, climb, embark, mount

get over *verb* RECOVER FROM, come round, get better, mend, pull through, rally, revive, survive

ghastly adjective HORRIBLE, dreadful, frightful, gruesome, hideous, horrendous, loathsome, shocking, terrible, terrifying

ghost noun 1 SPIRIT, apparition, phantom, poltergeist, soul, specter, spook (informal), wraith 2 TRACE, glimmer, hint, possibility, semblance, shadow, suggestion

ghostly adjective SUPERNATURAL, eerie, ghostlike, phantom, spectral, spooky (informal), unearthly, wraithlike

ghoulish adjective MACABRE, disgusting, grisly, gruesome, morbid, sick (informal), unwholesome

giant noun 1 OGRE, colossus, monster, titan ▶ adjective 2 HUGE, colossal, enormous, gargantuan, gigantic, immense, mammoth, titanic, vast

gibberish noun NONSENSE, babble, drivel, gobbledygook (informal), mumbo jumbo, twaddle

gibe, jibe verb 1 TAUNT, jeer, make fun of, mock, poke fun at, ridicule, scoff, scorn, sneer ▶ noun 2 TAUNT, barb, crack (slang), dig, jeer, sarcasm, scoffing, sneer

giddiness noun DIZZINESS, faintness, light-headedness, vertigo

giddy adjective DIZZY, dizzying, faint, light-headed, reeling, unsteady, vertiginous

gift noun 1 DONATION, bequest, bonus, contribution, grant, hand-out, legacy, offering,

present 2 TALENT, ability, capability, capacity, flair, genius, knack, power

gifted adjective TALENTED, able, accomplished, brilliant, capable, clever, expert, ingenious, masterly, skilled

gigantic adjective ENORMOUS, colossal, giant, huge, immense, mammoth, stupendous, titanic, tremendous

giggle verb, noun LAUGH, cackle, chortle, chuckle, snigger, titter, twitter

gild verb EMBELLISH, adorn, beautify, brighten, coat, dress up, embroider, enhance, ornament

gimmick noun STUNT, contrivance, device, dodge, ploy, scheme

gingerly adverb CAUTIOUSLY, carefully, charily, circumspectly, hesitantly, reluctantly, suspiciously, timidly, warily

gird verb SURROUND, encircle, enclose, encompass, enfold, hem in, ring

girdle noun 1 BELT, band, cummerbund, sash, waistband ▶ verb 2 SURROUND, bound, encircle, enclose, encompass, gird, ring

girl noun FEMALE CHILD, damsel (archaic), daughter, lass, maid (archaic), maiden (archaic), miss

girth noun CIRCUMFERENCE, bulk, measure, size

gist noun POINT, core, essence, force, idea, meaning, sense, significance, substance

give verb 1 PRESENT, award, contribute, deliver, donate, grant, hand over or out, provide, supply 2 ANNOUNCE, communicate, issue, notify, pronounce, transmit, utter **3** CONCEDE, grant, hand over, relinquish, surrender, yield **4** PRODUCE, cause, engender, make, occasion

give away verb REVEAL, betray, disclose, divulge, expose, leak, let out, let slip, uncover

give in verb ADMIT DEFEAT, capitulate, collapse, concede, quit, submit, succumb, surrender, yield

give off verb EMIT, discharge, exude, produce, release, send out, throw out

give out verb EMIT, discharge, exude, produce, release, send out, throw out

give up verb ABANDON, call it a day or night, cease, desist, leave off, quit, relinquish, renounce, stop, surrender

glad adjective **1** HAPPY, contented, delighted, gratified, joyful, overjoyed, pleased **2** PLEASING, cheerful, cheering, gratifying, pleasant

gladden verb PLEASE, cheer, delight, gratify, hearten

gladly adverb HAPPILY, cheerfully, freely, gleefully, readily, willingly, with pleasure

gladness noun HAPPINESS, cheerfulness, delight, gaiety, glee, high spirits, joy, mirth, pleasure

glamorous adjective ELEGANT, attractive, dazzling, exciting, fascinating, glittering, glossy, prestigious, smart

glamour noun CHARM, allure, appeal, attraction, beauty, enchantment, fascination, prestige

glance verb **1** LOOK, glimpse, peek, peep, scan, view **2** GLEAM, flash, glimmer, glint, glisten, glitter, reflect, shimmer, shine, twinkle ▸ noun **3** LOOK, glimpse, peek, peep, view

glare verb **1** SCOWL, frown, glower, look daggers, lour or lower **2** GLEAM, blaze, flame, flare ▸ noun **3** SCOWL, black look, dirty look, frown, glower, lour or lower **4** DAZZLE, blaze, brilliance, flame, glow

glaring adjective **1** CONSPICUOUS, blatant, flagrant, gross, manifest, obvious, outrageous, unconcealed **2** DAZZLING, blazing, bright, garish, glowing

glassy adjective **1** TRANSPARENT, clear, glossy, shiny, slippery, smooth **2** EXPRESSIONLESS, blank, cold, dull, empty, fixed, glazed, lifeless, vacant

glaze verb **1** COAT, enamel, gloss, lacquer, polish, varnish ▸ noun **2** COAT, enamel, finish, gloss, lacquer, luster, patina, polish, shine, varnish

gleam noun **1** GLOW, beam, flash, glimmer, ray, sparkle **2** TRACE, flicker, glimmer, hint, inkling, suggestion ▸ verb **3** SHINE, flash, glimmer, glint, glisten, glitter, glow, shimmer, sparkle

glee noun DELIGHT, elation, exhilaration, exuberance, exultation, joy, merriment, triumph

gleeful adjective DELIGHTED, elated, exuberant, exultant, joyful, jubilant, overjoyed, triumphant

glib adjective SMOOTH, easy,

fluent, insincere, plausible, quick, ready, slick, suave, voluble

glide verb SLIDE, coast, drift, float, flow, roll, run, sail, skate, slip

glimmer verb 1 FLICKER, blink, gleam, glisten, glitter, glow, shimmer, shine, sparkle, twinkle ▶noun 2 GLEAM, blink, flicker, glow, ray, shimmer, sparkle, twinkle 3 TRACE, flicker, gleam, hint, inkling, suggestion

glimpse noun 1 LOOK, glance, peek, peep, sight, sighting ▶verb 2 CATCH SIGHT OF, espy, sight, spot, spy, view

glint verb 1 GLEAM, flash, glimmer, glitter, shine, sparkle, twinkle ▶noun 2 GLEAM, flash, glimmer, glitter, shine, sparkle, twinkle, twinkling

glisten verb GLEAM, flash, glance, glare, glimmer, glint, glitter, shimmer, shine, sparkle, twinkle

glitch noun PROBLEM, blip, difficulty, gremlin, hitch, interruption, malfunction, snag

glitter verb 1 SHINE, flash, glare, gleam, glimmer, glint, glisten, shimmer, sparkle, twinkle ▶noun 2 SHINE, brightness, flash, glare, gleam, radiance, sheen, shimmer, sparkle 3 GLAMOUR, display, gaudiness, pageantry, show, showiness, splendor, tinsel

gloat verb RELISH, brag, crow, drool, exult, glory, revel in, rub it in (informal), triumph

global adjective 1 WORLDWIDE, international, planetary, universal, world 2 COMPREHENSIVE, all-inclusive, exhaustive, general, total,

unlimited

globe noun SPHERE, ball, earth, orb, planet, world

globule noun DROPLET, bead, bubble, drop, particle, pearl, pellet

gloom noun 1 DARKNESS, blackness, dark, dusk, murk, obscurity, shade, shadow, twilight 2 DEPRESSION, dejection, despondency, low spirits, melancholy, sorrow, unhappiness, woe

gloomy adjective 1 DARK, black, dim, dismal, dreary, dull, gray, murky, somber 2 DEPRESSING, bad, cheerless, disheartening, dispiriting, dreary, sad, somber 3 MISERABLE, crestfallen, dejected, dispirited, downcast, downhearted, glum, melancholy, morose, pessimistic, sad

glorify verb 1 ENHANCE, aggrandize, dignify, elevate, ennoble, magnify 2 WORSHIP, adore, bless, exalt, honor, idolize, pay homage to, revere, venerate 3 PRAISE, celebrate, eulogize, extol, sing or sound the praises of

glorious adjective 1 FAMOUS, celebrated, distinguished, eminent, honored, illustrious, magnificent, majestic, renowned 2 SPLENDID, beautiful, brilliant, dazzling, gorgeous, shining, superb 3 DELIGHTFUL, excellent, fine, gorgeous, marvelous, wonderful

glory noun 1 HONOR, dignity, distinction, eminence, fame, kudos, praise, prestige, renown 2 SPLENDOR, grandeur, greatness, magnificence, majesty, nobility, pageantry, pomp ▶ verb **3** TRIUMPH, boast, exult, pride oneself, relish, revel, take delight

gloss[1] noun SHINE, brightness, gleam, luster, patina, polish, sheen, veneer

gloss[2] noun **1** COMMENT, annotation; commentary, elucidation, explanation, footnote, interpretation, note, translation ▶ verb **2** INTERPRET, annotate, comment, elucidate, explain, translate

glossy adjective SHINY, bright, glassy, glazed, lustrous, polished, shining, silky

glow verb **1** SHINE, brighten, burn, gleam, glimmer, redden, smolder ▶ noun **2** LIGHT, burning, gleam, glimmer, luminosity, phosphorescence **3** RADIANCE, brightness, brilliance, effulgence, splendor, vividness

glower verb **1** SCOWL, frown, give a dirty look, glare, look daggers, lour or lower ▶ noun **2** SCOWL, black look, dirty look, frown, glare, lour or lower

glowing adjective **1** BRIGHT, aglow, flaming, luminous, radiant **2** COMPLIMENTARY, adulatory, ecstatic, enthusiastic, laudatory, rave (informal), rhapsodic

glue noun **1** ADHESIVE, cement, gum, paste ▶ verb **2** STICK, affix, cement, fix, gum, paste, seal

glum adjective GLOOMY, crestfallen, dejected, doleful, low, morose, pessimistic, sullen

glut noun **1** SURFEIT, excess, oversupply, plethora, saturation, superfluity, surplus

▶ verb **2** SATURATE, choke, clog, deluge, flood, inundate, overload, oversupply

glutton noun GOURMAND, pig (informal)

gluttonous adjective GREEDY, gormandizing, insatiable, piggish, ravenous, voracious

gluttony noun GREED, gormandizing, greediness, voracity

gnarled adjective TWISTED, contorted, knotted, knotty, rough, rugged, weather-beaten, wrinkled

gnaw verb BITE, chew, munch, nibble

go verb **1** MOVE, advance, journey, make for, pass, proceed, set off, travel **2** LEAVE, depart, make tracks, move out, slope off, withdraw **3** FUNCTION, move, operate, perform, run, work **4** CONTRIBUTE, lead to, serve, tend, work towards **5** HARMONIZE, agree, blend, chime, complement, correspond, fit, match, suit **6** ELAPSE, expire, flow, lapse, pass, slip away ▶ noun **7** ATTEMPT, bid, crack (informal), effort, shot (informal), try, turn **8** Informal ENERGY, drive, force, life, spirit, verve, vigor, vitality, vivacity

goad verb **1** PROVOKE, drive, egg on, exhort, incite, prod, prompt, spur ▶ noun **2** PROVOCATION, impetus, incentive, incitement, irritation, spur, stimulus, urge

goal noun AIM, ambition, end, intention, object, objective, purpose, target

gobble verb DEVOUR, bolt, cram,

gorge, gulp, guzzle, stuff, swallow, wolf

go-between noun INTERMEDIARY, agent, broker, dealer, mediator, medium, middleman

godforsaken adjective DESOLATE, abandoned, bleak, deserted, dismal, dreary, forlorn, gloomy, lonely, remote, wretched

godlike adjective DIVINE, celestial, heavenly, superhuman, transcendent

godly adjective DEVOUT, god-fearing, good, holy, pious, religious, righteous, saintly

godsend noun BLESSING, boon, manna, stroke of luck, windfall

go for verb 1 FAVOR, admire, be attracted to, be fond of, choose, like, prefer 2 ATTACK, assail, assault, launch oneself at, rush upon, set about or upon, spring upon

golden adjective 1 YELLOW, blond or blonde, flaxen 2 SUCCESSFUL, flourishing, glorious, halcyon, happy, prosperous, rich 3 PROMISING, excellent, favorable, opportune

gone adjective 1 FINISHED, elapsed, ended, over, past 2 MISSING, absent, astray, away, lacking, lost, vanished

good adjective 1 PLEASING, acceptable, admirable, excellent, fine, first-class, first-rate, great, satisfactory, splendid, superior 2 PRAISEWORTHY, admirable, ethical, honest, honorable, moral, righteous, trustworthy, upright, virtuous, worthy 3 EXPERT, able, accomplished, adept, adroit, clever,

competent, proficient, skilled, talented 4 BENEFICIAL, advantageous, convenient, favorable, fitting, helpful, profitable, suitable, useful, wholesome, win-win (informal) 5 KIND, altruistic, benevolent, charitable, friendly, humane, kind-hearted, kindly, merciful, obliging 6 VALID, authentic, bona fide, genuine, legitimate, proper, real, true 7 WELL-BEHAVED, dutiful, obedient, orderly, polite, well-mannered 8 FULL, adequate, ample, complete, considerable, extensive, large, substantial, sufficient ▶ noun 9 BENEFIT, advantage, gain, interest, profit, use, usefulness, welfare, wellbeing 10 VIRTUE, excellence, goodness, merit, morality, rectitude, right, righteousness, worth 11 **for good** PERMANENTLY, finally, for ever, irrevocably, once and for all

good-bye noun FAREWELL, adieu, leave-taking, parting

good-for-nothing noun 1 IDLER, couch potato (slang), slacker (informal), waster, wastrel ▶ adjective 2 WORTHLESS, feckless, idle, irresponsible, useless

goodly adjective CONSIDERABLE, ample, large, significant, sizable or sizeable, substantial, tidy (informal)

goodness noun 1 EXCELLENCE, merit, quality, superiority, value, worth 2 KINDNESS, benevolence, friendliness, generosity, goodwill, humaneness, kind-heartedness, kindliness, mercy 3 VIRTUE, honesty, honor, integrity,

merit, morality, probity,
rectitude, righteousness,
uprightness **4** BENEFIT,
advantage, salubriousness,
wholesomeness

goods plural noun **1** PROPERTY,
belongings, chattels, effects,
gear, paraphernalia,
possessions, things, trappings
2 MERCHANDISE, commodities,
stock, stuff, wares

goodwill noun FRIENDLINESS,
amity, benevolence, friendship,
heartiness, kindliness

go off verb **1** EXPLODE, blow up,
detonate, fire **2** LEAVE, decamp,
depart, go away, move out,
part, quit, slope off

go out verb **1** LEAVE, depart, exit
2 BE EXTINGUISHED, die out,
expire, fade out

go over verb EXAMINE, inspect,
rehearse, reiterate, review,
revise, study, work over

gore[1] noun BLOOD, bloodshed,
butchery, carnage, slaughter

gore[2] verb PIERCE, impale,
transfix, wound

gorge noun **1** RAVINE, canyon,
chasm, cleft, defile, fissure,
pass ▶ verb **2** OVEREAT, cram,
devour, feed, glut, gobble,
gulp, guzzle, stuff, wolf

gorgeous adjective **1** BEAUTIFUL,
dazzling, elegant, magnificent,
ravishing, splendid, stunning
(informal), sumptuous, superb
2 Informal PLEASING, delightful,
enjoyable, exquisite, fine,
glorious, good, lovely

gory adjective BLOODTHIRSTY,
blood-soaked, bloodstained,
bloody, murderous, sanguinary

gospel noun **1** TRUTH, certainty,
fact, the last word **2** DOCTRINE,

credo, creed, message, news,
revelation, tidings

gossip noun **1** IDLE TALK, blether,
chitchat, hearsay, scandal,
small talk, tittle-tattle
2 BUSYBODY, chatterbox
(informal), chatterer,
gossipmonger, scandalmonger,
tattler, telltale ▶ verb **3** CHAT,
blether, chew the fat (slang),
gabble, jaw (slang), prate,
prattle, tattle

go through verb **1** SUFFER, bear,
brave, endure, experience,
tolerate, undergo, withstand
2 EXAMINE, check, explore,
forage, hunt, look, search

gouge verb **1** SCOOP, chisel,
claw, cut, dig (out), hollow
(out) ▶ noun **2** GASH, cut,
furrow, groove, hollow, scoop,
scratch, trench

gourmet noun CONNOISSEUR, bon
vivant, epicure, foodie
(informal), gastronome

govern verb **1** RULE, administer,
command, control, direct,
guide, handle, lead, manage,
order **2** RESTRAIN, check, control,
curb, discipline, hold in check,
master, regulate, subdue, tame

government noun **1** RULE,
administration, authority,
governance, sovereignty,
statecraft **2** EXECUTIVE,
administration, ministry,
powers-that-be, regime

governor noun LEADER,
administrator, chief,
commander, controller,
director, executive, head,
manager, ruler

gown noun DRESS, costume,
frock, garb, garment, habit,
robe

grab verb SNATCH, capture, catch, catch or take hold of, clutch, grasp, grip, pluck, seize, snap up

grace noun 1 ELEGANCE, attractiveness, beauty, charm, comeliness, ease, gracefulness, poise, polish, refinement, tastefulness 2 GOODWILL, benefaction, benevolence, favor, generosity, goodness, kindliness, kindness 3 MANNERS, consideration, decency, decorum, etiquette, propriety, tact 4 INDULGENCE, mercy, pardon, reprieve 5 PRAYER, benediction, blessing, thanks, thanksgiving ▶verb 6 HONOR, adorn, decorate, dignify, embellish, enhance, enrich, favor, ornament, set off

graceful adjective ELEGANT, beautiful, charming, comely, easy, pleasing, tasteful

gracious adjective KIND, charitable, civil, considerate, cordial, courteous, friendly, polite, well-mannered

grade noun 1 LEVEL, category, class, degree, echelon, group, rank, stage ▶verb 2 CLASSIFY, arrange, class, group, order, range, rank, rate, sort

gradient noun SLOPE, bank, declivity, grade, hill, incline, rise

gradual adjective STEADY, gentle, graduated, piecemeal, progressive, regular, slow, unhurried

gradually adverb STEADILY, by degrees, gently, little by little, progressively, slowly, step by step, unhurriedly

graduate verb 1 MARK OFF, calibrate, grade, measure out,

proportion, regulate 2 CLASSIFY, arrange, grade, group, order, rank, sort

graft noun 1 SHOOT, bud, implant, scion, splice, sprout ▶verb 2 TRANSPLANT, implant, ingraft, insert, join, splice

grain noun 1 CEREALS, corn 2 SEED, grist, kernel 3 BIT, fragment, granule, modicum, morsel, particle, piece, scrap, speck, trace 4 TEXTURE, fiber, nap, pattern, surface, weave 5 As in **go against the grain** INCLINATION, character, disposition, humor, make-up, temper

grand adjective 1 IMPRESSIVE, dignified, grandiose, great, imposing, large, magnificent, regal, splendid, stately, sublime 2 EXCELLENT, cool (informal), fine, first-class, great (informal), outstanding, phat (slang), splendid, wonderful

grandeur noun SPLENDOR, dignity, magnificence, majesty, nobility, pomp, stateliness, sublimity

grandiose adjective 1 PRETENTIOUS, affected, bombastic, extravagant, flamboyant, high-flown, ostentatious, pompous, showy 2 IMPOSING, grand, impressive, lofty, magnificent, majestic, monumental, stately

grant verb 1 CONSENT TO, accede to, agree to, allow, permit 2 GIVE, allocate, allot, assign, award, donate, hand out, present 3 ADMIT, acknowledge, concede ▶noun 4 AWARD, allowance, donation, endowment, gift, hand-out, present, subsidy

granule noun GRAIN, atom, crumb, fragment, molecule, particle, scrap, speck

graphic adjective **1** VIVID, clear, detailed, explicit, expressive, lively, lucid, striking **2** PICTORIAL, diagrammatic, visual

grapple verb **1** GRIP, clutch, grab, grasp, seize, wrestle **2** DEAL WITH, address oneself to, confront, get to grips with, struggle, tackle, take on

grasp verb **1** GRIP, catch, clasp, clinch, clutch, grab, grapple, hold, lay or take hold of, seize, snatch **2** UNDERSTAND, catch on, catch or get the drift of, comprehend, get, realize, see, take in ▶noun **3** GRIP, clasp, clutches, embrace, hold, possession, tenure **4** CONTROL, power, reach, scope **5** UNDERSTANDING, awareness, comprehension, grip, knowledge, mastery

grasping adjective GREEDY, acquisitive, avaricious, covetous, rapacious

grate verb **1** SHRED, mince, pulverize, triturate **2** SCRAPE, creak, grind, rasp, rub, scratch **3** ANNOY, exasperate, get on one's nerves (informal), irritate, jar, rankle, set one's teeth on edge

grateful adjective THANKFUL, appreciative, beholden, indebted, obliged

gratification noun SATISFACTION, delight, enjoyment, fulfillment, indulgence, pleasure, relish, reward, thrill

gratify verb PLEASE, delight, give pleasure, gladden, humor,

requite, satisfy

grating[1] adjective IRRITATING, annoying, discordant, displeasing, harsh, jarring, offensive, raucous, strident, unpleasant

grating[2] noun GRILLE, grate, grid, gridiron, lattice, trellis

gratitude noun THANKFULNESS, appreciation, gratefulness, indebtedness, obligation, recognition, thanks

gratuitous adjective **1** FREE, complimentary, gratis, spontaneous, unasked-for, unpaid, unrewarded, voluntary **2** UNJUSTIFIED, baseless, causeless, groundless, needless, superfluous, uncalled-for, unmerited, unnecessary, unwarranted, wanton

gratuity noun TIP, bonus, donation, gift, largesse or largess, reward

grave[1] noun BURYING PLACE, crypt, mausoleum, pit, sepulcher, tomb, vault

grave[2] adjective **1** SOLEMN, dignified, dour, earnest, serious, sober, somber, unsmiling **2** IMPORTANT, acute, critical, dangerous, pressing, serious, severe, threatening, urgent

graveyard noun CEMETERY, burial ground, charnel house, churchyard, necropolis

gravity noun **1** IMPORTANCE, acuteness, momentousness, perilousness, seriousness, severity, significance, urgency, weightiness **2** SOLEMNITY, dignity, earnestness, gravitas, seriousness, sobriety

gray adjective **1** PALE, ashen,

pallid, wan **2** DISMAL, dark, depressing, dim, drab, dreary, dull, gloomy **3** CHARACTERLESS, anonymous, colorless, dull

graze[1] *verb* FEED, browse, crop, pasture

graze[2] *verb* **1** TOUCH, brush, glance off, rub, scrape, shave, skim **2** SCRATCH, abrade, chafe, scrape, skin ▶ *noun* **3** SCRATCH, abrasion, scrape

greasy *adjective* FATTY, oily, oleaginous, slimy, slippery

great *adjective* **1** LARGE, big, enormous, gigantic, huge, immense, prodigious, vast, voluminous **2** IMPORTANT, critical, crucial, momentous, serious, significant **3** FAMOUS, eminent, illustrious, noteworthy, outstanding, prominent, remarkable, renowned **4** *Informal* EXCELLENT, fantastic (*informal*), fine, marvelous, superb, terrific (*informal*), tremendous (*informal*), wonderful

greatly *adverb* VERY MUCH, considerably, enormously, exceedingly, hugely, immensely, remarkably, tremendously, vastly

greatness *noun* **1** IMMENSITY, enormity, hugeness, magnitude, prodigiousness, size, vastness **2** IMPORTANCE, gravity, momentousness, seriousness, significance, urgency, weight **3** FAME, celebrity, distinction, eminence, glory, grandeur, illustriousness, kudos, note, renown

greed, greediness *noun* **1** GLUTTONY, edacity, esurience,

gormandizing, hunger, voracity **2** AVARICE, acquisitiveness, avidity, covetousness, craving, desire, longing, selfishness

greedy *adjective* **1** GLUTTONOUS, gormandizing, hungry, insatiable, piggish, ravenous, voracious **2** GRASPING, acquisitive, avaricious, avid, covetous, craving, desirous, rapacious, selfish

green *adjective* **1** LEAFY, grassy, verdant **2** ECOLOGICAL, conservationist, environment-friendly, non-polluting, ozone-friendly **3** IMMATURE, gullible, inexperienced, naive, new, raw, untrained, wet behind the ears (*informal*) **4** JEALOUS, covetous, envious, grudging, resentful ▶ *noun* **5** LAWN, common, sward, turf

greet *verb* WELCOME, accost, address, compliment, hail, meet, receive, salute

greeting *noun* WELCOME, address, reception, salutation, salute

gregarious *adjective* OUTGOING, affable, companionable, convivial, cordial, friendly, sociable, social

gridlock *noun* STANDSTILL, deadlock, impasse, stalemate

grief *noun* SADNESS, anguish, distress, heartache, misery, regret, remorse, sorrow, suffering, woe

grievance *noun* COMPLAINT, ax to grind, gripe (*informal*), injury, injustice

grieve *verb* **1** MOURN, complain, deplore, lament, regret, rue, suffer, weep **2** SADDEN, afflict, distress, hurt, injure, pain, wound

grievous *adjective* **1** PAINFUL, dreadful, grave, harmful, severe **2** DEPLORABLE, atrocious, dreadful, monstrous, offensive, outrageous, shameful, shocking

grim *adjective* FORBIDDING, formidable, harsh, merciless, ruthless, severe, sinister, stern, terrible

grimace *noun* **1** SCOWL, face, frown, sneer ▶ *verb* **2** SCOWL, frown, lour *or* lower, make a face *or* faces, sneer

grime *noun* DIRT, filth, grease, smut, soot

grimy *adjective* DIRTY, filthy, foul, grubby, scuzzy (*slang*), soiled, sooty, unclean

grind *verb* **1** CRUSH, abrade, granulate, grate, mill, pound, powder, pulverize, triturate **2** SMOOTH, polish, sand, sharpen, whet **3** SCRAPE, gnash, grate ▶ *noun* **4** *Informal* HARD WORK, chore, drudgery, labor, sweat (*informal*), toil

grip *noun* **1** CLASP, hold **2** CONTROL, clutches, domination, influence, possession, power **3** UNDERSTANDING, command, comprehension, grasp, mastery ▶ *verb* **4** GRASP, clasp, clutch, hold, seize, take hold of **5** ENGROSS, absorb, enthrall, entrance, fascinate, hold, mesmerize, rivet

gripping *adjective* FASCINATING, compelling, engrossing, enthralling, entrancing, exciting, riveting, spellbinding, thrilling

grisly *adjective* GRUESOME,

appalling, awful, dreadful, ghastly, horrible, macabre, shocking, terrifying

grit *noun* **1** GRAVEL, dust, pebbles, sand **2** COURAGE, backbone, determination, fortitude, guts (*informal*), perseverance, resolution, spirit, tenacity ▶ *verb* **3** GRIND, clench, gnash, grate

gritty *adjective* **1** ROUGH, dusty, granular, gravelly, rasping, sandy **2** COURAGEOUS, brave, determined, dogged, plucky, resolute, spirited, steadfast, tenacious

groan *noun* **1** MOAN, cry, sigh, whine ▶ *verb* **2** MOAN, cry, sigh, whine

groggy *adjective* DIZZY, confused, dazed, faint, shaky, unsteady, weak, wobbly

groom *noun* **1** STABLEMAN, stableboy ▶ *verb* **2** SMARTEN UP, clean, preen, primp, spruce up, tidy **3** RUB DOWN, brush, clean, curry, tend **4** TRAIN, coach, drill, educate, make ready, nurture, prepare, prime, ready

groove *noun* INDENTATION, channel, cut, flute, furrow, hollow, rut, trench, trough

grope *verb* FEEL, cast about, fish, flounder, forage, fumble, scrabble, search

gross *adjective* **1** FAT, corpulent, hulking, obese, overweight **2** TOTAL, aggregate, before deductions, before tax, entire, whole **3** VULGAR, coarse, crude, indelicate, obscene, offensive **4** BLATANT, flagrant, grievous, heinous, rank, sheer, unmitigated, utter ▶ *verb* **5** EARN, bring in, make, rake in (*informal*), take

grotesque *adjective* UNNATURAL, bizarre, deformed, distorted, fantastic, freakish, outlandish, preposterous, strange

ground *noun* 1 EARTH, dry land, land, soil, terra firma, terrain, turf 2 STADIUM, arena, field, park, pitch 3 (often plural) LAND, estate, fields, gardens, terrain, territory 4 (usually plural) DREGS, deposit, lees, sediment 5 **grounds** REASON, basis, cause, excuse, foundation, justification, motive, occasion, pretext, rationale ▶ *verb* 6 BASE, establish, fix, found, set, settle 7 INSTRUCT, acquaint with, familiarize with, initiate, teach, train, tutor

groundless *adjective* UNJUSTIFIED, baseless, empty, idle, uncalled-for, unfounded, unwarranted

groundwork *noun* PRELIMINARIES, foundation, fundamentals, preparation, spadework, underpinnings

group *noun* 1 SET, band, bunch, cluster, collection, crowd, gang, pack, party ▶ *verb* 2 ARRANGE, bracket, class, classify, marshal, order, sort

grouse *verb* 1 COMPLAIN, bellyache (*slang*), carp, gripe (*informal*), grumble, moan, whine ▶ *noun* 2 COMPLAINT, grievance, gripe (*informal*), grouch (*informal*), grumble, moan, objection, protest

grove *noun* WOOD, coppice, copse, covert, plantation, spinney, thicket

grovel *verb* HUMBLE ONESELF,

abase oneself, bow and scrape, brown-nose (*slang*), crawl, creep, cringe, demean oneself, fawn, kiss ass (*slang*), kowtow, toady

grow *verb* 1 INCREASE, develop, enlarge, expand, get bigger, multiply, spread, stretch, swell 2 ORIGINATE, arise, issue, spring, stem 3 IMPROVE, advance, flourish, progress, prosper, succeed, thrive 4 BECOME, come to be, get, turn 5 CULTIVATE, breed, farm, nurture, produce, propagate, raise

grown-up *adjective* 1 MATURE, adult, fully-grown, of age ▶ *noun* 2 ADULT, man, woman

growth *noun* 1 INCREASE, development, enlargement, expansion, multiplication, proliferation, stretching 2 IMPROVEMENT, advance, expansion, progress, prosperity, rise, success 3 *Medical* TUMOR, lump

grub *noun* 1 LARVA, caterpillar, maggot 2 *Slang* FOOD, rations, sustenance, victuals ▶ *verb* 3 DIG UP, burrow, pull up, root (*informal*) 4 SEARCH, ferret, forage, hunt, rummage, scour, uncover, unearth

grubby *adjective* DIRTY, filthy, grimy, messy, mucky, scuzzy (*slang*), seedy, shabby, sordid, squalid, unwashed

grudge *verb* 1 RESENT, begrudge, complain, covet, envy, mind ▶ *noun* 2 RESENTMENT, animosity, antipathy, bitterness, dislike, enmity, grievance, rancor

grueling *adjective* EXHAUSTING, arduous, backbreaking,

demanding, laborious, punishing, severe, strenuous, taxing, tiring

gruesome adjective HORRIFIC, ghastly, grim, grisly, horrible, macabre, shocking, terrible

gruff adjective 1 SURLY, bad-tempered, brusque, churlish, grumpy, rough, rude, sullen, ungracious 2 HOARSE, croaking, guttural, harsh, husky, low, rasping, rough, throaty

grumble verb 1 COMPLAIN, bleat, carp, gripe (informal), grouch (informal), grouse, moan, whine 2 RUMBLE, growl, gurgle, murmur, mutter, roar ▶ noun 3 COMPLAINT, grievance, gripe (informal), grouch (informal), grouse, moan, objection, protest 4 RUMBLE, growl, gurgle, murmur, muttering, roar

grumpy adjective IRRITABLE, cantankerous, crotchety, ill-tempered, peevish, sulky, sullen, surly, testy

guarantee noun 1 ASSURANCE, bond, certainty, pledge, promise, security, surety, warranty, word of honor ▶ verb 2 MAKE CERTAIN, assure, certify, ensure, pledge, promise, secure, vouch for, warrant

guard verb 1 WATCH OVER, defend, mind, preserve, protect, safeguard, secure, shield ▶ noun 2 PROTECTOR, custodian, defender, lookout, picket, sentinel, sentry, warden, watch, watchman 3 PROTECTION, buffer, defense, safeguard, screen, security, shield 4 **off guard** UNPREPARED, napping, unready, unwary 5 **on guard** PREPARED, alert,

cautious, circumspect, on the alert, on the lookout, ready, vigilant, wary, watchful

guarded adjective CAUTIOUS, cagey (informal), careful, circumspect, noncommittal, prudent, reserved, reticent, suspicious, wary

guardian noun KEEPER, champion, curator, custodian, defender, guard, protector, warden

guerrilla noun FREEDOM FIGHTER, partisan, underground fighter

guess verb 1 ESTIMATE, conjecture, hypothesize, predict, speculate, work out 2 SUPPOSE, believe, conjecture, fancy, imagine, judge, reckon, suspect, think ▶ noun 3 PREDICTION, conjecture, hypothesis, shot in the dark, speculation, supposition, theory

guesswork noun SPECULATION, conjecture, estimation, supposition, surmise, theory

guest noun VISITOR, boarder, caller, company, lodger, visitant

guidance noun ADVICE, counseling, direction, help, instruction, leadership, management, teaching

guide noun 1 ESCORT, adviser, conductor, counselor, leader, mentor, teacher, usher 2 MODEL, example, ideal, inspiration, paradigm, standard 3 POINTER, beacon, guiding light, landmark, lodestar, marker, sign, signpost 4 GUIDEBOOK, Baedeker, catalog, directory, handbook, instructions, key, manual ▶ verb 5 LEAD, accompany, conduct, direct, escort, shepherd, show

the way, usher **6** STEER,
command, control, direct,
handle, manage, maneuver
7 SUPERVISE, advise, counsel,
influence, instruct, oversee,
superintend, teach, train

guild noun SOCIETY, association,
brotherhood, club, company,
corporation, fellowship,
fraternity, league, lodge, order,
organization, union

guile noun CUNNING, artifice,
cleverness, craft, deceit,
slyness, trickery, wiliness

guilt noun **1** CULPABILITY, blame,
guiltiness, misconduct,
responsibility, sinfulness,
wickedness, wrongdoing
2 REMORSE, contrition, guilty
conscience, regret,
self-reproach, shame, stigma

guiltless adjective INNOCENT,
blameless, clean (slang),
irreproachable, pure, sinless,
spotless, squeaky-clean,
untainted

guilty adjective **1** RESPONSIBLE, at
fault, blameworthy, culpable,
reprehensible, sinful, to blame,
wrong **2** REMORSEFUL, ashamed,
conscience-stricken, contrite,
regretful, rueful, shamefaced,
sheepish, sorry

guise noun FORM, appearance,
aspect, demeanor, disguise,
mode, pretense, semblance,
shape

gulf noun **1** BAY, bight, sea inlet
2 CHASM, abyss, gap, opening,
rift, separation, split, void

gullibility noun CREDULITY,
innocence, naivety, simplicity

gullible adjective NAIVE, born
yesterday, credulous, innocent,
simple, trusting, unsuspecting,

wet behind the ears (informal)

gully noun CHANNEL, ditch,
gutter, watercourse

gulp verb **1** SWALLOW, devour,
gobble, guzzle, quaff, swig
(informal), swill, wolf **2** GASP,
choke, swallow ▶ noun
3 SWALLOW, draft, mouthful,
swig (informal)

gum noun **1** GLUE, adhesive,
cement, paste, resin ▶ verb
2 STICK, affix, cement, glue,
paste

gun noun FIREARM, handgun,
piece (slang), pistol, revolver,
rifle, saturday night special
(slang)

gunman noun TERRORIST, bandit,
gunslinger (slang), killer

gurgle verb **1** MURMUR, babble,
bubble, lap, plash, purl, ripple,
splash ▶ noun **2** MURMUR,
babble, purl, ripple

guru noun TEACHER, authority,
leader, master, mentor, sage,
Svengali, tutor

gush verb **1** FLOW, cascade,
flood, pour, run, rush, spout,
spurt, stream **2** ENTHUSE,
babble, chatter, effervesce,
effuse, overstate, spout ▶ noun
3 STREAM, cascade, flood, flow,
jet, rush, spout, spurt, torrent

gust noun **1** BLAST, blow, breeze,
puff, rush, squall ▶ verb **2** BLOW,
blast, squall

gusto noun RELISH, delight,
enjoyment, enthusiasm, fervor,
pleasure, verve, zeal

gut noun **1** Informal PAUNCH,
belly, potbelly, spare tire
(slang) **2 guts: a** INTESTINES,
belly, bowels, entrails, innards
(informal), insides (informal),
stomach, viscera **b** Informal

COURAGE, audacity, backbone, daring, mettle, nerve, pluck, spirit ▶ verb **3** DISEMBOWEL, clean **4** RAVAGE, clean out, despoil, empty **5** *As in* **gut reaction** INSTINCTIVE, basic, heartfelt, intuitive, involuntary, natural, spontaneous, unthinking, visceral

gutsy *adjective* BRAVE, bold, courageous, determined, gritty, indomitable, plucky, resolute, spirited

gutter *noun* DRAIN, channel, conduit, ditch, sluice, trench, trough

guttural *adjective* THROATY, deep, gravelly, gruff, hoarse, husky, rasping, rough, thick

guy *noun Informal* MAN, chap, dude (*slang*), fellow, lad, person

guzzle *verb* DEVOUR, bolt, cram, drink, gobble, stuff (oneself), swill, wolf

Gypsy *noun* TRAVELER, Bohemian, nomad, rambler, roamer, Romany, rover, wanderer

—— **H h** ——

habit *noun* **1** MANNERISM, custom, practice, proclivity, propensity, quirk, tendency, way **2** ADDICTION, dependence

habitation *noun* **1** DWELLING, abode, domicile, home, house, living quarters, lodging, quarters, residence **2** OCCUPANCY, inhabitance, occupation, tenancy

habitual *adjective* CUSTOMARY, accustomed, familiar, normal,

regular, routine, standard, traditional, usual

hack[1] *verb* CUT, chop, hew, lacerate, mangle, mutilate, slash

hack[2] *noun* SCRIBBLER, literary hack, penny-a-liner **2** HORSE, crock, nag

hackneyed *adjective* UNORIGINAL, clichéd, commonplace, overworked, stale, stereotyped, stock, threadbare, tired, trite

hag *noun* WITCH, crone, harridan

haggard *adjective* GAUNT, careworn, drawn, emaciated, pinched, thin, wan

haggle *verb* BARGAIN, barter, beat down

hail[1] *noun* **1** BOMBARDMENT, barrage, downpour, rain, shower, storm, volley ▶ verb **2** RAIN DOWN ON, batter, beat down upon, bombard, pelt, rain, shower

hail[2] *verb* **1** GREET, acclaim, acknowledge, applaud, cheer, honor, salute, welcome **2** FLAG DOWN, signal to, wave down **3** **hail from** COME FROM, be a native of, be born in, originate in

hair *noun* LOCKS, head of hair, mane, mop, shock, tresses

hairdresser *noun* STYLIST, barber, coiffeur or coiffeuse

hair-raising *adjective* FRIGHTENING, alarming, bloodcurdling, horrifying, scary, shocking, spine-chilling, terrifying

hairstyle *noun* HAIRCUT, coiffure, cut, hairdo, style

hairy *adjective* SHAGGY, bushy, furry, hirsute, stubbly, unshaven, woolly

halcyon *adjective* **1** PEACEFUL,

calm, gentle, quiet, serene, tranquil, undisturbed **2** As in halcyon days HAPPY, carefree, flourishing, golden, palmy, prosperous

hale adjective HEALTHY, able-bodied, fit, flourishing, in the pink, robust, sound, strong, vigorous, well

half noun **1** EQUAL PART, fifty per cent, hemisphere, portion, section ▶ adjective **2** PARTIAL, halved, limited, moderate ▶ adverb **3** PARTIALLY, in part, partly

half-baked adjective ILL-JUDGED, ill-conceived, impractical, poorly planned, short-sighted, unformed, unthought out or through

half-hearted adjective UNENTHUSIASTIC, apathetic, indifferent, lackluster, listless, lukewarm, perfunctory, tame

halfway adverb **1** MIDWAY, to or in the middle ▶ adjective **2** MIDWAY, central, equidistant, intermediate, mid, middle

halfwit noun FOOL, airhead (slang), dork (slang), dunderhead, idiot, imbecile (informal), moron, schmuck (slang), simpleton

hall noun **1** ENTRANCE HALL, corridor, entry, foyer, hallway, lobby, passage, passageway, vestibule **2** MEETING PLACE, assembly room, auditorium, chamber, concert hall

hallmark noun **1** SEAL, device, endorsement, mark, sign, stamp, symbol **2** INDICATION, sure sign, telltale sign

hallucination noun ILLUSION, apparition, delusion, dream,

fantasy, figment of the imagination, mirage, vision

halo noun RING OF LIGHT, aura, corona, nimbus, radiance

halt verb **1** STOP, break off, cease, come to an end, desist, rest, stand still, wait **2** END, block, bring to an end, check, curb, cut short, nip in the bud, terminate ▶ noun **2** STOP, close, end, pause, standstill, stoppage

halting adjective FALTERING, awkward, hesitant, labored, stammering, stumbling, stuttering

halve verb BISECT, cut in half, divide equally, share equally, split in two

hammer verb **1** HIT, bang, beat, drive, knock, strike, tap **2** Informal DEFEAT, beat, drub, run rings around (informal), thrash, trounce, wipe the floor with (informal)

hamper verb HINDER, frustrate, hamstring, handicap, impede, interfere with, obstruct, prevent, restrict

hand noun **1** PALM, fist, mitt (slang), paw (informal) **2** HIRED MAN, artisan, craftsman, employee, laborer, operative, worker, workman **3** PENMANSHIP, calligraphy, handwriting, script **4** OVATION, clap, round of applause **5** at or on hand NEARBY, at one's fingertips, available, close, handy, near, ready, within reach ▶ verb **6** PASS, deliver, hand over

handbook noun GUIDEBOOK, Baedeker, guide, instruction book, manual

handcuff verb SHACKLE, fetter, manacle

handcuffs plural noun SHACKLES, cuffs (informal), fetters, manacles

handful noun FEW, small number, smattering, sprinkling

handicap noun 1 DISADVANTAGE, barrier, drawback, hindrance, impediment, limitation, obstacle, restriction, stumbling block 2 ADVANTAGE, head start 3 DISABILITY, defect, impairment ▶verb 4 RESTRICT, burden, encumber, hamper, hamstring, hinder, hold back, impede, limit

handicraft noun CRAFTSMANSHIP, art, craft, handiwork, skill, workmanship

handiwork noun CREATION, achievement, design, invention, product, production

handle noun 1 GRIP, haft, hilt, stock ▶verb 2 HOLD, feel, finger, grasp, pick up, touch 3 CONTROL, direct, guide, manage, maneuver, manipulate 4 DEAL WITH, cope with, manage

hand-out noun 1 CHARITY, alms 2 LEAFLET, bulletin, circular, literature (informal), mailshot, press release

handsome adjective 1 GOOD-LOOKING, attractive, comely, elegant, gorgeous, personable, well-proportioned 2 LARGE, abundant, ample, considerable, generous, liberal, plentiful, sizable or sizeable

handwriting noun PENMANSHIP, calligraphy, hand, scrawl, script

handy adjective 1 AVAILABLE, accessible, at hand, at one's fingertips, close, convenient, nearby, on hand, within reach 2 USEFUL, convenient, easy to use, helpful, manageable, neat, practical, serviceable, user-friendly 3 SKILLFUL, adept, adroit, deft, dexterous, expert, proficient, skilled

hang verb 1 SUSPEND, dangle, droop 2 EXECUTE, lynch, string up (informal) ▶noun 3 **get the hang of** GRASP, comprehend, understand

hang back verb HESITATE, be reluctant, demur, hold back, recoil

hangdog adjective GUILTY, cowed, cringing, defeated, downcast, furtive, shamefaced, wretched

hangover noun AFTEREFFECTS, crapulence, morning after (informal)

hang-up noun PREOCCUPATION, block, difficulty, inhibition, obsession, problem, thing (informal)

hank noun COIL, length, loop, piece, roll, skein

hanker verb (with for or after) DESIRE, crave, hunger, itch, long, pine, thirst, yearn

haphazard adjective DISORGANIZED, aimless, casual, hit or miss (informal), indiscriminate, random, slapdash

happen verb 1 OCCUR, come about, come to pass, develop, result, take place, transpire (informal) 2 CHANCE, turn out

happening noun EVENT, affair, episode, experience, incident, occurrence, proceeding

happily adverb 1 WILLINGLY, freely, gladly, with pleasure 2 JOYFULLY, blithely, cheerfully, gaily, gleefully, joyously,

merrily **3** LUCKILY, fortunately,
opportunely, providentially

happiness noun JOY, bliss,
cheerfulness, contentment,
delight, ecstasy, elation,
jubilation, pleasure, satisfaction

happy adjective **1** JOYFUL, blissful,
cheerful, content, delighted,
ecstatic, elated, glad, jubilant,
merry, overjoyed, pleased,
thrilled **2** FORTUNATE,
advantageous, auspicious,
favorable, lucky, timely,
win-win (informal)

happy-go-lucky adjective
CAREFREE, blithe, easy-going,
light-hearted, nonchalant,
unconcerned, untroubled

harangue verb **1** RANT, address,
declaim, exhort, hold forth,
lecture, spout (informal) ▶ noun
2 SPEECH, address, declamation,
diatribe, exhortation, tirade

harass verb ANNOY, bother,
harry, hassle (informal), hound,
persecute, pester, plague,
trouble, vex

harassed adjective WORRIED,
careworn, distraught, hassled
(informal), strained, tormented,
troubled, under pressure, vexed

harassment noun TROUBLE,
annoyance, bother, hassle
(informal), irritation, nuisance,
persecution, pestering

harbor noun **1** PORT, anchorage,
haven ▶ verb **2** SHELTER, hide,
protect, provide refuge, shield
3 MAINTAIN, cling to, entertain,
foster, hold, nurse, nurture,
retain

hard adjective **1** SOLID, firm,
inflexible, rigid, rocklike, stiff,
strong, tough, unyielding
2 STRENUOUS, arduous,

backbreaking, exacting,
exhausting, laborious, rigorous,
tough **3** DIFFICULT, complicated,
intricate, involved, knotty,
perplexing, puzzling, thorny
4 UNFEELING, callous, cold, cruel,
hardhearted, pitiless, stern,
unkind, unsympathetic
5 PAINFUL, disagreeable,
distressing, grievous,
intolerable, unpleasant ▶ adverb
6 ENERGETICALLY, fiercely,
forcefully, forcibly, heavily,
intensely, powerfully, severely,
sharply, strongly, vigorously,
violently, with all one's might,
with might and main
7 DILIGENTLY, doggedly,
industriously, persistently,
steadily, untiringly

hard-boiled adjective TOUGH,
cynical, hard-nosed (informal),
matter-of-fact, practical,
realistic, unsentimental

harden verb **1** SOLIDIFY, anneal,
bake, cake, freeze, set, stiffen
2 ACCUSTOM, habituate, inure,
season, train

hardened adjective **1** HABITUAL,
chronic, incorrigible,
inveterate, shameless
2 ACCUSTOMED, habituated,
inured, seasoned, toughened

hard-headed adjective SENSIBLE,
level-headed, practical,
pragmatic, realistic, shrewd,
tough, unsentimental

hardhearted adjective
UNSYMPATHETIC, callous, cold,
hard, heartless, insensitive,
uncaring, unkind

hardiness noun RESILIENCE,
resolution, robustness,
ruggedness, sturdiness,
toughness

hardly adverb BARELY, just, only just, scarcely, with difficulty

hardship noun SUFFERING, adversity, difficulty, misfortune, need, privation, tribulation

hard up adjective POOR, broke (informal), impecunious, impoverished, on the breadline, out of pocket, penniless, short, strapped for cash (informal)

hardy adjective STRONG, robust, rugged, sound, stout, sturdy, tough

harm verb 1 INJURE, abuse, damage, hurt, ill-treat, maltreat, ruin, spoil, wound ▸noun 2 INJURY, abuse, damage, hurt, ill, loss, mischief, misfortune

harmful adjective DESTRUCTIVE, damaging, deleterious, detrimental, hurtful, injurious, noxious, pernicious

harmless adjective INNOCUOUS, gentle, innocent, inoffensive, nontoxic, safe, unobjectionable

harmonious adjective
1 MELODIOUS, agreeable, concordant, consonant, dulcet, mellifluous, musical, sweet-sounding, tuneful
2 FRIENDLY, agreeable, amicable, compatible, congenial, cordial, sympathetic

harmonize verb BLEND, chime with, cohere, coordinate, correspond, match, tally, tone in with

harmony noun 1 AGREEMENT, accord, amicability, compatibility, concord, cooperation, friendship, peace, rapport, sympathy
2 TUNEFULNESS, euphony,

melody, tune, unison

harness noun 1 EQUIPMENT, gear, tack, tackle ▸verb 2 EXPLOIT, channel, control, employ, mobilize, utilize

harrowing adjective DISTRESSING, agonizing, disturbing, heart-rending, nerve-racking, painful, terrifying, tormenting, traumatic

harry verb PESTER, badger, bother, chivvy, harass, hassle (informal), molest, plague

harsh adjective 1 RAUCOUS, discordant, dissonant, grating, guttural, rasping, rough, strident 2 SEVERE, austere, cruel, draconian, drastic, pitiless, punitive, ruthless, stern

harshly adverb SEVERELY, brutally, cruelly, roughly, sternly, strictly

harshness noun SEVERITY, asperity, austerity, brutality, rigor, roughness, sternness

harvest noun 1 CROP, produce, yield ▸verb 2 GATHER, mow, pick, pluck, reap

hassle noun 1 ARGUMENT, bickering, disagreement, dispute, fight, quarrel, row, squabble 2 TROUBLE, bother, difficulty, grief (informal), inconvenience, problem ▸verb 3 BOTHER, annoy, badger, bug (informal), harass, hound, pester

haste noun 1 SPEED, alacrity, quickness, rapidity, swiftness, urgency, velocity 2 RUSH, hurry, hustle, impetuosity

hasten verb RUSH, dash, fly, hurry (up), make haste, race, scurry, speed

hastily adverb 1 SPEEDILY, promptly, quickly, rapidly
2 HURRIEDLY, impetuously,

precipitately, rashly

hasty *adjective* **1** SPEEDY, brisk, hurried, prompt, rapid, swift, urgent **2** IMPETUOUS, impulsive, precipitate, rash, thoughtless

hatch *verb* **1** INCUBATE, breed, bring forth, brood **2** DEVISE, conceive, concoct, contrive, cook up (*informal*), design, dream up (*informal*), think up

hate *verb* **1** DETEST, abhor, despise, dislike, loathe, recoil from **2** BE UNWILLING, be loath, be reluctant, be sorry, dislike, feel disinclined, shrink from ▶ *noun* **3** DISLIKE, animosity, antipathy, aversion, detestation, enmity, hatred, hostility, loathing

hateful *adjective* DESPICABLE, abhorrent, detestable, horrible, loathsome, lousy (*slang*), obnoxious, odious, offensive, repellent, repugnant, repulsive, scuzzy (*slang*)

hatred *noun* DISLIKE, animosity, antipathy, aversion, detestation, enmity, hate, repugnance, revulsion

haughty *adjective* PROUD, arrogant, conceited, contemptuous, disdainful, imperious, scornful, snooty (*informal*), stuck-up (*informal*), supercilious

haul *verb* **1** DRAG, draw, heave, lug, pull, tug ▶ *noun* **2** GAIN, booty, catch, harvest, loot, spoils, takings, yield

haunt *verb* **1** PLAGUE, obsess, possess, prey on, recur, stay with, torment, trouble, weigh on ▶ *noun* **2** MEETING PLACE, hangout (*informal*), rendezvous, stamping ground

haunted *adjective* **1** POSSESSED, cursed, eerie, ghostly, jinxed, spooky (*informal*) **2** PREOCCUPIED, obsessed, plagued, tormented, troubled, worried

haunting *adjective* POIGNANT, evocative, nostalgic, persistent, unforgettable

have *verb* **1** POSSESS, hold, keep, obtain, own, retain **2** RECEIVE, accept, acquire, gain, get, obtain, procure, secure, take **3** EXPERIENCE, endure, enjoy, feel, meet with, suffer, sustain, undergo **4** GIVE BIRTH TO, bear, beget, bring forth, deliver **5 have to** BE OBLIGED, be bound, be compelled, be forced, have got to, must, ought, should

haven *noun* SANCTUARY, asylum, refuge, retreat, sanctum, shelter

havoc *noun* DISORDER, chaos, confusion, disruption, mayhem, shambles

haywire *adjective* **As in go haywire** TOPSY-TURVY, chaotic, confused, disordered, disorganized, mixed up, out of order, shambolic (*informal*)

hazard *noun* **1** DANGER, jeopardy, peril, pitfall, risk, threat ▶ *verb* **2** JEOPARDIZE, endanger, expose, imperil, risk, threaten **3** **As in hazard a guess** CONJECTURE, advance, offer, presume, throw out, venture, volunteer

hazardous *adjective* DANGEROUS, difficult, insecure, perilous, precarious, risky, unsafe

haze *noun* MIST, cloud, fog, obscurity, vapor

hazy *adjective* **1** MISTY, cloudy, dim, dull, foggy, overcast

2 VAGUE, fuzzy, ill-defined, indefinite, indistinct, muddled, nebulous, uncertain, unclear

head noun **1** SKULL, crown, noodle (slang), nut (slang), pate **2** LEADER, boss (informal), captain, chief, commander, director, manager, master, principal, supervisor **3** TOP, crest, crown, peak, pinnacle, summit, tip **4** BRAIN, brains (informal), intellect, intelligence, mind, thought, understanding **5 go to one's head** EXCITE, intoxicate, make conceited, puff up **6 head over heels** UNCONTROLLABLY, completely, intensely, thoroughly, utterly, wholeheartedly ▶ adjective **7** CHIEF, arch, first, leading, main, pre-eminent, premier, prime, principal, supreme ▶ verb **8** LEAD, be or go first, cap, crown, lead the way, precede, top **9** CONTROL, be in charge of, command, direct, govern, guide, lead, manage, run **10** MAKE FOR, aim, go to, make a beeline for, point, set off for, set out, start towards, steer, turn

headache noun **1** MIGRAINE, neuralgia **2** PROBLEM, bane, bother, inconvenience, nuisance, trouble, vexation, worry

heading noun TITLE, caption, headline, name, rubric

headlong adverb, adjective **1** HEADFIRST, head-on ▶ adverb **2** HASTILY, heedlessly, helter-skelter, hurriedly, pell-mell, precipitately, rashly, thoughtlessly ▶ adjective **3** HASTY, breakneck, dangerous,

impetuous, impulsive, inconsiderate, precipitate, reckless, thoughtless

headstrong adjective OBSTINATE, foolhardy, heedless, impulsive, perverse, pig-headed, self-willed, stubborn, unruly, willful

headway noun PROGRESS, advance, improvement, progression, way

heady adjective **1** INEBRIATING, intoxicating, potent, strong **2** EXCITING, exhilarating, intoxicating, stimulating, thrilling

heal verb CURE, make well, mend, regenerate, remedy, restore, treat

health noun **1** WELLBEING, fitness, good condition, healthiness, robustness, soundness, strength, vigor **2** CONDITION, constitution, fettle, shape, state

healthy adjective **1** WELL, active, fit, hale and hearty, in fine fettle, in good shape (informal), in the pink, robust, strong **2** WHOLESOME, beneficial, hygienic, invigorating, nourishing, nutritious, salubrious, salutary

heap noun **1** PILE, accumulation, collection, hoard, lot, mass, mound, stack **2** (often plural) A LOT, great deal, lots (informal), mass, plenty, pot's (informal), stack(s), tons ▶ verb **3** PILE, accumulate, amass, collect, gather, hoard, stack **4** CONFER, assign, bestow, load, shower upon

hear verb **1** LISTEN TO, catch, overhear **2** LEARN, ascertain, discover, find out, gather, get

wind of (*informal*), pick up
3 *Law* TRY, examine,
investigate, judge

hearing noun INQUIRY, industrial
tribunal, investigation, review,
trial

hearsay noun RUMOR, gossip,
idle talk, report, talk,
tittle-tattle, word of mouth

heart noun **1** NATURE, character,
disposition, soul, temperament
2 BRAVERY, courage, fortitude,
pluck, purpose, resolution,
spirit, will **3** CENTER, core, hub,
middle, nucleus, quintessence
4 by heart BY MEMORY, by rote,
off pat, parrot-fashion
(*informal*), pat, word for word

heartache noun SORROW, agony,
anguish, despair, distress, grief,
heartbreak, pain, remorse,
suffering, torment, torture

heartbreak noun GRIEF, anguish,
desolation, despair, misery,
pain, sorrow, suffering

heartbreaking adjective TRAGIC,
agonizing, distressing,
harrowing, heart-rending,
pitiful, poignant, sad

heartbroken adjective MISERABLE,
brokenhearted, crushed,
desolate, despondent,
disconsolate, dispirited,
heartsick

heartfelt adjective SINCERE, deep,
devout, earnest, genuine,
honest, profound, unfeigned,
wholehearted

heartily adverb ENTHUSIASTICALLY,
eagerly, earnestly, resolutely,
vigorously, zealously

heartless adjective CRUEL,
callous, cold, hard,
hardhearted, merciless, pitiless,
uncaring, unfeeling

heart-rending adjective MOVING,
affecting, distressing,
harrowing, heartbreaking,
poignant, sad, tragic

hearty adjective **1** FRIENDLY,
back-slapping, ebullient,
effusive, enthusiastic, genial,
jovial, warm **2** SUBSTANTIAL,
ample, filling, nourishing,
sizable or sizeable, solid, square

heat verb **1** WARM UP, make hot,
reheat ▶ noun **2** HOTNESS, high
temperature, warmth
3 INTENSITY, excitement, fervor,
fury, passion, vehemence

heated adjective ANGRY, excited,
fierce, frenzied, furious,
impassioned, intense,
passionate, stormy, vehement

heathen noun **1** UNBELIEVER,
infidel, pagan ▶ adjective
2 PAGAN, godless, idolatrous,
irreligious

heave verb **1** LIFT, drag (up),
haul (up), hoist, pull (up),
raise, tug **2** THROW, cast, fling,
hurl, pitch, send, sling, toss
3 SIGH, groan, puff **4** VOMIT,
barf (*slang*), gag, retch, spew,
throw up (*informal*)

heaven noun **1** PARADISE, bliss,
Elysium or Elysian fields (*Greek
myth*), hereafter, life
everlasting, next world, nirvana
(*Buddhism, Hinduism*), Zion
(*Christianity*) **2** HAPPINESS, bliss,
ecstasy, paradise, rapture,
seventh heaven, utopia **3 the
heavens** SKY, ether, firmament

heavenly adjective **1** BEAUTIFUL,
blissful, delightful, divine
(*informal*), exquisite, lovely,
ravishing, sublime, wonderful
2 CELESTIAL, angelic, blessed,
divine, holy, immortal

heavily adverb **1** PONDEROUSLY, awkwardly, clumsily, weightily **2** DENSELY, closely, compactly, thickly **3** CONSIDERABLY, a great deal, copiously, excessively, to excess, very much

heaviness noun WEIGHT, gravity, heftiness, ponderousness

heavy adjective **1** WEIGHTY, bulky, hefty, massive, ponderous **2** CONSIDERABLE, abundant, copious, excessive, large, profuse

heckle verb JEER, boo, disrupt, interrupt, shout down, taunt

hectic adjective FRANTIC, animated, chaotic, feverish, frenetic, heated, turbulent

hedge noun **1** BARRIER, boundary, screen, windbreak ▶ verb **2** DODGE, duck, equivocate, evade, prevaricate, sidestep, temporize **3** INSURE, cover, guard, protect, safeguard, shield

heed noun **1** CARE, attention, caution, mind, notice, regard, respect, thought ▶ verb **2** PAY ATTENTION TO, bear in mind, consider, follow, listen to, note, obey, observe, take notice of

heedless adjective CARELESS, foolhardy, inattentive, oblivious, thoughtless, unmindful

heel noun Slang SWINE, louse, rat, scumbag, scuzzbucket (slang), skunk

heel over verb LEAN OVER, keel over, list, tilt

hefty adjective STRONG, big, burly, hulking, massive, muscular, robust, strapping

height noun **1** ALTITUDE, elevation, highness, loftiness, stature, tallness **2** PEAK, apex, crest, crown, pinnacle, summit, top, zenith **3** CULMINATION, climax, limit, maximum, ultimate

heighten verb INTENSIFY, add to, amplify, enhance, improve, increase, magnify, sharpen, strengthen

heir noun SUCCESSOR, beneficiary, heiress (fem.), inheritor, next in line

hell noun **1** UNDERWORLD, abyss, fire and brimstone, Hades (Greek myth), hellfire, inferno, nether world **2** TORMENT, agony, anguish, misery, nightmare, ordeal, suffering, wretchedness

hellish adjective DEVILISH, damnable, diabolical, fiendish, infernal

hello interjection WELCOME, good afternoon, good evening, good morning, greetings

helm noun **1** TILLER, rudder, wheel **2 at the helm** IN CHARGE, at the wheel, in command, in control, in the driving seat, in the saddle

help verb **1** AID, abet, assist, cooperate, lend a hand, succor, support **2** IMPROVE, alleviate, ameliorate, ease, facilitate, mitigate, relieve **3** REFRAIN FROM, avoid, keep from, prevent, resist ▶ noun **4** ASSISTANCE, advice, aid, cooperation, guidance, helping hand, support

helper noun ASSISTANT, adjutant, aide, ally, attendant, collaborator, helpmate, mate, partner, right-hand man, second, supporter

helpful *adjective* **1** USEFUL, advantageous, beneficial, constructive, practical, profitable, timely, win-win (*informal*) **2** COOPERATIVE, accommodating, considerate, friendly, kind, neighborly, supportive, sympathetic

helping *noun* PORTION, dollop (*informal*), piece, plateful, ration, serving

helpless *adjective* WEAK, challenged, disabled, impotent, incapable, infirm, paralyzed, powerless

helter-skelter *adjective* **1** HAPHAZARD, confused, disordered, hit-or-miss, jumbled, muddled, random, topsy-turvy ▶ *adverb* **2** CARELESSLY, anyhow, hastily, headlong, hurriedly, pell-mell, rashly, recklessly, wildly

hem *noun* **1** EDGE, border, fringe, margin, trimming ▶ *verb* **2 hem in** SURROUND, beset, circumscribe, confine, enclose, restrict, shut in

hence *conjunction* THEREFORE, ergo, for this reason, on that account, thus

henchman *noun* ATTENDANT, associate, bodyguard, follower, minder (*slang*), right-hand man, sidekick (*slang*), subordinate, supporter

henpecked *adjective* BULLIED, browbeaten, dominated, meek, subjugated, timid

herald *noun* **1** MESSENGER, crier **2** FORERUNNER, harbinger, indication, omen, precursor, sign, signal, token ▶ *verb* **3** INDICATE, foretoken, portend,

presage, promise, show, usher in

herd *noun* **1** MULTITUDE, collection, crowd, drove, flock, horde, mass, mob, swarm, throng ▶ *verb* **2** CONGREGATE, assemble, collect, flock, gather, huddle, muster, rally

hereafter *adverb* **1** IN FUTURE, from now on, hence, henceforth, henceforward ▶ *noun* **2** AFTERLIFE, life after death, next world

hereditary *adjective* **1** GENETIC, inborn, inbred, inheritable, transmissible **2** INHERITED, ancestral, traditional

heredity *noun* GENETICS, constitution, genetic make-up, inheritance

heresy *noun* DISSIDENCE, apostasy, heterodoxy, iconoclasm, unorthodoxy

heretic *noun* DISSIDENT, apostate, dissenter, nonconformist, renegade, revisionist

heretical *adjective* UNORTHODOX, heterodox, iconoclastic, idolatrous, impious, revisionist

heritage *noun* INHERITANCE, bequest, birthright, endowment, legacy, tradition

hermit *noun* RECLUSE, anchorite, eremite, loner (*informal*), monk

hero *noun* **1** IDOL, champion, conqueror, star, superstar, victor **2** LEADING MAN, protagonist

heroic *adjective* COURAGEOUS, brave, daring, fearless, gallant, intrepid, lion-hearted, valiant

heroine *noun* LEADING LADY, diva, prima donna, protagonist

heroism *noun* BRAVERY, courage, courageousness, fearlessness, gallantry, intrepidity, spirit, valor

hesitant *adjective* UNCERTAIN, diffident, doubtful, half-hearted, halting, irresolute, reluctant, unsure, vacillating, wavering

hesitate *verb* 1 WAVER, delay, dither, doubt, hum and haw, pause, vacillate, wait 2 BE RELUCTANT, balk, be unwilling, demur, hang back, scruple, shrink from, think twice

hesitation *noun* 1 INDECISION, delay, doubt, hesitancy, irresolution, uncertainty, vacillation 2 RELUCTANCE, misgiving(s), qualm(s), scruple(s), unwillingness

hew *verb* 1 CUT, ax, chop, hack, lop, split 2 CARVE, fashion, form, make, model, sculpt, sculpture, shape, smooth

heyday *noun* PRIME, bloom, pink, prime of life, salad days

hiatus *noun* PAUSE, break, discontinuity, gap, interruption, interval, respite, space

hidden *adjective* CONCEALED, clandestine, covert, latent, secret, under wraps, unseen, veiled

hide[1] *verb* 1 CONCEAL, secrete, stash (*informal*) 2 GO INTO HIDING, go to ground, go underground, hole up, lie low, take cover 3 DISGUISE, camouflage, cloak, conceal, cover, mask, obscure, shroud, veil 4 SUPPRESS, draw a veil over, hush up, keep dark, keep secret, keep under one's hat, withhold

hide[2] *noun* SKIN, pelt

hidebound *adjective* CONVENTIONAL, narrow-minded, rigid, set in one's ways, strait-laced, ultraconservative

hideous *adjective* UGLY, ghastly, grim, grisly, grotesque, gruesome, monstrous, repulsive, revolting, scuzzy (*slang*), unsightly

hideout *noun* HIDEAWAY, den, hiding place, lair, shelter

hierarchy *noun* GRADING, pecking order, ranking

high *adjective* 1 TALL, elevated, lofty, soaring, steep, towering 2 EXTREME, excessive, extraordinary, great, intensified, sharp, strong 3 IMPORTANT, arch, chief, eminent, exalted, powerful, superior 4 *Informal* INTOXICATED, stoned (*slang*), tripping (*informal*) 5 HIGH-PITCHED, acute, penetrating, piercing, piping, sharp, shrill, strident ▶ *adverb* 6 ALOFT, at great height, far up, way up

highbrow *noun* 1 INTELLECTUAL, aesthete, egghead (*informal*), scholar ▶ *adjective* 2 INTELLECTUAL, bookish, cultivated, cultured, sophisticated

high-flown *adjective* EXTRAVAGANT, elaborate, exaggerated, florid, grandiose, inflated, lofty, overblown, pretentious

high-handed *adjective* DICTATORIAL, despotic, domineering, imperious, oppressive, overbearing, tyrannical, willful

highlight *noun* 1 FEATURE, climax, focal point, focus, high point, high spot, peak ▶ *verb*

2 EMPHASIZE, accent, accentuate, bring to the fore, show up, spotlight, stress, underline

highly *adverb* EXTREMELY, exceptionally, greatly, immensely, tremendously, vastly, very, very much

highly strung *adjective* NERVOUS, edgy, excitable, neurotic, sensitive, stressed, temperamental, tense, twitchy (*informal*), wired (*slang*)

hijack *verb* SEIZE, commandeer, expropriate, take over

hike *noun* **1** WALK, march, ramble, tramp, trek ▶ *verb* **2** WALK, back-pack, ramble, tramp **3 hike up** RAISE, hitch up, jack up, lift, pull up

hilarious *adjective* FUNNY, amusing, comical, entertaining, humorous, rollicking, side-splitting, uproarious

hilarity *noun* LAUGHTER, amusement, exhilaration, glee, high spirits, jollity, merriment, mirth

hill *noun* MOUNT, fell, height, hillock, hilltop, knoll, mound, tor

hillock *noun* MOUND, hummock, knoll

hilly *adjective* MOUNTAINOUS, rolling, undulating

hilt *noun* HANDLE, grip, haft, handgrip

hinder *verb* OBSTRUCT, block, check, delay, encumber, frustrate, hamper, handicap, hold up *or* back, impede, interrupt, stop

hindmost *adjective* LAST, final, furthest, furthest behind, rearmost, trailing

hindrance *noun* OBSTACLE,

barrier, deterrent, difficulty, drawback, handicap, hitch, impediment, obstruction, restriction, snag, stumbling block

hinge *verb* DEPEND, be contingent, hang, pivot, rest, revolve around, turn

hint *noun* **1** INDICATION, allusion, clue, implication, innuendo, insinuation, intimation, suggestion **2** ADVICE, help, pointer, suggestion, tip **3** TRACE, dash, suggestion, suspicion, tinge, touch, undertone ▶ *verb* **4** SUGGEST, imply, indicate, insinuate, intimate

hippie *noun* BOHEMIAN, beatnik, dropout

hire *verb* **1** EMPLOY, appoint, commission, engage, sign up, take on **2** RENT, charter, engage, lease, let ▶ *noun* **3** RENTAL, charge, cost, fee, price, rent

hiss *noun* **1** SIBILATION, buzz, hissing **2** CATCALL, boo, jeer ▶ *verb* **3** WHISTLE, sibilate, wheeze, whirr, whiz **4** JEER, boo, deride, hoot, mock

historic *adjective* SIGNIFICANT, epoch-making, extraordinary, famous, ground-breaking, momentous, notable, outstanding, remarkable

historical *adjective* FACTUAL, actual, attested, authentic, documented, real

history *noun* **1** CHRONICLE, account, annals, narrative, recital, record, story **2** THE PAST, antiquity, olden days, yesterday, yesteryear

hit *verb* **1** STRIKE, bang, beat,

clout (*informal*), knock, slap, smack, thump, wallop (*informal*), whack **2** COLLIDE WITH, bang into, bump, clash with, crash against, run into, smash into **3** REACH, accomplish, achieve, arrive at, attain, gain **4** AFFECT, damage, devastate, impact on, influence, leave a mark on, overwhelm, touch **5 hit it off** *Informal* GET ON (WELL), be on good terms, click (*slang*), get on like a house on fire (*informal*) ▶ *noun* **6** STROKE, belt (*informal*), blow, clout (*informal*), knock, rap, slap, smack, wallop (*informal*) **7** SUCCESS, sensation, smash (*informal*), triumph, winner

hit-and-miss *adjective* HAPHAZARD, aimless, casual, disorganized, indiscriminate, random, undirected, uneven

hitch *noun* **1** PROBLEM, catch, difficulty, drawback, hindrance, hold-up, impediment, obstacle, snag ▶ *verb* **2** FASTEN, attach, connect, couple, harness, join, tether, tie **3** *Informal* HITCHHIKE, thumb a lift **4 hitch up** PULL UP, jerk, tug, yank

hitherto *adverb* PREVIOUSLY, heretofore, so far, thus far, until now

hit on *verb* THINK UP, arrive at, discover, invent, light upon, strike upon, stumble on

hoard *noun* **1** STORE, accumulation, cache, fund, pile, reserve, stockpile, supply, treasure-trove ▶ *verb* **2** SAVE, accumulate, amass, collect, gather, lay up, put by, keep, stash away (*informal*), stockpile, store

hoarse *adjective* RAUCOUS,

croaky, grating, gravelly, gruff, guttural, husky, rasping, rough, throaty

hoax *noun* **1** TRICK, con (*informal*), deception, fraud, practical joke, prank, spoof (*informal*), swindle ▶ *verb* **2** DECEIVE, con (*slang*), dupe, fool, hoodwink, swindle, trick

hobby *noun* PASTIME, diversion, (leisure) activity, leisure pursuit, relaxation

hobnob *verb* SOCIALIZE, associate, consort, fraternize, hang about, hang out (*informal*), keep company, mingle, mix

hoist *verb* **1** RAISE, elevate, erect, heave, lift ▶ *noun* **2** LIFT, crane, elevator, winch

hold *verb* **1** OWN, have, keep, maintain, occupy, possess, retain **2** GRASP, clasp, cling, clutch, cradle, embrace, enfold, grip **3** RESTRAIN, confine, detain, impound, imprison **4** CONSIDER, assume, believe, deem, judge, presume, reckon, regard, think **5** CONVENE, call, conduct, preside over, run **6** ACCOMMODATE, contain, have a capacity for, seat, take ▶ *noun* **7** GRIP, clasp, grasp **8** FOOTHOLD, footing, support **9** CONTROL, influence, mastery

holder *noun* **1** OWNER, bearer, keeper, possessor, proprietor **2** CASE, container, cover

hold forth *verb* SPEAK, declaim, discourse, go on, lecture, preach, spiel (*informal*), spout (*informal*)

hold-up *noun* **1** DELAY, bottleneck, hitch, setback, snag, stoppage, traffic jam, wait **2** ROBBERY, mugging (*informal*), stick-up (*slang*), theft

hold up *verb* **1** DELAY, detain, hinder, retard, set back, slow down, stop **2** SUPPORT, prop, shore up, sustain **3** ROB, mug (*informal*), waylay

hold with *verb* APPROVE OF, agree to *or* with, be in favor of, countenance, subscribe to, support

hole *noun* **1** OPENING, aperture, breach, crack, fissure, gap, orifice, perforation, puncture, tear, vent **2** CAVITY, cave, cavern, chamber, hollow, pit **3** BURROW, den, earth, lair, shelter **4** *Informal* HOVEL, dive (*slang*), dump (*informal*), slum

holiday *noun* **1** VACATION, break, leave, recess, time off **2** FESTIVAL, celebration, feast, fête, gala

holiness *noun* DIVINITY, godliness, piety, purity, righteousness, sacredness, saintliness, sanctity, spirituality

hollow *adjective* **1** EMPTY, unfilled, vacant, void **2** DEEP, dull, low, muted, reverberant **3** WORTHLESS, fruitless, futile, meaningless, pointless, useless, vain ▶ *noun* **4** CAVITY, basin, bowl, crater, depression, hole, pit, trough **5** VALLEY, dale, dell, dingle, glen ▶ *verb* **6** SCOOP, dig, excavate, gouge

holocaust *noun* GENOCIDE, annihilation, conflagration, destruction, devastation, massacre

holy *adjective* **1** DEVOUT, god-fearing, godly, pious, pure, religious, righteous, saintly, virtuous **2** SACRED, blessed, consecrated, hallowed,

sacrosanct, sanctified, venerable

homage *noun* RESPECT, adoration, adulation, deference, devotion, honor, reverence, worship

home *noun* **1** HOUSE, abode, domicile, dwelling, habitation, pad (*slang, dated*), residence **2** BIRTHPLACE, home town **3 at home:** **a** IN, available, present **b** AT EASE, comfortable, familiar, relaxed **4 bring home to** MAKE CLEAR, drive home, emphasize, impress upon, press home ▶ *adjective* **5** DOMESTIC, familiar, internal, local, native

homeboy *or* **home girl** *noun Slang* FRIEND, buddy (*informal*), chum (*slang*), comrade, crony, pal (*informal*)

homeland *noun* NATIVE LAND, country of origin, fatherland, mother country, motherland

homeless *adjective* **1** DESTITUTE, displaced, dispossessed, down-and-out, down on one's luck (*informal*) ▶ *noun* **2 the homeless** VAGRANTS, squatters

homely *adjective U.S.* DOWDY, dumpy (*informal*), frowzy, frumpy, ugly, unattractive, unfashionable

homespun *adjective* UNSOPHISTICATED, coarse, dumpy (*informal*), homely (*U.S.*), home-made, plain, rough

homey *adjective* COMFORTABLE, cozy, friendly, homespun, modest, ordinary, plain, simple, welcoming

homicidal *adjective* MURDEROUS, deadly, lethal, maniacal, mortal

homicide *noun* **1** MURDER, bloodshed, killing, manslaughter, slaying

2 MURDERER, killer, slayer

homily noun SERMON, address, discourse, lecture, preaching

homogeneity noun UNIFORMITY, consistency, correspondence, sameness, similarity

homogeneous adjective UNIFORM, akin, alike, analogous, comparable, consistent, identical, similar, unvarying

hone verb SHARPEN, edge, file, grind, point, polish, whet

honest adjective TRUSTWORTHY, ethical, honorable, law-abiding, reputable, scrupulous, truthful, upright, virtuous **2** OPEN, candid, direct, forthright, frank, plain, sincere, upfront (informal)

honestly adverb **1** ETHICALLY, by fair means, cleanly, honorably, lawfully, legally **2** FRANKLY, candidly, in all sincerity, plainly, straight (out), to one's face, truthfully

honesty noun **1** INTEGRITY, honor, incorruptibility, morality, probity, rectitude, scrupulousness, trustworthiness, truthfulness, uprightness, virtue **2** FRANKNESS, bluntness, candor, openness, outspokenness, sincerity, straightforwardness

honor noun **1** GLORY, credit, dignity, distinction, fame, kudos, prestige, renown, reputation **2** TRIBUTE, accolade, commendation, homage, praise, recognition **3** FAIRNESS, decency, goodness, honesty, integrity, morality, probity, rectitude **4** PRIVILEGE, compliment, credit, pleasure ▶ verb **5** RESPECT, adore,

appreciate, esteem, prize, value **6** FULFILL, be true to, carry out, discharge, keep, live up to, observe **7** ACCLAIM, commemorate, commend, decorate, praise **8** ACCEPT, acknowledge, pass, pay, take

honorable adjective RESPECTED, creditable, estimable, reputable, respectable, virtuous

honorary adjective NOMINAL, complimentary, in name or title only, titular, unofficial, unpaid

hoodwink verb DECEIVE, con (informal), delude, dupe, fool, mislead, swindle, trick

hook noun **1** FASTENER, catch, clasp, link, peg ▶ verb **2** FASTEN, clasp, fix, secure **3** CATCH, ensnare, entrap, snare, trap

hooked adjective **1** BENT, aquiline, curved, hook-shaped **2** ADDICTED, devoted, enamored, obsessed, taken, turned on (slang)

hooligan noun DELINQUENT, lager lout, ruffian, vandal

hooliganism noun DELINQUENCY, disorder, loutishness, rowdiness, vandalism, violence

hoop noun RING, band, circlet, girdle, loop, wheel

hoot noun **1** CRY, call, toot **2** CATCALL, boo, hiss, jeer ▶ verb **3** JEER, boo, hiss, howl down

hop verb **1** JUMP, bound, caper, leap, skip, spring, trip, vault ▶ noun **2** JUMP, bounce, bound, leap, skip, spring, step, vault

hope verb **1** DESIRE, aspire, cross one's fingers, long, look forward to, set one's heart on ▶ noun **2** DESIRE, ambition, assumption, dream, expectation, longing

hopeful *adjective* **1** OPTIMISTIC, buoyant, confident, expectant, looking forward to, sanguine **2** PROMISING, auspicious, bright, encouraging, heartening, reassuring, rosy

hopefully *adverb* OPTIMISTICALLY, confidently, expectantly

hopeless *adjective* POINTLESS, futile, impossible, no-win, unattainable, useless, vain

horde *noun* CROWD, band, drove, gang, host, mob, multitude, pack, swarm, throng

horizon *noun* SKYLINE, vista

horizontal *adjective* LEVEL, flat, parallel

horrible *adjective* **1** TERRIFYING, appalling, dreadful, frightful, ghastly, grim, grisly, gruesome, hideous, repulsive, revolting, shocking **2** UNPLEASANT, awful, cruel, disagreeable, dreadful, horrid, lousy (*slang*), mean, nasty, scuzzy (*slang*), terrible

horrid *adjective* **1** UNPLEASANT, awful, disagreeable, dreadful, horrible, terrible **2** UNKIND, beastly (*informal*), cruel, mean, nasty

horrific *adjective* TERRIFYING, appalling, awful, dreadful, frightful, ghastly, grisly, horrendous, horrifying, shocking

horrify *verb* **1** TERRIFY, alarm, frighten, intimidate, make one's hair stand on end, petrify, scare **2** SHOCK, appall, dismay, outrage, sicken

horror *noun* **1** TERROR, alarm, consternation, dread, fear, fright, panic **2** HATRED, aversion, detestation, disgust, loathing,

odium, repugnance, revulsion

horse *noun* NAG, colt, filly, mare, mount, stallion, steed (*archaic or literary*)

horseman *noun* RIDER, cavalier, cavalryman, dragoon, equestrian

horseplay *noun* BUFFOONERY, clowning, fooling around, high jinks, pranks, romping, rough-and-tumble, skylarking (*informal*)

hospitable *adjective* WELCOMING, cordial, friendly, generous, gracious, kind, liberal, sociable

hospitality *noun* WELCOME, conviviality, cordiality, friendliness, neighborliness, sociability, warmth

host[1] *noun* **1** MASTER OF CEREMONIES, entertainer, innkeeper, landlord *or* landlady, proprietor **2** PRESENTER, anchorman *or* anchorwoman ▶ *verb* **3** PRESENT, front (*informal*), introduce

host[2] *noun* MULTITUDE, army, array, drove, horde, legion, myriad, swarm, throng

hostage *noun* PRISONER, captive, pawn

hostile *adjective* **1** OPPOSED, antagonistic, belligerent, contrary, ill-disposed, rancorous **2** UNFRIENDLY, adverse, inhospitable, unsympathetic, unwelcoming

hostilities *plural noun* WARFARE, conflict, fighting, war

hostility *noun* OPPOSITION, animosity, antipathy, enmity, hatred, ill will, malice, resentment, unfriendliness

hot *adjective* **1** HEATED, boiling, roasting, scalding, scorching,

searing, steaming, sultry,
sweltering, torrid, warm
2 SPICY, biting, peppery,
piquant, pungent, sharp
3 FIERCE, fiery, intense,
passionate, raging, stormy,
violent **4** RECENT, fresh, just out,
latest, new, up to the minute
5 POPULAR, approved, favored,
in demand, in vogue,
sought-after

hot air noun EMPTY TALK,
bombast, claptrap (informal),
guff (slang), verbiage, wind

hot-blooded adjective
PASSIONATE, ardent, excitable,
fiery, impulsive, spirited,
temperamental, wild

hot-headed adjective RASH, fiery,
foolhardy, hasty,
hot-tempered, impetuous,
quick-tempered, reckless,
volatile

hot water noun (usually
preceded by in) Informal
PREDICAMENT, dilemma, fix
(informal), jam (informal), mess,
scrape (informal), spot
(informal), tight spot

hound verb HARASS, badger,
goad, harry, impel, persecute,
pester, provoke

house noun **1** HOME, abode,
domicile, dwelling, habitation,
homestead, pad (slang, dated),
residence **2** FAMILY, household
3 DYNASTY, clan, tribe **4** FIRM,
business, company,
organization, outfit (informal)
5 ASSEMBLY, Commons,
legislative body, parliament
6 on the house FREE, for
nothing, gratis ▶ verb
7 ACCOMMODATE, billet, harbor,
lodge, put up, quarter, take in
8 CONTAIN, cover, keep, protect,

sheathe, shelter, store

household noun FAMILY, home,
house

householder noun OCCUPANT,
homeowner, resident, tenant

housing noun **1** ACCOMMODATION,
dwellings, homes, houses
2 CASE, casing, container,
cover, covering, enclosure,
sheath

hovel noun HUT, cabin, den,
hole, shack, shanty, shed

hover verb **1** FLOAT, drift, flutter,
fly, hang **2** LINGER, hang about
3 WAVER, dither, fluctuate,
oscillate, vacillate

however adverb NEVERTHELESS,
after all, anyhow, but,
nonetheless, notwithstanding,
still, though, yet

howl noun **1** CRY, bawl, bay,
clamor, groan, roar, scream,
shriek, wail ▶ verb **2** CRY, bawl,
bellow, roar, scream, shriek,
wail, weep, yell

hub noun CENTER, core, focal
point, focus, heart, middle,
nerve center

huddle verb **1** CROWD, cluster,
converge, flock, gather, press,
throng **2** CURL UP, crouch,
hunch up ▶ noun **3** Informal
CONFERENCE, discussion,
meeting, powwow

hue noun COLOR, dye, shade,
tinge, tint, tone

hug verb **1** CLASP, cuddle,
embrace, enfold, hold close,
squeeze, take in one's arms
▶ noun **2** EMBRACE, bear hug,
clasp, clinch (slang), squeeze

huge adjective LARGE, colossal,
enormous, gigantic, immense,
mammoth, massive,
monumental, tremendous, vast

hulk *noun* **1** WRECK, frame, hull, shell, shipwreck **2** OAF, lout, lubber, lump (*informal*)

hull *noun* FRAME, body, casing, covering, framework

hum *verb* **1** MURMUR, buzz, drone, purr, throb, thrum, vibrate, whir **2** BE BUSY, bustle, buzz, pulsate, pulse, stir

human *adjective* **1** MORTAL, manlike ▸ *noun* **2** HUMAN BEING, creature, individual, man *or* woman, mortal, person, soul

humane *adjective* KIND, benign, compassionate, forgiving, good-natured, merciful, sympathetic, tender, understanding

humanitarian *adjective* **1** COMPASSIONATE, altruistic, benevolent, charitable, humane, philanthropic, public-spirited ▸ *noun* **2** PHILANTHROPIST, altruist, benefactor, Good Samaritan

humanity *noun* **1** HUMAN RACE, Homo sapiens, humankind, man, mankind, people **2** HUMAN NATURE, mortality **3** SYMPATHY, charity, compassion, fellow feeling, kind-heartedness, kindness, mercy, philanthropy

humanize *verb* CIVILIZE, educate, enlighten, improve, soften, tame

humble *adjective* **1** MODEST, meek, self-effacing, unassuming, unostentatious, unpretentious **2** LOWLY, mean, modest, obscure, ordinary, plebeian, poor, simple, undistinguished ▸ *verb* **3** HUMILIATE, chasten, crush, disgrace, put (someone) in their place, subdue, take down a peg (*informal*)

humbug *noun* **1** FRAUD, charlatan, con man (*informal*), faker, impostor, phoney *or* phony (*informal*), swindler, trickster **2** NONSENSE, baloney (*informal*), cant, claptrap (*informal*), hypocrisy, quackery, rubbish **3** KILLJOY, scrooge (*informal*), spoilsport, wet blanket (*informal*)

humdrum *adjective* DULL, banal, boring, dreary, monotonous, mundane, ordinary, tedious, tiresome, uneventful

humid *adjective* DAMP, clammy, dank, moist, muggy, steamy, sticky, sultry, wet

humidity *noun* DAMP, clamminess, dampness, dankness, moistness, moisture, mugginess, wetness

humiliate *verb* EMBARRASS, bring low, chasten, crush, degrade, humble, mortify, put down, put (someone) in their place, shame

humiliating *adjective* EMBARRASSING, crushing, degrading, humbling, ignominious, mortifying, shaming

humiliation *noun* EMBARRASSMENT, degradation, disgrace, dishonor, humbling, ignominy, indignity, loss of face, mortification, put-down, shame

humility *noun* MODESTY, humbleness, lowliness, meekness, submissiveness, unpretentiousness

humor *noun* **1** FUNNINESS, amusement, comedy, drollery, facetiousness, fun, jocularity, ludicrousness **2** JOKING, comedy, farce, jesting, pleasantry, wisecracks (*informal*), wit, witticisms **3** MOOD, disposition, frame of mind, spirits, temper ▶ *verb* **4** INDULGE, accommodate, flatter, go along with, gratify, mollify, pander to

humorist *noun* COMEDIAN, card (*informal*), comic, funny man, jester, joker, wag, wit

humorous *adjective* FUNNY, amusing, comic, comical, droll, entertaining, jocular, playful, waggish, witty

hump *noun* LUMP, bulge, bump, mound, projection, protrusion, protuberance, swelling

hunch *noun* **1** FEELING, idea, impression, inkling, intuition, premonition, presentiment, suspicion ▶ *verb* **2** DRAW IN, arch, bend, curve

hunger *noun* **1** FAMINE, starvation **2** APPETITE, emptiness, hungriness, ravenousness **3** DESIRE, ache, appetite, craving, itch, lust, thirst, yearning ▶ *verb* **4** WANT, ache, crave, desire, hanker, itch, long, thirst, wish, yearn

hungry *adjective* **1** EMPTY, famished, ravenous, starved, starving, voracious **2** EAGER, athirst, avid, covetous, craving, desirous, greedy, keen, yearning

hunk *noun* LUMP, block, chunk, mass, nugget, piece, slab, wedge

hunt *verb* **1** STALK, chase, hound, pursue, track, trail **2** SEARCH, ferret about, forage, look, scour, seek ▶ *noun* **3** SEARCH, chase, hunting, investigation,

pursuit, quest

hurdle *noun* **1** FENCE, barricade, barrier **2** OBSTACLE, barrier, difficulty, handicap, hazard, hindrance, impediment, obstruction, stumbling block

hurl *verb* THROW, cast, fling, heave, launch, let fly, pitch, propel, sling, toss

hurricane *noun* STORM, cyclone, gale, tempest, tornado, twister (*informal*), typhoon

hurried *adjective* HASTY, brief, cursory, perfunctory, quick, rushed, short, speedy, swift

hurry *verb* **1** RUSH, dash, fly, get a move on (*informal*), make haste, scoot, scurry, step on it (*informal*) ▶ *noun* **2** URGENCY, flurry, haste, quickness, rush, speed

hurt *verb* **1** HARM, bruise, damage, disable, impair, injure, mar, spoil, wound **2** ACHE, be sore, be tender, burn, smart, sting, throb **3** SADDEN, annoy, distress, grieve, pain, upset, wound ▶ *noun* **4** DISTRESS, discomfort, pain, pang, soreness, suffering ▶ *adjective* **5** INJURED, bruised, cut, damaged, harmed, scarred, wounded **6** OFFENDED, aggrieved, crushed, wounded

hurtful *adjective* UNKIND, cruel, cutting, damaging, destructive, malicious, nasty, spiteful, upsetting, wounding

hurtle *verb* RUSH, charge, crash, fly, plunge, race, shoot, speed, stampede, tear

husband *noun* **1** PARTNER, better half (*humorous*), mate, spouse ▶ *verb* **2** ECONOMIZE, budget, conserve, hoard, save, store

husbandry noun **1** FARMING, agriculture, cultivation, tillage **2** THRIFT, economy, frugality

hush verb **1** QUIETEN, mute, muzzle, shush, silence ▶ noun **2** QUIET, calm, peace, silence, stillness, tranquillity

hush-hush adjective SECRET, classified, confidential, restricted, top-secret, under wraps

husky adjective **1** HOARSE, croaky, gruff, guttural, harsh, raucous, rough, throaty **2** MUSCULAR, burly, hefty, powerful, rugged, stocky, strapping, thickset

hustle verb JOSTLE, elbow, force, jog, push, shove

hut noun SHED, cabin, den, hovel, lean-to, shanty, shelter

hybrid noun CROSSBREED, amalgam, composite, compound, cross, half-breed, mixture, mongrel

hygiene noun CLEANLINESS, sanitation

hygienic adjective CLEAN, aseptic, disinfected, germ-free, healthy, pure, sanitary, sterile

hymn noun ANTHEM, carol, chant, paean, psalm

hype noun PUBLICITY, ballyhoo (informal), brouhaha, plugging (informal), promotion, razzmatazz (slang)

hypnotic adjective MESMERIC, mesmerizing, sleep-inducing, soothing, soporific, spellbinding

hypnotize verb MESMERIZE, put in a trance, put to sleep

hypocrisy noun INSINCERITY, cant, deceitfulness, deception, duplicity, pretense

hypocrite noun FRAUD, charlatan, deceiver, impostor, phoney or phony (informal), pretender

hypocritical adjective INSINCERE, canting, deceitful, duplicitous, false, fraudulent, phoney or phony (informal), sanctimonious, two-faced

hypothesis noun ASSUMPTION, postulate, premise, proposition, supposition, theory, thesis

hypothetical adjective THEORETICAL, academic, assumed, conjectural, imaginary, putative, speculative, supposed

hysteria noun FRENZY, agitation, delirium, hysterics, madness, panic

hysterical adjective **1** FRENZIED, crazed, distracted, distraught, frantic, overwrought, raving **2** Informal HILARIOUS, comical, side-splitting, uproarious

I i

icy adjective **1** COLD, biting, bitter, chill, chilly, freezing, frosty, ice-cold, raw **2** SLIPPERY, glassy, slippy (informal or dialect) **3** UNFRIENDLY, aloof, cold, distant, frigid, frosty, unwelcoming

idea noun **1** THOUGHT, concept, impression, perception **2** BELIEF, conviction, notion, opinion, teaching, view **3** PLAN, aim, intention, object, objective, purpose

ideal adjective **1** PERFECT, archetypal, classic, complete, consummate, model,

quintessential, supreme ▶*noun*
2 MODEL, last word, paradigm,
paragon, pattern, perfection,
prototype, standard

idealist *noun* ROMANTIC,
dreamer, Utopian, visionary

idealistic *adjective* PERFECTIONIST,
impracticable, optimistic,
romantic, starry-eyed, Utopian,
visionary

idealize *verb* ROMANTICIZE,
apotheosize, ennoble, exalt,
glorify, magnify, put on a
pedestal, worship

ideally *adverb* IN A PERFECT WORLD,
all things being equal, if one
had one's way

identical *adjective* ALIKE,
duplicate, indistinguishable,
interchangeable, matching,
twin

identification *noun*
1 RECOGNITION, naming,
pinpointing **2** EMPATHY,
association, connection, fellow
feeling, involvement, rapport,
relationship, sympathy

identify *verb* **1** RECOGNIZE,
diagnose, make out, name,
pick out, pinpoint, place, point
out, put one's finger on
(*informal*), spot **2 identify with**
RELATE TO, associate with,
empathize with, feel for,
respond to

identity *noun* **1** EXISTENCE,
individuality, personality, self
2 SAMENESS, correspondence,
unity

idiocy *noun* FOOLISHNESS,
asininity, fatuousness,
imbecility, inanity, insanity,
lunacy, senselessness

idiom *noun* **1** PHRASE, expression,
turn of phrase **2** LANGUAGE,

jargon, parlance, style,
vernacular

idiosyncrasy *noun* PECULIARITY,
characteristic, eccentricity,
mannerism, oddity, quirk, trick

idiot *noun* FOOL, chump, cretin
(*offensive*), dork (*slang*),
dunderhead, halfwit, imbecile,
moron, schmuck (*slang*),
simpleton

idiotic *adjective* FOOLISH, asinine,
bonkers (*informal*), crazy, daft
(*informal*), foolhardy,
harebrained, insane, moronic,
senseless, stupid

idle *adjective* **1** INACTIVE,
redundant, unemployed,
unoccupied, unused, vacant
2 LAZY, good-for-nothing,
indolent, lackadaisical, shiftless,
slothful, sluggish **3** USELESS,
fruitless, futile, groundless,
ineffective, pointless,
unavailing, unsuccessful, vain,
worthless ▶*verb* **4** (often with
away) LAZE, dally, dawdle, kill
time, loaf, loiter, lounge, potter

idleness *noun* **1** INACTIVITY,
inaction, leisure, time on one's
hands, unemployment
2 LAZINESS, inertia, shiftlessness,
sloth, sluggishness, torpor

idol *noun* **1** GRAVEN IMAGE, deity,
god **2** HERO, beloved, darling,
favorite, pet, pin-up (*slang*)

idolatry *noun* ADORATION,
adulation, exaltation,
glorification

idolize *verb* WORSHIP, adore, dote
upon, exalt, glorify,
hero-worship, look up to, love,
revere, venerate

idyllic *adjective* IDEALIZED,
charming, halcyon, heavenly,
ideal, picturesque, unspoiled

if conjunction PROVIDED, assuming, on condition that, providing, supposing

ignite verb 1 CATCH FIRE, burn, burst into flames, flare up, inflame, take fire 2 SET FIRE TO, kindle, light, set alight, torch

ignominious adjective HUMILIATING, discreditable, disgraceful, dishonorable, indecorous, inglorious, shameful, sorry, undignified

ignominy noun DISGRACE, discredit, dishonor, disrepute, humiliation, infamy, obloquy, shame, stigma

ignorance noun UNAWARENESS, inexperience, innocence, unconsciousness, unfamiliarity

ignorant adjective 1 UNINFORMED, benighted, inexperienced, innocent, oblivious, unaware, unconscious, unenlightened, uninitiated, unwitting 2 UNEDUCATED, illiterate 3 INSENSITIVE, crass, half-baked (informal), rude

ignore verb OVERLOOK, blow off (slang), discount, disregard, neglect, pass over, reject, take no notice of, turn a blind eye to

ill adjective 1 UNWELL, ailing, diseased, indisposed, infirm, off-color, sick, under the weather (informal), unhealthy 2 HARMFUL, bad, damaging, deleterious, detrimental, evil, foul, injurious, unfortunate ▸ noun 3 HARM, affliction, hardship, hurt, injury, misery, misfortune, trouble, unpleasantness, woe ▸ adverb 4 BADLY, inauspiciously, poorly, unfavorably, unfortunately,

unluckily 5 HARDLY, barely, by no means, scantily

ill-advised adjective MISGUIDED, foolhardy, ill-considered, ill-judged, imprudent, incautious, injudicious, rash, reckless, thoughtless, unwise

ill-disposed adjective UNFRIENDLY, antagonistic, disobliging, hostile, inimical, uncooperative, unwelcoming

illegal adjective UNLAWFUL, banned, criminal, felonious, forbidden, illicit, outlawed, prohibited, unauthorized, unlicensed

illegality noun CRIME, felony, illegitimacy, lawlessness, wrong

illegible adjective INDECIPHERABLE, obscure, scrawled, unreadable

illegitimate adjective 1 UNLAWFUL, illegal, illicit, improper, unauthorized 2 BORN OUT OF WEDLOCK, bastard

ill-fated adjective DOOMED, hapless, ill-omened, ill-starred, luckless, star-crossed, unfortunate, unhappy, unlucky

illicit adjective 1 ILLEGAL, criminal, felonious, illegitimate, prohibited, unauthorized, unlawful, unlicensed 2 FORBIDDEN, clandestine, furtive, guilty, immoral, improper

illiterate adjective UNEDUCATED, ignorant, uncultured, untaught, untutored

ill-mannered adjective RUDE, badly behaved, boorish, churlish, discourteous, impolite, insolent, loutish, uncouth

illness noun DISEASE, affliction, ailment, disorder, infirmity, malady, sickness

illogical *adjective* IRRATIONAL, absurd, inconsistent, invalid, meaningless, senseless, unreasonable, unscientific, unsound

ill-treat *verb* ABUSE, damage, harm, injure, maltreat, mishandle, misuse, oppress

illuminate *verb* 1 LIGHT UP, brighten 2 EXPLAIN, clarify, clear up, elucidate, enlighten, interpret, make clear, shed light on

illuminating *adjective* INFORMATIVE, enlightening, explanatory, helpful, instructive, revealing

illumination *noun* 1 LIGHT, brightness, lighting, radiance 2 ENLIGHTENMENT, clarification, insight, revelation

illusion *noun* 1 FANTASY, chimera, daydream, figment of the imagination, hallucination, mirage, will-o'-the-wisp 2 MISCONCEPTION, deception, delusion, error, fallacy, misapprehension

illusory *adjective* UNREAL, chimerical, deceptive, delusive, fallacious, false, hallucinatory, mistaken, sham

illustrate *verb* DEMONSTRATE, bring home, elucidate, emphasize, explain, point up, show

illustrated *adjective* PICTORIAL, decorated, graphic

illustration *noun* 1 EXAMPLE, case, instance, specimen 2 PICTURE, decoration, figure, plate, sketch

illustrious *adjective* FAMOUS, celebrated, distinguished, eminent, glorious, great, notable, prominent, renowned

ill will *noun* HOSTILITY, animosity, bad blood, dislike, enmity, hatred, malice, rancor, resentment, venom

image *noun* 1 REPRESENTATION, effigy, figure, icon, idol, likeness, picture, portrait, statue 2 REPLICA, counterpart, (dead) ringer (*slang*), Doppelgänger, double, facsimile, spitting image (*informal*) 3 CONCEPT, idea, impression, mental picture, perception

imaginable *adjective* POSSIBLE, believable, comprehensible, conceivable, credible, likely, plausible

imaginary *adjective* FICTIONAL, fictitious, hypothetical, illusory, imagined, invented, made-up, nonexistent, unreal

imagination *noun* 1 CREATIVITY, enterprise, ingenuity, invention, inventiveness, originality, resourcefulness, vision 2 UNREALITY, illusion, supposition

imaginative *adjective* CREATIVE, clever, enterprising, ingenious, inspired, inventive, original

imagine *verb* 1 ENVISAGE, conceive, conceptualize, conjure up, picture, plan, think of, think up, visualize 2 BELIEVE, assume, conjecture, fancy, guess (*informal*), infer, suppose, surmise, suspect, take it, think

imbecile *noun* 1 IDIOT, chump, cretin (*offensive*), dork (*slang*), fool, halfwit, moron, schmuck (*slang*), thickhead ▸ *adjective* 2 STUPID, asinine, fatuous, feeble-minded, foolish, idiotic, moronic, thick, witless

imbibe verb **1** DRINK, consume, knock back (*informal*), quaff, sink (*informal*), swallow, swig (*informal*) **2** *Literary* ABSORB, acquire, assimilate, gain, gather, ingest, receive, take in

imbroglio noun COMPLICATION, embarrassment, entanglement, involvement, misunderstanding, quandary

imitate verb COPY, ape, echo, emulate, follow, mimic, mirror, repeat, simulate

imitation noun **1** MIMICRY, counterfeiting, duplication, likeness, resemblance, simulation **2** REPLICA, fake, forgery, impersonation, impression, reproduction, sham, substitution ▶ adjective **3** ARTIFICIAL, dummy, ersatz, man-made, mock, phoney or phony (*informal*), reproduction, sham, simulated, synthetic

imitative adjective DERIVATIVE, copycat (*informal*), mimetic, parrot-like, second-hand, simulated, unoriginal

imitator noun IMPERSONATOR, copier, copycat (*informal*), impressionist, mimic, parrot

immaculate adjective **1** CLEAN, neat, spick-and-span, spotless, spruce, squeaky-clean **2** FLAWLESS, above reproach, faultless, impeccable, perfect, unblemished, unexceptionable, untarnished

immaterial adjective IRRELEVANT, extraneous, inconsequential, inessential, insignificant, of no importance, trivial, unimportant

immature adjective **1** YOUNG,

adolescent, undeveloped, unformed, unripe **2** CHILDISH, callow, inexperienced, infantile, juvenile, puerile

immaturity noun **1** UNRIPENESS, greenness, imperfection, rawness, unpreparedness **2** CHILDISHNESS, callowness, inexperience, puerility

immediate adjective **1** INSTANT, instantaneous **2** NEAREST, close, direct, near, next

immediately adverb AT ONCE, directly, forthwith, instantly, now, promptly, right away, straight away, this instant, without delay

immense adjective HUGE, colossal, enormous, extensive, gigantic, great, massive, monumental, stupendous, tremendous, vast

immensity noun SIZE, bulk, enormity, expanse, extent, greatness, hugeness, magnitude, vastness

immerse verb **1** PLUNGE, bathe, dip, douse, duck, dunk, sink, submerge **2** ENGROSS, absorb, busy, engage, involve, occupy, take up

immersion noun **1** DIPPING, dousing, ducking, dunking, plunging, submerging **2** INVOLVEMENT, absorption, concentration, preoccupation

immigrant noun SETTLER, incomer, newcomer

imminent adjective NEAR, at hand, close, coming, forthcoming, gathering, impending, in the pipeline, looming

immobile adjective STATIONARY, at a standstill, at rest, fixed, immovable, motionless, rigid, rooted, static, still, stock-still, unmoving

immobility noun STILLNESS, fixity, inertness, motionlessness, stability, steadiness

immobilize verb PARALYZE, bring to a standstill, cripple, disable, freeze, halt, stop, transfix

immoderate adjective EXCESSIVE, exaggerated, exorbitant, extravagant, extreme, inordinate, over the top (slang), undue, unjustified, unreasonable

immoral adjective WICKED, bad, corrupt, debauched, depraved, dissolute, indecent, sinful, unethical, unprincipled, wrong

immorality noun WICKEDNESS, corruption, debauchery, depravity, dissoluteness, sin, vice, wrong

immortal adjective 1 ETERNAL, deathless, enduring, everlasting, imperishable, lasting, perennial, undying ▶ noun 2 GOD, goddess 3 GREAT, genius, hero

immortality noun 1 ETERNITY, everlasting life, perpetuity 2 FAME, celebrity, glory, greatness, renown

immortalize verb COMMEMORATE, celebrate, exalt, glorify

immovable adjective 1 FIXED, firm, immutable, jammed, secure, set, stable, stationary, stuck 2 INFLEXIBLE, adamant, obdurate, resolute, steadfast, unshakable, unwavering, unyielding

immune adjective EXEMPT, clear, free, invulnerable, proof (against), protected, resistant, safe, unaffected

immunity noun 1 EXEMPTION, amnesty, freedom, indemnity, invulnerability, license, release 2 RESISTANCE, immunization, protection

immunize verb VACCINATE, inoculate, protect, safeguard

imp noun 1 DEMON, devil, sprite 2 RASCAL, brat, minx, rogue, scamp

impact noun 1 COLLISION, blow, bump, contact, crash, jolt, knock, smash, stroke, thump 2 EFFECT, consequences, impression, influence, repercussions, significance ▶ verb 3 HIT, clash, collide, crash, crush, strike

impair verb WORSEN, blunt, damage, decrease, diminish, harm, hinder, injure, lessen, reduce, undermine, weaken

impaired adjective DAMAGED, defective, faulty, flawed, imperfect, unsound

impart verb 1 COMMUNICATE, convey, disclose, divulge, make known, pass on, relate, reveal, tell 2 GIVE, accord, afford, bestow, confer, grant, lend, yield

impartial adjective NEUTRAL, detached, disinterested, equitable, even-handed, fair, just, objective, open-minded, unbiased, unprejudiced

impartiality noun NEUTRALITY, detachment, disinterestedness, dispassion, equity, even-handedness, fairness, objectivity, open-mindedness

impassable adjective BLOCKED, closed, impenetrable, obstructed

impasse noun DEADLOCK, dead end, gridlock, stalemate, standoff, standstill

impassioned adjective INTENSE, animated, fervent, fiery, heated, inspired, passionate, rousing, stirring

impatience noun 1 HASTE, impetuosity, intolerance, rashness 2 RESTLESSNESS, agitation, anxiety, eagerness, edginess, fretfulness, nervousness, uneasiness

impatient adjective 1 HASTY, demanding, hot-tempered, impetuous, intolerant 2 RESTLESS, eager, edgy, fretful, straining at the leash

impeach verb CHARGE, accuse, arraign, indict

impeccable adjective FAULTLESS, blameless, flawless, immaculate, irreproachable, perfect, unblemished, unimpeachable

impecunious adjective POOR, broke (informal), destitute, down and out, down on one's luck (informal), indigent, insolvent, penniless, poverty-stricken

impede verb HINDER, block, check, disrupt, hamper, hold up, obstruct, slow (down), thwart

impediment noun OBSTACLE, barrier, difficulty, encumbrance, hindrance, obstruction, snag, stumbling block

impel verb FORCE, compel, constrain, drive, induce, oblige, push, require

impending adjective LOOMING, approaching, coming,

forthcoming, gathering, imminent, in the pipeline, near, upcoming

impenetrable adjective 1 SOLID, dense, impassable, impermeable, impervious, inviolable, thick 2 INCOMPREHENSIBLE, arcane, enigmatic, inscrutable, mysterious, obscure, unfathomable, unintelligible

imperative adjective URGENT, crucial, essential, pressing, vital

imperceptible adjective UNDETECTABLE, faint, indiscernible, microscopic, minute, slight, small, subtle, tiny

imperfect adjective FLAWED, damaged, defective, faulty, impaired, incomplete, limited, unfinished

imperfection noun FAULT, blemish, defect, deficiency, failing, flaw, frailty, shortcoming, taint, weakness

imperial adjective ROYAL, kingly, majestic, princely, queenly, regal, sovereign

imperil verb ENDANGER, expose, jeopardize, risk

impersonal adjective REMOTE, aloof, cold, detached, dispassionate, formal, inhuman, neutral

impersonate verb IMITATE, ape, do (informal), masquerade as, mimic, pass oneself off as, pose as (informal)

impersonation noun IMITATION, caricature, impression, mimicry, parody

impertinence noun RUDENESS, brazenness, cheek (informal), disrespect, effrontery, front, impudence, insolence, nerve (*informal*), presumption

impertinent *adjective* RUDE, brazen, cheeky (*informal*), disrespectful, impolite, impudent, insolent, presumptuous

imperturbable *adjective* CALM, collected, composed, cool, nerveless, self-possessed, serene, unexcitable, unflappable (*informal*), unruffled

impervious *adjective* 1 SEALED, impassable, impenetrable, impermeable, resistant 2 UNAFFECTED, immune, invulnerable, proof against, unmoved, untouched

impetuosity *noun* HASTE, impulsiveness, precipitateness, rashness

impetuous *adjective* RASH, hasty, impulsive, precipitate, unthinking

impetus *noun* 1 INCENTIVE, catalyst, goad, impulse, motivation, push, spur, stimulus 2 FORCE, energy, momentum, power

impinge *verb* 1 ENCROACH, infringe, invade, obtrude, trespass, violate 2 AFFECT, bear upon, have a bearing on, impact, influence, relate to, touch

impious *adjective* SACRILEGIOUS, blasphemous, godless, irreligious, irreverent, profane, sinful, ungodly, unholy, wicked

impish *adjective* MISCHIEVOUS, devilish, puckish, rascally, roguish, sportive, waggish

implacable *adjective* UNYIELDING, inflexible, intractable, merciless, pitiless, unbending,

uncompromising, unforgiving

implant *verb* 1 INSTILL, inculcate, infuse 2 INSERT, fix, graft

implement *verb* 1 CARRY OUT, bring about, complete, effect, enforce, execute, fulfill, perform, realize ▶ *noun* 2 TOOL, apparatus, appliance, device, gadget, instrument, utensil

implicate *verb* INCRIMINATE, associate, embroil, entangle, include, inculpate, involve

implication *noun* SUGGESTION, inference, innuendo, meaning, overtone, presumption, significance

implicit *adjective* 1 IMPLIED, inferred, latent, tacit, taken for granted, undeclared, understood, unspoken 2 ABSOLUTE, constant, firm, fixed, full, steadfast, unqualified, unreserved, wholehearted

implied *adjective* UNSPOKEN, hinted at, implicit, indirect, suggested, tacit, undeclared, unexpressed, unstated

implore *verb* BEG, beseech, entreat, importune, plead with, pray

imply *verb* 1 HINT, insinuate, intimate, signify, suggest 2 ENTAIL, indicate, involve, mean, point to, presuppose

impolite *adjective* BAD-MANNERED, discourteous, disrespectful, ill-mannered, insolent, loutish, rude, uncouth

impoliteness *noun* BAD MANNERS, boorishness, churlishness, discourtesy, disrespect, insolence, rudeness

import *verb* 1 BRING IN, introduce ▶ *noun* 2 MEANING,

drift, gist, implication, intention, sense, significance, thrust **3** IMPORTANCE, consequence, magnitude, moment, significance, substance, weight

importance noun **1** SIGNIFICANCE, concern, consequence, import, interest, moment, substance, usefulness, value, weight **2** PRESTIGE, distinction, eminence, esteem, influence, prominence, standing, status

important adjective **1** SIGNIFICANT, far-reaching, momentous, seminal, serious, substantial, urgent, weighty **2** POWERFUL, eminent, high-ranking, influential, noteworthy, pre-eminent, prominent

importunate adjective PERSISTENT, demanding, dogged, insistent, pressing, urgent

impose verb **1** ESTABLISH, decree, fix, institute, introduce, levy, ordain **2** INFLICT, appoint, enforce, saddle (someone) with

imposing adjective IMPRESSIVE, commanding, dignified, grand, majestic, stately, striking

imposition noun **1** APPLICATION, introduction, levying **2** INTRUSION, liberty, presumption

impossibility noun HOPELESSNESS, impracticability, inability

impossible adjective **1** UNATTAINABLE, impracticable, inconceivable, out of the question, unachievable, unobtainable, unthinkable **2** ABSURD, ludicrous, outrageous, preposterous, unreasonable

impostor noun IMPERSONATOR,

charlatan, deceiver, fake, fraud, phoney or phony (informal), pretender, sham, trickster

impotence noun POWERLESSNESS, feebleness, frailty, helplessness, inability, incapacity, incompetence, ineffectiveness, paralysis, uselessness, weakness

impotent adjective POWERLESS, feeble, frail, helpless, incapable, incapacitated, incompetent, ineffective, paralyzed, weak

impoverish verb **1** BANKRUPT, beggar, break, ruin **2** DIMINISH, deplete, drain, exhaust, reduce, sap, use up, wear out

impoverished adjective POOR, bankrupt, destitute, impecunious, needy, penurious, poverty-stricken

impracticable adjective UNFEASIBLE, impossible, out of the question, unachievable, unattainable, unworkable

impractical adjective **1** UNWORKABLE, impossible, impracticable, inoperable, nonviable, unrealistic, wild **2** IDEALISTIC, romantic, starry-eyed, unrealistic

imprecise adjective INDEFINITE, equivocal, hazy, ill-defined, indeterminate, inexact, inexplicit, loose, rough, vague, woolly

impregnable adjective INVULNERABLE, impenetrable, indestructible, invincible, secure, unassailable, unbeatable, unconquerable

impregnate verb **1** SATURATE, infuse, permeate, soak, steep, suffuse **2** FERTILIZE, inseminate, make pregnant

impress verb **1** EXCITE, affect,

inspire, make an impression, move, stir, strike, touch **2** STRESS, bring home to, emphasize, fix, inculcate, instill into **3** IMPRINT, emboss, engrave, indent, mark, print, stamp

impression noun **1** EFFECT, feeling, impact, influence, reaction **2** IDEA, belief, conviction, feeling, hunch, notion, sense, suspicion **3** MARK, dent, hollow, imprint, indentation, outline, stamp **4** IMITATION, impersonation, parody

impressionable adjective SUGGESTIBLE, gullible, ingenuous, open, receptive, responsive, sensitive, susceptible, vulnerable

impressive adjective GRAND, awesome, cool (informal), dramatic, exciting, moving, phat (slang), powerful, stirring, striking

imprint noun **1** MARK, impression, indentation, sign, stamp ▶ verb **2** FIX, engrave, etch, impress, print, stamp

imprison verb JAIL, confine, detain, incarcerate, intern, lock up, put away, send down (informal)

imprisoned adjective JAILED, behind bars, captive, confined, incarcerated, in jail, inside (slang), locked up, under lock and key

imprisonment noun CUSTODY, confinement, detention, incarceration

improbability noun DOUBT, dubiety, uncertainty, unlikelihood

improbable adjective DOUBTFUL, dubious, fanciful, far-fetched, implausible, questionable, unconvincing, unlikely, weak

impromptu adjective UNPREPARED, ad-lib, extemporaneous, improvised, offhand, off the cuff (informal), spontaneous, unrehearsed, unscripted

improper adjective **1** INDECENT, risqué, smutty, suggestive, unbecoming, unseemly, untoward, vulgar **2** UNWARRANTED, inappropriate, out of place, uncalled-for, unfit, unsuitable

impropriety noun INDECENCY, bad taste, incongruity, vulgarity

improve verb **1** ENHANCE, advance, better, correct, help, rectify, touch up, upgrade **2** PROGRESS, develop, make strides, pick up, rally, rise

improvement noun **1** ENHANCEMENT, advancement, betterment **2** PROGRESS, development, rally, recovery, upswing

improvident adjective IMPRUDENT, careless, negligent, prodigal, profligate, reckless, short-sighted, spendthrift, thoughtless, wasteful

improvisation noun **1** SPONTANEITY, ad-libbing, extemporizing, invention **2** MAKESHIFT, ad-lib, expedient

improvise verb **1** EXTEMPORIZE, ad-lib, busk, invent, play it by ear (informal), speak off the cuff (informal), wing it (informal) **2** CONCOCT, contrive, devise, throw together

imprudent adjective UNWISE, careless, foolhardy, ill-advised, ill-considered, ill-judged, injudicious, irresponsible, rash, reckless

impudence noun BOLDNESS, audacity, brazenness, cheek (informal), effrontery, impertinence, insolence, nerve (informal), presumption, shamelessness

impudent adjective BOLD, audacious, brazen, cheeky (informal), impertinent, insolent, pert, presumptuous, rude, shameless

impulse noun URGE, caprice, feeling, inclination, notion, whim, wish

impulsive adjective INSTINCTIVE, devil-may-care, hasty, impetuous, intuitive, passionate, precipitate, rash, spontaneous

impunity noun SECURITY, dispensation, exemption, freedom, immunity, liberty, license, permission

impure adjective **1** UNREFINED, adulterated, debased, mixed **2** CONTAMINATED, defiled, dirty, infected, polluted, tainted **3** IMMORAL, corrupt, indecent, lascivious, lewd, licentious, obscene, unchaste

impurity noun CONTAMINATION, defilement, dirtiness, infection, pollution, taint

imputation noun BLAME, accusation, aspersion, censure, insinuation, reproach, slander, slur

inability noun INCAPABILITY, disability, disqualification, impotence, inadequacy, incapacity, incompetence, ineptitude, powerlessness

inaccessible adjective OUT OF

REACH, impassable, out of the way, remote, unapproachable, unattainable, unreachable

inaccuracy noun ERROR, defect, erratum, fault, lapse, mistake

inaccurate adjective INCORRECT, defective, erroneous, faulty, imprecise, mistaken, out, unreliable, unsound, wrong

inactive adjective UNUSED, dormant, idle, inoperative, unemployed, unoccupied

inactivity noun IMMOBILITY, dormancy, hibernation, inaction, passivity, unemployment

inadequacy noun **1** SHORTAGE, dearth, insufficiency, meagerness, paucity, poverty, scantiness **2** INCOMPETENCE, deficiency, inability, incapacity, ineffectiveness **3** SHORTCOMING, defect, failing, imperfection, weakness

inadequate adjective **1** INSUFFICIENT, meager, scant, sketchy, sparse **2** INCOMPETENT, deficient, faulty, found wanting, incapable, lousy (slang), not up to scratch (informal), unqualified

inadmissible adjective UNACCEPTABLE, inappropriate, irrelevant, unallowable

inadvertently adverb UNINTENTIONALLY, accidentally, by accident, by mistake, involuntarily, mistakenly, unwittingly

inadvisable adjective UNWISE, ill-advised, impolitic, imprudent, inexpedient, injudicious

inane adjective SENSELESS, empty, fatuous, frivolous, futile, idiotic,

inanimate adjective LIFELESS, cold, dead, defunct, extinct, inert

inapplicable adjective IRRELEVANT, inappropriate, unsuitable

inappropriate adjective UNSUITABLE, improper, incongruous, out of place, unbecoming, unbefitting, unfitting, unseemly, untimely

inarticulate adjective FALTERING, halting, hesitant, poorly spoken

inattention noun NEGLECT, absent-mindedness, carelessness, daydreaming, inattentiveness, preoccupation, thoughtlessness

inattentive adjective PREOCCUPIED, careless, distracted, dreamy, negligent, unobservant, vague

inaudible adjective INDISTINCT, low, mumbling, out of earshot, stifled, unheard

inaugural adjective FIRST, initial, introductory, maiden, opening

inaugurate verb 1 LAUNCH, begin, commence, get under way, initiate, institute, introduce, set in motion 2 INVEST, induct, install

inauguration noun 1 LAUNCH, initiation, institution, opening, setting up 2 INVESTITURE, induction, installation

inauspicious adjective UNPROMISING, bad, discouraging, ill-omened, ominous, unfavorable, unfortunate, unlucky, unpropitious

inborn adjective NATURAL, congenital, hereditary, inbred, ingrained, inherent, innate, instinctive, intuitive, native

inbred adjective INNATE, constitutional, deep-seated, ingrained, inherent, native, natural

incalculable adjective COUNTLESS, boundless, infinite, innumerable, limitless, numberless, untold, vast

incantation noun CHANT, charm, formula, invocation, spell

incapable adjective 1 INCOMPETENT, feeble, inadequate, ineffective, inept, inexpert, insufficient, lousy (slang), unfit, unqualified, weak 2 UNABLE, helpless, impotent, powerless

incapacitate verb DISABLE, cripple, immobilize, lay up (informal), paralyze, put out of action (informal)

incapacitated adjective INDISPOSED, hors de combat, immobilized, laid up (informal), out of action (informal), unfit

incapacity noun INABILITY, impotence, inadequacy, incapability, incompetency, ineffectiveness, powerlessness, unfitness, weakness

incarcerate verb IMPRISON, confine, detain, impound, intern, jail, lock up, throw in jail

incarceration noun IMPRISONMENT, captivity, confinement, detention, internment

incarnate adjective PERSONIFIED, embodied, typified

incarnation noun EMBODIMENT, epitome, manifestation, personification, type

incense verb ANGER, enrage, inflame, infuriate, irritate, madden, make one's hackles rise, rile (informal)

incensed adjective ANGRY, enraged, fuming, furious, indignant, infuriated, irate, maddened, steamed up (slang), up in arms

incentive noun ENCOURAGEMENT, bait, carrot (informal), enticement, inducement, lure, motivation, spur, stimulus

inception noun BEGINNING, birth, commencement, dawn, initiation, origin, outset, start

incessant adjective ENDLESS, ceaseless, constant, continual, eternal, interminable, never-ending, nonstop, perpetual, twenty-four-seven (slang), unceasing, unending

incessantly adverb ENDLESSLY, ceaselessly, constantly, continually, eternally, interminably, nonstop, perpetually, persistently, twenty-four-seven (slang)

incident noun 1 HAPPENING, adventure, episode, event, fact, matter, occasion, occurrence 2 DISTURBANCE, clash, commotion, confrontation, contretemps, scene

incidental adjective SECONDARY, ancillary, minor, nonessential, occasional, subordinate, subsidiary

incidentally adverb PARENTHETICALLY, by the bye, by the way, in passing

incinerate verb BURN UP, carbonize, char, cremate, reduce to ashes

incipient adjective BEGINNING, commencing, developing, embryonic, inchoate, nascent, starting

incision noun CUT, gash, notch, opening, slash, slit

incisive adjective PENETRATING, acute, keen, perspicacious, piercing, trenchant

incite verb PROVOKE, encourage, foment, inflame, instigate, spur, stimulate, stir up, urge, whip up

incitement noun PROVOCATION, agitation, encouragement, impetus, instigation, prompting, spur, stimulus

incivility noun RUDENESS, bad manners, boorishness, discourteousness, discourtesy, disrespect, ill-breeding, impoliteness

inclement adjective STORMY, foul, harsh, intemperate, rough, severe, tempestuous

inclination noun 1 TENDENCY, disposition, liking, partiality, penchant, predilection, predisposition, proclivity, proneness, propensity 2 SLOPE, angle, gradient, incline, pitch, slant, tilt

incline verb 1 PREDISPOSE, influence, persuade, prejudice, sway 2 SLOPE, lean, slant, tilt, tip, veer ▶ noun 3 SLOPE, ascent, descent, dip, grade, gradient, rise

inclined adjective DISPOSED, apt, given, liable, likely, minded, predisposed, prone, willing

include verb 1 CONTAIN, comprise, cover, embrace, encompass, incorporate, involve, subsume, take in 2 INTRODUCE, add, enter, insert

inclusion noun ADDITION, incorporation, insertion

inclusive adjective COMPREHENSIVE, across-the-board,

all-embracing, blanket, general, global, sweeping, umbrella

incognito *adjective* IN DISGUISE, disguised, under an assumed name, unknown, unrecognized

incoherence *noun* UNINTELLIGIBILITY, disjointedness, inarticulateness

incoherent *adjective* UNINTELLIGIBLE, confused, disjointed, disordered, inarticulate, inconsistent, jumbled, muddled, rambling, stammering, stuttering

income *noun* REVENUE, earnings, pay, proceeds, profits, receipts, salary, takings, wages

incoming *adjective* ARRIVING, approaching, entering, homeward, landing, new, returning

incomparable *adjective* UNEQUALED, beyond compare, inimitable, matchless, peerless, superlative, supreme, transcendent, unmatched, unparalleled, unrivaled

incompatible *adjective* INCONSISTENT, conflicting, contradictory, incongruous, mismatched, unsuited

incompetence *noun* INEPTITUDE, inability, inadequacy, incapability, incapacity, ineffectiveness, unfitness, uselessness

incompetent *adjective* INEPT, bungling, floundering, incapable, ineffectual, inexpert, unfit, useless

incomplete *adjective* UNFINISHED, deficient, fragmentary, imperfect, partial, wanting

incomprehensible *adjective* UNINTELLIGIBLE, baffling, beyond

one's grasp, impenetrable, obscure, opaque, perplexing, puzzling, unfathomable

inconceivable *adjective* UNIMAGINABLE, beyond belief, incomprehensible, incredible, mind-boggling (*informal*), out of the question, unbelievable, unheard-of, unthinkable

inconclusive *adjective* INDECISIVE, ambiguous, indeterminate, open, unconvincing, undecided, up in the air (*informal*), vague

incongruity *noun* INAPPROPRIATENESS, conflict, discrepancy, disparity, incompatibility, inconsistency, unsuitability

incongruous *adjective* INAPPROPRIATE, discordant, improper, incompatible, out of keeping, out of place, unbecoming, unsuitable

inconsiderable *adjective* INSIGNIFICANT, inconsequential, minor, negligible, slight, small, trifling, trivial, unimportant

inconsiderate *adjective* SELFISH, indelicate, insensitive, rude, tactless, thoughtless, unkind, unthinking

inconsistency *noun* 1 INCOMPATIBILITY, disagreement, discrepancy, disparity, divergence, incongruity, variance 2 UNRELIABILITY, fickleness, instability, unpredictability, unsteadiness

inconsistent *adjective* 1 INCOMPATIBLE, at odds, conflicting, contradictory, discordant, incongruous, irreconcilable, out of step 2 CHANGEABLE, capricious, erratic, fickle, unpredictable, unstable, unsteady, variable

inconsolable adjective
HEARTBROKEN, brokenhearted, desolate, despairing

inconspicuous adjective
UNOBTRUSIVE, camouflaged, hidden, insignificant, ordinary, plain, unassuming, unnoticeable, unostentatious

incontrovertible adjective
INDISPUTABLE, certain, established, incontestable, indubitable, irrefutable, positive, sure, undeniable, unquestionable

inconvenience noun 1 TROUBLE, awkwardness, bother, difficulty, disadvantage, disruption, disturbance, fuss, hindrance, nuisance ▶verb 2 TROUBLE, bother, discommode, disrupt, disturb, put out, upset

inconvenient adjective
TROUBLESOME, awkward, bothersome, disadvantageous, disturbing, inopportune, unsuitable, untimely

incorporate verb INCLUDE, absorb, assimilate, blend, combine, integrate, merge, subsume

incorrect adjective FALSE, erroneous, faulty, flawed, inaccurate, mistaken, untrue, wrong

incorrigible adjective INCURABLE, hardened, hopeless, intractable, inveterate, irredeemable, unreformed

incorruptible adjective
1 HONEST, above suspicion, straight, trustworthy, upright
2 IMPERISHABLE, everlasting, undecaying

increase verb 1 GROW, advance,
boost, develop, enlarge, escalate, expand, extend, multiply, raise, spread, swell ▶noun 2 GROWTH, development, enlargement, escalation, expansion, extension, gain, increment, rise, upturn

increasingly adverb
PROGRESSIVELY, more and more

incredible adjective
1 IMPLAUSIBLE, beyond belief, far-fetched, improbable, inconceivable, preposterous, unbelievable, unimaginable, unthinkable 2 Informal AMAZING, astonishing, astounding, extraordinary, prodigious, sensational (informal), wonderful

incredulity noun DISBELIEF, distrust, doubt, skepticism

incredulous adjective
DISBELIEVING, distrustful, doubtful, dubious, skeptical, suspicious, unbelieving, unconvinced

increment noun INCREASE, accrual, addition, advancement, augmentation, enlargement, gain, step up, supplement

incriminate verb IMPLICATE, accuse, blame, charge, impeach, inculpate, involve

incumbent adjective OBLIGATORY, binding, compulsory, mandatory, necessary

incur verb EARN, arouse, bring (upon oneself), draw, expose oneself to, gain, meet with, provoke

incurable adjective FATAL, inoperable, irremediable, terminal

indebted adjective GRATEFUL, beholden, in debt, obligated, obliged, under an obligation

indecency noun OBSCENITY, immodesty, impropriety, impurity, indelicacy, lewdness, licentiousness, pornography, vulgarity

indecent adjective 1 LEWD, crude, dirty, filthy, immodest, improper, impure, licentious, pornographic, salacious, scuzzy (slang), X-rated 2 UNBECOMING, in bad taste, indecorous, unseemly, vulgar

indecipherable adjective ILLEGIBLE, indistinguishable, unintelligible, unreadable

indecision noun HESITATION, dithering, doubt, indecisiveness, uncertainty, vacillation, wavering

indecisive adjective HESITATING, dithering, faltering, in two minds (informal), tentative, uncertain, undecided, vacillating, wavering

indeed adverb REALLY, actually, certainly, in truth, truly, undoubtedly

indefensible adjective UNFORGIVABLE, inexcusable, unjustifiable, unpardonable, untenable, unwarrantable, wrong

indefinable adjective INEXPRESSIBLE, impalpable, indescribable

indefinite adjective UNCLEAR, doubtful, equivocal, ill-defined, imprecise, indeterminate, inexact, uncertain, unfixed, vague

indefinitely adverb ENDLESSLY, ad infinitum, continually, for ever

indelible adjective PERMANENT, enduring, indestructible,

ineradicable, ingrained, lasting

indelicate adjective OFFENSIVE, coarse, crude, embarrassing, immodest, off-color, risqué, rude, suggestive, tasteless, vulgar

indemnify verb 1 INSURE, guarantee, protect, secure, underwrite 2 COMPENSATE, reimburse, remunerate, repair, repay

indemnity noun 1 INSURANCE, guarantee, protection, security 2 COMPENSATION, redress, reimbursement, remuneration, reparation, restitution

independence noun FREEDOM, autonomy, liberty, self-reliance, self-rule, self-sufficiency, sovereignty

independent adjective 1 FREE, liberated, separate, unconstrained, uncontrolled 2 SELF-GOVERNING, autonomous, nonaligned, self-determining, sovereign 3 SELF-SUFFICIENT, liberated, self-contained, self-reliant, self-supporting

independently adverb SEPARATELY, alone, autonomously, by oneself, individually, on one's own, solo, unaided

indescribable adjective UNUTTERABLE, beyond description, beyond words, indefinable, inexpressible

indestructible adjective PERMANENT, enduring, everlasting, immortal, imperishable, incorruptible, indelible, indissoluble, lasting, unbreakable

indeterminate adjective UNCERTAIN, imprecise, indefinite, inexact, undefined, unfixed, unspecified, unstipulated, vague

indicate verb 1 SIGNIFY, betoken, denote, imply, manifest, point to, reveal, suggest 2 POINT OUT, designate, specify 3 SHOW, display, express, read, record, register

indication noun SIGN, clue, evidence, hint, inkling, intimation, manifestation, mark, suggestion, symptom

indicative adjective SUGGESTIVE, pointing to, significant, symptomatic

indicator noun SIGN, gauge, guide, mark, meter, pointer, signal, symbol

indict verb CHARGE, accuse, arraign, impeach, prosecute, summon

indictment noun CHARGE, accusation, allegation, impeachment, prosecution, summons

indifference noun DISREGARD, aloofness, apathy, coldness, coolness, detachment, inattention, negligence, nonchalance, unconcern

indifferent adjective 1 UNCONCERNED, aloof, callous, cold, cool, detached, impervious, inattentive, uninterested, unmoved, unsympathetic 2 MEDIOCRE, moderate, ordinary, passable, so-so (informal), undistinguished

indigestion noun HEARTBURN, dyspepsia, upset stomach

indignant adjective RESENTFUL, angry, disgruntled, exasperated, incensed, irate, peeved (informal), riled, scornful, ticked off (informal), up in arms (informal)

indignation noun RESENTMENT, anger, exasperation, pique, rage, scorn, umbrage

indignity noun HUMILIATION, affront, dishonor, disrespect, injury, insult, opprobrium, slight, snub

indirect adjective 1 CIRCUITOUS, long-drawn-out, meandering, oblique, rambling, roundabout, tortuous, wandering 2 INCIDENTAL, secondary, subsidiary, unintended

indiscreet adjective TACTLESS, impolitic, imprudent, incautious, injudicious, naive, rash, reckless, unwise

indiscretion noun MISTAKE, error, faux pas, folly, foolishness, gaffe, lapse, slip

indiscriminate adjective RANDOM, careless, desultory, general, uncritical, undiscriminating, unsystematic, wholesale

indispensable adjective ESSENTIAL, crucial, imperative, key, necessary, needed, requisite, vital

indisposed adjective ILL, ailing, sick, under the weather, unwell

indisposition noun ILLNESS, ailment, ill health, sickness

indisputable adjective UNDENIABLE, beyond doubt, certain, incontestable, incontrovertible, indubitable, irrefutable, unquestionable

indistinct adjective UNCLEAR, blurred, faint, fuzzy, hazy, ill-defined, indeterminate, shadowy, undefined, vague

individual adjective 1 PERSONAL, characteristic, distinctive, exclusive, idiosyncratic, own, particular, peculiar, singular, special, specific, unique ▸ noun **2** PERSON, being, character, creature, soul, unit

individualist noun MAVERICK, freethinker, independent, loner, lone wolf, nonconformist, original

individuality noun DISTINCTIVENESS, character, originality, personality, separateness, singularity, uniqueness

individually adverb SEPARATELY, apart, independently, one at a time, one by one, singly

indoctrinate verb TRAIN, brainwash, drill, ground, imbue, initiate, instruct, school, teach

indoctrination noun TRAINING, brainwashing, drilling, grounding, inculcation, instruction, schooling

indolent adjective LAZY, idle, inactive, inert, languid, lethargic, listless, slothful, sluggish, workshy

indomitable adjective INVINCIBLE, bold, resolute, staunch, steadfast, unbeatable, unconquerable, unflinching, unyielding

indubitable adjective CERTAIN, incontestable, incontrovertible, indisputable, irrefutable, obvious, sure, undeniable, unquestionable

induce verb **1** PERSUADE, convince, encourage, incite, influence, instigate, prevail upon, prompt, talk into **2** CAUSE, bring about, effect, engender, generate, give rise to, lead to, occasion, produce

inducement noun INCENTIVE, attraction, bait, carrot (informal), encouragement, incitement, lure, reward

indulge verb **1** GRATIFY, feed, give way to, pander to, satisfy, yield to **2** SPOIL, cosset, give in to, go along with, humor, pamper

indulgence noun **1** GRATIFICATION, appeasement, fulfillment, satiation, satisfaction **2** LUXURY, extravagance, favor, privilege, treat **3** TOLERANCE, forbearance, patience, understanding

indulgent adjective LENIENT, compliant, easy-going, forbearing, kindly, liberal, permissive, tolerant, understanding

industrialist noun CAPITALIST, big businessman, captain of industry, magnate, manufacturer, tycoon

industrious adjective HARD-WORKING, busy, conscientious, diligent, energetic, persistent, purposeful, tireless, zealous

industry noun **1** BUSINESS, commerce, manufacturing, production, trade **2** EFFORT, activity, application, diligence, labor, tirelessness, toil, zeal

inebriated adjective DRUNK, crocked (slang), intoxicated, paralytic (informal), plastered (slang), three sheets to the wind (slang), tipsy, under the influence (informal)

ineffective adjective USELESS, fruitless, futile, idle, impotent, inefficient, unavailing, unproductive, vain, worthless

ineffectual adjective WEAK,

inefficiency noun INCOMPETENCE, carelessness, disorganization, muddle, slackness, sloppiness

inefficient adjective INCOMPETENT, disorganized, ineffectual, inept, wasteful, weak

ineligible adjective UNQUALIFIED, disqualified, ruled out, unacceptable, unfit, unsuitable

inept adjective INCOMPETENT, bumbling, bungling, clumsy, inexpert, maladroit

ineptitude noun INCOMPETENCE, clumsiness, inexpertness, unfitness

inequality noun DISPARITY, bias, difference, disproportion, diversity, irregularity, prejudice, unevenness

inequitable adjective UNFAIR, biased, discriminatory, one-sided, partial, partisan, preferential, prejudiced, unjust

inert adjective INACTIVE, dead, dormant, immobile, lifeless, motionless, static, still, unreactive, unresponsive

inertia noun INACTIVITY, apathy, immobility, lethargy, listlessness, passivity, sloth, unresponsiveness

inescapable adjective UNAVOIDABLE, certain, destined, fated, ineluctable, inevitable, inexorable, sure

inestimable adjective INCALCULABLE, immeasurable, invaluable, precious, priceless, prodigious

inevitable adjective UNAVOIDABLE, assured, certain, destined, fixed, ineluctable, inescapable, inexorable, sure

inevitably adverb UNAVOIDABLY, as a result, automatically, certainly, necessarily, of necessity, perforce, surely, willy-nilly

inexcusable adjective UNFORGIVABLE, indefensible, outrageous, unjustifiable, unpardonable, unwarrantable

inexorable adjective UNRELENTING, inescapable, relentless, remorseless, unbending, unyielding

inexpensive adjective CHEAP, bargain, budget, economical, modest, reasonable

inexperience noun UNFAMILIARITY, callowness, greenness, ignorance, newness, rawness

inexperienced adjective IMMATURE, callow, green, new, raw, unpracticed, untried, unversed

inexpert adjective AMATEURISH, bungling, clumsy, inept, maladroit, unpracticed, unprofessional, unskilled

inexplicable adjective UNACCOUNTABLE, baffling, enigmatic, incomprehensible, insoluble, mysterious, mystifying, strange, unfathomable, unintelligible

inextricably adverb INSEPARABLY, indissolubly, indistinguishably, intricately, irretrievably, totally

infallibility noun PERFECTION, impeccability, omniscience, supremacy, unerringness

infallible adjective FOOLPROOF, certain, dependable, reliable, sure, sure-fire (informal), trustworthy, unbeatable, unfailing

infamous adjective NOTORIOUS, disreputable, ignominious, ill-famed

infancy noun BEGINNINGS, cradle, dawn, inception, origins, outset, start

infant noun BABY, babe, child, minor, toddler, tot

infantile adjective CHILDISH, babyish, immature, puerile

infatuate verb OBSESS, besot, bewitch, captivate, enchant, enrapture, fascinate

infatuated adjective OBSESSED, besotted, bewitched, captivated, carried away, enamored, enraptured, fascinated, possessed, smitten (*informal*), spellbound

infatuation noun OBSESSION, crush (*informal*), fixation, madness, passion, thing (*informal*)

infect verb CONTAMINATE, affect, blight, corrupt, defile, poison, pollute, taint

infection noun CONTAMINATION, contagion, corruption, defilement, poison, pollution, virus

infectious adjective CATCHING, communicable, contagious, spreading, transmittable, virulent

infer verb DEDUCE, conclude, derive, gather, presume, surmise, understand

inference noun DEDUCTION, assumption, conclusion, presumption, reading, surmise

inferior adjective 1 LOWER, lesser, menial, minor, secondary, subordinate, subsidiary ▶noun 2 UNDERLING, junior, menial, subordinate

inferiority noun 1 INADEQUACY, deficiency, imperfection, insignificance, mediocrity, shoddiness, worthlessness 2 SUBSERVIENCE, abasement, lowliness, subordination

infernal adjective DEVILISH, accursed, damnable, damned, diabolical, fiendish, hellish, satanic

infertile adjective BARREN, sterile, unfruitful, unproductive

infertility noun STERILITY, barrenness, infecundity, unproductiveness

infest verb OVERRUN, beset, invade, penetrate, permeate, ravage, swarm, throng

infested adjective OVERRUN, alive, crawling, ravaged, ridden, swarming, teeming

infiltrate verb PENETRATE, filter through, insinuate oneself, make inroads (into), percolate, permeate, pervade, sneak in (*informal*)

infinite adjective NEVER-ENDING, boundless, eternal, everlasting, illimitable, immeasurable, inexhaustible, limitless, measureless, unbounded

infinitesimal adjective MICROSCOPIC, insignificant, minuscule, minute, negligible, teeny, tiny, unnoticeable

infinity noun ETERNITY, boundlessness, endlessness, immensity, vastness

infirm adjective FRAIL, ailing, debilitated, decrepit, doddering, enfeebled, failing, feeble, weak

infirmity noun FRAILTY, decrepitude, ill health, sickliness, vulnerability

inflame verb ENRAGE, anger, arouse, excite, incense, infuriate, madden, provoke, rouse, stimulate

inflamed adjective SORE, fevered, hot, infected, red, swollen

inflammable adjective FLAMMABLE, combustible, incendiary

inflammation noun SORENESS, painfulness, rash, redness, tenderness

inflammatory adjective PROVOCATIVE, explosive, fiery, intemperate, like a red rag to a bull, rabble-rousing

inflate verb EXPAND, bloat, blow up, dilate, distend, enlarge, increase, puff up or out, pump up, swell

inflated adjective EXAGGERATED, ostentatious, overblown, swollen

inflation noun EXPANSION, enlargement, escalation, extension, increase, rise, spread, swelling

inflexibility noun OBSTINACY, intransigence, obduracy

inflexible adjective 1 OBSTINATE, implacable, intractable, obdurate, resolute, set in one's ways, steadfast, stubborn, unbending, uncompromising 2 INELASTIC, hard, rigid, stiff, taut

inflict verb IMPOSE, administer, apply, deliver, levy, mete or deal out, visit, wreak

infliction noun IMPOSITION, administration, perpetration, wreaking

influence noun 1 EFFECT, authority, control, domination, magnetism, pressure, weight 2 POWER, clout (informal), hold, importance, leverage, prestige, pull (informal) ▶ verb 3 AFFECT, control, direct, guide, manipulate, sway

influential adjective IMPORTANT, authoritative, instrumental, leading, potent, powerful, significant, telling, weighty

influx noun ARRIVAL, incursion, inrush, inundation, invasion, rush

inform verb 1 TELL, advise, communicate, enlighten, instruct, notify, teach, tip off 2 INCRIMINATE, betray, blow the whistle on (informal), denounce, inculpate, squeal (slang)

informal adjective RELAXED, casual, colloquial, cozy, easy, familiar, homey, natural, simple, unofficial

informality noun FAMILIARITY, casualness, ease, naturalness, relaxation, simplicity

information noun FACTS, data, intelligence, knowledge, message, news, notice, report

informative adjective INSTRUCTIVE, chatty, communicative, edifying, educational, enlightening, forthcoming, illuminating, revealing

informed adjective KNOWLEDGEABLE, enlightened, erudite, expert, familiar, in the picture, up to date, versed, well-read

informer noun BETRAYER, accuser, Judas, sneak, stool pigeon

infrequent adjective OCCASIONAL, few and far between, once in a blue moon, rare, sporadic, uncommon, unusual

infringe verb BREAK, contravene,

disobey, transgress, violate

infringement noun
CONTRAVENTION, breach,
infraction, transgression,
trespass, violation

infuriate verb ENRAGE, anger,
exasperate, incense, irritate,
madden, provoke, rile

infuriating adjective ANNOYING,
exasperating, galling, irritating,
maddening, mortifying,
provoking, vexatious

ingenious adjective CREATIVE,
bright, brilliant, clever, crafty,
inventive, original, resourceful,
shrewd

ingenuity noun ORIGINALITY,
cleverness, flair, genius, gift,
inventiveness, resourcefulness,
sharpness, shrewdness

ingenuous adjective NAIVE,
artless, guileless, honest,
innocent, open, plain, simple,
sincere, trusting,
unsophisticated

inglorious adjective
DISHONORABLE, discreditable,
disgraceful, disreputable,
ignoble, ignominious,
infamous, shameful, unheroic

ingratiate verb PANDER TO,
brown-nose (slang), crawl,
curry favor, fawn, flatter,
grovel, insinuate oneself, kiss
ass (slang), toady

ingratiating adjective
SYCOPHANTIC, crawling, fawning,
flattering, humble, obsequious,
servile, toadying, unctuous

ingratitude noun
UNGRATEFULNESS, thanklessness

ingredient noun COMPONENT,
constituent, element, part

inhabit verb LIVE, abide, dwell,
occupy, populate, reside

inhabitant noun DWELLER, citizen,
denizen, inmate, native,
occupant, occupier, resident,
tenant

inhabited adjective POPULATED,
colonized, developed,
occupied, peopled, settled,
tenanted

inhale verb BREATHE IN, draw in,
gasp, respire, suck in

inherent adjective INNATE,
essential, hereditary, inborn,
inbred, inbuilt, ingrained,
inherited, intrinsic, native,
natural

inherit verb BE LEFT, come into,
fall heir to, succeed to

inheritance noun LEGACY,
bequest, birthright, heritage,
patrimony

inhibit verb RESTRAIN, check,
constrain, curb, discourage,
frustrate, hinder, hold back or
in, impede, obstruct

inhibited adjective SHY,
constrained, guarded,
repressed, reserved, reticent,
self-conscious, subdued

inhibition noun SHYNESS, block,
hang-up (informal), reserve,
restraint, reticence,
self-consciousness

inhospitable adjective
1 UNWELCOMING, cool,
uncongenial, unfriendly,
unreceptive, unsociable,
xenophobic **2** BLEAK, barren,
desolate, forbidding,
godforsaken, hostile

inhuman adjective CRUEL,
barbaric, brutal, cold-blooded,
heartless, merciless, pitiless,
ruthless, savage, unfeeling

inhumane adjective CRUEL,
brutal, heartless, pitiless,

unfeeling, unkind, unsympathetic

inhumanity noun CRUELTY, atrocity, barbarism, brutality, heartlessness, pitilessness, ruthlessness, unkindness

inimical adjective HOSTILE, adverse, antagonistic, ill-disposed, opposed, unfavorable, unfriendly, unwelcoming

inimitable adjective UNIQUE, consummate, incomparable, matchless, peerless, unparalleled, unrivaled

iniquitous adjective WICKED, criminal, evil, immoral, reprehensible, sinful, unjust

iniquity noun WICKEDNESS, abomination, evil, injustice, sin, wrong

initial adjective FIRST, beginning, incipient, introductory, opening, primary

initially adverb AT FIRST, at or in the beginning, first, firstly, originally, primarily

initiate verb 1 BEGIN, commence, get under way, kick off (informal), launch, open, originate, set in motion, start 2 INDUCT, indoctrinate, introduce, invest 3 INSTRUCT, acquaint with, coach, familiarize with, teach, train ▶noun 4 NOVICE, beginner, convert, entrant, learner, member, probationer

initiation noun INTRODUCTION, debut, enrollment, entrance, inauguration, induction, installation, investiture

initiative noun 1 FIRST STEP, advantage, first move, lead 2 RESOURCEFULNESS, ambition, drive, dynamism, enterprise, get-up-and-go (informal), leadership

inject verb 1 VACCINATE, inoculate 2 INTRODUCE, bring in, infuse, insert, instill

injection noun 1 VACCINATION, inoculation, shot (informal) 2 INTRODUCTION, dose, infusion, insertion

injudicious adjective UNWISE, foolish, ill-advised, ill-judged, impolitic, imprudent, incautious, inexpedient, rash, unthinking

injunction noun ORDER, command, exhortation, instruction, mandate, precept, ruling

injure verb HURT, damage, harm, impair, ruin, spoil, undermine, wound

injured adjective HURT, broken, challenged, damaged, disabled, undermined, weakened, wounded

injury noun HARM, damage, detriment, disservice, hurt, ill, trauma (Pathology), wound, wrong

injustice noun UNFAIRNESS, bias, discrimination, inequality, inequity, iniquity, oppression, partisanship, prejudice, wrong

inkling noun SUSPICION, clue, conception, hint, idea, indication, intimation, notion, suggestion, whisper

inland adjective INTERIOR, domestic, internal, upcountry

inlet noun BAY, bight, creek, firth or frith (Scot.), fjord, passage

inmost or **innermost** adjective DEEPEST, basic, central, essential, intimate, personal, private, secret

innate adjective INBORN, congenital, constitutional, essential, inbred, ingrained, inherent, instinctive, intuitive, native, natural

inner adjective 1 INSIDE, central, interior, internal, inward, middle 2 PRIVATE, hidden, intimate, personal, repressed, secret, unrevealed

innkeeper noun PUBLICAN, host or hostess, hotelier, landlord or landlady, mine host

innocence noun 1 GUILTLESSNESS, blamelessness, clean hands, incorruptibility, probity, purity, uprightness, virtue 2 HARMLESSNESS, innocuousness, inoffensiveness 3 INEXPERIENCE, artlessness, credulousness, gullibility, ingenuousness, naivety, simplicity, unworldliness

innocent adjective 1 NOT GUILTY, blameless, guiltless, honest, in the clear, uninvolved 2 HARMLESS, innocuous, inoffensive, unobjectionable, well-intentioned, well-meant 3 NAIVE, artless, childlike, credulous, gullible, ingenuous, open, simple, unworldly

innovation noun MODERNIZATION, alteration, change, departure, introduction, newness, novelty, variation

innuendo noun INSINUATION, aspersion, hint, implication, imputation, intimation, overtone, suggestion, whisper

innumerable adjective COUNTLESS, beyond number, incalculable, infinite, multitudinous, myriad, numberless, numerous, unnumbered, untold

inoffensive adjective HARMLESS, innocent, innocuous, mild, quiet, retiring, unobjectionable, unobtrusive

inoperative adjective OUT OF ACTION, broken, defective, ineffective, invalid, null and void, out of order, out of service, useless

inopportune adjective INCONVENIENT, ill-chosen, ill-timed, inappropriate, unfavorable, unfortunate, unpropitious, unseasonable, unsuitable, untimely

inordinate adjective EXCESSIVE, disproportionate, extravagant, immoderate, intemperate, preposterous, unconscionable, undue, unreasonable, unwarranted

inorganic adjective ARTIFICIAL, chemical, man-made

inquest noun INQUIRY, inquisition, investigation, probe

inquire verb 1 INVESTIGATE, examine, explore, look into, make inquiries, probe, research 2 Also enquire ASK, query, question

inquiry noun 1 INVESTIGATION, examination, exploration, inquest, interrogation, probe, research, study, survey 2 Also enquiry QUESTION, query

inquisition noun INVESTIGATION, cross-examination, examination, grilling (informal), inquest, inquiry, questioning, third degree (informal)

inquisitive adjective CURIOUS, inquiring, nosy (informal), probing, prying, questioning

insane adjective 1 MAD, crazed, crazy, demented, deranged, mentally ill, out of one's mind, unhinged 2 STUPID, bonkers (informal), daft (informal), foolish, idiotic, impractical, irrational, irresponsible, preposterous, senseless

insanitary adjective UNHEALTHY, dirty, disease-ridden, filthy, infested, insalubrious, polluted, scuzzy (slang), unclean, unhygienic

insanity noun 1 MADNESS, delirium, dementia, mental disorder, mental illness 2 STUPIDITY, folly, irresponsibility, lunacy, senselessness

insatiable adjective UNQUENCHABLE, greedy, intemperate, rapacious, ravenous, voracious

inscribe verb CARVE, cut, engrave, etch, impress, imprint

inscription noun ENGRAVING, dedication, legend, words

inscrutable adjective 1 ENIGMATIC, blank, deadpan, impenetrable, poker-faced (informal) 2 MYSTERIOUS, hidden, incomprehensible, inexplicable, unexplainable, unfathomable, unintelligible

insecure adjective 1 ANXIOUS, afraid, uncertain, unsure 2 UNSAFE, defenceless, exposed, unguarded, unprotected, vulnerable, wide-open

insecurity noun ANXIETY, fear, uncertainty, worry

insensible adjective UNAWARE, impervious, oblivious, unaffected, unconscious, unmindful

insensitive adjective UNFEELING, callous, hardened, indifferent, thick-skinned, tough, uncaring, unconcerned

inseparable adjective 1 INDIVISIBLE, indissoluble 2 DEVOTED, bosom, close, intimate

insert verb ENTER, embed, implant, introduce, place, put, stick in

insertion noun INCLUSION, addition, implant, interpolation, introduction, supplement

inside adjective 1 INNER, interior, internal, inward 2 CONFIDENTIAL, classified, exclusive, internal, private, restricted, secret ▸adverb 3 INDOORS, under cover, within ▸noun 4 INTERIOR, contents 5 insides Informal STOMACH, belly, bowels, entrails, guts, innards (informal), viscera, vitals

insidious adjective STEALTHY, deceptive, sly, smooth, sneaking, subtle, surreptitious

insight noun UNDERSTANDING, awareness, comprehension, discernment, judgment, observation, penetration, perception, perspicacity, vision

insignia noun BADGE, crest, emblem, symbol

insignificance noun UNIMPORTANCE, inconsequence, irrelevance, meaninglessness, pettiness, triviality, worthlessness

insignificant adjective UNIMPORTANT, inconsequential, irrelevant, meaningless, minor, nondescript, paltry, petty, trifling, trivial

insincere adjective DECEITFUL,

dishonest, disingenuous, duplicitous, false, hollow, hypocritical, lying, two-faced, untruthful

insincerity noun DECEITFULNESS, dishonesty, dissimulation, duplicity, hypocrisy, pretense, untruthfulness

insinuate verb 1 IMPLY, allude, hint, indicate, intimate, suggest 2 INGRATIATE, curry favor, get in with, worm or work one's way in

insinuation noun IMPLICATION, allusion, aspersion, hint, innuendo, slur, suggestion

insipid adjective 1 BLAND, anemic, characterless, colorless, prosaic, uninteresting, vapid, wishy-washy (informal) 2 TASTELESS, bland, flavorless, unappetizing, watery

insist verb 1 DEMAND, lay down the law, put one's foot down (informal), require 2 ASSERT, aver, claim, maintain, reiterate, repeat, swear, vow

insistence noun PERSISTENCE, emphasis, importunity, stress

insistent adjective PERSISTENT, dogged, emphatic, importunate, incessant, persevering, unrelenting, urgent

insolence noun RUDENESS, boldness, cheek (informal), disrespect, effrontery, impertinence, impudence

insolent adjective RUDE, bold, contemptuous, impertinent, impudent, insubordinate, insulting

insoluble adjective INEXPLICABLE, baffling, impenetrable, indecipherable, mysterious, unaccountable, unfathomable,

unsolvable

insolvency noun BANKRUPTCY, failure, liquidation, ruin

insolvent adjective BANKRUPT, broke (informal), failed, gone bust (informal), gone to the wall, in receivership, ruined

insomnia noun SLEEPLESSNESS, wakefulness

inspect verb EXAMINE, check, go over or through, investigate, look over, scrutinize, survey, vet

inspection noun EXAMINATION, check, checkup, investigation, once-over (informal), review, scrutiny, search, survey

inspector noun EXAMINER, censor, investigator, overseer, scrutinizer, superintendent, supervisor

inspiration noun 1 INFLUENCE, muse, spur, stimulus 2 REVELATION, creativity, illumination, insight

inspire verb 1 STIMULATE, animate, encourage, enliven, galvanize, influence, spur 2 AROUSE, enkindle, excite, give rise to, produce

inspired adjective 1 BRILLIANT, cool (informal), dazzling, impressive, memorable, outstanding, phat (slang), superlative, thrilling, wonderful 2 UPLIFTED, elated, enthused, exhilarated, stimulated

inspiring adjective UPLIFTING, exciting, exhilarating, heartening, moving, rousing, stimulating, stirring

instability noun UNPREDICTABILITY, changeableness, fickleness, fluctuation, impermanence, inconstancy, insecurity, unsteadiness, variability, volatility, wavering

install verb 1 SET UP, fix, lay, lodge, place, position, put in, station 2 INDUCT, establish, inaugurate, institute, introduce, invest 3 SETTLE, ensconce, position

installation noun 1 SETTING UP, establishment, fitting, installment, placing, positioning 2 INDUCTION, inauguration, investiture 3 EQUIPMENT, machinery, plant, system

installment noun PORTION, chapter, division, episode, part, repayment, section

instance noun 1 EXAMPLE, case, illustration, occasion, occurrence, situation ▶ verb 2 QUOTE, adduce, cite, mention, name, specify

instant noun 1 SECOND, flash, jiffy (informal), moment, split second, trice, twinkling of an eye (informal) 2 JUNCTURE, moment, occasion, point, time ▶ adjective 3 IMMEDIATE, direct, instantaneous, on-the-spot, prompt, quick, split-second 4 PRECOOKED, convenience, fast, ready-mixed

instantaneous adjective IMMEDIATE, direct, instant, on-the-spot, prompt

instantaneously adverb IMMEDIATELY, at once, instantly, in the twinkling of an eye (informal), on the spot, promptly, straight away

instantly adverb IMMEDIATELY, at once, directly, instantaneously, now, right away, straight away, this minute

instead adverb 1 RATHER, alternatively, in lieu, in preference, on second thoughts, preferably 2 instead of IN PLACE OF, in lieu of, rather than

instigate verb PROVOKE, bring about, incite, influence, initiate, prompt, set off, start, stimulate, trigger

instigation noun PROMPTING, behest, bidding, encouragement, incentive, incitement, urging

instigator noun RINGLEADER, agitator, leader, motivator, prime mover, troublemaker

instill verb INTRODUCE, engender, imbue, implant, inculcate, infuse, insinuate

instinct noun INTUITION, faculty, gift, impulse, knack, predisposition, proclivity, talent, tendency

instinctive adjective INBORN, automatic, inherent, innate, intuitive, involuntary, natural, reflex, spontaneous, unpremeditated, visceral

instinctively adverb INTUITIVELY, automatically, by instinct, involuntarily, naturally, without thinking

institute noun 1 SOCIETY, academy, association, college, foundation, guild, institution, school ▶ verb 2 ESTABLISH, fix, found, initiate, introduce, launch, organize, originate, pioneer, set up, start

institution noun 1 ESTABLISHMENT, academy, college, foundation, institute, school, society 2 CUSTOM, convention, law, practice, ritual, rule, tradition

institutional adjective

CONVENTIONAL, accepted, established, formal, orthodox

instruct verb 1 ORDER, bid, charge, command, direct, enjoin, tell 2 TEACH, coach, drill, educate, ground, school, train, tutor

instruction noun 1 TEACHING, coaching, education, grounding, guidance, lesson(s), schooling, training, tuition 2 ORDER, command, demand, directive, injunction, mandate, ruling

instructions plural noun ORDERS, advice, directions, guidance, information, key, recommendations, rules

instructive adjective INFORMATIVE, edifying, educational, enlightening, helpful, illuminating, revealing, useful

instructor noun TEACHER, adviser, coach, demonstrator, guide, mentor, trainer, tutor

instrument noun 1 TOOL, apparatus, appliance, contraption (informal), device, gadget, implement, mechanism 2 MEANS, agency, agent, mechanism, medium, organ, vehicle

instrumental adjective ACTIVE, contributory, helpful, influential, involved, useful

insubordinate adjective DISOBEDIENT, defiant, disorderly, mutinous, rebellious, recalcitrant, refractory, undisciplined, ungovernable, unruly

insubordination noun DISOBEDIENCE, defiance, indiscipline, insurrection, mutiny, rebellion, recalcitrance, revolt

insubstantial adjective FLIMSY, feeble, frail, poor, slight, tenuous, thin, weak

insufferable adjective UNBEARABLE, detestable, dreadful, impossible, insupportable, intolerable, unendurable

insufficient adjective INADEQUATE, deficient, incapable, lacking, scant, short

insular adjective NARROW-MINDED, blinkered, circumscribed, inward-looking, limited, narrow, parochial, petty, provincial

insulate verb ISOLATE, close off, cocoon, cushion, cut off, protect, sequester, shield

insult verb 1 OFFEND, abuse, affront, call names, put down, slander, slight, snub ▸ noun 2 ABUSE, affront, aspersion, insolence, offense, put-down, slap in the face (informal), slight, snub

insulting adjective OFFENSIVE, abusive, contemptuous, degrading, disparaging, insolent, rude, scurrilous

insuperable adjective INSURMOUNTABLE, impassable, invincible, unconquerable

insupportable adjective 1 INTOLERABLE, insufferable, unbearable, unendurable 2 UNJUSTIFIABLE, indefensible, untenable

insurance noun PROTECTION, assurance, cover, guarantee, indemnity, safeguard, security, warranty

insure verb PROTECT, assure, cover, guarantee, indemnify, underwrite, warrant

insurgent noun 1 REBEL, , insurrectionist, mutineer, revolutionary, rioter ▶ adjective 2 REBELLIOUS, disobedient, insubordinate, mutinous, revolting, revolutionary, riotous, seditious

insurmountable adjective INSUPERABLE, hopeless, impassable, impossible, invincible, overwhelming, unconquerable

insurrection noun REBELLION, coup, insurgency, mutiny, revolt, revolution, riot, uprising

intact adjective UNDAMAGED, complete, entire, perfect, sound, unbroken, unharmed, unimpaired, unscathed, whole

integral adjective ESSENTIAL, basic, component, constituent, fundamental, indispensable, intrinsic, necessary

integrate verb COMBINE, amalgamate, assimilate, blend, fuse, incorporate, join, merge, unite

integration noun ASSIMILATION, amalgamation, blending, combining, fusing, incorporation, mixing, unification

integrity noun 1 HONESTY, goodness, honor, incorruptibility, principle, probity, purity, rectitude, uprightness, virtue 2 UNITY, coherence, cohesion, completeness, soundness, wholeness

intellect noun INTELLIGENCE, brains (informal), judgment, mind, reason, sense, understanding

intellectual adjective 1 SCHOLARLY, bookish, cerebral, highbrow, intelligent, studious, thoughtful ▶ noun 2 THINKER, academic, egghead (informal), highbrow

intelligence noun 1 UNDERSTANDING, acumen, brain power, brains (informal), cleverness, comprehension, intellect, perception, sense 2 INFORMATION, data, facts, findings, knowledge, news, notification, report

intelligent adjective CLEVER, brainy (informal), bright, enlightened, perspicacious, quick-witted, sharp, smart, well-informed

intelligentsia noun INTELLECTUALS, highbrows, literati

intelligible adjective UNDERSTANDABLE, clear, comprehensible, distinct, lucid, open, plain

intemperate adjective EXCESSIVE, extreme, immoderate, profligate, self-indulgent, unbridled, unrestrained, wild

intend verb PLAN, aim, have in mind or view, mean, propose, purpose

intense adjective 1 EXTREME, acute, deep, excessive, fierce, great, powerful, profound, severe 2 PASSIONATE, ardent, fanatical, fervent, fierce, heightened, impassioned, vehement

intensify verb INCREASE, add to, aggravate, deepen, escalate, heighten, magnify, redouble, reinforce, sharpen, strengthen

intensity noun FORCE, ardor, emotion, fanaticism, fervor, fierceness, passion, strength, vehemence, vigor

intensive adjective CONCENTRATED, comprehensive, demanding, exhaustive, in-depth, thorough, thoroughgoing

intent noun 1 INTENTION, aim, design, end, goal, meaning, object, objective, plan, purpose ▸adjective 2 ATTENTIVE, absorbed, determined, eager, engrossed, preoccupied, rapt, resolved, steadfast, watchful

intention noun PURPOSE, aim, design, end, goal, idea, object, objective, point, target

intentional adjective DELIBERATE, calculated, intended, meant, planned, premeditated, willful

intentionally adverb DELIBERATELY, designedly, on purpose, willfully

inter verb BURY, entomb, lay to rest

intercede verb MEDIATE, arbitrate, intervene, plead

intercept verb SEIZE, block, catch, cut off, head off, interrupt, obstruct, stop

interchange verb 1 SWITCH, alternate, exchange, reciprocate, swap ▸noun 2 JUNCTION, intersection

interchangeable adjective IDENTICAL, equivalent, exchangeable, reciprocal, synonymous

intercourse noun 1 COMMUNICATION, commerce, contact, dealings 2 SEXUAL INTERCOURSE, carnal knowledge, coitus, copulation, sex

interest noun 1 CURIOSITY, attention, concern, notice, regard 2 HOBBY, activity, diversion, pastime, preoccupation, pursuit 3 ADVANTAGE, benefit, good, profit 4 STAKE, claim, investment, right, share ▸verb 5 INTRIGUE, attract, catch one's eye, divert, engross, fascinate

interested adjective 1 CURIOUS, attracted, drawn, excited, fascinated, keen 2 INVOLVED, concerned, implicated

interesting adjective INTRIGUING, absorbing, appealing, attractive, compelling, engaging, engrossing, gripping, stimulating, thought-provoking

interface noun CONNECTION, border, boundary, frontier, link

interfere verb 1 INTRUDE, butt in, intervene, meddle, stick one's oar in (informal), tamper 2 (often with with) CONFLICT, clash, hamper, handicap, hinder, impede, inhibit, obstruct

interference noun 1 INTRUSION, intervention, meddling, prying 2 CONFLICT, clashing, collision, obstruction, opposition

interim adjective TEMPORARY, acting, caretaker, improvised, makeshift, provisional, stopgap

interior noun 1 INSIDE, center, core, heart ▸adjective 2 INSIDE, inner, internal, inward 3 MENTAL, hidden, inner, intimate, personal, private, secret, spiritual

interloper noun TRESPASSER, gate-crasher (informal), intruder, meddler

interlude noun INTERVAL, break, breathing space, delay, hiatus, intermission, pause, respite, rest, spell, stoppage

intermediary noun MEDIATOR,

agent, broker, go-between, middleman

intermediate *adjective* MIDDLE, halfway, in-between (*informal*), intervening, mid, midway, transitional

interment *noun* BURIAL, funeral

interminable *adjective* ENDLESS, ceaseless, everlasting, infinite, long-drawn-out, long-winded, never-ending, perpetual, protracted

intermingle *verb* MIX, blend, combine, fuse, interlace, intermix, interweave, merge

intermission *noun* INTERVAL, break, interlude, pause, recess, respite, rest, stoppage

intermittent *adjective* PERIODIC, broken, fitful, irregular, occasional, spasmodic, sporadic

intern *verb* IMPRISON, confine, detain, hold, hold in custody

internal *adjective* 1 INNER, inside, interior 2 DOMESTIC, civic, home, in-house, intramural

international *adjective* UNIVERSAL, cosmopolitan, global, intercontinental, worldwide

Internet *noun* INFORMATION SUPERHIGHWAY, cyberspace, the net (*informal*), the web (*informal*), World Wide Web

interpose *verb* INTERRUPT, insert, interject, put one's oar in

interpret *verb* EXPLAIN, construe, decipher, decode, elucidate, make sense of, render, translate

interpretation *noun* EXPLANATION, analysis, clarification, elucidation, exposition, portrayal, rendition, translation, version

interpreter *noun* TRANSLATOR, commentator

interrogate *verb* QUESTION, cross-examine, examine, grill (*informal*), investigate, pump, quiz

interrogation *noun* QUESTIONING, cross-examination, examination, grilling (*informal*), inquiry, inquisition, third degree (*informal*)

interrupt *verb* 1 INTRUDE, barge in (*informal*), break in, butt in, disturb, heckle, interfere (with) 2 SUSPEND, break off, cut short, delay, discontinue, hold up, lay aside, stop

interruption *noun* STOPPAGE, break, disruption, disturbance, hitch, intrusion, pause, suspension

intersection *noun* JUNCTION, crossing, crossroads, interchange

interval *noun* BREAK, delay, gap, interlude, intermission, pause, respite, rest, space, spell

intervene *verb* 1 INVOLVE ONESELF, arbitrate, intercede, interfere, intrude, lend a hand, mediate, step in (*informal*) 2 HAPPEN, befall, come to pass, ensue, occur, take place

intervention *noun* MEDIATION, agency, interference, intrusion

interview *noun* 1 MEETING, audience, conference, consultation, dialogue, press conference, talk ▸ *verb* 2 QUESTION, examine, interrogate, talk to

interviewer *noun* QUESTIONER, examiner, interrogator, investigator, reporter

intestines *plural noun* GUTS,

bowels, entrails, innards (*informal*), insides (*informal*), viscera

intimacy noun FAMILIARITY, closeness, confidentiality

intimate¹ adjective 1 CLOSE, bosom, buddy-buddy (*informal*), confidential, dear, near, thick (*informal*) 2 PERSONAL, confidential, private, secret 3 DETAILED, deep, exhaustive, first-hand, immediate, in-depth, profound, thorough 4 SNUG, comfy (*informal*), cozy, friendly, homey, warm ▶noun 5 FRIEND, close friend, confidant or (*fem.*) confidante, (constant) companion, crony, homeboy (*slang*), homegirl (*slang*), soul mate

intimate² verb 1 SUGGEST, hint, imply, indicate, insinuate 2 ANNOUNCE, communicate, declare, make known, state

intimately adverb 1 CONFIDINGLY, affectionately, confidentially, familiarly, personally, tenderly, warmly 2 IN DETAIL, fully, inside out, thoroughly, very well

intimation noun 1 HINT, allusion, indication, inkling, insinuation, reminder, suggestion, warning 2 ANNOUNCEMENT, communication, declaration, notice

intimidate verb FRIGHTEN, browbeat, bully, coerce, daunt, overawe, scare, subdue, terrorize, threaten

intimidation noun BULLYING, arm-twisting (*informal*), browbeating, coercion, menaces, pressure, terrorization, threat(s)

intolerable adjective UNBEARABLE, excruciating, impossible, insufferable, insupportable, painful, unendurable

intolerance noun NARROW-MINDEDNESS, bigotry, chauvinism, discrimination, dogmatism, fanaticism, illiberality, prejudice

intolerant adjective NARROW-MINDED, bigoted, chauvinistic, dictatorial, dogmatic, fanatical, illiberal, prejudiced, small-minded

intone verb RECITE, chant

intoxicated adjective 1 DRUNK, drunken, inebriated, paralytic (*informal*), plastered (*slang*), tipsy, under the influence (*informal*) 2 EUPHORIC, dizzy, elated, enraptured, excited, exhilarated, high (*informal*), wired (*slang*)

intoxicating adjective 1 ALCOHOLIC, strong 2 EXCITING, exhilarating, heady, thrilling

intoxication noun 1 DRUNKENNESS, inebriation, insobriety, tipsiness 2 EXCITEMENT, delirium, elation, euphoria, exhilaration

intransigent adjective UNCOMPROMISING, hardline, intractable, obdurate, obstinate, stiff-necked, stubborn, unbending, unyielding

intrepid adjective FEARLESS, audacious, bold, brave, courageous, daring, gallant, plucky, stouthearted, valiant

intricacy noun COMPLEXITY, complication, convolutions, elaborateness

intricate *adjective* COMPLICATED, complex, convoluted, elaborate, fancy, involved, labyrinthine, tangled, tortuous

intrigue *verb* **1** INTEREST, attract, fascinate, rivet, titillate **2** PLOT, connive, conspire, machinate, maneuver, scheme ▶ *noun* **3** PLOT, chicanery, collusion, conspiracy, machination, maneuver, scheme, stratagem, wile **4** AFFAIR, amour, intimacy, liaison, romance

intriguing *adjective* INTERESTING, beguiling, compelling, diverting, exciting, fascinating, tantalizing, titillating

intrinsic *adjective* INBORN, basic, built-in, congenital, constitutional, essential, fundamental, inbred, inherent, native, natural

introduce *verb* **1** PRESENT, acquaint, familiarize, make known **2** BRING IN, establish, found, initiate, institute, launch, pioneer, set up, start **3** BRING UP, advance, air, broach, moot, put forward, submit **4** INSERT, add, inject, put in, throw in (*informal*)

introduction *noun* **1** LAUNCH, establishment, inauguration, institution, pioneering **2** OPENING, foreword, intro (*informal*), lead-in, preamble, preface, prelude, prologue

introductory *adjective* PRELIMINARY, first, inaugural, initial, opening, preparatory

introspective *adjective* INWARD-LOOKING, brooding, contemplative, introverted, meditative, pensive

introverted *adjective* INTROSPECTIVE, inner-directed, inward-looking, self-contained, withdrawn

intrude *verb* INTERFERE, butt in, encroach, infringe, interrupt, meddle, push in, trespass

intruder *noun* TRESPASSER, gate-crasher (*informal*), infiltrator, interloper, invader, prowler

intrusion *noun* INVASION, encroachment, infringement, interference, interruption, trespass, violation

intrusive *adjective* INTERFERING, impertinent, importunate, meddlesome, nosy (*informal*), presumptuous, pushy (*informal*), uncalled-for, unwanted

intuition *noun* INSTINCT, hunch, insight, perception, presentiment, sixth sense

intuitive *adjective* INSTINCTIVE, innate, spontaneous, untaught

inundate *verb* FLOOD, drown, engulf, immerse, overflow, overrun, overwhelm, submerge, swamp

invade *verb* **1** ATTACK, assault, burst in, descend upon, encroach, infringe, make inroads, occupy, raid, violate **2** INFEST, overrun, permeate, pervade, swarm over

invader *noun* ATTACKER, aggressor, plunderer, raider, trespasser

invalid[1] *adjective* **1** DISABLED, ailing, bedridden, challenged, frail, ill, infirm, sick ▶ *noun* **2** PATIENT, convalescent, valetudinarian

invalid[2] *adjective* NULL AND VOID, fallacious, false, illogical, inoperative, irrational, unfounded, unsound, void, worthless

invalidate verb NULLIFY, annul, cancel, overthrow, undermine, undo

invaluable adjective PRECIOUS, inestimable, priceless, valuable, worth one's or its worth in gold

invariably adverb CONSISTENTLY, always, customarily, day in, day out, habitually, perpetually, regularly, unfailingly, without exception

invasion noun 1 ATTACK, assault, campaign, foray, incursion, inroad, offensive, onslaught, raid 2 INTRUSION, breach, encroachment, infraction, infringement, usurpation, violation

invective noun ABUSE, censure, denunciation, diatribe, tirade, tongue-lashing, vilification, vituperation

invent verb 1 CREATE, coin, conceive, design, devise, discover, formulate, improvise, originate, think up 2 MAKE UP, concoct, cook up (informal), fabricate, feign, forge, manufacture, trump up

invention noun 1 CREATION, brainchild (informal), contraption, contrivance, design, device, discovery, gadget, instrument 2 CREATIVITY, genius, imagination, ingenuity, inventiveness, originality, resourcefulness 3 FICTION, fabrication, falsehood, fantasy, forgery, lie, untruth, yarn

inventive adjective CREATIVE, fertile, imaginative, ingenious,

innovative, inspired, original, resourceful

inventor noun CREATOR, architect, author, coiner, designer, maker, originator

inventory noun LIST, account, catalog, file, record, register, roll, roster

inverse adjective OPPOSITE, contrary, converse, reverse, reversed, transposed

invert verb OVERTURN, reverse, transpose, upset, upturn

invest verb 1 SPEND, advance, devote, lay out, put in, sink 2 EMPOWER, authorize, charge, license, sanction, vest

investigate verb EXAMINE, explore, go into, inquire into, inspect, look into, probe, research, study

investigation noun EXAMINATION, exploration, inquest, inquiry, inspection, probe, review, search, study, survey

investigator noun EXAMINER, gumshoe (slang), inquirer, (private) detective, private eye (informal), researcher, sleuth

investiture noun INSTALLATION, enthronement, inauguration, induction, ordination

investment noun 1 TRANSACTION, speculation, venture 2 STAKE, ante (informal), contribution

inveterate adjective LONG-STANDING, chronic, confirmed, deep-seated, dyed-in-the-wool, entrenched, habitual, hardened, incorrigible, incurable

invidious adjective UNDESIRABLE, hateful

invigorate verb REFRESH, energize, enliven, exhilarate,

fortify, galvanize, liven up, revitalize, stimulate

invincible adjective UNBEATABLE, impregnable, indestructible, indomitable, insuperable, invulnerable, unassailable, unconquerable

inviolable adjective SACROSANCT, hallowed, holy, inalienable, sacred, unalterable

inviolate adjective INTACT, entire, pure, unbroken, undefiled, unhurt, unpolluted, unsullied, untouched, whole

invisible adjective UNSEEN, imperceptible, indiscernible

invitation noun REQUEST, call, invite (informal), summons

invite verb 1 REQUEST, ask, beg, bid, summon 2 ENCOURAGE, ask for (informal), attract, court, entice, provoke, tempt, welcome

inviting adjective TEMPTING, alluring, appealing, attractive, enticing, mouthwatering, seductive, welcoming

invocation noun APPEAL, entreaty, petition, prayer, supplication

invoke verb 1 CALL UPON, appeal to, beg, beseech, entreat, implore, petition, pray, supplicate 2 APPLY, implement, initiate, put into effect, resort to, use

involuntary adjective UNINTENTIONAL, automatic, instinctive, reflex, spontaneous, unconscious, uncontrolled, unthinking

involve verb 1 ENTAIL, imply, mean, necessitate, presuppose, require 2 CONCERN, affect, draw in, implicate, touch

involved adjective
1 COMPLICATED, complex, confusing, convoluted, elaborate, intricate, labyrinthine, tangled, tortuous 2 CONCERNED, caught (up), implicated, mixed up in or with, participating, taking part

involvement noun CONNECTION, association, commitment, interest, participation

invulnerable adjective SAFE, impenetrable, indestructible, insusceptible, invincible, proof against, secure, unassailable

inward adjective 1 INCOMING, entering, inbound, ingoing 2 INTERNAL, inner, inside, interior 3 PRIVATE, confidential, hidden, inmost, innermost, personal, secret

inwardly adverb PRIVATELY, at heart, deep down, inside, secretly

irate adjective ANGRY, annoyed, cross, enraged, furious, incensed, indignant, infuriated, livid

irksome adjective IRRITATING, annoying, bothersome, disagreeable, exasperating, tiresome, troublesome, trying, vexing, wearisome

iron adjective 1 FERROUS, chalybeate, ferric 2 INFLEXIBLE, adamant, hard, implacable, indomitable, rigid, steely, strong, tough, unbending, unyielding

ironic adjective 1 SARCASTIC, double-edged, mocking, sardonic, satirical, with tongue in cheek, wry 2 PARADOXICAL, incongruous

iron out verb SETTLE, clear up,

get rid of, put right, reconcile, resolve, smooth over, sort out, straighten out

irony noun 1 SARCASM, mockery, satire 2 PARADOX, incongruity

irrational adjective ILLOGICAL, absurd, crazy, nonsensical, preposterous, unreasonable

irrefutable adjective UNDENIABLE, certain, incontestable, incontrovertible, indisputable, indubitable, sure, unquestionable

irregular adjective 1 VARIABLE, erratic, fitful, haphazard, occasional, random, spasmodic, sporadic, unsystematic 2 UNCONVENTIONAL, abnormal, exceptional, extraordinary, peculiar, unofficial, unorthodox, unusual 3 UNEVEN, asymmetrical, bumpy, crooked, jagged, lopsided, ragged, rough

irregularity noun 1 UNCERTAINTY, desultoriness, disorganization, haphazardness 2 ABNORMALITY, anomaly, oddity, peculiarity, unorthodoxy 3 UNEVENNESS, asymmetry, bumpiness, jaggedness, lopsidedness, raggedness, roughness

irrelevant adjective UNCONNECTED, beside the point, extraneous, immaterial, impertinent, inapplicable, inappropriate, neither here nor there, unrelated

irreparable adjective BEYOND REPAIR, incurable, irremediable, irretrievable, irreversible

irrepressible adjective EBULLIENT, boisterous, buoyant, effervescent, unstoppable

irreproachable adjective BLAMELESS, beyond reproach, faultless, impeccable, innocent, perfect, pure, unimpeachable

irresistible adjective OVERWHELMING, compelling, compulsive, overpowering, urgent

irresponsible adjective IMMATURE, careless, reckless, scatterbrained, shiftless, thoughtless, unreliable, untrustworthy

irreverent adjective DISRESPECTFUL, cheeky (informal), flippant, iconoclastic, impertinent, impudent, mocking, tongue-in-cheek

irreversible adjective IRREVOCABLE, final, incurable, irreparable, unalterable

irrevocable adjective FIXED, fated, immutable, irreversible, predestined, predetermined, settled, unalterable

irrigate verb WATER, flood, inundate, moisten, wet

irritability noun BAD TEMPER, ill humor, impatience, irascibility, prickliness, testiness, tetchiness, touchiness

irritable adjective BAD-TEMPERED, cantankerous, crotchety, ill-tempered, irascible, oversensitive, prickly, testy, tetchy, touchy

irritate verb 1 ANNOY, anger, bother, exasperate, get on one's nerves (informal), infuriate, needle (informal), nettle, rankle with, try one's patience 2 RUB, chafe, inflame, pain

irritated adjective ANNOYED, angry, bothered, cross, exasperated, nettled, piqued, put out, vexed

irritating adjective ANNOYING, disturbing, infuriating, irksome, maddening, nagging, troublesome, trying

irritation noun 1 ANNOYANCE, anger, displeasure, exasperation, indignation, resentment, testiness, vexation 2 NUISANCE, drag (informal), irritant, pain in the neck (informal), thorn in one's flesh

island noun ISLE, atoll, cay or key, islet

isolate verb SEPARATE, cut off, detach, disconnect, insulate, segregate, set apart

isolated adjective REMOTE, hidden, lonely, off the beaten track, outlying, out-of-the-way, secluded

isolation noun SEPARATION, detachment, remoteness, seclusion, segregation, solitude

issue noun 1 TOPIC, bone of contention, matter, point, problem, question, subject 2 OUTCOME, consequence, effect, end result, result, upshot 3 EDITION, copy, number, printing 4 CHILDREN, descendants, heirs, offspring, progeny 5 take issue DISAGREE, challenge, dispute, object, oppose, raise an objection, take exception ▶verb 6 PUBLISH, announce, broadcast, circulate, deliver, distribute, give out, put out, release

isthmus noun STRIP, spit

itch noun 1 IRRITATION, itchiness, prickling, tingling 2 DESIRE, craving, hankering, hunger, longing, lust, passion, yearning, yen (informal) ▶verb

3 PRICKLE, irritate, tickle, tingle 4 LONG, ache, crave, hanker, hunger, lust, pine, yearn

itchy adjective IMPATIENT, eager, edgy, fidgety, restive, restless, unsettled

item noun 1 DETAIL, article, component, entry, matter, particular, point, thing 2 REPORT, account, article, bulletin, dispatch, feature, note, notice, paragraph, piece

itinerant adjective WANDERING, migratory, nomadic, peripatetic, roaming, roving, traveling, vagrant

itinerary noun SCHEDULE, program, route, timetable

J j

jab verb, noun POKE, dig, lunge, nudge, prod, punch, stab, tap, thrust

jabber verb CHATTER, babble, blether, gabble, mumble, ramble, yap (informal)

jacket noun COVERING, case, casing, coat, sheath, skin, wrapper, wrapping

jackpot noun PRIZE, award, bonanza, reward, winnings

jack up verb RAISE, elevate, hoist, lift, lift up

jaded adjective TIRED, exhausted, fatigued, spent, weary

jagged adjective UNEVEN, barbed, craggy, indented, ragged, serrated, spiked, toothed

jail noun 1 PRISON, penitentiary, reformatory, slammer (slang) ▶verb 2 IMPRISON, confine, detain, incarcerate, lock up, send down

jailer noun GUARD, keeper, warden

jam verb 1 PACK, cram, force, press, ram, squeeze, stuff, wedge 2 CROWD, crush, throng 3 CONGEST, block, clog, obstruct, stall, stick ▶ noun 4 PREDICAMENT, deep water, fix (informal), hot water, pickle (informal), tight spot, trouble

jamboree noun FESTIVAL, carnival, celebration, festivity, fête, revelry, spree

jangle verb RATTLE, chime, clank, clash, clatter, jingle, vibrate

janitor noun CARETAKER, concierge, custodian, doorkeeper, porter

jar¹ noun POT, container, crock, jug, pitcher, urn, vase

jar² verb 1 JOLT, bump, convulse, rattle, rock, shake, vibrate 2 IRRITATE, annoy, get on one's nerves (informal), grate, irk, nettle, offend ▶ noun 3 JOLT, bump, convulsion, shock, vibration

jargon noun PARLANCE, argot, idiom, usage

jaundiced adjective 1 CYNICAL, skeptical 2 BITTER, envious, hostile, jealous, resentful, spiteful, suspicious

jaunt noun OUTING, airing, excursion, expedition, ramble, stroll, tour, trip

jaunty adjective SPRIGHTLY, buoyant, carefree, high-spirited, lively, perky, self-confident, sparky

jaw verb TALK, chat, chatter, chew the fat (slang), gossip, spout

jaws plural noun OPENING, entrance, mouth

jazz up verb ENLIVEN, animate, enhance, improve

jazzy adjective FLASHY, fancy, gaudy, snazzy (informal)

jealous adjective 1 ENVIOUS, covetous, desirous, green, grudging, resentful 2 WARY, mistrustful, protective, suspicious, vigilant, watchful

jealousy noun ENVY, covetousness, mistrust, possessiveness, resentment, spite, suspicion

jeans plural noun DENIMS, Levis (Trademark)

jeer verb 1 SCOFF, barrack, deride, gibe, heckle, mock, ridicule, taunt ▶ noun 2 TAUNT, abuse, boo, catcall, derision, gibe, ridicule

jell verb 1 SOLIDIFY, congeal, harden, set, thicken 2 TAKE SHAPE, come together, crystallize, materialize

jeopardize verb ENDANGER, chance, expose, gamble, imperil, risk, stake, venture

jeopardy noun DANGER, insecurity, peril, risk, vulnerability

jerk verb, noun TUG, jolt, lurch, pull, thrust, twitch, wrench, yank

jerky adjective BUMPY, convulsive, jolting, jumpy, shaky, spasmodic, twitchy

jest noun 1 JOKE, bon mot, crack (slang), jape, pleasantry, prank, quip, wisecrack (informal), witticism ▶ verb 2 JOKE, kid (informal), mock, quip, tease

jester noun CLOWN, buffoon, fool, harlequin

jet¹ *adjective* BLACK, coal-black, ebony, inky, pitch-black, raven, sable

jet² *noun* **1** STREAM, flow, fountain, gush, spout, spray, spring **2** NOZZLE, atomizer, sprayer, sprinkler ▸ *verb* **3** FLY, soar, zoom

jettison *verb* ABANDON, discard, dump, eject, expel, scrap, throw overboard, unload

jetty *noun* PIER, breakwater, dock, groyne, mole, quay, wharf

jewel *noun* **1** GEMSTONE, ornament, rock (*slang*), sparkler (*informal*) **2** RARITY, collector's item, find, gem, pearl, treasure, wonder

jewelry *noun* JEWELS, finery, gems, ornaments, regalia, treasure, trinkets

jib *verb* REFUSE, balk, recoil, retreat, shrink, stop short

jibe see GIBE

jiffy *noun* Slang INSTANT, blink of an eye (*informal*), flash, heartbeat (*informal*), second, two shakes of a lamb's tail (*slang*)

jig *verb* SKIP, bob, bounce, caper, prance, wiggle

jingle *noun* **1** RATTLE, clang, clink, reverberation, ringing, tinkle **2** SONG, chorus, ditty, melody, tune ▸ *verb* **3** RING, chime, clatter, clink, jangle, rattle, tinkle

jinx *noun* **1** CURSE, evil eye (*informal*), hex (*informal*), hoodoo (*informal*), nemesis ▸ *verb* **2** CURSE, bewitch, hex (*informal*)

jitters *plural noun* NERVES, anxiety, butterflies (in one's stomach) (*informal*), cold feet (*informal*), fidgets, nervousness, the shakes (*informal*)

jittery *adjective* NERVOUS, agitated, anxious, fidgety, jumpy, shaky, trembling, twitchy (*informal*), wired (*slang*)

job *noun* **1** TASK, assignment, chore, duty, enterprise, errand, undertaking, venture **2** OCCUPATION, business, calling, career, employment, livelihood, profession, vocation

jobless *adjective* UNEMPLOYED, idle, inactive, out of work, unoccupied

jocular *adjective* HUMOROUS, amusing, droll, facetious, funny, joking, jovial, playful, sportive, teasing, waggish

jog *verb* **1** NUDGE, prod, push, shake, stir **2** RUN, canter, lope, trot

John Doe *noun* Informal MAN IN THE STREET, average guy, average person, know-nothing (*slang*)

joie de vivre *noun* ENTHUSIASM, ebullience, enjoyment, gusto, relish, zest

join *verb* **1** CONNECT, add, append, attach, combine, couple, fasten, link, unite **2** ENROLL, enlist, enter, sign up

joint *adjective* SHARED, collective, combined, communal, cooperative, joined, mutual, united ▸ *noun* **2** JUNCTION, connection, hinge, intersection, nexus, node ▸ *verb* **3** DIVIDE, carve, cut up, dissect, segment, sever

jointly *adverb* COLLECTIVELY, as one, in common, in conjunction, in league, in partnership, mutually, together

joke noun **1** JEST, gag (informal), jape, prank, pun, quip, wisecrack (informal), witticism **2** CLOWN, buffoon, laughing stock ▶ verb **3** JEST, banter, kid (informal), mock, play the fool, quip, taunt, tease

joker noun COMEDIAN, buffoon, clown, comic, humorist, jester, prankster, trickster, wag, wit

jolly adjective HAPPY, cheerful, chirpy (informal), genial, jovial, merry, playful, sprightly, upbeat (informal)

jolt noun **1** JERK, bump, jar, jog, jump, lurch, shake, start **2** SURPRISE, blow, bolt from the blue, bombshell, setback, shock ▶ verb **3** JERK, jar, jog, jostle, knock, push, shake, shove **4** SURPRISE, discompose, disturb, perturb, stagger, startle, stun

jostle verb PUSH, bump, elbow, hustle, jog, jolt, shake, shove

jot verb **1** NOTE DOWN, list, record, scribble ▶ noun **2** BIT, fraction, grain, morsel, scrap, speck

journal noun **1** NEWSPAPER, daily, gazette, magazine, monthly, periodical, weekly **2** DIARY, chronicle, log, record

journalist noun REPORTER, broadcaster, columnist, commentator, correspondent, hack, newsman or newswoman, pressman

journey noun **1** TRIP, excursion, expedition, odyssey, pilgrimage, tour, trek, voyage ▶ verb **2** TRAVEL, go, proceed, roam, rove, tour, traverse, trek, voyage, wander

jovial adjective CHEERFUL,

animated, cheery, convivial, happy, jolly, merry, mirthful

joy noun DELIGHT, bliss, ecstasy, elation, gaiety, glee, pleasure, rapture, satisfaction

joyful adjective DELIGHTED, elated, enraptured, glad, gratified, happy, jubilant, merry, pleased

joyless adjective UNHAPPY, cheerless, depressed, dismal, dreary, gloomy, miserable, sad

joyous adjective JOYFUL, festive, merry, rapturous

jubilant adjective OVERJOYED, elated, enraptured, euphoric, exuberant, exultant, thrilled, triumphant

jubilation noun JOY, celebration, ecstasy, elation, excitement, exultation, festivity, triumph

jubilee noun CELEBRATION, festival, festivity, holiday

judge noun **1** REFEREE, adjudicator, arbiter, arbitrator, moderator, umpire **2** CRITIC, arbiter, assessor, authority, connoisseur, expert **3** MAGISTRATE, justice ▶ verb **4** ARBITRATE, adjudicate, decide, mediate, referee, umpire **5** CONSIDER, appraise, assess, esteem, estimate, evaluate, rate, value

judgment noun **1** SENSE, acumen, discernment, discrimination, prudence, shrewdness, understanding, wisdom **2** VERDICT, arbitration, decision, decree, finding, ruling, sentence **3** OPINION, appraisal, assessment, belief, diagnosis, estimate, finding, valuation, view

judicial adjective LEGAL, official

judicious adjective SENSIBLE,

jug *noun* CONTAINER, carafe, crock, ewer, jar, pitcher, urn, vessel

juggle *verb* MANIPULATE, alter, change, maneuver, modify

juice *noun* LIQUID, extract, fluid, liquor, nectar, sap

juicy *adjective* 1 MOIST, lush, succulent 2 INTERESTING, colorful, provocative, racy, risqué, sensational, spicy (*informal*), suggestive, vivid

jumble *noun* 1 MUDDLE, clutter, confusion, disarray, disorder, mess, mishmash, mixture ▶*verb* 2 MIX, confuse, disorder, disorganize, mistake, muddle, shuffle

jumbo *adjective* GIANT, gigantic, huge, immense, large, oversized

jump *verb* 1 LEAP, bounce, bound, hop, hurdle, skip, spring, vault 2 RECOIL, flinch, jerk, start, wince 3 MISS, avoid, evade, omit, skip 4 INCREASE, advance, ascend, escalate, rise, surge ▶*noun* 5 LEAP, bound, hop, skip, spring, vault 6 INTERRUPTION, break, gap, hiatus, lacuna, space 7 RISE, advance, increase, increment, upsurge, upturn

jumped-up *adjective* CONCEITED, arrogant, insolent, overbearing, pompous, presumptuous

jumpy *adjective* NERVOUS, agitated, anxious, apprehensive, fidgety, jittery (*informal*), on edge, restless, tense, wired (*slang*)

junction *noun* CONNECTION, coupling, linking, union

juncture *noun* MOMENT, occasion, point, time

junior *adjective* MINOR, inferior, lesser, lower, secondary, subordinate, younger

junk *noun* RUBBISH, clutter, debris, litter, odds and ends, refuse, scrap, trash, waste

jurisdiction *noun* 1 AUTHORITY, command, control, influence, power, rule 2 RANGE, area, bounds, compass, field, province, scope, sphere

just *adverb* 1 EXACTLY, absolutely, completely, entirely, perfectly, precisely 2 RECENTLY, hardly, lately, only now, scarcely 3 MERELY, by the skin of one's teeth, only, simply, solely ▶*adjective* 4 FAIR, conscientious, equitable, fair-minded, good, honest, upright, virtuous 5 PROPER, appropriate, apt, deserved, due, fitting, justified, merited, rightful

justice *noun* 1 FAIRNESS, equity, honesty, integrity, law, legality, legitimacy, right 2 JUDGE, magistrate

justifiable *adjective* REASONABLE, acceptable, defensible, excusable, legitimate, sensible, understandable, valid, warrantable

justification *noun* 1 EXPLANATION, defense, excuse, rationalization, vindication 2 REASON, basis, grounds, warrant

justify *verb* EXPLAIN, defend, exculpate, excuse, exonerate, support, uphold, vindicate, warrant

justly *adverb* PROPERLY, correctly, equitably, fairly, lawfully

jut *verb* STICK OUT, bulge, extend, overhang, poke, project, protrude

juvenile *adjective* 1 YOUNG, babyish, callow, childish, immature, inexperienced, infantile, puerile, youthful ▶*noun* 2 CHILD, adolescent, boy, girl, infant, minor, youth

juxtaposition *noun* PROXIMITY, adjacency, closeness, contact, nearness, propinquity, vicinity

— K k —

kamikaze *adjective* SELF-DESTRUCTIVE, foolhardy, suicidal

keel over *verb* COLLAPSE, black out (*informal*), faint, pass out

keen *adjective* 1 EAGER, ardent, avid, enthusiastic, impassioned, intense, zealous 2 SHARP, cutting, incisive, razor-like 3 ASTUTE, canny, clever, perceptive, quick, shrewd, wise

keenness *noun* EAGERNESS, ardor, enthusiasm, fervor, intensity, passion, zeal, zest

keep *verb* 1 RETAIN, conserve, control, hold, maintain, possess, preserve 2 STORE, carry, deposit, hold, place, stack, stock 3 LOOK AFTER, care for, guard, maintain, manage, mind, protect, tend, watch over 4 SUPPORT, feed, maintain, provide for, subsidize, sustain 5 DETAIN, delay, hinder, hold back, keep back, obstruct, prevent, restrain ▶*noun* 6 BOARD, food, living,

maintenance 7 TOWER, castle

keeper *noun* GUARDIAN, attendant, caretaker, curator, custodian, guard, preserver, steward, warden

keeping *noun* 1 CARE, charge, custody, guardianship, possession, protection, safekeeping 2 As in **in keeping with** AGREEMENT, accord, balance, compliance, conformity, correspondence, harmony, observance, proportion

keepsake *noun* SOUVENIR, memento, relic, reminder, symbol, token

keep up *verb* MAINTAIN, continue, keep pace, preserve, sustain

keg *noun* BARREL, cask, drum, vat

kernel *noun* ESSENCE, core, germ, gist, nub, pith, substance

key *noun* 1 OPENER, latchkey 2 ANSWER, explanation, solution ▶*adjective* 3 ESSENTIAL, crucial, decisive, fundamental, important, leading, main, major, pivotal, principal

key in *verb* TYPE, enter, input, keyboard

keynote *noun* HEART, center, core, essence, gist, substance, theme

kick *verb* 1 BOOT, punt 2 *Informal* GIVE UP, abandon, desist from, leave off, quit, stop ▶*noun* 3 *Informal* THRILL, buzz (*slang*), pleasure, stimulation

kick off *verb* BEGIN, commence, get the show on the road, initiate, open, start

kick out *verb* DISMISS, eject, evict, expel, get rid of, remove, sack (*informal*)

kid¹ noun *Informal* CHILD, baby, infant, minor, teenager, tot, youngster, youth

kid² verb TEASE, delude, fool, hoax, jest, joke, pretend, trick

kidnap verb ABDUCT, capture, hijack, hold to ransom, seize

kill verb 1 SLAY, assassinate, butcher, destroy, execute, exterminate, liquidate, massacre, murder, slaughter 2 SUPPRESS, extinguish, halt, quash, quell, scotch, smother, stifle, stop

killer noun ASSASSIN, butcher, cut-throat, executioner, exterminator, gunman, hit man (*slang*), murderer, slayer

killing noun 1 SLAUGHTER, bloodshed, carnage, extermination, homicide, manslaughter, massacre, murder, slaying 2 *Informal* BONANZA, cleanup (*informal*), coup, gain, profit, success, windfall

killjoy noun SPOILSPORT, dampener, wet blanket (*informal*)

kin noun FAMILY, kindred, kinsfolk, relations, relatives

kind¹ adjective CONSIDERATE, benign, charitable, compassionate, courteous, friendly, generous, humane, kindly, obliging, philanthropic, tender-hearted

kind² noun CLASS, brand, breed, family, set, sort, species, variety

kind-hearted adjective SYMPATHETIC, altruistic, compassionate, considerate, generous, good-natured, helpful, humane, kind, tender-hearted

kindle verb 1 SET FIRE TO, ignite, inflame, light 2 AROUSE, awaken, induce, inspire, provoke, rouse, stimulate, stir

kindliness noun KINDNESS, amiability, benevolence, charity, compassion, friendliness, gentleness, humanity, kind-heartedness

kindly adjective 1 GOOD-NATURED, benevolent, benign, compassionate, helpful, kind, pleasant, sympathetic, warm ▶ adverb 2 POLITELY, agreeably, cordially, graciously, tenderly, thoughtfully

kindness noun GOODWILL, benevolence, charity, compassion, generosity, humanity, kindliness, philanthropy, understanding

kindred adjective 1 SIMILAR, akin, corresponding, like, matching, related ▶ noun 2 FAMILY, kin, kinsfolk, relations, relatives

king noun RULER, emperor, monarch, sovereign

kingdom noun COUNTRY, nation, realm, state, territory

kink noun 1 TWIST, bend, coil, wrinkle 2 QUIRK, eccentricity, fetish, foible, idiosyncrasy, vagary, whim

kinky adjective 1 *Slang* WEIRD, eccentric, odd, outlandish, peculiar, queer, quirky, strange 2 TWISTED, coiled, curled, tangled

kinship noun 1 RELATION, consanguinity, kin, ties of blood 2 SIMILARITY, affinity, association, connection, correspondence, relationship

kiosk noun BOOTH, bookstall,

counter, newsstand, stall, stand

kiss verb 1 OSCULATE, neck (informal), peck (informal) 2 BRUSH, glance, graze, scrape, touch ▶ noun 3 OSCULATION, peck (informal), smacker (slang), smooch (slang)

kit noun EQUIPMENT, apparatus, gear, paraphernalia, tackle, tools

knack noun SKILL, ability, aptitude, capacity, expertise, facility, gift, propensity, talent, trick

knave noun ROGUE, rascal, scoundrel, villain

knead verb SQUEEZE, form, manipulate, massage, mold, press, rub, shape, work

kneel verb GENUFLECT, get (down) on one's knees, stoop

knell noun RINGING, chime, peal, sound, toll

knick-knack noun TRINKET, bagatelle, bauble, bric-a-brac, plaything, trifle

knife noun 1 BLADE, cutter ▶ verb 2 CUT, lacerate, pierce, slash, stab, wound

knit verb 1 JOIN, bind, fasten, intertwine, link, tie, unite, weave 2 WRINKLE, crease, furrow, knot, pucker

knob noun LUMP, bump, hump, knot, projection, protrusion, stud

knock verb 1 HIT, belt (informal), cuff, punch, rap, smack, strike, thump 2 Informal CRITICIZE, abuse, belittle, censure, condemn, denigrate, deprecate, disparage, find fault, run down ▶ noun 3 BLOW, clip, clout (informal), cuff, rap, slap, smack, thump 4 SETBACK,

defeat, failure, rebuff, rejection, reversal

knock down verb DEMOLISH, destroy, fell, level, raze

knock off verb 1 STOP WORK, clock off, clock out, finish 2 STEAL, pinch, rob, thieve

knockout noun 1 KILLER BLOW, coup de grâce, KO or K.O. (slang) 2 SUCCESS, hit, sensation, smash, smash hit, triumph, winner

knot noun 1 CONNECTION, bond, joint, ligature, loop, tie 2 CLUSTER, bunch, clump, collection ▶ verb 3 TIE, bind, loop, secure, tether

know verb 1. REALIZE, comprehend, feel certain, notice, perceive, recognize, see, understand 2 BE ACQUAINTED WITH, be familiar with, have dealings with, have knowledge of, recognize

know-how noun CAPABILITY, ability, aptitude, expertise, ingenuity, knack, knowledge, savoir-faire, skill, talent

knowing adjective MEANINGFUL, expressive, significant

knowingly adverb DELIBERATELY, consciously, intentionally, on purpose, purposely, willfully, wittingly

knowledge noun 1 LEARNING, education, enlightenment, erudition, instruction, intelligence, scholarship, wisdom 2 ACQUAINTANCE, cognizance, familiarity, intimacy

knowledgeable adjective 1 WELL-INFORMED, au fait, aware, clued-up (informal), cognizant, conversant, experienced, familiar, in the know (informal)

2 INTELLIGENT, educated, erudite, learned, scholarly

known *adjective* **1** FAMOUS, acknowledged, avowed, celebrated, noted, recognized, well-known

knuckle under *verb* GIVE WAY, accede, acquiesce, capitulate, cave in (*informal*), give in, submit, succumb, surrender, yield

kudos *noun* PRAISE, acclaim, applause, credit, laudation, plaudits, recognition

—— **LI** ——

label *noun* **1** TAG, marker, sticker, ticket ▸ *verb* **2** MARK, stamp, tag

labor *noun* **1** WORK, industry, toil **2** WORKERS, employees, hands, laborers, workforce **3** CHILDBIRTH, delivery, parturition ▸ *verb* **4** WORK, endeavor, slave, strive, struggle, sweat (*informal*), toil **5** (*usually with* under) BE DISADVANTAGED, be a victim of, be burdened by, suffer **6** OVEREMPHASIZE, dwell on, elaborate, overdo, strain

labored *adjective* FORCED, awkward, difficult, heavy, stiff, strained

laborer *noun* WORKER, blue-collar worker, drudge, hand, manual worker

laborious *adjective* HARD, arduous, backbreaking, exhausting, onerous, strenuous, tiring, tough,

wearisome

labyrinth *noun* MAZE, intricacy, jungle, tangle

lace *noun* **1** NETTING, filigree, openwork **2** CORD, bootlace, shoelace, string, tie ▸ *verb* **3** FASTEN, bind, do up, thread, tie **4** MIX IN, add to, fortify, spike

lacerate *verb* TEAR, claw, cut, gash, mangle, rip, slash, wound

laceration *noun* CUT, gash, rent, rip, slash, tear, wound

lack *noun* **1** SHORTAGE, absence, dearth, deficiency, need, scarcity, want ▸ *verb* **2** NEED, be deficient in, be short of, be without, miss, require, want

lackadaisical *adjective* **1** LETHARGIC, apathetic, dull, half-hearted, indifferent, languid, listless **2** LAZY, abstracted, dreamy, idle, indolent, inert

lackey *noun* **1** HANGER-ON, brown-noser (*slang*), flatterer, minion, sycophant, toady, yes man **2** MANSERVANT, attendant, flunky, footman, valet

lackluster *adjective* FLAT, drab, dull, leaden, lifeless, muted, prosaic, uninspired, vapid

laconic *adjective* TERSE, brief, concise, curt, monosyllabic, pithy, short, succinct

lad *noun* BOY, fellow, guy (*informal*), juvenile, kid (*informal*), youngster, youth

laden *adjective* LOADED, burdened, charged, encumbered, full, weighed down

lady *noun* **1** GENTLEWOMAN, dame **2** WOMAN, female

ladylike *adjective* REFINED,

elegant, genteel, modest, polite, proper, respectable, sophisticated, well-bred

lag verb HANG BACK, dawdle, delay, linger, loiter, straggle, tarry, trail

laggard noun STRAGGLER, dawdler, idler, loiterer, slowpoke (*informal*), sluggard, snail

laid-back adjective RELAXED, casual, easy-going, free and easy, unflappable (*informal*), unhurried

lair noun NEST, burrow, den, earth, hole

laissez faire noun NONINTERVENTION, free enterprise, free trade

lake noun POND, basin, lagoon, mere, pool, reservoir, tarn

lame adjective 1 DISABLED, challenged, crippled, game, handicapped, hobbling, limping 2 UNCONVINCING, feeble, flimsy, inadequate, lousy (*slang*), pathetic, poor, thin, unsatisfactory, weak

lament verb 1 COMPLAIN, bemoan, bewail, deplore, grieve, mourn, regret, sorrow, wail, weep ▶ noun 2 COMPLAINT, lamentation, moan, wailing 3 DIRGE, elegy, requiem, threnody

lamentable adjective REGRETTABLE, deplorable, distressing, grievous, mournful, tragic, unfortunate, woeful

lampoon noun 1 SATIRE, burlesque, caricature, parody, spoof (*informal*) ▶ verb 2 RIDICULE, caricature, make fun of, mock, parody, satirize

land noun 1 GROUND, dry land, earth, terra firma 2 SOIL, dirt, ground, loam 3 COUNTRYSIDE, farmland 4 PROPERTY, estate, grounds, realty 5 COUNTRY, district, nation, province, region, territory, tract ▶ verb 6 ARRIVE, alight, come to rest, disembark, dock, touch down 7 END UP, turn up, wind up 8 *Informal* OBTAIN, acquire, gain, get, secure, win

landlord noun 1 INNKEEPER, host, hotelier 2 OWNER, freeholder, lessor, proprietor

landmark noun 1 FEATURE, monument 2 MILESTONE, turning point, watershed

landscape noun SCENERY, countryside, outlook, panorama, prospect, scene, view, vista

landslide noun 1 ROCKFALL, avalanche, landslip ▶ adjective 2 OVERWHELMING, conclusive, decisive, runaway

lane noun ROAD, alley, footpath, passageway, path, pathway, street, way

language noun 1 SPEECH, communication, discourse, expression, parlance, talk 2 TONGUE, dialect, patois, vernacular

languid adjective 1 LAZY, indifferent, lackadaisical, languorous, listless, unenthusiastic 2 LETHARGIC, dull, heavy, sluggish, torpid

languish verb 1 WEAKEN, decline, droop, fade, fail, faint, flag, wilt, wither 2 (often with *for*) PINE, desire, hanker, hunger, long, yearn 3 BE NEGLECTED, be abandoned, rot, suffer, waste away

lank *adjective* **1** LIMP, lifeless, straggling **2** THIN, emaciated, gaunt, lean, scrawny, skinny, slender, slim, spare

lanky *adjective* GANGLING, angular, bony, gaunt, rangy, spare, trail

lap[1] *noun* CIRCUIT, circle, loop, orbit, tour

lap[2] *verb* **1** RIPPLE, gurgle, plash, purl, splash, swish, wash **2** DRINK, lick, sip, sup

lapse *noun* **1** MISTAKE, error, failing, fault, indiscretion, negligence, omission, oversight, slip **2** INTERVAL, break, breathing space, gap, intermission, interruption, lull, pause **3** DROP, decline, deterioration, fall ▶ *verb* **4** DROP, decline, degenerate, deteriorate, fall, sink, slide, slip **5** END, expire, run out, stop, terminate

lapsed *adjective* OUT OF DATE, discontinued, ended, expired, finished, invalid, run out

large *adjective* **1** BIG, considerable, enormous, gigantic, great, huge, immense, massive, monumental, sizable *or* sizeable, substantial, vast **2 at large: a** FREE, at liberty, on the loose, on the run, unconfined **b** IN GENERAL, as a whole, chiefly, generally, in the main, mainly **c** AT LENGTH, exhaustively, greatly, in full detail

largely *adverb* MAINLY, as a rule, by and large, chiefly, generally, mostly, predominantly, primarily, principally, to a great extent

large-scale *adjective* WIDE-RANGING, broad, extensive, far-reaching, global, sweeping, vast, wholesale, wide

lark *noun* **1** PRANK, caper, escapade, fun, game, jape, mischief ▶ *verb* **2 lark about** PLAY, caper, cavort, have fun, make mischief

lash[1] *noun* **1** BLOW, hit, stripe, stroke, swipe (*informal*) ▶ *verb* **2** WHIP, beat, birch, flog, scourge, thrash **3** POUND, beat, buffet, dash, drum, hammer, smack, strike **4** SCOLD, attack, blast, censure, criticize, put down, upbraid

lash[2] *verb* FASTEN, bind, make fast, secure, strap, tie

lass *noun* GIRL, damsel, maid, maiden, young woman

last[1] *adjective* **1** HINDMOST, at the end, rearmost **2** MOST RECENT, latest **3** FINAL, closing, concluding, terminal, ultimate ▶ *adverb* **4** IN THE REAR, after, behind, bringing up the rear, in *or* at the end

last[2] *verb* CONTINUE, abide, carry on, endure, keep on, persist, remain, stand up, survive

lasting *adjective* CONTINUING, abiding, durable, enduring, long-standing, long-term, perennial, permanent

latch *noun* **1** FASTENING, bar, bolt, catch, hasp, hook, lock ▶ *verb* **2** FASTEN, bar, bolt, make fast, secure

late *adjective* **1** OVERDUE, behind, behindhand, belated, delayed, last-minute, tardy **2** RECENT, advanced, fresh, modern, new **3** DEAD, deceased, defunct, departed, former, past ▶ *adverb*

4 BELATEDLY, at the last minute, behindhand, behind time, dilatorily, tardily

lately adverb RECENTLY, in recent times, just now, latterly, not long ago, of late

lateness noun DELAY, belatedness, tardiness

latent adjective HIDDEN, concealed, dormant, invisible, potential, undeveloped, unrealized

later adverb AFTERWARDS, after, by and by, in a while, in time, later on, subsequently, thereafter

lateral adjective SIDEWAYS, edgeways, flanking

latest adjective UP-TO-DATE, cool (informal), current, fashionable, modern, most recent, newest, phat (slang), up-to-the-minute

lather noun 1 FROTH, bubbles, foam, soapsuds, suds ▶ verb 2 FROTH, foam, soap

latitude noun SCOPE, elbowroom, freedom, laxity, leeway, liberty, license, play

latter adjective LAST-MENTIONED, closing, concluding, last, second

latterly adverb RECENTLY, lately, of late

lattice noun GRID, grating, grille, trellis

laudable adjective PRAISEWORTHY, admirable, commendable, creditable, excellent, meritorious, of note, worthy

laugh verb 1 CHUCKLE, be in stitches, chortle, giggle, guffaw, snigger, split one's sides, titter ▶ noun 2 CHUCKLE, chortle, giggle, guffaw, snigger, titter 3 Informal JOKE,

hoot (informal), lark, scream (informal)

laughable adjective RIDICULOUS, absurd, derisory, farcical, ludicrous, nonsensical, preposterous, risible

laughing stock noun FIGURE OF FUN, butt, target, victim

laugh off verb DISREGARD, brush aside, dismiss, ignore, minimize, pooh-pooh, shrug off

laughter noun AMUSEMENT, glee, hilarity, merriment, mirth

launch verb 1 PROPEL, discharge, dispatch, fire, project, send off, set in motion 2 BEGIN, commence, embark upon, inaugurate, initiate, instigate, introduce, open, start

laurels plural noun GLORY, credit, distinction, fame, honor, kudos, praise, prestige, recognition, renown

lavatory noun TOILET, bathroom, latrine, powder room, (public) convenience, washroom, water closet, W.C.

lavish adjective 1 PLENTIFUL, abundant, copious, profuse, prolific 2 GENEROUS, bountiful, free, liberal, munificent, open-handed, unstinting 3 EXTRAVAGANT, exaggerated, excessive, immoderate, prodigal, unrestrained, wasteful, wild ▶ verb 4 SPEND, deluge, dissipate, expend, heap, pour, shower, squander, waste

law noun 1 CONSTITUTION, charter, code 2 RULE, act, command, commandment, decree, edict, order, ordinance, regulation, statute 3 PRINCIPLE, axiom, canon, precept

law-abiding *adjective* OBEDIENT, compliant, dutiful, good, honest, honorable, lawful, orderly, peaceable

law-breaker *noun* CRIMINAL, convict, crook (*informal*), culprit, delinquent, felon, miscreant, offender, villain, wrongdoer

lawful *adjective* LEGAL, authorized, constitutional, legalized, legitimate, licit, permissible, rightful, valid, warranted

lawless *adjective* DISORDERLY, anarchic, chaotic, rebellious, riotous, unruly, wild

lawlessness *noun* ANARCHY, chaos, disorder, mob rule

lawsuit *noun* CASE, action, dispute, industrial tribunal, litigation, proceedings, prosecution, suit, trial

lawyer *noun* LEGAL ADVISER, advocate, attorney, barrister (*chiefly Brit.*), counsel, counselor

lax *adjective* SLACK, careless, casual, lenient, negligent, overindulgent, remiss, slapdash, slipshod

lay¹ *verb* 1 PLACE, deposit, leave, plant, put, set, set down, spread 2 ARRANGE, organize, position, set out 3 PRODUCE, bear, deposit 4 PUT FORWARD, advance, bring forward, lodge, offer, present, submit 5 ATTRIBUTE, allocate, allot, ascribe, assign, impute 6 DEVISE, concoct, contrive, design, hatch, plan, plot, prepare, work out 7 BET, gamble, give odds, hazard, risk, stake, wager

lay² *adjective* 1 NONCLERICAL, secular 2 NONSPECIALIST, amateur, inexpert, nonprofessional

layer *noun* TIER, row, seam, stratum, thickness

layman *noun* AMATEUR, lay person, nonprofessional, outsider

layoff *noun* DISMISSAL, discharge, unemployment

lay off *verb* DISMISS, discharge, let go, pay off

lay on *verb* PROVIDE, cater (for), furnish, give, purvey, supply

layout *noun* ARRANGEMENT, design, formation, outline, plan

lay out *verb* 1 ARRANGE, design, display, exhibit, plan, spread out 2 *Informal* SPEND, disburse, expend, fork out (*slang*), invest, pay, shell out (*informal*) 3 *Informal* KNOCK OUT, knock for six (*informal*), knock unconscious, KO or K.O. (*slang*)

laziness *noun* IDLENESS, inactivity, indolence, slackness, sloth, sluggishness

lazy *adjective* 1 IDLE, inactive, indolent, inert, slack, slothful, slow, workshy 2 LETHARGIC, drowsy, languid, languorous, sleepy, slow-moving, sluggish, somnolent, torpid

lead *verb* 1 GUIDE, conduct, escort, pilot, precede, show the way, steer, usher 2 PERSUADE, cause, dispose, draw, incline, induce, influence, prevail, prompt 3 COMMAND, direct, govern, head, manage, preside over, supervise 4 BE AHEAD (OF), blaze a trail, come first, exceed, excel, outdo, outstrip, surpass, transcend 5 LIVE, experience, have, pass, spend, undergo

6 RESULT IN, bring on, cause, contribute, produce ▶ *noun* **7** FIRST PLACE, precedence, primacy, priority, supremacy, vanguard **8** ADVANTAGE, edge, margin, start **9** EXAMPLE, direction, guidance, leadership, model **10** CLUE, hint, indication, suggestion **11** LEADING ROLE, principal, protagonist, title role ▶ *adjective* **12** MAIN, chief, first, foremost, head, leading, premier, primary, prime, principal

leader *noun* PRINCIPAL, boss (*informal*), captain, chief, chieftain, commander, director, guide, head, ringleader, ruler

leadership *noun* **1** GUIDANCE, direction, domination, management, running, superintendency **2** AUTHORITY, command, control, influence, initiative, pre-eminence, supremacy

leading *adjective* MAIN, chief, dominant, first, foremost, greatest, highest, primary, principal

lead on *verb* ENTICE, beguile, deceive, draw on, lure, seduce, string along (*informal*), tempt

lead up to *verb* INTRODUCE, pave the way, prepare for

leaf *noun* **1** FROND, blade **2** PAGE, folio, sheet ▶ *verb* **3** **leaf through** BROWSE, flip, glance, riffle, skim, thumb (through)

leaflet *noun* BOOKLET, brochure, circular, pamphlet

leafy *adjective* GREEN, bosky (*literary*), shaded, shady, verdant

league *noun* **1** ASSOCIATION, alliance, coalition, confederation, consortium, federation, fraternity, group, guild, partnership, union **2** CLASS, category, level

leak *noun* **1** HOLE, aperture, chink, crack, crevice, fissure, opening, puncture **2** DRIP, leakage, percolation, seepage **3** DISCLOSURE, divulgence ▶ *verb* **4** DRIP, escape, exude, ooze, pass, percolate, seep, spill, trickle **5** DISCLOSE, divulge, give away, let slip, make known, make public, pass on, reveal, tell

leaky *adjective* PUNCTURED, cracked, holey, leaking, perforated, porous, split

lean¹ *verb* **1** REST, be supported, prop, recline, repose **2** BEND, heel, incline, slant, slope, tilt, tip **3** TEND, be disposed to, be prone to, favor, prefer **4** **lean on** DEPEND ON, count on, have faith in, rely on, trust

lean² *adjective* **1** SLIM, angular, bony, gaunt, rangy, skinny, slender, spare, thin, wiry **2** UNPRODUCTIVE, barren, meager, poor, scanty, unfruitful

leaning *noun* TENDENCY, bent, bias, disposition, inclination, partiality, penchant, predilection, proclivity, propensity

leap *verb* **1** JUMP, bounce, bound, hop, skip, spring ▶ *noun* **2** JUMP, bound, spring, vault **3** INCREASE, escalation, rise, surge, upsurge, upswing

learn *verb* **1** MASTER, grasp, pick up **2** MEMORIZE, commit to memory, get off pat, learn by heart **3** DISCOVER, ascertain, detect, discern, find out, gather, hear, understand

learned adjective SCHOLARLY, academic, erudite, highbrow, intellectual, versed, well-informed, well-read

learner noun BEGINNER, apprentice, neophyte, novice, tyro

learning noun KNOWLEDGE, culture, education, erudition, information, lore, scholarship, study, wisdom

lease verb HIRE, charter, let, loan, rent

leash noun LEAD, rein, tether

least adjective SMALLEST, fewest, lowest, meanest, minimum, poorest, slightest, tiniest

leathery adjective TOUGH, hard, rough

leave¹ verb 1 DEPART, decamp, disappear, exit, go away, make tracks, move, pull out, quit, retire, slope off, withdraw 2 FORGET, leave behind, mislay 3 CAUSE, deposit, generate, produce, result in 4 GIVE UP, abandon, drop, relinquish, renounce, surrender 5 ENTRUST, allot, assign, cede, commit, consign, give over, refer 6 BEQUEATH, hand down, will

leave² noun 1 PERMISSION, allowance, authorization, concession, consent, dispensation, freedom, liberty, sanction 2 HOLIDAY, furlough, leave of absence, sabbatical, time off, vacation 3 PARTING, adieu, departure, farewell, good-bye, leave-taking, retirement, withdrawal

leave out verb OMIT, blow off (slang), cast aside, disregard, exclude, ignore, neglect,

overlook, reject

lecherous adjective LUSTFUL, lascivious, lewd, libidinous, licentious, prurient, salacious

lecture noun 1 TALK, address, discourse, instruction, lesson, speech 2 REBUKE, reprimand, reproof, scolding, talking-to (informal), telling off (informal) ▶verb 3 TALK, address, discourse, expound, hold forth, speak, spout, teach 4 SCOLD, admonish, berate, castigate, censure, reprimand, reprove, tell off (informal)

ledge noun SHELF, mantle, projection, ridge, sill, step

leer noun, verb GRIN, gloat, goggle, ogle, smirk, squint, stare

lees plural noun SEDIMENT, deposit, dregs, grounds

leeway noun ROOM, elbowroom, latitude, margin, play, scope, space

left adjective 1 LEFT-HAND, larboard (Nautical), port, sinistral 2 Of politics SOCIALIST, leftist, left-wing, radical

leftover noun REMNANT, oddment, scrap

left-wing adjective SOCIALIST, communist, radical, red (informal)

leg noun 1 LIMB, lower limb, member, pin (informal), stump (informal) 2 SUPPORT, brace, prop, upright 3 STAGE, lap, part, portion, section, segment, stretch 4 **pull someone's leg** Informal TEASE, fool, kid (informal), make fun of, trick

legacy noun BEQUEST, estate, gift, heirloom, inheritance

legal *adjective* **1** LEGITIMATE, allowed, authorized, constitutional, lawful, licit, permissible, sanctioned, valid **2** JUDICIAL, forensic, juridical

legality *noun* LEGITIMACY, lawfulness, rightfulness, validity

legalize *verb* ALLOW, approve, authorize, decriminalize, legitimate, legitimize, license, permit, sanction, validate

legation *noun* DELEGATION, consulate, embassy, representation

legend *noun* **1** MYTH, fable, fiction, folk tale, saga, story, tale **2** CELEBRITY, luminary, megastar (*informal*), phenomenon, prodigy **3** INSCRIPTION, caption, motto

legendary *adjective* **1** MYTHICAL, apocryphal, fabled, fabulous, fictitious, romantic, traditional **2** FAMOUS, celebrated, famed, illustrious, immortal, renowned, well-known

legibility *noun* CLARITY, neatness, readability

legible *adjective* CLEAR, decipherable, distinct, easy to read, neat, readable

legion *noun* **1** ARMY, brigade, company, division, force, troop **2** MULTITUDE, drove, horde, host, mass, myriad, number, throng

legislation *noun* **1** LAWMAKING, enactment, prescription, regulation **2** LAW, act, bill, charter, measure, regulation, ruling, statute

legislative *adjective* LAW-MAKING, judicial, law-giving

legislator *noun* LAWMAKER, lawgiver

legislature *noun* PARLIAMENT, assembly, chamber, congress, senate

legitimate *adjective* **1** LEGAL, authentic, authorized, genuine, kosher (*informal*), lawful, licit, rightful **2** REASONABLE, admissible, correct, justifiable, logical, sensible, valid, warranted, well-founded ▶ *verb* **3** AUTHORIZE, legalize, legitimize, permit, pronounce lawful, sanction

legitimize *verb* LEGALIZE, authorize, permit, sanction

leisure *noun* SPARE TIME, ease, freedom, free time, liberty, recreation, relaxation, rest

leisurely *adjective* UNHURRIED, comfortable, easy, gentle, lazy, relaxed, slow

lend *verb* **1** LOAN, advance **2** ADD, bestow, confer, give, grant, impart, provide, supply **3 lend itself to** SUIT, be appropriate, be serviceable

length *noun* **1** *Of linear extent* DISTANCE, extent, longitude, measure, reach, span **2** *Of time* DURATION, period, space, span, stretch, term **3** PIECE, measure, portion, section, segment **4 at length: a** IN DETAIL, completely, fully, in depth, thoroughly, to the full **b** FOR A LONG TIME, for ages, for hours, interminably **c** AT LAST, at long last, eventually, finally, in the end

lengthen *verb* EXTEND, continue, draw out, elongate, expand, increase, prolong, protract, spin out, stretch

lengthy *adjective* LONG, drawn-out, extended, interminable, long-drawn-out, long-winded, prolonged, protracted, tedious

leniency noun TOLERANCE,
clemency, compassion,
forbearance, indulgence,
mercy, moderation, pity,
quarter

lenient adjective TOLERANT,
compassionate, forbearing,
forgiving, indulgent, kind,
merciful, sparing

lesbian adjective HOMOSEXUAL,
gay, sapphic

less adjective **1** SMALLER, shorter
▶preposition **2** MINUS, excepting,
lacking, subtracting, without

lessen verb REDUCE, contract,
decrease, diminish, ease, lower,
minimize, narrow, shrink

lesser adjective MINOR, inferior,
less important, lower, secondary

lesson noun **1** CLASS, coaching,
instruction, period, schooling,
teaching, tutoring **2** EXAMPLE,
deterrent, message, moral

let[1] verb **1** ALLOW, authorize,
entitle, give permission, give
the go-ahead, permit, sanction,
tolerate **2** LEASE, hire, rent

let[2] noun HINDRANCE, constraint,
impediment, interference,
obstacle, obstruction,
prohibition, restriction

letdown noun DISAPPOINTMENT,
anticlimax, blow, comedown
(informal), setback, washout
(informal)

let down verb DISAPPOINT,
disenchant, disillusion,
dissatisfy, fail, fall short, leave
in the lurch, leave stranded

lethal adjective DEADLY,
dangerous, destructive,
devastating, fatal, mortal,
murderous, virulent

lethargic adjective SLUGGISH,

apathetic, drowsy, dull,
languid, listless, sleepy, slothful

lethargy noun SLUGGISHNESS,
apathy, drowsiness, inertia,
languor, lassitude, listlessness,
sleepiness, sloth

let off verb **1** FIRE, detonate,
discharge, explode **2** EMIT,
exude, give off, leak, release
3 EXCUSE, absolve, discharge,
exempt, exonerate, forgive,
pardon, release, spare

let on verb REVEAL, admit,
disclose, divulge, give away, let
the cat out of the bag
(informal), make known, say

let out verb **1** EMIT, give vent
to, produce **2** RELEASE,
discharge, free, let go, liberate

letter noun **1** CHARACTER, sign,
symbol **2** MESSAGE,
communication, dispatch,
epistle, line, missive, note

let-up noun LESSENING, break,
breathing space, interval, lull,
pause, remission, respite,
slackening

let up verb STOP, abate,
decrease, diminish, ease (up),
moderate, relax, slacken,
subside

level adjective **1** HORIZONTAL, flat
2 EVEN, consistent, plain,
smooth, uniform **3** EQUAL,
balanced, commensurate,
comparable, equivalent, even,
neck and neck, on a level
playing field (informal), on a
par, proportionate ▶verb
4 FLATTEN, even off or out,
plane, smooth **5** EQUALIZE,
balance, even up **6** RAZE,
bulldoze, demolish, destroy,
devastate, flatten, knock down,
pull down, tear down **7** DIRECT,

aim, focus, point, train ▸*noun*
8 POSITION, achievement,
degree, grade, rank, stage,
standard, standing, status **9 on
the level** *Informal* HONEST,
above board, fair, genuine,
square, straight

level-headed *adjective* STEADY,
balanced, calm, collected,
composed, cool, sensible,
unflappable (*informal*)

lever *noun* **1** HANDLE, bar ▸*verb*
2 PRISE, force

leverage *noun* INFLUENCE,
authority, clout (*informal*), pull
(*informal*), weight

levity *noun* LIGHT-HEARTEDNESS,
facetiousness, flippancy,
frivolity, silliness, skittishness,
triviality

levy *verb* **1** IMPOSE, charge,
collect, demand, exact
2 CONSCRIPT, call up, mobilize,
muster, raise ▸*noun*
3 IMPOSITION, assessment,
collection, exaction, gathering
4 TAX, duty, excise, fee, tariff,
toll

lewd *adjective* INDECENT, bawdy,
lascivious, libidinous, licentious,
lustful, obscene, pornographic,
smutty, wanton, X-rated

lewdness *noun* INDECENCY,
bawdiness, carnality,
debauchery, depravity,
lasciviousness, lechery,
licentiousness, obscenity,
pornography, wantonness

liability *noun* **1** RESPONSIBILITY,
accountability, answerability,
culpability **2** DEBT, debit,
obligation **3** DISADVANTAGE,
burden, drawback,
encumbrance, handicap,
hindrance, inconvenience,

millstone, nuisance

liable *adjective* **1** RESPONSIBLE,
accountable, answerable,
obligated **2** VULNERABLE,
exposed, open, subject,
susceptible **3** LIKELY, apt,
disposed, inclined, prone,
tending

liaise *verb* LINK, communicate,
keep contact, mediate

liaison *noun* **1** COMMUNICATION,
connection, contact, hook-up,
interchange **2** AFFAIR, amour,
entanglement, intrigue, love
affair, romance

liar *noun* FALSIFIER, fabricator,
fibber, perjurer

libel *noun* **1** DEFAMATION,
aspersion, calumny,
denigration, smear ▸*verb*
2 DEFAME, blacken, malign,
revile, slur, smear, vilify

libelous *adjective* DEFAMATORY,
derogatory, false, injurious,
malicious, scurrilous, untrue

liberal *adjective* **1** PROGRESSIVE,
libertarian, radical, reformist
2 GENEROUS, beneficent,
bountiful, charitable, kind,
open-handed, open-hearted,
unstinting **3** TOLERANT,
broad-minded, indulgent,
permissive **4** ABUNDANT, ample,
bountiful, copious, handsome,
lavish, munificent, plentiful,
profuse, rich

liberality *noun* **1** GENEROSITY,
beneficence, benevolence,
bounty, charity, kindness,
largesse or largess,
munificence, philanthropy
2 TOLERATION,
broad-mindedness, latitude,
liberalism, libertarianism,
permissiveness

liberalize verb RELAX, ease, loosen, moderate, modify, slacken, soften

liberate verb FREE, deliver, emancipate, let loose, let out, release, rescue, set free

liberation noun DELIVERANCE, emancipation, freedom, freeing, liberty, release

liberator noun DELIVERER, emancipator, freer, redeemer, rescuer, savior

libertine noun REPROBATE, debauchee, lecher, profligate, rake, roué, sensualist, voluptuary, womanizer

liberty noun 1 FREEDOM, autonomy, emancipation, immunity, independence, liberation, release, self-determination, sovereignty 2 IMPERTINENCE, impropriety, impudence, insolence, presumption 3 **at liberty** FREE, on the loose, unrestricted

libidinous adjective LUSTFUL, carnal, debauched, lascivious, lecherous, sensual, wanton

license noun 1 CERTIFICATE, charter, permit, warrant 2 PERMISSION, authority, authorization, blank check, carte blanche, dispensation, entitlement, exemption, immunity, leave, liberty, right 3 LATITUDE, freedom, independence, leeway, liberty 4 LAXITY, excess, immoderation, indulgence, irresponsibility

license verb PERMIT, accredit, allow, authorize, certify, empower, sanction, warrant

licentious adjective PROMISCUOUS, abandoned, debauched, dissolute, immoral, lascivious, lustful, sensual, wanton

lick verb 1 TASTE, lap, tongue 2 *Of flames* FLICKER, dart, flick, play over, ripple, touch 3 *Slang* BEAT, defeat, master, outdo, outstrip, overcome, rout, trounce, vanquish ▶ noun 4 DAB, bit, stroke, touch 5 *Informal* PACE, clip (*informal*), rate, speed

lie¹ verb 1 FALSIFY, dissimulate, equivocate, fabricate, fib, prevaricate, tell untruths ▶ noun 2 FALSEHOOD, deceit, fabrication, fib, fiction, invention, prevarication, untruth

lie² verb 1 RECLINE, loll, lounge, repose, rest, sprawl, stretch out 2 BE SITUATED, be, be placed, exist, remain

life noun 1 BEING, sentience, vitality 2 EXISTENCE, being, lifetime, span, time 3 BIOGRAPHY, autobiography, confessions, history, life story, memoirs, story 4 BEHAVIOR, conduct, life style, way of life 5 LIVELINESS, animation, energy, high spirits, spirit, verve, vigor, vitality, vivacity, zest

lifeless adjective 1 DEAD, deceased, defunct, extinct, inanimate 2 DULL, colorless, flat, lackluster, lethargic, listless, sluggish, wooden 3 UNCONSCIOUS, comatose, dead to the world (*informal*), insensible

lifelike adjective REALISTIC, authentic, exact, faithful, natural, true-to-life, vivid

lifelong adjective LONG-STANDING, enduring, lasting, long-lasting, perennial, persistent

lifetime noun EXISTENCE, career, day(s), span, time

lift verb **1** RAISE, draw up, elevate, hoist, pick up, uplift, upraise **2** REVOKE, annul, cancel, countermand, end, remove, rescind, stop, terminate **3** DISAPPEAR, be dispelled, disperse, dissipate, vanish ▸ noun **4** RIDE, drive, run **5** BOOST, encouragement, pick-me-up, shot in the arm (*informal*)

light¹ noun **1** BRIGHTNESS, brilliance, glare, gleam, glint, glow, illumination, luminosity, radiance, shine **2** LAMP, beacon, candle, flare, lantern, taper, torch **3** ASPECT, angle, context, interpretation, point of view, slant, vantage point, viewpoint **4** MATCH, flame, lighter ▸ adjective **5** BRIGHT, brilliant, illuminated, luminous, lustrous, shining, well-lit **6** PALE, bleached, blond, faded, fair, pastel ▸ verb **7** IGNITE, inflame, kindle **8** ILLUMINATE, brighten, light up

light² adjective **1** INSUBSTANTIAL, airy, buoyant, flimsy, portable, slight, underweight **2** WEAK, faint, gentle, indistinct, mild, moderate, slight, soft **3** INSIGNIFICANT, inconsequential, inconsiderable, scanty, slight, small, trifling, trivial **4** NIMBLE, agile, graceful, lithe, sprightly, sylphlike **5** LIGHT-HEARTED, amusing, entertaining, frivolous, funny, humorous, witty **6** DIGESTIBLE, frugal, modest ▸ verb **7** SETTLE, alight, land, perch **8** light on *or* upon COME ACROSS, chance upon, discover, encounter, find, happen upon, hit upon, stumble on

lighten¹ verb BRIGHTEN, become light, illuminate, irradiate, light up

lighten² verb **1** EASE, allay, alleviate, ameliorate, assuage, lessen, mitigate, reduce, relieve **2** CHEER, brighten, buoy up, lift, perk up, revive

light-headed adjective FAINT, dizzy, giddy, hazy, vertiginous, woozy (*informal*)

light-hearted adjective CAREFREE, blithe, cheerful, happy-go-lucky, jolly, jovial, playful, upbeat (*informal*)

lightly adverb **1** GENTLY, delicately, faintly, slightly, softly **2** MODERATELY, sparingly, sparsely, thinly **3** EASILY, effortlessly, readily, simply **4** CARELESSLY, breezily, flippantly, frivolously, heedlessly, thoughtlessly

lightweight adjective UNIMPORTANT, inconsequential, insignificant, paltry, petty, slight, trifling, trivial, worthless

likable, likeable adjective ATTRACTIVE, agreeable, amiable, appealing, charming, engaging, nice, pleasant, sympathetic

like¹ adjective SIMILAR, akin, alike, analogous, corresponding, equivalent, identical, parallel, same

like² verb **1** ENJOY, be fond of, be keen on, be partial to, delight in, go for, love, relish, revel in **2** ADMIRE, appreciate, approve, cherish, esteem, hold dear, prize, take to **3** WISH, care to, choose, desire, fancy, feel inclined, prefer, want **4** *Informal* BE ATTRACTED TO, be captivated by, be turned on by (*informal*), lust after, take a liking to, take to

likelihood noun PROBABILITY, chance, possibility, prospect

likely adjective **1** INCLINED, apt, disposed, liable, prone, tending **2** PROBABLE, anticipated, expected, odds-on, on the cards, to be expected **3** PLAUSIBLE, believable, credible, feasible, possible, reasonable **4** PROMISING, hopeful, up-and-coming

liken verb COMPARE, equate, match, parallel, relate, set beside

likeness noun **1** RESEMBLANCE, affinity, correspondence, similarity **2** PORTRAIT, depiction, effigy, image, picture, representation

likewise adverb SIMILARLY, in like manner, in the same way

liking noun FONDNESS, affection, inclination, love, partiality, penchant, preference, soft spot, taste, weakness

limb noun **1** PART, appendage, arm, extremity, leg, member, wing **2** BRANCH, bough, offshoot, projection, spur

limelight noun PUBLICITY, attention, celebrity, fame, prominence, public eye, recognition, stardom, the spotlight

limit noun **1** BREAKING POINT, deadline, end, ultimate **2** BOUNDARY, border, edge, frontier, perimeter ▶ verb **3** RESTRICT, bound, check, circumscribe, confine, curb, ration, restrain

limitation noun RESTRICTION,

check, condition, constraint, control, curb, qualification, reservation, restraint

limited adjective RESTRICTED, bounded, checked, circumscribed, confined, constrained, controlled, curbed, finite

limitless adjective INFINITE, boundless, countless, endless, inexhaustible, unbounded, unlimited, untold, vast

limp^1 verb **1** HOBBLE, falter, hop, shamble, shuffle ▶ noun **2** LAMENESS, hobble

limp^2 adjective FLOPPY, drooping, flabby, flaccid, pliable, slack, soft

line noun **1** STROKE, band, groove, mark, score, scratch, streak, stripe **2** WRINKLE, crease, crow's foot, furrow, mark **3** BOUNDARY, border, borderline, edge, frontier, limit **4** STRING, cable, cord, rope, thread, wire **5** TRAJECTORY, course, direction, path, route, track **6** JOB, area, business, calling, employment, field, occupation, profession, specialization, trade **7** ROW, column, file, procession, queue, rank **8** in line for DUE FOR, in the running for ▶ verb **9** MARK, crease, furrow, rule, score **10** BORDER, bound, edge, fringe

lineaments plural noun FEATURES, countenance, face, physiognomy

lined adjective **1** RULED, feint **2** WRINKLED, furrowed, wizened, worn

lines plural noun WORDS, part, script

line-up noun ARRANGEMENT, array,

row, selection, team

linger verb 1 STAY, hang around, loiter, remain, stop, tarry, wait 2 DELAY, dally, dawdle, drag one's feet or heels, idle, take one's time

link noun 1 COMPONENT, constituent, element, member, part, piece 2 CONNECTION, affinity, association, attachment, bond, relationship, tie-up ▶ verb 3 FASTEN, attach, bind, connect, couple, join, tie, unite 4 ASSOCIATE, bracket, connect, identify, relate

lip noun 1 EDGE, brim, brink, margin, rim 2 Slang IMPUDENCE, backchat (informal), cheek (informal), effrontery, impertinence, insolence

liquid noun 1 FLUID, juice, solution ▶ adjective 2 FLUID, aqueous, flowing, melted, molten, running, runny 3 Of assets CONVERTIBLE, negotiable

liquidate verb 1 PAY, clear, discharge, honor, pay off, settle, square 2 DISSOLVE, abolish, annul, cancel, terminate 3 KILL, destroy, dispatch, eliminate, exterminate, get rid of, murder, wipe out (informal)

liquor noun 1 ALCOHOL, booze (informal), drink, hard stuff (informal), spirits, strong drink 2 JUICE, broth, extract, liquid, stock

list¹ noun 1 REGISTER, catalog, directory, index, inventory, record, roll, series, tally ▶ verb 2 TABULATE, catalog, enter, enumerate, itemize, record, register

list² verb 1 LEAN, careen, heel over, incline, tilt, tip ▶ noun 2 TILT, cant, leaning, slant

listen verb 1 HEAR, attend, lend an ear, prick up one's ears 2 PAY ATTENTION, heed, mind, obey, observe, take notice

listless adjective LANGUID, apathetic, indifferent, indolent, lethargic, sluggish

literacy noun EDUCATION, knowledge, learning

literal adjective 1 EXACT, accurate, close, faithful, strict, verbatim, word for word 2 ACTUAL, bona fide, genuine, plain, real, simple, true, unvarnished

literally adverb STRICTLY, actually, exactly, faithfully, precisely, really, to the letter, truly, verbatim, word for word

literary adjective WELL-READ, bookish, erudite, formal, learned, scholarly

literate adjective EDUCATED, informed, knowledgeable

literature noun WRITINGS, letters, lore

lithe adjective SUPPLE, flexible, limber, lissom(e), loose-limbed, pliable

litigant noun CLAIMANT, party, plaintiff

litigate verb SUE, go to court, press charges, prosecute

litigation noun LAWSUIT, action, case, prosecution

litter noun 1 RUBBISH, debris, detritus, garbage, muck, refuse, trash 2 BROOD, offspring, progeny, young ▶ verb 3 CLUTTER, derange, disarrange, disorder, mess up 4 SCATTER, strew

little *adjective* **1** SMALL, diminutive, miniature, minute, petite, short, tiny, wee **2** YOUNG, babyish, immature, infant, junior, undeveloped ▸ *adverb* **3** HARDLY, barely **4** RARELY, hardly ever, not often, scarcely, seldom ▸ *noun* **5** BIT, fragment, hint, particle, speck, spot, touch, trace

live[1] *verb* **1** EXIST, be, be alive, breathe **2** PERSIST, last, prevail **3** DWELL, abide, inhabit, lodge, occupy, reside, settle **4** SURVIVE, endure, get along, make ends meet, subsist, support oneself **5** THRIVE, flourish, prosper

live[2] *adjective* **1** LIVING, alive, animate, breathing **2** TOPICAL, burning, controversial, current, hot, pertinent, pressing, prevalent **3** BURNING, active, alight, blazing, glowing, hot, ignited, smoldering

livelihood *noun* OCCUPATION, bread and butter (*informal*), employment, job, living, work

liveliness *noun* ENERGY, animation, boisterousness, dynamism, spirit, sprightliness, vitality, vivacity

lively *adjective* **1** VIGOROUS, active, agile, alert, brisk, energetic, keen, perky, quick, sprightly **2** ANIMATED, cheerful, chirpy (*informal*), sparky, spirited, upbeat (*informal*), vivacious **3** VIVID, bright, colorful, exciting, forceful, invigorating, refreshing, stimulating

liven up *verb* STIR, animate, brighten, buck up (*informal*), enliven, perk up, rouse

liverish *adjective* **1** SICK, bilious,

queasy **2** IRRITABLE, crotchety, crusty, disagreeable, grumpy, ill-humored, irascible, splenetic, tetchy

livery *noun* COSTUME, attire, clothing, dress, garb, regalia, suit, uniform

livid *adjective* **1** *Informal* ANGRY, beside oneself, enraged, fuming, furious, incensed, indignant, infuriated, outraged **2** DISCOLORED, black-and-blue, bruised, contused, purple

living *adjective* **1** ALIVE, active, breathing, existing **2** CURRENT, active, contemporary, extant, in use ▸ *noun* **3** EXISTENCE, being, existing, life, subsistence **4** LIFE STYLE, way of life

load *noun* **1** CARGO, consignment, freight, shipment **2** BURDEN, albatross, encumbrance, millstone, onus, trouble, weight, worry ▸ *verb* **3** FILL, cram, freight, heap, pack, pile, stack, stuff **4** BURDEN, encumber, oppress, saddle with, weigh down, worry **5** *Of firearms* MAKE READY, charge, prime

loaded *adjective* **1** WEIGHTED, biased, distorted **2** TRICKY, artful, insidious, manipulative, prejudicial **3** *Slang* RICH, affluent, flush (*informal*), moneyed, wealthy, well-heeled (*informal*), well off, well-to-do

loaf[1] *noun* LUMP, block, cake, cube, slab

loaf[2] *verb* IDLE, laze, lie around, loiter, lounge around, take it easy

loan *noun* **1** ADVANCE, credit ▸ *verb* **2** LEND, advance, let out

loath, loth *adjective* UNWILLING,

averse, disinclined, opposed, reluctant

loathe verb HATE, abhor, abominate, despise, detest, dislike

loathing noun HATRED, abhorrence, antipathy, aversion, detestation, disgust, repugnance, repulsion, revulsion

loathsome adjective HATEFUL, abhorrent, detestable, disgusting, nauseating, obnoxious, odious, offensive, repugnant, repulsive, revolting, scuzzy (slang), vile

lobby noun 1 CORRIDOR, entrance hall, foyer, hallway, passage, porch, vestibule 2 PRESSURE GROUP ▶ verb 3 CAMPAIGN, influence, persuade, press, pressure, promote, push, urge

local adjective 1 REGIONAL, provincial 2 RESTRICTED, confined, limited ▶ noun 3 RESIDENT, inhabitant, native

locality noun 1 NEIGHBORHOOD, area, district, neck of the woods (informal), region, vicinity 2 SITE, locale, location, place, position, scene, setting, spot

localize verb RESTRICT, circumscribe, confine, contain, delimit, limit

locate verb 1 FIND, come across, detect, discover, pin down, pinpoint, track down, unearth 2 PLACE, establish, fix, put, seat, set, settle, situate

location noun POSITION, locale, place, point, site, situation, spot, venue

lock¹ noun 1 FASTENING, bolt,

clasp, padlock ▶ verb 2 FASTEN, bolt, close, seal, secure, shut 3 UNITE, clench, engage, entangle, entwine, join, link 4 EMBRACE, clasp, clutch, encircle, enclose, grasp, hug, press

lock² noun STRAND, curl, ringlet, tress, tuft

lockup noun PRISON, cell, jail

lock up verb IMPRISON, cage, confine, detain, incarcerate, jail, put behind bars, shut up

lodge noun 1 CABIN, chalet, cottage, gatehouse, hut, shelter 2 SOCIETY, branch, chapter, club, group ▶ verb 3 STAY, board, room 4 STICK, come to rest, imbed, implant 5 REGISTER, file, put on record, submit

lodger noun TENANT, boarder, paying guest, resident

lodging noun (often plural) ACCOMMODATION, abode, apartments, quarters, residence, rooms, shelter

lofty adjective 1 HIGH, elevated, raised, soaring, towering 2 NOBLE, dignified, distinguished, elevated, exalted, grand, illustrious, renowned 3 HAUGHTY, arrogant, condescending, disdainful, patronizing, proud, supercilious

log noun 1 STUMP, block, chunk, trunk 2 RECORD, account, journal, logbook ▶ verb 3 CHOP, cut, fell, hew 4 RECORD, chart, note, register, set down

loggerheads plural noun **at loggerheads** QUARRELING, at daggers drawn, at each other's throats, at odds, feuding, in dispute, opposed

logic noun REASON, good sense, sense

logical adjective **1** RATIONAL, clear, cogent, coherent, consistent, sound, valid, well-organized **2** REASONABLE, plausible, sensible, wise

loiter verb LINGER, dally, dawdle, dilly-dally (informal), hang about or around, idle, loaf, skulk

loll verb **1** LOUNGE, loaf, recline, relax, slouch, slump, sprawl **2** DROOP, dangle, drop, flap, flop, hang, sag

lone adjective SOLITARY, one, only, single, sole, unaccompanied

loneliness noun SOLITUDE, desolation, isolation, seclusion

lonely adjective **1** ABANDONED, destitute, forlorn, forsaken, friendless, lonesome **2** SOLITARY, alone, apart, companionless, isolated, lone, single, withdrawn **3** REMOTE, deserted, desolate, godforsaken, isolated, out-of-the-way, secluded, unfrequented, uninhabited

loner noun INDIVIDUALIST, lone wolf, maverick, outsider, recluse

lonesome adjective LONELY, companionless, desolate, dreary, forlorn, friendless, gloomy

long[1] adjective **1** ELONGATED, expanded, extended, extensive, far-reaching, lengthy, spread out, stretched **2** PROLONGED, interminable, lengthy, lingering, long-drawn-out, protracted, sustained

long[2] verb DESIRE, crave, hanker, itch, lust, pine, want, wish, yearn

longing noun DESIRE, ambition, aspiration, craving, hope, itch, thirst, urge, wish, yearning, yen (informal)

long-lived adjective LONG-LASTING, enduring

long shot noun OUTSIDER, dark horse

long-standing adjective ESTABLISHED, abiding, enduring, fixed, long-established, long-lasting, time-honored

long-suffering adjective UNCOMPLAINING, easy-going, forbearing, forgiving, patient, resigned, stoical, tolerant

long-winded adjective RAMBLING, lengthy, long-drawn-out, prolix, prolonged, repetitious, tedious, tiresome, verbose, wordy

look verb **1** SEE, contemplate, examine, eye, gaze, glance, observe, scan, study, survey, view, watch **2** SEEM, appear, look like, strike one as **3** FACE, front, overlook **4** HOPE, anticipate, await, expect, reckon on **5** SEARCH, forage, hunt, seek ▸ noun **6** VIEW, examination, gaze, glance, glimpse, inspection, observation, peek, sight **7** APPEARANCE, air, aspect, bearing, countenance, demeanor, expression, manner, semblance

look after verb TAKE CARE OF, attend to, care for, guard, keep an eye on, mind, nurse, protect, supervise, take charge of, tend

look down on verb DISDAIN, contemn, despise, scorn, sneer, spurn

look forward to verb ANTICIPATE, await, expect, hope for, long for, look for, wait for

lookout noun 1 VIGIL, guard, readiness, watch 2 WATCHMAN, guard, sentinel, sentry 3 WATCHTOWER, observation post, observatory, post

look out verb BE CAREFUL, beware, keep an eye out, pay attention, watch out

look up verb 1 RESEARCH, find, hunt for, search for, seek out, track down 2 IMPROVE, get better, perk up, pick up, progress, shape up (informal) 3 VISIT, call on, drop in on (informal), look in on 4 **look up to** RESPECT, admire, defer to, esteem, honor, revere

loom verb APPEAR, bulk, emerge, hover, impend, menace, take shape, threaten

loop noun 1 CURVE, circle, coil, curl, ring, spiral, twirl, twist, whorl ▶ verb 2 TWIST, coil, curl, knot, roll, spiral, turn, wind round

loophole noun LET-OUT, escape, excuse

loose adjective 1 UNTIED, free, insecure, unattached, unbound, unfastened, unfettered, unrestricted 2 SLACK, easy, relaxed, sloppy 3 VAGUE, ill-defined, imprecise, inaccurate, indistinct, inexact, rambling, random 4 PROMISCUOUS, abandoned, debauched, dissipated, dissolute, fast, immoral, profligate ▶ verb 5 FREE, detach, disconnect, liberate, release, set free, unfasten, unleash, untie

loosen verb 1 UNTIE, detach, separate, undo, unloose 2 FREE, liberate, release, set free 3 **loosen up** RELAX, ease up or off, go easy (informal), let up, soften

loot noun 1 PLUNDER, booty, goods, haul, prize, spoils, swag (slang) ▶ verb 2 PLUNDER, despoil, pillage, raid, ransack, ravage, rifle, rob, sack

lopsided adjective CROOKED, askew, asymmetrical, awry, cockeyed, disproportionate, squint, unbalanced, uneven, warped

lord noun 1 MASTER, commander, governor, leader, liege, overlord, ruler, superior 2 NOBLEMAN, earl, noble, peer, viscount 3 **Our Lord** or the **Lord** JESUS CHRIST, Christ, God, Jehovah, the Almighty ▶ verb 4 **lord it over** ORDER AROUND, boss around (informal), domineer, pull rank, put on airs, swagger

lordly adjective PROUD, arrogant, condescending, disdainful, domineering, haughty, high-handed, imperious, lofty, overbearing

lore noun TRADITIONS, beliefs, doctrine, sayings, teaching, wisdom

lose verb 1 MISLAY, be deprived of, drop, forget, misplace 2 FORFEIT, miss, pass up (informal), yield 3 BE DEFEATED, come to grief, lose out

loser noun 1 FAILURE, also-ran, dud (informal), flop (informal) 2 NERD, dork (slang), drip (informal), dweeb (slang), geek (slang)

loss noun 1 DEFEAT, failure, forfeiture, mislaying, squandering, waste 2 DAMAGE, cost, destruction, harm, hurt, injury, ruin 3 (sometimes plural) DEFICIT, debit, debt, deficiency, depletion 4 **at a loss** CONFUSED, at one's wits' end, baffled, bewildered, helpless, nonplussed, perplexed, puzzled, stumped

lost adjective 1 MISSING, disappeared, mislaid, misplaced, vanished, wayward 2 OFF-COURSE, adrift, astray, at sea, disoriented, off-track

lot noun 1 COLLECTION, assortment, batch, bunch (informal), consignment, crowd, group, quantity, set 2 DESTINY, accident, chance, doom, fate, fortune 3 **a lot** or **lots** PLENTY, abundance, a great deal, heap(s), masses (informal), piles (informal), scores, stack(s)

loth see LOATH

lotion noun CREAM, balm, embrocation, liniment, salve, solution

lottery noun 1 RAFFLE, drawing, sweepstakes 2 GAMBLE, chance, hazard, risk, toss-up (informal)

loud adjective 1 NOISY, blaring, booming, clamorous, deafening, ear-splitting, forte (Music), resounding, thundering, tumultuous, vociferous 2 GARISH, brash, flamboyant, flashy, gaudy, glaring, lurid, showy

loudly adverb NOISILY, deafeningly, fortissimo (Music), lustily, shrilly, uproariously, vehemently, vigorously,

vociferously

lounge verb RELAX, laze, lie about, loaf, loiter, loll, sprawl, take it easy

lousy adjective Informal CRUMMY, awful, crappy (slang), inadequate, inferior, shabby, shoddy, terrible

lout noun OAF, boor, dolt, lummox (informal)

lovable, loveable adjective ENDEARING, adorable, amiable, charming, cute, delightful, enchanting, likable or likeable, lovely, sweet

love verb 1 ADORE, cherish, dote on, hold dear, idolize, prize, treasure, worship 2 ENJOY, appreciate, delight in, like, relish, savor, take pleasure in ▶ noun 3 PASSION, adoration, affection, ardor, attachment, devotion, infatuation, tenderness, warmth 4 LIKING, devotion, enjoyment, fondness, inclination, partiality, relish, soft spot, taste, weakness 5 BELOVED, darling, dear, dearest, lover, sweetheart, truelove 6 **in love** ENAMORED, besotted, charmed, enraptured, infatuated, smitten

love affair noun ROMANCE, affair, amour, intrigue, liaison, relationship

lovely adjective 1 ATTRACTIVE, adorable, beautiful, charming, comely, exquisite, graceful, handsome, pretty 2 ENJOYABLE, agreeable, delightful, engaging, nice, pleasant, pleasing

lover noun SWEETHEART, admirer, beloved, boyfriend or girlfriend, flame (informal), mistress, suitor

loving *adjective* AFFECTIONATE, amorous, dear, devoted, doting, fond, tender, warm-hearted

low *adjective* **1** SMALL, little, short, squat, stunted **2** INFERIOR, deficient, inadequate, lousy (*slang*), poor, second-rate, shoddy **3** COARSE, common, crude, disreputable, rough, rude, undignified, vulgar **4** DEJECTED, depressed, despondent, disheartened, downcast, down in the dumps (*informal*), fed up, gloomy, glum, miserable **5** ILL, debilitated, frail, stricken, weak **6** QUIET, gentle, hushed, muffled, muted, soft, subdued, whispered

lowdown *noun Informal* INFORMATION, info (*informal*), inside story, intelligence

lower *adjective* **1** MINOR, inferior, junior, lesser, secondary, second-class, smaller, subordinate **2** REDUCED, curtailed, decreased, diminished, lessened ▶ *verb* **3** DROP, depress, fall, let down, sink, submerge, take down **4** LESSEN, cut, decrease, diminish, minimize, prune, reduce, slash

low-key *adjective* SUBDUED, muted, quiet, restrained, toned down, understated

lowly *adjective* HUMBLE, meek, mild, modest, unassuming

low-spirited *adjective* DEPRESSED, dejected, despondent, dismal, down, down-hearted, fed up, low, miserable, sad

loyal *adjective* FAITHFUL, constant, dependable, devoted, dutiful, staunch, steadfast, true, trustworthy, trusty, unwavering

loyalty *noun* FAITHFULNESS, allegiance, constancy, dependability, devotion, fidelity, staunchness, steadfastness, trustworthiness

lubricate *verb* OIL, grease, smear

lucid *adjective* **1** CLEAR, comprehensible, explicit, intelligible, transparent **2** TRANSLUCENT, clear, crystalline, diaphanous, glassy, limpid, pellucid, transparent **3** CLEAR-HEADED, all there, *compos mentis*, in one's right mind, rational, sane

luck *noun* **1** FORTUNE, accident, chance, destiny, fate **2** GOOD FORTUNE, advantage, blessing, godsend, prosperity, serendipity, success, windfall

luckily *adverb* FORTUNATELY, favorably, happily, opportunely, propitiously, providentially

luckless *adjective* ILL-FATED, cursed, doomed, hapless, hopeless, jinxed, unfortunate, unlucky

lucky *adjective* FORTUNATE, advantageous, blessed, charmed, favored, serendipitous, successful, win-win (*informal*)

lucrative *adjective* PROFITABLE, advantageous, fruitful, productive, remunerative, well-paid

lucre *noun* MONEY, gain, mammon, pelf, profit, riches, spoils, wealth

ludicrous *adjective* RIDICULOUS, absurd, crazy, farcical,

luggage *noun* BAGGAGE, bags, cases, gear, impedimenta, paraphernalia, suitcases, things

lugubrious *adjective* GLOOMY, doleful, melancholy, mournful, sad, serious, somber, sorrowful, woebegone

lukewarm *adjective* **1** TEPID, warm **2** HALF-HEARTED, apathetic, cool, indifferent, unenthusiastic, unresponsive

lull *verb* **1** CALM, allay, pacify, quell, soothe, subdue, tranquilize ▶ *noun* **2** RESPITE, calm, hush, let-up (*informal*), pause, quiet, silence

lumber *verb* PLOD, clump, shamble, shuffle, stump, trudge, trundle, waddle

lumbering *adjective* AWKWARD, clumsy, heavy, hulking, ponderous, ungainly

luminous *adjective* BRIGHT, glowing, illuminated, luminescent, lustrous, radiant, shining

lump *noun* **1** PIECE, ball, chunk, hunk, mass, nugget **2** SWELLING, bulge, bump, growth, hump, protrusion, tumor ▶ *verb* **3** GROUP, collect, combine, conglomerate, consolidate, mass, pool

lumpy *adjective* BUMPY, knobbly, uneven

lunacy *noun* **1** INSANITY, dementia, derangement, madness, mania, psychosis **2** FOOLISHNESS, absurdity, craziness, folly, foolhardiness, madness, stupidity

lunatic *adjective* **1** IRRATIONAL, bonkers (*informal*),

crackbrained (*informal*), crackpot (*informal*), crazy, daft, deranged, insane, mad ▶ *noun* **2** MADMAN, maniac, nutcase (*slang*), psychopath

lunge *noun* **1** THRUST, charge, jab, pounce, spring, swing ▶ *verb* **2** POUNCE, charge, dive, leap, plunge, thrust

lurch *verb* **1** TILT, heave, heel, lean, list, pitch, rock, roll **2** STAGGER, reel, stumble, sway, totter, weave

lure *verb* **1** TEMPT, allure, attract, draw, ensnare, entice, invite, seduce ▶ *noun* **2** TEMPTATION, allurement, attraction, bait, carrot (*informal*), enticement, incentive, inducement

lurid *adjective* **1** SENSATIONAL, graphic, melodramatic, shocking, vivid **2** GLARING, intense

lurk *verb* HIDE, conceal oneself, lie in wait, prowl, skulk, slink, sneak

luscious *adjective* DELICIOUS, appetizing, juicy, mouth-watering, palatable, succulent, sweet, toothsome, yummy (*informal*)

lush *adjective* **1** ABUNDANT, dense, flourishing, green, rank, verdant **2** LUXURIOUS, elaborate, extravagant, grand, lavish, opulent, ornate, palatial, plush (*informal*), sumptuous

lust *noun* **1** LECHERY, lasciviousness, lewdness, sensuality **2** APPETITE, craving, desire, greed, longing, passion, thirst ▶ *verb* **3** DESIRE, covet, crave, hunger for or after, want, yearn

luster *noun* **1** SPARKLE, gleam,

glint, glitter, gloss, glow, sheen, shimmer, shine **2** GLORY, distinction, fame, honor, kudos, prestige, renown

lusty adjective VIGOROUS, energetic, healthy, hearty, powerful, robust, strong, sturdy, virile

luxurious adjective SUMPTUOUS, comfortable, expensive, lavish, magnificent, opulent, plush (informal), rich, splendid

luxury noun **1** OPULENCE, affluence, hedonism, richness, splendor, sumptuousness **2** EXTRAVAGANCE, extra, frill, indulgence, treat

lying noun **1** DISHONESTY, deceit, mendacity, perjury, untruthfulness ▶ adjective **2** DECEITFUL, dishonest, false, mendacious, perfidious, treacherous, two-faced, untruthful

lyrical adjective ENTHUSIASTIC, effusive, impassioned, inspired, poetic, rhapsodic

M m

macabre adjective GRUESOME, dreadful, eerie, frightening, ghastly, ghostly, ghoulish, grim, grisly, morbid

machiavellian adjective SCHEMING, astute, crafty, cunning, cynical, double-dealing, opportunist, sly, underhand, unscrupulous

machine noun **1** APPLIANCE, apparatus, contraption, contrivance, device, engine,

instrument, mechanism, tool **2** SYSTEM, machinery, organization, setup (informal), structure

machinery noun EQUIPMENT, apparatus, gear, instruments, tackle, tools

macho adjective MANLY, chauvinist, macho, masculine, virile

mad adjective **1** INSANE, crazy (informal), demented, deranged, non compos mentis, nuts (slang), of unsound mind, out of one's mind, psychotic, raving, unhinged, unstable **2** FOOLISH, absurd, asinine, bonkers (informal), daft (informal), foolhardy, irrational, nonsensical, preposterous, senseless, wild **3** ANGRY, berserk, enraged, furious, incensed, livid (informal), wild **4** ENTHUSIASTIC, ardent, avid, crazy (informal), fanatical, impassioned, infatuated, wild **5** FRENZIED, excited, frenetic, uncontrolled, unrestrained, wild, wired (slang) **6 like mad** Informal ENERGETICALLY, enthusiastically, excitedly, furiously, rapidly, speedily, violently, wildly

madden verb INFURIATE, annoy, derange, drive one crazy, enrage, incense, inflame, irritate, upset

madly adverb **1** INSANELY, crazily, deliriously, distractedly, frantically, frenziedly, hysterically **2** FOOLISHLY, absurdly, irrationally, ludicrously, senselessly, wildly **3** ENERGETICALLY, excitedly, furiously, like mad (informal), recklessly, speedily, wildly **4** Informal PASSIONATELY, desperately, devotedly, intensely, to distraction

madman or **madwoman** noun LUNATIC, maniac, nutcase (slang), psycho (slang), psychopath

madness noun 1 INSANITY, aberration, craziness, delusion, dementia, derangement, distraction, lunacy, mania, mental illness, psychopathy, psychosis 2 FOOLISHNESS, absurdity, daftness (informal), folly, foolhardiness, idiocy, nonsense, preposterousness, wildness

maelstrom noun 1 WHIRLPOOL, vortex 2 TURMOIL, chaos, confusion, disorder, tumult, upheaval

maestro noun MASTER, expert, genius, virtuoso

magazine noun 1 JOURNAL, pamphlet, periodical 2 STOREHOUSE, arsenal, depot, store, warehouse

magic noun 1 SORCERY, black art, enchantment, necromancy, witchcraft, wizardry 2 CONJURING, illusion, legerdemain, prestidigitation, sleight of hand, trickery 3 CHARM, allurement, enchantment, fascination, glamour, magnetism, power ▶ adjective 4 Also **magical** MIRACULOUS, bewitching, charming, enchanting, entrancing, fascinating, marvelous, spellbinding

magician noun SORCERER, conjurer, enchanter or enchantress, illusionist, necromancer, warlock, witch, wizard

magisterial adjective AUTHORITATIVE, commanding, lordly, masterful

magistrate noun JUDGE, J.P., justice, justice of the peace

magnanimity noun GENEROSITY, benevolence, big-heartedness, largesse or largess, nobility, selflessness, unselfishness

magnanimous adjective GENEROUS, big-hearted, bountiful, charitable, kind, noble, selfless, unselfish

magnate noun TYCOON, baron, captain of industry, mogul, plutocrat

magnetic adjective ATTRACTIVE, captivating, charismatic, charming, fascinating, hypnotic, irresistible, mesmerizing, seductive

magnetism noun CHARM, allure, appeal, attraction, charisma, drawing power, magic, pull, seductiveness

magnification noun INCREASE, amplification, enhancement, enlargement, expansion, heightening, intensification

magnificence noun SPLENDOR, brilliance, glory, grandeur, majesty, nobility, opulence, stateliness, sumptuousness

magnificent adjective 1 SPLENDID, cool (informal), glorious, gorgeous, imposing, impressive, majestic, regal, sublime, sumptuous 2 EXCELLENT, brilliant, fine, outstanding, phat (slang), splendid, superb

magnify verb 1 ENLARGE, amplify, blow up (informal), boost, dilate, expand, heighten, increase, intensify 2 OVERSTATE, exaggerate, inflate, overemphasize, overplay

magnitude noun **1** IMPORTANCE, consequence, greatness, moment, note, significance, weight **2** SIZE, amount, amplitude, extent, mass, quantity, volume

maid noun **1** GIRL, damsel, lass, maiden, wench **2** SERVANT, housemaid, maidservant, serving-maid

maiden noun **1** GIRL, damsel, lass, maid, virgin, wench ▶ adjective **2** UNMARRIED, unwed **3** FIRST, inaugural, initial, introductory

maidenly adjective MODEST, chaste, decent, decorous, demure, pure, virginal

mail noun **1** LETTERS, correspondence, junk mail, post (chiefly Brit.) **2** POSTAL SERVICE, collection, delivery, post office ▶ verb **3** POST, dispatch, forward, send, transmit

maim verb CRIPPLE, disable, hurt, injure, mutilate, wound

main adjective **1** CHIEF, central, essential, foremost, head, leading, pre-eminent, primary, principal ▶ noun **2** CONDUIT, cable, channel, duct, line, pipe **3 in the main** ON THE WHOLE, for the most part, generally, in general, mainly, mostly

mainly adverb CHIEFLY, for the most part, in the main, largely, mostly, on the whole, predominantly, primarily, principally

mainstay noun PILLAR, anchor, backbone, bulwark, buttress, lynchpin, prop

mainstream adjective

CONVENTIONAL, accepted, current, established, general, orthodox, prevailing, received

maintain verb **1** KEEP UP, carry on, continue, perpetuate, preserve, prolong, retain, sustain **2** SUPPORT, care for, look after, provide for, supply, take care of **3** ASSERT, avow, claim, contend, declare, insist, profess, state

maintenance noun **1** CONTINUATION, carrying-on, perpetuation, prolongation **2** UPKEEP, care, conservation, keeping, nurture, preservation, repairs **3** ALLOWANCE, alimony, keep, support

majestic adjective GRAND, grandiose, impressive, magnificent, monumental, regal, splendid, stately, sublime, superb

majesty noun GRANDEUR, glory, magnificence, nobility, pomp, splendor, stateliness

major adjective **1** MAIN, bigger, chief, greater, higher, leading, senior, supreme **2** IMPORTANT, critical, crucial, great, notable, outstanding, serious, significant

majority noun **1** PREPONDERANCE, best part, bulk, greater number, mass, most **2** ADULTHOOD, manhood or womanhood, maturity, seniority

make verb **1** CREATE, assemble, build, construct, fashion, form, manufacture, produce, put together, synthesize **2** PRODUCE, accomplish, bring about, cause, create, effect, generate, give rise to, lead to **3** FORCE, cause, compel, constrain, drive, impel, induce, oblige, prevail upon, require **4** AMOUNT TO, add up to, compose, constitute, form **5** PERFORM, carry out, do, effect, execute **6** EARN, clear, gain, get, net, obtain, win **7 make it** *Informal* SUCCEED, arrive (*informal*), get on, prosper ▸ *noun* **8** BRAND, kind, model, sort, style, type, variety

make-believe *noun* FANTASY, imagination, play-acting, pretense, unreality

make for *verb* HEAD FOR, aim for, be bound for, head towards

make off *verb* **1** FLEE, bolt, clear out (*informal*), run away or off, take to one's heels **2 make off with** STEAL, abduct, carry off, filch, kidnap, pinch (*informal*), run away or off with

make out *verb* **1** SEE, detect, discern, discover, distinguish, perceive, recognize **2** UNDERSTAND, comprehend, decipher, fathom, follow, grasp, work out **3** WRITE OUT, complete, draw up, fill in or out **4** PRETEND, assert, claim, let on, make as if or though **5** FARE, get on, manage

maker *noun* MANUFACTURER, builder, constructor, producer

makeshift *adjective* TEMPORARY, expedient, provisional, stopgap, substitute

make-up *noun* **1** COSMETICS, face (*informal*), greasepaint (*Theatre*), paint (*informal*), powder **2** STRUCTURE, arrangement, assembly, composition, configuration, constitution, construction, format, organization **3** NATURE, character, constitution,

disposition, temperament

make up *verb* **1** FORM, compose, comprise, constitute **2** INVENT, coin, compose, concoct, construct, create, devise, dream up, formulate, frame, originate **3** COMPLETE, fill, supply **4** SETTLE, bury the hatchet, call it quits, reconcile **5 make up for** COMPENSATE FOR, atone for, balance, make amends for, offset, recompense

making *noun* CREATION, assembly, building, composition, construction, fabrication, manufacture, production

makings *plural noun* BEGINNINGS, capacity, ingredients, potential

maladjusted *adjective* DISTURBED, alienated, neurotic, unstable

maladministration *noun* MISMANAGEMENT, corruption, dishonesty, incompetence, inefficiency, malpractice, misrule

maladroit *adjective* CLUMSY, awkward, inept, inexpert, unskillful

malady *noun* DISEASE, affliction, ailment, complaint, disorder, illness, infirmity, sickness

malaise *noun* UNEASE, anxiety, depression, disquiet, melancholy

malcontent *noun* TROUBLEMAKER, agitator, mischief-maker, rebel, stirrer (*informal*)

male *adjective* MASCULINE, manly, virile

malefactor *noun* WRONGDOER, criminal, delinquent, evildoer, miscreant, offender, villain

malevolence *noun* MALICE, hate, hatred, ill will, rancor, spite, vindictiveness

malevolent *adjective* SPITEFUL, hostile, ill-natured, malicious, malign, vengeful, vindictive

malformation *noun* DEFORMITY, distortion, misshapenness

malformed *adjective* MISSHAPEN, abnormal, crooked, deformed, distorted, irregular, twisted

malfunction *verb* 1 BREAK DOWN, fail, go wrong ▶ *noun* 2 FAULT, breakdown, defect, failure, flaw, glitch

malice *noun* ILL WILL, animosity, enmity, evil intent, hate, hatred, malevolence, spite, vindictiveness

malicious *adjective* SPITEFUL, ill-disposed, ill-natured, malevolent, rancorous, resentful, vengeful

malign *verb* 1 DISPARAGE, abuse, defame, denigrate, libel, run down, slander, smear, vilify ▶ *adjective* 2 EVIL, bad, destructive, harmful, hostile, injurious, malevolent, malignant, pernicious, wicked

malignant *adjective* 1 HARMFUL, destructive, hostile, hurtful, malevolent, malign, pernicious, spiteful 2 *Medical* UNCONTROLLABLE, cancerous, dangerous, deadly, fatal, irremediable

malleable *adjective* 1 WORKABLE, ductile, plastic, soft, tensile 2 MANAGEABLE, adaptable, biddable, compliant, impressionable, pliable, tractable

malodorous *adjective* SMELLY, fetid, funky (*slang*), mephitic, nauseating, noisome, offensive, putrid, reeking, stinking

malpractice *noun* MISCONDUCT, abuse, dereliction, mismanagement, negligence

maltreat *verb* ABUSE, bully, harm, hurt, ill-treat, injure, mistreat

mammoth *adjective* COLOSSAL, enormous, giant, gigantic, huge, immense, massive, monumental, mountainous, prodigious

man *noun* 1 MALE, chap (*informal*), dude (*informal*), gentleman, guy (*informal*) 2 HUMAN, human being, individual, person, soul 3 MANKIND, Homo sapiens, humanity, humankind, human race, people 4 MANSERVANT, attendant, retainer, servant, valet ▶ *verb* 5 STAFF, crew, garrison, occupy, people

manacle *noun* 1 HANDCUFF, bond, chain, fetter, iron, shackle ▶ *verb* 2 HANDCUFF, bind, chain, fetter, put in chains, shackle

manage *verb* 1 ADMINISTER, be in charge (of), command, conduct, direct, handle, run, supervise 2 SUCCEED, accomplish, arrange, contrive, effect, engineer 3 HANDLE, control, manipulate, operate, use 4 COPE, carry on, get by (*informal*), make do, muddle through, survive

manageable *adjective* DOCILE, amenable, compliant, easy, submissive

management *noun* 1 DIRECTORS, administration, board, employers, executive(s) 2 ADMINISTRATION, command, control, direction, handling, operation, running, supervision

manager noun SUPERVISOR, administrator, boss (informal), director, executive, governor, head, organizer

mandate noun COMMAND, commission, decree, directive, edict, instruction, order

mandatory adjective COMPULSORY, binding, obligatory, required, requisite

maneuver noun 1 STRATAGEM, dodge, intrigue, machination, ploy, ruse, scheme, subterfuge, tactic, trick 2 MOVEMENT, exercise, operation ▶ verb 3 MANIPULATE, contrive, engineer, machinate, pull strings, scheme, wangle (informal) 4 MOVE, deploy, exercise

manfully adverb BRAVELY, boldly, courageously, determinedly, gallantly, hard, resolutely, stoutly, valiantly

mangle verb CRUSH, deform, destroy, disfigure, distort, mutilate, ruin, spoil, tear, wreck

mangy adjective DIRTY, moth-eaten, scuzzy (slang), seedy, shabby, shoddy, squalid

manhandle verb ROUGH UP, knock about or around, maul, paw (informal)

manhood noun MANLINESS, masculinity, virility

mania noun 1 MADNESS, delirium, dementia, derangement, insanity, lunacy 2 OBSESSION, craze, fad (informal), fetish, fixation, passion, preoccupation, thing (informal)

maniac noun 1 MADMAN or MADWOMAN, lunatic, psycho (slang), psychopath 2 FANATIC,

enthusiast, fan, fiend (informal), freak (informal)

manifest adjective 1 OBVIOUS, apparent, blatant, clear, conspicuous, evident, glaring, noticeable, palpable, patent ▶ verb 2 DISPLAY, demonstrate, exhibit, expose, express, reveal, show

manifestation noun DISPLAY, demonstration, exhibition, expression, indication, mark, show, sign, symptom

manifold adjective NUMEROUS, assorted, copious, diverse, many, multifarious, multiple, varied, various

manipulate verb 1 WORK, handle, operate, use 2 INFLUENCE, control, direct, engineer, maneuver

mankind noun PEOPLE, Homo sapiens, humanity, humankind, human race, man

manliness noun VIRILITY, boldness, bravery, courage, fearlessness, masculinity, valor, vigor

manly adjective VIRILE, bold, brave, courageous, fearless, manful, masculine, strapping, strong, vigorous

man-made adjective ARTIFICIAL, ersatz, manufactured, mock, synthetic

manner noun 1 BEHAVIOR, air, aspect, bearing, conduct, demeanor 2 STYLE, custom, fashion, method, mode, way 3 TYPE, brand, category, form, kind, sort, variety

mannered adjective AFFECTED, artificial, pretentious, stilted

mannerism noun HABIT, characteristic, foible,

idiosyncrasy, peculiarity, quirk, trait, trick

manners *plural noun* **1** BEHAVIOR, conduct, demeanor **2** POLITENESS, courtesy, decorum, etiquette, p's and q's, refinement

mansion *noun* RESIDENCE, hall, manor, seat, villa

mantle *noun* **1** CLOAK, cape, hood, shawl, wrap **2** COVERING, blanket, canopy, curtain, pall, screen, shroud, veil

manual *adjective* **1** HAND-OPERATED, human, physical ▶ *noun* **2** HANDBOOK, bible, instructions

manufacture *verb* **1** MAKE, assemble, build, construct, create, mass-produce, produce, put together, turn out **2** CONCOCT, cook up (*informal*), devise, fabricate, invent, make up, think up, trump up ▶ *noun* **3** MAKING, assembly, construction, creation, production

manufacturer *noun* MAKER, builder, constructor, creator, industrialist, producer

manure *noun* COMPOST, droppings, dung, excrement, fertilizer, muck, ordure

many *adjective* **1** NUMEROUS, abundant, countless, innumerable, manifold, myriad, umpteen (*informal*), various ▶ *noun* **2** A LOT, heaps (*informal*), lots (*informal*), plenty, scores

mar *verb* SPOIL, blemish, damage, detract from, disfigure, hurt, impair, ruin, scar, stain, taint, tarnish

maraud *verb* RAID, forage, loot, pillage, plunder, ransack, ravage

marauder *noun* RAIDER, bandit, buccaneer, outlaw, plunderer

march *verb* **1** WALK, file, pace, parade, stride, strut ▶ *noun* **2** WALK, routemarch, trek **3** PROGRESS, advance, development, evolution, progression

margin *noun* EDGE, border, boundary, brink, perimeter, periphery, rim, side, verge

marginal *adjective* **1** BORDERLINE, bordering, on the edge, peripheral **2** INSIGNIFICANT, minimal, minor, negligible, slight, small

marijuana *noun* CANNABIS, dope (*slang*), grass (*slang*), hemp, pot (*slang*)

marine *adjective* NAUTICAL, maritime, naval, seafaring, seagoing

mariner *noun* SAILOR, salt, sea dog, seafarer, seaman

marital *adjective* MATRIMONIAL, conjugal, connubial, nuptial

maritime *adjective* **1** NAUTICAL, marine, naval, oceanic, seafaring **2** COASTAL, littoral, seaside

mark *noun* **1** SPOT, blemish, blot, line, scar, scratch, smudge, stain, streak **2** SIGN, badge, device, emblem, flag, hallmark, label, symbol, token **3** CRITERION, measure, norm, standard, yardstick **4** TARGET, aim, goal, object, objective, purpose ▶ *verb* **5** SCAR, blemish, blot, scratch, smudge, stain, streak **6** CHARACTERIZE, brand, flag, identify, label, stamp **7** DISTINGUISH, denote, exemplify, illustrate, show

8 OBSERVE, attend, mind, note, notice, pay attention, pay heed, watch **9** GRADE, appraise, assess, correct, evaluate

marked adjective NOTICEABLE, blatant, clear, conspicuous, decided, distinct, obvious, patent, prominent, pronounced, striking

markedly adverb NOTICEABLY, clearly, considerably, conspicuously, decidedly, distinctly, obviously, strikingly

market noun **1** FAIR, bazaar, mart ▶ verb **2** SELL, retail, vend

marketable adjective SOUGHT AFTER, in demand, salable, wanted

marksman, markswoman noun SHARPSHOOTER, crack shot (informal), good shot

maroon verb ABANDON, desert, leave, leave high and dry (informal), strand

marriage noun WEDDING, match, matrimony, nuptials, wedlock

marry verb **1** WED, get hitched (slang), tie the knot (informal) **2** UNITE, ally, bond, join, knit, link, merge, unify, yoke

marsh noun SWAMP, bog, fen, morass, quagmire, slough

marshal verb **1** ARRANGE, align, array, deploy, draw up, group, line up, order, organize **2** CONDUCT, escort, guide, lead, shepherd, usher

marshy adjective SWAMPY, boggy, quaggy, waterlogged, wet

martial adjective MILITARY, bellicose, belligerent, warlike

martinet noun DISCIPLINARIAN, stickler

martyrdom noun PERSECUTION,

ordeal, suffering

marvel verb **1** WONDER, be amazed, be awed, gape ▶ noun **2** WONDER, miracle, phenomenon, portent, prodigy

marvelous adjective **1** AMAZING, astonishing, astounding, breathtaking, brilliant, extraordinary, miraculous, phenomenal, prodigious, spectacular, stupendous **2** EXCELLENT, fabulous (informal), fantastic (informal), great (informal), splendid, superb, terrific (informal), wonderful

masculine adjective MALE, manlike, manly, mannish, virile

mask noun **1** DISGUISE, camouflage, cover, façade, front, guise, screen, veil ▶ verb **2** DISGUISE, camouflage, cloak, conceal, cover, hide, obscure, screen, veil

masquerade noun **1** MASKED BALL, fancy dress party, revel **2** PRETENSE, cloak, cover-up, deception, disguise, mask, pose, screen, subterfuge ▶ verb **3** POSE, disguise, dissemble, dissimulate, impersonate, pass oneself off, pretend (to be)

mass noun **1** PIECE, block, chunk, hunk, lump **2** LOT, bunch, collection, heap, load, pile, quantity, stack **3** SIZE, bulk, greatness, magnitude ▶ adjective **4** LARGE-SCALE, extensive, general, indiscriminate, wholesale, widespread ▶ verb **5** GATHER, accumulate, assemble, collect, congregate, rally, swarm, throng

massacre noun **1** SLAUGHTER, annihilation, blood bath,

butchery, carnage,
extermination, holocaust,
murder ▶ verb 2 SLAUGHTER,
butcher, cut to pieces,
exterminate, kill, mow down,
murder, wipe out

massage noun 1 RUB-DOWN,
manipulation ▶ verb 2 RUB
DOWN, knead, manipulate

massive adjective HUGE, big,
colossal, enormous, gigantic,
hefty, immense, mammoth,
monumental, whopping
(informal)

master noun 1 RULER, boss
(informal), chief, commander,
controller, director, governor,
lord, manager 2 EXPERT, ace
(informal), doyen, genius,
maestro, past master, virtuoso,
wizard 3 TEACHER, guide, guru,
instructor, tutor ▶ adjective
4 MAIN, chief, foremost,
leading, predominant, prime,
principal ▶ verb 5 LEARN, get the
hang of (informal), grasp
6 OVERCOME, conquer, defeat,
tame, triumph over, vanquish

masterful adjective 1 SKILLFUL,
adroit, consummate, expert,
fine, first-rate, masterly,
superlative, supreme,
world-class 2 DOMINEERING,
arrogant, bossy (informal),
high-handed, imperious,
overbearing, overweening

masterly adjective SKILLFUL,
adroit, consummate, crack
(slang), expert, first-rate,
masterful, supreme, world-class

mastermind verb 1 PLAN,
conceive, devise, direct,
manage, organize ▶ noun
2 ORGANIZER, architect, brain(s)
(informal), director, engineer,
manager, planner

masterpiece noun CLASSIC,
jewel, magnum opus, pièce de
résistance, tour de force

mastery noun 1 EXPERTISE,
finesse, know-how (informal),
proficiency, prowess, skill,
virtuosity 2 CONTROL,
ascendancy, command,
domination, superiority,
supremacy, upper hand, whip
hand

match noun 1 GAME, bout,
competition, contest,
head-to-head, test, trial
2 EQUAL, counterpart, peer, rival
3 MARRIAGE, alliance, pairing,
partnership ▶ verb 4 CORRESPOND,
accord, agree, fit, go with,
harmonize, tally 5 RIVAL,
compare, compete, emulate,
equal, measure up to

matching adjective IDENTICAL,
coordinating, corresponding,
equivalent, like, twin

matchless adjective UNEQUALED,
incomparable, inimitable,
superlative, supreme,
unmatched, unparalleled,
unrivaled, unsurpassed

mate noun 1 PARTNER, husband
or wife, spouse 2 COLLEAGUE,
associate, companion
3 ASSISTANT, helper, subordinate
▶ verb 4 PAIR, breed, couple

material noun 1 SUBSTANCE,
matter, stuff 2 INFORMATION,
data, evidence, facts, notes
3 CLOTH, fabric ▶ adjective
4 PHYSICAL, bodily, concrete,
corporeal, palpable,
substantial, tangible
5 IMPORTANT, essential,
meaningful, momentous,
serious, significant, vital,
weighty 6 RELEVANT, applicable,
apposite, apropos, germane,

pertinent

materialize verb OCCUR, appear, come about, come to pass, happen, take shape, turn up

materially adverb SIGNIFICANTLY, essentially, gravely, greatly, much, seriously, substantially

maternal adjective MOTHERLY

maternity noun MOTHERHOOD, motherliness

matrimonial adjective MARITAL, conjugal, connubial, nuptial

matrimony noun MARRIAGE, nuptials, wedding ceremony, wedlock

matted adjective TANGLED, knotted, tousled, uncombed

matter noun 1 SUBSTANCE, body, material, stuff 2 SITUATION, affair, business, concern, event, incident, proceeding, question, subject, topic 3 As in **what's the matter?** PROBLEM, complication, difficulty, distress, trouble, worry ▶ verb 4 BE IMPORTANT, carry weight, count, make a difference, signify

matter-of-fact adjective UNSENTIMENTAL, deadpan, down-to-earth, emotionless, mundane, plain, prosaic, sober, unimaginative

mature adjective 1 GROWN-UP, adult, full-grown, fully fledged, mellow, of age, ready, ripe, seasoned ▶ verb 2 DEVELOP, age, bloom, blossom, come of age, grow up, mellow, ripen

maturity noun ADULTHOOD, experience, manhood or womanhood, ripeness, wisdom

maudlin adjective SENTIMENTAL, mawkish, overemotional, slushy (informal), tearful,

weepy (informal)

maul verb 1 ILL-TREAT, abuse, manhandle, molest, paw 2 TEAR, batter, claw, lacerate, mangle

maverick noun 1 REBEL, dissenter, eccentric, heretic, iconoclast, individualist, nonconformist, protester, radical ▶ adjective 2 REBEL, dissenting, eccentric, heretical, iconoclastic, individualistic, nonconformist, radical

mawkish adjective SENTIMENTAL, emotional, maudlin, schmaltzy (slang), slushy (informal)

maxim noun SAYING, adage, aphorism, axiom, dictum, motto, proverb, rule

maximum noun 1 TOP, ceiling, height, peak, pinnacle, summit, upper limit, utmost, zenith ▶ adjective 2 GREATEST, highest, most, paramount, supreme, topmost, utmost

maybe adverb PERHAPS, perchance (archaic), possibly

mayhem noun CHAOS, commotion, confusion, destruction, disorder, fracas, havoc, trouble, violence

maze noun 1 LABYRINTH 2 WEB, confusion, imbroglio, tangle

meadow noun FIELD, grassland, lea (poetic), pasture

meager adjective INSUBSTANTIAL, inadequate, lousy (slang), measly, paltry, poor, puny, scanty, slight, small

meal noun Informal FEAST, feed, repast, spread (informal)

mean¹ verb 1 SIGNIFY, convey, denote, express, imply, indicate, represent, spell, stand for, symbolize 2 INTEND, aim, aspire, design, desire, plan, set out, want, wish

mean[2] adjective **1** MISERLY, mercenary, niggardly, parsimonious, penny-pinching, stingy, tight-fisted, ungenerous **2** DESPICABLE, callous, contemptible, hard-hearted, lousy (slang), petty, scuzzy (slang), shabby, shameful, sordid, vile

mean[3] noun **1** AVERAGE, balance, compromise, happy medium, middle, midpoint, norm ▸adjective **2** AVERAGE, middle, standard

meander verb **1** WIND, snake, turn, zigzag **2** WANDER, ramble, stroll ▸noun **3** CURVE, bend, coil, loop, turn, twist, zigzag

meaning noun SENSE, connotation, drift, gist, message, significance, substance

meaningful adjective SIGNIFICANT, important, material, purposeful, relevant, useful, valid, worthwhile

meaningless adjective POINTLESS, empty, futile, inane, inconsequential, insignificant, senseless, useless, vain, worthless

meanness noun **1** MISERLINESS, niggardliness, parsimony, selfishness, stinginess **2** PETTINESS, disgracefulness, ignobility, narrow-mindedness, shabbiness, shamefulness

means plural noun **1** METHOD, agency, instrument, medium, mode, process, way **2** MONEY, affluence, capital, fortune, funds, income, resources, wealth, wherewithal **3** by all

means CERTAINLY, definitely, doubtlessly, of course, surely **4 by no means** IN NO WAY, definitely not, not in the least, on no account

meantime, meanwhile adverb AT THE SAME TIME, concurrently, in the interim, simultaneously

measly adjective MEAGER, miserable, paltry, pathetic, pitiful, poor, puny, scanty, skimpy

measurable adjective QUANTIFIABLE, assessable, perceptible, significant

measure noun **1** QUANTITY, allotment, allowance, amount, portion, quota, ration, share **2** GAUGE, meter, rule, scale, yardstick **3** ACTION, act, deed, expedient, maneuver, means, procedure, step **4** LAW, act, bill, resolution, statute **5** RHYTHM, beat, cadence, meter, verse ▸verb **6** QUANTIFY, assess, calculate, calibrate, compute, determine, evaluate, gauge, weigh

measured adjective **1** STEADY, dignified, even, leisurely, regular, sedate, slow, solemn, stately, unhurried **2** CONSIDERED, calculated, deliberate, reasoned, sober, studied, well-thought-out

measurement noun CALCULATION, assessment, calibration, computation, evaluation, mensuration, valuation

measure up to verb FULFILL THE EXPECTATIONS, be equal to, be suitable, come up to scratch (informal), fit or fill the bill, make the grade (informal)

meat noun FLESH

meaty adjective **1** BRAWNY, beefy (informal), burly, heavily built, heavy, muscular, solid, strapping, sturdy **2** INTERESTING, meaningful, profound, rich, significant, substantial

mechanical adjective **1** AUTOMATIC, automated **2** UNTHINKING, automatic, cursory, impersonal, instinctive, involuntary, perfunctory, routine, unfeeling

mechanism noun **1** MACHINE, apparatus, appliance, contrivance, device, instrument, tool **2** PROCESS, agency, means, method, operation, procedure, system, technique

meddle verb INTERFERE, butt in, intervene, intrude, pry, tamper

meddlesome adjective INTERFERING, intrusive, meddling, mischievous, officious, prying

mediate verb INTERVENE, arbitrate, conciliate, intercede, reconcile, referee, step in (informal), umpire

mediation noun ARBITRATION, conciliation, intercession, intervention, reconciliation

mediator noun NEGOTIATOR, arbiter, arbitrator, go-between, honest broker, intermediary, middleman, peacemaker, referee, umpire

medicinal adjective THERAPEUTIC, curative, healing, medical, remedial, restorative

medicine noun REMEDY, cure, drug, medicament, medication, nostrum

mediocre adjective SECOND-RATE, average, indifferent, inferior, middling, ordinary, passable, pedestrian, so-so (informal), undistinguished

mediocrity noun INSIGNIFICANCE, indifference, inferiority, ordinariness, unimportance

meditate verb **1** REFLECT, cogitate, consider, contemplate, deliberate, muse, ponder, ruminate, think **2** PLAN, have in mind, intend, purpose, scheme

meditation noun REFLECTION, cogitation, contemplation, musing, pondering, rumination, study, thought

medium adjective **1** MIDDLE, average, fair, intermediate, mean, median, mediocre, middling, midway ▶noun **2** MIDDLE, average, center, compromise, mean, midpoint **3** MEANS, agency, channel, instrument, mode, organ, vehicle, way **4** ENVIRONMENT, atmosphere, conditions, milieu, setting, surroundings **5** SPIRITUALIST

medley noun MIXTURE, assortment, farrago, jumble, mélange, miscellany, mishmash, mixed bag (informal), potpourri

meek adjective SUBMISSIVE, acquiescent, compliant, deferential, docile, gentle, humble, mild, modest, timid, unassuming, unpretentious

meekness noun SUBMISSIVENESS, acquiescence, compliance, deference, docility, gentleness, humility, mildness, modesty, timidity

meet verb **1** ENCOUNTER, bump into, chance on, come across, confront, contact, find, happen on, run across, run into

2 CONVERGE, come together, connect, cross, intersect, join, link up, touch **3** SATISFY, answer, come up to, comply with, discharge, fulfill, match, measure up to **4** GATHER, assemble, collect, come together, congregate, convene, muster **5** EXPERIENCE, bear, encounter, endure, face, go through, suffer, undergo

meeting noun **1** ENCOUNTER, assignation, confrontation, engagement, introduction, rendezvous, tryst **2** CONFERENCE, assembly, conclave, congress, convention, gathering, get-together (informal), reunion, session

melancholy noun **1** SADNESS, dejection, depression, despondency, gloom, low spirits, misery, sorrow, unhappiness ▶ adjective **2** SAD, depressed, despondent, dispirited, downhearted, gloomy, glum, miserable, mournful, sorrowful

melee, mêlée noun FIGHT, brawl, fracas, free-for-all (informal), rumpus, scrimmage, scuffle, skirmish, tussle

mellifluous adjective SWEET, dulcet, euphonious, honeyed, silvery, smooth, soft, soothing, sweet-sounding

mellow adjective **1** SOFT, delicate, full-flavored, mature, rich, ripe, sweet ▶ verb **2** MATURE, develop, improve, ripen, season, soften, sweeten

melodious adjective TUNEFUL, dulcet, euphonious, harmonious, melodic, musical, sweet-sounding

melodramatic adjective SENSATIONAL, blood-and-thunder, extravagant, histrionic, overdramatic, overemotional, theatrical

melody noun **1** TUNE, air, music, song, strain, theme **2** TUNEFULNESS, euphony, harmony, melodiousness, musicality

melt verb **1** DISSOLVE, fuse, liquefy, soften, thaw **2** (often with away) DISAPPEAR, disperse, dissolve, evanesce, evaporate, fade, vanish **3** SOFTEN, disarm, mollify, relax

member noun **1** REPRESENTATIVE, associate, fellow **2** LIMB, appendage, arm, extremity, leg, part

membership noun **1** MEMBERS, associates, body, fellows **2** PARTICIPATION, belonging, enrollment, fellowship

memento noun SOUVENIR, keepsake, memorial, relic, remembrance, reminder, token, trophy

memoir noun ACCOUNT, biography, essay, journal, life, monograph, narrative, record

memoirs plural noun AUTOBIOGRAPHY, diary, experiences, journals, life story, memories, recollections, reminiscences

memorable adjective NOTEWORTHY, celebrated, famous, historic, momentous, notable, remarkable, significant, striking, unforgettable

memorandum noun NOTE, communication, jotting, memo, message, minute, reminder

memorial noun 1 MONUMENT, memento, plaque, record, remembrance, souvenir
▶ adjective 2 COMMEMORATIVE, monumental

memorize verb REMEMBER, commit to memory, learn, learn by heart, learn by rote

memory noun 1 RECALL, recollection, remembrance, reminiscence, retention
2 COMMEMORATION, honor, remembrance

menace noun 1 THREAT, intimidation, warning
2 Informal NUISANCE, annoyance, pest, plague, troublemaker
▶ verb 3 THREATEN, bully, frighten, intimidate, loom, lour or lower, terrorize

menacing adjective THREATENING, forbidding, frightening, intimidating, looming, louring or lowering, ominous

mend verb 1 REPAIR, darn, fix, patch, refit, renew, renovate, restore, retouch 2 IMPROVE, ameliorate, amend, correct, emend, rectify, reform, revise 3 HEAL, convalesce, get better, recover, recuperate ▶ noun 4 REPAIR, darn, patch, stitch 5 on the mend CONVALESCENT, getting better, improving, recovering, recuperating

mendacious adjective LYING, deceitful, deceptive, dishonest, duplicitous, fallacious, false, fraudulent, insincere, untruthful

menial adjective 1 UNSKILLED, boring, dull, humdrum, low-status, routine ▶ noun 2 SERVANT, attendant, drudge, flunky, lackey, underling

mental adjective 1 INTELLECTUAL, cerebral 2 Informal INSANE, deranged, disturbed, mad, mentally ill, psychotic, unbalanced, unstable

mentality noun ATTITUDE, cast of mind, character, disposition, make-up, outlook, personality, psychology

mentally adverb IN THE MIND, in one's head, intellectually, inwardly, psychologically

mention verb 1 REFER TO, bring up, declare, disclose, divulge, intimate, point out, reveal, state, touch upon ▶ noun 2 ACKNOWLEDGMENT, citation, recognition, tribute 3 REFERENCE, allusion, indication, observation, remark

mentor noun GUIDE, adviser, coach, counselor, guru, instructor, teacher, tutor

menu noun BILL OF FARE, carte du jour

mercantile adjective COMMERCIAL, trading

mercenary adjective 1 GREEDY, acquisitive, avaricious, grasping, money-grubbing (informal), sordid, venal ▶ noun 2 HIRELING, soldier of fortune

merchandise noun GOODS, commodities, produce, products, stock, wares

merchant noun TRADESMAN, broker, dealer, purveyor, retailer, salesman, seller, shopkeeper, supplier, trader, trafficker, vendor, wholesaler

merciful adjective COMPASSIONATE, clement, forgiving, generous, gracious, humane, kind, lenient, sparing, sympathetic, tender-hearted

merciless *adjective* CRUEL, barbarous, callous, hard-hearted, harsh, heartless, pitiless, ruthless, unforgiving

mercurial *adjective* LIVELY, active, capricious, changeable, impulsive, irrepressible, mobile, quicksilver, spirited, sprightly, unpredictable, volatile

mercy *noun* **1** COMPASSION, clemency, forbearance, forgiveness, grace, kindness, leniency, pity **2** BLESSING, boon, godsend

mere *adjective* SIMPLE, bare, common, nothing more than, plain, pure, sheer

meretricious *adjective* TRASHY, flashy, garish, gaudy, gimcrack, showy, tawdry, tinsel

merge *verb* COMBINE, amalgamate, blend, coalesce, converge, fuse, join, meet, mingle, mix, unite

merger *noun* UNION, amalgamation, coalition, combination, consolidation, fusion, incorporation

merit *noun* **1** WORTH, advantage, asset, excellence, goodness, integrity, quality, strong point, talent, value, virtue ▶ *verb* **2** DESERVE, be entitled to, be worthy of, earn, have a right to, rate, warrant

meritorious *adjective* PRAISEWORTHY, admirable, commendable, creditable, deserving, excellent, good, laudable, virtuous, worthy

merriment *noun* FUN, amusement, festivity, glee, hilarity, jollity, joviality, laughter, mirth, revelry

merry *adjective* CHEERFUL, blithe, carefree, convivial, festive, happy, jolly, joyous

mesh *noun* **1** NET, netting, network, tracery, web ▶ *verb* **2** ENGAGE, combine, connect, coordinate, dovetail, harmonize, interlock, knit

mesmerize *verb* ENTRANCE, captivate, enthrall, fascinate, grip, hold spellbound, hypnotize

mess *noun* **1** DISORDER, chaos, clutter, confusion, disarray, disorganization, jumble, litter, shambles, untidiness **2** DIFFICULTY, dilemma, fix (*informal*), hot water, jam (*informal*), muddle, pickle (*informal*), plight, predicament, tight spot ▶ *verb* **3** (often with *up*) DIRTY, clutter, disarrange, dishevel, muddle, pollute, scramble **4** (often with *with*) INTERFERE, meddle, play, tamper, tinker

message *noun* **1** COMMUNICATION, bulletin, communiqué, dispatch, letter, memorandum, note, tidings, word **2** POINT, idea, import, meaning, moral, purport, theme

messenger *noun* COURIER, carrier, delivery boy, emissary, envoy, errand-boy, go-between, herald, runner

messy *adjective* UNTIDY, chaotic, cluttered, confused, dirty, disheveled, disordered, disorganized, muddled, scuzzy (*slang*), shambolic, sloppy (*informal*)

metamorphosis *noun* TRANSFORMATION, alteration, change, conversion, mutation, transmutation

metaphor noun FIGURE OF SPEECH, allegory, analogy, image, symbol, trope

metaphorical adjective FIGURATIVE, allegorical, emblematic, symbolic

mete verb DISTRIBUTE, administer, apportion, assign, deal, dispense, portion

meteoric adjective SPECTACULAR, brilliant, dazzling, fast, overnight, rapid, speedy, sudden, swift

method noun 1 MANNER, approach, mode, modus operandi, procedure, process, routine, style, system, technique, way 2 ORDERLINESS, order, organization, pattern, planning, purpose, regularity, system

methodical adjective ORDERLY, businesslike, deliberate, disciplined, meticulous, organized, precise, regular, structured, systematic

meticulous adjective THOROUGH, exact, fastidious, fussy, painstaking, particular, precise, punctilious, scrupulous, strict

mettle noun COURAGE, bravery, fortitude, gallantry, life, nerve, pluck, resolution, spirit, valor, vigor

microbe noun MICROORGANISM, bacillus, bacterium, bug (informal), germ, virus

microscopic adjective TINY, imperceptible, infinitesimal, invisible, minuscule, minute, negligible

midday noun NOON, noonday, twelve o'clock

middle adjective 1 CENTRAL, halfway, intermediate, intervening, mean, median, medium, mid ▸ noun 2 CENTER, focus, halfway point, heart, midpoint, midsection, midst

middle-class adjective BOURGEOIS, conventional, traditional

middling adjective 1 MEDIOCRE, indifferent, so-so (informal), tolerable, unexceptional, unremarkable 2 MODERATE, adequate, all right, average, fair, medium, modest, O.K. or okay (informal), ordinary, passable, serviceable

midget noun DWARF, pygmy or pigmy, shrimp (informal), Tom Thumb

midnight noun TWELVE O'CLOCK, dead of night, middle of the night, the witching hour

midst noun **in the midst of** AMONG, amidst, during, in the middle of, in the thick of, surrounded by

midway adjective, adverb HALFWAY, betwixt and between, in the middle

might noun 1 POWER, energy, force, strength, vigor 2 **with might and main** FORCEFULLY, lustily, manfully, mightily, vigorously

mightily adverb 1 VERY, decidedly, exceedingly, extremely, greatly, highly, hugely, intensely, much 2 POWERFULLY, energetically, forcefully, lustily, manfully, strongly, vigorously

mighty adjective POWERFUL, forceful, lusty, robust, strapping, strong, sturdy, vigorous

migrant noun WANDERER,

drifter, emigrant, immigrant, itinerant, nomad, rover, traveler ▸ adjective 2 TRAVELING, drifting, immigrant, itinerant, migratory, nomadic, roving, shifting, transient, vagrant, wandering

migrate verb MOVE, emigrate, journey, roam, rove, travel, trek, voyage, wander

migration noun WANDERING, emigration, journey, movement, roving, travel, trek, voyage

migratory adjective NOMADIC, itinerant, migrant, peripatetic, roving, transient

mild adjective 1 GENTLE, calm, docile, easy-going, equable, meek, peaceable, placid 2 BLAND, smooth 3 CALM, balmy, moderate, temperate, tranquil, warm

mildness noun GENTLENESS, calmness, clemency, docility, moderation, placidity, tranquillity, warmth

milieu noun SURROUNDINGS, background, element, environment, locale, location, scene, setting

militant adjective AGGRESSIVE, active, assertive, combative, vigorous

military adjective 1 WARLIKE, armed, martial, soldierly ▸ noun 2 ARMED FORCES, army, forces, services

militate verb **militate against** COUNTERACT, be detrimental to, conflict with, counter, oppose, resist, tell against, weigh against

milk verb EXPLOIT, extract, pump, take advantage of

mill noun 1 FACTORY, foundry, plant, works 2 GRINDER, crusher ▸ verb 3 GRIND, crush, grate, pound, powder 4 SWARM, crowd, throng

millstone noun 1 GRINDSTONE, quernstone 2 BURDEN, affliction, albatross, encumbrance, load, weight

mime verb ACT OUT, gesture, represent, simulate

mimic verb 1 IMITATE, ape, caricature, do (informal), impersonate, parody ▸ noun 2 IMITATOR, caricaturist, copycat (informal), impersonator, impressionist

mimicry noun IMITATION, burlesque, caricature, impersonation, mimicking, mockery, parody

mince verb 1 CUT, chop, crumble, grind, hash 2 As in **mince one's words** TONE DOWN, moderate, soften, spare, weaken

mincing adjective AFFECTED, camp (informal), dainty, effeminate, foppish, precious, pretentious, sissy

mind noun 1 INTELLIGENCE, brain(s) (informal), gray matter (informal), intellect, reason, sense, understanding, wits 2 MEMORY, recollection, remembrance 3 INTENTION, desire, disposition, fancy, inclination, leaning, notion, urge, wish 4 SANITY, judgment, marbles (informal), mental balance, rationality, reason, senses, wits 5 **make up one's mind** DECIDE, choose, determine, resolve ▸ verb 6 TAKE OFFENSE, be affronted, be bothered, care, disapprove, dislike, object, resent **7** PAY ATTENTION, heed, listen to, mark, note, obey, observe, pay heed to, take heed **8** GUARD, attend to, keep an eye on, look after, take care of, tend, watch **9** BE CAREFUL, be cautious, be on (one's) guard, be wary, take care, watch

mindful adjective AWARE, alert, alive to, careful, conscious, heedful, wary, watchful

mindless adjective STUPID, foolish, idiotic, inane, moronic, thoughtless, unthinking, witless

mine noun **1** PIT, colliery, deposit, excavation, shaft **2** SOURCE, abundance, fund, hoard, reserve, stock, store, supply, treasury, wealth ▶ verb **3** DIG UP, dig for, excavate, extract, hew, quarry, unearth

mingle verb **1** MIX, blend, combine, intermingle, interweave, join, merge, unite **2** ASSOCIATE, consort, fraternize, hang about or around, hobnob, rub shoulders (informal), socialize

miniature adjective SMALL, diminutive, little, minuscule, minute, scaled-down, tiny, toy

minimal adjective MINIMUM, least, least possible, nominal, slightest, smallest, token

minimize verb **1** REDUCE, curtail, decrease, diminish, miniaturize, prune, shrink **2** PLAY DOWN, belittle, decry, deprecate, discount, disparage, make light or little of, underrate

minimum adjective **1** LEAST, least possible, lowest, minimal, slightest, smallest ▶ noun

2 LEAST, lowest, nadir

minion noun FOLLOWER, flunky, hanger-on, henchman, hireling, lackey, underling, yes man

minister noun **1** CLERGYMAN, cleric, parson, pastor, preacher, priest, rector, vicar ▶ verb **2** ATTEND, administer, cater to, pander to, serve, take care of, tend

ministry noun **1** DEPARTMENT, bureau, council, office, quango **2** THE PRIESTHOOD, holy orders, the church

minor adjective SMALL, inconsequential, insignificant, lesser, petty, slight, trivial, unimportant ▶ noun UNDERAGE PERSON, adolescent, child, juvenile, teenager, youngster (informal), youth

minstrel noun MUSICIAN, bard, singer, songstress, troubadour

mint verb MAKE, cast, coin, produce, punch, stamp, strike

minuscule adjective TINY, diminutive, infinitesimal, little, microscopic, miniature, minute

minute[1] noun MOMENT, flash, instant, jiffy (informal), second, trice

minute[2] adjective **1** SMALL, diminutive, infinitesimal, little, microscopic, miniature, minuscule, tiny **2** PRECISE, close, critical, detailed, exact, exhaustive, meticulous, painstaking, punctilious

minutes plural noun RECORD, memorandum, notes, proceedings, transactions, transcript

minutiae plural noun DETAILS, finer points, ins and outs, niceties, particulars, subtleties, trifles, trivia

minx noun FLIRT, coquette, hussy

miracle noun WONDER, marvel, phenomenon, prodigy

miraculous adjective WONDERFUL, amazing, astonishing, astounding, extraordinary, incredible, phenomenal, prodigious, unaccountable, unbelievable

mirage noun ILLUSION, hallucination, optical illusion

mire noun 1 SWAMP, bog, marsh, morass, quagmire 2 MUD, dirt, muck, ooze, slime

mirror noun 1 LOOKING-GLASS, glass, reflector ▶ verb 2 REFLECT, copy, echo, emulate, follow

mirth noun MERRIMENT, amusement, cheerfulness, fun, gaiety, glee, hilarity, jollity, joviality, laughter, revelry

mirthful adjective MERRY, blithe, cheerful, cheery, festive, happy, jolly, jovial, light-hearted, playful, sportive

misadventure noun MISFORTUNE, accident, bad luck, calamity, catastrophe, debacle, disaster, mishap, reverse, setback

misanthropic adjective ANTISOCIAL, cynical, malevolent, unfriendly

misapprehend verb MISUNDERSTAND, misconstrue, misinterpret, misread, mistake

misapprehension noun MISUNDERSTANDING, delusion, error, fallacy, misconception, misinterpretation, mistake

misappropriate verb STEAL, embezzle, misspend, misuse, peculate, pocket

misbehave verb ACT UP, be disobedient, make a fuss, make trouble, make waves

miscalculate verb MISJUDGE, blunder, err, overestimate, overrate, slip up, underestimate, underrate

miscarriage noun FAILURE, breakdown, error, mishap, perversion

miscarry verb FAIL, come to grief, fall through, go awry, go wrong, misfire

miscellaneous adjective MIXED, assorted, diverse, jumbled, motley, sundry, varied, various

miscellany noun ASSORTMENT, anthology, collection, jumble, medley, mélange, mixed bag, mixture, potpourri, variety

mischance noun MISFORTUNE, accident, calamity, disaster, misadventure, mishap

mischief noun 1 TROUBLE, impishness, misbehavior, monkey business (informal), naughtiness, shenanigans (informal), waywardness 2 HARM, damage, evil, hurt, injury, misfortune, trouble

mischievous adjective 1 NAUGHTY, impish, playful, puckish, rascally, roguish, sportive, troublesome, wayward 2 MALICIOUS, damaging, destructive, evil, harmful, hurtful, spiteful, vicious, wicked

misconception noun DELUSION, error, fallacy, misapprehension, misunderstanding

misconduct noun IMMORALITY, impropriety, malpractice, mismanagement, wrongdoing

miscreant noun WRONGDOER,

criminal, rascal, reprobate, rogue, scoundrel, sinner, vagabond, villain

misdeed noun OFFENSE, crime, fault, misconduct, misdemeanor, sin, transgression, wrong

misdemeanor noun OFFENSE, fault, infringement, misdeed, peccadillo, transgression

miser noun SKINFLINT, cheapskate (informal), niggard, penny-pincher (informal), Scrooge

miserable adjective 1 UNHAPPY, dejected, depressed, despondent, disconsolate, forlorn, gloomy, sorrowful, woebegone, wretched 2 SQUALID, deplorable, lamentable, shameful, sordid, sorry, wretched

miserly adjective MEAN, avaricious, grasping, niggardly, parsimonious, penny-pinching (informal), stingy, tightfisted, ungenerous

misery noun UNHAPPINESS, anguish, depression, desolation, despair, distress, gloom, grief, sorrow, suffering, torment, woe

misfire verb FAIL, fall through, go wrong, miscarry

misfit noun NONCONFORMIST, eccentric, fish out of water (informal), oddball (informal), square peg (in a round hole) (informal)

misfortune noun 1 BAD LUCK, adversity, hard luck, ill luck, infelicity 2 MISHAP, affliction, calamity, disaster, reverse, setback, tragedy, tribulation, trouble

misgiving noun UNEASE, anxiety, apprehension, distrust, doubt, qualm, reservation, suspicion, trepidation, uncertainty, worry

misguided adjective UNWISE, deluded, erroneous, ill-advised, imprudent, injudicious, misplaced, mistaken, unwarranted

mishandle verb MISMANAGE, botch, bungle, make a mess of, mess up (informal), muff

mishap noun ACCIDENT, calamity, misadventure, mischance, misfortune

misinform verb MISLEAD, deceive, misdirect, misguide

misinterpret verb MISUNDERSTAND, distort, misapprehend, misconceive, misconstrue, misjudge, misread, misrepresent, mistake

misjudge verb MISCALCULATE, overestimate, overrate, underestimate, underrate

mislay verb LOSE, lose track of, misplace

mislead verb DECEIVE, delude, fool, hoodwink, misdirect, misguide, misinform

misleading adjective CONFUSING, ambiguous, deceptive, disingenuous, evasive, false

mismanage verb MISHANDLE, botch, bungle, make a mess of, mess up, misconduct, misdirect, misgovern

misplace verb LOSE, lose track of, mislay

misprint noun MISTAKE, corrigendum, erratum, literal, typo (informal)

misquote verb MISREPRESENT, falsify, twist

misrepresent *verb* DISTORT, disguise, falsify, misinterpret

misrule *noun* DISORDER, anarchy, chaos, confusion, lawlessness, turmoil

miss *verb* **1** OMIT, leave out, let go, overlook, pass over, skip **2** AVOID, escape, evade **3** LONG FOR, pine for, yearn for ▶ *noun* **4** MISTAKE, blunder, error, failure, omission, oversight

misshapen *adjective* DEFORMED, contorted, crooked, distorted, grotesque, malformed, twisted, warped

missile *noun* ROCKET, projectile, weapon

missing *adjective* ABSENT, astray, lacking, left out, lost, mislaid, misplaced, unaccounted-for

mission *noun* TASK, assignment, commission, duty, errand, job, quest, undertaking, vocation

missionary *noun* EVANGELIST, apostle, preacher

missive *noun* LETTER, communication, dispatch, epistle, memorandum, message, note, report

misspent *adjective* WASTED, dissipated, imprudent, profitless, squandered

mist *noun* FOG, cloud, film, haze, smog, spray, steam, vapor

mistake *noun* **1** ERROR, blunder, erratum, fault, faux pas, miscalculation, oversight, slip ▶ *verb* **2** MISUNDERSTAND, misapprehend, misconstrue, misinterpret, misjudge, misread **3** CONFUSE WITH, mix up with, take for

mistaken *adjective* WRONG, erroneous, false, faulty, inaccurate, incorrect, misguided, unsound, wide of the mark

mistakenly *adverb* INCORRECTLY, by mistake, erroneously, fallaciously, falsely, inaccurately, misguidedly, wrongly

mistimed *adjective* INOPPORTUNE, badly timed, ill-timed, untimely

mistreat *verb* ABUSE, harm, ill-treat, injure, knock about *or* around, maltreat, manhandle, misuse, molest

mistress *noun* LOVER, concubine, girlfriend, kept woman, paramour

mistrust *verb* **1** DOUBT, be wary of, distrust, fear, suspect ▶ *noun* **2** SUSPICION, distrust, doubt, misgiving, skepticism, uncertainty, wariness

mistrustful *adjective* SUSPICIOUS, chary, cynical, distrustful, doubtful, fearful, hesitant, skeptical, uncertain, wary

misty *adjective* FOGGY, blurred, cloudy, dim, hazy, indistinct, murky, obscure, opaque, overcast

misunderstand *verb* MISINTERPRET, be at cross-purposes, get the wrong end of the stick, misapprehend, misconstrue, misjudge, misread, mistake

misunderstanding *noun* MISTAKE, error, misconception, misinterpretation, misjudgment, mix-up

misuse *noun* **1** WASTE, abuse, desecration, misapplication, squandering ▶ *verb* **2** WASTE, abuse, desecrate, misapply, prostitute, squander

mitigate *verb* EASE, extenuate,

lessen, lighten, moderate, soften, subdue, temper

mitigation noun RELIEF, alleviation, diminution, extenuation, moderation, remission

mix verb **1** COMBINE, blend, cross, fuse, intermingle, interweave, join, jumble, merge, mingle **2** SOCIALIZE, associate, consort, fraternize, hang out (informal), hobnob, mingle ▶ noun **3** MIXTURE, alloy, amalgam, assortment, blend, combination, compound, fusion, medley

mixed adjective **1** COMBINED, amalgamated, blended, composite, compound, joint, mingled, united **2** VARIED, assorted, cosmopolitan, diverse, heterogeneous, miscellaneous, motley

mixed-up adjective CONFUSED, at sea, bewildered, distraught, disturbed, maladjusted, muddled, perplexed, puzzled, upset

mixture noun BLEND, amalgam, assortment, brew, compound, fusion, jumble, medley, mix, potpourri, variety

mix-up noun CONFUSION, mess, mistake, misunderstanding, muddle, tangle

mix up verb **1** COMBINE, blend, mix **2** CONFUSE, confound, muddle

moan noun **1** GROAN, lament, sigh, sob, wail, whine **2** Informal GRUMBLE, complaint, gripe (informal), grouch (informal), grouse, protest, whine ▶ verb **3** GROAN, lament, sigh, sob, whine **4** Informal GRUMBLE, bleat, carp, complain, groan, grouse, whine

mob noun **1** CROWD, drove, flock, horde, host, mass, multitude, pack, swarm, throng **2** Slang GANG, crew (informal), group, lot, set ▶ verb **3** SURROUND, crowd around, jostle, set upon, swarm around

mobile adjective MOVABLE, itinerant, moving, peripatetic, portable, traveling, wandering

mobilize verb PREPARE, activate, call to arms, call up, get or make ready, marshal, organize, rally, ready

mock verb **1** LAUGH AT, deride, jeer, make fun of, poke fun at, ridicule, scoff, scorn, sneer, taunt, tease **2** MIMIC, ape, caricature, imitate, lampoon, parody, satirize ▶ adjective **3** IMITATION, artificial, dummy, fake, false, feigned, phoney or phony (informal), pretended, sham, spurious

mockery noun **1** DERISION, contempt, disdain, disrespect, insults, jeering, ridicule, scoffing, scorn **2** FARCE, disappointment, joke, letdown

mocking adjective SCORNFUL, contemptuous, derisive, disdainful, disrespectful, sarcastic, sardonic, satirical, scoffing

mode noun **1** METHOD, form, manner, procedure, process, style, system, technique, way **2** FASHION, craze, look, rage, style, trend, vogue

model noun **1** REPRESENTATION, copy, dummy, facsimile, image, imitation, miniature, mock-up, replica **2** PATTERN, archetype, example, ideal, original, paradigm, paragon, prototype, standard **3** SITTER, poser, subject ▶ *verb* **4** SHAPE, carve, design, fashion, form, mold, sculpt **5** SHOW OFF, display, sport (*informal*), wear

moderate *adjective* **1** MILD, controlled, gentle, limited, middle-of-the-road, modest, reasonable, restrained, steady **2** AVERAGE, fair, indifferent, mediocre, middling, ordinary, passable, so-so (*informal*), unexceptional ▶ *verb* **3** REGULATE, control, curb, ease, modulate, restrain, soften, subdue, temper, tone down

moderately *adverb* REASONABLY, fairly, passably, quite, rather, slightly, somewhat, tolerably

moderation *noun* RESTRAINT, fairness, reasonableness, temperance

modern *adjective* CURRENT, contemporary, fresh, new, newfangled, novel, present-day, recent, up-to-date

modernity *noun* NOVELTY, currency, freshness, innovation, newness

modernize *verb* UPDATE, make over, rejuvenate, remake, remodel, renew, renovate, revamp

modest *adjective* **1** UNPRETENTIOUS, bashful, coy, demure, diffident, reserved, reticent, retiring, self-effacing, shy **2** MODERATE, fair, limited, middling, ordinary, small, unexceptional

modesty *noun* RESERVE, bashfulness, coyness, demureness, diffidence, humility, reticence, shyness, timidity

modicum *noun* LITTLE, bit, crumb, drop, fragment, scrap, shred, touch

modification *noun* CHANGE, adjustment, alteration, qualification, refinement, revision, variation

modify *verb* **1** CHANGE, adapt, adjust, alter, convert, reform, remodel, revise, rework **2** TONE DOWN, ease, lessen, lower, moderate, qualify, restrain, soften, temper

modish *adjective* FASHIONABLE, chic, contemporary, cool (*informal*), current, in, phat (*slang*), smart, stylish, trendy (*informal*), up-to-the-minute, voguish

modulate *verb* ADJUST, attune, balance, regulate, tune, vary

mogul *noun* TYCOON, baron, big cheese (*informal*), big shot (*informal*), magnate, V.I.P.

moist *adjective* DAMP, clammy, dewy, humid, soggy, wet

moisten *verb* DAMPEN, damp, moisturize, soak, water, wet

moisture *noun* DAMPNESS, dew, liquid, water, wetness

mold¹ *noun* **1** CAST, pattern, shape **2** DESIGN, build, construction, fashion, form, format, kind, pattern, shape, style **3** NATURE, caliber, character, kind, quality, sort, stamp, type ▶ *verb* **4** SHAPE, construct, create, fashion, forge, form, make, model, sculpt, work **5** INFLUENCE, affect, control, direct, form, make, shape

mold² *noun* FUNGUS, blight,

mildew, mustiness

moldy *adjective* STALE, bad, blighted, decaying, fusty, mildewed, musty, rotten

molecule *noun* PARTICLE, jot, speck

molest *verb* 1 ANNOY, badger, beset, bother, disturb, harass, persecute, pester, plague, torment, worry 2 ABUSE, attack, harm, hurt, ill-treat, interfere with, maltreat

mollify *verb* PACIFY, appease, calm, conciliate, placate, quiet, soothe, sweeten

moment *noun* 1 INSTANT, flash, jiffy (*informal*), second, split second, trice, twinkling 2 TIME, juncture, point, stage

momentarily *adverb* BRIEFLY, for a moment, temporarily

momentary *adjective* SHORT-LIVED, brief, fleeting, passing, short, temporary, transitory

momentous *adjective* SIGNIFICANT, critical, crucial, fateful, historic, important, pivotal, vital, weighty

momentum *noun* IMPETUS, drive, energy, force, power, propulsion, push, strength, thrust

monarch *noun* RULER, emperor *or* empress, king, potentate, prince *or* princess, queen, sovereign

monarchy *noun* 1 SOVEREIGNTY, autocracy, kingship, monocracy, royalism 2 KINGDOM, empire, principality, realm

monastery *noun* ABBEY, cloister, convent, friary, nunnery, priory

monastic *adjective* MONKISH, ascetic, cloistered,

contemplative, hermit-like, reclusive, secluded, sequestered, withdrawn

monetary *adjective* FINANCIAL, budgetary, capital, cash, fiscal, pecuniary

money *noun* CASH, capital, coin, currency, hard cash, legal tender, riches, silver, wealth

mongrel *noun* 1 HYBRID, cross, crossbreed, half-breed ▶*adjective* 2 HYBRID, crossbred

monitor *noun* 1 WATCHDOG, guide, invigilator, supervisor ▶*verb* 2 CHECK, follow, keep an eye on, keep tabs on, keep track of, observe, stalk, survey, watch

monk *noun* FRIAR, brother

monkey *noun* 1 SIMIAN, primate 2 RASCAL, devil, imp, rogue, scamp ▶*verb* 3 FOOL, meddle, mess, play, tinker

monolithic *adjective* HUGE, colossal, impenetrable, intractable, massive, monumental, solid

monologue *noun* SPEECH, harangue, lecture, sermon, soliloquy

monopolize *verb* CONTROL, corner the market in, dominate, hog (*slang*), keep to oneself, take over

monotonous *adjective* TEDIOUS, boring, dull, humdrum, mind-numbing, repetitive, tiresome, unchanging, wearisome

monotony *noun* TEDIUM, boredom, monotonousness, repetitiveness, routine, sameness, tediousness

monster *noun* 1 BRUTE, beast, demon, devil, fiend, villain

2 FREAK, monstrosity, mutant
3 GIANT, colossus, mammoth, titan ▶ *adjective* **4** HUGE, colossal, enormous, gigantic, immense, mammoth, massive, stupendous, tremendous

monstrosity *noun* EYESORE, freak, horror, monster

monstrous *adjective*
1 UNNATURAL, fiendish, freakish, frightful, grotesque, gruesome, hideous, horrible **2** OUTRAGEOUS, diabolical, disgraceful, foul, inhuman, intolerable, scandalous, shocking **3** HUGE, colossal, enormous, immense, mammoth, massive, prodigious, stupendous, tremendous

monument *noun* MEMORIAL, cairn, cenotaph, commemoration, gravestone, headstone, marker, mausoleum, shrine, tombstone

monumental *adjective*
1 IMPORTANT, awesome, enormous, epoch-making, historic, majestic, memorable, significant, unforgettable
2 *Informal* IMMENSE, colossal, great, massive, staggering

mood *noun* STATE OF MIND, disposition, frame of mind, humor, spirit, temper

moody *adjective* **1** SULLEN, gloomy, glum, ill-tempered, irritable, morose, sad, sulky, temperamental, touchy
2 CHANGEABLE, capricious, erratic, fickle, flighty, impulsive, mercurial, temperamental, unpredictable, volatile

moon *noun* **1** SATELLITE ▶ *verb*
2 IDLE, daydream, languish, mope, waste time

moor[1] *noun* MOORLAND, heath

moor[2] *verb* TIE UP, anchor, berth, dock, lash, make fast, secure

moot *adjective* **1** DEBATABLE, arguable, contestable, controversial, disputable, doubtful, undecided, unresolved, unsettled ▶ *verb*
2 BRING UP, broach, propose, put forward, suggest

mop *noun* **1** SQUEEGEE, sponge, swab **2** MANE, shock, tangle, thatch

mope *verb* BROOD, fret, languish, moon, pine, pout, sulk

mop up *verb* CLEAN UP, soak up, sponge, swab, wash, wipe

moral *adjective* **1** GOOD, decent, ethical, high-minded, honorable, just, noble, principled, right, virtuous
▶ *noun* **2** LESSON, meaning, message, point, significance

morale *noun* CONFIDENCE, esprit de corps, heart, self-esteem, spirit

morality *noun* **1** INTEGRITY, decency, goodness, honesty, justice, righteousness, virtue
2 STANDARDS, conduct, ethics, manners, morals, mores, philosophy, principles

morals *plural noun* MORALITY, behavior, conduct, ethics, habits, integrity, manners, mores, principles, scruples, standards

morass *noun* **1** MARSH, bog, fen, quagmire, slough, swamp
2 MESS, confusion, mix-up, muddle, tangle

moratorium *noun* POSTPONEMENT, freeze, halt, standstill, suspension

morbid adjective
1 UNWHOLESOME, ghoulish, gloomy, melancholy, sick, somber, unhealthy **2** GRUESOME, dreadful, ghastly, grisly, hideous, horrid, macabre

mordant adjective SARCASTIC, biting, caustic, cutting, incisive, pungent, scathing, stinging, trenchant

more adjective **1** EXTRA, added, additional, further, new, other, supplementary ▶ adverb **2** TO A GREATER EXTENT, better, further, longer

moreover adverb FURTHERMORE, additionally, also, as well, besides, further, in addition, too

morgue noun MORTUARY

moribund adjective DECLINING, on its last legs, stagnant, waning, weak

morning noun DAWN, a.m., break of day, daybreak, forenoon, morn (poetic), sunrise

moron noun FOOL, blockhead, cretin (offensive), dork (slang), dunce, dunderhead, halfwit, idiot, imbecile, oaf, schmuck (slang)

moronic adjective IDIOTIC, cretinous (offensive), foolish, halfwitted, imbecilic, mindless, stupid, unintelligent

morose adjective SULLEN, depressed, dour, gloomy, glum, ill-tempered, moody, sour, sulky, surly, taciturn

morsel noun PIECE, bit, bite, crumb, mouthful, part, scrap, soupçon, taste, tidbit

mortal adjective **1** HUMAN, ephemeral, impermanent, passing, temporal, transient, worldly **2** FATAL, deadly,

death-dealing, destructive, killing, lethal, murderous, terminal ▶ noun **3** HUMAN BEING, being, earthling, human, individual, man, person, woman

mortality noun **1** HUMANITY, impermanence, transience **2** KILLING, bloodshed, carnage, death, destruction, fatality

mortification noun
1 HUMILIATION, annoyance, chagrin, discomfiture, embarrassment, shame, vexation **2** DISCIPLINE, abasement, chastening, control, denial, subjugation **3** Medical GANGRENE, corruption, festering

mortified adjective HUMILIATED, ashamed, chagrined, chastened, crushed, deflated, embarrassed, humbled, shamed

mortify verb **1** HUMILIATE, chagrin, chasten, crush, deflate, embarrass, humble, shame **2** DISCIPLINE, abase, chasten, control, deny, subdue **3** Of flesh PUTREFY, deaden, die, fester

mortuary noun MORGUE, funeral parlour

mostly adverb GENERALLY, as a rule, chiefly, largely, mainly, on the whole, predominantly, primarily, principally, usually

moth-eaten adjective DECAYED, decrepit, dilapidated, ragged, shabby, tattered, threadbare, worn-out

mother noun **1** PARENT, dam, ma (informal), mama or mamma (old-fashioned informal), mater (old-fashioned informal, chiefly Brit.), mom (informal), mommy (informal), old lady (informal)

▶ *adjective* **2** NATIVE, inborn,
innate, natural ▶ *verb* **3** NURTURE,
care for, cherish, nurse,
protect, raise, rear, tend

motherly *adjective* MATERNAL,
affectionate, caring,
comforting, loving, protective,
sheltering

motif *noun* **1** THEME, concept,
idea, leitmotif, subject **2** DESIGN,
decoration, ornament, shape

motion *noun* **1** MOVEMENT, flow,
locomotion, mobility, move,
progress, travel **2** PROPOSAL,
proposition, recommendation,
submission, suggestion ▶ *verb*
3 GESTURE, beckon, direct,
gesticulate, nod, signal, wave

motionless *adjective* STILL, fixed,
frozen, immobile, paralyzed,
standing, static, stationary,
stock-still, transfixed, unmoving

motivate *verb* INSPIRE, arouse,
cause, drive, induce, move,
persuade, prompt, stimulate,
stir

motivation *noun* INCENTIVE,
incitement, inducement,
inspiration, motive, reason,
spur, stimulus

motive *noun* REASON, ground(s),
incentive, inducement,
inspiration, object, purpose,
rationale, stimulus

motley *adjective*
1 MISCELLANEOUS, assorted,
disparate, heterogeneous,
mixed, varied **2** MULTICOLORED,
checkered, variegated

mottled *adjective* BLOTCHY,
dappled, flecked, piebald,
speckled, spotted, stippled,
streaked

motto *noun* SAYING, adage,
dictum, maxim, precept,

proverb, rule, slogan,
watchword

mound *noun* **1** HEAP, drift, pile,
rick, stack **2** HILL, bank, dune,
embankment, hillock, knoll, rise

mount *verb* **1** CLIMB, ascend,
clamber up, go up, scale
2 BESTRIDE, climb onto, jump on
3 INCREASE, accumulate, build,
escalate, grow, intensify,
multiply, pile up, swell ▶ *noun*
4 BACKING, base, frame, setting,
stand, support **5** HORSE, steed
(*archaic or literary*)

mountain *noun* **1** PEAK, alp, fell
(*Brit.*), mount **2** HEAP,
abundance, mass, mound, pile,
stack, ton

mountainous *adjective* **1** HIGH,
alpine, highland, rocky,
soaring, steep, towering,
upland **2** HUGE, daunting,
enormous, gigantic, great,
immense, mammoth, mighty,
monumental

mourn *verb* GRIEVE, bemoan,
bewail, deplore, lament, rue,
wail, weep

mournful *adjective* **1** SAD,
melancholy, piteous, plaintive,
sorrowful, tragic, unhappy,
woeful **2** DISMAL, disconsolate,
downcast, gloomy, grieving,
heavy-hearted, lugubrious,
miserable, rueful, somber

mourning *noun* **1** GRIEVING,
bereavement, grief,
lamentation, weeping, woe
2 BLACK, sackcloth and ashes,
widow's weeds

mouth *noun* **1** LIPS, jaws, maw
2 OPENING, aperture, door,
entrance, gateway, inlet, orifice

mouthful *noun* TASTE, bit, bite,
little, morsel, sample,

spoonful, swallow

mouthpiece noun SPOKESPERSON, agent, delegate, representative, spokesman or spokeswoman

movable adjective PORTABLE, detachable, mobile, transferable, transportable

move verb **1** GO, advance, budge, proceed, progress, shift, stir **2** CHANGE, shift, switch, transfer, transpose **3** LEAVE, migrate, pack one's bags (informal), quit, relocate, remove **4** DRIVE, activate, operate, propel, shift, start, turn **5** TOUCH, affect, excite, impress **6** INCITE, cause, induce, influence, inspire, motivate, persuade, prompt, rouse **7** PROPOSE, advocate, put forward, recommend, suggest, urge ▶ noun **8** ACTION, maneuver, measure, ploy, step, stratagem, stroke, turn **9** TRANSFER, relocation, removal, shift

movement noun **1** MOTION, action, activity, change, development, flow, maneuver, progress, stirring **2** GROUP, campaign, crusade, drive, faction, front, grouping, organization, party **3** WORKINGS, action, machinery, mechanism, works ▶ Music SECTION, division, part, passage

movie noun FILM, feature, flick (slang), picture

moving adjective **1** EMOTIONAL, affecting, inspiring, pathetic, persuasive, poignant, stirring, touching **2** MOBILE, movable, portable, running, unfixed

mow verb CUT, crop, scythe, shear, trim

mow down verb MASSACRE, butcher, cut down, cut to pieces, shoot down, slaughter

much adjective **1** GREAT, abundant, a lot of, ample, considerable, copious, plenty of, sizable or sizeable, substantial ▶ noun **2** A LOT, a good deal, a great deal, heaps (informal), lots (informal), plenty ▶ adverb **3** GREATLY, a great deal, a lot, considerably, decidedly, exceedingly

muck noun **1** MANURE, dung, ordure **2** DIRT, filth, mire, mud, ooze, slime, sludge

mucky adjective DIRTY, begrimed, filthy, grimy, messy, muddy, scuzzy (slang)

mud noun DIRT, clay, mire, ooze, silt, slime, sludge

muddle verb **1** JUMBLE, disarrange, disorder, disorganize, mess, scramble, spoil, tangle **2** CONFUSE, befuddle, bewilder, confound, daze, disorient, perplex, stupefy ▶ noun **3** CONFUSION, chaos, disarray, disorder, disorganization, jumble, mess, mix-up, predicament, tangle

muddy adjective **1** DIRTY, bespattered, grimy, mucky, mud-caked, scuzzy (slang), soiled **2** BOGGY, marshy, quaggy, swampy

muffle verb **1** WRAP UP, cloak, cover, envelop, shroud, swaddle, swathe **2** DEADEN, muzzle, quieten, silence, soften, stifle, suppress

muffled adjective INDISTINCT, faint, muted, stifled, strangled, subdued, suppressed

mug[1] noun CUP, beaker, flagon,

pot, tankard

mug² noun FACE, countenance, features, visage **1** FOOL, dork (slang), schmuck (slang), sucker (slang) ▶ verb **2** ATTACK, assault, beat up, rob, set about or upon

muggy adjective HUMID, clammy, close, moist, oppressive, sticky, stuffy, sultry

mull verb PONDER, consider, contemplate, deliberate, meditate, reflect on, ruminate, think over, weigh

multifarious adjective DIVERSE, different, legion, manifold, many, miscellaneous, multiple, numerous, sundry, varied

multiple adjective MANY, manifold, multitudinous, numerous, several, sundry, various

multiply verb **1** INCREASE, build up, expand, extend, proliferate, spread **2** REPRODUCE, breed, propagate

multitude noun MASS, army, crowd, horde, host, mob, myriad, swarm, throng

munch verb CHEW, champ, chomp, crunch

mundane adjective **1** ORDINARY, banal, commonplace, day-to-day, everyday, humdrum, prosaic, routine, workaday **2** EARTHLY, mortal, secular, temporal, terrestrial, worldly

municipal adjective CIVIC, public, urban

municipality noun TOWN, borough, city, district, township

munificence noun GENEROSITY, beneficence, benevolence, bounty, largesse or largess, liberality, magnanimousness,
philanthropy

munificent adjective GENEROUS, beneficent, benevolent, bountiful, lavish, liberal, magnanimous, open-handed, philanthropic, unstinting

murder noun **1** KILLING, assassination, bloodshed, butchery, carnage, homicide, manslaughter, massacre, slaying ▶ verb **2** KILL, assassinate, bump off (slang), butcher, eliminate (slang), massacre, slaughter, slay

murderer noun KILLER, assassin, butcher, cut-throat, hit man (slang), homicide, slaughterer, slayer

murderous adjective DEADLY, bloodthirsty, brutal, cruel, cut-throat, ferocious, lethal, savage

murky adjective DARK, cloudy, dim, dull, gloomy, gray, misty, overcast

murmur verb **1** MUMBLE, mutter, whisper **2** GRUMBLE, complain, moan (informal) ▶ noun **3** DRONE, buzzing, humming, purr, rumble, whisper

muscle noun **1** TENDON, sinew **2** STRENGTH, brawn, clout (informal), forcefulness, might, power, stamina, weight

muscular adjective STRONG, athletic, powerful, robust, sinewy, strapping, sturdy, vigorous

muse verb PONDER, brood, cogitate, consider, contemplate, deliberate, meditate, mull over, reflect, ruminate

mushy adjective **1** SOFT, pulpy, semi-solid, slushy, squashy, squelchy **2** *Informal* SENTIMENTAL, maudlin, mawkish, saccharine, schmaltzy (*slang*), sloppy (*informal*), slushy (*informal*)

musical *adjective* MELODIOUS, dulcet, euphonious, harmonious, lyrical, melodic, sweet-sounding, tuneful

must *noun* NECESSITY, essential, fundamental, imperative, prerequisite, requirement, requisite, *sine qua non*

muster *verb* **1** ASSEMBLE, call together, convene, gather, marshal, mobilize, rally, summon ▶ *noun* **2** ASSEMBLY, collection, congregation, convention, gathering, meeting, rally, roundup

musty *adjective* STALE, airless, dank, funky (*slang*), fusty, mildewed, moldy, old, smelly, stuffy

mutability *noun* CHANGE, alteration, evolution, metamorphosis, transition, variation, vicissitude

mutable *adjective* CHANGEABLE, adaptable, alterable, fickle, inconsistent, inconstant, unsettled, unstable, variable, volatile

mutation *noun* CHANGE, alteration, evolution, metamorphosis, modification, transfiguration, transformation, variation

mute *adjective* SILENT, dumb, mum, speechless, unspoken, voiceless, wordless

mutilate *verb* **1** MAIM, amputate, cut up, damage, disfigure, dismember, injure, lacerate, mangle **2** DISTORT, adulterate, bowdlerize, censor, cut, damage, expurgate

mutinous *adjective* REBELLIOUS, disobedient, insubordinate, insurgent, refractory, riotous, subversive, unmanageable, unruly

mutiny *noun* **1** REBELLION, disobedience, insubordination, insurrection, revolt, revolution, riot, uprising ▶ *verb* **2** REBEL, disobey, resist, revolt, rise up

mutter *verb* GRUMBLE, complain, grouse, mumble, murmur, rumble

mutual *adjective* SHARED, common, interchangeable, joint, reciprocal, requited, returned

muzzle *noun* **1** JAWS, mouth, nose, snout **2** GAG, guard ▶ *verb* **3** SUPPRESS, censor, curb, gag, restrain, silence, stifle

myopic *adjective* SHORT-SIGHTED, near-sighted

myriad *adjective* **1** INNUMERABLE, countless, immeasurable, incalculable, multitudinous, untold ▶ *noun* **2** MULTITUDE, army, horde, host, swarm

mysterious *adjective* STRANGE, arcane, enigmatic, inexplicable, inscrutable, mystifying, perplexing, puzzling, secret, uncanny, unfathomable, weird

mystery *noun* PUZZLE, conundrum, enigma, problem, question, riddle, secret, teaser

mystic, mystical *adjective* SUPERNATURAL, inscrutable, metaphysical, mysterious, occult, otherworldly, paranormal, preternatural, transcendental

mystify *verb* PUZZLE, baffle, bewilder, confound, confuse, flummox, nonplus, perplex, stump

mystique noun FASCINATION, awe, charisma, charm, glamour, magic, spell

myth noun 1 LEGEND, allegory, fable, fairy story, fiction, folk tale, saga, story, urban legend or myth 2 ILLUSION, delusion, fancy, fantasy, figment, imagination, superstition, tall tale (informal)

mythical adjective 1 LEGENDARY, fabled, fabulous, fairy-tale, mythological 2 IMAGINARY, fabricated, fantasy, fictitious, invented, made-up, make-believe, nonexistent, pretended, unreal, untrue

mythological adjective LEGENDARY, fabulous, mythic, mythical, traditional

mythology noun LEGEND, folklore, lore, tradition

— N n —

nadir noun BOTTOM, depths, lowest point, minimum, rock bottom

nag[1] verb 1 SCOLD, annoy, badger, harass, hassle (informal), henpeck, irritate, pester, plague, upbraid, worry ▶ noun 2 SCOLD, harpy, shrew, tartar, virago

nag[2] noun HORSE, hack

nagging adjective IRRITATING, persistent, scolding, shrewish, worrying

nail verb FASTEN, attach, fix, hammer, join, pin, secure, tack

naive adjective 1 GULLIBLE, callow, credulous, green, unsuspicious, wet behind the ears (informal) 2 INNOCENT, artless, guileless, ingenuous, open, simple, trusting, unsophisticated, unworldly

naivety, naïveté noun 1 GULLIBILITY, callowness, credulity 2 INNOCENCE, artlessness, guilelessness, inexperience, ingenuousness, naturalness, openness, simplicity

naked adjective NUDE, bare, exposed, in one's birthday suit (informal), stripped, unclothed, undressed, without a stitch on (informal)

nakedness noun NUDITY, bareness, undress

name noun 1 TITLE, designation, epithet, handle (slang), moniker or monicker (slang), nickname, sobriquet, term 2 FAME, distinction, eminence, esteem, honor, note, praise, renown, repute ▶ verb 3 CALL, baptize, christen, dub, entitle, label, style, term 4 NOMINATE, appoint, choose, designate, select, specify

named adjective 1 CALLED, baptized, christened, dubbed, entitled, known as, labeled, styled, termed 2 NOMINATED, appointed, chosen, designated, mentioned, picked, selected, singled out, specified

nameless adjective 1 ANONYMOUS, unnamed, untitled 2 UNKNOWN, incognito, obscure, undistinguished, unheard-of, unsung 3 HORRIBLE, abominable, indescribable, unmentionable, unspeakable, unutterable

namely *adverb* SPECIFICALLY, to wit, viz.

nap[1] *noun* **1** SLEEP, catnap, forty winks (*informal*), rest, siesta ▶*verb* **2** SLEEP, catnap, doze, drop off (*informal*), nod off (*informal*), rest, snooze (*informal*)

nap[2] *noun* WEAVE, down, fiber, grain, pile

napkin *noun* CLOTH, linen, wipe

narcissism *noun* EGOTISM, self-love, vanity

narcotic *noun* **1** DRUG, analgesic, anesthetic, anodyne, opiate, painkiller, sedative, tranquilizer ▶*adjective* **2** SEDATIVE, analgesic, calming, hypnotic, painkilling, soporific

narrate *verb* TELL, chronicle, describe, detail, recite, recount, relate, report

narration *noun* TELLING, description, explanation, reading, recital, relation

narrative *noun* STORY, account, chronicle, history, report, statement, tale

narrator *noun* STORYTELLER, author, chronicler, commentator, reporter, writer

narrow *adjective* **1** THIN, attenuated, fine, slender, slim, spare, tapering **2** LIMITED, close, confined, constricted, contracted, meager, restricted, tight **3** INSULAR, dogmatic, illiberal, intolerant, narrow-minded, partial, prejudiced, small-minded ▶*verb* **4** TIGHTEN, constrict, limit, reduce

narrowly *adverb* JUST, barely, by the skin of one's teeth, only just, scarcely

narrow-minded *adjective* INTOLERANT, bigoted, hidebound, illiberal, opinionated, parochial, prejudiced, provincial, small-minded

nastiness *noun* UNPLEASANTNESS, malice, meanness, spitefulness

nasty *adjective* **1** OBJECTIONABLE, disagreeable, loathsome, obnoxious, offensive, unpleasant, vile **2** SPITEFUL, despicable, disagreeable, distasteful, lousy (*slang*), malicious, mean, scuzzy (*slang*), unpleasant, vicious, vile **3** PAINFUL, bad, critical, dangerous, serious, severe

nation *noun* COUNTRY, people, race, realm, society, state, tribe

national *adjective* **1** NATIONWIDE, countrywide, public, widespread ▶*noun* **2** CITIZEN, inhabitant, native, resident, subject

nationalism *noun* PATRIOTISM, allegiance, chauvinism, jingoism, loyalty

nationality *noun* RACE, birth, nation

nationwide *adjective* NATIONAL, countrywide, general, widespread

native *adjective* **1** LOCAL, domestic, home, indigenous **2** INBORN, congenital, hereditary, inbred, ingrained, innate, instinctive, intrinsic, natural ▶*noun* **3** INHABITANT, aborigine, citizen, countryman, dweller, national, resident

natty *adjective* SMART, dapper, elegant, fashionable, neat, phat (*slang*), snazzy (*informal*), spruce, stylish, trim

natural *adjective* **1** NORMAL,

common, everyday, legitimate, logical, ordinary, regular, typical, usual 2 UNAFFECTED, genuine, ingenuous, open, real, simple, spontaneous, unpretentious, unsophisticated 3 INNATE, characteristic, essential, inborn, inherent, instinctive, intuitive, native 4 PURE, organic, plain, unrefined, whole

naturalist noun BIOLOGIST, botanist, ecologist, zoologist

naturalistic adjective REALISTIC, lifelike, true-to-life

naturally adverb 1 OF COURSE, certainly 2 GENUINELY, normally, simply, spontaneously, typically, unaffectedly, unpretentiously

nature noun 1 CREATION, cosmos, earth, environment, universe, world 2 MAKE-UP, character, complexion, constitution, essence 3 KIND, category, description, sort, species, style, type, variety 4 TEMPERAMENT, disposition, humor, mood, outlook, temper

naughty adjective 1 DISOBEDIENT, bad, impish, misbehaved, mischievous, refractory, wayward, wicked, worthless 2 OBSCENE, improper, lewd, ribald, risqué, smutty, vulgar

nausea noun SICKNESS, biliousness, queasiness, retching, squeamishness, vomiting

nauseate verb SICKEN, disgust, offend, repel, repulse, revolt, turn one's stomach

nauseous adjective SICKENING, abhorrent, disgusting, distasteful, nauseating, offensive, repugnant, repulsive, revolting, scuzzy (slang)

nautical adjective MARITIME, marine, naval

naval adjective NAUTICAL, marine, maritime

navigable adjective 1 PASSABLE, clear, negotiable, unobstructed 2 SAILABLE, controllable, dirigible

navigate verb SAIL, drive, guide, handle, maneuver, pilot, steer, voyage

navigation noun SAILING, helmsmanship, seamanship, voyaging

navigator noun PILOT, mariner, seaman

navy noun FLEET, armada, flotilla

near adjective 1 CLOSE, adjacent, adjoining, nearby, neighboring 2 FORTHCOMING, approaching, imminent, impending, in the offing, looming, nigh, upcoming

nearby adjective NEIGHBORING, adjacent, adjoining, convenient, handy

nearly adverb ALMOST, approximately, as good as, just about, practically, roughly, virtually, well-nigh

nearness noun CLOSENESS, accessibility, availability, handiness, proximity, vicinity

near-sighted adjective SHORT-SIGHTED, myopic

neat adjective 1 TIDY, orderly, shipshape, smart, spick-and-span, spruce, systematic, trim 2 ELEGANT, adept, adroit, deft, dexterous, efficient, graceful, nimble, skillful, stylish 3 Of alcoholic drinks STRAIGHT, pure, undiluted, unmixed

neatly adverb 1 TIDILY, daintily, fastidiously, methodically, smartly, sprucely, systematically 2 ELEGANTLY, adeptly, adroitly, deftly, dexterously, efficiently, expertly, gracefully, nimbly, skillfully

neatness noun 1 TIDINESS, daintiness, orderliness, smartness, spruceness, trimness 2 ELEGANCE, adroitness, deftness, dexterity, efficiency, grace, nimbleness, skill, style

nebulous adjective VAGUE, confused, dim, hazy, imprecise, indefinite, indistinct, shadowy, uncertain, unclear

necessarily adverb CERTAINLY, automatically, compulsorily, incontrovertibly, inevitably, inexorably, naturally, of necessity, undoubtedly

necessary adjective 1 NEEDED, compulsory, essential, imperative, indispensable, mandatory, obligatory, required, requisite, vital 2 CERTAIN, fated, inescapable, inevitable, inexorable, unavoidable

necessitate verb COMPEL, call for, coerce, constrain, demand, force, impel, oblige, require

necessities plural noun ESSENTIALS, exigencies, fundamentals, needs, requirements

necessity noun 1 INEVITABILITY, compulsion, inexorableness, obligation 2 NEED, desideratum, essential, fundamental, prerequisite, requirement, requisite, sine qua non

necromancy noun MAGIC, black magic, divination, enchantment, sorcery, witchcraft, wizardry

necropolis noun CEMETERY, burial ground, churchyard, graveyard

need verb 1 REQUIRE, call for, demand, entail, lack, miss, necessitate, want ▶ noun 2 POVERTY, deprivation, destitution, inadequacy, insufficiency, lack, paucity, penury, shortage 3 REQUIREMENT, demand, desideratum, essential, requisite 4 EMERGENCY, exigency, necessity, obligation, urgency, want

needed adjective NECESSARY, called for, desired, lacked, required, wanted

needful adjective NECESSARY, essential, indispensable, needed, required, requisite, stipulated, vital

needle verb IRRITATE, annoy, get on one's nerves (informal), goad, harass, nag, pester, provoke, rile, taunt

needless adjective UNNECESSARY, gratuitous, groundless, pointless, redundant, superfluous, uncalled-for, unwanted, useless

needlework noun EMBROIDERY, needlecraft, sewing, stitching, tailoring

needy adjective POOR, deprived, destitute, disadvantaged, impoverished, penniless, poverty-stricken, underprivileged

nefarious adjective WICKED, criminal, depraved, evil, foul, heinous, infernal, villainous

negate verb 1 INVALIDATE, annul, cancel, countermand, neutralize, nullify, obviate, reverse, wipe out **2** DENY, contradict, disallow, disprove, gainsay (*archaic or literary*), oppose, rebut, refute

negation noun **1** CANCELLATION, neutralization, nullification **2** DENIAL, contradiction, converse, disavowal, inverse, opposite, rejection, renunciation, reverse

negative adjective **1** CONTRADICTORY, contrary, denying, dissenting, opposing, refusing, rejecting, resisting **2** PESSIMISTIC, cynical, gloomy, jaundiced, uncooperative, unenthusiastic, unwilling ▶noun **3** CONTRADICTION, denial, refusal

neglect verb **1** DISREGARD, blow off (*slang*), disdain, ignore, overlook, rebuff, scorn, slight, spurn **2** FORGET, be remiss, evade, omit, pass over, shirk, skimp ▶noun **3** DISREGARD, disdain, inattention, indifference **4** NEGLIGENCE, carelessness, dereliction, failure, laxity, oversight, slackness

neglected adjective **1** ABANDONED, derelict, overgrown **2** DISREGARDED, unappreciated, underestimated, undervalued

neglectful adjective CARELESS, heedless, inattentive, indifferent, lax, negligent, remiss, thoughtless, uncaring

negligence noun CARELESSNESS, dereliction, disregard, inattention, indifference, laxity, neglect, slackness, thoughtlessness

negligent adjective CARELESS, forgetful, heedless, inattentive, neglectful, remiss, slack,

slapdash, thoughtless, unthinking

negligible adjective INSIGNIFICANT, imperceptible, inconsequential, minor, minute, small, trifling, trivial, unimportant

negotiable adjective DEBATABLE, variable

negotiate verb **1** DEAL, arrange, bargain, conciliate, debate, discuss, haggle, mediate, transact, work out **2** GET ROUND, clear, cross, get over, get past, pass, surmount

negotiation noun BARGAINING, arbitration, debate, diplomacy, discussion, haggling, mediation, transaction, wheeling and dealing (*informal*)

negotiator noun MEDIATOR, ambassador, delegate, diplomat, honest broker, intermediary, moderator

neighborhood noun DISTRICT, community, environs, locale, locality, quarter, region, vicinity

neighboring adjective NEARBY, adjacent, adjoining, bordering, connecting, near, next, surrounding

neighborly adjective HELPFUL, considerate, friendly, harmonious, hospitable, kind, obliging, sociable

nemesis noun RETRIBUTION, destiny, destruction, fate, vengeance

nepotism noun FAVORITISM, bias, partiality, patronage, preferential treatment

nerd noun BORE, doofus (*slang*), dork (*slang*), drip (*informal*), dweeb (*slang*), egghead (*informal*), geek (*slang*), goober (*informal*)

nerve noun **1** BRAVERY, courage, daring, fearlessness, grit, guts (informal), pluck, resolution, will **2** IMPUDENCE, audacity, boldness, brazenness, cheek (informal), impertinence, insolence, temerity ▶verb **3 nerve oneself** BRACE ONESELF, fortify oneself, steel oneself

nerveless adjective CALM, composed, controlled, cool, impassive, imperturbable, self-possessed, unemotional

nerve-racking adjective TENSE, difficult, distressing, frightening, harrowing, stressful, trying, worrying

nerves plural noun TENSION, anxiety, butterflies (in one's stomach) (informal), cold feet (informal), fretfulness, nervousness, strain, stress, worry

nervous adjective APPREHENSIVE, anxious, edgy, fearful, jumpy, on edge, tense, uneasy, uptight (informal), wired (slang), worried

nervousness noun ANXIETY, agitation, disquiet, excitability, fluster, tension, touchiness, worry

nervy adjective ANXIOUS, agitated, fidgety, jittery, jumpy (informal), jumpy, nervous, on edge, tense, twitchy (informal), wired (slang)

nest noun REFUGE, den, haunt, hideaway, retreat

nest egg noun RESERVE, cache, deposit, fall-back, fund(s), savings, store

nestle verb SNUGGLE, cuddle, curl up, huddle, nuzzle

nestling noun CHICK, fledgling

net¹ noun **1** MESH, lattice, netting, network, openwork, tracery, web ▶verb **2** CATCH, bag, capture, enmesh, ensnare, entangle, trap

net² adjective **1** FINAL, after taxes, clear, take-home ▶verb **2** EARN, accumulate, bring in, clear, gain, make, realize, reap

nether adjective LOWER, below, beneath, bottom, inferior, under, underground

nettled adjective IRRITATED, annoyed, exasperated, galled, harassed, incensed, peeved, put out, riled, vexed

network noun SYSTEM, arrangement, complex, grid, labyrinth, lattice, maze, organization, structure, web

neurosis noun OBSESSION, abnormality, affliction, derangement, instability, maladjustment, mental illness, phobia

neurotic adjective UNSTABLE, abnormal, compulsive, disturbed, maladjusted, manic, nervous, obsessive, unhealthy

neuter verb CASTRATE, doctor (informal), emasculate, fix (informal), geld, spay

neutral adjective **1** UNBIASED, disinterested, even-handed, impartial, nonaligned, nonpartisan, uncommitted, uninvolved, unprejudiced **2** INDETERMINATE, dull, indistinct, intermediate, undefined

neutrality noun IMPARTIALITY, detachment, nonalignment, noninterference, noninvolvement, nonpartisanship

neutralize verb COUNTERACT,

cancel, compensate for, counterbalance, frustrate, negate, nullify, offset, undo

never adverb AT NO TIME, not at all, on no account, under no circumstances

nevertheless adverb
NONETHELESS, but, even so, (even) though, however, notwithstanding, regardless, still, yet

new adjective **1** MODERN, contemporary, current, fresh, ground-breaking, latest, novel, original, recent, state-of-the-art, unfamiliar, up-to-date **2** CHANGED, altered, improved, modernized, redesigned, renewed, restored **3** EXTRA, added, more, supplementary

newcomer noun NOVICE, arrival, beginner, Johnny-come-lately (*informal*), new kid in town (*informal*), parvenu

newfangled adjective NEW, contemporary, cool (*informal*), fashionable, gimmicky, modern, novel, phat (*slang*), recent, state-of-the-art

newly adverb RECENTLY, anew, freshly, just, lately, latterly

newness noun NOVELTY, freshness, innovation, oddity, originality, strangeness, unfamiliarity, uniqueness

news noun INFORMATION, bulletin, communiqué, exposé, gossip, hearsay, intelligence, latest (*informal*), report, revelation, rumor, story

newsworthy adjective
INTERESTING, important, notable, noteworthy, remarkable, significant, stimulating

next adjective **1** FOLLOWING, consequent, ensuing, later, subsequent, succeeding **2** NEAREST, adjacent, adjoining, closest, neighboring ▸ adverb **3** AFTERWARDS, following, later, subsequently, thereafter

nibble verb **1** BITE, eat, gnaw, munch, nip, peck, pick at ▸ noun **2** SNACK, bite, crumb, morsel, peck, soupçon, taste, tidbit

nice adjective **1** PLEASANT, agreeable, attractive, charming, delightful, good, pleasurable **2** KIND, courteous, friendly, likable or likeable, polite, well-mannered **3** NEAT, dainty, fine, tidy, trim **4** SUBTLE, careful, delicate, fastidious, fine, meticulous, precise, strict

nicely adverb **1** PLEASANTLY, acceptably, agreeably, attractively, charmingly, delightfully, pleasurably, well **2** KINDLY, amiably, commendably, courteously, politely **3** NEATLY, daintily, finely, tidily, trimly

nicety noun SUBTLETY, daintiness, delicacy, discrimination, distinction, nuance, refinement

niche noun **1** ALCOVE, corner, hollow, nook, opening, recess **2** POSITION, calling, pigeonhole (*informal*), place, slot (*informal*), vocation

nick verb **1** CUT, chip, dent, mark, notch, scar, score, scratch, snick ▸ noun **2** CUT, chip, dent, mark, notch, scar, scratch

nickname noun PET NAME, diminutive, epithet, label, moniker or monicker (*slang*), sobriquet

nifty *adjective* NEAT, attractive, chic, deft, pleasing, smart, stylish

niggard *noun* MISER, cheapskate (*informal*), Scrooge, skinflint

niggardly *adjective* STINGY, avaricious, frugal, grudging, mean, miserly, parsimonious, tightfisted, ungenerous

niggle *verb* 1 WORRY, annoy, irritate, rankle 2 CRITICIZE, carp, cavil, find fault, fuss

niggling *adjective* 1 PERSISTENT, gnawing, irritating, troubling, worrying 2 PETTY, finicky, fussy, nit-picking (*informal*), pettifogging, picky (*informal*), quibbling

night *noun* DARKNESS, dark, night-time

nightfall *noun* EVENING, dusk, sundown, sunset, twilight

nightly *adjective* 1 NOCTURNAL, night-time ▶ *adverb* 2 EVERY NIGHT, each night, night after night, nights (*informal*)

nightmare *noun* 1 BAD DREAM, hallucination 2 ORDEAL, horror, torment, trial, tribulation

nil *noun* NOTHING, love, naught, none, zero

nimble *adjective* AGILE, brisk, deft, dexterous, lively, quick, sprightly, spry, swift

nimbly *adverb* QUICKLY, briskly, deftly, dexterously, easily, readily, smartly, spryly, swiftly

nip¹ *verb* PINCH, bite, squeeze, tweak

nip² *noun* DRAM, draft, drop, mouthful, shot (*informal*), sip, snifter (*informal*)

nippy *adjective* CHILLY, biting, sharp, stinging

nirvana *noun* PARADISE, bliss, joy, peace, serenity, tranquillity

nit-picking *adjective* FUSSY, captious, carping, finicky, hairsplitting, pedantic, pettifogging, quibbling

nitty-gritty *noun* BASICS, brass tacks (*informal*), core, crux, essentials, fundamentals, gist, substance

nitwit *noun* Informal FOOL, dimwit (*informal*), doofus (*slang*), dork (*slang*), dummy (*slang*), halfwit, oaf, schmuck (*slang*), simpleton

no *interjection* 1 NEVER, nay, not at all, no way ▶ *noun* 2 REFUSAL, denial, negation

nobility *noun* 1 INTEGRITY, honor, incorruptibility, uprightness, virtue 2 ARISTOCRACY, elite, lords, nobles, patricians, peerage, upper class

noble *adjective* 1 WORTHY, generous, honorable, magnanimous, upright, virtuous 2 ARISTOCRATIC, blue-blooded, highborn, lordly, patrician, titled 3 GREAT, dignified, distinguished, grand, imposing, impressive, lofty, splendid, stately ▶ *noun* 4 LORD, aristocrat, nobleman, peer

nobody *pronoun* 1 NO-ONE ▶ *noun* 2 NONENTITY, cipher, lightweight (*informal*), menial

nocturnal *adjective* NIGHTLY, night-time

nod *verb* 1 ACKNOWLEDGE, bow, gesture, indicate, signal 2 SLEEP, doze, drowse, nap ▶ *noun* 3 GESTURE, acknowledgment, greeting, indication, sign, signal

noggin *noun* CUP, dram, mug,

nip, tot **2** *Informal* HEAD, block
(*informal*), noodle (*slang*), nut
(*slang*)

no go *adjective* IMPOSSIBLE, futile,
hopeless, vain

noise *noun* SOUND, clamor,
commotion, din, hubbub,
racket, row, uproar

noiseless *adjective* SILENT,
hushed, inaudible, mute, quiet,
soundless, still

noisome *adjective* **1** POISONOUS,
bad, harmful, pernicious,
pestilential, unhealthy,
unwholesome **2** OFFENSIVE,
disgusting, fetid, foul, funky
(*slang*), malodorous, noxious,
putrid, smelly, stinking

noisy *adjective* LOUD, boisterous,
cacophonous, clamorous,
deafening, ear-splitting,
strident, tumultuous,
uproarious, vociferous

nomad *noun* WANDERER, drifter,
itinerant, migrant, rambler,
rover, vagabond

nomadic *adjective* WANDERING,
itinerant, migrant, peripatetic,
roaming, roving, traveling,
vagrant

nom de plume *noun*
PSEUDONYM, alias, assumed
name, nom de guerre, pen
name

nomenclature *noun*
TERMINOLOGY, classification,
codification, phraseology,
taxonomy, vocabulary

nominal *adjective* **1** SO-CALLED,
formal, ostensible, professed,
puppet, purported, supposed,
theoretical, titular **2** SMALL,
inconsiderable, insignificant,
minimal, symbolic, token,
trifling, trivial

nominate *verb* NAME, appoint,
assign, choose, designate,
elect, propose, recommend,
select, suggest

nomination *noun* CHOICE,
appointment, designation,
election, proposal,
recommendation, selection,
suggestion

nominee *noun* CANDIDATE,
aspirant, contestant, entrant,
protégé, runner

nonaligned *adjective* NEUTRAL,
impartial, uncommitted,
undecided

nonchalance *noun* INDIFFERENCE,
calm, composure, equanimity,
imperturbability, sang-froid,
self-possession, unconcern

nonchalant *adjective* CASUAL,
blasé, calm, careless,
indifferent, insouciant,
laid-back (*informal*), offhand,
unconcerned, unperturbed

noncombatant *noun* CIVILIAN,
neutral, nonbelligerent

noncommittal *adjective* EVASIVE,
cautious, circumspect,
equivocal, guarded, neutral,
politic, temporizing, tentative,
vague, wary

non compos mentis *adjective*
INSANE, crazy, deranged,
mentally ill, unbalanced,
unhinged

nonconformist *noun* MAVERICK,
dissenter, eccentric, heretic,
iconoclast, individualist,
protester, radical, rebel

nonconformity *noun* DISSENT,
eccentricity, heresy, heterodoxy

nondescript *adjective* ORDINARY,
commonplace, dull, featureless,
undistinguished,
unexceptional, unremarkable

none *pronoun* NOT ANY, nil, nobody, no-one, nothing, not one, zero

nonentity *noun* NOBODY, cipher, lightweight (*informal*), mediocrity, small fry

nonessential *adjective* UNNECESSARY, dispensable, expendable, extraneous, inessential, peripheral, superfluous, unimportant

nonetheless *adverb* NEVERTHELESS, despite that, even so, however, in spite of that, yet

nonevent *noun* FLOP (*informal*), disappointment, dud (*informal*), failure, fiasco, washout

nonexistent *adjective* IMAGINARY, chimerical, fictional, hypothetical, illusory, legendary, mythical, unreal

nonsense *noun* RUBBISH, balderdash, claptrap (*informal*), drivel, gibberish, hot air (*informal*), stupidity, tripe (*informal*), twaddle

nonsensical *adjective* SENSELESS, absurd, crazy, foolish, inane, incomprehensible, irrational, meaningless, ridiculous, silly

nonstarter *noun* DEAD LOSS, dud (*informal*), lemon (*informal*), loser, no-hoper (*informal*), turkey (*informal*), washout (*informal*)

nonstop *adjective* **1** CONTINUOUS, constant, endless, incessant, interminable, relentless, twenty-four-seven (*slang*), unbroken, uninterrupted ▶ *adverb* **2** CONTINUOUSLY, ceaselessly, constantly, endlessly, incessantly, interminably, perpetually, relentlessly, twenty-four-seven

(*slang*), unremittingly

noodle *noun* Slang HEAD, common sense, gut feeling (*informal*), intuition, sense

nook *noun* NICHE, alcove, corner, cubbyhole, hideout, opening, recess, retreat

noon *noun* MIDDAY, high noon, noonday, noontide, twelve noon

norm *noun* STANDARD, average, benchmark, criterion, par, pattern, rule, yardstick

normal *adjective* **1** USUAL, average, common, conventional, natural, ordinary, regular, routine, standard, typical **2** SANE, rational, reasonable, well-adjusted

normality *noun* **1** REGULARITY, conventionality, naturalness **2** SANITY, balance, rationality, reason

normally *adverb* USUALLY, as a rule, commonly, generally, habitually, ordinarily, regularly, typically

north *adjective* **1** NORTHERN, Arctic, boreal, northerly, polar ▶ *adverb* **2** NORTHWARD(S), northerly

nose *noun* **1** SNOUT, beak, bill, honker (*slang*), proboscis ▶ *verb* **2** EASE FORWARD, nudge, nuzzle, push, shove **3** PRY, meddle, snoop (*informal*)

nosegay *noun* POSY, bouquet

nostalgia *noun* REMINISCENCE, homesickness, longing, pining, regretfulness, remembrance, wistfulness, yearning

nostalgic *adjective* SENTIMENTAL, emotional, homesick, longing, maudlin, regretful, wistful

nostrum *noun* MEDICINE, cure,

drug, elixir, panacea, potion, remedy, treatment

nosy adjective INQUISITIVE, curious, eavesdropping, interfering, intrusive, meddlesome, prying, snooping (informal)

notability noun FAME, celebrity, distinction, eminence, esteem, renown

notable adjective 1 REMARKABLE, conspicuous, extraordinary, memorable, noteworthy, outstanding, rare, striking, uncommon, unusual ▶ noun 2 CELEBRITY, big name, dignitary, personage, V.I.P.

notably adverb PARTICULARLY, especially, outstandingly, strikingly

notation noun SIGNS, characters, code, script, symbols, system

notch noun 1 CUT, cleft, incision, indentation, mark, nick, score 2 Informal LEVEL, degree, grade, step ▶ verb 3 CUT, indent, mark, nick, score, scratch

notch up verb REGISTER, achieve, gain, make, score

note noun 1 MESSAGE, comment, communication, epistle, jotting, letter, memo, memorandum, minute, remark, reminder 2 SYMBOL, indication, mark, sign, token ▶ verb 3 SEE, notice, observe, perceive 4 MARK, denote, designate, indicate, record, register 5 MENTION, remark

notebook noun JOTTER, diary, exercise book, journal, notepad

noted adjective FAMOUS, acclaimed, celebrated, distinguished, eminent,

illustrious, notable, prominent, renowned, well-known

noteworthy adjective REMARKABLE, exceptional, extraordinary, important, notable, outstanding, significant, unusual

nothing noun NOUGHT, emptiness, nada (informal), nil, nothingness, nullity, void, zero

nothingness noun 1 OBLIVION, nonbeing, nonexistence, nullity 2 INSIGNIFICANCE, unimportance, worthlessness

notice noun 1 OBSERVATION, cognizance, consideration, heed, interest, note, regard 2 ATTENTION, civility, respect 3 ANNOUNCEMENT, advice, communication, instruction, intimation, news, notification, order, warning ▶ verb 4 OBSERVE, detect, discern, distinguish, mark, note, perceive, see, spot

noticeable adjective OBVIOUS, appreciable, clear, conspicuous, evident, manifest, perceptible, plain, striking

notification noun ANNOUNCEMENT, advice, declaration, information, intelligence, message, notice, statement, warning

notify verb INFORM, advise, alert, announce, declare, make known, publish, tell, warn

notion noun 1 IDEA, belief, concept, impression, inkling, opinion, sentiment, view 2 WHIM, caprice, desire, fancy, impulse, inclination, wish

notional adjective SPECULATIVE, abstract, conceptual, hypothetical, imaginary, theoretical, unreal

notoriety noun SCANDAL, dishonor, disrepute, infamy, obloquy, opprobrium

notorious adjective INFAMOUS, dishonorable, disreputable, opprobrious, scandalous

notoriously adverb INFAMOUSLY, dishonorably, disreputably, opprobriously, scandalously

notwithstanding preposition DESPITE, in spite of

nought noun ZERO, nil, nothing

nourish verb 1 FEED, nurse, nurture, supply, sustain, tend 2 ENCOURAGE, comfort, cultivate, foster, maintain, promote, support

nourishing adjective NUTRITIOUS, beneficial, nutritive, wholesome

nourishment noun FOOD, nutriment, nutrition, sustenance

novel[1] noun STORY, fiction, narrative, romance, tale

novel[2] adjective NEW, different, fresh, innovative, original, strange, uncommon, unfamiliar, unusual

novelty noun 1 NEWNESS, freshness, innovation, oddity, originality, strangeness, surprise, unfamiliarity, uniqueness 2 GIMMICK, curiosity, gadget 3 KNICK-KNACK, bauble, memento, souvenir, trifle, trinket

novice noun BEGINNER, amateur, apprentice, learner, newcomer, probationer, pupil, trainee

now adverb 1 NOWADAYS, anymore, at the moment 2 IMMEDIATELY, at once, instantly, promptly, straightaway **3 now and then** or **again** OCCASIONALLY, from time to time, infrequently, intermittently, on and off, sometimes, sporadically

nowadays adverb NOW, anymore, at the moment, in this day and age, today

noxious adjective HARMFUL, deadly, destructive, foul, hurtful, injurious, poisonous, unhealthy, unwholesome

nuance noun SUBTLETY, degree, distinction, gradation, nicety, refinement, shade, tinge

nubile adjective MARRIAGEABLE, ripe (informal)

nucleus noun CENTER, basis, core, focus, heart, kernel, nub, pivot

nude adjective NAKED, bare, disrobed, in one's birthday suit, stark-naked, stripped, unclad, unclothed, undressed, without a stitch on (informal)

nudge verb PUSH, bump, dig, elbow, jog, poke, prod, shove, touch

nudity noun NAKEDNESS, bareness, deshabille, nudism, undress

nugget noun LUMP, chunk, clump, hunk, mass, piece

nuisance noun PROBLEM, annoyance, bother, drag (informal), hassle (informal), inconvenience, irritation, pain in the neck, pest, trouble

null adjective **null and void** INVALID, inoperative, useless, valueless, void, worthless

nullify verb CANCEL, counteract, invalidate, negate, neutralize, obviate, render null and void, veto

nullity noun NONEXISTENCE, invalidity, powerlessness, uselessness, worthlessness

numb *adjective* **1** UNFEELING, benumbed, dead, deadened, frozen, immobilized, insensitive, paralyzed, torpid ▶ *verb* **2** DEADEN, benumb, dull, freeze, immobilize, paralyze

number *noun* **1** NUMERAL, character, digit, figure, integer **2** QUANTITY, aggregate, amount, collection, crowd, horde, multitude, throng **3** ISSUE, copy, edition, imprint, printing ▶ *verb* **4** COUNT, account, add, calculate, compute, enumerate, include, reckon, total

numberless *adjective* INFINITE, countless, endless, innumerable, multitudinous, myriad, unnumbered, untold

numbness *noun* DEADNESS, dullness, insensitivity, paralysis, torpor

numeral *noun* NUMBER, digit, figure, integer

numerous *adjective* MANY, abundant, copious, plentiful, profuse, several, thick on the ground

nunnery *noun* CONVENT, abbey, cloister, house

nuptial *adjective* MARITAL, bridal, conjugal, connubial, matrimonial

nuptials *plural noun* WEDDING, marriage, matrimony

nurse *verb* **1** LOOK AFTER, care for, minister to, tend, treat **2** BREAST-FEED, feed, nourish, nurture, suckle, wet-nurse **3** FOSTER, cherish, cultivate, encourage, harbor, preserve, promote, succor, support

nursery *noun* CRECHE, kindergarten, playgroup

nurture *noun* **1** DEVELOPMENT,

discipline, education, instruction, rearing, training, upbringing ▶ *verb* **2** DEVELOP, bring up, discipline, educate, instruct, rear, school, train

nut *noun* **1** *Slang* MADMAN, crank (*informal*), lunatic, maniac, nutcase (*slang*), psycho (*slang*) **2** *Slang* HEAD, brain, mind, reason, senses

nutrition *noun* FOOD, nourishment, nutriment, sustenance

nutritious *adjective* NOURISHING, beneficial, health-giving, invigorating, nutritive, strengthening, wholesome

nuts *adjective Informal* INSANE, deranged, disturbed, mad, mentally ill, psychotic, unbalanced, unstable

nuzzle *verb* SNUGGLE, burrow, cuddle, fondle, nestle, pet

nymph *noun* SYLPH, dryad, girl, maiden, naiad

oaf *noun* IDIOT, blockhead, clod, dolt, dork (*slang*), dunce, fool, goon, lout, moron, schmuck (*slang*)

oafish *adjective* MORONIC, dense, dim-witted (*informal*), doltish, dumb (*informal*), loutish, stupid, thick

oath *noun* **1** PROMISE, affirmation, avowal, bond, pledge, vow, word **2** SWEARWORD, blasphemy, curse, expletive, profanity

obdurate *adjective* STUBBORN,

dogged, hard-hearted, immovable, implacable, inflexible, obstinate, pig-headed, unyielding

obedience noun RESPECT, acquiescence, compliance, docility, observance, reverence, submissiveness, subservience

obedient adjective RESPECTFUL, acquiescent, biddable, compliant, deferential, docile, dutiful, submissive, subservient, well-trained

obelisk noun COLUMN, monolith, monument, needle, pillar, shaft

obese adjective FAT, corpulent, gross, heavy, overweight, paunchy, plump, portly, rotund, stout, tubby

obesity noun FATNESS, bulk, corpulence, grossness, portliness, stoutness, tubbiness

obey verb CARRY OUT, abide by, act upon, adhere to, comply, conform, follow, heed, keep, observe

obfuscate verb CONFUSE, befog, cloud, darken, muddy the waters, obscure, perplex

object[1] noun 1 THING, article, body, entity, item, phenomenon 2 TARGET, focus, recipient, victim 3 PURPOSE, aim, design, end, goal, idea, intention, objective, point

object[2] verb PROTEST, argue against, demur, draw the line (at something), expostulate, oppose, take exception

objection noun PROTEST, counter-argument, demur, doubt, opposition, remonstrance, scruple

objectionable adjective UNPLEASANT, deplorable, disagreeable, intolerable, obnoxious, offensive, regrettable, repugnant, unseemly

objective noun 1 PURPOSE, aim, ambition, end, goal, intention, mark, object, target ▶ adjective 2 UNBIASED, detached, disinterested, dispassionate, even-handed, fair, impartial, open-minded, unprejudiced

objectively adverb IMPARTIALLY, disinterestedly, dispassionately, even-handedly, with an open mind

objectivity noun IMPARTIALITY, detachment, disinterestedness, dispassion

obligation noun DUTY, accountability, burden, charge, compulsion, liability, requirement, responsibility

obligatory adjective COMPULSORY, binding, de rigueur, essential, imperative, mandatory, necessary, required, requisite, unavoidable

oblige verb 1 COMPEL, bind, constrain, force, impel, make, necessitate, require 2 INDULGE, accommodate, benefit, gratify, please

obliged adjective 1 GRATEFUL, appreciative, beholden, indebted, in (someone's) debt, thankful 2 BOUND, compelled, forced, required

obliging adjective COOPERATIVE, accommodating, agreeable, considerate, good-natured, helpful, kind, polite, willing

oblique adjective 1 SLANTING, angled, aslant, sloping, tilted 2 INDIRECT, backhanded, circuitous, implied, roundabout, sidelong

obliterate verb DESTROY, annihilate, blot out, efface, eradicate, erase, expunge, extirpate, root out, wipe out

obliteration noun ANNIHILATION, elimination, eradication, extirpation, wiping out

oblivion noun 1 NEGLECT, abeyance, disregard, forgetfulness
2 UNCONSCIOUSNESS, insensibility, obliviousness, unawareness

oblivious adjective UNAWARE, forgetful, heedless, ignorant, insensible, neglectful, negligent, regardless, unconcerned, unconscious, unmindful

obloquy noun 1 ABUSE, aspersion, attack, blame, censure, criticism, invective, reproach, slander, vilification
2 DISCREDIT, disgrace, dishonor, humiliation, ignominy, infamy, shame, stigma

obnoxious adjective OFFENSIVE, disagreeable, insufferable, loathsome, nasty, nauseating, objectionable, odious, repulsive, revolting, scuzzy (slang), unpleasant

obscene adjective 1 INDECENT, dirty, filthy, immoral, improper, lewd, offensive, pornographic, salacious, scuzzy (slang), X-rated 2 SICKENING, atrocious, disgusting, evil, heinous, loathsome, outrageous, shocking, vile, wicked

obscenity noun 1 INDECENCY, coarseness, dirtiness, impropriety, lewdness, licentiousness, pornography,

smut **2** SWEARWORD, four-letter word, profanity, vulgarism
3 OUTRAGE, abomination, affront, atrocity, blight, evil, offense, wrong

obscure adjective 1 VAGUE, ambiguous, arcane, confusing, cryptic, enigmatic, esoteric, mysterious, opaque, recondite
2 INDISTINCT, blurred, cloudy, dim, faint, gloomy, murky, shadowy **3** LITTLE-KNOWN, humble, lowly, out-of-the-way, remote, undistinguished, unheard-of, unknown ▶ verb
4 CONCEAL, cover, disguise, hide, obfuscate, screen, veil

obscurity noun 1 DARKNESS, dimness, dusk, gloom, haze, shadows **2** INSIGNIFICANCE, lowliness, unimportance

obsequious adjective SYCOPHANTIC, cringing, deferential, fawning, flattering, grovelling, ingratiating, servile, submissive, unctuous

observable adjective NOTICEABLE, apparent, detectable, discernible, evident, obvious, perceptible, recognizable, visible

observance noun HONORING, carrying out, compliance, fulfillment, performance

observant adjective ATTENTIVE, alert, eagle-eyed, perceptive, quick, sharp-eyed, vigilant, watchful, wide-awake

observation noun 1 STUDY, examination, inspection, monitoring, review, scrutiny, surveillance, watching
2 REMARK, comment, note, opinion, pronouncement, reflection, thought, utterance

observe verb 1 SEE, detect,

discern, discover, note, notice, perceive, spot, witness **2** WATCH, check, keep an eye on (*informal*), keep track of, look at, monitor, scrutinize, study, survey, view **3** REMARK, comment, mention, note, opine, say, state **4** HONOR, abide by, adhere to, comply, conform to, follow, heed, keep, obey, respect

observer noun SPECTATOR, beholder, bystander, eyewitness, fly on the wall, looker-on, onlooker, viewer, watcher, witness

obsessed adjective PREOCCUPIED, dominated, gripped, haunted, hung up on (*slang*), infatuated, troubled

obsession noun PREOCCUPATION, complex, fetish, fixation, hang-up (*informal*), infatuation, mania, phobia, thing (*informal*)

obsessive adjective COMPULSIVE, besetting, consuming, gripping, haunting

obsolescent adjective WANING, ageing, declining, dying out, on the wane, on the way out, past its prime

obsolete adjective EXTINCT, antiquated, archaic, discarded, disused, old, old-fashioned, outmoded, out of date, passé

obstacle noun DIFFICULTY, bar, barrier, block, hindrance, hitch, hurdle, impediment, obstruction, snag, stumbling block

obstinacy noun STUBBORNNESS, doggedness, inflexibility, intransigence, obduracy, persistence, pig-headedness, tenacity, willfulness

obstinate adjective STUBBORN, determined, dogged, inflexible, intractable, intransigent, pig-headed, refractory, self-willed, strong-minded, willful

obstreperous adjective UNRULY, disorderly, loud, noisy, riotous, rowdy, turbulent, unmanageable, wild

obstruct verb BLOCK, bar, barricade, check, hamper, hinder, impede, restrict, stop, thwart

obstruction noun OBSTACLE, bar, barricade, barrier, blockage, difficulty, hindrance, impediment

obstructive adjective UNCOOPERATIVE, awkward, blocking, delaying, hindering, restrictive, stalling, unhelpful

obtain verb **1** GET, achieve, acquire, attain, earn, gain, land, procure, secure **2** EXIST, be in force, be prevalent, be the case, hold, prevail

obtainable adjective AVAILABLE, achievable, attainable, on tap (*informal*), to be had

obtrusive adjective NOTICEABLE, blatant, obvious, prominent, protruding, protuberant, sticking out

obtuse adjective SLOW, dense, dull, stolid, stupid, thick, uncomprehending

obviate verb PRECLUDE, avert, prevent, remove

obvious adjective EVIDENT, apparent, clear, conspicuous, distinct, indisputable, manifest, noticeable, plain, self-evident, undeniable, unmistakable

obviously adverb CLEARLY,

manifestly, of course, palpably, patently, plainly, undeniably, unmistakably, unquestionably, without doubt

occasion noun 1 TIME, chance, moment, opening, opportunity, window 2 EVENT, affair, celebration, experience, happening, occurrence 3 REASON, call, cause, excuse, ground(s), justification, motive, prompting, provocation ▸verb 4 CAUSE, bring about, engender, generate, give rise to, induce, inspire, lead to, produce, prompt, provoke

occasional adjective INFREQUENT, incidental, intermittent, irregular, odd, rare, sporadic, uncommon

occasionally adverb SOMETIMES, at times, from time to time, irregularly, now and again, once in a while, periodically

occult adjective SUPERNATURAL, arcane, esoteric, magical, mysterious, mystical

occupancy noun TENURE, possession, residence, tenancy, use

occupant noun INHABITANT, incumbent, indweller, inmate, lessee, occupier, resident, tenant

occupation noun 1 PROFESSION, business, calling, employment, job, line (of work), pursuit, trade, vocation, walk of life 2 POSSESSION, control, holding, occupancy, residence, tenancy, tenure 3 INVASION, conquest, seizure, subjugation

occupied adjective 1 BUSY, employed, engaged, working 2 IN USE, engaged, full, taken,

unavailable 3 INHABITED, lived-in, peopled, settled, tenanted

occupy verb 1 (often passive) TAKE UP, divert, employ, engage, engross, involve, monopolize, preoccupy, tie up 2 LIVE IN, dwell in, inhabit, own, possess, reside in 3 FILL, cover, permeate, pervade, take up 4 INVADE, capture, overrun, seize, take over

occur verb 1 HAPPEN, befall, come about, crop up (informal), take place, turn up (informal) 2 EXIST, appear, be found, be present, develop, manifest itself, show itself 3 **occur to** COME TO MIND, cross one's mind, dawn on, enter one's head, spring to mind, strike one, suggest itself

occurrence noun 1 INCIDENT, adventure, affair, circumstance, episode, event, happening, instance 2 EXISTENCE, appearance, development, manifestation, materialization

odd adjective 1 UNUSUAL, bizarre, extraordinary, freakish, irregular, peculiar, rare, remarkable, singular, strange 2 OCCASIONAL, casual, incidental, irregular, periodic, random, sundry, various 3 SPARE, leftover, remaining, solitary, surplus, unmatched, unpaired

oddity noun 1 IRREGULARITY, abnormality, anomaly, eccentricity, freak, idiosyncrasy, peculiarity, quirk 2 MISFIT, crank (informal), maverick, oddball (informal)

oddment noun LEFTOVER, bit, fag end, fragment, off cut, remnant, scrap, snippet

odds plural noun 1 PROBABILITY, chances, likelihood 2 **at odds** IN CONFLICT, at daggers drawn, at loggerheads, at sixes and sevens, at variance, out of line

odds and ends plural noun SCRAPS, bits, bits and pieces, debris, oddments, remnants

odious adjective OFFENSIVE, detestable, horrid, loathsome, obnoxious, repulsive, revolting, scuzzy (slang), unpleasant

odor noun SMELL, aroma, bouquet, essence, fragrance, perfume, redolence, scent, stench, stink

odyssey noun JOURNEY, crusade, pilgrimage, quest, trek, voyage

off adverb 1 AWAY, apart, aside, elsewhere, out ▶ adjective 2 UNAVAILABLE, canceled, finished, gone, postponed

offbeat adjective UNUSUAL, eccentric, left-field (informal), novel, outré, strange, unconventional, unorthodox, way-out (informal)

off color adjective ILL, out of sorts, peaky, poorly (informal), queasy, run down, sick, under the weather (informal), unwell

offend verb INSULT, affront, annoy, displease, hurt (someone's) feelings, outrage, slight, snub, upset, wound

offended adjective RESENTFUL, affronted, disgruntled, displeased, outraged, piqued, put out (informal), smarting, stung, upset

offender noun CRIMINAL, crook, culprit, delinquent, lawbreaker, miscreant, sinner, transgressor, villain, wrongdoer

offense noun 1 CRIME, fault,

misdeed, misdemeanor, sin, transgression, trespass, wrongdoing 2 SNUB, affront, hurt, indignity, injustice, insult, outrage, slight 3 ANNOYANCE, anger, displeasure, indignation, pique, resentment, umbrage, wrath

offensive adjective 1 INSULTING, abusive, discourteous, disrespectful, impertinent, insolent, objectionable, rude 2 DISAGREEABLE, disgusting, nauseating, obnoxious, odious, repellent, revolting, unpleasant, vile 3 AGGRESSIVE, attacking, invading ▶ noun 4 ATTACK, campaign, drive, onslaught, push (informal)

offer verb 1 BID, proffer, tender 2 PROVIDE, afford, furnish, present 3 PROPOSE, advance, submit, suggest 4 VOLUNTEER, come forward, offer one's services ▶ noun 5 BID, proposal, proposition, submission, suggestion, tender

offering noun DONATION, contribution, gift, hand-out, present, sacrifice, subscription

offhand adjective 1 CASUAL, aloof, brusque, careless, curt, glib ▶ adverb 2 IMPROMPTU, ad lib, extempore, off the cuff (informal)

office noun POST, function, occupation, place, responsibility, role, situation

officer noun OFFICIAL, agent, appointee, executive, functionary, office-holder, representative

official adjective 1 AUTHORIZED, accredited, authentic, certified, formal, legitimate, licensed,

proper, sanctioned ▶ *noun*
2 OFFICER, agent, bureaucrat, executive, functionary, office bearer, representative

officiate *verb* PRESIDE, chair, conduct, manage, oversee, serve, superintend

officious *adjective* INTERFERING, dictatorial, intrusive, meddlesome, obtrusive, overzealous, pushy (*informal*), self-important

offing *noun* **in the offing** IN PROSPECT, imminent, on the horizon, upcoming

offset *verb* CANCEL OUT, balance out, compensate for, counteract, counterbalance, make up for, neutralize

offshoot *noun* BY-PRODUCT, adjunct, appendage, development, spin-off

offspring *noun* **1** CHILD, descendant, heir, scion, successor **2** CHILDREN, brood, descendants, family, heirs, issue, progeny, young

often *adverb* FREQUENTLY, generally, repeatedly, time and again

ogle *verb* LEER, eye up (*informal*)

ogre *noun* MONSTER, bogeyman, bugbear, demon, devil, giant, specter

oil *verb* LUBRICATE, grease

oily *adjective* GREASY, fatty, oleaginous

ointment *noun* LOTION, balm, cream, embrocation, emollient, liniment, salve, unguent

O.K., okay *interjection* **1** ALL RIGHT, agreed, right, roger, very good, very well, yes ▶ *adjective* **2** ALL RIGHT, acceptable, adequate, fine, good, in order,

permitted, satisfactory, up to scratch (*informal*) ▶ *verb* **3** APPROVE, agree to, authorize, endorse, give the green light, rubber-stamp (*informal*), sanction ▶ *noun* **4** APPROVAL, agreement, assent, authorization, consent, go-ahead (*informal*), green light, permission, sanction, say-so (*informal*), seal of approval

old *adjective* **1** SENILE, aged, ancient, decrepit, elderly, mature, venerable **2** ANTIQUE, antediluvian, antiquated, dated, obsolete, timeworn **3** FORMER, earlier, erstwhile, one-time, previous

old-fashioned *adjective* OUT OF DATE, behind the times, dated, obsolescent, obsolete, old hat, outdated, outmoded, passé, unfashionable

omen *noun* SIGN, foreboding, indication, portent, premonition, presage, warning

ominous *adjective* SINISTER, fateful, foreboding, inauspicious, portentous, threatening, unpromising, unpropitious

omission *noun* EXCLUSION, failure, lack, neglect, oversight

omit *verb* LEAVE OUT, drop, eliminate, exclude, forget, neglect, overlook, pass over, skip

omnipotence *noun* SUPREMACY, invincibility, mastery

omnipotent *adjective* ALMIGHTY, all-powerful, supreme

omniscient *adjective* ALL-KNOWING, all-wise

once *adverb* **1** FORMERLY, at one

time, long ago, once upon a
time, previously **2 at once:
a** IMMEDIATELY, directly,
forthwith, instantly, now, right
away, straight away, this (very)
minute **b** SIMULTANEOUSLY, at the
same time, together

oncoming adjective APPROACHING,
advancing, forthcoming,
looming, onrushing

onerous adjective DIFFICULT,
burdensome, demanding,
exacting, hard, heavy,
laborious, oppressive, taxing

one-sided adjective BIASED,
lopsided, partial, partisan,
prejudiced, unfair, unjust

ongoing adjective EVOLVING,
continuous, developing,
progressing, unfinished,
unfolding

onlooker noun OBSERVER,
bystander, eyewitness,
looker-on, spectator, viewer,
watcher, witness

only adjective **1** SOLE, exclusive,
individual, lone, single, solitary,
unique ▶ adverb **2** MERELY,
barely, just, purely, simply

onset noun BEGINNING, inception,
outbreak, start

onslaught noun ATTACK, assault,
blitz, charge, offensive, onrush,
onset

onus noun BURDEN, liability, load,
obligation, responsibility, task

onward, onwards adverb
AHEAD, beyond, forth, forward,
in front, on

ooze[1] verb SEEP, drain, dribble,
drip, escape, filter, leak

ooze[2] noun MUD, alluvium, mire,
silt, slime, sludge

opaque adjective CLOUDY, dim,
dull, filmy, hazy, impenetrable,
muddy, murky

open adjective **1** UNFASTENED,
agape, ajar, gaping,
uncovered, unfolded, unfurled,
unlocked, yawning **2** ACCESSIBLE,
available, free, public,
unoccupied, unrestricted,
vacant **3** UNRESOLVED, arguable,
debatable, moot, undecided,
unsettled **4** FRANK, candid,
guileless, honest, sincere,
transparent ▶ verb **5** START,
begin, commence, inaugurate,
initiate, kick off (informal),
launch, set in motion
6 UNFASTEN, unblock, uncork,
uncover, undo, unlock, untie,
unwrap **7** UNFOLD, expand,
spread (out), unfurl, unroll

open-air adjective OUTDOOR,
alfresco

open-handed adjective
GENEROUS, bountiful, free, lavish,
liberal, munificent, unstinting

opening noun **1** HOLE, aperture,
chink, cleft, crack, fissure, gap,
orifice, perforation, slot, space
2 OPPORTUNITY, chance,
occasion, vacancy **3** BEGINNING,
commencement, dawn,
inception, initiation, launch,
outset, start ▶ adjective **4** FIRST,
beginning, inaugural, initial,
introductory, maiden, primary

openly adverb CANDIDLY,
forthrightly, frankly, overtly,
plainly, unhesitatingly,
unreservedly

open-minded adjective TOLERANT,
broad-minded, impartial,
liberal, reasonable, receptive,
unbiased, undogmatic,
unprejudiced

operate verb **1** WORK, act,
function, go, perform, run

2 HANDLE, be in charge of, manage, maneuver, use, work

operation noun PROCEDURE, action, course, exercise, motion, movement, performance, process

operational adjective WORKING, functional, going, operative, prepared, ready, up and running, usable, viable, workable

operative adjective 1 IN FORCE, active, effective, functioning, in operation, operational ▶ noun 2 WORKER, artisan, employee, laborer

operator noun WORKER, conductor, driver, handler, mechanic, operative, practitioner, technician

opinion noun BELIEF, assessment, feeling, idea, impression, judgment, point of view, sentiment, theory, view

opinionated adjective DOGMATIC, bigoted, cocksure, doctrinaire, overbearing, pig-headed, prejudiced, single-minded

opponent noun COMPETITOR, adversary, antagonist, challenger, contestant, enemy, foe, rival

opportune adjective TIMELY, advantageous, appropriate, apt, auspicious, convenient, favorable, fitting, suitable, well-timed

opportunism noun EXPEDIENCY, exploitation, pragmatism, unscrupulousness

opportunity noun CHANCE, moment, occasion, opening, scope, time

oppose verb FIGHT, block, combat, counter, defy, resist,

take issue with, take on, thwart, withstand

opposed adjective AVERSE, antagonistic, clashing, conflicting, contrary, dissentient, hostile

opposing adjective HOSTILE, conflicting, contrary, enemy, incompatible, opposite, rival

opposite adjective 1 FACING, fronting 2 DIFFERENT, antithetical, conflicting, contrary, contrasted, reverse, unlike ▶ noun 3 REVERSE, antithesis, contradiction, contrary, converse, inverse

opposition noun 1 HOSTILITY, antagonism, competition, disapproval, obstruction, prevention, resistance, unfriendliness 2 OPPONENT, antagonist, competition, foe, other side, rival

oppress verb 1 DEPRESS, afflict, burden, dispirit, harass, sadden, torment, vex 2 PERSECUTE, abuse, maltreat, subdue, subjugate, suppress, wrong

oppressed adjective DOWNTRODDEN, abused, browbeaten, disadvantaged, harassed, maltreated, tyrannized, underprivileged

oppression noun PERSECUTION, abuse, brutality, cruelty, injury, injustice, maltreatment, subjection, tyranny

oppressive adjective 1 TYRANNICAL, brutal, cruel, despotic, harsh, inhuman, repressive, severe, unjust 2 SULTRY, airless, close, muggy, stifling, stuffy

oppressor noun PERSECUTOR,

autocrat, bully, despot, scourge, slave-driver, tormentor, tyrant

opt verb (often with for) CHOOSE, decide (on), elect, go for, plump for, prefer

optimistic adjective HOPEFUL, buoyant, cheerful, confident, encouraged, expectant, positive, rosy, sanguine

optimum adjective IDEAL, best, highest, optimal, peak, perfect, superlative

option noun CHOICE, alternative, preference, selection

optional adjective VOLUNTARY, discretionary, elective, extra, open, possible

opulence noun 1 WEALTH, affluence, luxuriance, luxury, plenty, prosperity, riches 2 ABUNDANCE, copiousness, cornucopia, fullness, profusion, richness, superabundance

opulent adjective 1 RICH, affluent, lavish, luxurious, moneyed, prosperous, sumptuous, wealthy, well-off, well-to-do 2 ABUNDANT, copious, lavish, luxuriant, plentiful, profuse, prolific

opus noun WORK, brainchild, composition, creation, oeuvre, piece, production

oracle noun 1 PROPHECY, divination, prediction, prognostication, revelation 2 PUNDIT, adviser, authority, guru, mastermind, mentor, wizard

oral adjective SPOKEN, verbal, vocal

oration noun SPEECH, address, discourse, harangue, homily, lecture

orator noun PUBLIC SPEAKER, declaimer, lecturer, rhetorician, speaker

oratorical adjective RHETORICAL, bombastic, declamatory, eloquent, grandiloquent, high-flown, magniloquent, sonorous

oratory noun ELOQUENCE, declamation, elocution, grandiloquence, public speaking, rhetoric, speech-making

orb noun SPHERE, ball, circle, globe, ring

orbit noun 1 PATH, circle, course, cycle, revolution, rotation, trajectory 2 SPHERE OF INFLUENCE, ambit, compass, domain, influence, range, reach, scope, sweep ▶ verb 3 CIRCLE, circumnavigate, encircle, revolve around

orchestrate verb 1 SCORE, arrange 2 ORGANIZE, arrange, coordinate, put together, set up, stage-manage

ordain verb 1 APPOINT, anoint, consecrate, invest, nominate 2 ORDER, decree, demand, dictate, fix, lay down, legislate, prescribe, rule, will

ordeal noun HARDSHIP, agony, anguish, baptism of fire, nightmare, suffering, test, torture, trial, tribulation(s)

order noun 1 INSTRUCTION, command, decree, dictate, direction, directive, injunction, law, mandate, regulation, rule 2 SEQUENCE, arrangement, array, grouping, layout, line-up, progression, series, structure 3 TIDINESS, method, neatness, orderliness, organization, pattern, regularity, symmetry, system **4** DISCIPLINE, calm, control, law and order, peace, quiet, tranquillity **5** REQUEST, application, booking, commission, requisition, reservation **6** CLASS, caste, grade, position, rank, status **7** KIND, class, family, genre, ilk, sort, type **8** SOCIETY, association, brotherhood, community, company, fraternity, guild, organization ▸ *verb* **9** INSTRUCT, bid, charge, command, decree, demand, direct, require **10** REQUEST, apply for, book, reserve, send away for **11** ARRANGE, catalog, classify, group, marshal, organize, sort out, systematize

orderly *adjective* **1** WELL-ORGANIZED, businesslike, in order, methodical, neat, regular, scientific, shipshape, systematic, tidy **2** WELL-BEHAVED, controlled, disciplined, law-abiding, peaceable, quiet, restrained

ordinarily *adverb* USUALLY, as a rule, commonly, customarily, generally, habitually, in general, normally

ordinary *adjective* **1** USUAL, common, conventional, everyday, normal, regular, routine, standard, stock, typical **2** COMMONPLACE, banal, humble, humdrum, modest, mundane, plain, unremarkable, workaday

organ *noun* **1** PART, element, structure, unit **2** MOUTHPIECE, forum, medium, vehicle, voice

organic *adjective* **1** NATURAL, animate, biological, live, living **2** SYSTEMATIC, integrated, methodical, ordered,

organized, structured

organism *noun* CREATURE, animal, being, body, entity, structure

organization *noun* **1** GROUP, association, body, company, confederation, corporation, institution, outfit (*informal*), syndicate **2** MANAGEMENT, construction, coordination, direction, organizing, planning, running, structuring **3** ARRANGEMENT, chemistry, composition, format, make-up, pattern, structure, unity

organize *verb* ARRANGE, classify, coordinate, group, marshal, put together, run, set up, systematize, take care of

orgy *noun* **1** REVEL, bacchanalia, carousal, debauch, revelry, Saturnalia **2** SPREE, binge (*informal*), bout, excess, indulgence, overindulgence, splurge, surfeit

orient *verb* FAMILIARIZE, acclimatize, adapt, adjust, align, get one's bearings, orientate

orientation *noun* **1** POSITION, bearings, direction, location **2** FAMILIARIZATION, acclimatization, adaptation, adjustment, assimilation, introduction, settling in

orifice *noun* OPENING, aperture, cleft, hole, mouth, pore, rent, vent

origin *noun* **1** ROOT, base, basis, derivation, fount, fountainhead, source, wellspring **2** BEGINNING, birth, creation, emergence, foundation, genesis, inception, launch, start

original *adjective* **1** FIRST,

earliest, initial, introductory,
opening, primary, starting
2 NEW, fresh, ground-breaking,
innovative, novel, seminal,
unprecedented, unusual
3 CREATIVE, fertile, imaginative,
ingenious, inventive,
resourceful ▸ *noun* **4** PROTOTYPE,
archetype, master, model,
paradigm, pattern, precedent,
standard

originality *noun* NOVELTY,
creativity, freshness,
imagination, ingenuity,
innovation, inventiveness,
newness, unorthodoxy

originally *adverb* INITIALLY, at
first, first, in the beginning, to
begin with

originate *verb* **1** BEGIN, arise,
come, derive, emerge, result,
rise, spring, start, stem
2 INTRODUCE, bring about,
create, formulate, generate,
institute, launch, pioneer

originator *noun* CREATOR,
architect, author, father *or*
mother, founder, inventor,
maker, pioneer

ornament *noun* **1** DECORATION,
accessory, adornment, bauble,
embellishment, festoon,
knick-knack, trimming, trinket
▸ *verb* **2** DECORATE, adorn,
beautify, embellish, festoon,
grace, prettify

ornamental *adjective* DECORATIVE,
attractive, beautifying,
embellishing, for show, showy

ornamentation *noun*
DECORATION, adornment,
elaboration, embellishment,
embroidery, frills, ornateness

ornate *adjective* ELABORATE,
baroque, busy, decorated,

fancy, florid, fussy,
ornamented, overelaborate,
rococo

orthodox *adjective* ESTABLISHED,
accepted, approved,
conventional, customary,
official, received, traditional,
well-established

orthodoxy *noun* CONFORMITY,
authority, conventionality,
received wisdom, traditionalism

oscillate *verb* FLUCTUATE, seesaw,
sway, swing, vacillate, vary,
vibrate, waver

oscillation *noun* SWING,
fluctuation, instability,
vacillation, variation, wavering

ossify *verb* HARDEN, fossilize,
solidify, stiffen

ostensible *adjective* APPARENT,
outward, pretended, professed,
purported, seeming, so-called,
superficial, supposed

ostensibly *adverb* APPARENTLY, on
the face of it, professedly,
seemingly, supposedly

ostentation *noun* DISPLAY,
affectation, exhibitionism,
flamboyance, flashiness,
flaunting, parade, pomp,
pretentiousness, show,
showing off (*informal*)

ostentatious *adjective*
PRETENTIOUS, brash, conspicuous,
flamboyant, flashy, gaudy,
loud, obtrusive, showy

ostracism *noun* EXCLUSION,
banishment, exile, isolation,
rejection

ostracize *verb* EXCLUDE, banish,
cast out, cold-shoulder, exile,
give (someone) the cold
shoulder, reject, shun

other *adjective* **1** ADDITIONAL,
added, alternative, auxiliary,

extra, further, more, spare, supplementary **2** DIFFERENT, contrasting, dissimilar, distinct, diverse, separate, unrelated, variant

otherwise conjunction **1** OR ELSE, if not, or then ▶ adverb **2** DIFFERENTLY, any other way, contrarily

ounce noun SHRED, atom, crumb, drop, grain, scrap, speck, trace

oust verb EXPEL, depose, dislodge, displace, dispossess, eject, throw out, topple, turn out, unseat

out adjective **1** AWAY, abroad, absent, elsewhere, gone, not at home, outside **2** EXTINGUISHED, at an end, dead, ended, exhausted, expired, finished, used up

outbreak noun ERUPTION, burst, epidemic, explosion, flare-up, outburst, rash, upsurge

outburst noun OUTPOURING, eruption, explosion, flare-up, outbreak, paroxysm, spasm, surge

outcast noun PARIAH, castaway, exile, leper, persona non grata, refugee, vagabond, wretch

outclass verb SURPASS, eclipse, excel, leave standing (informal), outdo, outshine, outstrip, overshadow, run rings around (informal)

outcome noun RESULT, conclusion, consequence, end, issue, payoff (informal), upshot

outcry noun PROTEST, clamor, commotion, complaint, hue and cry, hullabaloo, outburst, uproar

outdated adjective

OLD-FASHIONED, antiquated, archaic, obsolete, outmoded, out of date, passé, unfashionable

outdo verb SURPASS, beat, best, eclipse, exceed, get the better of, outclass, outmaneuver, overcome, top, transcend

outdoor adjective OPEN-AIR, alfresco, out-of-door(s), outside

outer adjective EXTERNAL, exposed, exterior, outlying, outside, outward, peripheral, surface

outfit noun **1** COSTUME, clothes, ensemble, garb, get-up (informal), kit, suit **2** GROUP, company, crew, organization, setup (informal), squad, team, unit

outgoing adjective **1** LEAVING, departing, former, retiring, withdrawing **2** SOCIABLE, approachable, communicative, expansive, extrovert, friendly, gregarious, open, warm

outgoings plural noun EXPENSES, costs, expenditure, outlay, overheads

outing noun TRIP, excursion, expedition, jaunt, spin (informal)

outlandish adjective STRANGE, bizarre, exotic, fantastic, far-out (slang), freakish, outré, preposterous, unheard-of, weird

outlaw noun **1** BANDIT, desperado, fugitive, highwayman, marauder, outcast, robber ▶ verb **2** FORBID, ban, bar, disallow, exclude, prohibit, proscribe

outlay noun EXPENDITURE, cost, expenses, investment, outgoings, spending

outlet noun **1** RELEASE, avenue,

channel, duct, exit, opening, vent **2** SHOP, market, store

outline noun **1** SUMMARY, recapitulation, résumé, rundown, synopsis, thumbnail sketch **2** SHAPE, configuration, contour, delineation, figure, form, profile, silhouette ▶ verb **3** SUMMARIZE, adumbrate, delineate, draft, plan, rough out, sketch (in), trace

outlive verb SURVIVE, outlast

outlook noun **1** ATTITUDE, angle, frame of mind, perspective, point of view, slant, standpoint, viewpoint **2** PROSPECT, expectations, forecast, future

outlying adjective REMOTE, distant, far-flung, out-of-the-way, peripheral, provincial

outmoded adjective OLD-FASHIONED, anachronistic, antiquated, archaic, obsolete, out-of-date, outworn, passé, unfashionable

out-of-date adjective OLD-FASHIONED, antiquated, dated, expired, invalid, lapsed, obsolete, outmoded, outworn, passé

outpouring noun STREAM, cascade, effusion, flow, spate, spurt, torrent

output noun PRODUCTION, achievement, manufacture, productivity, yield

outrage noun **1** VIOLATION, abuse, affront, desecration, indignity, insult, offense, sacrilege, violence **2** INDIGNATION, anger, fury, hurt, resentment, shock, wrath ▶ verb **3** OFFEND, affront, incense,

infuriate, madden, scandalize, shock

outrageous adjective **1** OFFENSIVE, atrocious, disgraceful, flagrant, heinous, iniquitous, nefarious, unspeakable, villainous, wicked **2** SHOCKING, exorbitant, extravagant, immoderate, preposterous, scandalous, steep (*informal*), unreasonable

outré adjective ECCENTRIC, bizarre, fantastic, freakish, odd, off-the-wall (*slang*), outlandish, unconventional, weird

outright adjective **1** ABSOLUTE, complete, out-and-out, perfect, thorough, thoroughgoing, total, unconditional, unmitigated, unqualified **2** DIRECT, definite, flat, straightforward, unequivocal, unqualified ▶ adverb **3** ABSOLUTELY, completely, openly, overtly, straightforwardly, thoroughly, to the full

outset noun BEGINNING, commencement, inauguration, inception, kickoff (*informal*), onset, opening, start

outshine verb OVERSHADOW, eclipse, leave or put in the shade, outclass, outdo, outstrip, surpass, transcend, upstage

outside adjective **1** EXTERNAL, exterior, extraneous, outer, outward **2** As in **an outside chance** UNLIKELY, distant, faint, marginal, remote, slight, slim, small ▶ noun **3** SURFACE, exterior, façade, face, front, skin, topside

outsider noun INTERLOPER, incomer, intruder, newcomer,

odd man out, stranger

outsize *adjective* EXTRA-LARGE, giant, gigantic, huge, jumbo (*informal*), mammoth, monster, oversized

outskirts *plural noun* EDGE, boundary, environs, periphery, suburbia, suburbs

outspoken *adjective* FORTHRIGHT, abrupt, blunt, explicit, frank, open, plain-spoken, unceremonious, unequivocal

outstanding *adjective*
1 EXCELLENT, cool (*informal*), exceptional, great, important, impressive, phat (*slang*), special, superior, superlative
2 UNPAID, due, payable, pending, remaining, uncollected, unsettled

outstrip *verb* SURPASS, better, eclipse, exceed, excel, outdistance, outdo, overtake, transcend

outward *adjective* APPARENT, noticeable, observable, obvious, ostensible, perceptible, surface, visible

outwardly *adverb* OSTENSIBLY, apparently, externally, on the face of it, on the surface, seemingly, superficially, to all intents and purposes

outweigh *verb* OVERRIDE, cancel (out), compensate for, eclipse, prevail over, take precedence over, tip the scales

outwit *verb* OUTTHINK, cheat, dupe, fool, get the better of, outfox, outmaneuver, outsmart (*informal*), swindle

outworn *adjective* OUTDATED, antiquated, discredited, disused, hackneyed, obsolete, outmoded, out-of-date,
threadbare, worn-out

oval *adjective* ELLIPTICAL, egg-shaped, ovoid

ovation *noun* APPLAUSE, acclaim, acclamation, big hand, cheers, clapping, plaudits

over *preposition* **1** ON, above, on top of, upon **2** EXCEEDING, above, in excess of, more than
▸ *adverb* **3** ABOVE, aloft, on high, overhead **4** EXTRA, beyond, in addition, in excess, left over
▸ *adjective* **5** FINISHED, bygone, closed, completed, concluded, done (with), ended, gone, past

overact *verb* EXAGGERATE, ham *or* ham up (*informal*), overdo, overplay

overall *adjective* **1** TOTAL, all-embracing, blanket, complete, comprehensive, general, global, inclusive
▸ *adverb* **2** IN GENERAL, on the whole

overawe *verb* INTIMIDATE, abash, alarm, daunt, frighten, scare, terrify

overbalance *verb* OVERTURN, capsize, keel over, slip, tip over, topple over, tumble, turn turtle

overbearing *adjective* ARROGANT, bossy (*informal*), dictatorial, domineering, haughty, high-handed, imperious, supercilious, superior

overblown *adjective* EXCESSIVE, disproportionate, immoderate, inflated, overdone, over the top, undue

overcast *adjective* CLOUDY, dismal, dreary, dull, gray, leaden, louring *or* lowering, murky

overcharge *verb* CHEAT, fleece,

rip off (*slang*), short-change, sting (*informal*), surcharge

overcome verb **1** CONQUER, beat, defeat, master, overpower, overwhelm, prevail, subdue, subjugate, surmount, triumph over, vanquish ▸ adjective **2** AFFECTED, at a loss for words, bowled over (*informal*), overwhelmed, speechless, swept off one's feet

overconfident adjective BRASH, cocksure, foolhardy, overweening, presumptuous

overcrowded adjective CONGESTED, bursting at the seams, choked, jam-packed, overloaded, overpopulated, packed (out), swarming

overdo verb **1** EXAGGERATE, belabor, gild the lily, go overboard (*informal*), overindulge, overreach, overstate **2** overdo it OVERWORK, bite off more than one can chew, burn the candle at both ends (*informal*), overload, strain or overstrain oneself, wear oneself out

overdone adjective **1** EXCESSIVE, exaggerated, fulsome, immoderate, inordinate, overelaborate, too much, undue, unnecessary **2** OVERCOOKED, burnt, charred, dried up, spoiled

overdue adjective LATE, behindhand, behind schedule, belated, owing, tardy, unpunctual

overeat verb OVERINDULGE, binge (*informal*), gorge, gormandize, guzzle, pig out (*slang*), stuff oneself

overemphasize verb OVERSTRESS,

belabor, blow up out of all proportion, make a mountain out of a molehill (*informal*), overdramatize

overflow verb **1** SPILL, brim over, bubble over, pour over, run over, well over ▸ noun **2** SURPLUS, overabundance, spilling over

overhang verb PROJECT, extend, jut, loom, protrude, stick out

overhaul verb **1** REPAIR, check, do up (*informal*), examine, inspect, recondition, refurbish, restore, service **2** OVERTAKE, catch up with, get ahead of, pass ▸ noun **3** CHECKUP, check, examination, inspection, reconditioning, service

overhead adverb **1** ABOVE, aloft, in the sky, on high, skyward, up above, upward ▸ adjective **2** AERIAL, overhanging, upper

overheads plural noun RUNNING COSTS, operating costs

overindulgence noun EXCESS, immoderation, intemperance, overeating, surfeit

overjoyed adjective DELIGHTED, elated, euphoric, jubilant, on cloud nine (*informal*), over the moon (*informal*), thrilled

overload verb OVERBURDEN, burden, encumber, oppress, overtax, saddle (with), strain, weigh down

overlook verb **1** FORGET, disregard, miss, neglect, omit, pass **2** IGNORE, condone, disregard, excuse, forgive, make allowances for, pardon, turn a blind eye to, wink at **3** HAVE A VIEW OF, look over or out on

overpower verb OVERWHELM,

conquer, crush, defeat, master, overcome, overthrow, quell, subdue, subjugate, vanquish

overpowering adjective IRRESISTIBLE, forceful, invincible, irrefutable, overwhelming, powerful, strong

overrate verb OVERESTIMATE, exaggerate, overvalue

override verb OVERRULE, annul, cancel, countermand, nullify, outweigh, supersede

overriding adjective ULTIMATE, dominant, paramount, predominant, primary, supreme

overrule verb REVERSE, alter, annul, cancel, countermand, override, overturn, repeal, rescind, veto

overrun verb 1 INVADE, occupy, overwhelm, rout 2 INFEST, choke, inundate, permeate, ravage, spread over, swarm over 3 EXCEED, go beyond, overshoot, run over or on

overseer noun SUPERVISOR, boss (informal), chief, foreman, master, superintendent

overshadow verb 1 OUTSHINE, dominate, dwarf, eclipse, leave or put in the shade, surpass, tower above 2 SPOIL, blight, mar, put a damper on, ruin, temper

oversight noun MISTAKE, blunder, carelessness, error, fault, lapse, neglect, omission, slip

overt adjective OPEN, blatant, manifest, observable, obvious, plain, public, unconcealed, undisguised

overtake verb 1 PASS, catch up with, get past, leave behind, outdistance, outdo, outstrip,

overhaul 2 BEFALL, engulf, happen, hit, overwhelm, strike

overthrow verb 1 DEFEAT, bring down, conquer, depose, dethrone, oust, overcome, overpower, topple, unseat, vanquish ▶ noun 2 DOWNFALL, defeat, destruction, dethronement, fall, ousting, undoing, unseating

overtone noun CONNOTATION, hint, implication, innuendo, intimation, nuance, sense, suggestion, undercurrent

overture noun 1 Music INTRODUCTION, opening, prelude 2 overtures APPROACH, advance, invitation, offer, proposal, proposition

overturn verb 1 TIP OVER, capsize, keel over, overbalance, topple, upend, upturn 2 OVERTHROW, bring down, depose, destroy, unseat

overweight adjective FAT, bulky, chubby, chunky, corpulent, heavy, hefty, obese, plump, portly, stout, tubby (informal)

overwhelm verb 1 DEVASTATE, bowl over (informal), knock (someone) for six (informal), overcome, stagger, sweep (someone) off his or her feet, take (someone's) breath away 2 DESTROY, crush, cut to pieces, massacre, overpower, overrun, rout

overwhelming adjective DEVASTATING, breathtaking, crushing, irresistible, overpowering, shattering, stunning, towering

overwork verb 1 STRAIN, burn the midnight oil, sweat (informal), work one's fingers to the bone **2** OVERUSE, exhaust, exploit, fatigue, oppress, wear out, weary

overwrought *adjective* AGITATED, distracted, excited, frantic, keyed up, on edge, overexcited, tense, uptight (*informal*), wired (*slang*)

owe *verb* BE IN DEBT, be in arrears, be obligated or indebted

owing *adjective* UNPAID, due, outstanding, overdue, owed, payable, unsettled

owing to *preposition* BECAUSE OF, as a result of, on account of

own *adjective* **1** PERSONAL, individual, particular, private ▶*pronoun* **2** hold one's own COMPETE, keep going, keep one's end up, keep one's head above water **3** on one's own ALONE, by oneself, independently, singly, unaided, unassisted, under one's own steam ▶*verb* **4** POSSESS, be in possession of, enjoy, have, hold, keep, retain **5** ACKNOWLEDGE, admit, allow, concede, confess, grant, recognize **6 own up** CONFESS, admit, come clean, make a clean breast, tell the truth

owner *noun* POSSESSOR, holder, landlord or landlady, proprietor

ownership *noun* POSSESSION, dominion, title

—— **P p** ——

pace *noun* **1** STEP, gait, stride, tread, walk **2** SPEED, rate, tempo, velocity ▶*verb* **3** STRIDE, march, patrol, pound **4 pace out** MEASURE, count, mark out, step

pacifist *noun* PEACE LOVER, conscientious objector, dove

pacify *verb* CALM, allay, appease, assuage, mollify, placate, propitiate, soothe

pack *verb* **1** PACKAGE, bundle, load, store, stow **2** CRAM, compress, crowd, fill, jam, press, ram, stuff **3 pack off** SEND AWAY, dismiss, send packing (*informal*) ▶*noun* **4** BUNDLE, back pack, burden, kitbag, knapsack, load, parcel, rucksack **5** PACKET, package **6** GROUP, band, bunch, company, crowd, flock, gang, herd, mob, troop

package *noun* **1** PARCEL, box, carton, container, packet **2** UNIT, combination, whole ▶*verb* **3** PACK, box, parcel (up), wrap

packed *adjective* FULL, chock-a-block, chock-full, crammed, crowded, filled, jammed, jam-packed

packet *noun* PACKAGE, bag, carton, container, parcel

pack up *verb* **1** PUT AWAY, store **2** *Informal* STOP, finish, give up, pack it in (*informal*) **3** BREAK DOWN, conk out (*informal*), fail

pact *noun* AGREEMENT, alliance, bargain, covenant, deal, treaty, understanding

pad[1] *noun* **1** CUSHION, buffer, protection, stuffing, wad **2** NOTEPAD, block, jotter, writing pad **3** PAW, foot, sole **4** *Slang, dated* HOME, apartment, flat, place ▶*verb* **5** PACK, cushion, fill,

protect, stuff **6 pad out**
LENGTHEN, elaborate, fill out,
flesh out, protract, spin out,
stretch

pad² verb SNEAK, creep, go
barefoot, steal

padding noun **1** FILLING,
packing, stuffing, wadding
2 WORDINESS, hot air (informal),
verbiage, verbosity

paddle¹ noun **1** OAR, scull ▸ verb
2 ROW, propel, pull, scull

paddle² verb **1** WADE, slop,
splash (about) **2** DABBLE, stir

pagan adjective **1** HEATHEN,
idolatrous, infidel, polytheistic
▸ noun **2** HEATHEN, idolater,
infidel, polytheist

page¹ noun FOLIO, leaf, sheet,
side

page² noun **1** ATTENDANT,
pageboy, servant, squire ▸ verb
2 CALL, send for, summon

pageant noun SHOW, display,
parade, procession, spectacle,
tableau

pageantry noun SPECTACLE,
display, grandeur, parade,
pomp, show, splendor,
theatricality

pain noun **1** HURT, ache,
discomfort, irritation, pang,
soreness, tenderness, throb,
twinge **2** SUFFERING, agony,
anguish, distress, heartache,
misery, torment, torture ▸ verb
3 HURT, smart, sting, throb
4 DISTRESS, agonize, cut to the
quick, grieve, hurt, sadden,
torment, torture

pained adjective DISTRESSED,
aggrieved, hurt, injured,
offended, upset, wounded

painful adjective **1** DISTRESSING,
disagreeable, distasteful,

grievous, unpleasant **2** SORE,
aching, agonizing, smarting,
tender **3** DIFFICULT, arduous,
hard, laborious, troublesome,
trying

painfully adverb DISTRESSINGLY,
clearly, dreadfully, sadly,
unfortunately

painkiller noun ANALGESIC,
anesthetic, anodyne, drug

painless adjective SIMPLE, easy,
effortless, fast, quick

pains plural noun TROUBLE,
bother, care, diligence, effort

painstaking adjective THOROUGH,
assiduous, careful,
conscientious, diligent,
meticulous, scrupulous

paint noun **1** COLORING, color,
dye, pigment, stain, tint ▸ verb
2 DEPICT, draw, picture, portray,
represent, sketch **3** COAT, apply,
color, cover, daub

pair noun **1** COUPLE, brace, duo,
twins ▸ verb **2** COUPLE, bracket,
join, match (up), team, twin

pal noun Informal FRIEND, buddy
(informal), chum (informal),
companion, comrade, crony,
homeboy (slang), homegirl
(slang)

palatable adjective DELICIOUS,
appetizing, luscious,
mouthwatering, tasty, yummy
(informal)

palate noun TASTE, appetite,
stomach

palatial adjective MAGNIFICENT,
grand, imposing, majestic,
opulent, regal, splendid, stately

palaver noun FUSS, big deal
(informal), performance
(informal), rigmarole, song and
dance (informal), to-do

pale adjective **1** WHITE, ashen,

bleached, colorless, faded, light, pallid, pasty, wan ▸ verb **2** BECOME PALE, blanch, go white, lose color, whiten

pall¹ noun **1** CLOUD, mantle, shadow, shroud, veil **2** GLOOM, check, damp, damper

pall² verb BECOME BORING, become dull, become tedious, cloy, jade, sicken, tire, weary

pallid adjective PALE, anemic, ashen, colorless, pasty, wan

pallor noun PALENESS, lack of color, pallidness, wanness, whiteness

palm off verb FOB OFF, foist off, pass off

palpable adjective OBVIOUS, clear, conspicuous, evident, manifest, plain, unmistakable, visible

palpitate verb BEAT, flutter, pound, pulsate, throb, tremble

paltry adjective INSIGNIFICANT, contemptible, despicable, inconsiderable, lousy (slang), meager, mean, measly, minor, miserable, petty, poor, puny, scuzzy (slang), slight, small, trifling, trivial, unimportant, worthless

pamper verb SPOIL, cater to, coddle, cosset, indulge, overindulge, pet

pamphlet noun BOOKLET, brochure, circular, leaflet, tract

pan¹ noun **1** POT, container, saucepan ▸ verb **2** SIFT OUT, look for, search for **3** Informal CRITICIZE, censure, knock (informal), slam (slang)

pan² verb MOVE, follow, sweep, track

panacea noun CURE-ALL, nostrum, universal cure

panache noun STYLE, dash, élan, flamboyance

pandemonium noun UPROAR, bedlam, chaos, confusion, din, hullabaloo, racket, rumpus, turmoil

pander verb **pander to** INDULGE, cater to, gratify, play up to (informal), please, satisfy

pang noun TWINGE, ache, pain, prick, spasm, stab, sting

panic noun **1** FEAR, alarm, fright, hysteria, scare, terror ▸ verb **2** GO TO PIECES, become hysterical, lose one's nerve **3** ALARM, scare, unnerve

panic-stricken adjective FRIGHTENED, frightened out of one's wits, hysterical, in a cold sweat (informal), panicky, scared, scared stiff, terrified

panoply noun ARRAY, attire, dress, garb, regalia, trappings

panorama noun VIEW, prospect, vista

panoramic adjective WIDE, comprehensive, extensive, overall, sweeping

pant verb PUFF, blow, breathe, gasp, heave, wheeze

pants plural noun TROUSERS, slacks

paper noun **1** NEWSPAPER, daily, gazette, journal **2** ESSAY, article, dissertation, report, treatise **3** papers: **a** DOCUMENTS, certificates, deeds, records **b** LETTERS, archive, diaries, documents, dossier, file, records ▸ verb **4** WALLPAPER, hang

par noun AVERAGE, level, mean, norm, standard, usual

parable noun LESSON, allegory, fable, moral tale, story

parade noun **1** PROCESSION,

array, cavalcade, march,
pageant 2 SHOW, display,
spectacle ▶verb 3 FLAUNT,
display, exhibit, show off
(informal) 4 MARCH, process

paradigm noun MODEL,
example, ideal, pattern

paradise noun HEAVEN, Elysian
fields, Happy Valley, Promised
Land 2 BLISS, delight, felicity,
heaven, utopia

paradox noun CONTRADICTION,
anomaly, enigma, oddity,
puzzle

paradoxical adjective
CONTRADICTORY, baffling,
confounding, enigmatic,
puzzling

paragon noun MODEL, epitome,
exemplar, ideal, nonpareil,
pattern, quintessence

paragraph noun SECTION, clause,
item, part, passage, subdivision

parallel adjective 1 EQUIDISTANT,
alongside, side by side
2 MATCHING, analogous,
corresponding, like,
resembling, similar ▶noun
3 EQUIVALENT, analogue,
counterpart, equal, match,
twin 4 SIMILARITY, analogy,
comparison, likeness,
resemblance

paralysis noun 1 IMMOBILITY,
palsy 2 STANDSTILL, breakdown,
halt, stoppage

paralytic adjective PARALYZED,
challenged, crippled, disabled,
incapacitated, lame, palsied

paralyze verb 1 DISABLE, cripple,
incapacitate, lame 2 IMMOBILIZE,
freeze, halt, numb, petrify, stun

parameter noun LIMIT,
framework, limitation,
restriction, specification

paramount adjective PRINCIPAL,
cardinal, chief, first, foremost,
main, primary, prime, supreme

paranoid adjective 1 MENTALLY
ILL, deluded, disturbed, manic,
neurotic, paranoiac, psychotic
2 Informal SUSPICIOUS, fearful,
nervous, wired (slang), worried

paraphernalia noun EQUIPMENT,
apparatus, baggage,
belongings, effects, gear, stuff,
tackle, things, trappings

paraphrase noun 1 REWORDING,
rephrasing, restatement ▶verb
2 REWORD, express in other
words or one's own words,
rephrase, restate

parasite noun SPONGER
(informal), bloodsucker
(informal), hanger-on, leech,
scrounger (informal)

parasitic, parasitical adjective
SCROUNGING (informal),
bloodsucking (informal),
sponging (informal)

parcel noun 1 PACKAGE, bundle,
pack ▶verb 2 (often with up)
WRAP, do up, pack, package, tie
up

parch verb DRY UP, dehydrate,
desiccate, evaporate, shrivel,
wither

parched adjective DRIED OUT or
UP, arid, dehydrated, dry, thirsty

pardon verb 1 FORGIVE, absolve,
acquit, excuse, exonerate, let
off (informal), overlook ▶noun
2 FORGIVENESS, absolution,
acquittal, amnesty, exoneration

pardonable adjective FORGIVABLE,
excusable, minor,
understandable, venial

pare verb 1 PEEL, clip, cut,
shave, skin, trim 2 CUT BACK,
crop, cut, decrease, dock,

reduce

parent noun FATHER or MOTHER, procreator, progenitor, sire

parentage noun FAMILY, ancestry, birth, descent, lineage, pedigree, stock

pariah noun OUTCAST, exile, undesirable, untouchable

parish noun COMMUNITY, church, congregation, flock

parity noun EQUALITY, consistency, equivalence, uniformity, unity

park noun PARKLAND, estate, garden, grounds, woodland

parlance noun LANGUAGE, idiom, jargon, phraseology, speech, talk, tongue

parliament noun ASSEMBLY, congress, convention, council, legislature, senate

parliamentary adjective GOVERNMENTAL, law-making, legislative

parlor noun Old-fashioned SITTING ROOM, drawing room, front room, living room, lounge

parochial adjective PROVINCIAL, insular, limited, narrow, narrow-minded, petty, small-minded

parody noun 1 SATIRE (informal), burlesque, caricature, skit, spoof (informal) ▶verb 2 SATIRIZE (informal), burlesque, caricature

paroxysm noun OUTBURST, attack, convulsion, fit, seizure, spasm

parrot verb REPEAT, copy, echo, imitate, mimic

parry verb 1 WARD OFF, block, deflect, rebuff, repel, repulse 2 EVADE, avoid, dodge, sidestep

parsimonious adjective MEAN, close, frugal, miserly, niggardly, penny-pinching (informal), stingy, tightfisted

parson noun CLERGYMAN, churchman, cleric, minister, pastor, preacher, priest, vicar

part noun 1 PIECE, bit, fraction, fragment, portion, scrap, section, share 2 COMPONENT, branch, constituent, division, member, unit 3 Theatre ROLE, character, lines 4 SIDE, behalf, cause, concern, interest 5 (often plural) REGION, area, district, neighborhood, quarter, vicinity 6 **in good part** GOOD-NATUREDLY, cheerfully, well, without offense 7 **in part** PARTLY, a little, in some measure, partially, somewhat ▶verb 8 DIVIDE, break, come apart, detach, rend, separate, sever, split, tear 9 SEPARATE, depart, go, go away, leave, split up, withdraw

partake verb 1 **partake of** CONSUME, chow down (slang), eat, take 2 **partake in** PARTICIPATE IN, engage in, share in, take part in

partial adjective 1 INCOMPLETE, imperfect, uncompleted, unfinished 2 BIASED, discriminatory, one-sided, partisan, prejudiced, unfair, unjust

partiality noun 1 BIAS, favoritism, preference, prejudice 2 LIKING, fondness, inclination, love, penchant, predilection, taste, weakness

partially adverb PARTLY, fractionally, incompletely, in part, not wholly, somewhat

participant noun PARTICIPATOR,

contributor, member, player, stakeholder

participate verb TAKE PART, be involved in, join in, partake, perform, share

participation noun TAKING PART, contribution, involvement, joining in, partaking, sharing in

particle noun BIT, grain, iota, jot, mite, piece, scrap, shred, speck

particular adjective 1 SPECIFIC, distinct, exact, peculiar, precise, special 2 SPECIAL, especial, exceptional, marked, notable, noteworthy, remarkable, singular, uncommon, unusual 3 FUSSY, choosy (informal), demanding, fastidious, finicky, picky (informal) ▶ noun 4 (usually plural) DETAIL, circumstance, fact, feature, item, specification 5 **in particular** ESPECIALLY, distinctly, exactly, particularly, specifically

particularly adverb 1 ESPECIALLY, exceptionally, notably, singularly, uncommonly, unusually 2 SPECIFICALLY, distinctly, especially, explicitly, expressly, in particular

parting noun 1 GOING, farewell, good-bye 2 DIVISION, breaking, rift, rupture, separation, split

partisan noun 1 SUPPORTER, adherent, devotee, upholder 2 UNDERGROUND FIGHTER, guerrilla, resistance fighter ▶ adjective 3 PREJUDICED, biased, interested, one-sided, partial, sectarian

partition noun 1 SCREEN, barrier, wall 2 DIVISION, segregation, separation 3 ALLOTMENT, apportionment, distribution

▶ verb 4 SEPARATE, divide, screen

partly adverb PARTIALLY, slightly, somewhat

partner noun 1 SPOUSE, consort, husband or wife, mate, significant other (informal) 2 COMPANION, ally, associate, colleague, comrade, helper, mate

partnership noun COMPANY, alliance, cooperative, firm, house, society, union

party noun 1 GET-TOGETHER (informal), celebration, festivity, function, gathering, reception, social gathering 2 GROUP, band, company, crew, gang, squad, team, unit 3 FACTION, camp, clique, coterie, league, set, side 4 PERSON, individual, someone

pass verb 1 GO BY or PAST, elapse, go, lapse, move, proceed, run 2 QUALIFY, do, get through, graduate, succeed 3 SPEND, fill, occupy, while away 4 GIVE, convey, deliver, hand, send, transfer 5 APPROVE, accept, decree, enact, legislate, ordain, ratify 6 EXCEED, beat, go beyond, outdo, outstrip, surpass 7 END, blow over, cease, go ▶ noun 8 GAP, canyon, gorge, ravine, route 9 LICENSE, authorization, passport, permit, ticket, warrant

passable adjective ADEQUATE, acceptable, all right, average, fair, mediocre, so-so (informal), tolerable

passage noun 1 WAY, alley, avenue, channel, course, path, road, route 2 CORRIDOR, hall, lobby, vestibule 3 EXTRACT, excerpt, piece, quotation, reading, section, text 4 JOURNEY,

crossing, trek, trip, voyage
5 SAFE-CONDUCT, freedom,
permission, right

passageway noun CORRIDOR,
aisle, alley, hall, hallway, lane,
passage

pass away verb Euphemistic DIE,
expire, kick the bucket (*slang*),
pass on, pass over, shuffle off
this mortal coil, snuff it
(*informal*)

passé adjective OUT-OF-DATE,
dated, obsolete, old-fashioned,
old hat, outdated, outmoded,
unfashionable

passenger noun TRAVELER, fare,
rider

passer-by noun BYSTANDER,
onlooker, witness

passing adjective **1** MOMENTARY,
brief, ephemeral, fleeting,
short-lived, temporary,
transient, transitory
2 SUPERFICIAL, casual, cursory,
glancing, quick, short

passion noun **1** LOVE, ardor,
desire, infatuation, lust
2 EMOTION, ardor, excitement,
feeling, fervor, fire, heat,
intensity, warmth, zeal **3** RAGE,
anger, fit, frenzy, fury,
outburst, paroxysm, storm
4 MANIA, bug (*informal*),
craving, craze, enthusiasm,
fascination, obsession

passionate adjective **1** LOVING,
amorous, ardent, erotic, hot,
lustful **2** EMOTIONAL, ardent,
eager, fervent, fierce, heartfelt,
impassioned, intense, strong

passive adjective SUBMISSIVE,
compliant, docile, inactive,
quiescent, receptive

pass off verb FAKE, counterfeit,
make a pretense of, palm off

pass out verb FAINT, become
unconscious, black out
(*informal*), lose consciousness

pass over verb DISREGARD,
ignore, overlook, take no
notice of

pass up verb MISS, abstain,
decline, forgo, let slip, neglect

password noun SIGNAL, key
word, watchword

past adjective **1** FORMER, ancient,
bygone, early, olden, previous
2 OVER, done, ended, finished,
gone ▶ noun **3** BACKGROUND,
history, life, past life **4 the
past** FORMER TIMES, days gone
by, long ago, olden days
▶ preposition **5** AFTER, beyond,
later than **6** BEYOND, across, by,
over

paste noun **1** ADHESIVE, cement,
glue, gum ▶ verb **2** STICK,
cement, glue, gum

pastel adjective PALE, delicate,
light, muted, soft

pastiche noun MEDLEY, blend,
mélange, miscellany, mixture

pastime noun ACTIVITY,
amusement, diversion,
entertainment, game, hobby,
recreation

pastor noun CLERGYMAN,
churchman, ecclesiastic,
minister, parson, priest, rector,
vicar

pastoral adjective **1** RUSTIC,
bucolic, country, rural
2 ECCLESIASTICAL, clerical,
ministerial, priestly

pasture noun GRASSLAND, grass,
grazing, meadow

pasty adjective PALE, anemic,
pallid, sickly, wan

pat verb **1** STROKE, caress, fondle,
pet, tap, touch ▶ noun **2** STROKE,

clap, tap

patch noun **1** REINFORCEMENT **2** SPOT, bit, scrap, shred, small piece **3** PLOT, area, ground, land, tract ▶verb **4** MEND, cover, reinforce, repair, sew up

patchwork noun MIXTURE, jumble, medley, pastiche

patchy adjective UNEVEN, erratic, fitful, irregular, sketchy, spotty, variable

patent noun **1** COPYRIGHT, license ▶adjective **2** OBVIOUS, apparent, clear, evident, glaring, manifest

paternal adjective FATHERLY, concerned, protective, solicitous

paternity noun **1** FATHERHOOD **2** PARENTAGE, descent, extraction, family, lineage

path noun **1** WAY, footpath, road, track, trail **2** COURSE, direction, road, route, way

pathetic adjective SAD, affecting, distressing, heart-rending, moving, pitiable, plaintive, poignant, tender, touching

pathos noun SADNESS, pitifulness, plaintiveness, poignancy

patience noun **1** FORBEARANCE, calmness, restraint, serenity, sufferance, tolerance **2** ENDURANCE, constancy, fortitude, long-suffering, perseverance, resignation, stoicism, submission

patient adjective **1** LONG-SUFFERING, calm, enduring, persevering, philosophical, resigned, stoical, submissive, uncomplaining **2** FORBEARING, even-tempered, forgiving, indulgent, lenient, mild, tolerant, understanding ▶noun **3** SICK PERSON, case, invalid, sufferer

patriot noun NATIONALIST, chauvinist, loyalist

patriotic adjective NATIONALISTIC, chauvinistic, jingoistic, loyal

patriotism noun NATIONALISM, jingoism

patrol noun **1** POLICING, guarding, protecting, vigilance, watching **2** GUARD, patrolman, sentinel, watch, watchman ▶verb **3** POLICE, guard, inspect, keep guard, keep watch, safeguard

patron noun **1** SUPPORTER, backer, benefactor, champion, friend, helper, philanthropist, sponsor **2** CUSTOMER, buyer, client, frequenter, habitué, shopper

patronage noun **1** SUPPORT, aid, assistance, backing, help, promotion, sponsorship **2** CUSTOM, business, clientele, commerce, trade, trading, traffic

patronize verb **1** TALK DOWN TO, look down on **2** BE A CUSTOMER or CLIENT OF, do business with, frequent, shop at **3** SUPPORT, back, fund, help, maintain, promote, sponsor

patronizing adjective CONDESCENDING, disdainful, gracious, haughty, snobbish, supercilious, superior

patter[1] verb **1** TAP, beat, pat, pitter-patter **2** WALK LIGHTLY, scurry, scuttle, skip, trip ▶noun **3** TAPPING, pattering, pitter-patter

patter[2] noun **1** SPIEL (informal), line, pitch **2** CHATTER, gabble, jabber, nattering, prattle **3** JARGON, argot, cant, lingo (informal), patois, slang,

vernacular ▸ verb 4 CHATTER, jabber, prate, rattle on, spout (informal)

pattern noun **1** DESIGN, arrangement, decoration, device, figure, motif **2** ORDER, method, plan, sequence, system **3** PLAN, design, diagram, guide, original, stencil, template ▸ verb **4** MODEL, copy, follow, form, imitate, mold, style

paucity noun Formal SCARCITY, dearth, deficiency, lack, rarity, scantiness, shortage, sparseness

paunch noun BELLY, pot, potbelly, spare tire (slang)

pauper noun DOWN-AND-OUT, bankrupt, beggar, mendicant, poor person

pause verb **1** STOP BRIEFLY, break, cease, delay, halt, have a breather (informal), interrupt, rest, take a break, wait ▸ noun **2** STOP, break, breather (informal), cessation, gap, halt, interlude, intermission, interval, lull, respite, rest, stoppage

pave verb COVER, concrete, floor, surface, tile

paw verb MANHANDLE, grab, handle roughly, maul, molest

pawn¹ verb HOCK (informal), deposit, mortgage, pledge

pawn² noun TOOL, cat's-paw, instrument, plaything, puppet, stooge (slang)

pay verb **1** REIMBURSE, compensate, give, recompense, remit, remunerate, requite, reward, settle **2** GIVE, bestow, extend, grant, hand out, present **3** BENEFIT, be worthwhile, repay **4** BE PROFITABLE, make a return, make

money **5** YIELD, bring in, produce, return ▸ noun **6** WAGES, allowance, earnings, fee, income, payment, recompense, reimbursement, remuneration, reward, salary, stipend

payable adjective DUE, outstanding, owed, owing

pay back verb **1** REPAY, refund, reimburse, settle up, square **2** GET EVEN WITH (informal), hit back, retaliate

payment noun **1** PAYING, discharge, remittance, settlement **2** REMITTANCE, advance, deposit, installment, premium **3** WAGE, fee, hire, remuneration, reward

pay off verb **1** SETTLE, clear, discharge, pay in full, square **2** SUCCEED, be effective, work

pay out verb SPEND, disburse, expend, fork out or over or up (slang), shell out (informal)

peace noun **1** STILLNESS, calm, calmness, hush, quiet, repose, rest, silence, tranquillity **2** SERENITY, calm, composure, contentment, repose **3** HARMONY, accord, agreement, concord **4** TRUCE, armistice, treaty

peaceable adjective PEACE-LOVING, conciliatory, friendly, gentle, mild, peaceful, unwarlike

peaceful adjective **1** AT PEACE, amicable, friendly, harmonious, nonviolent **2** CALM, placid, quiet, restful, serene, still, tranquil, undisturbed **3** PEACE-LOVING, conciliatory, peaceable, unwarlike

peacemaker noun MEDIATOR, arbitrator, conciliator, pacifier

peak noun **1** POINT, apex, brow,

crest, pinnacle, summit, tip, top **2** HIGH POINT, acme, climax, crown, culmination, zenith ▶verb **3** CULMINATE, climax, come to a head

peal noun **1** RING, blast, chime, clang, clap, crash, reverberation, roar, rumble ▶verb **2** RING, chime, crash, resound, roar, rumble

peasant noun RUSTIC, countryman

peccadillo noun MISDEED, error, indiscretion, lapse, misdemeanor, slip

peck verb, noun PICK, dig, hit, jab, poke, prick, strike, tap

peculiar adjective **1** ODD, abnormal, bizarre, curious, eccentric, extraordinary, freakish, funny, offbeat, outlandish, outré, quaint, queer, singular, strange, uncommon, unconventional, unusual, weird **2** SPECIFIC, characteristic, distinctive, particular, special, unique

peculiarity noun **1** ECCENTRICITY, abnormality, foible, idiosyncrasy, mannerism, oddity, quirk **2** CHARACTERISTIC, attribute, feature, mark, particularity, property, quality, trait

pedagogue noun TEACHER, instructor, master or mistress, schoolmaster or schoolmistress

pedant noun HAIRSPLITTER, nit-picker (informal), quibbler

pedantic adjective HAIRSPLITTING, academic, bookish, donnish, formal, fussy, nit-picking (informal), particular, precise, punctilious

pedantry noun HAIRSPLITTING,

punctiliousness, quibbling

peddle verb SELL, hawk, market, push (informal), trade

peddler noun SELLER, door-to-door salesman, hawker, huckster, vendor

pedestal noun SUPPORT, base, foot, mounting, plinth, stand

pedestrian noun **1** WALKER, foot-traveler ▶adjective **2** DULL, banal, boring, commonplace, humdrum, mediocre, mundane, ordinary, prosaic, uninspired

pedigree noun **1** LINEAGE, ancestry, blood, breed, descent, extraction, family, family tree, genealogy, line, race, stock ▶adjective **2** PUREBRED, full-blooded, thoroughbred

peek verb **1** GLANCE, look, peep ▶noun **2** GLANCE, glimpse, look, look-see (slang), peep

peel verb **1** SKIN, flake off, pare, scale, strip off ▶noun **2** SKIN, peeling, rind

peep¹ verb **1** PEEK, look, sneak a look, steal a look ▶noun **2** LOOK, glimpse, look-see (slang), peek

peep² verb, noun TWEET, cheep, chirp, squeak

peephole noun SPYHOLE, aperture, chink, crack, hole, opening

peer¹ noun **1** NOBLE, aristocrat, lord, nobleman **2** EQUAL, compeer, fellow, like

peer² verb SQUINT, gaze, inspect, peep, scan, snoop, spy

peerage noun ARISTOCRACY, lords and ladies, nobility, peers

peerless adjective UNEQUALED,

beyond compare, excellent, incomparable, matchless, outstanding, unmatched, unparalleled, unrivaled

peevish adjective IRRITABLE, cantankerous, childish, churlish, cross, crotchety, fractious, fretful, grumpy, petulant, querulous, snappy, sulky, sullen, surly

peg verb FASTEN, attach, fix, join, secure

pejorative adjective DEROGATORY, deprecatory, depreciatory, disparaging, negative, uncomplimentary, unpleasant

pelt[1] verb 1 THROW, batter, bombard, cast, hurl, pepper, shower, sling, strike 2 RUSH, belt (slang), charge, dash, hurry, run fast, shoot, speed, tear 3 POUR, bucket down (informal), rain cats and dogs (informal), rain hard, teem

pelt[2] noun COAT, fell, hide, skin

pen[1] verb WRITE, compose, draft, draw up, jot down

pen[2] noun 1 ENCLOSURE, cage, coop, fold, hutch, pound, sty ▶verb 2 ENCLOSE, cage, confine, coop up, fence in, hedge, shut up or in

penal adjective DISCIPLINARY, corrective, punitive

penalize verb PUNISH, discipline, handicap, impose a penalty on

penalty noun PUNISHMENT, fine, forfeit, handicap, price

penance noun ATONEMENT, penalty, reparation, sackcloth and ashes

penchant noun LIKING, bent, bias, fondness, inclination, leaning, partiality, predilection, proclivity, propensity, taste, tendency

pending adjective UNDECIDED, awaiting, imminent, impending, in the balance, undetermined, unsettled

penetrate verb 1 PIERCE, bore, enter, go through, prick, stab 2 GRASP, comprehend, decipher, fathom, figure out (informal), get to the bottom of, work out

penetrating adjective 1 SHARP, carrying, harsh, piercing, shrill 2 PERCEPTIVE, acute, astute, incisive, intelligent, keen, perspicacious, quick, sharp, sharp-witted, shrewd

penetration noun 1 PIERCING, entrance, entry, incision, puncturing 2 PERCEPTION, acuteness, astuteness, insight, keenness, sharpness, shrewdness

penitence noun REPENTANCE, compunction, contrition, regret, remorse, shame, sorrow

penitent adjective REPENTANT, abject, apologetic, conscience-stricken, contrite, regretful, remorseful, sorry

pen name noun PSEUDONYM, nom de plume

pennant noun FLAG, banner, ensign, pennon, streamer

penniless adjective POOR, broke (informal), destitute, dirt-poor (informal), down and out, down on one's luck (informal), flat broke (informal), impecunious, impoverished, indigent, penurious, poverty-stricken

pension noun ALLOWANCE, annuity, benefit, superannuation

pensive adjective THOUGHTFUL, contemplative, dreamy, meditative, musing, preoccupied, reflective, sad, serious, solemn, wistful

pent-up adjective SUPPRESSED, bottled up, curbed, held back, inhibited, repressed, smothered, stifled

penury noun POVERTY, beggary, destitution, indigence, need, privation, want

people plural noun 1 PERSONS, humanity, mankind, men and women, mortals 2 NATION, citizens, community, folk, inhabitants, population, public 3 FAMILY, clan, race, tribe ▶verb 4 INHABIT, colonize, occupy, populate, settle

pepper noun 1 SEASONING, flavor, spice ▶verb 2 SPRINKLE, dot, fleck, spatter, speck 3 PELT, bombard, shower

perceive verb 1 SEE, behold, discern, discover, espy, make out, note, notice, observe, recognize, spot 2 UNDERSTAND, comprehend, gather, grasp, learn, realize, see

perceptible adjective VISIBLE, apparent, appreciable, clear, detectable, discernible, evident, noticeable, observable, obvious, recognizable, tangible

perception noun UNDERSTANDING, awareness, conception, consciousness, feeling, grasp, idea, impression, notion, sensation, sense

perceptive adjective OBSERVANT, acute, alert, astute, aware, percipient, perspicacious, quick, sharp

perch noun 1 RESTING PLACE,

branch, pole, post ▶verb 2 SIT, alight, balance, land, rest, roost, settle

percussion noun IMPACT, blow, bump, clash, collision, crash, knock, smash, thump

peremptory adjective
1 IMPERATIVE, absolute, binding, compelling, decisive, final, obligatory 2 IMPERIOUS, authoritative, bossy (informal), dictatorial, dogmatic, domineering, overbearing

perennial adjective LASTING, abiding, constant, continual, enduring, incessant, persistent, recurrent, twenty-four-seven (slang)

perfect adjective 1 COMPLETE, absolute, consummate, entire, finished, full, sheer, unmitigated, utter, whole 2 FAULTLESS, flawless, immaculate, impeccable, pure, spotless, unblemished 3 EXCELLENT, ideal, splendid, sublime, superb, superlative, supreme 4 EXACT, accurate, correct, faithful, precise, true, unerring ▶verb 5 IMPROVE, develop, polish, refine 6 ACCOMPLISH, achieve, carry out, complete, finish, fulfill, perform

perfection noun 1 COMPLETENESS, maturity 2 PURITY, integrity, perfectness, wholeness 3 EXCELLENCE, exquisiteness, sublimity, superiority 4 EXACTNESS, faultlessness, precision

perfectionist noun STICKLER, precisionist, purist

perfectly adverb 1 COMPLETELY, absolutely, altogether, fully,

quite, thoroughly, totally,
utterly, wholly **2** FLAWLESSLY,
faultlessly, ideally, impeccably,
superbly, supremely,
wonderfully

perfidious adjective Literary
TREACHEROUS, disloyal,
double-dealing, traitorous,
two-faced, unfaithful

perforate verb PIERCE, drill,
penetrate, punch, puncture

perform verb **1** CARRY OUT,
accomplish, achieve, complete,
discharge, do, execute, fulfill,
pull off, work **2** PRESENT, act,
enact, play, produce, put on,
represent, stage

performance noun **1** CARRYING
OUT, accomplishment,
achievement, act, completion,
execution, fulfillment, work
2 PRESENTATION, acting,
appearance, exhibition, gig
(informal), play, portrayal,
production, show

performer noun ARTISTE, actor or
actress, player, Thespian,
trouper

perfume noun FRAGRANCE,
aroma, bouquet, odor, scent,
smell

perfunctory adjective OFFHAND,
cursory, heedless, indifferent,
mechanical, routine, sketchy,
superficial

perhaps adverb MAYBE,
conceivably, feasibly, it may
be, perchance (archaic), possibly

peril noun DANGER, hazard,
jeopardy, menace, risk,
uncertainty

perilous adjective DANGEROUS,
hazardous, precarious, risky,
threatening, unsafe

perimeter noun BOUNDARY,

ambit, border, bounds,
circumference, confines, edge,
limit, margin, periphery

period noun TIME, interval,
season, space, span, spell,
stretch, term, while

periodic adjective RECURRENT,
cyclical, intermittent,
occasional, regular, repeated,
sporadic

periodical noun PUBLICATION,
journal, magazine, monthly,
paper, quarterly, weekly

peripheral adjective
1 INCIDENTAL, inessential,
irrelevant, marginal, minor,
secondary, unimportant
2 OUTERMOST, exterior, external,
outer, outside

perish verb **1** DIE, be killed,
expire, lose one's life, pass
away **2** BE DESTROYED, collapse,
decline, disappear, fall, vanish
3 ROT, decay, decompose,
disintegrate, molder, waste

perishable adjective SHORT-LIVED,
decaying, decomposable

perjure verb perjure oneself
Criminal law COMMIT PERJURY,
bear false witness, forswear,
give false testimony, lie under
oath, swear falsely

perjury noun LYING UNDER OATH,
bearing false witness, false
statement, forswearing, giving
false testimony

perk noun Informal BONUS,
benefit, extra, fringe benefit,
perquisite, plus

permanence noun CONTINUITY,
constancy, continuance,
durability, endurance, finality,
indestructibility, perpetuity,
stability

permanent adjective LASTING,

abiding, constant, enduring, eternal, everlasting, immutable, perpetual, persistent, stable, steadfast, twenty-four-seven (slang), unchanging

permeate verb PERVADE, charge, fill, imbue, impregnate, infiltrate, penetrate, saturate, spread through

permissible adjective PERMITTED, acceptable, allowable, all right, authorized, lawful, legal, legitimate, O.K. or okay (informal)

permission noun AUTHORIZATION, allowance, approval, assent, consent, dispensation, go-ahead (informal), green light, leave, liberty, license, sanction

permissive adjective TOLERANT, easy-going, forbearing, free, indulgent, lax, lenient, liberal

permit verb 1 ALLOW, authorize, consent, enable, entitle, give leave or permission, give the green light to, grant, let, license, sanction ▶noun 2 LICENSE, authorization, pass, passport, permission, warrant

permutation noun TRANSFORMATION, alteration, change, transposition

pernicious adjective WICKED, bad, damaging, dangerous, deadly, destructive, detrimental, evil, fatal, harmful, hurtful, malign, poisonous

perpendicular adjective UPRIGHT, at right angles to, on end, plumb, straight, vertical

perpetrate verb COMMIT, carry out, do, enact, execute, perform, wreak

perpetual adjective

1 EVERLASTING, endless, eternal, infinite, lasting, never-ending, perennial, permanent, unchanging, unending 2 CONTINUAL, constant, continuous, endless, incessant, interminable, never-ending, persistent, recurrent, repeated, twenty-four-seven (slang)

perpetuate verb MAINTAIN, immortalize, keep going, preserve

perplex verb PUZZLE, baffle, bewilder, confound, confuse, mystify, stump

perplexing adjective PUZZLING, baffling, bewildering, complex, complicated, confusing, difficult, enigmatic, hard, inexplicable, mystifying

perplexity noun 1 PUZZLEMENT, bafflement, bewilderment, confusion, incomprehension, mystification 2 PUZZLE, difficulty, fix (informal), mystery, paradox

perquisite noun Formal BONUS, benefit, dividend, extra, perk (informal), plus

persecute verb 1 VICTIMIZE, afflict, ill-treat, maltreat, oppress, torment, torture 2 HARASS, annoy, badger, bother, hassle (informal), pester, tease

perseverance noun PERSISTENCE, determination, diligence, doggedness, endurance, pertinacity, resolution, tenacity

persevere verb KEEP GOING, carry on, continue, go on, hang on, persist, remain, stick at or to

persist verb 1 CONTINUE, carry on, keep up, last, linger, remain 2 PERSEVERE, continue, insist, stand firm

persistence noun DETERMINATION, doggedness, endurance, grit, perseverance, pertinacity, resolution, tenacity, tirelessness

persistent adjective **1** CONTINUOUS, constant, continual, endless, incessant, never-ending, perpetual, repeated, twenty-four-seven (*slang*) **2** DETERMINED, dogged, obdurate, obstinate, persevering, pertinacious, steadfast, steady, stubborn, tenacious, tireless, unflagging

person noun **1** INDIVIDUAL, being, body, human, soul **2 in person** PERSONALLY, bodily, in the flesh, oneself

personable adjective PLEASANT, agreeable, amiable, attractive, charming, good-looking, handsome, likable or likeable, nice

personage noun PERSONALITY, big shot (*informal*), celebrity, dignitary, luminary, megastar (*informal*), notable, public figure, somebody, V.I.P.

personal adjective **1** PRIVATE, exclusive, individual, intimate, own, particular, peculiar, special **2** OFFENSIVE, derogatory, disparaging, insulting, nasty

personality noun **1** NATURE, character, disposition, identity, individuality, make-up, temperament **2** CELEBRITY, famous name, household name, megastar (*informal*), notable, personage, star

personally adverb **1** BY ONESELF, alone, independently, on one's own, solely **2** IN ONE'S OPINION, for one's part, from one's own

viewpoint, in one's books, in one's own view **3** INDIVIDUALLY, individualistically, privately, specially, subjectively

personification noun EMBODIMENT, epitome, image, incarnation, portrayal, representation

personify verb EMBODY, epitomize, exemplify, represent, symbolize, typify

personnel noun EMPLOYEES, helpers, human resources, people, staff, workers, workforce

perspective noun **1** OUTLOOK, angle, attitude, context, frame of reference **2** OBJECTIVITY, proportion, relation, relative importance, relativity

perspicacious adjective PERCEPTIVE, acute, alert, astute, discerning, keen, percipient, sharp, shrewd

perspiration noun SWEAT, moisture, wetness

perspire verb SWEAT, exude, glow, pour with sweat, secrete, swelter

persuade verb **1** TALK INTO, coax, entice, impel, incite, induce, influence, sway, urge, win over **2** CONVINCE, cause to believe, satisfy

persuasion noun **1** URGING, cajolery, enticement, inducement, wheedling **2** PERSUASIVENESS, cogency, force, potency, power **3** CREED, belief, conviction, credo, faith, opinion, tenet, views **4** FACTION, camp, denomination, party, school, school of thought, side

persuasive adjective CONVINCING, cogent, compelling, credible,

effective, eloquent, forceful,
influential, plausible, sound,
telling, valid, weighty

pert adjective IMPUDENT, bold,
cheeky, forward, impertinent,
insolent, sassy (informal), saucy

pertain verb RELATE, apply, befit,
belong, be relevant, concern,
refer, regard

pertinent adjective RELEVANT,
applicable, apposite,
appropriate, apt, fit, fitting,
germane, material, proper, to
the point

pertness noun IMPUDENCE,
audacity, cheek (informal),
cheekiness, effrontery,
forwardness, front,
impertinence, insolence,
sauciness

perturb verb DISTURB, agitate,
bother, disconcert, faze, fluster,
ruffle, trouble, unsettle, vex,
worry

perturbed adjective DISTURBED,
agitated, anxious,
disconcerted, flustered, shaken,
troubled, uncomfortable,
uneasy, worried

peruse verb READ, browse,
check, examine, inspect, scan,
scrutinize, study

pervade verb SPREAD THROUGH,
charge, fill, imbue, infuse,
penetrate, permeate, suffuse

pervasive adjective WIDESPREAD,
common, extensive, general,
omnipresent, prevalent, rife,
ubiquitous, universal

perverse adjective 1 ABNORMAL,
contrary, deviant, disobedient,
improper, rebellious, refractory,
troublesome, unhealthy
2 WILLFUL, contrary, dogged,
headstrong, intractable,

intransigent, obdurate,
wrong-headed 3 STUBBORN,
contrary, mulish, obstinate,
pig-headed, stiff-necked,
wayward 4 ILL-NATURED, churlish,
cross, fractious, ill-tempered,
peevish, surly

perversion noun 1 DEVIATION,
aberration, abnormality,
debauchery, depravity,
immorality, kink (informal),
kinkiness (slang),
unnaturalness, vice
2 DISTORTION, corruption,
falsification, misinterpretation,
misrepresentation, twisting

perversity noun CONTRARINESS,
contradictoriness,
intransigence, obduracy,
refractoriness, waywardness,
wrong-headedness

pervert verb 1 DISTORT, abuse,
falsify, garble, misrepresent,
misuse, twist, warp 2 CORRUPT,
debase, debauch, degrade,
deprave, lead astray ▶ noun
3 DEVIANT, degenerate, sicko
(informal), weirdo or weirdie
(informal)

perverted adjective UNNATURAL,
abnormal, corrupt, debased,
debauched, depraved, deviant,
kinky (slang), sick, twisted,
unhealthy, warped

pessimism noun GLOOMINESS,
dejection, depression, despair,
despondency, distrust, gloom,
hopelessness, melancholy

pessimist noun WET BLANKET
(informal), cynic, defeatist,
killjoy, prophet of doom,
worrier

pessimistic adjective GLOOMY,
bleak, cynical, dark, dejected,
depressed, despairing,

despondent, glum, hopeless, morose

pest noun 1 NUISANCE, annoyance, bane, bother, drag (informal), irritation, pain (informal), thorn in one's flesh, trial, vexation 2 INFECTION, blight, bug, epidemic, pestilence, plague, scourge

pester verb ANNOY, badger, bedevil, bother, bug (informal), harass, harry, hassle (informal), nag, plague, torment

pestilence noun PLAGUE, epidemic, visitation

pestilent adjective 1 ANNOYING, bothersome, irksome, irritating, tiresome, vexing 2 HARMFUL, detrimental, evil, injurious, pernicious 3 CONTAMINATED, catching, contagious, diseased, disease-ridden, infected, infectious

pestilential adjective DEADLY, dangerous, destructive, detrimental, harmful, hazardous, injurious, pernicious

pet noun 1 FAVORITE, darling, idol, jewel, treasure ▶ adjective 2 FAVORITE, cherished, dearest, dear to one's heart ▶ verb 3 PAMPER, baby, coddle, cosset, spoil 4 FONDLE, caress, pat, stroke 5 CUDDLE, kiss, make out, neck (informal), smooch (informal)

peter out verb DIE OUT, dwindle, ebb, fade, fail, run out, stop, taper off, wane

petite adjective SMALL, dainty, delicate, elfin, little, slight

petition noun 1 APPEAL, entreaty, plea, prayer, request, solicitation, suit, supplication ▶ verb 2 APPEAL, adjure, ask,

beg, beseech, entreat, plead, pray, solicit, supplicate

petrify verb 1 TERRIFY, horrify, immobilize, paralyze, stun, stupefy, transfix 2 FOSSILIZE, calcify, harden, turn to stone

petty adjective 1 TRIVIAL, contemptible, inconsiderable, insignificant, little, lousy (slang), measly (informal), negligible, paltry, slight, small, trifling, unimportant 2 SMALL-MINDED, mean, mean-minded, shabby, spiteful, ungenerous

petulance noun SULKINESS, bad temper, ill humor, irritability, peevishness, pique, sullenness

petulant adjective SULKY, bad-tempered, huffy, ill-humored, moody, peevish, sullen

phantom noun 1 SPECTER, apparition, ghost, phantasm, shade (literary), spirit, spook (informal), wraith 2 ILLUSION, figment of the imagination, hallucination, vision

phase noun STAGE, chapter, development, juncture, period, point, position, step, time

phase out verb WIND DOWN, close, ease off, eliminate, pull out, remove, run down, terminate, wind up, withdraw

phenomenal adjective EXTRAORDINARY, exceptional, fantastic, marvelous, miraculous, outstanding, prodigious, remarkable, unusual

phenomenon noun 1 OCCURRENCE, circumstance, episode, event, fact, happening, incident 2 WONDER, exception, marvel, miracle, prodigy, rarity, sensation

philanderer noun WOMANIZER
(*informal*), Casanova, Don Juan,
flirt, gigolo, ladies' man,
playboy, stud (*slang*), wolf
(*informal*)

philanthropic adjective
HUMANITARIAN, beneficent,
benevolent, charitable,
humane, kind, kind-hearted,
munificent, public-spirited

philanthropist noun
HUMANITARIAN, benefactor,
contributor, donor, giver,
patron

philanthropy noun
HUMANITARIANISM, almsgiving,
beneficence, benevolence,
brotherly love, charitableness,
charity, generosity,
kind-heartedness

philistine noun 1 BOOR,
barbarian, ignoramus, lout,
lowbrow, vulgarian, yahoo
▶ adjective 2 UNCULTURED,
boorish, ignorant, lowbrow,
tasteless, uncultivated,
uneducated, unrefined

philosopher noun THINKER,
logician, metaphysician, sage,
theorist, wise man

philosophical adjective 1 WISE,
abstract, logical, rational,
sagacious, theoretical,
thoughtful 2 STOICAL, calm,
collected, composed, cool,
serene, tranquil, unruffled

philosophy noun 1 THOUGHT,
knowledge, logic, metaphysics,
rationalism, reasoning,
thinking, wisdom 2 OUTLOOK,
beliefs, convictions, doctrine,
ideology, principles, tenets,
thinking, values, viewpoint,
world view 3 STOICISM,

calmness, composure,
equanimity, self-possession,
serenity

phlegmatic adjective
UNEMOTIONAL, apathetic,
impassive, indifferent, placid,
stoical, stolid,
undemonstrative, unfeeling

phobia noun TERROR, aversion,
detestation, dread, fear,
hatred, horror, loathing,
repulsion, revulsion, thing
(*informal*)

phone noun 1 TELEPHONE, blower
(*informal*), horn (*informal*)
2 CALL ▶ verb 3 CALL, get on the
blower (*informal*), get on the
horn (*informal*), give someone
a call, make a call, telephone

phony Informal ▶ adjective
1 FAKE, bogus, counterfeit,
ersatz, false, imitation, pseudo
(*informal*), sham ▶ noun 2 FAKE,
counterfeit, forgery, fraud,
impostor, pseud (*informal*),
sham

photograph noun 1 PICTURE,
photo (*informal*), print, shot,
snap (*informal*), snapshot,
transparency ▶ verb 2 TAKE A
PICTURE OF, film, record, shoot,
snap (*informal*), take
(someone's) picture

photographic adjective
1 LIFELIKE, graphic, natural,
pictorial, realistic, visual, vivid
2 Of a person's memory
ACCURATE, exact, faithful,
precise, retentive

phrase noun 1 EXPRESSION, group
of words, idiom, remark,
saying ▶ verb 2 EXPRESS, put, put
into words, say, voice, word

phraseology noun WORDING,
choice of words, expression,

idiom, language, parlance, phrase, phrasing, speech, style, syntax

physical adjective **1** BODILY, corporal, corporeal, earthly, fleshly, incarnate, mortal **2** MATERIAL, natural, palpable, real, solid, substantial, tangible

physician noun DOCTOR, doc (informal), doctor of medicine, general practitioner, G.P., M.D., medic (informal), medical practitioner

physique noun BUILD, body, constitution, figure, form, frame, shape, structure

pick verb **1** SELECT, choose, decide upon, elect, fix upon, hand-pick, opt for, settle upon, single out **2** GATHER, harvest, pluck, pull **3** NIBBLE, have no appetite, peck at, play or toy with, push the food round the plate **4** PROVOKE, incite, instigate, start **5** OPEN, break into, break open, crack, force ▶ noun **6** CHOICE, decision, option, preference, selection **7** THE BEST, crème de la crème, elect, elite, the cream

picket noun **1** PROTESTER, demonstrator, picketer **2** LOOKOUT, guard, patrol, sentinel, sentry, watch **3** STAKE, pale, paling, post, stanchion, upright ▶ verb **4** BLOCKADE, boycott, demonstrate

pickle noun **1** Informal PREDICAMENT, bind (informal), difficulty, dilemma, fix (informal), hot water (informal), jam (informal), quandary, scrape (informal), tight spot ▶ verb **2** PRESERVE, marinade, steep

pick-me-up noun Informal TONIC, bracer (informal), refreshment, restorative, shot in the arm (informal), stimulant

pick on verb TORMENT, badger, bait, bully, goad, hector, tease

pick out verb IDENTIFY, discriminate, distinguish, make out, perceive, recognize, tell apart

pick up verb **1** LIFT, gather, grasp, raise, take up, uplift **2** OBTAIN, buy, come across, find, purchase **3** RECOVER, be on the mend, get better, improve, mend, rally, take a turn for the better, turn the corner **4** LEARN, acquire, get the hang of (informal), master **5** COLLECT, call for, get

pick-up noun IMPROVEMENT, change for the better, rally, recovery, revival, rise, strengthening, upswing, upturn

picnic noun EXCURSION, outdoor meal, outing

pictorial adjective GRAPHIC, illustrated, picturesque, representational, scenic

picture noun **1** REPRESENTATION, drawing, engraving, illustration, image, likeness, painting, photograph, portrait, print, sketch **2** DESCRIPTION, account, depiction, image, impression, report **3** DOUBLE, carbon copy, copy, dead ringer (slang), duplicate, image, likeness, lookalike, replica, spitting image (informal), twin **4** PERSONIFICATION, embodiment, epitome, essence **5** FILM, flick (slang), motion picture, movie (informal) ▶ verb **6** IMAGINE, conceive of, envision, see, visualize **7** REPRESENT, depict, draw, illustrate, paint, photograph, show, sketch

picturesque *adjective* **1** PRETTY, attractive, beautiful, charming, quaint, scenic, striking **2** VIVID, colorful, graphic

piebald *adjective* PIED, black and white, brindled, dappled, flecked, mottled, speckled, spotted

piece *noun* **1** BIT, chunk, fragment, morsel, part, portion, quantity, segment, slice **2** WORK, article, composition, creation, item, study, work of art

piecemeal *adverb* BIT BY BIT, by degrees, gradually, little by little

pier *noun* **1** JETTY, landing place, promenade, quay, wharf **2** PILLAR, buttress, column, pile, post, support, upright

pierce *verb* PENETRATE, bore, drill, enter, perforate, prick, puncture, spike, stab, stick into

piercing *adjective* **1** *Usually of sound* PENETRATING, ear-splitting, high-pitched, loud, sharp, shrill **2** KEEN, alert, penetrating, perceptive, perspicacious, quick-witted, sharp, shrewd **3** *Usually of weather* COLD, arctic, biting, bitter, freezing, nippy, wintry **4** SHARP, acute, agonizing, excruciating, intense, painful, severe, stabbing

piety *noun* HOLINESS, faith, godliness, piousness, religion, reverence

pig *noun* **1** HOG, boar, porker, sow, swine **2** *Informal* SLOB (*slang*), boor, brute, glutton,

hog (*informal*), swine

pigeonhole *noun* **1** COMPARTMENT, cubbyhole, locker, niche, place, section ▶*verb* **2** CLASSIFY, categorize, characterize, compartmentalize, ghettoize, label, slot (*informal*) **3** PUT OFF, defer, postpone, shelve

pig-headed *adjective* STUBBORN, contrary, inflexible, mulish, obstinate, self-willed, stiff-necked, unyielding

pigment *noun* COLOR, coloring, dye, paint, stain, tincture, tint

pile¹ *noun* **1** HEAP, accumulation, collection, hoard, mass, mound, mountain, stack **2** BUILDING, edifice, erection, structure ▶*verb* **3** COLLECT, accumulate, amass, assemble, gather, heap, hoard, stack **4** CROWD, crush, flock, flood, jam, pack, rush, stream

pile² *noun* FOUNDATION, beam, column, pillar, post, support, upright

pile³ *noun* NAP, down, fiber, fur, hair, plush

pile-up *noun* *Informal* COLLISION, accident, crash, multiple collision, smash, smash-up (*informal*)

pilfer *verb* STEAL, appropriate, embezzle, filch, lift (*informal*), pinch (*informal*), purloin, swipe (*slang*), take

pilgrim *noun* TRAVELER, wanderer, wayfarer

pilgrimage *noun* JOURNEY, excursion, expedition, mission, tour, trip

pill *noun* **1** TABLET, capsule, pellet **2 the pill** ORAL CONTRACEPTIVE

pillage *verb* **1** PLUNDER, despoil,

loot, maraud, raid, ransack, ravage, sack ▸noun 2 PLUNDER, marauding, robbery, sack, spoliation

pillar noun 1 SUPPORT, column, pier, post, prop, shaft, stanchion, upright 2 SUPPORTER, follower, mainstay, upholder

pillory verb RIDICULE, brand, denounce, stigmatize

pilot noun 1 AIRMAN, aviator, flyer 2 HELMSMAN, navigator, steersman ▸adjective 3 TRIAL, experimental, model, test ▸verb 4 FLY, conduct, direct, drive, guide, handle, navigate, operate, steer

pimple noun SPOT, boil, pustule, zit (slang)

pin verb 1 FASTEN, affix, attach, fix, join, secure 2 HOLD FAST, fix, hold down, immobilize, pinion

pinch verb 1 SQUEEZE, compress, grasp, nip, press 2 HURT, cramp, crush, pain 3 Informal STEAL, filch, lift (informal), pilfer, purloin, swipe (slang) ▸noun 4 SQUEEZE, nip 5 DASH, bit, jot, mite, soupçon, speck 6 HARDSHIP, crisis, difficulty, emergency, necessity, plight, predicament, strait

pinched adjective THIN, drawn, gaunt, haggard, peaky, worn

pin down verb 1 FORCE, compel, constrain, make, press, pressurize 2 DETERMINE, identify, locate, name, pinpoint, specify

pine verb (often with for) 1 LONG, ache, crave, desire, eat one's heart out over, hanker, hunger for, thirst for, wish for, yearn for 2 WASTE, decline, fade, languish, sicken

pinion verb IMMOBILIZE, bind,

chain, fasten, fetter, manacle, shackle, tie

pink adjective ROSY, flushed, reddish, rose, roseate, salmon

pinnacle noun PEAK, apex, crest, crown, height, summit, top, vertex, zenith

pinpoint verb IDENTIFY, define, distinguish, locate

pioneer noun 1 SETTLER, colonist, explorer 2 FOUNDER, developer, innovator, leader, trailblazer ▸verb 3 DEVELOP, create, discover, establish, initiate, instigate, institute, invent, originate, show the way, start

pious adjective RELIGIOUS, devout, God-fearing, godly, holy, reverent, righteous, saintly

pipe noun 1 TUBE, conduit, duct, hose, line, main, passage, pipeline ▸verb 2 WHISTLE, cheep, peep, play, sing, sound, warble 3 CONVEY, channel, conduct

pipe down verb Informal BE QUIET, hold one's tongue, hush, quieten down, shush, shut one's mouth, shut up (informal)

pipeline noun TUBE, conduit, duct, passage, pipe

piquant adjective 1 SPICY, biting, pungent, savory, sharp, tangy, tart, zesty 2 INTERESTING, lively, provocative, scintillating, sparkling, stimulating

pique noun 1 RESENTMENT, annoyance, displeasure, huff, hurt feelings, irritation, offense, umbrage, wounded pride ▸verb 2 DISPLEASE, affront, annoy, get (informal), irk, irritate, nettle, offend, rile, sting 3 AROUSE, excite, rouse, spur, stimulate, stir, whet

piracy noun ROBBERY,

buccaneering, freebooting, stealing, theft

pirate noun **1** BUCCANEER, corsair, freebooter, marauder, raider **2** PLAGIARIST, infringer, plagiarizer ▶ verb **3** COPY, appropriate, plagiarize, poach, reproduce, steal

pit noun **1** HOLE, abyss, cavity, chasm, crater, dent, depression, hollow ▶ verb **2** SCAR, dent, indent, mark, pockmark

pitch verb **1** THROW, cast, chuck (informal), fling, heave, hurl, lob (informal), sling, toss **2** SET UP, erect, put up, raise, settle **3** FALL, dive, drop, topple, tumble **4** TOSS, lurch, plunge, roll ▶ noun **5** SPORTS FIELD, field of play, ground, park **6** LEVEL, degree, height, highest point, point, summit **7** SLOPE, angle, dip, gradient, incline, tilt **8** TONE, modulation, sound, timbre **9** SALES TALK, patter, spiel (informal)

pitch-black adjective JET-BLACK, dark, inky, pitch-dark, unlit

pitch in verb HELP, chip in (informal), contribute, cooperate, do one's bit, join in, lend a hand, participate

piteous adjective PATHETIC, affecting, distressing, harrowing, heartbreaking, heart-rending, moving, pitiable, pitiful, plaintive, poignant, sad

pitfall noun DANGER, catch, difficulty, drawback, hazard, peril, snag, trap

pith noun ESSENCE, core, crux, gist, heart, kernel, nub, point, quintessence, salient point

pithy adjective SUCCINCT, brief, cogent, concise, epigrammatic, laconic, pointed, short, terse, to the point, trenchant

pitiful adjective **1** PATHETIC, distressing, grievous, harrowing, heartbreaking, heart-rending, piteous, pitiable, sad, wretched **2** CONTEMPTIBLE, abject, base, lousy (slang), low, mean, miserable, paltry, shabby, sorry

pitiless adjective MERCILESS, callous, cold-blooded, cold-hearted, cruel, hardhearted, heartless, implacable, relentless, ruthless, unmerciful

pittance noun PEANUTS (slang), chicken feed (slang), drop, mite, slave wages, trifle

pity noun **1** COMPASSION, charity, clemency, fellow feeling, forbearance, kindness, mercy, sympathy **2** SHAME, bummer (slang), crying shame, misfortune, sin ▶ verb **3** FEEL SORRY FOR, bleed for, feel for, grieve for, have compassion for, sympathize with, weep for

pivot noun **1** AXIS, axle, fulcrum, spindle, swivel **2** HUB, center, heart, hinge, kingpin ▶ verb **3** TURN, revolve, rotate, spin, swivel, twirl **4** RELY, be contingent, depend, hang, hinge

pivotal adjective CRUCIAL, central, critical, decisive, vital

pixie noun ELF, brownie, fairy, sprite

placard noun NOTICE, advertisement, bill, poster

placate verb CALM, appease, assuage, conciliate, humor,

mollify, pacify, propitiate, soothe

place noun **1** SPOT, area, location, point, position, site, venue, whereabouts **2** REGION, district, locale, locality, neighborhood, quarter, vicinity **3** POSITION, grade, rank, station, status **4** SPACE, accommodation, room **5** HOME, abode, domicile, dwelling, house, pad (*slang, dated*), property, residence **6** DUTY, affair, charge, concern, function, prerogative, responsibility, right, role **7** JOB, appointment, employment, position, post **8** take place HAPPEN, come about, go on, occur, transpire (*informal*) ▶ verb **9** PUT, deposit, install, lay, locate, position, rest, set, situate, stand, station, stick (*informal*) **10** CLASSIFY, arrange, class, grade, group, order, rank, sort **11** IDENTIFY, know, put one's finger on, recognize, remember **12** ASSIGN, allocate, appoint, charge, entrust, give

placid adjective CALM, collected, composed, equable, even-tempered, imperturbable, serene, tranquil, unexcitable, unruffled, untroubled

plagiarism noun COPYING, borrowing, infringement, piracy, theft

plagiarize verb COPY, borrow, lift (*informal*), pirate, steal

plague noun **1** DISEASE, epidemic, infection, pestilence **2** AFFLICTION, bane, blight, curse, evil, scourge, torment ▶ verb **3** PESTER, annoy, badger, bother, harass, harry, hassle (*informal*), tease, torment, torture, trouble, vex

plain adjective **1** CLEAR, comprehensible, distinct, evident, manifest, obvious, overt, patent, unambiguous, understandable, unmistakable, visible **2** HONEST, blunt, candid, direct, downright, forthright, frank, open, outspoken, straightforward, upfront (*informal*) **3** UNADORNED, austere, bare, basic, severe, simple, Spartan, stark, unembellished, unfussy, unornamented **4** UGLY, dumpy (*informal*), frowzy, homely (*U.S.*), ill-favored, no oil painting (*informal*), not beautiful, unattractive, unlovely, unprepossessing **5** ORDINARY, common, commonplace, everyday, simple, unaffected, unpretentious ▶ noun **6** FLATLAND, grassland, plateau, prairie, steppe, veld

plain-spoken adjective BLUNT, candid, direct, downright, forthright, frank, outspoken

plaintive adjective SORROWFUL, heart-rending, mournful, pathetic, piteous, pitiful, sad

plan noun **1** SCHEME, design, method, plot, program, proposal, strategy, suggestion, system **2** DIAGRAM, blueprint, chart, drawing, layout, map, representation, sketch ▶ verb **3** DEVISE, arrange, contrive, design, draft, formulate, organize, outline, plot, scheme, think out **4** INTEND, aim, mean, propose, purpose

plane noun **1** AIRPLANE, aircraft, jet **2** FLAT SURFACE, level surface **3** LEVEL, condition, degree, position ▶ adjective **4** LEVEL, even, flat, horizontal, regular, smooth ▸ verb 5 SKIM, glide, sail, skate

plant noun 1 VEGETABLE, bush, flower, herb, shrub, weed 2 FACTORY, foundry, mill, shop, works, yard 3 MACHINERY, apparatus, equipment, gear ▸ verb 4 SOW, put in the ground, scatter, seed, transplant 5 PLACE, establish, fix, found, insert, put, set

plaster noun 1 MORTAR, gypsum, plaster of Paris, stucco 2 BANDAGE, adhesive plaster, dressing, Elastoplast (Trademark), sticking plaster ▸ verb 3 COVER, coat, daub, overlay, smear, spread

plastic adjective 1 MANAGEABLE, docile, malleable, pliable, receptive, responsive, tractable 2 PLIANT, ductile, flexible, moldable, pliable, soft, supple

plate noun 1 PLATTER, dish, trencher (archaic) 2 HELPING, course, dish, portion, serving 3 LAYER, panel, sheet, slab 4 ILLUSTRATION, lithograph, print ▸ verb 5 COAT, cover, gild, laminate, overlay

plateau noun 1 UPLAND, highland, table, tableland 2 LEVELLING OFF, level, stability, stage

platform noun 1 STAGE, dais, podium, rostrum, stand 2 POLICY, manifesto, objective(s), party line, principle, program

platitude noun CLICHÉ, banality, commonplace, truism

platoon noun SQUAD, company, group, outfit (informal), patrol, squadron, team

platter noun PLATE, dish, salver, tray, trencher (archaic)

plaudits plural noun APPROVAL, acclaim, acclamation, applause, approbation, praise

plausible adjective 1 REASONABLE, believable, conceivable, credible, likely, persuasive, possible, probable, tenable 2 GLIB, smooth, smooth-talking, smooth-tongued, specious

play verb 1 AMUSE ONESELF, entertain oneself, fool, have fun, revel, romp, sport, trifle 2 COMPETE, challenge, contend against, participate, take on, take part 3 ACT, act the part of, perform, portray, represent ▸ noun 4 DRAMA, comedy, dramatic piece, farce, pantomime, piece, show, stage show, tragedy 5 AMUSEMENT, diversion, entertainment, fun, game, pastime, recreation, sport 6 FUN, humor, jest, joking, lark (informal), prank, sport 7 SPACE, elbowroom, latitude, leeway, margin, room, scope

playboy noun WOMANIZER, ladies' man, philanderer, rake, roué

play down verb MINIMIZE, gloss over, make light of, make little of, underplay, underrate

player noun 1 SPORTSMAN or SPORTSWOMAN, competitor, contestant, participant 2 MUSICIAN, artist, instrumentalist, performer, virtuoso 3 PERFORMER, actor or actress, entertainer, Thespian, trouper

playful adjective LIVELY, frisky, impish, merry, mischievous, spirited, sportive, sprightly, vivacious

playmate noun FRIEND, chum (informal), companion, comrade, pal (informal), playfellow

play on or **upon** verb TAKE ADVANTAGE OF, abuse, capitalize on, exploit, impose on, trade on

plaything noun TOY, amusement, game, pastime, trifle

play up verb EMPHASIZE, accentuate, highlight, stress, underline

plea noun 1 APPEAL, entreaty, intercession, petition, prayer, request, suit, supplication 2 EXCUSE, defense, explanation, justification

plead verb APPEAL, ask, beg, beseech, entreat, implore, petition, request

pleasant adjective 1 PLEASING, agreeable, amusing, delightful, enjoyable, fine, lovely, nice, pleasurable 2 NICE, affable, agreeable, amiable, charming, congenial, engaging, friendly, genial, likable or likeable

pleasantry noun JOKE, badinage, banter, jest, quip, witticism

please verb DELIGHT, amuse, entertain, gladden, gratify, humor, indulge, satisfy, suit

pleased adjective HAPPY, contented, delighted, euphoric, glad, gratified, over the moon (informal), satisfied, thrilled

pleasing adjective ENJOYABLE, agreeable, charming, delightful, engaging, gratifying, likable or likeable, pleasurable, satisfying

pleasurable adjective ENJOYABLE,

agreeable, delightful, fun, good, lovely, nice, pleasant

pleasure noun HAPPINESS, amusement, bliss, delectation, delight, enjoyment, gladness, gratification, joy, satisfaction

plebeian adjective 1 COMMON, base, coarse, low, lower-class, proletarian, uncultivated, unrefined, vulgar, working-class ▶ noun 2 COMMONER, common man, man in the street, pleb, proletarian

pledge noun 1 PROMISE, assurance, covenant, oath, undertaking, vow, warrant, word 2 GUARANTEE, bail, collateral, deposit, pawn, security, surety ▶ verb 3 PROMISE, contract, engage, give one's oath, give one's word, swear, vow

plentiful adjective ABUNDANT, ample, bountiful, copious, generous, lavish, liberal, overflowing, plenteous, profuse

plenty noun 1 LOTS (informal), abundance, enough, great deal, heap(s) (informal), masses, pile(s) (informal), plethora, quantity, stack(s) 2 ABUNDANCE, affluence, copiousness, fertility, fruitfulness, plenitude, profusion, prosperity, wealth

plethora noun EXCESS, glut, overabundance, profusion, superabundance, surfeit, surplus

pliable adjective 1 FLEXIBLE, bendable, bendy, malleable, plastic, pliant, supple 2 IMPRESSIONABLE, adaptable, compliant, docile, easily led, pliant, receptive, responsive, susceptible, tractable

pliant adjective **1** FLEXIBLE, bendable, bendy, plastic, pliable, supple **2** IMPRESSIONABLE, biddable, compliant, easily led, pliable, susceptible, tractable

plight noun DIFFICULTY, condition, jam (informal), predicament, scrape (informal), situation, spot (informal), state, trouble

plod verb **1** TRUDGE, clump, drag, lumber, tramp, tread **2** SLOG, grind (informal), labor, persevere, plow through, soldier on, toil

plot[1] noun **1** PLAN, cabal, conspiracy, intrigue, machination, scheme, stratagem **2** STORY, action, narrative, outline, scenario, story line, subject, theme ▸ verb **3** PLAN, collude, conspire, contrive, intrigue, machinate, maneuver, scheme **4** DEVISE, conceive, concoct, contrive, cook up (informal), design, hatch, lay **5** CHART, calculate, locate, map, mark, outline

plot[2] noun PATCH, allotment, area, ground, lot, parcel, tract

plow verb **1** TURN OVER, cultivate, dig, till **2** (usually with through) FORGE, cut, drive, plunge, press, push, wade

ploy noun TACTIC, device, dodge, maneuver, move, ruse, scheme, stratagem, trick, wile

pluck verb **1** PULL OUT or OFF, collect, draw, gather, harvest, pick **2** TUG, catch, clutch, jerk, pull at, snatch, tweak, yank **3** STRUM, finger, pick, twang ▸ noun **4** COURAGE, backbone, boldness, bravery, grit, guts (informal), nerve

plucky adjective COURAGEOUS,

bold, brave, daring, game, gutsy (slang), intrepid

plug noun **1** STOPPER, bung, cork, spigot **2** Informal MENTION, advertisement, hype, publicity, push ▸ verb **3** SEAL, block, bung, close, cork, fill, pack, stop, stopper, stop up, stuff **4** Informal MENTION, advertise, build up, hype, promote, publicize, push

plum adjective CHOICE, best, first-class, prize

plumb verb **1** DELVE, explore, fathom, gauge, go into, penetrate, probe, unravel ▸ noun **2** WEIGHT, lead, plumb bob, plummet ▸ adverb **3** EXACTLY, bang, precisely, slap

plume noun FEATHER, crest, pinion, quill

plummet verb PLUNGE, crash, descend, dive, drop down, fall, nose-dive, tumble

plump adjective CHUBBY, corpulent, dumpy, fat, roly-poly, rotund, round, stout, tubby

plunder verb **1** LOOT, pillage, raid, ransack, rifle, rob, sack, strip ▸ noun **2** LOOT, booty, ill-gotten gains, pillage, prize, spoils, swag (slang)

plunge verb **1** THROW, cast, pitch **2** HURTLE, career, charge, dash, jump, rush, tear **3** DESCEND, dip, dive, drop, fall, nose-dive, plummet, sink, tumble ▸ noun **4** DIVE, descent, drop, fall, jump

plus preposition **1** AND, added to, coupled with, with ▸ adjective **2** ADDITIONAL, added, add-on, extra, supplementary ▸ noun **3** ADVANTAGE, asset, benefit, bonus, extra, gain, good point

plush adjective LUXURIOUS, deluxe, lavish, luxury, opulent, rich, sumptuous

ply verb 1 WORK AT, carry on, exercise, follow, practice, pursue 2 USE, employ, handle, manipulate, wield

poach verb ENCROACH, appropriate, infringe, intrude, trespass

pocket noun 1 POUCH, bag, compartment, receptacle, sack ▶verb 2 STEAL, appropriate, filch, lift (informal), pilfer, purloin, take ▶adjective 3 SMALL, abridged, compact, concise, little, miniature, portable

pod noun, verb SHELL, hull, husk, shuck

podium noun PLATFORM, dais, rostrum, stage

poem noun VERSE, lyric, ode, rhyme, song, sonnet

poet noun BARD, lyricist, rhymer, versifier

poetic adjective LYRICAL, elegiac, lyric, metrical

poetry noun VERSE, poems, rhyme, rhyming

poignancy noun 1 SADNESS, emotion, feeling, pathos, sentiment, tenderness 2 SHARPNESS, bitterness, intensity, keenness

poignant adjective MOVING, bitter, distressing, heart-rending, intense, painful, pathetic, sad, touching

point noun 1 ESSENCE, crux, drift, gist, heart, import, meaning, nub, pith, question, subject, thrust 2 AIM, end, goal, intent, intention, motive, object,

objective, purpose, reason 3 ITEM, aspect, detail, feature, particular 4 CHARACTERISTIC, aspect, attribute, quality, respect, trait 5 PLACE, location, position, site, spot, stage 6 FULL STOP, dot, mark, period, stop 7 END, apex, prong, sharp end, spike, spur, summit, tip, top 8 HEADLAND, cape, head, promontory 9 STAGE, circumstance, condition, degree, extent, position 10 MOMENT, instant, juncture, time, very minute 11 UNIT, score, tally ▶verb 12 INDICATE, call attention to, denote, designate, direct, show, signify 13 AIM, direct, level, train

point-blank adjective 1 DIRECT, blunt, downright, explicit, express, plain ▶adverb 2 DIRECTLY, bluntly, candidly, explicitly, forthrightly, frankly, openly, plainly, straight

pointed adjective 1 SHARP, acute, barbed, edged 2 CUTTING, acute, biting, incisive, keen, penetrating, pertinent, sharp, telling

pointer noun 1 HINT, advice, caution, information, recommendation, suggestion, tip 2 INDICATOR, guide, hand, needle

pointless adjective SENSELESS, absurd, aimless, fruitless, futile, inane, irrelevant, meaningless, silly, stupid, useless

point out verb MENTION, allude to, bring up, identify, indicate, show, specify

poise noun COMPOSURE, aplomb, assurance, calmness, cool (slang), dignity, presence, sang-froid, self-possession

poised *adjective* **1** READY, all set, prepared, standing by, waiting **2** COMPOSED, calm, collected, dignified, self-confident, self-possessed, together (*informal*)

poison *noun* **1** TOXIN, bane, venom ▸*verb* **2** MURDER, give (someone) poison, kill **3** CONTAMINATE, infect, pollute **4** CORRUPT, defile, deprave, pervert, subvert, taint, undermine, warp

poisonous *adjective* **1** TOXIC, deadly, fatal, lethal, mortal, noxious, venomous, virulent **2** EVIL, baleful, corrupting, malicious, noxious, pernicious

poke *verb* **1** JAB, dig, nudge, prod, push, shove, stab, stick, thrust ▸*noun* **2** JAB, dig, nudge, prod, thrust

poky *adjective* SMALL, confined, cramped, narrow, tiny

pole *noun* ROD, bar, mast, post, shaft, spar, staff, stick

police *noun* **1** THE LAW (*informal*), boys in blue (*informal*), constabulary, fuzz (*slang*), police force ▸*verb* **2** CONTROL, guard, patrol, protect, regulate, watch

policeman *noun* COP (*slang*), constable, copper (*slang*), fuzz (*slang*), officer

policy *noun* PROCEDURE, action, approach, code, course, custom, plan, practice, rule, scheme

polish *verb* **1** SHINE, brighten, buff, burnish, rub, smooth, wax **2** PERFECT, brush up, enhance, finish, improve, refine, touch up ▸*noun* **3** VARNISH, wax **4** SHEEN,

brightness, finish, glaze, gloss, luster **5** STYLE, breeding, class (*informal*), elegance, finesse, finish, grace, refinement

polished *adjective* **1** ACCOMPLISHED, adept, expert, fine, masterly, professional, skillful, superlative **2** SHINING, bright, burnished, gleaming, glossy, smooth **3** ELEGANT, cultivated, polite, refined, sophisticated, well-bred

polite *adjective* **1** MANNERLY, civil, complaisant, courteous, gracious, respectful, well-behaved, well-mannered **2** REFINED, civilized, cultured, elegant, genteel, polished, sophisticated, well-bred

politeness *noun* COURTESY, civility, courteousness, decency, etiquette, mannerliness

politic *adjective* WISE, advisable, diplomatic, expedient, judicious, prudent, sensible

political *adjective* GOVERNMENTAL, parliamentary, policy-making

politician *noun* STATESMAN, bureaucrat, congressman, legislator, office bearer, public servant, representative

politics *noun* STATESMANSHIP, affairs of state, civics, government, political science

poll *noun* **1** CANVASS, ballot, census, count, sampling, survey **2** VOTE, figures, returns, tally, voting ▸*verb* **3** TALLY, register **4** QUESTION, ballot, canvass, interview, sample, survey

pollute *verb* **1** CONTAMINATE, dirty, foul, infect, poison, soil, spoil, stain, taint **2** DEFILE, corrupt, debase, debauch, deprave, desecrate, dishonor, profane, sully

pollution noun CONTAMINATION, corruption, defilement, dirtying, foulness, impurity, taint, uncleanness

pomp noun 1 CEREMONY, flourish, grandeur, magnificence, pageant, pageantry, splendor, state 2 SHOW, display, grandiosity, ostentation

pomposity noun SELF-IMPORTANCE, affectation, airs, grandiosity, pompousness, portentousness, pretension, pretentiousness

pompous adjective 1 SELF-IMPORTANT, arrogant, grandiose, ostentatious, pretentious, puffed up, showy 2 GRANDILOQUENT, boastful, bombastic, high-flown, inflated

pond noun POOL, duck pond, fish pond, millpond, small lake, tarn

ponder verb THINK, brood, cogitate, consider, contemplate, deliberate, meditate, mull over, muse, reflect, ruminate

ponderous adjective 1 DULL, heavy, long-winded, pedantic, tedious 2 UNWIELDY, bulky, cumbersome, heavy, huge, massive, weighty 3 CLUMSY, awkward, heavy-footed, lumbering

pontificate verb EXPOUND, hold forth, lay down the law, preach, pronounce, sound off

pool[1] noun 1 POND, lake, mere, puddle, tarn 2 SWIMMING POOL, swimming bath

pool[2] noun 1 SYNDICATE,

collective, consortium, group, team, trust 2 KITTY, bank, funds, jackpot, pot ▶ verb 3 COMBINE, amalgamate, join forces, league, merge, put together, share

poor adjective 1 IMPOVERISHED, broke (informal), destitute, down and out, down on one's luck (informal), hard up (informal), impecunious, indigent, needy, on the breadline, penniless, penurious, poverty-stricken, short 2 INADEQUATE, deficient, incomplete, insufficient, lacking, lousy (slang), meager, measly, scant, scanty, skimpy 3 INFERIOR, below par, lousy (slang), low-grade, mediocre, rotten (informal), rubbishy, second-rate, substandard, unsatisfactory 4 UNFORTUNATE, hapless, ill-fated, luckless, pitiable, unhappy, unlucky, wretched

poorly adverb BADLY, inadequately, incompetently, inexpertly, insufficiently, unsatisfactorily, unsuccessfully

pop verb 1 BURST, bang, crack, explode, go off, snap 2 PUT, insert, push, shove, slip, stick, thrust, tuck ▶ noun 3 BANG, burst, crack, explosion, noise, report

pope noun HOLY FATHER, Bishop of Rome, pontiff, Vicar of Christ

populace noun PEOPLE, general public, hoi polloi, masses, mob, multitude

popular adjective 1 WELL-LIKED, accepted, approved, cool (informal), fashionable, favorite, in (informal), in demand, in favor, liked, phat (slang), sought-after **2** COMMON, conventional, current, general, prevailing, prevalent, universal

popularity noun FAVOR, acceptance, acclaim, approval, currency, esteem, regard, vogue

popularize verb MAKE POPULAR, disseminate, give currency to, give mass appeal, make available to all, spread, universalize

popularly adverb GENERALLY, commonly, conventionally, customarily, ordinarily, traditionally, universally, usually, widely

populate verb INHABIT, colonize, live in, occupy, settle

population noun INHABITANTS, community, denizens, folk, natives, people, residents, society

populous adjective POPULATED, crowded, heavily populated, overpopulated, packed, swarming, teeming

pore[1] verb **pore over** STUDY, examine, peruse, ponder, read, scrutinize

pore[2] noun OPENING, hole, orifice, outlet

pornographic adjective OBSCENE, blue, dirty, filthy, indecent, lewd, salacious, scuzzy (slang), smutty, X-rated

pornography noun OBSCENITY, dirt, filth, indecency, porn (informal), smut

porous adjective PERMEABLE, absorbent, absorptive, penetrable, spongy

port noun HARBOR, anchorage, haven, seaport

portable adjective LIGHT, compact, convenient, easily carried, handy, manageable, movable

portend verb FORETELL, augur, betoken, bode, foreshadow, herald, indicate, predict, prognosticate, promise, warn of

portent noun OMEN, augury, forewarning, indication, prognostication, sign, warning

portentous adjective **1** SIGNIFICANT, crucial, fateful, important, menacing, momentous, ominous **2** POMPOUS, ponderous, self-important, solemn

porter[1] noun BAGGAGE ATTENDANT, bearer, carrier

porter[2] noun DOORMAN, caretaker, concierge, gatekeeper, janitor

portion noun **1** PART, bit, fragment, morsel, piece, scrap, section, segment **2** SHARE, allocation, allotment, allowance, lot, measure, quantity, quota, ration **3** HELPING, piece, serving **4** DESTINY, fate, fortune, lot, luck ▸ verb **5 portion out** DIVIDE, allocate, allot, apportion, deal, distribute, dole out, share out

portly adjective STOUT, burly, corpulent, fat, fleshy, heavy, large, plump

portrait noun **1** PICTURE, image, likeness, painting, photograph, representation **2** DESCRIPTION, characterization, depiction, portrayal, profile, thumbnail sketch

portray verb **1** REPRESENT, depict, draw, figure, illustrate, paint, picture, sketch **2** DESCRIBE, characterize, depict, put in words **3** PLAY, act the part of, represent

portrayal noun REPRESENTATION, characterization, depiction, interpretation, performance, picture

pose verb 1 POSITION, model, sit 2 PUT ON AIRS, posture, show off (informal) 3 **pose as** IMPERSONATE, masquerade as, pass oneself off as, pretend to be, profess to be ▶ noun 4 POSTURE, attitude, bearing, position, stance 5 ACT, affectation, air, façade, front, mannerism, posturing, pretense

poser noun PUZZLE, enigma, problem, question, riddle

posit verb PUT FORWARD, advance, assume, postulate, presume, propound, state

position noun 1 PLACE, area, bearings, locale, location, point, post, situation, spot, station, whereabouts 2 POSTURE, arrangement, attitude, pose, stance 3 ATTITUDE, belief, opinion, outlook, point of view, slant, stance, view, viewpoint 4 STATUS, importance, place, prestige, rank, reputation, standing, station, stature 5 JOB, duty, employment, occupation, office, place, post, role, situation ▶ verb 6 PLACE, arrange, lay out, locate, put, set, stand

positive adjective 1 CERTAIN, assured, confident, convinced, sure 2 DEFINITE, absolute, categorical, certain, clear, conclusive, decisive, explicit, express, firm, real 3 HELPFUL, beneficial, constructive, practical, productive, progressive, useful

positively adverb DEFINITELY, absolutely, assuredly, categorically, certainly, emphatically, firmly, surely, unequivocally, unquestionably

possess verb 1 HAVE, enjoy, hold, own 2 CONTROL, acquire, dominate, hold, occupy, seize, take over

possessed adjective CRAZED, berserk, demented, frenzied, obsessed, raving

possession noun 1 OWNERSHIP, control, custody, hold, occupation, tenure, title 2 **possessions** PROPERTY, assets, belongings, chattels, effects, estate, things

possessive adjective JEALOUS, controlling, covetous, dominating, domineering, overprotective, selfish

possibility noun 1 FEASIBILITY, likelihood, potentiality, practicability, workableness 2 LIKELIHOOD, chance, hope, liability, odds, probability, prospect, risk 3 (often plural) POTENTIAL, capabilities, potentiality, promise, prospects, talent

possible adjective 1 CONCEIVABLE, credible, hypothetical, imaginable, likely, potential 2 LIKELY, hopeful, potential, probable, promising 3 FEASIBLE, attainable, doable, practicable, realizable, viable, workable

possibly adverb PERHAPS, maybe, perchance (archaic)

post¹ noun **keep someone posted** NOTIFY, advise, brief, fill in on (informal), inform, report to

post² noun 1 SUPPORT, column,

picket, pillar, pole, shaft, stake, upright ▶ *verb* **2** PUT UP, affix, display, pin up

post³ *noun* **1** JOB, appointment, assignment, employment, office, place, position, situation **2** STATION, beat, place, position ▶ *verb* **3** STATION, assign, place, position, put, situate

poster *noun* NOTICE, advertisement, announcement, bill, placard, public notice, sticker

posterity *noun* **1** FUTURE, succeeding generations **2** DESCENDANTS, children, family, heirs, issue, offspring, progeny

postpone *verb* PUT OFF, adjourn, defer, delay, put back, put on the back burner (*informal*), shelve, suspend

postponement *noun* DELAY, adjournment, deferment, deferral, stay, suspension

postscript *noun* P.S., addition, afterthought, supplement

postulate *verb* PRESUPPOSE, assume, hypothesize, posit, propose, suppose, take for granted, theorize

posture *noun* **1** BEARING, attitude, carriage, disposition, set, stance ▶ *verb* **2** SHOW OFF (*informal*), affect, pose, put on airs

pot *noun* CONTAINER, bowl, pan, vessel

potency *noun* POWER, effectiveness, force, influence, might, strength

potent *adjective* **1** POWERFUL, authoritative, commanding, dominant, dynamic, influential **2** STRONG, forceful, mighty, powerful, vigorous

potential *adjective* **1** POSSIBLE, dormant, future, hidden, inherent, latent, likely, promising ▶ *noun* **2** ABILITY, aptitude, capability, capacity, possibility, potentiality, power, wherewithal

potion *noun* CONCOCTION, brew, dose, draft, elixir, mixture, philtre

pottery *noun* CERAMICS, earthenware, stoneware, terracotta

pouch *noun* BAG, container, pocket, purse, sack

pounce *verb* **1** SPRING, attack, fall upon, jump, leap at, strike, swoop ▶ *noun* **2** SPRING, assault, attack, bound, jump, leap, swoop

pound¹ *verb* **1** BEAT, batter, belabor, clobber (*slang*), hammer, pummel, strike, thrash, thump **2** CRUSH, powder, pulverize **3** PULSATE, beat, palpitate, pulse, throb **4** STOMP (*informal*), march, thunder, tramp

pound² *noun* ENCLOSURE, compound, pen, yard

pour *verb* **1** FLOW, course, emit, gush, run, rush, spew, spout, stream **2** LET FLOW, decant, spill, splash **3** RAIN, bucket down (*informal*), pelt (down), teem **4** STREAM, crowd, swarm, teem, throng

pout *verb* **1** SULK, glower, look petulant, pull a long face ▶ *noun* **2** SULLEN LOOK, glower, long face

poverty *noun* **1** PENNILESSNESS, beggary, destitution, hardship, indigence, insolvency, need, penury, privation, want

2 SCARCITY, dearth, deficiency, insufficiency, lack, paucity, shortage

poverty-stricken *adjective* PENNILESS, broke (*informal*), destitute, down and out, down on one's luck (*informal*), flat broke (*informal*), impecunious, impoverished, indigent, poor

powder *noun* **1** DUST, fine grains, loose particles, talc ▸ *verb* **2** DUST, cover, dredge, scatter, sprinkle, strew

powdery *adjective* FINE, crumbly, dry, dusty, grainy, granular

power *noun* **1** ABILITY, capability, capacity, competence, competency, faculty, potential **2** CONTROL, ascendancy, authority, command, dominance, domination, dominion, influence, mastery, rule **3** AUTHORITY, authorization, license, prerogative, privilege, right, warrant **4** STRENGTH, brawn, energy, force, forcefulness, intensity, might, muscle, potency, vigor

powerful *adjective* **1** CONTROLLING, authoritative, commanding, dominant, influential, prevailing **2** STRONG, energetic, mighty, potent, strapping, sturdy, vigorous **3** PERSUASIVE, cogent, compelling, convincing, effectual, forceful, impressive, striking, telling, weighty

powerless *adjective* **1** DEFENSELESS, dependent, ineffective, subject, tied, unarmed, vulnerable **2** HELPLESS, challenged, debilitated, disabled, feeble, frail, impotent, incapable,

incapacitated, ineffectual, weak

practicability *noun* FEASIBILITY, advantage, possibility, practicality, use, usefulness, viability

practicable *adjective* FEASIBLE, achievable, attainable, doable, possible, viable

practical *adjective* **1** FUNCTIONAL, applied, empirical, experimental, factual, pragmatic, realistic, utilitarian **2** SENSIBLE, businesslike, down-to-earth, hard-headed, matter-of-fact, ordinary, realistic **3** FEASIBLE, doable, practicable, serviceable, useful, workable **4** SKILLED, accomplished, efficient, experienced, proficient

practically *adverb* **1** ALMOST, all but, basically, essentially, fundamentally, in effect, just about, nearly, very nearly, virtually, well-nigh **2** SENSIBLY, clearly, matter-of-factly, rationally, realistically, reasonably

practice *noun* **1** CUSTOM, habit, method, mode, routine, rule, system, tradition, usage, way, wont **2** REHEARSAL, drill, exercise, preparation, repetition, study, training **3** PROFESSION, business, career, vocation, work **4** USE, action, application, exercise, experience, operation ▸ *verb* **5** REHEARSE, drill, exercise, go over, go through, prepare, repeat, study, train **6** DO, apply, carry out, follow, observe, perform **7** WORK AT, carry on, engage in, pursue

practiced *adjective* SKILLED, able, accomplished, experienced, expert, proficient, seasoned, trained, versed

pragmatic *adjective* PRACTICAL, businesslike, down-to-earth, hard-headed, realistic, sensible, utilitarian

praise *verb* **1** APPROVE, acclaim, admire, applaud, cheer, compliment, congratulate, eulogize, extol, honor, laud **2** GIVE THANKS TO, adore, bless, exalt, glorify, worship ▶ *noun* **3** APPROVAL, acclaim, acclamation, approbation, commendation, compliment, congratulation, eulogy, kudos, plaudit, tribute **4** THANKS, adoration, glory, homage, kudos, worship

praiseworthy *adjective* CREDITABLE, admirable, commendable, laudable, meritorious, worthy

prance *verb* **1** DANCE, caper, cavort, frisk, gambol, romp, skip **2** STRUT, parade, show off (*informal*), stalk, swagger

prank *noun* TRICK, antic, escapade, jape, lark (*informal*), practical joke

pray *verb* **1** SAY ONE'S PRAYERS, offer a prayer, recite the rosary **2** BEG, adjure, ask, beseech, entreat, implore, petition, plead, request, solicit

prayer *noun* **1** ORISON, devotion, invocation, litany, supplication **2** PLEA, appeal, entreaty, petition, request, supplication

preach *verb* **1** DELIVER A SERMON, address, evangelize **2** LECTURE, advocate, exhort, moralize, sermonize

preacher *noun* CLERGYMAN, evangelist, minister, missionary, parson

preamble *noun* INTRODUCTION, foreword, opening statement or remarks, preface, prelude

precarious *adjective* DANGEROUS, hazardous, insecure, perilous, risky, shaky, tricky, unreliable, unsafe, unsure

precaution *noun* **1** SAFEGUARD, insurance, protection, provision, safety measure **2** FORETHOUGHT, care, caution, providence, prudence, wariness

precede *verb* GO BEFORE, antedate, come first, head, introduce, lead, preface

precedence *noun* PRIORITY, antecedence, pre-eminence, primacy, rank, seniority, superiority, supremacy

precedent *noun* INSTANCE, antecedent, example, model, paradigm, pattern, prototype, standard

preceding *adjective* PREVIOUS, above, aforementioned, aforesaid, earlier, foregoing, former, past, prior

precept *noun* RULE, canon, command, commandment, decree, instruction, law, order, principle, regulation, statute

precinct *noun* **1** ENCLOSURE, confine, limit **2** AREA, district, quarter, section, sector, zone

precious *adjective* VALUABLE, costly, dear, expensive, fine, invaluable, priceless, prized **2** LOVED, adored, beloved, cherished, darling, dear, prized, treasured **3** AFFECTED, artificial, overnice, overrefined

precipice *noun* CLIFF, bluff, crag, height, rock face

precipitate *verb* **1** QUICKEN, accelerate, advance, bring on, expedite, hasten, hurry, speed up, trigger **2** THROW, cast, fling, hurl, launch, let fly ▸ *adjective* **3** HASTY, heedless, impetuous, impulsive, precipitous, rash, reckless **4** SWIFT, breakneck, headlong, rapid, rushing **5** SUDDEN, abrupt, brief, quick, unexpected, without warning

precipitous *adjective* **1** SHEER, abrupt, dizzy, high, perpendicular, steep **2** HASTY, heedless, hurried, precipitate, rash, reckless

précis *noun* **1** SUMMARY, abridgment, outline, résumé, synopsis ▸ *verb* **2** SUMMARIZE, abridge, outline, shorten, sum up

precise *adjective* **1** EXACT, absolute, accurate, correct, definite, explicit, express, particular, specific, strict **2** STRICT, careful, exact, fastidious, finicky, formal, meticulous, particular, punctilious, rigid, scrupulous, stiff

precisely *adverb* EXACTLY, absolutely, accurately, correctly, just so, plumb (*informal*), smack (*informal*), square, squarely, strictly

precision *noun* EXACTNESS, accuracy, care, meticulousness, particularity, preciseness

preclude *verb* PREVENT, check, debar, exclude, forestall, inhibit, obviate, prohibit, rule out, stop

precocious *adjective* ADVANCED, ahead, bright, developed, forward, quick, smart

preconceived *adjective* PRESUMED, forejudged,

prejudged, presupposed

preconception *noun* PRECONCEIVED IDEA *or* NOTION, bias, notion, predisposition, prejudice, presupposition

precursor *noun* **1** HERALD, forerunner, harbinger, vanguard **2** FORERUNNER, antecedent, forebear, predecessor

predatory *adjective* HUNTING, carnivorous, predacious, raptorial

predecessor *noun* **1** PREVIOUS JOB HOLDER, antecedent, forerunner, precursor **2** ANCESTOR, antecedent, forebear, forefather

predestination *noun* FATE, destiny, foreordainment, foreordination, predetermination

predestined *adjective* FATED, doomed, meant, preordained

predetermined *adjective* PREARRANGED, agreed, fixed, preplanned, set

predicament *noun* FIX (*informal*), dilemma, jam (*informal*), mess, pinch, plight, quandary, scrape (*informal*), situation, spot (*informal*)

predict *verb* FORETELL, augur, divine, forecast, portend, prophesy

predictable *adjective* LIKELY, anticipated, certain, expected, foreseeable, reliable, sure

prediction *noun* PROPHECY, augury, divination, forecast, prognosis, prognostication

predilection *noun* LIKING, bias, fondness, inclination, leaning, love, partiality, penchant, preference, propensity, taste, weakness

predispose verb INCLINE, affect, bias, dispose, influence, lead, prejudice, prompt

predisposed adjective INCLINED, given, liable, minded, ready, subject, susceptible, willing

predominant adjective MAIN, ascendant, chief, dominant, leading, paramount, prevailing, prevalent, prime, principal

predominantly adverb MAINLY, chiefly, for the most part, generally, largely, mostly, primarily, principally

predominate verb PREVAIL, be most noticeable, carry weight, hold sway, outweigh, overrule, overshadow

pre-eminence noun SUPERIORITY, distinction, excellence, predominance, prestige, prominence, renown, supremacy

pre-eminent adjective OUTSTANDING, chief, distinguished, excellent, foremost, incomparable, matchless, predominant, renowned, superior, supreme

pre-empt verb ANTICIPATE, appropriate, assume, usurp

preen verb 1 Of birds CLEAN, plume 2 SMARTEN, dress up, spruce up, titivate 3 **preen oneself (on)** PRIDE ONESELF, congratulate oneself

preface noun 1 INTRODUCTION, foreword, preamble, preliminary, prelude, prologue ▶ verb 2 INTRODUCE, begin, open, prefix

prefer verb LIKE BETTER, be partial to, choose, desire, fancy, favor, go for, incline towards,

opt for, pick

preferable adjective BETTER, best, chosen, favored, more desirable, superior

preferably adverb RATHER, by choice, first, in or for preference, sooner

preference noun 1 FIRST CHOICE, choice, desire, favorite, option, partiality, pick, predilection, selection 2 PRIORITY, favored treatment, favoritism, first place, precedence

preferential adjective PRIVILEGED, advantageous, better, favored, special

preferment noun PROMOTION, advancement, elevation, exaltation, rise, upgrading

pregnant adjective 1 EXPECTANT, big or heavy with child, expecting (informal), with child 2 MEANINGFUL, charged, eloquent, expressive, loaded, pointed, significant, telling, weighty

prehistoric adjective EARLIEST, early, primeval, primitive, primordial

prejudge verb JUMP TO CONCLUSIONS, anticipate, presume, presuppose

prejudice noun 1 BIAS, partiality, preconceived notion, preconception, prejudgment 2 DISCRIMINATION, bigotry, chauvinism, injustice, intolerance, narrow-mindedness, unfairness ▶ verb 3 BIAS, color, distort, influence, poison, predispose, slant 4 HARM, damage, hinder, hurt, impair, injure, mar, spoil, undermine

prejudiced adjective BIASED,

bigoted, influenced, intolerant, narrow-minded, one-sided, opinionated, unfair

prejudicial *adjective* HARMFUL, damaging, deleterious, detrimental, disadvantageous, hurtful, injurious, unfavorable

preliminary *adjective* **1** FIRST, initial, introductory, opening, pilot, prefatory, preparatory, prior, test, trial ▶ *noun* **2** INTRODUCTION, beginning, opening, overture, preamble, preface, prelude, start

prelude *noun* INTRODUCTION, beginning, foreword, overture, preamble, preface, prologue, start

premature *adjective* **1** EARLY, forward, unseasonable, untimely **2** HASTY, ill-timed, overhasty, rash, too soon, untimely

premeditated *adjective* PLANNED, calculated, conscious, considered, deliberate, intentional, willful

premeditation *noun* PLANNING, design, forethought, intention, plotting, prearrangement, predetermination, purpose

premier *noun* **1** HEAD OF GOVERNMENT, chancellor, chief minister, chief officer, prime minister ▶ *adjective* **2** CHIEF, first, foremost, head, highest, leading, main, primary, prime, principal

premiere *noun* FIRST NIGHT, debut, opening

premise *noun* ASSUMPTION, argument, assertion, hypothesis, postulation, presupposition, proposition, supposition

premises *plural noun* BUILDING, establishment, place, property, site

premium *noun* **1** BONUS, bounty, fee, perk (*informal*), perquisite, prize, reward **2 at a premium** IN GREAT DEMAND, hard to come by, in short supply, rare, scarce

premonition *noun* FEELING, foreboding, hunch, idea, intuition, presentiment, suspicion

preoccupation *noun* **1** OBSESSION, bee in one's bonnet, fixation **2** ABSORPTION, absent-mindedness, abstraction, daydreaming, engrossment, immersion, reverie, woolgathering

preoccupied *adjective* ABSORBED, absent-minded, distracted, engrossed, immersed, lost in, oblivious, rapt, wrapped up

preparation *noun* **1** GROUNDWORK, getting ready, preparing **2** (often *plural*) ARRANGEMENT, measure, plan, provision **3** MIXTURE, compound, concoction, medicine

preparatory *adjective* INTRODUCTORY, opening, prefatory, preliminary, primary

prepare *verb* MAKE OR GET READY, adapt, adjust, arrange, practice, prime, train, warm up

prepared *adjective* **1** READY, arranged, in order, in readiness, primed, set **2** WILLING, disposed, inclined

preponderance *noun* PREDOMINANCE, dominance, domination, extensiveness, greater numbers, greater part, lion's share, mass, prevalence, supremacy

prepossessing adjective
ATTRACTIVE, appealing, charming, engaging, fetching, good-looking, handsome, likable or likeable, pleasing

preposterous adjective
RIDICULOUS, absurd, crazy, incredible, insane, laughable, ludicrous, nonsensical, out of the question, outrageous, unthinkable

prerequisite noun
1 REQUIREMENT, condition, essential, must, necessity, precondition, qualification, requisite, sine qua non
▶ adjective **2** REQUIRED, essential, indispensable, mandatory, necessary, obligatory, requisite, vital

prerogative noun RIGHT, advantage, due, exemption, immunity, liberty, privilege

presage verb PORTEND, augur, betoken, bode, foreshadow, foretoken, signify

prescience noun FORESIGHT, clairvoyance, foreknowledge, precognition, second sight

prescribe verb ORDER, decree, dictate, direct, lay down, ordain, recommend, rule, set, specify, stipulate

prescription noun
1 INSTRUCTION, direction, formula, recipe **2** MEDICINE, drug, mixture, preparation, remedy

presence noun **1** BEING, attendance, existence, inhabitance, occupancy, residence **2** PERSONALITY, air, appearance, aspect, aura,
bearing, carriage, demeanor, poise, self-assurance

presence of mind noun
LEVEL-HEADEDNESS, calmness, composure, cool (slang), coolness, self-possession, wits

present[1] adjective **1** HERE, at hand, near, nearby, ready, there **2** CURRENT, contemporary, existent, existing, immediate, present-day ▶ noun **3** the **present** NOW, here and now, the present moment, the time being, today **4** at present JUST NOW, at the moment, now, right now **5** for the present FOR NOW, for the moment, for the time being, in the meantime, temporarily

present[2] noun **1** GIFT, boon, donation, endowment, grant, gratuity, hand-out, offering ▶ verb **2** INTRODUCE, acquaint with, make known **3** PUT ON, display, exhibit, give, show, stage **4** GIVE, award, bestow, confer, grant, hand out, hand over

presentable adjective DECENT, acceptable, becoming, fit to be seen, O.K. or okay (informal), passable, respectable, satisfactory, suitable

presentation noun **1** GIVING, award, bestowal, conferral, donation, offering **2** PRODUCTION, demonstration, display, exhibition, performance, show

presently adverb SOON, anon (archaic), before long, by and by, shortly

preservation noun PROTECTION, conservation, maintenance, safeguarding, safekeeping, safety, salvation, support

preserve verb 1 SAVE, care for, conserve, defend, keep, protect, safeguard, shelter, shield 2 MAINTAIN, continue, keep, keep up, perpetuate, sustain, uphold ▶ noun 3 AREA, domain, field, realm, sphere

preside verb RUN, administer, chair, conduct, control, direct, govern, head, lead, manage, officiate

press verb 1 FORCE DOWN, compress, crush, depress, jam, mash, push, squeeze 2 HUG, clasp, crush, embrace, fold in one's arms, hold close, squeeze 3 SMOOTH, flatten, iron 4 URGE, beg, entreat, exhort, implore, petition, plead, pressurize 5 CROWD, flock, gather, herd, push, seethe, surge, swarm, throng ▶ noun 6 **the press: a** NEWSPAPERS, Fleet Street, fourth estate, news media, the papers **b** JOURNALISTS, columnists, correspondents, newsmen, pressmen, reporters

pressing adjective URGENT, crucial, high-priority, imperative, important, importunate, serious, vital

pressure noun 1 FORCE, compressing, compression, crushing, squeezing, weight 2 POWER, coercion, compulsion, constraint, force, influence, sway 3 STRESS, burden, demands, hassle (informal), heat, load, strain, urgency

prestige noun STATUS, credit, distinction, eminence, fame, honor, importance, kudos, renown, reputation, standing

prestigious adjective CELEBRATED,

eminent, esteemed, great, illustrious, important, notable, prominent, renowned, respected

presumably adverb IT WOULD SEEM, apparently, in all likelihood, in all probability, on the face of it, probably, seemingly

presume verb 1 BELIEVE, assume, conjecture, guess (informal), infer, postulate, suppose, surmise, take for granted, think 2 DARE, go so far, make so bold, take the liberty, venture

presumption noun 1 CHEEK (informal), audacity, boldness, effrontery, gall (informal), impudence, insolence, nerve (informal) 2 PROBABILITY, basis, chance, likelihood

presumptuous adjective PUSHY (informal), audacious, bold, forward, insolent, overconfident, too big for one's boots

presuppose verb PRESUME, assume, imply, posit, postulate, take as read, take for granted

presupposition noun ASSUMPTION, belief, preconception, premise, presumption, supposition

pretend verb 1 FEIGN, affect, allege, assume, fake, falsify, impersonate, profess, sham, simulate 2 MAKE BELIEVE, act, imagine, make up, suppose

pretended adjective FEIGNED, bogus, counterfeit, fake, false, phoney or phony (informal), pretend (informal), pseudo (informal), sham, so-called

pretender noun CLAIMANT, aspirant

pretense noun **1** DECEPTION, acting, charade, deceit, falsehood, feigning, sham, simulation, trickery **2** SHOW, affectation, artifice, display, façade, veneer

pretension noun **1** CLAIM, aspiration, assumption, demand, pretense, profession **2** AFFECTATION, airs, conceit, ostentation, pretentiousness, self-importance, show, snobbery, vanity

pretentious adjective AFFECTED, conceited, grandiloquent, grandiose, high-flown, inflated, mannered, ostentatious, pompous, puffed up, showy, snobbish

pretext noun GUISE, cloak, cover, excuse, ploy, pretense, ruse, show

pretty adjective **1** ATTRACTIVE, beautiful, bonny, charming, comely, fair, good-looking, lovely ▶ adverb **2** FAIRLY, kind of (informal), moderately, quite, rather, reasonably, somewhat

prevail verb **1** WIN, be victorious, overcome, overrule, succeed, triumph **2** BE WIDESPREAD, abound, be current, be prevalent, exist generally, predominate

prevailing adjective **1** WIDESPREAD, common, cool (informal), current, customary, established, fashionable, general, in vogue, ordinary, phat (slang), popular, prevalent, usual **2** PREDOMINATING, dominant, main, principal, ruling

prevalence noun COMMONNESS, currency, frequency, popularity, universality

prevalent adjective COMMON, current, customary, established, frequent, general, popular, universal, usual, widespread

prevaricate verb EVADE, beat about the bush, cavil, deceive, dodge, equivocate, hedge

prevent verb STOP, avert, avoid, foil, forestall, frustrate, hamper, hinder, impede, inhibit, obstruct, obviate, preclude, thwart

prevention noun ELIMINATION, avoidance, deterrence, precaution, safeguard, thwarting

preventive adjective **1** HINDERING, hampering, impeding, obstructive **2** PROTECTIVE, counteractive, deterrent, precautionary ▶ noun **3** HINDRANCE, block, impediment, obstacle, obstruction **4** PROTECTION, deterrent, prevention, remedy, safeguard, shield

preview noun ADVANCE SHOWING, foretaste, sneak preview, taster, trailer

previous adjective EARLIER, erstwhile, foregoing, former, past, preceding, prior

previously adverb BEFORE, beforehand, earlier, formerly, hitherto, in the past, once

prey noun **1** QUARRY, game, kill **2** VICTIM, dupe, fall guy (informal), mug (Brit. slang), target

price noun **1** COST, amount, charge, damage (informal), estimate, expense, fee, figure, rate, value, worth

2 CONSEQUENCES, cost, penalty, toll ▶ *verb* **3** EVALUATE, assess, cost, estimate, rate, value

priceless *adjective* **1** VALUABLE, costly, dear, expensive, invaluable, precious **2** *Informal* HILARIOUS, amusing, comic, droll, funny, rib-tickling, side-splitting

pricey *adjective* EXPENSIVE, costly, dear, high-priced, steep (*informal*)

prick *verb* **1** PIERCE, jab, lance, perforate, punch, puncture, stab **2** STING, bite, itch, prickle, smart, tingle ▶ *noun* **3** PUNCTURE, hole, perforation, pinhole, wound

prickle *noun* **1** SPIKE, barb, needle, point, spine, spur, thorn ▶ *verb* **2** TINGLE, itch, smart, sting **3** PRICK, jab, stick

prickly *adjective* **1** SPINY, barbed, bristly, thorny **2** ITCHY, crawling, scratchy, sharp, smarting, stinging, tingling

pride *noun* **1** SATISFACTION, delight, gratification, joy, pleasure **2** SELF-RESPECT, dignity, honor, self-esteem, self-worth **3** CONCEIT, arrogance, egotism, hubris, pretension, pretentiousness, self-importance, self-love, superciliousness, vanity **4** GEM, jewel, pride and joy, treasure

priest *noun* CLERGYMAN, cleric, curate, divine, ecclesiastic, father, minister, pastor, vicar

prig *noun* GOODY-GOODY (*informal*), prude, puritan, stuffed shirt (*informal*)

priggish *adjective* SELF-RIGHTEOUS, goody-goody (*informal*), holier-than-thou, prim,

prudish, puritanical

prim *adjective* PRUDISH, demure, fastidious, fussy, priggish, prissy (*informal*), proper, puritanical, strait-laced

prima donna *noun* DIVA, leading lady, star

primarily *adverb* **1** CHIEFLY, above all, essentially, fundamentally, generally, largely, mainly, mostly, principally **2** AT FIRST, at or from the start, first and foremost, initially, in the beginning, in the first place, originally

primary *adjective* **1** CHIEF, cardinal, first, greatest, highest, main, paramount, prime, principal **2** ELEMENTARY, introductory, rudimentary, simple

prime *adjective* **1** MAIN, chief, leading, predominant, pre-eminent, primary, principal **2** BEST, choice, excellent, first-class, first-rate, highest, quality, select, top ▶ *noun* **3** PEAK, bloom, flower, height, heyday, zenith ▶ *verb* **4** INFORM, brief, clue in (*informal*), fill in (*informal*), notify, tell **5** PREPARE, coach, get ready, make ready, train

primeval *adjective* EARLIEST, ancient, early, first, old, prehistoric, primal, primitive, primordial

primitive *adjective* **1** EARLY, earliest, elementary, first, original, primary, primeval, primordial **2** CRUDE, rough, rudimentary, simple, unrefined

prince *noun* RULER, lord, monarch, sovereign

princely *adjective* **1** REGAL,

imperial, majestic, noble, royal, sovereign **2** GENEROUS, bounteous, gracious, lavish, liberal, munificent, open-handed, rich

principal adjective **1** MAIN, cardinal, chief, essential, first, foremost, key, leading, paramount, pre-eminent, primary, prime ▶ noun **2** HEAD (informal), dean, headmaster or headmistress, superintendent **3** STAR, lead, leader **4** CAPITAL, assets, money

principally adverb MAINLY, above all, chiefly, especially, largely, mostly, predominantly, primarily

principle noun **1** RULE, canon, criterion, doctrine, dogma, fundamental, law, maxim, precept, scruples, standard, truth **2** MORALS, conscience, integrity, probity, scruples, sense of honor **3 in principle** IN THEORY, ideally, theoretically

print verb **1** PUBLISH, engrave, impress, imprint, issue, mark, stamp ▶ noun **2** PUBLICATION, book, magazine, newspaper, newsprint, periodical, printed matter **3** REPRODUCTION, copy, engraving, photo (informal), photograph, picture

prior adjective **1** EARLIER, foregoing, former, preceding, pre-existent, pre-existing, previous **2 prior to** BEFORE, earlier than, preceding, previous to

priority noun PRECEDENCE, pre-eminence, preference, rank, right of way, seniority

priory noun MONASTERY, abbey, convent, nunnery,

religious house

prison noun JAIL, clink (slang), confinement, cooler (slang), dungeon, lockup, penitentiary, slammer (slang)

prisoner noun **1** CONVICT, con (slang), jailbird, lag (slang) **2** CAPTIVE, detainee, hostage, internee

prissy adjective PRIM, old-maidish (informal), prim and proper, prudish, strait-laced

pristine adjective NEW, immaculate, pure, uncorrupted, undefiled, unspoiled, unsullied, untouched, virginal

privacy noun SECLUSION, isolation, retirement, retreat, solitude

private adjective **1** EXCLUSIVE, individual, intimate, own, personal, reserved, special **2** SECRET, clandestine, confidential, covert, hush-hush (informal), off the record, unofficial **3** SECLUDED, concealed, isolated, secret, separate, sequestered, solitary

privilege noun RIGHT, advantage, claim, concession, due, entitlement, freedom, liberty, prerogative

privileged adjective SPECIAL, advantaged, elite, entitled, favored, honored

privy adjective **1 privy to** INFORMED OF, apprised of, aware of, cognizant of, in on, in the know about (informal), wise to (slang) ▶ noun **2** LAVATORY, latrine, outside toilet

prize[1] noun **1** REWARD, accolade, award, honor, trophy **2** WINNINGS, haul, jackpot,

purse, stakes ▶ *adjective*
3 CHAMPION, award-winning,
best, first-rate, outstanding,
top, winning

prize² *verb* VALUE, cherish,
esteem, hold dear, treasure

probability *noun* LIKELIHOOD,
chance(s), expectation, liability,
likeliness, odds, prospect

probable *adjective* LIKELY,
apparent, credible, feasible,
plausible, possible, presumable,
reasonable

probably *adverb* LIKELY,
doubtless, maybe, most likely,
perchance (*archaic*), perhaps,
possibly, presumably

probation *noun* TRIAL PERIOD,
apprenticeship, trial

probe *verb* **1** EXAMINE, explore,
go into, investigate, look into,
scrutinize, search **2** EXPLORE, feel
around, poke, prod ▶ *noun*
3 EXAMINATION, detection,
exploration, inquiry,
investigation, scrutiny, study

problem *noun* **1** DIFFICULTY,
complication, dilemma,
dispute, predicament,
quandary, trouble **2** PUZZLE,
conundrum, enigma, poser,
question, riddle

problematic *adjective* TRICKY,
debatable, doubtful, dubious,
problematical, puzzling

procedure *noun* METHOD, action,
conduct, course, custom,
modus operandi, policy,
practice, process, routine,
strategy, system

proceed *verb* **1** GO ON, carry
on, continue, go ahead, move
on, press on, progress **2** ARISE,
come, derive, emanate, flow,
issue, originate, result,
spring, stem

proceeding *noun* **1** ACTION, act,
deed, measure, move,
procedure, process, step
2 proceedings BUSINESS,
account, affairs, archives,
doings, minutes, records,
report, transactions

proceeds *plural noun* INCOME,
earnings, gain, products, profit,
returns, revenue, takings, yield

process *noun* **1** PROCEDURE,
action, course, manner, means,
measure, method, operation,
performance, practice, system
2 DEVELOPMENT, advance,
evolution, growth, movement,
progress, progression ▶ *verb*
3 HANDLE, deal with, fulfill

procession *noun* PARADE,
cavalcade, cortege, file, march,
train

proclaim *verb* DECLARE, advertise,
announce, circulate, herald,
indicate, make known, profess,
publish

proclamation *noun* DECLARATION,
announcement, decree, edict,
notice, notification,
pronouncement, publication

procrastinate *verb* DELAY, dally,
drag one's feet (*informal*), gain
time, play for time, postpone,
put off, stall, temporize

procure *verb* OBTAIN, acquire,
buy, come by, find, gain, get,
pick up, purchase, score
(*slang*), secure, win

prod *verb* **1** POKE, dig, drive,
jab, nudge, push, shove
2 PROMPT, egg on, goad, impel,
incite, motivate, move, rouse,
spur, stimulate, urge ▶ *noun*
3 POKE, dig, jab, nudge, push,
shove **4** PROMPT, cue, reminder,

signal, stimulus

prodigal adjective EXTRAVAGANT, excessive, immoderate, improvident, profligate, reckless, spendthrift, wasteful

prodigious adjective **1** HUGE, colossal, enormous, giant, gigantic, immense, massive, monstrous, vast **2** WONDERFUL, amazing, exceptional, extraordinary, fabulous, fantastic (informal), marvelous, phenomenal, remarkable, staggering

prodigy noun **1** GENIUS, mastermind, talent, whizz (informal), wizard **2** WONDER, marvel, miracle, phenomenon, sensation

produce verb **1** CAUSE, bring about, effect, generate, give rise to **2** BRING FORTH, bear, beget, breed, deliver **3** SHOW, advance, demonstrate, exhibit, offer, present **4** MAKE, compose, construct, create, develop, fabricate, invent, manufacture **5** PRESENT, direct, do, exhibit, mount, put on, show, stage ▶ noun **6** FRUIT AND VEGETABLES, crop, greengrocery, harvest, product, yield

producer noun **1** DIRECTOR, impresario **2** MAKER, farmer, grower, manufacturer

product noun **1** GOODS, artefact, commodity, creation, invention, merchandise, produce, work **2** RESULT, consequence, effect, outcome, upshot

production noun **1** PRODUCING, construction, creation, fabrication, formation, making, manufacture, manufacturing

2 PRESENTATION, direction, management, staging

productive adjective **1** FERTILE, creative, fecund, fruitful, inventive, plentiful, prolific, rich **2** USEFUL, advantageous, beneficial, constructive, effective, profitable, rewarding, valuable, win-win (informal), worthwhile

productivity noun OUTPUT, production, work rate, yield

profane adjective **1** SACRILEGIOUS, disrespectful, godless, impious, impure, irreligious, irreverent, sinful, ungodly, wicked **2** CRUDE, blasphemous, coarse, filthy, foul, obscene, vulgar ▶ verb **3** DESECRATE, commit sacrilege, debase, defile, violate

profanity noun **1** SACRILEGE, blasphemy, impiety, profaneness **2** SWEARING, curse, cursing, irreverence, obscenity

profess verb **1** CLAIM, allege, fake, feign, make out, pretend, purport **2** STATE, admit, affirm, announce, assert, avow, confess, declare, proclaim, vouch

professed adjective **1** SUPPOSED, alleged, ostensible, pretended, purported, self-styled, so-called, would-be **2** DECLARED, avowed, confessed, confirmed, proclaimed, self-acknowledged, self-confessed

profession noun **1** OCCUPATION, business, calling, career, employment, office, position, sphere, vocation **2** DECLARATION, affirmation, assertion, avowal, claim, confession, statement

professional adjective **1** EXPERT, adept, competent, efficient, experienced, masterly, proficient, qualified, skilled ▶noun 2 EXPERT, adept, maestro, master, past master, pro (slang), specialist, virtuoso

professor noun TEACHER, don (Brit.), fellow (Brit.), prof (informal)

proficiency noun SKILL, ability, aptitude, competence, dexterity, expertise, knack, know-how (informal), mastery

proficient adjective SKILLED, able, accomplished, adept, capable, competent, efficient, expert, gifted, masterly, skillful

profile noun 1 OUTLINE, contour, drawing, figure, form, side view, silhouette, sketch 2 BIOGRAPHY, characterization, sketch, thumbnail sketch, vignette

profit noun 1 (often plural) EARNINGS, gain, proceeds, receipts, return, revenue, takings, yield 2 BENEFIT, advancement, advantage, gain, good, use, value ▶verb 3 BENEFIT, be of advantage to, gain, help, improve, promote, serve 4 MAKE MONEY, earn, gain

profitable adjective 1 MONEY-MAKING, commercial, cost-effective, fruitful, lucrative, paying, remunerative, worthwhile 2 BENEFICIAL, advantageous, fruitful, productive, rewarding, useful, valuable, win-win (informal), worthwhile

profiteer noun 1 RACKETEER, exploiter ▶verb 2 RACKETEER, exploit, make a quick buck (slang)

profligate adjective

1 EXTRAVAGANT, immoderate, improvident, prodigal, reckless, spendthrift, wasteful 2 DEPRAVED, debauched, degenerate, dissolute, immoral, licentious, shameless, wanton, wicked, wild ▶noun 3 SPENDTHRIFT, squanderer, waster, wastrel 4 DEGENERATE, debauchee, libertine, rake, reprobate, roué

profound adjective 1 WISE, abstruse, deep, learned, penetrating, philosophical, sagacious, sage 2 INTENSE, acute, deeply felt, extreme, great, heartfelt, keen

profuse adjective PLENTIFUL, abundant, ample, bountiful, copious, luxuriant, overflowing, prolific

profusion noun ABUNDANCE, bounty, excess, extravagance, glut, plethora, quantity, surplus, wealth

progeny noun CHILDREN, descendants, family, issue, lineage, offspring, posterity, race, stock, young

prognosis noun FORECAST, diagnosis, prediction, prognostication, projection

program noun 1 SCHEDULE, agenda, curriculum, line-up, list, listing, order of events, plan, syllabus, timetable 2 SHOW, broadcast, performance, presentation, production

progress noun 1 DEVELOPMENT, advance, breakthrough, gain, growth, headway, improvement 2 MOVEMENT, advance, course, passage, way 3 in progress GOING ON, being done, happening, occurring, proceeding, taking place, under way ▶ verb **4** DEVELOP, advance, gain, grow, improve **5** MOVE ON, advance, continue, go forward, make headway, proceed, travel

progression noun **1** PROGRESS, advance, advancement, furtherance, gain, headway, movement forward **2** SEQUENCE, chain, course, cycle, series, string, succession

progressive adjective **1** ENLIGHTENED, advanced, avant-garde, forward-looking, liberal, modern, radical, reformist, revolutionary **2** GROWING, advancing, continuing, developing, increasing, ongoing

prohibit verb **1** FORBID, ban, debar, disallow, outlaw, proscribe, veto **2** PREVENT, hamper, hinder, impede, restrict, stop

prohibition noun **1** PREVENTION, constraint, exclusion, obstruction, restriction **2** BAN, bar, boycott, embargo, injunction, interdict, proscription, veto

prohibitive adjective EXORBITANT, excessive, extortionate, steep (informal)

project noun **1** SCHEME, activity, assignment, enterprise, job, occupation, plan, task, undertaking, venture, work ▶ verb **2** FORECAST, calculate, estimate, extrapolate, gauge, predict, reckon **3** STICK OUT, bulge, extend, jut, overhang, protrude, stand out

projectile noun MISSILE, bullet,

rocket, shell

projection noun **1** PROTRUSION, bulge, ledge, overhang, protuberance, ridge, shelf **2** FORECAST, calculation, computation, estimate, estimation, extrapolation, reckoning

proletarian adjective **1** WORKING-CLASS, common, plebeian ▶ noun **2** WORKER, commoner, man of the people, pleb, plebeian

proletariat noun WORKING CLASS, commoners, hoi polloi, laboring classes, lower classes, plebs, the common people, the masses

proliferate verb INCREASE, breed, expand, grow rapidly, multiply

proliferation noun MULTIPLICATION, expansion, increase, spread

prolific adjective PRODUCTIVE, abundant, copious, fecund, fertile, fruitful, luxuriant, profuse

prologue noun INTRODUCTION, foreword, preamble, preface, preliminary, prelude

prolong verb LENGTHEN, continue, delay, drag out, draw out, extend, perpetuate, protract, spin out, stretch

promenade noun **1** WALKWAY, esplanade, parade, prom **2** STROLL, constitutional, saunter, turn, walk ▶ verb **3** STROLL, perambulate, saunter, take a walk, walk

prominence noun **1** CONSPICUOUSNESS, markedness **2** FAME, celebrity, distinction, eminence, importance, name, prestige, reputation

prominent adjective

1 NOTICEABLE, conspicuous, eye-catching, obtrusive, obvious, outstanding, pronounced **2** FAMOUS, distinguished, eminent, foremost, important, leading, main, notable, renowned, top, well-known

promiscuity noun LICENTIOUSNESS, debauchery, immorality, looseness, permissiveness, promiscuousness, wantonness

promiscuous adjective LICENTIOUS, abandoned, debauched, fast, immoral, libertine, loose, wanton, wild

promise verb **1** GUARANTEE, assure, contract, give an undertaking, give one's word, pledge, swear, take an oath, undertake, vow, warrant **2** SEEM LIKELY, augur, betoken, indicate, look like, show signs of, suggest ▶ noun **3** GUARANTEE, assurance, bond, commitment, oath, pledge, undertaking, vow, word **4** POTENTIAL, ability, aptitude, capability, capacity, flair, talent

promising adjective **1** ENCOURAGING, auspicious, bright, favorable, hopeful, likely, propitious, reassuring, rosy **2** TALENTED, able, gifted, rising

promontory noun POINT, cape, foreland, head, headland

promote verb **1** HELP, advance, aid, assist, back, boost, encourage, forward, foster, support **2** RAISE, elevate, exalt, upgrade **3** ADVERTISE, hype, plug (informal), publicize, push, sell

promotion noun **1** RISE, advancement, elevation, exaltation, honor, move up, preferment, upgrading **2** PUBLICITY, advertising, plugging (informal) **3** ENCOURAGEMENT, advancement, boosting, furtherance, support

prompt verb **1** CAUSE, elicit, give rise to, occasion, provoke **2** REMIND, assist, cue, help out ▶ adjective **3** IMMEDIATE, early, instant, quick, rapid, speedy, swift, timely ▶ adverb **4** Informal EXACTLY, on the dot, promptly, punctually, sharp

promptly adverb IMMEDIATELY, at once, directly, on the dot, on time, punctually, quickly, speedily, swiftly

promptness noun SWIFTNESS, briskness, eagerness, haste, punctuality, quickness, speed, willingness

promulgate verb MAKE KNOWN, broadcast, circulate, communicate, disseminate, make public, proclaim, promote, publish, spread

prone adjective **1** LIABLE, apt, bent, disposed, given, inclined, likely, predisposed, subject, susceptible, tending **2** FACE DOWN, flat, horizontal, prostrate, recumbent

prong noun POINT, spike, tine

pronounce verb **1** SAY, accent, articulate, enunciate, sound, speak **2** DECLARE, affirm, announce, decree, deliver, proclaim

pronounced adjective NOTICEABLE, conspicuous, decided, definite, distinct, evident, marked, obvious, striking

pronouncement noun
ANNOUNCEMENT, declaration,
decree, dictum, edict,
judgment, proclamation,
statement

pronunciation noun INTONATION,
accent, articulation, diction,
enunciation, inflection, speech,
stress

proof noun 1 EVIDENCE,
authentication, confirmation,
corroboration, demonstration,
substantiation, testimony,
verification ▶ *adjective*
2 IMPERVIOUS, impenetrable,
repellent, resistant, strong

prop verb 1 SUPPORT, bolster,
brace, buttress, hold up, stay,
sustain, uphold ▶ *noun*
2 SUPPORT, brace, buttress,
mainstay, stanchion, stay

propaganda noun INFORMATION,
advertising, disinformation,
hype, promotion, publicity

propagate verb 1 SPREAD,
broadcast, circulate,
disseminate, promote,
promulgate, publish, transmit
2 REPRODUCE, beget, breed,
engender, generate, increase,
multiply, procreate, produce

propel verb DRIVE, force, impel,
launch, push, send, shoot,
shove, thrust

propensity noun TENDENCY,
bent, disposition, inclination,
liability, penchant,
predisposition, proclivity

proper adjective 1 SUITABLE,
appropriate, apt, becoming,
befitting, fit, fitting, right
2 CORRECT, accepted,
conventional, established,
formal, orthodox, precise, right
3 POLITE, decent, decorous,

genteel, gentlemanly, ladylike,
mannerly, respectable, seemly

properly adverb 1 SUITABLY,
appropriately, aptly, fittingly,
rightly 2 CORRECTLY, accurately
3 POLITELY, decently, respectably

property noun 1 POSSESSIONS,
assets, belongings, capital,
effects, estate, goods, holdings,
riches, wealth 2 LAND, estate,
freehold, holding, real estate
3 QUALITY, attribute,
characteristic, feature,
hallmark, trait

prophecy noun PREDICTION,
augury, divination, forecast,
prognostication, second sight,
soothsaying

prophesy verb PREDICT, augur,
divine, forecast, foresee,
foretell, prognosticate

prophet noun SOOTHSAYER,
diviner, forecaster, oracle,
prophesier, seer, sibyl

prophetic adjective PREDICTIVE,
oracular, prescient, prognostic,
sibylline

propitious adjective FAVORABLE,
auspicious, bright,
encouraging, fortunate, happy,
lucky, promising

proportion noun 1 RELATIVE
AMOUNT, ratio, relationship
2 BALANCE, congruity,
correspondence, harmony,
symmetry 3 PART, amount,
division, fraction, percentage,
quota, segment, share
4 proportions DIMENSIONS,
capacity, expanse, extent, size,
volume

proportional, proportionate
adjective BALANCED,
commensurate, compatible,
consistent, corresponding,

equitable, even, in proportion

proposal noun SUGGESTION, bid, offer, plan, presentation, program, project, recommendation, scheme

propose verb 1 PUT FORWARD, advance, present, submit, suggest 2 NOMINATE, name, present, recommend 3 INTEND, aim, design, have in mind, mean, plan, scheme 4 OFFER MARRIAGE, ask for someone's hand (in marriage), pop the question (informal)

proposition noun 1 PROPOSAL, plan, recommendation, scheme, suggestion ▶ verb 2 MAKE A PASS AT, accost, make an improper suggestion, solicit

propound verb PUT FORWARD, advance, postulate, present, propose, submit, suggest

proprietor, proprietress noun OWNER, landlord or landlady, titleholder

propriety noun 1 CORRECTNESS, aptness, fitness, rightness, seemliness 2 DECORUM, courtesy, decency, etiquette, manners, politeness, respectability, seemliness

propulsion noun DRIVE, impetus, impulse, propelling force, push, thrust

prosaic adjective DULL, boring, everyday, humdrum, matter-of-fact, mundane, ordinary, pedestrian, routine, trite, unimaginative

proscribe verb 1 PROHIBIT, ban, embargo, forbid, interdict 2 OUTLAW, banish, deport, exclude, exile, expatriate, expel, ostracize

prosecute verb Law PUT ON TRIAL,

arraign, bring to trial, indict, litigate, sue, take to court, try

prospect noun 1 EXPECTATION, anticipation, future, hope, odds, outlook, probability, promise 2 (sometimes plural) LIKELIHOOD, chance, possibility 3 VIEW, landscape, outlook, scene, sight, spectacle, vista ▶ verb 4 LOOK FOR, search for, seek

prospective adjective FUTURE, anticipated, coming, destined, expected, forthcoming, imminent, intended, likely, possible, potential

prospectus noun CATALOG, list, outline, program, syllabus, synopsis

prosper verb SUCCEED, advance, do well, flourish, get on, progress, thrive

prosperity noun SUCCESS, affluence, fortune, good fortune, luxury, plenty, prosperousness, riches, wealth

prosperous adjective 1 WEALTHY, affluent, moneyed, rich, well-heeled (informal), well-off, well-to-do 2 SUCCESSFUL, booming, doing well, flourishing, fortunate, lucky, thriving

prostitute noun 1 WHORE, call girl, fallen woman, harlot, ho (slang), hooker (slang), loose woman, streetwalker, strumpet, tart (informal), trollop ▶ verb 2 CHEAPEN, debase, degrade, demean, devalue, misapply, pervert, profane

prostrate adjective 1 PRONE, flat, horizontal 2 EXHAUSTED, dejected, depressed, desolate, drained, inconsolable, overcome, spent, worn out ▶ *verb* **3** EXHAUST, drain, fatigue, sap, tire, wear out, weary **4** *prostrate oneself* BOW DOWN TO, abase oneself, fall at (someone's) feet, grovel, kiss ass (*slang*), kneel, kowtow

protagonist *noun* **1** SUPPORTER, advocate, champion, exponent **2** LEADING CHARACTER, central character, hero *or* heroine, principal

protect *verb* KEEP SAFE, defend, guard, look after, preserve, safeguard, save, screen, shelter, shield, stick up for (*informal*), support, watch over

protection *noun* **1** SAFETY, aegis, care, custody, defense, protecting, safeguard, safekeeping, security **2** SAFEGUARD, barrier, buffer, cover, guard, screen, shelter, shield

protective *adjective* PROTECTING, defensive, fatherly, maternal, motherly, paternal, vigilant, watchful

protector *noun* DEFENDER, bodyguard, champion, guard, guardian, patron

protest *noun* **1** OBJECTION, complaint, dissent, outcry, protestation, remonstrance ▶ *verb* **2** OBJECT, complain, cry out, demonstrate, demur, disagree, disapprove, express disapproval, oppose, remonstrate **3** ASSERT, affirm, attest, avow, declare, insist, maintain, profess

protestation *noun* DECLARATION, affirmation, avowal, profession, vow

protester *noun* DEMONSTRATOR, agitator, rebel

protocol *noun* CODE OF BEHAVIOR, conventions, customs, decorum, etiquette, manners, propriety

prototype *noun* ORIGINAL, example, first, model, pattern, standard, type

protracted *adjective* EXTENDED, dragged out, drawn-out, long-drawn-out, prolonged, spun out

protrude *verb* STICK OUT, bulge, come through, extend, jut, obtrude, project, stand out

protrusion *noun* PROJECTION, bulge, bump, lump, outgrowth, protuberance

protuberance *noun* BULGE, bump, excrescence, hump, knob, lump, outgrowth, process, prominence, protrusion, swelling

proud *adjective* **1** SATISFIED, content, glad, gratified, pleased, well-pleased **2** CONCEITED, arrogant, boastful, disdainful, haughty, imperious, lordly, overbearing, self-satisfied, snobbish, supercilious

prove *verb* **1** VERIFY, authenticate, confirm, demonstrate, determine, establish, justify, show, substantiate **2** TEST, analyze, assay, check, examine, try **3** TURN OUT, come out, end up, result

proven *adjective* ESTABLISHED, attested, confirmed, definite, proved, reliable, tested, verified

proverb *noun* SAYING, adage, dictum, maxim, saw

proverbial *adjective*
CONVENTIONAL, acknowledged, axiomatic, current, famed, famous, legendary, notorious, traditional, typical, well-known

provide *verb* **1** SUPPLY, cater, equip, furnish, outfit, purvey, stock up **2** GIVE, add, afford, bring, impart, lend, present, produce, render, serve, yield **3 provide for** *or* **against** TAKE PRECAUTIONS, anticipate, forearm, plan ahead, plan for, prepare for **4 provide for** SUPPORT, care for, keep, maintain, sustain, take care of

providence *noun* FATE, destiny, fortune

provident *adjective* **1** THRIFTY, economical, frugal, prudent **2** FORESIGHTED, careful, cautious, discreet, far-seeing, forearmed, shrewd, vigilant, well-prepared, wise

providential *adjective* LUCKY, fortuitous, fortunate, happy, heaven-sent, opportune, timely

provider *noun* **1** SUPPLIER, donor, giver, source **2** BREADWINNER, earner, supporter, wage earner

providing, provided *conjunction* ON CONDITION THAT, as long as, given

province *noun* **1** REGION, colony, department, district, division, domain, patch, section, zone **2** AREA, business, capacity, concern, duty, field, function, line, responsibility, role, sphere

provincial *adjective* **1** RURAL, country, hick (*informal*), homespun, local, rustic **2** NARROW-MINDED, insular, inward-looking, limited, narrow, parochial, small-minded, small-town, unsophisticated ▶ *noun* **3** YOKEL, country cousin, hayseed (*informal*), hick (*informal*), rustic

provision *noun* **1** SUPPLYING, catering, equipping, furnishing, providing **2** CONDITION, clause, demand, proviso, requirement, rider, stipulation, term

provisional *adjective* **1** TEMPORARY, interim **2** CONDITIONAL, contingent, limited, qualified, tentative

provisions *plural noun* FOOD, comestibles, eatables, edibles, fare, foodstuff, rations, stores, supplies, victuals

proviso *noun* CONDITION, clause, qualification, requirement, rider, stipulation

provocation *noun* **1** CAUSE, grounds, incitement, motivation, reason, stimulus **2** OFFENSE, affront, annoyance, challenge, dare, grievance, indignity, injury, insult, taunt

provocative *adjective* OFFENSIVE, annoying, galling, goading, insulting, provoking, stimulating

provoke *verb* **1** ANGER, aggravate (*informal*), annoy, enrage, hassle (*informal*), incense, infuriate, irk, irritate, madden, rile **2** CAUSE, bring about, elicit, evoke, incite, induce, occasion, produce, promote, prompt, rouse, stir

prowess *noun* **1** SKILL, accomplishment, adeptness, aptitude, excellence, expertise, genius, mastery, talent **2** BRAVERY, courage, daring, fearlessness, heroism, mettle, valiance, valor

prowl *verb* MOVE STEALTHILY, skulk,

slink, sneak, stalk, steal

proximity noun NEARNESS, closeness

proxy noun REPRESENTATIVE, agent, delegate, deputy, factor, substitute

prudence noun COMMON SENSE, care, caution, discretion, good sense, judgment, vigilance, wariness, wisdom

prudent adjective **1** SENSIBLE, careful, cautious, discerning, discreet, judicious, politic, shrewd, vigilant, wary, wise **2** THRIFTY, canny, careful, economical, far-sighted, frugal, provident, sparing

prudish adjective PRIM, old-maidish (informal), overmodest, priggish, prissy (informal), proper, puritanical, starchy (informal), strait-laced, stuffy, Victorian

prune verb CUT, clip, dock, reduce, shape, shorten, snip, trim

pry verb BE INQUISITIVE, be nosy (informal), interfere, intrude, meddle, poke, snoop (informal)

prying adjective INQUISITIVE, curious, interfering, meddlesome, meddling, nosy (informal), snooping (informal), spying

psalm noun HYMN, chant

pseudo- adjective FALSE, artificial, fake, imitation, mock, phoney or phony (informal), pretended, sham, spurious

pseudonym noun FALSE NAME, alias, assumed name, incognito, nom de plume, pen name

psyche noun SOUL, anima, individuality, mind, personality, self, spirit

psychiatrist noun PSYCHOTHERAPIST, analyst, headshrinker (slang), psychoanalyst, psychologist, shrink (slang), therapist

psychic adjective **1** SUPERNATURAL, mystic, occult **2** MENTAL, psychological, spiritual

psychological adjective **1** MENTAL, cerebral, intellectual **2** IMAGINARY, all in the mind, irrational, psychosomatic, unreal

psychology noun **1** BEHAVIORISM, science of mind, study of personality **2** WAY OF THINKING, attitude, mental make-up, mental processes, thought processes, what makes one tick

psychopath noun MADMAN, headcase (informal), lunatic, maniac, nutcase (slang), psychotic, sociopath

psychotic adjective MAD, certifiable, demented, deranged, insane, loony (informal), lunatic, non compos mentis, unbalanced

puberty noun ADOLESCENCE, pubescence, teens

public adjective **1** GENERAL, civic, common, national, popular, social, state, universal, widespread **2** COMMUNAL, accessible, open, unrestricted **3** WELL-KNOWN, important, prominent, respected **4** PLAIN, acknowledged, known, obvious, open, overt, patent ▶ noun **5** PEOPLE, citizens, community, electorate, everyone, nation, populace, society

publication noun **1** PAMPHLET, brochure, issue, leaflet, magazine, newspaper, periodical, title **2** ANNOUNCEMENT, broadcasting, declaration, disclosure, notification, proclamation, publishing, reporting

publicity noun ADVERTISING, attention, boost, hype, plug (*informal*), press, promotion

publicize verb ADVERTISE, hype, make known, play up, plug (*informal*), promote, push

public-spirited adjective ALTRUISTIC, charitable, humanitarian, philanthropic, unselfish

publish verb **1** PUT OUT, issue, print, produce **2** ANNOUNCE, advertise, broadcast, circulate, disclose, divulge, proclaim, publicize, reveal, spread

pucker verb **1** WRINKLE, contract, crease, draw together, gather, knit, purse, screw up, tighten ▶ noun **2** WRINKLE, crease, fold

puerile adjective CHILDISH, babyish, foolish, immature, juvenile, silly, trivial

puff noun **1** BLAST, breath, draft, gust, whiff **2** SMOKE, drag (*slang*), pull ▶ verb **3** BLOW, breathe, exhale, gasp, gulp, pant, wheeze **4** SMOKE, drag (*slang*), draw, inhale, pull at or on, suck **5** (usually with *up*) SWELL, bloat, dilate, distend, expand, inflate

puffy adjective SWOLLEN, bloated, distended, enlarged, puffed up

pugilist noun BOXER, fighter, prizefighter

pugnacious adjective AGGRESSIVE, belligerent, combative, hot-tempered, quarrelsome

pull verb **1** DRAW, drag, haul,

jerk, tow, trail, tug, yank **2** STRAIN, dislocate, rip, sprain, stretch, tear, wrench **3** EXTRACT, draw out, gather, pick, pluck, remove, take out, uproot ▶ noun **4** TUG, jerk, twitch, yank **5** PUFF, drag (*slang*), inhalation **6** *Informal* INFLUENCE, clout (*informal*), muscle, power, weight

pull down verb DEMOLISH, bulldoze, destroy, raze, remove

pull off verb SUCCEED, accomplish, carry out, do the trick, manage

pull out verb WITHDRAW, depart, evacuate, leave, quit, retreat

pull through verb SURVIVE, get better, rally, recover

pulp noun **1** PASTE, mash, mush **2** FLESH, soft part ▶ verb **3** CRUSH, mash, pulverize, squash ▶ adjective **4** CHEAP, lurid, rubbishy, trashy

pulsate verb THROB, beat, palpitate, pound, pulse, quiver, thump

pulse noun **1** BEAT, beating, pulsation, rhythm, throb, throbbing, vibration ▶ verb **2** BEAT, pulsate, throb, vibrate

pulverize verb **1** CRUSH, granulate, grind, mill, pound **2** DEFEAT, annihilate, crush, demolish, destroy, flatten, smash, wreck

pummel verb BEAT, batter, hammer, pound, punch, strike, thump

pump verb **1** (often with *into*) DRIVE, force, inject, pour, push, send, supply **2** INTERROGATE, cross-examine, probe, quiz

pun noun PLAY ON WORDS, double entendre, quip, witticism

punch[1] verb **1** HIT, belt (informal), bop (informal), box, pummel, smash, sock (slang), strike ▶noun **2** BLOW, bop (informal), hit, jab, sock (slang), wallop (informal) **3** Informal EFFECTIVENESS, bite, drive, forcefulness, impact, verve, vigor

punch[2] verb PIERCE, bore, cut, drill, perforate, prick, puncture, stamp

punctilious adjective PARTICULAR, exact, finicky, formal, fussy, meticulous, nice, precise, proper, strict

punctual adjective ON TIME, exact, on the dot, precise, prompt, timely

punctuality noun PROMPTNESS, promptitude, readiness

punctuate verb **1** INTERRUPT, break, intersperse, pepper, sprinkle **2** EMPHASIZE, accentuate, stress, underline

puncture noun **1** HOLE, break, cut, damage, leak, nick, opening, slit **2** FLAT TIRE, flat ▶verb **3** PIERCE, bore, cut, nick, penetrate, perforate, prick, rupture

pungent adjective STRONG, acrid, bitter, hot, peppery, piquant, sharp, sour, spicy, tart

punish verb DISCIPLINE, castigate, chasten, chastise, correct, penalize, sentence

punishable adjective CULPABLE, blameworthy, criminal, indictable

punishing adjective HARD, arduous, backbreaking, exhausting, grueling, strenuous, taxing, tiring, wearing

punishment noun PENALTY, chastening, chastisement, correction, discipline, penance, retribution

punitive adjective RETALIATORY, in reprisal, retaliative

punt verb **1** BET, back, gamble, lay, stake, wager ▶noun **2** BET, gamble, stake, wager

puny adjective FEEBLE, frail, little, sickly, stunted, tiny, weak

pupil noun LEARNER, beginner, disciple, novice, schoolboy or schoolgirl, student

puppet noun **1** MARIONETTE, doll, ventriloquist's dummy **2** PAWN, cat's-paw, instrument, mouthpiece, stooge, tool

purchase verb **1** BUY, acquire, come by, gain, get, obtain, pay for, pick up, score (slang) ▶noun **2** BUY, acquisition, asset, gain, investment, possession, property **3** GRIP, foothold, hold, leverage, support

pure adjective **1** UNMIXED, authentic, flawless, genuine, natural, neat, real, simple, straight, unalloyed **2** CLEAN, germ-free, sanitary, spotless, squeaky-clean, sterilized, uncontaminated, unpolluted, untainted, wholesome **3** INNOCENT, blameless, chaste, impeccable, modest, uncorrupted, unsullied, virginal, virtuous **4** COMPLETE, absolute, outright, sheer, thorough, unmitigated, unqualified, utter

purely adverb ABSOLUTELY, completely, entirely, exclusively, just, merely, only, simply, solely, wholly

purge verb **1** GET RID OF, do

away with, eradicate, expel,
exterminate, remove, wipe out
▶ *noun* 2 REMOVAL, ejection,
elimination, eradication,
expulsion

purify *verb* 1 CLEAN, clarify,
cleanse, decontaminate,
disinfect, refine, sanitize, wash
2 ABSOLVE, cleanse, redeem,
sanctify

purist *noun* STICKLER, formalist,
pedant

puritan *noun* 1 MORALIST,
fanatic, prude, rigorist, zealot
▶ *adjective* 2 STRICT, ascetic,
austere, moralistic,
narrow-minded, prudish,
severe, strait-laced

puritanical *adjective* STRICT,
ascetic, austere,
narrow-minded, proper,
prudish, puritan, severe,
strait-laced

purity *noun* 1 CLEANNESS,
cleanliness, faultlessness,
immaculateness, pureness,
wholesomeness 2 INNOCENCE,
chasteness, chastity, decency,
honesty, integrity, virginity,
virtue, virtuousness

purloin *verb* STEAL, appropriate,
filch, pilfer, pinch (*informal*),
swipe (*slang*), thieve

purport *verb* 1 CLAIM, allege,
assert, profess ▶ *noun*
2 SIGNIFICANCE, drift, gist, idea,
implication, import, meaning

purpose *noun* 1 REASON, aim,
idea, intention, object, point
2 AIM, ambition, desire, end,
goal, hope, intention, object,
plan, wish 3 DETERMINATION,
firmness, persistence,
resolution, resolve,
single-mindedness, tenacity,

will 4 on purpose DELIBERATELY,
designedly, intentionally,
knowingly, purposely

purposeless *adjective* POINTLESS,
aimless, empty, motiveless,
needless, senseless,
uncalled-for, unnecessary

purposely *adverb* DELIBERATELY,
consciously, expressly,
intentionally, knowingly, on
purpose, with intent

purse *noun* 1 POUCH,
money-bag, wallet 2 MONEY,
exchequer, funds, means,
resources, treasury, wealth
▶ *verb* 3 PUCKER, contract, pout,
press together, tighten

pursue *verb* 1 FOLLOW, chase,
dog, hound, hunt, hunt down,
run after, shadow, stalk, tail
(*informal*), track 2 TRY FOR, aim
for, desire, seek, strive for,
work towards 3 ENGAGE IN,
carry on, conduct, perform,
practice 4 CONTINUE, carry on,
keep on, maintain, persevere
in, persist in, proceed

pursuit *noun* 1 PURSUING, chase,
hunt, quest, search, seeking,
trailing 2 OCCUPATION, activity,
hobby, interest, line, pastime,
pleasure

purvey *verb* SUPPLY, cater, deal
in, furnish, provide, sell, trade
in

push *verb* 1 SHOVE, depress,
drive, press, propel, ram, thrust
2 MAKE *or* FORCE ONE'S WAY,
elbow, jostle, move, shoulder,
shove, squeeze, thrust 3 URGE,
encourage, hurry, impel, incite,
persuade, press, spur ▶ *noun*
4 SHOVE, butt, nudge, thrust
5 DRIVE, ambition, dynamism,
energy, enterprise, go

(*informal*), initiative, vigor, vitality

pushed *adjective* (often with *for*) SHORT OF, hurried, pressed, rushed, under pressure

pushover *noun* 1 PIECE OF CAKE (*informal*), breeze (*informal*), child's play (*informal*), cinch (*slang*), picnic (*informal*), plain sailing, walkover (*informal*) 2 SUCKER (*slang*), easy game (*informal*), easy or soft mark (*informal*), mug (*Brit. slang*), walkover (*informal*)

pushy *adjective* FORCEFUL, ambitious, assertive, bold, brash, bumptious, obtrusive, presumptuous, self-assertive

pussyfoot *verb* beat about the bush, be noncommittal, equivocate, hum and haw, prevaricate, sit on the fence

put *verb* 1 PLACE, deposit, lay, position, rest, set, settle, situate 2 EXPRESS, phrase, state, utter, word 3 THROW, cast, fling, heave, hurl, lob, pitch, toss

put across *or* **over** *verb* COMMUNICATE, convey, explain, get across, make clear, make oneself understood

put aside *or* **by** *verb* SAVE, deposit, lay by, stockpile, store

put away *verb* 1 SAVE, deposit, keep, put by 2 COMMIT, certify, institutionalize, lock up 3 CONSUME, devour, eat up, gobble, wolf down 4 PUT BACK, replace, tidy away

put down *verb* 1 RECORD, enter, set down, take down, write down 2 STAMP OUT, crush, quash, quell, repress, suppress 3 (usually with *to*) ATTRIBUTE,

ascribe, impute, set down 4 PUT TO SLEEP, destroy, do away with, put out of its misery 5 *Slang* HUMILIATE, disparage, mortify, shame, slight, snub

put forward *verb* RECOMMEND, advance, nominate, propose, submit, suggest; tender

put off *verb* 1 POSTPONE, defer, delay, hold over, put on the back burner (*informal*), take a rain check on (*informal*) 2 DISCONCERT, confuse, discomfit, dismay, faze, nonplus, perturb, throw (*informal*), unsettle 3 DISCOURAGE, dishearten, dissuade

put on *verb* 1 DON, change into, dress, get dressed in, slip into 2 FAKE, affect, assume, feign, pretend, sham, simulate 3 PRESENT, do, mount, produce, show, stage 4 ADD, gain, increase by

put out *verb* 1 ANNOY, anger, exasperate, irk, irritate, nettle, vex 2 EXTINGUISH, blow out, douse, quench 3 INCONVENIENCE, bother, discomfit, discommode, impose upon, incommode, trouble

putrid *adjective* ROTTEN, bad, decayed, decomposed, putrefied, rancid, rotting, spoiled

putter *verb* MESS AROUND, dabble, dawdle, monkey around (*informal*), tinker

put up *verb* 1 ERECT, build, construct, fabricate, raise 2 ACCOMMODATE, board, house, lodge, take in 3 RECOMMEND, nominate, offer, present,

propose, put forward, submit
4 put up with STAND, abide,
bear, endure, stand for,
swallow, take, tolerate

puzzle verb **1** PERPLEX, baffle,
bewilder, confound, confuse,
mystify, stump ▸noun
2 PROBLEM, conundrum,
enigma, mystery, paradox,
poser, question, riddle

puzzled adjective PERPLEXED, at a
loss, at sea, baffled,
bewildered, confused, lost,
mystified

puzzlement noun PERPLEXITY,
bafflement, bewilderment,
confusion, doubt, mystification

puzzling adjective PERPLEXING,
abstruse, baffling, bewildering,
enigmatic, incomprehensible,
involved, mystifying

— Q q —

quack noun CHARLATAN, fake,
fraud, humbug, impostor,
mountebank, phoney or phony
(informal), pretender

quaff verb DRINK, down, gulp,
imbibe, swallow, swig (informal)

quagmire noun BOG, fen,
marsh, mire, morass,
quicksand, slough, swamp

quail verb SHRINK, blanch,
blench, cower, cringe, falter,
flinch, have cold feet
(informal), recoil, shudder

quaint adjective **1** UNUSUAL,
bizarre, curious, droll,
eccentric, fanciful, odd,
old-fashioned, peculiar, queer,
singular, strange

2 OLD-FASHIONED, antiquated,
old-world, picturesque

quake verb SHAKE, move, quiver,
rock, shiver, shudder, tremble,
vibrate

qualification noun **1** ATTRIBUTE,
ability, aptitude, capability,
eligibility, fitness, quality, skill,
suitability **2** CONDITION, caveat,
limitation, modification,
proviso, requirement,
reservation, rider, stipulation

qualified adjective **1** CAPABLE,
able, adept, competent,
efficient, experienced, expert,
fit, practiced, proficient, skillful,
trained **2** RESTRICTED, bounded,
conditional, confined,
contingent, limited, modified,
provisional, reserved

qualify verb **1** CERTIFY, empower,
equip, fit, permit, prepare,
ready, train **2** MODERATE,
diminish, ease, lessen, limit,
reduce, regulate, restrain,
restrict, soften, temper

quality noun **1** EXCELLENCE,
caliber, distinction, grade,
merit, position, rank, standing,
status **2** CHARACTERISTIC, aspect,
attribute, condition, feature,
mark, property, trait **3** NATURE,
character, kind, make, sort

qualm noun MISGIVING, anxiety,
apprehension, compunction,
disquiet, doubt, hesitation,
scruple, twinge or pang of
conscience, uneasiness

quandary noun DIFFICULTY,
Catch-22, dilemma, impasse,
plight, predicament, puzzle,
strait

quantity noun **1** AMOUNT, lot,
number, part, sum, total **2** SIZE,
bulk, capacity, extent, length,

magnitude, mass, measure, volume

quarrel noun 1 DISAGREEMENT, argument, brawl, breach, contention, controversy, dispute, dissension, feud, fight, row, squabble, tiff ▶ verb 2 DISAGREE, argue, bicker, brawl, clash, differ, dispute, fall out (informal), fight, row, squabble

quarrelsome adjective ARGUMENTATIVE, belligerent, combative, contentious, disputatious, pugnacious

quarry noun PREY, aim, game, goal, objective, prize, victim

quarter noun 1 DISTRICT, area, locality, neighborhood, part, place, province, region, side, zone 2 MERCY, clemency, compassion, forgiveness, leniency, pity ▶ verb 3 ACCOMMODATE, billet, board, house, lodge, place, post, station

quarters plural noun LODGINGS, abode, barracks, billet, chambers, dwelling, habitation, residence, rooms

quash verb 1 ANNUL, cancel, invalidate, overrule, overthrow, rescind, reverse, revoke 2 SUPPRESS, beat, crush, overthrow, put down, quell, repress, squash, subdue

quasi- adjective PSEUDO-, apparent, seeming, semi-, so-called, would-be

quaver verb 1 TREMBLE, flicker, flutter, quake, quiver, shake, vibrate, waver ▶ noun 2 TREMBLING, quiver, shake, tremble, tremor, vibration

queasy adjective 1 SICK, bilious, green around the gills

(informal), ill, nauseated, off color, squeamish, upset 2 UNEASY, anxious, fidgety, ill at ease, restless, troubled, uncertain, worried

queen noun 1 SOVEREIGN, consort, monarch, ruler 2 IDEAL, mistress, model, star

queer adjective 1 STRANGE, abnormal, curious, droll, extraordinary, funny, odd, peculiar, uncommon, unusual, weird 2 FAINT, dizzy, giddy, light-headed, queasy

quell verb 1 SUPPRESS, conquer, crush, defeat, overcome, overpower, put down, quash, subdue, vanquish 2 ASSUAGE, allay, appease, calm, mollify, pacify, quiet, soothe

quench verb 1 SATISFY, allay, appease, sate, satiate, slake 2 PUT OUT, crush, douse, extinguish, smother, stifle, suppress

querulous adjective COMPLAINING, captious, carping, critical, discontented, dissatisfied, fault-finding, grumbling, peevish, whining

query noun 1 QUESTION, doubt, inquiry, objection, problem, suspicion ▶ verb 2 DOUBT, challenge, disbelieve, dispute, distrust, mistrust, suspect 3 ASK, inquire or enquire, question

quest noun SEARCH, adventure, crusade, enterprise, expedition, hunt, journey, mission

question noun 1 ISSUE, motion, point, point at issue, proposal, proposition, subject, theme, topic 2 DIFFICULTY, argument, contention, controversy, dispute, doubt, problem, query **3 in question** UNDER DISCUSSION, at issue, in doubt, open to debate **4 out of the question** IMPOSSIBLE, inconceivable, unthinkable ▶ verb **5** ASK, cross-examine, examine, inquire, interrogate, interview, probe, quiz **6** DISPUTE, challenge, disbelieve, doubt, mistrust, oppose, query, suspect

questionable adjective DUBIOUS, controversial, debatable, doubtful, iffy (informal), moot, suspect, suspicious

queue noun LINE, chain, file, sequence, series, string, train

quibble verb **1** SPLIT HAIRS, carp, cavil ▶ noun **2** OBJECTION, cavil, complaint, criticism, nicety, niggle

quick adjective **1** FAST, brisk, express, fleet, hasty, rapid, speedy, swift **2** BRIEF, cursory, hasty, hurried, perfunctory **3** SUDDEN, prompt **4** INTELLIGENT, acute, alert, astute, bright (informal), clever, perceptive, quick-witted, sharp, shrewd, smart **5** DEFT, adept, adroit, dexterous, skillful **6** EXCITABLE, irascible, irritable, passionate, testy, touchy

quicken verb **1** SPEED, accelerate, expedite, hasten, hurry, impel, precipitate **2** INVIGORATE, arouse, energize, excite, incite, inspire, revive, stimulate, vitalize

quickly adverb SWIFTLY, abruptly, apace, briskly, fast, hastily, hurriedly, promptly, pronto (informal), rapidly, soon, speedily

quick-tempered adjective HOT-TEMPERED, choleric, fiery,

irascible, irritable, quarrelsome, testy

quick-witted adjective CLEVER, alert, astute, bright (informal), keen, perceptive, sharp, shrewd, smart

quiet adjective **1** SILENT, hushed, inaudible, low, noiseless, peaceful, soft, soundless **2** CALM, mild, peaceful, placid, restful, serene, smooth, tranquil **3** UNDISTURBED, isolated, private, secluded, sequestered, unfrequented **4** RESERVED, gentle, meek, mild, retiring, sedate, shy ▶ noun **5** PEACE, calmness, ease, quietness, repose, rest, serenity, silence, stillness, tranquillity

quieten verb **1** SILENCE, compose, hush, muffle, mute, quell, quiet, stifle, still, stop, subdue **2** SOOTHE, allay, appease, blunt, calm, deaden, dull

quietly adverb **1** SILENTLY, in an undertone, inaudibly, in silence, mutely, noiselessly, softly **2** CALMLY, mildly, patiently, placidly, serenely

quietness noun PEACE, calm, hush, quiet, silence, stillness, tranquillity

quilt noun BEDSPREAD, continental quilt, counterpane, coverlet, duvet, eiderdown

quintessence noun ESSENCE, distillation, soul, spirit

quintessential adjective ULTIMATE, archetypal, definitive, prototypical, typical

quip noun JOKE, gibe, jest, pleasantry, retort, riposte, sally, wisecrack (informal), witticism

quirk noun PECULIARITY,

aberration, characteristic, eccentricity, foible, habit, idiosyncrasy, kink, mannerism, oddity, trait

quirky *adjective* ODD, eccentric, idiosyncratic, offbeat, peculiar, unusual

quit *verb* **1** STOP, abandon, cease, discontinue, drop, end, give up, halt **2** RESIGN, abdicate, go, leave, pull out, retire, step down (*informal*) **3** DEPART, go, leave, pull out

quite *adverb* **1** SOMEWHAT, fairly, moderately, rather, reasonably, relatively **2** ABSOLUTELY, completely, entirely, fully, perfectly, totally, wholly **3** TRULY, in fact, in reality, in truth, really

quiver *verb* **1** SHAKE, oscillate, quake, quaver, shiver, shudder, tremble, vibrate ▶ *noun* **2** SHAKE, oscillation, shiver, shudder, tremble, tremor, vibration

quixotic *adjective* UNREALISTIC, dreamy, fanciful, idealistic, impractical, romantic

quiz *noun* **1** EXAMINATION, investigation, questioning, test ▶ *verb* **2** QUESTION, ask, examine, interrogate, investigate

quizzical *adjective* MOCKING, arch, questioning, sardonic, teasing

quota *noun* SHARE, allowance, assignment, part, portion, ration, slice

quotation *noun* **1** PASSAGE, citation, excerpt, extract, quote (*informal*), reference **2** *Commerce* ESTIMATE, charge, cost, figure, price, quote (*informal*), rate, tender

quote *verb* REPEAT, cite, detail,

instance, name, recall, recite, recollect, refer to

—— R r ——

rabble *noun* MOB, canaille, crowd, herd, horde, swarm, throng

rabid *adjective* **1** FANATICAL, extreme, fervent, irrational, narrow-minded, zealous **2** MAD, hydrophobic

race[1] *noun* **1** CONTEST, chase, competition, dash, pursuit, rivalry ▶ *verb* **2** RUN, career, compete, contest, dart, dash, fly, gallop, hurry, speed, tear, zoom

race[2] *noun* PEOPLE, blood, folk, nation, stock, tribe, type

racial *adjective* ETHNIC, ethnological, folk, genealogical, genetic, national, tribal

rack *noun* **1** FRAME, framework, stand, structure ▶ *verb* **2** TORTURE, afflict, agonize, crucify, harrow, oppress, pain, torment

racket *noun* **1** NOISE, clamor, din, disturbance, fuss, outcry, pandemonium, row **2** FRAUD, scheme

racy *adjective* **1** RISQUÉ, bawdy, blue, naughty, smutty, suggestive **2** LIVELY, animated, energetic, entertaining, exciting, sparkling, spirited

radiance *noun* **1** HAPPINESS, delight, gaiety, joy, pleasure, rapture, warmth **2** BRIGHTNESS, brilliance, glare, gleam, glow, light, luster, shine

radiant adjective **1** HAPPY, blissful, delighted, ecstatic, glowing, joyful, joyous, on cloud nine (informal), rapturous **2** BRIGHT, brilliant, gleaming, glittering, glowing, luminous, lustrous, shining

radiate verb **1** SPREAD OUT, branch out, diverge, issue **2** EMIT, diffuse, give off or out, pour, scatter, send out, shed, spread

radical adjective **1** FUNDAMENTAL, basic, deep-seated, innate, natural, profound **2** EXTREME, complete, drastic, entire, extremist, fanatical, severe, sweeping, thorough ▶ noun **3** EXTREMIST, fanatic, militant, revolutionary

raffle noun DRAW, lottery, sweep, sweepstake

ragamuffin noun URCHIN, guttersnipe

rage noun **1** FURY, anger, frenzy, ire, madness, passion, rampage, wrath **2** As in all the rage CRAZE, enthusiasm, fad (informal), fashion, latest thing, trend, vogue ▶ verb **3** BE FURIOUS, blow one's top, blow up (informal), fly off the handle (informal), fume, go ballistic (slang), go up the wall (slang), see red, seethe, storm, wig out (slang)

ragged adjective **1** TATTERED, in rags, in tatters, shabby, tatty, threadbare, torn, unkempt **2** ROUGH, jagged, rugged, serrated, uneven, unfinished

raging adjective FURIOUS, beside oneself, enraged, fuming, incensed, infuriated, mad, raving, seething

rags plural noun TATTERS, castoffs, old clothes, tattered clothing

raid noun **1** ATTACK, foray, incursion, inroad, invasion, sally, sortie ▶ verb **2** ATTACK, assault, foray, invade, pillage, plunder, sack

raider noun ATTACKER, invader, marauder, plunderer, robber, thief

railing noun FENCE, balustrade, barrier, paling, rails

rain noun **1** RAINFALL, cloudburst, deluge, downpour, drizzle, fall, raindrops, showers, torrent ▶ verb **2** POUR, bucket down (informal), come down in buckets (informal), drizzle, pelt (down), rain cats and dogs, teem **3** FALL, deposit, drop, shower, sprinkle

rainy adjective WET, damp, drizzly, showery

raise verb **1** LIFT, build, elevate, erect, heave, hoist, rear, uplift **2** INCREASE, advance, amplify, boost, enhance, enlarge, heighten, inflate, intensify, magnify, strengthen **3** COLLECT, assemble, form, gather, mass, obtain, rally, recruit **4** CAUSE, create, engender, occasion, originate, produce, provoke, start **5** BRING UP, develop, nurture, rear **6** SUGGEST, advance, broach, introduce, moot, put forward

rake¹ verb **1** GATHER, collect, remove **2** SEARCH, comb, scour, scrutinize

rake² noun LIBERTINE, debauchee, lecher, playboy, roué

rakish adjective DASHING, dapper, debonair, devil-may-care, jaunty, raffish

rally noun **1** GATHERING, assembly, congress, convention, meeting **2** RECOVERY, improvement, recuperation, revival ▶ verb **3** REASSEMBLE, regroup, reorganize, unite **4** GATHER, assemble, collect, convene, marshal, muster, round up, unite **5** RECOVER, get better, improve, recuperate, revive

ram verb **1** HIT, butt, crash, dash, drive, force, impact, smash **2** CRAM, crowd, force, jam, stuff, thrust

ramble verb **1** WALK, range, roam, rove, saunter, stray, stroll, wander **2** BABBLE ▶ noun **3** WALK, hike, roaming, roving, saunter, stroll, tour

rambler noun WALKER, hiker, rover, wanderer, wayfarer

rambling adjective LONG-WINDED, circuitous, digressive, disconnected, discursive, disjointed, incoherent, wordy

ramification noun **ramifications** CONSEQUENCES, developments, results, sequel, upshot

ramp noun SLOPE, gradient, incline, rise

rampage verb **1** GO BERSERK, rage, run amok, run riot, storm ▶ noun **2 on the rampage** BERSERK, amok, out of control, raging, riotous, violent, wild

rampant adjective **1** WIDESPREAD, prevalent, profuse, rife, spreading like wildfire, unchecked, uncontrolled, unrestrained **2** Heraldry UPRIGHT, erect, rearing, standing

rampart noun DEFENSE, bastion, bulwark, fence, fortification, wall

ramshackle adjective RICKETY, crumbling, decrepit, derelict, flimsy, shaky, tumbledown, unsafe, unsteady

rancid adjective ROTTEN, bad, fetid, foul, putrid, rank, sour, stale, strong-smelling, tainted

rancor noun HATRED, animosity, bad blood, bitterness, hate, ill feeling, ill will

random adjective **1** CHANCE, accidental, adventitious, casual, fortuitous, haphazard, hit or miss, incidental ▶ noun **2 at random** HAPHAZARDLY, arbitrarily, by chance, randomly, unsystematically, willy-nilly

range noun **1** LIMITS, area, bounds, orbit, province, radius, reach, scope, sphere **2** SERIES, assortment, collection, gamut, lot, selection, variety ▶ verb **3** VARY, extend, reach, run, stretch **4** ROAM, ramble, rove, traverse, wander

rangy adjective LONG-LIMBED, gangling, lanky, leggy, long-legged

rank¹ noun **1** STATUS, caste, class, degree, division, grade, level, order, position, sort, type **2** ROW, column, file, group, line, range, series, tier ▶ verb **3** ARRANGE, align, array, dispose, line up, order, sort

rank² adjective **1** ABSOLUTE, arrant, blatant, complete, downright, flagrant, gross, sheer, thorough, total, utter **2** FOUL, bad, disgusting, funky (slang), noisome, noxious, offensive, rancid, revolting, smelly, stinking **3** ABUNDANT, dense, lush, luxuriant, profuse

rank and file noun GENERAL

PUBLIC, majority, mass, masses

rankle verb ANNOY, anger, gall, get on one's nerves (*informal*), irk, irritate, rile

ransack verb 1 SEARCH, comb, explore, go through, rummage, scour, turn inside out 2 PLUNDER, loot, pillage, raid, strip

ransom noun PAYMENT, money, payoff, price

rant verb SHOUT, cry, declaim, rave, roar, yell

rap verb 1 HIT, crack, knock, strike, tap ▶ noun 2 BLOW, clout (*informal*), crack, knock, tap 3 Slang PUNISHMENT, blame, responsibility

rapacious adjective GREEDY, avaricious, grasping, insatiable, predatory, preying, voracious

rape verb 1 SEXUALLY ASSAULT, abuse, force, outrage, ravish, violate ▶ noun 2 SEXUAL ASSAULT, outrage, ravishment, violation 3 DESECRATION, abuse, defilement, violation

rapid adjective QUICK, brisk, express, fast, hasty, hurried, prompt, speedy, swift

rapidity noun SPEED, alacrity, briskness, fleetness, haste, hurry, promptness, quickness, rush, swiftness, velocity

rapidly adverb QUICKLY, briskly, fast, hastily, hurriedly, in haste, promptly, pronto (*informal*), speedily, swiftly

rapport noun BOND, affinity, empathy, harmony, link, relationship, sympathy, tie, understanding

rapprochement noun RECONCILIATION, detente, reunion

rapt adjective SPELLBOUND,
absorbed, engrossed, enthralled, entranced, fascinated, gripped

rapture noun ECSTASY, bliss, delight, euphoria, joy, rhapsody, seventh heaven, transport

rapturous adjective ECSTATIC, blissful, euphoric, in seventh heaven, joyful, overjoyed, over the moon (*informal*), transported

rare adjective 1 UNCOMMON, few, infrequent, scarce, singular, sparse, strange, unusual 2 SUPERB, choice, excellent, fine, great, peerless, superlative

rarefied adjective EXALTED, elevated, high, lofty, noble, spiritual, sublime

rarely adverb SELDOM, hardly, hardly ever, infrequently

raring adjective As in **raring to** EAGER, desperate, enthusiastic, impatient, keen, longing, ready

rarity noun 1 CURIO, collector's item, find, gem, treasure 2 UNCOMMONNESS, infrequency, scarcity, shortage, sparseness, strangeness, unusualness

rascal noun ROGUE, devil, good-for-nothing, imp, scamp, scoundrel, villain

rash[1] adjective RECKLESS, careless, foolhardy, hasty, heedless, ill-advised, impetuous, imprudent, impulsive, incautious

rash[2] noun 1 OUTBREAK, eruption 2 SPATE, flood, outbreak, plague, series, wave

rashness noun RECKLESSNESS, carelessness, foolhardiness, hastiness, heedlessness, indiscretion, thoughtlessness

rate noun 1 SPEED, pace, tempo, velocity 2 DEGREE, proportion, ratio, scale, standard 3 CHARGE, cost, fee, figure, price 4 **at any rate** IN ANY CASE, anyhow, anyway, at all events ▸ verb 5 EVALUATE, consider, count, estimate, grade, measure, rank, reckon, value 6 DESERVE, be entitled to, be worthy of, merit

rather adverb 1 TO SOME EXTENT, a little, fairly, moderately, quite, relatively, somewhat, to some degree 2 PREFERABLY, more readily, more willingly, sooner

ratify verb APPROVE, affirm, authorize, confirm, endorse, establish, sanction, uphold

rating noun POSITION, class, degree, grade, order, placing, rank, rate, status

ratio noun PROPORTION, fraction, percentage, rate, relation

ration noun 1 ALLOWANCE, allotment, helping, measure, part, portion, quota, share ▸ verb 2 LIMIT, budget, control, restrict

rational adjective SANE, intelligent, logical, lucid, realistic, reasonable, sensible, sound, wise

rationale noun REASON, grounds, logic, motivation, philosophy, principle, raison d'être, theory

rationalize verb JUSTIFY, account for, excuse, vindicate

rattle verb 1 CLATTER, bang, jangle 2 SHAKE, bounce, jar, jolt, vibrate 3 Informal FLUSTER, disconcert, disturb, faze, perturb, shake, upset

raucous adjective HARSH, grating, hoarse, loud, noisy, rough, strident

raunchy adjective Slang SEXY, coarse, earthy, lusty, sexual, steamy (informal)

ravage verb 1 DESTROY, demolish, despoil, devastate, lay waste, ransack, ruin, spoil ▸ noun 2 **ravages** DAMAGE, destruction, devastation, havoc, ruin, ruination, spoliation

rave verb 1 RANT, babble, be delirious, go mad (informal), rage, roar 2 ENTHUSE, be excited about (informal), be wild about (informal), gush, praise

ravenous adjective STARVING, famished, starved

ravine noun CANYON, defile, gorge, gulch, gully, pass

raving adjective MAD, crazed, crazy, delirious, hysterical, insane, irrational, wild

ravish verb 1 ENCHANT, captivate, charm, delight, enrapture, entrance, fascinate, spellbind 2 RAPE, abuse, force, sexually assault, violate

ravishing adjective ENCHANTING, beautiful, bewitching, charming, entrancing, gorgeous, lovely

raw adjective 1 UNCOOKED, fresh, natural 2 UNREFINED, basic, coarse, crude, natural, rough, unfinished, unprocessed 3 INEXPERIENCED, callow, green, immature, new 4 CHILLY, biting, bitter, cold, freezing, piercing

ray noun BEAM, bar, flash, gleam, shaft

raze verb DESTROY, demolish, flatten, knock down, level, pull down, ruin

re preposition CONCERNING, about, apropos, regarding, with reference to, with regard to

reach verb 1 ARRIVE AT, attain, get to, make 2 TOUCH, contact, extend to, grasp, stretch to 3 CONTACT, communicate with, get hold of, get in touch with, get through to ▶noun 4 RANGE, capacity, distance, extension, extent, grasp, influence, power, scope, stretch

react verb 1 RESPOND, answer, reply 2 ACT, behave, function, operate, proceed, work

reaction noun 1 RESPONSE, answer, reply 2 RECOIL, counteraction 3 CONSERVATISM, the right

reactionary adjective 1 CONSERVATIVE, right-wing ▶noun 2 CONSERVATIVE, die-hard, right-winger

read verb 1 LOOK AT, peruse, pore over, scan, study 2 INTERPRET, comprehend, construe, decipher, discover, see, understand 3 REGISTER, display, indicate, record, show

readable adjective 1 ENJOYABLE, entertaining, enthralling, gripping, interesting 2 LEGIBLE, clear, comprehensible, decipherable

readily adverb 1 WILLINGLY, eagerly, freely, gladly, promptly, quickly 2 EASILY, effortlessly, quickly, smoothly, speedily, unhesitatingly

readiness noun 1 WILLINGNESS, eagerness, keenness 2 EASE, adroitness, dexterity, facility, promptness

reading noun 1 PERUSAL, examination, inspection, scrutiny, study 2 RECITAL, lesson, performance, sermon

3 INTERPRETATION, grasp, impression, version 4 LEARNING, education, erudition, knowledge, scholarship

ready adjective 1 PREPARED, arranged, fit, organized, primed, ripe, set 2 WILLING, agreeable, disposed, eager, glad, happy, inclined, keen, prone 3 PROMPT, alert, bright, clever, intelligent, keen, perceptive, quick, sharp, smart 4 AVAILABLE, accessible, convenient, handy, near, present

real adjective GENUINE, actual, authentic, factual, rightful, sincere, true, unfeigned, valid

realistic adjective 1 PRACTICAL, common-sense, down-to-earth, level-headed, matter-of-fact, real, sensible 2 LIFELIKE, authentic, faithful, genuine, natural, true, true to life

reality noun TRUTH, actuality, fact, realism, validity, verity

realization noun 1 AWARENESS, cognizance, comprehension, conception, grasp, perception, recognition, understanding 2 ACHIEVEMENT, accomplishment, fulfillment

realize verb 1 BECOME AWARE OF, comprehend, get the message, grasp, take in, understand 2 ACHIEVE, accomplish, carry out or through, complete, do, effect, fulfill, perform

really adverb TRULY, actually, certainly, genuinely, in actuality, indeed, in fact, positively, surely

realm noun 1 KINGDOM, country, domain, dominion, empire, land 2 SPHERE, area, branch, department, field, province, territory, world

reap verb 1 COLLECT, bring in, cut, garner, gather, harvest 2 OBTAIN, acquire, derive, gain, get

rear[1] noun 1 BACK, end, rearguard, stern, tail, tail end ▶ adjective 2 BACK, following, hind, last

rear[2] verb 1 BRING UP, breed, educate, foster, nurture, raise, train 2 RISE, loom, soar, tower

reason noun 1 CAUSE, aim, goal, grounds, incentive, intention, motive, object, purpose 2 SENSE(S), intellect, judgment, logic, mind, rationality, sanity, soundness, understanding ▶ verb 3 DEDUCE, conclude, infer, make out, think, work out 4 reason with PERSUADE, bring round (informal), prevail upon, talk into or out of, urge, win over

reasonable adjective 1 SENSIBLE, logical, plausible, practical, sane, sober, sound, tenable, wise 2 MODERATE, equitable, fair, fit, just, modest, O.K. or okay (informal), proper, right

reasoned adjective SENSIBLE, clear, logical, well-thought-out

reasoning noun THINKING, analysis, logic, thought

reassure verb ENCOURAGE, comfort, hearten, put or set one's mind at rest, restore confidence to

rebate noun REFUND, allowance, bonus, deduction, discount, reduction

rebel verb 1 REVOLT, mutiny, resist, rise up 2 DEFY, disobey, dissent ▶ noun 3 REVOLUTIONARY,

insurgent, revolutionist, secessionist 4 NONCONFORMIST, apostate, dissenter, heretic, schismatic ▶ adjective 5 REBELLIOUS, insurgent, insurrectionary, revolutionary

rebellion noun 1 RESISTANCE, mutiny, revolt, revolution, rising, uprising 2 NONCONFORMITY, defiance, heresy, schism

rebellious adjective 1 REVOLUTIONARY, disloyal, disobedient, disorderly, insurgent, mutinous, rebel, seditious, unruly 2 DEFIANT, difficult, refractory, resistant, unmanageable

rebound verb 1 BOUNCE, recoil, ricochet 2 MISFIRE, backfire, boomerang, recoil

rebuff verb 1 REJECT, cold-shoulder, cut, knock back (slang), refuse, repulse, slight, snub, spurn, turn down ▶ noun 2 REJECTION, cold shoulder, kick in the teeth (slang), knock-back (slang), refusal, repulse, slap in the face (informal), slight, snub

rebuke verb 1 SCOLD, admonish, castigate, censure, chide, reprimand, reprove, tell off (informal) ▶ noun 2 SCOLDING, admonition, censure, reprimand, row, telling-off (informal)

rebut verb DISPROVE, confute, invalidate, negate, overturn, prove wrong, refute

rebuttal noun DISPROOF, confutation, invalidation, negation, refutation

recalcitrant adjective DISOBEDIENT, defiant, insubordinate, refractory,

unmanageable, unruly,
wayward, willful

recall *verb* 1 RECOLLECT, bring or
call to mind, evoke, remember
2 ANNUL, cancel, countermand,
repeal, retract, revoke,
withdraw ▶ *noun* 3 RECOLLECTION,
memory, remembrance
4 ANNULMENT, cancellation,
repeal, rescindment, retraction,
withdrawal

recant *verb* WITHDRAW, disclaim,
forswear, renege, repudiate,
retract, revoke, take back

recapitulate *verb* REPEAT,
outline, recap (*informal*),
recount, restate, summarize

recede *verb* FALL BACK, abate,
ebb, regress, retire, retreat,
return, subside, withdraw

receipt *noun* 1 SALES SLIP,
counterfoil, proof of purchase
2 RECEIVING, acceptance,
delivery, reception

receive *verb* 1 GET, accept,
acquire, be given, collect,
obtain, pick up, take
2 EXPERIENCE, bear, encounter,
suffer, sustain, undergo
3 GREET, accommodate, admit,
entertain, meet, welcome

recent *adjective* NEW, current,
fresh, late, modern, novel,
present-day, up-to-date

recently *adverb* NEWLY,
currently, freshly, lately,
latterly, not long ago, of late

receptacle *noun* CONTAINER,
holder, repository

reception *noun* 1 PARTY,
function, levee, soirée
2 WELCOME, acknowledgment,
greeting, reaction, response,
treatment

receptive *adjective* OPEN,

amenable, interested,
open-minded, open to
suggestions, susceptible,
sympathetic

recess *noun* 1 ALCOVE, bay,
corner, hollow, niche, nook
2 BREAK, holiday, intermission,
interval, respite, rest, vacation

recession *noun* DEPRESSION,
decline, drop, slump

recipe *noun* 1 DIRECTIONS,
ingredients, instructions
2 METHOD, formula,
prescription, procedure,
process, technique

reciprocal *adjective* MUTUAL,
alternate, complementary,
correlative, corresponding,
equivalent, exchanged,
interchangeable

reciprocate *verb* RETURN,
exchange, reply, requite,
respond, swap, trade

recital *noun* 1 PERFORMANCE,
rehearsal, rendering
2 RECITATION, account, narrative,
reading, relation, statement,
telling

recitation *noun* RECITAL, lecture,
passage, performance, piece,
reading

recite *verb* REPEAT, declaim,
deliver, narrate, perform, speak

reckless *adjective* CARELESS,
hasty, headlong, heedless,
imprudent, mindless,
precipitate, rash, thoughtless,
wild

reckon *verb* 1 THINK, assume,
believe, guess (*informal*),
imagine, suppose 2 CONSIDER,
account, count, deem, esteem,
judge, rate, regard 3 COUNT,
add up, calculate, compute,
figure, number, tally, total

reckoning noun **1** COUNT, addition, calculation, estimate **2** BILL, account, charge, due, score

reclaim verb REGAIN, recapture, recover, redeem, reform, retrieve, salvage

recline verb LEAN, lie (down), loll, lounge, repose, rest, sprawl

recluse noun HERMIT, anchoress, anchorite, monk, solitary

reclusive adjective SOLITARY, hermit-like, isolated, retiring, withdrawn

recognition noun **1** IDENTIFICATION, discovery, recollection, remembrance **2** ACCEPTANCE, admission, allowance, confession **3** APPRECIATION, notice, respect

recognize verb **1** IDENTIFY, know, notice, place, recall, recollect, remember, spot **2** ACCEPT, acknowledge, admit, allow, concede, grant **3** APPRECIATE, notice, respect

recoil verb **1** JERK BACK, kick, react, rebound, spring back **2** DRAW BACK, falter, quail, shrink **3** BACKFIRE, boomerang, misfire, rebound ▶ noun **4** REACTION, backlash, kick, rebound, repercussion

recollect verb REMEMBER, place, recall, summon up

recollection noun MEMORY, impression, recall, remembrance, reminiscence

recommend verb **1** ADVISE, advance, advocate, counsel, prescribe, propose, put forward, suggest **2** PRAISE, approve, commend, endorse

recommendation noun **1** ADVICE, counsel, proposal, suggestion **2** PRAISE, advocacy, approval, commendation, endorsement, reference, sanction, testimonial

recompense verb **1** REWARD, pay, remunerate **2** COMPENSATE, make up for, pay for, redress, reimburse, repay, requite ▶ noun **3** COMPENSATION, amends, damages, payment, remuneration, reparation, repayment, requital, restitution **4** REWARD, payment, return, wages

reconcile verb **1** RESOLVE, adjust, compose, put to rights, rectify, settle, square **2** REUNITE, appease, conciliate, make peace between, propitiate **3** ACCEPT, put up with (informal), resign oneself, submit, yield

reconciliation noun REUNION, conciliation, pacification, reconcilement

recondite adjective OBSCURE, arcane, concealed, dark, deep, difficult, hidden, mysterious, occult, profound, secret

recondition verb RESTORE, do up (informal), overhaul, remodel, renew, renovate, repair, revamp

reconnaissance noun INSPECTION, exploration, investigation, observation, scan, survey

reconnoiter verb INSPECT, case (slang), explore, investigate, observe, scan, spy out, survey

reconsider verb RETHINK, reassess, review, revise, think again

reconstruct verb **1** REBUILD, recreate, regenerate, remake, remodel, renovate, restore

2 DEDUCE, build up, piece together

record noun **1** DOCUMENT, account, chronicle, diary, entry, file, journal, log, register, report **2** EVIDENCE, documentation, testimony, trace, witness **3** DISC, album, LP, single, vinyl **4** BACKGROUND, career, history, performance **5 off the record** CONFIDENTIAL, not for publication, private, unofficial ▸verb **6** WRITE DOWN, chronicle, document, enter, log, minute, note, register, set down, take down **7** TAPE, make a recording of, tape-record, video, video-tape **8** REGISTER, give evidence of, indicate, say, show

recorder noun CHRONICLER, archivist, clerk, diarist, historian, scribe

recording noun RECORD, disc, tape, video

recount verb TELL, depict, describe, narrate, recite, relate, repeat, report

recoup verb **1** REGAIN, recover, retrieve, win back **2** COMPENSATE, make up for, refund, reimburse, remunerate, repay, requite

recourse noun OPTION, alternative, choice, expedient, remedy, resort, resource, way out

recover verb **1** GET BETTER, convalesce, get well, heal, improve, mend, rally, recuperate, revive **2** REGAIN, get back, recapture, reclaim, redeem, repossess, restore, retrieve

recovery noun **1** IMPROVEMENT,

convalescence, healing, mending, recuperation, revival **2** RETRIEVAL, reclamation, repossession, restoration

recreation noun PASTIME, amusement, diversion, enjoyment, entertainment, fun, hobby, leisure activity, play, relaxation, sport

recrimination noun BICKERING, counterattack, mutual accusation, quarrel, squabbling

recruit verb **1** ENLIST, draft, enroll, levy, mobilize, muster, raise **2** WIN (OVER), engage, obtain, procure ▸noun **3** BEGINNER, apprentice, convert, helper, initiate, learner, novice, trainee

rectify verb CORRECT, adjust, emend, fix, improve, redress, remedy, repair, right

rectitude noun MORALITY, decency, goodness, honesty, honor, integrity, principle, probity, virtue

recuperate verb RECOVER, convalesce, get better, improve, mend

recur verb HAPPEN AGAIN, come again, persist, reappear, repeat, return, revert

recurrent adjective PERIODIC, continued, frequent, habitual, recurring

recycle verb REPROCESS, reclaim, reuse, salvage, save

red adjective **1** CRIMSON, carmine, cherry, coral, ruby, scarlet, vermilion **2** Of hair CHESTNUT, carroty, flame-colored, reddish, sandy, titian **3** FLUSHED, blushing, embarrassed, florid, shamefaced ▸noun **4 in the**

red Informal IN DEBT, in arrears, insolvent, overdrawn **5 see red** Informal LOSE ONE'S TEMPER, blow one's top, crack up (informal), fly off the handle (informal), go ballistic (slang), go mad (informal)

red-blooded adjective Informal VIGOROUS, lusty, robust, strong, virile

redden verb FLUSH, blush, color (up), crimson, go red

redeem verb 1 MAKE UP FOR, atone for, compensate for, make amends for 2 REINSTATE, absolve, restore to favor 3 SAVE, deliver, emancipate, free, liberate, ransom 4 BUY BACK, reclaim, recover, regain, repurchase, retrieve

redemption noun 1 COMPENSATION, amends, atonement, reparation 2 SALVATION, deliverance, emancipation, liberation, release, rescue 3 REPURCHASE, reclamation, recovery, repossession, retrieval

red-handed adjective IN THE ACT, (in) flagrante delicto

redolent adjective 1 REMINISCENT, evocative, suggestive 2 SCENTED, aromatic, fragrant, odorous, perfumed, sweet-smelling

redoubtable adjective FORMIDABLE, fearful, fearsome, mighty, powerful, strong

redress verb 1 MAKE AMENDS FOR, compensate for, make up for 2 PUT RIGHT, adjust, balance, correct, even up, rectify, regulate ▶noun 3 AMENDS, atonement, compensation, payment, recompense, reparation

reduce verb 1 LESSEN, abate, curtail, cut down, decrease, diminish, lower, moderate, shorten, weaken 2 DEGRADE, break, bring low, downgrade, humble

redundant adjective SUPERFLUOUS, extra, inessential, supernumerary, surplus, unnecessary, unwanted

reek verb 1 STINK, smell ▶noun 2 STINK, fetor, odor, smell, stench

reel verb 1 STAGGER, lurch, pitch, rock, roll, sway 2 WHIRL, revolve, spin, swirl

refer verb 1 ALLUDE, bring up, cite, mention, speak of 2 RELATE, apply, belong, be relevant to, concern, pertain 3 CONSULT, apply, go, look up, turn to 4 DIRECT, guide, point, send

referee noun 1 UMPIRE, adjudicator, arbiter, arbitrator, judge, ref (informal) ▶verb 2 UMPIRE, adjudicate, arbitrate, judge, mediate

reference noun 1 CITATION, allusion, mention, note, quotation 2 TESTIMONIAL, character, credentials, endorsement, recommendation 3 RELEVANCE, applicability, bearing, connection, relation

referendum noun PUBLIC VOTE, plebiscite, popular vote

refine verb 1 PURIFY, clarify, cleanse, distill, filter, process 2 IMPROVE, hone, perfect, polish

refined adjective 1 CULTURED, civilized, cultivated, elegant, polished, polite, well-bred 2 PURE, clarified, clean, distilled, filtered, processed, purified

3 DISCERNING, delicate, discriminating, fastidious, fine, precise, sensitive

refinement noun
1 SOPHISTICATION, breeding, civility, courtesy, cultivation, culture, discrimination, gentility, good breeding, polish, taste **2** SUBTLETY, fine point, nicety, nuance **3** PURIFICATION, clarification, cleansing, distillation, filtering, processing

reflect verb **1** THROW BACK, echo, mirror, reproduce, return **2** SHOW, demonstrate, display, indicate, manifest, reveal **3** THINK, cogitate, consider, meditate, muse, ponder, ruminate, wonder

reflection noun **1** IMAGE, echo, mirror image **2** THOUGHT, cogitation, consideration, contemplation, idea, meditation, musing, observation, opinion, thinking

reflective adjective THOUGHTFUL, contemplative, meditative, pensive

reform noun **1** IMPROVEMENT, amendment, betterment, rehabilitation ▸ verb **2** IMPROVE, amend, correct, mend, rectify, restore **3** MEND ONE'S WAYS, clean up one's act (informal), go straight (informal), shape up (informal), turn over a new leaf

refractory adjective UNMANAGEABLE, difficult, disobedient, headstrong, intractable, uncontrollable, unruly, willful

refrain[1] verb STOP, abstain, avoid, cease, desist, forbear, leave off, renounce

refrain[2] noun CHORUS, melody, tune

refresh verb **1** REVIVE, brace, enliven, freshen, reinvigorate, revitalize, stimulate **2** STIMULATE, jog, prompt, renew

refreshing adjective **1** STIMULATING, bracing, fresh, invigorating **2** NEW, novel, original

refreshment noun
refreshments FOOD AND DRINK, drinks, snacks, tidbits

refrigerate verb COOL, chill, freeze, keep cold

refuge noun SHELTER, asylum, haven, hideout, protection, retreat, sanctuary

refugee noun EXILE, displaced person, émigré, escapee

refund verb **1** REPAY, pay back, reimburse, restore, return ▸ noun **2** REPAYMENT, reimbursement, return

refurbish verb RENOVATE, clean up, do up (informal), mend, overhaul, repair, restore, revamp

refusal noun DENIAL, knock-back (slang), rebuff, rejection

refuse[1] verb REJECT, decline, deny, say no, spurn, turn down, withhold

refuse[2] noun RUBBISH, garbage, junk (informal), litter, trash, waste

refute verb DISPROVE, discredit, negate, overthrow, prove false, rebut

regain verb **1** RECOVER, get back, recapture, recoup, retrieve, take back, win back **2** GET BACK TO, reach again, return to

regal adjective ROYAL, kingly or

queenly, magnificent, majestic, noble, princely

regale verb ENTERTAIN, amuse, delight, divert

regalia plural noun EMBLEMS, accoutrements, decorations, finery, paraphernalia, trappings

regard verb 1 CONSIDER, believe, deem, esteem, judge, rate, see, suppose, think, view 2 LOOK AT, behold, check out (informal), eye, gaze at, observe, scrutinize, view, watch 3 HEED, attend, listen to, mind, pay attention to, take notice of 4 as regards CONCERNING, pertaining to, regarding, relating to ▸noun 5 HEED, attention, interest, mind, notice 6 RESPECT, care, concern, consideration, esteem, thought 7 LOOK, gaze, glance, scrutiny, stare

regarding preposition CONCERNING, about, as regards, in or with regard to, on the subject of, re, respecting, with reference to

regardless adjective 1 HEEDLESS, inconsiderate, indifferent, neglectful, negligent, rash, reckless, unmindful ▸adverb 2 ANYWAY, in any case, in spite of everything, nevertheless

regards plural noun GOOD WISHES, best wishes, compliments, greetings, respects

regenerate verb RENEW, breathe new life into, invigorate, reawaken, reinvigorate, rejuvenate, restore, revive

regime noun GOVERNMENT, leadership, management, reign, rule, system

regimented adjective CONTROLLED, disciplined, ordered, organized, regulated, systematized

region noun AREA, district, locality, part, place, quarter, section, sector, territory, tract, zone

regional adjective LOCAL, district, parochial, provincial, zonal

register noun 1 LIST, archives, catalog, chronicle, diary, file, log, record, roll, roster ▸verb 2 RECORD, catalog, chronicle, enlist, enroll, enter, list, note 3 SHOW, display, exhibit, express, indicate, manifest, mark, reveal

regress verb REVERT, backslide, degenerate, deteriorate, fall away or off, go back, lapse, relapse, return

regret verb 1 FEEL SORRY ABOUT, bemoan, bewail, deplore, grieve, lament, miss, mourn, repent, rue ▸noun 2 SORROW, bitterness, compunction, contrition, penitence, remorse, repentance, ruefulness

regretful adjective SORRY, apologetic, contrite, penitent, remorseful, repentant, rueful, sad, sorrowful

regrettable adjective UNFORTUNATE, disappointing, distressing, lamentable, sad, shameful

regular adjective 1 NORMAL, common, customary, habitual, ordinary, routine, typical, usual 2 EVEN, balanced, flat, level, smooth, straight, symmetrical, uniform 3 SYSTEMATIC, consistent, constant, even, fixed, ordered, set, stated, steady, uniform

regulate verb 1 CONTROL, direct, govern, guide, handle, manage, rule, run, supervise 2 ADJUST, balance, fit, moderate, modulate, tune

regulation noun 1 RULE, decree, dictate, edict, law, order, precept, statute 2 CONTROL, direction, government, management, supervision 3 ADJUSTMENT, modulation, tuning

regurgitate verb VOMIT, barf (slang), disgorge, puke (slang), spew (out or up), throw up (informal)

rehabilitate verb 1 REINTEGRATE, adjust 2 REDEEM, clear, reform, restore, save

rehash verb 1 REWORK, refashion, rejig (informal), reuse, rewrite ▶noun 2 REWORKING, new version, rearrangement, rewrite

rehearsal noun PRACTICE, drill, preparation, rehearsing, run-through

rehearse verb PRACTICE, drill, go over, prepare, recite, repeat, run through, train

reign noun 1 RULE, command, control, dominion, monarchy, power ▶verb 2 RULE, be in power, command, govern, influence 3 BE SUPREME, hold sway, predominate, prevail

reimburse verb PAY BACK, compensate, recompense, refund, remunerate, repay, return

rein verb 1 CONTROL, check, curb, halt, hold back, limit, restrain, restrict ▶noun 2 CONTROL, brake, bridle, check, curb, harness, hold, restraint

reincarnation noun REBIRTH, transmigration of souls

reinforce verb SUPPORT, bolster, emphasize, fortify, prop, strengthen, stress, supplement, toughen

reinforcement noun 1 STRENGTHENING, augmentation, fortification, increase 2 SUPPORT, brace, buttress, prop, stay 3 **reinforcements** RESERVES, additional or fresh troops, auxiliaries, support

reinstate verb RESTORE, recall, re-establish, replace, return

reiterate verb REPEAT, do again, restate, say again

reject verb 1 DENY, decline, disallow, exclude, renounce, repudiate, veto 2 REBUFF, jilt, refuse, repulse, say no to, spurn, turn down 3 DISCARD, eliminate, jettison, scrap, throw away or out ▶noun 4 CASTOFF, discard, failure, second

rejection noun 1 DENIAL, dismissal, exclusion, renunciation, repudiation, thumbs down, veto 2 REBUFF, brushoff (slang), kick in the teeth (slang), knock-back (slang), refusal

rejig verb REARRANGE, alter, juggle, manipulate, reorganize, tweak

rejoice verb BE GLAD, be happy, be overjoyed, celebrate, exult, glory

rejoicing noun HAPPINESS, celebration, elation, exultation, gladness, joy, jubilation, merrymaking

rejoin verb REPLY, answer, respond, retort, riposte

rejoinder noun REPLY, answer,

comeback (*informal*), response, retort, riposte

rejuvenate verb REVITALIZE, breathe new life into, refresh, regenerate, reinvigorate, renew, restore

relapse verb 1 LAPSE, backslide, degenerate, fail, regress, revert, slip back 2 WORSEN, deteriorate, fade, fail, sicken, sink, weaken ▶noun 3 LAPSE, backsliding, regression, retrogression 4 WORSENING, deterioration, turn for the worse, weakening

relate verb 1 CONNECT, associate, correlate, couple, join, link 2 CONCERN, apply, be relevant to, have to do with, pertain, refer 3 TELL, describe, detail, narrate, recite, recount, report

related adjective 1 AKIN, kindred 2 ASSOCIATED, affiliated, akin, connected, interconnected, joint, linked

relation noun 1 CONNECTION, bearing, bond, comparison, correlation, link 2 RELATIVE, kin, kinsman or kinswoman 3 KINSHIP, affinity, kindred

relations plural noun 1 DEALINGS, affairs, connections, contact, interaction, intercourse, relationship 2 FAMILY, clan, kin, kindred, kinsfolk, kinsmen, relatives, tribe

relationship noun 1 ASSOCIATION, affinity, bond, connection, kinship, rapport 2 AFFAIR, liaison 3 CONNECTION, correlation, link, parallel, similarity, tie-up

relative adjective 1 DEPENDENT, allied, associated, comparative, contingent, corresponding, proportionate, related 2 RELEVANT, applicable, apposite, appropriate, apropos, germane, pertinent ▶noun 3 RELATION, kinsman or kinswoman, member of one's or the family

relatively adverb COMPARATIVELY, rather, somewhat

relax verb 1 BE or FEEL AT EASE, calm, chill out (*slang*), lighten up (*slang*), rest, take it easy, unwind 2 LESSEN, abate, ease, ebb, let up, loosen, lower, moderate, reduce, relieve, slacken, weaken

relaxation noun LEISURE, enjoyment, fun, pleasure, recreation, rest

relaxed adjective EASY-GOING, casual, comfortable, easy, free and easy, homey, informal, laid-back (*informal*), leisurely

relay noun 1 SHIFT, relief, turn 2 MESSAGE, dispatch, transmission ▶verb 3 PASS ON, broadcast, carry, communicate, send, spread, transmit

release verb 1 SET FREE, discharge, drop, extricate, free, liberate, loose, unbridle, undo, unfasten 2 ACQUIT, absolve, exonerate, let go, let off 3 ISSUE, circulate, distribute, launch, make known, make public, publish, put out ▶noun 4 LIBERATION, deliverance, discharge, emancipation, freedom, liberty 5 ACQUITTAL, absolution, exemption, exoneration 6 ISSUE, proclamation, publication

relegate verb DEMOTE, downgrade

relent verb BE MERCIFUL, capitulate, change one's mind, come round, have pity, show mercy, soften, yield

relentless *adjective*
1 UNREMITTING, incessant, nonstop, persistent, unrelenting, unrelieved
2 MERCILESS, cruel, fierce, implacable, pitiless, remorseless, ruthless, unrelenting

relevant *adjective* SIGNIFICANT, apposite, appropriate, apt, fitting, germane, pertinent, related, to the point

reliable *adjective* DEPENDABLE, faithful, safe, sound, staunch, sure, true, trustworthy

reliance *noun* TRUST, belief, confidence, dependence, faith

relic *noun* REMNANT, fragment, keepsake, memento, souvenir, trace, vestige

relief *noun* **1** EASE, comfort, cure, deliverance, mitigation, release, remedy, solace **2** REST, break, breather (*informal*), relaxation, respite **3** AID, assistance, help, succor, support

relieve *verb* **1** EASE, alleviate, assuage, calm, comfort, console, cure, mitigate, relax, soften, soothe **2** HELP, aid, assist, succor, support, sustain

religious *adjective* **1** DEVOUT, devotional, faithful, godly, holy, pious, sacred, spiritual **2** CONSCIENTIOUS, faithful, meticulous, punctilious, rigid, scrupulous

relinquish *verb* GIVE UP, abandon, cede, drop, forsake, leave, let go, renounce, surrender

relish *verb* **1** ENJOY, delight in, fancy, like, revel in, savor ▶ *noun* **2** ENJOYMENT, fancy,

fondness, gusto, liking, love, partiality, penchant, predilection, taste **3** CONDIMENT, sauce, seasoning **4** FLAVOR, piquancy, smack, spice, tang, taste, trace

reluctance *noun* UNWILLINGNESS, aversion, disinclination, dislike, distaste, loathing, repugnance

reluctant *adjective* UNWILLING, disinclined, hesitant, loath, unenthusiastic

rely *verb* DEPEND, bank, bet, count, trust

remain *verb* **1** CONTINUE, abide, dwell, endure, go on, last, persist, stand, stay, survive **2** STAY BEHIND, be left, delay, linger, wait

remainder *noun* REST, balance, excess, leavings, remains, remnant, residue, surplus

remaining *adjective* LEFT-OVER, lingering, outstanding, persisting, surviving, unfinished

remains *plural noun* **1** REMNANTS, debris, dregs, leavings, leftovers, relics, residue, rest **2** BODY, cadaver, carcass, corpse

remark *verb* **1** COMMENT, declare, mention, observe, pass comment, reflect, say, state **2** NOTICE, espy, make out, mark, note, perceive, see ▶ *noun* **3** COMMENT, observation, reflection, statement, utterance

remarkable *adjective* EXTRAORDINARY, notable, outstanding, rare, singular, striking, surprising, uncommon, unusual, wonderful

remedy *noun* **1** CURE, medicine, nostrum, treatment ▶ *verb* **2** PUT RIGHT, correct, fix, rectify, set to rights

remember verb 1 RECALL, call to mind, commemorate, look back (on), recollect, reminisce, think back 2 BEAR IN MIND, keep in mind

remembrance noun 1 MEMORY, recall, recollection, reminiscence, thought 2 SOUVENIR, commemoration, keepsake, memento, memorial, monument, reminder, token

remind verb CALL TO MIND, jog one's memory, make (someone) remember, prompt

reminisce verb RECALL, hark back, look back, recollect, remember, think back

reminiscence noun RECOLLECTION, anecdote, memoir, memory, recall, remembrance

reminiscent adjective SUGGESTIVE, evocative, similar

remiss adjective CARELESS, forgetful, heedless, lax, neglectful, negligent, thoughtless

remission noun 1 PARDON, absolution, amnesty, discharge, exemption, release, reprieve 2 LESSENING, abatement, alleviation, ebb, lull, relaxation, respite

remit verb 1 SEND, dispatch, forward, mail, post, transmit 2 CANCEL, halt, repeal, rescind, stop 3 POSTPONE, defer, delay, put off, shelve, suspend ▸ noun 4 INSTRUCTIONS, brief, guidelines, orders

remittance noun PAYMENT, allowance, fee

remnant noun REMAINDER, end, fragment, leftovers, remains, residue, rest, trace, vestige

remonstrate verb ARGUE, dispute, dissent, object, protest, take issue

remorse noun REGRET, anguish, compunction, contrition, grief, guilt, penitence, repentance, shame, sorrow

remorseful adjective REGRETFUL, apologetic, ashamed, conscience-stricken, contrite, guilty, penitent, repentant, sorry

remorseless adjective 1 PITILESS, callous, cruel, inhumane, merciless, ruthless 2 RELENTLESS, inexorable

remote adjective 1 DISTANT, far, inaccessible, in the middle of nowhere, isolated, out-of-the-way, secluded 2 ALOOF, abstracted, cold, detached, distant, reserved, standoffish, uncommunicative, withdrawn 3 SLIGHT, doubtful, dubious, faint, outside, slender, slim, small, unlikely

removal noun 1 TAKING AWAY or OFF or OUT, dislodgment, ejection, elimination, eradication, extraction, uprooting, withdrawal 2 DISMISSAL, expulsion 3 MOVE, departure, relocation, transfer

remove verb 1 TAKE AWAY or OFF or OUT, abolish, delete, detach, displace, eject, eliminate, erase, excise, extract, get rid of, wipe from the face of the earth, withdraw 2 DISMISS, depose, dethrone, discharge, expel, oust, throw out 3 MOVE, depart, flit (Scot. & Northern English dialect), relocate

remunerate verb PAY, compensate, recompense,

reimburse, repay, requite, reward

remuneration noun PAYMENT, earnings, fee, income, pay, return, reward, salary, stipend, wages

remunerative adjective PROFITABLE, economic, lucrative, moneymaking, paying, rewarding, worthwhile

renaissance, renascence noun REBIRTH, reappearance, reawakening, renewal, restoration, resurgence, revival

rend verb TEAR, rip, rupture, separate, wrench

render verb 1 MAKE, cause to become, leave 2 PROVIDE, furnish, give, hand out, pay, present, submit, supply, tender 3 PORTRAY, act, depict, do, give, perform, play, represent

rendezvous noun 1 APPOINTMENT, assignation, date, engagement, meeting, tryst 2 MEETING PLACE, gathering point, venue ▶ verb 3 MEET, assemble, come together, gather, join up

rendition noun 1 PERFORMANCE, arrangement, interpretation, portrayal, presentation, reading, rendering, version 2 TRANSLATION, interpretation, reading, transcription, version

renegade noun 1 DESERTER, apostate, defector, traitor, turncoat ▶ adjective 2 REBELLIOUS, apostate, disloyal, traitorous, unfaithful

renege verb BREAK ONE'S WORD, back out, break a promise, default, go back

renew verb 1 RECOMMENCE, continue, extend, reaffirm,

recreate, reopen, repeat, resume 2 RESTORE, mend, modernize, overhaul, refit, refurbish, renovate, repair 3 REPLACE, refresh, replenish, restock

renounce verb GIVE UP, abjure, deny, disown, forsake, forswear, quit, recant, relinquish, waive

renovate verb RESTORE, do up (informal), modernize, overhaul, recondition, refit, refurbish, renew, repair

renown noun FAME, distinction, eminence, note, reputation, repute

renowned adjective FAMOUS, celebrated, distinguished, eminent, esteemed, notable, noted, well-known

rent[1] verb 1 HIRE, charter, lease, let ▶ noun 2 HIRE, fee, lease, payment, rental

rent[2] noun TEAR, gash, hole, opening, rip, slash, slit, split

renunciation noun GIVING UP, abandonment, abdication, abjuration, denial, disavowal, forswearing, rejection, relinquishment, repudiation

reorganize verb REARRANGE, reshuffle, restructure

repair verb 1 MEND, fix, heal, patch, patch up, renovate, restore ▶ noun 2 MEND, darn, overhaul, patch, restoration

reparation noun COMPENSATION, atonement, damages, recompense, restitution, satisfaction

repartee noun WIT, badinage, banter, riposte, wittiness, wordplay

repast noun MEAL, food

repay verb 1 PAY BACK, compensate, recompense, refund, reimburse, requite, return, square 2 GET EVEN WITH (informal), avenge, hit back, reciprocate, retaliate, revenge

repeal verb 1 ABOLISH, annul, cancel, invalidate, nullify, recall, reverse, revoke ▶noun 2 ABOLITION, annulment, cancellation, invalidation, rescindment

repeat verb 1 REITERATE, echo, replay, reproduce, rerun, reshow, restate, retell ▶noun 2 REPETITION, echo, reiteration, replay, rerun, reshowing

repeatedly adverb OVER AND OVER, frequently, many times, often

repel verb 1 DISGUST, gross out (slang), nauseate, offend, revolt, sicken 2 DRIVE OFF, fight, hold off, parry, rebuff, repulse, resist, ward off

repellent adjective 1 DISGUSTING, abhorrent, hateful, horrid, loathsome, nauseating, noxious, offensive, repugnant, repulsive, revolting, scuzzy (slang), sickening 2 PROOF, impermeable, repelling, resistant

repent verb REGRET, be sorry, feel remorse, rue

repentance noun REGRET, compunction, contrition, grief, guilt, penitence, remorse

repentant adjective REGRETFUL, contrite, penitent, remorseful, rueful, sorry

repercussion noun **repercussions** CONSEQUENCES, backlash, result, sequel, side effects

repertoire noun RANGE, collection, list, repertory, stock, store, supply

repetition noun REPEATING, echo, recurrence, reiteration, renewal, replication, restatement, tautology

repetitious adjective LONG-WINDED, prolix, tautological, tedious, verbose, wordy

repetitive adjective MONOTONOUS, boring, dull, mechanical, recurrent, tedious, unchanging, unvaried

rephrase verb REWORD, paraphrase, put differently

repine verb COMPLAIN, fret, grumble, moan

replace verb TAKE THE PLACE OF, follow, oust, substitute, succeed, supersede, supplant, take over from

replacement noun SUCCESSOR, double, proxy, stand-in, substitute, surrogate, understudy

replenish verb REFILL, fill, provide, reload, replace, restore, top up

replete adjective FULL, crammed, filled, full up, glutted, gorged, stuffed

replica noun DUPLICATE, carbon copy (informal), copy, facsimile, imitation, model, reproduction

replicate verb COPY, duplicate, mimic, recreate, reduplicate, reproduce

reply verb 1 ANSWER, counter, reciprocate, rejoin, respond, retaliate, retort ▶noun 2 ANSWER, counter, counterattack, reaction, rejoinder, response, retaliation, retort, riposte

report verb 1 COMMUNICATE, broadcast, cover, describe, detail, inform of, narrate, pass on, recount, relate, state, tell 2 PRESENT ONESELF, appear, arrive, come, turn up ▶ noun 3 ACCOUNT, communication, description, narrative, news, record, statement, word 4 ARTICLE, piece, story, write-up 5 RUMOR, buzz, gossip, hearsay, talk 6 BANG, blast, boom, crack, detonation, discharge, explosion, noise, sound

reporter noun JOURNALIST, correspondent, hack (derogatory), pressman, writer

repose noun 1 PEACE, ease, quietness, relaxation, respite, rest, stillness, tranquillity 2 COMPOSURE, calmness, poise, self-possession 3 SLEEP, slumber ▶ verb 4 REST, lie, lie down, recline, rest upon

repository noun STORE, depository, storehouse, treasury, vault

reprehensible adjective BLAMEWORTHY, bad, culpable, disgraceful, shameful, unworthy

represent verb 1 STAND FOR, act for, betoken, mean, serve as, speak for, symbolize 2 SYMBOLIZE, embody, epitomize, exemplify, personify, typify 3 PORTRAY, denote, depict, describe, illustrate, outline, picture, show

representation noun PORTRAYAL, account, depiction, description, illustration, image, likeness, model, picture, portrait

representative noun 1 DELEGATE, agent, deputy,

member, proxy, spokesman or spokeswoman 2 SALESMAN, agent, commercial traveler, rep ▶ adjective 3 TYPICAL, archetypal, characteristic, exemplary, symbolic

repress verb 1 INHIBIT, bottle up, check, control, curb, hold back, restrain, stifle, suppress 2 SUBDUE, quell, subjugate

repression noun SUBJUGATION, constraint, control, despotism, domination, restraint, suppression, tyranny

repressive adjective OPPRESSIVE, absolute, authoritarian, despotic, dictatorial, tyrannical

reprieve verb 1 GRANT A STAY OF EXECUTION TO, let off the hook (slang), pardon 2 RELIEVE, abate, allay, alleviate, mitigate, palliate ▶ noun 3 STAY OF EXECUTION, amnesty, deferment, pardon, postponement, remission 4 RELIEF, alleviation, mitigation, palliation, respite

reprimand verb 1 BLAME, censure, rap over the knuckles, rebuke, scold ▶ noun 2 BLAME, censure, rebuke, reproach, reproof, talking-to (informal)

reprisal noun RETALIATION, retribution, revenge, vengeance

reproach noun 1 BLAME, censure, condemnation, disapproval, opprobrium, rebuke ▶ verb 2 BLAME, censure, condemn, criticize, lambast(e), rebuke, reprimand, scold, upbraid

reproachful adjective CRITICAL, censorious, condemnatory, disapproving, fault-finding, reproving

reprobate noun 1 SCOUNDREL,

bad egg (*old-fashioned informal*), degenerate, evildoer, miscreant, profligate, rake, rascal, villain ▶ *adjective* **2** DEPRAVED, abandoned, bad, base, corrupt, degenerate, dissolute, immoral, sinful, wicked

reproduce *verb* **1** COPY, duplicate, echo, imitate, match, mirror, recreate, repeat, replicate **2** BREED, multiply, procreate, propagate, spawn

reproduction *noun* **1** BREEDING, generation, increase, multiplication **2** COPY, duplicate, facsimile, imitation, picture, print, replica

reproof *noun* REBUKE, blame, censure, condemnation, criticism, reprimand, scolding

reprove *verb* REBUKE, berate, blame, censure, condemn, reprimand, scold, tell off (*informal*)

repudiate *verb* REJECT, deny, disavow, disclaim, disown, renounce

repugnance *noun* DISTASTE, abhorrence, aversion, disgust, dislike, hatred, loathing

repugnant *adjective* DISTASTEFUL, abhorrent, disgusting, loathsome, nauseating, offensive, repellent, revolting, sickening, vile

repulse *verb* **1** DRIVE BACK, beat off, fight off, rebuff, repel, ward off **2** REBUFF, refuse, reject, snub, spurn, turn down

repulsion *noun* DISTASTE, abhorrence, aversion, detestation, disgust, hatred, loathing, repugnance, revulsion

repulsive *adjective* DISGUSTING,

abhorrent, foul, loathsome, nauseating, repellent, revolting, scuzzy (*slang*), sickening, vile

reputable *adjective* RESPECTABLE, creditable, excellent, good, honorable, reliable, trustworthy, well-thought-of, worthy

reputation *noun* ESTIMATION, character, esteem, name, renown, repute, standing, stature

repute *noun* REPUTATION, celebrity, distinction, eminence, fame, name, renown, standing, stature

reputed *adjective* SUPPOSED, alleged, believed, considered, deemed, estimated, held, reckoned, regarded

reputedly *adverb* SUPPOSEDLY, allegedly, apparently, seemingly

request *verb* **1** ASK (FOR), appeal for, demand, desire, entreat, invite, seek, solicit ▶ *noun* **2** ASKING, appeal, call, demand, desire, entreaty, suit

require *verb* **1** NEED, crave, desire, lack, miss, want, wish **2** DEMAND, ask, bid, call upon, command, compel, exact, insist upon, oblige, order

required *adjective* NEEDED, called for, essential, necessary, obligatory, requisite

requirement *noun* NECESSITY, demand, essential, lack, must, need, prerequisite, stipulation, want

requisite *adjective* **1** NECESSARY, called for, essential, indispensable, needed, needful, obligatory, required ▶ *noun* **2** NECESSITY, condition, essential, must, need, prerequisite, requirement

requisition verb 1 DEMAND, call for, request ▸ noun 2 DEMAND, call, request, summons

requital noun RETURN, repayment

requite verb RETURN, get even, give in return, pay (someone) back in his or her own coin, reciprocate, repay, respond, retaliate

rescind verb ANNUL, cancel, countermand, declare null and void, invalidate, repeal, set aside

rescue verb 1 SAVE, deliver, get out, liberate, recover, redeem, release, salvage ▸ noun 2 LIBERATION, deliverance, recovery, redemption, release, salvage, salvation, saving

research noun 1 INVESTIGATION, analysis, examination, exploration, probe, study ▸ verb 2 INVESTIGATE, analyze, examine, explore, probe, study

resemblance noun SIMILARITY, correspondence, kinship, likeness, parallel, sameness, similitude

resemble verb BE LIKE, bear a resemblance to, be similar to, look like, mirror, parallel

resent verb BE BITTER ABOUT, begrudge, grudge, object to, take exception to, take offense at

resentful adjective BITTER, angry, embittered, grudging, indignant, miffed (informal), offended, piqued, ticked off (informal)

resentment noun BITTERNESS, animosity, bad blood, grudge, ill feeling, ill will, indignation, pique, rancor, umbrage

reservation noun 1 DOUBT, hesitancy, scruple 2 CONDITION, proviso, qualification, rider, stipulation 3 RESERVE, preserve, sanctuary, territory

reserve verb 1 KEEP, hoard, hold, put by, retain, save, set aside, stockpile, store 2 BOOK, engage, prearrange, secure ▸ noun 3 STORE, cache, fund, hoard, reservoir, savings, stock, supply 4 RESERVATION, park, preserve, sanctuary, tract 5 SHYNESS, constraint, reservation, restraint, reticence, secretiveness, silence, taciturnity ▸ adjective 6 SUBSTITUTE, auxiliary, extra, fall-back, secondary, spare

reserved adjective 1 UNCOMMUNICATIVE, restrained, reticent, retiring, secretive, shy, silent, standoffish, taciturn, undemonstrative 2 SET ASIDE, booked, engaged, held, kept, restricted, retained, spoken for, taken

reservoir noun 1 LAKE, basin, pond, tank 2 STORE, pool, reserves, source, stock, supply

reshuffle noun 1 REORGANIZATION, change, rearrangement, redistribution, regrouping, restructuring, revision ▸ verb 2 REORGANIZE, change around, rearrange, redistribute, regroup, restructure, revise

reside verb LIVE, abide, dwell, inhabit, lodge, stay

residence noun HOME, abode, domicile, dwelling, flat, habitation, house, lodging, place

resident noun INHABITANT, citizen, local, lodger, occupant, occupier, tenant

residual adjective REMAINING, leftover, unconsumed, unused, vestigial

residue noun REMAINDER, dregs, excess, extra, leftovers, remains, remnant, rest, surplus

resign verb 1 QUIT, abdicate, give in one's notice, leave, step down (informal), vacate 2 GIVE UP, abandon, forgo, forsake, relinquish, renounce, surrender, yield 3 **resign oneself** ACCEPT, acquiesce, give in, submit, succumb, yield

resignation noun 1 LEAVING, abandonment, abdication, departure 2 ENDURANCE, acceptance, acquiescence, compliance, nonresistance, passivity, patience, submission, sufferance

resigned adjective STOICAL, compliant, long-suffering, patient, subdued, unresisting

resilient adjective 1 TOUGH, buoyant, hardy, irrepressible, strong 2 FLEXIBLE, elastic, plastic, pliable, rubbery, springy, supple

resist verb 1 OPPOSE, battle, combat, defy, hinder, stand up to 2 REFRAIN FROM, abstain from, avoid, forbear, forgo, keep from 3 WITHSTAND, be proof against

resistance noun FIGHTING, battle, defiance, fight, hindrance, impediment, obstruction, opposition, struggle

resistant adjective 1 IMPERVIOUS, hard, proof against, strong, tough, unaffected by 2 OPPOSED, antagonistic, hostile, intractable, intransigent, unwilling

resolute adjective DETERMINED, dogged, firm, fixed, immovable, inflexible, set, steadfast, strong-willed, tenacious, unshakable, unwavering

resolution noun 1 DETERMINATION, doggedness, firmness, perseverance, purpose, resoluteness, resolve, steadfastness, tenacity, willpower 2 DECISION, aim, declaration, determination, intent, intention, purpose, resolve

resolve verb 1 DECIDE, agree, conclude, determine, fix, intend, purpose 2 BREAK DOWN, analyze, reduce, separate 3 WORK OUT, answer, clear up, crack, fathom ▶noun 4 DETERMINATION, firmness, resoluteness, resolution, steadfastness, willpower 5 DECISION, intention, objective, purpose, resolution

resonant adjective ECHOING, booming, resounding, reverberating, ringing, sonorous

resort verb 1 **resort to** USE, employ, fall back on, have recourse to, turn to, utilize ▶noun 2 HOLIDAY CENTER, haunt, retreat, spot, tourist center 3 RECOURSE, reference

resound verb ECHO, re-echo, resonate, reverberate, ring

resounding adjective ECHOING, booming, full, powerful, resonant, reverberating, ringing, sonorous

resource noun 1 INGENUITY, ability, capability, cleverness, initiative, inventiveness 2 MEANS, course, device, expedient, resort

resourceful adjective INGENIOUS, able, bright, capable, clever, creative, inventive

resources plural noun RESERVES, assets, capital, funds, holdings, money, riches, supplies, wealth

respect noun 1 REGARD, admiration, consideration, deference, esteem, estimation, honor, recognition 2 POINT, aspect, characteristic, detail, feature, matter, particular, sense, way 3 RELATION, bearing, connection, reference, regard ▶verb 4 THINK HIGHLY OF, admire, defer to, esteem, have a good or high opinion of, honor, look up to, value 5 SHOW CONSIDERATION FOR, abide by, adhere to, comply with, follow, heed, honor, obey, observe

respectable adjective
1 HONORABLE, decent, estimable, good, honest, reputable, upright, worthy 2 REASONABLE, ample, appreciable, considerable, decent, fair, sizable or sizeable, substantial

respectful adjective POLITE, civil, courteous, deferential, mannerly, reverent, well-mannered

respective adjective SPECIFIC, individual, own, particular, relevant

respite noun PAUSE, break, cessation, halt, interval, lull, recess, relief, rest

resplendent adjective BRILLIANT, bright, dazzling, glorious, radiant, shining, splendid

respond verb ANSWER, counter, react, reciprocate, rejoin, reply, retort, return

response noun ANSWER, counterattack, feedback, reaction, rejoinder, reply, retort, return

responsibility noun 1 AUTHORITY, importance, power 2 FAULT, blame, culpability, guilt 3 DUTY, care, charge, liability, obligation, onus
4 LEVEL-HEADEDNESS, conscientiousness, dependability, rationality, sensibleness, trustworthiness

responsible adjective 1 IN CHARGE, in authority, in control 2 TO BLAME, at fault, culpable, guilty 3 ACCOUNTABLE, answerable, liable 4 SENSIBLE, dependable, level-headed, rational, reliable, trustworthy

responsive adjective SENSITIVE, alive, impressionable, open, reactive, receptive, susceptible

rest[1] noun 1 REPOSE, calm, inactivity, leisure, relaxation, relief, stillness, tranquillity
2 PAUSE, break, cessation, halt, interlude, intermission, interval, lull, respite, stop 3 SUPPORT, base, holder, prop, stand ▶verb
4 RELAX, be at ease, put one's feet up, sit down, take it easy
5 BE SUPPORTED, lean, lie, prop, recline, repose, sit

rest[2] noun REMAINDER, balance, excess, others, remains, remnants, residue, surplus

restaurant noun BISTRO, café, cafeteria, diner, eatery, tearoom

restful adjective RELAXING, calm, calming, peaceful, quiet, relaxed, serene, soothing, tranquil

restitution noun COMPENSATION, amends, recompense,

reparation, requital

restive *adjective* RESTLESS, edgy, fidgety, impatient, jumpy, nervous, on edge, wired (*slang*)

restless *adjective* **1** MOVING, nomadic, roving, transient, unsettled, unstable, wandering **2** UNSETTLED, antsy (*slang*), edgy, fidgeting, fidgety, jumpy, nervous, on edge, restive, wired (*slang*)

restlessness *noun* **1** MOVEMENT, activity, bustle, unrest, unsettledness **2** RESTIVENESS, edginess, jitters (*informal*), jumpiness, nervousness

restoration *noun* **1** REPAIR, reconstruction, renewal, renovation, revitalization, revival **2** REINSTATEMENT, re-establishment, replacement, restitution, return

restore *verb* **1** REPAIR, fix, mend, rebuild, recondition, reconstruct, refurbish, renew, renovate **2** REVIVE, build up, refresh, revitalize, strengthen **3** RETURN, bring back, give back, hand back, recover, reinstate, replace, send back **4** REINSTATE, reintroduce

restrain *verb* HOLD BACK, check, constrain, contain, control, curb, curtail, hamper, hinder, inhibit, restrict

restrained *adjective* CONTROLLED, calm, mild, moderate, self-controlled, undemonstrative

restraint *noun* **1** SELF-CONTROL, control, inhibition, moderation, self-discipline, self-possession, self-restraint **2** LIMITATION, ban, check, curb, embargo, interdict, limit, rein

restrict *verb* LIMIT, bound, confine, contain, hamper, handicap, inhibit, regulate, restrain

restriction *noun* LIMITATION, confinement, control, curb, handicap, inhibition, regulation, restraint, rule

result *noun* **1** CONSEQUENCE, effect, end, end result, outcome, product, sequel, upshot ▶ *verb* **2** HAPPEN, appear, arise, derive, develop, ensue, follow, issue, spring **3** result in END IN, culminate in, finish with

resume *verb* BEGIN AGAIN, carry on, continue, go on, proceed, reopen, restart

résumé *noun* SUMMARY, précis, recapitulation, rundown, synopsis

resumption *noun* CONTINUATION, carrying on, re-establishment, renewal, reopening, restart, resurgence

resurgence *noun* REVIVAL, rebirth, re-emergence, renaissance, resumption, resurrection, return

resurrect *verb* REVIVE, bring back, reintroduce, renew

resurrection *noun* REVIVAL, reappearance, rebirth, renaissance, renewal, restoration, resurgence, return

resuscitate *verb* REVIVE, bring round, resurrect, revitalize, save

retain *verb* **1** KEEP, hold, hold back, maintain, preserve, reserve, save **2** HIRE, commission, employ, engage, pay, reserve

retainer *noun* **1** FEE, advance, deposit **2** SERVANT, attendant, domestic

retaliate *verb* PAY (SOMEONE) BACK,

get even with (*informal*), hit back, reciprocate, strike back, take revenge

retaliation noun REVENGE, an eye for an eye, counterblow, reciprocation, repayment, reprisal, requital, vengeance

retard verb SLOW DOWN, arrest, check, delay, handicap, hinder, hold back *or* up, impede, set back

retch verb GAG, barf (*slang*), heave, puke (*slang*), regurgitate, spew, throw up (*informal*), vomit

reticence noun SILENCE, quietness, reserve, taciturnity

reticent adjective UNCOMMUNICATIVE, close-lipped, quiet, reserved, silent, taciturn, tight-lipped, unforthcoming

retinue noun ATTENDANTS, aides, entourage, escort, followers, servants

retire verb 1 STOP WORKING, give up work 2 WITHDRAW, depart, exit, go away, leave 3 GO TO BED, hit the hay (*slang*), hit the sack (*slang*), turn in (*informal*)

retirement noun WITHDRAWAL, privacy, retreat, seclusion, solitude

retiring adjective SHY, bashful, quiet, reserved, self-effacing, timid, unassertive, unassuming

retort verb 1 REPLY, answer, come back with, counter, respond, return, riposte ▶noun 2 REPLY, answer, comeback (*informal*), rejoinder, response, riposte

retract verb 1 WITHDRAW, deny, disavow, disclaim, eat one's words, recant, renege, renounce, revoke, take back

2 DRAW IN, pull back, pull in, sheathe

retreat verb 1 WITHDRAW, back away, back off, depart, draw back, fall back, go back, leave, pull back ▶noun 2 WITHDRAWAL, departure, evacuation, flight, retirement 3 REFUGE, haven, hideaway, sanctuary, seclusion, shelter

retrench verb CUT BACK, economize, make economies, save, tighten one's belt

retrenchment noun CUTBACK, cost-cutting, cut, economy, tightening one's belt

retribution noun PUNISHMENT, justice, Nemesis, reckoning, reprisal, retaliation, revenge, vengeance

retrieve verb GET BACK, recapture, recoup, recover, redeem, regain, restore, save, win back

retrograde adjective DECLINING, backward, degenerative, deteriorating, downward, regressive, retrogressive, worsening

retrogress verb DECLINE, backslide, deteriorate, go back, go downhill (*informal*), regress, relapse, worsen

retrospect noun HINDSIGHT, re-examination, review

return verb 1 COME BACK, go back, reappear, rebound, recur, retreat, revert, turn back 2 PUT BACK, re-establish, reinstate, replace, restore 3 GIVE BACK, pay back, recompense, refund, reimburse, repay 4 REPLY, answer, respond, retort 5 ELECT, choose, vote in ▶noun 6 RESTORATION, re-establishment, reinstatement **7** REAPPEARANCE, recurrence **8** RETREAT, rebound, recoil **9** PROFIT, gain, income, interest, proceeds, revenue, takings, yield **10** REPORT, account, form, list, statement, summary **11** REPLY, answer, comeback (*informal*), rejoinder, response, retort

revamp verb RENOVATE, do up (*informal*), overhaul, recondition, refurbish, restore

reveal verb **1** MAKE KNOWN, announce, disclose, divulge, give away, impart, let out, let slip, make public, proclaim, tell **2** SHOW, display, exhibit, manifest, uncover, unearth, unmask, unveil

revel verb **1** CELEBRATE, carouse, live it up (*informal*), make merry **2** revel in ENJOY, delight in, indulge in, lap up, luxuriate in, relish, take pleasure in, thrive on ▶*noun* **3** (*often plural*) MERRYMAKING, carousal, celebration, festivity, party, spree

revelation noun DISCLOSURE, exhibition, exposé, exposure, news, proclamation, publication, uncovering, unearthing, unveiling

reveller noun CAROUSER, merrymaker, partygoer

revelry noun FESTIVITY, carousal, celebration, fun, jollity, merrymaking, party, spree

revenge noun **1** RETALIATION, an eye for an eye, reprisal, retribution, vengeance ▶*verb* **2** AVENGE, get even, hit back, repay, retaliate, take revenge for

revenue noun INCOME, gain,

proceeds, profits, receipts, returns, takings, yield

reverberate verb ECHO, re-echo, resound, ring, vibrate

revere verb BE IN AWE OF, exalt, honor, look up to, respect, reverence, venerate, worship

reverence noun AWE, admiration, high esteem, honor, respect, veneration, worship

reverent adjective RESPECTFUL, awed, deferential, humble, reverential

reverie noun DAYDREAM, abstraction, brown study, woolgathering

reverse verb **1** TURN ROUND, invert, transpose, turn back, turn over, turn upside down, upend **2** CHANGE, annul, cancel, countermand, invalidate, overrule, overthrow, overturn, quash, repeal, rescind, revoke, undo **3** GO BACKWARDS, back, back up, move backwards, retreat ▶*noun* **4** OPPOSITE, contrary, converse, inverse **5** BACK, other side, rear, underside, wrong side **6** MISFORTUNE, adversity, affliction, blow, disappointment, failure, hardship, misadventure, mishap, reversal, setback ▶*adjective* **7** OPPOSITE, contrary, converse

revert verb RETURN, come back, go back, resume

review noun **1** CRITIQUE, commentary, criticism, evaluation, judgment, notice **2** MAGAZINE, journal, periodical **3** SURVEY, analysis, examination, scrutiny, study **4** Military

INSPECTION, march past, parade ▶ *verb* **5** ASSESS, criticize, evaluate, judge, study **6** RECONSIDER, reassess, re-evaluate, re-examine, rethink, revise, think over **7** LOOK BACK ON, recall, recollect, reflect on, remember **8** INSPECT, examine **9** STUDY, cram (*informal*), revise (*chiefly Brit.*)

reviewer *noun* CRITIC, commentator, judge

revile *verb* MALIGN, abuse, bad-mouth (*slang*), denigrate, knock (*informal*), reproach, run down, vilify

revise *verb* CHANGE, alter, amend, correct, edit, emend, redo, review, rework, update

revision *noun* CHANGE, amendment, correction, emendation, updating

revival *noun* RENEWAL, reawakening, rebirth, renaissance, resurgence, resurrection, revitalization

revive *verb* REVITALIZE, awaken, bring round, come round, invigorate, reanimate, recover, refresh, rekindle, renew, restore

revoke *verb* CANCEL, annul, countermand, disclaim, invalidate, negate, nullify, obviate, quash, repeal, rescind, retract, reverse, set aside, withdraw

revolt *noun* **1** UPRISING, insurgency, insurrection, mutiny, rebellion, revolution, rising *verb* **2** REBEL, mutiny, resist, rise **3** DISGUST, gross out (*slang*), make one's flesh creep, nauseate, repel, repulse, sicken, turn one's stomach

revolting *adjective* DISGUSTING, foul, horrible, horrid, nauseating, repellent, repugnant, repulsive, scuzzy (*slang*), sickening, yucky or yukky (*slang*)

revolution *noun* **1** REVOLT, coup, insurgency, mutiny, rebellion, rising, uprising **2** TRANSFORMATION, innovation, reformation, sea change, shift, upheaval **3** ROTATION, circle, circuit, cycle, lap, orbit, spin, turn

revolutionary *adjective* **1** REBEL, extremist, insurgent, radical, subversive **2** NEW, different, drastic, ground-breaking, innovative, novel, progressive, radical ▶ *noun* **3** REBEL, insurgent, revolutionist

revolutionize *verb* TRANSFORM, modernize, reform

revolve *verb* ROTATE, circle, go round, orbit, spin, turn, twist, wheel, whirl

revulsion *noun* DISGUST, abhorrence, detestation, loathing, repugnance, repulsion

reward *noun* **1** PAYMENT, bonus, bounty, premium, prize, recompense, repayment, return, wages **2** PUNISHMENT, just deserts, retribution ▶ *verb* **3** PAY, compensate, recompense, remunerate, repay

rewarding *adjective* WORTHWHILE, beneficial, enriching, fruitful, fulfilling, productive, profitable, satisfying, valuable

rhapsodize *verb* ENTHUSE, go into ecstasies, gush, rave (*informal*)

rhetoric *noun* **1** ORATORY, eloquence **2** HYPERBOLE,

bombast, grandiloquence,
magniloquence, verbosity,
wordiness

rhetorical adjective ORATORICAL,
bombastic, declamatory,
grandiloquent, high-flown,
magniloquent, verbose

rhyme noun **1** POETRY, ode,
poem, song, verse ▶ verb
2 SOUND LIKE, harmonize

rhythm noun BEAT, accent,
cadence, lilt, meter, pulse,
swing, tempo, time

rhythmic, rhythmical adjective
CADENCED, lilting, metrical,
musical, periodic, pulsating,
throbbing

ribald adjective RUDE, bawdy,
blue, broad, coarse, earthy,
naughty, obscene, racy,
smutty, vulgar

rich adjective **1** WEALTHY, affluent,
loaded (slang), moneyed,
prosperous, well-heeled
(informal), well-off, well-to-do
2 WELL-STOCKED, full, productive,
well-supplied **3** ABUNDANT,
abounding, ample, copious,
fertile, fruitful, lush, luxurious,
plentiful, productive, prolific
4 FULL-BODIED, creamy, fatty,
luscious, succulent, sweet, tasty

riches plural noun WEALTH,
affluence, assets, fortune,
plenty, resources, substance,
treasure

richly adverb **1** ELABORATELY,
elegantly, expensively,
exquisitely, gorgeously,
lavishly, luxuriously, opulently,
splendidly, sumptuously
2 FULLY, amply, appropriately,
properly, suitably, thoroughly,
well

rickety adjective SHAKY, insecure,

precarious, ramshackle,
tottering, unsound, unsteady,
wobbly

rid verb **1** FREE, clear, deliver,
disburden, disencumber, make
free, purge, relieve, unburden
2 get rid of DISPOSE OF, dump,
eject, eliminate, expel, remove,
throw away or out

riddle noun PUZZLE, conundrum,
enigma, mystery, poser,
problem

riddled adjective FILLED,
damaged, infested, permeated,
pervaded, spoilt

ride verb **1** CONTROL, handle,
manage **2** TRAVEL, be carried,
go, move ▶ noun **3** TRIP, drive,
jaunt, journey, lift, outing

ridicule noun **1** MOCKERY, chaff,
derision, gibe, jeer, laughter,
raillery, scorn ▶ verb **2** LAUGH AT,
chaff, deride, jeer, make fun of,
mock, poke fun at, sneer

ridiculous adjective LAUGHABLE,
absurd, comical, farcical,
funny, ludicrous, risible, silly,
stupid

rife adjective WIDESPREAD,
common, frequent, general,
prevalent, rampant, ubiquitous,
universal

riffraff noun RABBLE, dregs of
society (slang), hoi polloi, scum
of the earth (slang)

rifle verb RANSACK, burgle, go
through, loot, pillage, plunder,
rob, sack, strip

rift noun **1** BREACH,
disagreement, division, falling
out (informal), quarrel,
separation, split **2** SPLIT, break,
cleft, crack, crevice, fault,
fissure, flaw, gap, opening

rig verb **1** FIX (informal), arrange,

engineer, gerrymander, manipulate, tamper with **2** EQUIP, fit out, furnish, supply ▶ *noun* **3** APPARATUS, equipment, fittings, fixtures, gear, tackle

right *adjective* **1** JUST, equitable, ethical, fair, good, honest, lawful, moral, proper **2** CORRECT, accurate, exact, factual, genuine, precise, true, valid **3** PROPER, appropriate, becoming, desirable, done, fit, fitting, seemly, suitable ▶ *adverb* **4** CORRECTLY, accurately, exactly, genuinely, precisely, truly **5** PROPERLY, appropriately, aptly, fittingly, suitably **6** STRAIGHT, directly, promptly, quickly, straightaway **7** EXACTLY, precisely, squarely ▶ *noun* **8** CLAIM, authority, business, due, freedom, liberty, license, permission, power, prerogative, privilege ▶ *verb* **9** RECTIFY, correct, fix, put right, redress, settle, sort out, straighten

right away *adverb* IMMEDIATELY, at once, directly, forthwith, instantly, now, pronto (*informal*), straightaway

righteous *adjective* VIRTUOUS, ethical, fair, good, honest, honorable, just, moral, pure, upright

righteousness *noun* VIRTUE, goodness, honesty, honor, integrity, justice, morality, probity, purity, rectitude, uprightness

rightful *adjective* LAWFUL, due, just, legal, legitimate, proper, real, true, valid

rigid *adjective* **1** STRICT, exact, fixed, inflexible, rigorous, set, stringent, unbending,

uncompromising **2** STIFF, inflexible, unyielding

rigmarole *noun* PROCEDURE, bother, fuss, hassle (*informal*), nonsense, palaver

rigor *noun* **1** STRICTNESS, harshness, inflexibility, rigidity, sternness, stringency **2** HARDSHIP, ordeal, privation, suffering, trial

rigorous *adjective* STRICT, demanding, exacting, hard, harsh, inflexible, severe, stern, stringent, tough

rig-out *noun* OUTFIT, costume, dress, garb, gear, get-up (*informal*), togs

rig out *verb* **1** DRESS, array, attire, clothe, costume **2** EQUIP, fit, furnish, outfit

rig up *verb* SET UP, arrange, assemble, build, construct, erect, fix up, improvise, put together, put up

rile *verb* ANGER, aggravate (*informal*), annoy, get or put one's back up, irk, irritate

rim *noun* EDGE, border, brim, brink, lip, margin, verge

rind *noun* SKIN, crust, husk, outer layer, peel

ring¹ *verb* **1** CHIME, clang, peal, reverberate, sound, toll **2** PHONE, buzz (*informal*), call, telephone ▶ *noun* **3** CHIME, knell, peal **4** CALL, buzz (*informal*), phone call

ring² *noun* **1** CIRCLE, band, circuit, halo, hoop, loop, round **2** ARENA, circus, enclosure, rink **3** GANG, association, band, cartel, circle, group, mob, syndicate ▶ *verb* **4** ENCIRCLE, enclose, gird, girdle, surround

rinse *verb* **1** WASH, bathe, clean,

cleanse, dip, splash ▶ *noun*
2 WASH, bath, dip, splash

riot *noun* **1** DISTURBANCE,
anarchy, confusion, disorder,
lawlessness, strife, tumult,
turbulence, turmoil, upheaval
2 REVELRY, carousal, festivity,
frolic, high jinks, merrymaking
3 PROFUSION, display,
extravaganza, show, splash
4 run riot: a RAMPAGE, be out of
control, go wild **b** GROW
PROFUSELY, spread like wildfire
▶ *verb* **5** RAMPAGE, go on the
rampage, run riot

riotous *adjective* **1** UNRESTRAINED,
boisterous, loud, noisy,
uproarious, wild **2** UNRULY,
anarchic, disorderly, lawless,
rebellious, rowdy,
ungovernable, violent

rip *verb* **1** TEAR, burst, claw, cut,
gash, lacerate, rend, slash, slit,
split ▶ *noun* **2** TEAR, cut, gash,
hole, laceration, rent, slash, slit,
split

ripe *adjective* **1** MATURE, mellow,
ready, ripened, seasoned
2 SUITABLE, auspicious,
favorable, ideal, opportune,
right, timely

ripen *verb* MATURE, burgeon,
develop, grow ripe, season

rip-off *noun* SWINDLE, cheat, con
(*informal*), con trick (*informal*),
fraud, scam (*slang*), theft

rip off *verb Slang* SWINDLE, cheat,
con (*informal*), defraud, fleece,
rob

riposte *noun* **1** RETORT, answer,
comeback (*informal*), rejoinder,
reply, response, sally ▶ *verb*
2 RETORT, answer, come back,
reply, respond

rise *verb* **1** GET UP, arise, get to

one's feet, stand up **2** GO UP,
ascend, climb **3** ADVANCE, get
on, progress, prosper **4** GET
STEEPER, ascend, go uphill, slope
upwards **5** INCREASE, go up,
grow, intensify, mount **6** REBEL,
mutiny, revolt **7** ORIGINATE,
happen, issue, occur, spring
▶ *noun* **8** INCREASE, upsurge,
upswing, upturn
9 ADVANCEMENT, climb, progress,
promotion **10** UPWARD SLOPE,
ascent, elevation, incline
11 give rise to CAUSE, bring
about, effect, produce, result in

risk *noun* **1** DANGER, chance,
gamble, hazard, jeopardy,
peril, pitfall, possibility ▶ *verb*
2 DARE, chance, endanger,
gamble, hazard, imperil,
jeopardize, venture

risky *adjective* DANGEROUS,
chancy (*informal*), hazardous,
perilous, uncertain, unsafe

risqué *adjective* SUGGESTIVE,
bawdy, blue, improper,
indelicate, naughty, racy, ribald

rite *noun* CEREMONY, custom,
observance, practice,
procedure, ritual

ritual *noun* **1** CEREMONY,
observance, rite **2** CUSTOM,
convention, habit, practice,
procedure, protocol, routine,
tradition ▶ *adjective*
3 CEREMONIAL, conventional,
customary, habitual, routine

rival *noun* **1** OPPONENT,
adversary, competitor,
contender, contestant
▶ *adjective* **2** COMPETING,
conflicting, opposing ▶ *verb*
3 EQUAL, be a match for, come
up to, compare with, compete,
match

rivalry noun COMPETITION, conflict, contention, contest, opposition

river noun 1 STREAM, brook, creek, tributary, waterway 2 FLOW, flood, rush, spate, torrent

riveting adjective ENTHRALLING, absorbing, captivating, engrossing, fascinating, gripping, hypnotic, spellbinding

road noun WAY, course, highway, lane, motorway, path, pathway, roadway, route, track

roam verb WANDER, prowl, ramble, range, rove, stray, travel, walk

roar verb 1 CRY, bawl, bay, bellow, howl, shout, yell 2 GUFFAW, hoot, laugh heartily, split one's sides (informal) ▶noun 3 CRY, bawl, bellow, howl, outcry, shout, yell 4 GUFFAW, hoot

rob verb STEAL FROM, burgle, cheat, con (informal), defraud, deprive, dispossess, hold up, loot, mug (informal), pillage, plunder, raid

robber noun THIEF, bandit, burglar, cheat, con man (informal), fraud, looter, mugger (informal), plunderer, raider, stealer

robbery noun THEFT, burglary, hold-up, larceny, mugging (informal), pillage, plunder, raid, rip-off (slang), stealing, stick-up (slang), swindle

robe noun 1 GOWN, costume, habit ▶verb 2 CLOTHE, dress, garb

robot noun MACHINE, android, automaton, mechanical man

robust adjective STRONG, fit, hale, hardy, healthy, muscular, powerful, stout, strapping, sturdy, tough, vigorous

rock¹ noun STONE, boulder

rock² verb 1 SWAY, lurch, pitch, reel, roll, swing, toss 2 SHOCK, astonish, astound, shake, stagger, stun, surprise

rocky¹ adjective ROUGH, craggy, rugged, stony

rocky² adjective UNSTABLE, rickety, shaky, unsteady, wobbly

rod noun STICK, bar, baton, cane, pole, shaft, staff, wand

rogue noun SCOUNDREL, crook (informal), fraud, rascal, scamp, villain

role noun 1 JOB, capacity, duty, function, part, position, post, task 2 PART, character, portrayal, representation

roll verb 1 TURN, go round, revolve, rotate, spin, swivel, trundle, twirl, wheel, whirl 2 WIND, bind, enfold, envelop, furl, swathe, wrap 3 FLOW, run, undulate 4 LEVEL, even, flatten, press, smooth 5 TUMBLE, lurch, reel, rock, sway, toss ▶noun 6 TURN, cycle, reel, revolution, rotation, spin, twirl, wheel, whirl 7 REGISTER, census, index, list, record 8 RUMBLE, boom, reverberation, roar, thunder

rollicking adjective BOISTEROUS, carefree, devil-may-care, exuberant, hearty, jaunty, lively, playful

roly-poly adjective PLUMP, buxom, chubby, fat, rounded, tubby

romance noun 1 LOVE AFFAIR, affair, amour, attachment, liaison, relationship

2 EXCITEMENT, charm, color, fascination, glamour, mystery **3** STORY, fairy tale, fantasy, legend, love story, melodrama, tale

romantic *adjective* **1** LOVING, amorous, fond, passionate, sentimental, tender **2** IDEALISTIC, dreamy, impractical, starry-eyed, unrealistic **3** EXCITING, colorful, fascinating, glamorous, mysterious ▶ *noun* **4** IDEALIST, dreamer, sentimentalist

romp *verb* **1** FROLIC, caper, cavort, frisk, gambol, have fun, sport **2** WIN EASILY, walk it (*informal*), win by a mile (*informal*), win hands down ▶ *noun* **3** FROLIC, caper, lark (*informal*)

room *noun* **1** CHAMBER, apartment, office **2** SPACE, area, capacity, expanse, extent, leeway, margin, range, scope **3** OPPORTUNITY, chance, occasion, scope

roomy *adjective* SPACIOUS, ample, broad, capacious, commodious, extensive, generous, large, sizable *or* sizeable, wide

root[1] *noun* **1** STEM, rhizome, tuber **2** SOURCE, base, bottom, cause, core, foundation, heart, nucleus, origin, seat, seed **3 roots** SENSE OF BELONGING, birthplace, cradle, family, heritage, home, origins ▶ *verb* **4** ESTABLISH, anchor, fasten, fix, ground, implant, moor, set, stick

root[2] *verb* DIG, burrow, ferret

rooted *adjective* DEEP-SEATED, confirmed, deep, deeply felt,

entrenched, established, firm, fixed, ingrained

root out *verb* GET RID OF, abolish, do away with, eliminate, eradicate, exterminate, extirpate, remove, weed out

rope *noun* **1** CORD, cable, hawser, line, strand **2 know the ropes** BE EXPERIENCED, be an old hand, be knowledgeable

rope in *verb* PERSUADE, engage, enlist, inveigle, involve, talk into

roster *noun* ROTA, agenda, catalog, list, register, roll, schedule, table

rostrum *noun* STAGE, dais, platform, podium, stand

rosy *adjective* **1** PINK, red **2** GLOWING, blooming, healthy-looking, radiant, ruddy **3** PROMISING, auspicious, bright, cheerful, encouraging, favorable, hopeful, optimistic

rot *verb* **1** DECAY, crumble, decompose, deteriorate, go bad, molder, perish, putrefy, spoil **2** DETERIORATE, decline, waste away ▶ *noun* **3** DECAY, blight, canker, corruption, decomposition, mold, putrefaction

rotary *adjective* REVOLVING, rotating, spinning, turning

rotate *verb* **1** REVOLVE, go round, gyrate, pivot, reel, spin, swivel, turn, wheel **2** TAKE TURNS, alternate, switch

rotation *noun* **1** REVOLUTION, orbit, reel, spin, spinning, turn, turning, wheel **2** SEQUENCE, alternation, cycle, succession, switching

rotten *adjective* **1** DECAYING, bad, corrupt, crumbling,

decomposing, festering, funky
(*slang*), moldy, perished,
putrescent, rank, smelly, sour,
stinking **2** CORRUPT, crooked
(*informal*), dishonest,
dishonorable, immoral,
perfidious **3** *Informal* DESPICABLE,
base, contemptible, dirty, lousy
(*slang*), mean, nasty, scuzzy
(*slang*)

rotund *adjective* **1** ROUND,
globular, rounded, spherical
2 PLUMP, chubby, corpulent,
fat, fleshy, portly, stout, tubby

rough *adjective* **1** UNEVEN,
broken, bumpy, craggy,
irregular, jagged, rocky, stony
2 UNGRACIOUS, blunt, brusque,
coarse, impolite, rude,
unceremonious, uncivil,
uncouth, unmannerly
3 APPROXIMATE, estimated,
general, imprecise, inexact,
sketchy, vague **4** STORMY,
choppy, squally, turbulent,
wild **5** NASTY, cruel, hard,
harsh, tough, unfeeling,
unpleasant, violent **6** BASIC,
crude, imperfect, incomplete,
rudimentary, sketchy,
unfinished, unpolished,
unrefined **7** UNPLEASANT,
arduous, hard, tough,
uncomfortable ▶ **8 rough
out** OUTLINE, draft, plan, sketch
▶ *noun* **8** OUTLINE, draft,
mock-up, preliminary sketch

rough-and-ready *adjective*
MAKESHIFT, crude, improvised,
provisional, sketchy, stopgap,
unpolished, unrefined

round *adjective* **1** SPHERICAL,
circular, curved, cylindrical,
globular, rotund, rounded
2 PLUMP, ample, fleshy, full,
full-fleshed, rotund ▶ *verb* **3** GO

ROUND, bypass, circle, encircle,
flank, skirt, turn ▶ *noun*
4 SPHERE, ball, band, circle, disc,
globe, orb, ring **5** STAGE,
division, lap, level, period,
session, turn **6** SERIES, cycle,
sequence, session, succession
7 COURSE, beat, circuit, routine,
schedule, series, tour

roundabout *adjective* INDIRECT,
circuitous, devious, discursive,
evasive, oblique, tortuous

round off *verb* COMPLETE, close,
conclude, finish off

roundup *noun* GATHERING,
assembly, collection, herding,
marshalling, muster, rally

round up *verb* GATHER, collect,
drive, group, herd, marshal,
muster, rally

rouse *verb* **1** WAKE UP, awaken,
call, rise, wake **2** EXCITE, agitate,
anger, animate, incite, inflame,
move, provoke, stimulate, stir

rousing *adjective* LIVELY, exciting,
inspiring, moving, spirited,
stimulating, stirring

rout *noun* **1** DEFEAT, beating,
debacle, drubbing, overthrow,
thrashing ▶ *verb* **2** DEFEAT, beat,
conquer, crush, destroy, drub,
overthrow, thrash, trounce,
wipe the floor with (*informal*)

route *noun* WAY, beat, circuit,
course, direction, itinerary,
journey, path, road

routine *noun* **1** PROCEDURE,
custom, method, order,
pattern, practice, program
▶ *adjective* **2** USUAL, customary,
everyday, habitual, normal,
ordinary, standard, typical
3 BORING, dull, humdrum,
predictable, tedious, tiresome

rove *verb* WANDER, drift, ramble,

range, roam, stray, traipse (*informal*)

row¹ noun LINE, bank, column, file, range, series, string

row² noun 1 DISPUTE, brawl, quarrel, squabble, tiff, trouble 2 DISTURBANCE, commotion, noise, racket, rumpus, tumult, uproar ▸verb 3 QUARREL, argue, dispute, fight, squabble, wrangle

rowdy adjective 1 DISORDERLY, loud, noisy, rough, unruly, wild ▸noun 2 HOOLIGAN, lout, ruffian

royal adjective 1 REGAL, imperial, kingly, princely, queenly, sovereign 2 SPLENDID, grand, impressive, magnificent, majestic, stately

rub verb 1 POLISH, clean, scour, shine, wipe 2 CHAFE, abrade, fray, grate, scrape ▸noun 3 POLISH, shine, stroke, wipe 4 MASSAGE, caress, kneading

rubbish noun 1 WASTE, garbage, junk (*informal*), litter, lumber, refuse, scrap, trash 2 NONSENSE, claptrap (*informal*), garbage, hogwash, hot air (*informal*), trash, tripe (*informal*)

rub out verb ERASE, cancel, delete, efface, obliterate, remove, wipe out

ruckus noun Informal UPROAR, commotion, disturbance, fracas, fuss, hoopla, trouble

ruddy adjective ROSY, blooming, fresh, glowing, healthy, radiant, red, reddish, rosy-cheeked

rude adjective 1 IMPOLITE, abusive, cheeky, discourteous, disrespectful, ill-mannered, impertinent, impudent, insolent, insulting, uncivil,

unmannerly 2 VULGAR, boorish, brutish, coarse, graceless, loutish, oafish, rough, uncivilized, uncouth, uncultured 3 UNPLEASANT, abrupt, harsh, sharp, startling, sudden 4 ROUGHLY-MADE, artless, crude, inartistic, inelegant, makeshift, primitive, raw, rough, simple

rudimentary adjective BASIC, early, elementary, fundamental, initial, primitive, undeveloped

rudiments plural noun BASICS, beginnings, elements, essentials, foundation, fundamentals

rue verb REGRET, be sorry for, kick oneself for, lament, mourn, repent

rueful adjective REGRETFUL, contrite, mournful, penitent, remorseful, repentant, sorrowful, sorry

ruffian noun THUG, brute, bully, hoodlum, hooligan, tough

ruffle verb 1 DISARRANGE, dishevel, disorder, mess up, rumple, tousle 2 ANNOY, agitate, fluster, irritate, nettle, peeve (*informal*), tick off, upset

rugged adjective 1 ROUGH, broken, bumpy, craggy, difficult, irregular, jagged, ragged, rocky, uneven 2 STRONG-FEATURED, rough-hewn, weather-beaten 3 TOUGH, brawny, burly, husky (*informal*), muscular, robust, strong, sturdy, well-built

ruin verb 1 DESTROY, crush, defeat, demolish, devastate, lay waste, smash, wreck 2 BANKRUPT, impoverish, pauperize **3** SPOIL, blow (*slang*), botch, damage, make a mess of, mess up, screw up (*informal*) ▶ *noun* **4** DESTRUCTION, breakdown, collapse, defeat, devastation, downfall, fall, undoing, wreck **5** DISREPAIR, decay, disintegration, ruination, wreckage **6** BANKRUPTCY, destitution, insolvency

ruinous *adjective* **1** DEVASTATING, calamitous, catastrophic, destructive, dire, disastrous, shattering **2** EXTRAVAGANT, crippling, immoderate, wasteful

rule *noun* **1** REGULATION, axiom, canon, decree, direction, guideline, law, maxim, precept, principle, tenet **2** CUSTOM, convention, habit, practice, procedure, routine, tradition **3** GOVERNMENT, authority, command, control, dominion, jurisdiction, mastery, power, regime, reign **4 as a rule** USUALLY, generally, mainly, normally, on the whole, ordinarily ▶ *verb* **5** GOVERN, be in authority, be in power, command, control, direct, reign **6** BE PREVALENT, be customary, predominate, preponderate, prevail **7** DECREE, decide, judge, pronounce, settle

rule out *verb* EXCLUDE, ban, debar, dismiss, disqualify, eliminate, leave out, preclude, prohibit, reject

ruler *noun* **1** GOVERNOR, commander, controller, head of state, king or queen, leader, lord, monarch, potentate, sovereign **2** MEASURE, rule, yardstick

ruling *noun* **1** DECISION,

adjudication, decree, judgment, pronouncement, verdict ▶ *adjective* **2** GOVERNING, commanding, controlling, reigning **3** PREDOMINANT, chief, dominant, main, pre-eminent, preponderant, prevailing, principal

ruminate *verb* PONDER, cogitate, consider, contemplate, deliberate, mull over, muse, reflect, think, turn over in one's mind

rummage *verb* SEARCH, delve, forage, hunt, ransack, root

rumor *noun* STORY, buzz, dirt (*slang*), gossip, hearsay, news, report, talk, whisper, word

rump *noun* BUTTOCKS, backside (*informal*), bottom, buns (*slang*), butt (*informal*), derrière (*euphemistic*), hindquarters, posterior, rear, rear end, seat

rumpus *noun* COMMOTION, disturbance, furor, fuss, hue and cry, noise, row, uproar

run *verb* **1** RACE, bolt, dash, gallop, hurry, jog, lope, rush, scurry, sprint **2** FLEE, beat a retreat, beat it (*slang*), bolt, escape, make a run for it, take flight, take off (*informal*), take to one's heels **3** MOVE, course, glide, go, pass, roll, skim **4** WORK, function, go, operate, perform **5** MANAGE, administer, be in charge of, control, direct, handle, head, lead, operate **6** CONTINUE, extend, go, proceed, reach, stretch **7** FLOW, discharge, go, gush, leak, pour, spill, spout, stream **8** MELT, dissolve, go soft, liquefy **9** PUBLISH, display, feature, print **10** COMPETE, be a candidate, contend, put oneself up for, stand, take part **11** SMUGGLE, bootleg, traffic in ▶noun **12** RACE, dash, gallop, jog, rush, sprint, spurt **13** RIDE, drive, excursion, jaunt, outing, spin (informal), trip **14** SEQUENCE, course, period, season, series, spell, stretch, string **15** ENCLOSURE, coop, pen **16 in the long run** EVENTUALLY, in the end, ultimately

run across verb MEET, bump into, come across, encounter, run into

runaway noun **1** FUGITIVE, deserter, escapee, refugee, truant ▶adjective **2** ESCAPED, fleeing, fugitive, loose, wild

run away verb FLEE, abscond, bolt, escape, fly the coop (informal), make a run for it, scram (informal), take to one's heels

run-down adjective **1** EXHAUSTED, below par, debilitated, drained, enervated, unhealthy, weak, weary, worn-out **2** DILAPIDATED, broken-down, decrepit, ramshackle, seedy, shabby, worn-out

run down verb **1** CRITICIZE, bad-mouth (slang), belittle, decry, denigrate, disparage, knock (informal) **2** REDUCE, curtail, cut, cut back, decrease, downsize, trim **3** KNOCK DOWN, hit, knock over, run into, run over **4** WEAKEN, debilitate, exhaust

run into verb **1** MEET, bump into, come across or upon, encounter, run across **2** HIT, collide with, strike

runner noun **1** ATHLETE, jogger, sprinter **2** MESSENGER, courier,

dispatch bearer, errand boy

running adjective **1** CONTINUOUS, constant, incessant, perpetual, twenty-four-seven (slang), unbroken, uninterrupted **2** FLOWING, moving, streaming ▶noun **3** MANAGEMENT, administration, control, direction, leadership, organization, supervision **4** WORKING, functioning, maintenance, operation, performance

runny adjective FLOWING, fluid, liquefied, liquid, melted, watery

run off verb FLEE, bolt, escape, fly the coop (informal), make off, run away, take flight, take to one's heels

run out verb BE USED UP, be exhausted, dry up, end, fail, finish, give out

run over verb **1** KNOCK DOWN, hit, knock over, run down **2** GO THROUGH, check, go over, rehearse, run through

run through verb REHEARSE, go over, practise, read, run over

rupture noun **1** BREAK, breach, burst, crack, fissure, rent, split, tear ▶verb **2** BREAK, burst, crack, separate, sever, split, tear

rural adjective RUSTIC, agricultural, country, pastoral, sylvan

ruse noun TRICK, device, dodge, hoax, maneuver, ploy, stratagem, subterfuge

rush verb **1** HURRY, bolt, career, dash, fly, hasten, race, run, shoot, speed, tear **2** PUSH, hurry, hustle, press **3** ATTACK, charge, storm ▶noun **4** HURRY, charge, dash, haste, race, scramble, stampede, surge

5 ATTACK, assault, charge, onslaught ▸ *adjective* **6** HASTY, fast, hurried, quick, rapid, swift, urgent

rust *noun* **1** CORROSION, oxidation **2** MILDEW, blight, mold, must, rot ▸ *verb* **3** CORRODE, oxidize

rustic *adjective* **1** RURAL, country, pastoral, sylvan **2** UNCOUTH, awkward, coarse, crude, rough ▸ *noun* **3** YOKEL, boor, bumpkin, clod, clodhopper (*informal*), hick (*informal*), hillbilly, peasant, redneck (*slang*)

rustle *verb* **1** CRACKLE, crinkle, whisper ▸ *noun* **2** CRACKLE, crinkling, rustling, whisper

rusty *adjective* **1** CORRODED, oxidized, rust-covered, rusted **2** REDDISH, chestnut, coppery, reddish-brown, russet, rust-colored **3** OUT OF PRACTICE, stale, unpracticed, weak

rut *noun* **1** GROOVE, furrow, indentation, track, trough, wheel mark **2** HABIT, dead end, pattern, routine, system

ruthless *adjective* MERCILESS, brutal, callous, cruel, harsh, heartless, pitiless, relentless, remorseless

rutted *adjective* GROOVED, cut, furrowed, gouged, holed, indented, marked, scored

— S s —

sabotage *noun* **1** DAMAGE, destruction, disruption, subversion, wrecking ▸ *verb* **2** DAMAGE, destroy, disable,

disrupt, incapacitate, subvert, vandalize, wreck

saccharine *adjective* OVERSWEET, cloying, honeyed, nauseating, sickly, sugary, syrupy

sack¹ *noun* **1** the sack DISMISSAL, discharge, the ax (*informal*), the boot (*slang*) ▸ *verb* **2** DISMISS, ax (*informal*), discharge, fire (*informal*)

sack² *noun* **1** PLUNDERING, looting, pillage ▸ *verb* **2** PLUNDER, loot, pillage, raid, rob, ruin, strip

sacred *adjective* **1** HOLY, blessed, divine, hallowed, revered, sanctified **2** RELIGIOUS, ecclesiastical, holy **3** INVIOLABLE, protected, sacrosanct

sacrifice *noun* **1** SURRENDER, loss, renunciation **2** OFFERING, oblation ▸ *verb* **3** GIVE UP, forego, forfeit, let go, lose, say good-bye to, surrender **4** OFFER, immolate, offer up

sacrilege *noun* DESECRATION, blasphemy, heresy, impiety, irreverence, profanation, violation

sacrilegious *adjective* PROFANE, blasphemous, desecrating, impious, irreligious, irreverent

sacrosanct *adjective* INVIOLABLE, hallowed, inviolate, sacred, sanctified, set apart, untouchable

sad *adjective* **1** UNHAPPY, blue, dejected, depressed, doleful, down, low, low-spirited, melancholy, mournful, woebegone **2** TRAGIC, depressing, dismal, grievous, harrowing, heart-rending, moving, pathetic, pitiful, poignant, upsetting

3 DEPLORABLE, bad, lamentable, sorry, wretched

sadden verb UPSET, deject, depress, distress, grieve, make sad

saddle verb BURDEN, encumber, load

sadistic adjective CRUEL, barbarous, brutal, ruthless, vicious

sadness noun UNHAPPINESS, dejection, despondency, grief, melancholy, misery, poignancy, sorrow, the blues

safe adjective **1** SECURE, impregnable, in safe hands, out of danger, out of harm's way, protected, safe and sound **2** UNHARMED, all right, intact, O.K. or okay (informal), undamaged, unhurt, unscathed **3** RISK-FREE, certain, impregnable, secure, sound ▶noun **4** STRONGBOX, coffer, deposit box, repository, safe-deposit box, vault

safeguard verb **1** PROTECT, defend, guard, look after, preserve ▶noun **2** PROTECTION, defense, guard, security

safely adverb IN SAFETY, in one piece, safe and sound, with impunity, without risk

safety noun **1** SECURITY, impregnability, protection **2** SHELTER, cover, refuge, sanctuary

sag verb **1** SINK, bag, dip, droop, fall, give way, hang loosely, slump **2** TIRE, droop, flag, wane, weaken, wilt

saga noun TALE, epic, legend, narrative, story, yarn

sage noun **1** WISE MAN, elder,
guru, master, philosopher ▶adjective **2** WISE, judicious, sagacious, sapient, sensible

sail verb **1** EMBARK, set sail **2** GLIDE, drift, float, fly, skim, soar, sweep, wing **3** PILOT, steer

sailor noun MARINER, marine, sea dog, seafarer, seaman

saintly adjective VIRTUOUS, godly, holy, pious, religious, righteous, saintlike

sake noun **1** BENEFIT, account, behalf, good, interest, welfare **2** PURPOSE, aim, end, motive, objective, reason

salacious adjective LASCIVIOUS, carnal, erotic, lecherous, lewd, libidinous, lustful

salary noun PAY, earnings, income, wage, wages

sale noun **1** SELLING, deal, disposal, marketing, transaction **2 for sale** AVAILABLE, obtainable, on the market

salient adjective PROMINENT, conspicuous, important, noticeable, outstanding, pronounced, striking

sallow adjective WAN, anemic, pale, pallid, pasty, sickly, unhealthy, yellowish

salt noun **1** SEASONING, flavor, relish, savor, taste **2 with a grain** or **pinch of salt** SKEPTICALLY, cynically, disbelievingly, suspiciously, with reservations ▶adjective **3** SALTY, brackish, briny, saline

salty adjective SALT, brackish, briny, saline

salubrious adjective HEALTHY, beneficial, good for one, health-giving, wholesome

salutary adjective BENEFICIAL, advantageous, good for one, profitable, useful, valuable

salute noun 1 GREETING, address, recognition, salutation ▸ verb 2 GREET, acknowledge, address, hail, welcome 3 HONOR, acknowledge, pay tribute or homage to, recognize

salvage verb SAVE, recover, redeem, rescue, retrieve

salvation noun SAVING, deliverance, escape, preservation, redemption, rescue

salve noun OINTMENT, balm, cream, emollient, lotion

same adjective 1 AFOREMENTIONED, aforesaid 2 IDENTICAL, alike, corresponding, duplicate, equal, twin 3 UNCHANGED, changeless, consistent, constant, invariable, unaltered, unvarying

sample noun 1 SPECIMEN, example, instance, model, pattern ▸ verb 2 TEST, experience, inspect, taste, try ▸ adjective 3 TEST, representative, specimen, trial

sanctify verb CONSECRATE, cleanse, hallow

sanctimonious adjective HOLIER-THAN-THOU, hypocritical, pious, self-righteous, smug

sanction noun 1 PERMISSION, approval, authority, authorization, backing, O.K. or okay (informal), stamp or seal of approval 2 (often plural) BAN, boycott, coercive measures, embargo, penalty ▸ verb 3 PERMIT, allow, approve, authorize, endorse

sanctity noun 1 SACREDNESS, inviolability 2 HOLINESS, godliness, goodness, grace,

piety, righteousness

sanctuary noun 1 SHRINE, altar, church, temple 2 PROTECTION, asylum, haven, refuge, retreat, shelter 3 RESERVE, conservation area, national park, nature reserve

sane adjective 1 RATIONAL, all there (informal), compos mentis, in one's right mind, mentally sound, of sound mind 2 SENSIBLE, balanced, judicious, level-headed, reasonable, sound

sanguine adjective CHEERFUL, buoyant, confident, hopeful, optimistic

sanitary adjective HYGIENIC, clean, germ-free, healthy, wholesome

sanity noun 1 MENTAL HEALTH, normality, rationality, reason, saneness 2 GOOD SENSE, common sense, level-headedness, rationality, sense

sap[1] noun 1 VITAL FLUID, essence, lifeblood 2 Informal Slang FOOL, dork (slang), idiot, jerk (slang), ninny, schmuck (slang), simpleton

sap[2] verb WEAKEN, deplete, drain, exhaust, undermine

sarcasm noun IRONY, bitterness, cynicism, derision, mockery, satire

sarcastic adjective IRONIC, acid, biting, caustic, cutting, cynical, mocking, sardonic, satirical

sardonic adjective MOCKING, cynical, derisive, dry, ironic, sarcastic, sneering, wry

Satan noun THE DEVIL, Beelzebub, Lord of the Flies, Lucifer, Mephistopheles, Prince of Darkness, The Evil One

satanic adjective EVIL, black, demonic, devilish, diabolic, fiendish, hellish, infernal, wicked

satiate verb 1 GLUT, cloy, gorge, jade, nauseate, overfill, stuff, surfeit 2 SATISFY, sate, slake

satire noun MOCKERY, burlesque, caricature, irony, lampoon, parody, ridicule, spoof (informal)

satirical adjective MOCKING, biting, caustic, cutting, incisive, ironic

satirize verb RIDICULE, burlesque, deride, lampoon, parody, pillory

satisfaction noun 1 CONTENTMENT, comfort, content, enjoyment, happiness, pleasure, pride, repletion, satiety 2 FULFILLMENT, achievement, assuaging, gratification

satisfactory adjective ADEQUATE, acceptable, all right, average, fair, good enough, passable, sufficient

satisfy verb 1 CONTENT, assuage, gratify, indulge, pacify, pander to, please, quench, sate, slake 2 FULFILL, answer, do, meet, serve, suffice 3 PERSUADE, assure, convince, reassure

saturate verb SOAK, drench, imbue, souse, steep, suffuse, waterlog, wet through

saturated adjective SOAKED, drenched, dripping, soaking (wet), sodden, sopping (wet), waterlogged, wet through

saturnine adjective GLOOMY, dour, glum, grave, morose, somber

saucy adjective 1 IMPUDENT, cheeky (informal), forward, impertinent, insolent, pert, presumptuous, rude 2 JAUNTY,

dashing, gay, perky

saunter verb 1 STROLL, amble, meander, mosey (informal), ramble, roam, wander ▶ noun 2 STROLL, airing, amble, ramble, turn, walk

savage adjective 1 WILD, feral, undomesticated, untamed 2 UNCULTIVATED, rough, rugged, uncivilized 3 CRUEL, barbarous, bestial, bloodthirsty, brutal, ferocious, fierce, harsh, ruthless, sadistic, vicious 4 PRIMITIVE, rude, unspoilt ▶ noun 5 LOUT, boor, yahoo ▶ verb 6 ATTACK, lacerate, mangle, maul

savagery noun CRUELTY, barbarity, brutality, ferocity, ruthlessness, viciousness

save verb 1 RESCUE, deliver, free, liberate, recover, redeem, salvage 2 PROTECT, conserve, guard, keep safe, look after, preserve, safeguard 3 KEEP, collect, gather, hoard, hold, husband, lay by, put by, reserve, set aside, store

saving noun 1 ECONOMY, bargain, discount, reduction ▶ adjective 2 REDEEMING, compensatory, extenuating

savings plural noun NEST EGG, fund, reserves, resources, store

savior noun RESCUER, defender, deliverer, liberator, preserver, protector, redeemer

Savior noun CHRIST, Jesus, Messiah, Redeemer

savoir-faire noun SOCIAL KNOW-HOW (informal), diplomacy, discretion, finesse, poise, social graces, tact, urbanity, worldliness

savor verb 1 ENJOY, appreciate,

delight in, luxuriate in, relish, revel in **2** (often with *of*) SUGGEST, be suggestive, show signs, smack ▶*noun* **3** FLAVOR, piquancy, relish, smack, smell, tang, taste

savory *adjective* SPICY, appetizing, full-flavored, luscious, mouthwatering, palatable, piquant, rich, tasty

say *verb* **1** SPEAK, affirm, announce, assert, declare, maintain, mention, pronounce, remark, state, utter, voice **2** SUPPOSE, assume, conjecture, estimate, guess, imagine, presume, surmise **3** EXPRESS, communicate, convey, imply ▶*noun* **4** CHANCE TO SPEAK, voice, vote **5** INFLUENCE, authority, clout (*informal*), power, weight

saying *noun* PROVERB, adage, aphorism, axiom, dictum, maxim

scale¹ *noun* FLAKE, lamina, layer, plate

scale² *noun* **1** GRADUATION, gradation, hierarchy, ladder, progression, ranking, sequence, series, steps **2** RATIO, proportion **3** DEGREE, extent, range, reach, scope ▶*verb* **4** CLIMB, ascend, clamber, escalate, mount, surmount **5** ADJUST, proportion, regulate

scam *verb* Slang **1** CHEAT, cook the books (*informal*), diddle (*informal*), fix, swindle, wangle (*informal*) ▶*noun* **2** Slang FRAUD, fix, racket (*slang*), swindle

scamp *noun* RASCAL, devil, imp, monkey, rogue, scallywag (*informal*)

scamper *verb* RUN, dart, dash, hasten, hurry, romp, scoot,

scurry, scuttle

scan *verb* **1** GLANCE OVER, check, check out (*informal*), examine, eye, look through, run one's eye over, run over, skim **2** SCRUTINIZE, investigate, scour, search, survey, sweep

scandal *noun* **1** CRIME, disgrace, embarrassment, offense, sin, wrongdoing **2** SHAME, defamation, discredit, disgrace, dishonor, ignominy, infamy, opprobrium, stigma **3** GOSSIP, aspersion, dirt, rumors, slander, talk, tattle

scandalize *verb* SHOCK, affront, appall, horrify, offend, outrage

scandalous *adjective* **1** SHOCKING, disgraceful, disreputable, infamous, outrageous, shameful, unseemly **2** SLANDEROUS, defamatory, libelous, scurrilous, untrue

scant *adjective* MEAGER, barely sufficient, little, minimal, sparse

scanty *adjective* MEAGER, bare, deficient, inadequate, insufficient, lousy (*slang*), poor, scant, short, skimpy, sparse, thin

scapegoat *noun* WHIPPING BOY, fall guy (*informal*)

scar *noun* **1** MARK, blemish, injury, wound ▶*verb* **2** MARK, damage, disfigure

scarce *adjective* RARE, few, few and far between, infrequent, in short supply, insufficient, uncommon

scarcely *adverb* **1** HARDLY, barely **2** DEFINITELY NOT, hardly

scarcity *noun* SHORTAGE, dearth, deficiency, insufficiency, lack, paucity, rareness, want

scare verb 1 FRIGHTEN, alarm, dismay, intimidate, panic, shock, startle, terrify ▶ noun 2 FRIGHT, panic, shock, start, terror

scared adjective FRIGHTENED, fearful, panicky, panic-stricken, petrified, shaken, startled, terrified

scary adjective FRIGHTENING, alarming, chilling, creepy (informal), horrifying, spine-chilling, spooky (informal), terrifying

scathing adjective CRITICAL, biting, caustic, cutting, harsh, sarcastic, scornful, trenchant, withering

scatter verb 1 THROW ABOUT, diffuse, disseminate, fling, shower, spread, sprinkle, strew 2 DISPERSE, disband, dispel, dissipate

scatterbrain noun FEATHERBRAIN, butterfly, flibbertigibbet

scenario noun STORY LINE, outline, résumé, summary, synopsis

scene noun 1 SITE, area, locality, place, position, setting, spot 2 SETTING, backdrop, background, location, set 3 SHOW, display, drama, exhibition, pageant, picture, sight, spectacle 4 ACT, division, episode, part 5 VIEW, landscape, panorama, prospect, vista 6 FUSS, commotion, exhibition, performance, row, tantrum, to-do 7 Informal WORLD, arena, business, environment

scenery noun 1 LANDSCAPE, surroundings, terrain, view, vista 2 Theatre SET, backdrop,

flats, setting, stage set

scenic adjective PICTURESQUE, beautiful, panoramic, spectacular, striking

scent noun 1 FRAGRANCE, aroma, bouquet, odor, perfume, smell 2 TRAIL, spoor, track ▶ verb 3 DETECT, discern, nose out, sense, smell, sniff

scented adjective FRAGRANT, aromatic, odoriferous, perfumed, sweet-smelling

schedule noun 1 PLAN, agenda, calendar, catalog, inventory, list, program, timetable ▶ verb 2 PLAN, appoint, arrange, book, organize, program

scheme noun 1 PLAN, program, project, proposal, strategy, system, tactics 2 DIAGRAM, blueprint, chart, draft, layout, outline, pattern 3 PLOT, conspiracy, intrigue, maneuver, ploy, ruse, stratagem, subterfuge ▶ verb 4 PLAN, lay plans, project, work out 5 PLOT, collude, conspire, intrigue, machinate, maneuver

scheming adjective CALCULATING, artful, conniving, cunning, sly, tricky, underhand, wily

schism noun DIVISION, breach, break, rift, rupture, separation, split

scholar noun 1 INTELLECTUAL, academic, savant 2 STUDENT, disciple, learner, pupil, schoolboy or schoolgirl

scholarly adjective LEARNED, academic, bookish, erudite, intellectual, lettered, scholastic

scholarship noun 1 LEARNING, book-learning, education, erudition, knowledge 2 BURSARY, fellowship

scholastic adjective LEARNED, academic, lettered, scholarly

school noun 1 ACADEMY, college, faculty, institute, institution, seminary 2 GROUP, adherents, circle, denomination, devotees, disciples, faction, followers, set ▶verb 3 TRAIN, coach, discipline, drill, educate, instruct, tutor

schooling noun 1 TEACHING, education, tuition 2 TRAINING, coaching, drill, instruction

science noun 1 DISCIPLINE, body of knowledge, branch of knowledge 2 SKILL, art, technique

scientific adjective SYSTEMATIC, accurate, controlled, exact, mathematical, precise

scientist noun INVENTOR, technophile

scintillating adjective BRILLIANT, animated, bright, dazzling, exciting, glittering, lively, sparkling, stimulating

scoff[1] verb SCORN, belittle, deride, despise, jeer, knock (informal), laugh at, mock, pooh-pooh, ridicule, sneer

scoff[2] verb GOBBLE (UP), bolt, devour, gorge oneself on, gulp down, guzzle, wolf

scold verb REPRIMAND, berate, castigate, censure, chew out (slang), find fault with, lecture, rebuke, reproach, reprove, tell off (informal), upbraid

scolding noun REBUKE, lecture, row, telling-off (informal)

scoop noun 1 LADLE, dipper, spoon 2 EXCLUSIVE, exposé, revelation, sensation ▶verb 3 (often with up) LIFT, gather up, pick up, take up 4 (often with out) HOLLOW, bail, dig, empty,

excavate, gouge, shovel

scope noun 1 OPPORTUNITY, freedom, latitude, liberty, room, space 2 RANGE, area, capacity, orbit, outlook, reach, span, sphere

scorch verb BURN, parch, roast, sear, shrivel, singe, wither

scorching adjective BURNING, baking, boiling, fiery, flaming, red-hot, roasting, searing

score noun 1 POINTS, grade, mark, outcome, record, result, total 2 GROUNDS, basis, cause, ground, reason 3 GRIEVANCE, grudge, injury, injustice, wrong 4 **scores** LOTS, hundreds, masses, millions, multitudes, myriads, swarms ▶verb 5 GAIN, achieve, chalk up (informal), make, notch up (informal), win 6 KEEP COUNT, count, record, register, tally 7 CUT, deface, gouge, graze, mark, scrape, scratch, slash 8 (with out or through) CROSS OUT, cancel, delete, obliterate, strike out 9 Music ARRANGE, adapt, orchestrate, set

scorn noun 1 CONTEMPT, derision, disdain, disparagement, mockery, sarcasm ▶verb 2 DESPISE, be above, deride, disdain, flout, reject, scoff at, slight, spurn

scornful adjective CONTEMPTUOUS, derisive, disdainful, haughty, jeering, mocking, sarcastic, sardonic, scathing, scoffing, sneering

scoundrel noun ROGUE, bastard (offensive), good-for-nothing, heel (slang), miscreant, rascal, reprobate, scamp, swine, villain

scour[1] verb RUB, abrade, buff,

clean, polish, scrub, wash

scour² verb SEARCH, beat, comb, hunt, ransack

scourge noun 1 AFFLICTION, bane, curse, infliction, misfortune, pest, plague, terror, torment 2 WHIP, cat, lash, strap, switch, thong ▶ verb 3 AFFLICT, curse, plague, torment 4 WHIP, beat, cane, flog, horsewhip, lash, thrash

scout noun 1 VANGUARD, advance guard, lookout, outrider, precursor, reconnoiterer ▶ verb 2 RECONNOITER, investigate, observe, probe, spy, survey, watch

scowl verb 1 GLOWER, frown, lour or lower ▶ noun 2 GLOWER, black look, dirty look, frown

scrabble verb SCRAPE, claw, scramble, scratch

scraggy adjective SCRAWNY, angular, bony, lean, skinny

scram verb GO AWAY, abscond, beat it (slang), clear off (informal), get lost (informal), leave, make oneself scarce (informal), make tracks, vamoose (slang)

scramble verb 1 STRUGGLE, climb, crawl, scrabble, swarm 2 STRIVE, contend, jostle, push, run, rush, vie ▶ noun 3 CLIMB, trek 4 STRUGGLE, commotion, competition, confusion, melee or mêlée, race, rush, tussle

scrap¹ noun 1 PIECE, bit, crumb, fragment, grain, morsel, part, particle, portion, sliver, snippet 2 WASTE, junk, off cuts 3 scraps LEFTOVERS, bits, leavings, remains ▶ verb 4 DISCARD, abandon, ditch (slang), drop, jettison,

throw away or out, write off

scrap² Informal ▶ noun 1 FIGHT, argument, battle, disagreement, dispute, quarrel, row, squabble, wrangle ▶ verb 2 FIGHT, argue, row, squabble, wrangle

scrape verb 1 GRAZE, bark, rub, scratch, scuff, skin 2 RUB, clean, erase, remove, scour 3 GRATE, grind, rasp, scratch, squeak 4 SCRIMP, pinch, save, skimp, stint 5 scrape through GET BY (informal), just make it, struggle ▶ noun 6 Informal PREDICAMENT, awkward situation, difficulty, dilemma, fix (informal), mess, plight, tight spot

scrapheap noun on the scrapheap DISCARDED, ditched (slang), jettisoned, put out to pasture (informal), redundant

scrappy adjective FRAGMENTARY, bitty, disjointed, incomplete, piecemeal, sketchy, thrown together

scratch verb 1 MARK, claw, cut, damage, etch, grate, graze, lacerate, score, scrape 2 WITHDRAW, abolish, call off, cancel, delete, eliminate, erase, pull out ▶ noun 3 MARK, blemish, claw mark, gash, graze, laceration, scrape 4 up to scratch ADEQUATE, acceptable, satisfactory, sufficient, up to standard ▶ adjective 5 IMPROVISED, impromptu, rough-and-ready

scrawl verb SCRIBBLE, doodle, squiggle, writing

scrawny adjective THIN, bony, gaunt, lean, scraggy, skin-and-bones (informal), skinny, undernourished

scream verb 1 CRY, bawl, screech, shriek, yell ▸noun 2 CRY, howl, screech, shriek, yell, yelp

screech noun, verb CRY, scream, shriek

screen noun 1 COVER, awning, canopy, cloak, guard, partition, room divider, shade, shelter, shield 2 MESH, net ▸ verb 3 COVER, cloak, conceal, hide, mask, shade, veil 4 PROTECT, defend, guard, shelter, shield 5 VET, evaluate, examine, filter, gauge, scan, sift, sort 6 BROADCAST, present, put on, show

screw verb 1 TURN, tighten, twist 2 Informal, (often with out of) EXTORT, extract, wrest, wring

screw up verb 1 Informal BUNGLE, botch, make a mess of (slang), mess up, mishandle, spoil 2 DISTORT, contort, pucker, wrinkle

screwy adjective CRAZY, crackpot (informal), eccentric, loopy (informal), nutty (slang), odd, off-the-wall (slang), out to lunch (informal), weird

scribble verb SCRAWL, dash off, jot, write

scribe noun COPYIST, amanuensis, writer

scrimp verb ECONOMIZE, be frugal, save, scrape, skimp, stint, tighten one's belt

script noun 1 TEXT, book, copy, dialogue, libretto, lines, words 2 HANDWRITING, calligraphy, penmanship, writing

Scripture noun THE BIBLE, Holy Bible, Holy Scripture, Holy

Writ, The Good Book, The Gospels, The Scriptures

scrounge verb Informal CADGE, beg, bum (informal), freeload (slang), sponge (informal)

scrounger noun CADGER, freeloader (slang), parasite, sponger (informal)

scrub verb SCOUR, clean, cleanse, rub

scruple noun 1 MISGIVING, compunction, doubt, hesitation, qualm, reluctance, second thoughts, uneasiness ▸verb 2 HAVE MISGIVINGS ABOUT, demur, doubt, have qualms about, hesitate, think twice about

scrupulous adjective 1 MORAL, conscientious, honorable, principled, upright 2 CAREFUL, exact, fastidious, meticulous, precise, punctilious, rigorous, strict

scrutinize verb EXAMINE, explore, inspect, investigate, peruse, pore over, probe, scan, search, study

scrutiny noun EXAMINATION, analysis, exploration, inspection, investigation, perusal, search, study

scuffle verb 1 FIGHT, clash, grapple, jostle, struggle, tussle ▸noun 2 FIGHT, brawl, commotion, disturbance, fray, scrimmage, skirmish, tussle

sculpture verb SCULPT, carve, chisel, fashion, form, hew, model, mold, shape

scum noun 1 IMPURITIES, dross, film, froth 2 RABBLE, dregs of society, riffraff, trash

scurrilous adjective SLANDEROUS, abusive, defamatory, insulting, scandalous, vituperative

scurry verb 1 HURRY, dart, dash, race, scamper, scoot, scuttle, sprint ▶ noun 2 FLURRY, scampering, whirl

scuttle verb RUN, bustle, hasten, hurry, rush, scamper, scoot, scurry

sea noun 1 OCEAN, main, the deep, the waves 2 EXPANSE, abundance, mass, multitude, plethora, profusion 3 **at sea** BEWILDERED, baffled, confused, lost, mystified, puzzled

seafaring adjective NAUTICAL, marine, maritime, naval

seal noun 1 AUTHENTICATION, confirmation, imprimatur, insignia, ratification, stamp ▶ verb 2 CLOSE, bung, enclose, fasten, plug, shut, stop, stopper, stop up 3 AUTHENTICATE, confirm, ratify, stamp, validate 4 SETTLE, clinch, conclude, consummate, finalize 5 **seal off** ISOLATE, put out of bounds, quarantine, segregate

seam noun 1 JOINT, closure 2 LAYER, lode, stratum, vein 3 RIDGE, furrow, line, wrinkle

sear verb SCORCH, burn, sizzle

search verb 1 LOOK, comb, examine, explore, hunt, inspect, investigate, ransack, scour, scrutinize ▶ noun 2 LOOK, examination, exploration, hunt, inspection, investigation, pursuit, quest

searching adjective KEEN, close, intent, penetrating, piercing, probing, quizzical, sharp

season noun 1 PERIOD, spell, term, time ▶ verb 2 FLAVOR, enliven, pep up, salt, spice

seasonable adjective APPROPRIATE,

convenient, fit, opportune, providential, suitable, timely, well-timed

seasoned adjective EXPERIENCED, hardened, practiced, time-served, veteran

seasoning noun FLAVORING, condiment, dressing, relish, salt and pepper, sauce, spice

seat noun 1 CHAIR, bench, pew, settle, stall, stool 2 CENTER, capital, heart, hub, place, site, situation, source 3 RESIDENCE, abode, ancestral hall, house, mansion 4 MEMBERSHIP, chair, constituency, incumbency, place ▶ verb 5 SIT, fix, install, locate, place, set, settle 6 HOLD, accommodate, cater for, contain, sit, take

seating noun ACCOMMODATION, chairs, places, room, seats

secede verb WITHDRAW, break with, leave, pull out, quit, resign, split from

secluded adjective PRIVATE, cloistered, cut off, isolated, lonely, out-of-the-way, sheltered, solitary

seclusion noun PRIVACY, isolation, shelter, solitude

second¹ adjective 1 NEXT, following, subsequent, succeeding 2 ADDITIONAL, alternative, extra, further, other 3 INFERIOR, lesser, lower, secondary, subordinate ▶ noun 4 SUPPORTER, assistant, backer, helper ▶ verb 5 SUPPORT, approve, assist, back, endorse, go along with

second² noun MOMENT, flash, instant, jiffy (informal), minute, sec (informal), trice

secondary adjective

1 SUBORDINATE, inferior, lesser, lower, minor, unimportant **2** RESULTANT, contingent, derived, indirect **3** BACKUP, auxiliary, fall-back, reserve, subsidiary, supporting

second-class *adjective* INFERIOR, indifferent, mediocre, second-best, second-rate, undistinguished, uninspiring

second-hand *adjective* **1** USED, hand-me-down (*informal*), nearly new ▶ *adverb* **2** INDIRECTLY

second in command *noun* DEPUTY, number two, right-hand man

secondly *adverb* NEXT, in the second place, second

second-rate *adjective* INFERIOR, low-grade, low-quality, mediocre, poor, rubbishy, shoddy, substandard, tacky (*informal*), tawdry, two-bit (*slang*)

secrecy *noun* **1** MYSTERY, concealment, confidentiality, privacy, silence **2** SECRETIVENESS, clandestineness, covertness, furtiveness, stealth

secret *adjective* **1** CONCEALED, close, disguised, furtive, hidden, undercover, underground, undisclosed, unknown, unrevealed **2** STEALTHY, secretive, sly, underhand **3** MYSTERIOUS, abstruse, arcane, clandestine, cryptic, occult ▶ *noun* **4** MYSTERY, code, enigma, key **5 in secret** SECRETLY, slyly, surreptitiously

secrete[1] *verb* GIVE OFF, emanate, emit, exude

secrete[2] *verb* HIDE, cache, conceal, harbor, stash (*informal*), stow

secretive *adjective* RETICENT, close, deep, reserved, tight-lipped, uncommunicative

secretly *adverb* IN SECRET, clandestinely, covertly, furtively, privately, quietly, stealthily, surreptitiously

sect *noun* GROUP, camp, denomination, division, faction, party, schism

sectarian *adjective* **1** NARROW-MINDED, bigoted, doctrinaire, dogmatic, factional, fanatical, limited, parochial, partisan ▶ *noun* **2** BIGOT, dogmatist, extremist, fanatic, partisan, zealot

section *noun* **1** PART, division, fraction, installment, passage, piece, portion, segment, slice **2** DISTRICT, area, region, sector, zone

sector *noun* PART, area, district, division, quarter, region, zone

secular *adjective* WORLDLY, civil, earthly, lay, nonspiritual, temporal

secure *adjective* **1** SAFE, immune, protected, unassailable **2** SURE, assured, certain, confident, easy, reassured **3** FIXED, fast, fastened, firm, immovable, stable, steady ▶ *verb* **4** OBTAIN, acquire, gain, get, procure, score (*slang*) **5** FASTEN, attach, bolt, chain, fix, lock, make fast, tie up

security *noun* **1** PRECAUTIONS, defense, protection, safeguards, safety measures **2** SAFETY, care, custody, refuge, safekeeping, sanctuary **3** SURENESS, assurance, certainty, confidence, conviction, positiveness, reliance **4** PLEDGE, collateral, gage, guarantee, hostage, insurance, pawn, surety

sedate *adjective* CALM, collected, composed, cool, dignified, serene, tranquil

sedative *adjective* **1** CALMING, anodyne, relaxing, soothing, tranquilizing ▸ *noun* **2** TRANQUILIZER, anodyne, downer *or* down *(slang)*

sedentary *adjective* INACTIVE, desk, desk-bound, seated, sitting

sediment *noun* DREGS, deposit, grounds, lees, residue

sedition *noun* RABBLE-ROUSING, agitation, incitement to riot, subversion

seditious *adjective* REVOLUTIONARY, dissident, mutinous, rebellious, refractory, subversive

seduce *verb* **1** CORRUPT, debauch, deflower, deprave, dishonour **2** TEMPT, beguile, deceive, entice, inveigle, lead astray, lure, mislead

seduction *noun* **1** CORRUPTION **2** TEMPTATION, enticement, lure, snare

seductive *adjective* ALLURING, attractive, bewitching, enticing, inviting, provocative, tempting

seductress *noun* TEMPTRESS, enchantress, femme fatale, siren, succubus, vamp *(informal)*

see *verb* **1** PERCEIVE, behold, catch sight of, discern, distinguish, espy, glimpse, look, make out, notice, observe, sight, spot, witness **2** UNDERSTAND, appreciate, comprehend, fathom, feel, follow, get, grasp, realize **3** FIND OUT, ascertain, determine, discover, learn **4** MAKE SURE, ensure, guarantee, make certain, see to it **5** CONSIDER, decide, deliberate, reflect, think over **6** VISIT, confer with, consult, interview, receive, speak to **7** GO OUT WITH, court, date *(informal)*, go steady with *(informal)* **8** ACCOMPANY, escort, lead, show, usher, walk

seed *noun* **1** GRAIN, egg, embryo, germ, kernel, ovum, pip, spore **2** ORIGIN, beginning, germ, nucleus, source, start **3** OFFSPRING, children, descendants, issue, progeny **4 go** *or* **run to seed** DECLINE, decay, degenerate, deteriorate, go downhill *(informal)*, go to pot, let oneself go

seedy *Informal* ▸ *adjective* SHABBY, dilapidated, dirty, grubby, mangy, run-down, scuzzy *(slang)*, sleazy, squalid, tatty

seeing *conjunction* SINCE, as, inasmuch as, in view of the fact that

seek *verb* **1** LOOK FOR, be after, follow, hunt, pursue, search for, stalk **2** TRY, aim, aspire to, attempt, endeavor, essay, strive

seem *verb* APPEAR, assume, give the impression, look

seemly *adjective* FITTING, appropriate, becoming, correct, decent, decorous, fit, proper, suitable

seep *verb* OOZE, exude, leak, permeate, soak, trickle, well

seer *noun* PROPHET, sibyl, soothsayer

seesaw *verb* ALTERNATE, fluctuate,

oscillate, swing

seethe verb 1 BE FURIOUS, be livid, fume, go ballistic (*slang*), rage, see red (*informal*), simmer 2 BOIL, bubble, fizz, foam, froth

see through verb 1 BE UNDECEIVED BY, be wise to (*informal*), fathom, not fall for, penetrate 2 see (**something**) **through** PERSEVERE (WITH), keep at, persist, stick out (*informal*) 3 see (**someone**) **through** HELP OUT, stick by, support

segment noun SECTION, bit, division, part, piece, portion, slice, wedge

segregate verb SET APART, discriminate against, dissociate, isolate, separate

segregation noun SEPARATION, apartheid, discrimination, isolation

seize verb 1 GRAB, catch up, clutch, grasp, grip, lay hands on, snatch, take 2 CONFISCATE, appropriate, commandeer, impound, take possession of 3 CAPTURE, apprehend, arrest, catch, take captive

seizure noun 1 ATTACK, convulsion, fit, paroxysm, spasm 2 CAPTURE, apprehension, arrest 3 TAKING, annexation, commandeering, confiscation, grabbing

seldom adverb RARELY, hardly ever, infrequently, not often

select verb 1 CHOOSE, opt for, pick, single out ▶*adjective* 2 CHOICE, excellent, first-class, hand-picked, special, superior, top-notch (*informal*) 3 EXCLUSIVE, cliquish, elite, privileged

selection noun 1 CHOICE,

choosing, option, pick, preference 2 RANGE, assortment, choice, collection, medley, variety

selective adjective PARTICULAR, careful, discerning, discriminating

self-assurance noun CONFIDENCE, assertiveness, positiveness, self-confidence, self-possession

self-centered adjective SELFISH, egotistic, narcissistic, self-seeking

self-confidence noun SELF-ASSURANCE, aplomb, confidence, nerve, poise

self-confident adjective SELF-ASSURED, assured, confident, poised, sure of oneself

self-conscious adjective EMBARRASSED, awkward, bashful, diffident, ill at ease, insecure, nervous, uncomfortable, wired (*slang*)

self-control noun WILLPOWER, restraint, self-discipline, self-restraint

self-esteem noun SELF-RESPECT, confidence, faith in oneself, pride, self-assurance, self-regard

self-evident adjective OBVIOUS, clear, incontrovertible, inescapable, undeniable

self-important adjective CONCEITED, bigheaded, cocky, full of oneself, pompous, swollen-headed

self-indulgence noun INTEMPERANCE, excess, extravagance

selfish adjective SELF-CENTERED, egoistic, egoistical, egotistic, egotistical, greedy, self-interested, ungenerous

selfless adjective UNSELFISH,

altruistic, generous,
self-denying, self-sacrificing

self-possessed *adjective*
SELF-ASSURED, collected,
confident, cool, poised,
unruffled

self-reliant *adjective* INDEPENDENT,
self-sufficient, self-supporting

self-respect *noun* PRIDE, dignity,
morale, self-esteem

self-restraint *noun* SELF-CONTROL,
self-command, self-discipline,
willpower

self-righteous *adjective*
SANCTIMONIOUS, complacent,
holier-than-thou, priggish,
self-satisfied, smug, superior

self-sacrifice *noun* SELFLESSNESS,
altruism, generosity, self-denial

self-satisfied *adjective* SMUG,
complacent, pleased with
oneself, self-congratulatory

self-seeking *adjective* SELFISH,
careerist, looking out for
number one (*informal*), out for
what one can get,
self-interested, self-serving

sell *verb* 1 TRADE, barter,
exchange 2 DEAL IN, handle,
market, peddle, retail, stock,
trade in, traffic

seller *noun* DEALER, agent,
merchant, purveyor, retailer,
salesman *or* saleswoman,
supplier, vendor

selling *noun* DEALING, business,
trading, traffic

sell out *verb* 1 DISPOSE OF, be
out of stock of, get rid of, run
out of 2 *Informal* BETRAY,
double-cross (*informal*), sell
down the river (*informal*), stab
in the back

semblance *noun* APPEARANCE,
aspect, façade, mask, pretense,
resemblance, show, veneer

seminal *adjective* INFLUENTIAL,
formative, ground-breaking,
important, innovative, original

send *verb* 1 CONVEY, direct,
dispatch, forward, remit,
transmit 2 PROPEL, cast, fire,
fling, hurl, let fly, shoot

send for *verb* SUMMON, call for,
order, request

sendoff *noun* FAREWELL,
departure, leave-taking, start,
valediction

senile *adjective* DODDERING,
decrepit, doting, in one's
dotage

senility *noun* DOTAGE,
decrepitude, infirmity, loss of
one's faculties, senile dementia

senior *adjective* 1 HIGHER RANKING,
superior 2 OLDER, elder

senior citizen *noun* PENSIONER,
old fogey (*slang*), old or elderly
person, retired person

seniority *noun* SUPERIORITY,
precedence, priority, rank

sensation *noun* 1 FEELING,
awareness, consciousness,
impression, perception, sense
2 EXCITEMENT, commotion, furor,
stir, thrill

sensational *adjective*
1 DRAMATIC, amazing,
astounding, awesome,
exciting, melodramatic,
shock-horror (*facetious*),
shocking, thrilling 2 EXCELLENT,
awesome (*informal*), cool
(*informal*), fabulous (*informal*),
impressive, marvelous,
mind-blowing (*informal*), out of
this world (*informal*), phat
(*slang*), superb

sense *noun* 1 FACULTY, feeling,
sensation 2 FEELING,

atmosphere, aura, awareness, consciousness, impression, perception **3** (sometimes plural) INTELLIGENCE, brains (*informal*), cleverness, common sense, judgment, reason, sagacity, sanity, sharpness, understanding, wisdom, wit(s) **4** MEANING, drift, gist, implication, import, significance ▶ *verb* **5** PERCEIVE, be aware of, discern, feel, get the impression, pick up, realize, understand

senseless *adjective* **1** STUPID, asinine, bonkers (*informal*), crazy, daft (*informal*), foolish, idiotic, illogical, inane, irrational, mad, mindless, nonsensical, pointless, ridiculous, silly **2** UNCONSCIOUS, insensible, out, out cold, stunned

sensibility *noun* **1** (often plural) FEELINGS, emotions, moral sense, sentiments, susceptibilities **2** SENSITIVITY, responsiveness, sensitiveness, susceptibility

sensible *adjective* **1** WISE, canny, down-to-earth, intelligent, judicious, practical, prudent, rational, realistic, sage, sane, shrewd, sound **2** (usually with *of*) AWARE, conscious, mindful, sensitive to

sensitive *adjective* **1** EASILY HURT, delicate, tender **2** SUSCEPTIBLE, easily affected, impressionable, responsive, touchy-feely (*informal*) **3** TOUCHY, easily offended, easily upset, thin-skinned **4** RESPONSIVE, acute, fine, keen, precise

sensitivity *noun* SENSITIVENESS, delicacy, receptiveness, responsiveness, susceptibility

sensual *adjective* **1** PHYSICAL, animal, bodily, carnal, fleshly, luxurious, voluptuous **2** EROTIC, lascivious, lecherous, lewd, lustful, raunchy (*slang*), sexual

sensuality *noun* EROTICISM, carnality, lasciviousness, lecherousness, lewdness, sexiness (*informal*), voluptuousness

sensuous *adjective* PLEASURABLE, gratifying, hedonistic, sybaritic

sentence *noun* **1** PUNISHMENT, condemnation, decision, decree, judgment, order, ruling, verdict ▶ *verb* **2** CONDEMN, doom, penalize

sententious *adjective* POMPOUS, canting, judgmental, moralistic, preachifying (*informal*), sanctimonious

sentient *adjective* FEELING, conscious, living, sensitive

sentiment *noun* **1** EMOTION, sensibility, tenderness **2** (often plural) FEELING, attitude, belief, idea, judgment, opinion, view **3** SENTIMENTALITY, emotionalism, mawkishness, romanticism

sentimental *adjective* ROMANTIC, emotional, maudlin, nostalgic, overemotional, schmaltzy (*slang*), slushy (*informal*), soft-hearted, touching, weepy (*informal*)

sentimentality *noun* ROMANTICISM, corniness (*slang*), emotionalism, mawkishness, nostalgia, schmaltz (*slang*)

sentinel *noun* GUARD, lookout, sentry, watch, watchman

separable *adjective* DISTINGUISHABLE, detachable, divisible

separate *verb* **1** DIVIDE, come

apart, come away, detach, disconnect, disjoin, remove, sever, split, sunder **2** PART, break up, disunite, diverge, divorce, estrange, part company, split up **3** ISOLATE, segregate, single out ▶*adjective* **4** UNCONNECTED, detached, disconnected, divided, divorced, isolated, unattached **5** INDIVIDUAL, alone, apart, distinct, particular, single, solitary

separated *adjective* DISCONNECTED, apart, disassociated, disunited, divided, parted, separate, sundered

separately *adverb* INDIVIDUALLY, alone, apart, severally, singly

separation *noun* **1** DIVISION, break, disconnection, dissociation, disunion, gap **2** SPLIT-UP, break-up, divorce, parting, rift, split

septic *adjective* INFECTED, festering, poisoned, putrefying, putrid, suppurating

sepulcher *noun* TOMB, burial place, grave, mausoleum, vault

sequel *noun* FOLLOW-UP, continuation, development **2** CONSEQUENCE, conclusion, end, outcome, result, upshot

sequence *noun* SUCCESSION, arrangement, chain, course, cycle, order, progression, series

serene *adjective* CALM, composed, peaceful, tranquil, unruffled, untroubled

serenity *noun* CALMNESS, calm, composure, peace, peacefulness, quietness, stillness, tranquillity

series *noun* SEQUENCE, chain,

course, order, progression, run, set, string, succession, train

serious *adjective* **1** SEVERE, acute, critical, dangerous **2** IMPORTANT, crucial, fateful, grim, momentous, no laughing matter, pressing, significant, urgent, worrying **3** SOLEMN, grave, humorless, sober, unsmiling **4** SINCERE, earnest, genuine, honest, in earnest

seriously *adverb* **1** GRAVELY, acutely, badly, critically, dangerously, severely **2** SINCERELY, gravely, in earnest

seriousness *noun* **1** IMPORTANCE, gravity, significance, urgency **2** SOLEMNITY, earnestness, gravitas, gravity

sermon *noun* **1** HOMILY, address **2** LECTURE, harangue, talking-to (*informal*)

servant *noun* ATTENDANT, domestic, help, maid, retainer, slave

serve *verb* **1** WORK FOR, aid, assist, attend to, help, minister to, wait on **2** PERFORM, act, complete, discharge, do, fulfill **3** PROVIDE, deliver, dish up, present, set out, supply **4** BE ADEQUATE, answer the purpose, be acceptable, do, function as, satisfy, suffice, suit

service *noun* **1** HELP, assistance, avail, attend to, help, use, usefulness **2** WORK, business, duty, employment, labor, office **3** OVERHAUL, check, maintenance **4** CEREMONY, observance, rite, worship ▶*verb* **5** OVERHAUL, check, fine tune, go over, maintain, tune (up)

serviceable *adjective* USEFUL, beneficial, functional, helpful, operative, practical, profitable, usable, utilitarian

servile *adjective* SUBSERVIENT, abject, fawning, grovelling, obsequious, sycophantic, toadying

serving *noun* PORTION, helping

session *noun* MEETING, assembly, conference, congress, discussion, hearing, period, sitting

set[1] *verb* 1 PUT, deposit, lay, locate, place, plant, position, rest, seat, situate, station, stick 2 PREPARE, arrange, lay, make ready, spread 3 HARDEN, cake, congeal, crystallize, solidify, stiffen, thicken 4 ARRANGE, appoint, decide (upon), determine, establish, fix, fix up, resolve, schedule, settle, specify 5 ASSIGN, allot, decree, impose, ordain, prescribe, specify 6 GO DOWN, decline, dip, disappear, sink, subside, vanish ▶ *noun* 7 POSITION, attitude, bearing, carriage, posture 8 SCENERY, scene, setting, stage set ▶ *adjective* 9 FIXED, agreed, appointed, arranged, decided, definite, established, prearranged, predetermined, scheduled, settled 10 INFLEXIBLE, hard and fast, immovable, rigid, stubborn 11 CONVENTIONAL, stereotyped, stock, traditional, unspontaneous 12 **set on** or **upon** DETERMINED, bent, intent, resolute

set[2] *noun* 1 SERIES, assortment, batch, collection, compendium 2 GROUP, band, circle, clique, company, coterie, crowd, faction, gang

setback *noun* HOLD-UP, blow,

check, defeat, disappointment, hitch, misfortune, reverse

set back *verb* HOLD UP, delay, hinder, impede, retard, slow

set off *verb* 1 LEAVE, depart, embark, start out 2 DETONATE, explode, ignite

setting *noun* BACKGROUND, backdrop, context, location, scene, scenery, set, site, surroundings

settle *verb* 1 PUT IN ORDER, adjust, order, regulate, straighten out, work out 2 LAND, alight, come to rest, descend, light 3 MOVE TO, dwell, inhabit, live, make one's home, put down roots, reside, set up home, take up residence 4 COLONIZE, people, pioneer, populate 5 CALM, lull, pacify, quell, quiet, quieten, reassure, relax, relieve, soothe 6 PAY, clear, discharge, square (up) 7 (often with *on* or *upon*) DECIDE, agree, confirm, determine, establish, fix 8 RESOLVE, clear up, decide, put an end to, reconcile

settlement *noun* 1 AGREEMENT, arrangement, conclusion, confirmation, establishment, working out 2 PAYMENT, clearing, discharge 3 COLONY, community, encampment, outpost

settler *noun* COLONIST, colonizer, frontiersman, immigrant, pioneer

setup *noun* ARRANGEMENT, conditions, organization, regime, structure, system

set up *verb* 1 BUILD, assemble, construct, erect, put together, put up, raise 2 ESTABLISH, arrange, begin, found, initiate, institute, organize, prearrange, prepare

sever *verb* **1** CUT, cut in two, detach, disconnect, disjoin, divide, part, separate, split **2** BREAK OFF, dissociate, put an end to, terminate

several *adjective* SOME, different, diverse, manifold, many, sundry, various

severe *adjective* **1** STRICT, austere, cruel, drastic, hard, harsh, oppressive, rigid, unbending **2** GRIM, forbidding, grave, serious, stern, tight-lipped, unsmiling **3** INTENSE, acute, extreme, fierce **4** PLAIN, austere, classic, homely, restrained, simple, Spartan, unadorned, unembellished, unfussy

severely *adverb* **1** STRICTLY, harshly, sharply, sternly **2** SERIOUSLY, acutely, badly, extremely, gravely

severity *noun* STRICTNESS, hardness, harshness, severeness, sternness, toughness

sex *noun* **1** GENDER **2** (SEXUAL) INTERCOURSE, coition, coitus, copulation, fornication, lovemaking, sexual relations

sexual *adjective* **1** CARNAL, erotic, intimate, sensual, sexy **2** REPRODUCTIVE, genital, procreative, sex

sexual intercourse *noun* COPULATION, carnal knowledge, coition, coitus, sex, union

sexuality *noun* DESIRE, carnality, eroticism, lust, sensuality, sexiness (*informal*)

sexy *adjective* EROTIC, arousing, naughty, provocative, seductive, sensual, sensuous, suggestive, titillating

shabby *adjective* **1** TATTY, dilapidated, mean, ragged, run-down, seedy, tattered, threadbare, worn **2** MEAN, cheap, contemptible, despicable, dirty, dishonorable, lousy (*slang*), low, rotten (*informal*), scurvy, scuzzy (*slang*)

shack *noun* HUT, cabin, shanty

shackle *noun* **1** (often plural) FETTER, bond, chain, iron, leg-iron, manacle ▶ *verb* **2** FETTER, bind, chain, manacle, put in irons

shade *noun* **1** DIMNESS, dusk, gloom, gloominess, semidarkness, shadow **2** SCREEN, blind, canopy, cover, covering, curtain, shield, veil **3** COLOR, hue, tinge, tint, tone **4** DASH, hint, suggestion, trace **5** *Literary* GHOST, apparition, phantom, specter, spirit **6** put into the shade OUTSHINE, eclipse, outclass, overshadow ▶ *verb* **7** COVER, conceal, hide, obscure, protect, screen, shield, veil **8** DARKEN, cloud, dim, shadow

shadow *noun* **1** DIMNESS, cover, darkness, dusk, gloom, shade **2** TRACE, hint, suggestion, suspicion **3** CLOUD, blight, gloom, sadness ▶ *verb* **4** DARKEN, overhang, screen, shield **5** FOLLOW, stalk, tail (*informal*), trail

shadowy *adjective* **1** DARK, dim, dusky, gloomy, murky, shaded, shady **2** VAGUE, dim, dreamlike, faint, ghostly, nebulous, phantom, spectral, unsubstantial

shady *adjective* **1** SHADED, cool, dim **2** *Informal* CROOKED, disreputable, dubious, questionable, shifty, suspect, suspicious, unethical

shaft *noun* **1** HANDLE, pole, rod, shank, stem **2** RAY, beam, gleam

shaggy *adjective* UNKEMPT, hairy, hirsute, long-haired, rough, tousled, unshorn

shake *verb* **1** VIBRATE, bump, jar, jolt, quake, rock, shiver, totter, tremble **2** WAVE, brandish, flourish **3** UPSET, distress, disturb, frighten, rattle (*informal*), shock, unnerve ▶ *noun* **4** VIBRATION, agitation, convulsion, jerk, jolt, quaking, shiver, shudder, trembling, tremor

shake up *verb* **1** STIR (UP), agitate, churn (up), mix **2** UPSET, disturb, shock, unsettle

shaky *adjective* **1** UNSTEADY, faltering, precarious, quivery, rickety, trembling, unstable, weak **2** UNCERTAIN, dubious, iffy (*informal*), questionable, suspect

shallow *adjective* **1** SUPERFICIAL, empty, slight, surface, trivial **2** UNINTELLIGENT, foolish, frivolous, ignorant, puerile, simple

sham *noun* **1** PHONEY *or* PHONY (*informal*), counterfeit, forgery, fraud, hoax, humbug, imitation, impostor, pretense ▶ *adjective* **2** FALSE, artificial, bogus, counterfeit, feigned, imitation, mock, phoney *or* phony (*informal*), pretended, simulated ▶ *verb* **3** FAKE, affect, assume, feign, pretend, put on, simulate

shambles *noun* CHAOS,

confusion, disarray, disorder, havoc, madhouse, mess, muddle

shame *noun* **1** EMBARRASSMENT, abashment, humiliation, ignominy, mortification **2** DISGRACE, blot, discredit, dishonor, disrepute, infamy, reproach, scandal, smear ▶ *verb* **3** EMBARRASS, abash, disgrace, humble, humiliate, mortify **4** DISHONOR, blot, debase, defile, degrade, smear, stain

shamefaced *adjective* EMBARRASSED, abashed, ashamed, humiliated, mortified, red-faced, sheepish

shameful *adjective* **1** EMBARRASSING, humiliating, mortifying **2** DISGRACEFUL, base, dishonorable, low, mean, outrageous, scandalous, wicked

shameless *adjective* BRAZEN, audacious, barefaced, flagrant, hardened, insolent, unabashed, unashamed

shanty *noun* SHACK, cabin, hut, shed

shape *noun* **1** FORM, build, configuration, contours, figure, lines, outline, profile, silhouette **2** PATTERN, frame, model, mold **3** CONDITION, fettle, health, state, trim ▶ *verb* **4** FORM, create, fashion, make, model, mold, produce **5** DEVELOP, adapt, devise, frame, modify, plan

shapeless *adjective* FORMLESS, amorphous, irregular, misshapen, unstructured

shapely *adjective* WELL-FORMED, curvaceous, elegant, graceful, neat, trim, well-proportioned

share *noun* **1** PART, allotment,

curt, discourteous, impolite, sharp, terse, uncivil ▸ *adverb* **6** ABRUPTLY, suddenly, without warning

shortage *noun* DEFICIENCY, dearth, insufficiency, lack, paucity, scarcity, want

shortcoming *noun* FAILING, defect, fault, flaw, imperfection, weakness

shorten *verb* CUT, abbreviate, abridge, curtail, decrease, diminish, lessen, reduce

shortly *adverb* SOON, before long, in a little while, presently

short-sighted *adjective* **1** NEAR-SIGHTED, myopic **2** UNTHINKING, ill-advised, ill-considered, impolitic, impractical, improvident, imprudent, injudicious

short-tempered *adjective* QUICK-TEMPERED, hot-tempered, impatient, irascible, testy

shot *noun* **1** THROW, discharge, lob, pot shot **2** PELLET, ball, bullet, lead, projectile, slug **3** MARKSMAN, shooter **4** *Slang* ATTEMPT, effort, endeavor, go (*informal*), stab (*informal*), try, turn

shoulder *verb* **1** BEAR, accept, assume, be responsible for, carry, take on **2** PUSH, elbow, jostle, press, shove

shout *noun* **1** CRY, bellow, call, roar, scream, yell ▸ *verb* **2** CRY (OUT), bawl, bellow, call (out), holler (*informal*), roar, scream, yell

shout down *verb* SILENCE, drown, drown out, overwhelm

shove *verb* PUSH, drive, elbow, impel, jostle, press, propel, thrust

shovel *verb* MOVE, dredge, heap, ladle, load, scoop, toss

shove off *verb* GO AWAY, clear off (*informal*), depart, leave, push off (*informal*), scram (*informal*)

show *verb* **1** BE VISIBLE, appear **2** DISPLAY, exhibit, present **3** PROVE, clarify, demonstrate, elucidate, point out **4** INSTRUCT, demonstrate, explain, teach **5** DISPLAY, indicate, manifest, register, reveal **6** GUIDE, accompany, attend, conduct, escort, lead ▸ *noun* **7** ENTERTAINMENT, presentation, production **8** EXHIBITION, array, display, fair, pageant, parade, sight, spectacle **9** PRETENSE, affectation, air, appearance, display, illusion, parade, pose

showdown *noun* CONFRONTATION, clash, face-off (*slang*)

shower *noun* **1** DELUGE, barrage, stream, torrent, volley ▸ *verb* **2** INUNDATE, deluge, heap, lavish, pour, rain

showman *noun* PERFORMER, entertainer

show-off *noun* EXHIBITIONIST, boaster, braggart, poseur

show off *verb* **1** EXHIBIT, demonstrate, display, flaunt, parade **2** BOAST, blow one's own trumpet, brag, swagger

show up *verb* **1** STAND OUT, appear, be conspicuous, be visible **2** REVEAL, expose, highlight, lay bare **3** *Informal* EMBARRASS, let down, mortify, put to shame **4** ARRIVE, appear, come, turn up

showy *adjective* **1** OSTENTATIOUS, brash, flamboyant, flash (*informal*), flashy, over the top

shred (*informal*) **2** GAUDY, garish, loud

shred noun **1** STRIP, bit, fragment, piece, scrap, sliver, tatter **2** PARTICLE, atom, grain, iota, jot, scrap, trace

shrew noun NAG, harpy, harridan, scold, spitfire, vixen

shrewd adjective CLEVER, astute, calculating, canny, crafty, cunning, intelligent, keen, perceptive, perspicacious, sharp, smart

shrewdness noun ASTUTENESS, canniness, discernment, judgment, perspicacity, quick wits, sharpness, smartness

shriek verb, noun CRY, scream, screech, squeal, yell

shrill adjective PIERCING, high, penetrating, sharp

shrink verb **1** DECREASE, contract, diminish, dwindle, grow smaller, lessen, narrow, shorten **2** RECOIL, cower, cringe, draw back, flinch, quail

shrivel verb WITHER, dehydrate, desiccate, shrink, wilt, wizen

shroud noun **1** WINDING SHEET, grave clothes **2** COVERING, mantle, pall, screen, veil ▶ verb **3** CONCEAL, blanket, cloak, cover, envelop, hide, screen, veil

shudder verb **1** SHIVER, convulse, quake, quiver, shake, tremble ▶ noun **2** SHIVER, quiver, spasm, tremor

shuffle verb **1** SCUFFLE, drag, scrape, shamble **2** REARRANGE, disarrange, disorder, jumble, mix

shun verb AVOID, keep away from, steer clear of

shut verb CLOSE, fasten, seal, secure, slam

shut down verb **1** STOP, halt, switch off **2** CLOSE, shut up

shut out verb EXCLUDE, bar, debar, keep out, lock out

shuttle verb GO BACK AND FORTH, alternate, commute, go to and fro

shut up verb **1** *Informal* BE QUIET, fall silent, gag, hold one's tongue, hush, silence **2** CONFINE, cage, coop up, immure, imprison, incarcerate

shy¹ adjective **1** TIMID, bashful, coy, diffident, retiring, self-conscious, self-effacing, shrinking **2** CAUTIOUS, chary, distrustful, hesitant, suspicious, wary ▶ verb **3** (sometimes with *off* or *away*) RECOIL, balk, draw back, flinch, start

shy² verb THROW, cast, fling, hurl, pitch, sling, toss

shyness noun TIMIDNESS, bashfulness, diffidence, lack of confidence, self-consciousness, timidity, timorousness

sick adjective **1** NAUSEOUS, ill, nauseated, queasy **2** UNWELL, ailing, diseased, indisposed, poorly (*informal*), under the weather (*informal*) **3** *Informal* MORBID, black, ghoulish, macabre, sadistic **4 sick of** TIRED, bored, fed up, jaded, weary

sicken verb **1** DISGUST, gross out (*slang*), nauseate, repel, revolt, turn one's stomach **2** FALL ILL, ail, take sick

sickening adjective DISGUSTING, distasteful, foul, gross (*slang*), loathsome, nauseating, noisome, offensive, repulsive, revolting, scuzzy (*slang*), stomach-turning (*informal*), vile, yucky or yukky (*slang*)

sickly *adjective* **1** UNHEALTHY, ailing, delicate, faint, feeble, infirm, pallid, peaky, wan, weak **2** NAUSEATING, cloying, mawkish

sickness *noun* **1** ILLNESS, affliction, ailment, bug (*informal*), complaint, disease, disorder, malady **2** NAUSEA, queasiness, vomiting

side *noun* **1** BORDER, boundary, division, edge, limit, margin, perimeter, rim, sector, verge **2** PART, aspect, face, facet, flank, hand, surface, view **3** PARTY, camp, cause, faction, sect, team **4** POINT OF VIEW, angle, opinion, position, slant, stand, standpoint, viewpoint ▶ *adjective* **5** SUBORDINATE, ancillary, incidental, lesser, marginal, minor, secondary, subsidiary ▶ *verb* **6** (usually with *with*) SUPPORT, ally with, favor, go along with, take the part of

sidelong *adjective* SIDEWAYS, covert, indirect, oblique

sidestep *verb* AVOID, circumvent, dodge, duck (*informal*), evade, skirt

sidetrack *verb* DIVERT, deflect, distract

sideways *adverb* **1** OBLIQUELY, edgeways, laterally, sidelong, to the side ▶ *adjective* **2** OBLIQUE, sidelong

sidle *verb* EDGE, creep, inch, slink, sneak, steal

siesta *noun* NAP, catnap, doze, forty winks (*informal*), sleep, snooze (*informal*)

sieve *noun* **1** STRAINER, colander ▶ *verb* **2** SIFT, separate, strain

sift *verb* **1** SIEVE, filter, separate

2 EXAMINE, analyze, go through, investigate, research, scrutinize, work over

sight *noun* **1** VISION, eye, eyes, eyesight, seeing **2** VIEW, appearance, perception, range of vision, visibility **3** SPECTACLE, display, exhibition, pageant, scene, show, vista **4** EYESORE, mess, monstrosity **5** catch

sight of SPOT, espy, glimpse ▶ *verb* **6** SPOT, behold, discern, distinguish, make out, observe, perceive, see

sign *noun* **1** INDICATION, clue, evidence, hint, mark, proof, signal, symptom, token **2** NOTICE, board, placard, warning **3** SYMBOL, badge, device, emblem, logo, mark **4** OMEN, augury, auspice, foreboding, portent, warning ▶ *verb* **5** AUTOGRAPH, endorse, initial, inscribe **6** GESTURE, beckon, gesticulate, indicate, signal

signal *noun* **1** SIGN, beacon, cue, gesture, indication, mark, token ▶ *verb* **2** GESTURE, beckon, gesticulate, indicate, motion, sign, wave

significance *noun* **1** IMPORTANCE, consequence, moment, relevance, weight **2** MEANING, force, implication(s), import, message, point, purport, sense

significant *adjective* **1** IMPORTANT, critical, material, momentous, noteworthy, serious, vital, weighty **2** MEANINGFUL, eloquent, expressive, indicative, suggestive

signify *verb* **1** INDICATE, be a sign of, betoken, connote, denote, imply, intimate, mean, portend, suggest **2** MATTER, be important, carry weight, count

silence noun **1** QUIET, calm, hush, lull, peace, stillness **2** MUTENESS, dumbness, reticence, taciturnity ▶ verb **3** QUIETEN, cut off, cut short, deaden, gag, muffle, quiet, stifle, still, suppress

silent adjective **1** QUIET, hushed, muted, noiseless, soundless, still **2** MUTE, dumb, speechless, taciturn, voiceless, wordless

silently adjective QUIETLY, inaudibly, in silence, mutely, noiselessly, soundlessly, without a sound, wordlessly

silhouette noun **1** OUTLINE, form, profile, shape ▶ verb **2** OUTLINE, etch, stand out

silky adjective SMOOTH, silken, sleek, velvety

silly adjective FOOLISH, absurd, asinine, fatuous, idiotic, inane, ridiculous, senseless, stupid, unwise

silt noun **1** SEDIMENT, alluvium, deposit, ooze, sludge ▶ verb **2** silt up CLOG, choke, congest

similar adjective ALIKE, analogous, close, comparable, like, resembling

similarity noun RESEMBLANCE, affinity, agreement, analogy, closeness, comparability, correspondence, likeness, sameness

simmer verb FUME, be angry, rage, seethe, smolder

simmer down verb CALM DOWN, control oneself, cool off or down

simper verb SMILE COYLY, smile affectedly, smirk

simple adjective **1** EASY, clear,

intelligible, lucid, plain, straightforward, uncomplicated, understandable, uninvolved **2** PLAIN, classic, natural, unembellished, unfussy **3** PURE, elementary, unalloyed, uncombined, unmixed **4** ARTLESS, childlike, guileless, ingenuous, innocent, naive, natural, sincere, unaffected, unsophisticated **5** HONEST, bald, basic, direct, frank, naked, plain, sincere, stark **6** HUMBLE, dumpy (informal), homely, modest, unpretentious **7** FEEBLE-MINDED, foolish, half-witted, moronic, slow, stupid

simple-minded adjective FEEBLE-MINDED, backward, dim-witted, foolish, idiot, idiotic, moronic, retarded, simple, stupid

simpleton noun HALFWIT, doofus (slang), dork (slang), dullard, fool, idiot, imbecile (informal), moron, schmuck (slang)

simplicity noun **1** EASE, clarity, clearness, straightforwardness **2** PLAINNESS, lack of adornment, purity, restraint **3** ARTLESSNESS, candor, directness, innocence, naivety, openness

simplify verb MAKE SIMPLER, abridge, disentangle, dumb down, reduce to essentials, streamline

simply adverb **1** PLAINLY, clearly, directly, easily, intelligibly, naturally, straightforwardly, unpretentiously **2** JUST, merely, only, purely, solely **3** TOTALLY, absolutely, completely, really, utterly, wholly

simulate verb PRETEND, act,

affect, feign, put on, sham

simultaneous *adjective*
COINCIDING, at the same time,
coincident, concurrent,
contemporaneous, synchronous

simultaneously *adverb* AT THE
SAME TIME, concurrently, together

sin *noun* 1 WRONGDOING, crime,
error, evil, guilt, iniquity,
misdeed, offense, transgression
▶ *verb* 2 TRANSGRESS, err, fall, go
astray, lapse, offend

sincere *adjective* HONEST, candid,
earnest, frank, genuine,
guileless, heartfelt, real, serious,
true, unaffected

sincerely *adverb* HONESTLY,
earnestly, genuinely, in earnest,
seriously, truly, wholeheartedly

sincerity *noun* HONESTY, candor,
frankness, genuineness,
seriousness, truth

sinecure *noun* SOFT JOB
(*informal*), gravy train (*slang*),
money for jam or old rope
(*informal*), soft option

sinful *adjective* GUILTY, bad,
corrupt, criminal, erring,
immoral, iniquitous, wicked

sing *verb* 1 WARBLE, carol, chant,
chirp, croon, pipe, trill, yodel
2 HUM, buzz, purr, whine

singe *verb* BURN, char, scorch,
sear

singer *noun* VOCALIST, balladeer,
cantor, chorister, crooner,
minstrel, soloist

single *adjective* 1 ONE, distinct,
individual, lone, only, separate,
sole, solitary 2 INDIVIDUAL,
exclusive, separate, undivided,
unshared 3 SIMPLE, unblended,
unmixed 4 UNMARRIED, free,
unattached, unwed ▶ *verb* 5
(usually with *out*) PICK, choose,

distinguish, fix on, pick on *or*
out, select, separate, set apart

single-handed *adverb* UNAIDED,
alone, by oneself,
independently, on one's own,
solo, unassisted, without help

single-minded *adjective*
DETERMINED, dedicated, dogged,
fixed, unswerving

singly *adverb* ONE BY ONE,
individually, one at a time,
separately

singular *adjective* 1 SINGLE,
individual, separate, sole
2 REMARKABLE, eminent,
exceptional, notable,
noteworthy, outstanding
3 UNUSUAL, curious, eccentric,
extraordinary, odd, peculiar,
queer, strange

singularly *adverb* REMARKABLY,
especially, exceptionally,
notably, outstandingly,
particularly, uncommonly,
unusually

sinister *adjective* THREATENING,
dire, disquieting, evil, malign,
menacing, ominous

sink *verb* 1 DESCEND, dip, drop,
fall, founder, go down, go
under, lower, plunge,
submerge, subside 2 FALL,
abate, collapse, drop, lapse,
slip, subside 3 DECLINE, decay,
deteriorate, diminish, dwindle,
fade, fail, flag, lessen, weaken,
worsen 4 DIG, bore, drill, drive,
excavate 5 STOOP, be reduced
to, lower oneself

sink in *verb* BE UNDERSTOOD, get
through to, penetrate, register
(*informal*)

sinner *noun* WRONGDOER,
evildoer, malefactor, miscreant,
offender, transgressor

sip verb **1** DRINK, sample, sup, taste ▶noun **2** SWALLOW, drop, taste, thimbleful

sissy noun **1** WIMP (informal), coward, mama's boy, softie (informal), weakling ▶adjective **2** WIMPISH OR WIMPY (informal), cowardly, effeminate, feeble, soft (informal), unmanly, weak

sit verb **1** REST, perch, settle **2** CONVENE, assemble, deliberate, meet, officiate, preside

site noun **1** LOCATION, place, plot, position, setting, spot ▶verb **2** LOCATE, install, place, position, set, situate

situation noun **1** STATE OF AFFAIRS, case, circumstances, condition, plight, state **2** LOCATION, place, position, setting, site, spot **3** STATUS, rank, station **4** JOB, employment, office, place, position, post

sizable, sizeable adjective LARGE, considerable, decent, goodly, largish, respectable, substantial

size noun DIMENSIONS, amount, bulk, extent, immensity, magnitude, mass, proportions, range, volume

size up verb ASSESS, appraise, evaluate, take stock of

sizzle verb HISS, crackle, frizzle, fry, spit

skedaddle verb Slang RUN AWAY, abscond, beat it (slang), clear off (informal), disappear, flee, run for it, scram (informal), take to one's heels

skeleton noun FRAMEWORK, bare bones, draft, frame, outline, sketch, structure

skeptic noun DOUBTER, cynic,

disbeliever, doubting Thomas

skeptical adjective DOUBTFUL, cynical, disbelieving, dubious, incredulous, mistrustful, unconvinced

skepticism noun DOUBT, cynicism, disbelief, incredulity, unbelief

sketch noun **1** DRAWING, delineation, design, draft, outline, plan ▶verb **2** DRAW, delineate, depict, draft, outline, represent, rough out

sketchy adjective INCOMPLETE, cursory, inadequate, perfunctory, rough, scrappy, skimpy, superficial

skill noun EXPERTISE, ability, art, cleverness, competence, craft, dexterity, facility, knack, proficiency, skillfulness, talent, technique

skilled adjective EXPERT, able, masterly, professional, proficient, skillful

skillful adjective EXPERT, able, adept, adroit, clever, competent, dexterous, masterly, practiced, professional, proficient, skilled

skim verb **1** SEPARATE, cream **2** GLIDE, coast, float, fly, sail, soar **3** (usually with through) SCAN, glance, run one's eye over

skimp verb STINT, be mean with, be sparing with, cut corners, scamp, scrimp

skin noun **1** HIDE, fell, pelt **2** COATING, casing, crust, film, husk, outside, peel, rind ▶verb **3** PEEL, flay, scrape

skin alive verb Informal ATTACK, assail, assault, let have it (informal), let loose on (informal)

skinflint noun MISER, niggard,

penny-pincher (*informal*), Scrooge

skinny *adjective* THIN, emaciated, lean, scrawny, undernourished

skip *verb* **1** HOP, bob, bounce, caper, dance, flit, frisk, gambol, prance, trip **2** PASS OVER, eschew, give (something) a miss, leave out, miss out, omit

skirmish *noun* **1** FIGHT, battle, brush, clash, conflict, encounter, fracas, scrap (*informal*) ▶ *verb* **2** FIGHT, clash, collide

skirt *verb* **1** BORDER, edge, flank **2** (often with *around* or *round*) AVOID, circumvent, evade, steer clear of

skit *noun* **1** PARODY, burlesque, sketch, spoof (*informal*) **2** PLAY, comedy, drama, performance

skittish *adjective* LIVELY, excitable, fidgety, highly strung, jumpy, nervous, restive, wired (*slang*)

skulk *verb* LURK, creep, prowl, slink, sneak

sky *noun* HEAVENS, firmament

slab *noun* PIECE, chunk, lump, portion, slice, wedge

slack *adjective* **1** LOOSE, baggy, lax, limp, relaxed **2** NEGLIGENT, idle, inactive, lax, lazy, neglectful, remiss, slipshod **3** SLOW, dull, inactive, quiet, slow-moving, sluggish ▶ *noun* **4** ROOM, excess, give (*informal*), leeway ▶ *verb* **5** SHIRK, dodge, idle

slacken *verb* (often with *off*) LESSEN, abate, decrease, diminish, drop off, moderate, reduce, relax

slacker *noun* IDLER, couch

potato (*slang*), dodger, loafer, shirker

slake *verb* SATISFY, assuage, quench, sate

slam *verb* BANG, crash, dash, fling, hurl, smash, throw

slander *noun* **1** DEFAMATION, calumny, libel, scandal, smear ▶ *verb* **2** DEFAME, blacken (someone's) name, libel, malign, smear

slanderous *adjective* DEFAMATORY, damaging, libelous, malicious

slant *verb* **1** SLOPE, bend, bevel, cant, heel, incline, lean, list, tilt **2** BIAS, angle, color, distort, twist ▶ *noun* **3** SLOPE, camber, gradient, incline, tilt **4** BIAS, angle, emphasis, one-sidedness, point of view, prejudice

slanting *adjective* SLOPING, angled, at an angle, bent, diagonal, inclined, oblique, tilted, tilting

slap *noun* **1** SMACK, blow, cuff, spank ▶ *verb* **2** SMACK, clap, cuff, paddle (*U.S. & Canad.*), spank

slapdash *adjective* CARELESS, clumsy, hasty, hurried, messy, slipshod, sloppy (*informal*)

slash *verb* **1** CUT, gash, hack, lacerate, rend, rip, score, slit **2** REDUCE, cut, drop, lower ▶ *noun* **3** CUT, gash, incision, laceration, rent, rip, slit

slaughter *verb* **1** MURDER, butcher, kill, massacre, slay ▶ *noun* **2** MURDER, bloodshed, butchery, carnage, killing, massacre, slaying

slaughterhouse *noun* ABATTOIR

slave *noun* **1** SERVANT, drudge, serf, vassal ▶ *verb* **2** TOIL, drudge, slog

slavery noun ENSLAVEMENT, bondage, captivity, servitude, subjugation

slavish adjective 1 SERVILE, abject, base, cringing, fawning, grovelling, obsequious, submissive, sycophantic 2 IMITATIVE, second-hand, unimaginative, unoriginal

slay verb KILL, butcher, massacre, mow down, murder, slaughter

sleaze noun CORRUPTION, bribery, dishonesty, extortion, fraud, unscrupulousness, venality

sleazy adjective SORDID, disreputable, low, run-down, scuzzy (slang), seedy, squalid

sleek adjective GLOSSY, lustrous, shiny, smooth

sleep noun 1 SLUMBER(S), doze, forty winks (informal), hibernation, nap, siesta, snooze (informal) ▶ verb 2 SLUMBER, catnap, doze, drowse, hibernate, snooze (informal), take a nap

sleepless adjective WAKEFUL, insomniac, restless

sleepy adjective DROWSY, dull, heavy, inactive, lethargic, sluggish

slender adjective 1 SLIM, lean, narrow, slight, willowy 2 FAINT, poor, remote, slight, slim, tenuous, thin 3 MEAGRE, little, scant, scanty, small

sleuth noun DETECTIVE, gumshoe (slang), private eye (informal), (private) investigator

slice noun 1 SHARE, cut, helping, portion, segment, sliver, wedge ▶ verb 2 CUT, carve, divide, sever

slick adjective 1 GLIB, plausible,

polished, smooth, specious 2 SKILLFUL, adroit, deft, dexterous, polished, professional ▶ verb 3 SMOOTH, plaster down, sleek

slide verb SLIP, coast, glide, skim, slither

slight adjective 1 SMALL, feeble, insignificant, meager, measly, minor, paltry, scanty, trifling, trivial, unimportant 2 SLIM, delicate, feeble, fragile, lightly-built, small, spare ▶ verb 3 SNUB, affront, blow off (slang), disdain, ignore, insult, scorn ▶ noun 4 SNUB, affront, insult, neglect, rebuff, slap in the face (informal), (the) cold shoulder

slightly adverb A LITTLE, somewhat

slim adjective 1 SLENDER, lean, narrow, slight, svelte, thin, trim 2 SLIGHT, faint, poor, remote, slender ▶ verb 3 LOSE WEIGHT, diet, reduce

slimy adjective 1 VISCOUS, clammy, glutinous, oozy 2 OBSEQUIOUS, creeping, grovelling, oily, servile, smarmy (Brit. informal), unctuous

sling verb 1 THROW, cast, chuck (informal), fling, heave, hurl, lob (informal), shy, toss 2 HANG, dangle, suspend

slink verb CREEP, prowl, skulk, slip, sneak, steal

slinky adjective FIGURE-HUGGING, clinging, close-fitting, skintight

slip verb 1 FALL, skid 2 SLIDE, glide, skate, slither 3 SNEAK, conceal, creep, hide, steal 4 (sometimes with up) MAKE A MISTAKE, blunder, err, miscalculate 5 let slip GIVE

AWAY, disclose, divulge, leak, reveal ▶ *noun* **6** MISTAKE, blunder, error, failure, fault, lapse, omission, oversight
7 give (someone) the slip ESCAPE FROM, dodge, elude, evade, get away from, lose (someone)

slippery *adjective* **1** SMOOTH, glassy, greasy, icy, slippy (*informal or dialect*), unsafe **2** DEVIOUS, crafty, cunning, dishonest, evasive, shifty, tricky, untrustworthy

slipshod *adjective* CARELESS, casual, slapdash, sloppy (*informal*), slovenly, untidy

slit *noun* **1** CUT, gash, incision, opening, rent, split, tear ▶ *verb* **2** CUT (OPEN), gash, knife, lance, pierce, rip, slash

slither *verb* SLIDE, glide, slink, slip, snake, undulate

sliver *noun* SHRED, fragment, paring, shaving, splinter

slobber *verb* DROOL, dribble, drivel, salivate, slaver

slobbish *adjective* MESSY, slovenly, unclean, unkempt, untidy

slog *verb* **1** WORK, labor, plod, plow through, slave, toil **2** TRUDGE, tramp, trek **3** HIT, punch, slug, sock (*slang*), strike, thump, wallop (*informal*) ▶ *noun* **4** LABOR, effort, exertion, struggle **5** TRUDGE, hike, tramp, trek

slogan *noun* CATCH PHRASE, catchword, motto

slop *verb* **1** SPILL, overflow, slosh (*informal*), splash ▶ *noun* **2** *Informal* FOOD, grub (*slang*), mess (*slang*)

slope *noun* **1** INCLINATION, gradient, incline, ramp, rise, slant, tilt ▶ *verb* **2** SLANT, drop away, fall, incline, lean, rise, tilt **3** slope off SLINK AWAY, creep away, slip away

sloping *adjective* SLANTING, inclined, leaning, oblique

sloppy *adjective* **1** CARELESS, messy, slovenly, slovenly, untidy **2** SENTIMENTAL, gushing, mawkish, slushy (*informal*)

slot *noun* **1** OPENING, aperture, groove, hole, slit, vent **2** *Informal* PLACE, position, space, time, vacancy ▶ *verb* **3** FIT IN, fit, insert

sloth *noun* LAZINESS, idleness, inactivity, inertia, slackness, sluggishness, torpor

slothful *adjective* LAZY, idle, inactive, indolent, workshy

slouch *verb* SLUMP, droop, loll, stoop

slovenly *adjective* CARELESS, disorderly, negligent, slack, slapdash, slipshod, sloppy (*informal*), untidy

slow *adjective* **1** PROLONGED, gradual, lingering, long-drawn-out, protracted **2** UNHURRIED, dawdling, lackadaisical, laggard, lazy, leisurely, ponderous, sluggish **3** LATE, backward, behind, delayed, tardy **4** STUPID, braindead (*informal*), dense, dim, dull-witted, obtuse, retarded, thick ▶ *verb* **5** (often with *up* or *down*) REDUCE SPEED, brake, decelerate, handicap, hold up, retard, slacken (off)

slowly *adverb* GRADUALLY, leisurely, unhurriedly

sludge *noun* SEDIMENT, mire, muck, mud, ooze, residue,

silt, slime

sluggish adjective INACTIVE, dull, heavy, indolent, inert, lethargic, slothful, slow, torpid

slum noun GHETTO

slumber verb SLEEP, doze, drowse, nap, snooze (informal)

slump verb 1 FALL, collapse, crash, plunge, sink, slip 2 SAG, droop, hunch, loll, slouch ▸noun 3 FALL, collapse, crash, decline, downturn, drop, reverse, trough 4 RECESSION, depression

slur noun INSULT, affront, aspersion, calumny, innuendo, insinuation, smear, stain

slut noun Offensive TART, ho (slang), trollop, whore

sly adjective 1 CUNNING, artful, clever, crafty, devious, scheming, secret, shifty, stealthy, subtle, underhand, wily 2 ROGUISH, arch, impish, knowing, mischievous ▸noun 3 **on the sly** SECRETLY, covertly, on the quiet, privately, surreptitiously

smack verb 1 SLAP, clap, cuff, hit, paddle (U.S. & Canad.), spank, strike ▸noun 2 SLAP, blow ▸adverb 3 Informal DIRECTLY, exactly, precisely, right, slap (informal), squarely, straight

small adjective 1 LITTLE, diminutive, mini, miniature, minute, petite, pygmy or pigmy, teeny, teeny-weeny, tiny, undersized, wee 2 UNIMPORTANT, insignificant, minor, negligible, paltry, petty, trifling, trivial 3 PETTY, base, mean, narrow 4 MODEST, humble, unpretentious

small-minded adjective PETTY, bigoted, intolerant, mean, narrow-minded, ungenerous

small-time adjective MINOR, insignificant, of no account, petty, unimportant

smarmy adjective Brit. informal OBSEQUIOUS, crawling, ingratiating, servile, smooth, suave, sycophantic, toadying, unctuous

smart adjective 1 CLEVER, acute, astute, bright, canny, ingenious, intelligent, keen, quick, sharp, shrewd 2 BRISK, lively, quick, vigorous ▸verb 3 STING, burn, hurt ▸noun 4 STING, pain, soreness

smart aleck noun Informal KNOW-ALL (informal), smarty pants (informal), wise guy (informal)

smarten verb TIDY, groom, put in order, put to rights, spruce up

smash verb 1 BREAK, crush, demolish, pulverize, shatter 2 COLLIDE, crash 3 DESTROY, lay waste, ruin, trash (slang), wreck ▸noun 4 DESTRUCTION, collapse, downfall, failure, ruin 5 COLLISION, accident, crash

smattering noun MODICUM, bit, rudiments

smear verb 1 SPREAD OVER, bedaub, coat, cover, daub, rub on 2 DIRTY, smudge, soil, stain, sully 3 SLANDER, besmirch, blacken, malign ▸noun 4 SMUDGE, blot, blotch, daub, splotch, streak 5 SLANDER, calumny, defamation, libel

smell verb 1 SNIFF, scent 2 STINK, reek ▸noun 3 ODOR, aroma, bouquet, fragrance, perfume, scent 4 STINK, fetor, stench

smelly adjective 1 STINKING, fetid, foul, foul-smelling, funky (slang), malodorous, noisome, reeking

smirk noun SMUG LOOK, simper

smitten adjective 1 AFFLICTED, laid low, plagued, struck 2 INFATUATED, beguiled, bewitched, captivated, charmed, enamored

smolder verb SEETHE, boil, fume, rage, simmer

smooth adjective 1 EVEN, flat, flush, horizontal, level, plane 2 SLEEK, glossy, polished, shiny, silky, soft, velvety 3 EASY, effortless, well-ordered 4 FLOWING, regular, rhythmic, steady, uniform 5 SUAVE, facile, glib, persuasive, slick, smarmy (Brit. informal), unctuous, urbane 6 MELLOW, agreeable, mild, pleasant ▶verb 7 FLATTEN, iron, level, plane, press 8 CALM, appease, assuage, ease, mitigate, mollify, soften

smother verb 1 SUFFOCATE, choke, stifle, strangle 2 SUPPRESS, conceal, hide, muffle, repress, stifle

smudge verb 1 SMEAR, daub, dirty, mark, smirch ▶noun 2 SMEAR, blemish, blot

smug adjective SELF-SATISFIED, complacent, conceited, superior

smuggler noun TRAFFICKER, bootlegger, runner

smutty adjective OBSCENE, bawdy, blue, coarse, crude, dirty, indecent, indelicate, suggestive, vulgar

snack noun LIGHT MEAL, bite, refreshment(s)

snag noun 1 DIFFICULTY, catch, complication, disadvantage, downside, drawback, hitch, obstacle, problem ▶verb 2 CATCH, rip, tear

snap verb 1 BREAK, crack, separate 2 CRACKLE, click, pop 3 BITE AT, bite, nip, snatch 4 SPEAK SHARPLY, bark, jump down (someone's) throat (informal), lash out at ▶noun 5 CRACKLE, pop 6 BITE, grab, nip ▶adjective 7 INSTANT, immediate, spur-of-the-moment, sudden

snappy adjective 1 IRRITABLE, cross, edgy, testy, touchy 2 SMART, chic, cool (informal), dapper, fashionable, phat (slang), stylish

snap up verb SEIZE, grab, pounce upon, take advantage of

snare noun 1 TRAP, gin, net, noose, wire ▶verb 2 TRAP, catch, entrap, net, seize, wire

snarl verb (often with up) TANGLE, entangle, entwine, muddle, ravel

snarl-up noun TANGLE, confusion, entanglement, muddle

snatch verb 1 SEIZE, clutch, grab, grasp, grip ▶noun 2 BIT, fragment, part, piece, snippet

sneak verb 1 SLINK, lurk, pad, skulk, slip, steal 2 SLIP, smuggle, spirit ▶noun 3 INFORMER, telltale

sneaking adjective 1 NAGGING, persistent, uncomfortable, worrying 2 SECRET, hidden, private, undivulged, unexpressed, unvoiced

sneaky adjective SLY, deceitful, devious, dishonest, double-dealing, down and dirty (*informal*), furtive, low, mean, shifty, untrustworthy

sneer noun 1 SCORN, derision, gibe, jeer, mockery, ridicule ▶verb 2 SCORN, deride, disdain, jeer, laugh, mock, ridicule

snide adjective NASTY, cynical, disparaging, hurtful, ill-natured, malicious, sarcastic, scornful, sneering, spiteful

sniff verb INHALE, breathe, smell

snigger noun, verb LAUGH, giggle, snicker, titter

snip verb 1 CUT, clip, crop, dock, shave, trim ▶noun 2 BIT, clipping, fragment, piece, scrap, shred

snipe verb CRITICIZE, carp, denigrate, disparage, jeer, knock (*informal*), put down

snippet noun PIECE, fragment, part, scrap, shred

snitch verb 1 Informal INFORM ON, grass on (*Brit. slang*), tattle on, tell on (*informal*), tell tales ▶noun 2 INFORMER, tattletale, telltale

snivel verb WHINE, cry, moan, sniffle, whimper

snob noun ELITIST, highbrow, prig

snobbery noun ARROGANCE, airs, pretension, pride, snobbishness

snobbish adjective SUPERIOR, arrogant, patronizing, pretentious, snooty (*informal*), stuck-up (*informal*)

snoop verb PRY, interfere, poke one's nose in (*informal*), spy

snooper noun NOSY ROSY (*U.S. informal*), busybody, meddler, snoop (*informal*)

snooze verb 1 DOZE, catnap, nap, take forty winks (*informal*) ▶noun 2 DOZE, catnap, forty

winks (*informal*), nap, siesta

snub verb 1 PUT DOWN, avoid, blow off (*slang*), cold-shoulder, cut (*informal*), humiliate, ignore, rebuff, slight ▶noun 2 INSULT, affront, put-down, slap in the face

snug adjective COZY, comfortable, comfy (*informal*), homey, warm

snuggle verb NESTLE, cuddle, nuzzle

soak verb 1 WET, bathe, damp, drench, immerse, moisten, saturate, steep 2 PENETRATE, permeate, seep 3 soak up ABSORB, assimilate

soaking adjective SOAKED, drenched, dripping, saturated, sodden, sopping, streaming, wet through, wringing wet

soar verb 1 ASCEND, fly, mount, rise, wing 2 RISE, climb, escalate, rocket, shoot up

sob verb CRY, howl, shed tears, weep

sober adjective 1 ABSTINENT, abstemious, moderate, temperate 2 SERIOUS, composed, cool, grave, level-headed, rational, reasonable, sedate, solemn, staid, steady 3 PLAIN, dark, drab, dumpy (*informal*), frowzy, homely (*U.S.*), quiet, somber, subdued

sobriety noun 1 ABSTINENCE, abstemiousness, moderation, nonindulgence, soberness, temperance 2 SERIOUSNESS, gravity, level-headedness, solemnity, staidness, steadiness

so-called adjective ALLEGED, pretended, professed, self-styled, supposed

sociable *adjective* FRIENDLY, affable, companionable, convivial, cordial, genial, gregarious, outgoing, social, warm

social *adjective* 1 COMMUNAL, collective, common, community, general, group, public ▶*noun* GET-TOGETHER (*informal*), gathering, party

socialize *verb* MIX, fraternize, get about or around, go out

society *noun* 1 MANKIND, civilization, humanity, people, the community, the public 2 ORGANIZATION, association, circle, club, fellowship, group, guild, institute, league, order, union 3 UPPER CLASSES, beau monde, elite, gentry, high society 4 COMPANIONSHIP, company, fellowship, friendship

sodden *adjective* SOAKED, drenched, saturated, soggy, sopping, waterlogged

sofa *noun* COUCH, chaise longue, divan, settee

soft *adjective* 1 PLIABLE, bendable, elastic, flexible, malleable, moldable, plastic, supple 2 YIELDING, elastic, gelatinous, pulpy, spongy, squashy 3 VELVETY, downy, feathery, fleecy, silky, smooth 4 QUIET, dulcet, gentle, murmured, muted, soft-toned 5 PALE, bland, light, mellow, pastel, subdued 6 DIM, dimmed, faint, restful 7 MILD, balmy, temperate 8 LENIENT, easy-going, indulgent, lax, overindulgent, permissive, spineless 9 OUT OF CONDITION, effeminate, flabby, flaccid, limp, weak 10 *Informal* EASY, comfortable, undemanding

11 KIND, compassionate, gentle, sensitive, sentimental, tenderhearted, touchy-feely (*informal*)

soften *verb* LESSEN, allay, appease, cushion, ease, mitigate, moderate, mollify, still, subdue, temper

softhearted *adjective* KIND, charitable, compassionate, sentimental, sympathetic, tender, tenderhearted, warm-hearted

soggy *adjective* SODDEN, dripping, moist, saturated, soaked, sopping, waterlogged

soil[1] *noun* 1 EARTH, clay, dirt, dust, ground 2 LAND, country

soil[2] *verb* DIRTY, befoul, besmirch, defile, foul, pollute, spot, stain, sully, tarnish

solace *noun* 1 COMFORT, consolation, relief ▶*verb* 2 COMFORT, console

soldier *noun* FIGHTER, man-at-arms, serviceman, trooper, warrior

sole *adjective* ONLY, alone, exclusive, individual, one, single, solitary

solely *adverb* ONLY, alone, completely, entirely, exclusively, merely

solemn *adjective* 1 FORMAL, ceremonial, dignified, grand, grave, momentous, stately 2 SERIOUS, earnest, grave, sedate, sober, staid

solemnity *noun* 1 SERIOUSNESS, earnestness, gravity 2 FORMALITY, grandeur, impressiveness, momentousness

solicitous *adjective* CONCERNED, anxious, attentive, careful

solicitude *noun* CONCERN,

anxiety, attentiveness, care, consideration, regard

solid adjective 1 FIRM, compact, concrete, dense, hard 2 STRONG, stable, sturdy, substantial, unshakable 3 SOUND, genuine, good, pure, real, reliable 4 RELIABLE, dependable, trusty, upright, upstanding, worthy

solidarity noun UNITY, accord, cohesion, concordance, like-mindedness, team spirit, unanimity, unification

solidify verb HARDEN, cake, coagulate, cohere, congeal, jell, set

solitary adjective 1 UNSOCIABLE, cloistered, isolated, reclusive, unsocial 2 SINGLE, alone, lone, sole 3 LONELY, companionless, friendless, lonesome 4 ISOLATED, hidden, out-of-the-way, remote, unfrequented

solitude noun ISOLATION, loneliness, privacy, retirement, seclusion

solution noun 1 ANSWER, explanation, key, result 2 Chemistry MIXTURE, blend, compound, mix, solvent

solve verb ANSWER, clear up, crack, decipher, disentangle, get to the bottom of, resolve, unravel, work out

somber adjective 1 DARK, dim, drab, dull, gloomy, sober 2 GLOOMY, dismal, doleful, grave, joyless, lugubrious, mournful, sad, sober

somebody noun CELEBRITY, dignitary, household name, luminary, megastar (informal), name, notable, personage, star

someday adverb EVENTUALLY, one

day, one of these (fine) days, sooner or later

somehow adverb ONE WAY OR ANOTHER, by fair means or foul, by hook or (by) crook, by some means or other, come hell or high water (informal), come what may

sometimes adverb OCCASIONALLY, at times, now and then

song noun BALLAD, air, anthem, carol, chant, chorus, ditty, hymn, number, psalm, tune

soon adverb BEFORE LONG, in the near future, shortly

soothe verb 1 CALM, allay, appease, hush, lull, mollify, pacify, quiet, still 2 RELIEVE, alleviate, assuage, ease

soothing adjective CALMING, emollient, palliative, relaxing, restful

soothsayer noun PROPHET, diviner, fortune-teller, seer, sibyl

sophisticated adjective 1 CULTURED, cosmopolitan, cultivated, refined, urbane, worldly 2 COMPLEX, advanced, complicated, delicate, elaborate, intricate, refined, subtle

sophistication noun SAVOIR-FAIRE, finesse, poise, urbanity, worldliness, worldly wisdom

soporific adjective 1 SLEEP-INDUCING, sedative, somnolent, tranquilizing ▶ noun 2 SEDATIVE, narcotic, opiate, tranquilizer

sorcerer noun MAGICIAN, enchanter, necromancer, warlock, witch, wizard

sorcery noun BLACK MAGIC, black art, enchantment, magic, necromancy, witchcraft, wizardry

sordid *adjective* **1** DIRTY, filthy, foul, mean, scuzzy (*slang*), seedy, sleazy, squalid, unclean **2** BASE, debauched, degenerate, low, shabby, shameful, vicious, vile **3** MERCENARY, avaricious, covetous, grasping, selfish

sore *adjective* **1** PAINFUL, angry, burning, inflamed, irritated, raw, sensitive, smarting, tender **2** ANNOYING, severe, sharp, troublesome **3** ANNOYED, aggrieved, angry, cross, hurt, irked, irritated, pained, resentful, stung, upset **4** URGENT, acute, critical, desperate, dire, extreme, pressing

sorrow *noun* **1** GRIEF, anguish, distress, heartache, heartbreak, misery, mourning, regret, sadness, unhappiness, woe **2** AFFLICTION, hardship, misfortune, trial, tribulation, trouble, woe ▶ *verb* **3** GRIEVE, agonize, bemoan, be sad, bewail, lament, mourn

sorrowful *adjective* SAD, dejected, dismal, doleful, grieving, miserable, mournful, sorry, unhappy, woebegone, woeful, wretched

sorry *adjective* **1** REGRETFUL, apologetic, conscience-stricken, contrite, penitent, remorseful, repentant, shamefaced **2** SYMPATHETIC, commiserative, compassionate, full of pity, moved **3** WRETCHED, deplorable, mean, miserable, pathetic, pitiful, poor, sad

sort *noun* **1** KIND, brand, category, class, ilk, make, nature, order, quality, style, type, variety ▶ *verb* **2** ARRANGE,

categorize, classify, divide, grade, group, order, put in order, rank

sort out *verb* **1** RESOLVE, clarify, clear up **2** ORGANIZE, tidy up

soul *noun* **1** SPIRIT, essence, life, vital force **2** PERSONIFICATION, embodiment, epitome, essence, quintessence, type **3** PERSON, being, body, creature, individual, man *or* woman

sound¹ *noun* **1** NOISE, din, report, reverberation, tone **2** IMPRESSION, drift, idea, look ▶ *verb* **3** RESOUND, echo, reverberate **4** SEEM, appear, look **5** PRONOUNCE, announce, articulate, declare, express, utter

sound² *adjective* **1** PERFECT, fit, healthy, intact, solid, unhurt, unimpaired, uninjured, whole **2** SENSIBLE, correct, logical, proper, prudent, rational, reasonable, right, trustworthy, valid, well-founded, wise **3** DEEP, unbroken, undisturbed, untroubled

sound³ *verb* FATHOM, plumb, probe

sound out *verb* PROBE, canvass, pump, question, see how the land lies

sour *adjective* **1** SHARP, acetic, acid, bitter, pungent, tart **2** GONE OFF, curdled, gone bad, turned **3** ILL-NATURED, acrimonious, disagreeable, embittered, ill-tempered, peevish, tart, ungenerous, waspish

source *noun* **1** ORIGIN, author, beginning, cause, derivation, fount, originator **2** INFORMANT, authority

souvenir noun KEEPSAKE, memento, reminder

sovereign noun 1 MONARCH, chief, emperor or empress, king or queen, potentate, prince, ruler ▶ adjective 2 SUPREME, absolute, imperial, kingly or queenly, principal, royal, ruling 3 EXCELLENT, effectual, efficacious, efficient

sovereignty noun SUPREME POWER, domination, kingship, primacy, supremacy

sow verb SCATTER, implant, plant, seed

space noun 1 ROOM, capacity, elbowroom, expanse, extent, leeway, margin, play, scope 2 GAP, blank, distance, interval, omission 3 TIME, duration, interval, period, span, while

spacious adjective ROOMY, ample, broad, capacious, commodious, expansive, extensive, huge, large, sizable or sizeable

spadework noun PREPARATION, donkey-work, groundwork, labor

span noun 1 EXTENT, amount, distance, length, reach, spread, stretch 2 PERIOD, duration, spell, term ▶ verb 3 EXTEND ACROSS, bridge, cover, cross, link, traverse

spank verb SMACK, cuff, paddle (U.S. & Canad.), slap

spar verb ARGUE, bicker, row, scrap (informal), squabble, wrangle

spare adjective 1 EXTRA, additional, free, leftover, odd, over, superfluous, surplus, unoccupied, unused, unwanted

2 THIN, gaunt, lean, meager, wiry 3 HAVE MERCY ON, be merciful to, go easy on (informal), leave, let off (informal), pardon, save from 4 AFFORD, do without, give, grant, let (someone) have, manage without, part with

spare time noun LEISURE, free time, odd moments

sparing adjective ECONOMICAL, careful, frugal, prudent, saving, thrifty

spark noun 1 FLICKER, flare, flash, gleam, glint 2 TRACE, atom, hint, jot, scrap, vestige ▶ verb 3 (often with off) START, inspire, precipitate, provoke, set off, stimulate, trigger (off)

sparkle verb 1 GLITTER, dance, flash, gleam, glint, glisten, scintillate, shimmer, shine, twinkle ▶ noun 2 GLITTER, brilliance, flash, flicker, gleam, glint, twinkle 3 VIVACITY, dash, élan, life, spirit, vitality

sparse adjective SCATTERED, few and far between, meager, scanty, scarce

spartan adjective AUSTERE, ascetic, disciplined, frugal, plain, rigorous, self-denying, severe, strict

spasm noun 1 CONVULSION, contraction, paroxysm, twitch 2 BURST, eruption, fit, frenzy, outburst, seizure

spasmodic adjective SPORADIC, convulsive, erratic, fitful, intermittent, irregular, jerky

spate noun FLOOD, deluge, flow, outpouring, rush, torrent

speak verb 1 TALK, articulate, converse, express, pronounce, say, state, tell, utter 2 LECTURE,

address, declaim, discourse,
hold forth

speaker noun LECTURER, orator,
public speaker, spokesman or
spokeswoman, spokesperson

speak out or **up** verb SPEAK ONE'S
MIND, have one's say, make
one's position plain, voice
one's opinions

spearhead verb LEAD, head,
initiate, launch, pioneer, set in
motion, set off

special adjective **1** EXCEPTIONAL,
extraordinary, important,
memorable, significant,
uncommon, unique, unusual
2 PARTICULAR, appropriate,
distinctive, individual, precise,
specific

specialist noun EXPERT,
authority, buff (informal),
connoisseur, consultant,
master, professional

speciality noun FORTE, bag
(slang, dated), métier, pièce de
résistance, specialty

species noun KIND, breed,
category, class, group, sort,
type, variety

specific adjective **1** PARTICULAR,
characteristic, distinguishing,
special **2** DEFINITE, clear-cut,
exact, explicit, express, precise,
unequivocal

specification noun REQUIREMENT,
condition, detail, particular,
qualification, stipulation

specify verb STATE, define,
designate, detail, indicate,
mention, name, stipulate

specimen noun SAMPLE,
example, exemplification,
instance, model, pattern,
representative, type

speck noun **1** MARK, blemish,

dot, fleck, mote, speckle, spot,
stain **2** PARTICLE, atom, bit,
grain, iota, jot, mite, shred

speckled adjective FLECKED,
dappled, dotted, mottled,
spotted, sprinkled

spectacle noun **1** SIGHT,
curiosity, marvel,
phenomenon, scene, wonder
2 SHOW, display, event,
exhibition, extravaganza,
pageant, performance

spectacular adjective
1 IMPRESSIVE, cool (informal),
dazzling, dramatic, grand,
magnificent, phat (slang),
sensational, splendid, striking,
stunning (informal) ▶ noun
2 SHOW, display, spectacle

spectator noun ONLOOKER,
bystander, looker-on, observer,
viewer, watcher

specter noun GHOST, apparition,
phantom, spirit, vision, wraith

speculate verb **1** CONJECTURE,
consider, guess, hypothesize,
suppose, surmise, theorize,
wonder **2** GAMBLE, hazard, risk,
venture

speculation noun **1** GUESSWORK,
conjecture, hypothesis,
opinion, supposition, surmise,
theory **2** GAMBLE, hazard, risk

speculative adjective
HYPOTHETICAL, academic,
conjectural, notional,
suppositional, theoretical

speech noun **1** COMMUNICATION,
conversation, dialogue,
discussion, talk **2** TALK, address,
discourse, homily, lecture,
oration, spiel (informal)
3 LANGUAGE, articulation,
dialect, diction, enunciation,
idiom, jargon, parlance, tongue

speechless adjective **1** MUTE, dumb, inarticulate, silent, wordless **2** ASTOUNDED, aghast, amazed, dazed, shocked

speed noun **1** SWIFTNESS, haste, hurry, pace, quickness, rapidity, rush, velocity ▶ verb **2** RACE, career, gallop, hasten, hurry, make haste, rush, tear, zoom **3** HELP, advance, aid, assist, boost, expedite, facilitate

speed up verb ACCELERATE, gather momentum, increase the tempo

speedy adjective QUICK, express, fast, hasty, headlong, hurried, immediate, precipitate, prompt, rapid, swift

spell¹ verb INDICATE, augur, imply, mean, point to, portend, signify

spell² noun **1** INCANTATION, charm **2** FASCINATION, allure, bewitchment, enchantment, glamour, magic

spell³ noun PERIOD, bout, course, interval, season, stretch, term, time

spellbound adjective ENTRANCED, bewitched, captivated, charmed, enthralled, fascinated, gripped, mesmerized, rapt

spend verb **1** PAY OUT, disburse, expend, fork out (slang) **2** PASS, fill, occupy, while away **3** USE UP, consume, dissipate, drain, empty, exhaust, run through, squander, waste

spendthrift noun **1** SQUANDERER, big spender, profligate, spender, waster ▶ adjective **2** WASTEFUL, extravagant, improvident, prodigal, profligate

spew verb VOMIT, barf (slang), disgorge, puke (slang), regurgitate, throw up (informal)

sphere noun **1** BALL, circle, globe, globule, orb **2** FIELD, capacity, department, domain, function, patch, province, realm, scope, territory, turf (slang)

spherical adjective ROUND, globe-shaped, globular, rotund

spice noun **1** SEASONING, relish, savor **2** EXCITEMENT, color, pep, piquancy, zest, zing (informal)

spicy adjective **1** HOT, aromatic, piquant, savory, seasoned **2** Informal SCANDALOUS, hot (informal), indelicate, racy, ribald, risqué, suggestive, titillating

spike noun **1** POINT, barb, prong, spine ▶ verb **2** IMPALE, spear, spit, stick

spill verb **1** POUR, discharge, disgorge, overflow, slop over ▶ noun **2** FALL, tumble

spin verb **1** REVOLVE, gyrate, pirouette, reel, rotate, turn, twirl, whirl **2** REEL, swim, whirl ▶ noun **3** REVOLUTION, gyration, roll, whirl **4** Informal DRIVE, joy ride (informal), ride

spine noun **1** BACKBONE, spinal column, vertebrae, vertebral column **2** BARB, needle, quill, ray, spike, spur

spine-chilling adjective FRIGHTENING, bloodcurdling, eerie, horrifying, scary (informal), spooky (informal), terrifying

spineless adjective WEAK, cowardly, faint-hearted, feeble, gutless (informal), lily-livered, soft, weak-kneed (informal)

spin out verb PROLONG, amplify, delay, drag out, draw out, extend, lengthen

spiral noun 1 COIL, corkscrew, helix, whorl ▶ adjective 2 COILED, helical, whorled, winding

spirit noun 1 LIFE FORCE, life, soul, vital spark 2 FEELING, atmosphere, gist, tenor, tone 3 TEMPERAMENT, attitude, character, disposition, outlook, temper 4 LIVELINESS, animation, brio, energy, enthusiasm, fire, force, life, mettle, vigor, zest 5 COURAGE, backbone, gameness, grit, guts (informal), spunk (informal) 6 ESSENCE, intention, meaning, purport, purpose, sense, substance 7 GHOST, apparition, phantom, specter 8 spirits MOOD, feelings, frame of mind, morale ▶ verb 9 (with away or off) REMOVE, abduct, abstract, carry, purloin, seize, steal, whisk

spirited adjective LIVELY, active, animated, energetic, feisty (informal), mettlesome, vivacious

spiritual adjective SACRED, devotional, divine, holy, religious

spit verb 1 EJECT, expectorate, splutter, throw out ▶ noun 2 SALIVA, dribble, drool, slaver, spittle

spite noun 1 MALICE, animosity, hatred, ill will, malevolence, spitefulness, spleen, venom 2 in spite of DESPITE, (even) though, notwithstanding, regardless of ▶ verb 3 HURT, annoy, harm, injure, vex

spiteful adjective MALICIOUS, bitchy (informal), ill-natured, malevolent, nasty, vindictive

splash verb 1 SCATTER, shower, slop, spatter, spray, sprinkle, wet 2 PUBLICIZE, broadcast, tout, trumpet ▶ noun 3 DASH, burst, patch, spattering, touch 4 Informal DISPLAY, effect, impact, sensation, stir

splash out verb Informal SPEND, be extravagant, spare no expense, splurge

splendid adjective 1 MARVELOUS, fantastic (informal), first-class, glorious, great (informal), wonderful 2 MAGNIFICENT, cool (informal), costly, gorgeous, impressive, lavish, luxurious, ornate, phat (slang), resplendent, rich, sumptuous, superb

splendor noun MAGNIFICENCE, brightness, brilliance, display, glory, grandeur, pomp, richness, show, spectacle, sumptuousness

splinter noun 1 SLIVER, chip, flake, fragment ▶ verb 2 SHATTER, disintegrate, fracture, split

split verb 1 BREAK, burst, come apart, come undone, crack, give way, open, rend, rip 2 SEPARATE, branch, cleave, disband, disunite, diverge, fork, part 3 SHARE OUT, allocate, allot, apportion, distribute, divide, halve, partition ▶ noun 4 CRACK, breach, division, fissure, gap, rent, rip, separation, slit, tear 5 DIVISION, breach, break-up, discord, dissension, estrangement, rift, rupture, schism ▶ adjective 6 DIVIDED, broken, cleft, cracked, fractured, ruptured

split up verb SEPARATE, break up,

divorce, part

spoil verb 1 RUIN, damage, destroy, disfigure, harm, impair, injure, mar, mess up, trash (slang), wreck 2 OVERINDULGE, coddle, cosset, indulge, pamper 3 GO BAD, addle, curdle, decay, decompose, rot, turn

spoils plural noun BOOTY, loot, plunder, prey, swag (slang), treasure

spoilsport noun KILLJOY, damper, misery (informal), sourpuss, wet blanket (informal)

spoken adjective SAID, expressed, oral, told, unwritten, uttered, verbal, viva voce, voiced

spokesperson noun SPEAKER, mouthpiece, official, spin doctor (informal), spokesman or spokeswoman, voice

spongy adjective POROUS, absorbent

sponsor noun 1 BACKER, patron, promoter ▶verb 2 BACK, finance, fund, patronize, promote, subsidize

spontaneous adjective UNPLANNED, impromptu, impulsive, instinctive, natural, unprompted, voluntary, willing

spoof noun Informal PARODY, burlesque, caricature, mockery, satire

spooky adjective EERIE, chilling, creepy (informal), frightening, scary (informal), spine-chilling, uncanny, unearthly, weird

sporadic adjective INTERMITTENT, irregular, occasional, scattered, spasmodic

sport noun 1 GAME, amusement, diversion, exercise, pastime,

play, recreation 2 FUN, badinage, banter, jest, joking, teasing ▶verb 3 Old-fashioned, Informal WEAR, display, exhibit, show off

sporting adjective FAIR, game (informal), sportsmanlike

sporty adjective ATHLETIC, energetic, outdoor

spot noun 1 MARK, blemish, blot, blotch, scar, smudge, speck, speckle, stain 2 PLACE, location, point, position, scene, site 3 Informal PREDICAMENT, difficulty, hot water (informal), mess, plight, quandary, tight spot, trouble ▶verb 4 SEE, catch a glimpse of, catch sight of, detect, discern, espy, make out, observe, recognize, sight 5 MARK, dirty, fleck, mottle, smirch, soil, spatter, speckle, splodge, splotch, stain

spotless adjective CLEAN, flawless, gleaming, immaculate, impeccable, pure, shining, unblemished, unstained, unsullied, untarnished

spotlight noun 1 ATTENTION, fame, limelight, public eye ▶verb 2 HIGHLIGHT, accentuate, draw attention to

spotted adjective SPECKLED, dappled, dotted, flecked, mottled

spouse noun PARTNER, consort, husband or wife, mate, significant other (informal)

spout verb STREAM, discharge, gush, shoot, spray, spurt, surge

sprawl verb LOLL, flop, lounge, slouch, slump

spray¹ noun 1 DROPLETS, drizzle, fine mist 2 AEROSOL, atomizer, sprinkler ▶ *verb* **3** SCATTER, diffuse, shower, sprinkle

spray² *noun* SPRIG, branch, corsage, floral arrangement

spread *verb* **1** OPEN (OUT), broaden, dilate, expand, extend, sprawl, stretch, unfold, unroll, widen **2** PROLIFERATE, escalate, multiply **3** CIRCULATE, broadcast, disseminate, make known, propagate ▶ *noun* **4** INCREASE, advance, development, dispersal, dissemination, expansion, proliferation **5** EXTENT, span, stretch, sweep

spree *noun* BINGE (*informal*), bacchanalia, carousal, fling, orgy, revel

sprightly *adjective* LIVELY, active, agile, brisk, energetic, nimble, spirited, spry, vivacious

spring *verb* **1** JUMP, bounce, bound, leap, vault **2** (often with *from*) ORIGINATE, arise, come, derive, descend, issue, proceed, start, stem **3** (often with *up*) APPEAR, develop, mushroom, shoot up ▶ *noun* **4** JUMP, bound, leap, vault **5** ELASTICITY, bounce, buoyancy, flexibility, resilience

springy *adjective* ELASTIC, bouncy, buoyant, flexible, resilient, rubbery

sprinkle *verb* SCATTER, dredge, dust, pepper, powder, shower, spray, strew

sprinkling *noun* SCATTERING, dash, dusting, few, handful, sprinkle

sprint *verb* RACE, dart, dash, shoot, tear

sprite *noun* SPIRIT, brownie, elf, fairy, goblin, imp, pixie

sprout *verb* GROW, bud, develop, shoot, spring

spruce *adjective* SMART, dapper, neat, trim, well-groomed, well turned out

spruce up *verb* SMARTEN UP, tidy, titivate

spry *adjective* ACTIVE, agile, nimble, sprightly, supple

spur *noun* **1** STIMULUS, impetus, impulse, incentive, incitement, inducement, motive **2** GOAD, prick **3 on the spur of the moment** ON IMPULSE, impromptu, impulsively, on the spot, without planning ▶ *verb* **4** INCITE, animate, drive, goad, impel, prick, prod, prompt, stimulate, urge

spurious *adjective* FALSE, artificial, bogus, fake, phoney or phony (*informal*), pretended, sham, specious, unauthentic

spurn *verb* REJECT, despise, disdain, rebuff, repulse, scorn, slight, snub

spurt *verb* **1** GUSH, burst, erupt, shoot, squirt, surge ▶ *noun* **2** BURST, fit, rush, spate, surge

spy *noun* **1** UNDERCOVER AGENT, mole ▶ *verb* **2** CATCH SIGHT OF, espy, glimpse, notice, observe, spot

squabble *verb* **1** QUARREL, argue, bicker, dispute, fight, row, wrangle ▶ *noun* **2** QUARREL, argument, disagreement, dispute, fight, row, tiff

squad *noun* TEAM, band, company, crew, force, gang, group, troop

squalid *adjective* DIRTY, filthy, scuzzy (*slang*), seedy, sleazy, slummy, sordid, unclean

squalor *noun* FILTH, foulness,

sleaziness, squalidness

squander *verb* WASTE, blow (*slang*), expend, fritter away, misspend, misuse, spend

square *adjective* 1 HONEST, above board, ethical, fair, genuine, kosher (*informal*), straight 2 *Informal* UNCOOL, dorky (*slang*), nerdy, unhip ▶ *verb* 3 EVEN UP, adjust, align, level 4 (sometimes with *up*) PAY OFF, settle 5 (often with *with*) AGREE, correspond, fit, match, reconcile, tally

squash *verb* 1 CRUSH, compress, distort, flatten, mash, press, pulp, smash 2 SUPPRESS, annihilate, crush, humiliate, quell, silence

squashy *adjective* SOFT, mushy, pulpy, spongy, yielding

squawk *verb* CRY, hoot, screech

squeak *verb* PEEP, pipe, squeal

squeal *noun, verb* SCREAM, screech, shriek, wail, yell

squeamish *adjective* 1 DELICATE, fastidious, prudish, strait-laced 2 SICK, nauseous, queasy

squeeze *verb* 1 PRESS, clutch, compress, crush, grip, pinch, squash, wring 2 CRAM, pack, press, ram, stuff 3 HUG, clasp, cuddle, embrace, enfold 4 EXTORT, milk, pressurize, wrest ▶ *noun* 5 HUG, clasp, embrace 6 CRUSH, congestion, crowd, jam, press, squash

squirm *verb* WRIGGLE, twist, writhe

squirt *noun* *Informal* CHILD, baby, boy, girl, infant, kid (*informal*), minor, toddler, tot, whippersnapper (*old-fashioned*), youngster

stab *verb* 1 PIERCE, impale, jab, knife, spear, stick, thrust, transfix, wound ▶ *noun* 2 WOUND, gash, incision, jab, puncture, thrust 3 TWINGE, ache, pang, prick 4 **make** or **have a stab at** *Informal* ATTEMPT, endeavor, have a go, try

stability *noun* FIRMNESS, solidity, soundness, steadiness, strength

stable *adjective* 1 FIRM, constant, established, fast, fixed, immovable, lasting, permanent, secure, sound, strong 2 STEADY, reliable, staunch, steadfast, sure

stack *noun* 1 PILE, heap, load, mass, mound, mountain ▶ *verb* 2 PILE, accumulate, amass, assemble, heap up, load

staff *noun* 1 WORKERS, employees, personnel, team, workforce 2 STICK, cane, crook, pole, rod, scepter, stave, wand

stage *noun* POINT, division, juncture, lap, leg, level, period, phase, step

stagger *verb* 1 TOTTER, lurch, reel, sway, wobble 2 ASTOUND, amaze, astonish, confound, overwhelm, shake, shock, stun, stupefy 3 OVERLAP, alternate, step

stagnant *adjective* STALE, quiet, sluggish, still

stagnate *verb* VEGETATE, decay, decline, idle, languish, rot, rust

staid *adjective* SEDATE, calm, composed, grave, serious, sober, solemn, steady

stain *verb* 1 MARK, blemish, blot, dirty, discolor, smirch, soil, spot, tinge ▶ *noun* 2 MARK, blemish, blot, discoloration, smirch, spot 3 STIGMA, disgrace, dishonor, shame, slur

stake[1] noun POLE, pale, paling, palisade, picket, post, stick

stake[2] noun 1 BET, ante, pledge, wager 2 INTEREST, concern, investment, involvement, share ▶ verb 3 BET, chance, gamble, hazard, risk, venture, wager

stale adjective 1 OLD, decayed, dry, flat, fusty, hard, musty, sour 2 UNORIGINAL, banal, hackneyed, overused, stereotyped, threadbare, trite, worn-out

stalk verb PURSUE, follow, haunt, hunt, shadow, track

stall verb PLAY FOR TIME, hedge, temporize

stalwart adjective STRONG, staunch, stout, strapping, sturdy

stamina noun STAYING POWER, endurance, energy, force, power, resilience, strength

stammer verb STUTTER, falter, hesitate, pause, stumble

stamp noun 1 IMPRINT, brand, earmark, hallmark, mark, signature ▶ verb 2 TRAMPLE, crush 3 IDENTIFY, brand, categorize, label, mark, reveal, show to be 4 IMPRINT, impress, mark, print

stampede noun RUSH, charge, flight, rout

stamp out verb ELIMINATE, crush, destroy, eradicate, put down, quell, scotch, suppress

stance noun 1 ATTITUDE, position, stand, standpoint, viewpoint 2 POSTURE, bearing, carriage, deportment

stand verb 1 BE UPRIGHT, be erect, be vertical, rise 2 PUT, mount, place, position, set

3 EXIST, be valid, continue, hold, obtain, prevail, remain 4 TOLERATE, abide, allow, bear, brook, countenance, deal with (slang), endure, handle, put up with (informal), stomach, take ▶ noun 5 STALL, booth, table 6 POSITION, attitude, determination, opinion, stance 7 SUPPORT, base, bracket, dais, platform, rack, stage, tripod

standard noun 1 BENCHMARK, average, criterion, gauge, grade, guideline, measure, model, norm, yardstick 2 (often plural) PRINCIPLES, ethics, ideals, morals 3 FLAG, banner, ensign ▶ adjective 4 USUAL, average, basic, customary, normal, orthodox, regular, typical 5 ACCEPTED, approved, authoritative, definitive, established, official, recognized

standardize verb BRING INTO LINE, institutionalize, regiment

stand by verb 1 BE PREPARED, wait 2 SUPPORT, back, be loyal to, champion, take (someone's) part

stand for verb 1 REPRESENT, betoken, denote, indicate, mean, signify, symbolize 2 Informal TOLERATE, bear, brook, endure, put up with

stand-in noun SUBSTITUTE, deputy, locum, replacement, reserve, stopgap, surrogate, understudy

stand in for verb BE A SUBSTITUTE FOR, cover for, deputize for, represent, take the place of

standing adjective 1 PERMANENT, fixed, lasting, regular 2 UPRIGHT, erect, vertical ▶ noun 3 STATUS, eminence, footing, position,

rank, reputation, repute **4** DURATION, continuance, existence

standoffish *adjective* RESERVED, aloof, cold, distant, haughty, remote, unapproachable, unsociable

stand out *verb* BE CONSPICUOUS, be distinct, be obvious, be prominent

standpoint *noun* POINT OF VIEW, angle, position, stance, viewpoint

stand up for *verb* SUPPORT, champion, defend, stick up for (*informal*), uphold

staple *adjective* PRINCIPAL, basic, chief, fundamental, key, main, predominant

star *noun* **1** HEAVENLY BODY **2** CELEBRITY, big name, luminary, main attraction, megastar (*informal*), name, superstar (*informal*) ▸ *adjective* **3** LEADING, brilliant, celebrated, major, prominent, well-known

stare *verb* GAZE, eyeball (*slang*), gape, gawk, goggle, look, watch

stark *adjective* **1** HARSH, austere, bare, barren, bleak, grim, hard, homely, plain, severe **2** ABSOLUTE, blunt, downright, out-and-out, pure, sheer, unmitigated, utter ▸ *adverb* **3** ABSOLUTELY, altogether, completely, entirely, quite, utterly, wholly

start *verb* **1** BEGIN, appear, arise, commence, issue, originate **2** SET ABOUT, embark upon, make a beginning, take the first step **3** SET IN MOTION, activate, get going, initiate, instigate, kick-start, open,

originate, trigger **4** JUMP, flinch, jerk, recoil, shy **5** ESTABLISH, begin, create, found, inaugurate, initiate, institute, launch, pioneer, set up ▸ *noun* **6** BEGINNING, birth, dawn, foundation, inception, initiation, onset, opening, outset **7** ADVANTAGE, edge, head start, lead **8** JUMP, convulsion, spasm

startle *verb* SURPRISE, frighten, make (someone) jump, scare, shock

starving *adjective* HUNGRY, famished, ravenous, starved

state *noun* **1** CONDITION, circumstances, position, predicament, shape, situation **2** FRAME OF MIND, attitude, humor, mood, spirits **3** COUNTRY, commonwealth, federation, government, kingdom, land, nation, republic, territory **4** CEREMONY, display, glory, grandeur, majesty, pomp, splendor, style ▸ *verb* **5** EXPRESS, affirm, articulate, assert, declare, expound, present, say, specify, utter, voice

stately *adjective* GRAND, august, dignified, lofty, majestic, noble, regal, royal

statement *noun* ACCOUNT, announcement, communication, communiqué, declaration, proclamation, report

state-of-the-art *adjective* LATEST, newest, up-to-date, up-to-the-minute

static *adjective* STATIONARY, fixed, immobile, motionless, still, unmoving

station noun 1 HEADQUARTERS, base, depot 2 PLACE, location, position, post, seat, situation 3 POSITION, post, rank, situation, standing, status ▶ verb 4 ASSIGN, establish, install, locate, post, set

stationary adjective MOTIONLESS, fixed, parked, standing, static, stock-still, unmoving

statuesque adjective WELL-PROPORTIONED, imposing, Junoesque

stature noun IMPORTANCE, eminence, prestige, prominence, rank, standing

status noun POSITION, condition, consequence, eminence, grade, prestige, rank, standing

staunch[1] adjective LOYAL, faithful, firm, sound, stalwart, steadfast, true, trusty

staunch[2] verb STOP, check, dam, halt, stay, stem

stay verb 1 REMAIN, abide, continue, halt, linger, loiter, pause, stop, tarry, wait ▶ noun 2 VISIT, holiday, sojourn, stop, stopover 3 POSTPONEMENT, deferment, delay, halt, stopping, suspension

steadfast adjective FIRM, faithful, fast, fixed, intent, loyal, resolute, stalwart, staunch, steady, unswerving, unwavering

steady adjective 1 FIRM, fixed, safe, stable 2 SENSIBLE, balanced, calm, dependable, equable, level-headed, reliable, sober 3 CONTINUOUS, ceaseless, consistent, constant, incessant, nonstop, persistent, regular, twenty-four-seven (slang), unbroken, uninterrupted ▶ verb 4 STABILIZE, balance, brace,

secure, support

steal verb 1 TAKE, appropriate, embezzle, filch, lift (informal), misappropriate, pilfer, pinch (informal), purloin, thieve 2 SNEAK, creep, slink, slip, tiptoe

stealth noun SECRECY, furtiveness, slyness, sneakiness, stealthiness, surreptitiousness, unobtrusiveness

stealthy adjective SECRET, furtive, secretive, sneaking, surreptitious

steep[1] adjective 1 SHEER, abrupt, precipitous 2 HIGH, exorbitant, extortionate, extreme, overpriced, unreasonable

steep[2] verb 1 SOAK, drench, immerse, macerate, marinate (Cookery), moisten, souse, submerge 2 SATURATE, fill, imbue, infuse, permeate, pervade, suffuse

steer verb DIRECT, conduct, control, guide, handle, pilot

stem[1] noun 1 STALK, axis, branch, shoot, trunk ▶ verb 2 **stem from** ORIGINATE IN, arise from, be caused by, derive from

stem[2] verb STOP, check, curb, dam, hold back, staunch

stench noun STINK, foul smell, reek, whiff

step noun 1 FOOTSTEP, footfall, footprint, pace, print, stride, track 2 STAGE, move, phase, point 3 ACTION, act, deed, expedient, means, measure, move 4 DEGREE, level, rank ▶ verb 5 WALK, move, pace, tread

step in verb INTERVENE, become involved, take action

step up verb INCREASE, intensify, raise

stereotype noun 1 FORMULA, pattern ▶ verb 2 CATEGORIZE,

pigeonhole, standardize, typecast

sterile *adjective* 1 GERM-FREE, aseptic, disinfected, sterilized 2 BARREN, bare, dry, empty, fruitless, unfruitful, unproductive

sterilize *verb* DISINFECT, fumigate, purify

sterling *adjective* EXCELLENT, fine, genuine, sound, superlative, true

stern *adjective* SEVERE, austere, forbidding, grim, hard, harsh, inflexible, rigid, serious, strict

stick[1] *noun* 1 CANE, baton, crook, pole, rod, staff, twig 2 *Brit. slang* ABUSE, criticism, flak (*informal*)

stick[2] *verb* 1 POKE, dig, jab, penetrate, pierce, prod, puncture, spear, stab, thrust, transfix 2 FASTEN, adhere, affix, attach, bind, bond, cling, fix, glue, hold, join, paste, weld 3 (with *out, up*, etc.) PROTRUDE, bulge, extend, jut, obtrude, poke, project, show 4 PUT, deposit, lay, place, set 5 STAY, linger, persist, remain 6 *Slang* TOLERATE, abide, stand, stomach, take 7 **stick up for** DEFEND, champion, stand up for, support

stickler *noun* PERFECTIONIST, fanatic, fusspot (*informal*), purist

sticky *adjective* 1 TACKY, adhesive, clinging, gluey, glutinous, gooey (*informal*), gummy, viscid, viscous 2 *Informal* DIFFICULT, awkward, delicate, embarrassing, nasty, tricky, unpleasant 3 HUMID, clammy, close, muggy, oppressive, sultry, sweltering

stiff *adjective* 1 INFLEXIBLE, firm, hard, inelastic, rigid, solid, taut, tense, tight, unbending, unyielding 2 AWKWARD, clumsy, graceless, inelegant, jerky (*informal*), ungainly, ungraceful 3 DIFFICULT, arduous, exacting, hard, tough 4 SEVERE, drastic, extreme, hard, harsh, heavy, strict 5 UNRELAXED, artificial, constrained, forced, formal, stilted, unnatural

stiffen *verb* 1 BRACE, reinforce, tauten, tense 2 SET, congeal, crystallize, harden, jell, solidify, thicken

stifle *verb* 1 SUPPRESS, check, hush, repress, restrain, silence, smother, stop 2 SUFFOCATE, asphyxiate, choke, smother, strangle

stigma *noun* DISGRACE, dishonor, shame, slur, smirch, stain

still *adjective* 1 MOTIONLESS, calm, peaceful, restful, serene, stationary, tranquil, undisturbed 2 SILENT, hushed, quiet ▸ *verb* 3 QUIETEN, allay, calm, hush, lull, pacify, quiet, settle, silence, soothe ▸ *conjunction* 4 HOWEVER, but, nevertheless, notwithstanding, yet

stilted *adjective* STIFF, constrained, forced, unnatural, wooden

stimulant *noun* PICK-ME-UP (*informal*), restorative, tonic, upper (*slang*)

stimulate *verb* AROUSE, encourage, fire, impel, incite, prompt, provoke, rouse, spur

stimulating *adjective* EXCITING, exhilarating, inspiring, provocative, rousing, stirring

stimulus noun INCENTIVE, encouragement, goad, impetus, incitement, inducement, spur

sting verb 1 HURT, burn, pain, smart, tingle, wound 2 *Informal* CHEAT, defraud, fleece, overcharge, rip off (*slang*), swindle

stingy adjective MEAN, miserly, niggardly, parsimonious, penny-pinching (*informal*), tightfisted, ungenerous

stink verb 1 STENCH, fetor, foul smell ▶ verb 2 REEK

stint verb 1 BE MEAN, be frugal, be sparing, hold back, skimp on ▶ noun 2 SHARE, period, quota, shift, spell, stretch, term, time, turn

stipulate verb SPECIFY, agree, contract, covenant, insist upon, require, settle

stipulation noun SPECIFICATION, agreement, clause, condition, precondition, proviso, qualification, requirement

stir verb 1 MIX, agitate, beat, shake 2 STIMULATE, arouse, awaken, excite, incite, provoke, rouse, spur ▶ noun 3 COMMOTION, activity, bustle, disorder, disturbance, excitement, flurry, fuss

stock noun 1 GOODS, array, choice, commodities, merchandise, range, selection, variety, wares 2 SUPPLY, fund, hoard, reserve, stockpile, store 3 PROPERTY, assets, capital, funds, investment 4 LIVESTOCK, beasts, cattle, domestic animals ▶ adjective 5 STANDARD, conventional, customary, ordinary, regular, routine, usual

6 HACKNEYED, banal, overused, trite ▶ verb 7 SELL, deal in, handle, keep, supply, trade in 8 PROVIDE WITH, equip, fit out, furnish, supply 9 stock up STORE (UP), accumulate, amass, gather, hoard, lay in, put away, save

stocky adjective THICKSET, chunky, dumpy, solid, stubby, sturdy

stodgy adjective 1 HEAVY, filling, leaden, starchy 2 DULL, boring, heavy going, staid, stuffy, tedious, unexciting

stoical adjective RESIGNED, dispassionate, impassive, long-suffering, philosophical, phlegmatic, stoic, stolid

stoicism noun RESIGNATION, acceptance, forbearance, fortitude, impassivity, long-suffering, patience, stolidity

stolid adjective APATHETIC, dull, lumpish, unemotional, wooden

stomach noun 1 BELLY, abdomen, gut (*informal*), pot, tummy (*informal*) 2 INCLINATION, appetite, desire, relish, taste ▶ verb 3 BEAR, abide, endure, swallow, take, tolerate

stony adjective COLD, blank, chilly, expressionless, hard, hostile, icy, unresponsive

stoop verb 1 BEND, bow, crouch, duck, hunch, lean 2 stoop to SINK TO, descend to, lower oneself to, resort to ▶ noun 3 SLOUCH, bad posture, round-shoulderedness

stop verb 1 HALT, cease, conclude, cut short, desist, discontinue, end, finish, pause, put an end to, quit, refrain,

shut down, terminate
2 PREVENT, arrest, forestall, hinder, hold back, impede, repress, restrain **3** PLUG, block, obstruct, seal, staunch, stem **4** STAY, lodge, rest ▶ noun **5** END, cessation, finish, halt, standstill **6** STAY, break, rest **7** STATION, depot, terminus

stopgap noun MAKESHIFT, improvisation, resort, substitute

stoppage noun STOPPING, arrest, close, closure, cutoff, halt, hindrance, shutdown, standstill

store verb **1** PUT BY, deposit, garner, hoard, keep, put aside, reserve, save, stockpile ▶ noun **2** SHOP, market, mart, outlet **3** SUPPLY, accumulation, cache, fund, hoard, quantity, reserve, stock, stockpile **4** REPOSITORY, depository, storeroom, warehouse

storm noun **1** TEMPEST, blizzard, gale, hurricane, squall **2** OUTBURST, agitation, commotion, disturbance, furor, outbreak, outcry, row, rumpus, strife, tumult, turmoil ▶ verb **3** ATTACK, assail, assault, charge, rush **4** RAGE, bluster, rant, rave, thunder **5** RUSH, flounce, fly, stamp

stormy adjective WILD, blustery, inclement, raging, rough, squally, turbulent, windy

story noun **1** TALE, account, anecdote, history, legend, narrative, romance, yarn **2** REPORT, article, feature, news, news item, scoop

stout adjective **1** FAT, big, bulky, burly, corpulent, fleshy, heavy, overweight, plump, portly, rotund, tubby **2** STRONG,

able-bodied, brawny, muscular, robust, stalwart, strapping, sturdy **3** BRAVE, bold, courageous, fearless, gallant, intrepid, plucky, resolute, valiant

stow verb PACK, bundle, load, put away, stash (informal), store

straight adjective **1** DIRECT, near, short **2** LEVEL, aligned, even, horizontal, right, smooth, square, true **3** UPRIGHT, erect, plumb, vertical **4** HONEST, above board, accurate, fair, honorable, just, law-abiding, trustworthy, upright **5** FRANK, blunt, bold, candid, forthright, honest, outright, plain, straightforward **6** SUCCESSIVE, consecutive, continuous, nonstop, running, solid **7** UNDILUTED, neat, pure, unadulterated, unmixed **8** ORDERLY, arranged, in order, neat, organized, shipshape, tidy **9** Slang CONVENTIONAL, bourgeois, conservative ▶ adverb **10** DIRECTLY, at once, immediately, instantly

straight away adverb IMMEDIATELY, at once, directly, instantly, now, right away

straighten verb NEATEN, arrange, order, put in order, tidy (up)

straightforward adjective **1** HONEST, candid, direct, forthright, genuine, open, sincere, truthful, upfront (informal) **2** EASY, elementary, routine, simple, uncomplicated

strain¹ verb **1** STRETCH, distend, draw tight, tauten, tighten **2** OVEREXERT, injure, overtax, overwork, pull, sprain, tax, tear, twist, wrench **3** STRIVE, bend over backwards

(*informal*), endeavor, give it
one's best shot (*informal*), go
for it (*informal*), knock oneself
out (*informal*), labor, struggle
4 SIEVE, filter, purify, sift ▶ *noun*
5 STRESS, anxiety, burden,
pressure, tension **6** EXERTION,
effort, force, struggle **7** INJURY,
pull, sprain, wrench

strain² *noun* **1** BREED, ancestry,
blood, descent, extraction,
family, lineage, race **2** TRACE,
streak, suggestion, tendency

strained *adjective* **1** FORCED,
artificial, false, put on,
unnatural **2** TENSE, awkward,
difficult, embarrassed, stiff,
uneasy

strait *noun* **1** (often plural)
CHANNEL, narrows, sound
2 straits DIFFICULTY, dilemma,
extremity, hardship, plight,
predicament

strait-laced *adjective* STRICT,
moralistic, narrow-minded,
prim, proper, prudish,
puritanical

strand *noun* FILAMENT, fiber,
string, thread

stranded *adjective* **1** BEACHED,
aground, ashore, grounded,
marooned, shipwrecked
2 HELPLESS, abandoned, high
and dry

strange *adjective* **1** ODD,
abnormal, bizarre, curious,
extraordinary, peculiar, queer,
uncommon, weird, wonderful
2 UNFAMILIAR, alien, exotic,
foreign, new, novel, unknown,
untried

stranger *noun* NEWCOMER, alien,
foreigner, guest, incomer,
outlander, visitor

strangle *verb* **1** THROTTLE,

asphyxiate, choke, strangulate
2 SUPPRESS, inhibit, repress, stifle

strap *noun* **1** BELT, thong, tie
▶ *verb* **2** FASTEN, bind, buckle,
lash, secure, tie

strapping *adjective* WELL-BUILT,
big, brawny, husky (*informal*),
powerful, robust, sturdy

stratagem *noun* TRICK, device,
dodge, maneuver, plan, ploy,
ruse, scheme, subterfuge

strategic *adjective* **1** TACTICAL,
calculated, deliberate,
diplomatic, planned, politic
2 CRUCIAL, cardinal, critical,
decisive, important, key, vital

strategy *noun* PLAN, approach,
policy, procedure, scheme

stray *verb* **1** WANDER, drift, err,
go astray **2** DIGRESS, deviate,
diverge, get off the point
▶ *adjective* **3** LOST, abandoned,
homeless, roaming, vagrant
4 RANDOM, accidental, chance

streak *noun* **1** BAND, layer, line,
slash, strip, stripe, stroke, vein
2 TRACE, dash, element, strain,
touch, vein ▶ *verb* **3** SPEED, dart,
flash, fly, hurtle, sprint, tear,
whizz (*informal*), zoom

stream *noun* **1** RIVER, bayou,
beck, brook, rivulet, tributary
2 FLOW, course, current, drift,
run, rush, surge, tide, torrent
▶ *verb* **3** FLOW, cascade, course,
flood, gush, issue, pour, run,
spill, spout

streamlined *adjective* EFFICIENT,
organized, rationalized, slick,
smooth-running

street *noun* ROAD, avenue,
boulevard, lane, parkway,
roadway, row, terrace

strength *noun* **1** MIGHT, brawn,
courage, fortitude, muscle,

robustness, stamina, sturdiness, toughness **2** INTENSITY, effectiveness, efficacy, force, potency, power, vigor **3** ADVANTAGE, asset, strong point

strengthen *verb* **1** FORTIFY, brace up, consolidate, harden, invigorate, restore, stiffen, toughen **2** REINFORCE, augment, bolster, brace, build up, buttress, harden, intensify, support

strenuous *adjective* DEMANDING, arduous, hard, laborious, taxing, tough, uphill

stress *noun* **1** STRAIN, anxiety, burden, pressure, tension, trauma, worry **2** EMPHASIS, force, significance, weight **3** ACCENT, accentuation, beat, emphasis ▶*verb* **4** EMPHASIZE, accentuate, dwell on, underline

stretch *verb* **1** EXTEND, cover, put forth, reach, spread, unroll **2** PULL, distend, draw out, elongate, expand, strain, tighten ▶*noun* **3** EXPANSE, area, distance, extent, spread, tract **4** PERIOD, space, spell, stint, term, time

strict *adjective* **1** SEVERE, authoritarian, firm, harsh, stern, stringent **2** EXACT, accurate, close, faithful, meticulous, precise, scrupulous, true **3** ABSOLUTE, total, utter

strident *adjective* HARSH, discordant, grating, jarring, raucous, screeching, shrill

strife *noun* CONFLICT, battle, clash, discord, dissension, friction, quarrel

strike *verb* **1** WALK OUT, down tools, mutiny, revolt **2** HIT, beat, clobber (*slang*), clout

(*informal*), cuff, hammer, knock, punch, slap, smack, thump, wallop (*informal*) **3** COLLIDE WITH, bump into, hit, run into **4** ATTACK, assail, assault, hit **5** OCCUR TO, come to, dawn on or upon, hit, register (*informal*)

striking *adjective* IMPRESSIVE, conspicuous, cool (*informal*), dramatic, noticeable, outstanding, phat (*slang*)

string *noun* **1** CORD, fiber, twine **2** SERIES, chain, file, line, procession, row, sequence, succession

stringent *adjective* STRICT, inflexible, rigid, rigorous, severe, tight, tough

stringy *adjective* FIBROUS, gristly, sinewy, tough

strip[1] *verb* **1** UNDRESS, disrobe, unclothe **2** PLUNDER, despoil, divest, empty, loot, pillage, ransack, rob, sack

strip[2] *noun* PIECE, band, belt, shred

strive *verb* TRY, attempt, bend over backwards (*informal*), break one's neck (*informal*), do one's best, give it one's best shot (*informal*), go all out (*informal*), knock oneself out (*informal*), labor, make an all-out effort (*informal*), struggle, toil

stroke *verb* **1** CARESS, fondle, pet, rub ▶*noun* **2** APOPLEXY, attack, collapse, fit, seizure **3** BLOW, hit, knock, pat, rap, thump

stroll *verb* **1** WALK, amble, promenade, ramble, saunter ▶*noun* **2** WALK, breath of air, constitutional, promenade, ramble, turn

strong *adjective* **1** POWERFUL, athletic, brawny, burly, hardy, lusty, muscular, robust, strapping, sturdy, tough **2** DURABLE, hard-wearing, heavy-duty, sturdy, substantial, well-built **3** PERSUASIVE, compelling, convincing, effective, potent, sound, telling, weighty, well-founded **4** INTENSE, acute, deep, fervent, fervid, fierce, firm, keen, vehement, violent, zealous **5** EXTREME, drastic, forceful, severe **6** BRIGHT, bold, brilliant, dazzling

stronghold *noun* FORTRESS, bastion, bulwark, castle, citadel, fort

structure *noun* **1** BUILDING, construction, edifice, erection **2** ARRANGEMENT, configuration, construction, design, form, formation, make-up, organization ▶ *verb* **3** ARRANGE, assemble, build up, design, organize, shape

struggle *verb* **1** STRIVE, exert oneself, give it one's best shot (*informal*), go all out (*informal*), knock oneself out (*informal*), labor, make an all-out effort (*informal*), strain, toil, work **2** FIGHT, battle, compete, contend, grapple, wrestle ▶ *noun* **3** EFFORT, exertion, labor, pains, scramble, toil, work **4** FIGHT, battle, brush, clash, combat, conflict, contest, tussle

strut *verb* SWAGGER, parade, peacock, prance

stub *noun* **1** BUTT, end, remainder, remnant, stump, tail, tail end **2** COUNTERFOIL

stubborn *adjective* OBSTINATE, dogged, headstrong, inflexible, intractable, obdurate, persistent, pig-headed, recalcitrant, tenacious, unyielding

stubby *adjective* STOCKY, chunky, dumpy, short, squat, thickset

stuck *adjective* **1** FASTENED, cemented, fast, glued, joined **2** *Informal* BAFFLED, beaten, stumped

stuck-up *adjective* SNOBBISH, arrogant, bigheaded (*informal*), conceited, haughty, proud, snooty (*informal*)

stud *verb* ORNAMENT, bejewel, dot, spangle, spot

student *noun* LEARNER, apprentice, disciple, pupil, scholar, trainee, undergraduate

studied *adjective* PLANNED, conscious, deliberate, intentional, premeditated

studio *noun* WORKSHOP, atelier

studious *adjective* SCHOLARLY, academic, assiduous, bookish, diligent, hard-working, intellectual

study *verb* **1** CONTEMPLATE, consider, examine, go into, ponder, pore over, read **2** LEARN, cram (*informal*), read up, review **3** EXAMINE, analyze, investigate, look into, research, scrutinize, survey ▶ *noun* **4** LEARNING, application, lessons, reading, research, school work **5** EXAMINATION, analysis, consideration, contemplation, inquiry, inspection, investigation, review, scrutiny, survey

stuff *noun* **1** THINGS, belongings, effects, equipment, gear, kit, objects, paraphernalia, possessions, tackle **2** SUBSTANCE, essence, matter **3** MATERIAL, cloth, fabric, textile ▶*verb* **4** CRAM, crowd, fill, force, jam, pack, push, ram, shove, squeeze

stuffing *noun* FILLING, packing, wadding

stuffy *adjective* **1** AIRLESS, close, frowsty, heavy, muggy, oppressive, stale, stifling, sultry, unventilated **2** *Informal* STAID, dreary, dull, pompous, priggish, prim, stodgy

stumble *verb* **1** TRIP, fall, falter, lurch, reel, slip, stagger **2** (with *across*, *on* or *upon*) DISCOVER, chance upon, come across, find

stump *verb* BAFFLE, bewilder, confuse, flummox, mystify, nonplus, perplex, puzzle

stumpy *adjective* STOCKY, dumpy, short, squat, stubby, thickset

stun *verb* OVERCOME, astonish, astound, bewilder, confound, confuse, overpower, shock, stagger, stupefy

stunning *adjective* WONDERFUL, beautiful, cool (*informal*), dazzling, gorgeous, impressive, lovely, marvelous, phat (*slang*), sensational (*informal*), spectacular, striking

stunt *noun* FEAT, act, deed, exploit, trick

stunted *adjective* UNDERSIZED, diminutive, little, small, tiny

stupefy *verb* ASTOUND, amaze, daze, dumbfound, shock, stagger, stun

stupendous *adjective* **1** WONDERFUL, amazing, astounding, breathtaking, marvelous, overwhelming, sensational (*informal*), staggering, superb **2** HUGE, colossal, enormous, gigantic, mega (*slang*), vast

stupid *adjective* **1** UNINTELLIGENT, brainless, dense, dim, dumb (*informal*), half-witted, moronic, obtuse, simple, simple-minded, slow, slow-witted, thick **2** FOOLISH, asinine, bonkers (*informal*), daft (*informal*), idiotic, imbecilic, inane, nonsensical, pointless, rash, senseless, unintelligent **3** DAZED, groggy, insensate, semiconscious, stunned, stupefied

stupidity *noun* **1** LACK OF INTELLIGENCE, brainlessness, denseness, dimness, dullness, imbecility, obtuseness, slowness, thickness **2** FOOLISHNESS, absurdity, fatuousness, folly, idiocy, inanity, lunacy, madness, silliness

stupor *noun* DAZE, coma, insensibility, stupefaction, unconsciousness

sturdy *adjective* **1** ROBUST, athletic, brawny, hardy, lusty, muscular, powerful **2** WELL-BUILT, durable, solid, substantial, well-made

stutter *verb* STAMMER, falter, hesitate, stumble

style *noun* **1** DESIGN, cut, form, manner **2** MANNER, approach, method, mode, technique, way **3** ELEGANCE, chic, élan, flair, panache, polish, smartness, sophistication, taste **4** TYPE, category, genre, kind, sort, variety **5** FASHION, mode, rage, trend, vogue **6** LUXURY, affluence, comfort, ease, elegance, grandeur ▶ *verb* **7** DESIGN, adapt, arrange, cut, fashion, shape, tailor **8** CALL, designate, dub, entitle, label, name, term

stylish *adjective* SMART, chic, cool (*informal*), dressy (*informal*), fashionable, modish, phat (*slang*), trendy (*informal*), voguish

suave *adjective* SMOOTH, charming, courteous, debonair, polite, sophisticated, urbane

subconscious *adjective* HIDDEN, inner, intuitive, latent, repressed, subliminal

subdue *verb* **1** OVERCOME, break, conquer, control, crush, defeat, master, overpower, quell, tame, vanquish **2** MODERATE, mellow, quieten down, soften, suppress, tone down

subdued *adjective* **1** QUIET, chastened, crestfallen, dejected, downcast, down in the mouth, sad, serious **2** SOFT, dim, hushed, muted, quiet, subtle, toned down, unobtrusive

subject *noun* **1** TOPIC, affair, business, issue, matter, object, point, question, substance, theme **2** CITIZEN, national, subordinate ▶ *adjective* **3** SUBORDINATE, dependent, inferior, obedient, satellite **4 subject to: a** LIABLE TO, exposed to, in danger of, open to, prone to, susceptible to, vulnerable to **b** CONDITIONAL ON, contingent on, dependent on ▶ *verb* **5** PUT THROUGH, expose, lay open, submit, treat

subjective *adjective* PERSONAL,

biased, nonobjective, prejudiced

subjugate *verb* CONQUER, enslave, master, overcome, overpower, quell, subdue, suppress, vanquish

sublime *adjective* NOBLE, elevated, exalted, glorious, grand, great, high, lofty

submerge *verb* IMMERSE, deluge, dip, duck, engulf, flood, inundate, overflow, overwhelm, plunge, sink, swamp

submission *noun* **1** SURRENDER, assent, capitulation, giving in, yielding **2** PRESENTATION, entry, handing in, tendering **3** MEEKNESS, compliance, deference, docility, obedience, passivity, resignation

submissive *adjective* MEEK, accommodating, acquiescent, amenable, compliant, docile, obedient, passive, pliant, tractable, unresisting, yielding

submit *verb* **1** SURRENDER, accede, agree, capitulate, comply, endure, give in, succumb, tolerate, yield **2** PUT FORWARD, hand in, present, proffer, table, tender

subordinate *adjective* **1** LESSER, dependent, inferior, junior, lower, minor, secondary, subject ▶ *noun* **2** INFERIOR, aide, assistant, attendant, junior, second

subordination *noun* INFERIORITY, inferior *or* secondary status, servitude, subjection

subscribe *verb* **1** DONATE, contribute, give **2** SUPPORT, advocate, endorse

subscription *noun* **1** MEMBERSHIP FEE, annual payment, dues

2 DONATION, contribution, gift

subsequent adjective FOLLOWING, after, ensuing, later, succeeding, successive

subsequently adverb LATER, afterwards

subservient adjective SERVILE, abject, deferential, obsequious, slavish, submissive, sycophantic

subside verb **1** DECREASE, abate, diminish, ease, ebb, lessen, quieten, slacken, wane **2** SINK, cave in, collapse, drop, lower, settle

subsidence noun **1** SINKING, settling **2** DECREASE, abatement, easing off, lessening, slackening

subsidiary adjective LESSER, ancillary, auxiliary, minor, secondary, subordinate, supplementary

subsidize verb FUND, finance, promote, sponsor, support

subsidy noun AID, allowance, assistance, grant, help, support

substance noun **1** MATERIAL, body, fabric, stuff **2** MEANING, essence, gist, import, main point, significance **3** REALITY, actuality, concreteness **4** WEALTH, assets, estate, means, property, resources

substantial adjective BIG, ample, considerable, important, large, significant, sizable or sizeable

substantiate verb SUPPORT, authenticate, confirm, establish, prove, verify

substitute verb **1** REPLACE, change, exchange, interchange, swap, switch ▶noun **2** REPLACEMENT, agent, deputy, locum, proxy, reserve, sub, surrogate ▶adjective **3** REPLACEMENT, alternative,

fall-back, proxy, reserve, second, surrogate

substitution noun REPLACEMENT, change, exchange, swap, switch

subterfuge noun TRICK, deception, dodge, maneuver, ploy, ruse, stratagem

subtle adjective **1** SOPHISTICATED, delicate, refined **2** FAINT, delicate, implied, slight, understated **3** CRAFTY, artful, cunning, devious, ingenious, shrewd, sly, wily

subtlety noun **1** SOPHISTICATION, delicacy, refinement **2** CUNNING, artfulness, cleverness, craftiness, deviousness, ingenuity, slyness, wiliness

subtract verb TAKE AWAY, deduct, diminish, remove, take from, take off

subversive adjective **1** SEDITIOUS, riotous, treasonous ▶noun **2** DISSIDENT, fifth columnist, saboteur, terrorist, traitor

subvert verb OVERTURN, sabotage, undermine

succeed verb **1** MAKE IT (informal), be successful, flourish, make good, make the grade (informal), prosper, thrive, triumph, work **2** FOLLOW, come next, ensue, result

success noun **1** LUCK, fame, fortune, happiness, prosperity, triumph **2** HIT (informal), celebrity, megastar (informal), sensation, smash (informal), star, superstar, winner

successful adjective THRIVING, booming, flourishing, fortunate, fruitful, lucky, profitable, prosperous, rewarding, top, victorious

successfully adverb WELL, favorably, victoriously, with flying colors

succession noun **1** SERIES, chain, course, cycle, order, progression, run, sequence, train **2** TAKING OVER, accession, assumption, inheritance

successive adjective CONSECUTIVE, following, in succession

succinct adjective BRIEF, compact, concise, laconic, pithy, terse

succor noun **1** HELP, aid, assistance ▸ verb **2** HELP, aid, assist

succulent adjective JUICY, luscious, lush, moist

succumb verb **1** SURRENDER, capitulate, give in, submit, yield **2** DIE, fall

sucker noun Slang FOOL, dork (slang), dupe, mug (Brit. slang), pushover (slang), schmuck (slang), victim

sudden adjective QUICK, abrupt, hasty, hurried, rapid, rash, swift, unexpected

suddenly adverb ABRUPTLY, all of a sudden, unexpectedly

sue verb Law TAKE (SOMEONE) TO COURT, charge, indict, prosecute, summon

suffer verb **1** UNDERGO, bear, endure, experience, go through, sustain **2** TOLERATE, put up with (informal)

suffering noun PAIN, agony, anguish, discomfort, distress, hardship, misery, ordeal, torment

suffice verb BE ENOUGH, be adequate, be sufficient, do, meet requirements, serve

sufficient adjective ADEQUATE, enough, satisfactory

suffocate verb CHOKE, asphyxiate, smother, stifle

suggest verb **1** RECOMMEND, advise, advocate, prescribe, propose **2** BRING TO MIND, evoke **3** HINT, imply, indicate, intimate

suggestion noun **1** RECOMMENDATION, motion, plan, proposal, proposition **2** HINT, breath, indication, intimation, trace, whisper

suggestive adjective SMUTTY, bawdy, blue, indelicate, provocative, racy, ribald, risqué, rude

suit noun **1** OUTFIT, clothing, costume, dress, ensemble, habit **2** LAWSUIT, action, case, cause, proceeding, prosecution, trial ▸ verb **3** BE ACCEPTABLE TO, do, gratify, please, satisfy **4** BEFIT, agree, become, go with, harmonize, match, tally

suitability noun APPROPRIATENESS, aptness, fitness, rightness

suitable adjective APPROPRIATE, apt, becoming, befitting, fit, fitting, proper, right, satisfactory

suite noun ROOMS, apartment

suitor noun Old-fashioned ADMIRER, beau (old-fashioned), young man

sulk verb BE SULLEN, be in a huff, pout

sulky adjective HUFFY, cross, disgruntled, in the sulks, moody, petulant, querulous, resentful, sullen

sullen adjective MOROSE, cross, dour, glowering, moody, sour, surly, unsociable

sully verb DEFILE, besmirch, disgrace, dishonor, smirch, stain, tarnish ,

sultry adjective **1** HUMID, close, hot, muggy, oppressive, sticky, stifling **2** SEDUCTIVE, provocative, sensual, sexy (informal)

sum noun TOTAL, aggregate, amount, tally, whole

summarize verb SUM UP, abridge, condense, encapsulate, epitomize, précis

summary noun SYNOPSIS, abridgment, outline, précis, résumé, review, rundown

summit noun PEAK, acme, apex, head, height, pinnacle, top, zenith

summon verb SEND FOR, bid, call, invite **2** (often with up) GATHER, draw on, muster

sumptuous adjective LUXURIOUS, gorgeous, grand, lavish, opulent, splendid, superb

sum up verb SUMMARIZE, put in a nutshell, recapitulate, review

sunburned adjective TANNED, bronzed, brown, burnt, peeling, red

sundry adjective VARIOUS, assorted, different, miscellaneous, several, some

sunken adjective **1** HOLLOW, drawn, haggard **2** LOWER, buried, recessed, submerged

sunny adjective **1** BRIGHT, clear, fine, radiant, summery, sunlit, unclouded **2** CHEERFUL, buoyant, cheery, happy, joyful, light-hearted

sunrise noun DAWN, break of day, cockcrow, daybreak

sunset noun NIGHTFALL, close of (the) day, dusk, eventide

super adjective Informal EXCELLENT, glorious, magnificent, marvelous, outstanding, sensational (informal), superb, terrific (informal), wonderful

superb adjective SPLENDID, excellent, exquisite, fine, first-rate, grand, magnificent, marvelous, superior, superlative, world-class

supercilious adjective SCORNFUL, arrogant, contemptuous, disdainful, haughty, lofty, snooty (informal), stuck-up (informal)

superficial adjective **1** HASTY, casual, cursory, desultory, hurried, perfunctory, sketchy, slapdash **2** SHALLOW, empty-headed, frivolous, silly, trivial **3** SURFACE, exterior, external, on the surface, slight

superfluous adjective EXCESS, extra, left over, redundant, remaining, spare, supernumerary, surplus

superhuman adjective **1** HEROIC, phenomenal, prodigious **2** SUPERNATURAL, paranormal

superintendence noun SUPERVISION, charge, control, direction, government, management

superintendent noun SUPERVISOR, chief, controller, director, governor, inspector, manager, overseer

superior adjective **1** BETTER, grander, greater, higher, surpassing, unrivaled **2** SUPERCILIOUS, condescending, disdainful, haughty, lofty, lordly, patronizing, pretentious, snobbish **3** FIRST-CLASS, choice, deluxe, excellent, exceptional,

exclusive, first-rate ▶noun
4 BOSS (*informal*), chief,
director, manager, principal,
senior, supervisor

superiority noun SUPREMACY,
advantage, ascendancy,
excellence, lead, predominance

superlative adjective
OUTSTANDING, excellent,
supreme, unparalleled,
unrivaled, unsurpassed

supernatural adjective
PARANORMAL, ghostly, hidden,
miraculous, mystic, occult,
psychic, spectral, uncanny,
unearthly

supersede verb REPLACE,
displace, oust, supplant, take
the place of, usurp

supervise verb OVERSEE, control,
direct, handle, look after,
manage, run, superintend

supervision noun
SUPERINTENDENCE, care, charge,
control, direction, guidance,
management

supervisor noun BOSS (*informal*),
administrator, chief, foreman,
inspector, manager, overseer

supplant verb REPLACE, displace,
oust, supersede, take the place
of

supple adjective FLEXIBLE, limber,
lissom(e), lithe, pliable, pliant

supplement noun **1** ADDITION,
add-on, appendix, extra, insert,
postscript, pull-out ▶verb
2 ADD, augment, complement,
extend, reinforce

supplementary adjective
ADDITIONAL, add-on, ancillary,
auxiliary, extra, secondary

supplication noun PLEA, appeal,
entreaty, petition, prayer,
request

supply verb **1** PROVIDE,
contribute, endow, equip,
furnish, give, grant, produce,
stock, yield ▶noun **2** STORE,
cache, fund, hoard, quantity,
reserve, source, stock **3** (usually
plural) PROVISIONS, equipment,
food, materials, necessities,
rations, stores

support verb **1** BEAR, brace,
buttress, carry, hold, prop,
reinforce, sustain **2** PROVIDE FOR,
finance, fund, keep, look after,
maintain, sustain **3** HELP, aid,
assist, back, champion, defend,
second, side with **4** BEAR OUT,
confirm, corroborate,
substantiate, verify ▶noun
5 HELP, aid, assistance, backing,
encouragement, loyalty **6** PROP,
brace, foundation, pillar, post
7 SUPPORTER, backer, mainstay,
prop, second, tower of
strength **8** UPKEEP, keep,
maintenance, subsistence,
sustenance

supporter noun FOLLOWER,
adherent, advocate, champion,
fan, friend, helper, patron,
sponsor, well-wisher

supportive adjective HELPFUL,
encouraging, sympathetic,
understanding

suppose verb **1** PRESUME,
assume, conjecture, expect,
guess (*informal*), imagine, think
2 IMAGINE, conjecture, consider,
hypothesize, postulate, pretend

supposed adjective **1** PRESUMED,
accepted, alleged, assumed,
professed **2** (usually with *to*)
MEANT, expected, obliged,
required

supposedly adverb ALLEGEDLY,
hypothetically, ostensibly,
presumably, theoretically

supposition noun GUESS, conjecture, hypothesis, presumption, speculation, surmise, theory

suppress verb **1** STOP, check, conquer, crush, overpower, put an end to, quash, quell, subdue **2** RESTRAIN, conceal, contain, curb, hold in or back, repress, silence, smother, stifle

suppression noun ELIMINATION, check, crushing, quashing, smothering

supremacy noun DOMINATION, mastery, predominance, primacy, sovereignty, supreme power, sway

supreme adjective HIGHEST, chief, foremost, greatest, head, leading, paramount, pre-eminent, prime, principal, top, ultimate

sure adjective **1** CERTAIN, assured, confident, convinced, decided, definite, positive **2** RELIABLE, accurate, dependable, foolproof, infallible, undeniable, undoubted, unerring, unfailing **3** INEVITABLE, assured, bound, guaranteed, inescapable

surely adverb UNDOUBTEDLY, certainly, definitely, doubtlessly, indubitably, unquestionably, without doubt

surface noun **1** OUTSIDE, covering, exterior, face, side, top, veneer ▸ verb **2** APPEAR, arise, come to light, come up, crop up (informal), emerge, materialize, transpire

surfeit noun EXCESS, glut, plethora, superfluity

surge noun **1** RUSH, flood, flow, gush, outpouring **2** WAVE,

billow, roller, swell ▸ verb **3** RUSH, gush, heave, rise, roll

surly adjective ILL-TEMPERED, churlish, cross, grouchy (informal), morose, sulky, sullen, uncivil, ungracious

surmise verb **1** GUESS, conjecture, imagine, presume, speculate, suppose ▸ noun **2** GUESS, assumption, conjecture, presumption, speculation, supposition

surpass verb OUTDO, beat, eclipse, exceed, excel, outshine, outstrip, transcend

surpassing adjective SUPREME, exceptional, extraordinary, incomparable, matchless, outstanding, unrivaled

surplus noun **1** EXCESS, balance, remainder, residue, surfeit ▸ adjective **2** EXCESS, extra, odd, remaining, spare, superfluous

surprise noun **1** SHOCK, bombshell, eye-opener (informal), jolt, revelation **2** AMAZEMENT, astonishment, incredulity, wonder ▸ verb **3** AMAZE, astonish, stagger, stun, take aback **4** CATCH UNAWARES or OFF-GUARD, discover, spring upon, startle

surprised adjective AMAZED, astonished, speechless, taken by surprise, thunderstruck

surprising adjective AMAZING, astonishing, extraordinary, incredible, remarkable, staggering, unexpected, unusual

surrender verb **1** GIVE IN, capitulate, give way, submit, succumb, yield **2** GIVE UP, abandon, cede, concede, part with, relinquish, renounce,

waive, yield ▶ *noun*
3 SUBMISSION, capitulation,
relinquishment, renunciation,
resignation

surreptitious *adjective* SECRET,
covert, furtive, sly, stealthy,
underhand

surrogate *noun* SUBSTITUTE,
proxy, representative, stand-in

surround *verb* ENCLOSE, encircle,
encompass, envelop, hem in,
ring

surroundings *plural noun*
ENVIRONMENT, background,
location, milieu, setting

surveillance *noun* OBSERVATION,
inspection, scrutiny,
supervision, watch

survey *verb* **1** LOOK OVER,
contemplate, examine, inspect,
observe, scan, scrutinize, view
2 ESTIMATE, appraise, assess,
measure, plan, plot, size up
▶ *noun* **3** EXAMINATION,
inspection, scrutiny **4** STUDY,
inquiry, review

survive *verb* REMAIN ALIVE,
endure, last, live on, outlast,
outlive

susceptible *adjective* **1** (usually
with *to*) LIABLE, disposed, given,
inclined, prone, subject,
vulnerable **2** IMPRESSIONABLE,
receptive, responsive, sensitive,
suggestible

suspect *verb* **1** BELIEVE, consider,
feel, guess, speculate, suppose
2 DISTRUST, doubt, mistrust
▶ *adjective* **3** DUBIOUS, doubtful,
iffy (*informal*), questionable

suspend *verb* **1** HANG, attach,
dangle **2** POSTPONE, cease, cut
short, defer, discontinue,
interrupt, put off, shelve

suspense *noun* UNCERTAINTY,

anxiety, apprehension, doubt,
expectation, insecurity,
irresolution, tension

suspension *noun* POSTPONEMENT,
abeyance, break, breaking off,
deferment, discontinuation,
interruption

suspicion *noun* **1** DISTRUST,
doubt, dubiety, misgiving,
mistrust, qualm, skepticism,
wariness **2** IDEA, guess, hunch,
impression, notion **3** TRACE,
hint, shade, *soupçon*, streak,
suggestion, tinge, touch

suspicious *adjective*
1 DISTRUSTFUL, doubtful,
skeptical, unbelieving, wary
2 SUSPECT, doubtful, dubious,
fishy (*informal*), questionable

sustain *verb* **1** MAINTAIN,
continue, keep up, prolong,
protract **2** KEEP ALIVE, aid, assist,
help, nourish **3** WITHSTAND,
bear, endure, experience, feel,
suffer, undergo **4** SUPPORT, bear,
uphold

sustained *adjective* CONTINUOUS,
constant, nonstop, perpetual,
prolonged, steady,
twenty-four-seven (*slang*),
unremitting

swagger *verb* SHOW OFF
(*informal*), boast, brag, parade

swallow *verb* GULP, chow down
(*slang*), consume, devour,
drink, eat, swig (*informal*)

swamp *noun* **1** BOG, fen, marsh,
mire, morass, quagmire,
slough ▶ *verb* **2** FLOOD, capsize,
engulf, inundate, sink,
submerge **3** OVERWHELM, flood,
inundate, overload

swarm *noun* **1** MULTITUDE, army,
crowd, flock, herd, horde,
host, mass, throng ▶ *verb*

2 CROWD, flock, mass, stream, throng **3** TEEM, abound, bristle, crawl

swarthy adjective DARK-SKINNED, black, brown, dark, dark-complexioned, dusky

swashbuckling adjective DASHING, bold, daredevil, flamboyant

swathe verb WRAP, bundle up, cloak, drape, envelop, shroud

sway verb **1** LEAN, bend, rock, roll, swing **2** INFLUENCE, affect, guide, induce, persuade ▶noun **3** POWER, authority, clout (informal), control, influence

swear verb **1** CURSE, be foul-mouthed, blaspheme **2** DECLARE, affirm, assert, attest, promise, testify, vow

swearing noun BAD LANGUAGE, blasphemy, cursing, foul language, profanity

swearword noun OATH, curse, expletive, four-letter word, obscenity, profanity

sweat noun **1** PERSPIRATION **2** Informal LABOR, chore, drudgery, toil **3** Informal WORRY, agitation, anxiety, distress, panic, strain ▶verb **4** PERSPIRE, glow **5** Informal WORRY, agonize, fret, suffer, torture oneself

sweaty adjective PERSPIRING, clammy, sticky

sweep verb **1** CLEAR, brush, clean, remove **2** SAIL, fly, glide, pass, skim, tear, zoom ▶noun **3** ARC, bend, curve, move, stroke, swing **4** EXTENT, range, scope, stretch

sweeping adjective **1** WIDE-RANGING, all-embracing, all-inclusive, broad,

comprehensive, extensive, global, wide **2** INDISCRIMINATE, blanket, exaggerated, overstated, unqualified, wholesale

sweet adjective **1** SUGARY, cloying, saccharine **2** CHARMING, agreeable, appealing, cute, delightful, engaging, kind, likable or likeable, lovable, winning **3** MELODIOUS, dulcet, harmonious, mellow, musical **4** FRAGRANT, aromatic, clean, fresh, pure ▶noun **5** (usually plural) CONFECTIONERY, bonbon

sweeten verb **1** SUGAR **2** MOLLIFY, appease, pacify, soothe

sweetheart noun LOVER, beloved, boyfriend or girlfriend, darling, dear, love

swell verb **1** EXPAND, balloon, bloat, bulge, dilate, distend, enlarge, grow, increase, rise ▶noun **2** WAVE, billow, surge

swelling noun ENLARGEMENT, bulge, bump, inflammation, lump, protuberance

sweltering adjective HOT, boiling, burning, oppressive, scorching, stifling

swerve verb VEER, bend, deflect, deviate, diverge, stray, swing, turn, turn aside

swift adjective QUICK, fast, hurried, prompt, rapid, speedy

swiftly adverb QUICKLY, fast, hurriedly, promptly, rapidly, speedily

swiftness noun SPEED, promptness, quickness, rapidity, speediness, velocity

swindle verb **1** CHEAT, con, defraud, fleece, rip (someone) off (slang), sting (informal),

trick ▶ noun 2 FRAUD, con trick
(*informal*), deception, racket,
rip-off (*slang*), scam (*slang*)

swindler noun CHEAT, con man
(*informal*), fraud, rogue, shark,
trickster

swing verb 1 SWAY, oscillate,
rock, veer, wave 2 (usually
with *round*) TURN, curve, pivot,
rotate, swivel 3 HANG, dangle,
suspend ▶ noun 4 SWAYING,
oscillation

swipe verb 1 HIT, lash out at,
slap, strike, wallop (*informal*)
2 *Slang* STEAL, appropriate, filch,
lift (*informal*), pinch (*informal*),
purloin ▶ noun 3 BLOW, clout
(*informal*), cuff, slap, smack,
wallop (*informal*)

swirl verb WHIRL, churn, eddy,
spin, twist

switch noun 1 CHANGE, reversal,
shift 2 EXCHANGE, substitution,
swap ▶ verb 3 CHANGE, deflect,
deviate, divert, shift
4 EXCHANGE, substitute, swap

swivel verb TURN, pivot, revolve,
rotate, spin

swollen adjective ENLARGED,
bloated, distended, inflamed,
puffed up

swoop verb 1 POUNCE, descend,
dive, rush, stoop, sweep ▶ noun
2 POUNCE, descent, drop, lunge,
plunge, rush, stoop, sweep

swop verb EXCHANGE, barter,
interchange, switch, trade

sycophant noun CRAWLER,
brown-noser (*slang*), fawner,
flatterer, toady, yes man

sycophantic adjective
OBSEQUIOUS, crawling, fawning,
flattering, grovelling,
ingratiating, servile, slimy,
smarmy (*Brit. informal*),
toadying, unctuous

syllabus noun COURSE OF STUDY,
curriculum

symbol noun SIGN, badge,
emblem, figure, icon, image,
logo, mark, representation,
token

symbolic adjective REPRESENTATIVE,
allegorical, emblematic,
figurative

symbolize verb REPRESENT,
denote, mean, personify,
signify, stand for, typify

symmetrical adjective BALANCED,
in proportion, regular

symmetry noun BALANCE,
evenness, order, proportion,
regularity

sympathetic adjective 1 CARING,
compassionate, concerned,
interested, kind, pitying,
supportive, understanding,
warm 2 LIKE-MINDED, agreeable,
companionable, compatible,
congenial, friendly

sympathize verb 1 FEEL FOR,
commiserate, condole, pity
2 AGREE, side with, understand

sympathizer noun SUPPORTER,
partisan, well-wisher

sympathy noun 1 COMPASSION,
commiseration, pity,
understanding 2 AGREEMENT,
affinity, fellow feeling, rapport

symptom noun SIGN,
expression, indication, mark,
token, warning

symptomatic adjective
INDICATIVE, characteristic,
suggestive

synthetic adjective ARTIFICIAL,
fake, man-made

system noun 1 METHOD,
practice, procedure, routine,

technique 2 ARRANGEMENT, classification, organization, scheme, structure

systematic *adjective* METHODICAL, efficient, orderly, organized

T t

table *noun* 1 COUNTER, bench, board, stand 2 LIST, catalog, chart, diagram, record, register, roll, schedule, tabulation ▶*verb* 3 SUBMIT, enter, move, propose, put forward, suggest

tableau *noun* PICTURE, representation, scene, spectacle

taboo *noun* 1 PROHIBITION, anathema, ban, interdict, proscription, restriction ▶*adjective* 2 FORBIDDEN, anathema, banned, outlawed, prohibited, proscribed, unacceptable, unmentionable

tacit *adjective* IMPLIED, implicit, inferred, undeclared, understood, unexpressed, unspoken, unstated

taciturn *adjective* UNCOMMUNICATIVE, quiet, reserved, reticent, silent, tight-lipped, unforthcoming, withdrawn

tack¹ *noun* 1 NAIL, drawing pin, pin ▶*verb* 2 FASTEN, affix, attach, fix, nail, pin 3 STITCH, baste 4 tack on APPEND, add, attach, tag

tack² *noun* COURSE, approach, direction, heading, line, method, path, plan, procedure, way

tackle *verb* 1 DEAL WITH, attempt, come or get to grips with, embark upon, get stuck into (*informal*), set about, undertake 2 CONFRONT, challenge, grab, grasp, halt, intercept, seize, stop ▶*noun* 3 CHALLENGE, block 4 EQUIPMENT, accouterments, apparatus, gear, paraphernalia, tools, trappings

tacky¹ *adjective* STICKY, adhesive, gluey, gummy, wet

tacky² *adjective* Informal VULGAR, cheap, off-color, scuzzy (*slang*), seedy, shabby, shoddy, sleazy, tasteless, tatty

tact *noun* DIPLOMACY, consideration, delicacy, discretion, sensitivity, thoughtfulness, understanding

tactful *adjective* DIPLOMATIC, considerate, delicate, discreet, polite, politic, sensitive, thoughtful, understanding

tactic *noun* 1 POLICY, approach, maneuver, method, move, ploy, scheme, stratagem 2 **tactics** STRATEGY, campaigning, generalship, maneuvers, plans

tactical *adjective* STRATEGIC, cunning, diplomatic, shrewd, smart

tactician *noun* STRATEGIST, general, mastermind, planner

tactless *adjective* INSENSITIVE, impolite, impolitic, inconsiderate, indelicate, indiscreet, thoughtless, undiplomatic, unsubtle

tag *noun* 1 LABEL, flap, identification, mark, marker, note, slip, tab, ticket ▶*verb* 2 LABEL, mark 3 (with *along* or on) ACCOMPANY, attend, follow, shadow, stalk, tail (*informal*), trail

tail noun 1 EXTREMITY, appendage, end, rear end, tailpiece 2 **turn tail** RUN AWAY, cut and run, flee, retreat, run off, take to one's heels ▶verb 3 *Informal* FOLLOW, shadow, stalk, track, trail

tailor noun 1 OUTFITTER, clothier, costumier, couturier, dressmaker, seamstress ▶verb 2 ADAPT, adjust, alter, customize, fashion, modify, mold, shape, style

taint verb 1 SPOIL, blemish, contaminate, corrupt, damage, defile, pollute, ruin, stain, sully, tarnish ▶noun 2 STAIN, black mark, blemish, blot, defect, demerit, fault, flaw, spot

take verb 1 CAPTURE, acquire, catch, get, grasp, grip, obtain, secure, seize 2 ACCOMPANY, bring, conduct, convoy, escort, guide, lead, usher 3 CARRY, bear, bring, convey, ferry, fetch, haul, transport 4 STEAL, appropriate, misappropriate, pinch (*informal*), pocket, purloin 5 REQUIRE, call for, demand, necessitate, need 6 TOLERATE, abide, bear, endure, put up with (*informal*), stand, stomach, withstand 7 HAVE ROOM FOR, accept, accommodate, contain, hold 8 SUBTRACT, deduct, eliminate, remove 9 ASSUME, believe, consider, perceive, presume, regard, understand

take in verb 1 UNDERSTAND, absorb, assimilate, comprehend, digest, get the hang of (*informal*), grasp

2 DECEIVE, cheat, con (*informal*), dupe, fool, hoodwink, mislead, swindle, trick

takeoff noun DEPARTURE, launch, liftoff

take off verb 1 REMOVE, discard, peel off, strip off 2 LIFT OFF, take to the air 3 *Informal* DEPART, abscond, decamp, disappear, go, leave, slope off

takeover noun MERGER, coup, incorporation

take up verb 1 OCCUPY, absorb, consume, cover, extend over, fill, use up 2 START, adopt, become involved in, engage in

taking adjective 1 CHARMING, attractive, beguiling, captivating, enchanting, engaging, fetching (*informal*), likable *or* likeable, prepossessing ▶noun 2 **takings** REVENUE, earnings, income, proceeds, profits, receipts, returns, take

tale noun STORY, account, anecdote, fable, legend, narrative, saga, yarn (*informal*)

talent noun ABILITY, aptitude, capacity, flair, genius, gift, knack

talented adjective GIFTED, able, brilliant

talisman noun CHARM, amulet, fetish, lucky charm, mascot

talk verb 1 SPEAK, chat, chatter, chew the fat (*slang*), communicate, converse, gossip, natter, utter 2 NEGOTIATE, confabulate, confer, parley 3 INFORM, blab, give the game away, let the cat out of the bag, tell all ▶noun 4 SPEECH, address, discourse, disquisition, lecture, oration, sermon

talkative adjective LOQUACIOUS, chatty, effusive, garrulous, gossipy, long-winded, mouthy, verbose, voluble, wordy

talker noun SPEAKER, chatterbox, conversationalist, lecturer, orator

talking-to noun REPRIMAND, criticism, lecture, rebuke, reproach, reproof, scolding, telling-off (informal)

tall adjective 1 HIGH, big, elevated, giant, lanky, lofty, soaring, towering 2 As in **tall tale** Informal IMPLAUSIBLE, absurd, cock-and-bull (informal), exaggerated, far-fetched, incredible, preposterous, unbelievable 3 As in **tall order** DIFFICULT, demanding, hard, unreasonable, well-nigh impossible

tally verb 1 CORRESPOND, accord, agree, coincide, concur, conform, fit, harmonize, match, square ▶ noun 2 RECORD, count, mark, reckoning, running total, score, total

tame adjective 1 DOMESTICATED, amenable, broken, disciplined, docile, gentle, obedient, tractable 2 SUBMISSIVE, compliant, docile, manageable, meek, obedient, subdued, unresisting 3 UNINTERESTING, bland, boring, dull, humdrum, insipid, unexciting, uninspiring, vapid ▶ verb 4 DOMESTICATE, break in, house-train, train 5 DISCIPLINE, bring to heel, conquer, humble, master, subdue, subjugate, suppress

tamper verb INTERFERE, alter, fiddle (informal), fool about

(informal), meddle, mess about, tinker

tangible adjective DEFINITE, actual, concrete, material, palpable, perceptible, positive, real

tangle noun 1 KNOT, coil, entanglement, jungle, twist, web 2 CONFUSION, complication, entanglement, fix (informal), imbroglio, jam, mess, mix-up ▶ verb 3 TWIST, coil, entangle, interweave, knot, mat, mesh, ravel 4 (often with with) COME INTO CONFLICT, come up against, contend, contest, cross swords, dispute, lock horns

tangled adjective 1 TWISTED, entangled, jumbled, knotted, matted, messy, snarled, tousled 2 COMPLICATED, complex, confused, convoluted, involved, knotty, messy, mixed-up

tangy adjective SHARP, piquant, pungent, spicy, tart

tantalize verb TORMENT, frustrate, lead on, taunt, tease, torture

tantamount adjective EQUIVALENT, commensurate, equal, synonymous

tantrum noun OUTBURST, fit, flare-up, hysterics, temper

tap¹ verb 1 KNOCK, beat, knock, pat, rap, strike, touch ▶ noun 2 KNOCK, pat, rap, touch

tap² noun 1 VALVE, stopcock 2 **on tap**: a Informal AVAILABLE, at hand, in reserve, on hand, ready b ON DRAFT ▶ verb 3 LISTEN IN ON, bug (informal), eavesdrop on 4 DRAW OFF, bleed, drain, siphon off

tape noun 1 STRIP, band, ribbon

▶ *verb* 2 RECORD, tape-record, video 3 BIND, seal, secure, stick, wrap

taper *verb* 1 NARROW, come to a point, thin 2 *taper off* LESSEN, decrease, die away, dwindle, fade, reduce, subside, wane, wind down

target *noun* 1 GOAL, aim, ambition, end, intention, mark, object, objective 2 VICTIM, butt, scapegoat

tariff *noun* TAX, duty, excise, levy, toll

tarnish *verb* 1 STAIN, blacken, blemish, blot, darken, discolor, sully, taint ▶ *noun* 2 STAIN, blemish, blot, discoloration, spot, taint

tart¹ *noun* PIE, pastry, tartlet

tart² *adjective* SHARP, acid, bitter, piquant, pungent, sour, tangy, vinegary

tart³ *noun* SLUT, call girl, floozy (*slang*), ho (*slang*), prostitute, trollop, whore

task *noun* 1 JOB, assignment, chore, duty, enterprise, exercise, mission, undertaking 2 *take to task* CRITICIZE, blame, censure, reprimand, reproach, reprove, scold, tell off (*informal*), upbraid

taste *noun* 1 FLAVOR, relish, savor, smack, tang 2 BIT, bite, dash, morsel, mouthful, sample, *soupçon*, spoonful, tidbit 3 LIKING, appetite, fancy, fondness, inclination, partiality, penchant, predilection, preference 4 REFINEMENT, appreciation, discernment, discrimination, elegance, judgment, sophistication, style ▶ *verb* 5 DISTINGUISH, differentiate, discern, perceive 6 SAMPLE, savor, sip, test, try 7 HAVE A FLAVOR OF, savor of, smack of 8 EXPERIENCE, encounter, know, meet with, partake of, undergo

tasteful *adjective* REFINED, artistic, cultivated, cultured, discriminating, elegant, exquisite, in good taste, polished, stylish

tasteless *adjective* 1 INSIPID, bland, boring, dull, flat, flavorless, mild, thin, weak 2 VULGAR, crass, crude, gaudy, gross, inelegant, off-color, tacky (*informal*), tawdry

tasty *adjective* DELICIOUS, appetizing, delectable, full-flavored, luscious, palatable, savory, toothsome, yummy (*informal*)

tatters *noun* *in tatters* RAGGED, down at heel, in rags, in shreds, ripped, tattered, threadbare, torn

tatty *adjective* RAGGED, bedraggled, dilapidated, down at heel, neglected, run-down, shabby, threadbare, worn

taunt *verb* 1 TEASE, deride, insult, jeer, mock, provoke, ridicule, torment ▶ *noun* 2 JEER, derision, dig, gibe, insult, provocation, ridicule, sarcasm, teasing

taut *adjective* TIGHT, flexed, rigid, strained, stressed, stretched, tense

tavern *noun* INN, alehouse (*archaic*), bar, hostelry, public house

tawdry *adjective* VULGAR, cheap, flashy, gaudy, gimcrack, tacky (*informal*), tasteless, tatty, tinselly

tax noun **1** CHARGE, duty, excise, levy, tariff, tithe, toll ▶ verb **2** CHARGE, assess, rate **3** STRAIN, burden, exhaust, load, stretch, test, try, weaken, weary

taxing adjective DEMANDING, exacting, exhausting, onerous, punishing, sapping, stressful, tiring, tough, trying

teach verb INSTRUCT, coach, drill, educate, enlighten, guide, inform, show, train, tutor

teacher noun INSTRUCTOR, coach, educator, guide, lecturer, master or mistress, mentor, schoolteacher, trainer, tutor

team noun **1** GROUP, band, body, bunch, company, gang, line-up, set, side, squad ▶ verb **2** (often with up) JOIN, band together, cooperate, couple, get together, link, unite, work together

teamwork noun COOPERATION, collaboration, coordination, esprit de corps, fellowship, harmony, unity

tear verb **1** RIP, claw, lacerate, mangle, mutilate, pull apart, rend, rupture, scratch, shred, split **2** RUSH, bolt, charge, dash, fly, hurry, race, run, speed, sprint, zoom ▶ noun **3** HOLE, laceration, rent, rip, rupture, scratch, split

tearful adjective WEEPING, blubbering, crying, in tears, lachrymose, sobbing, weepy (informal), whimpering

tears plural noun **1** CRYING, blubbering, sobbing, wailing, weeping **2** in tears CRYING, blubbering, distressed, sobbing, weeping

tease verb MOCK, goad, lead on, provoke, pull someone's leg (informal), tantalize, taunt, torment

technical adjective SCIENTIFIC, hi-tech or high-tech, skilled, specialist, specialized, technological

technique noun **1** METHOD, approach, manner, means, mode, procedure, style, system, way **2** SKILL, artistry, craft, craftsmanship, execution, performance, proficiency, touch

tedious adjective BORING, drab, dreary, dull, humdrum, irksome, laborious, mind-numbing, monotonous, tiresome, wearisome

tedium noun BOREDOM, drabness, dreariness, dullness, monotony, routine, sameness, tediousness

teeming[1] adjective FULL, abundant, alive, brimming, bristling, bursting, crawling, overflowing, swarming, thick

teeming[2] adjective POURING, pelting, raining cats and dogs (informal)

teenager noun YOUTH, adolescent, boy, girl, juvenile, minor

teeter verb WOBBLE, rock, seesaw, stagger, sway, totter, waver

teetotaler noun ABSTAINER, nondrinker

telepathy noun MIND-READING, E.S.P., sixth sense

telephone noun **1** PHONE, handset, line ▶ verb **2** CALL, dial, phone

telescope noun **1** GLASS, spyglass ▶ verb **2** SHORTEN, abbreviate, abridge, compress, condense, contract, shrink

television noun TV, small screen (*informal*), the tube (*slang*)

tell verb 1 INFORM, announce, communicate, disclose, divulge, express, make known, notify, proclaim, reveal, state 2 INSTRUCT, bid, call upon, command, direct, order, require, summon 3 DESCRIBE, chronicle, depict, narrate, portray, recount, relate, report 4 DISTINGUISH, differentiate, discern, discriminate, identify 5 CARRY WEIGHT, count, have or take effect, make its presence felt, register, take its toll, weigh

telling adjective EFFECTIVE, considerable, decisive, forceful, impressive, influential, marked, powerful, significant, striking

telling-off noun REPRIMAND, criticism, lecture, rebuke, reproach, reproof, scolding, talking-to

tell off verb REPRIMAND, berate, censure, chide, lecture, rebuke, reproach, scold

temerity noun BOLDNESS, audacity, chutzpah (*informal*), effrontery, front, impudence, nerve (*informal*), rashness, recklessness

temper noun 1 RAGE, bad mood, fury, passion, tantrum 2 IRRITABILITY, hot-headedness, irascibility, passion, petulance, resentment, surliness 3 SELF-CONTROL, calmness, composure, cool (*slang*), equanimity 4 FRAME OF MIND, constitution, disposition, humor, mind, mood, nature, temperament ▶verb 5 MODERATE,

assuage, lessen, mitigate, mollify, restrain, soften, soothe, tone down 6 STRENGTHEN, anneal, harden, toughen

temperament noun 1 NATURE, bent, character, constitution, disposition, humor, make-up, outlook, personality, temper 2 EXCITABILITY, anger, hot-headedness, moodiness, petulance, volatility

temperamental adjective 1 MOODY, capricious, emotional, excitable, highly strung, hypersensitive, irritable, sensitive, touchy, volatile 2 UNRELIABLE, erratic, inconsistent, inconstant, unpredictable

temperance noun 1 MODERATION, continence, discretion, forbearance, restraint, self-control, self-discipline, self-restraint 2 TEETOTALISM, abstemiousness, abstinence, sobriety

temperate adjective 1 MILD, calm, cool, fair, gentle, moderate, pleasant 2 SELF-RESTRAINED, calm, composed, dispassionate, even-tempered, mild, moderate, reasonable, self-controlled, sensible

tempest noun GALE, cyclone, hurricane, squall, storm, tornado, typhoon

tempestuous adjective 1 STORMY, blustery, gusty, inclement, raging, squally, turbulent, windy 2 VIOLENT, boisterous, emotional, furious, heated, intense, passionate, stormy, turbulent, wild

temple noun SHRINE, church,

place of worship, sanctuary

temporarily adverb BRIEFLY, fleetingly, for the time being, momentarily, pro tem

temporary adjective IMPERMANENT, brief, ephemeral, fleeting, interim, momentary, provisional, short-lived, transitory

tempt verb ENTICE, allure, attract, coax, invite, lead on, lure, seduce, tantalize

temptation noun ENTICEMENT, allurement, inducement, lure, pull, seduction, tantalization

tempting adjective ENTICING, alluring, appetizing, attractive, inviting, mouthwatering, seductive, tantalizing

tenable adjective SOUND, arguable, believable, defensible, justifiable, plausible, rational, reasonable, viable

tenacious adjective 1 FIRM, clinging, forceful, immovable, iron, strong, tight, unshakable 2 STUBBORN, adamant, determined, dogged, obdurate, obstinate, persistent, resolute, steadfast, unswerving, unyielding

tenacity noun PERSEVERANCE, application, determination, doggedness, obduracy, persistence, resolve, steadfastness, stubbornness

tenancy noun LEASE, occupancy, possession, renting, residence

tenant noun LEASEHOLDER, inhabitant, lessee, occupant, occupier, renter, resident

tend¹ verb 1 BE INCLINED, be apt, be liable, gravitate, have a tendency, incline, lean 2 GO, aim, bear, head, lead,

make for, point

tend² verb TAKE CARE OF, attend, cultivate, keep, look after, maintain, manage, nurture, watch over

tendency noun INCLINATION, disposition, leaning, liability, proclivity, proneness, propensity, susceptibility

tender¹ adjective 1 GENTLE, affectionate, caring, compassionate, considerate, kind, loving, sympathetic, tenderhearted, warm-hearted 2 VULNERABLE, immature, impressionable, inexperienced, raw, sensitive, young, youthful 3 SENSITIVE, bruised, inflamed, painful, raw, sore

tender² verb 1 OFFER, give, hand in, present, proffer, propose, put forward, submit, volunteer ▶ noun 2 OFFER, bid, estimate, proposal, submission 3 As in **legal tender** CURRENCY, money, payment

tenderness noun 1 GENTLENESS, affection, care, compassion, consideration, kindness, love, sentimentality, sympathy, warmth 2 SORENESS, inflammation, pain, sensitivity

tense adjective 1 NERVOUS, anxious, apprehensive, edgy, jumpy, keyed up, on edge, on tenterhooks, strained, uptight (informal), wired (slang) 2 STRESSFUL, exciting, nerve-racking, worrying 3 TIGHT, rigid, strained, stretched, taut ▶ verb 4 TIGHTEN, brace, flex, strain, stretch

tension noun 1 SUSPENSE, anxiety, apprehension, hostility, nervousness, pressure,

strain, stress, unease
2 TIGHTNESS, pressure, rigidity, stiffness, stress, stretching, tautness

tentative adjective
1 EXPERIMENTAL, conjectural, indefinite, provisional, speculative, unconfirmed, unsettled **2** HESITANT, cautious, diffident, doubtful, faltering, timid, uncertain, undecided, unsure

tenuous adjective SLIGHT, doubtful, dubious, flimsy, insubstantial, nebulous, shaky, sketchy, weak

tepid adjective **1** LUKEWARM, warmish **2** HALF-HEARTED, apathetic, cool, indifferent, lukewarm, unenthusiastic

term noun **1** WORD, expression, name, phrase, title **2** PERIOD, duration, interval, season, span, spell, time, while ▶ verb **3** CALL, designate, dub, entitle, label, name, style

terminal adjective **1** DEADLY, fatal, incurable, killing, lethal, mortal **2** FINAL, concluding, extreme, last, ultimate, utmost ▶ noun **3** TERMINUS, depot, end of the line, station

terminate verb END, abort, cease, close, complete, conclude, discontinue, finish, stop

termination noun ENDING, abortion, cessation, completion, conclusion, discontinuation, end, finish

terminology noun LANGUAGE, jargon, nomenclature, phraseology, terms, vocabulary

terminus noun END OF THE LINE, depot, garage, last stop, station

terms plural noun **1** CONDITIONS, particulars, provisions, provisos, qualifications, specifications, stipulations **2** RELATIONSHIP, footing, relations, standing, status

terrain noun GROUND, country, going, land, landscape, topography

terrestrial adjective EARTHLY, global, worldly

terrible adjective **1** SERIOUS, dangerous, desperate, extreme, severe **2** BAD, abysmal, awful, dire, dreadful, poor, rotten (informal) **3** FEARFUL, dreadful, frightful, horrendous, horrible, horrifying, monstrous, shocking, terrifying

terribly adverb EXTREMELY, awfully (informal), decidedly, desperately, exceedingly, seriously, thoroughly, very

terrific adjective **1** GREAT, enormous, fearful, gigantic, huge, intense, tremendous **2** Informal EXCELLENT, amazing, brilliant, fantastic (informal), magnificent, marvelous, outstanding, sensational (informal), stupendous, superb, wonderful

terrified adjective FRIGHTENED, alarmed, appalled, horrified, horror-struck, panic-stricken, petrified, scared

terrify verb FRIGHTEN, alarm, appall, horrify, make one's hair stand on end, scare, shock, terrorize

territory noun DISTRICT, area, country, domain, land, patch, province, region, zone

terror noun **1** FEAR, alarm, anxiety, dread, fright, horror, panic, shock **2** SCOURGE, bogeyman, bugbear, devil, fiend, monster

terrorize verb OPPRESS, browbeat, bully, coerce, intimidate, menace, threaten

terse adjective **1** CONCISE, brief, condensed, laconic, monosyllabic, pithy, short, succinct **2** CURT, abrupt, brusque, short, snappy

test verb **1** CHECK, analyze, assess, examine, experiment, investigate, put to the test, research, try out ▶ noun **2** EXAMINATION, acid test, analysis, assessment, check, evaluation, investigation, research, trial

testament noun **1** PROOF, demonstration, evidence, testimony, tribute, witness **2** WILL, last wishes

testify verb BEAR WITNESS, affirm, assert, attest, certify, corroborate, state, swear, vouch

testimonial noun TRIBUTE, commendation, endorsement, recommendation, reference

testimony noun **1** EVIDENCE, affidavit, deposition, statement, submission **2** PROOF, corroboration, demonstration, evidence, indication, manifestation, support, verification

testing adjective DIFFICULT, arduous, challenging, demanding, exacting, rigorous, searching, strenuous, taxing, tough

tether noun **1** ROPE, chain, fetter, halter, lead, leash **2 at the end of one's tether** EXASPERATED, at one's wits' end,

exhausted ▶ verb **3** TIE, bind, chain, fasten, fetter, secure

text noun **1** CONTENTS, body **2** WORDS, wording

texture noun FEEL, consistency, grain, structure, surface, tissue

thank verb SAY THANK YOU, show one's appreciation

thankful adjective GRATEFUL, appreciative, beholden, indebted, obliged, pleased, relieved

thankless adjective UNREWARDING, fruitless, unappreciated, unprofitable, unrequited

thanks plural noun **1** GRATITUDE, acknowledgment, appreciation, credit, gratefulness, kudos, recognition **2 thanks to** BECAUSE OF, as a result of, due to, owing to, through

thaw verb MELT, defrost, dissolve, liquefy, soften, unfreeze, warm

theatrical adjective **1** DRAMATIC, Thespian **2** EXAGGERATED, affected, dramatic, histrionic, mannered, melodramatic, ostentatious, showy, stagy

theft noun STEALING, embezzlement, fraud, larceny, pilfering, purloining, robbery, thieving

theme noun **1** SUBJECT, idea, keynote, subject matter, topic **2** MOTIF, leitmotif

theological adjective RELIGIOUS, doctrinal, ecclesiastical

theoretical adjective ABSTRACT, academic, conjectural, hypothetical, notional, speculative

theorize verb SPECULATE, conjecture, formulate, guess, hypothesize, project, propound, suppose

theory *noun* SUPPOSITION, assumption, conjecture, hypothesis, presumption, speculation, surmise, thesis

therapeutic *adjective* BENEFICIAL, corrective, curative, good, healing, remedial, restorative, salutary

therapist *noun* HEALER, physician

therapy *noun* REMEDY, cure, healing, treatment

therefore *adverb* CONSEQUENTLY, accordingly, as a result, ergo, hence, so, then, thence, thus

thesis *noun* 1 DISSERTATION, essay, monograph, paper, treatise 2 PROPOSITION, contention, hypothesis, idea, opinion, proposal, theory, view

thick *adjective* 1 WIDE, broad, bulky, fat, solid, substantial 2 DENSE, close, compact, concentrated, condensed, heavy, impenetrable, opaque 3 *Informal* FRIENDLY, close, devoted, familiar, inseparable, intimate, pally (*informal*) 4 FULL, brimming, bristling, bursting, covered, crawling, packed, swarming, teeming 5 **a bit thick** UNFAIR, unjust, unreasonable

thicken *verb* SET, clot, coagulate, condense, congeal, jell

thicket *noun* WOOD, brake, coppice, copse, covert, grove

thickset *adjective* WELL-BUILT, bulky, burly, heavy, muscular, stocky, strong, sturdy

thief *noun* ROBBER, burglar, embezzler, housebreaker, pickpocket, pilferer, plunderer, shoplifter, stealer

thieve *verb* STEAL, filch, pilfer, pinch (*informal*), purloin, rob, swipe (*slang*)

thin *adjective* 1 NARROW, attenuated, fine 2 SLIM, bony, emaciated, lean, scrawny, skeletal, skinny, slender, slight, spare, spindly 3 MEAGER, deficient, scanty, scarce, scattered, skimpy, sparse, wispy 4 DELICATE, diaphanous, filmy, fine, flimsy, gossamer, sheer, unsubstantial 5 UNCONVINCING, feeble, flimsy, inadequate, lame, lousy (*slang*), poor, superficial, weak

thing *noun* 1 OBJECT, article, being, body, entity, something, substance 2 *Informal* OBSESSION, bee in one's bonnet, fetish, fixation, hang-up (*informal*), mania, phobia, preoccupation 3 **things** POSSESSIONS, belongings, effects, equipment, gear, luggage, stuff

think *verb* 1 BELIEVE, consider, deem, estimate, imagine, judge, reckon, regard, suppose 2 PONDER, cerebrate, cogitate, contemplate, deliberate, meditate, muse, reason, reflect, ruminate

thinker *noun* PHILOSOPHER, brain (*informal*), intellect (*informal*), mastermind, sage, theorist, wise man

thinking *noun* 1 REASONING, conjecture, idea, judgment, opinion, position, theory, view
▶*adjective* 2 THOUGHTFUL, contemplative, intelligent, meditative, philosophical, rational, reasoning, reflective

think up *verb* DEVISE, come up with, concoct, contrive, create, dream up, invent, visualize

thirst noun 1 THIRSTINESS, drought, dryness 2 CRAVING, appetite, desire, hankering, keenness, longing, passion, yearning

thirsty adjective 1 PARCHED, arid, dehydrated, dry 2 EAGER, avid, craving, desirous, greedy, hungry, longing, yearning

thorn noun PRICKLE, barb, spike, spine

thorny adjective PRICKLY, barbed, bristly, pointed, sharp, spiky, spiny

thorough adjective 1 CAREFUL, assiduous, conscientious, efficient, exhaustive, full, in-depth, intensive, meticulous, painstaking, sweeping 2 COMPLETE, absolute, out-and-out, outright, perfect, total, unmitigated, unqualified, utter

thoroughbred adjective PUREBRED, pedigree

thoroughfare noun ROAD, avenue, highway, passage, passageway, street, way

thoroughly adverb 1 CAREFULLY, assiduously, conscientiously, efficiently, exhaustively, from top to bottom, fully, intensively, meticulously, painstakingly, scrupulously 2 COMPLETELY, absolutely, downright, perfectly, quite, totally, to the hilt, utterly

though conjunction 1 ALTHOUGH, even if, even though, notwithstanding, while ▶ adverb 2 NEVERTHELESS, for all that, however, nonetheless, notwithstanding, still, yet

thought noun 1 THINKING, brainwork, cogitation, consideration, deliberation, meditation, musing, reflection, rumination 2 IDEA, concept, judgment, notion, opinion, view 3 CONSIDERATION, attention, heed, regard, scrutiny, study 4 INTENTION, aim, design, idea, notion, object, plan, purpose 5 EXPECTATION, anticipation, aspiration, hope, prospect

thoughtful adjective 1 CONSIDERATE, attentive, caring, helpful, kind, kindly, solicitous, unselfish 2 WELL-THOUGHT-OUT, astute, canny, prudent 3 REFLECTIVE, contemplative, deliberative, meditative, pensive, ruminative, serious, studious

thoughtless adjective INCONSIDERATE, impolite, insensitive, rude, selfish, tactless, uncaring, undiplomatic, unkind

thrash verb 1 BEAT, belt (informal), cane, flog, paddle (U.S. & Canad.), scourge, spank, whip 2 DEFEAT, beat, crush, run rings around (informal), slaughter (informal), trounce, wipe the floor with (informal) 3 THRESH, flail, jerk, toss and turn, writhe

thrashing noun 1 BEATING, belting (informal), flogging, punishment, whipping 2 DEFEAT, beating, hammering (informal), trouncing

thrash out verb SETTLE, argue out, debate, discuss, have out, resolve, solve, talk over

thread noun 1 STRAND, fiber, filament, line, string, yarn 2 THEME, direction, drift, plot, story line, train of thought

▶ *verb* **3** PASS, ease, pick (one's way), squeeze through

threadbare *adjective* **1** SHABBY, down at heel, frayed, old, ragged, tattered, tatty, worn **2** HACKNEYED, commonplace, conventional, familiar, overused, stale, stereotyped, tired, trite, well-worn

threat *noun* **1** WARNING, foreboding, foreshadowing, omen, portent, presage, writing on the wall **2** DANGER, hazard, menace, peril, risk

threaten *verb* **1** INTIMIDATE, browbeat, bully, lean on (*slang*), menace, pressurize, terrorize **2** ENDANGER, imperil, jeopardize, put at risk, put in jeopardy, put on the line **3** FORESHADOW, forebode, impend, portend, presage

threatening *adjective* **1** MENACING, bullying, intimidatory **2** OMINOUS, forbidding, grim, inauspicious, sinister

threshold *noun* **1** ENTRANCE, door, doorstep, doorway **2** START, beginning, brink, dawn, inception, opening, outset, verge **3** MINIMUM, lower limit

thrift *noun* FRUGALITY, carefulness, economy, parsimony, prudence, saving, thriftiness

thrifty *adjective* ECONOMICAL, careful, frugal, parsimonious, provident, prudent, saving, sparing

thrill *noun* **1** PLEASURE, buzz (*slang*), kick (*informal*), stimulation, tingle, titillation ▶ *verb* **2** EXCITE, arouse, electrify, move, stimulate, stir, titillate

thrilling *adjective* EXCITING, electrifying, gripping, riveting, rousing, sensational, stimulating, stirring

thrive *verb* PROSPER, boom, develop, do well, flourish, get on, grow, increase, succeed

thriving *adjective* PROSPEROUS, blooming, booming, burgeoning, flourishing, healthy, successful, well

throb *verb* **1** PULSATE, beat, palpitate, pound, pulse, thump, vibrate ▶ *noun* **2** PULSE, beat, palpitation, pounding, pulsating, thump, thumping, vibration

throng *noun* **1** CROWD, crush, horde, host, mass, mob, multitude, pack, swarm ▶ *verb* **2** CROWD, congregate, converge, flock, mill around, pack, swarm around

throttle *verb* STRANGLE, choke, garrotte, strangulate

through *preposition* **1** BETWEEN, by, past **2** BECAUSE OF, by means of, by way of, using, via **3** DURING, in, throughout ▶ *adjective* **4** FINISHED, completed, done, ended ▶ *adverb* **5** through and through COMPLETELY, altogether, entirely, fully, thoroughly, totally, utterly, wholly

throughout *adverb* EVERYWHERE, all over, from start to finish, right through

throw *verb* **1** HURL, cast, chuck (*informal*), fling, launch, lob (*informal*), pitch, send, sling, toss **2** *Informal* CONFUSE, astonish, baffle, confound, disconcert, dumbfound, faze ▶ *noun* **3** TOSS, fling, heave, lob (*informal*), pitch, sling

throwaway *adjective* CASUAL, careless, offhand, passing, understated

throw away *verb* DISCARD, dispense with, dispose of, ditch (*slang*), dump (*informal*), get rid of, jettison, reject, scrap, throw out

thrust *verb* **1** PUSH, drive, force, jam, plunge, propel, ram, shove ▶ *noun* **2** PUSH, drive, lunge, poke, prod, shove, stab **3** MOMENTUM, impetus

thud *noun, verb* THUMP, clunk, crash, knock, smack

thug *noun* RUFFIAN, bruiser (*informal*), bully boy, gangster, hooligan, tough

thump *noun* **1** CRASH, bang, clunk, thud, thwack **2** BLOW, clout (*informal*), knock, punch, rap, smack, wallop (*informal*), whack ▶ *verb* **3** STRIKE, beat, clobber (*slang*), clout (*informal*), hit, knock, pound, punch, smack, wallop (*informal*), whack

thunder *noun* **1** RUMBLE, boom, crash, explosion ▶ *verb* **2** RUMBLE, boom, crash, peal, resound, reverberate, roar **3** SHOUT, bark, bellow, roar, yell

thunderous *adjective* LOUD, booming, deafening, ear-splitting, noisy, resounding, roaring, tumultuous

thunderstruck *adjective* AMAZED, astonished, astounded, dumbfounded, flabbergasted (*informal*), open-mouthed, shocked, staggered, stunned, taken aback

thus *adverb* **1** THEREFORE, accordingly, consequently,

ergo, for this reason, hence, on that account, so, then **2** IN THIS WAY, as follows, like this, so

thwart *verb* FRUSTRATE, foil, hinder, obstruct, outwit, prevent, snooker, stymie

tick¹ *noun* **1** MITE, bug, insect **2** TAPPING, clicking, ticktock

tick² *noun* CREDIT, account

ticket *noun* **1** VOUCHER, card, certificate, coupon, pass, slip, token **2** LABEL, card, docket, marker, slip, sticker, tab, tag

tidbit *noun* DELICACY, dainty, morsel, snack, treat

tide *noun* **1** CURRENT, ebb, flow, stream, tideway, undertow **2** TENDENCY, direction, drift, movement, trend

tidy *adjective* **1** NEAT, clean, methodical, orderly, shipshape, spruce, well-kept, well-ordered **2** *Informal* CONSIDERABLE, ample, generous, goodly, handsome, healthy, large, sizable *or* sizeable, substantial ▶ *verb* **3** NEATEN, clean, groom, order, spruce up, straighten

tie *verb* **1** FASTEN, attach, bind, connect, join, knot, link, secure, tether **2** RESTRICT, bind, confine, hamper, hinder, limit, restrain **3** DRAW, equal, match ▶ *noun* **4** BOND, affiliation, allegiance, commitment, connection, liaison, relationship **5** FASTENING, bond, cord, fetter, knot, ligature, link **6** DRAW, dead heat, deadlock, gridlock, stalemate

tier *noun* ROW, bank, layer, level, line, rank, story, stratum

tight *adjective* **1** STRETCHED, close, constricted, cramped, narrow, rigid, snug, taut

2 *Informal* MISERLY, grasping, mean, niggardly, parsimonious, stingy, tightfisted **3** CLOSE, even, evenly-balanced, well-matched

tighten *verb* SQUEEZE, close, constrict, narrow

till¹ *verb* CULTIVATE, dig, plow, work

till² *noun* CASH REGISTER, cash box

tilt *verb* **1** SLANT, heel, incline, lean, list, slope, tip ▶ *noun* **2** SLOPE, angle, inclination, incline, list, pitch, slant **3** *Medieval history* JOUST, combat, duel, fight, lists, tournament **4** (at) full tilt FULL SPEED, for dear life, headlong

timber *noun* WOOD, beams, boards, logs, planks, trees

timbre *noun* TONE, color, resonance, ring

time *noun* **1** PERIOD, duration, interval, space, span, spell, stretch, term **2** OCCASION, instance, juncture, point, stage **3** *Music* TEMPO, beat, measure, rhythm ▶ *verb* **4** SCHEDULE, set

timeless *adjective* ETERNAL, ageless, changeless, enduring, everlasting, immortal, lasting, permanent

timely *adjective* OPPORTUNE, appropriate, convenient, judicious, propitious, seasonable, suitable, well-timed

timetable *noun* SCHEDULE, agenda, calendar, curriculum, diary, list, program

timid *adjective* FEARFUL, apprehensive, bashful, coy, diffident, faint-hearted, shrinking, shy, timorous

timorous *adjective* TIMID, apprehensive, bashful, coy, diffident, faint-hearted, fearful, shrinking, shy

tinge *noun* **1** TINT, color, shade **2** BIT, dash, drop, smattering, sprinkling, suggestion, touch, trace ▶ *verb* **3** TINT, color, imbue, suffuse

tingle *verb* **1** PRICKLE, have goose pimples, itch, sting, tickle ▶ *noun* **2** QUIVER, goose pimples, itch, pins and needles (*informal*), prickling, shiver, thrill

tinker *verb* MEDDLE, dabble, fiddle (*informal*), mess about, play, potter

tint *noun* **1** SHADE, color, hue, tone **2** DYE, rinse, tincture, tinge, wash ▶ *verb* **3** DYE, color

tiny *adjective* SMALL, diminutive, infinitesimal, little, microscopic, miniature, minute, negligible, petite, slight

tip¹ *noun* **1** END, extremity, head, peak, pinnacle, point, summit, top ▶ *verb* **2** CAP, crown, finish, surmount, top

tip² *noun* **1** GRATUITY, gift **2** HINT, clue, pointer, suggestion, warning ▶ *verb* **3** REWARD, remunerate **4** ADVISE, caution, forewarn, suggest, warn

tip³ *verb* **1** TILT, incline, lean, list, slant **2** DUMP, empty, pour out, unload ▶ *noun* **3** DUMP, refuse heap, rubbish heap

tipple *verb* **1** DRINK, imbibe, indulge (*informal*), quaff, swig, tope (*informal*) ▶ *noun* **2** ALCOHOL, booze (*informal*), drink, liquor

tipsy *adjective* DRUNK, fuzzy, happy, mellow, three sheets to the wind

tirade *noun* OUTBURST, diatribe, fulmination, harangue, invective, lecture

tire verb 1 FATIGUE, drain, exhaust, wear out, weary 2 BORE, exasperate, irk, irritate, weary

tired adjective 1 EXHAUSTED, drained, drowsy, fatigued, flagging, jaded, sleepy, weary, worn out 2 BORED, fed up, sick, weary 3 HACKNEYED, clichéd, corny (slang), old, outworn, stale, threadbare, trite, well-worn

tireless adjective ENERGETIC, indefatigable, industrious, resolute, unflagging, untiring, vigorous

tiresome adjective BORING, dull, irksome, irritating, tedious, trying, vexatious, wearing, wearisome

tiring adjective EXHAUSTING, arduous, demanding, exacting, laborious, strenuous, tough, wearing

titillate verb EXCITE, arouse, interest, stimulate, tantalize, tease, thrill

titillating adjective EXCITING, arousing, interesting, lurid, provocative, stimulating, suggestive, teasing

title noun 1 NAME, designation, handle (slang), moniker or monicker (slang), term 2 CHAMPIONSHIP, crown 3 OWNERSHIP, claim, entitlement, prerogative, privilege, right

titter verb LAUGH, chortle, chuckle, giggle, snigger

tizzy noun Informal PANIC, agitation, commotion, fluster, state (informal), sweat (informal)

toady noun 1 SYCOPHANT, brown-noser (slang), creep (slang), flatterer, flunkey, hanger-on, lackey, minion, scuzzbucket (slang), yes man ▶verb 2 FLATTER, brown-nose (slang), fawn on, grovel, kiss ass (slang), kowtow to, pander to, suck up to (informal)

toast¹ verb WARM, brown, grill, heat, roast

toast² noun 1 TRIBUTE, compliment, health, pledge, salutation, salute 2 FAVORITE, darling, hero or heroine ▶verb 3 DRINK TO, drink (to) the health of, salute

together adverb 1 COLLECTIVELY, as one, hand in glove, in concert, in unison, jointly, mutually, shoulder to shoulder, side by side 2 AT THE SAME TIME, at one fell swoop, concurrently, contemporaneously, simultaneously ▶adjective 3 Informal WELL-ORGANIZED, composed, well-adjusted, well-balanced

toil noun 1 HARD WORK, application, drudgery, effort, elbow grease (informal), exertion, slog, sweat ▶verb 2 WORK, drudge, labor, slave, slog, strive, struggle, sweat (informal), work one's fingers to the bone

toilet noun LAVATORY, bathroom, convenience, gents (Brit. informal), ladies' room, latrine, privy, urinal, water closet, W.C.

token noun 1 SYMBOL, badge, expression, indication, mark, note, representation, sign ▶adjective 2 NOMINAL, hollow, minimal, perfunctory, superficial, symbolic

tolerable *adjective* **1** BEARABLE, acceptable, allowable, endurable, sufferable, supportable **2** FAIR, acceptable, adequate, all right, average, O.K. or okay (*informal*), passable

tolerance *noun* **1** BROAD-MINDEDNESS, forbearance, indulgence, open-mindedness, permissiveness **2** ENDURANCE, fortitude, hardiness, resilience, resistance, stamina, staying power, toughness

tolerant *adjective* BROAD-MINDED, catholic, forbearing, liberal, long-suffering, open-minded, understanding, unprejudiced

tolerate *verb* ALLOW, accept, brook, condone, endure, permit, put up with (*informal*), stand, stomach, take

toleration *noun* ACCEPTANCE, allowance, endurance, indulgence, permissiveness, sanction

toll¹ *verb* **1** RING, chime, clang, knell, peal, sound, strike ▶ *noun* **2** RINGING, chime, clang, knell, peal

toll² *noun* **1** CHARGE, duty, fee, levy, payment, tariff, tax **2** DAMAGE, cost, loss, penalty

tomb *noun* GRAVE, catacomb, crypt, mausoleum, sarcophagus, sepulcher, vault

tombstone *noun* GRAVESTONE, headstone, marker, memorial, monument

tomfoolery *noun* FOOLISHNESS, buffoonery, clowning, fooling around (*informal*), horseplay, shenanigans (*informal*), silliness, skylarking (*informal*), stupidity

ton *noun* (often plural) *Informal*

A LOT, great deal, ocean, quantity, stacks

tone *noun* **1** PITCH, inflection, intonation, modulation, timbre **2** CHARACTER, air, attitude, feel, manner, mood, spirit, style, temper **3** COLOR, hue, shade, tinge, tint ▶ *verb* **4** HARMONIZE, blend, go well with, match, suit

tone down *verb* MODERATE, play down, reduce, restrain, soften, subdue, temper

tongue *noun* LANGUAGE, dialect, parlance, speech

tonic *noun* STIMULANT, boost, pick-me-up (*informal*), restorative, shot in the arm (*informal*)

too *adverb* **1** ALSO, as well, besides, further, in addition, likewise, moreover, to boot **2** EXCESSIVELY, extremely, immoderately, inordinately, overly, unduly, unreasonably, very

tool *noun* **1** IMPLEMENT, appliance, contraption, contrivance, device, gadget, instrument, machine, utensil **2** PUPPET, cat's-paw, creature, flunkey, hireling, lackey, minion, pawn, stooge (*slang*)

top *noun* **1** PEAK, apex, crest, crown, culmination, head, height, pinnacle, summit, zenith **2** FIRST PLACE, head, lead **3** LID, cap, cover, stopper ▶ *adjective* **4** LEADING, best, chief, elite, finest, first, foremost, head, highest, pre-eminent, principal, uppermost ▶ *verb* **5** COVER, cap, crown, finish, garnish **6** LEAD, be first, head **7** SURPASS, beat, best, better, eclipse, exceed, excel, outstrip, transcend

topic noun SUBJECT, issue, matter, point, question, subject matter, theme

topical adjective CURRENT, contemporary, newsworthy, popular, up-to-date, up-to-the-minute

topmost adjective HIGHEST, dominant, foremost, leading, paramount, principal, supreme, top, uppermost

topple verb 1 FALL OVER, collapse, fall, keel over, overbalance, overturn, totter, tumble 2 OVERTHROW, bring down, bring low, oust, overturn, unseat

topsy-turvy adjective CONFUSED, chaotic, disorderly, disorganized, inside-out, jumbled, messy, mixed-up, upside-down

torment verb 1 TORTURE, crucify, distress, rack 2 TEASE, annoy, bother, harass, hassle (informal), irritate, nag, pester, vex ▶ noun 3 SUFFERING, agony, anguish, distress, hell, misery, pain, torture

torn adjective 1 CUT, lacerated, ragged, rent, ripped, slit, split 2 UNDECIDED, in two minds (informal), irresolute, uncertain, unsure, vacillating, wavering

tornado noun WHIRLWIND, cyclone, gale, hurricane, squall, storm, tempest, typhoon

torpor noun INACTIVITY, apathy, drowsiness, indolence, laziness, lethargy, listlessness, sloth, sluggishness

torrent noun STREAM, cascade, deluge, downpour, flood, flow, rush, spate, tide

torrid adjective 1 ARID, dried, parched, scorched 2 PASSIONATE, ardent, fervent, intense, steamy (informal)

tortuous adjective 1 WINDING, circuitous, convoluted, indirect, mazy, meandering, serpentine, sinuous, twisting, twisty 2 COMPLICATED, ambiguous, convoluted, devious, indirect, involved, roundabout, tricky

torture verb 1 TORMENT, afflict, crucify, distress, persecute, put on the rack, rack ▶ noun 2 AGONY, anguish, distress, pain, persecution, suffering, torment

toss verb 1 THROW, cast, fling, flip, hurl, launch, lob (informal), pitch, sling 2 THRASH, rock, roll, shake, wriggle, writhe ▶ noun 3 THROW, lob (informal), pitch

tot noun INFANT, baby, child, mite, toddler

total noun 1 WHOLE, aggregate, entirety, full amount, sum, totality ▶ adjective 2 COMPLETE, absolute, comprehensive, entire, full, gross, thoroughgoing, undivided, utter, whole ▶ verb 3 AMOUNT TO, come to, mount up to, reach 4 ADD UP, reckon, tot up

totalitarian adjective DICTATORIAL, authoritarian, despotic, oppressive, tyrannous, undemocratic

totality noun WHOLE, aggregate, entirety, sum, total

totally adverb COMPLETELY, absolutely, comprehensively, entirely, fully, one hundred per cent, thoroughly, utterly, wholly

totter verb STAGGER, falter, lurch,

reel, stumble, sway

touch verb 1 HANDLE, brush, caress, contact, feel, finger, fondle, stroke, tap 2 MEET, abut, adjoin, be in contact, border, contact, graze, impinge upon 3 AFFECT, disturb, impress, influence, inspire, move, stir 4 EAT, chow down (slang), consume, drink, partake of 5 MATCH, compare with, equal, hold a candle to (informal), parallel, rival 6 **touch on** REFER TO, allude to, bring in, cover, deal with, mention, speak of ▶ noun 7 FEELING, handling, physical contact 8 TAP, brush, contact, pat, stroke 9 BIT, dash, drop, jot, small amount, smattering, soupçon, spot, trace 10 STYLE, manner, method, technique, trademark, way

touch and go adjective RISKY, close, critical, near, nerve-racking, precarious

touching adjective MOVING, affecting, emotive, pathetic, pitiable, poignant, sad, stirring

touchstone noun STANDARD, criterion, gauge, measure, norm, par, yardstick

touchy adjective OVERSENSITIVE, irascible, irritable, querulous, quick-tempered, testy, tetchy, thin-skinned

tough adjective 1 RESILIENT, durable, hard, inflexible, leathery, resistant, rugged, solid, strong, sturdy 2 STRONG, hardy, seasoned, stout, strapping, sturdy, vigorous 3 ROUGH, hard-boiled, pugnacious, ruthless, violent 4 STRICT, firm, hard, merciless, resolute, severe, stern,

unbending 5 DIFFICULT, arduous, exacting, hard, laborious, strenuous, troublesome, uphill 6 Informal UNLUCKY, lamentable, regrettable, unfortunate ▶ noun

tour noun 1 JOURNEY, excursion, expedition, jaunt, outing, trip ▶ verb 2 VISIT, explore, go round, journey, sightsee, travel through

tourist noun TRAVELER, excursionist, globetrotter, holiday-maker, sightseer, tripper, voyager

tournament noun COMPETITION, contest, event, meeting, series

tow verb DRAG, draw, haul, lug, pull, tug

towards preposition 1 IN THE DIRECTION OF, en route for, for, on the way to to 2 REGARDING, about, concerning, for, with regard to, with respect to

tower noun COLUMN, belfry, obelisk, pillar, skyscraper, steeple, turret

towering adjective HIGH, colossal, elevated, imposing, impressive, lofty, magnificent, soaring, tall

toxic adjective POISONOUS, deadly, harmful, lethal, noxious, pernicious, pestilential, septic

toy noun 1 PLAYTHING, doll, game ▶ verb 2 PLAY, amuse oneself, dally, fiddle (informal), fool (about or around), trifle

trace verb 1 FIND, detect, discover, ferret out, hunt down, track, unearth 2 COPY, draw, outline, sketch ▶ noun 3 TRACK, footmark, footprint, footstep, path, spoor, trail 4 BIT, drop, hint, shadow, suggestion, suspicion, tinge, touch, whiff **5** INDICATION, evidence, mark, record, remnant, sign, survival, vestige

track noun **1** PATH, course, line, orbit, pathway, road, trajectory, way **2** TRAIL, footmark, footprint, footstep, mark, path, spoor, trace, wake **3** LINE, permanent way, rails ▶verb **4** FOLLOW, chase, hunt down, pursue, shadow, stalk, tail (informal), trace, trail

track down verb FIND, dig up, discover, hunt down, run to earth or ground, sniff out, trace, unearth

tract[1] noun AREA, district, expanse, extent, plot, region, stretch, territory

tract[2] noun TREATISE, booklet, dissertation, essay, homily, monograph, pamphlet

tractable adjective MANAGEABLE, amenable, biddable, compliant, docile, obedient, submissive, tame, willing, yielding

traction noun GRIP, friction, pull, purchase, resistance

trade noun **1** COMMERCE, barter, business, dealing, exchange, traffic, transactions, truck **2** JOB, business, craft, employment, line of work, métier, occupation, profession ▶verb **3** DEAL, bargain, do business, have dealings, peddle, traffic, transact, truck **4** EXCHANGE, barter, swap, switch

trader noun DEALER, merchant, purveyor, seller, supplier

tradesman noun **1** CRAFTSMAN, artisan, journeyman, workman **2** SHOPKEEPER, dealer, merchant,

purveyor, retailer, seller, supplier, vendor

tradition noun CUSTOM, convention, folklore, habit, institution, lore, ritual

traditional adjective CUSTOMARY, accustomed, conventional, established, old, time-honored, usual

traffic noun **1** TRANSPORT, freight, transportation, vehicles **2** TRADE, business, commerce, dealings, exchange, peddling, truck ▶verb **3** TRADE, bargain, deal, do business, exchange, have dealings, peddle

tragedy noun DISASTER, adversity, calamity, catastrophe, misfortune

tragic adjective DISASTROUS, appalling, calamitous, catastrophic, deadly, dire, dreadful, miserable, pathetic, sad, unfortunate

trail noun **1** PATH, footpath, road, route, track, way **2** TRACKS, footprints, marks, path, scent, spoor, trace, wake ▶verb **3** DRAG, dangle, draw, haul, pull, tow **4** LAG, dawdle, follow, hang back, linger, loiter, straggle, traipse (informal) **5** FOLLOW, chase, hunt, pursue, shadow, stalk, tail (informal), trace, track

train verb **1** INSTRUCT, coach, drill, educate, guide, prepare, school, teach, tutor **2** EXERCISE, prepare, work out **3** AIM, direct, focus, level, point ▶noun **4** SEQUENCE, chain, progression, series, set, string, succession

trainer noun COACH, handler

training noun **1** INSTRUCTION, coaching, discipline, education, grounding, schooling, teaching, tuition 2 EXERCISE, practice, preparation, working out

traipse verb TRUDGE, drag oneself, footslog, slouch, trail, tramp

trait noun CHARACTERISTIC, attribute, feature, idiosyncrasy, mannerism, peculiarity, quality, quirk

traitor noun BETRAYER, apostate, back-stabber, defector, deserter, Judas, quisling, rebel, renegade, turncoat

trajectory noun PATH, course, flight path, line, route, track

tramp verb 1 HIKE, footslog, march, ramble, roam, rove, slog, trek, walk 2 TRUDGE, plod, stump, toil, traipse (informal) ▶ noun 3 VAGRANT, derelict, down-and-out, drifter 4 HIKE, march, ramble, slog, trek 5 TREAD, footfall, footstep, stamp

trample verb CRUSH, flatten, run over, squash, stamp, tread, walk over

trance noun DAZE, abstraction, dream, rapture, reverie, stupor, unconsciousness

tranquil adjective CALM, peaceful, placid, quiet, restful, sedate, serene, still, undisturbed

tranquilize verb CALM, lull, pacify, quell, quiet, relax, sedate, settle one's nerves, soothe

tranquilizer noun SEDATIVE, barbiturate, bromide, downer (slang), opiate

tranquillity noun CALM, hush, peace, placidity, quiet, repose, rest, serenity, stillness

transaction noun DEAL, bargain,

business, enterprise, negotiation, undertaking

transcend verb SURPASS, eclipse, exceed, excel, go beyond, outdo, outstrip, rise above

transcendent adjective UNPARALLELED, consummate, incomparable, matchless, pre-eminent, sublime, unequaled, unrivaled

transcribe verb WRITE OUT, copy out, reproduce, take down, transfer

transcript noun COPY, duplicate, manuscript, record, reproduction, transcription

transfer verb 1 MOVE, change, convey, hand over, pass on, relocate, shift, transplant, transport, transpose ▶ noun 2 MOVE, change, handover, relocation, shift, transference, translation, transmission, transposition

transfix verb 1 STUN, engross, fascinate, hold, hypnotize, mesmerize, paralyze 2 PIERCE, impale, puncture, run through, skewer, spear

transform verb CHANGE, alter, convert, remodel, revolutionize, transmute

transformation noun CHANGE, alteration, conversion, metamorphosis, revolution, sea change, transmutation

transgress verb OFFEND, break the law, contravene, disobey, encroach, infringe, sin, trespass, violate

transgression noun OFFENSE, contravention, crime, encroachment, infraction, infringement, misdeed, misdemeanor, sin, trespass, violation, wrongdoing

transgressor noun OFFENDER, criminal, culprit, lawbreaker, miscreant, sinner, trespasser, villain, wrongdoer

transient adjective TEMPORARY, brief, ephemeral, fleeting, impermanent, momentary, passing, short-lived, transitory

transit noun MOVEMENT, carriage, conveyance, crossing, passage, transfer, transport, transportation

transition noun CHANGE, alteration, conversion, development, metamorphosis, passing, progression, shift, transmutation

transitional adjective CHANGING, developmental, fluid, intermediate, passing, provisional, temporary, unsettled

transitory adjective SHORT-LIVED, brief, ephemeral, fleeting, impermanent, momentary, passing, short, temporary, transient

translate verb INTERPRET, construe, convert, decipher, decode, paraphrase, render

translation noun INTERPRETATION, decoding, paraphrase, rendering, rendition, version

transmission noun 1 TRANSFER, conveyance, dissemination, sending, shipment, spread, transference 2 BROADCASTING, dissemination, putting out, relaying, sending, showing 3 PROGRAM, broadcast, show

transmit verb 1 PASS ON, bear, carry, convey, disseminate, hand on, impart, send, spread, transfer 2 BROADCAST,

disseminate, radio, relay, send out

transparency noun 1 CLARITY, clearness, limpidity, pellucidness, translucence 2 PHOTOGRAPH, slide

transparent adjective 1 CLEAR, crystalline, diaphanous, limpid, lucid, see-through, sheer, translucent 2 PLAIN, evident, explicit, manifest, obvious, patent, recognizable, unambiguous, undisguised

transpire verb 1 EMERGE, become known, come out, come to light 2 Informal HAPPEN, arise, befall, chance, come about, occur, take place

transplant verb TRANSFER, displace, relocate, remove, resettle, shift, uproot

transport verb 1 CONVEY, bear, bring, carry, haul, move, take, transfer 2 EXILE, banish, deport 3 ENRAPTURE, captivate, delight, enchant, entrance, move, ravish ▶ noun 4 VEHICLE, conveyance, transportation 5 TRANSFERENCE, conveyance, shipment, transportation 6 ECSTASY, bliss, delight, enchantment, euphoria, heaven, rapture, ravishment

transpose verb INTERCHANGE, alter, change, exchange, move, reorder, shift, substitute, swap, switch, transfer

trap noun 1 SNARE, ambush, gin, net, noose, pitfall 2 TRICK, ambush, deception, ruse, stratagem, subterfuge, wile ▶ verb 3 CATCH, corner, enmesh, ensnare, entrap, snare, take 4 TRICK, ambush, beguile, deceive, dupe, ensnare, inveigle

trappings plural noun
ACCESSORIES, accoutrements, equipment, finery, furnishings, gear, panoply, paraphernalia, things, trimmings

trash noun 1 NONSENSE, drivel, hogwash, moonshine, rot, rubbish, tripe (informal), twaddle 2 LITTER, dross, garbage, junk (informal), refuse, rubbish, waste ▶ verb 3 DESTROY, defeat, demolish, put paid to, ruin, torpedo, trounce, wreck

trashy adjective WORTHLESS, cheap, inferior, rubbishy, shabby, shoddy, tawdry

trauma noun SUFFERING, agony, anguish, hurt, ordeal, pain, shock, torture

traumatic adjective SHOCKING, agonizing, damaging, disturbing, hurtful, injurious, painful, scarring, upsetting, wounding

travel verb 1 GO, journey, move, progress, roam, tour, trek, voyage, wander ▶ noun 2 (usually plural) WANDERING, excursion, expedition, globetrotting, journey, tour, trip, voyage

traveler noun WANDERER, explorer, globetrotter, gypsy, holiday-maker, tourist, voyager, wayfarer

traveling adjective MOBILE, itinerant, migrant, nomadic, peripatetic, roaming, roving, touring, wandering, wayfaring

traverse verb CROSS, go over, span, travel over

travesty noun 1 MOCKERY, burlesque, caricature, distortion, lampoon, parody,

perversion ▶ verb 2 MOCK, burlesque, caricature, distort, lampoon, make a mockery of, parody, ridicule

treacherous adjective 1 DISLOYAL, deceitful, double-dealing, duplicitous, faithless, false, perfidious, traitorous, unfaithful, untrustworthy 2 DANGEROUS, deceptive, hazardous, icy, perilous, precarious, risky, slippery, unreliable, unsafe, unstable

treachery noun BETRAYAL, disloyalty, double-dealing, duplicity, faithlessness, infidelity, perfidy, treason

tread verb 1 STEP, hike, march, pace, stamp, stride, walk 2 TRAMPLE, crush underfoot, squash ▶ noun 3 STEP, footfall, footstep, gait, pace, stride, walk

treason noun DISLOYALTY, duplicity, lese-majesty, mutiny, perfidy, sedition, traitorousness, treachery

treasonable adjective DISLOYAL, mutinous, perfidious, seditious, subversive, traitorous, treacherous

treasure noun 1 RICHES, cash, fortune, gold, jewels, money, valuables, wealth 2 DARLING, apple of one's eye, gem, jewel, nonpareil, paragon, pride and joy ▶ verb 3 PRIZE, adore, cherish, esteem, hold dear, idolize, love, revere, value

treasury noun STOREHOUSE, bank, cache, hoard, repository, store, vault

treat verb 1 HANDLE, act towards, behave towards, consider, deal with, look upon, manage, regard, use 2 ATTEND

TO, care for, nurse **3** ENTERTAIN, lay on, provide, regale, stand (informal) ▶ noun **4** ENTERTAINMENT, banquet, celebration, feast, gift, party, refreshment **5** PLEASURE, delight, enjoyment, fun, joy, satisfaction, surprise, thrill

treatise noun ESSAY, dissertation, monograph, pamphlet, paper, study, thesis, tract, work

treatment noun **1** CARE, cure, healing, medication, medicine, remedy, surgery, therapy **2** HANDLING, action, behavior, conduct, dealing, management, manipulation

treaty noun PACT, agreement, alliance, compact, concordat, contract, convention, covenant, entente

trek noun **1** JOURNEY, expedition, hike, march, odyssey, safari, slog, tramp ▶ verb **2** JOURNEY, footslog, hike, march, rove, slog, traipse (informal), tramp, trudge

tremble verb **1** SHAKE, quake, quiver, shiver, shudder, totter, vibrate, wobble ▶ noun **2** SHAKE, quake, quiver, shiver, shudder, tremor, vibration, wobble

tremendous adjective **1** HUGE, colossal, enormous, formidable, gigantic, great, immense, stupendous, terrific **2** Informal EXCELLENT, amazing, brilliant, exceptional, extraordinary, fantastic (informal), great, marvelous, sensational (informal), wonderful

tremor noun **1** SHAKE, quaking, quaver, quiver, shiver, trembling, wobble **2** EARTHQUAKE, quake (informal),

shock

trench noun DITCH, channel, drain, excavation, furrow, gutter, trough

trenchant adjective **1** INCISIVE, acerbic, caustic, cutting, penetrating, pointed, pungent, scathing **2** EFFECTIVE, energetic, forceful, potent, powerful, strong, vigorous

trend noun **1** TENDENCY, bias, current, direction, drift, flow, inclination, leaning **2** FASHION, craze, fad (informal), mode, rage, style, thing, vogue

trendy adjective Informal FASHIONABLE, cool (informal), in fashion, in vogue, modish, phat (slang), stylish, voguish, with it (informal)

trepidation noun ANXIETY, alarm, apprehension, consternation, disquiet, dread, fear, nervousness, uneasiness, worry

trespass verb **1** INTRUDE, encroach, infringe, invade, obtrude ▶ noun **2** INTRUSION, encroachment, infringement, invasion, unlawful entry

trespasser noun INTRUDER, interloper, invader, poacher

trial noun **1** HEARING, litigation, tribunal **2** TEST, audition, dry run (informal), experiment, probation, test-run **3** HARDSHIP, adversity, affliction, distress, ordeal, suffering, tribulation, trouble

tribe noun RACE, clan, family, people

tribunal noun HEARING, court, trial

tribute noun **1** ACCOLADE, commendation, compliment, eulogy, panegyric, recognition, testimonial **2** TAX, charge, homage, payment, ransom

trick noun 1 DECEPTION, fraud, hoax, maneuver, ploy, ruse, stratagem, subterfuge, swindle, trap, wile 2 JOKE, antic, jape, practical joke, prank, stunt 3 SECRET, hang (informal), knack, know-how (informal), skill, technique 4 MANNERISM, characteristic, foible, habit, idiosyncrasy, peculiarity, practice, quirk, trait ▶ verb 5 DECEIVE, cheat, con (informal), dupe, fool, hoodwink, kid (informal), mislead, swindle, take in (informal), trap

trickery noun DECEPTION, cheating, chicanery, deceit, dishonesty, guile, monkey business (informal)

trickle verb 1 DRIBBLE, drip, drop, exude, ooze, run, seep, stream ▶ noun 2 DRIBBLE, drip, seepage

tricky adjective 1 DIFFICULT, complicated, delicate, knotty, problematic, risky, thorny, ticklish 2 CRAFTY, artful, cunning, deceitful, devious, scheming, slippery, sly, wily

trifle noun 1 KNICK-KNACK, bagatelle, bauble, plaything, toy ▶ verb 2 TOY, dally, mess about, play

trifling adjective INSIGNIFICANT, measly, negligible, paltry, trivial, unimportant, worthless

trigger verb SET OFF, activate, cause, generate, produce, prompt, provoke, set in motion, spark off, start

trim adjective 1 NEAT, dapper, shipshape, smart, spruce, tidy, well-groomed 2 SLENDER, fit, shapely, sleek, slim,
streamlined, svelte, willowy ▶ verb 3 CUT, clip, crop, even up, pare, prune, shave, tidy 4 DECORATE, adorn, array, beautify, deck out, dress, embellish, ornament ▶ noun 5 DECORATION, adornment, border, edging, embellishment, frill, ornamentation, piping, trimming 6 CONDITION, fettle, fitness, health, shape (informal), state 7 CUT, clipping, crop, pruning, shave, shearing, tidying up

trimming noun 1 DECORATION, adornment, border, edging, embellishment, frill, ornamentation, piping 2 trimmings EXTRAS, accessories, accompaniments, frills, ornaments, paraphernalia, trappings

trinity noun THREESOME, triad, trio, triumvirate

trinket noun ORNAMENT, bagatelle, bauble, knick-knack, toy, trifle

trio noun THREESOME, triad, trilogy, trinity, triumvirate

trip noun 1 JOURNEY, errand, excursion, expedition, foray, jaunt, outing, run, tour, voyage 2 STUMBLE, fall, misstep, slip ▶ verb 3 STUMBLE, fall, lose one's footing, misstep, slip, tumble 4 CATCH OUT, trap 5 SKIP, dance, gambol, hop

triple adjective 1 THREEFOLD, three-way, tripartite ▶ verb 2 TREBLE, increase threefold

trite adjective UNORIGINAL, banal, clichéd, commonplace, hackneyed, stale, stereotyped, threadbare, tired

triumph noun 1 JOY, elation,

exultation, happiness, jubilation, pride, rejoicing **2** SUCCESS, accomplishment, achievement, attainment, conquest, coup, feat, victory ▶*verb* **3** (often with *over*) WIN, overcome, prevail, prosper, succeed, vanquish **4** REJOICE, celebrate, crow, exult, gloat, glory, revel

triumphant *adjective* VICTORIOUS, celebratory, conquering, elated, exultant, jubilant, proud, successful, winning

trivia *plural noun* MINUTIAE, details, trifles, trivialities

trivial *adjective* UNIMPORTANT, incidental, inconsequential, insignificant, meaningless, minor, petty, small, trifling, worthless

triviality *noun* INSIGNIFICANCE, meaninglessness, pettiness, unimportance, worthlessness

trivialize *verb* UNDERVALUE, belittle, laugh off, make light of, minimize, play down, scoff at, underestimate, underplay

troop *noun* **1** GROUP, band, body, company, crowd, horde, multitude, squad, team, unit **2 troops** SOLDIERS, armed forces, army, men, servicemen, soldiery ▶*verb* **3** FLOCK, march, stream, swarm, throng, traipse (*informal*)

trophy *noun* PRIZE, award, booty, cup, laurels, memento, souvenir, spoils

tropical *adjective* HOT, steamy, stifling, sultry, sweltering, torrid

trot *verb* **1** RUN, canter, jog, lope, scamper ▶*noun* **2** RUN, canter, jog, lope

trouble *noun* **1** DISTRESS, anxiety,

disquiet, grief, misfortune, pain, sorrow, torment, woe, worry **2** DISEASE, ailment, complaint, defect, disorder, failure, illness, malfunction **3** DISORDER, agitation, bother (*informal*), commotion, discord, disturbance, strife, tumult, unrest **4** EFFORT, care, exertion, inconvenience, labor, pains, thought, work ▶*verb* **5** WORRY, bother, disconcert, distress, disturb, pain, perturb, plague, sadden, upset **6** TAKE PAINS, exert oneself, make an effort, take the time **7** INCONVENIENCE, bother, burden, disturb, impose upon, incommode, put out

troublesome *adjective* **1** WORRYING, annoying, demanding, difficult, inconvenient, irksome, taxing, tricky, trying, vexatious **2** DISORDERLY, rebellious, rowdy, turbulent, uncooperative, undisciplined, unruly, violent

trough *noun* **1** MANGER, water trough **2** CHANNEL, canal, depression, ditch, duct, furrow, gully, gutter, trench

trounce *verb* THRASH, beat, crush, drub, hammer (*informal*), rout, slaughter (*informal*), wipe the floor with (*informal*)

troupe *noun* COMPANY, band, cast

truancy *noun* ABSENCE, absence without leave, malingering, shirking

truant *noun* ABSENTEE, malingerer, runaway, shirker

truce *noun* CEASEFIRE, armistice, cessation, let-up (*informal*), lull, moratorium, peace, respite

truculent *adjective* HOSTILE, aggressive, bellicose, belligerent, defiant, ill-tempered, obstreperous, pugnacious

trudge *verb* 1 PLOD, footslog, lumber, slog, stump, traipse (*informal*), tramp, trek ▶ *noun* 2 HIKE, footslog, march, slog, traipse (*informal*), tramp, trek

true *adjective* 1 CORRECT, accurate, authentic, factual, genuine, precise, real, right, truthful, veracious 2 FAITHFUL, dedicated, devoted, dutiful, loyal, reliable, staunch, steady, trustworthy 3 EXACT, accurate, on target, perfect, precise, unerring

truism *noun* CLICHÉ, axiom, bromide, commonplace, platitude

truly *adverb* 1 CORRECTLY, authentically, exactly, factually, genuinely, legitimately, precisely, rightly, truthfully 2 FAITHFULLY, devotedly, dutifully, loyally, sincerely, staunchly, steadily 3 REALLY, extremely, greatly, indeed, of course, very

trumpet *noun* 1 HORN, bugle, clarion ▶ *verb* 2 PROCLAIM, advertise, announce, broadcast, shout from the rooftops, tout (*informal*)

trump up *verb* FABRICATE, concoct, contrive, cook up (*informal*), create, fake, invent, make up

truncate *verb* SHORTEN, abbreviate, curtail, cut short, dock, lop, pare, prune, trim

truncheon *noun* CLUB, baton, cudgel, staff

trunk *noun* 1 STEM, bole, stalk 2 CHEST, box, case, casket, coffer, crate 3 BODY, torso 4 SNOUT, proboscis

truss *verb* 1 TIE, bind, fasten, make fast, secure, strap, tether ▶ *noun* 2 *Medical* SUPPORT, bandage 3 JOIST, beam, brace, buttress, prop, stanchion, stay, strut, support

trust *verb* 1 BELIEVE IN, bank on, count on, depend on, have faith in, rely upon 2 CONSIGN, assign, commit, confide, delegate, entrust, give 3 EXPECT, assume, hope, presume, suppose, surmise ▶ *noun* 4 CONFIDENCE, assurance, belief, certainty, conviction, credence, credit, expectation, faith, reliance

trustful, trusting *adjective* UNWARY, credulous, gullible, naive, unsuspecting, unsuspicious

trustworthy *adjective* HONEST, dependable, honorable, principled, reliable, reputable, responsible, staunch, steadfast, trusty

trusty *adjective* FAITHFUL, dependable, reliable, solid, staunch, steady, strong, trustworthy

truth *noun* TRUTHFULNESS, accuracy, exactness, fact, genuineness, legitimacy, precision, reality, validity, veracity

truthful *adjective* HONEST, candid, frank, precise, sincere, straight, true, trustworthy

try *verb* 1 ATTEMPT, aim, endeavor, have a go, make an effort, seek, strive, struggle

2 TEST, appraise, check out, evaluate, examine, investigate, put to the test, sample, taste ▶noun **3** ATTEMPT, crack (*informal*), effort, go (*informal*), shot (*informal*), stab (*informal*), whack (*informal*)

trying *adjective* ANNOYING, bothersome, difficult, exasperating, hard, stressful, taxing, tiresome, tough, wearisome

tubby *adjective* FAT, chubby, corpulent, obese, overweight, plump, portly, stout

tuck *verb* **1** PUSH, fold, gather, insert ▶noun **2** FOLD, gather, pinch, pleat

tuft *noun* CLUMP, bunch, cluster, collection, knot, tussock

tug *verb* **1** PULL, jerk, wrench, yank ▶noun **2** PULL, jerk, yank

tuition *noun* TRAINING, education, instruction, lessons, schooling, teaching, tutelage, tutoring

tumble *verb* **1** FALL, drop, flop, plummet, stumble, topple ▶noun **2** FALL, drop, plunge, spill, stumble, trip

tumbledown *adjective* DILAPIDATED, crumbling, decrepit, ramshackle, rickety, ruined

tumor *noun* GROWTH, cancer, carcinoma (*Pathology*), lump, sarcoma (*Medical*), swelling

tumult *noun* COMMOTION, clamor, din, hubbub, pandemonium, riot, row, turmoil, upheaval, uproar

tumultuous *adjective* WILD, boisterous, excited, noisy, riotous, rowdy, turbulent, unruly, uproarious, wired (*slang*)

tune *noun* **1** MELODY, air, song,

strain, theme **2** PITCH, concord, consonance, euphony, harmony ▶verb **3** ADJUST, adapt, attune, harmonize, pitch, regulate

tuneful *adjective* MELODIOUS, catchy, euphonious, harmonious, mellifluous, melodic, musical, pleasant

tuneless *adjective* DISCORDANT, atonal, cacophonous, dissonant, harsh, unmusical

tunnel *noun* **1** PASSAGE, burrow, channel, hole, passageway, shaft, subway, underpass ▶verb **2** DIG, burrow, excavate, mine, scoop out

turbulence *noun* CONFUSION, agitation, commotion, disorder, instability, tumult, turmoil, unrest, upheaval

turbulent *adjective* AGITATED, blustery, choppy, foaming, furious, raging, rough, tempestuous, tumultuous

turf *noun* **1** GRASS, sod, sward **2 the turf** HORSE-RACING, racing, the flat

turmoil *noun* CONFUSION, agitation, chaos, commotion, disarray, disorder, tumult, upheaval, uproar

turn *verb* **1** CHANGE COURSE, move, shift, swerve, switch, veer, wheel **2** ROTATE, circle, go round, gyrate, pivot, revolve, roll, spin, twist, whirl **3** CHANGE, alter, convert, mold, mutate, remodel, shape, transform **4** SHAPE, fashion, frame, make, mold **5** GO BAD, curdle, sour, spoil, taint ▶noun **6** ROTATION, circle, cycle, gyration, revolution, spin, twist, whirl **7** SHIFT, departure, deviation

8 OPPORTUNITY, chance, crack (informal), go, stint, time, try **9** DIRECTION, drift, heading, tendency, trend **10** As in **good turn** ACT, action, deed, favor, gesture, service

turncoat noun TRAITOR, apostate, backslider, defector, deserter, renegade

turn down verb **1** LOWER, lessen, muffle, mute, quieten, soften **2** REFUSE, decline, rebuff, reject, repudiate, spurn

turn in verb **1** GO TO BED, go to sleep, hit the sack (slang) **2** HAND IN, deliver, give up, hand over, return, submit, surrender, tender

turning noun JUNCTION, bend, crossroads, curve, side road, turn, turn-off

turning point noun CROSSROADS, change, crisis, crux, moment of truth

turn off verb STOP, cut out, put out, shut down, switch off, turn out, unplug

turn on verb **1** START, activate, ignite, kick-start, start up, switch on **2** ATTACK, assail, assault, fall on, round on **3** Informal EXCITE, arouse, attract, please, stimulate, thrill, titillate

turnout noun ATTENDANCE, assembly, audience, congregation, crowd, gate, number, throng

turnover noun **1** OUTPUT, business, productivity **2** MOVEMENT, change, coming and going

turn up verb **1** ARRIVE, appear, attend, come, put in an appearance, show one's face,

show up (informal) **2** FIND, dig up, disclose, discover, expose, reveal, unearth **3** COME TO LIGHT, crop up (informal), pop up **4** INCREASE, amplify, boost, enhance, intensify, raise

tussle noun **1** FIGHT, battle, brawl, conflict, contest, scrap (informal), scuffle, struggle ▶ verb **2** FIGHT, battle, grapple, scrap (informal), scuffle, struggle, vie, wrestle

tutor noun **1** TEACHER, coach, educator, guardian, guide, guru, instructor, lecturer, mentor ▶ verb **2** TEACH, coach, drill, educate, guide, instruct, school, train

twaddle noun NONSENSE, claptrap (informal), drivel, garbage (informal), gobbledegook (informal), poppycock (informal), rubbish

tweak verb, noun TWIST, jerk, pinch, pull, squeeze

twig noun BRANCH, shoot, spray, sprig, stick

twilight noun DUSK, dimness, evening, gloaming (Scot. or poetic), gloom, half-light, sundown, sunset

twin noun **1** DOUBLE, clone, counterpart, duplicate, fellow, likeness, lookalike, match, mate ▶ verb **2** PAIR, couple, join, link, match, yoke

twine noun **1** STRING, cord, yarn ▶ verb **2** COIL, bend, curl, encircle, loop, spiral, twist, wind

twinge noun PAIN, pang, prick, spasm, stab, stitch

twinkle verb **1** SPARKLE, blink, flash, flicker, gleam, glint, glisten, glitter, shimmer, shine ▶ noun **2** FLICKER, flash, gleam, glimmer, shimmer, spark, sparkle

twirl verb **1** TURN, pirouette, pivot, revolve, rotate, spin, twist, wheel, whirl, wind ▶ noun **2** TURN, pirouette, revolution, rotation, spin, twist, wheel, whirl

twist verb **1** WIND, coil, curl, screw, spin, swivel, wrap, wring **2** DISTORT, contort, screw up ▶ noun **3** WIND, coil, curl, spin, swivel **4** DEVELOPMENT, change, revelation, slant, surprise, turn, variation **5** CURVE, arc, bend, meander, turn, undulation, zigzag **6** DISTORTION, defect, deformation, flaw, imperfection, kink, warp

twitch verb **1** JERK, flutter, jump, squirm ▶ noun **2** SPASM, flutter, jerk, jump, tic

two-faced adjective HYPOCRITICAL, deceitful, dissembling, duplicitous, false, insincere, treacherous, untrustworthy

tycoon noun MAGNATE, baron, capitalist, fat cat (slang), financier, industrialist, mogul, plutocrat

type noun CATEGORY, class, genre, group, kind, order, sort, species, style, variety

typhoon noun STORM, cyclone, squall, tempest, tornado

typical adjective CHARACTERISTIC, archetypal, average, classic, model, normal, orthodox, representative, standard, stock, usual

typify verb SYMBOLIZE, characterize, embody, epitomize, exemplify, illustrate, personify, represent, sum up

tyrannical adjective OPPRESSIVE, authoritarian, autocratic, cruel, despotic, dictatorial, domineering, high-handed, imperious, overbearing, tyrannous

tyranny noun OPPRESSION, absolutism, authoritarianism, autocracy, cruelty, despotism, dictatorship, high-handedness, imperiousness

tyrant noun DICTATOR, absolutist, authoritarian, autocrat, bully, despot, martinet, oppressor, slave-driver

U u

ubiquitous adjective EVERYWHERE, ever-present, omnipresent, pervasive, universal

ugly adjective **1** UNATTRACTIVE, dumpy (informal), frowzy, hideous, homely (U.S.), ill-favored, plain, unlovely, unprepossessing, unsightly **2** UNPLEASANT, disagreeable, distasteful, horrid, objectionable, shocking, terrible **3** OMINOUS, baleful, dangerous, menacing, sinister

ulcer noun SORE, abscess, boil, gumboil, peptic ulcer, pustule

ulterior adjective HIDDEN, concealed, covert, secret, undisclosed

ultimate adjective **1** FINAL, end, last **2** SUPREME, extreme, greatest, highest, paramount, superlative, utmost

ultimately adverb FINALLY, after all, at last, eventually, in due time, in the end, sooner or later

umpire noun **1** REFEREE, arbiter, arbitrator, judge ▶ verb **2** REFEREE, adjudicate, arbitrate, judge

unabashed adjective UNEMBARRASSED, blatant, bold, brazen

unable adjective INCAPABLE, impotent, ineffectual, powerless, unfit, unqualified

unabridged adjective UNCUT, complete, full-length, unexpurgated, whole

unacceptable adjective UNSATISFACTORY, displeasing, objectionable

unaccompanied adjective **1** ALONE, by oneself, lone, on one's own, solo, unescorted **2** Music A CAPPELLA

unaccountable adjective **1** INEXPLICABLE, baffling, mysterious, odd, puzzling, unexplainable, unfathomable **2** NOT ANSWERABLE, exempt, not responsible

unaccustomed adjective **1** UNFAMILIAR, new, strange, unwonted **2** unaccustomed to NOT USED TO, inexperienced at, unfamiliar with, unused to

unaffected[1] adjective NATURAL, artless, genuine, plain, simple, sincere, unpretentious

unaffected[2] adjective IMPERVIOUS, proof, unmoved, unresponsive, untouched

unafraid adjective FEARLESS, daring, dauntless, intrepid

unalterable adjective UNCHANGEABLE, fixed, immutable, permanent

unanimity noun AGREEMENT, accord, assent, concord,

concurrence, consensus, harmony, like-mindedness, unison

unanimous adjective AGREED, common, concerted, harmonious, in agreement, like-minded, united

unanimously adverb WITHOUT EXCEPTION, as one, in concert, of one mind, with one accord

unanswerable adjective CONCLUSIVE, absolute, incontestable, incontrovertible, indisputable

unanswered adjective UNRESOLVED, disputed, open, undecided

unappetizing adjective UNPLEASANT, distasteful, repulsive, scuzzy (slang), unappealing, unattractive, unpalatable

unapproachable adjective **1** UNFRIENDLY, aloof, chilly, cool, distant, reserved, standoffish **2** INACCESSIBLE, out of reach, remote

unarmed adjective DEFENSELESS, exposed, helpless, open, unprotected, weak

unassailable adjective IMPREGNABLE, invincible, invulnerable, secure

unassuming adjective MODEST, humble, quiet, reserved, retiring, self-effacing, unassertive, unobtrusive, unpretentious

unattached adjective **1** FREE, independent **2** SINGLE, available, not spoken for, unengaged, unmarried

unattended adjective **1** ABANDONED, unguarded, unwatched **2** ALONE, on one's own, unaccompanied

unauthorized adjective ILLEGAL, unlawful, unofficial, unsanctioned

unavoidable adjective INEVITABLE, certain, fated, inescapable

unaware adjective IGNORANT, oblivious, unconscious, uninformed, unknowing

unawares adverb **1** BY SURPRISE, off guard, suddenly, unexpectedly **2** UNKNOWINGLY, accidentally, by accident, inadvertently, unwittingly

unbalanced adjective **1** BIASED, one-sided, partial, partisan, prejudiced, unfair **2** SHAKY, lopsided, uneven, unstable, wobbly **3** DERANGED, crazy, demented, disturbed, eccentric, insane, irrational, mad, non compos mentis, not all there, unhinged, unstable

unbearable adjective INTOLERABLE, insufferable, too much (informal), unacceptable

unbeatable adjective INVINCIBLE, indomitable

unbeaten adjective UNDEFEATED, triumphant, victorious

unbecoming adjective **1** UNSIGHTLY, unattractive, unbefitting, unflattering, unsuitable **2** UNSEEMLY, discreditable, improper, offensive

unbelievable adjective INCREDIBLE, astonishing, far-fetched, implausible, impossible, improbable, inconceivable, preposterous, unconvincing, unimaginable

unbending adjective INFLEXIBLE, firm, intractable, resolute, rigid, severe, strict, stubborn, tough, uncompromising

unbiased adjective FAIR, disinterested, equitable, impartial, just, neutral, objective, unprejudiced

unblemished adjective SPOTLESS, flawless, immaculate, impeccable, perfect, pure, untarnished

unborn adjective EXPECTED, awaited, embryonic, fetal

unbreakable adjective INDESTRUCTIBLE, durable, lasting, rugged, strong

unbridled adjective UNRESTRAINED, excessive, intemperate, licentious, riotous, unchecked, unruly, wanton

unbroken adjective **1** INTACT, complete, entire, whole **2** CONTINUOUS, constant, incessant, twenty-four-seven (slang), uninterrupted

unburden verb CONFESS, confide, disclose, get (something) off one's chest (informal), reveal

uncalled-for adjective UNJUSTIFIED, gratuitous, needless, undeserved, unnecessary, unwarranted

uncanny adjective **1** WEIRD, mysterious, strange, supernatural, unearthly, unnatural **2** EXTRAORDINARY, astounding, exceptional, incredible, miraculous, remarkable, unusual

unceasing adjective CONTINUAL, constant, continuous, endless, incessant, nonstop, perpetual, twenty-four-seven (slang)

uncertain adjective **1** UNPREDICTABLE, doubtful, indefinite, questionable, risky, speculative **2** UNSURE, dubious, hazy, irresolute, unclear, unconfirmed, undecided, vague

uncertainty noun DOUBT, ambiguity, confusion, dubiety, hesitancy, indecision, unpredictability

unchangeable adjective UNALTERABLE, constant, fixed, immutable, invariable, irreversible, permanent, stable

unchanging adjective CONSTANT, continuing, enduring, eternal, immutable, lasting, permanent, perpetual, twenty-four-seven (slang), unvarying

uncharitable adjective UNKIND, cruel, hardhearted, unfeeling, ungenerous

uncharted adjective UNEXPLORED, strange, undiscovered, unfamiliar, unknown

uncivil adjective IMPOLITE, bad-mannered, discourteous, ill-mannered, rude, unmannerly

uncivilized adjective 1 PRIMITIVE, barbarian, savage, wild 2 UNCOUTH, boorish, coarse, philistine, uncultivated, uneducated

unclean adjective DIRTY, corrupt, defiled, evil, filthy, foul, impure, polluted, scuzzy (slang), soiled, stained

unclear adjective 1 INDISTINCT, blurred, dim, faint, fuzzy, hazy, obscure, shadowy, undefined, vague 2 DOUBTFUL, ambiguous, indefinite, indeterminate, vague

uncomfortable adjective 1 AWKWARD, cramped, painful, rough 2 UNEASY, awkward, discomfited, disturbed, embarrassed, troubled

uncommitted adjective UNINVOLVED, floating, free,

neutral, nonaligned, not involved, unattached

uncommon adjective 1 RARE, infrequent, novel, odd, peculiar, queer, scarce, strange, unusual 2 EXTRAORDINARY, distinctive, exceptional, notable, outstanding, remarkable, special

uncommonly adverb 1 RARELY, hardly ever, infrequently, occasionally, seldom 2 EXCEPTIONALLY, particularly, very

uncommunicative adjective RETICENT, close, reserved, secretive, silent, taciturn, tight-lipped, unforthcoming

uncompromising adjective INFLEXIBLE, firm, inexorable, intransigent, rigid, strict, tough, unbending

unconcern noun INDIFFERENCE, aloofness, apathy, detachment, lack of interest, nonchalance

unconcerned adjective INDIFFERENT, aloof, apathetic, cool, detached, dispassionate, distant, uninterested, unmoved

unconditional adjective ABSOLUTE, complete, entire, full, outright, positive, total, unlimited, unqualified, unreserved

unconnected adjective 1 SEPARATE, detached, divided 2 MEANINGLESS, disjointed, illogical, incoherent, irrelevant

unconscious adjective 1 SENSELESS, insensible, knocked out, out, out cold, stunned 2 UNAWARE, ignorant, oblivious, unknowing 3 UNINTENTIONAL, accidental, inadvertent, unwitting

uncontrollable adjective WILD,

frantic, furious, mad, strong, unruly, violent

uncontrolled *adjective*
UNRESTRAINED, rampant, riotous, unbridled, unchecked, undisciplined

unconventional *adjective*
UNUSUAL, eccentric, individual, irregular, nonconformist, odd, offbeat, original, outré, unorthodox

unconvincing *adjective*
IMPLAUSIBLE, dubious, feeble, flimsy, improbable, lame, questionable, suspect, thin, unlikely, weak

uncooperative *adjective*
UNHELPFUL, awkward, difficult, disobliging, obstructive

uncoordinated *adjective* CLUMSY, awkward, bungling, graceless, lumbering, maladroit, ungainly, ungraceful

uncouth *adjective* COARSE, boorish, crude, graceless, ill-mannered, loutish, oafish, rough, rude, vulgar

uncover *verb* 1 REVEAL, disclose, divulge, expose, make known 2 OPEN, bare, show, strip, unwrap

uncritical *adjective*
UNDISCRIMINATING, indiscriminate, undiscerning

undecided *adjective* 1 UNSURE, dithering, hesitant, in two minds, irresolute, torn, uncertain 2 UNSETTLED, debatable, iffy (*informal*), indefinite, moot, open, unconcluded, undetermined

undefined *adjective*
1 UNSPECIFIED, imprecise, inexact, unclear 2 INDISTINCT, formless, indefinite, vague

undeniable *adjective* CERTAIN, clear, incontrovertible, indisputable, obvious, sure, unquestionable

under *preposition* 1 BELOW, beneath, underneath 2 SUBJECT TO, governed by, secondary to, subordinate to ▶ *adverb* 3 BELOW, beneath, down, lower

underclothes *plural noun*
UNDERWEAR, lingerie, undergarments, undies (*informal*)

undercover *adjective* SECRET, concealed, covert, hidden, private

undercurrent *noun* 1 UNDERTOW, riptide 2 UNDERTONE, atmosphere, feeling, hint, overtone, sense, suggestion, tendency, tinge, vibes (*slang*)

underdog *noun* OUTSIDER, little fellow (*informal*)

underestimate *verb* UNDERRATE, belittle, minimize, miscalculate, undervalue

undergo *verb* EXPERIENCE, bear, endure, go through, stand, suffer, sustain

underground *adjective*
1 SUBTERRANEAN, buried, covered 2 SECRET, clandestine, covert, hidden ▶ *noun* 3 **the underground** THE RESISTANCE, partisans

undergrowth *noun* SCRUB, bracken, briars, brush, underbrush

underhand, underhanded *adjective* SLY, crafty, deceitful, devious, dishonest, down and dirty (*informal*), furtive, secret, sneaky, stealthy

underline *verb* 1 UNDERSCORE, mark 2 EMPHASIZE, accentuate, highlight, stress

underlying adjective
FUNDAMENTAL, basic, elementary, intrinsic, primary, prime

undermine verb WEAKEN, disable, sabotage, sap, subvert

underprivileged adjective
DISADVANTAGED, deprived, destitute, impoverished, needy, poor

underrate verb UNDERESTIMATE, belittle, discount, undervalue

undersized adjective STUNTED, dwarfish, miniature, pygmy or pigmy, small

understand verb 1 COMPREHEND, conceive, fathom, follow, get, grasp, perceive, realize, see, take in 2 BELIEVE, assume, gather, presume, suppose, think

understandable adjective
REASONABLE, justifiable, legitimate, natural, to be expected

understanding noun
1 PERCEPTION, appreciation, awareness, comprehension, discernment, grasp, insight, judgment, knowledge, sense 2 INTERPRETATION, belief, idea, judgment, notion, opinion, perception, view 3 AGREEMENT, accord, pact ▶ adjective 4 SYMPATHETIC, compassionate, considerate, kind, patient, sensitive, tolerant

understood adjective 1 IMPLIED, implicit, inferred, tacit, unspoken, unstated 2 ASSUMED, accepted, taken for granted

understudy noun STAND-IN, replacement, reserve, substitute

undertake verb AGREE, bargain, contract, engage, guarantee, pledge, promise

undertaking noun 1 TASK, affair, attempt, business, effort, endeavor, enterprise, operation, project, venture 2 PROMISE, assurance, commitment, pledge, vow, word

undertone noun 1 MURMUR, whisper 2 UNDERCURRENT, hint, suggestion, tinge, touch, trace

undervalue verb UNDERRATE, depreciate, hold cheap, minimize, misjudge, underestimate

underwater adjective SUBMERGED, submarine, sunken

under way adjective BEGUN, going on, in progress, started

underwear noun UNDERCLOTHES, lingerie, undergarments, underthings, undies (informal)

underweight adjective SKINNY, emaciated, half-starved, puny, skin and bone (informal), undernourished, undersized

underworld noun 1 CRIMINALS, gangland (informal), gangsters, organized crime 2 NETHER WORLD, Hades, nether regions

underwrite verb 1 FINANCE, back, fund, guarantee, insure, sponsor, subsidize 2 SIGN, endorse, initial

undesirable adjective
OBJECTIONABLE, disagreeable, distasteful, unacceptable, unattractive, unsuitable, unwanted, unwelcome

undeveloped adjective
POTENTIAL, immature, latent

undignified adjective UNSEEMLY, improper, indecorous, inelegant, unbecoming, unsuitable

undisciplined adjective

UNCONTROLLED, obstreperous, unrestrained, unruly, wayward, wild, willful

undisguised adjective OBVIOUS, blatant, evident, explicit, open, overt, patent, unconcealed

undisputed adjective ACKNOWLEDGED, accepted, certain, indisputable, recognized, unchallenged, undeniable, undoubted

undistinguished adjective ORDINARY, everyday, mediocre, unexceptional, unimpressive, unremarkable

undisturbed adjective 1 QUIET, tranquil 2 CALM, collected, composed, placid, sedate, serene, tranquil, unfazed (informal), unperturbed, untroubled

undivided adjective COMPLETE, entire, exclusive, full, solid, thorough, undistracted, united, whole

undo verb 1 OPEN, disentangle, loose, unbutton, unfasten, untie 2 REVERSE, annul, cancel, invalidate, neutralize, offset 3 RUIN, defeat, destroy, overturn, quash, shatter, subvert, undermine, upset, wreck

undoing noun DOWNFALL, collapse, defeat, disgrace, overthrow, reversal, ruin, shame

undone adjective UNFINISHED, left, neglected, omitted, unfulfilled, unperformed

undoubted adjective CERTAIN, acknowledged, definite, indisputable, indubitable, sure, undisputed, unquestioned

undoubtedly adverb CERTAINLY, assuredly, definitely, doubtless,

surely, without doubt

undress verb 1 STRIP, disrobe, shed, take off one's clothes ▶ noun 2 NAKEDNESS, nudity

undue adjective EXCESSIVE, extreme, improper, needless, uncalled-for, unnecessary, unwarranted

unduly adverb EXCESSIVELY, overly, unnecessarily, unreasonably

undying adjective ETERNAL, constant, deathless, everlasting, infinite, permanent, perpetual, twenty-four-seven (slang), unending

unearth verb 1 DISCOVER, expose, find, reveal, uncover 2 DIG UP, dredge up, excavate, exhume

unearthly adjective EERIE, ghostly, phantom, spectral, spooky (informal), strange, supernatural, uncanny, weird

uneasiness noun ANXIETY, disquiet, doubt, misgiving, qualms, trepidation, worry

uneasy adjective 1 ANXIOUS, disturbed, edgy, nervous, on edge, perturbed, troubled, twitchy (informal), uncomfortable, wired (slang), worried 2 AWKWARD, insecure, precarious, shaky, strained, tense, uncomfortable

uneconomic adjective UNPROFITABLE, loss-making, nonpaying

uneducated adjective 1 IGNORANT, illiterate, unlettered, unschooled, untaught 2 LOWBROW, uncultivated, uncultured

unemotional adjective IMPASSIVE, apathetic, cold, cool, phlegmatic, reserved, undemonstrative, unexcitable

unemployed *adjective* OUT OF WORK, idle, jobless, laid off, redundant

unending *adjective* PERPETUAL, continual, endless, eternal, everlasting, interminable, unceasing

unendurable *adjective* UNBEARABLE, insufferable, insupportable, intolerable

unenthusiastic *adjective* INDIFFERENT, apathetic, half-hearted, nonchalant

unenviable *adjective* UNPLEASANT, disagreeable, uncomfortable, undesirable

unequal *adjective* **1** DIFFERENT, differing, disparate, dissimilar, unlike, unmatched, varying **2** DISPROPORTIONATE, asymmetrical, ill-matched, irregular, unbalanced, uneven

unequaled *adjective* INCOMPARABLE, matchless, paramount, peerless, supreme, unparalleled, unrivaled

unequivocal *adjective* CLEAR, absolute, certain, definite, explicit, incontrovertible, indubitable, manifest, plain, unambiguous

unerring *adjective* ACCURATE, exact, infallible, perfect, sure, unfailing

unethical *adjective* DISHONEST, disreputable, illegal, immoral, improper, shady (*informal*), unprincipled, unscrupulous, wrong

uneven *adjective* **1** ROUGH, bumpy **2** VARIABLE, broken, fitful, irregular, jerky, patchy, spasmodic **3** UNBALANCED, lopsided, odd **4** UNEQUAL,

ill-matched, unfair

uneventful *adjective* HUMDRUM, boring, dull, ho-hum (*informal*), monotonous, routine, tedious, unexciting

unexceptional *adjective* ORDINARY, commonplace, conventional, mediocre, normal, pedestrian, undistinguished, unremarkable

unexpected *adjective* UNFORESEEN, abrupt, chance, fortuitous, sudden, surprising, unanticipated, unlooked-for, unpredictable

unfailing *adjective* **1** CONTINUOUS, boundless, endless, persistent, unflagging **2** RELIABLE, certain, dependable, faithful, loyal, staunch, sure, true

unfair *adjective* **1** BIASED, bigoted, one-sided, partial, partisan, prejudiced, unjust **2** UNSCRUPULOUS, dishonest, unethical, unsporting, wrongful

unfaithful *adjective* FAITHLESS, adulterous, two-timing (*informal*), untrue **2** DISLOYAL, deceitful, faithless, false, traitorous, treacherous, untrustworthy

unfamiliar *adjective* STRANGE, alien, different, new, novel, unknown, unusual

unfashionable *adjective* PASSÉ, antiquated, dated, dumpy (*informal*), frowzy, homely (*U.S.*), obsolete, old-fashioned, old hat

unfasten *verb* UNDO, detach, let go, loosen, open, separate, unlace, untie

unfathomable *adjective* **1** BAFFLING, deep, impenetrable, incomprehensible, indecipherable, inexplicable, profound **2** IMMEASURABLE, bottomless, unmeasured

unfavorable *adjective* **1** ADVERSE, contrary, inauspicious, unfortunate, unlucky, unpropitious **2** HOSTILE, inimical, negative, unfriendly

unfeeling *adjective* **1** HARDHEARTED, apathetic, callous, cold, cruel, heartless, insensitive, pitiless, uncaring **2** NUMB, insensate, insensible

unfinished *adjective* **1** INCOMPLETE, half-done, uncompleted, undone **2** ROUGH, bare, crude, natural, raw, unrefined

unfit *adjective* **1** INCAPABLE, inadequate, incompetent, lousy (*slang*), no good, unqualified, useless **2** UNSUITABLE, inadequate, ineffective, unsuited, useless **3** OUT OF SHAPE, feeble, flabby, in poor condition, unhealthy

unflappable *adjective* IMPERTURBABLE, calm, collected, composed, cool, impassive, level-headed, self-possessed

unflattering *adjective* **1** BLUNT, candid, critical, honest **2** UNATTRACTIVE, dumpy (*informal*), frowzy, homely (*U.S.*), plain, unbecoming

unflinching *adjective* DETERMINED, firm, immovable, resolute, staunch, steadfast, steady, unfaltering

unfold *verb* **1** OPEN, expand, spread out, undo, unfurl, unravel, unroll, unwrap **2** REVEAL, disclose, divulge, make known, present, show, uncover

unforeseen *adjective* UNEXPECTED, accidental, sudden, surprising, unanticipated, unpredicted

unforgettable *adjective* MEMORABLE, exceptional, impressive, notable

unforgivable *adjective* INEXCUSABLE, deplorable, disgraceful, shameful, unpardonable

unfortunate *adjective* **1** DISASTROUS, adverse, calamitous, ill-fated **2** UNLUCKY, cursed, doomed, hapless, unhappy, unsuccessful, wretched **3** REGRETTABLE, deplorable, lamentable, unsuitable

unfounded *adjective* GROUNDLESS, baseless, false, idle, spurious, unjustified

unfriendly *adjective* **1** HOSTILE, aloof, chilly, cold, distant, uncongenial, unsociable **2** UNFAVORABLE, alien, hostile, inhospitable

ungainly *adjective* AWKWARD, clumsy, inelegant, lumbering, ungraceful

ungodly *adjective* **1** UNREASONABLE, dreadful, intolerable, outrageous, unearthly **2** WICKED, corrupt, depraved, godless, immoral, impious, irreligious, profane, sinful

ungracious *adjective* BAD-MANNERED, churlish, discourteous, impolite, rude, uncivil, unmannerly

ungrateful *adjective* UNAPPRECIATIVE, unmindful, unthankful

unguarded *adjective* **1** UNPROTECTED, defenseless,

undefended, vulnerable
2 CARELESS, heedless,
ill-considered, imprudent,
incautious, rash, thoughtless,
unthinking, unwary

unhappiness *noun* SADNESS,
blues, dejection, depression,
despondency, gloom,
heartache, low spirits,
melancholy, misery, sorrow,
wretchedness

unhappy *adjective* **1** SAD, blue,
dejected, depressed,
despondent, downcast,
melancholy, miserable,
mournful, sorrowful **2** UNLUCKY,
cursed, hapless, ill-fated,
unfortunate, wretched

unharmed *adjective* UNHURT,
intact, safe, sound,
undamaged, unscathed, whole

unhealthy *adjective* **1** HARMFUL,
detrimental, insalubrious,
insanitary, unwholesome
2 SICK, ailing, delicate, feeble,
frail, infirm, invalid, sickly,
unwell

unheard-of *adjective*
1 UNPRECEDENTED, inconceivable,
new, novel, singular, unique
2 SHOCKING, disgraceful,
outrageous, preposterous
3 OBSCURE, unfamiliar, unknown

unhesitating *adjective* **1** INSTANT,
immediate, prompt, ready
2 WHOLEHEARTED, resolute,
unfaltering, unquestioning,
unreserved

unholy *adjective* EVIL, corrupt,
profane, sinful, ungodly, wicked

unhurried *adjective* LEISURELY,
easy, sedate, slow

unidentified *adjective* UNNAMED,
anonymous, nameless,
unfamiliar, unrecognized

unification *noun* UNION, alliance,
amalgamation, coalescence,
coalition, confederation,
federation, uniting

uniform *noun* **1** OUTFIT,
costume, dress, garb, habit,
livery, regalia, suit ▶*adjective*
2 UNVARYING, consistent,
constant, even, regular,
smooth, unchanging **3** ALIKE,
equal, like, on a level playing
field (*informal*), same, similar

uniformity *noun* **1** REGULARITY,
constancy, evenness,
invariability, sameness,
similarity **2** MONOTONY, dullness,
flatness, sameness, tedium

unify *verb* UNITE, amalgamate,
combine, confederate,
consolidate, join, merge

unimaginable *adjective*
INCONCEIVABLE, fantastic,
impossible, incredible,
unbelievable

unimaginative *adjective*
UNORIGINAL, banal, derivative,
dull, hackneyed, ordinary,
pedestrian, predictable,
prosaic, uncreative, uninspired

unimportant *adjective*
INSIGNIFICANT, inconsequential,
irrelevant, minor, paltry, petty,
trifling, trivial, worthless

uninhabited *adjective* DESERTED,
barren, desolate, empty,
unpopulated, vacant

uninhibited *adjective*
1 UNSELFCONSCIOUS, free,
liberated, natural, open,
relaxed, spontaneous,
unrepressed, unreserved
2 UNRESTRAINED, free, unbridled,
unchecked, unconstrained,
uncontrolled, unrestricted

uninspired *adjective*

UNIMAGINATIVE, banal, dull, humdrum, ordinary, prosaic, unexciting, unoriginal

unintelligent *adjective* STUPID, braindead (*informal*), brainless, dense, dull, foolish, obtuse, slow, thick

unintelligible *adjective* INCOMPREHENSIBLE, inarticulate, incoherent, indistinct, jumbled, meaningless, muddled

unintentional *adjective* ACCIDENTAL, casual, inadvertent, involuntary, unconscious, unintended

uninterested *adjective* INDIFFERENT, apathetic, blasé, bored, listless, unconcerned

uninteresting *adjective* BORING, drab, dreary, dry, dull, flat, humdrum, monotonous, tedious, unexciting

uninterrupted *adjective* CONTINUOUS, constant, nonstop, steady, sustained, unbroken

union *noun* **1** JOINING, amalgamation, blend, combination, conjunction, fusion, mixture, uniting **2** ALLIANCE, association, coalition, confederacy, federation, league **3** AGREEMENT, accord, concord, harmony, unanimity, unison, unity

unique *adjective* **1** SINGLE, lone, only, solitary **2** UNPARALLELED, incomparable, inimitable, matchless, unequaled, unmatched, unrivaled

unison *noun* AGREEMENT, accord, accordance, concert, concord, harmony, unity

unit *noun* **1** ITEM, entity, whole **2** PART, component, constituent, element, member,

section, segment **3** SECTION, detachment, group **4** MEASURE, measurement, quantity

unite *verb* **1** JOIN, amalgamate, blend, combine, couple, fuse, link, merge, unify **2** COOPERATE, ally, band, join forces, pool

united *adjective* **1** COMBINED, affiliated, allied, banded together, collective, concerted, pooled, unified **2** IN AGREEMENT, agreed, of one mind, of the same opinion, unanimous

unity *noun* **1** WHOLENESS, entity, integrity, oneness, singleness, union **2** AGREEMENT, accord, assent, concord, consensus, harmony, solidarity, unison

universal *adjective* WIDESPREAD, common, general, total, unlimited, whole, worldwide

universally *adverb* EVERYWHERE, always, invariably, without exception

universe *noun* COSMOS, creation, macrocosm, nature

unjust *adjective* UNFAIR, biased, one-sided, partial, partisan, prejudiced, wrong, wrongful

unjustifiable *adjective* INEXCUSABLE, indefensible, outrageous, unacceptable, unforgivable, unpardonable, wrong

unkempt *adjective* **1** UNCOMBED, shaggy, tousled **2** UNTIDY, disheveled, disordered, messy, slovenly, ungroomed

unkind *adjective* CRUEL, harsh, malicious, mean, nasty, spiteful, uncharitable, unfeeling, unfriendly, unsympathetic

unknown *adjective* **1** HIDDEN, concealed, dark, mysterious, secret, unrevealed **2** STRANGE, alien, new **3** UNIDENTIFIED, anonymous, nameless, uncharted, undiscovered, unexplored, unnamed **4** OBSCURE, humble, unfamiliar

unlawful *adjective* ILLEGAL, banned, criminal, forbidden, illicit, outlawed, prohibited

unleash *verb* RELEASE, free, let go, let loose

unlike *adjective* DIFFERENT, dissimilar, distinct, diverse, not alike, opposite, unequal

unlikely *adjective* **1** IMPROBABLE, doubtful, faint, remote, slight **2** UNBELIEVABLE, implausible, incredible, questionable

unlimited *adjective* **1** INFINITE, boundless, countless, endless, extensive, great, immense, limitless, unbounded, vast **2** COMPLETE, absolute, full, total, unqualified, unrestricted

unload *verb* EMPTY, discharge, dump, lighten, relieve, unpack

unlock *verb* OPEN, release, undo, unfasten, unlatch

unlooked-for *adjective* UNEXPECTED, chance, fortuitous, surprising, unanticipated, unforeseen, unpredicted

unloved *adjective* NEGLECTED, forsaken, loveless, rejected, spurned, unpopular, unwanted

unlucky *adjective* **1** UNFORTUNATE, cursed, hapless, luckless, miserable, unhappy, wretched **2** ILL-FATED, doomed, inauspicious, ominous, unfavorable

unmarried *adjective* SINGLE, bachelor, maiden, unattached, unwed

unmask *verb* REVEAL, disclose,

discover, expose, lay bare, uncover

unmentionable *adjective* TABOO, forbidden, indecent, obscene, scandalous, shameful, shocking, unspeakable

unmerciful *adjective* MERCILESS, brutal, cruel, hard, implacable, pitiless, remorseless, ruthless

unmistakable *adjective* CLEAR, certain, distinct, evident, manifest, obvious, plain, sure, unambiguous

unmitigated *adjective* **1** UNRELIEVED, intense, persistent, unalleviated, unbroken, undiminished **2** COMPLETE, absolute, arrant, downright, outright, sheer, thorough, utter

unmoved *adjective* UNAFFECTED, cold, impassive, indifferent, unimpressed, unresponsive, untouched

unnatural *adjective* **1** STRANGE, extraordinary, freakish, outlandish, queer **2** ABNORMAL, anomalous, irregular, odd, perverse, perverted, unusual **3** FALSE, affected, artificial, feigned, forced, insincere, phoney *or* phony (*informal*), stiff, stilted

unnecessary *adjective* NEEDLESS, expendable, inessential, redundant, superfluous, unneeded, unrequired

unnerve *verb* INTIMIDATE, demoralize, discourage, dishearten, dismay, faze, fluster, frighten, psych out (*informal*), rattle (*informal*), shake, upset

unnoticed *adjective* UNOBSERVED, disregarded, ignored, neglected, overlooked, unheeded, unperceived, unrecognized, unseen

unobtrusive *adjective*
INCONSPICUOUS, low-key, modest, quiet, restrained, retiring, self-effacing, unassuming

unoccupied *adjective* EMPTY, uninhabited, vacant

unofficial *adjective* UNAUTHORIZED, informal, private, unconfirmed

unorthodox *adjective*
UNCONVENTIONAL, abnormal, irregular, off-the-wall (*slang*), unusual

unpaid *adjective* **1** VOLUNTARY, honorary, unsalaried **2** OWING, due, outstanding, overdue, payable, unsettled

unpalatable *adjective*
UNPLEASANT, disagreeable, distasteful, horrid, offensive, repugnant, unappetizing, unsavory

unparalleled *adjective*
UNEQUALED, incomparable, matchless, superlative, unique, unmatched, unprecedented, unsurpassed

unpardonable *adjective*
UNFORGIVABLE, deplorable, disgraceful, indefensible, inexcusable

unperturbed *adjective* CALM, as cool as a cucumber, composed, cool, placid, unfazed (*informal*), unruffled, untroubled, unworried

unpleasant *adjective* NASTY, bad, disagreeable, displeasing, distasteful, horrid, objectionable

unpopular *adjective* DISLIKED, rejected, shunned, unwanted, unwelcome

unprecedented *adjective*
EXTRAORDINARY, abnormal, new,

novel, original, remarkable, singular, unheard-of

unpredictable *adjective*
INCONSTANT, chance, changeable, doubtful, erratic, random, unforeseeable, unreliable, variable

unprejudiced *adjective* IMPARTIAL, balanced, fair, just, objective, open-minded, unbiased

unprepared *adjective* **1** TAKEN OFF GUARD, surprised, unaware, unready **2** IMPROVISED, ad-lib, off the cuff (*informal*), spontaneous

unpretentious *adjective* MODEST, dumpy (*informal*), homely, humble, plain, simple, straightforward, unaffected, unassuming, unostentatious

unprincipled *adjective* DISHONEST, amoral, crooked, devious, immoral, underhand, unethical, unscrupulous

unproductive *adjective*
1 USELESS, fruitless, futile, idle, ineffective, unprofitable, unrewarding, vain **2** BARREN, fruitless, sterile

unprofessional *adjective*
1 UNETHICAL, improper, lax, negligent, unprincipled **2** AMATEURISH, incompetent, inefficient, inexpert

unprotected *adjective*
VULNERABLE, defenseless, helpless, open, undefended

unqualified *adjective* **1** UNFIT, ill-equipped, incapable, incompetent, ineligible, unprepared **2** TOTAL, absolute, complete, downright, outright, thorough, utter

unquestionable *adjective*
CERTAIN, absolute, clear, conclusive, definite,

unravel verb 1 UNDO, disentangle, free, separate, untangle, unwind 2 SOLVE, explain, figure out (informal), resolve, work out

unreal adjective 1 IMAGINARY, dreamlike, fabulous, fanciful, illusory, make-believe, visionary 2 INSUBSTANTIAL, immaterial, intangible, nebulous 3 FAKE, artificial, false, insincere, mock, pretended, sham

unrealistic adjective IMPRACTICAL, impracticable, improbable, romantic, unworkable

unreasonable adjective
1 EXCESSIVE, extortionate, immoderate, undue, unfair, unjust, unwarranted 2 BIASED, blinkered, opinionated

unrelated adjective 1 DIFFERENT, unconnected, unlike
2 IRRELEVANT, extraneous, inapplicable, inappropriate, unconnected

unreliable adjective
1 UNDEPENDABLE, irresponsible, treacherous, untrustworthy
2 UNCERTAIN, deceptive, fallible, false, implausible, inaccurate, unsound

unrepentant adjective
IMPENITENT, abandoned, callous, hardened, incorrigible, shameless, unremorseful

unreserved adjective 1 TOTAL, absolute, complete, entire, full, unlimited, wholehearted
2 OPEN, demonstrative, extrovert, free, outgoing, uninhibited, unrestrained

unresolved adjective UNDECIDED, doubtful, moot, unanswered, undetermined, unsettled, unsolved, vague

unrest noun DISCONTENT, agitation, discord, dissension, protest, rebellion, sedition, strife

unrestrained adjective
UNCONTROLLED, abandoned, free, immoderate, intemperate, unbounded, unbridled, unchecked, uninhibited

unrestricted adjective
1 UNLIMITED, absolute, free, open, unbounded, unregulated 2 OPEN, public

unrivaled adjective UNPARALLELED, beyond compare, incomparable, matchless, supreme, unequaled, unmatched, unsurpassed

unruly adjective UNCONTROLLABLE, disobedient, mutinous, rebellious, wayward, wild, willful

unsafe adjective DANGEROUS, hazardous, insecure, perilous, risky, unreliable

unsatisfactory adjective
UNACCEPTABLE, deficient, disappointing, inadequate, insufficient, lousy (slang), not good enough, not up to scratch (informal), poor

unsavory adjective 1 UNPLEASANT, distasteful, nasty, obnoxious, offensive, repellent, repulsive, revolting, scuzzy (slang)
2 UNAPPETIZING, nauseating, sickening, unpalatable

unscathed adjective UNHARMED, safe, unhurt, uninjured, unmarked, whole

unscrupulous adjective
UNPRINCIPLED, corrupt, dishonest, dishonorable, immoral,

improper, unethical

unseat *verb* **1** THROW, unhorse, unsaddle **2** DEPOSE, dethrone, displace, oust, overthrow, remove

unseemly *adjective* IMPROPER, inappropriate, indecorous, unbecoming, undignified, unsuitable

unseen *adjective* UNOBSERVED, concealed, hidden, invisible, obscure, undetected, unnoticed

unselfish *adjective* GENEROUS, altruistic, kind, magnanimous, noble, selfless, self-sacrificing

unsettle *verb* DISTURB, agitate, bother, confuse, disconcert, faze, fluster, perturb, ruffle, trouble, upset

unsettled *adjective* **1** UNSTABLE, disorderly, insecure, shaky, unsteady **2** RESTLESS, agitated, anxious, confused, disturbed, flustered, restive, shaken, tense, wired (*slang*) **3** CHANGING, inconstant, uncertain, variable

unshakable *adjective* FIRM, absolute, fixed, immovable, staunch, steadfast, sure, unswerving, unwavering

unsightly *adjective* UGLY, disagreeable, dumpy (*informal*), hideous, homely (*U.S.*), horrid, repulsive, scuzzy (*slang*), unattractive

unskilled *adjective* UNPROFESSIONAL, amateurish, inexperienced, unqualified, untrained

unsociable *adjective* UNFRIENDLY, chilly, cold, distant, hostile, retiring, unforthcoming, withdrawn

unsolicited *adjective*

UNREQUESTED, gratuitous, unasked for, uncalled-for, uninvited, unsought

unsophisticated *adjective* **1** NATURAL, artless, childlike, guileless, ingenuous, unaffected **2** SIMPLE, dumpy (*informal*), frowzy, homely (*U.S.*), plain, uncomplicated, unrefined, unspecialized

unsound *adjective* **1** UNHEALTHY, ailing, defective, diseased, ill, unbalanced, unstable, unwell, weak **2** UNRELIABLE, defective, fallacious, false, flawed, illogical, shaky, specious, weak

unspeakable *adjective* **1** INDESCRIBABLE, inconceivable, unbelievable, unimaginable **2** DREADFUL, abominable, appalling, awful, heinous, horrible, monstrous, shocking

unspoiled, unspoilt *adjective* **1** PERFECT, intact, preserved, unchanged, undamaged, untouched **2** NATURAL, artless, innocent, unaffected

unspoken *adjective* TACIT, implicit, implied, understood, unexpressed, unstated

unstable *adjective* **1** INSECURE, precarious, shaky, tottering, unsettled, unsteady, wobbly **2** CHANGEABLE, fitful, fluctuating, inconstant, unpredictable, variable, volatile **3** UNPREDICTABLE, capricious, changeable, erratic, inconsistent, irrational, temperamental

unsteady *adjective* **1** UNSTABLE, infirm, insecure, precarious, shaky, unsafe, wobbly **2** CHANGEABLE, erratic, inconstant, temperamental, unsettled, volatile

unsuccessful adjective **1** USELESS, failed, fruitless, futile, unavailing, unproductive, vain **2** UNLUCKY, hapless, luckless, unfortunate

unsuitable adjective INAPPROPRIATE, improper, inapposite, inapt, ineligible, unacceptable, unbecoming, unfit, unfitting, unseemly

unsure adjective **1** UNCONFIDENT, insecure, unassured **2** DOUBTFUL, distrustful, dubious, hesitant, mistrustful, skeptical, suspicious, unconvinced

unsuspecting adjective TRUSTING, credulous, gullible, trustful, unwary

unswerving adjective CONSTANT, firm, resolute, single-minded, staunch, steadfast, steady, true, unwavering

unsympathetic adjective HARD, callous, cold, cruel, harsh, heartless, insensitive, unfeeling, unkind, unmoved

untangle verb DISENTANGLE, extricate, unravel, unsnarl

untenable adjective UNSUSTAINABLE, groundless, illogical, indefensible, insupportable, shaky, unsound, weak

unthinkable adjective **1** IMPOSSIBLE, absurd, out of the question, unreasonable **2** INCONCEIVABLE, implausible, incredible, unimaginable

untidy adjective MESSY, chaotic, cluttered, disarrayed, disordered, jumbled, littered, muddled, shambolic, unkempt

untie verb UNDO, free, loosen, release, unbind, unfasten,

unknot, unlace

untimely adjective **1** EARLY, premature **2** ILL-TIMED, awkward, inappropriate, inconvenient, inopportune, mistimed

untiring adjective TIRELESS, constant, determined, dogged, persevering, steady, unflagging, unremitting

untold adjective **1** INDESCRIBABLE, inexpressible, undreamed of, unimaginable, unthinkable, unutterable **2** COUNTLESS, incalculable, innumerable, myriad, numberless, uncountable

untouched adjective UNHARMED, intact, undamaged, unhurt, uninjured, unscathed

untoward adjective **1** ANNOYING, awkward, inconvenient, irritating, troublesome, unfortunate **2** UNLUCKY, adverse, inauspicious, inopportune, unfavorable

untrained adjective AMATEUR, green, inexperienced, raw, uneducated, unqualified, unschooled, unskilled, untaught

untroubled adjective UNDISTURBED, calm, cool, peaceful, placid, tranquil, unfazed (informal), unperturbed, unworried

untrue adjective **1** FALSE, deceptive, dishonest, erroneous, inaccurate, incorrect, lying, mistaken, wrong **2** UNFAITHFUL, deceitful, disloyal, faithless, false, inconstant, treacherous, untrustworthy

untrustworthy adjective UNRELIABLE, deceitful, devious,

dishonest, disloyal, false, slippery, treacherous, tricky

untruth noun LIE, deceit, falsehood, fib, story, white lie

untruthful adjective DISHONEST, deceitful, deceptive, false, lying, mendacious

unusual adjective EXTRAORDINARY, curious, different, exceptional, odd, queer, rare, remarkable, singular, strange, uncommon, unconventional

unveil verb REVEAL, disclose, divulge, expose, make known, uncover

unwanted adjective UNDESIRED, outcast, rejected, uninvited, unneeded, unsolicited, unwelcome

unwarranted adjective UNNECESSARY, gratuitous, groundless, indefensible, inexcusable, uncalled-for, unjustified, unprovoked

unwavering adjective STEADY, consistent, determined, immovable, resolute, staunch, steadfast, unshakable, unswerving

unwelcome adjective
1 UNWANTED, excluded, rejected, unacceptable, undesirable
2 DISAGREEABLE, displeasing, distasteful, undesirable, unpleasant

unwell adjective ILL, ailing, sick, sickly, under the weather (informal), unhealthy

unwholesome adjective
1 HARMFUL, deleterious, noxious, poisonous, unhealthy **2** WICKED, bad, corrupting, degrading, demoralizing, evil, immoral

unwieldy adjective **1** AWKWARD, cumbersome, inconvenient,

unmanageable **2** BULKY, clumsy, hefty, massive, ponderous

unwilling adjective RELUCTANT, averse, disinclined, grudging, indisposed, loath, resistant, unenthusiastic

unwind verb **1** UNRAVEL, slacken, uncoil, undo, unroll, untwine, untwist **2** RELAX, loosen up, take it easy, wind down

unwise adjective FOOLISH, foolhardy, improvident, imprudent, inadvisable, injudicious, rash, reckless, senseless, silly, stupid

unwitting adjective
1 UNINTENTIONAL, accidental, chance, inadvertent, involuntary, unplanned
2 UNKNOWING, ignorant, innocent, unaware, unconscious, unsuspecting

unworldly adjective **1** SPIRITUAL, metaphysical, nonmaterialistic **2** NAIVE, idealistic, innocent, unsophisticated

unworthy adjective
1 UNDESERVING, not fit for, not good enough **2** DISHONORABLE, base, contemptible, degrading, discreditable, disgraceful, disreputable, ignoble, lousy (slang), shameful **3 unworthy of** UNBEFITTING, beneath, inappropriate, unbecoming, unfitting, unseemly, unsuitable

unwritten adjective **1** ORAL, vocal **2** CUSTOMARY, accepted, tacit, understood

unyielding adjective FIRM, adamant, immovable, inflexible, obdurate, obstinate, resolute, rigid, stiff-necked, stubborn, tough, uncompromising

upbeat adjective CHEERFUL, cheery, encouraging, hopeful, optimistic, positive

upbraid verb SCOLD, admonish, berate, rebuke, reprimand, reproach, reprove

upbringing noun EDUCATION, breeding, raising, rearing, training

update verb REVISE, amend, bring up to date, modernize, renew

upgrade verb PROMOTE, advance, better, elevate, enhance, improve, raise

upheaval noun DISTURBANCE, disorder, disruption, revolution, turmoil

uphill adjective 1 ASCENDING, climbing, mounting, rising 2 ARDUOUS, difficult, exhausting, grueling, hard, laborious, strenuous, taxing, tough

uphold verb SUPPORT, advocate, aid, back, champion, defend, endorse, maintain, promote, sustain

upkeep noun 1 MAINTENANCE, keep, repair, running, subsistence 2 OVERHEADS, expenditure, expenses, running costs

uplift verb 1 RAISE, elevate, hoist, lift up 2 IMPROVE, advance, better, edify, inspire, raise, refine ▶ noun 3 IMPROVEMENT, advancement, edification, enhancement, enlightenment, enrichment, refinement

upmarket adjective Informal UPPER-CLASS, classy (informal), grand, high-class, luxurious, smart, stylish, swanky (informal)

upper adjective 1 HIGHER, high, loftier, top, topmost 2 SUPERIOR, eminent, greater, important

upper-class adjective ARISTOCRATIC, blue-blooded, highborn, high-class, noble, patrician

upper hand noun CONTROL, advantage, ascendancy, edge, mastery, supremacy

uppermost adjective 1 TOP, highest, loftiest, topmost 2 SUPREME, chief, dominant, foremost, greatest, leading, main, principal

uppity adjective Informal CONCEITED, bumptious, cocky, full of oneself, impertinent, self-important

upright adjective 1 VERTICAL, erect, perpendicular, straight 2 HONEST, conscientious, ethical, good, honorable, just, principled, righteous, virtuous

uprising noun REBELLION, disturbance, insurgence, insurrection, mutiny, revolt, revolution, rising

uproar noun COMMOTION, din, furor, mayhem, noise, outcry, pandemonium, racket, riot, turmoil

uproarious adjective 1 HILARIOUS, hysterical, rib-tickling, rip-roaring (informal), side-splitting, very funny 2 LOUD, boisterous, rollicking, unrestrained

uproot verb 1 PULL UP, dig up, rip up, root out, weed out 2 DISPLACE, exile

upset adjective 1 SICK, ill, queasy 2 DISTRESSED, agitated, bothered, dismayed, disturbed, grieved, hurt, put out, troubled, worried 3 DISORDERED, chaotic, confused, disarrayed,

in disarray, muddled
4 OVERTURNED, capsized, spilled,
upside down ▸verb **5** TIP OVER,
capsize, knock over, overturn,
spill **6** MESS UP, change,
disorder, disorganize, disturb,
spoil **7** DISTRESS, agitate, bother,
disconcert, disturb, faze,
fluster, grieve, perturb, ruffle,
trouble ▸noun **8** REVERSAL,
defeat, shake-up (*informal*)
9 ILLNESS, bug (*informal*),
complaint, disorder, malady,
sickness **10** DISTRESS, agitation,
bother, disturbance, shock,
trouble, worry

upshot noun RESULT,
culmination, end, end result,
finale, outcome, sequel

upside down adjective
1 INVERTED, backward,
overturned, upturned
2 CONFUSED, chaotic,
disordered, muddled,
topsy-turvy

upstanding adjective HONEST,
ethical, good, honorable,
incorruptible, moral,
principled, upright

upstart noun SOCIAL CLIMBER,
arriviste, nouveau riche, parvenu

uptight adjective Informal TENSE,
anxious, edgy, on edge,
uneasy, wired (*slang*)

up-to-date adjective MODERN,
cool (*informal*), current,
fashionable, in vogue, phat
(*slang*), stylish, trendy
(*informal*), up-to-the-minute

upturn noun RISE, advancement,
improvement, increase,
recovery, revival, upsurge,
upswing

urban adjective CIVIC, city,
metropolitan, municipal, town

urbane adjective SOPHISTICATED,
courteous, cultivated, cultured,
debonair, polished, refined,
smooth, suave, well-bred

urchin noun RAGAMUFFIN, brat,
gamin, waif

urge noun **1** IMPULSE,
compulsion, desire, drive, itch,
longing, thirst, wish, yearning
▸verb **2** BEG, beseech, entreat,
exhort, implore, plead
3 ADVOCATE, advise, counsel,
recommend, support **4** DRIVE,
compel, force, goad, impel,
incite, induce, press, push, spur

urgency noun IMPORTANCE,
extremity, gravity, hurry,
necessity, need, pressure,
seriousness

urgent adjective CRUCIAL,
compelling, critical, immediate,
imperative, important, pressing

usable adjective SERVICEABLE,
available, current, functional,
practical, utilizable, valid,
working

usage noun **1** USE, control,
employment, handling,
management, operation,
running **2** PRACTICE, convention,
custom, habit, method, mode,
procedure, regime, routine

use verb **1** EMPLOY, apply,
exercise, exert, operate,
practice, utilize, work **2** TAKE
ADVANTAGE OF, exploit,
manipulate **3** CONSUME,
exhaust, expend, run through,
spend ▸noun **4** USAGE,
application, employment,
exercise, handling, operation,
practice, service **5** GOOD,
advantage, avail, benefit, help,
point, profit, service,
usefulness, value **6** PURPOSE,

end, object, reason

used adjective SECOND-HAND, cast-off, nearly new, shopsoiled

used to adjective ACCUSTOMED TO, familiar with

useful adjective HELPFUL, advantageous, beneficial, effective, fruitful, practical, profitable, serviceable, valuable, win-win (informal), worthwhile

usefulness noun HELPFULNESS, benefit, convenience, effectiveness, efficacy, practicality, use, utility, value, worth

useless adjective 1 WORTHLESS, fruitless, futile, impractical, ineffectual, pointless, unproductive, vain, valueless 2 Informal INEPT, hopeless, incompetent, ineffectual, no good

use up verb CONSUME, absorb, drain, exhaust, finish, run through

usher noun 1 ATTENDANT, doorkeeper, doorman, escort, guide ▶ verb 2 ESCORT, conduct, direct, guide, lead

usual adjective NORMAL, common, customary, everyday, general, habitual, ordinary, regular, routine, standard, typical

usually adverb NORMALLY, as a rule, commonly, generally, habitually, mainly, mostly, on the whole

usurp verb SEIZE, appropriate, assume, commandeer, take, take over, wrest

utility noun USEFULNESS, benefit, convenience, efficacy, practicality, serviceableness

utilize verb USE, avail oneself of, employ, make use of, put to use, take advantage of, turn to account

utmost adjective 1 GREATEST, chief, highest, maximum, paramount, pre-eminent, supreme 2 FARTHEST, extreme, final, last ▶ noun 3 GREATEST, best, hardest, highest

Utopia noun PARADISE, bliss, Eden, Garden of Eden, heaven, Shangri-la

Utopian adjective PERFECT, dream, fantasy, ideal, idealistic, imaginary, romantic, visionary

utter[1] verb EXPRESS, articulate, pronounce, say, speak, voice

utter[2] adjective ABSOLUTE, complete, downright, outright, sheer, thorough, total, unmitigated

utterance noun SPEECH, announcement, declaration, expression, remark, statement, words

utterly adverb TOTALLY, absolutely, completely, entirely, extremely, fully, perfectly, thoroughly

vacancy noun JOB, opening, opportunity, position, post, situation

vacant adjective 1 UNOCCUPIED, available, empty, free, idle, unfilled, untenanted, void 2 VAGUE, absent-minded, abstracted, blank, dreamy, idle, inane, vacuous

vacate verb LEAVE, evacuate, quit

vacuous adjective UNINTELLIGENT, blank, inane, stupid, uncomprehending, vacant

vacuum noun EMPTINESS, gap, nothingness, space, vacuity, void

vagabond noun BEGGAR, down-and-out, itinerant, rover, tramp, vagrant

vagrant noun 1 TRAMP, drifter, hobo, itinerant, rolling stone, wanderer ▶ adjective 2 ITINERANT, nomadic, roaming, rootless, roving, unsettled, vagabond

vague adjective UNCLEAR, equivocal, hazy, ill-defined, imprecise, indefinite, indeterminate, indistinct, loose, nebulous, uncertain, unspecified

vain adjective 1 PROUD, arrogant, conceited, egotistical, narcissistic, self-important, swaggering ▶ adjective 2 FUTILE, abortive, fruitless, idle, pointless, senseless, unavailing, unprofitable, useless, worthless ▶ noun 3 **in vain** TO NO AVAIL, fruitless(ly), ineffectual(ly), unsuccessful(ly), useless(ly), vain(ly)

valiant adjective BRAVE, bold, courageous, fearless, gallant, heroic, intrepid, lion-hearted

valid adjective 1 LOGICAL, cogent, convincing, good, sound, telling, well-founded, well-grounded 2 LEGAL, authentic, bona fide, genuine, lawful, legitimate, official

validate verb CONFIRM, authenticate, authorize, certify, corroborate, endorse, ratify, substantiate

validity noun 1 SOUNDNESS, cogency, force, power, strength, weight 2 LEGALITY, authority, lawfulness, legitimacy, right

valley noun HOLLOW, dale, dell, depression, glen, vale

valor noun BRAVERY, boldness, courage, fearlessness, gallantry, heroism, intrepidity, spirit

valuable adjective 1 PRECIOUS, costly, dear, expensive, high-priced 2 USEFUL, beneficial, helpful, important, prized, profitable, worthwhile ▶ noun 3 **valuables** TREASURES, heirlooms

value noun 1 IMPORTANCE, advantage, benefit, desirability, merit, profit, usefulness, utility, worth 2 COST, market price, rate 3 **values** PRINCIPLES, ethics, (moral) standards ▶ verb 4 EVALUATE, appraise, assess, estimate, price, rate, set at 5 RESPECT, appreciate, cherish, esteem, hold dear, prize, regard highly, treasure

vandal noun HOOLIGAN, delinquent, rowdy

vanguard noun FORERUNNERS, cutting edge, forefront, front line, leaders, spearhead, trailblazers, trendsetters, van

vanish verb DISAPPEAR, dissolve, evanesce, evaporate, fade (away), melt (away)

vanity noun PRIDE, arrogance, conceit, conceitedness, egotism, narcissism

vanquish verb Literary DEFEAT, beat, conquer, crush, master, overcome, overpower, overwhelm, triumph over

vapid adjective DULL, bland, boring, flat, insipid, tame, uninspiring, uninteresting, weak, wishy-washy (*informal*)

vapor noun MIST, exhalation, fog, haze, steam

variable adjective CHANGEABLE, flexible, fluctuating, inconstant, mutable, shifting, temperamental, uneven, unstable, unsteady

variance noun at variance IN DISAGREEMENT, at loggerheads, at odds, conflicting, out of line

variant adjective DIFFERENT, alternative, divergent, modified ▶noun 2 VARIATION, alternative, development, modification

variation noun DIFFERENCE, change, departure, deviation, diversity, innovation, modification, novelty, variety

varied adjective DIFFERENT, assorted, diverse, heterogeneous, miscellaneous, mixed, motley, sundry, various

variety noun 1 DIVERSITY, change, difference, discrepancy, diversification, multifariousness, variation 2 RANGE, array, assortment, collection, cross section, medley, miscellany, mixture 3 TYPE, brand, breed, category, class, kind, sort, species, strain

various adjective DIFFERENT, assorted, disparate, distinct, diverse, miscellaneous, several, sundry, varied

varnish noun, verb POLISH, glaze, gloss, lacquer

vary verb CHANGE, alter, differ, disagree, diverge, fluctuate

vast adjective HUGE, boundless, colossal, enormous, gigantic, great, immense, massive, monumental, wide

vault¹ noun 1 STRONGROOM,

depository, repository 2 CRYPT, catacomb, cellar, charnel house, mausoleum, tomb, undercroft

vault² verb JUMP, bound, clear, hurdle, leap, spring

vaulted adjective ARCHED, cavernous, domed

veer verb SWERVE, change course, change direction, sheer, shift, turn

vegetate verb STAGNATE, deteriorate, go to seed, idle, languish, loaf

vehemence noun FORCEFULNESS, ardor, emphasis, energy, fervor, force, intensity, passion, vigor

vehement adjective STRONG, ardent, emphatic, fervent, fierce, forceful, impassioned, intense, passionate, powerful

vehicle noun 1 TRANSPORT, conveyance, transportation 2 MEDIUM, apparatus, channel, means, mechanism, organ

veil noun 1 COVER, blind, cloak, curtain, disguise, film, mask, screen, shroud ▶verb 2 COVER, cloak, conceal, disguise, hide, mask, obscure, screen, shield

veiled adjective DISGUISED, concealed, covert, hinted at, implied, masked, suppressed

vein noun 1 BLOOD VESSEL 2 SEAM, course, current, lode, stratum, streak, stripe 3 MOOD, mode, note, style, temper, tenor, tone

velocity noun SPEED, pace, quickness, rapidity, swiftness

velvety adjective SMOOTH, delicate, downy, soft

vendetta noun FEUD, bad blood, quarrel

veneer noun MASK, appearance, façade, front, guise, pretense, semblance, show

venerable adjective RESPECTED, august, esteemed, honored, revered, sage, wise, worshipped

venerate verb RESPECT, adore, esteem, honor, look up to, revere, reverence, worship

vengeance noun REVENGE, reprisal, retaliation, retribution

venom noun 1 MALICE, acrimony, bitterness, hate, rancor, spite, spleen, virulence 2 POISON, bane, toxin

venomous adjective 1 MALICIOUS, hostile, malignant, rancorous, savage, spiteful, vicious, vindictive 2 POISONOUS, mephitic, noxious, toxic, virulent

vent noun 1 OUTLET, aperture, duct, opening, orifice ▶verb 2 EXPRESS, air, discharge, emit, give vent to, pour out, release, utter, voice

venture noun 1 UNDERTAKING, adventure, endeavor, enterprise, gamble, hazard, project, risk ▶verb 2 RISK, chance, hazard, speculate, stake, wager 3 DARE, hazard, make bold, presume, take the liberty, volunteer 4 GO, embark on, plunge into, set out

verbal adjective SPOKEN, oral, unwritten, word-of-mouth

verbatim adverb EXACTLY, precisely, to the letter, word for word

verbose adjective LONG-WINDED, circumlocutory, diffuse, periphrastic, prolix, tautological, windy, wordy

verbosity noun LONG-WINDEDNESS, loquaciousness, prolixity, verboseness, wordiness

verdant adjective GREEN, flourishing, fresh, grassy, leafy, lush

verdict noun DECISION, adjudication, conclusion, finding, judgment, opinion, sentence

verge noun 1 BORDER, boundary, brim, brink, edge, limit, margin, threshold ▶verb 2 verge on BORDER, approach, come near

verification noun PROOF, authentication, confirmation, corroboration, substantiation, validation

verify verb CHECK, authenticate, bear out, confirm, corroborate, prove, substantiate, support, validate

vernacular noun DIALECT, idiom, parlance, patois, speech

versatile adjective ADAPTABLE, adjustable, all-purpose, all-round, flexible, multifaceted, resourceful, variable

versed adjective KNOWLEDGEABLE, acquainted, conversant, experienced, familiar, practiced, proficient, seasoned, well informed

version noun 1 FORM, design, model, style, variant 2 ACCOUNT, adaptation, interpretation, portrayal, rendering

vertical adjective UPRIGHT, erect, on end, perpendicular

vertigo noun DIZZINESS, giddiness, light-headedness

verve noun ENTHUSIASM, animation, energy, gusto,

very adverb 1 EXTREMELY, acutely, decidedly, deeply, exceedingly, greatly, highly, profoundly, uncommonly, unusually ▶ adjective 2 EXACT, precise, selfsame

vessel noun 1 SHIP, boat, craft 2 CONTAINER, pot, receptacle, utensil

vest verb (with in or with) PLACE, bestow, confer, consign, endow, entrust, invest, settle

vestibule noun HALL, anteroom, foyer, lobby, porch, portico

vestige noun TRACE, glimmer, indication, remnant, scrap, suspicion

vet verb CHECK, appraise, examine, investigate, review, scrutinize

veteran noun 1 OLD HAND, old stager, past master, warhorse (informal) ▶ adjective 2 LONG-SERVING, battle-scarred, old, seasoned

veto noun 1 BAN, boycott, embargo, interdict, prohibition ▶ verb 2 BAN, boycott, disallow, forbid, prohibit, reject, rule out, turn down

vex verb ANNOY, bother, distress, exasperate, irritate, plague, trouble, upset, worry

vexation noun 1 ANNOYANCE, chagrin, displeasure, dissatisfaction, exasperation, frustration, irritation, pique 2 PROBLEM, bother, difficulty, hassle (informal), headache (informal), nuisance, trouble, worry

viable adjective WORKABLE, applicable, feasible, operable, practicable, usable

vibrant adjective ENERGETIC, alive, animated, dynamic, sparkling, spirited, vigorous, vivacious, vivid

vibrate verb SHAKE, fluctuate, oscillate, pulsate, quiver, reverberate, shudder, sway, throb, tremble

vibration noun TREMOR, oscillation, pulsation, quiver, reverberation, shake, shudder, throbbing, trembling

vicarious adjective INDIRECT, delegated, substituted, surrogate

vice noun 1 WICKEDNESS, corruption, depravity, evil, immorality, iniquity, sin, turpitude 2 FAULT, blemish, defect, failing, imperfection, shortcoming, weakness

vice versa adverb CONVERSELY, contrariwise, in reverse, the other way round

vicinity noun NEIGHBORHOOD, area, district, environs, locality, neck of the woods (informal), proximity

vicious adjective 1 VIOLENT, barbarous, cruel, ferocious, savage, wicked 2 MALICIOUS, cruel, mean, spiteful, venomous, vindictive

victim noun CASUALTY, fatality, martyr, sacrifice, scapegoat, sufferer

victimize verb PERSECUTE, discriminate against, pick on

victor noun WINNER, champion, conqueror, prizewinner, vanquisher

victorious adjective WINNING, champion, conquering, first, prizewinning, successful, triumphant, vanquishing

victory noun WIN, conquest, success, triumph

vie verb COMPETE, contend, strive, struggle

view noun **1** (sometimes plural) OPINION, attitude, belief, conviction, feeling, impression, point of view, sentiment **2** SCENE, landscape, outlook, panorama, perspective, picture, prospect, spectacle, vista **3** VISION, sight ▶ verb **4** REGARD, consider, deem, look on

viewer noun WATCHER, observer, onlooker, spectator

vigilance noun WATCHFULNESS, alertness, attentiveness, carefulness, caution, circumspection, observance

vigilant adjective WATCHFUL, alert, attentive, careful, cautious, circumspect, on one's guard, on the lookout, wakeful

vigor noun ENERGY, animation, dynamism, forcefulness, gusto, liveliness, power, spirit, strength, verve, vitality

vigorous adjective ENERGETIC, active, dynamic, forceful, lively, lusty, powerful, spirited, strenuous, strong

vigorously adverb ENERGETICALLY, forcefully, hard, lustily, strenuously, strongly

vile adjective **1** WICKED, corrupt, degenerate, depraved, evil, nefarious, perverted **2** DISGUSTING, foul, horrid, nasty, nauseating, offensive, repugnant, repulsive, revolting, scuzzy (slang), sickening

vilify verb MALIGN, abuse, berate, denigrate, disparage, revile, slander, smear

villain noun **1** EVILDOER, criminal, miscreant, reprobate, rogue, scoundrel, wretch **2** ANTIHERO, baddy (informal)

villainous adjective WICKED, bad, cruel, degenerate, depraved, evil, fiendish, nefarious, vicious, vile

villainy noun WICKEDNESS, delinquency, depravity, devilry, iniquity, turpitude, vice

vindicate verb **1** CLEAR, absolve, acquit, exculpate, exonerate, rehabilitate **2** JUSTIFY, defend, excuse

vindication noun **1** EXONERATION, exculpation, rehabilitation **2** JUSTIFICATION, defense, excuse

vindictive adjective VENGEFUL, implacable, malicious, resentful, revengeful, spiteful, unforgiving, unrelenting

vintage adjective BEST, choice, classic, prime, select, superior

violate verb **1** BREAK, contravene, disobey, disregard, encroach upon, infringe, transgress **2** DESECRATE, abuse, befoul, defile, dishonor, pollute, profane **3** RAPE, abuse, assault, debauch, ravish

violation noun **1** INFRINGEMENT, abuse, breach, contravention, encroachment, infraction, transgression, trespass **2** DESECRATION, defilement, profanation, sacrilege, spoliation

violence noun **1** FORCE, bloodshed, brutality, cruelty, ferocity, fighting, savagery, terrorism **2** INTENSITY, abandon, fervor, force, severity, vehemence

violent adjective DESTRUCTIVE, brutal, cruel, hot-headed, murderous, riotous, savage, uncontrollable, unrestrained, vicious

V.I.P. noun CELEBRITY, big name, luminary, somebody, star

virgin noun 1 MAIDEN, girl ▶ adjective 2 PURE, chaste, immaculate, uncorrupted, undefiled, vestal, virginal

virginity noun CHASTITY, maidenhood

virile adjective MANLY, lusty, macho, manlike, masculine, red-blooded, strong, vigorous

virility noun MASCULINITY, machismo, manhood, vigor

virtual adjective PRACTICAL, essential, in all but name

virtually adverb PRACTICALLY, almost, as good as, in all but name, in effect, in essence, nearly

virtue noun 1 GOODNESS, incorruptibility, integrity, morality, probity, rectitude, righteousness, uprightness, worth 2 MERIT, advantage, asset, attribute, credit, good point, plus (informal), strength

virtuosity noun MASTERY, brilliance, craft, expertise, flair, panache, polish, skill

virtuoso noun MASTER, artist, genius, maestro, magician

virtuous adjective GOOD, ethical, honorable, incorruptible, moral, praiseworthy, righteous, upright, worthy

virulent adjective POISONOUS, deadly, lethal, pernicious, toxic, venomous

viscous adjective THICK, gelatinous, sticky, syrupy

visible adjective APPARENT, clear, discernible, evident, in view,

manifest, observable, perceptible, unconcealed

vision noun 1 SIGHT, eyesight, perception, seeing, view 2 IMAGE, concept, conception, daydream, dream, fantasy, idea, ideal 3 HALLUCINATION, apparition, chimera, delusion, illusion, mirage, revelation 4 FORESIGHT, discernment, farsightedness, imagination, insight, intuition, penetration, prescience

visionary adjective 1 PROPHETIC, mystical 2 IMPRACTICAL, idealistic, quixotic, romantic, speculative, starry-eyed, unrealistic, unworkable, utopian ▶ noun 3 PROPHET, mystic, seer

visit verb 1 CALL ON, drop in on (informal), look (someone) up, stay with, stop by ▶ noun 2 CALL, sojourn, stay, stop

visitation noun 1 INSPECTION, examination, visit 2 CATASTROPHE, blight, calamity, cataclysm, disaster, ordeal, punishment, scourge

visitor noun GUEST, caller, company

vista noun VIEW, panorama, perspective, prospect

visual adjective 1 OPTICAL, ocular, optic 2 OBSERVABLE, discernible, perceptible, visible

visualize verb PICTURE, conceive of, envisage, imagine

vital adjective 1 ESSENTIAL, basic, fundamental, imperative, indispensable, necessary, requisite 2 IMPORTANT, critical, crucial, decisive, key, life-or-death, significant, urgent 3 LIVELY, animated, dynamic, energetic, spirited, vibrant, vigorous, vivacious, zestful

vitality *noun* ENERGY, animation, exuberance, life, liveliness, strength, vigor, vivacity

vitriolic *adjective* BITTER, acerbic, caustic, envenomed, sardonic, scathing, venomous, virulent, withering

vivacious *adjective* LIVELY, bubbling, ebullient, high-spirited, sparkling, spirited, sprightly, upbeat (*informal*), vital

vivacity *noun* LIVELINESS, animation, ebullience, energy, gaiety, high spirits, sparkle, spirit, sprightliness

vivid *adjective* 1 BRIGHT, brilliant, clear, colorful, glowing, intense, rich 2 LIFELIKE, dramatic, graphic, memorable, powerful, realistic, stirring, telling, true to life

vocabulary *noun* WORDS, dictionary, glossary, language, lexicon

vocal *adjective* 1 SPOKEN, oral, said, uttered, voiced 2 OUTSPOKEN, articulate, eloquent, expressive, forthright, frank, plain-spoken, strident, vociferous

vocation *noun* PROFESSION, calling, career, job, mission, pursuit, trade

vociferous *adjective* NOISY, clamorous, loud, outspoken, strident, uproarious, vehement, vocal

vogue *noun* 1 FASHION, craze, custom, mode, style, trend, way 2 *As in* **in vogue** POPULARITY, acceptance, currency, favor, prevalence, usage, use

voice *noun* 1 SOUND, articulation, tone, utterance 2 SAY, view, vote, will, wish ▶ *verb* 3 EXPRESS, air, articulate, declare, enunciate, utter

void *noun* 1 EMPTINESS, blankness, gap, lack, space, vacuity, vacuum ▶ *adjective* 2 INVALID, ineffective, inoperative, null and void, useless, vain, worthless 3 EMPTY, bare, free, tenantless, unfilled, unoccupied, vacant ▶ *verb* 4 INVALIDATE, cancel, nullify, rescind 5 EMPTY, drain, evacuate

volatile *adjective* 1 CHANGEABLE, explosive, inconstant, unsettled, unstable, unsteady, variable 2 TEMPERAMENTAL, erratic, fickle, mercurial, up and down (*informal*)

volition *noun* FREE WILL, choice, choosing, discretion, preference, will

volley *noun* BARRAGE, blast, bombardment, burst, cannonade, fusillade, hail, salvo, shower

voluble *adjective* TALKATIVE, articulate, fluent, forthcoming, glib, loquacious

volume *noun* 1 CAPACITY, compass, dimensions 2 AMOUNT, aggregate, body, bulk, mass, quantity, total 3 BOOK, publication, title, tome, treatise

voluminous *adjective* LARGE, ample, capacious, cavernous, roomy, vast

voluntarily *adverb* WILLINGLY, by choice, freely, off one's own bat, of one's own accord

voluntary *adjective* UNFORCED, discretionary, free, optional, spontaneous, willing

volunteer verb OFFER, step forward

voluptuous adjective **1** BUXOM, ample, curvaceous (informal), enticing, seductive, shapely **2** SENSUAL, epicurean, hedonistic, licentious, luxurious, self-indulgent, sybaritic

vomit verb RETCH, barf (slang), disgorge, emit, heave, regurgitate, spew out or up, throw up (informal)

voracious adjective **1** GLUTTONOUS, greedy, hungry, insatiable, omnivorous, ravenous **2** AVID, hungry, insatiable, rapacious, uncontrolled, unquenchable

vortex noun WHIRLPOOL, eddy, maelstrom

vote noun **1** POLL, ballot, franchise, plebiscite, referendum, show of hands ▶verb **2** ELECT, cast one's vote, opt

voucher noun TICKET, coupon, token

vouch for verb **1** GUARANTEE, answer for, certify, give assurance of, stand witness, swear to **2** CONFIRM, affirm, assert, attest to, support, uphold

vow noun **1** PROMISE, oath, pledge ▶verb **2** PROMISE, affirm, pledge, swear

voyage noun JOURNEY, crossing, cruise, passage, trip

vulgar adjective CRUDE, coarse, common, impolite, indecent, off-color, ribald, risqué, rude, tasteless, uncouth, unrefined

vulgarity noun CRUDENESS, bad

taste, coarseness, indelicacy, ribaldry, rudeness, tastelessness

vulnerable adjective **1** WEAK, sensitive, susceptible, tender, thin-skinned **2** EXPOSED, accessible, assailable, defenseless, unprotected, wide open

— W w —

wacky adjective Informal FOOLISH, absurd, asinine, crackpot (informal), crazy, idiotic, silly, stupid, witless

wad noun MASS, bundle, hunk, roll

waddle verb SHUFFLE, sway, toddle, totter, wobble

wade verb **1** WALK THROUGH, ford, paddle, splash **2 wade through** PLOW THROUGH, drudge at, labor at, peg away at, toil at, work one's way through

waft verb CARRY, bear, convey, drift, float, transport

wag verb **1** WAVE, bob, nod, quiver, shake, stir, vibrate, wiggle ▶noun **2** WAVE, bob, nod, quiver, shake, vibration, wiggle

wage noun **1** Also **wages** PAYMENT, allowance, emolument, fee, pay, recompense, remuneration, reward, stipend ▶verb **2** ENGAGE IN, carry on, conduct, practice, proceed with, prosecute, pursue, undertake

wager noun **1** BET, gamble ▶verb **2** BET, chance, gamble, lay, pledge, risk, speculate, stake, venture

waif *noun* STRAY, foundling, orphan

wail *verb* **1** CRY, bawl, grieve, howl, lament, weep, yowl ▶*noun* **2** CRY, complaint, howl, lament, moan, weeping, yowl

wait *verb* **1** REMAIN, hang fire, hold back, linger, pause, rest, stay, tarry ▶*noun* **2** DELAY, halt, hold-up, interval, pause, rest, stay

waiter, waitress *noun* ATTENDANT, server, steward *or* stewardess

wait on *or* **upon** *verb* SERVE, attend, minister to, tend

waive *verb* SET ASIDE, abandon, dispense with, forgo, give up, relinquish, remit, renounce

wake[1] *verb* **1** AWAKEN, arise, awake, bestir, come to, get up, rouse, stir **2** ACTIVATE, animate, arouse, excite, fire, galvanize, kindle, provoke, stimulate, stir up ▶*noun* **3** VIGIL, deathwatch, funeral, watch

wake[2] *noun* SLIPSTREAM, aftermath, backwash, path, track, trail, train, wash, waves

wakeful *adjective* **1** SLEEPLESS, insomniac, restless **2** WATCHFUL, alert, alive, attentive, observant, on guard, vigilant, wary

waken *verb* AWAKEN, activate, arouse, awake, rouse, stir

walk *verb* **1** GO, amble, hike, march, move, pace, step, stride, stroll **2** ESCORT, accompany, convoy, take ▶*noun* **3** STROLL, hike, march, promenade, ramble, saunter, trek, trudge **4** GAIT, carriage, step **5** PATH, alley, avenue,

esplanade, footpath, lane, promenade, trail **6** walk of life PROFESSION, calling, career, field, line, trade, vocation

walker *noun* PEDESTRIAN, hiker, rambler, wayfarer

walkout *noun* STRIKE, industrial action, protest, stoppage

walkover *noun* PUSHOVER (*slang*), breeze (*informal*), cakewalk (*informal*), child's play (*informal*), picnic (*informal*), piece of cake (*informal*)

wall *noun* **1** PARTITION, enclosure, screen **2** BARRIER, fence, hedge, impediment, obstacle, obstruction

wallet *noun* HOLDER, case, pocketbook, pouch, purse

wallop *verb* **1** HIT, batter, beat, clobber (*slang*), pound, pummel, strike, thrash, thump, whack ▶*noun* **2** BLOW, bash, punch, slug, smack, thump, thwack

wallow *verb* **1** REVEL, bask, delight, glory, luxuriate, relish, take pleasure **2** ROLL ABOUT, splash around

wan *adjective* PALE, anemic, ashen, pallid, pasty, sickly, washed out, white

wand *noun* STICK, baton, rod

wander *verb* **1** ROAM, drift, meander, ramble, range, rove, stray, stroll **2** DEVIATE, depart, digress, diverge, err, go astray, swerve, veer ▶*noun* **3** EXCURSION, cruise, meander, ramble

wanderer *noun* TRAVELER, drifter, gypsy, nomad, rambler, rover, vagabond, voyager

wandering *adjective* NOMADIC, itinerant, migratory,

peripatetic, rootless, roving, traveling, vagrant, wayfaring

wane verb 1 DECLINE, decrease, diminish, dwindle, ebb, fade, fail, lessen, subside, taper off, weaken ▶noun 2 **on the wane** DECLINING, dwindling, ebbing, fading, obsolescent, on the decline, tapering off, weakening

wangle verb CONTRIVE, arrange, engineer, fix (*informal*), maneuver, manipulate, pull off

want verb 1 DESIRE, covet, crave, hanker after, hope for, hunger for, long for, thirst for, wish, yearn for 2 NEED, call for, demand, lack, miss, require ▶noun 3 WISH, appetite, craving, desire, longing, need, requirement, yearning 4 LACK, absence, dearth, deficiency, famine, insufficiency, paucity, scarcity, shortage 5 POVERTY, destitution, neediness, penury, privation

wanting adjective 1 LACKING, absent, incomplete, missing, short, shy 2 INADEQUATE, defective, deficient, faulty, imperfect, lousy (*slang*), poor, substandard, unsound

wanton adjective 1 UNPROVOKED, arbitrary, gratuitous, groundless, motiveless, needless, senseless, uncalled-for, unjustifiable, willful 2 PROMISCUOUS, dissipated, dissolute, immoral, lecherous, libidinous, loose, lustful, shameless, unchaste

war noun 1 FIGHTING, battle, combat, conflict, enmity, hostilities, struggle, warfare ▶verb 2 FIGHT, battle, campaign against, clash, combat, take up arms, wage war

warble verb SING, chirp, trill, twitter

ward noun 1 ROOM, apartment, cubicle 2 DISTRICT, area, division, precinct, quarter, zone 3 DEPENDANT, charge, minor, protégé, pupil

warden noun KEEPER, administrator, caretaker, curator, custodian, guardian, ranger, superintendent

ward off verb REPEL, avert, avoid, deflect, fend off, parry, stave off

wardrobe noun 1 CLOTHES CUPBOARD, closet 2 CLOTHES, apparel, attire

warehouse noun STORE, depository, depot, stockroom, storehouse

wares plural noun GOODS, commodities, merchandise, produce, products, stock, stuff

warfare noun WAR, arms, battle, combat, conflict, fighting, hostilities

warily adverb CAUTIOUSLY, carefully, charily, circumspectly, distrustfully, gingerly, suspiciously, vigilantly, watchfully, with care

warlike adjective BELLIGERENT, aggressive, bellicose, bloodthirsty, hawkish, hostile, martial, warmongering

warlock noun MAGICIAN, conjurer, enchanter, sorcerer, wizard

warm adjective 1 HEATED, balmy, lukewarm, pleasant, sunny, tepid, thermal 2 AFFECTIONATE, amorous, cordial, friendly, hospitable, kindly, loving, tender ▶verb 3 HEAT, heat up, melt, thaw, warm up

warmonger noun HAWK, belligerent, militarist, saber-rattler

warmth noun 1 HEAT, hotness, warmness 2 AFFECTION, amorousness, cordiality, heartiness, kindliness, love, tenderness

warn verb NOTIFY, advise, alert, apprise, caution, forewarn, give notice, inform, make (someone) aware, tip off

warning noun CAUTION, advice, alarm, alert, notification, omen, sign, tip-off

warp verb 1 TWIST, bend, contort, deform, distort ▶ noun 2 TWIST, bend, contortion, distortion, kink

warrant noun 1 AUTHORIZATION, authority, license, permission, permit, sanction ▶ verb 2 CALL FOR, demand, deserve, excuse, justify, license, necessitate, permit, require, sanction 3 GUARANTEE, affirm, attest, certify, declare, pledge, vouch for

warranty noun GUARANTEE, assurance, bond, certificate, contract, covenant, pledge

warrior noun SOLDIER, combatant, fighter, gladiator, man-at-arms

wary adjective CAUTIOUS, alert, careful, chary, circumspect, distrustful, guarded, suspicious, vigilant, watchful

wash verb 1 CLEAN, bathe, cleanse, launder, rinse, scrub 2 SWEEP AWAY, bear away, carry off, move 3 Informal BE PLAUSIBLE, bear scrutiny, be convincing, carry weight, hold up, hold water, stand up, stick ▶ noun 4 CLEANING, cleansing, laundering, rinse, scrub 5 COAT, coating, film, layer, overlay 6 SWELL, surge, wave

washout noun FAILURE, disappointment, disaster, dud (informal), fiasco, flop (informal)

waste verb 1 MISUSE, blow (slang), dissipate, fritter away, lavish, squander, throw away 2 waste away DECLINE, atrophy, crumble, decay, dwindle, fade, wane, wear out, wither ▶ noun 3 MISUSE, dissipation, extravagance, frittering away, prodigality, squandering, wastefulness 4 RUBBISH, debris, dross, garbage, leftovers, litter, refuse, scrap, trash 5 wastes DESERT, wasteland, wilderness ▶ adjective 6 UNWANTED, leftover, superfluous, supernumerary, unused, useless, worthless 7 UNCULTIVATED, bare, barren, desolate, empty, uninhabited, unproductive, wild

wasteful adjective EXTRAVAGANT, lavish, prodigal, profligate, spendthrift, thriftless, uneconomical

waster noun IDLER, couch potato (slang), good-for-nothing, loafer, shirker, wastrel

watch verb 1 LOOK AT, contemplate, view, observe, regard, see, view 2 GUARD, keep, look after, mind, protect, superintend, take care of, tend ▶ noun 3 WRISTWATCH, chronometer, timepiece 4 LOOKOUT, observation, surveillance, vigil

watchdog noun 1 GUARD DOG 2 GUARDIAN, custodian, monitor, protector, scrutineer

watchful adjective ALERT, attentive, observant, on the lookout, suspicious, vigilant, wary, wide awake

watchman noun GUARD, caretaker, custodian, security guard

watchword noun MOTTO, battle cry, byword, catch phrase, catchword, maxim, rallying cry, slogan

water noun 1 LIQUID, H₂O ▶verb 2 MOISTEN, dampen, douse, drench, hose, irrigate, soak, spray

water down verb DILUTE, thin, water, weaken

waterfall noun CASCADE, cataract, fall

watertight adjective 1 WATERPROOF 2 FOOLPROOF, airtight, flawless, impregnable, sound, unassailable

watery adjective 1 WET, aqueous, damp, fluid, liquid, moist, soggy 2 DILUTED, runny, thin, washy, watered-down, weak

wave verb 1 SIGNAL, beckon, direct, gesticulate, gesture, indicate, sign 2 FLAP, brandish, flourish, flutter, oscillate, shake, stir, swing, wag ▶noun 3 RIPPLE, billow, breaker, ridge, roller, swell, undulation 4 OUTBREAK, flood, rash, rush, stream, surge, upsurge

waver verb 1 HESITATE, dither, falter, fluctuate, hum and haw, seesaw, vacillate 2 TREMBLE, flicker, quiver, shake, totter, wobble

wax verb INCREASE, develop, enlarge, expand, grow, magnify, swell

way noun 1 METHOD, fashion, manner, means, mode, procedure, process, system, technique 2 STYLE, custom, habit, manner, nature, personality, practice, wont 3 ROUTE, channel, course, direction, path, pathway, road, track, trail 4 JOURNEY, approach, march, passage 5 DISTANCE, length, stretch

wayfarer noun TRAVELER, gypsy, itinerant, nomad, rover, voyager, wanderer

wayward adjective ERRATIC, capricious, inconstant, ungovernable, unmanageable, unpredictable, unruly

weak adjective 1 FEEBLE, debilitated, effete, fragile, frail, infirm, puny, sickly, unsteady 2 UNSAFE, defenseless, exposed, helpless, unguarded, unprotected, vulnerable 3 UNCONVINCING, feeble, flimsy, hollow, lame, pathetic, unsatisfactory 4 TASTELESS, diluted, insipid, runny, thin, watery

weaken verb 1 LESSEN, diminish, dwindle, fade, flag, lower, moderate, reduce, sap, undermine, wane 2 DILUTE, thin out, water down

weakling noun SISSY, baby (informal), drip (informal), wimp (informal)

weakness noun 1 FRAILTY, decrepitude, feebleness, fragility, infirmity, powerlessness, vulnerability 2 FAILING, blemish, defect, deficiency, fault, flaw, imperfection, lack, shortcoming 3 LIKING, fondness, inclination, partiality, passion, penchant, soft spot

wealth noun 1 RICHES, affluence, capital, fortune, money, opulence, prosperity 2 PLENTY, abundance, copiousness, cornucopia, fullness, profusion, richness

wealthy adjective RICH, affluent, flush (informal), moneyed, opulent, prosperous, well-heeled (informal), well-off, well-to-do

wear verb 1 BE DRESSED IN, don, have on, put on, sport (informal) 2 SHOW, display, exhibit 3 DETERIORATE, abrade, corrode, erode, fray, grind, rub ▶ noun 4 CLOTHES, apparel, attire, costume, dress, garb, garments, gear (informal), things 5 DAMAGE, abrasion, attrition, corrosion, deterioration, erosion, wear and tear

weariness noun TIREDNESS, drowsiness, exhaustion, fatigue, languor, lassitude, lethargy, listlessness

wearing adjective TIRESOME, exasperating, fatiguing, irksome, oppressive, trying, wearisome

wearisome adjective TEDIOUS, annoying, boring, exhausting, fatiguing, irksome, oppressive, tiresome, troublesome, trying, wearing

wear off verb SUBSIDE, decrease, diminish, disappear, dwindle, fade, peter out, wane

weary adjective 1 TIRED, done in (informal), drained, drowsy, exhausted, fatigued, flagging, jaded, sleepy, worn out 2 TIRING, arduous, laborious,

tiresome, wearisome ▶ verb 3 TIRE, drain, enervate, fatigue, sap, take it out of (informal), tax, tire out, wear out

weather noun 1 CLIMATE, conditions ▶ verb 2 WITHSTAND, brave, come through, endure, overcome, resist, ride out, stand, survive

weave verb 1 KNIT, braid, entwine, interlace, intertwine, plait 2 CREATE, build, construct, contrive, fabricate, make up, put together, spin 3 ZIGZAG, crisscross, wind

web noun 1 SPIDER'S WEB, cobweb 2 NETWORK, lattice, tangle

wed verb 1 MARRY, get married, take the plunge (informal), tie the knot (informal) 2 UNITE, ally, blend, combine, interweave, join, link, merge

wedding noun MARRIAGE, nuptials, wedlock

wedge noun 1 BLOCK, chunk, lump ▶ verb 2 SQUEEZE, cram, crowd, force, jam, lodge, pack, ram, stuff, thrust

wedlock noun MARRIAGE, matrimony

weed out verb ELIMINATE, dispense with, eradicate, get rid of, remove, root out, uproot

weedy adjective WEAK, feeble, frail, ineffectual, puny, skinny, thin

weep verb CRY, blubber, lament, mourn, shed tears, snivel, sob, whimper

weepy adjective Informal SENTIMENTAL, overemotional, schmaltzy (slang), slushy (informal)

weigh verb 1 HAVE A WEIGHT OF,

tip the scales at (*informal*)
2 CONSIDER, contemplate, deliberate upon, evaluate, examine, meditate upon, ponder, reflect upon, think over **3** MATTER, carry weight, count

weight *noun* **1** HEAVINESS, load, mass, poundage, tonnage **2** IMPORTANCE, authority, consequence, impact, import, influence, power, value ▶ *verb* **3** LOAD, freight **4** BIAS, load, slant, unbalance

weighty *adjective* **1** IMPORTANT, consequential, crucial, grave, momentous, portentous, serious, significant, solemn **2** HEAVY, burdensome, cumbersome, hefty (*informal*), massive, ponderous

weird *adjective* STRANGE, bizarre, creepy (*informal*), eerie, freakish, mysterious, odd, queer, spooky (*informal*), unnatural

welcome *verb* **1** GREET, embrace, hail, meet, receive ▶ *noun* **2** GREETING, acceptance, hospitality, reception, salutation ▶ *adjective* **3** ACCEPTABLE, agreeable, appreciated, delightful, desirable, gratifying, pleasant, refreshing **4** FREE, under no obligation

weld *verb* JOIN, bind, bond, connect, fuse, link, solder, unite

welfare *noun* **1** WELLBEING, advantage, benefit, good, happiness, health, interest, prosperity **2** BENEFIT, allowance, gift, grant, handout

well[1] *adverb* **1** SATISFACTORILY, agreeably, nicely, pleasantly,

smoothly, splendidly, successfully **2** SKILLFULLY, ably, adeptly, adequately, admirably, correctly, efficiently, expertly, proficiently, properly **3** PROSPEROUSLY, comfortably **4** SUITABLY, fairly, fittingly, justly, properly, rightly **5** INTIMATELY, deeply, fully, profoundly, thoroughly **6** FAVORABLY, approvingly, glowingly, highly, kindly, warmly **7** CONSIDERABLY, abundantly, amply, fully, greatly, heartily, highly, substantially, thoroughly, very much ▶ *adjective* **8** HEALTHY, fit, in fine fettle, sound **9** SATISFACTORY, agreeable, fine, pleasing, proper, right, thriving

well[2] *noun* **1** HOLE, bore, pit, shaft ▶ *verb* **2** FLOW, gush, jet, pour, spout, spring, spurt, surge

well-known *adjective* FAMOUS, celebrated, familiar, noted, popular, renowned

well-off *adjective* RICH, affluent, comfortable (*informal*), moneyed, prosperous, wealthy, well-heeled (*informal*), well-to-do

well-to-do *adjective* RICH, affluent, comfortable (*informal*), moneyed, prosperous, wealthy, well-heeled (*informal*), well-off

well-worn *adjective* STALE, banal, commonplace, hackneyed, overused, stereotyped, trite

welt *noun* MARK, contusion, streak, stripe, wale, weal

welter *noun* JUMBLE, confusion, mess, muddle, tangle, web

wet *adjective* **1** DAMP, dank, moist, saturated, soaking, sodden, soggy, sopping, waterlogged, watery **2** RAINY, drizzling, pouring, raining, showery, teeming ▶ *noun* **3** RAIN, drizzle **4** MOISTURE, condensation, damp, dampness, humidity, liquid, water, wetness ▶ *verb* **5** MOISTEN, dampen, douse, irrigate, saturate, soak, spray, water

whack *verb* **1** STRIKE, bang, belt (*informal*), clobber (*slang*), hit, smack, thrash, thump, thwack, wallop (*informal*) ▶ *noun* **2** BLOW, bang, belt (*informal*), hit, smack, stroke, thump, thwack, wallop (*informal*) **3** *Informal* SHARE, bit, cut (*informal*), part, portion, quota **4** *As in* **have a whack** ATTEMPT, bash (*informal*), crack (*informal*), go (*informal*), shot (*informal*), stab (*informal*), try, turn

wharf *noun* DOCK, jetty, landing stage, pier, quay

wheedle *verb* COAX, cajole, entice, inveigle, persuade

wheel *noun* **1** CIRCLE, gyration, pivot, revolution, rotation, spin, turn ▶ *verb* **2** TURN, gyrate, pirouette, revolve, rotate, spin, swing, swivel, twirl, whirl

wheeze *verb* **1** GASP, cough, hiss, rasp, whistle ▶ *noun* **2** GASP, cough, hiss, rasp, whistle **3** *Brit. slang* TRICK, idea, plan, ploy, ruse, scheme, stunt

whereabouts *noun* POSITION, location, site, situation

wherewithal *noun* RESOURCES, capital, funds, means, money, supplies

whet *verb* **1** *As in* **whet someone's appetite** STIMULATE,

arouse, awaken, enhance, excite, kindle, quicken, rouse, stir **2** SHARPEN, hone

whiff *noun* SMELL, aroma, hint, odor, scent, sniff

whim *noun* IMPULSE, caprice, fancy, notion, urge

whimper *verb* **1** CRY, moan, snivel, sob, weep, whine ▶ *noun* **2** SOB, moan, snivel, whine

whimsical *adjective* FANCIFUL, curious, eccentric, freakish, funny, odd, playful, quaint, unusual

whine *noun* **1** CRY, moan, sob, wail, whimper **2** COMPLAINT, gripe (*informal*), grouch (*informal*), grouse, grumble, moan

whip *noun* **1** LASH, birch, cane, cat-o'-nine-tails, crop, scourge ▶ *verb* **2** LASH, beat, birch, cane, flagellate, flog, paddle (*U.S. & Canad.*), scourge, spank, strap, thrash **3** *Informal* DASH, dart, dive, fly, rush, shoot, tear, whisk **4** BEAT, whisk **5** INCITE, agitate, drive, foment, goad, spur, stir, work up

whirl *verb* **1** SPIN, pirouette, revolve, roll, rotate, swirl, turn, twirl, twist **2** FEEL DIZZY, reel, spin ▶ *noun* **3** REVOLUTION, pirouette, roll, rotation, spin, swirl, turn, twirl, twist **4** BUSTLE, flurry, merry-go-round, round, series, succession **5** CONFUSION, daze, dither, giddiness, spin

whirlwind *noun* **1** TORNADO, waterspout ▶ *adjective* **2** RAPID, hasty, quick, short, speedy, swift

whisk *verb* **1** FLICK, brush, sweep, whip **2** BEAT, fluff up, whip ▶ *noun* **3** FLICK, brush, sweep, whip **4** BEATER

whisper verb **1** MURMUR, breathe
2 RUSTLE, hiss, sigh, swish
▶ noun **3** MURMUR, undertone
4 RUSTLE, hiss, sigh, swish

white adjective PALE, ashen,
pallid, pasty, wan

white-collar adjective CLERICAL,
nonmanual, professional,
salaried

whiten verb PALE, blanch,
bleach, fade

whitewash noun **1** COVER-UP,
camouflage, concealment,
deception ▶ verb **2** COVER UP,
camouflage, conceal, gloss
over, suppress

whittle verb **1** CARVE, cut, hew,
pare, shape, shave, trim
2 whittle down or **away**
REDUCE, consume, eat away,
erode, wear away

whole adjective **1** COMPLETE,
entire, full, total, unabridged,
uncut, undivided **2** UNDAMAGED,
in one piece, intact, unbroken,
unharmed, unscathed,
untouched ▶ noun **3** TOTALITY,
ensemble, entirety **4 on the
whole: a** ALL IN ALL, all things
considered, by and large **b**
GENERALLY, as a rule, in general,
in the main, mostly,
predominantly

wholehearted adjective SINCERE,
committed, dedicated,
determined, devoted,
enthusiastic, unstinting, zealous

wholesale adjective **1** EXTENSIVE,
broad, comprehensive,
far-reaching, indiscriminate,
mass, sweeping, wide-ranging
▶ adverb **2** EXTENSIVELY,
comprehensively,
indiscriminately

wholesome adjective
1 BENEFICIAL, good, healthy,
nourishing, nutritious,
salubrious **2** MORAL, decent,
edifying, improving, respectable

wholly adverb COMPLETELY,
altogether, entirely, fully, in
every respect, perfectly,
thoroughly, totally, utterly

whopper noun **1** GIANT,
colossus, crackerjack (informal),
jumbo (informal), leviathan,
mammoth, monster **2** BIG LIE,
fabrication, falsehood, tall tale
(informal), untruth

whopping adjective GIGANTIC,
big, enormous, giant, great,
huge, mammoth, massive

whore noun PROSTITUTE, call girl,
ho (slang), streetwalker, tart
(informal)

wicked adjective **1** BAD, corrupt,
depraved, devilish, evil,
fiendish, immoral, sinful,
vicious, villainous **2** MISCHIEVOUS,
impish, incorrigible, naughty,
rascally, roguish

wide adjective **1** BROAD,
expansive, extensive,
far-reaching, immense, large,
sweeping, vast **2** SPACIOUS,
baggy, capacious,
commodious, full, loose,
roomy **3** EXPANDED, dilated,
distended, outspread,
outstretched **4** DISTANT, off
course, off target, remote
▶ adverb **5** FULLY, completely
6 OFF TARGET, astray, off course,
off the mark, out

widen verb BROADEN, dilate,
enlarge, expand, extend,
spread, stretch

widespread adjective COMMON,
broad, extensive, far-reaching,

general, pervasive, popular, universal

width noun BREADTH, compass, diameter, extent, girth, scope, span, thickness

wield verb 1 BRANDISH, employ, flourish, handle, manage, manipulate, ply, swing, use 2 As in wield power EXERT, exercise, have, possess

wife noun SPOUSE, better half (humorous), bride, mate, partner

wiggle verb, noun JERK, flutter, jiggle, oscillate, shake, shimmy, squirm, twitch, wag, wave, writhe

wild adjective 1 UNTAMED, feral, ferocious, fierce, savage, unbroken, undomesticated 2 UNCULTIVATED, free, natural 3 UNCIVILIZED, barbaric, barbarous, brutish, ferocious, fierce, primitive, savage 4 UNCONTROLLED, disorderly, riotous, rowdy, turbulent, undisciplined, unfettered, unmanageable, unrestrained, unruly, wayward 5 STORMY, blustery, choppy, raging, rough, tempestuous, violent 6 EXCITED, crazy (informal), enthusiastic, hysterical, raving, wired (slang) ▶noun 7 wilds WILDERNESS, back of beyond (informal), desert, middle of nowhere (informal), wasteland

wilderness noun DESERT, jungle, wasteland, wilds

wiles plural noun TRICKERY, artfulness, chicanery, craftiness, cunning, guile, slyness

will noun 1 DETERMINATION, purpose, resolution, resolve, willpower 2 WISH, desire, fancy,

inclination, mind, preference, volition 3 TESTAMENT, last wishes ▶verb 4 WISH, desire, prefer, see fit, want 5 BEQUEATH, confer, give, leave, pass on, transfer

willful adjective 1 OBSTINATE, determined, headstrong, inflexible, intransigent, obdurate, perverse, pig-headed, stubborn, uncompromising 2 INTENTIONAL, conscious, deliberate, intended, purposeful, voluntary

willing adjective READY, agreeable, amenable, compliant, consenting, game (informal), inclined, prepared

willingly adverb READILY, by choice, cheerfully, eagerly, freely, gladly, happily, of one's own accord, voluntarily

willingness noun INCLINATION, agreement, consent, volition, will, wish

willowy adjective SLENDER, graceful, lithe, slim, supple, svelte, sylphlike

willpower noun SELF-CONTROL, determination, drive, grit, resolution, resolve, self-discipline, single-mindedness

wilt verb 1 DROOP, sag, shrivel, wither 2 WEAKEN, fade, flag, languish, wane

wily adjective CUNNING, artful, astute, crafty, guileful, sharp, shrewd, sly, tricky

wimp noun Informal WEAKLING, coward, drip (informal), loser (slang), mouse, sissy, softy or softie

wimpy adjective Informal FEEBLE, effete, ineffectual, soft, spineless, timorous, weak, weedy (*informal*)

win verb **1** TRIUMPH, come first, conquer, overcome, prevail, succeed, sweep the board **2** GAIN, achieve, acquire, attain, earn, get, land, obtain, procure, secure ▶ *noun* **3** VICTORY, conquest, success, triumph

wince verb **1** FLINCH, blench, cower, cringe, draw back, quail, recoil, shrink, start ▶ *noun* **2** FLINCH, cringe, start

wind[1] noun **1** AIR, blast, breeze, draft, gust, zephyr **2** BREATH, puff, respiration **3** FLATULENCE, gas **4** TALK, babble, blather, bluster, boasting, hot air, humbug **5** As in **get wind of** HINT, inkling, notice, report, rumor, suggestion, warning, whisper

wind[2] verb **1** COIL, curl, encircle, loop, reel, roll, spiral, twist **2** MEANDER, bend, curve, ramble, snake, turn, twist, zigzag

windfall noun GODSEND, bonanza, find, jackpot, manna from heaven

wind up verb **1** END, close, conclude, finalize, finish, settle, terminate, wrap up **2** END UP, be left, finish up

windy adjective BREEZY, blowy, blustery, gusty, squally, stormy, wild, windswept

wing noun **1** FACTION, arm, branch, group, section ▶ *verb* **2** FLY, glide, soar **3** WOUND, clip, hit

wink verb **1** BLINK, bat, flutter **2** TWINKLE, flash, gleam, glimmer, sparkle ▶ *noun* **3** BLINK, flutter

winner noun VICTOR, champ (*informal*), champion, conqueror, master

winning adjective **1** VICTORIOUS, conquering, successful, triumphant **2** CHARMING, alluring, attractive, cute, disarming, enchanting, endearing, engaging, likable *or* likeable, pleasing

winnings plural noun SPOILS, gains, prize, proceeds, profits, takings

winnow verb SEPARATE, divide, select, sift, sort out

win over verb CONVINCE, bring or talk round, convert, influence, persuade, prevail upon, sway

wintry adjective COLD, chilly, freezing, frosty, frozen, icy, snowy

wipe verb **1** CLEAN, brush, mop, rub, sponge, swab **2** ERASE, remove ▶ *noun* **3** RUB, brush

wipe out verb DESTROY, annihilate, eradicate, erase, expunge, exterminate, massacre, obliterate

wiry adjective LEAN, sinewy, strong, tough

wisdom noun UNDERSTANDING, discernment, enlightenment, erudition, insight, intelligence, judgment, knowledge, learning, sense

wise adjective SENSIBLE, clever, discerning, enlightened, erudite, intelligent, judicious, perceptive, prudent, sage

wisecrack noun *Informal* **1** JOKE, jest, jibe, quip, witticism ▶ *verb* **2** JOKE, jest, jibe, quip

wish verb **1** WANT, aspire, crave, desire, hanker, hope, long,

yearn ▸ *noun* 2 DESIRE, aspiration, hope, intention, urge, want, whim, will

wispy *adjective* THIN, attenuated, delicate, fine, flimsy, fragile, frail

wistful *adjective* MELANCHOLY, contemplative, dreamy, longing, meditative, pensive, reflective, thoughtful

wit *noun* 1 HUMOR, badinage, banter, drollery, jocularity, raillery, repartee, wordplay 2 HUMORIST, card (*informal*), comedian, joker, wag 3 CLEVERNESS, acumen, brains, common sense, ingenuity, intellect, sense, wisdom

witch *noun* ENCHANTRESS, crone, hag, magician, sorceress

witchcraft *noun* MAGIC, enchantment, necromancy, occultism, sorcery, the black art, voodoo, wizardry

withdraw *verb* REMOVE, draw back, extract, pull out, take away, take off

withdrawal *noun* REMOVAL, extraction

withdrawn *adjective* UNCOMMUNICATIVE, distant, introverted, reserved, retiring, shy, taciturn, unforthcoming

wither *verb* WILT, decay, decline, disintegrate, fade, perish, shrivel, waste

withering *adjective* SCORNFUL, devastating, humiliating, hurtful, mortifying, snubbing

withhold *verb* KEEP BACK, conceal, hide, hold back, refuse, reserve, retain, suppress

withstand *verb* RESIST, bear, cope with, endure, hold off, oppose, stand up to, suffer, tolerate

witless *adjective* FOOLISH, halfwitted, idiotic, inane, moronic, senseless, silly, stupid

witness *noun* 1 OBSERVER, beholder, bystander, eyewitness, looker-on, onlooker, spectator, viewer, watcher 2 TESTIFIER, corroborator ▸ *verb* 3 SEE, note, notice, observe, perceive, view, watch 4 SIGN, countersign, endorse

wits *plural noun* INTELLIGENCE, acumen, brains (*informal*), cleverness, comprehension, faculties, ingenuity, reason, sense, understanding

witticism *noun* QUIP, bon mot, one-liner (*slang*), pun, riposte

witty *adjective* HUMOROUS, amusing, clever, droll, funny, piquant, sparkling, waggish, whimsical

wizard *noun* MAGICIAN, conjurer, magus, necromancer, occultist, shaman, sorcerer, warlock, witch

wizardry *noun* MAGIC, sorcery, voodoo, witchcraft

wizened *adjective* WRINKLED, dried up, gnarled, lined, shriveled, shrunken, withered

wobble *verb* 1 SHAKE, rock, sway, teeter, totter, tremble ▸ *noun* 2 UNSTEADINESS, shake, tremble, tremor

wobbly *adjective* UNSTEADY, rickety, shaky, teetering, tottering, uneven

woe *noun* GRIEF, agony, anguish, distress, gloom, misery, sadness, sorrow, unhappiness, wretchedness

woeful *adjective* 1 SAD, deplorable, dismal, distressing, grievous, lamentable, miserable, pathetic, tragic, wretched **2** PITIFUL, abysmal, appalling, bad, deplorable, dreadful, feeble, pathetic, poor, sorry

woman noun LADY, female, girl

womanizer noun PHILANDERER, Casanova, Don Juan, lecher, seducer

womanly adjective FEMININE, female, ladylike, matronly, motherly, tender, warm

wonder verb **1** THINK, conjecture, meditate, ponder, puzzle, query, question, speculate **2** BE AMAZED, be astonished, gape, marvel, stare ▶ noun **3** PHENOMENON, curiosity, marvel, miracle, prodigy, rarity, sight, spectacle **4** AMAZEMENT, admiration, astonishment, awe, bewilderment, fascination, surprise, wonderment

wonderful adjective **1** EXCELLENT, brilliant, fabulous (informal), fantastic (informal), great (informal), magnificent, marvelous, outstanding, superb, terrific (informal), tremendous **2** REMARKABLE, amazing, astonishing, extraordinary, incredible, miraculous, phenomenal, staggering, startling, unheard-of

woo verb COURT, cultivate, pursue

wood noun **1** TIMBER **2** WOODLAND, coppice, copse, forest, grove, thicket

wooded adjective TREE-COVERED, forested, sylvan (poetic), timbered, tree-clad

wooden adjective **1** WOODY, ligneous, timber **2** EXPRESSIONLESS, deadpan,

lifeless, unresponsive

wool noun FLEECE, hair, yarn

woolly adjective **1** FLEECY, hairy, shaggy, woollen **2** VAGUE, confused, hazy, ill-defined, indefinite, indistinct, muddled, unclear

word noun **1** TERM, expression, name **2** CHAT, confab (informal), consultation, discussion, talk, tête-à-tête **3** REMARK, comment, utterance **4** MESSAGE, communiqué, dispatch, information, intelligence, news, notice, report **5** PROMISE, assurance, guarantee, oath, pledge, vow **6** COMMAND, bidding, decree, mandate, order ▶ verb **7** EXPRESS, couch, phrase, put, say, state, utter

wording noun PHRASEOLOGY, language, phrasing, terminology, words

wordy adjective LONG-WINDED, diffuse, prolix, rambling, verbose, windy

work noun **1** EFFORT, drudgery, elbow grease (facetious), exertion, industry, labor, sweat, toil **2** EMPLOYMENT, business, duty, job, livelihood, occupation, profession, trade **3** TASK, assignment, chore, commission, duty, job, stint, undertaking **4** CREATION, achievement, composition, handiwork, opus, piece, production ▶ verb **5** LABOR, drudge, exert oneself, peg away, slave, slog (away), sweat, toil **6** BE EMPLOYED, be in work **7** OPERATE, control, drive, handle, manage, manipulate, move, use **8** FUNCTION, go, operate, run **9** CULTIVATE, dig, farm, till **10** MANIPULATE, fashion, form, knead, mold, shape

workable *adjective* VIABLE, doable, feasible, possible, practicable, practical

worker *noun* EMPLOYEE, artisan, craftsman, hand, laborer, tradesman, workman

working *adjective* 1 EMPLOYED, active, in work 2 FUNCTIONING, going, operative, running

workman *noun* LABORER, artisan, craftsman, employee, hand, journeyman, mechanic, operative, tradesman, worker

workmanship *noun* SKILL, artistry, craftsmanship, expertise, handiwork, technique

work out *verb* 1 SOLVE, calculate, figure out, find out 2 HAPPEN, develop, evolve, result, turn out 3 EXERCISE, practice, train, warm up

works *plural noun* 1 FACTORY, mill, plant, workshop 2 WRITINGS, canon, oeuvre, output 3 MECHANISM, action, machinery, movement, parts, workings

workshop *noun* STUDIO, factory, mill, plant, workroom

world *noun* 1 EARTH, globe 2 MANKIND, everybody, everyone, humanity, humankind, man, the public 3 SPHERE, area, domain, environment, field, realm

worldly *adjective* 1 EARTHLY, physical, profane, secular, temporal, terrestrial 2 MATERIALISTIC, grasping, greedy, selfish 3 WORLDLY-WISE, blasé, cosmopolitan, experienced, knowing, sophisticated, urbane

worldwide *adjective* GLOBAL,

general, international, omnipresent, pandemic, ubiquitous, universal

worn *adjective* RAGGED, frayed, shabby, tattered, tatty, the worse for wear, threadbare

worn-out *adjective* 1 RUN-DOWN, on its last legs, ragged, shabby, threadbare, used-up, useless, worn 2 EXHAUSTED, dead-tired, done in (*informal*), fatigued, ready to drop, spent, tired out, weary

worried *adjective* ANXIOUS, afraid, apprehensive, concerned, fearful, frightened, nervous, perturbed, tense, troubled, uneasy, wired (*slang*)

worry *verb* 1 BE ANXIOUS, agonize, brood, fret 2 TROUBLE, annoy, bother, disturb, perturb, pester, unsettle, upset, vex ▶ *noun* 3 ANXIETY, apprehension, concern, fear, misgiving, trepidation, trouble, unease 4 PROBLEM, bother, care, hassle (*informal*), trouble

worsen *verb* 1 AGGRAVATE, damage, exacerbate 2 DETERIORATE, decay, decline, degenerate, get worse, go downhill (*informal*), sink

worship *verb* 1 PRAISE, adore, exalt, glorify, honor, pray to, revere, venerate 2 LOVE, adore, idolize, put on a pedestal ▶ *noun* 3 PRAISE, adoration, adulation, devotion, glory, honor, kudos, regard, respect, reverence

worth *noun* 1 VALUE, cost, price, rate, valuation 2 EXCELLENCE, goodness, importance, merit, quality, usefulness, value, worthiness

worthless adjective 1 USELESS, ineffectual, rubbishy, unimportant, valueless 2 GOOD-FOR-NOTHING, contemptible, despicable, lousy (*slang*), scuzzy (*slang*), vile

worthwhile adjective USEFUL, beneficial, constructive, expedient, helpful, productive, profitable, valuable

worthy adjective PRAISEWORTHY, admirable, creditable, deserving, laudable, meritorious, valuable, virtuous, worthwhile

would-be adjective BUDDING, self-appointed, self-styled, unfulfilled, wannabe (*informal*)

wound noun 1 INJURY, cut, gash, hurt, laceration, lesion, trauma (*Pathology*) 2 INSULT, offense, slight ▶ verb 3 INJURE, cut, gash, hurt, lacerate, pierce, wing 4 OFFEND, annoy, cut (someone) to the quick, hurt, mortify, sting

wrangle verb 1 ARGUE, bicker, contend, disagree, dispute, fight, quarrel, row, squabble ▶ noun 2 ARGUMENT, altercation, bickering, dispute, quarrel, row, squabble, tiff

wrap verb 1 COVER, bind, bundle up, encase, enclose, enfold, pack, package, shroud, swathe ▶ noun 2 CLOAK, cape, mantle, shawl, stole

wrapper noun COVER, case, envelope, jacket, packaging, wrapping

wrap up verb 1 GIFTWRAP, bundle up, pack, package 2 *Informal* END, conclude, finish off, polish off, round off, terminate, wind up

wrath noun ANGER, displeasure, fury, indignation, ire, rage, resentment, temper

wreath noun GARLAND, band, chaplet, crown, festoon, ring

wreck verb 1 DESTROY, break, demolish, devastate, ruin, shatter, smash, spoil ▶ noun 2 SHIPWRECK, hulk

wreckage noun REMAINS, debris, fragments, pieces, rubble, ruin

wrench verb 1 TWIST, force, jerk, pull, rip, tear, tug, yank 2 SPRAIN, Rick, strain ▶ noun 3 TWIST, jerk, pull, rip, tug, yank 4 SPRAIN, strain, twist 5 BLOW, pang, shock, upheaval 6 SPANNER, adjustable spanner

wrest verb SEIZE, extract, force, take, win, wrench

wrestle verb FIGHT, battle, combat, grapple, scuffle, struggle, tussle

wretch noun SCOUNDREL, good-for-nothing, miscreant, rascal, rogue, swine, worm

wretched adjective 1 UNHAPPY, dejected, depressed, disconsolate, downcast, forlorn, hapless, miserable, woebegone 2 WORTHLESS, inferior, miserable, paltry, pathetic, poor, sorry

wriggle verb 1 TWIST, jerk, jiggle, squirm, turn, wiggle, writhe 2 CRAWL, slink, snake, worm, zigzag 3 As in **wriggle out of** MANEUVER, dodge, extricate oneself ▶ noun 4 TWIST, jerk, jiggle, squirm, turn, wiggle

wring verb TWIST, extract, force, screw, squeeze

wrinkle noun 1 CREASE, corrugation, crinkle, crow's-foot, crumple, fold, furrow, line ▶ *verb* **2** CREASE, corrugate, crumple, fold, furrow, gather, pucker, rumple

writ *noun* SUMMONS, court order, decree, document

write *verb* RECORD, draft, draw up, inscribe, jot down, pen, scribble, set down

writer *noun* AUTHOR, hack, novelist, penpusher, scribbler, scribe, wordsmith

writhe *verb* SQUIRM, jerk, struggle, thrash, thresh, toss, twist, wiggle, wriggle

writing *noun* **1** SCRIPT, calligraphy, hand, handwriting, penmanship, scrawl, scribble **2** DOCUMENT, book, composition, opus, publication, work

wrong *adjective* **1** INCORRECT, erroneous, fallacious, false, inaccurate, mistaken, untrue, wide of the mark **2** BAD, criminal, dishonest, evil, illegal, immoral, sinful, unjust, unlawful, wicked, wrongful **3** INAPPROPRIATE, incongruous, incorrect, unacceptable, unbecoming, undesirable, unseemly, unsuitable **4** DEFECTIVE, amiss, askew, awry, faulty ▶ *adverb* **5** INCORRECTLY, badly, erroneously, inaccurately, mistakenly, wrongly **6** AMISS, askew, astray, awry ▶ *noun* **7** OFFENSE, crime, error, injury, injustice, misdeed, sin, transgression, wickedness ▶ *verb* **8** MISTREAT, abuse, cheat, dishonor, harm, hurt, malign, oppress, take advantage of

wrongdoer *noun* OFFENDER, criminal, culprit, delinquent, evildoer, lawbreaker, miscreant,

sinner, villain

wrongful *adjective* IMPROPER, criminal, evil, illegal, illegitimate, immoral, unethical, unjust, unlawful, wicked

wry *adjective* **1** IRONIC, droll, dry, mocking, sarcastic, sardonic **2** CONTORTED, crooked, twisted, uneven

Xmas *noun* CHRISTMAS, festive season, Noel, Yule, Yuletide

X-rated *adjective* PORNOGRAPHIC, adult, dirty, graphic, hardcore (*slang*), obscene, scuzzy (*slang*)

X-rays *plural noun* RÖNTGEN RAYS (*old name*)

yank *verb, noun* PULL, hitch, jerk, snatch, tug, wrench

yardstick *noun* STANDARD, benchmark, criterion, gauge, measure, par, touchstone

yarn *noun* **1** THREAD, fiber **2** Old-fashioned, informal STORY, anecdote, cock-and-bull story (*informal*), fable, tale, tall tale (*informal*)

yawning *adjective* GAPING, cavernous, vast, wide

yearly *adjective* **1** ANNUAL ▶ *adverb* **2** ANNUALLY, every year, once a year, per annum

yearn *verb* LONG, ache, covet,

crave, desire, hanker, hunger, itch

yell verb 1 SCREAM, bawl, holler (informal), howl, screech, shout, shriek, squeal ▶ noun 2 SCREAM, cry, howl, screech, shriek, whoop

yell at verb Informal CRITICIZE, censure, rebuke, scold, tear into (informal)

yelp verb CRY, yap, yowl

yen noun LONGING, ache, craving, desire, hankering, hunger, itch, passion, thirst, yearning

yes man noun SYCOPHANT, brown-noser (slang), minion, timeserver, toady

yet conjunction 1 NEVERTHELESS, however, notwithstanding, still ▶ adverb 2 SO FAR, as yet, thus far, until now, up to now 3 STILL, besides, in addition, into the bargain, to boot 4 NOW, just now, right now, so soon

yield verb 1 PRODUCE, bear, bring forth, earn, generate, give, net, provide, return, supply 2 SURRENDER, bow, capitulate, give in, relinquish, resign, submit, succumb ▶ noun 3 PROFIT, crop, earnings, harvest, income, output, produce, return, revenue, takings

yielding adjective 1 SUBMISSIVE, accommodating, acquiescent, biddable, compliant, docile, flexible, obedient, pliant 2 SOFT, elastic, pliable, spongy, springy, supple, unresisting

yoke verb BURDEN, encumber, land, load, saddle

yokel noun PEASANT, (country)

bumpkin, countryman, hick (informal, chiefly U.S. & Canad.), hillbilly, redneck (slang), rustic

young adjective 1 IMMATURE, adolescent, callow, green, infant, junior, juvenile, little, youthful 2 NEW, early, fledgling, recent, undeveloped ▶ plural noun 3 OFFSPRING, babies, brood, family, issue, litter, progeny

youngster noun YOUTH, boy, girl, juvenile, kid (informal), lad, lass, teenager

youth noun 1 IMMATURITY, adolescence, boyhood, girlhood, salad days 2 BOY, adolescent, kid (informal), lad, stripling, teenager, young man, youngster

youthful adjective YOUNG, boyish, childish, fresh-faced, girlish, immature, inexperienced, juvenile, rosy-cheeked

— Z z —

zany adjective COMICAL, clownish, crazy, eccentric, goofy (informal), wacky (slang)

zeal noun ENTHUSIASM, ardor, eagerness, fanaticism, fervor, gusto, keenness, passion, spirit, verve, zest

zealot noun FANATIC, bigot, enthusiast, extremist, militant

zealous adjective ENTHUSIASTIC, ardent, devoted, eager, fanatical, fervent, impassioned, keen, passionate

zenith noun HEIGHT, acme, apex,

apogee, climax, crest, high point, peak, pinnacle, summit, top

zero noun **1** NOTHING, nada (*informal*), nil, nought, zilch (*informal*) **2** BOTTOM, nadir, rock bottom

zest noun **1** ENJOYMENT, appetite, gusto, keenness, relish, zeal **2** FLAVOR, charm, interest, piquancy, pungency, relish, spice, tang, taste

zip noun **1** *Informal* ENERGY, drive, gusto, liveliness, verve, vigor, zest ▶verb **2** SPEED, flash, fly, shoot, whizz (*informal*), zoom

zone noun AREA, belt, district, region, section, sector, sphere

zoom verb SPEED, dash, flash, fly, hurtle, pelt, rush, shoot, whizz (*informal*)